EMPIRE

STANOVOI MTS

(Acquired by Russia, 1858-1860)

Lake
Baikal

Amur R.

MANCHURIA

OUTER
MONGOLIA

JAPAN

INNER MONGOLIA

GREAT WALL

SHANSI

CHIHLI

Peking

Tientsin

SHANTUNG

KIANGSU

KOREA

Yalu R.

Lanchow

SHENSI

Yellow R.

HONAN

HUPEH

Hankow

ANHWEI

Nanking

Shanghai

CHINA

Chengtu
SZECHWAN

Yangtze R.

KIANGSI

CHEKIANG

FUKIEN

HUNAN

KWEICHOW

KWANGSI

Canton

KWANGTUNG

Hong Kong
(Br. 1842)

TAIWAN
(FORMOSA)

RYUKYU IS.

Ocean

Pacific

Mekong R.

YUNNAN

TONKIN

VIETNAM

HAINAN

South China
Sea

PHILIPPINE IS.

LAOS

SIAM

ANNAM

CAMBODIA

COCHIN CHINA

Lanchow

U

The Rise of Modern China

中國近代史

The Rise of
MODERN CHINA

IMMANUEL C. Y. HSÜ

New York
OXFORD UNIVERSITY PRESS
London   1970   Toronto

Copyright © 1970 by Oxford University Press, Inc.
Fourth Printing, 1973
Library of Congress Catalogue Card Number: 78-83022
Printed in the United States of America

To
John King Fairbank

Preface

This comprehensive history conveys primarily a Chinese view of the evolution of Modern China, reinforced by the fruits of Western and Japanese scholarship which has been considerable in the past three decades. We see here a turbulent era of Chinese history in which domestic and foreign forces interacted to transform the Confucian universal empire into a modern national state. The metamorphosis was labored, slow, and at times painful; an inside view of the process promises to shed light on the contemporary behavior of China, both Communist and Nationalist.

As the present volume represents the author's long time study of history, both Western and Chinese, he is deeply grateful to many of his former professors at Harvard who taught him the historical discipline: Drs. John K. Fairbank, L. S. Yang, Edwin O. Reischauer, William L. Langer, and Serge Elisséeff. To Harvard-Yenching Institute he is indebted for four years of fellowship which enabled him to pursue graduate studies in a most stimulating atmosphere. He is also thankful to the numerous authors whose works have directly or indirectly benefitted him in the preparation of this volume. While it is impossible to acknowledge them all here, he should like to mention a few of the most helpful scholars and research centers. Hsiao I-shan's monumental work, *Ch'ing-tai t'ung-shih* (A general history of the Ch'ing period), which first appeared in two volumes in 1927-28 and was enlarged into a five-volume set in 1963, is truly a mine of information, which materially enriched this work. The writings of John K. Fairbank have been a source of inspiration to a generation of students, and under his resourceful directorship the Harvard

East Asian Research Center has published several dozen monographs which have significantly elevated the level of scholarship on Modern China. The series of publications by the Institute of Modern History, Academia Sinica, on Taiwan, the Toyo Bunko in Tokyo, and the Historical Research Association on mainland China, have all been useful in various ways. Special thanks are due Dr. S. Y. Teng, University Professor at Indiana University, for his perceptive comments on the manuscript which enabled the author to make numerous corrections and improvements. To his many students over the past decade, the author is indebted for their stimulating questions which alerted him to their needs and frequently opened new vistas for discussion. Thanks are also due Mrs. Alice Kladnik for her typing of the manuscript and to Mr. En-han Lee for preparing the index. Last but not least, the author's wife, Dolores, deserves a special word of appreciation: but for her constant encouragement, moral support, and loving companionship, this work would not have been possible.

Despite all the help and inspiration he has received, the author alone is responsible for all the inadequacies of the book. He submits it to the public with the sincere hope that it will prompt other scholars to make worthier contributions, in the spirit of the Chinese saying: "May the brick I have thrown attract jade from others" (*p'ao-chuan yin-yü*).

Santa Barbara, California   I. C. Y. H.
New Year's Day, 1970

Contents

Maps

ALL MAPS HAVE BEEN PREPARED BY VAUGHN GRAY

A Note on the Text

1. All translations from the Chinese, unless otherwise indicated, are by the author.

2. Footnotes, usually considered superfluous in a work of synthesis, are nonetheless given, where essential, to indicate the sources of direct quotations and important statements, and thus facilitate the reader's further study.

3. A reading list appears at the end of each chapter, consisting mostly of easily available Western works. A few important Chinese and Japanese works are included for the advanced student. These reading lists are not intended to be exhaustive bibliographies of the chapters, but merely aids to further reading.

4. All Chinese, Japanese, and Russian dates have been transcribed to correspond with the Western dates according to the Gregorian calendar.

5. Chinese place names are given in accordance with the Chinese Postal Atlas; hence many of them appear in Anglicized forms such as Peking, rather than Pei-ching, and Nanking, rather than Nan-ching.

6. Chinese personal names are usually given in their original order, with the family name preceding the given name, such as Li Hung-chang, Mao Tse-tung. However, where a man is better known under some other form, such as Confucius rather than K'ung-fu-tzu, Chiang Kai-shek rather than Chiang Chung-cheng, T. V. Soong rather than Sung Tzu-wen, the more familiar form is adopted.

7. Transliteration of Chinese names follows the Wade-Giles system, originally devised by the British diplomat-linguist, Thomas F. Wade, for

his Peking *Syllabary* of 1859. Wade became the first professor of Chinese (1888-95) at Cambridge University after his retirement from the foreign service. The system was slightly revised by Herbert A. Giles, another British consular officer and Sinologue, for his *Chinese-English Dictionary* of 1912. The Wade-Giles system is designed to achieve pronunciation in the official Peking dialect (*Mandarin*); since many of the Chinese sounds have no exact counterpart in English, a number of letters used in the system are pronounced in a "peculiar" manner to approximate the Chinese sound. Though not perfect by modern linguistic standards, the Wade-Giles system has been widely followed by the Sinologists for many decades, and it is used here for convenience and consistency. Its main features may be summarized as follows:

VOWELS

a is pronounced as in f*a*ther   *ai* as "i" in i*ce*   *ao* as in c*ow*
e as in *e*bb
i as in mach*i*ne
o as in s*aw* or oft
u as in l*u*nar   *ü* as the German ü

CONSONANTS

Unaspirated	*Aspirated, as marked by an apostrophe*
ch as J in Joe	*ch'* as in *ch*in
j as in *r*um	*k'* as in *k*ing
k as in *g*ive	*p'* as in *p*an
p as in *b*an	*t'* as in *t*ip
t as in *d*ip	*ts'* or *tz'* as in Bet*sy*
ts or *tz* as *dz*	
ss as in hi*ss*	

8. Japanese names are transliterated according to the Hepburn system in which:
a is pronounced as ä in f*a*r
i as e in m*e*te
u as oo in f*oo*d
e as e in b*e*t
o as o in h*o*me

Major Chronological Periods

The Ch'ing Dynasty (1644-1911)

      Shun-chih   1644-61

      K'ang-hsi   1662-1722

      Yung-cheng   1723-35

      Ch'ien-lung   1736-95

      Chia-ch'ing   1796-1820

      Tao-kuang   1821-50

      Hsien-feng   1851-61

      T'ung-chih   1862-74

      Kuang-hsü   1875-1908

      Hsüan-t'ung   1909-11

The Republic of China (1912-)

The People's Republic of China (1949-)

Conversion Tables
of Currencies, Weights, and Measures

CURRENCIES (1600-1814)

1 tael 兩 = 1 Chinese ounce, or 1.208 English ounce, of pure silver
$\quad$ = £⅓ = 6s. 8d. (6 shillings and 8 pence)
$\quad$ = U.S. $1.63
$\quad$ = Spanish $1.57

(In 1894 the value of tael dropped to 3s. 2d., and in 1904, 2s. 10d.)

1£ = 3 taels (Tls.) = Spanish $4
1 Spanish $ = 0.72 tael or 5s.

WEIGHTS

1 picul (*shih* 石) = 100 catties (*chin* 斤)
$\quad$ = 133⅓ lbs.
$\quad$ = 60.453 kilograms
1 catty (*chin*) = 16 taels (*liang* 兩)
$\quad$ = 1⅓ lbs.
$\quad$ = 604.53 grams
1 tael (*liang*) = 1⅓ oz.
$\quad$ = 37.783 grams
16.8 piculs = 1 long ton
16.54 piculs = 1 metric ton

MEASURES

1 *li* 里 = ⅓ mile = ½ kilometer
1 *ch'ih* 尺 = 1 Chinese foot or cubit = 14.1 inches

The Rise of Modern China

1

Prologue: A Conceptual Framework
of Modern China

With a recorded history of nearly 4,000 years, Chinese civilization is one of the oldest in the world. Until modern times its development had been largely indigenous, partly because of the independent spirit of the Chinese people and partly because of China's isolation from the other great civilizations. However, with the advent of the Age of Discovery a drastically different situation set in. Portuguese and Spanish explorers and envoys began to arrive in South China via the new sea routes in the 16th century, and in their wake came the traders and missionaries. Shortly afterwards, the Russians marched across Siberia and reached the Manchurian border in the mid-17th century. These events were nothing less than epochal for China, for they broke her age-old isolation and initiated the beginning of direct East-West contact, which, though weak and faltering at first, was to grow to such force in the 19th century as to effect a head-on collision between China and the West. Moreover, when viewed in the context of China's domestic development, the arrival of the Europeans takes on added significance: it coincided with the rise of the Manchus and the establishment of the alien Ch'ing dynasty. These momentous foreign and domestic developments left behind far-reaching consequences which endowed the period that followed with characteristics markedly different from earlier times.

First and foremost, the convergence of Chinese and Western history ended China's seclusion and resulted in her increasing involvement in world affairs, until today what happens in one immediately affects the other. Secondly, the interplay of foreign and domestic elements gave rise

3

to revolutionary changes in the Chinese political system, economic institutions, social structure, and intellectual attitudes. "Change" thus became a key feature of the period, making it far more complex than ever
before. Thirdly, the forcible injection of alien elements into Chinese
life—the Westerners from without and the Manchus from within—generated a strong sense of nationalistic-racial consciousness, which was to
influence deeply the future course of Chinese history. So distinct is this
period from earlier ones that it justifiably forms a separate period of
historical investigation.

WHEN DOES MODERN CHINA BEGIN?

Although the meeting of Western and Chinese history began in the 16th
century, its effect did not become significant until the middle of the 19th
century, when the intensified activities of the West led to radical changes
in China. Scholars therefore have differed on whether the 16th century
or the 19th should be regarded as the beginning of modern China. One
influential school, consisting mostly of Western historians and political
scientists, Marxist scholars, and many Western-trained Chinese scholars,
take the Opium War of 1839-42 as the point of departure. For the
Chinese historians of this school, the war marked the beginning of foreign imperialism in their country, and Chinese history thereafter was
largely one of imperialism in China. For the Western historians, the war
signified the acceleration of foreign activities which shattered Chinese
isolation and ushered in a period of revolutionary changes in China. For
Marxist historians, the war was the epitome of the evils of capitalism
and imperialism, which plunged the "semifeudal" Chinese state into the
abyss of "semicolonialism."

A second school, consisting mostly of the more traditional Chinese
historians[1] (who are beginning to win converts among Western scholars),
disputes the propriety of regarding the Opium War as the beginning of
a new era. They consider the arrival of European explorers and missionaries during the transitional period from the Ming (1368-1643) to the
Ch'ing (1644-1911) as a more justifiable starting point, for internally
it was the time of the rise of the Manchus and the establishment of the
Ch'ing dynasty, and externally it was the period when Western learning

1. Such as Hsiao I-shan, *Ch'ing-tai t'ung-shih* (A general history of the Ch'ing period), rev. ed. (Taipei, 1962); Li Shou-k'ung, *Chung-kuo chin-tai shih* (Chinese
modern history), (Taipei, 1961); Li Fang-ch'en, *Chung-kuo chin-tai shih* (Chinese
modern history), (Taipei, 1960).

was first introduced into China. They argue that for all its spectacular effects the Western impact in the 19th century was only an extension and intensification of a process already set in motion two and one half centuries earlier, and that the hundred or so years since the Opium War is scarcely enough time to represent the modern period of a 4,000-year-old history. Moreover, to date modern China from the 16th-17th centuries is to place it more in congruity with the beginning of modern Europe.

Both approaches are valid, and both have certain shortcomings. From the standpoint of effects, the burgeoning of the Western impact in the 19th century certainly was more instrumental in transforming traditional China into modern China than the arrival of the European explorers and missionaries in the 16th and 17th centuries. To be sure, the Jesuits introduced the Western sciences of astronomy, mathematics, geography, cartography, and architecture, but their influence was limited to a small group of Chinese scholars and officials in the ruling circles. They left little imprint on China's political institutions, social structure, and economic systems, which remained much as they were before the coming of the missionaries. From this point of view, the first school would seem to have a strong claim.

Yet no one can fully appreciate the changes in the 19th and 20th centuries without knowing the institutions of the earlier period. The study of the Western impact must be preceded by a knowledge of what that impact was on. Furthermore, in view of the crucial role that the West and Russia played on influencing the destiny of modern China, one should not lose sight of the import of the early contacts, nor the manner of their advance—the Western maritime powers pushed from the south upward and the Russian land power thrust from the north downward, constituting something of a pincer movement pointing at the heart of China, Peking.[2] Indeed, from a historical standpoint the arrival of the western Europeans and the Russians in the 16th and 17th centuries paved the way for the intensified activity of the West in the 19th century. For these reasons, the second school would seem to have a plausible argument.

2. Immanuel C. Y. Hsü, *China's Entrance into the Family of Nations: The Diplomatic Phase, 1858-1880*, 2nd printing (Cambridge, Mass., 1968), 108. See also T. F. Tsiang, "Chung-kuo yü chin-tai shih-chieh ti ta-pien-chü" (China and the great changes of the modern world), *Tsing-hua hsüeh-pao* (The Tsing-hua Journal), 9:4: 783-828 (Oct. 1934); "China and European Expansion," *Politica*, 2:5:1-18 (March 1936).

However, I believe that the two schools can be reconciled through the development of an eclectic approach. Even accrediting the Opium War as a viable point of departure, one still needs to be familiar with the traditional Chinese state and society, which conditioned China's reaction to the foreign challenge of the 19th century. The intrusion of the West can be construed as a kind of catalyst, precipitating traditional China into its modern counterpart. Hence, one can hardly understand the result of the transformation without a fair knowledge of the mother institutions.

Consequently, a general discussion of the major developments in domestic and foreign affairs from 1600 to 1800 will provide the background information necessary for a sound understanding of modern China. During this period, China's political system, social structure, economic institutions, and intellectual atmosphere remained substantially what they had been during the previous 2,000 years. The polity was a dynasty ruled by an imperial family; the economy was basically agrarian and self-sufficient; the society centered around the gentry; and the dominant ideology was Confucianism. With a knowledge of this traditional complexion of China one can more readily appreciate Chinese conduct vis-à-vis the accelerated Western activity in the 19th century. Hence, this eclectic approach preserves the historical completeness of the second school without sacrificing the realistic considerations of the first.

The questions may be asked, why did the convergence of Chinese and Western history not begin before the 16th century, and why did the Western influence not intensify before the 19th? To answer these questions, one must remember that for over two millennia before the last century, the main streams of Chinese and Western civilizations moved in divergent directions. Western civilization originated in Greece, moved westward to Rome, and spread over western Europe and into America, while Chinese civilization developed in the Yellow River valley, moved southward toward the Yangtze River valley, and then to other parts of China. The major currents of the two civilizations thus moved farther and farther apart rather than toward each other. They could not meet until one of them had developed sufficient power and technology, coupled with interest, to reach the other.

To be sure, there were intermittent contacts between the two civilizations before the Age of Discovery. The Han dynasty (202 B.C.-A.D. 220) and its European contemporary, the Roman Empire, knew something of each other. The Chinese addressed the Roman Empire with the honorable title of *Ta-Ch'in*, the Great Ch'in state. The famous general, Pan Ch'ao, active in Central Asia from A.D. 73 to 102, even sent an envoy[3] to look for the Roman Empire, and he reached as far as the Persian Gulf. Other contacts included the importation of Chinese silk to Rome, and the arrival in China of Roman jugglers and merchants in A.D. 120 and A.D. 166. During the T'ang period (618-907), Nestorian Christianity and Mohammedanism entered China, and the Arabs were active in Chinese foreign trade during both the T'ang and Sung (960-1279) periods. The Yüan period (1280-1367) witnessed the coming of the Venetian merchants, Maffio and Niccolo Polo and the latter's famous son, Marco, as well as many Franciscan monks. The Ming period (1368-1643) saw the rise of the great maritime expeditions conducted by Cheng Ho, who reached as far as the eastern coast of Africa, and in the 15th century the Chinese technique of blockprinting was transmitted to Europe. Thus, for many centuries before the Age of Discovery, there were sporadic contacts between China and the West, but a direct confrontation of the two had to wait until one of them could make a *sustained* drive to reach the other.

By the time of the Age of Discovery, Europe had developed enough geographical knowledge and technical skill in shipbuilding to be able to reach the East. Portuguese oceanic expeditions carried explorers and empire-builders to Asia, followed immediately by traders and missionaries, bringing with them the new scientific knowledge of the Western world. The beginnings of a more than occasional East-West contact were established, but it was still not powerful enough to bring the two civilizations face to face. Europe had to wait until after the Industrial Revolution to generate power sufficient to make a vigorous and sustained effort to reach China. It is no accident that England, as the cradle of the Industrial Revolution, took the lead in this drive. Clearly, the convergence of Chinese and Western history could not have occurred before the Age of Discovery, and the direct confrontation of the two civilizations could not have occurred before the Industrial Revolution.

THE SHAPING FORCES OF MODERN CHINA

The key to an understanding of any period of history lies in the discovery of its major shaping forces. In the case of modern China, we discern

3. Kan Ying.

several powerful forces at work, some overt and some covert. First was of course the government's policies and institutions which to a large extent determined the ebb and flow of the country's fortune. During the Ch'ing period, the overriding consideration of the dynasty was to maintain itself. To win Chinese good will and acceptance, it identified itself with the traditional order, kept the Ming government and social institutions, embraced Neo-Confucianism as a state philosophy, and absorbed the Chinese into its bureaucracy to work alongside the Manchus in a sort of dyarchy. It carried out ruthless literary inquisitions to punish critics of the alien rule. It strove to preserve the Manchu identity through the establishment of the Imperial Clan Court to supervise the births, education, and marriages of the Manchu nobles, the prohibition of Manchu-Chinese intermarriages, and the ban on Chinese immigration to Manchuria. New government offices were created to suit its particular needs, such as the *Li-fan yüan* in 1638 to manage affairs relating to Tibet, Mongolia, and the Western Region (Sinkiang); the Grand Council in 1729 to centralize the decision-making process; and the Tsungli Yamen in 1861 to direct foreign relations with the Western powers. Military expeditions were dispatched to the far corners of the empire to quell revolts and expand frontiers, making the dynasty the second largest in Chinese history. After the mid-19th century, many foreigners were appointed to government services, thereby enlarging the Manchu-Chinese dyarchy into a Manchu-Chinese-Western *synarchy*.[4] All these policies and undertakings as well as a host of others, designed to ensure the permanence of the Ch'ing rule, strongly influenced and guided the main streams of the country's political life from 1644 to 1911. After the fall of the Manchu dynasty, the primary concern of the republican government was to unify the country internally and abolish the unequal treaties externally. Coming down to the Communist period since 1949, we notice an intense drive toward socialist transformation, rapid industrialization, and big-power status. These overriding policies of the government in power obviously played a major role in guiding the destiny of the country and the people and should therefore earn the unremitting attention of the historian.

Yet we must not ignore the more elusive subterranean currents of

4. John K. Fairbank, "Synarchy under the Treaties" in John K. Fairbank (ed.), *Chinese Thought and Institutions* (Chicago, 1957), 204-31; "The Early Treaty System in the Chinese World Order" in John K. Fairbank (ed.), *The Chinese World Order: Traditional China's Foreign Relations* (Cambridge, Mass., 1968), 257-75.

history as a shaping force. Indeed, in an autocracy like the Ch'ing where no legal or loyal opposition was allowed, underground activities at times played a vital role in the unfolding of history. While many Chinese joined the Manchu government and tacitly accepted the Ch'ing rule, a great many more remained in silent opposition. The very fact that the Ch'ing was an alien dynasty continuously evoked Chinese protest in the form of secret society activities and nationalistic-racial revolt and revolution. Initially, the anti-Ch'ing sentiment was accompanied by a desire to revive the Ming—as witness the various Ming loyalist movements, the resistance of Koxinga and his son on Taiwan, and the Revolt of the Three Feudatories (San-Fan). When these movements failed, the "Anti-Ch'ing, Revive-Ming" (Fan-Ch'ing fu-Ming) idea was covertly preserved and nurtured among the secret societies such as the Heaven and Earth Society (T'ien-ti hui) and the White Lotus Sect (Pai-lien chiao), waiting for a chance to burst out. It was no coincidence that when the central vigilance laxed toward the end of the Ch'ien-lung reign (1736-95), the White Lotus Rebellion broke out in 1796 and lasted until 1804. After its pacification, the nationalistic-racial protest once again subsided, only to be revived by the Taipings in 1850-64. However, the Taipings kept only the "Anti-Ch'ing" portion of the slogan and dropped the idea of reviving the Ming, since they wanted to create a kingdom of their own. After the failure of the Taipings in 1864, the nationalistic-racial revolution again subsided into secret society activities, giving inspiration to later revolutionaries such as Dr. Sun Yat-sen. By then the scope of revolutionary aspirations was broadened to include a vendetta against foreign imperialism as well. With the downfall of the Manchu dynasty in 1912, the original "Anti-Ch'ing" objective had been realized, and the nationalistic revolution turned against foreign imperialism, with European colonial powers as the chief target in the 1910's and 20's, Japan in the 1930's and first half of the 40's, and Russia in the 1950's and 1960's—the last, it may be observed, as much the target of the Chinese Nationalists as of the Communists.

Thus, throughout the three-hundred-odd years of modern China, the thread of nationalistic-racial protest against foreign elements in Chinese life formed a distinct theme of history, now coming to the surface and now going underground. So persistent was this force that a noted historian remarks, perhaps somewhat exaggeratedly, that the history of modern China may be construed as a history of nationalistic revolution.[5]

5. Hsiao I-shan, I, 15.

The third shaping force was the search for a way to survival in the new world that had been forcibly thrust upon China by the West after the mid-19th century. Ironically, Western civilization, so creative and vital elsewhere, proved more destructive than constructive in its immediate confrontation with China. It precipitated the breakdown of the old order without substituting another, leaving the Chinese the difficult task of forging a new order out of the ruins of the old. Burdened by tradition and heritage, and as yet ignorant of the nature of the Western world, the Chinese groped in the dark, looking for a way to live with what the great statesman Li Hung-chang described as "a great change in more than three thousand years of history."[6] They were faced with the agonizing problem of deciding how much of Old China must be discarded and how much of the modern West must be accepted in order for China to exist and win a respectable place in the community of nations.

The search for a new order involved an extremely hard struggle against the weight of pride, disdain for things foreign, and the inveterate belief that the bountiful Middle Kingdom had nothing to learn from the outlandish barbarians and little to gain from their association. However, after China's second defeat in war and the Anglo-French occupation of Peking in 1860, the more progressive mandarins[7] realized that the Western challenge was inescapable and that China must change if she was to survive. They initiated what was known as the Self-strengthening Movement in the early 1860's, invoking the slogan of the famous scholar Wei Yüan, "learn the superior barbarian technique with which to repel the barbarians." In this spirit, translation bureaus were established, and arsenals and dockyards were created after the Western models, supported by military industries. The movement, which lasted some thirty-five years, was a superficial attempt at modernization; only those aspects having immediate usefulness were adopted, while the more commendable parts of the Western civilization—political systems, economic institutions, philosophy, literature, and the arts—were totally ignored. Even the progressive Chinese at the time believed that China had little to learn from the West except weaponry.

The Self-strengthening Movement was proved totally inadequate by the defeat in the Japanese war in 1895. Realizing the limited scope of

6. Li Hung-chang, *Li Wen-chung-kung ch'üan-chi* (Complete works of Li Hung-chang), (Shanghai, 1921), "Tsou-kao" (Memorials), 19:45. Memorial dated June 20, 1872.
7. Such as Prince Kung, Wen-hsiang, Tseng Kuo-fan, Tso Tsung-t'ang, and Li Hung-chang.

their movement, Chinese scholars and officials determined that they must broaden the modernization program to include political reform as well. K'ang Yu-wei, an assertive thinker, and his famous student, Liang Ch'i-ch'ao, urged the emperor to make institutional reform after the fashion of Peter the Great and Emperor Meiji. However, even at this late stage reformers did not advocate complete Westernization but rather the creation of a hybrid polity containing both Chinese and Western elements. The spirit of the movement was "Chinese learning for fundamentals, Western learning for practical application," as described by the famous scholar-official Chang Chih-tung. The result of K'ang's program was the "Hundred-Day" Reform of 1898, which ended abruptly in failure.

Meanwhile, secret revolutionary activities were initiated by Dr. Sun Yat-sen, a Western-trained physician, who believed that China's problems could not be remedied by a partial institutional reform, but only by a complete revolution. Carrying the torch of nationalistic-racial revolution, he advocated overthrow of the Manchu rule. Operating on the fringes of society, he won support from the secret societies, the lower classes, and the overseas Chinese, but not from the scholars and the gentry, who generally followed K'ang and Liang. But after the Boxer Rebellion of 1900, which severely discredited the dynasty, an increasing number of educated people joined Dr. Sun's cause, and his earlier image of disloyal rebel was transformed into that of patriotic revolutionary. The success of the revolution in 1911 was followed by the establishment of a Western-style republic the next year, and the dynasty was abolished for the first time in 4,000 years.

Although a break was made with the outdated political system, the hand of the past continued to weigh heavily in social habits and intellectual life. The government had had a face-lifting but its spirit remained the same; corruption, warlordism, attempts at reviving monarchism, and disorder were rife. The institution of the republic was not accompanied by the expected peace and order, and Chinese intellectuals became convinced that without a thorough thought-reform no good government and no social improvement were possible. Those who had studied in Japan, Europe, and the United States—men such as Ch'en Tu-hsiu, Ts'ai Yüan-p'ei, and Hu Shih—returned home in the second half of the 1910's to promote a New Cultural Movement and an intellectual revolution, culminating in the May Fourth Movement of 1919. The spirit of the age opposed traditionalism and Confucianism and advocated complete Westernization, "science," and "democracy." In this period of ideological ferment, two main philosophies emerged. John Dewey's pragmatism, espousing an evolutionary approach to social improvement, was introduced by his student Hu Shih, while the Marxist revolutionary approach was propagated by Ch'en Tu-hsiu and Li Ta-chao under the influence of the Bolshevik Revolution.

China had come a long way from a sneering rejection of the West in the early 19th century to the worship of it by 1920. A learned political scientist summarizes the sequence of change in the following words: "First, technologies affecting material existence; then principles concerning state and society; and finally, ideas touching the inner core of intellectual life. The Self-strengthening Movement of the T'ung-chih period, the reform movement of 1898, and the May Fourth movement of 1919 marked the climactic points of these three stages."[8] One could add a fourth stage as following the May Fourth Movement: the period of Contemporary China, which is generally not considered separately from the Age of Modern China.

The dominant theme of Contemporary China has been the struggle between the Nationalists and the Communists for the supreme power of state. The Chinese Communist Party was founded in 1921 amidst the intellectual revolution surrounding the May Fourth Movement. Under the guidance of the Comintern, it began to collaborate with the Nationalist Party in 1923. Dr. Sun, impressed by the success of the Bolshevik Revolution and desirous of Soviet assistance in reorganizing his party and army, was anxious to cooperate with the Soviets and the Chinese Communists. However, his death in 1925 doomed the alliance, and an open split came in 1927. Chiang Kai-shek, the Nationalist military leader, emerged as the new strong man, with a Nationalist government established in Nanking in 1928.

After the split, Mao Tse-tung and Chu Teh formed their own soviets in Kiangsi, virtually independent of the underground central party organization in Shanghai. Chiang launched five campaigns against them, routing them from southeastern China late in 1934. The Communists embarked upon the epic Long March of 25,000 *li*[9] (actually 6,000 miles) to the Northwest, where they re-established themselves. But hardly had the Communist problem been resolved when the Japanese struck in 1937. Facing a common enemy, the Nationalists and the Communists formed a United Front, though neither trusted the other. No sooner had the

8. Kung-chuan Hsiao, "The Philosophical Thought of K'ang Yu-wei—An Attempt at a New Synthesis," *Monumenta Serica*, XXI (1962), 129-30.
9. *Li* is one-third of a mile.

Japanese war ended in 1945 than civil strife erupted again. Depleted by the long foreign war, threatened by runaway inflation, burdened by the age-old problem of landlordism, and weary of fratricidal fighting, the Nationalists, despite their apparent military superiority and American aid, lost the mainland and took refuge on Taiwan. Mao established the Chinese People's Republic in 1949, after more than twenty years of struggle.

This cursory survey reveals several important stages in the development of modern China: from rejection of the West in the pre-Opium War period to the Self-strengthening Movement of 1861-95, to political reform and revolution of 1898-1912, to intellectual revolution around 1917-23, and finally to the rise of Chinese Communism in 1949. While history seldom moves in a simple linear fashion, the general pattern of development and major landmarks nevertheless serve as useful guideposts in evolving a conceptual framework.

Accompanying the great political changes described above was a fundamental transformation of the economy and the society. During the 16th and 17th centuries, the traditional agrarian economy first witnessed the emergence of an incipient proto-capitalism, which in the view of Chinese Marxist scholars would have led the country onto the road of capitalism even in the absence of foreign stimuli. Be that as it may, modern industries and enterprises did spring up, though under different circumstances, during the Self-Strengthening Movement in the second half of the 19th century, while foreigners operated manufacturing, shipping, banking, and trading firms in the treaty ports under the protection of the "unequal treaties." The juxtaposition of these different types of activity gave rise to a mixed economy, tinted with a semicolonial flavor, which characterized the Chinese economic scene for nearly a century.

Socially, the gentry who dominated Chinese society for centuries began to fade away after the abolition of the civil service examinations in 1905. The traditional social stratification of the four classes—scholar-official, farmer, artisan, and merchant—also crumbled in the face of two rising groups: the compradores and the militarists, who represented the new rich and the new power. Moreover, the influx of the Western ideas of individualism, freedom, and equality of the sexes eroded the Confucian precepts of family loyalty, filial piety, the Three Bonds, and the Five Relations.[10] When the individual rose to assert his status as the member of

10. The Three Bonds are those between the ruler and the subjects, father and son, and husband and wife. The Five Relations include two more: between brothers and between friends.

the state rather than of the family, the kinship society disintegrated. The pace of social changes accelerated after the Communist take-over in 1949, and the most dramatic change of all was perhaps the transformation of the peasant from an inert entity to an activist member of the state.

Modern China represents such a broad spectrum of kaleidoscopic change that I believe it cannot be satisfactorily explained by the restrictive theories of foreign imperialism, Western impact, or capitalistic and feudal exploitation. The dynamics of change suggests that modern Chinese history is not characterized by a passive response to the West, but by an active struggle of the Chinese to meet the foreign and domestic challenges in an effort to regenerate and transform their country from an outdated Confucian universal empire to a modern national state, with a rightful place in the family of nations. This view removes the pitfall of "foreign causation" of Chinese history and the unavoidable implication that China merely "reacted."

TOWARD A NEW SYNTHESIS

I propose to open the study of modern China with a survey of the "traditional" state and society during the years 1600-1800 as a prerequisite to the discussion of the above-mentioned stages of development. This approach differs notably from several that have been attempted in the past. Pioneer Western scholars of the World War I vintage tended to favor general works on Chinese foreign relations and relied almost exclusively on Western sources; they ignored or treated superficially the internal conditions. Scholars of the next generation shifted their focus from general works to monographic studies, taking China's response to the West as a main theme of investigation. Works of this period strove to see history from the Chinese side, and made much use of Chinese materials along with Western sources. They forged a new trend in research and enriched considerably our knowledge of modern China. More recently, there have been attempts to probe basic Chinese, social, economic, and intellectual forces independent of the Western impact, or to examine the changes in terms of the domestic milieu, all of which result in a more sophisticated scholarship.

The study of modern China has also been pursued with great zeal by Communist historians on the mainland, apparently in response to Mao's call that special attention be devoted to the modern period of Chinese history. They approach the subject from the standpoint of dialectical materialism, class struggle, and the changing nature of the society. While no consensus has been reached, there seems to be some tentative agreement among a majority of them on the question of periodization: (1) the period of the invasion of foreign capitalism and of peasant revolution, 1840-64; (2) the period of semicolonialism and semifeudalism, 1864-95; (3) the period of deepening national crises and the emergence of patriotic movements, 1895-1905; and (4) the period of the rise and fall of the bourgeois revolution, 1905-19. These four periods of modern Chinese history are said to constitute "The Age of the Old Democratic Revolution," as opposed to the period of contemporary Chinese history from 1919 to 1949, which constitutes "The Age of the New Democratic Revolution."[11]

The increased sophistication of Chinese, Western, and Japanese scholarship on modern China, and the flurry of activity among the Marxist writers lead one to think that the relatively young field of modern Chinese studies is coming of age. Through the application of new methodologies of the social sciences and the humanities, and the employment of multiarchival and interdisciplinary approaches, a great many sound and perceptive monographs have appeared in several major languages over the past three decades. Productive research and the general elevation of scholarship encourage the appearance of a comprehensive history, which should include the distillation of Chinese, Japanese, Western, and, where applicable, Marxist scholarship. China's deep involvement with the West makes it highly desirable, if not imperative, that her modern history be written in such a way as to reflect both the insight of Chinese scholarship and the kind of objectivity that only foreign scholars can bring to bear from without. Such a synthesis promises to place modern China in a proper historical perspective.

FURTHER READING

Chung-kuo chin-tai shih fen-ch'i wen-ti t'ao-lun chi 中國近代史分期問題討論集 (A collection of papers on the question of periodizing modern Chinese history), compiled by the editorial department of Li-shih yen-chiu (Historical Research), (Peking, 1957).

Feuerwerker, Albert, Rhoads Murphey, and Mary C. Wright (eds.), Approaches to Modern Chinese History (Berkeley, 1967), Introduction, 1-14.

11. Chung-kuo chin-tai shih fen-ch'i wen-t'i t'ao-lun chi (A collection of papers on the question of periodizing modern Chinese history), compiled by the editorial department of Li-shih yen-chiu (Historical Research), (Peking, 1957).

Hsiao, I-shan 蕭一山, *Ch'ing-tai t'ung-shih* 清代通史 (A general history of the Ch'ing period), revised edition (Taipei, 1962), I, chapter 1.

Li, Fang-ch'en 李方晨, *Chung-kuo chin-tai shih* 中國近代史 (Chinese modern history), (Taipei, 1960), Introduction.

Morse, H. B., *International Relations of the Chinese Empire* (London, 1910-18), 3 vols.

Teng, S. Y., and John K. Fairbank, *China's Response to the West* (Cambridge, Mass., 1954).

Tsiang, T. F., "China and European Expansion," *Politica*, 2:5:1-18 (March 1935).

———— "Chung-kuo yü chin-tai shih-chieh ti ta pien-chu" 中國與近代世界的大變局 (China and the great changes of the modern world), *Tsinghua hsüeh-pao*, 9:4:783-828 (Oct. 1934).

PART I

The Persistence of Traditional Institutions
1600-1800

2

The Rise and Splendor of the Ch'ing Empire

By 1600 a new age was about to dawn in China. For the first time western European explorers, traders, and missionaries began to arrive by sea in considerable numbers, bringing with them the seeds of a new civilization, while the Russians, having marched across Siberia, were pushing toward the Manchurian border. In time these two external forces, one from the south and the other from the north, were to influence greatly the course of history in China. Domestically, a momentous transition was also in the offing. The Ming dynasty, which came into power in 1368, had long since passed its zenith[1] and entered a state of rapid decline, beset with problems usually associated with the end of a "dynastic cycle"— eunuch domination of the court, moral degradation, political corruption, intellectual irresponsibility, high taxes, and famine. In this period of decadence, two devastating peripatetic rebel bands under Chang Hsien-chung and Li Tzu-ch'eng overran the greater part of the country for nearly twenty years (1628-47), generating untold misery and causing widespread unrest. Taking advantage of this dynastic decline and general disorder, an alien frontier tribe in the Northeast, the Manchus, rose to challenge the central power, ultimately succeeding to establish a new dynasty in China.

THE FOUNDING OF THE CH'ING DYNASTY

Historically, the Manchus[2] were a hardy stock of the nomadic Jurched tribe, living in what is today's Manchuria where they subsisted by hunting and fishing. During the 12th century they founded the Chin (Gold)

1. Reached during the Yung-lo period (1403-24).
2. Known in ancient times as Su-shen.

dynasty (1115-1234), which had subjugated the Khitans and even threatened the existence of the Southern Sung dynasty (1127-1279). Though conquered by the Mongols in the 13th century, they regained something of their former independence under the Ming (1368-1643) emperors, who divided them into three commanderies: Chien-chou, Hai-hsi, and Yeh-jen. They sent horses, furs, and ginseng[3] as tribute to the Ming court, and received Chinese agricultural products as gifts in return.

Geopolitics played an important part in the future development of the Jurched tribes. They lived in an area north of Korea and east and northeast of Liaotung where the Chinese had already settled, and were thus in a position to observe and profit from the Chinese experience and institutions.[4] Increasingly they came under the Chinese influence in modes of dwelling, eating, and drinking. After the mid-16th century, a growing number of Chinese had crossed the frontier and taught the Jurcheds to farm and to build castles and fortresses. The resultant economic and technological advancement considerably altered the character of the once nomadic society, and historical hindsight reveals that the time was propitious for the appearance of a great leader to lift the Jurcheds out of their feudal frontier existence.[5]

As reward for having assisted China in smoothing eastern border hostilities, the head of the Chien-chou commandery was made a frontier officer of the Ming with an imperially bestowed name, Li. This commandery was divided into the Left Branch (Tso-wei) and Right Branch (Yu-wei), both under the Chinese commander in Liaotung. In 1574 the chieftain of the Left Branch, Giocangga, and his son Taksi, allied themselves with the Chinese commander, Li Ch'eng-liang, in a campaign to chastise the unruly chieftain of the Right Branch. A second campaign was launched in 1582 against the son of the said chieftain, and in the melee that followed Giocangga and Taksi were killed. The manner in which they met death was a mystery; some accounts say that Giocangga was burned to death in the enemy fortress while Taksi was killed by a Chinese by mistake; others say that they were both captured and then executed,

---

3. A kind of root which the Chinese considered an elixir with rejuvenating properties.
4. Franz Michael, The Origin of Manchu Rule in China (Baltimore, 1942), 3, 11; Wada Sei, Tōashi kenkyū-Manshū hen (Studies on the history of the Far East-Manchurian volume), (Tokyo, 1955), Chapters 15-16.
5. Wada Sei, "Some Problems Concerning the Rise of T'ai-tsu, the Founder of Manchu Dynasty," Memoirs of the Research Department of the Toyo Bunko, Tokyo, 16:71-73 (1957); David M. Farquhar, "The Origins of the Early Manchu State." Paper read before the 62nd annual meeting of the Pacific Coast Branch, American Historical Association, San Diego, August 28, 1969.

or both were killed in action by firearms.[6] What followed was an intense internecine struggle within the household of the deceased, and in 1583 Taksi's 25-*sui*-old son,[7] Nurhaci, emerged victorious and won the right to succeed his father as a chieftain.[8]

The Ascent of Nurhaci. In his youth Nurhaci (1559-1626) is said to have frequented the house of General Li, the Chinese commander, and developed an interest in the Chinese novels *Romance of the Three Kingdoms* (*San-kuo yen-i*) and *All Men Are Brothers* (*Shui-hu chuan*). Well acquainted with frontier affairs, this ambitious Jurched chieftain was determined to avenge the deaths of his father and grandfather and was equally set on advancing his own cause. But for the moment his innate shrewdness dictated that he recognize his limitations and suppress his hostility toward the Ming court. It was clear to him that the unification of the Jurched tribes must be achieved before any projected attack on China. By two skillfully contrived marriages and a series of successful military campaigns, he rose rapidly in power and status. A Chinese captive, Kung Cheng-liu, originally of Chekiang, became his trusted adviser and handled documents and correspondence for him.[9] During all these years of preparation, Nurhaci showed the greatest fealty and respect toward the Ming court. In fact, in 1590 he personally brought his tribute to Peking, and in 1592-93 offered to lead an army to defend Korea against the Japanese invasion under Toyotomi Hideyoshi. In appreciation the Ming emperor bestowed on him the coveted title of "Dragon-Tiger General," the highest designation granted to a Jurched chief.

As a prospective empire-builder, Nurhaci sought the economic foundations of military conquest, drawing upon his earlier business experience to monopolize the trade in pearls, furs, and ginseng. He succeeded in amassing a considerable fortune, and by 1599 he was sufficiently prepared to start his campaign by attacking his neighbors while befriending the distant tribes. One by one the various Jurched tribes fell to him. His position had become so strong by 1607 that the Mongols conferred on him the title of Kundulen Han (The Respected Emperor); and in 1608, by a

6. Wada Sei, "Some Problems," 36, 40.
7. *Sui*, the Chinese age, is counted from the day of conception; hence, 25 *sui* is actually 24 years of age in Western calculation.
8. Wada Sei, "Some Problems," 41-50. Nurhaci's surname in Manchu, Aisin Gioro, means the "Golden (Chin) Clan." See Inaba Iwakichi, *Shinchō zenshi* (A history of the Ch'ing dynasty), (Tokyo, 1914), Chinese tr. by Tan T'ao, *Ch'ing-chao ch'üan-shih*, reprinted, (Taipei, 1960), chapter 7, p. 71.
9. Wada Sei, *Tōashi kenkyū*, 637-49.

formal agreement with the Ming general in Liaotung, he was able to fix the boundary of his domain and forbid any Chinese to cross it. By 1613 Nurhaci had conquered all the Jurched tribes except one, the Yehe of the Hai-hsi commandery, which resisted him with the aid of the Ming troops.

As a step toward creating a new state, in 1599 Nurhaci caused a Jurched alphabet to be created to replace the Mongolian script which had hitherto been used among the Jurched peoples since at least 1444.[10] In 1601 he invented the ingenious military "Banner System," whereby his warriors were organized into four companies (*niru*) of 300 men each, represented by banners of four different colors: yellow, white, blue, and red. By 1615 the number of companies had grown to 200,[11] and four more banners were created, with the same four colors but bordered in red, except for the red banner itself, which had a white fringe. Later, the size of the banner (*gūsa* or *gusai*) grew to 7,500 men, divided into five regiments (*jalan*), each of which commanded five companies (*niru*).

The Eight Banners were more than a simple military organization; they functioned as rudimentary administrative units during the transition from tribal feudalism to military administration and proto-nationhood. Everyone under Nurhaci, except for a few princes, belonged to a banner. Registration, taxation, conscription, and mobilization of the members were all managed by the banner organization. In time of peace the bannermen and their families engaged in farming and craftsmanship, and in time of war each banner contributed a certain number of men who fought under it. With this system Nurhaci organized his people into a war machine, which proved to be most effective. Chinese captured in the early campaigns were made bondservants, who were also organized into companies after the banner fashion, although probably they did not participate in actual fighting.[12] Eight Mongol and Eight Chinese Banners were

10. David M. Farquhar, "The Origins of the Manchus' Mongolian Policy" in Fairbank (ed.), *The Chinese World Order*, 203.

11. The figure 400 is given in many accounts, such as the *Great Ch'ing Collected Statutes*, the *Veritable Records* of the Ch'ien-lung Period, and Meng Shen, *Ch'ing-tai shih* (A history of the Ch'ing period), (Taipei, 1960), 21-22. But it has been found unreliable. See Chaoying Fang, "A Technique for Estimating the Numerical Strength of the Early Manchu Military Forces," *Harvard Journal of Asiatic Studies*, 13:195, 208 (1950); a recent study suggests that the banner system was a mixed product of Mongol influence and Manchu hunting tradition, and that the size of the *niru* was not fixed at 300 until 1615. See Farquhar, "The Origins of the Early Manchu State." Cited with permission.

12. For a succinct description of the bondservant system, see Jonathan D. Spence, *Ts'ao Yin and the K'ang-hsi Emperor: Bondservant and Master* (New Haven, 1966), 1-18.

added in 1634 and 1642 respectively, bringing the total number to twenty-four.

In 1616 Nurhaci boldly announced the establishment of the Chin state, and proclaimed himself "the Heaven-designated" emperor (*T'ien-ming*). Two years later, with the aid of the Qalqa Mongols he was ready to attack China. He enumerated seven grievances against the Ming, including the murder of his father and grandfather, the aid given to the Yehe tribe against him, the fact that Chinese subjects were permitted to cross over his border, and that the Ming had sent an inferior envoy to him.[13] This public airing of complaints was in fact a feudal declaration of war. Nurhaci swiftly advanced to the Chinese border and took the important city of Fu-shun. He captured a Chinese scholar, Fan Wen-ch'eng, whom he persuaded to change sides and who became his and his successors' trusted adviser.

The Ming court sent General Yang Hao and 90,000 soldiers to chastise Nurhaci but met with a disastrous defeat at Sarhu, east of Fu-shun. Having annihilated the main forces of the Ming, Nurhaci, riding the tide of victory, swept into the recalcitrant Yehe tribe and conquered it in September 1619. In the ensuing campaign against the Ming, he was stalled for over a year by the Chinese commander in Liaotung, Hsiung T'ing-pi. But when Hsiung was removed and executed by the court on false charges, Nurhaci advanced again and took the important cities of Liao-yang and Mukden in May 1621. Later, seventy cities east of the Liao River fell to him, and in 1625 Nurhaci moved his capital to Mukden. A year later, at the crest of his success, he led a vehement attack on Ning-yüan. The defending Ming general Yüan Ch'ung-huan, using cannons cast by Jesuit missionaries, for once repelled the invader. In this first major defeat of his life, Nurhaci was wounded but his pride was hurt even more; seven months later he died.

Abahai (1592-1643), eighth son of Nurhaci, carried on his father's unfinished work. He attacked Korea first to safeguard his rear and to force the Koreans to send him annual tribute in silver. He then turned on Ning-yüan, where General Yüan once again repulsed the enemy. Twice defeated by Yüan, the Manchus decided to avoid further direct confrontation with him; instead, they employed the circuitous tactic of finding a way into China through the friendly territories of the Mongols. A breakthrough was made in the Great Wall at Hsi-feng-k'ou, and Abahai advanced

13. Arthur W. Hummel (ed.), *Eminent Chinese of the Ch'ing Period* (Washington, D.C., 1943-44), I, 597.

to Peking. General Yüan hurriedly returned to defend the capital, only to discover that Abahai's spies had spread the rumor that a seditious relationship secretly existed between him and the Manchus. The young, suspicious Ming emperor fell into the trap and threw the general into prison, enabling Abahai to loot Peking and return to Mukden with rich spoils. There, in 1631, Abahai set up a civil administration with six boards, patterned after the Ming court, thus marking a further constitutional transition from the banner-style military administration to the Chinese-style civil administration. However, the organization of the boards was different—there were no presidents or vice-presidents as in the Ming system. Each board was put under the nominal direction of a Manchu prince (*beile*), who was usually away in the battlefield, leaving the actual administration to three to five assistants (*ch'eng-cheng*), including one Mongol and one Chinese except for the Board of Punishments which kept two Chinese assistants, presumably due to the greater need for experienced Chinese to handle complicated legal matters. Herein lay the origin of the Manchu-Chinese dyarchy, or rather Manchu-Mongol-Chinese synarchy, which later characterized the Ch'ing administration for 268 years.[14]

Following the establishment of the civil administration at Mukden, Abahai continued his work of conquest by attacking Inner Mongolia, Shansi, and Chihli. As a result of his many successes and in response to his rising reputation, many Chinese came over to him: in 1633 the Ming generals K'ung Yu-te and Keng Chung-ming joined him, and in the following year Shang K'o-hsi also came to surrender his services. In 1635 Abahai subdued the Hurkas of the Amur Region.

The Meaning of Manchu and Ch'ing. On the advice of his Chinese collaborators, Abahai in 1635 barred the use of "Jurched" and "Chien-chou," in favor of the term "Manchu." On May 14, 1636, he changed the dynastic title "Chin" to "Ch'ing" and proclaimed himself emperor. The motives behind these changes were never officially disclosed, but there are many interpretations and speculations. Abahai, aiming at the creation of a new empire, apparently wanted to obliterate anything reminiscent of Chinese suzerainty and to obscure the vassal status the tribes had endured under the Ming.

The origin of "Manchu" is of some interest. According to Emperor Ch'ien-lung, Manchu 滿洲 was the Chinese corruption of Man-chu 滿珠,

14. Piero Corradini, "Civil Administration at the Beginning of the Manchu Dynasty," *Oriens Extremus*, 9:2:136-38 (Dec. 1962).

which was the old name of the Jurched state in the beginning.[15] The noted Japanese scholar, Inaba Iwakichi, agreed with this explanation, and suggested further that Man-chu 滿珠 was an honorable and respected designation among the Jurched, Tibetans, and Mongolians.[16] Another interpretation is that Manchu came from a similarly pronounced Buddhist term Man-chu 曼珠, meaning "wonderful luck" 妙吉祥, which appeared in Tibetan Buddhist scriptures that were sent to the Jurched tribes. A fourth interpretation, rather mystical in nature, holds that Manchu is derived from the first character of Nurhaci's honorable designation Man-chu 滿柱 and the second character in Chien-chou 建州, to which the water-radical 氵 is appended to make it 洲. That these characters—Manchu 滿洲 and Ch'ing 清—contain the same water radical is no mere coincidence, but a deliberate creation according to the principles of Yin-yang and Five Elements. The character for the Ming 明 dynasty means "bright," and that for the surname of the imperial family, Chu 朱, means "red." The combined image of "bright" and "red" is "fire," which can melt gold, the character indicated by the Chin 金 dynasty. An inauspicious name such as Chin, then, must be changed. The creation of the terms Manchu and Ch'ing, all written with the water radical, augured the future quenching of the Ming fire.[17] Though possibly farfetched, this speculative interpretation ought not to be overlooked, inasmuch as it applies to a country in an age in which calendar-making, geomancy, and the ideas of Yin-yang and Five Elements figured prominently in public life.

Political expedience provided yet another motive for the change of dynastic title. Nurhaci had first adopted the title "Chin" in 1616 to arouse the nostalgia of the Jurched tribes and to prompt them toward the creation of a new empire like the Chin state of the 12th century. By Abahai's time in the 1630's, this emotional appeal was no longer useful. Many Chinese had come over to join his ranks and the objective of the new regime was no longer to unify the Jurched tribes but to overthrow the Ming dynasty. It was therefore necessary to win Chinese support and avoid offending their sensibilities. The dynastic name Chin could not serve this purpose, for the Chinese associated it with the killing, pillaging, and invasion of their country by the old Chin state in the 12th century. To expunge this odious connotation, Abahai dropped the name Chin in favor of Ch'ing 清, meaning "pure." The two characters are pronounced

15. Hsiao I-shan, I, 49.
16. Inaba Iwakichi (Chinese translation), chapter 18, pp. 58-61.
17. Li Fang-ch'en, 16.

nearly alike, but their meanings are vastly different. Furthermore, Ch'ing sounds more like Chinese and could more easily win Chinese acceptance.

Another theory is based on the historical fact that the old Chin state had conquered only the northern half of China, not all of it. The ambitious Abahai could not be satisfied with this imperfect record and so determined to make a fresh start with a new dynastic name. Finally, there is the interpretation, supplied by Emperor Ch'ien-lung, that Great Ch'ing meant Great East—if one matches the five directions with five colors, one finds the color for East is azure, or Ch'ing 青, from which the character 清 is derived.[18] If this interpretation is correct, then Ch'ing has little connection with the name of the old Jurched state Chin.

By assuming the title of emperor and adopting the new dynastic name, Abahai made apparent his intent to overthrow the Ming dynasty. Late in 1636 he sent two armies to invade China; they pillaged Pao-ting and many other cities and returned with great quantities of booty. Meanwhile, Abahai demanded vassal status of Korea in place of the existing "brotherly relationship." When Korea refused, he led a personal expedition and forced the Korean king to break off relations with the Ming court and accept the Ch'ing suzerainty. The *Li-fan yüan* (Court of Colonial Affairs) was then set up (1638) to take charge of Korean and Mongolian affairs.

The Seizure of Peking. Abahai now prepared to invade North China. Late in 1638 two armies were dispatched to attack the Great Wall. They looted more than sixty cities in Chihli and Shantung and penetrated as far as Tsinan, then retreated with rich spoil. In 1640 Abahai attacked Chinchow with a large force. In defense, the Ming court appointed Hung Ch'eng-ch'ou commander in Liaotung, transferring eight generals, including Wu San-kuei, and 130,000 troops to reinforce the city. Abahai routed more than 50,000 Ming troops and overpowered stubborn resistance. Chinchow fell and Hung was captured in 1642. He was treated with honor, and subsequently capitulated and joined the Ch'ing cause. Abahai now extended his territory to the key pass in the Great Wall, Shanhaikuan (Mountain and Sea Pass), but for the time being, he chose to avoid a direct confrontation with heavy Ming forces there. He turned instead to Northern Manchuria, and by 1643 he had brought the whole Amur Region under the Ch'ing rule. At this point his health failed, and he died at the age of fifty-one. His ninth son, Fu-lin (1638-61), a boy of six *sui*,

18. Hsiao I-shan, I, 186. The five directions are East, West, North, South, and Central.

was chosen to succeed him, under the regency of Jirgalang, a nephew of Nurhaci, and Dorgan, Nurhaci's fourteenth son.

The Ming court was not only threatened by the rising power of the Manchus but also by devastating internal rebellions. Dorgan had intended to make connections with some of the rebels, but before his plans matured the swift-moving rebel leader Li Tzu-ch'eng (1605?-45), nicknamed the "Dashing King" (Ch'uang Wang), advanced to Peking in late April 1644. Wu San-kuei, the brigade-general of Liaotung and commander of large forces at Shanhaikuan, was ordered by the Ming emperor to come to the rescue, but the city fell before his arrival. The rebel leader Li entered Peking on April 25, and the Ming emperor hanged himself on Prospect Hill, overlooking the Forbidden City. The rebels captured Wu's father, then in Peking, and forced him to urge his son to surrender. Afraid for his father's safety and apprehensive of fighting a losing battle with the high-riding rebels, Wu seemed inclined to surrender. However, when the news came that his favorite concubine (Ch'en Yüan-yüan) had been kidnapped by the rebel general, Wu changed his mind and beat a hasty retreat to Shanhaikuan. Now the troops under Li advanced on him. Caught between the rebels and the Manchus, Wu decided to invite the latter to join him.

Dorgan, who on the advice of his Chinese counsellor, Fan Wen-ch'eng, had encamped near Sanhaikuan to await developments in China, was delighted with the invitation. Manchu troops poured through the opened gates of Shanhaikuan, where Wu welcomed Dorgan in person. The combined armies of Dorgan and Wu dealt a crushing blow to Li, who retreated to Peking. There he killed Wu's father and the latter's entire family to avenge himself, looted the palace, and proclaimed himself emperor. As the Ch'ing forces advanced toward Peking, Li burned part of the palaces and the towers of the nine gates of the city. At daybreak on June 4, 1644, he escaped westward before the approaching Ch'ing forces, which entered Peking on June 6.

To win the support and confidence of the Chinese, Dorgan buried the Ming emperor and empress with honors, and paid tribute to those Ming officials who had lost their lives in the turmoil. Piously he declared that the Manchus had come to save the country from the rebels. Forces were sent out under Wu San-kuei and several Manchu generals to exterminate Li, who was killed in June or July of 1645, not by the forces but reputedly by villagers in Hupeh province while he was making a desperate attempt to raid for food. The other rebel leader, Chang Hsien-chung, notorious for his reckless killing of millions, was defeated and killed in Szechwan in 1647 by the Ch'ing forces. Thus, the two largest rebellions that had troubled China for nearly two decades were suppressed.

Although the Manchus had announced that they had entered China to avenge the death of the Ming emperor and to save the country from destruction at the hands of the rebels, it was evident that their motives were not entirely noble. They cleverly defended their occupation of Peking by announcing that they had recovered it from the rebels rather than having seized it from the Ming rulers. In October 1644 the Ch'ing court was moved from Mukden to Peking, marking the beginning of a new dynasty in China—one which was to last until 1911. The first emperor of the dynasty was Fu-lin. In accordance with the practice which discouraged use of the ruler's personal name, he was better known by his reign title, Shun-chih. The power of state was in the hands of Regent Dorgan, who decided state policies and directed the unfinished task of the conquest of China.

MING LOYALIST MOVEMENT

Though the Manchus had established a court in Peking, South China remained in the hands of Ming loyalists. In 1645 these loyalists set up Prince Fu as emperor in Nanking, the subsidiary capital of the Ming dynasty, to continue their resistance. However, he proved to be a feeble ruler, who displayed more interest in the pursuit of pleasure than in state affairs. Doting on watching frogs play, he was nicknamed the "frog emperor," while his chief minister, Ma Shih-ying, who was partial to crickets, was dubbed the "cricket premier." The only outstanding official in Nanking, Shih K'o-fa, who had been minister of war in the subsidiary capital, was not tolerated by Ma and was sent away to guard Yangchow. Dorgan, who admired men of talent and character, had tried to win Shih over, but the latter would not join the Manchu cause under any circumstance.

The Ch'ing forces advanced south, reaching the outskirts of Yangchow in early 1645. Shih resisted courageously, but the city could not be saved; the Ch'ing army under Dodo besieged it for seven days in mid-May 1645. Shih vowed that he would die with the city, and begged his officers that should he be captured before he could kill himself, one of them might do him the honor of taking his life. His aide-de-camp boldly offered his service. The city fell on May 20, but when Shih pulled his sword, intending to kill himself, his officers, who loved him deeply, could not bear the sight and rushed forward to hold him from hurting himself. The aide-de-camp was overcome by emotion and could not honor his pledge. The officers swept Shih along in their hurried flight but were intercepted outside the city. The Ch'ing commanding general treated Shih with great respect and offered him all kinds of amity to induce him to surrender, but the Ming loyalist could not be moved and was finally put to death. Then Manchus plundered the city of Yangchow for ten days (May 20-29) and massacred the people as a punishment for their stubborn resistance.

Several other uncoordinated resistance movements came into being to continue the Ming cause. One group of loyalists proclaimed Prince Lu their new leader in Shao-hsin, while another group established Prince T'ang in Foochow. The two princes were uncle and nephew, but could not stand one another. In the end both were defeated by the Ch'ing army: Prince Lu managed to escape to Amoy, while Prince T'ang was killed by the Ch'ing forces in 1646. Prince T'ang's brother, known as the New Prince T'ang, was then proclaimed emperor in Canton by still another faction of Ming loyalists. His rule lasted only forty days when the Ch'ing army took Canton (1646). All these movements having fizzled, a new and more durable loyalist regime under Prince Kuei, a grandson of Emperor Wan-li (1573-1619), came into being in Chao-ch'ing, Kwang-tung province. His fluctuating fortune need not be pursued in detail; suffice it to note that despite the many flights he had to make under the pressure of enemy attack, Prince Kuei succeeded in regaining control of seven southern and southwestern provinces by 1648. For a while it looked as though he might even stem the tide of Manchu conquest and restore the Ming dynasty. But ultimately the movement collapsed under powerful attacks from several directions by Chinese collaborators of the Manchus. Wu San-kuei drove Prince Kuei to seek refuge in Burma in 1659, and then crossed the border to force the Burmese king to surrender the prince, who was put to death by strangulation in 1662.

While these movements rose and fell in rapid succession, a more sustained resistance was organized along the coast by the Ming loyalist Cheng Ch'eng-kung, better known as Koxinga (1624-62). He was the son of Cheng Chih-lung, a onetime supporter of Prince T'ang, and a Japanese woman of the Tagawa family. Prince T'ang, much taken with young Cheng, had bestowed on him the imperial surname Chu in 1645; hence he was popularly known as the "Lord of the Imperial Surname" (*Kuo-hsing-yeh*), from which the Dutch derivation "Koxinga" comes. Prince

T'ang made him assistant controller of the Imperial Clan Court and treated him as an imperial agnate. In early 1646 the prince further favored him with the rank of earl and the title "Field Marshal of the Punitive Expedition" against the Ch'ing. In grateful acknowledgment of the imperial grace, Koxinga pledged lifelong allegiance to the Ming cause. However, late in 1646, his father, whom he could not dissuade, defected to the Ch'ing, thus providing a way for Ch'ing forces to attack Prince T'ang. In disgust Koxinga burned his scholar's vestments in a Confucian temple to mark the end to his civilian life and the beginning of a new military career. He gathered a following of several thousand men and took Amoy and Quemoy as his bases, declaring his support of Prince Kuei, who was then fighting the Manchus. For his continuous raiding of the southeastern coast of China, Prince Kuei rewarded him with the titles of marquis and later duke (1649). Early in 1655 he established seventy-two military stations and six civil bureaus in Fukien, thus perfecting his military and civil organization, which had a total strength estimated at 100,000 to 170,000 men. Koxinga patronized Ming officials and scholars, and engaged in foreign trade to raise revenue for his movement. The Ch'ing court, working through his father, urged him to surrender and gave him very favorable terms, but he remained adamant.

In 1658-59 Koxinga raided Chekiang and Kiangsu from the sea and took the key city of Chinkiang. He could have taken Yangchow and cut off the supply lines of the Ch'ing army, but instead he decided, against his generals' counsel, to advance to Nanking. There he suffered a fatal defeat in September 1659, and saw five hundred of his ships burned. He had to retreat to Amoy to recoup. With this fiasco the prospect for restoring the Ming was dimmed. He now found Amoy and Quemoy too restricted as operational bases, and turned his attention to Taiwan, or Formosa ("beautiful" in Portuguese), which was then under Dutch occupation. Having learned that the Batavian fleet under Jan van der Laan had left Taiwan and that only a small garrison was guarding the island, Koxinga launched an all-out attack in 1661 with 900 ships and 25,000 marines. The Dutch defenders were overpowered, and on February 1, 1662, a treaty was concluded between Koxinga and Governor Frederick Coyett, ending Dutch rule on Taiwan. With Taiwan as his new base, Koxinga was prepared for a long drawn-out struggle against the Ch'ing, who were virtually helpless to stop him. They could do no more than to have his father and brothers executed (1661), order the coastal inhabitants to move inland by 30 to 50 *li* (1662), and forbid fishing boats and commercial vessels to sail from the coast, thus cutting off Koxinga's sources of supply. Koxinga now represented the only thread of hope for the Ming loyalists. But he died suddenly on June 23, 1662, at the age of 38, reputedly of malaria but possibly by his own hand. The resistance movement was carried on by his son Cheng Ching, but the spirit was no longer the same, and there was continuous internal dissension. In 1683 Taiwan fell to the Ch'ing forces and a year later was made a prefecture of the Fukien province. With the defeat of this last loyalist group, the Ch'ing had completed the conquest of all China.

DYNASTIC CONSOLIDATION AND SPLENDOR

The Reign of Emperor Shun-chih, 1644-61. Shun-chih became emperor of China on October 30, 1644, at the age of seven *sui.* The power of state was exercised by his uncle Dorgan, who was given the affectionate title "Uncle Prince Regent." In late 1644 Dorgan reduced Jirgalang, the other regent, to the capacity of assistant regent with a stipend half the size of his own, and in 1647 dismissed him altogether. In 1645 Dorgan's title was expanded and raised to "Imperial Uncle Prince Regent" and in 1648 or 1649 to the most exalted "Imperial Father Prince Regent." Dorgan was the most powerful man in the country; his word was law. All high policies were made by him and the imperial seals were kept in his residence. Court officials sought only him and slighted the boy emperor. Those who memorialized[19] the emperor sent duplicate copies to Dorgan and awaited his reaction. On New Year's Day or other festive occasions, officials hastened to his residence to pay respect. So imposing was his position that he was excused from kowtowing to the emperor during audience. Princes and high officials whom he found unacceptable were dismissed, humiliated, or executed.

Dorgan no doubt derived immense pleasure from exercising the supreme authority of state; however, that he had in fact usurped the powers of the throne seems to have made him self-conscious. In a gesture toward setting things right, he admonished the court officials:

> Among the princes, nobles, and high officials today, I see only those who ingratiate themselves with me but none who respects the emperor. How can I accept this situation? Formerly, when T'ai-tsung [Abahai] died and a successor had not yet been chosen, the princes, nobles, and

19. A memorial was a minister's report to the emperor.

high ministers all urged me to take over the throne. I said, "If you people speak in this manner, I will commit suicide." I vowed that I would rather die than take it, and I supported the present emperor to succeed to the throne. If I rejected the throne at that critical moment, how can I accept you people who do not respect the emperor but who flatter me? From now on, those who are loyal to the emperor will be loved and used by me, while those who are disloyal and disrespectful to him will not be forgiven by me, even if they flatter me.[20]

That Dorgan was able to give such an admonishment served only to demonstrate how powerful he indeed was, and no courtier dared stand any the less in fear of him.

Dorgan's contribution to the young dynasty cannot be ignored, however. Under his direction, the Ch'ing forces took the provinces of Shensi, Honan, and Shantung; and in 1645 Kiangnan, Kiangsi, Hupeh, and part of Chekiang. In 1646 Szechwan and Fukien were added. In civil administration he retained most of the Ming institutions and practices, and welcomed Chinese officials into the government service, even permitting them the privilege of wearing the Ming costumes. He retained the service of the German Jesuit Adam Schall von Bell as director of the Imperial Board of Astronomy. Two of Dorgan's orders, however, greatly irritated Chinese sensibilities: the compulsory pigtail after the Manchu fashion and the encircling of rich Chinese farms for allotment to Manchu princes, nobles, and bannermen.

In reaching the summit of power at a relatively early age, Dorgan in effect halted his own career; he seems to have experienced the frustration of having no higher estate to reach for. He began to indulge himself in pleasure-seeking. When his wife died in 1650 he married the widow of his nephew Haoge, and ordered the Korean king to send him beauties for concubines. He had planned to build a city with a palace in the southern part of Jehol for his retirement, but toward the end of 1650, before this plan was realized, he died suddenly during a hunting trip at Kharahotun, near the Great Wall. He was only thirty-nine sui. His funeral was conducted with the honors and rituals due an emperor. The following year Emperor Shun-chih began his personal rule at the age of fourteen sui.

Now Jirgalang, the deposed regent, returned to power and the systematic vilification of Dorgan began. Other princes and high officials who had suffered during Dorgan's dictatorial days openly accused the dead man of having usurped the powers of the throne. Dorgan's honors were with-

20. Hsiao I-shan, I, 379. Translation mine.

drawn and he was posthumously denounced in a decree of March 12, 1651. Dorbo, his adopted son, was disinherited, and many of his henchmen were condemned and executed. Even his tomb was allowed to fall into disrepair. It was not until 1778 when Emperor Ch'ien-lung (1736-95) re-examined the merits and faults of the dynasty's founders that his good name was restored and he was exonerated.

When Emperor Shun-chih took over the reins of the government in 1651, he continued the same policy that Dorgan had found successful, of using Chinese assistance in the civil administration. He himself made diligent efforts to learn Chinese so that he could read Chinese memorials without relying on Manchu translations. He continued the "single-whip taxation system"[21] and improved the accounting system to reduce corruption and abuse. Irregularities were dealt with severely. To forestall secret opposition among the Chinese scholars, literary societies were forbidden. In institutions he made several innovations, among them the Imperial Clan Court and the positions of sub-chancellors of the Grand Secretariat, chancellors of the Hanlin Academy, and readers, expositors, as well as sub-readers and sub-expositors, of the same organization. The Ministry of Imperial Household was abolished in 1653 and in its place were established thirteen departments in the palace, run by the eunuchs, who wielded considerable influence over the young emperor. Although he warned them not to interfere with politics, it was impossible to keep them out of public affairs altogether, and in 1660 these departments were abolished.

The emperor had an academic interest in religion. From 1651 to 1657 he was in close contact with the Jesuit father Adam Schall von Bell, who failed, nevertheless, to convert him. After 1657 Shun-chih became deeply interested in Buddhism, especially the Ch'an (Zen) sect. Three great masters were invited to converse with him about Buddhism, calligraphy, novels and dramas, etc. Impressed and charmed with their wisdom and knowledge, he conferred on each an honorable title, while he himself humbly took a Buddhist name.[22]

Shun-chih's private life had not been a happy one. His empress, picked for him by Dorgan, did not please him, and after Dorgan's death and disgrace he felt the choice a shameful reflection on himself. In 1653 he reduced her status to consort and sent her away to a minor palace, and

21. Consolidation of all taxes into one general sum; hence the name. For details, see Chapter 3.
22. Hsing-ch'ih.

in the following year took another empress. In 1656 he became deeply enamored of the wife of his youngest half-brother Bombogor. When the latter died of anger and shame, his widow Donggo was made imperial consort of the first class. The emperor was very devoted to her for four years until her premature death in 1660, which caused him such grief that he did not attend to state affairs for five days. At one point he even considered committing suicide. He went so far as to tonsure his hair in preparation for entering the clergy, but was dissuaded by a monk whose wisdom he admired. As a token of his love, he had Donggo posthumously canonized as Empress Hsiso-hsien. On February 2, 1661, the emperor contracted smallpox and three days later died at the age of twenty-four *sui*.[23]

The Reign of Emperor K'ang-hsi, 1662-1722. Emperor Shun-chih was succeeded by his third son Hsüan-yeh, better known by his reign title K'ang-hsi, a boy of eight *sui*. He was selected primarily because he had already survived the dreaded smallpox and was in that measure more nearly certain of longevity. During his minority four regents were appointed: Soni, Suksaha, Ebilun, and Oboi. Of the four the last named was the most aggressive and domineering, ever ready to wield his dictatorial power and to place his own men in key positions. He intimidated Ebilun into submission, while Soni was too old and feeble to offer any resistance. Only Suksaha had the temerity to oppose him, and Oboi accordingly had him put to death by strangulation. Emperor K'ang-hsi, though a mere boy, resented Oboi's dictatorship; nor did the latter make any secret of his contempt for the young ruler. Even after K'angi-hsi had assumed personal rule in 1667, Oboi still refused to curb his scorn. One day, on the pretext of illness, he did not attend the court and asked the emperor to visit him. K'ang-hsi did so, and as he approached the sickbed the imperial complexion suddenly changed. Sensing some emergency the emperor's bodyguards rushed forward and retrieved a knife from under the mattress. K'ang-hsi dismissed the incident with a smile, remarking that it was not unusual for a Manchu to keep his weapon with him all the time. But the incident settled the young sovereign's determination to get rid of Oboi. With the help of Songgotu, the uncle of his empress, he hatched a secret plot. When Oboi visited the emperor a few days later, there was a group of Manchu boys playing games in the palace. Suspecting nothing,

23. There was an unofficial rumor that he had not actually died but had joined a Buddhist monastery, either at the T'ien-t'ai Ssu southwest of Peking or at the Wu-t'ai Mountain in Shansi, to free himself from the pain of losing his consort and to pray for the repose of her soul.

he took no special notice of the fact until he found himself suddenly seized and taken captive by these "boys," who turned out to be imperial guards in disguise. Charged with thirty high crimes, Obio was sent to prison. Ebilun, who had been his puppet, was demoted. This incident, taking place when K'ang-hsi was only sixteen *sui*, demonstrated the courage, determination, and quick action that were to characterize his long reign of sixty-one years.

As a ruler K'ang-hsi approached the ideal. He was intelligent, understanding, lenient, diligent, conscientious, and attentive to state affairs. He often admonished himself: "One act of negligence may cause sorrow all through the country, and one moment of negligence may result in trouble for hundreds and thousands of generations." His reign was marked by careful performance of official duties and frugal living in the court. It was under K'ang-hsi that the insecure Manchu rule was turned into a stable and prosperous state.

In civil administration K'ang-hsi performed a number of laudable works. Mindful of the suffering of the people, he put an end to the unscrupulous practice which had allowed the Manchus to take over good Chinese farms in desirable locations in exchange for their poor and badly located farms. He was concerned over the flooding of the Yellow and Huai rivers, and accordingly made personal inspections of the conservancy work being done there. Six times he toured the southern provinces of Kiangsu and Chekiang; four times he went beyond the passes in the north; and four times he visited the Wu-t'ai Mountain in Shansi. These tours served to acquaint the ruler with the local conditions and strengthen the ties between the central government and the various parts of the country.

K'ang-hsi also appointed a number of his trusted Chinese bondservants to various provincial posts as financial, textile, salt, or judicial commis sioners to insure the flow of funds to the Imperial Household and the transmission of confidential information to himself. He issued them secret instructions and they furnished him with information in "secret palace memorials" (*mi-che*) on which the emperor marked his endorsements. In this manner, K'ang-hsi built up a personal bureaucracy as well as an intelligence network.[24]

To demonstrate his benevolence toward his people K'ang-hsi reduced the land and grain taxes countless times; during his first forty-four years (1662-1705) of reign he remitted some 90 million taels of taxes, and in

24. Spence, 14-16, 222-40.

1712 alone, some 33 million. In that latter year, he issued the famous decree that the tax quota was to be based on the population of that year, and that no more taxes would be imposed on the basis of the number born after that year. He cleaned up corruption in government by a relentless application of justice; irregularities in civil service examinations were punished with particular severity. Justice was carried out regardless of person; as important an official as the Grand Secretary Songgotu, who had helped in disposing of Oboi, was imprisoned in the Imperial Clan Court and allowed to die in 1703, charged with having wrongly advised the crown prince and having unduly interfered in state affairs.

K'ang-hsi was a dedicated patron of learning. He was said to be well versed in Chinese classics and philosophical writings. In 1679 he called for a *Po-hsüeh hung-ts'u* special examination to recruit fifty learned men to compile the *History of the Ming* (*Ming-shih*). They were given preferred posts in the Hanlin Academy, to the jealousy of those who had risen from the regular examinations, who therefore called the fifty fortunate men "Wild Hanlin." K'ang-hsi's Imperial Study (*Nan shu-fang*) was filled with literary men, artists, and calligraphers. Frequently he gave banquets in honor of famous scholars and artists, and on those occasions they would drink and compose poems with great ease.

The emperor was particularly fond of the great Sung Neo-Confucian scholar Chu Hsi, whose commentaries on the classics he regarded as "the grand synthesis of hundreds and thousands of years of untransmitted learning, capable of opening the minds of fools and children and of establishing the ultimate goal (truth) for a myriad of generations." He honored Chu Hsi as one of the Ten Great Philosophers and promoted the Neo-Confucian metaphysical ideas of "Human Nature" (*hsing*) and "Rational Principle" (*li*). To be sure, K'ang-hsi's sponsoring of Neo-Confucianism was not without political motive, for Chu Hsi's ideas of Grand Unification and the importance of honoring the ruler made his own domination of the state a matter of course. Opportunistic scholars in the country therefore flocked to the Sung Learning, i.e. the Neo-Confucian School, while anti-Manchu scholars, favoring Han Learning, maintained an opposition.

As a result of K'ang-hsi's patronage of learning, several monumental works were compiled; of these, the most famous are the *K'ang-hsi Dictionary*, the important phrase dictionary called *P'ei-wen yün-fu*, the *Complete Works of Chu Hsi*, and a grand encyclopedia called *Ku-chin t'u-shu chi-ch'eng*, which dealt with ancient and modern books and comprised 5,020 volumes (*ts'e*). Many of these works contained a preface written by the emperor himself, and therefore bore the impressive and authoritative mark "Imperial Edition"; but apparently most of the prefaces came from the hands of his learned Chinese scribes.

The emperor's widely acknowledged fondness for learning naturally included an extensive interest in the arts and sciences. He had an impressive collection of paintings and calligraphy, and his imperial kilns turned out many beautiful pieces of porcelain which today are priceless. Many Chinese and European artists worked in his palace; the *Jui-i kuan* (Hall of Satisfaction) was said to be filled with artistic Jesuit missionaries who drew, painted, and engraved for the emperor. With the missionaries he studied mathematics and his accomplishments were described by his admirers as quite remarkable. It was said that K'ang-hsi so loved learning that "his hands were never free from books." But the extent of his accomplishments was probably exaggerated. His "vermilion remarks"[25] on the memorials have been found rather childish in style and poor in calligraphy.[26] Father Matteo Ripa, who served in the court for thirteen years and who engraved a map of China for K'ang-hsi in 1718, remarked in his memoirs: "The emperor supposed himself to be an excellent musician and a still better mathematician, but though he had a taste for the sciences and other acquirements in general, he knew nothing of music and scarcely understood the first elements of mathematics."[27] Nonetheless, K'ang-hsi was a conscientious ruler of unusually broad interests. He regarded learning as the basis of good government, and people's welfare as the root of peace and order. Constantly he scrutinized himself and his administration in the light of these two standards. A noted scholar of Ch'ing history characterized K'ang-hsi's reign of sixty-one years aphoristically: "Diligence in administration, concern for people, and orthodoxy in thought."[28] K'ang-hsi was truly one of the greatest and most admirable of emperors in the history of China. Some have compared him to Louis XIV and Peter the Great.

In military conquest K'ang-hsi completed the unfinished work of his

25. Marginal or interlinear comments written in vermilion ink.
26. Jonathan Spence, "The Seven Ages of K'ang-hsi (1654-1722)," *The Journal of Asian Studies*, XXVI: 2:206 (Feb. 1967).
27. Matteo Ripa, *Memoirs of Father Ripa, during Thirteen Years' Residence at the Court of Peking in the Service of the Emperor of China*, tr. from the Italian by Fortunato Prandi (London, 1855), 63.
28. Hsiao I-shan, *Ch'ing-tai shih* (A history of the Ch'ing dynasty), (Chungking, 1945), 64.

predecessors and laid the foundations of an empire which turned out to be the largest in China since the Mongols. His greatest accomplishment was the suppression of the Rebellion of the Three Feudatories (San-Fan). It will be recalled that the Ch'ing conquered China with the help of many Chinese defectors. General Wu San-kuei, who opened the gates at Sanhaikuan to welcome Dorgan's army into China proper and who later fought all over the country for the Manchus and drove Prince Kuei into Burma, was rewarded with the title of West-Suppressing Prince (P'ing-hsi wang) and given jurisdiction over Yunnan. Shang K'o-hsi and Keng Chi-mao, commanders of Ming forces in Liaotung who had surrendered to the Manchus, were made, respectively, South-Suppressing Prince (P'ing-nan wang) in Kwangtung and South-Pacifying Prince (Ching-nan wang) in Fukien. These were known as the Three Feudatories. Wu controlled an army of over 100,000 men while the other two princes maintained forces of 20,000 each. The military forces of the Three Feudatories cost the Ch'ing court some 20 million taels annually by 1667 —more than half the total state expenditures—while at the same time they were virtually independent within their own realms. Wu built a palace for himself in Yunnan, collected taxes, increased trade with Tibet, imported thousands of horses annually from Mongolia, and established monopolies on salt wells and gold and copper mines. So powerful and independent was he that his expenditures were not subject to examination or auditing by the Board of Revenue in Peking. His selection of civil and military personnel for appointments in Yunnan as well as in other provinces—Kweichow, Hunan, Szechwan, Shensi, and Kansu—could not be rejected by the Board of Civil Office or Board of War. This freedom to choose whom he wished without fear of interference from Peking became known as the "Western Selection" (Hsi-hsüan), i.e., the selection of officials by the West-Suppressing Prince.

The Three Feudatories were a source of great irritation to the Ch'ing dynasty. Emperor Shun-chih had put up with them because the new regime had not dared risk a civil war, but when K'ang-hsi came to power, the dynasty had been considerably consolidated and he decided to abolish the feudatories and cut the military power of the three princes. In 1673 Shäng K'o-hsi (the South-Suppressing Prince) was forced by his intractable son Shang Chih-hsin to request permission to retire to Liaotung. Taking advantage of this fortuitous occasion, K'ang-hsi not only granted the request but also used the pretext of the prince's retirement to order the abolition of the Feudatory in Kwangtung. Made uneasy by this act, Wu San-kuei and Keng Ching-chung, son of Keng Chi-mao, decided to feel out the court's intention by requesting the abolition of their feudatories and the complete transference of their troops, too, to see how Peking would respond. The court was divided: the majority of cautious officials preferred that Wu and his troops remain stationed in Yunnan, but a powerful minority consisting of the presidents of the boards of War, Revenue, and Punishments energetically called for the transfer of Wu and his troops to Shanhaikuan and the dispatching of the Manchu army to guard Yunnan. K'ang-hsi, then twenty *sui*, sagaciously reasoned that since Wu had been building up his resources for many years he would sooner or later rebel for reasons quite apart from the issue of abolishing the feudatories, and that his request to have his feudatory dissolved was, in a sense, his way of testing the firmness of the court. A decision was then made in Peking to accept the request for the abolition of the feudatories, and high emissaries were sent to the three princes to arrange the takeover.

Wu reacted by an open rebellion on December 28, 1673, calling himself generalissimo of all the forces of the country and proclaiming the establishment of a new dynasty, the Chou. He ordered the restoration of Ming style costumes and haircut; his army used white flags and his soldiers wore white caps.[29] He announced to the country his intention of overthrowing the Ch'ing and reviving the Ming. The other two feudatories joined him, and for a time it looked as if the Ch'ing dynasty might be toppled. The Manchu bannermen were unable to suppress them. K'ang-hsi used a number of Chinese generals in the campaign, and in 1681, after eight years of hard fighting, the Three Feudatories were finally put down. Two years later (see previous section) Taiwan under Koxinga's grandson[30] was also taken and turned into a prefecture of the Fukien province.

Once freed from the civil war, K'ang-hsi turned to the two problems posed by the Ölöd Mongols in the Northwest and the Russians in the Northeast. These two problems in fact directly involved one another, for there seemed to be a good possibility that the Ölöd and the Russians might form an alliance against the Ch'ing dynasty: both were in a position that made such a move feasible. The Russians had conquered Siberia and reached the Amur River; and during the 1640's and 1650's the

29. White, the funeral color, was presumably being worn to mourn the passing of the Ming dynasty.
30. Cheng K'o-shuang.

Cossacks from Siberia had made repeated raids on the Amur Region. In 1666 they founded Albazin (Ya-k'e-sa) as an advance base, threatening the Manchu homeland. Nearly simultaneously with this, during the 1670's, Galdan (1644?-97), khan of the Dzungars (West Mongols), a tribe of the Ölöd, had risen to power and aspired to build a Central Asian empire. He conquered Eastern Turkestan in 1679, invaded Outer Mongolia in 1687, routed the Qalqa (Khalkha, East Mongols), and penetrated as far as the Kerulen River. Thus an alliance with the Russians seemed nearly inevitable.

To prevent this, K'ang-hsi's strategy was first to crush the Russians at Albazin and then propose them a liberal treaty as a kind of sop. His general Pengcun attacked Albazin in 1685, ruthlessly demolishing it. Russian reinforcements were sent in the following year and new fortifications were constructed. A Ch'ing expedition was dispatched to besiege Albazin. Informed that a Russian diplomatic mission under Fedor A. Golovin was on its way, K'ang-hsi, with an eye to winning Russian good will, lifted the siege and prepared to enter negotiations with the envoy.

The result was the signing of the Treaty of Nerchinsk in 1689, China's first agreement with a "Western" power. In the treaty, Russia agreed to destroy her fortresses at Albazin and evacuate her subjects, while China agreed to cede some territory along the undecided frontiers and extend certain trade privileges to Russia. With this diplomatic exchange, K'ang-hsi felt relatively assured of Russian neutrality in his war against Galdan, whom, in 1696, after many years of inconclusive fighting, he finally defeated at Jao Modo. The following year the Ölöd chieftain died, and K'ang-hsi extended the Ch'ing rule to Outer Mongolia and Hami, clearing the way for his grandson, Emperor Ch'ien-lung, to complete the conquest of Chinese Turkestan in the 1750's.[31]

Galdan's death did not spell an end to the Ölöd problem, however. His nephew Cewang Arabdan gradually built up his power and in the early 1710's became a new threat to the Ch'ing. Cewang had married the daughter of Ayüki, chief of the Türgüd tribe which had migrated to Russia in 1630. This marriage made it quite possible that Cewang and Ayüki might join forces against the Ch'ing. To forestall this possibility and strengthen the Ch'ing tie with the Türgüd—and possibly to persuade the Türgüd tribe to return to China—K'ang-hsi dispatched a mission in 1712 to Ayüki. The mission, under the leadership of Tulisen, traveled through

31. For details of K'ang-hsi's war against Galdan and the early Russian-Chinese relations, see Chapter 5.

Siberia and reached the Volga in 1714. Tulisen met with Ayüki and presumably accomplished the objectives. He returned with an account of his travels which was entitled *I-yü lu* (Description of a foreign land), probably the first authentic Chinese work written on Russia during the Ch'ing period.

In both internal and external affairs, K'ang-hsi truly had accomplished much. He had developed a stable, frugal, and efficient civil administration, patronized learning, suppressed the Rebellion of the Three Feudatories, crushed the resistance movement on Taiwan, established diplomatic relations with Russia, and defeated the Ölöd under Galdan. Dynastic splendor had replaced the earlier insecurity, and the country took on the appearance of an empire. K'ang-hsi closed his reign a contented ruler. In 1722 he gave a banquet for all civil and military officials 65 years of age or older. One hundred eighty Manchus and 340 Chinese were entertained in the palace in two lots. The occasion was grandly described as "A Thousand Elders' Banquet" (*Ch'ien-sou yen*).

One matter, however, was of lasting regret to the old ruler, and that was the fate of his heir-apparent. Of his twenty sons who survived infancy, only the second—Yin-jeng—was born of the empress; all the others were children of consorts. Accordingly, Yin-jeng was designated crown prince, but he frequently exhibited a violent temper and such a degree of mental instability that finally, in 1712, K'ang-hsi was forced to strip him of the title and send him into confinement. The other sons plotted against each other to win the coveted designation, but K'ang-hsi never again named an heir. During the last years of his life, he seemed to show preference for his fourteenth son, who had been sent to Sining to fight the Ölöd leader Cewang Arabdan. It was said that on his deathbed K'ang-hsi designated him the successor, but that the ambitious and scheming fourth son, Yin-chen, with the help of General Lungkodo, commander of the Peking gendarmerie, secretly altered "the fourteenth son" to "the fourth son," who became Emperor Yung-cheng.

The Reign of Emperor Yung-cheng, 1723-35. Yung-cheng ascended the throne at the age of 46 *sui*. By nature he was severe, suspicious, and jealous, but extremely capable and resourceful; these characteristics were clearly exhibited in his administration. Five of his brothers who had opposed him in the struggle for succession were imprisoned and allowed to die there, and the Jesuit missionaries who had taken sides with his opponents during the struggle were deported. Even General Lungkodo, who had helped him attain the throne, was eliminated. Material in the court records of the K'ang-hsi period unfavorable to him was edited out. Throughout his reign he was busy suppressing evidence that suggested he might have usurped the throne. Yet in the administration of state affairs, he was a hard-working and conscientious ruler, who did much to consolidate the dynasty.

Yung-cheng felt that his father's rule, especially during the last years, had been too relaxed. He therefore began his reign by centralizing power in his own hands. Not only did he reject the request of the various princes that they be established as feudal lords with territories of their own, but he went further to deprive them of their military power. Whereas in the early Ch'ing period the emperor had directly controlled only the three superior Manchu banners—yellow, bordered yellow, and white—Yung-cheng took over control of all eight banners. He sent young princes to a special palace school called the *Shang shu-fang* to learn the virtues of loyalty and obedience, and forbade imperial clansmen to develop connections with provincial authorities. The bannermen were not allowed to establish clandestine relations among themselves.

In civil administration Yung-cheng was indefatigable. He personally read and commented on numerous memorials daily, working late at night to deliberate over state policies. He was probably the hardest-working man in the empire. His control of the officials was tight and autocratic; enforcement of law was carried out inexorably and vigorously, and spies were sent out all over the empire to inform on officials' dereliction of duty. To prevent any possibility of secret opposition, associations and cliques among officials and scholars were emphatically prohibited; the emperor himself in 1725 wrote "A Discourse on Parties and Cliques" (*P'eng-tang lun*) to warn the more venturesome against attempts in this direction. In financial matters, he combined the poll tax with the land tax. He also instituted the practice of granting officials liberal stipends called "anti-corruption fund" (*yang-lien chin*, lit., integrity-nourishing allowance) while prohibiting them from charging surtax or practicing irregularities, which, when discovered, were severely punished. Socially, he took the egalitarian step of raising beggars, hereditary servants, and boatmen from the despised status of "mean people" to that of the common people.

Institutionally, he brought in two innovations. One was the practice of depositing the name of the heir-apparent in a sealed box to prevent tampering with the machinery of succession. The box was placed behind a big tablet that was hung in his palace. Copies of the secret designation were locked in other safe places so that the authenticity of the selection could be double-checked upon the death of the reigning emperor. This practice was observed until the last decades of the Ch'ing dynasty. The other institutional contribution was the creation of the Grand Council (*Chün-chi ch'u*) in 1729 to assist the emperor in drafting edicts and offering him advice on military and state policy during the campaign against the Ölöd. The Grand Council originally had three members who stayed within the palace grounds so as to be available for service at any time. This small, tightly knit group could reach fast decisions, offer quick counsel, and guard secrets. Because it proved so useful, the Grand Council continued to exist even after peace was restored. It pre-empted the powers of the Great Secretariat, which was reduced to handling only routine matters.[32]

Military and diplomatic matters had not changed much from K'ang-hsi's reign: the twofold threat from the Ölöd and the Russians continued to trouble China. The Treaty of Nerchinsk with Russia had not settled the boundary between Siberia and Outer Mongolia, and the traffic between the Ölöd leader Cewang Arabdan and the Russians renewed Chinese fears of secret plotting between them. To carry out his father's policy of isolating Mongolia from the Russians in order to avert such an alliance, Yung-cheng was anxious to settle all pending issues with Russia by a new agreement. The resultant Treaty of Kiakhta of 1727 secured for China a clear delineation of the Mongolian-Siberian frontier, while Russia gained territorial concessions of nearly 40,000 square miles between the Upper Irtysh and the Sayan Mountains as well as land south and southwest of Lake Baikal. In addition, Russia was granted trade privileges and permitted to establish a religious mission in Peking.

Having settled the Russian problem, Yung-cheng sent an expedition to the Ölöd. During the campaign, however, reports came of complaints made by the Russians over Mongolian border raids: the Mongolian bandits had been looting horses, camels, oxen, and sheep. Wanting Sino-Russian relations to remain unimpaired and desirous of keeping Russia neutral, Yung-cheng dispatched T'o-shih, a vice-president of one of the boards, on a diplomatic mission to Russia in 1729—the first official Chi-

32. Alfred K. L. Ho, "The Grand Council in the Ch'ing Dynasty," *The Far Eastern Quarterly*, XI:2:167-82 (Feb. 1952). See also Silas Hsiu-liang Wu, "The Memorial System of the Ch'ing Dynasty (1644-1911)," *Harvard Journal of Asiatic Studies*, 27:30 (1967).

nese mission to a "Western" state. The mission was sent on the pretext of congratulating Peter the Second on his coronation, but upon his arrival in St. Petersburg, T'o-shih learned that the tsar had died and that the new ruler was Anna Ivanovna, a niece of Peter the Great. The Manchu envoy returned to Peking to obtain new credentials and in 1731 set out for Russia again. To St. Petersburg he suggested that if the Chinese attack drove the Ölöd to seek refuge in Russia, the Russian government should extradite their rulers and nobles but should keep the tribesmen in the country, under control, and prevent them from troubling China; in return China would give Russia part of the land that should be seized from the Ölöd. The Russian government was noncommittal, replying that it would discuss the question of extradition when it arose. Although the mission achieved no concrete results, it soon became clear that Russia, then fighting the Polish Succession War, was in no position to aid the Ölöd anyway. The Ch'ing forces sent to fight the Ölöd were at first defeated by Galdan Cereng, the son of Cewang Arabdan, who had died in 1727, but were able to score a victory in 1732 at Erdeni Tsu, making possible a negotiated peace at no great loss of prestige to China.

Yung-cheng's military and diplomatic careers, then, were not a resounding success; but that he sent a diplomatic mission to Russia and permitted the establishment of a Russian religious mission in Peking against all precedent amply illustrate his daring spirit and his absolute control of the state.

Yung-cheng had often been accused of being excessively autocratic and despotic, particularly in his literary inquisitions. In 1727 Hsieh Chi-shih was sentenced to hard labor for his criticism of the Neo-Confucianists Chu Hsi and the Ch'eng brothers, whom the dynasty held in high regard. A more celebrated case involved Lü Liu-liang, who was accused of having written an anti-Manchu book which stressed the differences between the Chinese and the barbarians (i.e. Manchus). Lü was put to the most severe punishment—the "lingering death"—and his son and students were all beheaded. Emperor Yung-cheng himself even wrote a treatise[33] to justify the Manchu rule in China and to warn against the danger of advocating racial revolution by the Chinese.

If K'ang-hsi's reign was characterized by tolerance, leniency, and liberality, Yung-cheng's was marked by strict control, severe punishment, and high efficiency. The spirit of his administration was reflected in the manner of his favorite grand secretary and president of the Board of War,

33. *Ta-i chüeh-mi lu.*

O-erh-t'ai, who was noted for his unbending, high-handed measures. To be sure, the emperor himself declared that a proper balance between strictness and leniency was essential to good government; but he did not take this to mean the tempering of justice with mercy. Rather it meant that a careful weighing of a given situation should elicit a clear picture of whether severity or leniency was called for and to what degree of either the administrator should resort. When strictness was needed, he should be strict; when leniency was warranted, he should be lenient. But there was no profit in mixing the two; the important consideration in each situation was "appropriateness" (*i*).

Yung-cheng could accurately be described as a Legalist statesman. Under him the highest form of absolute monarchy was achieved. All powers of state were concentrated in his hands. His reign was sometimes described as cruel, despotic, and autocratic—the opposite of K'ang-hsi's; but the opposites apparently supplemented each other and made possible the glorious reign of the next emperor, Ch'ien-lung.

After thirteen years of reign, Yung-cheng died suddenly at the age of 58 *sui*. He had been interested in the longevity theories of the Taoists, and it is possible that he died from the effects of the drugs he took. There was also a widespread belief that he was murdered by a female knight-assassin, the granddaughter of Lü Liu-liang, whom he had killed in the literary inquisition.

The Reign of Emperor Ch'ien-lung, 1736-95. Emperor Yung-cheng was succeeded by his fourth son, Hung-li, whose reign title was Ch'ien-lung. As a boy Ch'ien-lung had been a favorite of his grandfather, K'ang-hsi, after whom he sought to model himself. In disposition the two were in fact much alike, both straightforward, open-minded, and rather lenient. When Ch'ien-lung ascended the throne late in 1735 at the age of 25 *sui*, he prayed to heaven that he might be granted a reign almost as long as, but no longer than, his grandfather's, which had been sixty-one years. His prayer evidently was answered, for Ch'ien-lung did enjoy a prosperous rule of comparable length, and he, on his part, also honored his pledge by abdicating at the end of his sixtieth year on the throne—a complete cycle of life according to Chinese calculation.

Ch'ien-lung was well prepared for the throne, for during his prince-hood he had been given a rigorous indoctrination in the idealized role of the sovereign. When barely ten and a half years old, he was ordered by K'ang-hsi to come to the Palace School for Princes (*Shang shu-fang*), where ten Chinese and five Manchu tutors eagerly taught him the Confucian ethics and the Manchu military arts. Class hours lasted from dawn till mid- or late afternoon, and the curriculum included the study of the classics, history, literature, philosophy, court manners, filial duties, ritual performances, and later, administrative techniques. Riding and archery were also practiced. Ch'ien-lung showed little aptitude for Neo-Confucian metaphysics and classical literature, but was a keen student of history, especially of the chronicles that provided historical models of imperial perfection. His paragon and all-time favorite was the martial and heroic emperor, T'ang T'ai-tsung (A.D. 627-47), whose reign of military splendor and material prosperity, tempered by a studied humility and benevolence, was a source of inspiration to the young prince.[34]

During his years of study, Ch'ien-lung learned that the ideal ruler was one who had the "ability and desire to discover, select, and use ministers of high talent" and to "exhaust their talent in the service of the state." He was also taught to shun favoritism, to beware of clique machination and eunuch dominance, and to treat the lowly "according to their merits" and the superior talent with the respect due a teacher, with ample material rewards.[35]

Thus, when ascending the throne, Ch'ien-lung was thoroughly grounded in the art of emperorship. He was conscientious and responsible, if somewhat pompous and ostentatious. He thought his father's rule too severe just as the latter had thought K'ang-hsi's too indulgent, and he deliberately announced his own preference for the "middle road," i.e. the golden mean. During the early years of his reign he was assisted by experienced statesmen like O-erh-t'ai (1680-1745) and Chang T'ing-yu (1672-1755), whom he inherited from his father. The work begun by his predecessors now reached fruition. The country enjoyed peace and prosperity; the treasury was full; the dynasty glowed with an opulence and affluence it had never known before. And, as if to demonstrate his benevolence and the country's prosperity, Ch'ien-lung exempted the people from land-poll (*ti-ting*) taxes and tribute grains on several occasions.

After O-erh-t'ai's death in 1745 and Chang's retirement four years later, Ch'ien-lung came into his own. Like the son of a rich man, he enjoyed luxury and extravagance. After the pattern of his grandfather, he

34. Harold L. Kahn, "Some Mid-Ch'ing Views of the Monarchy," *The Journal of Asian Studies*, XXIV:2:230-31 (Feb. 1965).
35. Harold L. Kahn, "The Education of a Prince: The Emperor Learns His Roles" in Albert Feuerwerker, Rhoads Murphey, and Mary C. Wright (eds.), *Approaches to Modern Chinese History* (Berkeley, 1967), 15-44.

made elaborate tours of the country. Six times he journeyed to the south, ostensibly to inspect the water conservancy, but actually to enjoy the wealth and luxury of the southern provinces. Four times he toured the east; five times he went to the west; and numerous times he visited the birthplace of Confucius in Shantung. Frequently, he was accompanied by his mother, to whom he showed great deference in a studied display of filial piety.[36] Wherever they went, elaborate preparations were made to welcome them, and a trend of luxury set in. Ch'ien-lung derived genuine pleasure from observing the demonstrated wealth of his empire, and it displeased him to be cautioned about imposing burdens on the people.

Ch'ien-lung considered himself the lord-patron of letters. He revived special examinations for erudite men, of the type that K'ang-hsi had given, and invited famous scholars and recluses to join his government. His own accomplishments in the arts and letters were not particularly impressive, although he boasted of having composed 43,000 poems—a prolificness that defies credulity. A number of them have been termed doggerel, while some of his prose writings have been dismissed as "rubbish."[37] Doubtless, the better pieces were accomplished with the assistance of his Chinese secretaries. Moreover, Ch'ien-lung's penchant for displaying his calligraphy and seals on old master paintings raised the question of good taste, and when he jotted down 54 inscriptions on one handscroll and fixed 13 seals on another, he did not endear himself to the artistic world.[38] Nonetheless, Ch'ien-lung exhibited a great interest in the arts and maintained exquisite collections of paintings, calligraphy, porcelain, and cloisonné. His imperial kilns produced some of the most elegant porcelain and cloisonné the world has ever known, with designs that occasionally reveal European influence, for many missionaries taught Western drawing to Chinese court artists and amused the emperor with their accomplishments. For instance, in 1747 Michel Benoist built a Western-style fountain for him, and a number of Italian-style buildings were designed by G. Castiglione in the Summer Palace, called the Yüan-ming Yüan, located about five miles to the northwest of Peking.

The greatest literary project sponsored by Ch'ien-lung was the compilation of the *Complete Library of the Four Treasuries* (*Ssu-k'u ch'üan-shu*), which contained more than 36,000 volumes, arranged in the four

36. Harold L. Kahn, "The Politics of Filiality: Justification for Imperial Action in Eighteenth-Century China," *The Journal of Asian Studies*, XXVI:2:197-203 (Feb. 1967).
37. Kahn, "Some Mid-Ch'ing Views," 233.
38. Kahn, "The Education of a Prince," 30-31.

main categories of the literature: classics (*ching*), history (*shih*), philosophy (*tzu*), and belles-lettres (*chi*). Even the printed catalogue of this monumental library was an impressive work of scholarship: it consisted of succinct comments on 10,230 titles of works. Seven sets of the *Four Treasuries* were made and deposited in different parts of the empire.

It must be stated that Ch'ien-lung's sponsoring of literary projects was to some degree prompted by political motives: it provided the means to control virtually everything that was written and to expunge seditious references to the Manchus. Suspect and heretical views could be discovered and suppressed and their authors brought to account. According to the reports of the Board of War, the destruction of "unacceptable" books took place 24 times between 1774 and 1782, amounting to 13,862 works in 538 titles. Many considered his destruction of books the greatest catastrophe since the book-burning of the First Ch'in Emperor in 213 B.C. Indeed, the imperial control of learning led to more than sixty cases of literary inquisition during the Ch'ien-lung era. Wang Hsi-hou, who criticized the *K'ang-hsi Dictionary*, and whose own dictionary ignored the official proscription of forbidden characters for the names of Confucius and the Ch'ing rulers, was beheaded, and his two sons and three grandsons were sent into slavery. Ch'i Ts'e-shih, who had attempted to defend the Lü Liu-liang case of the Yung-cheng inquisition, was killed; and a Chinese scholar whose poem dealt with late Ming events and carried overtones of sarcasm regarding the Ch'ing was put to death.

Ch'ien-lung's military record was splendid. He solved once and for all the Ölöd problem, which had troubled the dynasty since its early days. So confident was he, in fact, of defeating the Ölöd that he did not even consider the possibility of Russian intervention. Nevertheless the victory did not come easily. It will be noted that Galdan Cereng, the powerful Ölöd leader, died in 1745. There followed several years of succession struggle between his two sons, a result of which was that the Dzungar tribe of the Ölöd was greatly weakened. Seizing upon this advantage, Ch'ien-lung sent an expedition to Ili in the Western Region (Hsi-yü). He enlisted the help of Amursana, the *taisha* of the Khoits (another branch of the Ölöd), and with Amursana the Ch'ing forces defeated the Dzungars and occupied Ili in June 1755. Amursana was rewarded with the title of prince and given a double stipend; but he was not satisfied. No sooner had the Chinese troops withdrawn than he started a rebellion of his own, proclaiming himself khan of all Ölöd. Once again Ch'ien-lung sent an expedition and in March 1756 retook Ili. Amursana fled to

the Kazaks. The Ch'ing forces then established a garrison in Ili and began colonization. But late in 1756 Amursana succeeded in instigating the
Dzungars to start an insurrection, and a third Ch'ing expedition was sent,
restoring order in Ili in 1757. This time Amursana fled to Siberia, where
he died of smallpox in the autumn of that year. To punish the Dzungars
for having twice rebelled under Amursana, the Ch'ing army massacred
them in great numbers, nearly depopulating Dzungaria. The tribal name
Dzungar was dropped in favor of the generic name Ölöd.

Following the Dzungar insurrection, the Moslems in southern Sinkiang
started their own rebellion under Khozi Khan, nicknamed the Little
Hodja, and his brother Durhan-al-din, nicknamed the Big Hodja. This
was suppressed by Generals Chao-hui and A-kuei in 1759. The whole of
Chinese Turkestan was thus pacified, and a military occupation followed.
A military governor was stationed in Ili, with jurisdiction over the northern and southern sides of the T'ien-shan Mountains. Large columns of
troops and a number of imperial agents and councillors were stationed in
key points. In 1768 the area known as the Hsi-yü, or Chinese Turkestan,
was renamed Sinkiang, meaning "New Dominion" or "New Territory."
The Ch'ing dynasty now joined the ranks of the three great dynasties
before it—the Han, the T'ang, and the Yüan—in the distinction of
having extended the Chinese rule into the Tarim Basin in the heart of
Central Asia.

In addition to the conquest of Sinkiang, Ch'ien-lung was notably successful in a number of lesser campaigns. Enormously proud of these
feats, he composed a eulogy of them in 1792 and called it *A Record of
Ten Complete Accomplishments (Shih-ch'üan chi)*. This *Record* included two campaigns against the Dzungars in northern Sinkiang (1755,
1756-57), the pacification of the Moslems in southern Sinkiang (1758-
59), the annihilation of the Chin-ch'uan rebels in two campaigns (1747-
49, 1771-76), the suppression of a rebellion on Taiwan (1787-88), the
subjugation of Burma (1766-70), the subjection of the Annamese to his
suzerainty (1788-89), and two separate conquests of the Gurkhas. To
give things their proper perspective it must be noted that except for the
conquest of Sinkiang, which was a great military accomplishment by any
standard, the other victories enumerated in the *Record* were only police
actions or localized campaigns which deserved little special recognition.
But in the very act of compiling such a record and calling himself the
"Old Man of Ten Complete Accomplishments" (*Shih-ch'üan lao-jen*),
Ch'ien-lung demonstrated his self-satisfaction and love of show. A similar

spirit was shown when, in studied emulation of K'ang-hsi, he gave a grand banquet in honor of 3,000 elderly (aged 60 or above) officials. He even composed a poem himself to celebrate the occasion:

> Grandfather and grandson
> Twice feasted with thousands of elders
> In all of history
> There is no parallel.

Indeed, Ch'ien-lung had much to be proud of and much to be grateful for. He ruled over an empire that stretched from Outer Mongolia in the north to Kwangtung in the south, and from the coast in the east to Central Asia in the west. Peace and prosperity prevailed within the country, and numerous peripheral states came to pay tribute. Dozens of nations in East, Southeast, and Central Asia acknowledged Chinese suzerainty over them: from Korea in the northeast, to Annam, Burma, and Siam in the south; Bhutan, Nepal, and the Gurkhas in the southwest; and a number of khanates in Central Asia such as Khokand, Bukhara, Burut, Badakshan, Afghanistan, and the Kazaks. Ch'ien-lung proudly presided over this vast empire, which was larger than those of the Han and T'ang and second only to the Mongol Empire of the 13th century. It was a golden era in Ch'ing—and Chinese—history.

But in the very splendor of the dynasty the elements of ultimate ruin were already present. Ch'ien-lung's senility and the degeneration of his judgment had much to do with the decline. At the age of 65, he noticed a 25-year-old imperial bodyguard called Ho-shen (1750-99). Handsome and intelligent, the young man's facial features were said to resemble those of one of Emperor Yung-cheng's consorts with whom Ch'ien-lung had unsuccessfully attempted a liaison.[39] Within a year of his discovery by the emperor, Ho-shen was promoted to vice-president of the Board of Revenue, two months later was made a grand councillor, and a month after that a minister of the Imperial Household—posts usually filled by the most meritorious and venerable officials. In 1777, when barely 27, Ho-shen was given the unusual privilege of riding a horse in the Forbidden City, a favor reserved for the highest officials who were too old to walk. Later he was given control of the Boards of Revenue and of Civil Office, enabling him to control the revenue of the empire and appoint his henchmen to important and lucrative positions. His hold on the

39. The consort was later sent to death by Ch'ien-lung's empress. See Kahn, "Some Mid-Ch'ing Views," 239.

senile emperor was further strengthened when in 1790 his son was married to Ch'ien-lung's youngest daughter. Secure of the emperor's favor and approbation, Ho-shen enjoyed complete freedom of action. He was openly corrupt and practiced extortion on a large scale. His satellites in the government followed suit, and his associates in the military service unnecessarily prolonged campaigns so as to have the benefit of additional official funds.

The question naturally arises, why did not some upright officials impeach Ho-shen? Large-scale organized attack was precluded by the standing Ch'ing injunction against "clique formation," while direct individual attack was also considered inadvisable because it could be construed as an implied criticism of the emperor. Ch'ien-lung was extremely sensitive as to his fitness to rule, and any criticism of his choice of ministers would reflect badly on his judgment. Moreover, Ho-shen's hold on the aged sovereign and the latter's weakness for him was too obvious to escape notice. Ho-shen's accusers, therefore, chose not to attack him directly but to accuse his subordinates and servants of corruption and irregularities, in hopes of implicating him. But Ho-shen was too clever to be trapped. When investigations took place, frequently he was tipped off in advance by some court sources and managed to hide evidence of misconduct or to replace the embezzled funds in time to avoid discovery. When the accusers could not prove their case, they became the accused and were punished. However, Ch'ien-lung sometimes commuted the sentences or exonerated the accusers. It was, in a sense, the imperial way of admitting Ho-shen's guilt.[40]

The last years of Ch'ien-lung's reign were indeed shameful. Although he retired in 1795 after sixty years of reign, he still ruled behind the scenes as Super Emperor (*T'ai shang-huang*). Not until his death in 1799 was his son, Emperor Chia-ch'ing, able to execute Ho-shen. From the time he caught Ch'ien-lung's attention in 1775 until his death in 1799, Ho-shen plundered the state and amassed an incredible fortune. His confiscated property was estimated at 800,000,000 taels—nearly one and a half billion dollars!

The influence of Ho-shen spread like a dye. There was corruption at different levels within and without the capital, among civil as well as military personnel. Bannermen developed licentious habits and became

40. For details, see David S. Nivison, "Ho-shen and His Accusers: Ideology and Political Behavior in the Eighteenth Century" in David S. Nivison and Arthur F. Wright (eds.), *Confucianism in Action* (Stanford, 1959), 209-43.

totally useless as a military force. The Chinese Green Standard army was beset with irregular practice and lost much of its earlier fighting spirit. Military defense of the frontiers was neglected. The habit of luxury and big spending contributed to moral degradation and a general decline of the dynasty. Ch'ien-lung's six tours to the south cost at least 20 million taels, while the expenditures of his other tours to the east, west and north were not even known. His Ten Complete Accomplishments were made at great cost to the state: the Sinkiang campaigns, 23,110,000 taels; the first and second Chin-ch'uan campaigns, 7,750,000 and 63,700,000 taels respectively; the Burmese campaign, 9,110,000 taels; the Taiwan campaign, 10,000,000 taels; the Annam campaign, 1,000,000 taels; and the figures for the Gurkhas campaigns were unknown.[41] All told, the Ten Complete Accomplishments cost about 120 million taels, against an average annual revenue of some 40 million taels. These massive spendings and the general trend toward luxury which he had inculcated in the empire set the machinery in motion for great financial difficulties in the future.

Thus as Ch'ien-lung's reign drew to a close, China was experiencing the beginning of a dynastic decline characterized by official corruption, a degraded military, and fiscal imbalance. The splendor of past glory remained on the surface, but beneath it the substance of grandeur was gone. It was at this juncture that the Westerners began to intensify their bid to open China to trade and diplomacy, and a new phase of history began.

FURTHER READING

A-kuei 阿桂 (ed.), *Huang-ch'ao k'ai-kuo fang-lüeh* 皇朝開國方略 (A brief account of the founding of our imperial dynasty), (1887), 6 ts'e.

Corradini, Piero, "Civil Administration at the Beginning of the Manchu Dynasty," *Oriens Extremus*, 9:2:133-38 (Dec. 1962).

Fang, Chaoying, "A Technique for Estimating the Numerical Strength of the Early Manchu Military Forces," *Harvard Journal of Asiatic Studies*, 13:192-215 (1950).

Hsiao, I-shan 蕭一山, *Ch'ing-tai shih* 清代史 (A history of the Ch'ing dynasty), (Chungking, 1945), chapters 3-4.

————, *Ch'ing-tai t'ung-shih* 清代通史 (A general history of the Ch'ing period), revised edition (Taipei, 1962), I, chapters 1-5, 8-21, 26-30; II, chapters 1-4.

Huang, Pei, "Five Major Sources for the Yung-cheng Period, 1723-1735," *The Journal of Asian Studies*, XXVII:4:847-57 (Aug. 1968).

41. Hsiao I-shan, II, 233-34.

Hummel, Arthur W., *Eminent Chinese of the Ch'ing Period* (Washington, D.C., 1943-44). Biographies of Nurhaci, Abahai, Dorgan, Shun-chih (Fu-lin), K'ang-hsi (Hsüan-yeh), Yung-cheng (Yin-chen), and Ch'ien-lung (Hung-li).

Inaba, Iwakichi 稻葉岩吉, *Shinchō zenshi* 清朝全史 (A history of the Ch'ing dynasty), (Tokyo, 1914), Chinese tr. by Tan T'ao under the title, *Ch'ing-ch'ao ch'üan-shih* 清朝全史 (Taipei, 1960), chapters 1-2, 7-12, 17-18, 24-32, 39-43, 47-48.

Ishida, Mikinosuke, "A Biographical Study of Giuseppe Castiglione (Lang Shih-ning), A Jesuit Painter in the Court of Peking under the Ch'ing Dynasty," *Memoirs of the Research Department of the Toyo Bunko*, 19:79-121 (Tokyo, 1960).

Kahn, Harold L., "The Education of a Prince: The Emperor Learns His Roles" in Albert Feuerwerker, Rhoads Murphey, and Mary C. Wright (eds.), *Approaches to Modern Chinese History* (Berkeley, 1967), 15-44.

———, "Some Mid-Ch'ing Views of the Monarch," *The Journal of Asian Studies*, XXIV:2:29-43 (Feb. 1965).

———, "The Politics of Filiality: Justification for Imperial Action in Eighteenth-Century China," *The Journal of Asian Studies*, XXVI:2:197-203 (Feb. 1967).

K'ang-hsi, *The Sacred Edict, Containing Sixteen Maxims of Emperor Kang-hi*, tr. by the Rev. William Milne, second edition (Shanghai, 1870).

Meng, Shen 孟森, *Ch'ing-tai shih* 清代史 (A history of the Ch'ing period), (Taipei, 1960), chapters 1-3.

Michael, Franz, *The Origin of Manchu Rule in China* (Baltimore, 1942).

Miyazaki, Ichisada 宮崎市定, *Yō sei-tei, Chūgoku no dokusai kunshu* 雍正帝, 中國の獨裁君主 (The Yung-cheng Emperor, China's autocratic ruler), (Tokyo, 1950).

Naitō, Torajirō 內藤虎次郎, *Shinchōshi tsuron* 清朝史通論 (A survey of the history of the Ch'ing dynasty), (Tokyo, 1944).

Nivison, David S., "Ho-shen and His Accusers: Ideology and Political Behavior in the Eighteenth Century" in David S. Nivison and Arthur F. Wright (eds.), *Confucianism in Action* (Stanford, 1959), 209-43.

Ripa, Matteo, *Memoirs of Father Ripa, during Thirteen Years' Residence at the Court of Peking in the Service of the Emperor of China*, tr. from the Italian by Fortunato Prandi (London, 1855).

Shen, Yün 沈雲, *Tai-wan Cheng-shih shih-mo* 台灣鄭氏始末 (A complete account of the Koxinga family on Taiwan), (1836), 6 *chüan*.

Spence, Jonathan D., *Ts'ao Yin and the K'ang-hsi Emperor: Bondservant and Master* (New Haven, 1966).

———, "The Seven Ages of K'ang-hsi (1654-1722)" *The Journal of Asian Studies*, XXVI:2:205-11 (Feb. 1967).

Sugimura, Yūzō 杉村勇造, *Ken-ryū kotei* 乾隆皇帝 (Emperor Ch'ien-lung), (Tokyo, 1961).

Wada, Sei 和田清, *Tōashi kenkyū—Manshū hen* 東亞史研究(滿洲篇) (Studies

on the history of the Far East—Manchurian volume), (Tokyo, 1955).
————, "Some Problems Concerning the Rise of T'ai-tsu, the Founder of
Manchu Dynasty," *Memoirs of the Research Department of the Toyo
Bunko* (Tokyo, 1956).
Yang, Lu-jung 楊陸榮, *San-Fan chi-shih pen-mo* 三藩記事本末 (A complete ac-
count of the Three Feudatories), (1717), 4 *chüan*.

3

Political and Economic Institutions

POLITICAL STRUCTURE

Though the Ch'ing was an alien dynasty, it accepted the traditional Confucian order and recruited Chinese scholars into the officialdom to work side by side with the Manchus, forming a kind of ethnic dyarchy within a political monarchy. The government was essentially an autocracy. There was no division of power in the Western sense; the emperor was the absolute ruler in every branch of the regime, whether executive, legislative, or judicial. He governed without even a prime minister, and was truly qualified to pronounce: "L'état, c'est moi!" This high concentration of power placed far more and far greater demands on the emperor than on any other man in the empire; K'ang-hsi once remarked that though his ministers were free to come and go, he was not. Ch'ing absolutism was doubtless an inheritance from the Ming, as indeed were most of its institutions and practices; only a few additions were made to suit special occasions and needs.

The Emperor and the Nobility. The emperor, at the summit of the hierarchy, gave to state affairs a personal attention seldom tendered by earlier rulers. He read all the memorials from every corner of the empire—from 50 or 60 to 100 daily—and wrote marginal or interlinear comments on each of them in vermilion ink. In his executive capacity he decided all important state policies, made appointments, conferred titles, approved promotions, demotions, and dismissals, awarded pensions, commanded the army, and ratified treaties with foreign powers. As the supreme legislator he enacted, annulled, and amended laws by decrees and edicts. Judicially, he was the highest court of appeal, granting pardons and reprieves as a mark of favor. Indeed, the highest form of absolute monarchism was reached under the Ch'ing.

The emperor was the religious head, too. He sanctioned the Dalai Lama, the chief Taoist, and the Duke K'ung (direct descendants of Confucius), and offered sacrifices to heaven, earth, Confucius, Buddha, and other focuses of reverence. In times of natural calamities—manifestations of nature's anger—he made offerings to heaven to expiate his sins, which were considered to be the cause.

Finally, in his sponsoring of the compilation and publication of books and encyclopedias, and in his patronage of learning generally, he showed himself the intellectual leader of his people. He ordered the administering of provincial and metropolitan examinations and conducted the palace examinations himself. Often he personally questioned the candidates and decided the ranking of the first ten successful ones; and occasionally he would even lecture to the Imperial College (*Kuo-tzu chien*). All degrees were conferred in his name.

For all of his near-omnipotence, the emperor was nevertheless subject to some restrictions. The Confucian cult demanded that he be moral, virtuous, and attentive to the needs of his subjects; and it bound him to be respectful on ceremonial occasions and to follow the good precedents of the past, setting a living example for the millions. He should not run counter to traditions and social customs, nor should he ignore the "public opinion" of the literati and the gentry. Except in great emergency he could not call into service officials who were in mourning. When he referred cases to his high ministers—the Six Boards (*Liu-pu*) and the Nine Ministers (*Chiu-ch'ing*)—he was morally bound by their unanimous recommendations. As a member of the imperial household, he could not ignore the imperial family law or take lightly the admonitions and instructions of his ancestors, which were considered sacred and inviolable. To neglect these restraints would be to justify remonstration by the censors or a *coup d'état* or even a rebellion. Rebellion—a corollary of the Mencius idea of the popular right to revolt—was the strongest check on a ruler's conduct. If the emperor exercised his supreme powers conscientiously and at the same time honored these provisions, he could be reasonably sure of his ministers' admiration and the support of his subjects, and could thereby justify his exercising of the fictitious Mandate of Heaven in his role as the Son of Heaven (*T'ien-tzu*) and mediator between man and nature.

The nobility in the Ch'ing system consisted of three categories: the imperial clansmen, the titular nobles, and the bannermen. The clansmen were the direct male descendants of Nurhaci, numbering about 700 from the late 16th century through the end of the 19th. They were governed by an Imperial Clan Court (*Tsung-jen fu*) whose function it was to keep their identity. This Court kept records of them from birth to death, including marriages, appointments, promotions, demotions, dismissals, or whatever. It also operated their schools, conducted separate examinations for literary degrees, tried them for offenses, and in general supervised their activities. The emperor gave them land, official residences, and annual silver and rice allowances. But they were kept more or less isolated: they were not allowed to communicate with the provincial authorities, and as a rule were not appointed to the all-important Grand Secretariat or, later, to the Grand Council. Exceptions were made only rarely during the 17th and 18th centuries, though in the last decades of the dynasty the restriction was relaxed somewhat: Prince Kung, for instance, was appointed to the Grand Council in 1853.

The titular nobility were divided into five classes, each of which was further divided into various grades. There were three grades of duke (*kung*), four each of marquis (*hou*), earl (*po*), viscount (*tzu*), and baron (*nan*). These nobles, in addition to their rice stipends, received silver and land from the emperor commensurate with their respective rank and grade, ranging from 700 taels annually for a first-grade duke to 260 taels for a fourth-grade baron. Most of these titles were accorded civil and military officers who had merited such honor. The titular nobility did not function as a class by itself, and as a group had little influence in the society.

The bannermen, the third type of nobility, were also given preferential treatment by the emperor in the form of annual pensions, land for cattle-raising, and allotments of rice and cloth. The Manchu bannermen usually received more favorable treatment than their Mongol and Chinese counterparts. A Manchu bannerman, for instance, might receive 50 *mou* of land (*mou* = ⅓ acre), while a Mongol would get 35 *mou* and a Chinese only 25. To preserve their dignity and special status all bannermen were excluded from participation in trade and labor. Should a bannerman wish so to engage himself, however, he could petition to debannerize himself. Offenses committed by the bannermen were tried not by the ordinary civil magistrates but by the Tartar General (Manchu General-in-Chief). A large portion of the bannermen were stationed in Peking and its vicinity, while the rest were assigned garrison duties throughout the country.

Central Government Organizations. Before 1729 the most important organ in the central government was the Grand Secretariat (*Nei-ko*),
which the first Ming emperor had instituted after he abolished the office
of prime minister in 1380.[1] The Ch'ing dynasty inherited this institution
and appointed four grand secretaries and two associate grand secretaries
to comprise it, half of whom were Manchus and half Chinese. They
formed an advisory group to the emperor and were the closest equivalent
to the old office of prime minister, but there was no leader among them
officially, and they could not issue orders directly to the Six Boards or
provincial governments: only the emperor could do that. The grand secretaries drafted edicts, declarations, and manifestos for the emperor and
assisted him in deciding high policies. As they controlled access of memorials and were able to pass judgment on them before submitting them
to the emperor, they had the power to influence his decisions. In addition they performed a number of strictly ceremonial functions, such as
preparing eulogies and prayers for use in state sacrifices, presenting new
metropolitan graduates (*chin-shih*) to the emperor, and recommending
posthumous titles be bestowed upon deceased emperors, empresses, and
noteworthy officials and scholars. Because they were close to the source
of power, they commanded great prestige and were regarded as the highest officials in the empire. Only holders of the *chin-shih* degree could be
appointed grand secretaries, who enjoyed an indefinite tenure in this office, simply because there existed no higher one for them to be advanced
to. The average length of tenure was eight years and nine months, but between 1644 and 1773 one grand secretary held office for more than 30
years, and twenty-four lasted more than 10 years.[2] All the grand secretaries held concurrent appointments either as presidents of the Six
Boards or other important offices.

Though it was considered the most exalted organization in the empire,
the Grand Secretariat suffered some loss of power during K'ang-hsi's
reign, when the emperor came to rely on his own secretaries in the Imperial Study (*Nan shu-fang*) to draft edicts and decrees for him in preference to the grand secretaries. And in 1729 came the really severe blow:
the establishment of the Grand Council (*Chün-chi ch'u*). This new organization pre-empted the Grand Secretariat's role as the closest adviser
to the sovereign and usurped most of its original functions, leaving it

1. S. Y. Teng, "Ming T'ai-tsu's Destructive and Constructive Work," *Chinese Culture,* VIII:3:20 (Sept. 1967).
2. Pao Chao Hsieh, *The Government of China* (1644-1911), (Baltimore, 1925),
74-75.

only routine matters to handle. Grand secretaryships then became merely honorary titles granted to meritorious high civil officials; they did not require attendance to any regular business.

The Grand Council, established during a military campaign against the Ölöd in the Northwest, was conceived as a result of Emperor Yung-cheng's need for a small, tightly knit group of aides to help him draft edicts and to offer counsel. The decision-making power remained with the emperor, but the grand councillors, because of their proximity to the ruler, were in a position to influence the formation of policies. The councillors numbered three at the outset but increased to ten in 1745; their average number, however, was five or six, divided between Manchus and Chinese. Officially they were equals, but unofficially there was always a ranking member (*ling-pan chün-chi ta-ch'en*), who was usually a Manchu grand secretary in the early period or a Manchu prince of the blood after the mid-19th century. They were stationed within the palace precincts (as opposed to the grand secretaries, who maintained offices outside the palace), and were therefore in a position to respond immediately to imperial summons. They followed the emperor wherever he went, even on furloughs, hunting trips, and visits. They read, transmitted, and kept memorials for the master, wrote rescripts, and recommended and executed policies for him; they suggested appointments and dismissals, and at times even prepared the palace examinations. But, like the grand secretaries, they had no authority to issue orders directly to the Six Boards or the provinces, such power belonging to the emperor alone. The terms of the grand councillors were indefinite: one served as long as thirty-one years (Tung Kao, 1779-91, 1799-1818) while others served as short as a few months. Of the 145 grand councillors appointed during the Ch'ing period, 72 were Manchus, six Mongols, 3 Chinese bannermen, and 64 Han Chinese.

Under the grand councillors were 32 secretaries—16 Chinese and 16 Manchus. They worked in shifts around the clock, half of them working by day and the other half by night. They performed the regular administrative and secretarial work in the Council, and were the couriers of memorials and other state documents between the emperor and the grand councillors. Being well informed on all important state affairs, these secretaries were known as the Little Councillors (*Hsiao chün-chi*).

Because it was a small body the Grand Council could reach decisions quickly and keep them secret. Its jurisdiction was not limited to military affairs as its Chinese name, *Chün-chi ch'u* (Military Strategy Office), might suggest, but extended to all important state affairs. Because it had proved so useful it remained in service, permanently replacing the Grand Secretariat as the most powerful body in the central government.[3]

Next to the Grand Secretariat and the Grand Council were the Six Boards, which formed the backbone of the central administration. These were the boards of Civil Office (*Li-pu*), Revenue (*Hu-pu*), Rites (*Li-pu*), War (*Ping-pu*), Punishments (*Hsing-pu*), and Public Works (*Kung-pu*). Each Board had two presidents and four vice-presidents, the offices being equally divided between the Manchus and the Chinese, and each board had four bureaus, except for the Board of Revenue which had fourteen bureaus and the Board of Punishments which had eighteen. Conspicuously absent in the central government was the Foreign Office, for the Confucian universal empire traditionally maintained no equal diplomatic relations as understood in the West; it recognized no foreign affairs but only tributary, or barbarian, or trading, affairs.

Of the Six Boards, that of Civil Office headed the list. Its four bureaus were appointments, examinations, records, and titles. The Board of Civil Office was the administrative body of the civil service; to it fell the responsibility of giving appointments and making dismissals, and of conferring ranks, merits, titles, and rewards. It authorized leaves of absence, recommended officials, and conducted examinations of those officials already in the service of the emperor. People wishing to purchase a rank or an advancement did so through the Board of Civil Office. It did not, however, administer the regular literary examinations by which candidates for government service were selected, this being the function of the Board of Rites.

Appointments, except those of the grand secretaries and grand councillors, were usually made for three years, at the end of which time a nominal examination was held to determine promotion or demotion. Four factors were decisive at this point in an appointee's career: personal conduct, executive ability, service record, and age. The "Law of Avoidance" required that no one be appointed to high positions in his native province and no two members of the same family be allowed to work in the same locality or service, so as to prevent nepotism and the forming of cliques. There were exceptions to these rules, but they were rare.[4] Retirement age was fixed at 55 *sui* in 1757 and raised to 65 in 1768, but this rule was not strictly enforced.

3. Alfred K. L. Ho, "The Grand Council."
4. In 1865, for instance, Li Hung-chang was appointed acting governor-general of

Accordingly as a given appointment in the Ch'ing civil service was attended by greater or less prestige, it came from one of three sources. The emperor himself appointed high officials such as the grand secretaries, the grand councillors, presidents and vice-presidents of the Six Boards, senior presidents and vice-presidents of the Censorate, governors-general, governors, and financial, judicial, and educational commissioners of the provinces, as well as the salt controllers. Intermediate appointments such as secretaries in the several boards, directors of minor organizations, officials from the fourth to the seventh rank, and circuit intendants and district magistrates were also made by the emperor, but on the recommendation of the Board of Civil Office. Appointments below the seventh rank were made by the respective boards themselves.

Official appointments might be obtained in five ways, of which the most common was to pass the civil service examinations and win the degrees. Another was through the recommendation of an official of the third rank or above (lower-ranking officials being unqualified to make such recommendations); this was not too frequently done because the man making the recommendation was held responsible for the conduct of the man recommended. A third way was to secure an appointment from the emperor by virtue of one's father's excellent services, but the rank thus obtained was usually four steps lower; that is, the son of a first-rank official could secure only a fifth-rank position for himself. One could, however, obtain a higher rank than his own for his father or grandfather: a second-rank official, for instance, could secure a first-rank place for his father. One could also (the fourth method) obtain a rank, an appointment, or an advancement by purchasing it, a method innocently described as "contribution for appointment to public office." The highest rank open to purchase was 1-b (first rank, second grade). In 1843 the cost of the office of assistant controller of salt, at 4-b, was 15,000 taels; that of circuit intendant, at 4-a, was 30,000 taels—roughly the sum total of ten years' salary and allowance. Finally, the fifth path to official appointment was through promotion from the rank of underclerk in the yamen, but this did not occur very often.

The Board of Revenue was second in rank to that of Civil Office. Like every other Board it had its two presidents and four vice-presidents, but in addition it retained a general superintendent, usually a Manchu but occasionally a Chinese. Under this Board's custody, naturally enough,

---

Liang-kiang, with jurisdiction over Kiangsu, Kiangsi, and Anhwei, the last-named being his native province.

came the collection of taxes and, since the biggest single tax was the land tax, the management of land registration. It controlled the transportation of taxes and tributes from the provinces to the government offices, regulated payment to nobles and government employees; it audited the accounts of the central and provincial treasuries, and maintained control of the customs houses. It governed currency and coinage, took the census, and kept up the records of the empire's territory and provincial boundaries. Under the Board of Revenue there were fourteen bureaus, each corresponding to a province: the Bureau of Chekiang, of Fukien, etc., though a few of them had jurisdiction over more than one province. The primary function of these bureaus was the auditing of the combined land and poll taxes in the provinces.

The Board of Rites attended, as might be supposed, to rituals. These included obvious things like court ceremonies, state sacrifices, official costumes, wedding and funeral rites; but under the same rubric came, perhaps surprisingly, tributary affairs, education, and the administering of the civil service examinations. Its four bureaus were ceremonies, sacrifices, reception, and banquet. There was also a department of music, which determined the music, singing, and posturing for sacrifices and other solemn occasions. An Office of Engraving was attached to the Board of Rites to supervise the casting of seals for governmental agencies. A Residence for Envoys from Tributary States was maintained by the Board to lodge the missions from Korea, Siam, Burma, Annam, and other tributary states.

Education represented a highly important part of the Board's province, for it involved not only schooling for the young but also the cultivation and selection of educated men for public service. The Board saw to it that the educational commissioners in the provinces properly superintended the education of young men, and it administered examinations at the district, provincial, and metropolitan levels. The successful candidates became degree-holders, the *shen-shih*, who formed a privileged class, from which the government selected its officials.

The Board of War concerned itself with military policies, controlled the appointments and dismissals of officers, conferred ranks and titles to military personnel, conducted military examinations and ceremonies, kept the census of the imperial army, and maintained the relay system of communication. However, it did not exercise jurisdiction over the Imperial Bodyguard, whose 8,646 officers were directly under the control of the emperor. The four bureaus of the Board were military selection, discipline, communication (remount), and commissariat.

In the provinces, there were three separate channels of military command. The provincial commander-in-chief (*t'i-tu*) was the highest military authority, but the governor-general and the governor each controlled several thousand independent troops as well. The military commissioners in the various circuits, though they ranked under the provincial commander-in-chief, were not obliged to take his orders. That this arrangement sometimes caused the various authorities to be at cross purposes is to be expected; the system was designed to achieve the maximum effect of checks and balances so that no one could gather enough power to threaten the central government.

An interesting feature of the Board was its control of official communication. It raised horses and supplied them to the relay teams throughout the country which carried messages between the capital and the provinces. High provincial and military authorities were given a certain number of credentials to use the teams. According to the importance of a document that was to be delivered, one or another statutory speed was required of the relay teams in transmitting it. The highest statutory speed was 600 *li* a day ordinarily, although 800 *li* a day was occasionally required of the teams. Other speeds ranged from 500 to 300 *li* a day; and routine communications were forwarded by foot couriers at 100 *li* a day. Thus a routine report from Nanking to Peking (2,300 *li* or 766 miles) was 23 days in transit, and from Canton to Peking it was 56 days.

The Board of Punishments directed matters of law, including punishments, pardons, and confiscation, and in conjunction with the Censorate and the Court of Judicature and Revision (*Ta-li ssu*) it reviewed cases in which the provincial judges had issued the death sentence. There were eighteen bureaus within the Board, seventeen of which tallied off to the provinces, while the other was a Bureau of Search and Arrest, which concerned itself with the recovery of convicted bannermen who had escaped. Fourteen of the seventeen bureaus exercised jurisdiction over one province, while the Bureau of Shensi had authority also over Kansu; the Bureau of Hukwang, over Hunan and Hupeh; and the Bureau of Fengtien, Manchuria (Fengtien, Kirin, and Heilungkiang).

The legal philosophy and practice of the Ch'ing were markedly different from those of the West. The judiciary was not independent of the executive branch—it was merely a part of it. There was no such thing as due process of law or advice of counsel in a trial. The judges were not protected by lifelong tenure of office. A case would more likely be tried on the basis of its moral implications than on any consideration of legality. Lawsuits and litigations were regarded as manifestations of unvirtuous behavior—therefore an appearance in court was a blow to one's social prestige. Only as a last resort—after all persuasion and ethical appeal had failed—would a man take recourse to law.

The lowest court was the office of the district magistrate or sub-prefect, who tried cases of the first instance. The decisions of this court were subject to review by the prefect if one party in a dispute was not satisfied with the verdict. The next level of appeal was the circuit intendant or the provincial judicial commissioner. The last named was appointed by the emperor as the highest judicial authority in the province, but even his decision could be reviewed by the governor or governor-general. If all the provincial courts failed to bring justice or to give a satisfactory verdict, the case could be brought to the Three Supreme Tribunals in Peking: the Board of Punishments, the Censorate, and the Court of Judicature and Revision. Working by the rule of unanimity, these three decided all appellate cases and reviewed all cases involving capital punishment. Should they not reach a unanimous decision, the case went to the emperor, who would usually appoint some grand secretary or grand councillor to decide for him.

The Board of Public Works was the lowest in rank of the Six Boards. It controlled the construction and repair of public buildings, purchased and sold properties for the government, maintained the streets and ditches in the capital, supplied materials for official construction, regulated the architecture and styles of residences belonging to the titular nobles and officials, and made annual inspections of such things as the imperial tombs, the city walls, palaces, temples, offices, warehouses, rivers, and canals. The repair of river dikes, dams, and irrigation systems were an important part of its works. Its four bureaus were construction, weights and measures, rivers and canals, and imperial tombs.

The Grand Secretariat, the Grand Council, and the Six Boards were the essential organs of the central government, but there were several other important "coordinate" offices that should be mentioned; two in particular were the Li-fan yüan (Court of Colonial Affairs) and the Censorate.

The Li-fan yüan ranked directly after the Six Boards and just ahead of the Censorate. Unlike many Ch'ing institutions, this one was not inherited from the Ming dynasty, nor had it any other historical precedent. It was established about 1636 as the Mongolian Office, (*Meng-ku ya-men*), and its chief function at that time was the management of relations with the Mongols. As the Ch'ing demesne expanded, however, the office took over the relations with Tibet, Sinkiang, and Russia as well; and two years after its inception its name was changed to the Li-fan yüan. Except for a brief period (1658-61) during which it was part of the Board of Rites, it was an independent organ in the central government. Its duties included the custodianship of the complete records of Mongolia, Sinkiang, and Tibet, and the appointment of civil and military officials to those special administrative areas. It regulated trade between those areas and the provinces and trained the princes, nobles, and officials of these areas in the performance of court ceremonies; and, as mentioned, it managed the relations with Russia until 1861.

The Li-fan yüan was headed by a president and a senior and a junior vice-president, and during the Ch'ien-lung period a supernumerary vice-president—usually a Mongol Prince—was added. The presidency and the two regular vice-presidencies were usually held by Manchus but occasionally by Mongol bannermen, until the Ch'ien-lung period; thereafter they went to Manchus exclusively. No Chinese were ever appointed.

There were six departments or bureaus within the Li-fan yüan. The Bureau of Inner Mongolia issued feudal ranks, organized the assemblies of Inner Mongolian princes, registered the population, and took charge of the defense of banner territories. Next to this was the Bureau for the Reception of the Princes of Inner Mongolia, which concerned itself exclusively with the visits of Inner Mongolian princes to the court, their offering of tributes, and the banquets held for them. The Bureau of Outer Mongolia did for Outer Mongolia what its counterpart bureau did for Inner Mongolia; in addition it managed the affairs relating to Tibet and Russia. Among other things, it took charge of the Russians who came to China, and issued food, clothing, and allowances to students in the Russian School that was attached to the Russian religious mission in Peking. It also granted permits to Chinese merchants to trade in Outer Mongolia, Tibet, and at Kiakhta. The Bureau for the Reception of the Princes of Outer Mongolia had functions similar to those of the second

Bureau listed above except that its services were performed for Princes of Outer Mongolia rather than of Inner Mongolia. Next came the Bureau of Eastern Turkestan, which was concerned with relations with the Moslem *begs* (chieftains) in Sinkiang. The last was the Judicial Bureau, which took charge of civil and criminal cases in Inner and Outer Mongolia. The Li-fan yüan also maintained a number of appendages such as the Mongolian School for Officials, the Tibetan Language School, the Oirat (Ölöd) Language School, and the Office of Lama Seal Affairs.[5]

The Li-fan yüan was an organization unique to the Ch'ing dynasty. Its special emphasis on Mongolian affairs showed the cultural affinity and peculiar relationship that existed between the Manchus and the Mongols. It is also noteworthy that relations with Russia were regulated by this office, although Russia was clearly not in the same category as Mongolia, Tibet, and Sinkiang. Li-fan yüan, however, was the logical and convenient choice of organization to deal with Russia, partly because Russian affairs could not be administered by the Board of Rites inasmuch as Russia was not a regular tributary state, and partly because she was located in the north, close to Mongolia.

The Ch'ing Censorate (*Tu-ch'a yüan*) was headed by two senior presidents (Left Grand Censors) and four senior vice-presidents (Associate Left Grand Censors)—offices equally divided between the Manchus and Chinese. The titles of junior president (Right Grand Censor) and junior vice-presidents (Associate Right Grand Censor) were usually conferred concurrently on the governors-general and governors respectively. There were 24 censors for the Six Boards and 56 for the provinces, likewise composed of equal numbers of Manchu and Chinese.

The censors were known as the speech officials (*yen-kuan*) because they supposedly enjoyed freedom of speech: they were allowed to address the emperor on any subject. They served as his "eyes and ears," entrusted with the duty of discovering secret opposition. They could impeach, attack, criticize, or praise any official and any policy, openly or secretly as they saw fit. Although their institutional functions were to detect dereliction of duties among the officials and not to concern themselves with policies, nevertheless through their watchful supervision of the execution of policies and their readiness to impeach or attack the officials in charge, they actually exerted an influence on both the administration of current

5. For details, see David Miller Farquhar, "The Ch'ing Administration of Mongolia up to the Nineteenth Century," Ph. D. thesis, Harvard University, 1960.

policies and the formulation of new ones. They considered themselves guardians of the Confucian principle of propriety (*li*), and sometimes their straightforward admonition or remonstration of the emperor cost them their jobs or lives.[6] One censor was exiled by Emperor Yung-cheng, three were dismissed by Ch'ien-lung, while Chia-ch'ing had one demoted, four dismissed, and one executed.

Another remarkable feature of the central government was the Hanlin Academy. This was originally a part of the Grand Secretariat, but it became independent in 1659, and after a short second amalgamation of the two, it separated again in 1670. The Academy's function was primarily literary; its two chancellors—one Manchu and one Chinese—lectured on the classics to the emperor, or recommended lecturers to do so. They prepared edicts and manuscripts for imperial lectures, and officiated at the sacrificial offerings to Confucius. They were assisted by six readers, six expositors, six sub-readers and as many sub-expositors, comprising equal numbers of Chinese and Manchus. In addition there were a number of compilers and correctors. Members of the Academy lectured on the classics daily to the emperor for five months each year, from the second to the fourth month and from the eighth to the eleventh. They drafted sacrificial eulogies and speeches for conferring titles and ranks, wrote memoranda for tablets, and edited or compiled books which were later to bear the imperial imprint.

The Hanlin Academy maintained a magnificent library which contained duplicates of all the books in the Imperial Library and held as well a great stock of memorials and documents. The State Historiographer's Office within the Academy prepared a chronicle of each reign called the veritable records (*shih lu*), which was not made public until after the death of the reigning emperor. It also collected materials and drafted manuscripts for the biographies of emperors, empresses, nobles, officials, and scholars; but it never wrote out the history of the ruling dynasty: this was a task reserved for the next dynasty.

Membership in the Academy was limited to metropolitan graduates of the highest honors. It was a haven for the bright young talents and was an excellent training center for their political careers. Within a term of three years they could expect to win good appointments and rapid promotion in the official hierarchy. It was not infrequent that a member rose to the highest rung of the official ladder within ten years.

6. Hsü, *China's Entrance*, 200-201.

Two other organizations were significant in handling the flow of documents. The Office of Transmission (*T'ung-cheng ssu*) received the "routine memorials" (*pen-chang*) from the provinces and was empowered to open them to see whether their delivery had been delayed by the relay teams and whether all the proper forms of elevation and phraseology were observed. If all were found proper, the memorials were forwarded to the Grand Secretariat, which also received "routine memorials" from government offices in Peking directly. The Grand Secretariat prepared drafts of replies to these memorials in accordance with the established regulations before submitting them to the emperor. After the imperial decisions were made, the memorials were returned to the Grand Secretariat and "copied out" by the respective boards for implementation.

Another organ, the Chancery of Memorials (*Tsou-shih ch'u*), received special "palace memorials" (*tsou-che*) from civil and military officials above the rank of 4-a, whether in the capital or in the provinces. In the latter case, the memorials were usually sent by the horse post or by special messengers of the memorialists. If sent by the former means, the memorials were locked in special boxes given to the memorialists by the emperor, and if delivered by the latter, they were accompanied by official papers to identify the messengers. In no case was the Chancery allowed to open the "palace memorials," but only the accompanying papers to identify the couriers and to ascertain their masters' qualifications to address the emperor. If all the credentials were in order, the Chancery quickly transmitted the memorials to the chancery eunuchs for presentation to the emperor, who was the first to read the "palace memorials." Frequently he wrote interlinear remarks on the memorials; other times he gave oral instructions to the grand councillors on the drafting of replies. The memorials were then returned to the original senders, who read the imperial comments and returned the memorials to the capital. In this manner, the emperor kept himself well informed on the conditions of the country.

The "routine memorial" system, however, fell increasingly into disuse after the Chia-ch'ing period (1796-1820), when the urgency of domestic rebellions, foreign aggression, and modernization projects necessitated the constant use of "palace memorials." In 1901 the "routine memorial" system was finally abolished and five months later the Office of Transmission went out of existence.[7]

There were a number of lesser organizations in the capital—many of

7. Silas Hsiu-liang Wu, "The Memorial System," 8, 13, 24, 27-30, 55-56.

Ch'ing Central Government

Principal Offices
- Grand Secretariat (*Nei-ko*)
- Grand Council (*Chün-chi ch'u*)
- Six Boards
  - The Board of Civil Office (*Li-pu*)
  - The Board of Revenue (*Hu-pu*)
  - The Board of Rites (*Li-pu*)
  - The Board of War (*Ping-pu*)
  - The Board of Punishments (*Hsing-pu*)
  - The Board of Public Work (*Kung-pu*)

Coordinate Offices
- The Censorate (*Tu-ch'a yüan*)
- The Court of Judicature and Revision (*Ta-li ssu*)
- The Court of Colonial Affairs (*Li-fan yüan*)
- The Hanlin Academy (*Han-lin yüan*)
- The Office of Transmission (*T'ung-cheng ssu*)
- The Imperial College (*Kuo-tzu chien*)
- The Imperial Board of Astronomy (*Ch'in-t'ien chien*)

Imperial Departments
- The Imperial Clan Court (*Tsung-jen fu*)
- The Imperial Household (*Nei-wu fu*)
- The Supervisorate of Imperial Instruction (*Chan-shih fu*)
- The Court of Sacrificial Worship (*T'ai-ch'ang ssu*)
- The Banqueting Court (*Kuang-lu ssu*)
- The Imperial Stud (*T'ai-p'u ssu*)
- The Court of State Ceremonial (*Hung-lu ssu*)
- The Imperial Medical Department (*T'ai-i yüan*)

Adapted from Hsiao I-shan, I, 503, table 1.

which were concerned with the imperial household. The preceding chart gives their names along with those offices already discussed.

Local Administration. China's local administration—exclusive of special administrative areas such as Mongolia, Manchuria, Sinkiang, Tibet, and Chinghai—was of four kinds: province, circuit, prefecture, and district. There were altogether, 18 provinces,[8] 92 circuits, between 177 and 185 prefectures, and about 1,500 districts and departments.

The eighteen regular provinces were put under the control of governors-general and governors (numbering eight and fifteen respectively during the Ch'ien-lung reign, but varying from one reign to the next). Two of the governors-general controlled only one province each—Chihli and Szechwan—but the other six usually had jurisdiction over two or three provinces.[9] The fifteen governors each controlled one province, and in the remaining three provinces, Chihli, Szechwan, and Kansu, the governors-general performed the duties of governor. The ranks for governor-general and governor were 2-a and 2-b respectively.

The governor-general—sometimes called viceroy by the Westerner— was the highest authority in the province (or provinces). He ruled over all the people and controlled all of the civil and military officials within his jurisdiction. There were essentially eight acts that his office empowered him to do; these were to (1) memorialize the emperor, (2) issue orders and regulations for officials and subjects within his jurisdiction, (3) promote, demote, and dismiss civil officials of the rank of circuit intendant or below and military officers of the rank of colonel or below, (4) evaluate the work of civil officials every three years and military officers every five, (5) keep control of the Green Standard (Chinese) army within his realm, (6) supervise the provincial treasury and report to the emperor on provincial finances, (7) judge cases of the fourth instances after the district, prefectural, and circuit officials had passed

8. Chihli, Shantung, Shansi, Honan, Kiangsu, Anhwei, Kiangsi, Chekiang, Fukien, Hupeh, Hunan, Shensi, Kansu, Szechwan, Kwangtung, Kwangsi, Yünnan, and Kweichow. Actually, at the beginning of the Ch'ing dynasty there were only 15 provinces. Because of their large size, Emperor K'ang-hsi (1662-1722) split Kiangnan into Kiangsu and Anhwei, Shensi into Shensi and Kansu, and Hukwang into Hunan and Hupeh, making a total of 18 provinces, as stated. Later in 1884 and 1887, Sinkiang and Taiwan were respectively made provinces, but Taiwan was ceded to Japan in 1895. In 1907 Manchuria was turned into three provinces: Fengtien, Kirin, and Heilungkiang, making a total of 22 provinces by the end of the dynasty.
9. These were the governors-general of Liang-Kiang (Kiangsu-Anhwei-Kiangsi), Min-che (Fukien-Chekiang), Liang-Kwang (Kwangtung and Kwangsi), Hu-Kwang (Hupeh-Hunan), Shen-Kan (Shensi-Kansu), and Yün-Kwei (Yunnan-Kweichow).

judgment on them, and (8) transact business with foreign representatives when the need arose. The ´governor-general was not provided with an official staff to do these things; usually he kept a private staff of secretaries, scribes, and a number of assistants whom he put in charge of military affairs, honor guards, police, attendants, seals, and dispatches.

In his own province, the governor had more or less the same powers as the governor-general, but he had four additional duties: (1) to supervise the customs house, (2) to take general charge of the salt administration, (3) to superintend district literary examinations, and (4) to superintend the management of tribute grains. The governor was not provided with an official staff either; but like the governor-general he maintained a private staff of secretaries and scribes, and had a stable of advisers in judicial, financial, educational, and military matters. Both he and the governor-general could impeach officials anywhere in the country, and thus they acted as censors. In fact, the governor-general bore the concurrent title of junior president of the Censorate, and the governor that of junior vice-president.

Naturally the governor-general and the governor duplicated many of each other's functions; conflict was bound to arise, particularly if they resided in the same city. But this collision was a deliberately built-in part of the system—a kind of debilitating check and balance—so that no one would become strong enough to threaten the central government. This apparently worked better in theory than in practice, however. A noted publicist[10] of the late Ch'ing period made the penetrating observation that if the governor-general and the governor were both bad they would conceal each other's faults; if both were good, there was no need for two of them. And if one was good and the other bad, the bad would undermine the work of the good. The original purpose of mutual check and balance was therefore unlikely to be served. However, the court in Peking seemed to derive some sense of security in interposing Manchus with Chinese in these high provincial posts; whenever a Manchu was appointed governor-general, the governors under him were usually Chinese, and vice versa. During the first two centuries of the dynasty (1644-1850), Manchus (including Mongols and Chinese bannermen) accounted for 63.9 per cent of the governor-generalships and 56.5 per cent of the governorships, while Han Chinese occupied 36.1 per cent and 43.5 per cent respectively. Taking the Ch'ing period as a whole, the ethnic distri-

10. Hsüeh Fu-ch'eng, an associate of Li Hung-chang and minister to England and France, 1876-78.

bution was fairly even: 57 per cent of the governors-general and 48.4 per cent of the governors were Manchus, as compared with 43 per cent and 51.6 per cent, respectively, Han Chinese.[11]

Under each governor was a financial, a judicial, and an educational commissioner—all appointed by the emperor. The government supplied them with a staff, but usually they maintained their private staffs, too. Besides those just listed, there were a number of special commissioners who were placed in charge of salt, grain transport, customs, rivers and waterways, and postroads. A provincial commander-in-chief took charge of military affairs.

Further down the ladder in the provincial administration came the intermediary offices of the circuit intendants and prefects, and at the bottom was the district (*hsien*). Some large districts were bigger than the small states in the United States; the average population of a district was 200,000. The district magistrate collected taxes, settled litigations, and generally maintained peace and order in the locality. He was known as the "father-mother official" (*fu-mu kuan*) because he dealt directly with the people and was supposed to take care of them.[12] He was aided by an official staff made up of an assistant magistrate (*hsien-ch'eng*), a registrar (*chu-pu*), a jail warden (*tien-shih*), and a group of miscellaneous officials such as postmaster, tax collector, granary supervisor—all of whom the magistrate tended to ignore, preferring to rely on his private staff which consisted primarily of a treasurer, a legal expert, and a tax specialist. Yet even with their assistance, the magistrate could not adequately discharge all his duties without seeking additional help. Usually, upon assumption of office he entered into some kind of understanding or contractual relationship with a local group well conversant with the affairs of the district. This group functioned as an unofficial local permanent civil service, organizing itself into six "houses" (*fang*): (1) civil and administrative affairs; (2) census and taxation; (3) protocol and ceremonies; (4) militia; (5) crime or constabulary; and (6) public works. Members of this extralegal bureaucracy received no pay from the magistrate but were allowed to collect surcharges in his name. They were required to hand over a pre-fixed amount of their collections while keeping the rest for themselves. It is this little-publicized body which per-

11. Lawrence D. Kessler, "Ethnic Composition of Provincial Leadership during the Ch'ing Dynasty," *The Journal of Asian Studies*, XXVIII:3:496, 500 (May 1969); Hsiao I-shan, I, 533-37; Pao Chao Hsieh, 294.
12. For details, see T'ung-tsu Ch'ü, *Local Government in China Under the Ch'ing* (Cambridge, Mass., 1962), 14.

formed the bulk of the day-to-day operation of the magistrate's yamen.[13]

At the same level as the district were some slightly larger administrative units called department (*chou*) and subprefecture (*t'ing*). Some departments were under the direct control of the provincial government, in which case they enjoyed a higher status than the regular department. There were a total of 154 departments and 1,282 districts in the whole country during the Ch'ien-lung period.

Subadministrative Rural Control. In each district there were a number of villages (*ts'un* or *chuang*), cities (*ch'eng*), towns (*cheng*), countryside settlements (*hsiang*), and rural markets (*shih, chi, ch'ang*). Operation of these rural divisions was left to the local inhabitants rather than to government officials, as the imperial administration stopped at the district level. Imperial control, however, was still made manifest through the development of two neighborhood organization systems called the *pao-chia* and the *li-chia*. The former was established in 1644 to facilitate police control and the latter in 1648 to help with tax collection.

In the *pao-chia* system every ten households (*hu*) formed a *p'ai*, with a headman called the *p'ai-chang*; every ten *p'ai* constituted a *chia*, for which there was a headman called *chia-chang* (or *chia-t'ou*); and every ten *chia* in turn made up a *pao*, headed by a *pao-chang*. Each *pao* thus consisted of 1,000 households. Each household hung on its door an official placard bearing the names of its members. Those who made trips had to indicate where they were going, and those who came to visit for any length of time had to show where they had come from. Strangers or suspicious characters were not allowed into the house. The *pao-chia* maintained a census, kept track of the movements of individuals, and made periodic recounts of the local population. Members of the *pao-chia* were supposed to watch for and report crimes and criminals in the neighborhoods to the heads of the *pao-chia*, who relayed the information to the district magistrate. Every member of the *pao-chia* was therefore a potential informer on every other member. The fear and suspicion thus created inhibited the villagers from entering into seditious plots with their fellow citizens, and thus reduced the chances of uprisings or revolts. Failure to report crimes and secret plots would bring collective punishment. At the end of the month the head of each *pao* was required to submit a "voluntary bond" (*kan-chieh*) to the district magistrate to assure that everything was well in his neighborhood.

13. K. C. Wu, "Local Government in Imperial China" in his *Why Is America Not Better Informed on Asian Affairs* (Savannah, Georgia, 1968), 8-9.

The *li-chia*, often confused with the *pao-chia*, was a totally different system. Every 110 households in the *rural* area constituted a *li*, and the ten households within it which contained the largest number of tax-paying adults were chosen heads of the *li* (*li-chang*). The 100 households that remained were divided into ten *chia*, each with a head. To every 110 households in the *cities*, the term *fang*, rather than *li*, was applied; and in the suburban areas the same unit was designated by the term *hsiang*. The head of each *chia* collected the tax records of the 11 households under his supervision and submitted them to the head of the *li* (or *fang* or *hsiang*), who in turn forwarded them to the local magistrate. Every three, and after 1656 every five, years a census was taken as the basis of the land and poll taxes. The function of the *li-chia* was to assist in the registration of the local inhabitants, to assess and collect the land (*ti*) and poll (*ting*) imposts, and to help in compiling the Yellow Register,[14] which recorded all taxable individuals in the area.

The nature of the *li-chia*, however, underwent some change after 1712, when Emperor K'ang-hsi froze the *ting* (labor service) quota as it was established in that year and announced that no more new imposts would be made on the population increase thereafter. By 1740 the labor service impost had been merged into the land tax in nearly all the provinces, and the Yellow Register had virtually lost its original usefulness. The *li-chia* compilation of taxable adult records was discontinued in favor of the more general *pao-chia* census registration. In 1772 the practice of quinquennial register of the *ting* was abolished altogether. The main function of the *li-chia* now changed from providing materials for the compilation of the Yellow Register to the urging of prompt tax payments. Not infrequently the *li-chia* heads were held responsible for the failure of the villagers to honor their tax obligations.

By using the local inhabitants to control themselves at the subadministrative level, the Ch'ing government exercised an ingenious means of extending imperial control to the very root of the society, at the same time obviating the expenses of local government and the need to appoint officials. Yet the *pao-chia* and *li-chia* systems had their shortcomings too. For one thing, the door placards on which the names of the household members were inscribed were expensive to procure and their accuracy was hard to verify. The gentry in general were loath to post their names and whereabouts openly on these placards. Individuals of the *pao-chia* were reluctant to report crimes because of fear of involvement

14. So called because of its yellow covers.

and of revenge at the hands of the criminals' accomplices. Moreover, the *pao-chia* and *li-chia* heads were overworked: twice a month, on the first and fifteenth, they had to report to the magistrates, even when no untoward incidents had occurred. Twenty-four times a year, hundreds of them would wait at the gate of the local government office, and the yamen clerks assigned to receive them often demanded bribery to facilitate their reports. Men of education and self-respect managed to avoid the job of heading the *pao-chia* and *li-chia*, and this opened the way for the unscrupulous individuals and local scoundrels, who often resorted to petty extortion and blackmail in dealing with the members of the neighborhood organizations. The heads of *pao-chia* and *li-chia* were not respected; yet many of them made personal sacrifices because of the heavy duties imposed upon them—frequently even being forced to postpone the wedding of a son or daughter for a year.[15]

On the other hand, the headship of a village—the basic unit of rural community life—commanded much greater respect. It was usually filled by a leading local gentry or the elder of the largest or richest household in the area. He was often chosen by public acclaim, and the local magistrate recognized the position thus gotten. The village head ran the general affairs of the village, settled litigations by persuasion and took the lead in repairing roads, bridges, temples, schools, and shrines.

At the very bottom of the rural community was the docile, passive, and hard-working peasant, who worked all year round for a hand-to-mouth subsistence. The peasants were mostly resigned to their fate and accepted the social circumstances as the yoke they had to bear. Nevertheless, if the taxes became too onerous and their living too hard, they would, despite their inertia in political matters, accept the leadership of more venturesome scholars or members of the gentry to rebel. The government therefore saw to it that periodic favors were extended to them, these usually took the form of tax remission in years of bumper crops. A good government was one which could provide the peasantry with a passable living and at the same time temper control with a certain degree of latitude.

ECONOMIC INSTITUTIONS

In a predominantly agrarian country such as China, soil and human labor constituted the economic foundations of state. The bulk of the revenue

15. For details of the *pao-chia* and *li-chia* systems, see Kung-ch'üan Hsiao, *Rural China: Imperial Control in the Nineteenth Century* (Seattle, 1960), chapters 2-4.

came from the land and poll taxes (*ti-ting*), supplemented by incomes from the salt tax, tea tax, the native customs houses, the commercial license tax, and others. On the whole, revenue did not increase notably during the first century and a half of the dynasty. During the Shun-chih period (1644-61), the annual income was about 28 million taels; during the K'ang-hsi period (1662-1722), about 35 million; during the Yung-cheng period (1723-35), 40 million; and during the Ch'ien-lung period (1736-95), between 43 and 48 million, against an annual expenditure of roughly 35 million (1765). The slow rise in income was largely a result of the modest increase in land cultivation; in 1661 there was a total of 549 million *mou* of arable land and in 1766 it rose to only 741 million.

The Land and Taxation Systems. To understand the country's economy it is essential that one understand the Ch'ing land system, which was an extremely complex institution. There existed four categories under which the land might be generally classified: (1) the people's land (which can be further divided into 22 types, such as land owned by private citizens, mulberry land, marsh land, the aborigines' land); (2) official villas and fields allotted to the imperial household, imperial clansmen, and the bannermen; (3) public land—such as "educational" land, whose income went to the provincial treasuries to defray educational expenses; sacrificial land, whose income went to the descendants of Confucius and was used to support sacrificial expenses; horse-breeding land, and the emperor's own tilling land; (4) land for the military colonies in Sinkiang and the provinces. The total cultivated land of China proper and Manchuria, exclusive of Mongolia, Sinkiang, Tibet, and Chinghai, may be seen in the following list:[16]

1661	549,357,640 *mou* (1 *mou* = 1/6 acre)
1685	607,843,001
1724	683,791,427
1753	708,114,288
1766	741,449,550
1812	791,525,100
1833	737,512,900

In view of the primitive, unscientific methods of survey by which they were obtained, the accuracy of these figures is open to doubt; but they

16. Hsiao I-shan, II, 364-65. The decrease in arable land in 1833 was caused by natural disasters.

are nevertheless viable indicators of the slow increases in land cultivation.

The land tax was by far the greatest of all taxes in the early and middle Ch'ing periods. The basis of its collection was the 1646 edition of the *Fu-i ch'üan-shu* (Complete text of land and labor), in which were spelled out the total amount of cultivated land in the country, the quotas of land (*ti*) and labor (*ting*) imposts in the various provinces, the number of persons liable to the labor impost, and the quotas of the revenue to be sent to the imperial treasury. The regular land tax came from the people's land, with the rates contingent upon the fertility of the soil and the size of the property. Odd bits of people's land too small to be worth assessment were exempt from taxes, as were the official lands and public lands assigned for sacrificial and educational purposes, and those lands allotted to the imperial household or bannermen. The land measurement registers, called the Fish-scale Registers (*Yü-lin ts'e*)[17] showed the total land area in each locality, and the Yellow Registers (*Huang-ts'e*) gave the total number of taxable adults in the area.

In 1712 K'ang-hsi issued his well-known edict, which was to have far-reaching consequences, that the *ti* and *ting* taxes would be permanently based on the quotas of 1712. This document read in part as follows:

> In looking over the reports concerning the number of inhabitants and tax-liable persons made by the governors-general and governors of the various provinces, we perceived that they have not included all the population increases currently accrued. The empire has enjoyed continued peace for a long time, and the number of households and inhabitants has been multiplying daily. If additional taxes are assessed on the basis of the current population figures, it is really quite improper. For although there is an increase in population, there is no increase in the amount of cultivated land. We deem it fit, therefore, to instruct governors-general and governors of the provinces to take the number of registered *ting* listed in the *current registers*, which number is not to be augmented or diminished, *as the permanent, fixed quota* [for collecting the *ting* imposts]. *All inhabitants born hereafter shall be exempted from [additional] imposts.* In taking the census it will be necessary merely to ascertain the actual amount of population increase and report it in separate registers.[18]

17. So called because of its fish-scale design on the covers, supposedly symbolic of plots of land.
18. Kung-ch'üan Hsiao, 89-90. Italics added.

This freezing of the *ting* quota rendered the poll tax meaningless, and it was gradually merged into the land tax. In 1716, with K'ang-hsi's approval of the merger in Kwangtung province, the precedent was set, fixing the poll tax at .1064 tael for each tael of the land tax. Other provinces followed suit until by the early 19th century the combination of the two taxes became standard practice throughout the country. As a rule, the poll tax was light where the land tax was heavy, and vice versa. After the merging of the two taxes, the usefulness of the Yellow Registers decreased, whereas that of the Fish-scale Registers increased.

The method of collection was the "Single-whip system" (first begun in 1581), which consolidated all taxes into one compound sum to be paid twice a year, in summer and autumn. The summer payment was generally made between the second and fifth months, and the autumn payment between the eighth and eleventh months.[19] These two periods of payment were popularly known as "The Upper Busy (Season)" and "The Lower Busy (Season)."

About a month before the semiannual collection, the district government issued an "Easy-Comprehension Notice" (*I-chih yu-tan*) to all taxpayers, informing them of the exact amount of their payment and the date it was due. But in 1687 this practice was discontinued and the *li-chia* heads—whose original function had been to help compile the Yellow Registers—took over the job of reminding the taxpayers of their obligations, a process known as "prompting the payment" (*ts'ui-k'o*). The taxpayers deposited the money in a wooden box in front of the district government office, and sent the grain tax (in kind) to a designated warehouse. They received in return one section of a three-sectioned receipt (the second section being kept by the district office while the third was pasted in the book of receipts). Every ten days during the collection period the district magistrate reported to his superior the amount received. At the end of the collection period part of the revenue was kept for the district government's expenses and the rest was sent to the provincial treasury. Reports were then sent to the provincial financial commissioner. At the end of each year, the prefect and circuit intendant audited the accounts of the district magistrates and made a report to the governor. And the following year, before the fourth (sometimes sixth)

19. There were minor variations to this schedule in various provinces; in Kwangtung, for instance, they were paid during the seventh and eighth months, and during the twelfth month and the first month of the following year. In Kiangsu, Shensi, and Szechwan the schedule ran from the second to the seventh months, and from the eighth to the twelfth—all according to the lunar calendar.

month, copies of these provincial accounts were dispatched to the emperor and the Board of Revenue. The following table shows the land-poll tax in money and in grain during different years:[20]

Year	Tax in taels	Tax in shih (133⅓ lbs.) of grain
1661	21,576,006	6,479,465
1685	24,449,724	4,331,131
1724	26,362,541	4,731,400
1753	29,611,201	8,406,422
1766	29,917,761	8,318,735
1812	32,845,474	4,356,382

State Revenue and Expenditures. In addition to the land-poll tax, a number of other smaller taxes made up a considerable part of the revenue. The surtax called *huo-hao*, or allowance for wastage in silver-melting, was originally collected by district magistrates illegally, but since it could not be stopped in spite of repeated warning, Emperor Yung-cheng decided that the government should take it over. The rate of *huo-hao* varied in different provinces but it ranged for the most part between 4 per cent or 5 per cent to 20 per cent of the regular (i.e. land) tax. From this source the government derived an annual income of about four and a half million taels during the Ch'ien-lung period. Other taxes included tribute grain, rents from educational and weed lands, income from the salt gabelle, the customs houses, the tea tax, commercial license tax, etc. The total revenue of state toward the end of the 18th century may be summarized as follows:[21]

1.	Land-poll tax	approximately 30,000,000	taels
2.	Wastage allowance (*huo-hao*)	4,600,000	"
3.	Miscellaneous surtax on tribute grain	2,000,000	"
4.	Salt tax quota	7,500,000	"
5.	Customs dues	4,000,000	"
6.	Land rents	260,000	"
7.	Tea tax	70,000	"
8.	Tribute grain for Peking	4,000,000	shih

According to these figures, the total income of state should have been around 48 million taels and 4 million *shih* of grain, but since the salt tax

20. Hsiao I-shan, II, 386-87.
21. Hsiao I-shan, II, 432.

quota of seven and a half million taels was often filled only 50 per cent to 60 per cent, the actual revenue was around 43 or 44 million.

Against this income, the largest items of debit were military expenditures and officials' salaries and allowances. The Manchu banners and the Chinese Green Standard Army, totaling more than 200,000 and 600,000 men respectively, represented some 20 million taels of the expenditure. The stipends for the nobles and the salaries of the officials are shown in the following selective scale:[22]

Post	Annual Salary (taels)	Rice stipend (shih)
Prince of the Blood	10,000	5,000
Duke, First Grade	700	350
Earl, " "	610	305
Count, " "	510	255
Viscount, " "	410	205
Baron, " "	310	155
Civil official, Grade 1-a, b	180	90
" " " 2-a, b	155	77.5
" " " 3-a, b	130	65
" " " 4-a, b	105	52.5
" " " 5-a, b	80	40
" " " 6-a, b	60	30
" " " 7-a, b	45	22.5
" " " 8-a, b	40	20
" " " 9-a	33.114	16.557
" " " 9-b	31.5	15.75

It will be noted that the civil officials received very meager salaries indeed. A grand secretary at the rank of 1-a received only 180 taels a year, and a governor-general, whose rank was 2-a, received only 155 taels. To compensate for the low salary scale, officials were given what was euphemistically called "integrity-nourishing allowances" (yang-lien fei),[23] which were frequently a hundred times the amount of the regular pay. These allowances varied slightly in different provinces, as shown in the table on the facing page.

A governor-general whose regular salary was 155 taels received an "integrity-nourishing allowance" of 13,000 to 20,000 taels; and in addition he

22. Hsiao I-shan, II, 411-16.
23. Sometimes translated as "anti-corruption fee" or "honesty-fostering allowance."
24. Hsiao I-shan, II, 416-18.

Post	Annual Integrity-nourishing Allowance (*taels*)
Governor-general (Chihli)	15,000
” ” (Kiangsu)	18,000
” ” (Fukien)	13,000
” ” (Yunnan)	20,000
Governor (Shantung)	15,000
” (Kiangsu)	12,000
” (Fukien)	13,000
” (Yunnan)	10,000
Financial Commissioner (Chihli)	9,000
” ” (Kiangsu)	9,000
” ” (Fukien)	8,000
” ” (Yunnan)	8,000
District magistrate (Chihli)	1,200
” ” (Kiangsu)	1,800
” ” (Fukien)	1,600
” ” (Yunnan)	1,200

was given some "official expenses." The total "integrity-nourishing allow-ances" for all civil and military officials amounted to more than four million taels a year, while "official expenses" ran to a quarter of a million.

Other state expenses included repair works for rivers and ponds, main-tenance of postal stations, relief for victims of natural disasters, charitable establishments, public worship, public schools and scholarships, etc. A breakdown of the approximate expenditures of the central and local gov-ernments of the year 1765 is shown as follows:

Central Government Expenditures:

1. Salaries for princes, nobles, and officials	930,000
2. Military expenses	6,000,000
3. Military expenses in Mukden and Jehol	1,400,000
4. Stipends for Mongolian and Moslem nobles	120,000
5. Office and food expenses for metropolitan officials	110,000
6. Mess allowances for the Grand Secretariat, etc.	18,000
7. "Integrity-nourishing allowances" for the Boards of Civil Office and Rites	15,000
8. Gifts to Mongolian and Korean tribute bearers	10,000
9. Miscellaneous	900,000
	9,503,000

Local Government Expenditures:

1. Military expenses	15,000,000
2. Salaries of officials	1,000,000
3. "Integrity-nourishing allowances"	4,220,000
4. "Expense" allowances	200,000
5. Repairs of rivers and ponds	4,000,000
6. Miscellaneous (post stations, charity, etc.)	1,400,000
	25,820,000

The total expenses of the central government were approximately 9.5 million taels, and those of the local government about 25.8 million, making a grand total of 35 million taels, against a revenue of 43 or 44 million taels. The government during the Ch'ien-lung period enjoyed a surplus of eight or nine million taels annually.[25]

Population. In an agricultural economy land and population cannot be considered separately: the merging of the land and poll taxes was a recognition of this. Every three or five years during the early Ch'ing period, the *li-chia* heads conducted a census of taxable adult males between the ages of 16 and 60 (*sui*); it was on the basis of their investigation that the provincial financial commissioners compiled the Yellow Registers. Taxable individuals attempted to avoid being included in these registers, and for good reason: the poll (*ting*) tax actually consisted of a certain number of compulsory labor services commuted into money payment, which might be as high as eight or nine taels a year in some localities. Emperor K'ang-hsi reported in 1712 that during his tours of the country he frequently found only one out of five or six persons in a household who paid taxes, and sometimes in households of nine or ten members only one or two were paying taxes. Provincial authorities did not report the actual population for fear of increases in their tax quotas. K'ang-hsi's 1712 decree that froze the poll tax quotas to the population figure for that year somewhat alleviated the popular fear of registration, but the habit of avoiding the census was deep-rooted. With the increasing merging of the poll tax into the land tax during the Yung-cheng period, the Yellow Registers became more and more superfluous. On the other hand, the *pao-chia* census-taking took on a much greater importance. But the rate of increase in the population was not marked until the Ch'ien-lung period (1736-95). The difference is shown roughly in the following listing:[26]

25. Hsiao I-shan, II, 432-35.
26. Ping-ti Ho, *Studies on the Population of China, 1368-1953* (Cambridge, Mass., 1959), 281-82.

1660	19,088,000 *ting*
1670	19,396,000
1680	17,095,000
1690	20,364,000
1700	20,411,000
1710	23,312,000
1720	24,710,000
1730	25,480,080

1741 (first year of figures based on *pao-chia* census)	143,411,559 *k'ou* (mouths)
1749	177,495,039
1753	183,678,259
1757	190,348,328
1767	209,839,546
1779	275,042,916
1790	301,487,114
1800	295,273,311
1812	361,691,431
1821	355,540,258
1830	394,784,681
1841	413,457,311
1850	429,913,034

One sees from this that the figures in the early Ch'ing period rose only slightly between 1660 and 1730, but jumped abruptly in 1741 when the census came to be based on the *pao-chia* figures; thereafter the increase was steady. Actually, the figures for 1660-1730 represented neither the entire population nor returns of households nor tax-paying adult males, but were rather "tax-paying units" or *ting*—which were quotas of compulsory labor service commuted into money.[27] The figures for 1741 and thereafter were those of the individuals (*k'ou*, mouths) of every status.

The steady increase since 1741 may be explained in several ways, though the absolute figures themselves may not. For one thing, the merging of the land and poll taxes, whereby land and not person became the basis of taxation, erased much of the fear the people had had about reporting the actual numbers. Another possible reason to account for it is Emperor Ch'ien-lung's natural ostentatiousness and love of grandeur. He was fond of large figures as they attested to the prosperity of his reign,

27. Ping-ti Ho, 35. Thus, although the official figure for 1660 was 19 million, the actual population was probably somewhere around 100-150 million.

and he repeatedly warned the local officials not to conceal the true census figures. People who were formerly excluded from the census—women, old people, children, slaves, and mean persons—now were all included. Hence the sudden increase in 1741.

Chinese historians and demographers tend to believe that if the census figures after 1741 erred, they erred on the conservative side—that is, they were under- rather than over-reported; for a large section of the gentry harbored an inveterate resentment of being made to reveal the size of their households, and misrepresented wherever possible. One modern demographer suggests that the under-reporting of the census between 1741 and 1775 might be as high as 20 per cent of the total.[28] It is perhaps more reliable to derive census figures not from the number of individuals reported by the *pao-chia* but from the numbers of households registered, for one might conceal family members from the *pao-chia* registration but it would be difficult to hide the existence of a household. Take, for instance, the 38,845,354 households registered in 1753; multiplied by five, which was the average size of a household,[29] it comes to a figure of more than 190 million, which was very close to the figure of 1757 given above, but a considerable cut above the figure given for 1753.

Actually, the growth of population from 275 million in 1779 to 430 million in 1850 represented an increase of 56.3 per cent at an annual rate of 0.63 per cent, which is much lower than the 2 per cent annual increase in many of the rapidly expanding industrialized countries today.[30] The sharp increase from 1741 to 1779 might be ascribable to the generally favorable economic and political conditions and the long period of peace during the Ch'ien-lung era. Moreover, the increase of arable land and the introduction of foreign food products like maize, sweet potatoes, and peanuts from America in the 16th or 17th century also contributed to population increase. One is inclined to the opinion of the well-informed scholar, Wang Ch'ing-yün, that Ch'ing population figures showed less, rather than more, of the total picture.

Beginnings of Proto-Capitalism. Although the Ch'ing economy was predominantly agrarian, an incipient form of capitalism, which began to germinate during the 15th and 16th centuries, was slowly developing during the Ch'ien-lung period in the 18th century. Many small and

28. Ping-ti Ho, 46.
29. Ping-ti Ho gives 5.33 as the national average of a household; *ibid.*, 56.
30. *Ibid.*, 64.

medium-sized handicraft workshops had sprung up and an increasing commercialization of agricultural products was evident in the market. Communist historians on mainland China today, following the lead of Mao Tse-tung, assert that even in the absence of the intensified Western impact in the 19th century, China would have gone capitalist by herself.[31]

Workshops of considerable number and size could be found in weaving and porcelain, and in salt-, iron-, and copper-mining "industries." The silk-weaving business had its centers in Nanking, Soochow, Hangchow, and Huchow. In Nanking 30,000 looms were in operation during the Ch'ien-lung and Chia-ch'ing periods (1736-1820). Some workshops operated 400 to 600 looms, employing more than a thousand workers. Soochow, with more than 10,000 looms in operation, had a temporary employment agency to enlist the service of skilled or unskilled labor on a daily basis. Chengtu (in Szechwan) and Canton (in Kwangtung) were famous for brocade-weaving, with a considerable number of looms in each place. The silk products of Nanking were sold in great quantities throughout the country.

Porcelain was another handicraft industry that enjoyed a high degree of development during the 18th century. The famous chinaware center, Ching-te Chen, in Kiangsi had 200 to 300 privately owned kilns which employed hundreds of thousands of workers. Between 70 per cent and 80 per cent of the townsmen were engaged either in manufacturing or in trading porcelain. Fine divisions of labor were maintained between the workers and between the kilns. There was a careful distinction made among temporarily and regularly employed workers. Conflict between the workers and the employers, and strikes by disgruntled workers were already known to exist.

Salt manufacture was another enterprise that employed large numbers of workers. There were 2,319 salt wells in Szechwan province in 1730, and during the Ch'ien-lung period (1736-95) their number rose to 3,000. The digging and operation of the salt wells required a large capital outlay, and it is reported that some large salt plants involved as many as 300,000 or 400,000 men.[32]

Other enterprises existed, hiring great numbers of workers. The thirteen iron-mining houses in Hankow employed more than 5,000, for example.

31. Mao Tse-tung, *Mao Tse-tung hsüan-chi* (Selected works of Mao Tse-tung), 10th printing (Peking, 1963), II, 620; Tai I, *Chung-kuo chin-tai shih-kao* (A draft history of Chinese modern history), (Peking, 1961), I, chapter 1.
32. Tai I, 27.

And the copper mines in Yunnan were regularly run by twenty to thirty companies during the 18th century, producing 14,000,000 *chin* of copper annually. Larger copper mines employed 70,000 or 80,000 men, and smaller ones around 10,000. The total number of copper workers in Yunnan was in the neighborhood of 1,100,000. As with the porcelain artisans, there was a fine division of labor between them. The capital required for each of these mining operations was somewhere between 100,000 and 200,000 taels, and only the very wealthy merchants could afford to operate them.[33]

It is clear, then, that on the eve of the intensified Western impact, there had already emerged an incipient native capitalism in China. The various workshops, though still relying on handicraft skill as the basic mode of production, were already in possession of considerable capital and employed a sizable number of workers to produce commodities for the consumer market. Their stage of development was just one step before the appearance of the large-scale machine factories, a chronology characteristic of modern capitalistic enterprises.

Another sign of the development of this proto-capitalism was the commercialization of agricultural products. Plants that could be used as raw materials for handicraft industries gained increasing popularity. Cotton, for instance, was in great demand in the consumer market. In the cotton-producing areas in Sungkiang, T'ai-ts'ang, and T'ung-chou, 70 per cent to 80 per cent of the villagers were engaged in cotton planting and only 20 per cent to 30 per cent in rice. Cotton became an extremely active commercial item in the market. The planting of mulberry trees for silk-worm-feeding was the occupation of 100,000 households in Kwangtung because of its commercial profitability. Tobacco plantation was yet another major enterprise: half of the families in the tobacco-producing areas in Kwangsi were engaged in it, and 60 per cent to 70 per cent of the land in Fukien was reportedly given over to this crop. Sugar cane in Taiwan was still another agricultural product sold as a commercial commodity with a good profit.

Nevertheless, in the total picture of the Chinese economy the commercialization of agricultural products and the handicraft workshops of the various types made up a very small part. The country was still overwhelmingly agrarian, but the seeds of proto-capitalism were already sown. That the development of capitalism was retarded is partially ascribable to the heavy weight of traditional agrarian economy and to the unfavorable attitude of the Ch'ing government. There was fear that the employment

33. Tai I, 28-29.

of large numbers of workers in mining and other enterprises—some of them tucked away in the mountains and valleys, out of sight—might give rise to mass organizations in opposition to the government, similar to the "clique formation" of the scholars and officials. The court therefore discouraged the growth of capitalistic activities in favor of the safer agrarian kind. Nonetheless, the beginnings of capitalism were already evident, and a new economic force had been set in motion, however weak it may have been at its inception.

FURTHER READING

Backhouse, Edmund, and J. O. P. Bland, *Annals and Memoirs of the Court of Peking from the 16th to the 20th Century* (Boston, 1914).

Bodde, Derk, and Clarence Morris, *Law in Imperial China* (Cambridge, Mass., 1967).

Chen, Shao-kwan, *The System of Taxation in China in the Tsing Dynasty, 1644-1911* (New York, 1914).

Chi, Ch'ao-ting, *Key Economic Areas in Chinese History, as Revealed in the Development of Public Works for Water Control* (London, 1936).

Ch'ü, T'ung-tsu, *Local Government in China Under the Ch'ing* (Cambridge, Mass., 1962).

Cressey, George B., *Land of the 500 Million* (New York, 1955).

Fairbank, John K., and S. Y. Teng, *Ch'ing Administration: Three Studies* (Cambridge, Mass., 1960).

Farquhar, David Miller, "The Ch'ing Administration of Mongolia up to the Nineteenth Century" (Ph.D. thesis, Harvard University, 1960).

Hinton, Harold, *The Grain Tribute System of China, 1845-1911* (Cambridge, Mass., 1961).

Ho, Alfred K. L., 'The Grand Council in the Ch'ing Dynasty," *The Far Eastern Quarterly*, XI:2:167-82 (Feb. 1952).

Ho, Ping-ti, *Studies on the Population of China, 1368-1953* (Cambridge, Mass., 1959).

Hsiao, I-shan 蕭一山, *Ch'ing-tai t'ung-shih* 清代通史 (A general history of the Ch'ing period), revised edition (Taipei, 1962), I, chapters 19-21; II, chapters 7-9.

Hsiao, Kung-chüan, *Rural China: Imperial Control in the Nineteenth Century* (Seattle, 1960).

Hsieh, Pao Chao, *The Government of China (1644-1911)* (Baltimore, 1925).

Hucker, Charles O., *The Censorial System of Ming China* (Stanford, 1966).

Kessler, Lawrence D., "Ethnic Composition of Provincial Leadership during the Ch'ing Dynasty," *The Journal of Asian Studies*, XXVIII:3:489-511 (May 1969).

Liang, Fang-chung, *The Single Whip Method of Taxation in China* (Cambridge, Mass., 1961).

Mao Tse-tung, *Mao Tse-tung hsüan-chi* (Selected works of Mao Tse-tung), tenth printing, (Peking, 1963), II.

Mayers, W. F., *The Chinese Government* (Shanghai, 1897).

Morse, H. B., *The Trade and Administration of the Chinese Empire* (London, 1908).

Sprenkel, Sybille van der, *Legal Institutions in Manchu China, A Sociological Analysis* (London, 1962).

Sun, E-tu Zen, "Ch'ing Government and the Mineral Industries before 1800," *The Journal of Asian Studies*, XXVII:4:835-45 (Aug. 1968).

————, "The Board of Revenue in Nineteenth-Century China," *Harvard Journal of Asiatic Studies*, 24:175-228 (1962-63).

Taeuber, Irene B., and Wang Nai-chi, "Population Reports in the Ch'ing Dynasty," *Journal of Asian Studies*, XIX:403-17 (1959-60).

Tai I 戴逸, *Chung-kuo chin-tai shih-kao* 中國近代史稿 (A draft history of Chinese modern history), (Peking, 1961), third printing I, chapter 1.

Tang, Edgar C., "The Censorial Institution in China, 1644-1911" (Ph.D. thesis, Harvard University, 1932).

Teng, Ssu-yü, "Ming T'ai-tsu's Destructive and Constructive Work," *Chinese Culture*, VIII:3:14-38 (Sept. 1967).

Williams, S. Wells, *The Middle Kingdom* (New York, 1883), 2 vols.

Wu, Silas Hsiu-liang, "The Memorial Systems of the Ch'ing Dynasty (1644-1911)" *Harvard Journal of Asiatic Studies*, 27:7-75 (1967).

4

Social and Intellectual Conditions

THE CHINESE SOCIETY

The nature of Chinese society has been an object of keen interest to historians and sociologists. Marxist scholars have pointed to the combined exploitation of the peasantry by the landlords, usurers, and reactionary Manchu overlords, and have damned the Ch'ing society as feudal and bureaucratic. Others have emphasized the gentry as the dominant feature of the society. A more recent view appraises the Chinese society as an archetype of "Oriental despotism," characterized by a centralized monolithic government which kept the peasant masses in line by controlling the large-scale public projects, such as the building of roads and the raising of defensive walls along the frontiers, and especially the vast system of waterworks which the peasants needed for irrigation, flood control, drainage, and canalization.[1]

These three views—that of a feudal bureaucracy, a gentry-based elite, and an "Oriental despotism"—may at first glance appear contradictory, but they really are not, for each stresses an important aspect of Chinese society without canceling out the other two: the Ch'ing state was indeed a despotic autocracy, in which the bureaucrats within the government and the gentry outside of it dominated the political and social worlds; likewise, it was the peasant who paid the greatest part of the taxes to the government, the highest rents to the landlords, and the most exorbitant interest rates to the usurers. Each of these appraisals adumbrates a

1. Karl A. Wittfogel, *Oriental Despotism: A Comparative Study of Total Power* (New Haven, 1957).

characteristic of the state which existed side by side with the others; taken together they provide us with a fuller picture of the Chinese society.

The Family. The basic unit of the Chinese society was the family rather than the individual. The average size of the family was five members, contrary to the common belief that Chinese families were unusually large. The notion that several generations lived in one big household is true only in the case of the well-to-do; ordinary families could not afford that luxury. Within the family, respect was claimed and given according to age and sex, the older members enjoying a status superior to the younger ones, and the male members to the female. The family head was the father, who had complete authority over the other members. He decided all family issues, arranged his children's marriages, disciplined the unfilial and disobedient, and could even sell them if necessary. Yet for all his authority, he still had to act within the moral code of Confucianism and behave like a father—strict yet benevolent, authoritative yet paternalistic—so that his children would likewise behave in their expected roles. Status-consciousness led the father to speak respectfully to his own parents and authoritatively to his children. In the same vein, an elder brother conducted himself submissively toward his father but confidently before his younger brother. Indeed, the Chinese family was a laboratory of human relationships.

The status of women was very unlike that of the Western world. The wife was supposed to be obedient to her husband. She had no property rights and enjoyed no economic independence. Girls of good families had their feet bound at an early age in order to mold them to the ideal size and shape of a "three-inch golden lily"—a custom instituted by the men to prevent their women from running away from home, to enhance their feminine fragility, and to add to their erotic appeal. The widow was generally expected not to remarry, although the husband could take a concubine even if his legal wife was still alive.

Social Stratification. Chinese society was highly stratified. Among the many criteria for social classification, a very common one separated the farmers who constituted some 80 per cent of the population, from the other 20 per cent of the population, who lived in the urban areas and represented a composite stratum of scholars, gentry, officials, absentee landlords, artisans, merchants, militarists, etc. Another method of classification is to follow the Confucian principle of distinguishing the ruling group from the ruled on the basis of mental as opposed to menial work. "Those who labor with their minds rule others," the philosopher Mencius postulated, "and those who labor with their physical strength are ruled by others." Yet in reality not all brain workers were members of the ruling bureaucracy; at any given time during the Ch'ing period only a very small fraction of the 1.1 million degree-holders held the 27,000 official positions. Scientifically speaking, Chinese society has never been a simple, bipolarized structure of the ruling and the ruled, but always a multiclass one in which four major "functional orders"[2] coexisted: scholars, farmers, artisans, and tradesmen. Above them were the government bureaucrats, and below them were the "declassed" or "degraded" people,[3] who constituted a fraction of one per cent of the population and who, until their legal emancipation by Emperor Yung-cheng (1723-35), were denied the rights enjoyed by the common people.

Though stratified, the society was egalitarian in that there was no caste system. Except for the degraded, whose descendants for three generations were barred from the civil service examinations, the ladder of success was available to everyone, regardless of family, birth, or religion. There was in fact considerable movement up and down among the different social groups: powerful or high-status families could fall because of incompetent offspring, while men of humble circumstances rose through their successes in the open competitive government examinations and in receiving official appointments. More than anything else, individual merit based on literary excellence, as evidenced by the successful passing of the examinations, formed the basis of recognition.

The scholars, who occupied the top social stratum, included both those who passed the government examinations and those who did not. The latter included the literati who either failed or refused to take the examinations; they were known as the *pu-i* ("men wearing cotton clothes"). Those who passed the examinations or purchased an academic degree or official rank were called the *shen-shih,* usually translated as the gentry, and were divided into two groups: those who became government officials—the "official gentry"—and those who were not part of the bureauc-

2. Ping-ti Ho, *The Ladder of Success in Imperial China: Aspects of Social Mobility,* 1368-1911 (New York, 1962), 18.
3. These traditionally included the singers, dancers, entertainers, beggars, the "lazy people" of Chekiang, the boatmen, the hereditary servants, the bonded servants, prostitutes, actors, entertainers, and certain types of menial workers in government called the "runners."

racy—the scholar-gentry. The scholar-gentry were an intermediary group between the ruling class and the ruled, and were potential members of the ruling—a kind of reserve. They usually resided in their native places as community leaders until they were appointed to official posts in some area other than their own.

It must be explained that the term "gentry" is used here in a very different sense from what is meant by the Tudor English gentry, who owned large land estates, dominated country administration, and enjoyed fox hunts. In the Chinese context it applies to an elite social group who had acquired literary degrees, academic titles, or official ranks. Nothing could be further in spirit from the genteel, scholarly Chinese gentry than the hard-riding, rustic Tudor sort; nevertheless, the term is adopted here largely because it is an established English term which has more meaning for Western readers than another term might, and because many members of the Chinese gentry (in the predominantly agrarian Chinese society) did come from landed families, though this by itself was not the qualifying factor. Neither education nor ownership of land alone was sufficient to establish one's special status. Frequently a member of the gentry owned land after he had acquired his wealth from holding office, but the absence of primogeniture rule in China meant that no large landholdings could last very long, for the land was continually being divided among the offspring. Thus the gentry had no permanent hold on large land estates. As a rule they did not depend on land for the greater part of their income anyway: only about 30 per cent came from landholdings, while 50 per cent came from their government services; the remainder came from business enterprises of one sort or another. Property ownership, therefore, was almost incidental to one's status. It was literary excellence as demonstrated in the successful passing of the civil service examinations that provided the privileged position in the society. From this elite group came the country's public functionaries, artists, poets, philosophers, and thinkers.

The farmers, who were next in importance to the scholar-gentry, made up the bulk (80 per cent) of the population. Their great numbers gave them an added importance, for, besides raising the country's food, they were also the principal source of taxes, manpower for the public works, and military conscription. Their indispensable position in the agrarian society qualified them for a higher status than those of artisans and merchants. The farmers were not bound to the soil as were their counterparts in many parts of feudal Europe, but were free to move about, to buy and sell their land. They lived in small villages rather than on separate homesteads, and as long as they paid their taxes, performed the *corvée* labor, and accepted the obligations of the *pao-chia* and *li-chia* systems, they were left pretty much to themselves.

This relative freedom and comparatively high status in the establishment did not mean, however, that they had a comfortable life. Although most of them owned and cultivated their own plots of land, their average holdings were quite small—the equivalent of three acres in North China and an acre and a half in South China. The smallness of the individual plots was due in part to the absence of primogeniture rule, and in part to the limited physical capacity of a farm family to till. The farmer worked all year round to get the maximum production out of his diminutive acreage, and even then the yield was hardly enough to sustain an average family of five. But hard as it was for those who owned their land, it was worse for those who rented, for they had to pay as much as 40 to 70 per cent of the main crop to the landlords. It is perhaps ironic that the second most important member of the society should chronically be posed on the brink of disaster; very often, when faced with a tax deadline or some pressing family need, he had no choice but to turn to the usurers. As a result of high taxes, irregular levies, exorbitant rents, and the usurious interests which he was forced to accrue in order to meet the other payments, the farmer was continuously reduced to near starvation, and his life was a perennial struggle for survival. Occasionally a bright boy would surmount all the obstacles and obtain for himself an education which would qualify him to pass the competitive examinations and win degrees. He would then be admitted to the gentry membership and could acquire official appointments, bringing honor to his family and lifting it from poverty.

The artisans, who came third in the social stratification, included carpenters, masons, ironsmiths, coppersmiths, tinsmiths, tailors, painters, shoemakers, barbers, and the like. They formed guilds according to their respective trades, and the guilds regulated prices, standards, and quality of works. Artisans of the same trade tended to run their shops in the same quarters of the towns. In addition to the regular handicraft artisans, there was also in the same social category an emerging group of proto-industrial workers in such enterprises as weaving, mining, porcelain-making, paper-making, etc., as noted in the preceding chapter. The average income of an artisan was somewhat higher than that of a farmer, notwithstanding his lower status; a carpenter or a bricklayer before the mid-Ch'ing period earned about .05 or .06 tael a day; his annual income was somewhere between 10 and 20 taels. This was not much, to be sure, but the cost of living was correspondingly low. An ordinary meal, or a catty of chicken or duck, cost about .01 to .02 tael, and a picul of fine rice cost roughly one tael in the early Ch'ing period.[4] In times of peace and prosperity, such as the K'ang-hsi and Ch'ien-lung periods, the artisans could eke out a modest living, but in times of unrest, when the cost of living climbed, their meager income was scarcely sufficient to make ends meet.

The merchants were at the bottom of the social scale. They included not only the wealthy monopolistic traders but also the small shopkeepers and the clerks and apprentices. Their income varied with their work and the range was very wide indeed. Powerful tea and silk merchants who controlled the distribution of these commodities throughout the country were enormously rich. The salt merchants of Yangchow were particularly noted for their great wealth and luxurious living; their estimated aggregate profit in the second half of the 18th century was something like 250,000,000 taels.[5] The various houses of foreign trade were likewise famous for their riches; Howqua of Canton, for instance, built up a fortune of 26 million silver dollars in 1834 which was, according to H. B. Morse, the largest mercantile fortune on earth.[6]

However, wealth alone did not bring honor, or position, or security in the society. The merchants were not protected from official interference;

---

4. Hsiao I-shan, *Ch'ing-tai shih* (A history of the Ch'ing dynasty), 116. To be sure, there were yearly and even monthly fluctuations in prices of commodities, but the variations did not seem to be large except in years of droughts and floods. The following list shows the range of the fine rice prices in Kiangsu:

1693	(7th month)	0.9 tael per picul (133.33 lbs.)
	(10th month)	1.0
1698	(11th month)	1.0
1706	(3rd month)	1.43 ⎫
1707	(8th month)	1.47 ⎬ years of drought and floods
1710	(3rd month)	1.2
	(9th month)	0.7
1716	(2nd month)	1.0
1720	(6th month)	0.95

For details, see Spence, *Ts'ao Yin*, Appendix B, 297-99.
5. Ping-ti Ho, "The Salt Merchants of Yang-chow: A Study of Commercial Capitalism in Eighteenth-Century China," *Harvard Journal of Asiatic Studies*, 17:149 (1954).
6. H. B. Morse, *The International Relations of the Chinese Empire* (London, 1910), I, 86. Twenty-six million silver dollars was the equivalent of US $52 million. See Frederic Wakeman, Jr., *Strangers at the Gate: Social Disorder in South China, 1839-1861* (Berkeley, 1966), 44.

their security depended on the whim of the government. The officials could descend on them at any time to exact contributions or make irregular levies. Those merchants who worked with government monopolies such as salt and foreign trade could lose their franchise at the slightest provocation of official displeasure. Out of prudence, rich merchants tended to invest their surplus assets in land and acquired the more stable and respectable status of landlords. The more aggressive ones would purchase degrees for themselves or their sons so as to acquire the coveted gentry status. Of course the sons of rich merchant families could always manage to get a good education and try their luck in the competitive examinations. There was no social or legal barrier to the rise of merchant families to a higher status in the society. With land possession and a son in the government or in the gentry group, the merchant obtained the needed protection.

The merchants formed their guilds by trade much in the same way as the artisans, the greatest difference being that the merchant guilds were considerably richer. The guilds set prices and rules for business practice, arbitrated disputes among members, and provided aid in case of insolvency. The guild of the thirteen monopolistic merchants of foreign trade in Canton was particularly influential. But by and large commercial activities were regarded as beneath the dignity of the scholar-gentry, and the pursuit of profit was frowned upon by correct Confucianists. Such an attitude inhibited the growth of business enterprises.

The Gentry: Their Privileges and Functions. The gentry, or *shen-shih*—those scholars who had passed the government examinations—occupied a dominant role in the society and enjoyed many unique privileges. Only they, for instance, could attend official ceremonies in the Confucian temples, and it was usually they who led the ancestral rituals that were performed in clans. The gentry were distinguished from the commoners in style of dress and in embellishments. They wore black gowns with blue borders, and decorated their saddles and reins with splendid articles such as fur, brocade, and fancy embroidery. None of the commoners, no matter how rich, were allowed the same privilege. The *sheng-yüan* wore buttons of plain silver on their hats, and the *chü-jen* and *chin-shih* wore plain gold buttons.[7] When a degree-holder rose to an official position of

7. These were the scholars who had passed, the district, provincial, and metropolitan examinations, respectively, upon which their status as "lower" or "upper" gentry depended. The examinations and degrees are discussed in some detail in the next section.

the first rank, his gold button had a flower design added to it, with a ruby on top and a pearl in the middle, and his robe was embroidered with nine pythons.

Then gentry were protected against insults from commoners and interference from officials. A commoner who offended a gentry member would be punished more severely than one who had committed the same offense to another commoner. Furthermore, ordinary people were not allowed to involve the gentry as witnesses in lawsuits. If a member of the gentry was involved in such a suit himself, he was not required to appear before the court in person but could send a servant instead. A member of this upper class who had committed a crime presented an awkward problem, for gentry status made one immune to action by the local magistrate. In order to be prosecuted, such a person had first to be stripped of his gentry status. But the district magistrate could not perform this act, because the gentry member was his social equal. The divesting could be performed only by the educational commissioner, and it was he whom the magistrate had to consult before any punishment could be issued. Violation of this rule could bring about the impeachment of the magistrate.

The gentry were exempt from *corvée* labor service, for their station and cultural refinement forbade them to engage in manual labor. They were also excused from paying the poll tax in order that they might devote themselves to the studies that would qualify them for future government examinations and service. When the poll and land taxes were merged in 1727, the gentry managed to pay less of the combined assessment than did the commoners. They called their houses "scholar households" (*ju-hu*), or "gentry households" (*shen-hu*), or "big households" (*ta-hu*), as distinguished from the "commoner households" (*min-hu*) or "small households" (*hsiao-hu*), so as to make differentiations in tax payments. The gentry household might pay as little as 2,000 or 3,000 cash (copper coins) for each picul (133⅓ lbs) of rice that was collected as tax, or sometimes no grain tribute at all, whereas the commoner's household had to pay 6,000 or 7,000 cash for each picul.[8] Not infrequently the commoner and the gentry colluded to falsify land registration: the farmer would use the gentry member's name for the farmland and thus pay a lower tax and avoid labor conscription. Sometimes the gentry avoided the onerous surtaxes and delayed paying regular taxes in hopes that eventually they would not have to pay at all. In times of hardship or poor

8. Chung-li Chang, *The Chinese Gentry* (Seattle, 1955), 43.

harvest the gentry often asked for official remission or reduction of taxes in the name of the people; when the request was granted, it was they and not the people who benefited the most.

Privileged as they were, the scholar-gentry were not part of the ruling bureaucracy; they were the intermediary agent between the local magistrate and the people. The magistrate had to rely on them for information and advice on local affairs, and they in turn promoted the welfare and interest of their locality. The magistrate, usually a degree-holder from another province, had no great interest in local affairs and was reluctant to start long-term projects that would not yield results during his term of office, which was quite short.[9] Such projects therefore customarily fell to the gentry. They financed the construction and repair of public works, such as the bridges and ferries; in the Hui-chow prefecture, Kwangtung, for instance, the gentry constructed and repaired thirty-four bridges and seventeen ferries during the Ch'ing period, as opposed to the ten bridges and one ferry taken care of by the officials. The gentry also raised funds for dredging rivers, building dikes and dams, and improving irrigation systems, and they contributed to the upkeep of local temples, shrines, and memorial arches. Often they were involved in local charity and welfare cases such as the organizing of rice distribution centers for the poor.

A major function performed by the gentry in the local community was the settlement out of court of civil disputes between individuals and communities, using persuasion and arbitration rather than law. Since appearance in court was detrimental to one's reputation, disputes were more frequently settled privately, under the direction of the gentry, than in court, under the magistrate.

The gentry considered themselves guardians of the cultural heritage. They took it upon themselves to disseminate moral principle and they contributed heavily to the establishment of private academies. Twice a month they expounded K'ang-hsi's Sacred Edict of Sixteen Politico-moral Maxims[10] to the villagers in their respective prefectures. They supported

9. Averaging 1.7 to 4.5 years before 1800, and .9 to 1.7 years afterward; *ibid.*, 53.
10. Issued by Emperor K'ang-hsi in the eleventh year (1672) of his reign. They were read to students and expounded to the people on the 1st and 15th of each lunar month:
1. Stress filial piety and brotherly love to exalt human relations.
2. Be sincere to your kindred to manifest the virtue of harmony.
3. Maintain peace in your local communities to absolve quarrels and litigations.
4. Emphasize agriculture and sericulture to insure a full supply of food and clothing.
5. Promote thrift to save expenditures.

the examination system and often contributed money for the construction and repair of the local examination halls. Because the examples of loyal, filial, chaste, and virtuous persons were considered beneficial to public morality, the gentry compiled local gazetteers, which recorded the history of the localities and the biographies of prominent figures of the area.

In times of turmoil and unrest, when government troops were unable to afford protection to the local areas, the gentry would organize militia and at times even lead the fighting themselves. They raised funds to construct or repair the fortresses or city walls, and so strengthened the defense of their localities.

From arbitration of disputes to the sponsorship of public works to the organization of local defense, the gentry performed an indispensable function in their home areas. They served as a link between the government and the people: on the one hand they advised the officials on local affairs, and on the other they promoted the local interests to the officials as the commoners could not do. Because they were the social equal of the magistrates they could communicate freely, without the fear and diffidence of the commoner; thus they enjoyed the best of both worlds. The district magistrate, ever conscious of the gentry's possible connections with authorities higher than himself, and mindful that some members of the gentry might in fact rise above himself, saw to it that the gentry's position was respected. If the magistrates represented the formal power, the gentry represented the informal. In normal times the power of both derived from the same political order, and hence their interests

---

6. Expand schools to rectify the behavior of scholars.
7. Reject heterodox doctrines to honor the orthodox learning.
8. Make known the laws to warn the foolish and obstinate.
9. Manifest propriety and righteousness to cultivate good customs.
10. Accept your own calling to the end that the minds of all may be stabilized.
11. Admonish your children and youngsters against evil-doing.
12. Eliminate false accusations to preserve the good and innocent.
13. Refrain from protecting fugitives to avoid collective punishment.
14. Complete tax payments to dispense with official prompting.
15. Cooperate with the *pao-chia* neighborhood organizations to forestall burglary and thievery.
16. Resolve vengeance and animosities to guard your own lives.

The above is my own translation. Cf. three other versions: Rev. William Milne, *The Sacred Edit, Containing Sixteen Maxims of Emperor Kang-hi*, 2nd ed. (Shanghai, 1870); John K. Fairbank, Edwin O. Reischauer, and Albert M. Craig, *East Asia: The Modern Transformation* (Boston, 1965), 85; and Dun J. Li, *The Ageless Chinese: A History* (New York, 1965), 323.

coincided. But at other times, when their interests collided, the gentry could remonstrate with the officials with impunity, because they were the only pressure group in the locality. And if the worst should come, the gentry might organize an uprising in righteous protest of government oppression. Without question, the gentry were the most important single group in Chinese society. It is not without good reason that China was sometimes described as a "gentry state."

The Government Examinations. After observing the enormously influential stature of the gentry in the society, it is imperative to investigate the procedure by which one became a member of this group. Gentry status was conferred upon one, as mentioned in the last section, largely as a result of one's winning a literary degree in the civil service examinations. The ability to compose what was called the "eight-legged (i.e. eight-paragraphed) essay" (*pa-ku wen*) was essential to success in the examinations. This essay demonstrated a formal and rigid style of writing, requiring great literary skills but no profound knowledge. The candidate's ability, furthermore, had to manifest itself within a tight, prefabricated framework which allowed for only a minimum of creativity, and that only in minute details. The essay opens with two sentences of preliminary remarks, which are followed by three sentences of introduction and a short paragraph of general discussion. Then comes a short paragraph composed of one to three sentences that deal specifically with the subject matter, followed by two verse-paragraphs—a short one and a long one—composed of phrases of four or six words each, in rhymed couplets. The essay moves gradually into a preliminary closing paragraph, and perorates in a final paragraph of conclusions. The length of this performance ranges between 360 and 720 words. Successful writers had to excel in rhyme and diction as well as in calligraphy and poetical expressions. Poor phraseology or slipshod calligraphy reflected an unsound training in fundamentals or even "village mediocrity," which could doom the candidate from the start.

The examinations were conducted on the district, provincial, and metropolitan levels. In order to qualify for the first of these, the preliminary district examination (*t'ung-shih*), the candidate had to present a guarantee of his origin and character from a member of the gentry. This examination was held twice every three years and consisted of three sessions. The first session, conducted by the district magistrate for candidates of his locality, required two "eight-legged essays" on subjects taken from the Confucian Four Books[11] and a short poem of six couplets, with five characters to the line. Many candidates were eliminated in this first session for such things as the wrong use of words, violation of the rules of rhyme, and poor calligraphy; the successful candidates (*t'ung-sheng*) proceeded to the second session. This was given by the prefect or independent department (*chou*) magistrate. A test similar to the first one was administered to make sure that no one had passed the first one by luck, and then the candidate was asked to write from memory one or two hundred words from the Annotations of the Sixteen Politico-moral Maxims of K'ang-hsi's Sacred Edict. The candidates who passed this hurdle then took the *yüan* examination given by the provincial educational commissioner (whose title was *hsüeh-yüan*, whence the name of the examination). The dates set for this third session varied from place to place according to how the educational commissioner decided to schedule it. The number of candidates who could emerge successfully from the sessions was prearranged by quotas set by the government. In the entire country, for instance, only 25,089 were allowed for each *yüan* examination. Of this number, Chihli was alloted the highest provincial quota (2,845) and Kweichow the lowest (753.)[12] Only about one or two per cent of the candidates passed the *yüan* examination, taking the degree or title of *sheng-yüan* (government student), more commonly called *hsiu-ts'ai* (beautiful talent). With this degree they were admitted to membership among the gentry, but they were only the "lower gentry." Their average age was 24. Given a life expectancy of 57, they enjoyed gentry status for 33 years. At any given time before 1850 there were about 526,869 civil *sheng-yüan* and 212,330 military *sheng-yüan* in the whole country, i.e., a total of 740,000 extant at any one time.[13]

The *sheng-yüan*, or government students, became members of the district college and received allowances from the provincial government with which to prepare themselves for the higher examinations. The local gentry gave them travel subsidies to the provincial capital for the next examinations. These were conducted triennially by a chief examiner and an associate examiner, whom the emperor appointed from among the officials holding the metropolitan degree. By the "law of avoidance" these examiners had to come from other provinces than the one in which the exam-

11. *The Analects, The Book of the Mean, The Book of Mencius,* and *The Great Learning.*
12. Chung-li Chang, 73, 141-42.
13. *Ibid.,* 97-98.

inations were being held. They were aided by eight to eighteen assistant examiners, appointed by the governor-general or governor from among the provincial officials who held at least the provincial degree, i.e., *chü-jen*. As the government allowed a quota of only 1,400 successful candidates for the whole country, the competition in the provincial examination was very keen.

Like the district examination, the provincial examination consisted of three sessions. The sessions began usually on the ninth day of the eighth lunar month. On the day before, the candidates entered the examination halls; they were locked up in cells for three days to write three essays on subjects chosen from the Confucian Four Books and to compose an eight-couplet poem with five words to each line. Released from their cells on the tenth of the month, they re-entered them on the eleventh for the second session, this time to compose five essays on the Five Classics.[14] They were let out again on the 13th, only to return once more on the 14th for the third session, in which five more essays were required, these to be on government. They came out of the cells on the 16th, exhausted. The results of the examination were announced in 45 days if the province happened to be a large one; if it was a medium-size one they were given out in 40 days, and if a small one, in 30 days.

Extreme care was taken in the examination hall to avoid corruption in its various forms, especially favoritism. All papers written by the candidates were anonymous, and all the assistant examiners were held incommunicado while they were grading the papers. They recommended the better papers to the chief and associate examiners, who made the final decision. On the day the results were to be announced, the chief examiner, accompanied by the governor or governor-general, conferred the degree of *chü-jen* (employable men) to the successful candidates in the emperor's name, and on the following day the governor-general or governor gave a banquet in honor of the new degree-holders.

The examination papers were then forwarded to the Board of Rites in Peking for scrutiny and safekeeping. Those who failed in the provincial examinations but who otherwise showed high scholastic promise were given the title of *kung-sheng* (senior licentiates) and retired to their home towns as local community leaders or teachers, to await the next examination. The successful provincial graduates returned home in glory, for they reflected honor on their families and their districts. These for-

14. *The Book of Odes, The Book of History, The Book of Changes, The Book of Rites,* and *The Spring and Autumn Annals.*

tunates became members of the "upper gentry"; their average age was 31. They were given traveling expenses by the provincial government so that they might compete in the triennial metropolitan examination in Peking, usually given in the third month of the following year.

The metropolitan examination was also in three sessions. In the first, the candidates wrote four essays—three expository and one critical—on historical subjects; in the second, four expository essays on the classics and one short poem of eight rhymes, five characters per line; and in the third session, an essay on a current political topic.

The results of this examination were known in thirty days. Successful candidates were designated *kung-shih* (presentable scholars) and were qualified to take the palace examination a month and a half later, of which the emperor, with the assistance of fourteen ranking officials, took personal charge. There was only one session to this examination. The candidates wrote an essay of a thousand or more words on current problems. Although the substance of the essay was important, artistic penmanship and an exceptional literary style could catch the attention of the graders and create a good impression at the start. The fourteen examiners selected the ten best papers for the emperor, who indicated his preferences and his ranking of the candidates with a vermilion brush. The successful candidates of the palace examination were given the degree of *chin-shih* (advanced scholar). They were divided into three ranks: the first consisted of the three candidates with the highest honors, the second contained roughly the next 30 per cent of the candidates, and the third held the remainder. An imperial banquet was given in their honor; a gift of 80 taels was bestowed on the three in the first rank, and 30 taels were given each of the rest. The average age of the *chin-shih* was 34 or 35. The government quota allowed only one out of ten to succeed in the metropolitan examination. From 1644 to 1911, a total of 112 such examinations were held and 26,747 *chin-shih* degrees granted: an average of 238 degrees per examination and about 100 per year.[15]

It is often assumed, with some justification, that only the children of the very rich could afford the prolonged years of education necessary to prepare for the examinations. Of course the rich could meet the costs of education more easily; nevertheless, a good many of the poorer families managed to produce successful candidates. Recent research has revealed a considerable social spread among the degree-holders during the Ming (1368-1643) and Ch'ing (1644-1911) periods. During the Ming rule,

15. Ping-ti Ho, *The Ladder of Success*, 189.

47.5 per cent of the *chin-shih* came from families which had had no degree holders at all for the preceding three generations, and 2.5 per cent came from families whose past three generations had producd no one holding a degree higher than the elementary *sheng-yüan;* about 50 per cent came from families having holders of higher degrees in the last three generations. During the Ch'ing times, 19.1 per cent of the *chin-shih* came of families who were degreeless for three generations back; 18.1 per cent came from families that had had one or more *sheng-yüan* but no holders of higher degrees. What these figures show is that a total of 37.2 per cent of the *chin-shih* came from families whose educational background for the preceding three generations had been low or nil, while 62.8 per cent came from families with holders of higher degrees or offices for the same three generations.[16]

The provinces which were most prolific were Kiangsu and Chekiang—accounting for 2,920 and 2,808 *chin-shih*, respectively, out of a total of 26,747 granted during the entire Ch'ing period—followed by Chihli (with 2,701), Shantung (2,260), and Kiangsi (1,895). There were approximately 130 *chin-shih* per million people in Chekiang and 93 per million in Kiangsu. Within the provinces, the most successful prefectures were Hangchow in Chekiang, with 1,004 *chin-shih* during the Ch'ing period, and Suchow in Kiangsu, with 785.[17]

Since success and honor in the Ch'ing system was based so predominantly upon scholarship, an attitude came to prevail in the society that "all activities are unworthy; only learning is lofty." A student spent his entire youth getting ready for the examinations, and it was not unusual for an unlucky one to fail a dozen times or more in the triennial event—thereby virtually forfeiting his entire lifetime. Even the successful ones were marked by the exhaustion imposed on them by the unremitting intellectual strain. They were stunned into submissiveness and became cautious and meek officials of the court, offering little threat of inciting a rebellion. No wonder the ruler could remark with satisfaction: "All the brilliant men of the world have been trapped in my bag!"

The greatest shortcomings of the examination system were its narrow scope and impractical nature. Literary excellence and administrative ability were quite different matters: proficiency in one did not necessarily imply competence in the other. Conformity to the rigid pattern of the "eight-legged essay" tended to stifle free expression and encourage ortho-

16. Ping-ti Ho, 114.
17. Ping-ti Ho, 228-29, 247.

doxy of thought. What is perhaps most important, the examination system stressed the Confucian values only and rewarded literary and humanistic accomplishments at the expense of science, technology, commerce, and industry.

On the other hand, the system had its good points. It selected men of superior intelligence and common sense for public service. It set up objective and impartial standards for social advancement and reduced the chances for nepotism and other forms of favoritism. It made the society more egalitarian by permitting nearly all its members to rise to the top through individual merit rather than through birth and wealth. It encouraged social flexibility and tended to blur class distinctions. The convergence in government of educated men from all walks of life and all parts of the country created a force of unity. The intellectuals of the country formed an educated bureaucracy which assisted the government rather than criticized it, as opposed to bureaucratic habits in the West. Put on the scales, the advantages of the examination system probably outweighed the disadvantages.

Though passing the civil service examinations was the regular way to acquire gentry membership, it was not the only way. The academic title of *chien-sheng*—student status in the Imperial College—could also be bought. Occasionally, so could the title *kung-sheng*. The purchasers were usually literate men of means who had failed to win a regular degree or who wished to attain the coveted gentry status by short cut. The purchasers were "irregular" members of the gentry; they did not enjoy the same prestige as the regular members, and their appointments were usually made at a low level. However, they could regularize their status by passing the provincial and metropolitan examinations. Some perfectly intelligent students who also happened to be wealthy bought the *chien-sheng* title to qualify for the provincial examinations, without going through the pains of the district examinations.

It should be mentioned that there was a complete set of military degrees, corresponding to the civil ones, which could be won either by examination or by purchase, but most of the army officers rose from the ranks rather than through the examinations. Their official position gave them the status of gentry, too.

At any one time before 1850 the total number of the gentry was about 1.1 million, of whom 4,000 were civil and military *chin-shih*, and the rest were holders of other degrees and titles. There were, at the same time, only 27,000 official positions to be had in the whole country—

20,000 civil and 7,000 military. Regular degree-holders occupied the more important half of the 20,000 civil jobs, while the less important half went to the holders of purchased degrees. Since there were so many more successful candidates than available positions, the greater part of the degree-holders had to stay out of the government. But nearly all the metropolitan graduates and about one-third to one-half of the provincial graduates won appointments, while a small percentage of the *kung-sheng* and *sheng-yüan* were also able to step into official posts.[18] Those who were not part of the bureaucracy became the gentry and community leaders in the society at large.

INTELLECTUAL TRENDS

Early Ch'ing Reaction Against Ming Idealism. The early Ch'ing intellectual world was split into two circles. The government officially sponsored the Sung school of Neo-Confucianism as it had been taught in the 11th and 12th centuries by the Ch'eng brothers[19] and Chu Hsi. Chinese officials who served in the government and scholars who wished to do so attached themselves to this "Sung learning" (*Sung-hsüeh*) as to a kind of state philosophy. On the other hand, there were in the country a great many Ming loyalists who refused to serve the Manchus and who rejected Neo-Confucianism in favor of the so-called "Han learning" (*Han-hsüeh*), by which they hoped to create a new intellectual climate that would help topple the Ch'ing dynasty and restore the Ming.

The Ch'ing rulers used Neo-Confucianism as an instrument to win control over the intellectuals, the habitual ruling class in China, and through them over the people. K'ang-hsi's Sacred Edict of Sixteen Maxims, a required reading for all subjects, was full of the Confucian ideas of loyalty, obedience, duty, morality, and propriety. The task of the government, it was reasoned, would be facilitated if everyone followed these maxims and if the scholars and officials could set an example for the rest of the empire. K'ang-hsi was particularly impressed with the Sung philosopher Chu Hsi for his balance and proper interpretation of the Confucian classics. Every question and every answer on the Four Books and

18. Chung-li Chang, 116-18. The majority of the degree-holders had to wait ten to twenty years before they received appointments. John R. Watt, "Leadership Criteria in Late Imperial China." Paper read before the 62nd annual meeting of the Pacific Coast Branch, American Historical Association, San Diego, August 28, 1969.
19. Ch'eng Hao and Ch'eng I.

Five Classics in the civil service examinations had to conform to Chu's commentaries, which, as noted earlier, K'ang-hsi had praised as the "grand synthesis of hundreds and thousands of years of untransmitted learning, capable of opening the minds of fools and children and of establishing the ultimate goal (truth) for a myriad of generations."

The Sung school of Rationalism (li-hsüeh), commonly known in the Western world as Neo-Confucianism, was a syncretic philosophy which contained elements of Confucianism, Buddhism, and Taoism, and which provided a system of metaphysics to sanction the old Confucian moral order. Its most eminent apostles were Ch'eng Hao (1031-85), Ch'eng I (1032-1107), and Chu Hsi (1130-1200). These Sung scholars advanced the dual concepts of the rational principle (li) and its material manifestation (ch'i). According to this school, everything has a rational principle for its being. "All things under heaven," Ch'eng I wrote, "can be understood in the light of their (rational) principle. As there are things, there must be their specific (rational) principles. One thing necessarily has one principle."[20] Thus, a tree or a blade of grass has its own rational principle which makes it what it is. There is only one universal rational principle, although there are many manifestations of it. For instance, the concept of jen, often translated as humanity or benevolence, is manifested in filial piety, in affection to one's children, in loyalty to one's ruler, etc. Thus, there is only one jen but many manifestations.

Chu Hsi synthesized the Neo-Confucian ideas into a systematized school of philosophy. He reaffirmed the idea of one principle and many manifestations and called the sum total of all rational principles the "Supreme Ultimate" (T'ai-chi). With regard to the dual concepts of li and ch'i, he said, "There has never been any material force [ch'i] without the [rational] principle, nor [rational] principle without the material force . . . [Rational] principle is not a separate entity. It exists right in the material force. Without the material force, [rational] principle would have nothing to adhere to."[21] To Chu's mind, rational principle was immanent in the material force; the two did not exist separately, or independently of each other, much less in opposition. It is clear that although Chu advanced the dual concepts of li and ch'i, he did not preach the dualistic nature of things, as many assumed he did.

The Sung Neo-Confucianists, though metaphysically oriented, did not

20. Wing-tsit Chan, "The Evolution of the Neo-Confucian Concept Li as Principle," Tsing Hua Journal of Chinese Studies, New Series, IV:2:139 (Feb. 1964).
21. Wing-tsit Chan, 141.

lose sight of the practical aspects of Confucianism. They regarded the rational principle as the moral law that must be followed, and declared that an understanding of it could be achieved through the investigation of the nature of things and the study of history and the classics. They continued to stress the cultivation of the self and the management of the family in preparation for service to the state and the world at large. Even in their abstract discourses on the rational principle they emphasized the importance of book-reading and nature-investigating—both pursuits involving substantial effort. Nevertheless, it was the fresh and stimulating metaphysical side of Neo-Confucianism, rather than the practical side, that caught the attention of their disciples.

In time, Neo-Confucianism became rarefied. As the school entered the Ming period (1368-1643), the scholars persisted in the general tendency toward abstract discourse and metaphysical argumentation. The practical aspects of Confucianism were neglected and the classics went untouched. Students drifted in su'lime philosophizing of Mind (*hsin*) and Nature (*hsing*) without finding it necessary to read books; they had only to follow the Yung-lo *Hsing-li ta-ch'iian* (Encyclopedia on human nature and rational principle) to pass the civil service examinations and win official appointments, and that was the extent of their academic commitments.

The philosopher Wang Yang-ming (1472-1529) rose to propound his own idealistic school of Neo-Confucianism (*hsin-hsüeh*) as a revolt against Chu Hsi's rationalistic school. Wang was influenced by the meditative Ch'an (Zen) sect of Buddhism and by the Sung philosopher Lu Hsiang-shan (1139-93), who took the view that "the universe is my mind, and my mind is the universe. . . . What permeates the mind, what emanates from it and extends to fill the universe, is nothing but the principle." Wang found very congenial the idea that "the mind is the universe," and he argued further that when the mind was cleared of selfish desires it would be congruent with the principle of nature and hence would know the good from the evil. From this came Wang's theory of the "intuitive knowledge" (*liang-chih*, literally, "good innate knowledge"), which held that all things were complete within oneself; one needed only to search inwardly through meditation to discover the good "intuitive knowledge." Thus, instead of Chu Hsi's "extension of knowledge through the investigation of things," Wang stressed the nurture of intuitive knowledge through meditation and introspection. It should be noted, however, that even Wang did not neglect the importance of practical action. The mind, which is supreme, must "always be doing something," that is, must be actively engaged in human affairs. A sincere innate knowledge of filial piety was not its own end; rather it was desirable insofar as it would lead a man to serve his parents filially. Hence it was important to unite knowledge with action: "Knowledge is the beginning of action," he maintained, "and action the completion of knowledge." The unity of the two could be achieved through self-discipline and self-cultivation.[22]

In spite of his underscoring the importance of action, Wang's philosophy further strengthened rather than weakened the general tendency toward metaphysical discourse. Students packed books away as if reading were anathema and languished in the opiate of aimless abstract dialogue. The latter-day followers of Wang abused his teachings to the point of proclaiming that wine, women, wealth, and anger were not obstacles to Enlightenment. Uninhibited sexual freedom and unabashed drinking orgies were celebrated as free exercise of the "intuitive knowledge." Some disciples went so far as to insist that a sinner was also a sage, quoting out of context the master's statement that "all people in the street are sages." To maneuver themselves into official positions they took to currying favor with the court eunuchs. When social and moral behavior reached such a nadir, as a result of the Wang school of thought, a reaction against that school was bound to arise.

A group of serious scholars at the Tung-lin Academy in Wusih, Kiangsu, attempted to turn the tide of intellectual irresponsibility and moral degradation by shifting attention from the abstract back to the practical, and from individual introspection to engagement in public affairs. In their "moral crusade," they visited an ungenerous attack on political corruption which led, unfortunately, to their political destruction at the hands of the powerful eunuch Wei Chung-hsien; but they succeeded at least in arousing an interest in public affairs among scholars.[23]

Toward the end of the Ming dynasty a general weariness of the Wang philosophy had set in, and scholars began to react against the superficial and abstract discourse on Mind and Nature in which the school indulged. Liu Tsung-chou (1578-1645), a onetime follower of Wang, turned to attack the doctrine of intuitive knowledge. He de-emphasized the metaphysical elements of the Wang school and favored practical deeds over

22. Wing-tsit Chan, 142, 213.
23. For a study of the Tung-lin movement, see Charles O. Hucker, "The Tung-lin Movement of the late Ming Period" in Fairbank (ed.) *Chinese Thought and Institutions*, 132-62.

idle talk. Hsü Hung-tsu (1585-1641)[24] made a nationwide geographical survey and recorded his findings in his famous *Travelogue*, published posthumously in 1776. Sung Ying-hsing (born *ca.* 1600), compiled a compendium in applied science in 1637 called the *T'ien-kung k'ai-wu* (The ingenious creation of things by nature), which contained eighteen sections of discussion on such practical subjects as weaving, hydraulics, coinage, and gold-mining.[25] To conjur up an interest in old (and therefore good) books, a group of seven scholars[26] advocated the study of Ch'in (221-206 B.C.) and Han (202 B.C.-A.D. 220) works and urged that no books be read that had been written subsequent to the T'ang (A.D. 618-907) era. These activities pointed up a growing trend away from the kind of introspective meditation and metaphysical discussion that feeds only on itself, and return to more practical subjects and the more solid learning of the pre-T'ang era.

The great scholars of the early Ch'ing period who survived the dynastic change were mostly products of this new intellectual climate. They reacted vigorously against the Ming intellectuals, whom they held accountable for the moral and social degradation and the ultimate collapse of the dynasty. They called upon scholars to free themselves of the shackles imposed on them by the Sung and Ming learning and to seek truth directly from the old classics. Their advocating of practical studies and serious scholarship had itself a realistic purpose: to create a healthy intellectual atmosphere which would contribute to the overthrow of the Manchus.

Ku Yen-wu (1613-82) of Kunshan, Kiangsu, was the first to launch a powerful attack on the unhealthy Ming intellectual disposition. He censured Wang Yang-ming for gathering disciples to engage in "lofty and esoteric" doctrines of Mind and Nature without extensive study of the classics and history and without giving any concern to the problems of the society. He chided the Wang followers specifically as "unlettered men who borrow accepted sayings to hide their ignorance," and ridiculed Ming intellectuals in general by calling their works "nothing but plagiarism." The theory of "intuitive knowledge" he attacked as the basic cause of confusion and disorder. The Wang school of idealism never recovered from his attack.

24. Better known as Hsü Hsia-k'e.
25. For an English rendition of his work, see E-tu Zen Sun and Shiou-chuan Sun, *T'ien-kung k'ai-wu: Chinese Technology in the Seventeenth Century* (University Park, Pa., 1966).
26. Led by Li Meng-yang and Ho Ching-ming.

Refusing to accept the independence of Neo-Confucianism from classical study, Ku asked rhetorically, "From ancient until modern times, how could there be a separate entity called the philosophy of rational principle? Classical learning is itself a study of rational principle. Ever since men started to discuss the philosophy of rational principle apart from classical learning, heterodoxy has arisen."[27] The correctness of his assertion that "classical learning is itself a study of rational principle" is open to question, for Neo-Confucianism is a philosophy which should be divorced from classical learning and treated as a separate field of investigation. Yet Ku's forceful promotion of his view and his audacious attack shattered the sanctity and the inviolability of Neo-Confucianism. As a result the intellectual air was cleared and a new trend of classical studies set in. It should be noted that Ku did not attack Chu Hsi and the Ch'eng brothers personally, for he still had a high regard for their encouragement of book-reading and their exhortation to investigate the nature of things.

Ku traveled widely in North China and studied the practical problems of geography, frontier defense, farming, and trade. From his geographical investigations he drafted two treatises based on practical applications: *On the Strategic and Economic Advantages and Disadvantages of the Counties and States of the Empire* (*T'ien-hsia chün-kuo li-ping-shu*), and his *Local Geography* (*Chao-yü chih*). Both were documents of great scope, but they were only rough drafts, not finished products. Of the dozen or so works to his name, only one, the *Five Books on Phonology* (*Yin-hsüeh wu-shu*) was a systematic and finished work; all the rest were left in the form of drafts, notebooks, or monographs. Even his famous *Record of Daily Knowledge* (*Jih-chih lu*), which was a crystalization of his lifelong devotion, was in the form of a notebook.

Ku's chief contribution to the Ch'ing school of learning was his construction of a revolutionary research methodology distinguished by three characteristics: (1) *Originality:* In his preface to the *Jih-chih lu*, Ku wrote, "Since my childhood studies, I have always noted down what I perceived ... If earlier men had said it before me, I omitted it entirely." It is certain that Ku's writings did not contain a single point that was borrowed. (2) *Utility:* Just as Confucius had edited the Six Classics in order that they might keep people out of trouble, Ku decided "not to do any writing unless it had a relation to the actual affairs of the contem-

27. Liang Ch'i-ch'ao, *Intellectual Trends in the Ch'ing Period* tr. from the Chinese by Immanuel C. Y. Hsü (Cambridge, Mass., 1959), 30.

porary world as indicated in the Six Classics." His emphasis on utility brought knowledge and society into a closer relationship, in contrast to the Ming habit of abstract discussion totally divorced from social reality. (3) *Extensive Evidence*: Ku would not write a page without scrutinizing every fact thoroughly and supporting it with solid evidence. Consequently, citations in his work were numerous and extensive, and his writings were sound, broad, and consistent. His study of phonology relied on primary and secondary sources of evidence; only when these were lacking would he fall back on evidence at several removes. His research method approached the standards of modern historical investigation.[28]

For his generally destructive influence upon the Ming intellectual trends and for his constructive development of a new research methodology, Ku was honored as the founder of the Ch'ing school of learning. It was from his initial efforts that a new trend of "sound learning" (or "unadorned learning") (*p'u-hsüeh*) and textual criticism evolved.

Two other scholars also contributed substantially to the liberation of thought. Yen Jo-chu (1636-1704), after studying for thirty years the time-honored *Book of History (Shang-shu)*, wrote a devastating treatise entitled *Shang-shu ku-wen shu-cheng* (Commentary according to evidence on the *Book of History in Ancient Text*), in which he exposed as forgeries the sixteen chapters of the *Book of History in Ancient Text* and a *Commentary* attributed to Confucius's descendant K'ung An-kuo. The enormity of such an act was staggering. These two works had been studied by every student and every scholar in China for nearly two thousand years and were accepted as sacred writ, sacrosanct and inviolable. Citation and exegesis had been the only liberties that could be taken with them; actual criticism was unthinkable. The barest hint of doubt or of criticism of a word in their texts would be sufficient cause for intellectual suspicion and social stigma. Thus, despite the fact that the authenticity of these two works had been in doubt since the Sung period, such was their traditional awesomeness that no one had dared pass judgment on them. But now Yen courageously revealed that what had been previously honored as sacred was—at least in part—sheer fraud. With this powerful exposé and its consequent caving-in of intellectual barriers generally, the Ch'ing scholars could re-examine all classical and philosophical texts without the fear that they would become social and intellectual pariahs by so doing.

The other revolutionary figure following hard in Ku's wake was Hu

28. Liang Ch'i-ch'ao, 31-32.

Wei (1633-1714), whose work, *I-t'u ming-pien* (A clarification of the diagrams in the *Book of Changes*), dealt a crippling blow to Sung Neo-Confucianism. His principal object of attack was the "River Chart and Lo Writing," a mystic art of divination which was a basic theme in the Sung learning and which Chu Hsi and the Ch'eng brothers had considered to contain the very essence of the "true orthodox doctrine." Hu coolly traced its origin to the Taoist priest Ch'en T'uan (*ca.* 906-989), pronounced it entirely unrelated to the Duke of Chou or Confucius, contrary to all suppositions, and added that it was totally irrelevant to the tenets of the *Book of Changes.* Hu's research proved that Sung teachings were in fact quite different from Confucius's teachings and that the two ought to be kept clearly distinguished from one another. In other words, he showed that the pursuit of truth could be conducted in ways other than the Sung way—a revelation that severely undermined the foundation of the Neo-Confucian metaphysical philosophy.

The works of Yen and Hu were approximately the same kind of bombshell to the early Ch'ing intellectual world that Darwin's *Origin of Species* was to the 19th-century European world: both discredited and cast aside well-established beliefs; both recast the contours of thought in such a way as to provide new areas for consideration. Together with Ku Yen-wu, Yen and Hu carried out an intellectual revolution against the Sung-Ming Neo-Confucian oligarchy and reduced it to a position of disrepute. They corrected the trend toward aimless drifting and established a solid atmosphere of serious scholarship based on the revival of classical studies and the practical application of knowledge to society (*ching-shih chih-yung*).

Two other scholars also contributed to this trend. Huang Tsung-hsi (1610-95), the great historian, like Yen was once a student of Ming thought, and like Yen made an abrupt about-face to criticize it sharply: "The Ming scholars patched together their lectures from the dregs of [Sung] dialogues, with no roots in the Six Classics. They packed their books away and engaged in idle talk, giving rise to even more errors. Therefore, scholars must first exhaust the classics. However, to adhere exclusively to classical learning is impractical. To avoid pedantry it is necessary to study history as well."[29] He strongly urged extensive reading and proper application of knowledge to public affairs.

The problem of government was central to Huang as a historian— and especially as a nationalistic one. He lashed out at despotism in his

29. Liang Ch'i-chao, 36.

influential work *Ming-i tai-fang lu,* often translated as "A Plan for the Prince."[30] Pointing out the discrepancy between the Confucian ideal ruler and the actual despotism of sovereigns, he deplored the continuous deterioration of the conduct of later sovereigns, and favored the rule of law as a means to check their selfish and arbitrary behavior: "People say that when there is the rule of [good] man, there is no need for law, but I say that until there is the rule of law there is no rule of man."[31] Huang was generally recognized as the father of Ch'ing historical studies. His *Ming-ju hsüeh-an* (Survey of Ming Confucian philosophers) was considered by some as the first intellectual history in China. His student, Wan Ssu-t'ung of Ningpo, singlehandedly completed the *Draft History of the Ming (Ming-shih kao),* and was possibly the only one who had written a complete dynastic history since Ssu-ma Ch'ien and Pan Ku of the Han period.

Another important figure was Wang Fu-chih (1619-92), who, despite a lack of formal schooling under famous teachers, emerged as a scholar of considerable achievement. In philosophy he made a very perceptive statement on the relations between human desire and the rational principle: "The rational principle of nature resides in human desires; without human desires there can be no discovery of the rational principle of nature." It is from this line of thinking that Tai Chen (1724-77), perhaps the greatest of all Ch'ing scholars and thinkers, later developed his famous doctrine on human feelings and desires.

Wang's views on history and politics seem startlingly refreshing and modern. He denied that supernatural forces, mysticism, fate, or luck could influence the course of history, and boldly advanced the evolutionary and progressive view that history unfolds itself unceasingly in an orderly direction which perforce makes later periods better than earlier ones. Hence there was no point to revive ancient institutions and ways for modern application, inasmuch as each age has its own characteristics and needs. This view of continuous societal advancement contradicted the traditional cyclical theory of history, which asserts that a period of order is always followed by a period of disorder, and vice versa. Pointedly Wang asked, order might indeed grow out of disorder, but how could disorder emerge from order?

Wang has been described as a materialist in that he believed that

30. For a study of his work, see W. T. de Barry, "Chinese Despotism and the Confucian Ideal: A Seventeenth-Century View" in Fairbank (ed.), *Chinese Thought and Institutions,* 162-203.
31. Liang Ch'i-ch'ao, 37, with minor changes.

progress could best be achieved under conditions of economic well-being. He advocated the security of life and satisfaction of basic needs; development of natural resources; and encouragement of domestic and foreign trade. The state should consider the people's welfare as its chief occupation, and it should belong to the people and not to any one hero or any one dynasty, much less a foreign dynasty. Alien domination of China was utterly insufferable and illegitimate; hence the Chinese could justifiably cheat or kill barbarians.

Because of their nationalistic and anti-Manchu overtones, Wang's voluminous writings were not published for two hundred years. It was not until the late 19th century that reformers and revolutionaries publicly distributed them. T'an Ssu-t'ung, the martyr of the 1898 reform movement, is said to have derived much of his inspiration from Wang. Today, the Chinese Communists honor Wang as a "great patriot and nationalist."[32]

These early Ch'ing masters—from Ku Yen-wu to Wang Fu-chih—reacted vigorously against the abstract and metaphysical intellectual trends of the Ming, and created a new climate of learning, in which stress was laid on the study of the old classics, textual research based on extensive evidence, and practical application of knowledge to society. All of them exhibited a strong spirit of doubt which led them to scrutinize works which had been accepted for ages, if their authenticity seemed at all in doubt. Their revival of the old classics confronted them with problems of correctly understanding the ancient texts. To clarify the meaning of ancient words and phrases as well as the pronunciation of words so as to reconstruct the rhymes, they devoted themselves to the study of phonology, philology, the semantics of technical terms, and ancient regulations and institutions, as prerequisites to their classical studies. Their investigations led them deeper and deeper into antiquarian textural studies, and paved the way for the emergence of the School of Empirical Research (*K'ao-cheng hsüeh*) in the middle Ch'ing period.

Middle Ch'ing Empirical Research. The term *k'ao-cheng hsüeh*, literally "search for evidence," has sometimes been translated as "textual criticism." But since the activities of those engaged in this type of research included the examination of artifacts as well as textual study of ancient works it is more appropriate to give the term the broader translation,

32. For details, see S. Y. Teng, "Wang Fu-chih's Views on History and Historical Writing," *The Journal of Asian Studies*, XXVIII:1:111-123 (Nov. 1968).

School of Empirical Research. Scholars of this discipline employed the inductive method of investigation, collecting evidence from a wide range of sources and testing their various hypotheses against it. Their motto was to get at the truth through concrete proof and to hold to no belief without it. This school, which made a tentative beginning in the early Ch'ing period, grew to its full stature during the middle period, and came to dominate the entire intellectual world of China; even the court no longer sponsored Neo-Confucianism. Among the many scholars of empirical research, two were particularly outstanding: Hui Tung of the Soochow group and Tai Chen of the Anhwei group. Strictly speaking, Ch'ing scholars regarded each other as friends and teachers, and there were no schools or factions to speak of; yet Hui and Tai did differ fundamentally in their respective approaches to learning.

Hui Tung (1697-1758) came from a family with a scholarly tradition. His approach to scholarship was characterized by extensive reading and a ready acceptance of Han works, which were considered authentic because the Han was not far removed from antiquity. The guiding spirit of the Hui school was, "That which is ancient must be authentic and that which is of the Han must be good." In this vein, Hui Tung made a number of studies of ancient works.[33] His worship of Han scholarship prompted his attempt to elevate the views of the Han masters to the rank of the classics.

Hui's extreme reverence for the Han learning made it difficult for him to be impartial and discriminating; as a result his school lacked disciplined judgment. A work or an evidence was scrutinized not by the standard of whether it was authentic or not but whether it was Han or not. Those who dared to criticize Han doctrines were held as infirm believers. The Hui school unequivocally shifted the intellectual focus from the Sung and T'ang further back to the Han, and set up the scope and method of the Han learning for its own. Among the more famous students of this school were Chiang Sheng (1721-99) and Yü Hsiao-k'o (1729-77). The Ch'ing learning has often been labeled the Han learning; actually only the Hui school deserved the description. Those before Hui Tung, such as Ku Yen-wu, and those after him, such as Tai Chen, did not adhere strictly to the Han discipline.

Tai Chen (1724-77) of Siuning, Anhwei, was probably the greatest

33. Including the *Ancient Interpretation of the Nine Classics* (*Chiu-ching ku-i*), *Studies of the Book of Changes According to Han Tradition* (*I Han-hsüeh*), *A Study of the Book of History in Ancient Text* (*Ku-wen Shang-shu k'ao*).

of all Ch'ing scholars. He regarded Hui Tung as a teacher and friend, but his approach to learning was vastly different. Whereas Hui was partial to the Han learning to the exclusion of anything else, Tai would not let himself be bound by any school. Imbued with a strong spirit of doubt, he would not accept any statement—be it from the sage, or his father, or his teacher—without conclusive evidence. He maintained a high degree of objectivity in his work and sought truth by investigating the facts without patronizing any school. His guiding principle in research was "not to be deluded by others and not to be deluded by oneself." Tai wanted to liberate scholars from dependence of all kinds. For his own part, he respected the methodology of the Han scholars but would not ask anyone to follow it blindly. When he had doubts about a point, he had no peace with himself until he had repeatedly checked the references and evidence to his satisfaction. By virtue of his ability to make incisive observations and critical judgments in his investigation, he was able to elevate the standards of research to a new height. The thoroughness of his scholarship is illustrated in his statement: "Having an inaccurate understanding of ten [things] is worth less than having a true understanding of one."

Tai's learning was extensive, yet by no means superficial. His areas of specialization were traditional Chinese linguistics, the calendar and mathematics, and waterworks and geography.[34] In late life Tai went beyond the realm of empirical research to evolve a philosophy of his own. He completed a masterwork called *The Elucidation of the Meaning of Words in the Book of Mencius* (*Meng-tzu tzu-i shu-cheng*), by which he intended to substitute his own "philosophy of feeling" for the "philosophy of rational principle" which the Ch'eng brothers and Chu Hsi had evolved. He attacked the Sung philosophers for the two sins of adulterating Confucianism with Taoism and Buddhism, and of ignoring desires in favor of rational principle:

> The way of the sages was to see to it that there were no unexpressed feelings in the world; it sought to realize desires so that the world could be governed well. Later scholars did not understand that it is precisely when feelings reach their fullest and most unreserved ex-

34. Among his numerous accomplishments, the following works were particularly noteworthy: *A Study of Phonetics* (*Sheng-yün k'ao*), *A Study of the Language in the Erh-ya* (*Erh-ya wen-tzu k'ao*), *An Inquiry into the Origin of Astrology* (*Yüan-hsiang*), *A Study of Ancient Calendar* (*Ku-li k'ao*), *A Record of Waterworks and Geography* (*Shui-ti chi*), and *Collation of the Commentary on the Water Classics* (*Chiao Shui-ching chu*).

pression that the "rational principle" is fulfilled. Their so-called "rational principle" was similar to what cruel officials call "law": cruel officials killed men with their "law," and later scholars killed men with their "rational principle."

The Ch'eng [brothers] and Chu Hsi regarded "rational principle" as an entity of heavenly derivation yet immanent in human hearts, which opened the way for people of later generations the world over to rely on their own opinions and to insist on them as the "rational principle," to the detriment of the rest of men. They created further confusion with their doctrine of "Do away with desires," and became even farther removed from the [true] "rational principle," more insistent on maintaining their own opinion, and more disastrous to the people. Is it really "rational principle" that is detrimental to the people? It is rather that they were not conscious of the fact that it was their own opinion!

When the superior man governs the world, he makes it possible for everyone to express his feelings and satisfy his desires, not contradicting "truth" [tao] and righteousness. In governing himself, the superior man unifies feelings and desires in truth and righteousness. The evil of suppressing desires is even worse than that of blocking a river; it kills feelings and eradicates intelligence as well as stifles benevolence and righteousness.[35]

Tai's "philosophy of feeling" was undoubtedly influenced by Wang Fu-chih's statement quoted above, "the rational principle of nature resides in human desires; without human desires there can be no discovery of the rational principle of nature." Tai himself was very proud of his philosophy and spoke of his *Elucidation* as his greatest work. But unfortunately most of his students could not understand it and failed to take it seriously. Even though this work had little influence during the middle Ch'ing period, Tai's contributions to research methodology and linguistics, calendar and mathematics, and waterworks, were overwhelming. His investigations far exceeded the scope of the Han learning. Therefore, rather than call it "Han learning," it is both more accurate and more appropriate to refer to Tai's school as the "Ch'ing learning."

There were many prominent members of the Tai school: the best known were Tuan Yü-ts'ai (1735-1815), Wang Nien-sun (1744-1832), and his son Wang Yin-chih (1766-1834). They followed the rigorous re-

35. Liang Ch'i-ch'ao, 59-61.

search method of the master and extended further the works of empirical research. They, along with their mentor, were collectively known to the world as Tai, Tuan, and the two Wangs.

The School of Empirical Research reached its zenith during the middle Ch'ing period and dominated the intellectual horizon of the country. Even the court ceased to sponsor the now outmoded Sung learning. Emperor Ch'ien-lung's bureau for the compilation of *The Complete Works of the Four Treasuries* (*Ssu-k'u ch'üan-shu*) was in fact the headquarters of some 300 Han scholars, including Tai Chen. They edited 3,457 works in 79,070 *chüan* (tomes). The synopsis of each entry in the printed catalogue represented the crystallization of the Han school approach to the subject. Many high officials—among them Chi Yün (1724-1805), Wang Ch'ang (1725-1806), and Juan Yüan (1764-1849) —supported the school openly and eagerly. It became fashionable for men of talent to flock to the school and to consider it reproachable not to be a part of it.

Scholars of empirical research re-examined nearly every aspect of the Chinese cultural heritage with thoroughness, objectivity, alertness, and open-mindedness. Because of their solid research and unpretentious style of writing, they described their works as "unadorned learning" or "solid scholarship" (*p'u-hsüeh*). The core of their study was still the classics, but they extended their activities into such fields as traditional linguistics, phonology, history, astronomy and mathematics, geography, government institutions, and artifacts. The great corpus of Chinese classical literature since the Han (and even earlier) was put through a rigorous examination, with the result that difficult ancient books could be read and understood, forgeries were exposed, and lost subjects were restored.

Ch'ing scholars often called themselves Han scholars and their learning the Han learning. Doubtless they used the impressive name of Han in order to eclipse the Sung learning. But actually their reverence for the classics and their habit of extensive reading and the writing of commentary were very much in line with the spirit of the Sung scholars. In all fairness, one cannot say that the Ch'ing learning stood diametrically opposed to the Sung; the difference between the two lay chiefly in research methodology rather than in any essential difference in the spirit of learning. Nor can one equate Ch'ing learning with Han learning, for the Ch'ing was much broader in scope than the Han. It has been suggested that Ch'ing learning was established under the Han banner but in the Sung spirit.

Examining the merits and demerits of the School of Empirical Research, one is struck by the radical shift in its objective. Whereas in the early Ch'ing period the masters advocated the pursuit of knowledge for practical use, in the middle period knowledge was pursued for its own sake. The idea of utility was totally cast aside. Of course, such a turn of attitude could be ascribed in great part to the frequent literary inquisitions that were instigated as a result of anti-Manchu writings. Scholars found refuge in pure scholarship and antiquarian research, which was politically safe and at the same time intellectually rewarding. Empirical research, which had been a means by which the early Ch'ing scholars hoped to create the intellectual climate that would restore the Ming, became an end in itself during the middle period. When men of talents immersed themselves in ancient textual research and writing exegeses and commentaries, they lost contact with the reality of the society and deprived the country of practical leadership. It became again an intellectual irresponsibility which indirectly fostered the growth of political corruption—precisely the situation that the early Ch'ing scholars were anxious to correct.

Moreover, the Ch'ing learning had replaced the Ming learning because the Ch'ing was concrete and the Ming was abstract. But when Ch'ing scholars themselves became entangled in the minutiae of textual research, arguing about the indefinable technical terms of ancient times and writing long essays on the meaning of one or two ancient words, they, too, had become abstract. Furthermore, the Ch'ing learning rose as a protest against the Ming Neo-Confucian intellectual oligarchy, but by the middle period the scholars of empirical research had themselves become an imposing intellectual oligarchy, re-creating the very evil they had set out to destroy. A new cycle of reaction was bound to arise.

On balance, the Ch'ing scholars re-eveluated and reordered the rich Chinese cultural heritage, but they created no new strands of thought or major schools of philosophy. They were diligent interpreters and devoted editors of Chinese culture but they were not its creative builders. Liang Ch'i-ch'ao, observing the step-by-step revival of ancient studies from the Ming to the Sung to the Han and the pre-Han periods, remarked that the Ch'ing learning was "a reverse development of the intellectual trends of the previous two thousand years. It was like peeling a spring bamboo-shoot: the more it is peeled, the closer one gets to the core."[36] Liang compared the revival of antiquity to the European Ren-

36. Liang Ch'i-ch'ao, 14.

aissance. Such a comparison is of course forced, but it is undeniable that access to the treasury of Chinese cultural heritage was made much easier by the endeavors of the Ch'ing scholars.

FURTHER READING

Ayscough, Florence, *Chinese Women Yesterday and Today* (Boston, 1937).

Chan, Wing-tsit, "The Evolution of the Neo-Confucian Concept Li as Principle," *Tsing Hua Journal of Chinese Studies*, New Series, IV:2:123-49 (Feb. 1964).

———, "How Buddhistic Is Wang Yang-ming," *Philosophy East and West*, 12:3:203-14 (Oct. 1962).

Chang, Chung-li, *The Chinese Gentry* (Seattle, 1955).

———, *The Income of the Chinese Gentry* (Seattle, 1962).

Chow, Yung-teh, *Social Mobility in China: Status Careers among the Gentry in a Chinese Community* (New York, 1966).

Chü, T'ung-tsu, *Local Government in China under the Ch'ing* (Cambridge, Mass., 1962), chapter 10.

Creel, H. G., *Chinese Thought from Confucius to Mao Tse-tung* (Chicago, 1953).

de Bary, William Theodore, "Chinese Despotism and the Confucian Ideal: A Seventeenth-Century View" in John K. Fairbank (ed.), *Chinese Thought and Institutions* (Chicago, 1957), 163-203.

———, Wing-tsit Chan, and Burton Watson, *Sources of Chinese Tradition* (New York, 1960), chapters 19-22.

Fei, Hsiao-tung, *China's Gentry* (Chicago, 1953).

———, *Peasant Life in China* (London, 1945).

Freedman, Maurice (ed.), *Family and Kinship in Chinese Society* (Stanford, 1969).

———, *Chinese Lineage and Society* (London, 1966).

Fried, Morton H., *Fabric of Chinese Society* (New York, 1953).

Fung, Yu-lan, *A History of Chinese Philosophy*, tr. by Dark Bodde (Princeton, 1953).

Goodrich, L. Carrington, *The Literary Inquisition of Ch'ien-lung* (Baltimore, 1935).

Ho, Ping-ti, *The Ladder of Success in Imperial China: Aspects of Social Mobility, 1368-1911* (New York, 1962).

———, "The Salt Merchants of Yang-chow: A Study of Commercial Capitalism in Eighteenth-Century China," *Harvard Journal of Asiatic Studies*, 17:130-68 (1954).

Hsiao, I-shan 蕭一山, *Ch'ing-tai t'ung-shih* 清代通史 (A general history of the Ch'ing period), revised edition (Taipei, 1962), I, chapters 21, 31-33; II, chapters 7-15.

Hsiao, Kung-ch'üan, *Rural China: Imperial Control in the Nineteenth Century* (Seattle, 1960).

Hsieh, Pao-chao, *The Government of China (1644-1911)* (Baltimore, 1925), chapter 6.

Hucker, Charles O., "The Tung-lin Movement of the Late Ming Period," in John K. Fairbank (ed.), *Chinese Thought and Institutions* (Chicago, 1957), 132-62.

K'ang-hsi, *The Sacred Edict, Containing Sixteen Maxims of Emperor Kang-hi*, tr. by the Rev. William Milne, second edition (Shanghai, 1870).

Lang, Olga, *Chinese Family and Society* (New Haven, 1946).

Leong, Y. K. and L. K. Tao, *Village and Town Life in China* (London, 1915).

Levenson, Joseph R., *Confucian China and Its Modern Fate*, Vol. I: *The Problem of Intellectual Continuity* (Berkeley, 1958), chapters 1-2.

Liang, Ch'i-ch'ao, *Intellectual Trends in the Ch'ing Period (Ch'ing-tai hsüeh-shu kai-lun)*, tr. by Immanuel C. Y. Hsü, (Cambridge, Mass., 1959) Parts I and II.

Liu, Hui-chen (Wang), *The Traditional Chinese Clan Rules* (Locust Valley, N.Y., 1959).

Marsh, Robert M., *The Mandarins, the Circulation of Elites in China, 1600-1900* (Glencoe, Ill., 1961).

Milne, William, *The Sacred Edict, Containing Sixteen Maxims of Emperor Kang-hi*, second edition (Shanghai, 1870). (See also entry under K'ang-hsi.)

Moore, Charles A. (ed.), *The Chinese Mind* (Honolulu, 1967).

Nivison, David S., *The Life and Thought of Chang Hsüeh-ch'eng (1738-1801)*, (Standford, 1966).

Peterson, Williard J., "The Life of Ku Yen-wu (1613-1682)," Part I, *Harvard Journal of Asiatic Studies*, 28:114-56 (1968).

Shang, Yen-liu 商衍鎏, *Ch'ing-tai k'o-chü k'ao-shih shu-lu* 清代科舉考試述錄 (A study of the civil service examinations system of the Ch'ing period), (Peking, 1958).

Teng, S. Y., "Wang Fu-chih's Views on History and Historical Writing," *The Journal of Asian Studies*, XXVIII:1:111-23 (Nov. 1968).

Weber, Max, *The Religion of China: Confucianism and Taoism*, tr. by Hans H. Gerth (Glencoe, Ill., 1951).

Wittfogel, Karl A., *Oriental Despotism: A Comparative Study of Total Power* (New Haven, 1957).

Wright, Arthur F. (ed.), *Studies in Chinese Thought* (Chicago, 1953).

5

Foreign Relations

During the transitional period from late Ming to early Ch'ing, the western Europeans began to arrive in China—and almost simultaneously with them, though independently, the Russians were marching across Siberia toward the Manchurian border. With this unprecedented confrontation of the East and the West, there began a new era in China's relations with the outside world.

THE ARRIVAL OF THE WESTERN EUROPEANS

Europe during the Age of Discovery was suffused with a new spirit of adventure, fed by the lust for empire, by the evangelical zeal to spread Christianity to the heathen (i.e. non-Western) world, and by the mercantile search for the spice trade. Under the patronage of Prince Henry the Navigator (1394-1460), Portuguese captains set out for the vaguely known continent of Africa, and in 1487 Bartholomeo Dias rounded the Cape of Good Hope. Only a few years later, in 1492, Spain, moving in a different direction, sponsored Columbus's voyage which inadvertently led to the discovery of America. Competition between the Portuguese and the Spaniards was so fierce that Pope Alexander VI intervened and issued the famous Bulls of May 3 and 4, 1493 (ratified a year later at the Convention of Tordesillas), dividing the as yet unexplored world between them for future expeditions—Portugal taking Brazil and most of the non-Christian world of the East and Spain taking most of the Americas, the Pacific, the Philippines, and the Moluccas. With this division of sphere of operation, Vasco da Gama reached India in 1498 via the Cape, and the route to the East was thereupon carved out; Portuguese, Spaniard, Dutch, and English, one after another, arrived in Asia.

The Explorers and the Traders. In those days little distinction existed between geographical explorers and empire-builders. When Alfonso d'Albuquerque captured Goa in 1510 and Malacca in 1511, he broke the ground for the Portuguese empire in the East and also gained control of the gateway to the spice land of Malaya and the East Indies. At Malacca the Portuguese met Chinese traders, who had come with silk, satins, chinaware, and pearls to exchange for spices, ginger, incense, and gold thread. Intrigued by the presence of these Chinese traders, the Portuguese began to think about reaching China itself. In 1516 Rafael Perestrello sailed there in a European vessel, made a handsome profit from his trade, and probably established himself as the first Portuguese to appear in China. The Chinese called the Portuguese "Fo-lang-chi," a corruption of the Arabic name for the Europeans, "Feringhi," which in turn was derived from the name "Franks" of the Crusades.

In 1517 Tomé Pires was sent by the king of Portugal as ambassador to the Ming court, and the mayor of Goa, Fernao d'Andrade, was given command of an exploratory mission along the China coast. Together they arrived in Canton in September of that year in eight ships, from which they fired a thunderous gun salute—their first act, and a cause of great alarm to the Chinese, who could not understand the meaning of the fusillade. However, the governor-general[1] received them with some courtesy and allowed them to anchor at St. John's Island (*Shang-ch'uan*). A year later they were joined by Fernao's brother, Simon, who forcibly occupied Tamao, built fortified posts there, and mounted guns in open violation of Chinese laws. Rumors began to circulate that the Portuguese raped Chinese women, kidnapped Chinese men for enslavement, and ate Chinese children.

The Portuguese made a very unfavorable impression on the Chinese, who considered them no better than the Japanese pirates (*Wo-k'ou*) who disturbed the China coast, and Chinese courtiers proposed a motion to expel them. Pires, after a visit to Peking (permission for which he had had to secure, incidentally, by bribery), was thrown into prison in Canton, where he died in disgrace. The Portuguese fortified base on Tamao was besieged by Chinese forces, and after three or four months'

1. Ch'en Chin.

fighting Simon was expelled. The bad behavior of the Portuguese was confirmed by reports from the king of Malacca, who received his investiture from the Ming dynasty and who sent an envoy in 1521 to seek Chinese aid against Portuguese rapacity in his domain. In that year a general order was issued by the Ming court to expel all Portuguese, but it was relaxed almost immediately, and large contingents of Portuguese gradually came to settle on St. John's Island, on Lambacao, and on Macao (which shortly became the chief place of residency.) In 1535 the Portuguese secured, by way of bribery, official Chinese permission to dry their cargoes in Macao, thus winning legal sanction to reside and trade there. They agreed to pay an annual customs dues of 20,000 taels on ships and commodities and an annual 1,000 taels rent, which was reduced in 1582(?) to 500 taels at their repeated request.[2] China did not cede the territory of Macao, but by 1557 the Portuguese appointed officials themselves to govern the area, as though it were a colony. The Ming court did not protest this conduct but instead in 1573 constructed a wall along the narrow isthmus of Macao, guarded by soldiers, ostensibly to check the kidnapping of Chinese coolies but actually to keep a close watch over the Portuguese and limit their expansion. This act was tantamount to extending recognition of the Portuguese occupation, and with the firmness of their entrenchment thus established in Macao, the Portuguese monopolized China's foreign trade at Canton and strove to exclude other foreigners from sharing the profit.

The fortunes brought back by the Portuguese flotillas from the spice trade in Malacca and the East Indies kindled the jealousy of the Spaniards, who were determined to share in the profit. Columbus's discovery of America convinced the Spaniards that they could reach the East by sailing west, skirting the American continent via its southernmost tip. In 1519 Ferdinand Magellan, a Portuguese navigator in the service of the Spanish King Charles V, led an expedition of five ships along the eastern coast of South America and emerged into the Pacific. After thirty-three months of navigation he reached the Luzon (later known as the Philippine Islands), completing the first voyage of a European ship from America to the East. Magellan and most of his followers were killed by the natives, and the survivors returned to Spain by way of the Indian Ocean and the Cape of Good Hope in 1522.

2. Kuo T'ing-i, *Chin-tai Chung-kuo shih* (Modern Chinese history), (Taipei, 1963), I, 117-18.

With Cortés's conquest of Mexico, the Spaniards had a point from which to embark for Asia. In 1545, from the port of Acapulco on the Pacific coast, Ruy Lopez de Villalobos led a fleet to attack the Portuguese in the Moluccas, but was defeated. In 1564 Miguel Lopez de Legazpi, sent from Mexico by Philip II, seized the Luzon, which was renamed the Philippine Islands, with Manila as the capital.

Meantime, many Chinese were engaged in lucrative trade in this very area which the Spaniards had taken over. The problem of piracy became increasingly serious. In 1574 a Chinese pirate fleet of 62 armed vessels and 2,000 men under Lin Feng (Limahong) attacked Manila. The Spaniards repulsed them and followed up by burning their fleet, thereby earning the gratitude of the Chinese fleet commander from Fukien, who had been sent to chastise the pirates. The Spaniards seized this opportunity to develop relations with China and invited the Chinese commander to Manila. A Spanish deputation, consisting of two Augustinian friars[3] returned with the Chinese fleet to Fukien in 1575—the first official contact between the two countries. The Chinese authorities treated the delegates well and allowed the Spaniards to trade along the Fukien and Chekiang coast, but not to maintain a settlement such as the Portuguese had done in Macao. From then on trade flourished between Foochow, Amoy, Ch'uan-chow (Zayton) and Manila, Mexico, and Spain.

The medium of exchange was the Mexican dollar, since the Philippines were under the administrative jurisdiction of Mexico. Spanish and Peruvian dollars were also used but to a lesser extent. This was the beginning of the influx of Mexican dollars into Chinese ports. The Chinese called the Spaniards "men of Luzon" since they came from the Luzon; and often they were known as the "Fo-lang-chi" (Franks), as the Chinese did not distinguish them from the Portuguese.

Chinese immigration to Manila at this time reached considerable proportions, causing alarm among the community of Spanish colonists, who frequently persecuted these immigrants out of fear that they might be agents of the Chinese government. In 1603 a large-scale massacre of the Chinese occurred. The Ming government, which had no conception of protecting its overseas subjects, did not protest the incident. Another massacre followed in 1639, after a number of Chinese immigrants had staged a demonstration against high taxes, during which they had killed a number of Spanish officials. Out of 33,000 Chinese in Manila, 20,000 reportedly perished. Nevertheless, there was no letup in Chinese immigra-

3. Geromine Marin and Martin de Rada.

tion to the Philippines, largely because of the disorder in the Fukien area during the last decades of the Ming dynasty.

In 1626 the Spaniards descended upon Keelung, Taiwan, and established a base at Tamsui for trade and the propagation of religion. There they remained until they were expelled in 1642 by the Dutch.

The Dutch arrived in China in 1604, some thirty years after the Spaniards and ninety years behind the Portuguese. Though latecomers into the East, they achieved a remarkable success in trade as well as in empire-building. The forces behind their vigorous push were their nationalistic sentiments and their spirit of Protestant Reformation. The Dutch had been under Spanish rule but had succeeded in throwing it off in 1581; for this action King Philip II of Spain, who also ruled Portugal, punished them by barring them from the port of Lisbon in 1594, thereby depriving them of their share of the spice trade. The Dutch then determined to reach the East Indies themselves and the needed information on the trade possibilities was provided by J. H. van Linschoten, a Dutchman who had spent many years of service with the Portuguese in the East. In 1595 the merchants of Amsterdam organized a private East India Company to explore the routes to the East, and Cornelius Houtman spearheaded the first voyage to Sumatra and Java in 1596. A number of expeditions followed in the next years. In 1601 a fleet under van Neck reached Macao but was repulsed by the Portuguese, who kept him from trading with Canton.

In 1602 the Netherlands East India Company was officially established, with authority from the government to maintain troops, colonize overseas territories, declare war, and conclude peace with countries in the East. Two years later Admiral Wijbrand van Waerwijek arrived in Canton for trade but, as before, found the Portuguese in Macao blocking his contact with the Chinese. Rejected by the Canton authorities, he retreated to the Pescadores and constructed fortified posts as a base of operations. After four months of futile attempts to open trade with Fukien, the Dutch left the Pescadores. In other areas of the East, however, they scored remarkable successes. From the Portuguese they seized Sumatra, Java, and the Moluccas, and won the right to trade with Japan under the Tokugawa Bakufu. In 1619 the great organizer and empire-builder Jan Pieterszoon Coen established the Batavian government on Java, which became the center of Dutch enterprise in the East, covering a vast area from India to Japan.

To the Dutch empire-builders the Portuguese at Macao proved to be an infuriating thwart, and in 1622 a fleet of seventeen vessels under C. Reijerszoon set out from Batavia for Macao. The expedition was not a success; one-third of the 800 Dutchmen landed were killed by the Portuguese and the Chinese troops who had come to help. In frustration the Dutch again retreated to the Pescadores and attempted to open trade with Fukien. They met with no success, and, possibly out of sheer spite, they interfered with the Chinese trade at Manila and the South China Sea islands, and launched forays into Fukien ports, making themselves a nuisance to the Ming court. It was not until 1624 that the Chinese succeeded in driving them to Taiwan (Formosa), where they built up a new base and by 1642 had expelled the Spaniards at Tamsui and Keelung; a year earlier, they had also seized Malacca from the Portuguese.

With the establishment of the Ch'ing dynasty in 1644, the Dutch, who had been barred from Canton by the Portuguese during the Ming era, had their hopes for trade revived. In 1656 two envoys[4] were dispatched from Java to Peking. They accepted the role of tributary envoys, performed the full kowtow to Emperor Shun-chih, and presented gifts as tribute. The Ch'ing court permitted the Dutch to send a tributary mission by way of Canton every eight years. The size of the mission was limited to four ships and 100 men, of whom twenty were allowed to come to Peking.

The Dutch rule on Taiwan, which began in 1624, came to a sudden end in 1661, when Koxinga, the Ming loyalist who had been raiding the China coast from Amoy, descended on the island and drove them out. The Dutch retaliated by assisting the Ch'ing to seize Amoy and Quemoy from Koxinga's son in 1664. Seeking reward for their services, a second Dutch mission came to Peking in that year under Pieter van Hoorn, who performed the kowtow to Emperor K'ang-hsi and accepted the role of tributary envoy, but achieved little satisfaction in his request for trade. After the pacification of Taiwan in 1683, the Chinese granted the Dutch permission to trade in Kwangtung and Fukien and pay tribute every five instead of every eight years.

The expansive Elizabethan Englishmen naturally would not fall far behind in the race for the spice trade. Even before the defeat of the Spanish Armada in 1588, Francis Drake and Thomas Cavendish had

4. Pieter de Goyer and Jacon de Keyser.

made voyages to the Pacific through the Straits of Magellan and returned home with much new information. In 1589 a group of London merchants applied to the Privy Council for a license to dispatch a trading expedition to the East. In 1591 a fleet of three ships set out under James Lancaster, rounding the Cape of Good Hope and reaching Ceylon, Malacca, and Sumatra. New vistas of trade with India were opened, and a formal application was filed with the government by the merchants to form a company for trading with the East. In 1600 the queen of England granted a charter for fifteen years to "The Governor and Merchants of London trading into the East Indies"—the coterie that was the origin of the British East India Company. A fleet of five ships under James Lancaster and John Davis then set out for Sumatra and Java, marking the beginning of the English commercial empire in the East. In the following years the Company rapidly established a number of agencies, called "factories," in key points of trade: seven in India, two in Siam, three in Sumatra, two in Java, two in Borneo, one each at Macassar, the Banda islands, and Hirado, Japan. Because of conflicts of interest with the Dutch in the East Indies and with the Portuguese in Macao, the British focused their attention on India.

Just as the Portuguese and the Spaniards were indiscriminately called "Fo-lang-chi" (Franks), the British and the Dutch, so far as the Chinese were concerned, were both the "Red Hair." As a result, predatory activities committed by the Dutch on the high seas caused Chinese resentment to be directed against the Englishmen as well. Added to this, the Portuguese in Macao, who intended to monopolize the Canton trade as long as possible, did their best to denigrate the English. The Chinese therefore had a very poor image of the English from the start.

King Charles I of England, hoping to replenish his treasury, ignored the Company's monopoly of the Eastern trade, and in 1635 authorized Sir William Courteen and others "to undertake a voyage to Goa, the parts of Mallahar, the coast of China and Japan, there to trade." A fleet of four ships and two pinnaces under the command of Captain John Weddell reached Goa in 1636 and Macao in 1637. Frustrated by Portuguese intrigues and obstruction, Weddell sailed straight into the Bogue in an attempt to make direct contact with the Canton authorities, in open violation of the established regulations. After overcoming Chinese resistance, Weddell succeeded in carrying out some desultory transactions of trade, and left. The mission left behind a bad impression, but the Chinese mistook Weddell for a Dutchman.

The attempt of the English to reach China suffered a temporary lapse due to unsettled domestic conditions between 1649 and 1660. When they resumed activities in 1664—seven years after Cromwell had granted a new charter to the East India Company—they turned their attention to areas north of Canton and entered into relations with Koxinga's son, to whom they sold ammunitions. They won the right to trade at Amoy and on Taiwan. After the Ch'ing pacification of Taiwan, K'ang-hsi lifted the ban on sea trade; in 1685 customs houses were opened at four places: Canton, Chang-chou (in Fukien), Ningpo, and Yün-t'ai-shan (in Kiangsu). Among the ports Canton was the most prosperous because of its proximity to Southeast Asia, and in 1699 an English factory was formally established there.

France's attempt to establish its interests in the East was beset with internal dissension. In 1604 King Henri IV, following the Dutch and English examples, granted a charter of fifteen years of monopolistic trade with the East Indies to La Compagnie française des Indes. The company did little, and soon a rival organization—employing mostly Dutchmen for its fleet—came into existence. In 1660 yet another Compagnie de Chine was formed by noblemen and merchants, to propagate Catholicism and promote trade with China, Tonking, Cochin China, and adjacent islands. But insufficient capital and the untimely death in 1661 of its patron, Cardinal Mazarin, spelled an end to its activities. In 1664 a new Compagnie pour la commerce des Indes Orientales was created at the instance of Colbert, but it remained inactive. A rich merchant, Jean Jourdan, won permission from the company to send a ship to Canton and Ningpo. The success of the journey led Jourdan to secure an agreement from the Company that he be given the monopoly of the China trade. However, his company, registered as Compagnie Royale de la Chine, went into debt. By 1719 all eastern trade was given to a new organization called Compagnie des Indes. A factory was established at Canton in 1728, but French trade remained insignificant throughout the 18th century.

On the whole, foreign traders in China, who were mostly profit-seeking adventurers and uncouth men of little culture, made a poor show of themselves. Their violent and reckless conduct confirmed the Chinese view of foreigners as barbarians. They were not welcomed but only tolerated in China as a mark of favor from the emperor for men from afar. The proud and self-sufficient Chinese simply refused to admit of a need for foreign products. Quarantined in a few pockets along the coast, the foreign traders made little constructive impact on the Chinese state and society. Of far greater importance were the missionaries, particularly the Jesuits.

The Missionary Activities. After the middle of the 16th century, close on the heels of the explorers, conquerors, and traders, came the missionaries. This was not, however, the first time that Christianity had been introduced to China. As early as the T'ang period (A.D. 618-907) the Nestorian Sect of Christianity had entered China, and during the Mongol period a number of Catholic friars came, the most famous of whom was John of Monte Corvino, sent by Pope Nicolas IV in 1290. Once John had secured permission to propagate Catholicism in Peking, he established four churches, converted some six thousand Chinese, and was made archbishop of Peking. But after the fall of the Mongol power, Catholicism in China declined.

With the discovery of the new sea route to the East, members of the Catholic Church—which had weakened since the Reformation—looked to foreign lands for spreading the faith. The Society of Jesus, founded by St. Ignatius of Loyola in 1540, in particular was fired with the zeal natural to a new order to evangelize the East. St. Francis Xavier, having opened Japan to Catholicism, came to China with the dream of converting the Chinese, only to die in 1552 at the gates of his promised land. In 1573 Alessandro Valignano, an Italian Jesuit with a degree of doctor of civil law, who had served in the court of Pope Paul IV, was made Superior of all the Jesuit missions in the East Indies, which included China and Japan. With forty-one Jesuits he left Lisbon in 1574 and arrived in Macao in 1577. A man of rare intellectual and spiritual gifts, he charted a new course of action in China. Instead of imposing Christianity as a foreign religion and forcing the converts to take up Christian names and a foreign style of dress, as was the habit of missionary activity at the time, he decided that Christianity should function like a leaven, entering China quietly and transforming it from within. "Europeanism" was to be replaced by cultural adaptation. The Jesuits in China were instructed to learn to read, write, and speak Chinese, to "Sinicize" themselves rather than to "Portugalize" the converts.[5] Two Italian priests, Michele Ruggieri and Matteo Ricci, were sent as pioneer missionaries to carry out this policy and to continue the unfinished work of Xavier.

5. George H. Dunne, S.J., *Generations of Giants: The Story of the Jesuits in China in the Last Decades of the Ming Dynasty* (Notre Dame, 1962), 17.

Ruggieri and Ricci settled in Chaoching, Kwangtung, in 1583. To lay the groundwork of an effective apostolate, they changed into Chinese attire, studied the Chinese language, adopted Chinese mannerisms, and learned the moral doctrines of Confucianism.[6] Their first aim was not to win converts but to earn for Christianity an accepted place in Chinese society. They did not work toward the statistical and dubious success of multiplying baptisms each year, but instead concentrated on diffusing Christian ideals and ideas through a widening circle of sympathetic contacts. Through their knowledge of the Chinese language and culture, and their astronomical, mathematical, geographical, and other scientific achievements, they made friends with the more open-minded Chinese scholars and officials. The Chinese were impressed with European mechanical devices such as clocks and solar quadrants, and with the technique of perspective drawing, as well as European cartography. Ricci, conscious of the Chinese ignorance of cosmography, constructed a map of the world, but unthinkingly placed America on the left side, Europe in the center, and Asia on the right. This was a tactical error, for it challenged the concept of China as the Middle Kingdom, and the map understandably did not win immediate acceptance. Fortunately the mistake was an easy one to set right; with the new knowledge that the earth is round rather than flat—as the Chinese still believed—Ricci revised the map, placing China at the center. The map then won high praises from the Chinese and was widely circulated in the country, earning much credit for the missionaries.

Ruggieri, on his part, had written in Latin a work of apologetics which he called a catechism. With the help of Ricci and a Chinese scholar it was translated into Chinese and published in 1584 under the title *T'ien-chu sheng-chiao shih-lu* (A true account of God and the Sacred Religion). This work, probably the first Christian literature to appear in China, discussed the existence and the attributes of God, the immortality of the soul, the natural law, the sacrament of baptism, etc.

Though they discussed religion with their Chinese visitors with full integrity, Ruggieri and Ricci were careful to present themselves initially as scholars and scientists; conversion naturally was the ultimate end, but they realized that it could not be hurried until the ground had been prepared. Ricci successfully established himself as a learned scholar of Chi-

6. However, it should be noted that they rejected the Sung school of Neo-Confucianism on the grounds that it was an adulterated form of philosophy which distorted the teachings of Confucius.

nese culture, maker of the famous world map, teacher of mathematics, astronomy, and other scientific truths, and only lastly as a missionary of Catholicism. After spending fifteen years in Chaoching and Shaochow and five years in Nanchang and Nanking, and having made many friends among leading Chinese scholars and officials, Ricci went to Peking in 1601, to seek imperial patronage. He presented to the throne many gifts, including a reproduction of the famous painting of the Madonna attributed to St. Luke, a painting of the Blessed Mother with the infant Jesus and John the Baptist, a Roman breviary, a reliquary in the form of a cross, two glass prisms, a spinet, two clocks, and a map of the world. Accompanying the gifts was a memorial in highly polished Chinese drafted by a friend and admirer.[7] In the memorial, beautifully copied out by the best calligrapher available, Ricci stated that, attracted by Chinese civilization to leave his own country, he had spent three years traveling to Kwangtung, had studied the Chinese language and the classics, had spent twenty years in various parts of China; and had now come to the capital to pay his respects and to offer his service. He also wrote that as a religious who had never married he had no family burden and sought no favor; that he was an established scholar in his own country well conversant with astronomy, geography, map-making, calendar, and mathematics; that it would indeed be a great honor if the emperor chose to enlist his service.

The emperor was greatly pleased with the memorial and the gifts, particularly with the clock that sounded the hour. While lodged in the Forbidden City for several days, Ricci and his associate de Pantoia taught four eunuchs how to regulate the clock; and for a month, de Pantoia went daily to the palace to instruct them in the art of spinet-playing. Ricci even composed eight simple motets for them with lyrics dealing with Christian moral doctrine. Attempts made by conservative officials to expel the Jesuits failed to win imperial support, and Ricci and his associates were well treated in the Residence for the Tributary Envoys. They never saw the emperor in person, but that they were allowed to reside in Peking implied imperial sanction of Christian activities in China.

Ricci's strategy was pacific penetration, cultural adaptation, and the avoidance of needless conflicts with Chinese prejudices and suspicions —methods calculated to win good Christians rather than a horde of in-

7. Liu Tung-hsing, who held the title of president of the Board of Public Works and president of the Censorate.

different baptisms. To his realistic mind, God's grace did not operate in a vacuum but through human instrumentalities. It was not improper, therefore, that he compose the motets for the eunuchs, since to do so was to help the cause of Christianity. With this approach, Ricci quickly won friends and admirers among prominent officials and scholars in Peking, among whom were dignitaries no less than a grand secretary,[8] a president of the Civil Office,[9] and a president of the Board of Rites.[10] The most famous converts were of course (Leo) Li Chih-tsao (d. 1630), a director in the Board of Public Works, and (Paul) Hsü Kuang-ch'i (1562-1633), a member of the Hanlin Academy who later rose to be a grand secretary.

Ricci's fame as a scholar and scientist drew a great number of admirers to his residence to hear him discourse on science, philosophy, and religion. From twenty to a hundred visitors came to him daily, and the street outside his home was always filled with carriages. The last nine years of his life were especially gratifying: he had become so familiar to —and popular with—the Chinese that they ceased to regard him as a foreigner but rather as one of themselves. His fame and popularity came at a price, however; the schedule he was forced to maintain in Peking eventually undermined his health, and in 1610 he died. His work was carried on by generations of dedicated Jesuits.[11]

So great had been the personal appeal of Ricci that his death caused a serious setback to the cause of Catholicism in China. The Jesuits came under a renewed attack by antiforeign elements among Chinese officialdom, and in 1616 Emperor Wan-li was moved to expel them. Many of the banished missionaries, however, managed to carry on their work in secret in the provinces; and in 1622—when the rising Manchu threat created an urgent need for Western cannon—the ban was lifted. The Ming court sent for the Jesuits from Macao to cast guns. The Jesuits came, as did a great many other foreigners from Macao, and Catholicism in China once again enjoyed a boom: in 1640 the total number of converts was between 60,000 and 70,000 and by 1651 it had risen to 150,000.[12] In 1642 fifty of the high-ranking ladies in the palaces became Christians, and when Prince Kuei was established emperor to continue the fight

8. Shen Yi-kuan.
9. Li T'ai-tsai.
10. Feng Ch'i.
11. Among whom the most famous were Diego de Pantoia, Sabbathinus de Ursis, Julius Aleni, Adam Schall von Bell, Ferdinand Verbiest, Thomas Pereira, Jean-François Gerbillon, and Michel Benoist.
12. Dunne, 212, 314.

against the Manchus, his empress, the crown prince, both dowagers, and several high officials all accepted Catholicism. One of the dowagers—christened Helena—even sent a message to Pope Innocent X in 1650, and another to the general of the Society of Jesus, asking for prayers for the Ming cause.[13] The papal state, observing that the Ming cause was virtually lost and not wishing to offend the new dynasty, delayed its reply until 1655; by then the dowager had died and the Ming resistance movement (except that under Koxinga) was all but defunct.[14]

The Ch'ing dynasty was not vindictive toward the Jesuits for their services to the Ming court; in fact, Emperor Shun-chih, who was religiously inclined, was very much drawn to the missionaries for several years. He was fond of Adam Schall von Bell, whom he appointed court astronomer and to whom he gave numerous favors and honors. In 1653 Adam Schall was given the title "Master of Universal Mysteries" and in 1657 the title "President of the Imperial Chancery." Between 1656 and 1657 the emperor visited him twenty-four times, even celebrating his own birthday in 1657 in Schall's home. The following year Schall was made a mandarin of the first class with the title of Imperial Chamberlain. He wore a red button on his hat and an official tunic with a gold-embroidered crane on it. His associate Verbiest observed: "Schall has more influence upon the emperor than any viceroy, or than the most respected prince, and the name of Father Adam is better known in China than the name of any famous man in Europe."[15] But Father Adam never succeeded in converting the emperor, who reputedly was unable to "overcome the lusts of the flesh." After 1658 the emperor's interest shifted to Buddhism, and the Jesuits lost some standing.

Another setback came during the early years of K'ang-hsi's reign when the Regent Oboi, sharing the native technicians' resentment of foreigners holding high posts in China, replaced Schall with the Chinese calendar-maker Yang Kuang-hsien as the court astronomer. However, after Emperor K'ang-hsi had begun his personal rule, he dismissed Yang in 1669, and appointed F. Verbiest as court astronomer. Keenly interested in Western science and mathematics, K'ang-hsi often asked the Jesuits to lecture on these subjects. It was a period of triumph for Western learning and for Christianity in China: churches were established in various parts of the country and the number of converts grew steadily. The

13. The Polish Jesuit, Michael Boym, was the courier.
14. Hsiao I-shan, I, 745-46.
15. Dunne, 348.

prospect was indeed promising, but shortly it was to meet the elements of discord from within the Church that would bring it to ruin.

The Decline of the Jesuit Influence: The Rites Controversy. As a matter of strategic policy Ricci and his followers had avoided conflict with Chinese sensibilities and customs as long as these customs did not contradict the basic teachings of the Church. They accepted established Chinese terms to express Christian ideas, related Confucian moral concepts to Christian teachings, refrained from interfering with Chinese rites honoring Confucius and one's ancestors, and allowed the converts to perform the kowtow as a form of civil obeisance. In short, they accepted the principle of cultural accommodation and rejected the spirit of "Europeanism" prevalent among many other religious orders since the Age of Discovery.

The "Europeanist" orders, such as the Franciscan and the Dominican, looked upon non-Christian cultures as the work of the devil and tolerance of these cultures as betrayal of Christian principles. Their missionaries, who arrived in China later than the Jesuits and whose works were overshadowed by the Jesuit success, attacked the Jesuits for compromising the integrity of the Roman Catholic faith and for misleading the Christians in China. The Franciscan and Dominican monks would not make concessions to Chinese susceptibilities or to local conditions, but sought to impose upon the converts the doctrine of faith as well as all ecclesiastical laws and customs as observed in Europe and in the Spanish possessions.

In 1634 Francisco Dias, a Dominican, and Francisco de la Madre de Dios, a Franciscan, arrived in China, and were joined three years later by another Franciscan, Gaspar Alexda. They were horrified by what they saw: the painting of Christ and the Twelve Apostles, hung in the Jesuit chapel in Peking, showed the figures with shoes on their feet; and the chapel itself maintained two "altars," one for the Christ and the other for the emperor. They charged the Jesuits with distorting the picture of Christ and the Apostles and of raising the pagan emperor to a rank coequal with the Savior's. They took no cognizance of Chinese feelings on the subject of bare feet; nor did they care to know that the chapel was a gift of the emperor in honor of Ricci, and that in acknowledgment of the imperial grace the Jesuits had placed a wooden plaque on a table with an inscription equivalent to "Long live the emperor." The Dominicans and the Franciscans attacked the Jesuits for their (1) improper use of Christian terminology, (2) tolerance of questionable Chinese rites honoring ancestors, the recently deceased, and Confucius, (3) refusal to say that Confucius was in hell, and (4) failure to promulgate the church laws and to preach the crucifixion of Christ. They also charged that the Jesuits "in baptizing women fail to apply saliva to their ears, salt to their mouths, and oil to the breast and head."[16]

The question of expressing Christian ideas in the Chinese language was a major point of contention. Ricci had chosen to find the closest existing Chinese concepts to express Christian ideas rather than to transliterate Western terms. The Latin word "gratia," for example, was not transliterated as "ke-la-chi-a" but rendered *t'ien-en* (heavenly grace) or *sheng-en* (sacred grace). He equated the Chinese concept of *t'ien* (heaven) with the Christian concept of God; hence *T'ien-chu* (Lord of Heaven) or *Shang-ti* (Lord on High) for God or Lord, *t'ien-shen* for angel, and *ling-hun* for soul.[17]

The problem of rites was even more controversial. Ricci and the Jesuits regarded the rites performed before ancestral tablets as expressions of reverence and respect. They permitted the keeping of a tablet in the house with names of the family ancestors inscribed on it surrounded by flowers, candles, and incense. They did not believe that the Chinese supposed their ancestors to dwell in these tablets; ancestral rites were accepted as nothing more than a civil role expressing one's respect and filial piety, with superstition having very little part. Likewise, Ricci considered the burning of incense a social custom without religious connotation. The kowtow before the ancestral tablets and the coffins of the recently deceased, which to many missionaries of other orders was an act of adoration which should be reserved for the Divinity alone, was construed by the Jesuits as a symbol of ceremonial obeisance and civil rites intended to console the afflicted and to manifest sorrow, without religious significance. They saw nothing religious or blasphemous in children kowtowing to their parents or officials to the emperor; the Jesuits themselves performed the kowtow when receiving imperial gifts or emissaries. They also tolerated simple ceremonies in honor of Confucius during the conferring of the *hsiu-ts'ai* degree as an expression of customary obeisance to the Master. Past a certain point, however, even the Jesuits drew a line: in matters of solemn ceremonies in honor of

---

16. Dunne, 249, 272.
17. This approach, it might be added, ran into some opposition even within his own order: a few Jesuits themselves, such as Longobardo, would rather have had a transliterated form of the Latin *Deus* for God.

Confucius, Chinese converts were not permitted to take part because such occasions took on the appearance of a sacrifice. Solemn rites observed in honor of familial ancestors were permitted only on condition that there be no burning of paper money,[18] no prayers or petition to the dead, and no expression to the effect that the spirits of the dead derived sustenance from the food offerings.[19]

The Jesuits had come to these decisions because they believed that the majority of the Chinese scholar class observed ritual as a part of good citizenship. Prohibition of the rites would make it impossible for them to become Christians and would render the policy of peaceful penetration unworkable: Christianity, instead of becoming a leaven working quietly from within the Chinese society, would be hostile to the Chinese way of life. Accordingly, the papal decree of 1656 allowed the practice of rites under the conditions observed by the Jesuits.

However, the matter of rites was not put to rest; it continued to plague the European intellectual and religious world and became a *cause célèbre*, with leading theologians and philosophers taking part in the debate. More than 262 works were published on the subject, in addition to a hundred or so that remained unpublished. In 1704 the Pope reversed the church stand and banned the rites, prohibiting the use of *T'ien* or *Shang-ti* for God, while approving the term *T'ien-chu* (Lord of Heaven).

Even as this new stand was taken, a papal legate was on his way to China. In December 1701 Carlo Tommaso Maillard de Tournon, at 33, was consecrated Patriarch of Antioch and Apostolic Visitor to the East Indies and the Chinese Empire. Arriving in Peking in December 1705, de Tournon entertained the grand hope of conciliating the "Emperor-Pope" relations by (1) establishing direct diplomatic relations between the Holy See and China through the appointment of a Papal Nuncio in Peking, and (2) designating this nuncio superior-general, with jurisdiction over all missionaries in China. Though K'ang-hsi treated de Tournon with courtesy and cordiality at first, he changed his attitude when he read the latter's written representation—translated into Chinese by the court Jesuits—in which the second request seemed to take precedence over the first, which was not de Tournon's intention. The papal legate angrily held the Jesuits, especially Pereira, responsible for the emperor's change of heart, despite their protestation of innocence.

18. It supposedly provided the departed spirits with means.
19. Dunne, 292.

K'ang-hsi could not accept the papal authority to regulate religious matters in his domain, and having sanctioned the Jesuit approach to the rites question, he would tolerate no change. In no uncertain terms he told de Tournon that there was no need for a Papal Nuncio to facilitate the communication between Rome and Peking, since any Jesuit in his service could perform this function well; that the superior-general, if appointed, had to be a man of long-standing experience in China, such as one of the Jesuit fathers. Already suspicious of the latter, de Tournon considered them unfit for the appointment because they were "wholly ignorant of the Roman Curio" and not "trusted agents of communications." His inflexibility killed any chance of a direct link between China and the Papacy.[20]

De Tournon left Peking on August 28, 1706, for the south, where he hoped to catch a ship home. On February 7, 1707, he announced the "Decree of Nanking" which condemned the ancestor worship and was critical of the emperor's views on religion. K'ang-hsi angrily remarked: "These people stand outside the door and discuss the affairs of the house. How can we accept it!"[21] He sent de Tournon to Macao for detention, while dispatching two Jesuits to Rome with bulky dossiers highly critical of the legate's behavior. However, both messengers were killed in separate shipwrecks near the coast of Portugal. For three years de Tournon spent his life in sickness and depression at Macao, and finally on June 10, 1710, passed away at the age of 41. Only six months earlier he had received the red hat of a cardinal.

In 1715 Pope Clement XI issued the bull *Ex Illa Die* to reaffirm the anti-rites stand of 1704 and warn violators of excommunication. It further strained the "Emperor-Pope" relations. Another papal mission was sent to China in 1721 to attempt a conciliation, but it failed. K'ang-hsi decided that to avoid further complication all missionaries would be repatriated except those who were scientists and technicians, such as court astronomers. Although the order was not strictly enforced, the status of the missionaries was slipping badly, and during the Yung-cheng period it deteriorated further. The new ruler was unfavorably disposed toward the Jesuits for their support of K'ang-hsi's ninth son against him in the succession struggle. He stated: "China has her religions and the Western

20. For details of the Tournon mission, see Francis A. Rouleau, S.J., "Maillard de Tournon, Papal Legate to the Court of Peking," *Archivum Historicum Societatis Iesu*, 31:264-323 (1962).
21. Li Shou-k'ung, 26.

1. Nurhaci (1559–1626),
founder of the Ch'ing dynasty.

2. Emperor K'ang-hsi (1662–1722).

3. Emperor Yung-cheng (1723–1735).

4. Emperor Ch'ien-lung (1736–1795).

5. A feast given to the old men by Emperor Ch'ien-lung on 14 February 1785.

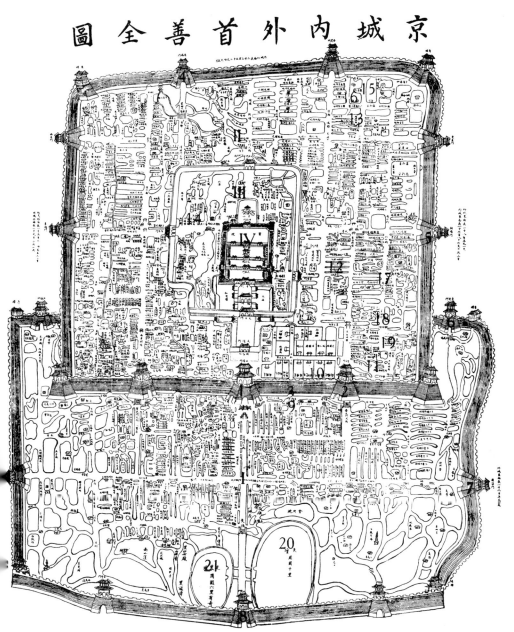

京城內外首善全圖

MAP OF PEKING

| I. | Native City. | III. | Imperial City. |
| II. | Tartar City. | IV. | Forbidden City. |

Ch'ienmen.
Hatamen.
Wall between the two gates fortified by the besieged.
Te-shengmen. (Court fled through this gate August 15, 1900.)
Ch'i Huamen. (Russian and Japanese relief entered at this gate in 1900.)
Tungpienmen. (The gate through which the Americans entered in 1900.)

7. Shakuomen. (Where the British entered in 1900.)
8. Yungtingmen. (Gate leading into the city from the station.)
9. Water Gate. (Here the relief troops entered the Legation.)
10. Legation quarters.
11. Methodist Mission.
12. American Board Mission.
13. Presbyterian Mission.

14. Peitang.
15. Lama temple.
16. Confucian temple.
17. Tsung Li Yamen.
18. Examination Halls.
19. Imperial Observatory.
20. Temple of Heaven, British headquarters in 1900.
21. Temple of Agriculture, American headquarters in 1900.

6. Map of Peking.

7. An outer view of the Imperial Palace, Peking.

8. The inner court of the Imperial Palace, Peking.

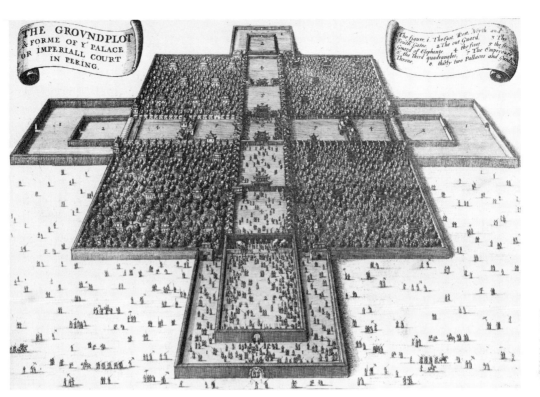

THE GROVNDPLOT & FORME OF Y PALACE OR IMPERIALL COURT IN PEKING.

9. The ground plot of the Imperial Palace.

10. The Temple of Heaven where the emperors worshiped.

11. The Yüan-ying Kuan at the Yüan-ming Yüan (Imperial Summer Palace).

12. The emperor of China in procession.

13. Ku Yen-wu, great early Ch'ing scholar.

14. Matteo Ricci and Paul Hsü.

15. Adam Schall von Bell.

world has its religions. Western religions need not propagate in China, just as Chinese religions cannot prevail in the Western world."[22] Prohibition of Christianity was much more strictly enforced under Emperor Yung-cheng.

In 1742 Pope Benedict XIV reiterated the anti-rites stand of the church, and the missionaries in China were put in an extremely difficult, if not impossible, position. Their work and influence fell to a low ebb. And with the dissolution of the Society of Jesus in 1773, the moving spirit of Catholicism in China was gone.

Introduction of Western Science and Technology. From the late Ming period until the middle Ch'ing, a total of about 500 Jesuits came to China, of whom 80 made substantial contributions to cultural exchange. From them the Chinese learned the Western methods of cannon-casting, calendar-making, cartography, mathematics, astronomy, algebra, geometry, geography, art, architecture, and music. At the same time, the Jesuits introduced Chinese civilization to Europe. It was the initial meeting of China and the West in modern times, and provided China with the chance to modernize herself. Some of the major Jesuit contributions to science and technology were as follows:

(1) Cannon-making. From the Dutch the Chinese first learned about the cannon, which they promptly dubbed *Hung-I p'ao* (Cannon of the Red-haired Barbarians). Too proud to adopt this foreign weapon, they were taught a lesson by the Japanese invaders of Korea in 1592-97, who used the cannon. Later, threatened by the rising power of the Manchus, the Ming court swallowed its pride and in 1622 sent for the Jesuits in Macao to cast guns for its army. Joannes de Rocha, Emmanuel Diaz, and Nicolo Longobardo answered the call, and in the following year Julius Aleni and Franciscus Sambiaso came to Peking. The ban on Catholicism was, perforce, automatically relaxed. In 1639 Sambiaso presented a memorial to Emperor Ch'ung-chen calling for a good reformed calendar, the mining of ores, international trade with the Western countries, and the purchase of foreign cannon. The Ming court, pressed by the Manchus, was interested only in the cannon. In 1642 Adam Schall was asked to cast guns and teach the technique to the Chinese officials in charge of gun-making. He made twenty probational guns and, having won imperial praises for them, was commissioned to make 500 more. Schall also wrote a book on the manufacture and operation of guns, balls,

22. Li Shou-k'ung, 27.

mines, and rockets. Under his instruction, (Paul) Hsü Kuang-ch'i, (Leo) Li Chih-tsao, and a few others among the Chinese mastered the technique of gun-making.

(2) Calendar-making. Besides the cannon, the Jesuits brought to China new knowledge of astronomy and calendar-making. The two existing Chinese almanacs—the Grand Calendar (*Ta-t'ung*) of Liu Chi based on a Yüan calendar, and the Moslem calendar (*Hui-li*)—were both exposed by Ricci as inaccurate and obsolete. Several of Ricci's associates—de Pantoia, de Ursis, and Terrenz—were well conversant with the technique of calendar-making. In 1629, on recommendation of (Paul) Hsü Kuang-ch'i, the court appointed the Jesuits Longobardo and Terrenz to the Calendrical Bureau (*Li-chü*). When Terrenz died in the spring of 1630, Adam Schall was named as his successor and proved to be even more highly skilled than his predecessor. With the help of Giacomo Rho, Schall completed 137 *chüan* of *Ch'ung-chen li-shu* (Ch'ung-chen astronomy book), 100 *chüan* of translation of astronomical subjects, and constructed a table of fixed stars under the title *Hsin-fa suan-shu* (New method of calculation).

The missionaries made astronomical instruments and directed Chinese officials to translate astronomical and logarithmic tables. During the eclipse of 1643, their calculations proved much more accurate than those of the official astronomer, and consequently the court agreed to accept the Jesuit calendar; but there was secret opposition among the courtiers.

When the Ming dynasty was replaced by the Ch'ing, the first emperor of the new regime, Shun-chih, appointed Schall court astronomer, and the Calendrical Bureau merged with the Imperial Board of Astronomy. The Jesuits holding these positions were given stipends and official residences, and Schall enjoyed the trust and respect of the emperor for several years, as noted before. A calamity befell him, however, when he presented to Emperor K'ang-hsi a 200-year calendar. The antiforeign astronomer Yang Kuang-hsien accused Schall of implying by this act that the dynasty could last only 200 years; using this pretext as a *point d'appui*, Yang went on to charge Schall with errors in his astronomical calculations and with indoctrinating people with false ideas. Oboi, the dictatorial regent during K'ang-hsi's minority, pronounced Schall's action "highly improper" and threw him into prison late in 1664; his life was spared only because the empress dowager interceded. Yang now became the court astronomer and the old calendar was revived, but shortly thereafter he made an erroneous calculation of the solar eclipse. Though released in May 1665, Schall, now old and paralyzed, died a year later. The post of the court astronomer, after Yang's downfall in 1669, went to Verbiest, and from that time until 1838 it remained occupied by foreigners exclusively.[23]

(3) Geographic Survey and Map-making. Under the patronage of K'ang-hsi, Joachin Bouvet, a French Jesuit, led a group of missionaries in a geographical exploration of the empire between 1708 and 1715. From the data they gathered, an atlas of China was completed in 1716, with detailed maps of the provinces. K'ang-hsi proudly bestowed on it the title *Huang-yü ch'üan-lan t'u* (A complete map of the Imperial Dynasty). This was the first map of China to be marked with the longitudes and latitudes.

(4) Other Activities. The Jesuits introduced a number of other elements of Western learning, too. Ricci and (Paul) Hsü Kuang-ch'i translated Euclid's *Elements of Geometry*, and Ricci and (Leo) Li Chih-tsao translated a work on mathematics. Rho and Hsü translated Archimedes' plane and spherical trigonometry; Aleni wrote on geometry, trigonometry, and geography; Terrenz wrote on human physiology; T. Pereira wrote on music; and Schall wrote on the principle of the spectrum and telescope. Aristotelian philosophy and perspective drawing were also brought in.

By the same token, the missionaries transmitted Chinese learning back to Europe. An Italian translation of the Confucian Four Books by Ricci was followed by a Latin version by Ignatius de Costa, Prosper Intorcenta, and Philippus Couplet, published in Paris in 1687. To the Pope in 1682 Couplet presented Jesuit translations of more than 400 Chinese works. For the first time Europe was learning something of the richness of Chinese culture, and great scholars and thinkers such as Spinoza, Leibniz, Goethe, Voltaire, and Adam Smith became admirers of Chinese civilization. During the Age of Enlightenment, the Chinese rational approach to life and the secular government—totally divorced from church—won praise from Voltaire, Holbach, and Diderot. In art, the Rococo movement, which liberated Europe from the stilted Baroque art

23. Yang made a defense of his stand in a treatise called *Pu-te-i* (*I could not do otherwise*) in which he bluntly stated that "he would rather have no good calendar than have foreigners in China" and that "it is exactly because of their excellent instruments and excellent weapons that they are a potential enemy." (Hsiao I-shan, I, 680-81) The apparently unreasoning petulance of these xenophobic outbursts can be understood in the light of the Spanish conquest of the Philippines and the rapid rise of the Catholic influence in Japan during the early Tokugawa period.

form of Louis XIV, was also in part a product of Chinese influence. Chinese porcelain was imitated by the Italians, the Dutch, and the Germans. French brocade with Chinese designs became a vogue. The Chinese garden, with its stone bridges, artificial hills, and goldfish, was much admired, and the Garden at Kew of the Duke of Kent was particularly famous for its good Chinese taste.

China's Lost Chance for Modernization. In spite of the samplings of Western civilization which they carried in, the Jesuits had not been the catalysts for modernization in China. While some Chinese historians assert that the Jesuit emphasis on science and practical studies influenced the development among the Ch'ing scholars of the practical approach to learning and the "scientific" research methodology, the fact remains that the total Jesuit impact on the Chinese state and society was relatively small. The missionaries represented a thin ray of Western learning which shone feebly among a small coterie of progressive Chinese scholars and officials, but it never penetrated beyond the surface. They caused at best a slight tremor in the otherwise immutable Sinic civilization. Chinese scholars and officials on the whole were too proud of their cultural heritage to admit of the need for foreign learning.

Moreover, the Jesuits who came with this new knowledge of science and technology were basically men of religion rather than men of science. Apart from the several dozen very gifted, most of the missionaries were severely limited in their capacity as cultural transmitters. Rather than presenting a broad front of European civilization, they merely introduced a few branches of Western science that happened to attract Chinese attention. Even this partial introduction was interrupted when the missionary movement was put to an end in the 18th century. Thus, the feebleness of the Jesuit efforts, the ethnocentric complacency of Confucian intellectuals, and the imperviousness of Chinese culture to outside stimuli inhibited any process of modernization of China at this point.[24]

24. The limitations of the missionaries were only too obvious to themselves. Repeated efforts were made by Sabbathinus de Ursis and Nicolo Longobardo to secure the services of famed astronomers and mathematicians, but the General of the Society felt that Europe could not spare such talents. In rejecting the applications of three noted mathematicians for missionary work in China—Gregory St. Vincent (1584-1667), Christopher Scheiner (1575-1650), and John Cysat (1588-1657)—the General stated that "for the greater glory of God and for the good of Society it was preferrable for them to stay in Europe, and energetically promote mathematical studies. Thus, they will be able to do by means of their disciples in China what they will not be able to do themselves." For details, see Pasquale M. D'Elia, *Galileo in China* (Cambridge, Mass., 1960), 21-24.

Ironically, it was precisely after this disruption of Western learning in China that the great leap in progress was made in Western political, economic, social, and scientific fields. The American Revolution, the French Revolution, and the great reforms in England set the stage for the rise of modern democracy, while the Industrial Revolution ushered in a new age of technological development, nationalism, expansion, capitalism, and imperialism. The shibboleth of progress permeated the air of Europe. In contrast, Chinese intellectuals still looked to their "golden past" for guidance and absorbed themselves in antiquarian textual research. Europe surged ahead in its search for progress, while China slept in her dream of glory. To jostle her out of her sleep would require efforts far more bombastic and powerful than the Jesuits had been able to provide. Britain, the front-runner in the Industrial Revolution, unhesitatingly accepted the challenge, as we will see in later chapters.

THE RUSSIAN ADVANCE

At about the same time the western Europeans were reaching China via the sea route, the Russians were marching toward her across Siberia. China's confrontation with the European world, then, was on two fronts. The seafaring European explorers and traders from the south and the land-based Russians from the north closed in on the previously impervious empire like a pair of pincers, and China's destiny was never afterwards quite the same. If the influence of the western Europeans was minimal for the first two centuries, it was different with the Russians, who constituted a threat to the Ch'ing dynasty and figured prominently in the strategic planning of Emperor K'ang-hsi and Emperor Yung-cheng.

The March Across Siberia. Russian interest in China was a logical extension of her interest in Siberia. First and last, the conquest of Siberia was largely the work of explorers, adventurers, hunters, and trappers. The promise of sable and other furs prompted the first incursions into the area, and traders from Novgorod had appeared in West Siberia as early as the 11th century. But it was not until the middle of the 16th century that a sustained drive to conquer the vast territory was begun. By then the Russians had reached the Urals and won submission from some of the tribal chieftains such as Ediger (khan of Sibir) and Kuchun Khan, and in 1554 Ivan the Terrible had assumed the title "Lord of all Sibir." In 1558 the rich merchant family of Stroganov secured permission from the tsar to explore beyond the Urals. In 1581 Yermak (Vasili Timofeiev), a onetime brigand and a chieftain in Stroganov's private army, led 800 Cossacks in an eastward drive and reached the Irtysh the following year, taking possession of the town of Sibir, from which the name Siberia was derived. The territory he occupied was offered to the tsar, along with a tribute of furs which he sent to redeem his past misconduct. Awarded a medal and made a hero, Yermak carried on his trek along the Irtysh and the Ob. He was drowned in 1584 but the march went on. In 1587 the town of Tobolsk was established and in 1590 the Russian government settled 3,000 peasant families in West Siberia. In 1604 Tomsk was founded on the Ob as the seat of government for Siberia, and in 1619 Yenisseisk was established. By 1628 the Cossacks had reached the Lena River in East Siberia. In 1632 and 1638 were founded Yakutsk and Okhotsk, respectively, from which a number of expeditions were sent still further east. Reaching Kamchatka and what is today's Bering Strait in 1648, the Russians had completed the march to the Pacific within seventy years of Yermak's drive from the Urals (1581), conquering more than four million square miles. In 1651 Lake Baikal was reached and the town of Irkutsk founded.

From the Siberian tribes the Cossacks first learned of the rumored riches of the Amur Region—the "Eldorado of Eastern Asia"—where gold and silver, cotton and silk, cattle and grains, were said to abound. A number of exploratory expeditions were sent into this unknown but promising land. In 1643 V. Poiarkov (Poyarkov), commissioned by the governor of Yakutsk, reached the mouth of the Dzeya and discovered the Sungari River. He pillaged the Amur Region for three years, returning to Yakutsk in 1646 with a creditable load of spoils and the conviction that 300 select Cossacks could conquer the whole region. From 1647 to 1652 the raid was continued by E. (Y.) Khabarov, who, except for some initial losses at the hands of Manchu troops from Ninguta, was as successful as his predecessor had been. Khabarov was recalled by the government in 1652 and richly rewarded, and under his successor O. Stepanov the Amur raid went on, to the great annoyance of the newly established Ch'ing dynasty. Manchu troops were sent out again from Ninguta to chastise the Cossacks. Faced with forty-seven armed vessels and overwhelming Manchu forces, Stepanov was badly beaten and possibly killed in 1658. But the Russians were not totally exterminated in the Amur Region; that same year Pashkov, the governor of Yenisseisk, penetrated to the Shilka, a tributary of the Amur, and founded Nerchinsk.

In 1666 Nikitor Chernigovskii, a Polish exile, built the fort of Albazin (Ya-k'e-sa or Yacsa), and was appointed governor by the tsar in 1669. Now firmly entrenched in the Amur Region, the Cossacks, known to the Chinese as the *Lo-ch'a*, were determined to push further into Manchuria.

The advance of the Russians coincided with the rise of the Manchus in China. The founders of the Ch'ing dynasty, though troubled and worried about the Russian threat, had to postpone any large-scale punitive action because of their preoccupation with the conquest of China and the consolidation of the dynasty. It was not until the suppression of the "Revolt of the Three Feudatories" (*San-Fan*) in 1681 that Emperor K'ang-hsi was free to deal with the Russian problem.

Early Diplomatic Missions to China. Along with their conquest of Siberia and penetration into the Amur Region, the Russians sent a number of exploratory and diplomatic missions to China. Russian knowledge of China at this point was pitifully limited; some believed that China was neither big nor rich—"completely surrounded by a brick wall, from which it is evident that it is no large place."[25] The first Russians to appear in Peking, so the account goes, were two Cossacks, I. Petrov and B. Iallyshev (Yallysheff), who arrived in 1567, claiming to be envoys of Ivan the Terrible. As they brought no tribute to the Ming court, they were not granted an audience with the emperor. In 1618 Tsar Mikhail Theodorovich dispatched Ivan Petlin of Tomsk to Peking to seek information about this strange country. Like the first two travelers, he brought no tribute and was refused an audience. However, he was told that Russian envoys and traders were welcome but because of the great distance between the two countries China would not send any envoys herself. Petlin returned with a letter from the Ming emperor Wan-li—which nobody in Russia could translate—and a map of China as well as some interesting (if somewhat condescending) descriptions of the people:

> The people of both sexes in China are clean; they wear clothes of their own fashion, with wide sleeves like those of our lietniks [light, summer women's gowns with wide sleeves] and, underneath, half-caftan, Russian fashion. There are many merchants and soldiers in China, and they use firearms; and they wage war with the Yellow Mongols; and the Mongols use bows for fighting; and in China the people are timid. . . . the people of China are not warlike; very good at trading . . .[26]

25. John F. Baddeley, *Russia, Mongolia, China* (London, 1919), II, 67-68.
26. *Ibid.*, 83.

The first Russian ambassador, Feodor Baikov, was sent off in 1654 to find out the best routes to reach China, the distance involved, and the kinds of goods the Chinese had to trade. He was also to look into the Chinese military and economic strength, and to investigate the local agricultural products and precious stones. He brought a letter from the tsar to the Bogdikhan (Great Khan), a designation for the Manchu emperor which the Russians had learned from the Mongols. Baikov was instructed to present the letter to no one but the Bogdikhan himself and during the audience he was not to perform the kowtow. Somewhat amusingly, his instructions went on to state: "he is by no means to kiss the Bogdikhan's foot [as the Chinese do]; but if he is called upon to kiss hands he need not refuse."[27] An advance emissary, Setkul Ablin, was sent to announce the mission, which arrived in Peking in 1656. Because of his adamant refusal to comply with Chinese ceremonies, Baikov was not granted an audience, and his gifts, first forcibly taken from him, were peremptorily returned. Though a failure as a diplomat, Baikov brought back "valuable" information on China:[28]

> The houses [in Peking] are all of stone [brick], built simply, roofed with glazed pentiles of different colours; and the houses are low, except those of the Emperor . . . The main streets are paved; the stone is natural granite; and on either side of the street a great ditch is dug, leading to the small river and to the lakes . . . the water in kanbalik [Peking] is very unhealthy . . . And between the dwelling houses and the yards all is garden. The Chinese and Mongols [Manchus] state that there are no large rivers in or near the capital except one river . . .

> All the people in the Chinese capital of both sexes are well-grown and clean; but the Chinese women have little feet, like those of children and it is said that they squeeze them on purpose, and they wear short dresses after their fashion with slits, and the sleeves wide, as in lietniks and the hair on their heads like the Germans. And the men wear long robes with buttons, and they fasten them under the armpit. Both sexes dress quietly; only the courtiers and uvans [wangs, princes] wear bright colours . . . And the religion of the Chinese is this: they pray to idols, and the idols are made of clay . . . every temple has one bell—the bells are of bronze or of iron like our Russian ones . . .

27. Baddeley, 134, 442.
28. *Ibid.*, II, 147-49.

And in the Chinese capital there are people of many countries: Niemtsi [Dutch], French, Livonians [Poles], Spaniards, and Italians; and they followed their own religions . . .

Another Russian envoy, Ivan Perfiliev, arrived in Peking in 1660. Because the tsar's letter was arrogant in tone and did not conform to the established Chinese way of address, there was a move on the part of Ch'ing courtiers to expel him. Emperor Shun-chih, however, decided that some forbearance should be shown, because Russia was a distant state on the frontier which had not participated in the blessings of civilization. He announced that the very fact of her sending a mission was proof of her submissiveness and her good intentions. The Russian envoy was therefore treated courteously and his presents were accepted as tribute. The emperor in return bestowed gifts upon the White Khan (the tsar) and his envoy, but no audience was given and no return mission was sent.

In 1670, another mission, under Ignashka Milovanov, was sent by the governor of Nerchinsk, Danilo Arshinskii. The envoy was instructed to demand that the Bogdikhan submit and pay tribute to the tsar. Once in Peking, Milovanov and his associates lost their nerve and decided to kowtow to Emperor K'ang-hsi rather than make the demand. They were allowed to tarry in the capital for thirty-eight days, were given gifts, and were treated on the whole rather well. They returned with a letter from the emperor, asking the governor of Nerchinsk to stop the disturbing activities of the Cossacks in Albazin and to hand over Ghantimur, a Manchu tribal chieftain who had defected to the Russians in 1666. As it happened, Ghantimur had since accepted the Orthodox faith and become a Russian noble, and the Russians refused to extradite him.

In 1675 the flamboyant envoy, Nikolai G. Spathary, whose original family name was Milescu, was sent to find out the best routes to China, feel out her reaction toward relations with Russia, and learn something about the type of people dwelling between Siberia and China. In contrast to his predecessors who were mostly illiterate, Spathary was a man of vast erudition, prepared to defend the honor of his master without compromise. He would not hand over the tsar's letter to Chinese officials but insisted on its personal delivery to the emperor, and protested strongly that China should not treat him and his sovereign in the same way as they did the envoys and rulers of Portugal and Holland, which were but petty states compared with Russia. He refused to have his gifts designated as tribute. After twenty-six days of contention with the Board of Rites, he finally gave in and performed the kowtow to K'ang-hsi, who then favored him with a dinner in the palace. However, Spathary's request for trade, friendly relations, and the release of Russian prisoners of war was not granted because he rejected the Chinese demands that (1) Russia extradite Ghantimur; and (2) Russian envoys accept Chinese etiquette, including the kowtow, as well as the designation of Russian gifts as tribute and the designation of Chinese gifts as gratuities for services rendered to the Chinese emperor by the tsar and his envoy. Moreover, Spathary declined to accept K'ang-hsi's "gratuities" to the tsar on his knees. Because of this disobedience and Russia's refusal to extradite Ghantimur, K'ang-hsi did not send a reply to the tsar. Spathary was in Peking for three and a half months without accomplishing his mission, but he did learn the important information from the Jesuit, F. Verbiest, that K'ang-hsi would go to war to demand the return of Ghantimur and the destruction of Albazin and Nerchinsk; that although the Chinese were in some measure afraid of the Russians, they believed that Moscow was too far away to reinforce effectively the small number of Cossacks in the Amur Region, while China had the advantage of geographical proximity and numerical superiority of her armed forces.[29] It was clear that the Ch'ing court was planning a campaign against the Russians sooner or later and was now merely biding its time.

The Treaty of Nerchinsk, 1689. With the "Revolt of the Three Feudatories" put down (1681), the Ming loyalist movement on Taiwan suppressed (1683), and the dynastic hold on the country made fast, K'anghsi was ready to take on the Russian problem. As noted briefly in Chapter 2, he ordered that an expedition be organized against the Russians in Albazin. In 1685, after several years of elaborate preparation, General Pengcun marched from Tsitsihar with 10,000 soldiers, 5,000 sailors, and 200 pieces of artillery. Against these numbers, the 450 Cossack defenders under Aleksei Tolbuzin stood very little chance, and were, predictably, completely overpowered. Forty-five Russians were taken prisoner, and Albazin was reduced to ashes. Tolbuzin, however, managed to escape to Nerchinsk. At the news of this total victory K'ang-hsi proudly announced the reasons for the campaign:[30]

29. Baddeley, 395-411.
30. Ho Ch-iu-t'ao (ed.), *Shuo-fang pei-sheng* (A manual of northern places), (Peking?, 1881), 6:16b-17.

The aim of government is enduring peace and order, not temporary expediency . . . The present campaign against the Russians, for example, does not look very important on the surface but it is actually of the greatest significance. For more than thirty years the Russians have disturbed our Amur and Sungari Rivers and have stolen an outpost [Albazin] which is very close to the original home of our imperial dynasty. If we do not eradicate them, I am afraid that there will be no place for our people on the frontiers. Ever since I personally assumed power at thirteen *sui*, I have always been alert to this problem, carefully examining [the enemy's] topography, the distance of the [Russian] position, their people and their customs, in order that I might take the necessary steps, moving ahead with ammunition at the opportune moment; and in the face of opposition by many people, I determinedly sent my generals on an expedition, striking deeply [into their positions].

After having leveled Albazin, Pengcun returned home; but Tolbuzin, with the help of 336 Cossacks, soon re-established himself on the ruins. New fortifications were erected, and in March 1686, Tolbuzin renewed his raids on the Amur. K'ang-hsi once again dispatched an expedition to Albazin. This time the Russians resisted the Chinese seige for more than a year, but, as before, the sides were hopelessly mismatched. Tolbuzin was killed in action and many of his men died of disease. At last, in mid-1687, when only 66 Cossacks were left and when one more concerted attack would have given Albazin to the Chinese, K'ang-hsi suddenly ordered the siege lifted. His general Sabsu even offered provisions to the starving Cossacks. Ostensibly, the emperor was acting in deference to the request of the tsar, who had sent two emissaries to Peking to announce that a diplomatic mission was on its way, by which it was hoped —the differences between the two countries could be settled. Actually, he had been looking for a chance to win Russian good will, and this move by the tsar provided just such an opportunity. It may seem paradoxical that he fought the Russians on the one hand and on the other wanted to cultivate their friendship. The fact was that he did not want to goad them into an alliance with the still unpacified Western Mongols, the Olöd. Moreover, China needed a rest after years of internal campaigns expended against the Three Feudatories: it was not in her own interest to prolong hostilities against the Russians.

Nor was Russia in any position to make war: Peter, not yet "the Great," was in his early teens sharing a shaky throne with his invalid brother;

the country itself was preoccupied with military affairs in the Baltic; and the treasury was depleted by military expenses and internal economic depression. It was far preferable for Russia to follow a policy of *peaceful penetration* of China through trade contact than one of naked aggression and *territorial expansion* along the Amur. For this reason peace with China was imperative; hence the diplomatic mission. It was dispatched under Fedor A. Golovin, the son of the Tobolsk governor. He was instructed to meet the Chinese at Selinginsk and to try to set the boundary line along the Amur and Bystra, or, failing that, at least along the Amur and the Dzeya. His other instructions were to negotiate for official regulation of trade, to collect information on the various water routes to China, and to request Chinese embassies to Russia. En route in 1687, he received additional instructions that in the interest of avoiding further bloodshed he might agree to cede Albazin in exchange for greater commercial privileges. On October 22, 1687, Golovin reached Selinginsk.

The Chinese delegation was led by Prince Songgotu (So-o-t'u) and a number of high dignitaries, and with them as interpreters two Jesuit priests, Jean-François Gerbillon and Thomas Pereira. They left Peking in May 1688, but found the road to Selinginsk blocked because of the Ölöd chieftain Galdan's invasion of the Eastern Mongols, the Qalqa (Khalkha). Nerchinsk was then selected as an alternative site for the diplomatic negotiations. Emperor K'ang-hsi, anxious to win Russian good will and prevent a unity between Galdan and the Russians, had instructed Songgotu that China might grant Nerchinsk to Russia and accept the boundary at the Argun River. At the conference, Golovin proposed to fix the boundary along the Amur, while Songgotu pressed for Russian evacuation of Nerchinsk and Albazin as well as relinquishment of the land beyond Selinginsk. With both sides insisting on their demands, a deadlock resulted. The two Jesuit priests shuttled between the two camps as mediators, while the Chinese delegation threatened to use force.[31] They had 10,000 soldiers and 90 armed vessels as support, while Golovin had only 1,500 troops at his disposal. The Russians gave in at last. The Treaty of Nerchinsk (Ni-pu-ch'u) was signed on September 7, 1689; it was drawn up in five languages: Chinese, Russian, Manchu, Mongolian, and Latin—the Latin version serving as the official text. It contained six articles:

---

31. For a study of the role of the Jesuits in the treaty negotiations, see Joseph Sebes, S.J., *The Jesuits and the Sino-Russian Treaty of Nerchinsk* (1689), (Rome, 1961).

1. The Siberian-Manchurian border would be set along the Argun, would continue along the Amur to the mouth of the Kerbechi, and along the Outer Hsing-an (Stenovoi) Mountains to the sea.
2. Albazin would be demolished and its Russian residents repatriated with their properties, and hunters who transgressed the boundary line would be punished.
3. Subjects of the two countries with passports could freely enter each other's territory for trade.
4. Deserters and fugitives would be extradited, and under no condition given refuge.
5. Citizens of either country now residing in the other should be allowed to remain.
6. With this peace settlement all past incidents should be disregarded.

This treaty—China's first such agreement with a "Western" power—was reached on the basis of equality between China and Russia, and on the whole both countries found it satisfactory. Russia gained control of Nerchinsk and some 93,000 square miles of undecided territory and was given a number of commercial privileges into the bargain, while China had the satisfaction of seeing the Russian problem at Albazin eliminated and the likelihood increased that Russia would remain neutral during China's struggle with Galdan. There was a noticeable gap in the treaty, however; the frontier between Mongolia and Siberia remained unsettled, for Golovin insisted that the issue was beyond his authority to negotiate. It was apparent that Russia was hedging from any settlement of this problem, because the Ch'ing dynasty was not in full control of Outer Mongolia.

K'ang-hsi demonstrated farsighted statesmanship in this diplomatic exchange, for shortly after it was concluded, Galdan did in fact send agents to Russia in search of aid or alliance. One agent met Golovin in Irkutsk in March 1690, another went to Tobolsk in August of the same year, and still another went to Nerchinsk. But Russia, having just concluded a treaty of peace with China, was in no mood to rock the boat with an alliance with the Ölöd. While it is impossible to say whether the Russians would have given Galdan assistance if K'ang-hsi had not lifted the Albazin siege and signed the Treaty of Nerchinsk, or whether such assistance, if given, could have altered the course of events, it is nevertheless a matter of admirable statesmanship that K'ang-hsi's maneuver anticipated and stifled any such possibility before it arose.

With the Treaty of Nerchinsk signed and out of the way, K'ang-hsi turned to the problem of the Ölöd. Several years of warfare followed, in which the imperial forces sustained considerable losses, both of men and ground—at one point Galdan penetrated as far as Ulan Butung, within 80 leagues (240 miles) of Peking. But the fighting remained for the most part inconclusive, neither side gaining much advantage. Finally, determined to crush Galdan, K'ang-hsi after several years of preparation sent out a grand expedition of 80,000 men in 1696. It was deployed in three divisions, the emperor himself commanding the central army, Generalissimo Fiyanggu the western one, and General Sabsu the eastern one, which was sent to guard the eastern borders of Mongolia. The imperial forces advanced with great difficulty in the Mongolian deserts, threatened by starvation and faced with what seemed insuperable logistic problems. In the midst of all this came the disquieting rumor—apparently originated by Galdan himself—that the Ölöd now had 60,000 Russians allied with them. K'ang-hsi brushed off the rumor as nothing more than hearsay, and when finally, on June 12, 1696, Galdan was drawn into a confrontation with Fiyanggu at Jau Modo, it was clearly evident that he had no such aid. His horsemen were completely overpowered by the Ch'ing artillery and musketeers, and Galdan, too proud to surrender, fled with a handful of loyal followers. He died the next year, 1697, of a sudden illness—possibly he took his own life with poison. K'ang-hsi thus extended his rule to Outer Mongolia and Hami, and laid the foundation for his grandson, Emperor Ch'ien-lung, to complete the conquest of the entire Western Region (Hsi-yü)[32] in the 1750's.

The most significant fact about the Treaty of Nerchinsk was that it regularized Sino-Russian relations. A number of Russian trade and diplomatic missions entered China after its enactment. The mission under E. Izbrandt Ides in 1693 won permission for Russian caravans to be sent to Peking once every three years. These caravans were restricted to 200 men and their stay was limited to 80 days; their goods—whether imports or exports—were exempt from customs duties. Between 1698 and 1718 ten such caravans made the journey. In 1720 a diplomatic mission under Ambassador Leon V. Izmailov arrived in Peking. The envoy performed the full kowtow—three kneelings and nine knockings of the head on the ground—on condition that future Chinese envoys to Russia would likewise conform to Russian court ceremonies.[33] He was favorably treated by

32. Renamed Sinkiang, or New Territory, in 1768.
33. Ripa, 105-07.

K'ang-hsi, but his request for the extension of trade and the establishment of a consulate-general in Peking did not evoke a sympathetic response. After three months in Peking he returned home, leaving his
attaché Lorentz Lange to continue the negotiations; seventeen months
later (in 1722) Lange was expelled for arrogant behavior.

Tulisen's Mission to the Tūrgūd Tribe in Russia, 1714. If Russia sent a
number of missions to China, China also sent a couple to Russia. The
first of these was not to the court at St. Petersburg, however, but to the
Tūrgūd tribe on the Volga. The Tūrgūd were an Ölöd tribe which originally lived in the Tarbagatai area but had migrated to Russia in 1630. By
1654 they had become Russian vassals, although their chieftains continued to send periodic tribute to China. In 1712 a Tūrgūd tributary mission came to Peking from the chief Ayüki, whose daughter was married
to the new Ölöd leader, Cewang Arabdan, Galdan's nephew. K'ang-hsi
decided to send a return mission, ostensibly to express his appreciation
of Ayüki's loyalty but in fact to strengthen China's ties with the Tūrgūd
and to forestall any alliance between Ayüki and Cewang Arabdan. Very
likely K'ang-hsi also wanted to persuade the Tūrgūd tribe to return to
China (as eventually it did, in 1770-71).

The mission was put under the charge of Tulisen, an assistant reader
in the Grand Secretariat. He left in 1712 and passed through Mongolia
and Siberia, where he was well received by Prince Gargarin, the governor
of Siberia. In June 1714 the mission reached the Volga, where Tulisen
and Ayüki met. Except that their exchange of good will was friendly
and that they talked about returning Ayüki's nephew from China, little
is known of their meeting. It is presumed that Ayüki secretly pledged his
friendship with China and promised that he would not enter into an
alliance with Cewang Arabdan. Tulisen returned with an account of his
travels, entitled *I-yü lu* (Description of a foreign land).

Even though this was not a diplomatic mission to Russia in the strict
sense of the term—in that it was sent not to the Russian court but to a
Mongol tribe in a remote province—K'ang-hsi nevertheless hoped to
make some use of it toward establishing closer ties with Russia. Such
intention was obvious from his instructions to Tulisen that if the tsar
would see him he was to go to St. Petersburg for an audience. However,
as Peter the Great was then engaged in an expedition to Sweden, Tulisen returned home without going to the Russian capital.

The Treaty of Kiakhta, 1727. Tulisen's mission apparently succeeded in what it proposed to do: it strengthened China's ties with the Türgüd and possibly prevented an alliance between Ayüki and Cewang Arabdan. But the Ölöd threat to the Ch'ing dynasty was still present. The traffic that persisted between Cewang Arabdan and the Russians caused renewed fear among the Chinese that there might be secret plotting between them. In this light, the question of fixing the boundary between Outer Mongolia and Siberia—an issue which the Treaty of Nerchinsk had left unresolved—became doubly important. During the year 1720 K'ang-hsi repeatedly impressed upon the Russian envoy Ismailov the need for delimiting the Mongolian-Siberian frontier. The Chinese concern was not unwarranted, for the Russians were in fact sanguine about exploiting China's trouble with the Ölöd. A mission under Ivan Unkovskii was sent to Cewang Arabdan in 1722, proposing that if the Ölöd chose to accept the status of a vassal, Russia would take a strong stand toward China and might even be talked into making a military demonstration against her. However, the death of K'ang-hsi that year made the Ölöd less anxious for Russian aid, especially if it would involve entering vassal status. The new emperor in China, Yung-cheng, carrying on his father's policy to isolate Mongolia from Russia, decided it was necessary to settle all pending issues with Russia in a new treaty and thereby remove any excuse she might use for aiding the Ölöd or entering into an alliance with them.

The Russians, on their part, were also anxious to settle a number of issues with China, such as frontier delimitation, extension of the overland trade, and the establishment of a religious mission in Peking. On pretext of congratulating Yung-cheng on his ascension to the throne in 1723, Catherine I, who succeeded Peter the Great in 1725, sent Sava Vladislavich Ruguzinskii as envoy extraordinary to China. The embassy, 100 men strong and escorted by 1,500 soldiers, arrived in Peking on October 21, 1726, after thirteen months of travel. Sava, a man of tact, patience, and vision, met with the Chinese negotiators—Tulisen and three others—thirty times in the six months between October 1726 and April 1727. The French Jesuit, Parrenin, served as a liaison between the two delegations and kept Sava informed of the current sentiments in the Chinese camp. Since there was no precedent for signing treaties in Peking—the first treaty with Russia was signed at the frontier town of Nerchinsk—the delegations moved to the border of the Boura River, a tributary of the Selinginsk, and there concluded a preliminary convention known as the Boura Agreement, which, when put into its final form on October

21, 1727, became the Treaty of Kiakhta. The important terms of this eleven-article treaty were as follows:

1. The Mongolian-Siberian frontier would be delimited by a joint Sino-Russian commission. The boundary was to run from the Sayan Mountains and Sapintabakha in the west to the Argun River in the east. The area from the Uda to the Stone Mountains in the east was to remain undecided because of the lack of accurate information about it, but elsewhere the commission would demarcate the boundary on the spot.

2. In addition to the existing trade at Nerchinsk, the Russians were allowed to trade at Kiakhta on the frontier.

3. Deserters and fugitives from either country would be extradited.

4. Russian caravans of not more than 200 men would be allowed to come to Peking once every three years, free from import and export duties.

5. Russia would be permitted to maintain a religious mission with its own church in Peking, and Russian priests and students would be permitted to live in Peking.

6. Communications between China and Russia would bear the seals of both governments—in China that of the Li-fan yüan, and in Russia that of both the Senate and the governor of Tobolsk.

In the territorial settlement China lost some 40,000 square miles between the Upper Irtysh and the Sayan Mountains and in the area south and southwest of Lake Baikal, but she gained the security of seeing Russia now partitioned off from the tribes of Mongolia. On the other hand Russia gained a number of trade concessions and the authorization to open a religious mission in China, but limited her border trade, hitherto conducted freely with the Mongols, to Nerchinsk and Kiakhta.

The T'o-shih Mission to Russia, 1729-32. Although the Treaty of Kiakhta settled many important issues, it raised a number of new problems because of the increased contacts which it permitted between the two countries. There were constant complaints from Russia of border raids by Mongolian bandits who were stealing horses, camels, oxen, and sheep; there were outcries over debts owed by Chinese merchants to Russian traders. Naturally this caused uneasiness over the question of whether Russia would remain neutral during the Ch'ing campaign against the new Ölöd leader, Galdan Cereng, a son of Cewang Arabdan, who had died in 1727. Seeking reassurance, Emperor Yung-cheng dispatched an embassy to Russia in 1729. As opposed to the one made to the Türgüd in

1714, this was a genuine diplomatic mission, accredited to the court at St. Petersburg, and as such was the first ever sent by China to a "Western" state.[34]

The mission, led by T'o-shih, a vice-president of one of the Boards, went with the formal purpose of congratulating Peter II on his coronation. However, upon reaching St. Petersburg in 1731 T'o-shih found that the tsar had died and that the new ruler was Anna Ivanovna, a niece of Peter the Great. His credentials had to be changed, necessitating a return to China. Back in St. Petersburg in 1732 once more, with the new credentials, he proposed to the Russians that if the Chinese attack were to drive the Ölöd into Russia for refuge, the Russian government should extradite the Ölöd rulers and nobles to China but might keep the tribesmen in Russia, under strict control, so as to prevent them from troubling China in the future. In return for this cooperation, China would give Russia part of the land seized from the Ölöd. The Russian government expressed willingness to discuss the question of extradition amicably when it arose, but refused to make any other commitments. T'o-shih's mission therefore did not seem to be much of a success. But as it turned out this was of no great consequence; Russia was preoccupied at the moment in the war of the Polish Succession and could not have helped the Ölöd in any event, and the Ch'ing expeditionary forces, after suffering an upset at the beginning of the campaign, finally defeated the Ölöd in 1732 at Erdeni Tsu, enabling China to negotiate a peace settlement at no great loss of prestige.

Russia's Special Position in China. Sino-Russian relations during the early Ch'ing period were markedly different from China's relations with western European maritime states. Russia, in fact, occupied a very special position in China. She was the only foreign country with which China maintained treaty relations, the only "Western" state to which China sent diplomatic missions, and the only foreign power granted religious, commercial, and educational privileges in Peking. The early Ch'ing rulers recognized that Russian neutrality was essential to China's consolidation of her northern and northwestern frontiers, and that to gain this neutrality it was necessary to grant Russia certain considerations and privileges denied to other foreign states.[35]

34. Mark Mancall, "China's First Missions to Russia, 1729-1731," *Papers on China,* East Asia Regional Studies Seminar, Harvard University, Vol. 9, 1955.
35. Immanuel C. Y. Hsü, "Russia's Special Position in China during the Early Ch'ing Period," *Slavic Review,* 13:4:688 (Dec. 1964).

Although the Ch'ing court insisted that Russian envoys kowtow to the Chinese emperor, and although Chinese records consistently described Russian emissaries as tribute bearers, Russia was not officially listed as a tributary state in any of the five editions of the *Collected Statutes of the Great Ch'ing Empire* (*Ta-Ch'ing hui-tien*). In fact, K'ang-hsi explicitly noted that Russia should not be classified as such: "Although tribute from a foreign country [Russia] would be a magnificent thing, I am afraid that when it is carried on into later generations it may become a source of trouble." On many occasions K'ang-hsi extended Russia the consideration due an independent state. When he sent Tulisen to Russia in 1712, for example, he ordered him "to act in accordance with the ceremonies of that country." No such instructions had ever been given any Chinese emissary to the tributary states; on the contrary, all tributary kings were required to conform to Chinese etiquette when receiving a Chinese envoy. Again, this peculiar deference to Russia was manifested in K'ang-hsi's exchange with the Russian envoy Leon V. Izmailov in 1720. If he complied with Chinese court ceremonies, the emperor told him, and performed the kowtow, the Ch'ing government would see to it that future Chinese envoys to Russia would follow Russian ceremonies and perform whatever rituals were required of them. Upon Izmailov's compliance, K'ang-hsi favored him with a dozen audiences in three months, during which he alluded to Peter the Great as "his equal," "his good neighbor," and "a most great and honorable ruler in possession of a vast territory."[36] No such expressions—indeed, no such sentiments—had ever been applied to China's tributary kings or to any other foreign rulers. When T'o-shih went to Russia in 1732 he actually knelt before the tsarina, as no Chinese envoy had done before a tributary king.

One interesting ramification of China's special consideration for Russia was the treatment of Russian prisoners of war. These prisoners, about one hundred in all, taken in several battles before and during the Albazin siege, were pardoned and organized into a unit of the Ch'ing army—the Eleventh Company of the Fourth Regiment of the Manchu Bordered Yellow Banner. As bannermen, they were given the favor of ranks and the privilege of living in quarters by themselves. They received annual pensions and were allowed complete religious freedom. Emperor K'ang-hsi gave them a Buddhist temple, on the site of which they built an Orthodox church known as the Church of St. Nicolas, later renamed the

36. Gaston Cahen, *Histoire des relations de la Russia avec la Chine, 1869-1730* (Paris, 1912), 165.

Church of the Assumption. To the Chinese it was known as the *Lo-ch'a miao* (Temple of the Russians), more often called, incorrectly, the Northern Russian Hostel.

Russian traders also fared well. Beginning with the Ides mission in 1693, they were allowed to come to Peking every three years in groups of two hundred, and although they paid their own way, their goods were brought in duty-free. While in Peking they were lodged in the Southern Russian Hostel—the old *Hui-t'ung kuan* (Common Residence for Envoys) of the Ming dynasty. Officially they were supposed to conclude their business and leave Peking within eighty days, but this regulation was scarcely more than a token. The caravan under Liangusov and Savatiev in 1698, for instance, consisted of nearly 300 merchants and 200 secretaries, servants and employees. Between 1698 and 1718 ten such caravans came to Peking, averaging one every two, instead of every three, years as officially stipulated, and they were often permitted to remain in the capital longer than the legal eighty days. At times the Chinese court even advanced loans to distressed Russian merchants.

After the Treaty of Kiakhta in 1727, groups of Russian priests were allowed to come every ten years to minister to the Russians in Peking, and the Chinese government paid their traveling and living expenses. From 1729 to 1859 thirteen of these missions came to the capital. The priests lived in the Southern Russian Hostel, where they maintained a church called the Convent of Candlemas, later renamed the Church of the Purification of the Virgin. After 1729 the priests of the religious mission also conducted services at the Church of St. Nicolas.

The Treaty of Kiakhta permitted Russia to send students to Peking to learn Chinese and Manchu. In 1728 a language school for Russians was inaugurated as a separate institution within the Southern Russian Hostel. The students came for a ten-year period and the Chinese subsidized their traveling and living costs. They were required to wear Chinese clothes supplied them by the Li-fan yüan; the Board of Rites provided them with food, and the Imperial Academy (*Kuo-tzu chien*) assigned a Chinese and a Manchu instructor to teach them the languages. There were also private tutors attached to the school. By the same token the Chinese government felt the need for instruction in Russian. Twenty-four students were chosen by the Li-fan yüan from members of the Eight Banners to study Russian and Latin for five years. At the end of the period, examinations were held and the two best candidates were given official appointments of the eighth or ninth rank.

By virtue of these religious, educational, and commercial privileges, Russia, alone among nations, had an established foothold in the Chinese capital. These privileges, and their attendant special status, were not revoked even after Ch'ien-lung's successful consolidation of the empire in the 1750's made Russian neutrality no longer necessary. It was not until 1861, when Peking was opened to the diplomatic representatives of Britain, France, and the United States, that Russia's monopolistic position was broken.

The significance of Russia's special position in China cannot be overemphasized. Members of the Russian religious mission and the language school in Peking were able to see China from within and study her language, politics, and social and economic structure firsthand. They were able to detect the strength and weakness of the Ch'ing dynasty long before other Westerners. Possibly they were the only foreigners who understood the Chinese mentality. They witnessed the progressive decline of the Manchu power, and their reports to the home government helped guide Russia's policy toward China. When they returned home they started what was probably the first systematic Sinological study in Europe, preceding that of any other Western state by many decades.[37]

FURTHER READING

Baddeley, John F., *Russia, Mongolia, China* (London, 1919), II.

Bernard, Henri, S. J., *Matteo Ricci's Scientific Contributions to China*, tr. by Edward C. Werner (Peiping, 1935).

Cahen, Gaston, *Histoire des relations de la Russie avec la Chine, 1689-1730* (Paris, 1912).

Chang, T'ien-tse, *Sino-Portuguese Trade from 1514 to 1644: A Synthesis of Portuguese and Chinese Sources*, reprinted (Leiden, 1969).

Chang, Yin-lin 張蔭麟, "Ming-Ch'ing chih-chi Hsi-hsüeh shu-ju Chung-kuo k'ao-lüeh" 明清之際西學輸入中國考略 (A brief study of the introduction of Western learning into China during the Ming-Ch'ing transitional period), *Tsing-hua hsüeh-pao*, 1:1:38-69 (June 1923).

Ch'en, Agnes Fang-chih, "Chinese Frontier Diplomacy: the Coming of the Russians and the Treaty of Nerchinsk," *The Yenching Journal of Social Studies*, 4:2:99-149 (Feb. 1949).

———, "Chinese Frontier Diplomacy: Kiakhta Boundary Treaties and Agreements," *The Yenching Journal of Social Studies*, 4:2:151-205 (Feb. 1949).

37. R. K. I. Quested, *The Expansion of Russia in East Asia, 1857-1860* (Kuala Lumpur, 1968), 24-29; Wu Hsiang-hsiang, *O-ti ch'in-lüeh Chung-kuo shih* (A history of the Russian imperialist aggression in China), (Taipei, 1957), 20-21.

Ch'en, Fu-kuang 陳復光, *Yu-Ch'ing i-tai chih Chung-O kuan-hsi* 有清一代之中俄關係 (Sino-Russian relations during the Ch'ing period exclusively), (Kunming, 1947), chapters 1-2.

Ch'en, Kenneth, "Matteo Ricci's Contribution to and Influence on Geographical Knowledge in China," *Journal of the American Oriental Society*, 59:325-59, 509 (1939).

Ch'en, Shou-yi 陳受頤, "Ming-mo Ch'ing-ch'u Yeh-su-hui-shih ti Ju-chiao-kuan chi ch'i fan-ying" 明末清初耶穌會士的儒教觀及其反應 (The Jesuits' conception of Confucianism in the late Ming and early Ch'ing and its repercussions in China), *Kuo-hsüeh chi-k'an* 國學季刊, 5:2:1-64 (1935).

———, "The Religious Influence of Early Jesuits on Emperor Ch'ung-cheng of the Ming Dynasty," *T'ien-hsia Monthly*, 8:5:397-419 (May 1939); 9:1:35-47 (Aug. 1939).

Ch'en, Teng-yüan 陳登元, "Hsi-hsüeh lai-Hua shih kuo-jen chih wu-tuan t'ai-tu" 西學來華時國人之武斷態度 (The Chinese dogmatic attitude toward Western learning when it was first introduced into China), *Tung-fang tsa-chih* 東方雜誌, 27:8:61-76 (April 1930).

Ch'en, Vincent, *Sino-Russian Relations in the Seventeenth Century* (The Hague, 1966).

Cheng, Tien-fong, *A History of Sino-Russian Relations* (Washington, D.C., 1957), chapters 2-3.

Chu, Ch'ien-chih 朱謙之, *Chung-kuo ssu-hsiang tui-yü Ou-chou wen-hua chih ying-hsiang* 中國思想對於歐洲文化之影响 (The influence of Chinese thought on European civilization), (Changsha, 1940).

Cranmer-Byng, J. L., "The Chinese Attitude Towards External Relations," *Internationl Journal* (Canada), XXI-1:57-77 (1966).

Dunne, George H., S.J., *Generation of Giants: The Story of the Jesuits in China in the Last Decades of the Ming Dynasty* (Notre Dame, 1962).

Fang, Hao 方豪, *Li Chih-tsao yen-chiu* 李之藻研究 (A study of Li Chih-tsao), (Taipei, 1966).

Fu, Lo-shu, *A Documentary Chronicle of Sino-Western Relations, 1644-1820* (Tucson, 1966), 2 vols.

Gallagher, Louis J., S.J., *China in the Sixteenth Century: The Journal of Matthew Ricci, 1583-1610* (New York, 1953).

Golder, F. A., *Russian Expansion on the Pacific, 1641-1850* (Cleveland, 1914).

Hibbert, Eloise T., *Jesuit Adventure in China During the Reign of K'ang Hsi* (New York, 1941).

Hsiao, I-shan 蕭一山, *Ch'ing-tai t'ung-shih* 清代通史 (A general history of the Ch'ing period), revised edition (Taipei, 1962), I, chapters 22-25.

Hsü, Immanuel C. Y., "Russia's Special Position in China during the Early Ch'ing Period," *Slavic Review*, 13:4:688-700 (Dec. 1964).

Hsü, Tsung-tse 徐宗澤, *Ming-Ch'ing chien Yeh-su-hui-shih i-chu t'i-yao* 明清間耶穌會士譯著提要 (A synopsis of translations and writings of the Jesuits during the transitional period from the Ming to the Ch'ing), (Taipei, 1958).

Lach, Donald F., *Asia in the Making of Europe,* Vol. I: *The Century of Discovery* (Chicago, 1965).

Liu, Hsüan-min 劉選民, "Chung-O tsao-ch'i mao-i k'ao" 中俄早期貿易考 (A study of early Russo-Chinese commercial relations), *Yen-ching hsüeh-pao* (Yenching Journal of Chinese Studies), 25:151-212 (June 1939).

Meng, Ssu-ming, "The E-lo-ssu Kuan [Russian Hostel] in Peking," *Harvard Journal of Asiatic Studies,* 23:19-46 (1960-61).

Parry, John H., *The Age of Reconnaissance* (London and Cleveland, 1963).

Quested, R. K. I., *The Expansion of Russia in East Asia, 1857-1860* (Kuala Lumpur, 1968), chapter 1.

Ravenstein, E. G., *The Russians on the Amur; Its Discovery, Conquest, and Colonization* (London, 1861).

Rosso, A. S., O.F.M., *Apostolic Legations to China of the Eighteenth Century* (South Pasadena, 1948).

Rouleau, Francis A., S.J., "Maillard de Tournon, Papal Legate at the Court of Peking," *Archivum Historicum Societatis Iesu,* 31:264-323 (1962).

Rowbotham, Arnold H., *Missionary and Mandarin: The Jesuits at the Court of China* (Berkeley, 1942).

Sebes, Joseph, S.J., *The Jesuits and the Sino-Russian Treaty of Nerchinsk (1689),* (Rome, 1961).

Wang, Chih-hsiang 王之相, and Liu Tse-jung 劉澤榮, *Ku-kung O-wen shih-liao* 故宮俄文史料 (Documents in Russian preserved in the National Palace Museum of Pciping), (Peiping, 1936).

Wu, Aitchen K., *China and the Soviet Union: A Study of Sino-Russian Relations* (New York, 1950).

Wu, Hsiang-hsiang 吳相湘, *O-ti ch'in lüeh Chung-kuo shih* 俄帝侵略中國史 (A history of the Russian imperialist aggression in China), (Taipei, 1957), chapters 1-2.

6

The Turn of Dynastic Fortune:
From Prosperity to Decline

We have noted that China before 1800 was a vast empire which stood resplendent and unrivaled in East Asia. Her territory stretched from the Central Asian massif to the coast of the China Sea, and from the Mongolian desert to the jungles and shores of the south. Politically, she was an absolute monarchy, ruled by alien Manchu conquerors, who had adopted the Confucian ideology and who continued to use the Chinese institutions that had come with the country. Economically she was self-sufficient—predominantly agrarian but with a rudimentary capitalism developing in isolated pockets of the country. The social scene was dominated by the gentry, who supplied the government officials and local community leaders; the intellectual climate was characterized by the textual and antiquarian scholars of the School of Empirical Research. In foreign relations, contacts with western Europe and Russia had begun but had not yet made any appreciable difference in Chinese life. The power and prosperity of the empire attracted tributary missions from dozens of peripheral countries in Asia as well as trade and diplomatic missions from Europe and Russia. China in the middle and late 18th century was doubtless one of the most advanced countries on earth, and her secular political and social systems had won the admiration of not a few famous European philosophers.[1] It is therefore not without good reason that the Chinese regarded their country as the Middle Kingdom on earth and the center of the known civilized world.

1. Spinoza, Leibniz, Goethe, Voltaire, and Adam Smith.

162

CAUSES FOR THE MANCHU SUCCESS

Circumstances had favored the Manchus right from the start. Their geographical proximity to the Chinese settlement in Liaotung had enabled them to learn the technique of government and had shown them how to turn their tribal structure into a civil bureaucracy. There were also a considerable number of Chinese defectors who became their helpful advisers. The appearance of a host of resourceful leaders among the Manchus—such as Nurhaci, Abahai, and Dorgan—coincided with the internal rebellions and political corruption of the Ming dynasty and the consequent feeling of unrest among the Chinese. Oppressive taxes and political corruption had become extremely wearisome to the greater part of the population, and the continuous internal rebellions added to the instability of the country and the disaffection of the people. To be sure, no one of the Chinese expected a complete takeover by the alien Manchus; nevertheless, the squalidness of life under Ming rule created a psychological longing for a change of some kind, and the atmosphere thus created was favorable for dynastic change. It is fair to say that although the Manchu conquest of China was a military feat, it was expedited by a general sense of ennui among the Chinese during the last decades of Ming rule.

Once established in China the Manchus were blessed with a succession of capable rulers. K'ang-hsi, Yung-cheng, and Ch'ien-lung consolidated the dynasty and expanded its territory to an extent second only to that of the Mongol empire of the 13th century, and while doing so initiated a number of policies which were calculated to keep it safe and intact. They aligned themselves with the established Confucian order and appointed Chinese and Mongol officials to work side by side with the Manchus in the government, but at the same time they took measures to preserve the Manchu identity. These measures included the establishment of an Imperial Clan Court to supervise virtually every activity of the imperial members from birth to death, especially in such areas as education and marriage. There was no permission for intermarriage between Manchu and Chinese, or Mongol and Chinese. This proscription was reinforced even by such things as geographical restrictions. A willow palisade was planted in southern Manchuria to mark off the statutory limit beyond which no Chinese were allowed to emigrate. Similarly, Chinese emigration to Mongolia, or Mongol residence in China proper, was forbidden; Mongol princes had to secure the approval of the court before they could even visit China proper. By this separatist policy, plotting and intrigue between the different ethnic groups were minimized if not eliminated.

To centralize power the court saw to it that imperial princes and nobles were not allowed either to establish themselves as feudal lords in the provinces, or to develop connections with provincial governors and governors-general. In principle, imperial relatives were not appointed to the Grand Secretariat or Grand Council. Provisions were also made to keep the eunuchs and the imperial distaff from usurping power. To forestall organized opposition by Chinese officials—whom the Manchu overlords, in general, held suspect—no cliques, factions, or even large literary societies were permitted to exist. Moreover, by the "law of avoidance" an official could not serve in his native province, and the tenure of office where he was allowed to serve was usually limited to three years—theoretically too little time for him to develop local ties. Scholars were kept in line on the one hand by intimidation (namely the endless literary inquisitions) and on the other by the offer of attractive government posts.

In the actual mechanics of the government, the principle of balance of weakness was cardinal. Chinese and Manchu were appointed jointly in the central government and were alternated between the governorships and governor-generalships, so as to effect a general check and balance and to permit them to keep an eye on one another. Each of them could memorialize the throne directly, separately, and secretly, and anyone could impeach anyone else. High provincial officials, after a tour of duty for three years, usually reported their missions to the emperor in a confidential audience before being appointed to another post. In this way the ruler learned of the local conditions firsthand, and by personal contact with the official in question reinforced that official's commitment to the throne and therefore his loyalty. Censors and spies were dispatched into every corner of the empire to ferret out secret opposition, and the *paochia* police control sifted through the lowest level of the society in search of seditious plotting. The fear and suspicion thus generated in the official and unofficial circles helped to ensure the permanence of imperial control. Last but not least, the Manchu-Mongol-Chinese Banners and the Green Standard army were stationed in strategic spots all over the country to guard against uprising and unrest.

With these measures the Manchus succeeded in maintaining peace and order in China for a century and a half. But no regulation is effective for all times; and these, conceived in response to conditions peculiar to a particular time, necessarily outlived their usefulness with the passage of time. By the late 18th century it was all too obvious that the country was beset with troubles which the Chinese had come to associate with dynastic decline.

THE DECLINE OF THE MANCHU POWER

When Emperor Ch'ien-lung abdicated the throne in 1795, the dynasty had already passed its apogee and the seeds of decay had long since been sown. His fifteenth son, who became Emperor Chia-ch'ing, inherited a country that was "externally strong but internally shriveled" (*wai-ch'iang chung-kan*). Indeed, Chia-ch'ing's twenty-five year reign (1796-1820) was plagued with serious administrative, military, and moral problems which were unmistakable indices of the falling dynastic fortune.

Administrative Inefficiency. The suspicion which the Manchu court entertained toward Chinese officials and the resultant policy of mutual check undermined administrative efficiency. A noted contemporary political scientist has remarked on this crippling effect: "Public functionaries were rarely given an opportunity to show initiative, independent judgment, or satisfactory performance of tasks through the exercising of adequate authority. On the contrary, all officials were subjected to a tight net of regulations, restrictions, and checks, and threatened with punishment for derelictions or offenses even in matters beyond their individual control. A situation eventually prevailed in which the most prudent thing for the average official to do was to assume as little responsibility as possible—to pay greater attention to formal compliance with written rules than to undertakings that were useful to the sovereign or beneficial to the people."[2] The accuracy of this observation can be seen in a piece of advice given by K'ang-hsi himself to a governor in 1711: "Now that the country is at peace, it is advisable that you avoid trouble. An act that is beneficial in one way may be harmful in another. The ancients said, 'More commitment is not as good as less commitment.' "[3] Thus the guiding principle in the officialdom was to avoid issues. A highly placed courtier once confided that the secret of success in govern-

2. Kung-ch'üan Hsiao, *Rural China*, 504.
3. Wang Hsien-ch'ien, *Tung-hua lu* (Tung-hua records), K'ang-hsi, 50th year (1711), 18:2b, edict to Governor Fan Tsung-lo.

ment was to "kowtow more and talk less." It is therefore understandable that there developed a tendency toward compromise, superficiality, temporization—anything so as not to disturb the *status quo*. That these characters strangled the capacity of officials for energetic action and imaginative response to challenge did not trouble the court, for its primary concern was not for dynamic or even efficient administration, but for the dynasty's security. Large decisions were not the province of administrators, but the prerogative of the emperor alone. Under these conditions the state could prosper only in direct proportion to the emperor's capacity. Such a high concentration of power worked well-enough with resourceful rulers such as K'ang-hsi, Yung-cheng, and Ch'ien-lung, but once leadership faltered, the ship of state drifted. After Ch'ien-lung, there was no great emperor.

Widespread Corruption. The last twenty years of Ch'ien-lung's reign were very corrupt. Ho-shen, the imperial bodyguard whose meteoric rise to power was discussed in Chapter 2, bled the state for nearly a quarter of a century and amassed an incredible fortune of 800 million taels (about $1.5 billion), reputedly more than half the *actual* total state income for twenty years. The inventory of his estate revealed some interesting entries: 4,288 gold bowls and dishes, 600 silver pots, 119 gold wash basins, 5.8 million ounces of gold, 75 pawnshops with a capital of 30 million taels, 42 moneyshops with a capital of 40 million taels, and 800,-000 *mou* of land at an estimated value of 8 million taels.[4] When Emperor Chia-ch'ing executed him in 1799, a popular saying circulated: "When Ho-shen fell, Chia-ch'ing feasted."[5]

It should be noted, however, that Ho-shen was an acute symptom rather than the cause of the widespread corruption, which was evident even before his rise. Nonetheless, he accentuated the trend and his evil influence continued to haunt the country. Graft, extortion, and irregular levies in both the civil government and the military services became commonplace, almost *de rigeur*. Metropolitan officials openly accepted "presents" from provincial officials, who in turn required them of their own subordinates. These officials led a way of life far beyond their salaries; many maintained luxurious residences with private staffs of servants, guards, and sedan-carriers, entertained permanent houseguests,

4. Hsiao I-shan, II, 264-67.
5. Actually only a small portion of Ho-shen's property was confiscated by the government and parceled out to the princes and nobles as gifts of the emperor. *Ibid.*, II, 268.

and supported poor relatives. Their positions made demands which could not be met by their low salaries—which ranged from 180 taels annually for a first-rank official to 33 taels for a ninth-rank official—unless the salaries were supplemented by graft. Even the awarding of "anti-corruption fees" of 50 to 100 times the amount of a salary could not stop the practice of the "squeeze," which was, in fact, institutionalized. For instance, in the collection of the land-poll (*ti-ting*) tax, each locality was given a certain quota, any amount over which the magistrate could keep for himself. It was not uncommon for the tax collected to be many times the official quota. The major brunt of payment fell on the peasant, who under the pressure of the tax collector and local gentry often had to pay 50 per cent to 80 per cent more than the stated tax in cash and as high as 250 per cent more in grain. Small wonder that an official who levied only 10 per cent surtax was considered a good conscientious official. It was commonly estimated that a prefect's three-year term could, under normal conditions, yield a handsome 100,000 taels.

A few concrete cases will illustrate the degree and the extent of corruption at the beginning of the 19th century. In 1809 a district magistrate, in applying for disaster relief funds from the government, falsified the census of his area and pocketed some 30,000 taels. The governor-general sent an investigator to look into the case and the magistrate approached the latter with a bribe. When the investigator refused to cooperate, the magistrate got a prefect friend to mediate, but to no avail. The servants of both the magistrate and the investigator then got together and poisoned the investigator. The magistrate burned the investigatory documents and reports, paid off the prefect with a thousand taels, and reported to the governor-general that the investigator had committed suicide out of insanity. The case was later exposed and the magistrate, the prefect, and the servants were all arrested and executed. Another case involved the bookkeepers in the office of the financial commissioner of Chihli in 1809. These clerks colluded with district magistrates to fabricate official seals and falsify tax receipts. A third case involved a secretary in the Board of Public Works in 1812, who falsified seals to obtain government funds for alleged repairs of public works; he pulled this off fourteen times and obtained funds amounting to more than 10 million taels. Corruption in the Yellow River Conservancy and the Grand Canal Administration was even more brazen. Funds for repairs of dikes, dams, and such were mostly pocketed by the officials in charge, with the result that between 1797 and 1819 the rivers flooded seventeen times. The government wasted a total of 40 million taels in the few years immediately before 1811. Investigators carried out their missions perfunctorily and never reported the real situation to the court.

Degradation of the Manchus and the Bannermen. The Manchus, as befitted the status of conquerors, were not permitted to engage in trade or farming, regardless of birth and social position. They hired the Chinese to till their land and received income from the rents. Their leisure and dependence on others bred laziness and irresponsibility. The bannermen, who constituted the backbone of the Manchu military power at the beginning of the dynasty, received stipends three times as high as those of the Chinese soldiers. Their privileged position and its corollary soft life caused a marked flaccidity of their original martial spirit, and by the Yung-cheng period (1723-35) they had already degenerated to a point where they could no longer fight. Instead of studying military arts, they led a debauched life of gambling, theater-going, watching the cock-fights, and ran usury and mortgaging businesses on the side. Unskilled in their military profession, they were good for nothing but consuming their government stipends. Not only could they not fulfill the duty of defending the dynasty, they had even become a burden to it. They were parasites on the society, and a great many parasites at that: the total number of Manchu, Mongol, and Chinese bannermen and their families was in the neighborhood of 1.5 million.

Corruption in the army was appalling. The Manchu general Fu-k'ang-an, reputedly a bastard son of Emperor Ch'ien-lung, deliberately prolonged his campaigns against the Chin-ch'uan rebels to increase his chances for embezzlement. Corruption was also rampant in the Chinese Green Standard army. Military funds for the suppression of the White Lotus Rebellion (1796-1804) went mostly into the private coffers of the officers in charge. The story has it that a certain circuit intendant[6] pocketed 500,000 taels of military funds and then entertained the officers with lavish banquets, each consisting of thirty to forty courses! He also made General Fu-k'ang-an a present of three pecks[7] of pearls and 10,000 rolls of Szechwan brocade. Manchu officers of such breed, laden with wealth and accustomed to soft living, naturally did not relish fighting. They sent local militia—which consisted mostly of country lads—to the front line; the Chinese Green Standard army marched behind these,

6. Shih Tso-jui.
7. One peck = 316 cubic inches.

while the Manchu bannermen remained in the rear. The rebels, who were too wise to miss this line-up, also held back their regular forces, and sent forward ragtag units made up of refugees. Thus the fighting was largely between the striplings in the militia and the refugees. When the militia appeared to score a good blow, the Manchu generals quickly reported victory to the court and claimed the credit for it. The rebels, needless to say, were a long time in being defeated, and the expenditures piled up. The length of the campaigns and the size of the expenditures were true testimonies to the degree of corruption and incompetence that prevailed in the army.

Financial Stringency. The early Ch'ing rulers had laid very sound economic foundations for the empire. K'ang-hsi left behind 8 million taels, Yung-cheng 24 million, and Ch'ien-lung 70 million. But even while Ch'ien-lung was ruling, the trend toward luxury and massive spending had started. His Ten Complete Accomplishments cost the state 120 million taels, and Chia-ch'ing's nine-year campaign against the White Lotus Sect and other secret societies cost 200 million. These inordinate military expenses plus the graft and corruption in the civil administration drained the treasury, resulting in a steady rise in the value of silver. Whereas in the early Ch'ien-lung period (1736-95) a tael of silver exchanged for 700 cash (copper coins), in the Chia-ch'ing period (1796-1820) it shot to 1,300 or 1,400 cash. By 1800 the economic foundation of the Ch'ing empire had been badly weakened.

Population Pressure. Ch'ing population increased much faster than did the land acreage, causing a decline in the standard of living. In 1660 the population of China was probably somewhere around 100 to 150 million, and it rose to 300 million by 1800. Arable land, however, had not increased correspondingly. In 1661 there were 549 million *mou* of land and in 1812 only 791 million. The land increase, then, was less than 50 per cent, whereas the population had increased by more than 100 per cent. The displaced, the poor, and the unemployed often turned to banditry or became recruits for rebel outfits.

Intellectual Irresponsibility. Although the Ch'ing court promoted the Sung school of Neo-Confucianism, it never subscribed to Chu Hsi's adminition that scholars should consider it their duty to govern the state. Under the threat of frequent literary inquisitions, scholars shied away from politics and sought refuge in antiquarian studies, where learning could remain safely divorced from reality. They prided themselves on pursuing knowledge for its own sake and ceased to apply their knowledge to society. Those who did join the government through the civil service examinations had received their training in this atmosphere, and many of them were all too often spineless creatures without the potential to be statesmen. In 1799 Hung Liang-chi, a second-class compiler in the Han-lin Academy, sent off a memorial to the emperor in which he bluntly described the moral degradation of scholars and officials. He cited cases of high officials such as board presidents and vice-presidents kowtowing to grand councillors and grand secretaries in order to curry favor, of scholars befriending the servants of dignitaries for the same purpose, and of officials shamelessly bribing palace attendants and guards in hopes of gaining imperial attention. When intellectual irresponsibility and moral degradation fell to this level, it meant that scholars had become oblivious to their duties to the society and had lost track of the importance of the unity of knowledge and action. In this sense, the Han scholars and empirical researchers failed to serve as leaders of society, and were remiss in their duty to cultivate men of character for public service. The society was thus deprived of real leadership. That the general decline of morality in the government was due at least in part to this very intellectual delinquency is an unavoidable conclusion.

All of these signs—administrative inefficiency, intellectual irresponsibility, widespread corruption, debasement of the military, pressures of a rising population, and a strained treasury—reflected the inner workings of the phenomenon known as "dynastic cycle." Indeed, by 1800 the ruling power had passed its peak and started to decline, making the country vulnerable to the twin evils of internal rebellion and external invasion (*nei-luan wai-ho*), so characteristic of dynasties in their later years.

REBELLIONS BY SECRET SOCIETIES

In an autocracy such as the Ch'ing, where no "loyal opposition" was permitted, the only form of organized resistance apart from open rebellion was secret societies. After the suppression of the anti-Manchu movement on Taiwan in 1683, Ming loyalists went underground to form or join secret organizations by which to continue their fight. Foremost among them were (1) the Heaven and Earth Society (*T'ien-ti hui*), also known as the Triad Society (*San-ho hui* or *San-tien hui*); (2) the Ko-lao Brotherhood Association (*Ko-lao hui*) in South China; and (3) the White Lotus Sect (*Pai-lien chiao*), and its branch the Heavenly Reason Sect (*T'ien-li chiao*) in North China.[8] Generally, the secret societies in South China called themselves *hui*, and those in the North called themselves *chiao*. The *hui* were secret political organizations with religious overtones, while the *chiao* were secret religious bodies with a nationalistic cast. They were all anti-Manchu.

The Heaven and Earth Society had its origin in the 1670's. Many of the Ming loyalists, convinced that their cause was lost, had retreated to the Shao-lin Monastery in Fukien as monks. In 1674 five of them—the "Five Former Progenitors"—secretly organized the Heaven and Earth Society to promote the overthrow of the Ch'ing and restoration of the Ming. The name of the society was derived from the saying, "Heaven is the father and earth the mother." The initiation oath went, "As ageless as the heaven and as lasting as the earth, we shall revenge even if it takes 10,000 years." In Western literature this organization was sometimes called the Triad Society because of its emphasis on the harmony of Heaven, Earth, and Man. The Triads maintained Five Grand Lodges and Five Minor Lodges, somewhat like those of Freemasonry, in the provinces.[9] Branches and affiliates of the Triads soon sprang up in the coastal areas—Taiwan, Kiangsu, Chekiang, Hunan, and Kwantung—using secret names written with the three-dot "water radical 氵"; hence they were also known as the Three Dots Society (*San-tien hui*). Significantly, this three-dot radical also formed a component of the character *Hung*, which was part of the reign title of the first Ming emperor, Hung-wu.[10] Small wonder that members of the Heaven and Earth Society called their organization the Hung League (*Hung-men*).

These secret societies, bent on overthrowing Ch'ing rule and restoring

8. Since the XVIIth International Congress of Chinese Studies held at Leeds, England in July 1965, there has been organized an international project of studying Chinese secret societies, with Jean Chesneaux of the Paris Center as coordinator. A volum of essays by international scholars is expected shortly. Cf. *Ch'ing-shih wen-ti*, I:4: 13-18 (Nov. 1966).
9. Jean Chesneaux, *Les sociétés secrètes en Chine* (*XIXe et XXe siècles*), (Paris, 1965), 50. (Avec la collaboration de Marianne Rochline.)
10. Wei Chü-hsien, *Chung-kuo ti pang-hui* (China's secret societies), (Chungking, 1945), Part II, 2-3. However, another interpretation suggests that the character *hung* is Han 漢 minus 里 (central land), signifying that these Ming loyalists considered themselves Han (Chinese) men deprived of the heartland of China, which had been stolen by the Manchus.

the Ming, vowed to avenge the killing of Chinese by the Manchus. Whoever embraced these objectives was welcome to join, regardless of birth, education, and social position, but on the whole the societies attracted only the lower classes. New members were introduced by old members and had to learn the secret signs and esoteric language of the society. At the initiation the candidates were led through three portals: (1) the Hung Door; (2) the Door of the Hall of Loyalty and Righteousness (which was a shrine of Kuan Kung, the god of war and patron of the secret societies); and (3) the Door of the City Willows (which was the Triad Lodge), leading to the Red Flower Pavilion where, among other things, the inscription "Overthrow the Ch'ing and Restore the Ming" was displayed. The candidates were questioned at each of the gates, and had to answer according to the secret instructions of the society. When all was in order, they vowed to keep the secrets of the fraternity, and read thirty-six oaths from a paper which was then burned and mixed into a bowl of chicken blood, tinted with wine, and sugar. They next pricked their left middle fingers, squeezed some blood into the bowl, and drank from it. With this, all became blood brothers, and after paying dues according to financial ability each received a membership card.[11]

The Ko-lao Brotherhood Association came into being during the Ch'ien-lung period (1736-95). Slightly more finicky than the Heaven and Earth Society, it denied membership to barbers, actors, sedan-carriers, and people born of "unclean blood," but otherwise accepted anyone whose interest was to destroy the Ch'ing and restore the Ming. The headman, or Dragon Head (*Lung-t'ou*), had complete authority over members, who were bound together as brothers. They pledged mutual support and whenever possible organized uprisings.

A much older cabal was the White Lotus Sect, first organized around A.D. 1250, or perhaps even earlier, as a quasi-religious secret body.[12] During the Yüan period (1280-1368), it dedicated itself to the objective of overturning the Mongol dynasty and restoring the Sung. Surviving into the Ch'ing period, it vowed to topple the Manchu dynasty and return the Ming to power. Members adopted Buddhistic as well as Taoistic ideas to win popular support. In 1781 one of its leaders, Liu Sung, was arrested and banished to the frontier; thereafter the government

---

11. For details, see L. F. Comber, *Chinese Secret Societies in Malaya: A Survey of the Triad Society from 1800 to 1900* (Locust Valley, N.Y., 1959), chapter 1; Chesneaux, 29-43.
12. Comber, 19-20; Chesneaux, 57.

pursued a program of continuous harassment of the sect members which finally goaded them into revolt in 1793. This touched off a succession of mass arrests and persecution, against which White Lotus members in Central China rose up in protest in 1796, using as a pretext "official oppression forced people into revolt" (*kuan-pi min-fan*). The movement quickly spread to Szechwan, Hupeh, Shensi, Kansu, and Honan. Government troops were too corrupt to suppress the revolt, and out of self-defense the local gentry and officials organized militia and constructed fortresses of their own. The court adopted four principles in dealing with the rebels: (1) pardon those who were forced to join the revolt, (2) encourage the rebels to surrender, (3) reward the militia, and (4) construct stockaded posts and clear the countryside of food supplies. The campaign reached a turning point after the fall of Ho-shen in 1799, when able generals[13] finally could obtain greater support from the court. The rebellion at length was suppressed, in 1804, after nine years of ineffectual and expensive campaigning.

About the time the White Lotus Revolt was raging in interior China, the southeastern coast was being mauled by pirates. In 1800 a large pirate fleet of a hundred or so vessels attacked the Chekiang coast. The situation was saved largely by a timely hurricane, which capsized most of the pirate vessels. In 1810 the pirates were finally suppressed.

But no sooner had peace been restored on the coast than another rebellion started in the interior, this time under the aegis of the Heavenly Reason Sect (*T'ien-li chiao*), a branch of the White Lotus. Also known as the Eight-trigram Sect (*Pa-kua chiao*), the Heavenly Reason Sect had a large following in North China (Chihli, Honan, Shantung, and Shansi provinces). Leaders of this sect practiced divination and astrology, and correlated natural signs with human events. In 1812 its leader, Li Wen ch'eng, announced that he was a "True Lord of the Ming" and secretly designated 1813 as the year for action. Members were given small white flags to be displayed on their doors when the revolt took place so that they would not be attacked. The sect managed to win support even from some of the eunuchs, who agreed to guide an attack on the palace during the emperor's hunting trip. The plot was uncovered and the rebels were goaded into action. The revolt was suppressed after more than 20,000 members of the sect had been killed.

There were a number of other uprisings on a smaller scale, such as

13. Such as E-le-teng-pao.

the revolt of the Miao aborigines in Hunan and Kweichow provinces in 1799 under the influence of the Heaven and Earth Society; the rising of the firewood cutters and peddlers in Shensi province during 1813 and 1814; and the revolt of the Yunnan aborigines in 1818. Indeed, throughout the 25-year reign of Chia-ch'ing, not a day passed without some trouble in the country. It was in this state of dynastic disrepair that the Western powers, particularly Britain, with surplus energies generated by the Industrial Revolution, intensified their efforts to open China to international commerce and diplomacy.

THE WESTERN ADVANCE AND THE TRIBUTARY SYSTEM

The Ch'ing dynasty, though weakened by internal decay, still kept up the face of a great empire and cherished the glory of its former years. It clung to the fond, if fictitious, notion that China, as the Middle Kingdom on earth, was the center of the known civilized world and that all countries which desired relations with her must accept the tributary status.[14] The theory and practice of the tributary system reflected China's world view, and were highly significant in conditioning her relations with the advancing West.

By virtue of her cultural excellence, economic affluence, military power, and vast territorial expanse, China stood pre-eminent in East Asia for two millenia. Since early Ming times (1368-1643) there had been instituted a hierarchical system of "international relations" in East and Southeast Asia, with China occupying the position of leadership and Korea, Liu-ch'iu (Ryūkyū), Annam (Vietnam), Siam, Burma, and a host of other peripheral states in Southeast and Central Asia accepting the status of junior members.[15] The European term "family of nations" would appear to apply more aptly to this China-centered community of nations than to the Western international society, for in the former "international relations" were based on an extension of the Confucian idea of proper relations between individuals: just as every person in a domestic society had his specific status, so every state in an "international society" had its proper station. Two Korean terms illustrate the idea well: relations with China were described as *sadae*, serving the great, whereas relations with Japan were termed *kyorin*, neighborly intercourse. Thus

14. For an excellent new study of the Chinese view of the world, see John K. Fairbank (ed.), *The Chinese World Order: Traditional China's Foreign Relations* (Cambridge, Mass., 1968).
15. Japan also paid tribute to China for a short period—1404-1549.

the basic principle underlying this China-oriented family of nations was inequality of states rather than equality of states as in the modern West, and relations between the members were not governed by international law but by what is known as the tributary system.[16]

The tributary system is reminiscent of the ancient Chinese practice that the emperor "invested" (feng) the feudal lords and vassals (fan) both inside and outside China, and received in return their offerings of local products (fang-wu) as "tribute" (kung), which was a sort of modified tax payments.[17] During Ming and Ch'ing times, tributary relations had been refined into a highly ritualistic performance, with clearly defined rights and duties on the part of each participant. To China fell the duty of keeping proper order in the East and Southeast Asian family of nations. She recognized the legitimacy of tributary kings by sending envoys to officiate at their investitures and by conferring on them the imperial patents of appointment. She went to their aid in times of foreign invasion, and sent relief missions and commiserative messages in times of disaster. On their part, the tributary states honored China as the superior state by sending periodic tribute, by requesting the investiture of their kings, and by adopting the Chinese calendar, i.e. recording events of their countries by the day, month, and year of the reign of the Chinese emperor.

The size, frequency, and route of the tributary mission were fixed by China—usually the closer the relationship the larger and more frequent the mission. For instance, Korea paid tribute four times a year, presenting all at once at the end of the year, Liu-ch'iu twice every three years, Annam once every two years, Siam every three years, and Burma and Laos every ten years. Large numbers of traders were attached to the tributary missions, and their goods were brought into China duty-free. All travel expenses and maintenance of the missions in China were borne by the Chinese government, and when they arrived in Peking the members were lodged in the Common Residence for Tributary Envoys (Hui-t'ung ssu-i kuan). A felicitous day was chosen for the envoys to present the tribute and local products to the emperor, at which time they performed the full ceremony of the kowtow—three kneelings and nine knockings of the head on the ground. The envoys and the merchants were then allowed to open a market at their hostel for a few days—usually three to

16. For details, see Immanuel C. Y. Hsü, China's Entrance into the Family of Nations, chapter 1; John K. Fairbank and S. Y. Teng, "On the Ch'ing Tributary System," Harvard Journal of Asiatic Studies, 6:2:135-246 (June 1941).
17. Fairbank (ed.), The Chinese World Order, 7.

five—to sell their goods. The commercial transactions were as a rule highly profitable for the tributary missions. In addition, the emperor showed his benevolence by bestowing handsome gifts on the tributary kings and members of the missions. But on the whole, the value of his gifts was considerably less than the tribute and presents he received.

Tributary relations were costly to maintain. The dispatch of a mission to China was an arduous and expensive task. For instance, the Koreans had to make elaborate preparation in organizing a mission of 200 to 300 men and moving them 750 miles from Seoul to Peking, which took forty to sixty days. The tribute and gifts of "local products" in 1808 came to 100,000 copper taels,[18] roughly ten times as much as the Chinese emperor's bestowals to the Korean king and his family. Even more expensive was the reception of the Chinese investiture missions. As a rule, after his succession to the throne the tributary king dispatched a special envoy to Peking to request investiture. Imperial missions would then be sent, but only to the three important states of Korea, Liu-ch'iu, and Annam; lesser tributary kings received only the imperial patents of appointment carried back by their own envoys. The investiture mission usually consisted of 400 to 500 persons, for whose reception the Korean court spent an average of 230,000 copper taels, which was equal to one-sixth of its central government's annual expenses![19] The burden was proportionately even more onerous for a smaller state, such as Liu-ch'iu, where the Chinese mission usually stayed for five months at the sumptuous Residence for the Celestial Envoy (T'ien-shih kuan). The Liu-ch'iuan government had to strain itself to meet the 320,000-silver tael expense involved in each investiture. During the ceremonies, the king had to perform no less than seven full kowtows—when he welcomed the imperial patent, when he greeted the imperial calligraphy housed in a moving pavilion, when he saluted the emperor, when he received the imperial gifts, when he offered thanks for the imperial grace, etc. But before the entire ceremony was over, he had yet to perform one more simple kowtow—one kneeling and three knockings of the head—to the Chinese envoy, who of course reciprocated the courtesy. The elaborate preparation and the vast expense involved in each investiture were so exacting that the Liu-ch'iuan king usually delayed the ceremonies until

18. A copper tael was equal to one-third silver tael at the time; it was worth one-half silver tael during 1725-76.
19. Hae-jong Chun, "Sino-Korean Tributary Relations in the Ch'ing Period" in Fairbank (ed.), The Chinese World Order, 95-97, 104-06.

two years after his actual accession, and some waited as long as seventeen or eighteen years![20]

Tributary relations, in effect, entailed very considerable financial strain and physical exhaustion on the part of the smaller states, with no appreciable economic benefit for China. The expenses of maintaining the tributary missions—and there were many—while they were in China certainly outweighed the excess value of the tribute and gifts the emperor received. Why then the system? There had to be reasons other than purely economic motivation. For the tributary king, the investiture legitimized his rule, raised his prestige before his people, offered him protection in times of foreign invasion and aid in times of natural disasters, brought him luxury articles from the emperor, heightened the cultural link between his country and China, and allowed him to conduct profitable trade with the Middle Kingdom. For the Chinese emperor, it was an immense pleasure and satisfaction to see the myth of his universal overlordship acknowledged and to know that these peripheral states willingly served as an "outer fence" to shield China from barbarian attacks. All in all, tributary relations were maintained primarily to manifest the Confucian concept of propriety and to affirm the hierarchical world order in which China was assued of a superior status, security, and inviolability.[21]

It was this system of international relations that the West encountered when it intruded into East Asia. The Ch'ing court insisted that the tributary system applied not only to the peripheral states of Asia but also to all other states that wanted to establish relations with China. Indeed, during the splendid reigns of K'ang-hsi, Yung-cheng, and Ch'ien-lung, dozens of Asian states were enrolled in the system, and envoys from Portugal, Holland, and Russia kowtowed, albeit reluctantly, to the Chinese emperor. Although Russia and the Western European nations were not formally included in the system, the Chinese treated their missions as though they were tributary missions. To account for the sporadic nature of these missions (unbecoming a tributary state), it was explained in the *Collected Statutes of the Great Ch'ing Empire* that their great distance from China precluded the Western trading nations from maintaining a fixed schedule for bringing tribute. It is interesting to note that of the seventeen missions from the West between 1655 and 1795, all

20. Ta-tuan Ch'en, "Investiture of Liu-ch'iu Kings in the Ch'ing Period" in Fairbank (ed.), *The Chinese World Order*, 136-37, 144, 148.
21. Wang Kungwu, "Early Ming Relations with Southeast Asia: A Background Essay" in Fairbank (ed.), *The Chinese World Order*, 61. See also 110-11, 160.

but one yielded to the Chinese demand and performed the kowtow to the emperor.[22] Ch'ing policy toward *official* missions from foreign countries was thus very strict, but its attitude toward *private* Western traders was more flexible. Private traders were allowed to reside in Macao and trade at Canton (after 1757) as a mark of imperial favor toward men from afar. These traders reaped quick and large profits from their transactions, but they were subject to a number of restrictive regulations regarding their movements and trade procedures (details will be given in the next chapter).

By the early 19th century both the governments and the private traders of the Western nations could no longer countenance the straitjacket of the Chinese system. The traders wanted greater freedom of action, and the Western governments, newly released from the Napoleonic Wars and greatly strengthened by the Industrial Revolution, would not suffer the tributary treatment. They insisted on international relations according to the law and diplomacy of Europe; but the Chinese would not sacrifice their cherished system. In effect they said, "We have not asked you to come; if you come you must accept our ways," to which the West's reply was, "You cannot stop us from coming and we will come on our terms." The story of Sino-Western relations thereafter is one of continuous conflict, leading to the ultimate humiliation of the Ch'ing empire.

Actually, by the time the West made a concerted effort to break down the Chinese institution of foreign relations, the tributary system had already worn itself out to a large extent. Since the middle of the 18th century it had been exposed to two disruptive influences: the rise of the Chinese junk trade with Southeast Asia (*Nan-yang*) and the growth of the European trade at Canton—both outside the range of the tributary system. Hundreds of Chinese junks, averaging 150 tons apiece, with the largest approaching 1,000 tons, sailed to Siam, Annam, the Malay Peninsula, Java, and the Moluccas to negotiate their own business. Many of the petty tributary states in these areas found that they no longer needed the tributary system to get along, and thereupon stopped sending tribute to China.[23] The independent European trade that had been permitted to

22. John K. Fairbank, *Trade and Diplomacy on the China Coast: The Opening of the Treaty Ports, 1842-1854* (Cambridge, Mass., 1953), I, 14.
23. For details of the Chinese junk trade, see T'ien Ju-k'ang, "Shih-ch'i shih-chi chih shih-chiu shih-chi chung-yeh Chung-kuo fan-ch'uan tsai Tung-nan Ya-chou hang-yün ho shang-yeh shang te ti-wei" (The position of Chinese junks in shipping and trade with Southeast Asia from the 17th century to the middle of the 19th century), *Li-shih yen-chiu*, 8:1-21 (1956).

go on at Canton was the other disruptive influence, and it was growing rapidly. Britain, the foremost industrial power and the leader of foreign trade, did the most to break down the existing Chinese system.

FURTHER READING

Abe, Takeo 安部健夫, *Chūgokujin no tenka kannen* 中國人の天下觀念 (The Chinese world view), (Kyoto, 1956).

Chesneaux, Jean, *Les sociétés secrètes en Chine, XIXe et XXe siècles)*, avec la collaboration de Marianne Rochline (Paris, 1965).

Chu, Lin 朱琳, *Hung-men chih* 洪門誌 (A record of the Hung Society), (Shanghai, 1947)

Comber, L. F., *Chinese Secret Societies in Malaya: A Survey of the Triad Society from 1800 to 1900* (Locust Valley, N.Y., 1959).

Fairbank, John K. (ed.), *The Chinese World Order: Traditional China's Foreign Relations* (Cambridge, Mass., 1968).

————, and S. Y. Teng, "On the Ch'ing Tributary System," *Harvard Journal of Asiatic Studies*, 6:2:135-246 (June 1941).

Hirayama, Amane 平山周, *Chung-kuo mi-mi she-hui shih* 中國秘密社會 (A history of Chinese secret societies), (Shanghai, 1935).

Hsiao, I-shan 蕭一山, *Ch'ing-tai t'ung-shih* 清代通史 (A general history of the Ch'ing period), revised edition (Taipei, 1962), II, chapters 4-6.

————, *Chin-tai mi-mi she-hui shih-liao* 近代秘密社會史料 (Historical materials on the secret societies of modern times), (Peiping, 1935).

Inaba, Iwakichi 稻葉岩吉, *Shinchō zenshi* 清朝全史 (A complete history of the Ch'ing dynasty), (Tokyo, 1914), Chinese tr. by Tan T'ao under the title, *Ch'ing-ch'ao ch'üan-shih* 清朝全史 (Taipei, 1960), chapters 49-52.

Morgan, W. P., *Triad Societies in Hong Kong* (Hong Kong, 1960).

Schlegel, Gustave, *Thian Ti Hwui: The Hung League or Heaven-Earth League* (Batavia, 1866).

T'ien, Ju-k'ang 田汝康, "Shih-ch'i shih-chi chih shih-chiu shih-chi chung-yeh Chung-kuo fan-ch'uan tsai Tung nan Ya-chou hang-yün ho shang-yeh shang ti ti-wei" 十七世紀至十九世紀中葉中國帆船在東南亞洲航運和商業上的地位 (The position of Chinese junks in shipping and trade with Southeast Asia from the 17th century to the middle of the 19th century), *Li-shih yen-chiu*, 8: 1-21 (1956).

Ward, J. S. M., and W. G. Stirling, *The Hung Society or the Society of Heaven and Earth* (London, 1925-26), 3 vols.

Wei, Chü-hsien 衛聚賢, *Chung-kuo ti pang-hui* 中國的幫會 (China's secret societies), (Chungking, 1946).

PART II

Foreign Aggression and Domestic Rebellions
1800-1864

7

The Canton System of Trade

During the eighty-five years preceding China's opening to the West in 1842, Canton was the only port open to foreign trade, and Chinese foreign relations of this period essentially concerned Canton trade.

THE ORIGIN OF THE SINGLE-PORT TRADE

Canton, located at the southern tip of the empire, had been an historic center of foreign trade since the T'ang period (A.D. 618-907). Subsequently, during the late Ming and early Ch'ing periods, its trade was virtually monopolized by the Portuguese, who had established themselves at Macao, as noted in Chapter 5. Ships and traders of other nationalities were denied admittance, only rarely succeeding in gaining entry as did the Englishman Weddell in 1637. Barred from Canton, enterprising English traders sought opportunities elsewhere. They developed relations with the Ming loyalist Koxinga and his son on Taiwan, selling them munitions in exchange for trading rights there and at Amoy.

The Ch'ing court, troubled by Koxinga's raids along the coast, in 1662 ordered all ports closed to foreign trade and all coastal inhabitants evacuated to a distance of 30 to 50 *li* inland so as to cut off his sources of supply. Macao, however, was exempted from this rule as a favor to foreign traders, and Canton, though officially closed, was not strictly held to it. With the successful pacification of Taiwan in 1683, the court lifted the ban on foreign trade and in 1685 opened customs houses at Canton, Chang-chou (in Fukien), Ningpo, and Yün-t'ai-shan (in Kiangsu). Among

183

the ports, Canton was the most flourishing not only because it had the longest history of foreign trade, but also because it lay closest to Southeast Asia, which the Chinese called Nan-yang.

An old port, Canton was tradition-bound and corruption-ridden. The first ship of the East India Company that called in 1689 was assessed an exorbitant measurement fee of 2,484 taels. After much dickering with customs officials, it was whittled down to 1,500 taels, of which 1,200 represented the measurement fee and 300 a gratuity to the Hoppo, the superintendent of maritime customs. Such irregular exactions and the small demand for English woolens in semitropical Canton prompted the Company to seek trade at other ports to the north. It was thought that if trade were possible in the tea- and silk-producing areas of Kiangsu and Chekiang, their procurement costs might be lowered. So in 1698 the Company created a factory—a trading agency or business establishment —at Ting-hai, near Ningpo, with Allen Catchpoole as president. Ningpo, though, turned out no better than Canton, plagued as it also was by official interference, unreasonable levies, lack of demand for woolens, and, furthermore, the local traders' insufficient funds for conducting business. Shifting its interest back to Canton, where another factory had been established in 1699, the Company decided around 1715 to regularize its trade. A council of supercargoes was organized as the permanent staff of the factory until 1758, when it was replaced by a smaller and more efficient permanent Select Committee—composed of three senior super-cargoes—which coordinated and directed the Company's business in China.

The arbitrary and whimsical exactions and the high costs of tea and silk at Canton once again renewed the Company's interest in Ningpo around 1753. Two ships were dispatched to Ting-hai in 1755 under Samuel Harrison and James Flint, the latter having learned Chinese. They were well treated by the local dignitaries, and the provincial authorities of Chekiang recommended to the court that since the ships of the "Red Hair"—the nickname for the English and Dutch—had not come for many years they should be received "with compassion."

The shift of business to Ningpo naturally reduced the calls of English ships at Canton: 27 in 1754, 22 in 1755, 15 in 1756, and 7 in 1757. The governor-general at Canton, fearful of deflection of trade to the north, petitioned the court in 1757 to increase the duties at Ningpo 100 per cent. Though indifferent to occasional calls by foreign ships at Ningpo, Peking was concerned lest frequent visits turn it into another Macao.

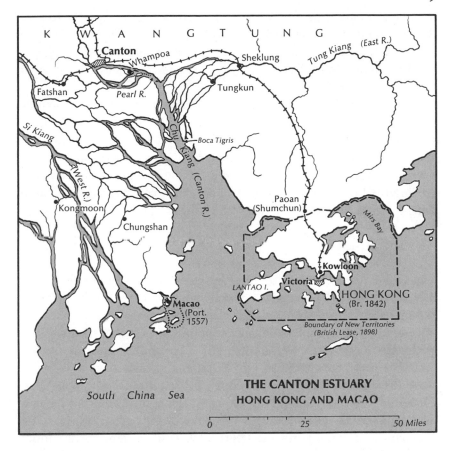

K   W   A   N   G   T   U   N   G

Canton
Whampoa
Sheklung
Tung Kiang (East R.)
Fatshan
Pearl R.
Tungkun
Si Kiang
Chu Kiang
Boca Tigris
(West R.)
Kongmoon
Paoan
(Shumchun)
Mirs Bay
Chungshan
Chu Kiang (Canton R.)
Kowloon
LANTAO I.   Victoria
HONG KONG
(Br. 1842)
Macao
(Port.
1557)
Boundary of New Territories
(British Lease, 1898)

South   China   Sea

**THE CANTON ESTUARY
HONG KONG AND MACAO**

0   25   50 Miles

Moreover, the court feared, the northern ports at Ningpo, Shanghai, and
Amoy, being more accessible from the ocean than Canton, would have
difficulty in controlling the movement of foreign ships, thus contributing
to collusion between the aliens and traitorous natives; whereas at Canton, the established forts at Whampoa and the Bogue enabled the government to watch the foreigners and their ships. Furthermore, a substantial portion of the Canton populace traditionally lived on foreign trade;
any shift of commerce to the north would seriously jeopardize their livelihood. With all these considerations, the court decided to increase the
customs duties at Ningpo and the other northern ports, making them
enough heavier than at Canton to discourage future trade. Foreigners
were urged to desist from going north. Thus, although trade was not
officially prohibited at Ningpo, Amoy, and Shanghai, the only port really

left open to foreign trade after 1757 was Canton. It was a *de facto* if not *de jure* prohibition of trade in the north (*pu-chin chih-chin* 不禁之禁).

However, in 1759 James Flint defied custom and visited Ningpo on his own. When refused admission, he went to Tientsin to complain of the corruption and irregular exactions at Canton. For his temerity the court threw him into prison in Macao for three years, but also appointed an investigatory commission to Canton and dismissed the Hoppo. A more serious consequence of the Flint incident, however, was a new, explicit court decree (1759) that henceforth Canton was the only port open to foreign commerce. This order eliminated all possibility of extending the trade to other parts of China, thus perpetuating the Canton system until the end of the Opium War in 1842.

THE CANTON TRADE

The Chinese attitude toward foreign trade was an outgrowth of their tributary mentality. It postulated that the bountiful Middle Kingdom had no need for things foreign, but that the benevolent emperor allowed trade as a mark of favor to foreigners and as a means of retaining their gratitude. Hence, trade was not a right to be insisted upon, but a privilege that could be withdrawn by China for any misbehavior. Moreover, since the Canton trade was conducted between private foreign and Chinese citizens, it required no formal diplomatic relations, only unofficial commercial transactions. Therefore, no direct contact was permitted between the foreign traders and Chinese government officials; the former could only *petition* the governor-general, governor, or Hoppo (customs superintendent) at Canton through the Chinese monopolistic merchants assigned to do business with them.

The chief characteristic of the Canton trade was its monopolistic structure. The court authorized "thirteen" commercial firms known as the *hongs* (a corruption of *yang-hang*) as sole agents of foreign trade. The proprietors, known as the hong (*hang*) merchants, secured their monopolistic privilege through handsome contributions to the court, reputedly in the neighborhood of 200,000 taels, or £55,000.

The origin of the hong merchants has sometimes been placed, erroneously, in 1720, which was actually the year they formed a guild in Canton; the hong merchants had existed long before. It is known that during the Wan-li period (1573-1619) of the Ming dynasty, some thirty-six hongs were trading with fourteen countries. The number of hongs dropped to thirteen toward the end of the Ming period (1368-1644), creating the designation of "The Thirteen Hongs," which persisted into the Ch'ing period. Actually the number of the hong merchants during the Ch'ing period fluctuated considerably, and only twice—in 1813 and 1837—actually totaled thirteen.[1]

Among the hongs there were three different groups: those specializing in European and American trade, called the *Wai-yang hang;* those specializing in trade with Southeast Asia, called the *Peng-kang hang;* and those trading with Fukien and Ch'ao-chow, called the *Ch'ao-Fu hang.* Our discussion here is mainly concerned with the first group.

Juxtaposed with the Thirteen Hongs were the thirteen foreign "factories," or agencies, located outside the Canton city walls on the bank of the Pearl River. The factory grounds and buildings, spread over some twenty-one acres, were rented from the hong merchants at an average annual fee of 600 taels. The Chinese commonly dubbed these British, American, French, Dutch, Belgian, Swedish, Danish, Spanish, and other miscellaneous factories the "Barbarian Houses" (*I-kuan*).

The British trade, predominant over that of all other Western countries, was monopolized by the East India Company. Yet there was quite an active private English venture, too. The Company granted charters to private ships to sail from India to China under its license. This trade was known as the "country trade," and the ships "country ships," as opposed to the "Company ships." Six out of every ten of the country ships originated from Bombay, and two each from Bengal and Madras. The country traders were mostly Englishmen doing business in India, judging from their names; but they also included some Indians and Parsees. This country trade accounted for 30 per cent of the total British trade at Canton between 1764 and 1800.

Another source of private trade originated from the Company's policy of allowing its ships' officers to carry a specified amount of gold and goods, supposedly to compensate for their small salaries—the captain's pay being only £10 a month, the first mate's £5. The captain of a 495-ton ship, for example, was allowed thirteen tons of private goods in 1730. In reality, the Company believed that when the ships' officers had a personal stake in the cargo, they would strive more diligently to make a speedy and successful voyage. Furthermore, they realized that no one could prevent the carrying of private goods anyway, so it seemed better to regulate than prohibit it. In addition to this type of private trade, the

1. Sixteen in 1720, 20 in 1757, 4 in 1781, and 5 in 1790.

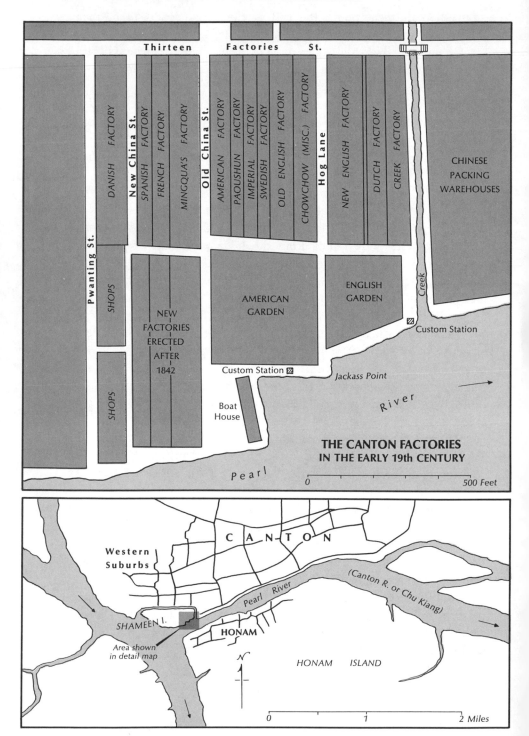

THE CANTON FACTORIES
IN THE EARLY 19th CENTURY

Company also allowed its junior supercargoes at Canton to engage in private transactions to compensate for their insubstantial wages. This private trade accounted for about 15 per cent of the total British trade at Canton between 1764 and 1800, but it increased rapidly after the opening of the 19th century.[2]

The Hong Merchants. The hong merchants rose to prominence only after much arduous struggling. At one point they were nearly driven out of business by the so-called "Emperor's Merchants" (*Huang-shang*), who, empowered to monopolize foreign trade, appeared in 1702 at Canton, Amoy, and Chusan. As it happened, the Emperor's Merchant at Canton—reputedly a former salt official who secured his new status from the crown prince through a donation of 42,000 taels—apparently possessed neither great capital nor a large stock of goods ready for delivery. Unable to fill orders without delay, he elicited complaints from foreign traders, which were echoed by hong merchants excluded from the profitable commerce. In 1704, five arriving English ships refused to deal with him, entering into clandestine arrangements with the hong merchants, who, having bribed the Hoppo, now openly competed with the Emperor's Merchant and eased him out of business. To strengthen their position, the hong merchants organized a guild in 1720 called the Co-hong (*Kung-hang*) and adopted a code of thirteen articles to regulate the prices and practices of transaction. The original membership consisted of sixteen hong merchants divided into three classes, stipulating that new members could join upon payment of 1,000 taels. Out of all business transactions, three per cent was set aside as a reserve, called the Consoo fund, against cases of insolvency. The guild, though a private organization, received official patronage, for it served as a convenient buffer between the government and the foreign traders. Thus, the government officials, who did not understand foreign languages, and the foreign traders, who did not understand Chinese regulations, could avoid personal encounters. Upon the guild fell the double task of collecting customs duties for the government and of paying fees for the foreign merchants.

The guild monopolized the Canton trade to the exclusion of all non-members. The latter naturally protested, while some foreign traders also

2. Earl H. Pritchard, *The Crucial Years of Early Anglo-Chinese Relations, 1750-1800* (Pullman, Washington, 1936), 170-74; "Private Trade between England and China in the 18th Century (1680-1833)" *Journal of Economic and Social History of the Orient,* I, 109 (Aug. 1957-Apr. 1958).

resented the strait-jacket arrangement. In the face of this opposition the guild disbanded after a year. In 1745 the Hoppo selected the five most substantial of the twenty or so hong merchants as "security merchants," to assume responsibility for all business transactions and to secure the proper conduct of all foreigners. By 1754 all hong merchants had become security merchants. On petition of the rich hong merchant Puankhequa, the Co-hong was revived in 1760, but it soon became ridden with serious problems of dissension and of debts to foreign traders. In 1771, by giving Puankhequa 100,000 taels to bribe the Chinese authorities, the East India Company succeeded in getting it disbanded, only to see it resurrected again in 1782, this time to survive until the end of the Opium War in 1842.[3]

Among the hong merchants, the richest and most famous during the 18th and early 19th centuries were Puankhequa of the Tung-foo Company, Mowqua of the Kwonglei Company, and Howqua of the Ewo Company. Incidentally, the suffix to their names, *qua*, was a corruption of the character *kuan*, meaning official, which was an honorary designation acquired through notable contributions to the court in exchange for a brevet title. The staff of the hongs was comprised of (1) compradores, who served at once as brokers, accountants, and cashiers; (2) linguists, the indispensable go-betweens who actually, by foreign description, "knew no language but their own;" (3) schroffs, the silvermasters who assayed the quality of silver, ingots, or dollars, in their capacity of "teller"; and (4) scribes and clerks.

The rich hong merchants were not permitted to reap their profits unhampered; they were subjected to merciless exploitation by officialdom. From 1786 on, they were required to pay a regular annual tribute of 55,000 taels and had, besides, to collect foreign clocks and watches to give to the governor and the Hoppo, who in turn presented them to the court. They were expected to proffer gifts on such festive occasions as imperial birthdays and marriages: on Emperor Chia-ch'ing's fiftieth birthday, for instance, they presented him with 120,000 taels. Frequently they were asked to contribute to military and river conservancy operations—such as Puankhequa's 200,000 tael donation in 1773 to the Chin-chu'an campaign and another 300,000 in 1787 toward the suppression of a Taiwan rebellion. For the campaign against the White Lotus Rebellion (1796-1804) the hong merchants collectively contributed 600,000 taels, and later an equal sum toward the suppression of the Moslem Rebellion

3. Kuo T'ing-i, I, 343.

under Jihangir in Sinkiang in the 1820's. Contributions for river conservancy included 550,000 taels in 1801, 200,000 in 1804, and 600,000 in 1811 and again in 1820. Between 1773 and 1832 they "contributed" nearly four million taels.[4] In addition, as rich residents of the province, these hong merchants were frequently called upon to donate to educational institutions, public charity, hospitals, and even clinics for smallpox vaccinations. And at times, they, as security merchants, were fined for crimes and uncivil acts of the foreign traders. The constant demands on the hong merchants and the high risks of their commercial ventures could well drive them into bankruptcy. Yet they could not easily quit business, because they were government-appointed agents for foreign trade. Many survived only through foreign loans.[5] On the whole, however, they fared quite well, and a number of them succeeded in amassing great wealth, as seen in the cases of Puankhequa, Mowqua, and Howqua.

The Trading Procedure. The trading season began before the end of the southwest monsoon in the early fall and ended during the northeast monsoon in the winter, lasting roughly the three to four months from October through January. At the opening of the season the incoming ship had first to go to Macao to employ a pilot, a linguist, and a compradore who purveyed the ship and crew provisions. Then it proceeded to the Bogue for measurement and payment of fees, and thence, cleared of all obligations, it was permitted to anchor at Whampoa. Here the cargo was handed over to one of the hong merchants, who fixed the commodity prices without competition from others; similarly, foreign traders purchased goods only through the assigned hong merchant. All contracts for sales and purchases were made a year in advance.

The hong merchant taking the foreign consignment bore complete responsibility for the foreign ship. He undertook settling the traders in the proper factory and recommended to them the compradore, linguists, schroffs, and servants. He was not obligated to sell the complete consigned stock, but could take a part of it while farming out the remainder to other hong merchants. In fact, according to the original agreement of the Co-hong, a hong merchant could not acquire more than half of the total cargo of a foreign ship. For instance, Howqua, in dealing with the East India Company, usually took fourteen shares of the stock, leaving

4. Liang Chia-pin, *Kuang-tung shih-san-hang k'ao* (A study of the Thirteen Hongs of Canton), (Shanghai, 1937), 368 ff.
5. In 1782 their debts to foreign traders amounted to $3,808,075. Morse, I, 68.

the rest to the others, some of whom took only one share or even half a share.[6] Conceivably, if the itinerary were followed strictly, a foreign ship could discharge its cargo and stow a new one within three weeks; but with the procedure described above, more often it would take a month or two. Once their business was concluded, the foreigners were required to leave Canton immediately, either returning home or going to Macao for the winter. However, for a consideration paid to "proper persons," some foreign traders were allowed to remain in Canton after the trading season.

Exactions and Fees. An incoming ship was subject to a variety of dues and levies, which fell into three major categories: the measurement fee, the presents and other gratuities (*kuei-li*), and the tariff on goods. The ship measurement was derived by multiplying the length between the mizzenmast and the foremast by the breadth of the ship at the gangway, and dividing the product by ten. According to this standard, ships were divided into three classes, with the large ones taxed at 7.777 taels per unit of measurement, medium ones at 7.142, and small ones at 5. The presents, on the other hand, were highly irregular levies of a very complex nature, including fees for opening the ship's hull, examining the hull, allowance for differences in scales and purity of silver, and a host of other impositions. Until 1726, when the government took over these fees, they went into the pockets of the Hoppo, the examining officers, the scribes, and the attendants—which accounted for their irregularity. In 1727, though, the gratuities were consolidated at 1,950 taels, where they remained for about a century. The gratuities and the measurement fee cost a first-class ship in 1810 something like 3,315 taels, and a second-class ship 2,666 taels. Ships going directly to Macao without anchoring at Canton paid about one half the measurement fees and gratuities, but had to pay an additional 2,520 taels to the Co-hong for trading privileges outside its territory. There were, in addition, all types of minor fees, such as $60 for the pilot for each of the inbound and outbound trips in the harbor, $400 for the compradore, $200 "expense money" for the linguist above his regular $75 pay and an allowance of $50 or $60 from the ship captain. Thus the total payment of a first-class ship during a three month stay in Canton ran to about 4,500 taels.[7]

The regular customs dues were reasonably low, somewhere between

6. Li Shou-k'ung, 82.
7. Morse, I, 77-78; Kuo T'ing-i, I, 457-72.

2 per cent and 4 per cent ad valorem, but frequently the customs officials charged twice as much, and not infrequently three or four times as much. The payment was usually made by the hong merchants for the foreign traders.

Articles of Trade. By the late 18th century there was a flourishing triangular trade between Canton, India, and England. The most important exports to England were tea (accounting for 90 per cent to 95 per cent of the total), raw silk, chinaware, rhubarb, lacquered ware, and cassia; while imports from England included woolens, lead, tin, iron, copper, furs, linen, and various knicknacks. Exports to India consisted of nankeen cloth, alum, camphor, pepper, vermilion, sugar, sugar candy, drugs, and chinaware; while imports included raw cotton, ivory, sandlewood, silver, and opium.

The large volume of tea export may have resulted from several causes. The prohibition of rice export and the limitation of silk outflow to 140 piculs (175 bales) per ship made tea the logical staple item of export. There was a growing demand for tea in Europe, especially in England, since Europe produced no tea, having no idea of it until 1550. The first small quantity of Chinese black tea was brought to Europe by Dutch merchants in 1640 and soon appeared in England. Beginning in 1684 the East India Company annually purchased five to six chests of teas from Canton for presents in England, and in 1705 green tea made its initial London appearance. Gradually, during the first quarter of the 18th century, the Company increased its tea purchase to 400,000 pounds a year, from which samples were presented to the crown and the nobles. Soon tea-drinking became a fetish among the polite society, later spreading to the populace—who drank it as a substitute for the heavily taxed liquor. So great was the national demand, that in 1800 the Company shipped 23 million pounds of tea, and after 1808 the annual British import averaged 26 million pounds, twice as much tea as shipped by other countries. By this time tea-drinking had become a national habit of England, and tea lovers went so far as to assert that its mild nature exercised a civilizing influence on character, whereas liquor often led to violence and misconduct. As its use increased, so did the English import duty—to an outrageous 100 per cent, a rate sufficient to encourage smuggling from the continent (especially from Holland), reputedly in the neighborhood of 7 million pounds a year. Finally, in 1784, the Commutation Act reduced the tea import duty to 12.5 per cent, putting an end to the lucrative smuggling. Even so, Chinese tea provided one-tenth of the English revenue.[8]

The tea-producing areas in China were Fukien (black tea), Anhwei (green tea), and Kiangsi (both). In February of each year, a thousand or more tea merchants came to Canton to make arrangements with the hong merchants for delivery. In 1755 a hundred catties[9] (*chin*) of tea cost 19 taels. It took a month or two to transport tea overland from its producing areas to Canton, roughly 2,400 *li*, or 800 miles, but much less time to ship along the coast. In 1813 some British steamers shipped a million pounds of teas from Foochow to Canton in thirteen days.

The flourishing state of the Canton trade is seen from the increasing number of ships that called, from 19 in 1751 to 81 in 1787 and then back to 57 in 1792, as shown in the following chart:

| | BRITISH | | | | | | | | |
| | *Company* | *Country* | | | | | | | |
YEAR	ships	ships	FRENCH	DUTCH	SWEDISH	DANISH	AMERICAN	OTHERS	TOTAL
1751	7	3	2	4	2	1	—	—	19
1780	12	12	—	4	3	3	—	—	34
1787	29	33	3	5	2	2	2	5	81
1792	16	23	2	3	1	1	6	5	57

Evident in the last two decades of the 18th century was the increasing activity of the country trade, and the entry of the Americans into the China trade, signaled by the arrival of the *Empress of China* from New York in 1784. The Americans were free traders, as opposed to the monopolistic East India Company.

The balance of trade at Canton during the 18th century was very much in China's favor, because she needed few foreign products, while Western traders purchased large quantities of tea, silk, and rhubarb. Foreign ships had to bring silver bullion to purchase Chinese products; at times the cargo of the East India Company's ships from London consisted of 90 per cent bullion. During 1775 and 1795 the Company's imports of goods and bullion into China amounted to 31.5 million taels, against an export of 56.6 million taels. The 25.1 million-tael deficit was partially relieved by the country trade and the private trade which en-

8. Michael Greenberg, *British Trade and the Opening of China* (Cambridge, 1951), 3.
9. About 133⅓ lbs.

joyed a favorable balance, the former showing a surplus of 13.6 million and the latter 1.7 million in the same period.[10] The proceeds from the country and private trade were transferred to the Company's treasury at Canton in return for bills of exchange payable in London. In the period mentioned above, the Company derived roughly a third of its funds for Canton purchases from the country trade.

FOREIGN LIFE AT CANTON

Since the Canton authorities governed aliens under the notion that trade was a privilege and not a right of foreigners, and since enjoyment of this imperial favor was contingent upon their good behavior, the foreigners were obliged to submit to certain rules of conduct periodically announced at the factories as a reminder. Violation of these rules could entail the stoppage of trade.

Rules of Behavior. A set of Five Regulations was first promulgated by Governor-general Li Ssu-yao in 1759 in the wake of the Flint incident. It underwent many subsequent additions and revisions until it finally assumed the form of the following code of behavior in the early 19th century:

1. No foreign warships may sail inside the Bogue.
2. Neither foreign women nor firearms may be brought into the factories.
3. All pilots and compradores must register with the Chinese authorities in Macao; foreign ships must not enter into direct communication with Chinese people and merchants without the immediate supervision of the compradore.
4. Foreign factories shall employ no maids and no more than eight Chinese male servants.
5. Foreigners may not communicate with Chinese officials except through the proper channel of the Co-hong.
6. Foreigners are not allowed to row boats freely in the river. They may, however, visit the Flower Gardens (*Hua-ti*) and the temple opposite the river in groups of ten or less three times a month— on the 8th, 18th, and 28th. They shall not visit other places.
7. Foreigners may not sit in sedan-chairs, or use the sanpan boats with flags flying; they may ride only in topless small boats.

10. Pritchard, *Crucial Years*, 180.

8. Foreign trade must be conducted through the hong merchants. Foreigners living in the factories must not move in and out too frequently, although they may walk freely within a hundred yards of their factories. Clandestine transactions between them and traitorous Chinese merchants must be prevented.

9. Foreign traders must not remain in Canton after the trading season; even during the trading season when the ship is laden, they should return home or go to Macao.

10. Foreign ships may anchor at Whampoa but nowhere else.

11. Foreigners may neither buy Chinese books, nor learn Chinese.

12. The hong merchants shall not go into debt to foreigners.[11]

Except for item 4 regarding the employment of servants, all the rest were strictly enforced, particularly the regulation on women. In 1830 when three foreign women sneaked into the English factory, the Chinese authorities threatened to stop trade, and the women had to leave for Macao. In consequence of this strict rule against women in Canton, foreign traders usually left their families in Macao. Of the 4,480 foreigners in Macao in 1830, 2,149 were white females against 1,201 white males, the rest being slaves and servants. The foreign community in Canton, in contrast, consisted entirely of males; in 1836 there were 307 foreign men, of whom 213 were non-Asian.

The regulations governing foreign behavior doubtless caused discomfort to the traders, but the momentary pains were assuredly somewhat alleviated by the prospect of quick monetary gains. On the whole, life in the factories, with their spacious drawing rooms, was rather pleasant, and the relations between the foreign traders and the hong merchants were harmonious and friendly. William C. Hunter, an American who went to Canton in 1825 and stayed for many years, spoke of the hong merchants as a body of men "honourable and reliable in all their dealings, faithful to their contracts, and large-minded."[12] They shared a spirit of camaraderie with the foreign traders, each helping the other out in times of difficulty and insolvency. Howqua, who led a frugal life himself, was particularly known for his munificence and generosity. Once, when it came to his knowledge that an American trader who had suffered business reverses was stranded in Canton for three years and unable to return to his family, he called the American in and tore up his promissory note

11. Hsiao I-shan, II, 836-37.
12. William C. Hunter, *The Fan Kwae" at Canton before Treaty Days, 1825-1844* (Shanghai, 1911), 40.

of $72,000, declaring the account settled. In his pidgin English—the business language—Howqua announced: "You and I are No. 1 'olo flen'; you belong honest man, only got no chance."[13] ("You and I are No. 1 old friends; you are an honest man; only you were unlucky.")

Pidgin—or pigeon—English was the *lingua franca* of the China coast trading communities. A mixture of English, Portuguese, and Indian words, it was spoken more or less in Chinese syntax without regard to English grammatical rules. Of Portuguese origin were such words as *mandarin*, from *mandar*, meaning to order; *compradore*, from *compra*, to buy; *maskee*, from *masque*, never mind. Of Indian origin were *bazaar*, a market; *schroff*, a money-dealer; *go-down*, a corruption of *ka-dang*, a warehouse; *lac*, one-hundred thousand; and *cooly* (coolie), a laborer. A typical sentence of pidgin English, as spoken by Howqua as he tore up the promissory note, was "Just now have settee counter, alln finishee; you go, you please."[14] ("Just now we have settled our account. All is finished. You may go as you please.")

The Problem of Jurisdiction. The various restrictions upon foreign activities were one source of conflict; the problem of law enforcement was another. Chinese legal concepts and practices differed greatly from those of the West. There was no "due process of law" as understood by Westerners, nor advice of counsel in court. The judiciary was not an independent arm of government, the local judge being none other than the magistrate. Lawsuit and litigation were thought to be manifestations of one's lack of virtue, rather than assertions of one's legal rights. In a criminal case a defendant was considered guilty until proven innocent, and in cases of homicide the principle of "a life for a life" was followed. The Chinese sense of justice permitted a father to shield his son from justice, and vice versa, rather than surrendering him to judgment; and several families in a neighborhood might be held responsible for the crime of one. All this was "strange" and "barbarous" to foreigners at Canton and Macao.

The "doctrine of responsibility" was another source of friction. Just as the emperor was theoretically responsible for all that happened under the sun, so the governor-general was culpable for all incidents within his jurisdiction, including the flooding of the river or disturbance of the

13. H. F. MacNair, *Modern Chinese History: Selected Readings* (Shanghai, 1913), I, 42.
14. MacNair, I, 42-43.

peace by foreigners. To protect himself, he mercilessly governed foreigners with the strictest regulations. Extending the application of this doctrine, the hong merchants were responsible for "securing" the good behavior of the foreign traders, and the headmen of foreign communities were obliged to control their nationals and hand over criminals when demanded by the Chinese authorities, regardless of their personal judgments in the particular case.

The Chinese government insisted that foreigners committing crimes in China be tried according to Chinese law. On the other hand, foreigners demanded exemption from Chinese law. This was not so much because they denied the universal principle of territorial jurisdiction, but because of the "strange" way the Chinese court dispensed justice and because of the harshness of the sentences. Actually, civil cases involving foreigners were rare, as there was little contact between foreign traders and the Chinese public. Disputes between the hong merchants and the foreigners were mostly settled by negotiation and arbitration. Also, very few, if any, foreign traders were involved in criminal cases, as these seemed to be the specialty of the sailors. When criminal cases did occur, those involving foreigners in both parties were settled in one of three ways: (1) the Chinese court tried the case, but sent the convicted to his own country for punishment, as in the case of a Frenchman, who, having killed an English sailor in 1754, was sentenced by a Chinese court to death by strangulation, the execution being left to the French government after he had been returned home; (2) the Chinese court tried the case and executed the sentence in China, as it carried out the strangulation execution of an English sailor sentenced for the slaying of a Portuguese sailor; (3) where the guilty had fled, the Chinese court would pass sentence on him, forwarding it to the home country for execution, as in the case in 1830 of a group of Englishmen who had beaten a Dutch sailor to death and then fled to India. In this instance the governor-general at Canton sentenced the chief offender to death by strangulation and his accomplices to a hundred lashes each, but the sentence was transmitted to Britain for its execution.

In mixed cases, where the criminal was Chinese, justice was inexorably carried out with consummate speed and equity. A case in point was the killing of an English seaman in 1785 by a Chinese, who was summarily sentenced to death by strangulation. The same practice held if the culprit was a foreigner, as in the case of the British ship *Lady Hughes* in 1784. On November 24 of that year, this country ship fired a salute and accidentally wounded three minor mandarins, two of whom subsequently died. The Canton authorities demanded the surrender of the gunner, and when told that he had absconded, seized George Smith, the supercargo of the ship, besieged the factory, and stopped trade. It was not until the gunner was found, on the *Lady Hughes,* and surrendered to the Chinese authorities that the supercargo was released and trade resumed. They then strangled the gunner.

The *Lady Hughes* incident, plus the Chinese explanation that the sentence was light because it only demanded one life for two, shocked the foreign community into a seizure of terror. Foreigners feared for their personal safety in future cases and deeply resented the Chinese practice of holding the supercargo or community chief responsible for crimes committed by others. Moreover, the harshness and apparent inhumaneness of Chinese sentences (*vide* the numerous "death by strangulation" penalties), the lack of a proper trial according to European justice, and the capricious stopping of trade or refusal of clearance to departing ships in order to force the surrender of the guilty—such irritants to the foreign sensibilities produced great anxiety and endless protest against the Canton authorities.

BRITISH ATTEMPTS TO CHANGE THE CANTON SYSTEM

The *Lady Hughes* incident climaxed the foreigners' feeling of insecurity and heightened the general dissatisfaction with the Canton system of trade, i.e., the limitation to one port, the humiliating restrictions on personal freedom, and the numerous irregular exactions. The British felt that much of the abuse at Canton was unknown to Peking. With a view to reducing the irritations, widening the trade, and placing British Chinese relations on a regular diplomatic footing through direct contact with the central power, London decided to dispatch an official mission to China. Instrumental in this decision was Henry Dundas, president of the Pitt government's newly founded Board of Control in India. The East India Company, while not wholly pleased with this move lest it jeopardize the existing trade, agreed to bear the expense of the embassy and to furnish presents to the Chinese court. The ambassadorship went to Lieutenant Colonel Charles Cathcart, member of Parliament, quartermaster-general to the Bengal army, and a friend of Dundas. His instructions called for the improvement of British trade with China and removal of the present restrictions, dispersion of Chinese fears of British territorial designs and the assurance of the peaceful intention of trade, and acquisition of "a small tract of ground or detached island in some more convenient situation than Canton" as a depot for commerce under British jurisdiction. Failing in these objectives, he was to work toward relieving the immediate difficulties and embarrassments at Canton. But if his mission should terminate successfully, he was to request an exchange of permanent envoys between Britain and China.[15]

The embassy, which sailed December 21, 1787, struck an unpropitious note at its beginning. Cathcart was seriously ill with consumption, and the ship ran into a storm and unfavorable winds. In February and March of the following year dysentery plagued the sailors, and the ambassador in the last stage of consumption wrote of his inability to shake his cough. Still insisting that the constant change of air at sea would enhance his recovery, Cathcart succumbed on June 10 during the journey. The aborted mission returned to England.

Talks of a second mission failed to produce government action because of the East India Company's lukewarm attitude, the unsettled conditions in Europe caused by the French Revolution, the outbreak of war in India with the Tippoo Sultan in late 1789, and the difficulty of finding a man suitable to head such a mission. Not until June 1791, when Henry Dundas was promoted to Home Secretary in addition to his old position on the Board of Control, did the idea of another embassy revive. With the support of Pitt, who wished to satisfy the growing demands of industrialists for a wider market in China, Dundas chose his friend Lord Macartney, Baron of Lissanoure and a cousin of the Crown, to be ambassador to China.

The Macartney Mission, 1793. Born near Belfast on May 14, 1737, Lord Macartney was a man of learning and dignity. An experienced colonial administrator and diplomat, he had been ambassador to Russia, member of the Irish and British Parliaments, chief secretary for Ireland, governor of the West Indian Island of Grenada, and governor of Madras. Having declined the post of governor-general of Bengal, he had been without a position since 1786. He was doubtless the best qualified and the most eligible man in England for the China mission. On May 3, 1792, he was officially designated "Ambassador Extraordinary and Plenipotentiary from the King of Great Britain to the Emperor of China." To add dignity to his mission, he was given the title of privy councillor and the rank of

15. Pritchard, *Crucial Years*, 255-58.

viscount. His lifelong friend, Sir George L. Staunton, was made "Secretary to the embassy and Minister Plenipotentiary in the absence of the Ambassador," with authorization to carry on the mission in the event of the death or incapacity of the leader. Macartney was stipulated a yearly compensation of £15,000 and Staunton £3,000.

On September 26, 1792, the mission set out from London with eighty-four members, including a machinist, a painter, a draftsman, an artificer, six musicians, and a number of military and naval officers. Impressive presents, costing £15,610, were prepared for the Chinese court, including a planetarium, globes, mathematical instruments, chronometers, a telescope, measuring instruments, chemical and electrical instruments, window and plate glass, carpets, Birmingham goods, Sheffield goods, copperware, and Wedgwood pottery.

In addition to collecting all available information about China—intellectual, political, military, social, economic, and philosophical—Macartney was instructed to achieve six specific objectives:

1. To acquire one or two places near the tea- and silk-producing and the woolens-consuming areas, where British traders might reside and English jurisdiction be exercised.
2. To negotiate a commercial treaty with a view to extending trade throughout China if possible.
3. To relieve existing abuses at Canton.
4. To create a desire in China for British products.
5. To arrange diplomatic representation at Peking.
6. To open Japan, Cochin China, and the Eastern Islands to British commerce.

In short, the mission was entrusted with the task of opening the whole East to British trade and of placing relations with China on a regular treaty basis.

Macartney was instructed to conform to all the ceremonials of the Chinese court which did not compromise the honor of his king and the dignity of himself. To prepare for the arrival of this embassy, the East India Company dispatched a Secret and Superintending Committee to Canton in September 1792 to inform the governor-general of the event. Under the pretext of presenting felicitations of the English king to Emperor Ch'ien-lung on his eighty-third birthday, the mission arrived off Canton shores on June 19, 1793, in a man-of-war, the *Lion*, a brig, the *Jackal*, and a Company steamer, the *Hindustan*. It then proceeded north to Chusan and Taku.

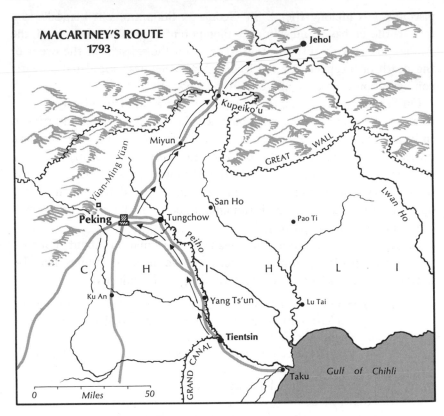

Flattered by the first English "tributary" mission, which had come to admire his Celestial Empire and help celebrate his birthday, Emperor Ch'ien-lung was much pleased and ordered that the embassy be accorded an honorable welcome. An edict of July 24, 1793, stated that although the reception of the English envoy need not be excessively elaborate, nevertheless—because it was his first visit and in view of his long ocean voyage —he should be treated differently from the tributary envoys of Burma and Annam. An order was issued[16] that Macartney be accorded proper courtesy and be given a reasonably good reception. Another edict, of August 1, reiterated the importance of receiving him in an appropriate manner—i.e. neither too servile nor too overbearing—so as to show China's benevolence toward men from afar. The court allocated a liberal daily allowance of 5,000 taels for the mission during its journey to Peking,

16. To Governor-general Liang K'en-t'ang at Tientsin, and to the Ch'ang-lu Salt Controller, Cheng-jui.

and a daily maintenance subsidy of 1,500 taels while it stayed in the capital.[17]

At Tientsin the mission was warmly welcomed by the governor-general, and the 600 cases of presents were carried to Peking on an impressive train of wagons, barrows, horses, and coolies. Though a flag bearing the characters of "Tributary Envoy from England" was placed on his boat, Macartney chose not to protest. At Peking he was lodged in the Summer Palace for five days, and on September 2 he left for Jehol, about a hundred miles north of Peking beyond the Great Wall, where the emperor was spending the summer.

An ostentatious and pompous old ruler, Emperor Ch'ien-lung was gratified at the coming of the English mission, but a little piqued at news that Macartney was reluctant to perform the kowtow. In an edict of August 14 he had announced that not only all tributary envoys but even their kings, when coming to China, must perform the kowtow; therefore Macartney, who had been sent by his king to congratulate the emperor on his birthday, should not resist the Chinese ceremony lest he fail to carry out his sovereign's intentions. The Chinese escorts of the mission were instructed to suggest that if the English envoys were perhaps physically unable to bend because of their knee buckles and garters, they should remove them temporarily in order to perform the kowtow. Macartney himself seemed to have no strong feelings about the kowtow, but he would do nothing that would compromise the dignity of his country or suggest a vassal status to China. He let it be known that he would pay the emperor the same obeisance which he did the English sovereign and that he would perform the kowtow only if an equally high ranking Chinese would perform the same ritual before the portrait of the English king. In the end Emperor Ch'ien-lung, who was in a good mood, yielded the point and allowed Macartney to fall on one knee during the audience as he would do to his own king, but exempted him from the English custom of kissing the hand of the monarch.

The celebrated audience took place on September 14, 1793, in a magnificient tent intended for extensive assemblies. Macartney and Staunton presented themselves in brilliant official costumes—the former wearing the mantle of the Order of the Bath over a rich embroidered velvet, with the collar and diamond badge and a diamond star, and the latter also wearing a rich embroidered velvet in addition to the scarlet silk habit of the Doctor of Laws of Oxford. They performed the modified

17. Kuo T'ing-i, I, 231-32; Hsiao I-shan, II, 811.

ritual as agreed upon—kneeling on one knee—although Chinese records later bemusedly reported that Macartney, overcome by awe and excitement in the imposing presence of the emperor, "unconsciously fell on his two knees." Then came the presentation of the English king's letter, which Macartney personally delivered in a gold box to the emperor. Exchange of gifts followed, with the emperor bestowing on the English king, through Macartney, a whitish jade scepter (ju-i) about a foot and a half long, as a symbol of peace and prosperity, remarking that he hoped that the English king might live as long as he himself. The aged ruler then gave the two envoys a greenish carved agate each as a special mark of favor. In return Macartney presented him with a pair of beautiful enameled watches set with diamonds, while Staunton proffered a pair of elegant air guns. Imperial gifts were also bestowed on other members of the delegation. A most sumptuous banquet followed in honor of the visitors, at which time the emperor solicitously offered the envoys dishes from his own table and went so far as to personally pour them each a cup of warm wine. Macartney found Ch'ien-lung a bit condescending, but very affable, dignified, and vigorous, looking more like a man of sixty than eighty-three. The grandeur, luxury, and elegance of Ch'ien-lung's summer court called to Macartney's mind "King Solomon in all his glory."[18] Emperor Ch'ien-lung, on his part, celebrated the occasion with a poem of his own composition:[19]

> Formerly Portugal presented tribute;
> Now England is paying homage.
> They have out-traveled Shu-hai and Heng-chang;[20]
> My Ancestors' merit and virtue must have reached their
>   distant shores.
> Though their tribute is commonplace, my heart approves
>   sincerely.
> Curios and the boasted ingenuity of their devices I
>   prize not.
> Though what they bring is meagre, yet,
> In my kindness to men from afar I make generous return,
> Wanting to preserve my good health and power.

On the following day Macartney was given a tour of the imperial Garden of Ten Thousand Trees (Wan-shu yüan) and another audience. In the

18. J. L. Cranmer-Byng, "Lord Macartney's Embassy to Peking in 1793," *Journal of Oriental Studies* (Hong Kong), IV: 1-2:163 (1957-58).
19. Tr. by J. L. Cranmer-Byng, 164.
20. Mythological travelers.

next two days he was again taken sight-seeing, given presents, and invited to a puppet show and a comic drama. On September 17, the imperial birthday, Macartney was admitted to the full company of Chinese and Manchu courtiers to present his felicitations to the emperor. On September 26 the mission returned to Peking, four days before the emperor himself.

Macartney had attempted in vain to open discussion with Ho-shen, the powerful grand councillor and chief minister of state, about the extension of trade and an exchange of envoys. In both Jehol and Peking, Ho-shen was unresponsive, parrying all attempts at negotiation. Finally, when pressed by Macartney, who by this time was quite worn out and sick with the gout and rheumatism, Ho-shen vaguely indicated that the English envoy might present his requests in a note. This Macartney readily did on October 3 in the name of the Crown, requesting:

1. To extend trade to Chusan, Ningpo, and Tientsin.
2. To allow English traders a warehouse in Peking for the sale of their goods, as the Russians formerly had.
3. To assign a small unfortified island near Chusan for the residence of English traders, storage of goods, and outfitting of ships.
4. To assign a small place near Canton for the residence of English traders, and allow them freedom of movement between Canton and Macao.
5. To abolish the transit dues between Macao and Canton, or at least to reduce them to the tariff of 1782.
6. To prohibit the exaction of duties from English merchants over and above the rates set by the imperial tariff, a copy of which should be made available to them.

The Ch'ing court considered diplomatic negotiations completely out of order. As far as it was concerned, Macartney had come to congratulate the emperor on his birthday and his mission was accomplished when he had done so. As he had been well treated, he should be satisfied to return home with gratitude. Since no tributary mission ever tarried in Peking for more than forty days, the court was anxious that Macartney leave before October 9. Ho-shen intimated to him that with severe winter descending soon, the emperor was concerned about the ambassador's health. It was obvious that the host was hinting that the guest should leave. Macartney realized that any further attempt to remain would serve no useful purpose. Disappointed, he noted in his Journal: " . . . having been selected for this Commission to China, the first of its kind from

Great Britain, of which considerable expectations of success had been formed by many, and by none more than by myself, I cannot help feeling the disappointment most severely. I cannot lose sight of my first prospects without infinite regret."[21]

The mission left Peking on October 7. Macartney remained in Canton from December 19, 1793, to January 10, 1794, then went to Macao, where he stayed until March 8, and finally returned to London on the following September 4. The whole experience of the embassy was wittily summed up in an epigram collected by Peter Auber, secretary to the Court of Directors of the East India Company: "It has just been observed that the Ambassador was received with the utmost politeness, treated with the utmost hospitality, watched with the utmost vigilance, and dismissed with the utmost civility."[22]

Although no reply had been made to Macartney directly, two edicts were issued to King George III. In the first celebrated message, dated October 3, 1793, Emperor Ch'ien-lung pompously stated that while China appreciated the English intention "to partake of the benefits" of Chinese civilization by displatching a mission, the request for diplomatic residence in Peking could not be granted because it was contrary to the established practice of China: "Europe consists of many other nations besides your own: if each and all demanded to be represented at our court, how could we possibly consent? The thing is utterly impracticable. How can our dynasty alter its whole procedure and system of etiquette, established for more than a century, in order to meet your individual view?" Moreover, an envoy in Peking would be too far from Canton to control the traders. "If you assert that your reverence for Our Celestial dynasty fills you with a desire to acquire the rudiments of our civilization, you could not possibly transplant our manners and customs to your alien soil. Therefore, however adept the Envoy might become, nothing would be gained thereby." Apropos of the request for the extension of trade, Ch'ien-lung announced: "We possess all things. I set no value on objects strange or ingenious, and have no use for your country's manufactures." The message closed with the imperious statement: "It behooves you, O King, to respect my sentiments and to display even greater devotion and loyalty in future, so that, by perpetual submission to our Throne, you may secure peace and prosperity for your country thereafter."[23]

21. Cranmer-Byng, 176.
22. Cranmer-Byng, 183.
23. MacNair, I, 2-4.

These were strong and provocative words to be addressed to the sovereign of a state which boasted of being the mistress of the seas, yet they unmistakably evinced the Chinese mentality on foreign relations at the close of the 18th century. "No one understands China until this document has ceased to seem absurd," remarked Bertrand Russell.[24]

In a separate mandate to George III, Ch'ien-lung rejected all six of Macartney's requests as impractical and unproductive of good results.

> It may be, O King, that the above proposals have been wantonly made by your ambassador on his own responsibility; or peradventure you yourself are ignorant of our dynastic regulations and had no intention of transgressing them when you expressed these wild ideas and hopes . . . Above all, upon you, who live in a remote and inaccessible region, far across the spaces of ocean, but who have shown your submissive loyalty by sending this tribute mission, I have heaped benefits far in excess of those I have accorded to other nations. But the demands presented by your embassy are not only a contravention of dynastic tradition, but would be unproductive of good results to yourself, besides being quite impracticable . . . It is your bounden duty reverently to appreciate my feelings and to obey these instructions henceforth for all times, so that you may enjoy the blessings of perpetual peace.[25]

The mission, which cost the British £78,522, was a complete diplomatic failure. It had achieved neither representation at Peking, nor the extension of trade, nor the opening of Japan, Cochin China, and the Eastern Islands. Nevertheless, it succeeded in collecting valuable firsthand information about the mysterious land called China. Macartney discovered the low state of her scientific and medical knowledge, the indifference of the literati class to material progress, the backwardness of an army which still used bows and arrows and lacked modern firearms, the poverty of the masses, and the widespread corruption and graft in government. Disbelieving, for example, that his mission had consumed the 1,500-tael daily allowance allocated by the court, Macartney surmised that part of it must have gone into the pockets of the officials in charge of his reception. The offspring of Confucius, he concluded, were no different from the descendants of Mammon. In regard to the future of the dynasty, he ventured a penetrating remark: "The empire of China is an

24. Cranmer-Byng, 182.
25. MacNair, I, 4-9.

old, crazy, first-rate Man of War, which a succession of able and vigilant officers have contrived to keep afloat for these hundred and fifty years past, and to overawe their neighbors merely by her bulk and appearance. But whenever an insufficient man happens to have the command on deck, adieu to the discipline and safety of the ship. She may, perhaps, not sink outright; she may drift some time as a wreck, and will then be dashed to pieces on the shores; but she can never be rebuilt on the old bottom."[26] Whatever the diplomatic results, a leading officer of the East India Company remarked that "the information alone to be acquired from the embassy would far more than compensate for the expense."[27]

As for the British government, it was clearly disappointed at the lackluster outcome of the mission, though it placed neither censure nor honor on the ambassador. Macartney had done his best and failed; his only fault, perhaps, was the persistent view that the Chinese government was not disinclined toward foreign intercourse. He now recommended that Staunton be sent on a follow-up legation to China as the king's minister and concurrent chief of the British supercargoes at Canton. Although the government was favorably disposed to the idea and steps were taken to put it into practice, Staunton's attack of paralysis and subsequent death in 1801 shelved the project. The lack of a suitable leader for the embassy and Britain's involvement in the Napoleonic Wars indefinitely postponed any move in that direction.

The Amherst Mission, 1816. In the period that followed, the Canton trade continued much as before, but Sino-British relations were strained by several new incidents. The first arose out of British fear of a French seizure of Macao from the Portuguese, a move which would win for France a commanding position in Southeast Asian trade. To forestall this possibility, twice—in 1802 and 1808—British forces occupied Macao, despite Chinese protests that Macao was Chinese territory and not in danger of French seizure. The first British withdrawal was achieved with the news of the Peace of Amiens in 1802, but the second was much more complicated. When the British commander, Admiral Drury, refused to evacuate, the governor-general at Canton retaliated with a stoppage of trade, causing inconveniences and widespread complaint among all foreigners. Drury then proposed an interview with the governor-general, and when refused, defiantly forced his way past the Bogue in three

26. Cranmer-Byng, 181.
27. Pritchard, *Crucial Years*, 375.

warships, cast anchor at Whampoa, and demanded the interview. There followed an armed conflict with the Chinese, in which the British suffered some casualties. The situation remained tense until the Select Committee of the Company secured British withdrawal from Macao in December of that year by getting the Portuguese to pay a ransom of $600,000.

Other issues that strained Sino-British rapport included the British attack on the Chinese tributary of Nepal, and the seizure of the American steamer *Hunter* off Canton waters (by the British warship *Doris*) in April 1814, Britain then being at war with the United States. The Canton authorities protested the violation of Chinese jurisdiction and threatened to cut off the British trade unless the *Doris* left port. The British community at Canton refused to give in, and the Chinese bluff failed.

These incidents, along with the growing dissatisfaction over the Canton trade system, prompted the Company to request that London send another deputation to Peking. The restoration of peace in Europe after the Congress of Vienna in 1815 freed Britain from its European involvement. It decided to send Lord Amherst, the ex-governor of India, on a mission to the Ch'ing court, accompanied by two associate envoys, Henry Ellis and Sir George Thomas Staunton, son of Macartney's secretary and president of the Select Committee in Canton. Lord Amherst's instructions called for the removal of grievances at Canton, the establishment of free trade between Chinese and British merchants, the abolition of the Co-hong system, freedom to reside at the factory without time limit and to employ Chinese servants, the establishment of direct communications between the factory and Chinese officials, the opening of more ports north of Canton, and the right to diplomatic representation in Peking. He was to remove Chinese misgivings about the British action in Nepal and explain the reasons for the *Doris* incident. Leaving Portsmouth on February 8, 1816, the delegation sailed straight to Tientsin without stopping at Canton, where it was feared the Chinese might block it from proceeding northward.

Unlike his expansive father Ch'ien-lung, Emperor Chia-ch'ing was reserved and hesitant to receive foreign envoys. Apprehensive of new British demands, he responded to the new embassy with the unenthusiastic comment: "All in all, I am not glad of this event." An order was issued that the reception of the mission need not be extravagant; that if Amherst was submissive, he might be allowed to come to Peking for an audience; but if he was headstrong and resistant to the ceremony of kowtow, he should be given a local reception at Tientsin only, and told that the emperor had gone on a hunting trip and would not return for several months.

On August 13, 1816, Amherst and his fifty-two pieces of "tribute" arrived in Tientsin, where he was received by the president of the Board of Public Works, who gave a dinner in his honor. When asked to express his thanks to the emperor by performing the kowtow, Amherst replied that he could not comply, but would remove his hat three times and bow his head nine times. Endless argument followed, but led to no solution. While the procession was en route to Peking, word came from the court that "if the English envoy refuses to comply with the ceremony no audience will be allowed." The procession stopped at Tungchow, about ten miles from Peking, and two high officials from the capital, the presidents of the Li-fan yüan and of the Board of Rites, came to reason with Amherst concerning the importance of kowtow. Amherst himself actually did not care one way or the other about the matter; he had been instructed in London to consider the kowtow as a matter of expediency and to perform it if it would expedite his mission. But the directors of the East India Company had advised him to resist the Chinese ritual lest it compromise the dignity and prestige of Britain. Division of opinion also existed between his associate envoys: Ellis favored accepting the Chinese demand, while Staunton firmly opposed it. Caught between contrary views, Amherst momentarily hesitated and wavered, but ultimately decided against the kowtow. He told the Chinese that he would bend one knee and bow his head three times, and repeat the performance three times so as to approximate the three kneelings and nine knockings of the head that were required. This the Chinese would not accept. The mission was stalled at Tungchow for ten days. Then an ameliorating order came from the court to the effect that since "outer barbarians" were unused to the kowtow, it should not matter too much if the envoy in question had not mastered the proper manner of kneeling and rising. Anxious to please the emperor, the president of the Li-fan yüan, who had been arguing with Amherst, reported on August 27 that "although his [Amherst's] kneeling and rising are somewhat unnatural, the ceremony may yet be performed."

On the evening of August 28 the mission was allowed to proceed to Peking. Emperor Chia-ch'ing, satisfied with the report of Amherst's "progress" in learning the kowtow, decided to accord him an audience the following day. The embassy was hurried on all night, and upon arrival in Peking early the next morning Amherst was told that the emperor was ready to receive him immediately at the Summer Palace. Exhausted from the bumpy journey and the summer heat, and unaccompanied by his credentials and costumes which had lagged behind, he pleaded for time to rest. After a heated argument with his Chinese escorts, Amherst left in anger. Presently the emperor sent for him. The president of the Li-fan yüan, unable to produce Amherst, falsely reported that the English envoy had fallen sick. The emperor then asked for the associate envoy, and was informed that he too was ill. Suspecting the envoys of falsehood, the exasperated ruler declared: "China is the universal overlord. How can she willingly submit to this kind of insult and insolence?" An edict was issued expelling the English embassy from the capital, rejecting its "tribute," and canceling the audience.

When the actual plight of the envoys became known to the emperor the next day, he was a little mollified, agreeing to recall part of the tribute and send some gifts to the king of England. He also sent an order to the governor-general at Nanking to avoid insulting Amherst, treating him with the courtesy due his rank. The embassy finally left for England from Canton on January 28, 1817.

Amherst's refusal to comply with Chinese ceremonies—the sole cause for his expulsion—received considerable attention in Europe. Napoleon Bonaparte, then in exile, chided him for applying the ceremonies of the court of St. James to the court at Peking. An envoy, in Napoleon's view, should respect the ceremonies and customs of the country to which he is accredited and should realize that he does not have the same privilege of discrimination as the sovereign who sent him; he should be satisfied with the treatment due a man of comparable rank at the local court. Hence, British and Russian envoys, in his view, should accept the Chinese ceremonies if the Chinese government agreed to instruct its future deputies to comply with the practices of London and St. Petersburg.

Since both the Macartney and Amherst attempts at peaceful negotiation had failed, the British throne faced three alternatives of action: (1) abandon the China trade, (2) submit to the Chinese treatment, or (3) change the situation by military means. For Britain, the most powerful state on earth and the mistress of the seas, the first two courses were unthinkable, leaving only the third alternative—force. On China's part, the disrespect displayed by Amherst was utterly intolerable and wholly incompatible with her claim to universal overlordship. Emperor Chia-ch'ing even considered severing relations with Britain and stopping the

Canton trade altogether, but was dissuaded from it by the governor-general at Canton, who feared reprisals and possible war with Britain. The time was fast approaching for a showdown between the two countries.

Meanwhile, the Canton trade had been undergoing a drastic metamorphosis in character as a result of the rapid growth of the private and country trade and the phenomenal rise of opium-smuggling from India to China. The private trade at Canton had risen from 688,880 taels in 1780-81 to 992,444 taels in 1799-1800, and the country trade from 1,020,-012 to 3,743,158 in the same period.[28] Their growth was even more rapid after the turn of the century. By 1817-1834 they accounted for three-quarters of the total British imports to China. Many of the private traders, to avoid the Company's intervention, secured consulships of other European countries, and managed to stay in Canton and expand their business. They served as agency houses for firms in London and India and engaged in the lucrative illicit traffic of opium-smuggling at "outside" anchorages, such as Lintin and Hong Kong, making transactions with "outside" (i.e. non-hong) merchants for quick profit. So powerful had the private traders become that they began to agitate for the abolition of the Company's monopoly. By 1820 the complexion of the Canton trade had changed: private trade had surpassed the company trade, and opium had superceded regular articles as a chief item of import. These two developments contributed to the breakdown of the outworn Canton system and precipitated the long-delayed clash between Britain and China. A new page of history was about to be written.

FURTHER READING

Chang, Hsin-pao, *Commissioner Lin and the Opium War* (Cambridge, Mass., 1964), chapter 1.

Chang, Te-ch'ang 張德昌, "Ch'ing-tai Ya-p'ien chan-cheng ch'ien chih Chung-Hsi yen-hai t'ung-shang" 清代鴉片戰爭前之中西沿海通商 (Sino-Western coastal trade in the Ch'ing period before the Opium War), *Tsing-hua hsüeh-pao*, 10:1:97-145 (Jan. 1935).

Cranmer-Byng, J. L., "Lord Macartney's Embassy to Peking in 1793," *Journal of Oriental Studies*, IV:1-2:117-183 (1957-58).

Danton, G. H., *The Cultural Contacts of the United States and China: The Earliest Sino-American Culture Contact, 1784-1844* (New York, 1931).

28. Pritchard, *Crucial Years*, 401-2.

Greenberg, Michael, *British Trade and the Opening of China, 1800-42* (Cambridge, 1951).

Hou, Hou-p'ei 侯厚培, "Wu-k'ou t'ung-shang i-ch'ien o-kuo kuo-chi mao-i chih kai-k'uang" 五口通商以前我國國際貿易之概況 (The general condition of our country's international trade before the five-port trading period), *Tsing-hua hsüeh-pao*, 4:1:1,217-1,264 (June 1927).

Hunter, William O., *The "Fan Kwae" at Canton before Treaty Days, 1825-44* (Shanghai, 1911).

Liang, Chia-pin 梁嘉彬, *Kuang-tung shih-san-hang k'ao* 廣東十三行考 (A study of the Thirteen Hongs of Canton), (Shanghai, 1937).

MacNair, H. F., *Modern Chinese History: Selected Readings* (Shanghai, 1913) chapter 2.

Morse, H. B., *The International Relations of the Chinese Empire* (London, 1910), I, chapters 3-6.

——, *The Chronicles of the East India Company Trading to China, 1635-1834* (Oxford, 1926-29), 5 vols.

P'eng, Tse-i 彭澤一, "Ch'ing-tai Kwang-tung yang-hang chih-tu ti ch'i yüan" 清代廣東洋行制度的起源 (The Rise of the hongs in Kwangtung during the Ch'ing Dynasty), *Li-shih yen-chiu*, 1:1-24 (1957).

Pritchard, Earl H., *Anglo-Chinese Relations during the Seventeenth and Eighteenth Centuries*, University of Illinois Studies in the Social Sciences, 17:1-2:1-244 (March-June 1929).

——, *The Crucial Years of Early Anglo-Chinese Relations, 1750-1800*, Research Studies of the State College of Washington, 4:3-4:95-442 (Sept.-Dec. 1936).

——, "The Kowtow in the Macartney Embassy to China in 1793," *Far Eastern Quarterly*, II:2:163-203 (Feb. 1943).

——, "Private Trade Between England and China in the 18th Century (1680-1833)" *Journal of Economic and Social History of the Orient*, I, Parts 1-2 (Aug. 1957-April 1958).

Staunton, Sir George, *An Authentic Account of an Embassy from the King of Great Britain to the Emperor of China* (London, 1797), 2 vols.

8

The Opium War

The Canton trade in the 18th century, as already noted, was heavily one-sided in China's favor. Foreign traders came to purchase tea, silk, rhubarb, and other articles, but they paid in gold and silver, the Chinese finding little need for the industrial products of the West—"We possess all things," as Emperor Ch'ien-lung told King George III. Frequently 90 per cent—and sometimes as high as 98 per cent—of the East India Company's shipment to China was gold, and only 10 per cent commodities. Between 1781 and 1790, 16.4 million taels of silver flowed into China, and between 1800 and 1810, 26 million. This balance in China's favor continued until the mid-1820's when it settled into an equilibrium. After 1826 the balance began to slip the other way: between 1831 and 1833 nearly 10 million taels flowed out of China.[1] The reversal gathered further momentum as time went on. What could cause such a phenomenal inversion in a trade balance? One factor: opium.

THE OPIUM TRADE

The opium poppy was first introduced into China by the Arabs and the Turks in the late 7th or early 8th century. The Chinese called it *ying-su*, or *mi-nang*, or *a-fu-yung*, or simply *po-pi* (poppy), and used it chiefly as medicine to relieve pain and reduce tension; opium-smoking for pleasure was unknown until much later. In 1620 some Formosans were said to

1. Hsin-pao Chang, *Commissioner Lin and the Opium War* (Cambridge, Mass. 1964), 41.

have mixed tobacco with opium for smoking, and the practice spread in the 1660's to Fukien and Kwangtung, where the method of smoking was refined: the smoker burned the opium over a lamp and inhaled its fumes through a pipe. It rapidly became a fad with the leisure classes, and before long even the poor took it up. The demand for opium led to increased foreign importation and to native cultivation in Szechwan, Yunnan, Fukien, Chekiang, and Kwangtung. From a moral concern Emperor Yung-cheng (1723-35) prohibited the sale and smoking of opium in 1729, and Emperor Chia-ch'ing (1796-1820) outlawed its importation and cultivation in 1796. Later, in the 1820's and 1830's, economic considerations also entered the picture, for the trade was causing a rapid outflow of silver.

The British took over the lead in opium importation from the Portuguese in 1773, when the East India Company established a monopoly of the opium cultivation—from seedling to sale of the finished product by auction in Calcutta—under the Bengal government. But knowing the Chinese prohibition, the Company disengaged itself officially from the opium trade by leaving its distribution to the country ships which sailed under the Company's license. In the license a clause required such ships to carry the Company's opium, but in the public sailing order there was always a statement of prohibition against carrying opium "lest the Company be implicated."[2] Thus the East India Company perfected the technique of growing opium cheaply and abundantly in India, while piously disowning it in China. Legally and officially, it was not involved in the illicit trade.

In general there were three types of opium: the Patna (Bengal opium), the Malwa (West Indian opium), and the Turkish opium. Their prices varied with time and place. A chest[3] of Patna cost $560 to $590 in Macao in 1801, $2,075 in 1821, and $744 in 1835; a chest of Malwa cost about $400, $1,325, and $602 in the corresponding years. The annual importation of opium at the time of the first prohibition in 1729 was 200 chests, but by 1767 it rose to 1,000. The import growth was rapid and steady: between 1800 and 1820, the average annual importation was 4,500 chests, and between 1820 and 1830, over 10,000 chests. In the 1830's the volume rose enormously, reaching a peak of 40,000 chests in 1838-39. This sharp rise was caused by the abolition of the Company's monopoly of the China

2. Greenberg, 110.
3. Opium was packed in chests, which weighed approximately 100 catties (*chin*), or 133⅓ lbs., for the Malwa, and 120 catties, or 160 lbs., for the Patna.

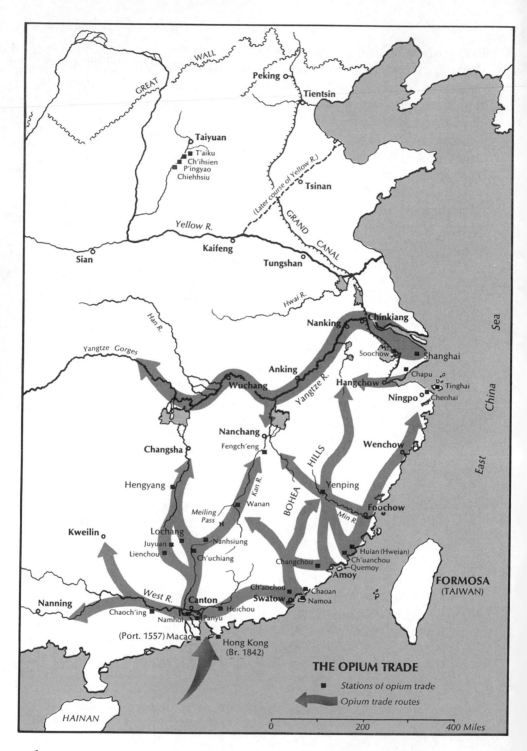

THE OPIUM TRADE

■ Stations of opium trade

Opium trade routes

0   200   400 Miles

THE OPIUM WAR 217

trade in 1834, the influx of private traders, and the extension of traffic beyond the Canton waters to the entire southeastern coast of China.

In contrast to the regular trade which was carried on by barter or on credit, the opium trade—forced into a subterranean existence because of its illicit nature—was conducted on a cash basis. The lucrativeness of the trade drew nearly all foreign traders, except men like D. W. C. Olyphant, a "pious, devoted servant of Christ, and a friend of China." The leading British private firm, Jardine, Matheson and Company, handled 5,000 chests in 1829-30, roughly one-third of the opium total in China. But, said Jardine in 1839, "the father of all smuggling and smugglers is the East India Company."[4]

The American traders handled Turkish as well as Indian opium, but it was the latter which made up most of their total commodity—around 95 per cent. Between 1800 and 1839 the Americans shipped 10,000 chests into China.

The opium-dealing organizations, known as the *yao-k'ao*, usually had capital anywhere from twenty thousand to one million dollars. They paid for the opium at the foreign factories and picked up the drug from the foreign "receiving ships" at Lintin by fast-moving small crafts called "smug boats," which were also known by such names as "fast crabs" (*k'uai-hsieh*) and "scrambling dragons" (*p'a-lung*). They were fully armed, rowed by sixty to seventy sailors, with twenty or more oars on each side, and they moved at an amazing speed. In 1831 there were something like a hundred or two hundred of them shuttling around the Canton waters. From there the opium was transported westward to Kwangsi and Kweichow, eastward to Fukien, and northward to Hunan, Kiangsi, Anhwei, and as far as Shensi. Opium dealers often maintained relations with the underworld—secret societies and brigands—as well as with the Shansi bankers for transmission of funds.

The rapid rise in opium imports naturally was connected with the growing demand for the drug in China. The addicts in the early 19th century were mostly young men of rich families, but gradually the habit spread to people of other walks of life: government officials, merchants, literati, women, servants, soldiers, and even monks, nuns, and priests. In 1838, nine out of ten people in Kwangtung and Fukien provinces were addicts, and opium shops in their towns were as common as gin shops in England. The addict went to any length to acquire the drug, for its deprivation would cause restlessness, chills, hot flashes, nausea, muscle

4. Hsin-pao Chang, 31, 49; Greenberg, 137.

twitch, and bone aches. Though hungry, he could not eat, and though drowsy, he could not sleep. A common laborer made one-tenth to two-tenths of a tael a day; half of it would be spent on the drug if he was an addict. An average smoker consumed .05 of a Chinese ounce[5] of opium extract daily, while a good many smoked twice as much. The 40,000 chests imported in 1838-39 yielded 2.4 million catties of extract and supplied about 2.1 million consumers. It was said that between 10 per cent to 20 per cent of the central government officials and 20 per cent to 30 per cent of the local officials smoked opium. The total number of smokers was estimated at somewhere between two and ten million. The famous statesman Lin Tse-hsü stated that if one out of a hundred people in China smoked opium there would be four million addicts. Chinese estimates put the annual consumption of opium at 17 to 18 million taels between 1823 and 1831, 20 million taels between 1831 and 1834, and 30 million between 1834 and 1838.[6]

The economic repercussions of opium-smoking were most serious. Spending on opium caused a stagnation in the demand for other commodities, with a consequent general sluggishness in the market. Moreover, the constant inflow of opium caused a continuous outflow of silver. Between 1828 and 1836, the British exported $37.9 million from Canton, and in the year beginning July 1, 1837 they took $8.9 million. However, there was an offsetting factor: the Americans and other foreign traders brought silver and gold into China. Between 1818 and 1834 the Americans brought in $60 million of silver against $50 million shipped out by the British. But as the opium trade grew, less American cash flowed in, while more Chinese silver was taken out; between 1828 and 1833 the British shipped out $29.6 million of specie against the American inflow of $15.8 million. The drain was most acute in the middle and late 1830's, somewhere between 4 and 5 million dollars annually.[7] The silver depletion upset the domestic economy and rocked the exchange rate between silver and copper in the market. Whereas a tael of silver in 1740 exchanged for 800 copper coins, in 1828 it was worth 2,500 in Chihli and 2,600 in Shantung. To meet the economic crisis, the government debased the copper coins and increased their annual minting.

In spite of these serious economic repercussions, the opium traffic could not be stopped for lack of a well-organized customs service, an ef-

5. One Chinese ounce was about 1⅓ English ounces.
6. Hsin-pao Chang, 35, 40; Kuo T'ing-i, II, 104-05.
7. Greenberg, 142; Hsin-pao Chang, 42.

fective navy, and a sense of moral responsibility in public administration. Too often officials charged with suppressing the drug traffic connived with the smugglers and turned over "free samples" of opium to the government as intercepted contraband.

The ineffectiveness of the Chinese prohibition was matched by the enterprising promotion of the trade by the British. In 1832 the East India Company made 10 million rupees from its opium production, in 1837, 20 million, and in 1838, 30 million. Opium provided over 5 per cent of the Company's revenue in India in 1826-27, 9 per cent in 1828-29, and 12 per cent in the 1850's, a sum close to £4 million sterling. The House of Commons' Select Committee reported in 1830 and 1832 that "it does not seem advisable to abandon so important a source of revenue as the East India Company's monopoly of opium in Bengal." In 1836 the British sold $18 million worth of opium in China as against the $17 million worth of Chinese tea and silk which they bought. Obviously, without the opium trade they would have suffered a severe deficit; opium had therefore become the economic panacea for the British trade doldrums. Small wonder that the astute and perceptive Duke of Wellington declared in May 1838 that Parliament had not only refused to frown upon the opium traffic but cherished it, extended it, and promoted it.[8]

THE NAPIER MISSION, 1834

A far-reaching event occurred in 1834 which greatly aggravated the Sino-British relations: the abolition of the East India Company's monopoly of the China trade. The doctrines of *laissez faire* and free trade had been gathering momentum in England since the middle of the 18th century, and the East India Company's monopolistic rights came under severe attack by the rising merchant class, which had been shut out of the lucrative Asiatic trade. When the Company's charter was up for renewal in 1813, Parliament, taking into consideration the clamor for liberation of trade, threw the Indian trade open to everyone, but continued the Company's monopoly of the China trade for another twenty years. This partial concession did not satisfy the increasingly influential manufacturers and entrepreneurs of Manchester, Glasgow, and London; the private traders in Canton also renewed their demand for free trade, citing the success of the American free traders as an example. There were debates in Parliament, and in 1830 a Select Committee was appointed to investigate the problem.

8. Hsin-pao Chang, 48.

The news of the forthcoming expiration of the Company's monopoly reached Canton in 1830. The prospect of the dissolution of a Company which had operated in China for more than a century troubled the local authorities. They were concerned about the future control of foreign traders, who were supposedly greedy, violent, and unfathomable like "dogs and sheep." The governor-general at Canton[9] therefore asked in 1831 that England send a *taipan* (head merchant) to Canton when the Company's monopoly ended. The British Parliament, however, decided on August 28, 1833, that three superintendents of trade should be appointed. Resolutions were adopted to end the Company's monopoly of the China trade formally on April 22, 1834; to grant to all British subjects free trade between the Cape of Good Hope and the Straits of Magellan; and to create a court of justice for the trial of offenses committed by British subjects in China and within a hundred miles of the coast. On December 10, 1833, Lord William John Napier, a Scottish peer, was appointed chief superintendent of the British trade in China, with H. C. Plowden and John Francis Davis, the last president of the Company's Select Committee in Canton, as the second and third chiefs. Plowden did not take up the assignment, and Davis succeeded as the second chief, while Sir George B. Robinson, another Company man, became the third chief. Captain Charles Elliot was made Master Attendant to take charge of "all British ships and crews within the Boca Tigris (Bogue)."

These measures resulted in a fundamental change in Sino-British relations. The British government had replaced the East India Company in dealing with China, and official relations had been substituted for private relations. While commercial interests continued to dominate policy, considerations of national honor and prestige now assumed a greater importance than ever. This turn of events dealt a severe blow to the already faltering and disintegrating Canton system. The extension of the private opium trade along the coast had in fact spelled an end to single-port trade and to the monopolistic Canton trade system. The Co-hong and the East India Company no longer controlled the expanded commercial activity, and now the Select Committee had been replaced by newly appointed officials of the British Crown. Unfortunately, the full significance of these changes had eluded the Chinese, who made no preparations to meet the new situation.

It was under these conditions that Lord Napier set out on his mission.

9. Li Hung-pin.

His instructions stressed a conciliatory and moderate approach to the Chinese problem. He was to "study . . . all practical methods to maintain a good and friendly understanding," to impress upon the British subjects their "duty of conforming to the laws and usages of the Chinese empire, so long as such laws shall be administered toward (British subjects) with justice and good faith and in the same manner" as toward the Chinese and the other foreigners. Specifically he was told (1) not to employ menacing language nor to offend Chinese sensibilities, (2) not to use military force unless absolutely necessary, and (3) to adjudicate cases involving British subjects in China. On January 25, 1834, Lord Palmerston, the foreign secretary, further instructed him to announce his arrival to the governor-general at Canton by letter, and to study the possibility of extending the trade beyond Canton. In short, Napier was given the contradictory orders of placing Britain on an equal footing with China, while adopting conciliatory and friendly methods.

However, the instructions were not alone self-defeating—Napier's haughty character and limited perception sufficed to foredoom the mission. As an officer of the Crown, he was overly anxious to defend his dignity and his country's honor. Arriving in China, he went straight to Canton, took up residence at the British factory, and dispatched a letter to the governor-general announcing his arrival. In doing so he violated the Chinese regulations on several counts: he did not wait in Macao for permission to come to Canton; he did not secure permission to move into the factory, and he did not address the governor-general by a "petition" (*ping*) through the hong merchants.

As expected, the governor-general[10] rejected his letter and ordered him to leave Canton at once. Taking this as an insult, Napier accused the governor-general of "ignorance and obstinacy," and announced that while Britain had no desire for war she was "perfectly prepared" for it; he added that it would be as difficult to stop his work as "to stop the current of the Canton river." The governor-general reacted by withdrawing all Chinese employees from the British factory, cutting off its food supply, and stopping trade. Napier called in two British frigates, threatening to move them right "under the wall of the town." To Earl Grey of India he wrote: "What can an army of bows and arrows and pikes and shields do against a handful of British veterans? I am sure they would never for a moment dare to show a front. The batteries at the Bogue are contemptible; and not a man to be seen within them." Napier fancied he would

10. Lu K'un.

"hand his name down to posterity as the man who had thrown open the wide field of the Chinese Empire to the British Spirit and Industry."[11]

The governor-general sent troops to surround the factory, declaring that Napier alone was the culprit and that his departure would restore trade to normalcy. This divide-and-rule policy proved effective—a group of English traders from Whiteman, Dent, and Brightman privately requested the Hoppo to reopen the trade. Feeling deserted and betrayed by his countrymen, Napier on September 11 retreated to Macao, where he fell ill, and died on October 11, 1834. The "Napier fizzle"—as it was called at the time—having spent itself, the trade ban was lifted.

Napier's failure was caused as much by his personal pretensions as by his contradictory instructions. He behaved as if he were a royal emissary, whereas his title was only superintendent of trade. He did not comprehend that the Chinese had not asked for a British official to come to Canton, but only a *taipan*, a head merchant. The Chinese could not see why Napier should behave differently from the past presidents of the Select Committee. They could not see how the new *taipan* Napier dared to defy the established regulations and demand an equality of status with the governor-general. On Napier's part, his readiness to use force contradicted his instructions, which called for a conciliatory approach; and his ambitious desire to acquire fame in China drove him to precipitous actions which obviated any possibility of compromise. The Duke of Wellington aptly ascribed Napier's fiasco to "an attempt . . . to force upon the Chinese authorities at Canton, an unaccustomed mode of communication with an authority, with whose power and of whose nature they had no knowledge, which commenced its proceedings by an assumption of power hitherto unadmitted."[12]

THE LULL BEFORE THE STORM

John Francis Davis assumed the superintendency of trade and pursued a quiescent policy. A long-time employee of the Company and the last president of its Select Committee in Canton, he had no sympathy for the free trade movement. Private traders lost no time in ridiculing and attacking him, asserting that "One brought up in the late School of monopoly can never . . . be a fit Representative and controller of the free

11. Hsin-pao Chang, 54-57.
12. Hsin-pao Chang, 61.

traders." Before the end of 1834 some eighty-five merchants had petitioned London to send a diplomat to China, accompanied by warships
and soldiers, to demand reparation for the insults to Lord Napier. Davis
resigned under pressure, after having been in office but a hundred days.

Sir George B. Robinson became the new superintendent in January
1835. Also a Company man, he was never known for vigor or shrewdness,
or even intelligence. To avoid running into trouble with the Chinese,
Robinson moved his office aboard the *Louisa* at Lintin on November
25, 1835. His policy of "not rocking the boat" pleased the Canton
authorities and the trade was regular, undisturbed, and prosperous. But
Robinson's inactivity was not generally appreciated by the British traders,
and consequently pressure was brought for his ouster. Elliot, who had
been master attendant under Napier and third chief under Davis, became
the logical choice as replacement.

Captain Charles Elliot, son of a Madras governor, was not satisfied
with Napier's uncompromising, pretentious attitude; nor did he approve
Robinson's meek, undynamic policy. He believed that a middle-of-the-
road policy of confidence and strength combined with caution and conciliation, calculated to convince the Canton authorities that Britain
meant no trouble for China and had no territorial designs, would win
acceptance. He had been secretly communicating his views to the Foreign Office, which was impressed and so appointed him Chief Superintendent of Trade in June 1836. He was instructed to strive for direct
and equal official communication with Chinese dignitaries, and to refrain
from employing the humiliating superscription *ping*, or petition, in addressing them. However, Elliot deliberately used the petition form in his
first message to the governor-general, Teng T'ing-chen, in order to create
a good impression and to show British "magnanimity." The Chinese
found his phraseology palatable and submissive, and allowed him to come
to Canton.

Having won a foothold, Elliot proceeded to fight for direct and equal
communication with the Canton authorities, and in this he partially
succeeded. The governor-general allowed him to send and receive sealed
documents via the hong merchants rather than through the Co-hong,
and to come to Canton from Macao on business any time he wished, provided he notified the subprefect of Macao first. Elliot was elated to report
to London that these arrangements put him in a different position from
any foreigner in China before. However, his fight for the abolition of
petition was unsuccessful; he rationalized his failure by noting that Chi-

nese officers of his own rank also addressed the governor-general in the form of *ping*.

Early in his tenure of office, Elliot learned of a move on the part of some Chinese to legalize the opium trade. The idea originated with a group of scholars at the famous academy in Canton, the *Hsüeh-hai t'ang*, who were distressed with the ineffectiveness of the prohibitory law on the one hand and the drain of silver on the other. On May 17, 1836, Hsü Nai-chi, a subdirector of the Court of Sacrificial Worship and onetime associate of the academy, boldly proposed to the court that a legal tariff be imposed on opium imports as medicine, which should be purchased by barter in order to stop the silver outflow; and that domestic cultivation of opium be permitted to slacken the demand for foreign imports. While rather unconcerned with opium-smoking by common people, he urged that scholars, officials, and soldiers be strictly prohibited from smoking. Governor-general Teng, who had also been exposed to the views of the academy, supported the legalization of opium. Foreign traders on the whole were excited by this possibility, except for a few leading opium smugglers such as Jardine, who dryly admitted: "I do not think well of the plan as far as our interests are concerned." The prospect of legalization prompted foreign traders to intensify their opium imports.

Meanwhile, two powerful memorials against legalization reached the emperor. The first[13] argued that inability to suppress opium was no justification for lifting the ban. Laws were like dikes which should not be cast away simply because parts were broken. Indeed, prostitution, gambling, treason, and robbery existed in spite of prohibitory laws. The second memorial[14] contended that legalization would make it impossible to ban smoking among the populace. It recommended that severe punishment be meted to the hong merchants, opium dealers and brokers, operators of the "fast crabs," and military officers who accepted bribes from them. The memorialist identified nine foreign opium traders—Jardine, Innes, Dent, and others—and asked for their arrest. The emperor, though having no definite view of his own, was prompted by these two papers to reject the idea of legalizing opium. On September 19, 1836, he ordered Governor-general Teng to stamp out opium and to devise a long-range plan of control. The movement for legalization, which lasted from May to September 1836, came to an abrupt halt. Foreign traders, who had

13. By Chu Tsun, a subchancellor of the Grand Secretariat and vice-president of the Board of Rites.
14. By Hsü Ch'iu, a supervising censor of the Board of War.

anticipated the legalization, suddenly found themselves stuck with an oversupply of opium for which they had sent from India during the interval.

Governor-general Teng, who assumed office in February 1836, was a hard-working and incorruptible official. He allowed the nine foreign traders, mentioned in the second memorial, four months in which to leave Canton. Prosecuting Chinese opium dealers and addicts inexorably, he succeeded in destroying all "fast crabs" and all native smuggling networks outside Canton by the end of 1837. As a result of his suppression, the price of opium in Canton fell off sharply: in February 1838, a chest of Patna cost only $450, and Benares and Malwa, $400. Opium export from Bombay dropped from 24.2 million rupees in 1836-37 to 11.2 million in 1837-38. By December 1838, two thousand Chinese opium dealers, brokers, and smokers had been imprisoned, and executions of addicts took place daily. Jardine reported that the governor-general had been "seizing, trying, and strangling the poor devils without mercy . . . We have never seen so serious a persecution, or one so general." The *Canton Press Price Current* of January 1839 reported that "There is absolutely nothing doing, and we therefore withdraw our quotations."[15] Foreign smuggling boats disappeared by the end of 1838, and as the new year began Canton was virtually cleared of all opium traffic. The stagnation of the opium traffic produced a disastrous effect on the British traders, but they would not easily concede so lucrative a trade.

COMMISSIONER LIN AT CANTON

As Governor-general Teng carried out his vigorous campaign in Canton, a grand debate erupted in Peking as to the best way to stamp out the illicit traffic, which had such a deleterious effect on the morality and health of the people and caused such a drain of silver from China. In a powerful memorial of June 2, 1838, Huang Chüeh-tze, director of the Court of State Ceremonial, demanded capital punishment for all addicts who did not reform within a year. The suggestion was judged too severe by most officials, but it won the support of a small minority including Lin Tse-hsü, governor-general of Hu-Kwang. In a hortatory memorial, which has been admired by patriots for over a century, Lin warned that in a few decades, if opium was not suppressed, China would have no soldiers to fight the enemy and no funds to support an army. "When I think of

15. Hsin-pao Chang, 111.

this, I cannot but tremble!" said Lin. He proposed a concrete six-point program for the destruction of the smoking equipment, the reform of the smokers within a set time limit, and the punishment of native opium dealers, traders, and consumers. Only about foreign smugglers was he rather reticent. Lin was not a talker, but a man of action. In his own jurisdiction of Hupeh and Hunan, he successfully enforced the program, confiscating 5,500 pipes and 12,000 ounces of the drug. Impressed with his arguments and achievements, the emperor appointed him imperial commissioner (*ch'in-ch'ai ta-ch'en*) on December 31, 1838, charging him with suppression of the Canton opium traffic.

Commissioner Lin (1785-1850) of Hou-kuan, Fukien, was an exemplary product of Old China. A holder of the *chü-jen* degree in 1804 and the *chin-shih* in 1811, he served in various official capacities—among them that of Hanlin compiler, supervisor of the Yunnan provincial examination, circuit intendant and salt controller in Chekiang, judicial and financial commissioner in Kiangsu, governor of Kiangsu, and finally, in 1837, governor-general of Hu-Kwang. His uprightness and incorruptibility won him the honorable nickname of "Lin the Blue Sky" (*Lin Ch'ing-t'ien*). Appointed imperial commissioner at fifty-four, Lin was a man of wide experience and proven probity. Nineteen times the troubled emperor conferred with him on the opium problem. On January 8, 1839, Lin set out from Peking, reaching Canton on March 10.

Having established his headquarters at the Yüeh-hua Academy, Lin vowed that he would not quit until the opium problem had been solved. His policy was to deal severely and aggressively with Chinese opium dealers, brokers, and consumers, and to confront forbearingly, yet firmly, the foreign traders. He was aware of the prestige and power of Britain, and hoped to avoid a clash with her if possible; but opium had to be suppressed, even at the risk of war. His campaign against Chinese opium dealers was remarkably successful: by May 12, 1839, 1,600 violators of the prohibitory laws had been arrested and 42,741 pipes and 28,845 catties of opium confiscated. He tried and severely punished corrupt officers who connived with the smugglers.

Foreign smugglers posed a more difficult problem. Lin had sought to learn about the West by making translations of foreign newspapers in Macao and of foreign geographical works. He had also asked the American medical missionary, Dr. Peter Parker, to translate for him three paragraphs of Vattel's *Le Droit des gens* (International Law) dealing with the right of states to prohibit contraband and to declare war. Twice he wrote to Queen Victoria to seek her intercession. In his first letter, which was distributed to the Canton foreign community but which probably did not reach England, Lin urged the queen to stop poppy cultivation and manufacture. In his second and more well known letter, he stated in part:

> There appear among the crowd of barbarians both good persons and bad, unevenly. Consequently, there are those who smuggle opium to seduce the Chinese people and so cause the spread of the poison to all provinces. . . . The wealth of China is used to profit the barbarians . . . By what right do they in return use the poisonous drug to injure the Chinese people? . . . Let us ask, where is their conscience? I have heard that the smoking of opium is very strictly forbidden by your country . . . Why do you let it be passed on to the harm of other countries? Suppose there were people from another country who carried opium for sale to England and seduced your people into buying and smoking it; certainly your honorable ruler would deeply hate it and be bitterly aroused . . . Naturally you would not wish to give unto others what you yourself do not want . . . May you, O Queen, check your wicked and sift your vicious people before they come to China, in order to guarantee the peace of your nation, to show further the sincerity of your politeness and submissiveness.[16]

The letter was carried by Captain Warner of the *Thomas Coutts* in January 1840 to London, but the Foreign Office refused to recognize him (Warner).

Lin admonished foreign traders in Canton from the standpoints of natural law (*t'ien-li*), common sense, Chinese prohibitory regulations, and government policy. He announced that having come from the seacoast of Fukien himself, he was well aware of the barbarian's tricks and would not fall into their traps. On March 18, 1839, he ordered them to surrender all their opium in three days and sign a bond pledging not to engage in the illicit traffic in the future; violation of the bond would result in the death penalty and the confiscation of the drug. Lin offered a reward of five catties of tea for each chest of opium surrendered, but he never once mentioned monetary compensation; nor did he ever consider the British government's economic interest in the opium trade.

16. S. Y. Teng and John K. Fairbank, *China's Response to the West: A Documentary Survey, 1839-1923* (Cambridge, Mass., 1954), 24-27, with minor changes. The excerpts throughout this book from *China's Response to the West* are reprinted by permission of Harvard University Press.

When the foreigners ignored his deadline of March 21, Lin threatened to decapitate two hong security merchants. The foreign traders surrendered 1,036 chests of opium as a token, which was, of course, unsatisfactory to the commissioner. Howqua and the elder Mowqua, the two leading hong merchants, were made to wear chains, and the former's son and the latter's brother were thrown into prison. Lin then turned to the British trader Dent, who was said to have been involved in more than half of the opium imports and silver exports. Dent was asked to surrender himself to the prefect of Canton, but he refused to do so unless the commissioner guaranteed him safe return. Howqua pleaded with the foreign merchants, reminding them that he would surely lose his head if Dent continued to resist. On March 23, Elliot came from Macao to join the traders at the factory; and on the 24th Lin ordered the stoppage of trade, the withdrawal of Chinese compradores and servants, and the siege of the British factory. Three hundred and fifty foreigners were confined to the factory compounds, inconvenienced by the loss of cooks, porters, and servants but never suffering from the lack of important provisions. Frequently the hong merchants, linguists, and former servants smuggled in bread, fowls, mutton, eggs, oil, and sugar. The greatest discomforts were the monotony, the muggy weather, and the uncertainty of the future. The detention lasted for six weeks. To Elliot, it was a piratical act against British lives, liberty, and property; but to Lin it was a rightful enforcement of Chinese laws and a just punishment for depraved smugglers.

Lin let it be known that when the first quarter of the opium was surrendered, the compradores, servants, and cooks would be returned; when the second quarter was surrendered, the passage boats between Whampoa and Macao would be allowed to resume activity; when the third quarter was surrendered, the siege of the factory would be lifted; and when the last quarter was given up, trade would be resumed.

It must be noted that there had been a stagnation of the opium trade for several months before the detention. On March 22, 1839, Matheson recorded that "not a chest of opium had been sold in Canton for the last five months." Some fifty thousand chests lay waiting for outlet, and more were on their way from Bombay. It occurred to Elliot that to surrender the opium to Lin would relieve the stagnant trade and would be a good way to hold the Chinese responsible for the cost. On March 27, 1839, he issued a notice in the name of his government ordering all British traders to surrender their opium to him for deliverance to Lin:

Now I, the said Chief Superintendent . . . do hereby, in the name and on the behalf of Her Britannic Majesty's Government, enjoin and require all Her Majesty's subjects now present in Canton, forthwith to make a surrender to me, for the service of Her Said Majesty's Government, to be delivered over to the Government of China, of all the opium belonging to them or British opium under their control . . . and I . . . do now, in the most full and unreserved manner, hold myself responsible, for and on the behalf of Her Britannic Majesty's Government, to all and each of Her Majesty's subjects surrendering the said British-owned opium into my hands to be delivered over to the Chinese Government.[17]

With this proclamation the ownership of the opium changed hands: it was no longer the private property of the traders, but the public property of the British government. Elliot's decision was praised as "a large and statesmanlike measure" by Matheson, who also confessed that "the Chinese have fallen into the snare of rendering themselves directly liable to the British Crown. Had the Chinese declined receiving it . . . our position would have been far less favourable."[18] Elliot pledged to surrender 20,306 chests of opium to Lin, but he actually delivered 21,306 chests by May 18. Lin had originally planned to send the opium to Peking for inspection and destruction, but the complexity of transporting such a large amount caused the emperor to order him to destroy it locally. Three large trenches—150 feet long, 75 feet wide, and 7 feet deep—were dug for the purpose. Beginning June 3, in the presence of high officials and foreign spectators, opium balls were crushed to pieces and thrown into the trenches, where a profuse amount of salt and lime was scattered over two feet of water. The laborers stirred the opium in the mixture until it was completely dissolved and then flushed it to a nearby creek, which carried the last shred of debris to the ocean.[19] Lin, it seemed, had scored a complete moral and legal victory over opium, but the victory was chimerical, for Britain would never be content to rest her case there.

After their liberation from detention, Elliot and the entire British community left for Macao on May 24, 1839, rather than accept Lin's demand for the bond. Elliot lost no time in urging London to start "prompt and vigorous proceedings" against China, and the traders also jointly petitioned Palmerston to protect British interests and to take steps

17. Hsin-pao Chang, 264-65.
18. *Ibid.*, 166.
19. The destruction lasted twenty-three days, until June 25.

to fulfill Elliot's promise of reimbursement for the surrendered opium. A special deputation under Jardine was sent to London to promote these views. Meanwhile, nearly three hundred firms in London, Manchester, and Liverpool connected with the China trade started a campaign for action. Numerous pamphlets and stories were circulated condemning the Chinese insult to the British subjects. One pamphleteer said: "You take my opium; I take your island in return, we are therefore quits; and henceforth, if you please, let us live in friendly communion and good fellowship."[20] On October 18, 1839, without prior consultation with Parliament, Palmerston informed Elliot that the government had decided to send an expeditionary force to blockade Canton and the Pei-ho.

The tense situation in the Canton-Macao area was further strained by the killing of a Chinese villager[21] by a group of English seamen in Kowloon on July 12, 1839. Commissioner Lin demanded the surrender of the culprits, stating: "He who kills a man must pay the penalty with his life; whether he be a native or a foreigner, the statute is in this respect quite the same." Elliot refused to submit British subjects to Chinese law; he tried the six suspects himself aboard the *Fort William*, sentencing two of them to three months' imprisonment at hard labor in England and a fifteen-pound fine, three more to six months' imprisonment and a twenty-five-pound fine, and acquitting the last. But in fact, when the sailors returned to England they went unpunished, because the government ruled that Elliot had no authority to try them. Commissioner Lin, on his part, was irritated with Elliot's refusal to cooperate, and brought pressure to bear on the Portuguese authorities at Macao to expel the British. On August 26, 1839, all British subjects left for Hong Kong, a small barren island of some thirty square miles, about ninety miles from Canton. Commissioner Lin and Governor-general Teng then made a triumphant tour of Macao. Up to this point Lin had won at every stage of the conflict.

However, one issue remained unresolved: the signing of the bond. Elliot had persistently resisted it on the ground that the death penalty without a fair trial for the violators was uncivilized and contrary to the British concept of justice. In point of fact, the British had refused to submit to Chinese jurisdiction since 1784, and the Americans since 1821. While Elliot remained adamant, some British traders felt that he had no right to stop them from accepting the bond. Accordingly, the captains of the *Thomas Coutts* and the *Royal Saxon* signed it on their own, in

20. Hsin-pao Chang, 192.
21. Lin Wei-hsi.

defiance of Elliot's order. On November 3, 1839, when the *Royal Saxon* approached the Bogue in hopes of trading with the Chinese, Captain H. Smith of H.M.S. *Volage* fired a shot across her bow. In an attempt to protect the *Royal Saxon*, the Chinese navy under Admiral Kuan engaged the British ships at Ch'uan-pi. Of the twenty-nine Chinese war junks, one was blown to pieces immediately, three were sunk, and several more were seriously damaged. War had now broken out, although there was no formal declaration by the Chinese, but the Indian government did issue one on behalf of the British Crown on January 31, 1840.

The trade with the British was stopped "forever" on December 6, 1839, but certain venturesome British traders managed to continue business under the American flag. Many American firms had accepted the bond; Robert Forbes of Russell and Company declared that "I had not come to China for my health or pleasure, and . . . I shall remain at my post as long as I could sell a yard of goods or buy a pound of tea . . . We Yankees had no Queen to guarantee our losses."[22] It was not until June 1840, when the British reinforcement had arrived to renew the fighting, that the Americans left Canton for Macao.

THE OPIUM WAR

The British expeditionary force arrived under Real Admiral George Elliot. It consisted of sixteen warships mounting 540 guns, four armed steamers, twenty-seven transports, one troop ship, and 4,000 soldiers. For the British, the war was one of reprisal, a necessary action to defend their right to trade, to uphold their national honor, to correct the injustice inflicted upon the British officials and subjects in China, and to secure an open future. For the Chinese, the war was primarily a crusade against opium.

Admiral Elliot was appointed first commissioner, procurator, and plenipotentiary, while his cousin, Captain Elliot, assumed the second in command. Their instructions called for (1) satisfaction for the illegal detention of the British Superintendent of Trade and of British subjects generally; (2) the return of the surrendered opium or suitable compensation; (3) satisfaction for the affront and indignity heaped upon the British superintendent and subjects, and assurance of future security; (4) the cession of one or more islands; and (5) abolition of the monopolistic system of trade at Canton and repayment of the hong merchants' debts.

22. Hsin-pao Chang, 206.

Palmerston ordered the expedition to blockade all principal ports of China so as to impress the Chinese with British might; to demand compensation of military expenses; to occupy Chusan until the indemnity was fully paid; and to demand the reply of the Chinese government at the Pei-ho, although negotiations might be conducted elsewhere. Admiral Elliot was also instructed to deliver a letter from Palmerston to the Chinese officials at either Amoy, or Ningpo, or the Pei-ho, for transmission to the court.

The First Stage. The war itself can be divided into three stages. The first lasted from the arrival of Admiral Elliot in June 1840 to the conclusion of the Ch'uan-pi Convention in January 1841. Commissioner Lin, in anticipation of an attack on Canton, had gathered a "water force" of some sixty warjunks, fortified the batteries at the Bogue with more than two hundred newly purchased foreign guns, and blockaded the river with huge iron chains. The British, however, did not attack Canton; they merely blockaded it and sailed north. The two Elliots attempted to deliver Palmerston's letter at Amoy on July 2, but were fired upon in spite of the white flag, which the Chinese apparently did not comprehend. They proceeded north and occupied Tinghai on the Chusan Islands on July 5. Unable to deliver the letter at Ningpo on July 10, they blockaded it, too, and sailed further north to the Pei-ho on August 29. There the letter was received by the governor-general, Ch'i-shan (Kishen).

Up to now, the emperor had had complete trust in Lin and endorsed his undertakings with the encouraging remark: "I do not worry about your aggressive prowess, but I admonish you against timidity." After the fall of Chusan and the blockade of the ports from Ningpo to the mouth of the Yangtze River, provincial officials began to criticize Lin for provoking the British into action, and the Manchu grand secretary and grand councillor, Mu-chang-a, also disapproved of Lin's hard, coercive policy. The emperor's confidence in Lin faltered, and when the British advanced to the Pei-ho, near Tientsin, threatening directly the security of Peking, his faith in Lin collapsed. Blaming him for creating complications without solving the opium problem, the emperor scolded Lin sternly: "Externally you wanted to eliminate the [opium] trade, but it has not been cut off; internally, you wanted to arrest the outlaws [smugglers], but they have not been cleared away. You have produced nothing more than empty excuses. Not only have you really accomplished nothing, you have, on the contrary, created many troubles. When I think of this, how angry

I become! Let me see what explanation you have to make!" Lin sent a memorial saying that if China had used one-tenth of the customs revenue for making gunboats she would have no difficulty tackling the barbarian problem; to which the imperial reply was: "All nonsense." Since Palmerston's letter had complained, among other things, of Lin's injurious proceedings at Canton and demanded "from the emperor satisfaction and redress," the emperor took it to mean that he needed only to redress their grievances to reach a settlement. He authorized Ch'i-shan at Tientsin to receive the two Elliots and determine precisely what they wanted.

Ch'i-shan, a sly politician and a wily diplomat, knew well Peking's veiled anxieties over the British naval demonstration. As governor-general of the capital province of Chihli, he was responsible for safeguarding Peking; yet he was without means of defense. Chinese guns were obsolescent; those found at Shanhaikuan were left over from the Ming dynasty. In contrast, the British possessed powerful guns and speedy ships. With such inequality in weaponry and equipment, and with the disheartening news that the Yangtze and coast areas had all been blockaded, Ch'i-shan concluded not only that it was senseless to fight, but that it was essential to appease the barbarians. In view of the British complaint about Lin's mistreatment in Canton, Ch'i-shan, grasping at straws, came to believe that possibly the British had come north not to fight, but simply to plead a redress of grievances. In his mind the situation was not unlike a litigation between Captain Elliot and Commissioner Lin, awaiting adjudication by the emperor. On the basis of this diagnosis, Ch'i-shan treated Captain Elliot courteously, and, employing mollifying tactics and flattery, told him that the emperor, having learned of the British grievances, had dispatched a high official to Canton to investigate; and that it would be best for the British to return south, where the truth of the dispute could be ascertained and negotiations taken up. Encouraged by the prospects of negotiations and settlement, the two Elliots left the Pei-ho on September 15. Thus, without firing a gun or losing a soldier, Ch'i-shan rid North China of the enemy.[23] Impressed with his diplomacy, the emperor appointed him as imperial commissioner, while Lin was dismissed in disgrace and exiled to Ili, Sinkiang.

In the British hierarchy there was a change of command, too. Captain Elliot rose in power until he replaced Admiral Elliot as the first pleni-

23. T. F. Tsiang, "New Light on Chinese Diplomacy, 1836-49," *The Journal of Modern Histroy,* 3:4:578-91 (Dec. 1931); "Ch'i-shan yü Ya-p'ien chan-cheng" (Ch'i-shan and the Opium War), *Tsing-hua hsüeh-pao,* 6:3:1-26 (Oct. 1931).

potentiary on November 29, 1840, the latter said to have contracted a "sudden and severe illness." In his negotiation with Ch'i-shan at Canton during the latter part of December 1840, Captain Elliot demanded the cession of Hong Kong and an indemnity. Ch'i-shan realized that the situation was far more serious than a simple case of litigation between Eliot and Lin. Though conciliatory, he would not yield, for he knew the court would not approve the territorial cession. Captain Elliot then attacked the forts at Ch'uan-pi and threatened to take the Bogue. On January 20, 1841, he forced Ch'i-shan to agree to draft a "Ch'uan-pi Convention," which provided: (1) cession of Hong Kong, though the customs dues were still to be collected by the Chinese government; (2) an indemnity of $6 million; (3) direct, equal intercourse between the officials of the two countries; and (4) reopening of Canton to trade within ten days of the Chinese New Year, i.e., before February 1.

Ch'i-shan did not affix his seal to the convention but agreed to memorialize the throne for its approval. Meanwhile, he secured the British consent to evacuate Tinghai, return the forts near the Bogue, and limit trade to Canton. However, the British occupied Hong Kong even before the convention was ratified by the court. The emperor, so enraged by the terms of the convention, deposed Ch'i-shan and recalled him in chains to stand trial for his unauthorized cession of territory and agreement to pay an indemnity. According to the court, Ch'i-shan had been sent to Canton to investigate the situation caused by Lin's mismanagement and to correct the wrongs; he had no power to sign any agreement with foreigners. His punishment was confiscation of family property (estimated at £10 million) and death, which was later commuted to exile to the Amur in May 1842.

The British government was equally displeased with the terms of the convention. The indemnity was considered too small to cover the value of the surrendered opium; the evacuation of Tinghai was thought premature; and the cession of the sovereignty of Hong Kong was deemed incomplete. Palmerston informed the queen that Captain Elliot had not made full use of the military force at his disposal, and that he had accepted the "lowest" possible terms. On April 21, 1841, he administered a stern reprimand to Elliot: "You have disobeyed and neglected your instructions . . . Throughout the whole course of your proceedings, you seemed to have considered that my instructions were waste paper . . . and that you were at full liberty to deal with the interests of your country according to your own fancy. . . . You have agreed to evacuate the Island

16. View of Canton showing foreign factories
(lacquered and painted tray made for the American market *circa* 1825).

17. The house of a Chinese merchant near Canton.

18. The opium fleet at Lintin, with an opium boat, "fast dragon," in the foreground.

19. Howqua, a leading hong merchant (oil painting by George Chinnery R.H.A., 1852).

林文忠公燒燬鴉片

迨道光十九年林文忠公督同廣州至。洋商所藏之鴉片即查得二萬二百八十三箱盡燒之于海口。時中輸入之鴉片有泊舟黑湖退潮時。公乘月黑以援之復燃其八者。後有出奇兵以撲之者。船二十三艘于長沙灣。逐以此醸成交沙之進口日多。今則英國收政府已樂賫成。煙毒由今思昔有令人傳成為欣願除者。

20. Commissioner Lin superintending
the destruction of opium, 1839.

21. Chinese painting of the arrival of one of the early European steamboats and her passengers in Canton, *circa* 1840.

TARTAR AND ENGLISH SOLDIERS FIGHTING.

ENGLISH FORAGING PARTY.

CHINESE CARICATURES.

22. Chinese caricatures of British soldiers.

23. Sir Henry Pottinger.

24. Ch'i-ying, imperial commissioner and signer of China's first treaties with the West.

26. Lord Elgin.

25. Commissioner Yeh (*Illustrated London News*, 13 February 1858, from a painting by a Chinese artist).

27. Sir Frederick Bruce.

28. Kuei-liang.

29. The signing of the peace treaty at Tientsin on 26 June 1858.

30. Prince Kung.

immediately. . . . You have obtained the cession of Hong Kong, a barren island with hardly a house upon it; and even this cession as it is called, seems to me, from the condition with which it is clogged, not to be a cession of the sovereignty of the island, which could only be made by the signature of the Emperor, but to be a permission to us to make a settlement there, upon the same footing on which the Portuguese have an establishment at Macao."[24]

That Elliot dared to ignore his instructions may be explained by the fact that for three years he had not had any and was forced to act on his own in situations of great difficulty and much delicacy. So used was he to freedom of action that when he at last was given specific instructions, he did not realize that he had to follow them explicitly. Elliot defended his position by saying that the evacuation of Tinghai was made necessary by the high rates of sickness and death among soldiers from dysentery, fever, and diarrhea; that the resumption of trade, after the conclusion of the draft convention, released 20,000 tons of shipping that had been held up, including the shipment of 30 million pounds of tea, which should net the British customs £3 million; that the restoration of commerce would promote an atmosphere of peace and demonstrate British magnanimity. However, before his defense reached London, the cabinet had decided on April 30, 1841, to dismiss him, disavow the convention, and appoint Colonel Sir Henry Pottinger as the new plenipotentiary to China.

The Second Stage. The repudiation of the Ch'uan-pi Convention by both governments ushered in a new phase of the war. The emperor appointed his nephew, I-shan, as imperial commissioner and barbarian-suppressing general in command of a large force against the British. Seizing the initiative, Captain Elliot, still in command before the arrival of Pottinger, took the Bogue forts in late February 1841, destroyed the Chinese defenses, occupied all the strategic points in the Pearl River, and besieged the city of Canton, where large Chinese forces were trapped. The hong merchants and the prefect of Canton offered a "ransom" of $6 million to save the city from destruction. Elliot accepted it to free his troops for the northern expedition, as he believed that pressure should be put on the court directly and not dissipated on the fringes of the empire. A second truce was reached on May 27, 1841, on the following

24. George H. C. Wong, "The Ch'i-shan-Elliot Negotiations Concerning an Offshore Entrepot and a Re-Evaluation of the Abortive Chuenpi Convention," *Monumenta Serica*, 14:539-73 (1949-55).

terms: (1) payment of $6 million within one week to the British; (2) withdrawal of Chinese troops sixty miles outside of Canton within six days; (3) evacuation of the British troops from the Bogue; (4) exchange of prisoners of war; and (5) postponement of the question of the cession of Hong Kong. With the complete payment of the ransom, the British forces began to withdraw on May 31, 1841. At this point, a body of 10,000 irate Cantonese, who had been organized by local gentry, launched a sudden attack at San-yüan-li, causing surprise but no great damage to the retreating British.[25] Marxist historians have hailed this incident as the first sign of Chinese nationalism.

The Third Stage. The arrival of Sir Henry Pottinger in Macao and the departure of Captain Elliot for England in August 1841, marked the beginning of the third stage of the war. Pottinger had been instructed to bypass Canton and go north to reoccupy Tinghai; to seize the important places on the Yangtze River; and if necessary to push north to the Pei-ho to open negotiations, at which time he was to demand monetary compensation, extension of trading ports, security of British subjects in China, and outright cession of Hong Kong. These terms were to be included in a formal treaty, which was to be approved by the Chinese emperor before being sent to the queen.

Pottinger carried out his instructions meticulously. After leaving a few ships to guard Hong Kong, he moved north on August 21, 1841, with 10 ships and 4 steamers carrying 336 guns and 2,519 men. Amoy was occupied on August 26, Tinghai on October 1, and Ningpo on October 13. As the alarmed court mobilized more troops and militia from the provinces, Pottinger had also received reinforcements from India in the spring of 1842: 25 warships carrying 668 guns, 14 steamers carrying 56 guns, 9 hospital and surveying ships, and troops for a total strength of 10,000 men, besides artillery. Moving swiftly, the British occupied Woosung on June 16, 1842, Shanghai on June 19, and Chinkiang on July 21—the last an important communication center at the crux of the Grand Canal and the Yangtze River, from which grains were shipped to North China. Its loss caused great anxiety among the provincial officials, who now requested the emperor to permit peace negotiations. The futility of war was obvious; furthermore it was imperative that the Manchu dynasty not lose any more face before the Chinese, lest they be encouraged to revolt.

25. One British private was killed, one officer and fourteen men wounded. For details of this incident, see Wakeman, *Strangers at the Gate*, 11-21.

Ch'i-ying (Kiying), Tartar-General of Canton, was made imperial commissioner, and together with I-li-pu, the Deputy Lieutenant General of Chapu and former imperial commissioner, was ordered by the court to start peace negotiations. Pottinger, refusing to negotiate until Ch'i-ying produced his "full powers," poised his ships for an attack on Nanking on August 9. On the 17th the peace terms were accepted in principle by Ch'i-ying and I-li-pu, and after several more days of settling details and translating the text into Chinese, the formal Treaty of Nangking, consisting of thirteen articles, was signed on the *Cornwallis*, on August 29, 1842, the general tenor of which follows:

1. An indemnity of $21 million: $12 million for military expenses, $6 million for the destroyed opium, and $3 million for the repayment of the hong merchants' debts to British traders.
2. Abolition of the Co-hong monopolistic system of trade.
3. Opening of five ports to trade and residence of British consuls and merchants and their families: Canton, Amoy, Foochow, Ningpo, and Shanghai.
4. Cession of Hong Kong. (The Chinese text of the treaty euphemistically states that the emperor graciously grants a place of rest and storage to the British after their long voyage to China.)
5. Equality in official correspondence.
6. A fixed tariff, to be established shortly afterwards.

This treaty was imposed by the victor upon the vanquished at gunpoint, without the careful deliberation usually accompanying international agreements in Europe and America. A most ironic point was that opium, the immediate cause of the war, was not even mentioned—the question of its future status cautiously avoided by both sides. The emperor painfully approved the treaty on September 15, and Queen Victoria's ratification came on December 28, 1842.

A supplementary Treaty of the Bogue was signed on October 18, 1843, which fixed the import duty from 4 per cent to 13 per cent ad valorem, averaging 5 per cent, and the export duty from 1.5 per cent to 10.75 per cent.[26] It also allowed British consuls to try their own subjects (i.e., extraterritoriality); allowed British warships to anchor at the five ports to protect commerce and control sailors; and gave Britain the most-favored-nation treatment, whereby China would grant Britain whatever rights that might be conceded to other powers later.

26. Stanley F. Wright, *Hart and the Chinese Customs* (Belfast, 1950), 58.

Close on the heels of the British came the Americans and the French, requesting similar treaties. Needless to say, after their defeat in the Opium War the Chinese were anxious to avoid new conflicts. They reasoned that denial of these requests would drive the Americans and French to seek trade under British auspices, in which case the Chinese would have difficulty distinguishing them, since they all looked alike and spoke equally unintelligible languages. Added to this concern was the fear that the French and Americans would be grateful to the British for the privileges and not to the Chinese, who felt that American and French good will might in the future protect China from collusion among the three powers, and perhaps even obtain their aid against further foreign encroachments. Moreover, the struggle for profits among the foreigners might lead to conflict among themselves, which fitted well into the traditional Chinese policy of playing off the barbarians against one another (*i-i chih-i*). Since there was a limit to China's foreign trade potential, it mattered little whether the whole profit went to the British alone or was shared with the others. Granting the American and French demands would allow them to cut into British profit without injuring China. Because the British had confidently declared that they did "not desire to obtain for British subjects any exclusive privileges of trade which should not be equally extended to the subjects of any other Power," the Chinese saw no reason to deny France and America a share in the fruits of British labors. For all these reasons, China decided to comply with the American and French requests for treaties. On July 3, 1844, Caleb Cushing signed the Treaty of Wanghsia for the United States, and Théodore de Lagréné signed the Treaty of Whampoa for France on October 24, 1844. The American treaty specified the prohibition of the opium trade, extraterritoriality, the most-favored-nation treatment, the right to maintain churches and hospitals in the five ports, and treaty revision in twelve years. The French treaty stipulated in addition the free propagation of Catholicism.[27]

In these treaties three stipulations were particularly injurious to China —the fixed tariff, extraterritoriality, and the most-favored-nation clause. They were granted partly out of expediency and partly out of ignorance

27. T. F. Tsiang, "The Extension of Equal Commercial Privileges to Other Nations than the British after the Treaty of Nanking," *The Chinese Social and Political Science Review* (CSPSR), 15:3:422-44 (Oct. 1931); Thomas Kearny, "The Tsiang Document, Elipoo, Keying, Pottinger, and Kearny and the Most Favored Nation and Open Door Policy in China in 1842-1844, An American View," CSPSR, 16:1:75-104 (April, 1932).

of international law and the concept of national sovereignty. The fixed tariff of 5 per cent ad valorem, as suggested by the British, was readily accepted by the Chinese for the simple reason that it was higher than the existing imperial tariff, which averaged only 2 per cent to 4 per cent ad valorem, although the irregular fees had been high. Little did the Chinese realize that their assent to a fixed rate precluded a protective tariff in the future. Extraterritoriality was signed away under the expedient notion that the barbarians, who spoke different languages and had strange customs, should be allowed to govern themselves—to show Chinese magnanimity and to ease the task of governing them.[28] The most-favored-nation treatment was granted *pro forma* on the ground that the emperor looked upon men from afar with equal benevolence. The more practical considerations have been discussed in the preceding paragraph.

These British, American, and French treaties reinforced each other and formed the beginning of a treaty system, which was further enriched and enlarged by later agreements. Because they were not negotiated by nations treating each other as equals but were imposed on China after a war, and because they encroached upon China's sovereign rights, they have been dubbed "unequal treaties," which reduced her to semicolonial status. The Opium War introduced a century of humiliation for the Chinese people.

The outcome of the war was inevitable, considering the decay of the Ch'ing dynasty and the new power achieved by Britain after the Industrial Revolution. But in the conduct of the war, the emperor's vacillation between resistance and concession, war and peace; the erroneous assessment of London's commitment to overseas interests; and the lack of accurate information about the enemy—all these presaged defeat. Commissioner Lin was convinced that London would not support its traders over so vicious and infamous an issue as the opium trade. But he did not realize that without the illicit traffic the British could not conduct regular trade without incurring a tremendous deficit; nor did he know that the expansionist Victorian government was keen on defending its foreign interests. Some of the Chinese misconceptions of the enemy were appalling and ludicrous. Lin believed that the British could not live without tea and rhubarb, and that their soldiers' legs could not stretch because of the puttees. A censor suggested that any attack on their feet

28. There was the precedent of Arab traders at Zayton (Ch'üan-chou) and at Canton during medieval times, when they were governed by their own chieftains.

would be fatal, while Ch'i-ying reported that the barbarians could see but poorly at night!

In retrospect, it is apparent that opium was the immediate, but not the ultimate, cause of the war. Without it a conflict between China and the West would still have erupted as a result of their differing conceptions of international relations, trade, and jurisprudence. Far deeper than the opium question was the incompatibility of the Chinese claim to universal overlordship with the Western idea of national sovereignty; the conflict between the Chinese system of tributary relationships and the Western system of diplomatic intercourse; and the confrontation between self-sufficient, agrarian China and expansive, industrial Britain. Indeed, the Smithsonian idea of free trade and the Chinese contempt for trade could not coexist. The power generated from the Industrial Revolution and the idea of progress through change propelled the West into overseas expansion. There was no way to stop it. It was unfortunate that the Manchu court and the Chinese scholars and officials had absolutely no recognition of these facts, and consequently China's confrontation with the West was rendered extremely painful.

The Opium War touched off explosive matters with far-reaching consequences. Politically, the cession of Hong Kong gave Britain a foothold in China for further advancement; the opening of the five ports extended foreign, particularly British, influence to the entire Eastern coast of China; and the loss of the three national rights mentioned above relegated China to a semicolonial state. Militarily, permission for foreign gunboats to anchor at the five ports, a concession later extended to the other ports opened along the Yangtze River, enabled foreign warships to navigate freely and legally in Chinese inland waterways, exposing the interior of the country mercilessly to alien powers. Economically, the fixed customs rates deprived China of a protective tariff and allowed an overabundant influx of foreign goods, which reduced Chinese handicraft industries to penury, causing social unrest and rebellion. Socially, the continuation of the illicit traffic deepened the opium problem, and the growth of foreign trade in the five ports introduced a new class of business entrepreneurs, sometimes derogatorily called the "compradore" class, who came to wield an increasing influence upon society. Diplomatically, China entered into official contacts with the Western maritime powers and took the first step in her long journey to membership in the international society.

But the Opium War did not shock the Chinese people into realizing their backwardness. The fact that Commissioner Lin was dismissed before he had a chance to fight the enemy led many to believe that the defeat was an historical accident. They refused to acknowledge China's military inferiority and political retrogressiveness, and so allowed themselves to sleep another twenty years.

Only a few exceptionally alert men realized the need to learn about the West. Wei Yüan, an associate of Lin and an eminent scholar of the Modern Text School of classical learning, compiled the famous *Illustrated Gazetteer of the Maritime Countries* (*Hai-kuo t'u-chih*) in 1844, which was revised and enlarged in 1847 and 1852 into a hundred tomes (*chüan*). Another important work on world geography was compiled by the governor of Fukien, Hsü Chi-yü, in 1850, under the title, *A Brief Survey of the Maritime Circuit* (*Ying-huan chih-lüeh*). A humble beginning in Western studies was thus made, but greater efforts had to wait until more intense shocks stunned the Middle Kingdom.

FURTHER READING

Chang, Hsin-pao, *Commissioner Lin and the Opium War* (Cambridge, Mass., 1964).
Ch'i, Ssu-ho 齊思和, *et al.* (eds.), *Ya-p'ien chan-cheng* 鴉片戰爭 (The Opium War), (Shanghai, 1954), 6 vols.
Fairbank, J. K., "Chinese Diplomacy and the Treaty of Nanking," *Journal of Modern History*, 12:1:1-30 (March 1940).
———, "The Manchu Appeasement Policy of 1843," *Journal of the American Oriental Society*, 59:4:469-84 (Dec. 1939).
———, *Trade and Diplomacy on the China Coast* (Cambridge, Mass., 1953), 2 vols.
Fox, Grace, *British Admirals and Chinese Pirates, 1832-1869* (London, 1940).
Greenberg, Michael, *British Trade and the Opening of China, 1800-42* (Cambridge, 1951).
Grosse-Aschhoff, Angelus, *Negotiations between Ch'i-ying and Lagrené, 1844-1846* (New York, 1950).
Holt, Edgar, *The Opium Wars in China* (Chester Springs, Pa., 1964).
Kearny, Thomas, "The Tsiang Document, Elipoo, Keying, Pottinger and Kearny and the Most Favored Nation and Open Door Policy in China in 1842-1844, an American View," *The Chinese Social and Political Science Review*, 16:1:75-104 (April 1932).
Kuo, P. C., *A Critical Study of the First Anglo-Chinese War, with Documents* (Shanghai, 1935).
MacNair, H. F., *Modern Chinese History, Selected Readings* (Shanghai, 1913), chapters 3-5.
Morse, H. B., *The International Relations of the Chinese Empire* (London, 1910), I, chapters 6-12.

Owen, David E., *British Opium Policy in India and China* (New Haven, 1934).

Teng, Ssu-yü, *Chang Hsi and the Treaty of Nanking, 1842* (Chicago, 1944).

Tsiang, T. F., "New Light on Chinese Diplomacy, 1836-49," *The Journal of Modern History*, 3:4:578-91 (Dec. 1931).

————, "The Extension of Equal Commercial Privileges to Other Nations than the British after the Treaty of Nanking," *The Chinese Social and Political Science Review*, 15:3:422-44 (Oct. 1931).

————, "Difficulties of Reconstruction after the Treaty of Nanking," *The Chinese and Social and Political Science* Review, 16:2:319-27 (July 1932).

————, *Chung-kuo chin-tai shih ta-kang* 中國近代史大綱 (An outline of Chinese modern history), (Taipei, 1959), chapter 1.

————, "Ch'i-shan yü Ya-p'ien chan-cheng" 琦善與鴉片戰爭 (Ch'i-shan and the Opium War), *Tsing-hua hsüeh-pao*, 6:3:1-26 (Oct. 1931).

————, *Chin-tai Chung-kuo wai-chiao shih-tzu-liao chi-yao* 近代中國外交史資料輯要 (A collection of essential sources of modern Chinese diplomatic history), (Taipei, 1958), I, chapters 1-2.

Waley, Arthur, *The Opium War Through Chinese Eyes* (London, 1958).

Wong, George, H. C., "The Ch'i-shan-Elliot Negotiations Concerning an Off-shore Entrepôt and a Re-Evaluation of the Abortive Chuenpi Convention," *Monumenta Serica*, 14:539-73 (1949-55).

Wright, Stanley F., *Hart and the Chinese Customs* (Belfast, 1950), chapter 2.

9

The Second Treaty Settlement

In the postwar period, Ch'i-ying (Kiying, Keying), the signer of China's first treaties with the West, emerged as the most colorful, spirited, and successful figure in Chinese foreign relations. Having pacified the British and saved the dynasty from a disastrous barbarian onslaught, he and his senior colleague, I-li-pu, enjoyed the illustrious reputation of being the foremost experts on barbarian affairs. The court at Peking came to respect and rely upon them for management of the barbarians. On October 17, 1842, I-li-pu was made imperial commissioner and Tartar-general of Kwangtung, and Ch'i-ying was given the influential and lucrative post of governor-general of Liang-Kiang. That Ch'i-ying was kept at Nanking, rather than sent to Canton, indicated the need for a man of his experience to take charge of the opening of the ports, the development of trade regulations, and the general superintendence of Sino-Western relations in Kiangsu, Chekiang, and Fukien. His position was further enhanced upon the death of I-li-pu on March 4, 1843. The coveted title of imperial commissioner was conferred on him on April 6, and in this capacity he took over the general direction of Chinese foreign relations at Canton. Until his retirement in 1848, he was, in effect, China's "foreign minister."

CH'I-YING'S NEW DIPLOMACY

Desiring power and responsibility, Ch'i-ying actually had projected himself into the imperial commissionership. To the court he had maximized

British confidence in him as a negotiator, claiming that there were matters only he could settle with them. Indeed, Ch'i-ying had evolved a new approach to foreign affairs which proved quite effective at times: the policy of friendship and personal diplomacy. Every effort was made to impress the foreign representatives of his sincerity, trustworthiness, and cooperation. In June 1843, shortly after his appointment as imperial commissioner, he was taken at his own request in a British gunboat to Hong Kong, where he wined and dined and engaged in cordial social intercourse with the British. Meeting Pottinger again, he embraced him "with all the warmth and sincerity of an old friend and was even visibly affected by the strength of his emotion."[1] Ch'i-ying fulsomely praised the British gunboat and its captain, visited the admiral's flagship, participated in various banquets, sang operatic airs, played the "game of finger-guessing," drank to everybody's health, and showered affection on Pottinger. In his encounter with Western-style dining, he did well with the soup and fish but had difficulty handling the knife when cutting up the meat.[2]

Friendship with Pottinger. His policy of friendship and personal diplomacy, while it was applied to foreign representatives in general, found its highest expression in his dealings with Pottinger. Having discovered that the British chieftain had an annual salary of $10,000, Ch'i-ying surmised that he must be a man of considerable importance to his own country, one who enjoyed great discretionary power in China and one who could probably exercise great influence in the high councils when he returned home. The cultivation of friendship and confidence with such a man was not only expedient, but essential. Ch'i-ying seized every opportunity to develop an intimate relationship with him. When shown a portrait of Pottinger's family, Ch'i-ying admired his son and declared that he should like to adopt him, as he had no son of his own. He then proposed to exchange his wife's picture for Lady Pottinger's—a most unusual gesture for a Manchu, prompted probably by his recent discovery that foreigners esteemed women. Not wishing to offend, Pottinger yielded on both counts, and his son's name became "Frederick Keying Pottinger." Following the establishment of this family relationship, Ch'i-ying exchanged gifts with Pottinger, giving him a gold bracelet and receiving in return an English sword and a belt. Ch'i-ying went so far as to say that when he himself returned to Peking in three or four years, he would recom-

1. Fairbank, *Trade and Diplomacy*, I, 110.
2. *Ibid.*, I, 110, footnote *f*.

mend to the emperor that the famous Pottinger be invited back from England to receive the imperial favor of a double-eyed peacock feather! In their subsequent correspondence, the Manchu diplomat addressed the British chieftain as "my intimate friend." Excerpts from Ch'i-ying's farewell letter to Pottinger after the Treaty of the Bogue, October 8, 1843, give a glimpse of his personal diplomacy in action—the free use of hyperbole and the outpouring of solicitous sentiment into which was worked a tactful request that Pottinger mediate in China's struggle with other Western powers:

> We two have now been engaged in the same work for upward of a year . . . In speaking or transacting business, our hearts appear to be stamped with each other's impress, so that there is nothing which we may not consult about; in fine, it may be said of us, tho' our persons seem *two*, yet our hearts are absolutely as *one*.

> . . . the time of parting is at hand, and I know not in what year or in what spot, I may again have the pleasure of meeting you face to face, the thought of which is almost insupportable . . . I shall therefore take certain parting words . . .

> First—I beg to present you with a trifle at parting; it is however the choicest production of our Northern Region [i.e. ginseng] and will suffice to manifest the strength of our attachment to each other and afterwards, looking at this trifling present will be as looking upon him who gave it; when we have parted you will think of me, and that will be some small consolation.

> Secondly—The climate in these seas, now hot, now cold, is most variable; you are a single individual from whom many most important duties are required; you must therefore from the time of rising till going to rest, be attentive to your comfort, be more guarded in your diet and particularly careful in all that concerns you. This is most important. . . .

> Fourthly— . . . Also in the case of foreign nations: if they have any differences of opinion with us [or if their ideas of right and wrong jar with ours] I hope that you will act the part of peacemaker, and set the matter at rest, thus avoiding the evil of losing that while we are taking care of this . . . I do urgently enjoin this upon you. . . .

> Sixthly—If you should have a favor for any of the productions of our Northern Regions whether articles of food, or clothing, or any-

thing else, just send me a letter and let me know and they will be immediately sent to you; you must not look upon me as a stranger, or in any way different from yourself.[3]

The Memorial of 1844. Ch'i-ying's policy of appeasement, friendship, and personal diplomacy was designed to disarm foreigners' suspicion, to win their confidence and trust, and to subject them to a sort of psychological obligation to him. While it did reduce tension and friction here and there, it could not change the basic objectives of the foreigners. From Ch'i-ying's assumption of power in 1843 until his retirement in 1848, this approach was at its apogee, successfully maintaining relative peace and order in Chinese foreign relations. However, in the eyes of anti-foreign, conservative officials, such a policy was obsequiousness to and ingratiation with the former enemy. Such opposition constrained Ch'i-ying to justify his action to the court in a memorial in November 1844, in which he stated that to make the outlandish barbarians conform to the requirements of Chinese civilization and ceremonies was to seek trouble unnecessarily, for they did not understand and could not appreciate such niceties; rather, it was necessary to humor them with material favors and outward sincerity, so as to win their trust and avoid quarrels:

> Throughout this period of three years the barbarian situation has undergone deceptive changes in many respects and has not produced a unified development. The methods by which to conciliate the barbarians and get them under control similarly could not but shift about and change their form. Certainly we have to curb them by skillful methods. There are times when it is possible to have them follow our directions but not let them understand the reasons. Sometimes we expose everything so that they will not be suspicious, whereupon we can dissipate their rebellious restlessness. Sometimes we have given them receptions and entertainment, after which they have had a feeling of appreciation. And at still other times we have shown trust in them in a broad-minded way and deemed it unnecessary to go deeply into minute discussions with them, whereupon we have been able to get their help in the business at hand.
>
> This is because the barbarians are born and grow up outside the frontiers of China, so that there are many things in the institutional system of the Celestial Dynasty with which they are not fully acquainted. Moreover, they are constantly making arbitrary interpreta-

3. Fairbank, I, 111-12, footnote *d*.

tions of things, and it is difficult to enlighten them by means of reason . . .

Moreover, the barbarians commonly lay great stress on their women. Whenever they have a distinguished guest, the wife is certain to come out to meet him . . . Your slave [minister] was confounded and ill at ease, while they on the other hand were deeply honored and delighted. Thus in actual fact the customs of the various Western countries cannot be regulated according to the ceremonies of the Middle Kingdom. If we should abruptly rebuke them, it would be no way of shattering their stupidity and might give rise to their suspicion and dislike . . .

With this type of people from outside the bounds of civilization, who are blind and unawakened in styles of address and forms of ceremony, if we adhered to the proper forms in official documents and let them be weighed according to the status of superior and inferior, even though our tongues were dry and our throats parched [from urging them to follow our way], still they could not avoid closing their ears and acting as if deaf. Not only would there be no way to bring them to their senses, but also it would immediately cause friction. Truly it would be of no advantage in the essential business of subduing and conciliating them. To fight with them over empty names and get no substantial result would not be so good as to pass over these small matters and achieve our larger scheme.[4]

Ch'i-ying's methods worked well enough with Pottinger, who became rather proud of his own ability to make friends in China. Not being a merchant and therefore free from considerations of profit, Pottinger could take a more objective and sometimes even magnanimous attitude toward Sino-British relations. He saw the general tendency among foreigners to infringe upon Chinese rights in a way not tolerated elsewhere, and he declared to London that he would take "the most decided measures" to enforce the treaties on British subjects; he cautioned, moreover, that British officials in China should guard against the inclination to take advantage of the Chinese, lest the latter lose faith in British justice and moderation. The Foreign Office approved of this view and asked the Colonial Office, Admiralty, and India Board to instruct their servants in China accordingly. Thus, with Ch'i-ying's policy of friendship and Pottinger's sense of moderation, a period of relative harmony reigned over Sino-British relations.

4. Teng and Fairbank, *China's Response*, 38-40.

The situation changed considerably when Pottinger was replaced in the middle of 1844 by John Davis, an old Company man and the former second superintendent of trade under Lord Napier. With characteristic Anglo-Indian arrogance toward the natives of the East, Davis spoke disparagingly of the Chinese "inability to comprehend the observance of good faith on the part of the strongest." He found Ch'i-ying's diplomacy "tiresome" and "childish," and was generally so unresponsive that Ch'i-ying finally gave it up in 1846.[5]

The "Canton City Question." The most knotty issue in the postwar period was the question of the British right to enter the city of Canton. Of the five ports, all except Canton were opened on schedule to foreign trade, residence, and consulates: Shanghai in November and Ningpo in December, 1843, and Fuchow and Amoy in June 1844. The residents of Canton, however, steadfastly refused to admit the British into the city, allowing them to live only in the old factory area. They argued that although the treaty opened Canton, it did not specify that foreigners be allowed inside the city. Indeed, the treaty text did not spell out the point clearly, but none of the other four ports ever contested the British right to enter their walled cities. In fact, the foreigners at Shanghai, after having gained entry into the city, found the hygienic conditions and living quarters so undesirable that they voluntarily moved out of the city to found their own settlements. But in Canton the more they met resistance, the more the British insisted on their right of entry. The local populace would not yield; they considered the British entry an insult to their city. Hence the "Canton city question" became a point of disruptive contention.

Historically, Canton had a reputation for conflicts with foreigners: cases of massacre of the Arabs were known to exist in medieval times. More recently, during the Opium War, its people were subjected to British humiliation more than those of any of the other cities, and they were also the object of a "ransom" in 1841. In the postwar period, Canton suffered from losing part of the foreign trade to Shanghai, owing to the latter's proximity to the tea- and silk-producing areas. The volume of tea export from Canton declined from 69 million pounds in 1844 to 27 million in 1860; whereas that from Shanghai increased from 1.1 million pounds to 53 million in the corresponding period. Silk export from Canton dropped from 6,787 bales in 1845 to 1,200 in 1847; that from

5. Fairbank, *Trade and Diplomacy*, I, 269-70.

Shanghai increased from 6,433 bales to 21,176 in the same years.[6] The decline of the Canton trade adversely affected the livelihood of the local people, so they transferred their resentment to the British, the largest group of foreign traders. This popular discontent became a considerable force when organized by the gentry and armed with weapons originally supplied to the local militia by Commissioner Lin during the Opium War.

Ch'i-ying, as imperial commissioner and governor-general at Canton, was caught between the ever-increasing pressure of the British to enter the city and the stubborn resistance of the gentry and the people of Canton. He knew, if the local populace did not, China's treaty obligations; and in January 1846, he boldly proclaimed the opening of the city. In doing so he exposed himself to public condemnation; numerous placards and notices were circulated to attack his appeasement policy and ridicule his ingratiation with the enemy. The mob staged an attack on the Canton prefect, who was supposedly pro-British, and burned his yamen (office building), plunging the city into disorder and confusion. Faced with this outburst of public wrath, Ch'i-ying had to modify his order. Fortunately, the British government did not want an immediate clash over the "Canton city question." In April 1846, Davis and Ch'i-ying reached an agreement: the British would postpone their entry into the city in exchange for a Chinese promise of nonalienation of the Chusan Islands to any other power (to block the rumored French design).

Elated by the British concession, the Canton populace became bolder than ever. Incidents of stoning and insulting British excursionists occurred repeatedly. In April 1847, Davis retaliated with his "famous" raid of Canton; with 900 soldiers in three armed steamers and a brig, he captured the Bogue forts, spiked 827 cannon, and occupied the Canton factories. Ch'i-ying hurriedly arranged an agreement with him on April 6, promising British entry to the city at the end of two years, and punishment of those Chinese who had offended the British. Other items gave British traders and missionaries the right to build warehouses and churches.

By his concessions to the British, Ch'i-ying's public image was irreparably damaged. Sensing that the "Canton city question" would sooner or later precipitate a clash which he was unable to prevent, and knowing his inability to cope with the growing problem of piracy along the coast, Ch'i-ying schemed to get out of the fix before it became un-

6. Morse, I, 366.

controllable. He asked the court that he be recalled on grounds of old age and infirmity. The request was granted, and in March 1848, Ch'i-ying left for Peking. The post of imperial commissioner and governor-general went to a xenophobic official, Hsü Kuang-chin (*ca.* 1786-1858), while the governorship of Kwangtung went to another, Yeh Ming-ch'en (1807-59). The appointment of these two, following Ch'i-ying's recall, marked the re-emergence in the government of the antiforeign element, which had been in eclipse since the defeat. Hsü and Yeh formed a team at Canton, adopting an unyielding and arrogant attitude toward foreigners, and secretly promoting antiforeign sentiment among the populace and encouraging them to block the British entry. There were frequent incidents of attacks, insults, stonings, and even killing of the British. Sino-British relations deteriorated rapidly.

THE HARD LINE AT CANTON, 1848-56

The change of Chinese personnel at Canton was paralleled on the English side. Davis was replaced by Sir S. George Bonham (1803-63) as governor of Hong Kong, envoy-extraordinary and minister-plenipotentiary, and superintendent of trade in China. Son of an East India Company ship captain, Bonham rose high early in his career. While still in his twenties, he was appointed resident councillor of Singapore, and in 1837 became governor of the Incorporated Settlement of Prince of Wales Island, Singapore, and Malacca. With some knowledge of the Chinese language, customs, and habits, and with a reputation for "practical common sense," he was appointed by Palmerston as governor of Hong Kong in 1848.

His first interview with the new Imperial Commissioner Hsü took place on April 29, 1848. While satisfied with the ceremonial, Bonham found Hsü "somewhat taciturn." On June 7 he wrote to Hsü suggesting preliminary arrangements be made to give effect to the Ch'i-ying-Davis agreement permitting British entry into Canton in 1849. Hsü replied that in view of the strong local opposition, the "temporary arrangement [of 1847] was by no means the way to insure perpetual protection or to secure lasting tranquillity to both sides." Palmerston, while not willing to give up the right of entry, doubted the practical value of going into a hostile city, and suggested that the right might be restricted to the British plenipotentiary or the consul, escorted by Chinese officials, when making business visits to the governor-general. On December 30, 1848, he authorized Bonham, in effect, to evade the issue.

On April 1, 1849, the Chinese commissioner communicated to Bonham an imperial rescript stating that the emperor could not ignore the spontaneous and unanimous opinion of the people of Canton. When all attempts by Bonham to see the commissioner failed, he informed the Chinese authorities on April 9, by letter, that "the question at issue rests where it was, and must remain in abeyance." The Cantonese believed that the awesome magnitude of their public demonstrations, involving a mob and militia of some 100,000, had intimidated the British into relinquishing the demand. When the jubilant Hsü and Yeh reported to the court that Bonham had agreed that "hereafter there will be no further discussion of entering the city," the delighted monarch rewarded Hsü with the title of viscount and Yeh with that of baron, and commended the people of Canton for their patriotism. Palmerston's wrath was irrepressible. He instructed Bonham to send Peking a message in which he reminded the high officials of the "mistake which was committed by their predecessors in 1839," and warned that "the forbearance which the British government has hitherto displayed arises, not from a sense of weakness, but from the consciousness of superior strength. The British government well knows that, if occasion required it, a British military force would be able to destroy the town of Canton, not leaving one single house standing, and could thus inflict the most signal chastisement upon the people of that city." The court contemptuously dismissed the warning with the remark that such a contumacious and insulting letter did not deserve a reply, lest the barbarians be encouraged to further insolence. Bonham then personally delivered a formal protest on August 24, 1849, in which he recited the whole series of events connected with the "Canton city question" and warned that "whatever may happen in future between the two countries that may be disagreeable to China, the fault thereof will lie upon the Chinese government."[7]

In 1850 the recalcitrant Emperor Tao-kuang died and was succeeded by his twenty-year-old son, Emperor Hsien-feng, who followed an even more uncompromising foreign policy. Advocates of appeasement, such as Mu-chang-a and Ch'i-ying, were dismissed, demoted, or replaced by stridently antiforeign officials. A xenophobic official suggested to the emperor that the hero of the Opium War, Lin Tse-hsü, be summoned to serve in the capital as a warning to the British: "The management of

7. Morse, I, 395-98, 402.

the barbarian affairs at Canton were begun by Lin and concluded by Hsü; both were most feared and respected by the British." However, Lin had been in bad health since the summer of 1849, and died on November 22 of the following year en route to Kwangsi to accept the new post as acting governor and imperial commissioner. When Hsü was transferred in 1852 to fight the Taipings (see next chapter), Yeh, who was even more antiforeign, stubborn, and arrogant, filled his office. Openly contemptuous of aliens, he refused to answer their communications or to meet with them, announcing that high officials of the Celestial Empire ought not debase themselves by receiving foreigners, but should preserve the dignity of their state by avoiding them. The French minister was unable to arrange an interview with him for fifteen months.

The stiffening of the Chinese attitude, however, was not reciprocated by the British. The new Liberal government was committed to a course of moderation, which was further confirmed when Bonham, having been granted a leave of absence, was replaced by John Bowring (1792-1872) in 1852. Bowring, a man of great learning and stature, had been a strong advocate of free trade, an editor of the *Westminster Review*, a private secretary of Jeremy Bentham, and an intimate friend of George Villiers, later Lord Clarendon, the foreign secretary. Toward the end of his long career Bowring found himself financially straitened and applied for the post of consul in Canton. He won the appointment in 1849 and subsequently became fascinated with Chinese civilization as he saw it at Canton. When he replaced Bonham as superintendent and plenipotentiary in 1852, he was cautioned by Lord Granville not to begin irritating discussions with the Chinese authorities and not to use force without prior approval from home. When his request for an interview with Yeh ran into a stone wall—not unexpectedly—London instructed him "not to raise any question as to the admission of British subjects into the city of Canton, and not to attempt yourself to enter it."[8]

In addition to the "Canton city question," a number of other issues also strained Sino-Western relations: the ever-present foreign desire to extend trade beyond the five ports to all parts of China, the demand for resident ministers in Peking to bypass the stubborn Canton authorities, and the drive to reduce customs dues as a result of the general decline of commodity prices in the postwar period. These issues converged to generate a strong impetus among the foreigners for a treaty revision. According to the American and French treaties of 1844, a revision might

8. Fairbank, *Trade and Diplomacy*, I, 278; Morse, I, 403.

take place in twelve years, i.e. 1856. Although the Treaty of Nanking of 1842 made no provision for treaty revision, the British claimed that their most-favored-nation treatment entitled them to similar revision in twelve years, i.e. 1854. Out of common interest the American and French ministers supported the British claim, and in 1854 the three ministers proposed discussion with Yeh about it. Yeh replied point-blank that there was no need for discussion. After having failed to move Yeh at Canton or to open negotiations at Shanghai, the British and American represent-atives went north in October 1854, to demand satisfaction. At Taku they were met, not by the governor-general of Chihli, who was ordered by the court not to personally receive the barbarians, but by a lesser figure, Ch'ung-lun, the Ch'ang-lu Salt Controller. The two ministers demanded tariff revision, establishment of legations in Peking, opening of Tientsin, the right to purchase land in the interior, legalization of opium import, and abolition of the inland transit dues (*likin*). The court rejected these demands as unreasonable and urged the ministers to return to Canton.

In 1856, the ministers of the three powers once again raised the ques-tion of treaty revision. The court intimated that minor changes of a reasonable nature might be allowed, but no major items could be con-sidered, lest the Treaty of Eternal Peace (Treaty of Nanking) should lose its meaning. However, Yeh at Canton persistently refused to nego-tiate, even on minor issues, insisting that if he gave an inch the foreign-ers would want a foot. The American commissioner, Peter Parker, un-willing to concede, made a solo attempt to reach Peking. At Shanghai the Chinese frustrated his efforts to continue further. Under these con-ditions, foreign, and particularly British, patience approached exhaustion. Even the peaceful-minded Bowring was compelled to inform London that extension and improvement of British relations with China would re-quire ships of war.

THE ARROW WAR

The occasion that provoked Britain into venting her wrath was the *Arrow* incident of 1856. The *Arrow* was a lorcha, a hybrid vessel with a Euro-pean hull and Chinese sails; it was owned by a Chinese resident[9] of Hong Kong and registered with the British authorities of that Crown Colony for protection from coastal piracy, which the Chinese govern-ment was unable to suppress. On October 8, 1856, while lying off the

9. Fong Ah-ming.

city of Canton with British flags flying, between eight and eight-thirty in the morning, the *Arrow* was boarded by four Chinese officers and sixty soldiers for the alleged purpose of searching out one notorious pirate who was said to be aboard. They arrested twelve Chinese crew members, and in the turmoil the British flag was hauled down. The British consul at Canton, Harry Parkes, under instructions from Bowring, protested strongly on October 12 against the insult to the flag and the arrest of the crew without a warrant from the British consul. He demanded future respect to the flag, release of all twelve crewmen, and a written apology from the governor-general within forty-eight hours. Yeh caustically denied there was any flag flying at the time and questioned the right of the consul to intervene in a case which involved the arrest of Chinese nationals by Chinese police on a Chinese-owned vessel in a Chinese harbor. He might have added, but he did not know then, that the registration of the *Arrow* had lapsed at the time of the incident. Bowring was himself of the opinion that "after the expiry of the license, [British] protection could not be legally granted." However, an ordinance of Hong Kong provided that if the expiry occurred while the vessel was at sea, the registration remained valid until its return to Hong Kong. On the basis of this ordinance, Parkes insisted that the *Arrow*, while at Canton and before returning to Hong Kong, was still entitled to British protection, and that any British ship in Chinese waters was British soil, with full extraterritorial privileges. Yeh's reply was deemed unsatisfactory, and Parkes ordered the seizure of a Chinese war junk to enforce redress. After prolonged bickering, Yeh returned the twelve crewmen on October 22, but he emphatically refused to apologize. On October 23, British gunboats under Admiral Seymour moved in to bombard the city of Canton. Except for Sunday, October 26, which was declared a day of rest, the shelling continued with humiliating regularity: shots were fired at ten-minute intervals on Yeh's yamen. On the 28th, Yeh ordered an all-out attack on the barbarians; the British responded by marching through his yamen on the 29th. The aroused people of Canton, utterly powerless before the British armed forces, vented their wrath by burning the foreign factories on December 14 and 15.

In London, Her Majesty's Loyal Opposition severely criticized Parkes and Bowring for dragging Britain into a foreign war. Gladstone grandiloquently declared in Parliament on March 3, 1857: "You have turned a consul into a diplomatist, and that metamorphosed counsul is forsooth to be at liberty to direct the whole might of England against the lives of a defenceless people."[10] In the House of Commons the Opposition succeeded in unseating the government by a vote of 263 to 247. Palmerston called an election, in which he stressed the importance of upholding British honor and overseas interests. He was returned with a majority of 85 in Parliament. His China policy having been vindicated, Palmerston sent Lord Elgin (1811-63), who had been governor-general of Canada in 1846, as plenipotentiary and the leader of an expedition to China.

The French government, capitalizing on the murder of a missionary, Abbé Auguste Chapdelaine, in February 1856, in Kwangsi province (which was not yet opened to the West), decided on a joint expedition with Britain by dispatching a task force under the command of Baron Gros, a veteran diplomat of thirty years' experience. The American and Russian governments abstained from joining this Anglo-French venture, but they sent representatives to participate in a "peaceful demonstration."

Lord Elgin's instructions called for (1) reparations of injuries to British subjects; (2) execution of treaty stipulations at Canton and other ports; (3) compensation to British subjects for losses sustained in the recent disturbances; (4) diplomatic representation at Peking, or at least the right to an occasional visit by a British minister, as well as the right of the British plenipotentiary to direct communication with high officials at Peking; and (5) revision of the treaties with a view to extending trade to the cities on the great rivers. Lord Clarendon, the foreign secretary, emphasized to Elgin that his chief mission was to liberate the trade from existing restrictions, and—since it was uncertain whether Yeh's conduct reflected his own xenophobia or orders from Peking—the matter of direct contact with Peking through diplomatic representation was also of utmost importance. Baron Gros' instructions required much the same things—including extension of trade, freedom for religious propagation, and diplomatic representation at Peking.

The plenipotentiary from the United States was William B. Reed, a politician from Philadelphia who had held state offices and taught American history at the University of Pennsylvania. He was told to cooperate with the French and British peacefully, but to make it clear to the Chinese that the United States had no territorial or political designs on China. His directives called for diplomatic residence in Peking, new ports, reduction of the domestic tariff, religious freedom, suppression of piracy, and extension of treaty benefits to all civilized nations. The other neutral state, Russia, sent Admiral Putiatin. Publicly he was

10. *Hansard Parliamentary Debate*, 144:1802 (1857).

to dissociate himself, before the Chinese, from the Anglo-French interventionists and emphasize the age-old friendship between Russia and China. But secretly he was to play the role of mediator between the Manchu empire and the European powers, so as to prevent the fall of the dynasty and the shifting of the political gravity from North China to South China—a shift which, if materialized, would benefit the British.

Lord Elgin arrived in Hong Kong on July 2, 1857, only to discover that the Sepoy Mutiny required diversion of his troops to India. Completing his Indian mission, he returned to Hong Kong in September and received authorization from Lord Clarendon to take Canton by force. Some delay in working out details of joint operations with the French ensued, but by early December 1857, the allied forces were ready for action. On December 12, Elgin and Gros demanded that Yeh peremptorily agree to direct negotiation and payment of an indemnity. Yeh was defiant. When the Allied ultimatum of the 24th went unanswered, the Anglo-French forces stormed the city on December 28, captured Yeh, and put him aboard H.M.S. *Inflexible.* Soon the British realized that this move rendered the warship useless for combat; they shipped him to Calcutta, where he died a year later. For governance of the city an Allied commission was established, with Harry Parkes as presiding officer, while the daily routines were left to the Manchu governor, Po-kuei. This puppet regime, which lasted for three years until the final treaty settlement in 1860, was probably the first of its kind in modern history.

The ease with which the Allies took Canton indicated that Yeh had made no special effort to strengthen its defenses. Story has it that he, a believer in oracular divination, consulted the planchette (*fu-chi,* a sort of ouija board) and was informed that the British would leave in fifteen days. Consequently he made no preparations for long-term resistance. After his fall a jingle appeared satirizing his superstitious approach to affairs of state: "He would not make war, would not make peace, would not make a defense, would not die, would not surrender, and would not flee." Actually Yeh was not the fool people believed. A calculating politician, Yeh's obduracy was the cover for his inward insecurity. He knew that militarily China could not withstand Britain. If he used force and brought on a disastrous war, he would end up in exile like Commissioner Lin; contrarily, if he followed a policy of appeasement, he might incur imperial displeasure, public condemnation, disgrace, and even banishment, such as befell Ch'i-shan and Ch'i-ying. Caught in a dilemma, he straddled the gulf of indecision, while erecting a façade of indifference, arrogance, and haughty contempt for the foreigners. Secretly he hoped the profit-minded barbarians would not prolong the disturbance at the expense of their trade. The price of his superstition and misjudgment was captivity, exile, and death in an alien land.[11]

The Tientsin Negotiations. Having settled the Canton question, Elgin and Gros proceeded north to demand satisfaction from the court. They arrived at the Gulf of Pechili off Tientsin in mid-April 1858, and after some preliminary encounters with the governor-general of Chihli, who was found unequipped with the "full powers" to negotiate, they took the Taku Forts and Tientsin. Shocked by the rapid enemy advance, the court at Peking hurriedly sent Kuei-liang, a 73-year-old grand secretary, and Hua-sha-na, a 52-year-old president of the Board of Civil Office, duly provided with the "full powers," to meet with Elgin and Gros. They arrived in Tientsin on June 3, and were shortly afterwards joined by a third negotiator, none other than the famous Ch'i-ying.

As may be recalled, Ch-i-ying returned to Peking in 1848, and was demoted to a fifth-grade mandarin in disgrace in 1850, upon the ascension to the throne of Emperor Hsien-feng. He lived in obscurity until 1858, when the resurgence of the insoluble barbarian trouble recalled to people's minds his clever diplomacy. The emperor summoned him from disgrace and sent him to Tientsin to manage the barbarians. Ch'i-ying, much deteriorated physically during his years of eclipse, and half blind, arrived in Tientsin on June 9. His presence caused concern among the Allies who rightly suspected a ruse, knowing, as Elgin did from the captured documents in Yeh's yamen, how Ch'i-ying boasted to the court of his skills in managing the unfathomable barbarians. Intuitively Elgin discerned that Ch'i-ying had come with the knavish intention of reviving the old stratagem of "caressing" and "restraining" the barbarians; therefore he must not be allowed in Tientsin. Two young assistants, Horatio Lay and Thomas Wade, were sent by Elgin to see him. When Ch'i-ying began playing his old game of gentle restraint, personal charm, and endless praises for the two Englishmen, Lay dramatically produced a document—Ch'i-ying's famous memorial of 1844—and made Hua-sha-na read it aloud. The situation was embarrassing in the extreme, and Ch-i-ying could only respond in confusion with tears of shame, while the English-

11. Yen-yü Huang, "Viceroy Yeh Ming-ch'en and the Canton Episode (1856-1861)," *Harvard Journal of Asiatic Studies*, 6:1:37-127 (March 1941).

men left laughing elatedly. Finding himself unacceptable to the British, Ch'i-ying left the negotiations without imperial permission. For his unauthorized leave, he was taken to Peking in chains, given a trial, and sentenced to death by suicide. So ended the life of China's most colorful diplomat in the mid-19th century: one who strutted into the limelight in the 1840's because of his canny ability to manage the foreigners, then lost his life when this ability no longer charmed his wary adversaries.

The Treaty of Tientsin, 1858. The negotiations at Tientsin focused on four major issues: a resident minister in Peking, the opening of new ports along the Yangtze River, foreign travel in interior China, and the indemnity. Of the four, the resident minister issue was central in Elgin's thinking, for he had come to believe that pacific relations with China were impossible without abolishing the imperial commissioner at Canton as China's "foreign minister" and forcing the court at Peking to take up foreign affairs itself so as to spare the local officials the dilemma of reporting unwelcome truths. His assistant, Horatio Lay, who carried on the major burden of negotiations, was even more emphatic about this point, insisting that the Canton system was the cause of foreigners' being "tossed to and fro like a shuttle between Imperial and Provincial authorities" and that without the right of diplomatic representation at Peking the new treaty "would not be worth the paper it was written upon."[12] The Chinese negotiators argued that diplomatic residence was incompatible with the established institutions of China (*t'i-chih*), whereupon Lay announced bluntly: "The provision will be for your good as well as ours, as you will surely see. The medicine may be unpleasant but the aftereffects will be grand. The more stern my attitude, the greater the service I render to you." He kept threatening, bullying, and insulting the Chinese negotiators. Totally helpless before Lay's truculence, Kueiliang pleaded for commiseration, saying that his acceptance of the term would cost him his head at the age of seventy-three. Lord Elgin could not help having some pity on the Manchu grandee, but in the end resolved not to relax his stand. "Being in the vicinity of Peking with an armed force," declared Elgin, "I might so demean myself as to make the Emperor think that he was under an obligation to his Plenipotentiaries for having made peace with me even on terms objected to."[13] On June

12. Horatio N. Lay, *Our Interests in China* (London, 1864), 49; and *Note on the Opium Question* (London, 1893), 12.
13. Hsü, *China's Entrance*, 52-54.

11, 1858, Lay warned that unless the term was accepted that day there would be a march on Peking. Kuei-liang had no alternative but to accede to British diplomatic representation at Peking. His last-minute tactics were to reach a settlement by whatever means, get the enemies out of North China, and then devise means to retrieve the lost rights.

Kuei-liang had made the concession without the prior approval of the court. The emperor, who viewed diplomatic representation as the end of the tributary system and a denial of China's universal overlordship, remained violently opposed to it. It taxed all the skills, courage, and manipulation of a deft and experienced politician such as Kuei-liang to convince him that there was no escape from the labyrinth. To the troubled ruler he divulged his secret tactics: "At present the peace treaties with the two nations of England and France should not be taken as true certificates and real contracts, but just a few pieces of paper by which the [enemy] warships could be made to withdraw temporarily from the harbor. In the future if the renouncement of the treaties and friendship is desired, your Highness needs only to charge your slaves [servants] with the crime of mismanagement: [the treaties] will immediately become waste paper." On another occasion he drolly told the throne that the barbarian envoys, once established in Peking, might not want to stay: "Barbarians dread most to spend money. Let them pay their own expenses. Furthermore, they fear wind and dust. With no advantages from residence [in Peking], they inevitably will leave on their own."[14]

On June 26, 1858, Frederick Bruce, Elgin's brother, warned that if the treaty were not signed by night, it would have to be signed in Peking itself. With a "knife" at their throats, Kuei-liang and Hua-sha-na concluded the Treaty of Tientsin with Britain that day, and with France a day later. The Treaties of Tientsin with Russia and the United States had been concluded earlier, on June 13 and 18 respectively. The French, Russian, and American treaties specified occasional visits of their diplomats to Peking, rather than the permanent-residence stipulation contained in the British treaty. But because of the most-favored-nation treatment, they equally shared the fruits of the British labors. Other important items in the Treaties of Tientsin included (1) opening of ten new ports;[15] (2) foreign travel in all parts of China under passport issued by the consul and countersigned by Chinese authorities, but no passport

14. Hsü, China's Entrance, 67-68.
15. Nanking, Newchwang, Tengchow, Hankow, Kiukiang, Chinkiang, Taiwanfu, Tamsui, Swatow, and Kiungchow.

required for travel within 100 *li* (33 miles) of the ports; (3) inland transit dues (*likin*) for foreign imports not to exceed 2.5 per cent ad valorem; (4) indemnity of 4 million taels for Britain and 2 million taels for France; and (5) freedom of movement in all China for missionaries, Catholic and Protestant alike.

After the conclusion of the treaties, Frederick Bruce returned home as courier of the treaty for the queen's ratification. The exchange of the ratifications was to take place in China a year from the date of signing. The Allied troops withdrew from North China, and Lord Elgin sailed for Japan to negotiate a treaty. But he promised to return to Shanghai in a few months for the tariff conference, as stipulated in Article 26 of the Treaty of Tientsin.

The Shanghai Tariff Conference. During Elgin's absence, the emperor devised a secret plan by which he would offer to exempt the British from all customs dues in exchange for the abrogation of the Treaty of Tientsin, or at least its four most objectionable items: diplomatic representation, trade along the Yangtze, inland travel, and indemnity. One reason for the emperor's resistance to diplomatic residence was his ridiculous apprehension that the barbarian envoys would construct tall buildings from which they could spy on the activities of the palace through binoculars! He instructed Kuei-liang and Ho Kuei-ch'ing (1816-62), governor-general at Nanking, to propose the plan to Lord Elgin at the forthcoming Shanghai Tariff Conference. Shocked by this impractical plan, they vigorously opposed it, arguing that foreign traders and foreign officials were two distinctly separate entities; exemption of customs dues would win the gratitude of the former, but not necessarily of the latter, who would still insist on complete execution of the treaty. Artfully they pleaded that the barbarians, who paid no tribute, should pay taxes as a kind of offering, which could then be used to defray the indemnity costs. Furthermore, if tax exemption were allowed foreign traders but not Chinese merchants, the former would have an unfair advantage, driving the latter into bankruptcy. Because of their remonstration, the emperor finally relinquished his secret strategy.[16]

The Shanghai Tariff Conference of October 1858 was conducted in a totally different atmosphere from the Tientsin negotiations four months earlier. Elgin was in a good mood, having returned from a triumphant

16. Hsü, *China's Entrance*, 71-75; T. F. Tsiang, "The Secret Plan of 1858," *CSPSR*, 15:2:291-99 (July 1931).

mission to Japan. There was no Lay bullying nor Bruce threatening a march on Peking. Because Shanghai was more than 800 miles removed from the capital, there was no sense of the urgency from foreign threat, either. Under these relaxed conditions, Kuei-liang found a chance to display his diplomatic talents. By blending frank persuasion and earnest pleading, he succeeded in committing Elgin to a gentleman's agreement that, if the future British envoy bearing the ratification of the Treaty of Tientsin were properly received at Peking, Elgin would see that he resided in a place other than Peking and that his visits to the capital would be periodic business trips only.

As regards the new tariff, the principle of 5 per cent ad valorem for both imports and exports was reaffirmed, except for opium, tea, and silk. The negotiations legalized opium importation at 30 taels per picul, which was about 7 per cent to 8 per cent of the average value. The existing tariff on tea, 2.5 taels per picul, which was about 15 per cent to 20 per cent ad valorem, was retained, as it represented only 1.5 pence per pound, in contrast to the much higher import duty of 1 shilling, 5 pence per pound in England. The agreement also maintained the old tariff of 10 taels per picul of silk, roughly below 5 per cent of the value.

THE SECOND SETTLEMENT

The Taku Repulse. Frederick Bruce was appointed British Envoy Extraordinary and Minister Plenipotentiary to China on March 1, 1859. He was instructed to exchange the ratifications at Peking, but to make his residence at Shanghai. On arrival in China in May 1859, Bruce found the Chinese trying to oblige him to exchange the ratifications at Shanghai. Irritated by this stratagem, he declared that his visit to Peking was "a matter of right, not of favor." With ships and troops he charged to the north, reaching the Pei-ho on June 18. Having now resigned themselves to his journey to Peking, the Chinese asked him to take the back route via Pei-t'ang, north of Taku, but Bruce insisted that only the main route from Tientsin befitted his honor. The Chinese warned that the river leading to Tientsin had been blockaded with iron spikes, chains, and solid rafts, and that the forts on the two shores would permit no passage. The obstructions in the river were clearly visible, but Bruce could hardly take the Chinese warning too seriously. He ordered Admiral Hope to clear the blockade so as to open a way for him to proceed to Tientsin. On June 25, 1859, some 600 marines and an engineer company were sent

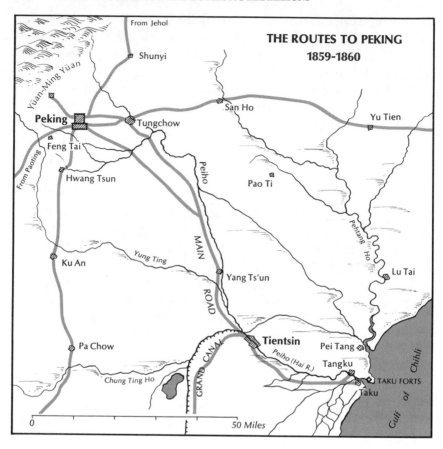

**THE ROUTES TO PEKING
1859-1860**

to remove the obstructions. Because of low tide and the soft deep mud, they were stuck and could not land. Suddenly the Chinese forts on the two shores opened fire with surprising accuracy, inflicting heavy losses on the British: 434 casualties, four ships sunk and two badly damaged, and Admiral Hope himself severely wounded. Commodore Tattnall of the United States fleet, a neutral observer of the scene, went to their aid in the belief that "blood is thicker than water." The Chinese suffered only nominal losses. The Taku repulse dealt a severe blow to British prestige and lent encouragement to antiforeign elements in China.

The British and French ministers retreated to Shanghai; but the American minister, John E. Ward, who had replaced William B. Reed, decided to accept the Chinese-assigned route to Peking. His party of twenty Americans and ten Chinese were conveyed in carts to Pei-t'ang, on July

20, 1859, and were then transferred to commodious boats which took them to Tungchow, whence they continued the journey by cart again, reaching Peking on July 27. The springless cart did not make for comfortable travel over stony roads, but the Americans were allowed the relief of riding horses from time to time. At Peking they were lodged in large, ostentatious houses, and their wants were provided for with "imperial munificence." They were, however, denied freedom of movement about the city, nor could they meet with the Russian ambassador, Nikolai Ignatiev, who had already established himself there. An audience with the emperor was arranged, but because of Ward's refusal to kowtow—he would kneel only to God and women—it did not materialize. President Buchanan's letter to the emperor was delivered to Kuei-liang for conveyance to the throne, and the exchange of the ratifications of the Treaty of Tientsin took place later at Pei t'ang with the governor-general of Chihli.[17] On the whole the Chinese reception was "courteous rather than cordial or open." Ward himself said that he was treated with "high consideration and respect, with unceasing attention and courtesy" throughout the journey, and the American government also pronounced itself satisfied with the treatment. However, the British insisted that the American reception in Peking was not honorable.[18]

Bruce came under severe criticism in England for having exhibited "too much precipitancy" in his use of force. Foreign Secretary Lord Russell conceded that the Treaty of Tientsin did not specify the route to Peking for the exchange of the ratifications, and according to normal international usage, the inland rivers were not open to foreign warships in time of peace. On November 10, 1859, a reprimand was administered to Bruce: "Although the denial of a passage to the capital by the usual and most convenient route would have been evidence of an unfriendly disposition, yet it was a matter upon which you might have remonstrated and negotiated, without having recourse to force to clear the passage." Bruce acknowledged his poor judgment, admitting that he had no right to go to Peking under the old treaty, and, though the new treaty did give him the right, it was not yet operative.[19]

The Conventions of Peking. In spite of British recognition of Bruce's tactical blunders, the Crown determined to enforce ratification at Peking.

17. Heng-fu.
18. S. W. Williams, "Narrative of the American Embassy to Peking," *Journal of the North-China Branch of the Royal Asiatic Society*, 3:315-49 (Dec. 1859).
19. Hsü, *China's Entrance*, 95.

Its confidence in Bruce having been shaken, London decided to commit Lord Elgin to a second China mission, which he reluctantly accepted. His spirit was further dampened by a shipwreck at the Point de Galle en route. Rescue operations recovered some cases of champagne but not his credentials and decorations, which had to be sent for from London again. His expeditionary force consisted of 41 warships, 143 transports, and some 11,000 soldiers under the command of General Sir Hope Grant, Elgin's brother-in-law, in conjunction with 6,700 French troops under General de Montaubon.

The Allied forces skirted South China and pushed north to attack Pei-t'ang and the Pei-ho in August 1860, threatening once again the security of Peking. Kuei-liang was rushed to Tientsin, but he was unable to save the situation. Lord Elgin insisted on exchanging the ratifications in Peking in the company of 400 to 500 soldiers, and to prepare for his reception he sent a party under Harry Parkes to inspect the roads and living quarters. At Tungchow, some ten miles from Peking, Parkes ran into the new imperial commissioner, Prince I, whom he insulted in an argument. At this juncture, news arrived that the prefect of Tientsin had been kidnapped by the British soldiers. In retaliation, Prince I ordered the arrest of Parkes, who, in Chinese eyes, was the chief instigator of trouble in Canton, the specter of British imperialism, and probably the most hated foreigner in China. Elgin lost all patience and charged into Peking with his forces, driving the emperor to seek refuge in Jehol, Manchuria. Finding no court to negotiate with, Elgin toyed with the idea of replacing the Manchu dynasty with a Chinese one, and of burning the palaces as a punishment for the illegal detention of Parkes and the mistreatment of the prisoners of war. In the end he was persuaded by the Russian and French diplomats, General Ignatiev and Baron Gros, to abandon both ideas, burning the Summer Palace instead.[20]

In these critical days, the Russian ambassador Nikolai Ignatiev played an active role as mediator (*posrednik*) between the Anglo-French plenipotentiaries and Prince Kung, the emperor's younger brother who had been left in Peking to take charge of the peace settlement. When Kung was so terrified by the burning of the Summer Palace that he sought to flee the capital, it was Ignatiev who persuaded him to remain and accept the Allied terms, so as to avoid total destruction. Ignatiev's diplomacy will be discussed in the next section; suffice it to say here that by ma-

20. China: *Dispatches*, Vol. 19, Doc. 26, Ward to Cass, Nov. 28, 1860 (National Archives, Washington, D.C.); Quested, *The Expansion of Russia*, 260-62.

neuvering at both ends he scored a great victory for Russia. On October 24, 1860, Lord Elgin dictated to Prince Kung the Convention of Peking, which established once and for all the British right to diplomatic representation in the Chinese capital. The indemnity was increased to 8 million taels for Britain and France each, and Tientsin was opened to foreign trade and residence. In addition, Britain acquired Kowloon Peninsula opposite Hong Kong, while France secured the right for Catholic missionaries to own properties in interior China. With this peace settlement, the Allied troops, urged by the Russian diplomat, left Peking around November 8, 1860.

The Russian Advance. On November 14, 1860, within a week of Allied evacuation of Peking, Ignatiev secured, as a reward for his mediation, a Supplementary Treaty of Peking, by which Russia won new territorial concessions east of the Ussuri River and legalized her previous acquisitions under the Treaty of Aigun of 1858. Ignatiev's work successfully crowned nearly two decades of Russian advance in the Amur Region under Nikolai Muraviev. Encouraged by the British success in the Opium War to intensify their own activities in China, the Russians under Nicholas I (1825-55) carried out a double-barreled penetration into Chinese Turkestan and the Amur Region. They secured a foothold in northern Sinkiang by the Treaty of Ili in 1851, which granted Russia the right to trade, to build warehouses, and to establish consulates in Ili (Kuldja) and Tarbagatai (Chuguchak). In the Amur Region, the advance was carried out by Muraviev, governor-general of Eastern Siberia since 1847. With headquarters at Irkutsk, Muraviev launched his forays into the Amur River, constructing fortified posts in strategic points and occupying its lower reaches. By 1858 he was in a position sufficiently powerful to intimidate the meek Manchu general I-shan into signing the Treaty of Aigun, which gave Russia the territory on the northern banks of the Amur and Sungari rivers, and joint possession with China of the land east of the Ussuri River to the sea. These three rivers were closed to ships of all nationalities except those of China and Russia. However, as this treaty completely ignored the boundaries established by the Treaty of Nerchinsk of 1689, the Ch'ing court adamantly refused to ratify it.

Ignatiev, once an aide-de-camp to the tsar, had succeeded Putiatin as ambassador to China in the summer of 1859. A shrewd schemer and a wily diplomat, he had been sent to perform the delicate task of seizing international leadership for Russia in Chinese affairs, getting the Treaty

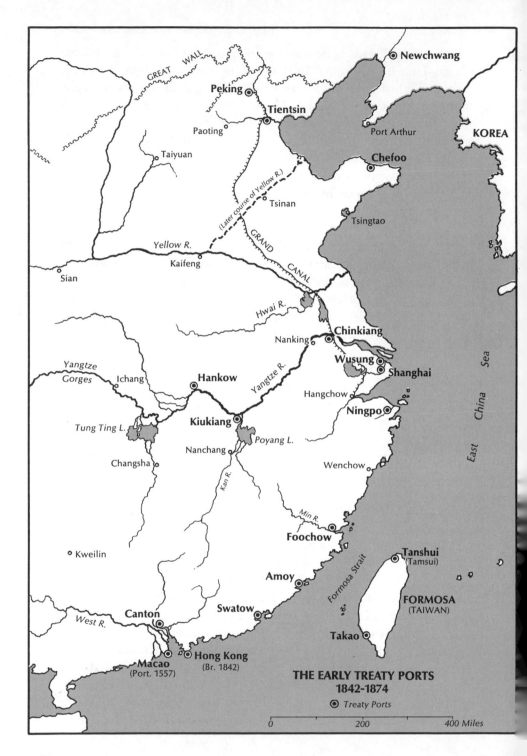

THE EARLY TREATY PORTS
1842-1874

⊙ Treaty Ports

0   200   400 Miles

Newchwang

Peking
Tientsin
Paoting
Taiyuan

GREAT WALL

Port Arthur

KOREA

Chefoo

(Later course of Yellow R.)
Tsinan

Tsingtao

Yellow R.
Kaifeng

Sian

GRAND CANAL

Hwai R.

Chinkiang
Nanking
Wusung
Shanghai

Yangtze Gorges
Ichang

Hankow

Yangtze R.

Hangchow

Ningpo

East China Sea

Tung Ting L.

Kiukiang

Nanchang

Poyang L.

Changsha

Kan R.

Wenchow

Min R.

Foochow

Kweilin

Tanshui
(Tamsui)

Amoy

Formosa Strait

FORMOSA
(TAIWAN)

Canton
Swatow

West R.

Takao

Macao
(Port. 1557)

Hong Kong
(Br. 1842)

of Aigun approved, and preventing the downfall of the Manchu dynasty, with which Russia maintained favorable treaty arrangements. The ingenious means of achieving these objectives was to act as mediator between the Chinese and the Anglo-French interventionists. Arriving in Peking via the land route over Kiakhta, he first engaged in protracted and fruitless negotiations with Su-shun, president of the Li-fan yüan,[21] who steadfastly refused to accept the Treaty of Aigun, the extension of trade to interior China, and the re-demarcation of the Sinkiang border. In disgust, Ignatiev left Peking in May 1860 and went to Shanghai to denounce the Chinese obstructionist tactics to the Anglo-French plenipotentiaries, urging them to be positive and unyielding toward Peking. Ingratiating himself with the British, he informed them of the conditions in the Chinese capital, later guided them to land at Pei-t'ang, and provided General Grant with a map of Peking to facilitate the British attack.

Then returning to Peking on the heels of the Allies, Ignatiev cunningly presented himself to the Chinese as a needed friend. To Prince Kung he offered to mediate China's troubles with the Allies, to work toward a reduction of the indemnity, and to effect an early evacuation of the Allied troops from Peking, if Kung agreed to the following terms: (1) to approve the Treaty of Aigun; (2) to settle an eastern border along the Ussuri River to the limits of Korea, and in the north along the permanent Chinese picket line; and (3) to allow Russian consulates in Kashgar, Urga, and Tsitsikhar. Quite aware of the Russian's duplicity, Prince Kung was indisposed toward such expensive Russian mediation, yet he was apprehensive lest his refusal should drive the Russians into the Anglo-French camp and thus make China face three enemies simultaneously. In his desire to rid Peking of Allied troops, he succumbed to Ignatiev's offer of mediation.

After Lord Elgin had dictated the Convention of Peking on October 24, 1860, Ignatiev spared no efforts in promoting the idea that the severe winter of North China would soon descend to freeze the Pei-ho, in which case all foreigners would be trapped and exposed to possible Chinese mob attacks; he assured all that he would shortly leave for Tientsin to spend the winter. Under his influence, General Grant clamored for an early exodus from Peking, setting November 8 as the deadline.

Within a few days of the Allied evacuation, Ignatiev, now freed from all possible intervention, secured the Supplementary Treaty of Peking on November 14 as the reward for his service to China. Not only did it

21. From July to September 1859 and from December 1859 to April 1860.

affirm the Russian gains in the Treaty of Aigun, including the land north of the Amur River, which had since become the Amur Province, but it went beyond to give Russia exclusive ownership of the land east of the Ussuri River to the sea, which had since become the Maritime Province. In addition, Urga and Kashgar were opened to Russian trade, consulates, and residences. Without a soldier or a shot, the Russians gained some 300,000 to 400,000 square miles of territory, plus impressive commercial concessions. Moreover, by the most-favored-nation treatment, they also shared the benefits of the British and French treaties.[22]

The second set of treaties reinforced the first signed after the Opium War, to form an iron-clad treaty system, from which China was not freed until 1943. Beyond a doubt, by 1860 the ancient civilization that was China was thoroughly defeated and humiliated by the West. The maritime powers of Europe and America advanced, step by step, northward from Canton to Shanghai to Peking, while the Russian land power thrust southward from the Siberian-Manchurian border toward Peking. The Western states sought commercial interest and economic concessions through the creation of treaty ports and the extension of trade. The Russians stressed territorial acquisitions as well as commercial gains. The advance of the two from the south and from the north truly constituted a pincers movement, closing in ever more tightly on the declining Ch'ing dynasty. For the century that followed, the West and Russia constituted the two major sources of foreign impact, the effects of which are still discernible today in China.

22. For Russian activities in China during this period, see Quested, chapters 2-4; A. Buksgevden, *Russkii Kitai: Ocherki diplomaticheskikh snoshenii Rossii s Kitaem—Pekinskii dogovor 1860 g.* (Russia's China: An account of the diplomatic relations between Russia and China—the Treaty of Peking, 1860), (Port Arthur, 1902). See also Hsü, *China's Entrance*, 103-05.

FURTHER READING

Bonner-Smith, D., and W. R. Lumby, *The Second China War, 1856-1860* (London, 1954).

Buksgevden (Boxhowden), Baron A., *Russkii Kitai: Ocherki diplomaticheskikh snoshenii Rossii s Kitaem—Pekinskii dogovor 1860 g.* (Russia's China: an account of the diplomatic relations between Russia and China—the Treaty of Peking, 1860), (Port Arthur, 1902).

Ch'en, Fu-kuang, *Yu-Ch'ing i-tai chih Chung-O kuan-hsi* (Sino-Russian relations during the Ch'ing period exclusively), (Kunming, 1947), chapter 3.

Costin, W. C., *Great Britain and China, 1833-1860* (Oxford, 1937).

Dennett, Tyler, *Americans in Eastern Asia* (New York, 1941), chapters 17-18.

Fairbank, John K., *Trade and Diplomacy on the China Coast: The Opening of the Treaty Ports, 1842-1854* (Cambridge, Mass., 1953), 2 vols.

———, "The Manchu Appeasement Policy of 1843," *Journal of the American Oriental Society*, 59:4:469-84 (Dec. 1939).

———, "The Manchu-Chinese Dyarchy in the 1840's and '50's," *The Far Eastern Quarterly*, XII:3:265-78 (May 1953).

———, "Synarchy under the Treaties" in John K. Fairbank (ed.), *Chinese Thought and Institutions* (Chicago, 1957), 204-31.

Hsü, Immanuel C. Y., *China's Entrance into the Family of Nations: The Diplomatic Phase, 1858-1880* (Cambridge, Mass., 1968), chapters 2-7.

Huang, Yen-yü, "Viceroy Yeh Ming-ch'en and the Canton Episode (1856-1861)" *Harvard Journal of Asiatic Studies*, 6:1:37-127 (March 1941).

Lane-Poole, Stanley, and Frederick V. Dickins, *The Life of Sir Harry Parkes* (London, 1894) Vol. 1.

Lay, Horatio N., *Our Interests in China* (London, 1864).

Lin, T. C., "The Amur Frontier Questions between China and Russia, 1850-1860," *Pacific Historical Review*, 3:1-27 (1934).

Mancall, Mark, "Major-General Ignatiev's Mission to Peking, 1859-1860," *Papers on China*, 10:55-96, Center for East Asian Studies, Harvard University, 1956.

Quested, R. K. I., *The Expansion of Russia in East Asia, 1857-1860* (Kuala Lumpur, 1968).

Shen, Wei-tai, *China's Foreign Policy, 1839-1960* (New York, 1932).

Tong, Te-kong, *United States Diplomacy in China, 1844-1860* (Seattle, 1964).

Tsiang, T. F., *Chung-kuo chin-tai shih ta-kang* (An outline of Chinese modern history), (Taipei, 1959), chapter 1.

——— "Tsui-chin san-pai-nien Tung-pei wai-chiao shih" 最近三百年東北外交史 (Diplomatic history of Manchuria in the last three hundred years), *Tsing hua hsüeh-pao*, 8;1:1-70 (1932).

———, "The Secret Plan of 1858," *The Chinese Social and Political Science Review*, 15:2:291-99 (July 1931).

Wong, George H. C., and Allan B. Cole, "Sino-Russian Border Relations, 1850-1860," *The Chung Chi Journal* (Hong Kong), 5:2:109-25 (May 1966).

Wu, Hsiang-hsiang 吳相湘, *O-ti chin-lüeh Chung-kuo shih* 俄帝侵略中國史 (A history of the Russian imperialist aggression in China), (Taipei, 1957), chapter 2.

10

The Taiping Revolution and the
Nien and Moslem Rebellions

Mid-19-century China was troubled not only by external wars, as noted in the previous chapters, but also by a series of debilitating internal convulsions. The Opium and the *Arrow* wars brought disasters and humiliation from the outside, while the domestic revolution and rebellions dealt serious blows to the ruling power from within. The largest of these upheavals, the Taiping Revolution, nearly toppled the dynasty. It lasted from 1850 to 1864, raging over sixteen provinces and destroying more than 600 cities. The Nien Rebellion lasted from 1851 to 1868, spreading over eight provinces. The Moslem Rebellion in Yunnan continued from 1855 until 1873, while that in the Northwest, known as the Tungan Rebellion, extended from 1862 to 1878. The fortune of the Ch'ing regime had reached its lowest point.

CAUSES FOR SOCIAL UPHEAVAL

Traditional Chinese subscribed to the theory that domestic rebellion and foreign invasion occurred when the central power declined; they appeared together as symptoms of serious and upsetting internal weakness. If the ruling power had been strong, these troubles could have been met and stopped out of hand. Nowhere was this theory better manifested than in the case of the Manchu government in the middle of the 19th century. It had inherited many deep-rooted social and economic problems from earlier periods which made domestic convulsion well-nigh inevitable.

Social and Economic Factors. For two thousand years preceding the mid-19th century the social structure and the mode of production in China had scarcely changed. It was for the most part an agrarian society, and social order and disorder depended to a great extent on the proper distribution of land. After each major disorder, enough people had been killed so that there was sufficient land for the survivors, but after a period of peace the population increase inevitably resulted in a decrease in per capita land cultivation. This caused difficulties in earning a livelihood, which led to banditry and uprisings, and these upsetting conditions were usually accompanied by administrative inefficiency, political corruption, and moral degeneration. A period of disorder followed, whereby the population was once again drastically reduced until, theoretically, a new balance was achieved between land and people. A period of peace and order then set in, signaling the beginning of a new cycle. In short, the alternation of order and disorder was nature's way of maintaining social equilibrium, and the Chinese had been at the mercy of this process since time immemorial. The philosopher Mencius (373-288 B.C.) perceptively observed that a period of order was perforce followed by a period of disorder, and the Chinese believed generally that a minor disturbance was to be expected every thirty years and a major one every hundred years. Western scholars sometimes described this phenomenon as "dynastic cycle," although it should more properly be called the theory of "natural evolution of history."

Applying this concept to the Ch'ing period, we find that the 150 years of peace and prosperity under K'ang-hsi, Yung-cheng, and Ch'ien-lung had nurtured a rapid growth in population, but that the land had not increased correspondingly. The population rose from 143 million in 1741 to 430 million in 1850, a gain of 200 per cent, whereas land rose from 549 million mou (mou = 1/6 acre) in 1661 to 737 (742?) million in 1833, an increase of only 35 per cent. The discrepancy between population and land growth resulted in a sharp decrease in per capita cultivation. With 708 million mou in 1753, each individual could theoretically be allotted 3.86 mou, but with 791 million mou in 1812, only 2.19 mou per person could be figured. It became even worse: between 1812 and 1833 not only was there no increase but due to natural calamities there was actually a decrease in arable land, from 791 million mou to 737 (742?) million, whereas the population increased from 361 million to 398 million, lowering the per capita cultivation further to only 1.86 mou.[1]

1. Lo Erh-kang, "T'ai-p'ing t'ien-kuo ko-ming ch'ien te jen-k'ou ya-p'o wen-t'i" (The population pressure in the pre-Taiping Rebellion years), *Chung-kuo she-hui ching-chi chi-k'an* (Collected writings on Chinese society and economics), Academia Sinica, 8:1:39 (Jan. 1939); also George Taylor, "The Taiping Rebellion: Its Economic Background and Social Theory," *The Chinese Social and Political Science Review*, 32:545-614 (1932-33); Ping-Ti Ho, *Studies on the Population of China*, 282.

Continuous shrinkage of individual landholdings could mean only increasing hardship for the peasant. When the yield of the small acreage could no longer sustain his life, he sold the land and became the tenant of a landlord. Once the land was sold, the peasant was not likely to buy it back, because the rich owner would not sell except at a very good price, which the peasant could not meet. The result of this spiral was the ever-increasing concentration of land among the rich. The Ho family of Chihli possessed a million *mou* in 1766, roughly 1/700 of the total arable land of the country. Not only the landlords, but wealthy rice merchants, usurers, and pawnshop owners also manipulated land ownership, with the result that the land value increased several fold. A *mou* of land that used to cost one or two taels in the early Ch'ing period rose to seven or eight taels in the middle period.

The high concentration of arable land is illustrated by the fact that 50 per cent to 60 per cent of it was in the hands of the rich families. Another 10 per cent was possessed by the bannermen and official villas, leaving only 30 per cent for the rest of the 400 million. Sixty to 90 per cent of the people had no land at all. The life of the landless peasant was wretched. He had to pay 50 per cent of the yield for rent; and as the rent was not paid in kind but in commuted money, in the process of commutation usually another 30 per cent was levied. For instance, a *mou* of land which produced 3 *shih* (*shih* = 133⅓ lbs.) should normally cost 1.5 *shih* for rent, but when commuted to money payment at 30 per cent extra, the rent actually amounted to 1.95 *shih*, leaving the tiller only 1.05 *shih* for himself. Naturally he could not eke out a subsistence but had to borrow from usurers.[2] Many displaced and unemployed peasants drifted to the cities as porters, dockhands, and sailors, while others went abroad to seek a new life, and still others became idlers, rascals, and bandits. Had there been large-scale industries or big enterprises in China at the time, these surplus persons might have found their way into productive channels, but unfortunately there were no such industries, and the jobless became a source of unrest in the society.[3] They were ready material for uprising or revolution.

The Effects of the Opium War. Taking advantage of the fact that the Treaty of Nanking made no provisions against the import of opium, the

2. P'eng Tse-i, *T'ai-p'ing t'ien-kuo ko-ming ssu-ch'ao* (The revolutionary thought-tide of the Heavenly Kingdom of Great Peace), (Shanghai, 1946), 14-15; Hsiao I-shan, III, 38-39.
3. Lo Erh-kang, 35.

foreign traders intensified their activities in this illicit but lucrative trade. The Chinese government, which had lost the war, dared not stop it. As a result, opium traffic practically became unrestrained and the volume of import rose from 33,000 chests in 1842 to 46,000 chests in 1848, and to 52,929 chests in 1850. The year 1848 alone witnessed the outflow of more than 10 million taels of silver, accentuating the already grave economic dislocation and copper-silver exchange rate. A tael of silver, which had exchanged for 1,000 copper coins in the 18th century, had a market value of more than 2,000 in 1845. This 100 per cent rise in the exchange rate virtually reduced a man's income by half, for although the silver tael and the copper coin were both common currencies of the state, it was the latter that was the basic medium of exchange in the market: rice was bought and wages were paid with the copper coin. A *shih* of rice formerly sold for 3,000 cash, which exchanged for 3 taels at the old rate of 1,000 to 1, but in 1851 it could only exchange for 1.5 taels at the inflated rate of 2,000 to 1. In effect, this meant that the farmer's land tax burden was doubled.[4] The wages of a common laborer or a house servant were about 10,000 cash a year, or 5 taels at the new inflated rate of exchange. He could not possibly maintain his family with that sum; accordingly, he had to go to the usurers for loans, which only plunged him hopelessly into debt, or he had to flee from his home town to avoid oppressive officials and tax collectors.

The disruptive economic consequence of opium importation was further confounded by the general influx of foreign goods in the treaty port areas. Canton was particularly hard hit, because it had the longest history of foreign trade and the widest foreign contact. Local household industries were swept away and the self-sufficient agrarian economy suffered dislocation. Those who were adversely affected became a potential source of trouble.

Political Corruption. Political corruption has been discussed in Chapter 6. It will just be reiterated here that government officials were characterized by superficiality, temporization, and irresponsibility. Little or no attention was paid to people's welfare. Among the more "conscientious" officials who were relatively free from irregularities, some passed their time in literary activities, while others read Buddhist scriptures and dabbled in philanthropic works. They considered themselves lofty and refined, regarding those officials who busied themselves with administration

4. Li Shou-k'ung, 143.

as vulgar. Official irresponsibility was also reflected in the rampant selling of offices and extorted contributions. With 3,000 taels a man could purchase a magistracy; it would be rare that such a man did not try to recover this sum during his incumbency. A popular saying had it that even a "clean" (i.e. honest) magistrate or prefect could net 100,000 taels during his three-year term of office; how much more might the grasping one make!

Military Degradation. The bannermen, who contributed much to the founding of the dynasty, had long since become enervated. As early as the K'ang-hsi period, they had degenerated to such a point as to be unable to suppress the Revolt of the Three Feudatories (1673-81), and the court had had to rely on the Chinese Green Standard army. By the time of the White Lotus Rebellion in 1796-1804, the Green Standard had lost its vigor, too, and the court was forced to use local militia. The bannermen and the Green Standard had forfeited the respect and fear of the people. Moreover, defeat in the Opium War exposed the military weakness of the dynasty. Secret societies and ambitious Chinese were encouraged to intensify their nationalistic and racial revolution against the Manchus.

Natural Disasters. The decades of the 1840's and '50's were full of natural calamities. Among the major ones were the severe draught in Honan in 1847, the flooding of the Yangtze River over the four provinces of Hupeh, Anhwei, Kiangsu, and Chekiang, the famine in Kwangsi in 1849, and the shifting of the course of the Yellow River from the southern to the northern route in Shantung in 1852, flooding a large area. Millions of people suffered from these natural disasters. Government relief at best was perfunctory, with much of the funds being embezzled at the same time. In disgust and desperation, the suffering masses were easily swayed to join a rebellion or uprising.

The Hakka and Christianity. The area in the south, the last to be conquered by the Ch'ing dynasty, was particularly vulnerable to uprising, because it was farthest from the seat of government (Peking) and because it had been exposed longest to foreign influence and contact. After the Opium War, many in the Canton area suffered by the shifting of foreign trade to Shanghai; former transportation workers connected with the shipment of tea and silk were thrown out of work.

The economic distress in the south was complicated and sharpened by the social conflict between the "natives" (original settlers) and the "guest settlers" known as the Hakka (*k'o-chia*) or *lai-jen* (men who had come). The Hakka were originally residents of Central China who had migrated to Kwangtung and Kwangsi during the Southern Sung (A.D. 1127-1278) period when the dynasty moved south under the barbarian threat. They were the social "out-group" and their different dialects, habits, and mode of life made it difficult for them to mix or assimilate with the natives. Collision between the two groups was bound to occur, and in areas where the "guest settlers" had gained ascendancy over the natives, conflict was exacerbated to the point of brutal fighting. By the middle of the 19th century, a new factor of friction was introduced: many Hakka took up Christianity, while the natives persisted in their worship of idols and spirits. The Hakka attacked the natives for their superstition, and the natives despised the Hakka for accepting a heterodox foreign faith. The tension between the two sharpened.

Men without deep social roots, the Hakka were on the whole more independent, daring, and prone to action than were the natives. Their major occupations were small farming, charcoal-making, and mining. It is here that potential revolutionary leaders recruited their followers.

From this description we get a picture of a country beset with social and economic problems, military degradation, political corruption, population pressure, natural calamities, and an explosive situation in Kwangtung. The country was ripe for an upheaval, and it is no coincidence that the largest and most significant convulsion, the Taiping Revolution, broke out in the south.

THE OUTBREAK OF THE TAIPING REVOLUTION

Hung Hsiu-ch'üan (1814-64), leader of the Taiping Revolution, was the third son of a Hakka farming family in Hua-hsien, Kwangtung, located some thirty miles from Canton. As a boy he was proud, domineering, irritable, and short-tempered, but showed considerable promise in learning. His teachers and elders had hoped that he could bring honor to his family and home town through success in the civil service examinations, but at sixteen *sui* he had to leave his studies to help with the family farming. Shortly afterwards, however, he was given the post of village teacher so that he could continue to improve himself and prepare for the examinations. Four times in his life—in 1828, 1836, 1837, and 1843—he tried for the *hsiu-ts'ai* examinations at Canton, but each time he failed.

During his second attempt, in 1836, two events took place that were to greatly influence his life later: (1) he became impressed with Confucian utopianism as envisaged in "The Evolution of Li" (*Li-yün*) and "The Grand Union" (*Ta-t'ung*), on which the famous scholar Chu Tz'u-ch'i was then lecturing in Canton; and (2) he met two Protestant missionaries in the street. One of them (Edwin Stevens) wore a robe and a long beard; the other handed Hung a set of nine tracts called "Good Words Exhorting the Age" (*Ch'üan-shih liang-yen*), prepared by the early convert Liang A-fa (1789-1855), an assistant of Dr. Robert Morrison of the London Missionary Society, who had settled at Canton to translate the Bible and spread the gospel. Preoccupied with his failure at the examinations, Hung gave no more than a casual glance at the tracts.

After his third failure in 1837, Hung became so distressed that he fell seriously ill. In his delirium he saw visions in which he was cleansed by an old woman, the Heavenly Mother, who told him: "Son of mine, you are filthy after your descent on earth. Let me wash you in the river before you are permitted to see your father."[5] Later, he was taken to heaven where a golden-bearded, venerable old man in a black robe gave him a sword to exterminate demons and a seal to overcome evil spirits. During similar visitations, he saw a middle-aged man, whom he called his Elder Brother, who instructed him in the annihilation of demons. Hung also saw Confucius confessing to the venerable old man his sin of not having explained the Truth clearly in his Classics. The delirium and visions went on intermittently for forty days; neither doctors nor sorcerers could cure him. During this period Hung often sang, announcing that he had been appointed emperor; the villagers considered him insane. His father one day discovered a slip of paper on which it was written: "Hung, the Heavenly King and Emperor of the Great Way [Truth]." Another time Hung told his sister: "I am the Emperor of Great Peace, with sun in my left hand and moon in my right."

When he came out of the delirium, Hung's personality and appearance had drastically changed. He seemed larger in stature and his steps were more solemn, while his disposition had become much milder, more friendly and tolerant—he was, in fact, a different man. A modern psychologist who has studied Hung's visions suggests that the golden-bearded man in the dream must have been the missionary whom he had met earlier in the Canton street, and that the forty-day delirium was cor-

---

5. Hsiang Ta, *et al.* (eds.) *T'ai-p'ing t'ien-kuo* (The Taiping Heavenly Kingdom), (Shanghai, 1952), II, 632; see also Wakeman, chapter 12.

related to the period of Jesus' temptation in the wilderness, which Hung must have learned from the Christian tracts.[6]

For the next six years Hung continued his career as a village teacher. He abstained from smoking and drinking in order to serve as an example, winning the praise and admiration of many. In 1843 he applied for the examinations for the fourth time, and again he failed. This occurred at a time when popular sentiments were running high over the "Canton city question." Hung's sympathy with this show of "nationalism" and his disgust with the existing system, which offered him no prospect for success, generated in him a strong incentive to foment a nationalistic-racial revolution against the Manchu dynasty. Yet, as with many revolutions in Chinese history, a religious aura would be helpful in sustaining such a movement.

One day, a cousin, Li Ching-fang, visited Hung and out of curiosity borrowed the Christian tracts on the shelves. Impressed with their unusual nature, Li urged Hung to read them. Hung did so, and came to believe that these tracts contained the key to his visions of six years before: the old man was God the Father, the middle-aged man was Jesus the Elder Brother, and Hung himself was the younger son of God and brother of Jesus. A new Trinity was born—at least in Hung's mind. He decided that the devils in his visions were the idols in the temples. Excited and overjoyed by this revelation, Hung and Li baptized themselves in the manner described in the tracts, promised God that they would abstain from idol-worship, and pledged to honor his Commandments. Among his first converts were a cousin, Hung Jen-kan (1822-64), and a neighbor and schoolmate, Feng Yün-shan (1822-52)—also a frustrated scholar. Shortly afterwards Hung's family was converted.

Hung Hsiu-ch'üan and Feng avidly studied the Christian tracts but could not fully understand many of the expressions. They took "the Heavenly Kingdom" to mean China, and "God's selected people" to mean Hung himself and his countrymen. They went about to destroy idols in the temples and remove Confucian tablets from the schools; as a result they lost their positions as teachers in 1844. Influenced by the biblical statement that a prophet is not without honor save in his own country and in his own house, they went to the neighboring province, Kwangsi, to preach. They ignored the warning that their Christianity was based on a limited and private interpretation of a small part of the Bible

6. P. M. Yap, "The Mental Illness of Hung Hsiu-ch'uan, Leader of the Taiping Rebellion," *The Far Eastern Quarterly*, 13:3:287-304 (May 1954).

and some tracts. A few months later, Hung returned to his home town, and during the next two years he continued to teach and to prepare religious tracts and odes, drawing ideas freely from the Bible and from the Confucian utopian writings, "The Evolution of Li" and "The Grand Union." He attacked opium-smoking, gambling, and drinking, and emphasized the egalitarian idea that all men were brothers and all women sisters. There is no doubt that Hung was using his new religion to build up a following for his revolutionary cause. Meanwhile, at Tzu-chin-shan (Thistlemont), some fifty *li* north of Kuei-ping, Kwangsi, Feng had organized an Association of the God Worshippers (*Pai Shang-ti hui*).

In 1847 Hung and his cousin Hung Jen-kan went to Canton to seek instruction in the Bible, as well as in Christian rituals and church organization from the Rev. Issachar J. Roberts (1802-71), an American Southern Baptist missionary. Hung's rapid progress aroused the jealousy of two of Roberts' Chinese assistants, who feared that they might be replaced by Hung. Taking advantage of Hung's naïveté, they persuaded him to ask Roberts for a subsidy for his baptism. Offended by Hung's venality, the missionary refused to baptize him, and Hung, conscious that he had been tricked, returned to Kwangsi without the baptism. By this time the Association of God Worshippers had already won more than 3,000 converts among the miners, charcoal-workers, and poor peasants, most of whom were Hakka. As the movement expanded, better educated and wealthier men also came into the fold. Among the first to join were Yang Hsiu-ch'ing, a charcoal-worker; Hsiao Ch'ao-kuei, a farmer and later brother-in-law to Hung; Wei Ch'ang-hui, a farmer of some education who had had previous experience in dealing with local officials; and Shih Ta-k'ai, a man of means, education, and fighting spirit. These four, together with Hung and Feng, formed the nucleus of a new religious and revolutionary movement. Hung, the second son of God, was acknowledged as the leader, while Feng was regarded as the third son of God; Yang, the fourth son; Hsiao, the fifth son. Ten Commandments, after Moses', were composed by Hung: (1) Thou shalt worship God; (2) Thou shalt not worship evil spirits; (3) Thou shalt not mention God's name superfluously; (4) Thou shalt worship God and praise him on the seventh day of the week; (5) Thou shalt have filial piety; (6) Thou shalt not kill or harm people; (7) Thou shalt not commit adultery and treachery; (8) Thou shalt not steal and rob; (9) Thou shalt not lie; and (10) Thou shalt not covet.[7] Hung's order of Christianity was primarily Protestant rather than Catholic, because Protestantism fitted better the

7. Li Shou-k'ung, 161.

nature of their movement, which was basically a "protest" against the existing order.

The God Worshippers went about destroying temples, shrines, and idols. They ran into trouble with local gentry but not with government authorities, who construed their religion as a kind of Catholicism, which the treaties permitted to be propagated. The governor of Kwangsi at this time,[8] an old Buddhist who resented killing and violence, followed a "live and let live" attitude toward bandits, robbers, the God Worshippers, and members of the secret societies.

During the great famine of 1849-50, members of the Heaven and Earth Society (T'ien-ti hui) in Kwangsi rose to action under the pretext of "robbing the rich to aid the poor." Their brothers in Hunan struck a sympathetic response and invaded Kwangsi. Taking advantage of this situation, thirty different companies of bandits burst out over 70 per cent of the province. The God Worshippers were not involved with the bandits, but they benefited from the disturbance. More Hakka joined them to seek refuge from the natives, and more poor people came to get protection from bandits and oppressive officials. Many naively believed that with their foreign religion the God Worshippers were immune to official intervention. By the spring of 1850 Hung had built up a following of 10,000. He picked the strategically located village of Chin-t'ien, Kwangsi, for his headquarters and sent for his family. In June 1850 all God Worshippers in the different areas were asked to sell their properties and bring the proceeds to a public treasury at Chin-t'ien, from which all drew their sustenance. The idea of mutual sharing had a great appeal to the poor.

Hung and his associates had by now completed their secret preparations for the revolution. In November 1850, when the government troops attempted to make irregular exaction from certain charcoal-workers who were God Worshippers, conflict broke out. On Hung's thirty-seventh birthday (38 sui), January 11, 1851, the God Worshippers celebrated the occasion at Chin-t'ien with a formal declaration of revolution. Hung was proclaimed "Heavenly King" (T'ien-wang) of a new "Heavenly Kingdom of Great Peace" (T'ai-p'ing t'ien-kuo), and his five senior associates were given the rank of king, though without specific title.[9] The term T'ai-p'ing (Great Peace) appeared in the Chinese classics and had

8. Cheng Tsu-ch'en.
9. The older accounts, that these terms were not adopted until the Taipings had taken Yung-an in September 1851, have been refuted by more recent research; see S. Y. Teng, New Light on the History of the Taiping Rebellion (Cambridge, Mass., 1950).

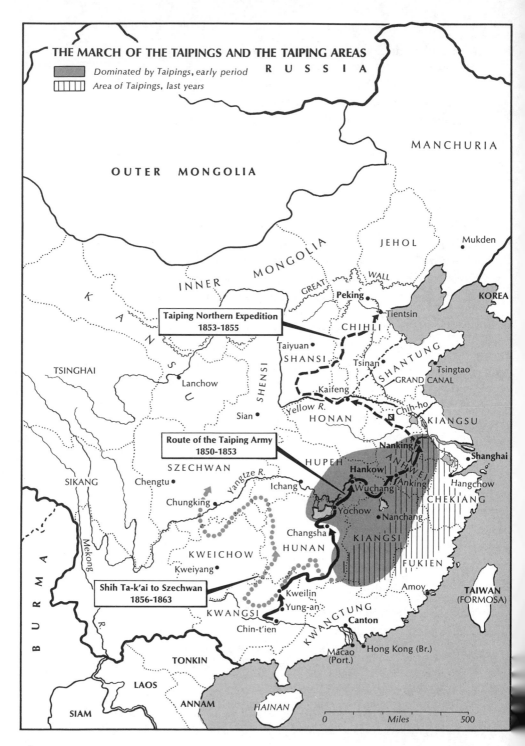

THE MARCH OF THE TAIPINGS AND THE TAIPING AREAS

Dominated by Taipings, early period
Area of Taipings, last years

RUSSIA

MANCHURIA

OUTER MONGOLIA

INNER MONGOLIA

JEHOL

• Mukden

GREAT WALL

Peking •

KOREA

Taiping Northern Expedition
1853-1855

→ Tientsin

CHIHLI

Taiyuan •

SHANSI

Tsinan •

SHANTUNG

• Tsingtao

TSINGHAI

• Lanchow

SHENSI

Kaifeng •

GRAND CANAL

Yellow R.

Chih-ho

Sian •

HONAN

KIANGSU

Route of the Taiping Army
1850-1853

HUPEH

Nanking •

• **Shanghai**

SZECHWAN

Chengtu •

Ichang •

Hankow

Wuchang

Anking

ANHWEI

Hangchow

Chungking •

Yangtze R.

Yochow

Nanchang •

CHEKIANG

Changsha •

KIANGSI

Shih Ta-k'ai to Szechwan
1856-1863

KWEICHOW

HUNAN

FUKIEN

Kweiyang •

Kweilin

Amoy •

TAIWAN
(FORMOSA)

KWANGSI

Yung-an

Chin-t'ien •

KWANGTUNG

Canton

BURMA

Mekong

TONKIN

Macao
(Port.)

• Hong Kong (Br.)

LAOS

SIAM

ANNAM

HAINAN

0   Miles   500

been the reign titles of several emperors before, while the term *"t'ien-kuo"* (heavenly kingdom) was taken from the Bible. Put together, *T'ai-p'ing t'ien-kuo* means a heavenly kingdom of great peace on earth, or more fully, "a new heaven, a new earth, a new people, and a new world," as the Taipings themselves interpreted it.

The Taipings maintained a delicate relationship with the secret societies. Hung found their idol-worship reprehensible and regarded their objective of restoring the Ming at cross purposes with his own scheme of creating a kingdom. However, their anti-Manchu stand was consonant with his revolutionary aim. Hung wanted to use them to advance his own cause without being used by them. He decided that members of the secret societies might join the Taipings provided they renounced idol-worship, took up God-worship, and accepted the Taiping Commandments and discipline. Many secret society members who joined the Taipings found it hard to live up to these demands and withdrew, but a number of them remained, includnig the fierce fighters Lo Ta-kang and Lin Feng-hsiang. Another figure of even greater stature was Hung Ta-ch'üan (no kin to the Taiping leader), who was a brilliant military strategist and a leader of the Heaven and Earth Society.

The Taipings wore their hair long, in contrast to the prevailing style of shaving the front part of the head while keeping a long queue in the back; hence they were known as the "Long-haired banditti" or simply "Long Hair." The Taiping forces fought with all the vigor and spirit of religious zealots, and the imperial army, provincial forces, and local militia melted away before them. From their base at Chin-t'ien, the Taipings charged north to take the important city of Yung-an on September 25, 1851, as a new base. There they halted for almost half a year to accumulate enough provisions for three or four months and expand their army to 37,000 men. The various senior associates of Hung, who had been called kings, were now given specific titles: Yang became the East King, Feng the South King, Hsiao the West King, Wei the North King, and Shih the Assistant King. Various offices of the new kingdom were also set up, after the institutions of the Chou dynasty 3,000 years earlier. Most accounts state that it was at Yung-an that the establishment of the Heavenly Kingdom of Great Peace was formally proclaimed, though this has been disputed by recent research.[10] The Taipings adopted a new calendar and issued a formal proclamation to the country, in which they denounced the Manchu oppression of the Chinese, attacked corruption

10. Teng, *New Light*.

within this alien rule, and called for the overthrow of the Ch'ing dynasty.

At Yung-an, the imperial forces laid a strong siege from which the Taipings could not break out for nearly half a year. At one point the morale sank so low that the movement might well have gone under had it not been for the clever tricks of the East King, who announced that God had revealed to him that the danger would pass after a hundred days. On April 3, 1852, the Taipings broke the siege and swept north. On the way the Heavenly Virtuous King (Hung Ta-ch'üan) was captured and taken to Peking, where he was executed at the age of thirty *sui*. The revolutionary army, however, moved on to attack Kueilin, the capital of Kwangsi, but failed to take it. The Taipings then broke into Hunan with a view to taking the provincial capital of Changsha. In this campaign, they suffered two major losses in the deaths of the South King and the West King—the former an originator of the movement and the latter Hung's brother-in-law. Nevertheless the revolutionary forces rolled on, taking Yochow on December 13, 1852, where they discovered a huge arsenal of munitions and cannon sequestered more than a century and a half earlier by General Wu San-kuei. In addition they confiscated more than 5,000 vessels. Thus fortified, the Taipings moved on to the key triple cities of Wuhan[11] on the Yangtze River, where theiy seized 10,000 vessels, a million taels of silver from the provincial and granary treasuries, and a great supply of provisions and ammunitions. Now boasting half a million men, the Taipings were poised for an advance to Nanking, the capital of many dynasties and the base from which the first Ming emperor expelled the Mongol conquerors. Having looted Wuhan, the Taipings charged eastward along the Yangtze and swept into Nanking on March 19-21, 1853. Hung entered the city triumphantly in a sedan-chair carried by thirty-six men, as if he were emperor, while the East King's chair was carried by sixteen men.

The Taiping success had been nothing less than spectacular. Within two and a half years they had moved from the small Chin-t'ien village in the south to Nanking in the rich Yangtze valley. They had followed a strategy mapped out by Yang at the very outset of the revolution. It called for the renunciation of Kwangtung and Kwangsi, and charging north along the rivers to take important cities if possible and to skirt them if not, with a view to taking Nanking at the earliest possible time. With Nanking as the permanent base, expeditionary forces would then be sent to the north, south, and west to conquer all of China, or at least

11. Wuchang, Hankow, and Hanyang.

the area south of the Yellow River. The East King had hoped that he could remain to rule Nanking while Hung led an army to invade Honan, the heartland of China from which the revolutionary forces could advance to attack Peking or retreat to defend Wuhan and Szechwan. Hung was said to be initially inclined to this undertaking but changed his mind on the advice of an old sailor, who impressed upon him that Honan was a relatively poor place in comparison with the Yangtze valley and that Nanking, with its strategic position and high walls, could be better defended than the open space of Honan.[12] There was also the popular story that the idea of staying at Nanking was suggested by a scholar, Ch'ien Chiang, but this has been disputed by recent research. For whichever reason, Hung settled down in Nanking, which he renamed the Heavenly Capital, and set about establishing a theocracy.

The imperial forces could do no more than set up two large camps to threaten the security of the Taiping capital: one in the eastern suburb of Nanking called the Great Camp on the South of the River (*Chiang-nan ta-ying*), and the other in the outskirts of Yangchow called the Great Camp on the North of the River (*Chiang-pei ta-ying*).

Although Hung gave up the idea of a personal expedition, he did send an army to Northern China under Lin Feng-hsiang and Li K'ai fang, and another under Lo Ta-kang westward to Anhwei, Kiangsi, Hupeh, and Hunan. These generals, all former members of secret societies, were fierce fighters but were not close associates of Hung's. Possibly Hung intended to send them away to reduce the influence of secret societies in the Taiping movement.[13] The northern expedition got within twenty miles of Tientsin, but ultimately failed for lack of support; both leaders were captured and executed in Peking in 1855. The western expedition also ran into stiff resistance by the scholar-general Tseng Kuo-fan, as we will soon see.

TAIPING INSTITUTIONS

The Taiping kingdom was a theocracy, in which religion, civil and military administration, culture, and society in general were all interwoven. The capital was called the Heavenly Capital, the leader the Heavenly

12. The story of the old sailor cannot be verified, but it has been widely circulated and cited in many accounts on the Taipings.
13. His decision to dissociate the Taipings from the secret societies offers an explanation for his refusal to aid the Small Sword Society, an offshoot of the Triad Society, which seized the walled city of Shanghai for a year and a half in 1853-54.

King, his palace the Heavenly Palace, his orders Heavenly Rescripts, and his treasury the Sacred Treasury. Opium-smoking, the use of tobacco and wine, prostitution, foot-binding, sale of slaves, gambling, and polygamy were all prohibited. There was a definite puritanical spirit in the early period of the Taipings, and the leaders conceived of many worthy institutions and innovations. The East King, a charcoal-worker by origin, contributed a great deal to the creation of the Taiping systems, as Hung had ensconced himself in the palaces and left the job of administration to him. The basic document of state was called "The Land System of the Heavenly Kingdom" (*T'ien-ch'ao t'ien-mou chih-tu*), which spelled out not only the land system, but also the military, civil, financial, judicial, and educational institutions. It was a sort of Taiping constitution.

1. *The Land System.* Perhaps the most drastic of the Taiping innovations was the abolition of the private ownership of land and property, and the introduction of a primitive communism. The spirit behind it was that all children of God must share his blessings, must be free from want, must have land to till, rice to eat, clothes to wear, and money to spend. To achieve this idealistic state, a basic change in the existing land system was imperative. The Taipings therefore divided land into nine classes according to yield.[14] The distribution of land was based not on the family as a unit but on the number of people in it. All men and women over sixteen *sui* received a share of land, and everyone under sixteen received half a share. Thus, if a man received one *mou* of A+ land, his children up through the age of fifteen received half a *mou* of the same quality land. A family of six received an equal amount of good and poor land, that is, three members received good land and three received poor.[15] The distributed land did not become the property of the recipient; he was merely given the right to use it for production. All surplus products beyond one's needs had to be surrendered to the public storehouse. Savings and private property were prohibited.

The idea of communal utilization of land can be found in the ancient

14. A *mou* of land with a yield of 1,200 chin (*chin* = 1⅓ lbs.) of product was classified as A+ (*shang-shang*), that with a yield of 1,100 *chin*, A (*shang-chung*); 1,000 *chin*, A— (*shang-hsia*); 900 *chin*, B+ (*chung-shang*); 800 *chin*, B (*chung-chung*); 700 *chin*, B— (*chung-hsia*); 600 *chin*, C+ (*hsia-shang*); 500 *chin*, C (*hsia-chung*); and 400 *chin*, C— (*hsia-hsia*).

15. One *mou* of the A+ land was equivalent to 1.1 *mou* of the A land, 1.2 *mou* of the A— land, 1.35 *mou* of the B+ land, 1.5 *mou* of the B land, 1.75 *mou* of the B— land, 2 *mou* of the C+ land, 2.4 *mou* of the C class, and 3 *mou* of the C— class.

Chinese work *The Rites of Chou*, and the usurper of the Han power, Wang Mang, had put this into practice during his short-lived Hsin dynasty (A.D. 8-23). The Taipings revived the doctrine with great visionary idealism, but unfortunately, due to incessant warfare and the unsettled conditions in the countryside they could not put it into practice except in a few experimental pockets.

2. *The Unity of the Military and Civil Administration.* The Taiping military institutions were derived from *The Rites of Chou* and the systems developed by the Ming general Ch'i Chi-kuang. The peculiar feature was the unity of the military with the civilian administration. Soldiers were farmers, and officers were assigned civil as well as military duties. For each 13,156 families there was an army commander, who was in charge of five divisions, each of which consisted of five brigades. Under each brigade commander were five captains, each of whom commanded four master sergeants, who in turn were in charge of five corporals each, who controlled four soldiers. An army thus consisted of 10,000 soldiers and 3,156 officers, making a total of 13,156 men. When more families were formed, new army units were organized. For instance, with each five new families, a new corporal was appointed, and with twenty-five new families a master sergeant was commissioned. In this progressive manner, a new army was formed when there were 13,156 new families.

The military officers were also civil administrators. Every twenty-five families formed a basic social unit, each with a public storehouse and a church under the charge of the master sergeant. He administered the civil, educational, religious, financial, and judicial matters of his twenty-five families and took charge of their litigations, marriages, and funerals. All the expenses of these affairs were paid out of the public storehouse, but there was a limit to what each event could cost. In time of peace the soldiers and corporals performed public works. The children of the twenty-five families went to church daily to receive instructions from the master sergeant on the Old and New Testaments and Christian tracts written by Hung. On Sunday the corporals led the people to church, where the master sergeant preached, and the men and women were seated separately. The hymnal was different from the Protestant hymnal, and although the ritual of the service in general followed the Protestant tradition, there were deviations, too, such as the use of drums and firecrackers and the serving of cakes and fruits, much as the Buddhists and the Taoists did.

The Taipings forbade ancestor-worship, and destroyed idols and temples whenever they were discovered. The officers usually preached to the inhabitants of any new area their army reached.

3. *Unity of Culture and Religion.* In the Taiping kingdom, the inculcation of Christian ideas among the people was a primary undertaking. A new *Three-Character Classics* of 478 sentences and 1,434 words, based on Hung's interpretation of the Bible, was compiled for the children, with opening passages as: "God our Lord, creates Heaven [and] Earth, creates mountains [and] seas, provides all things; within six days, all was done . . ." There were also *Odes for Youths* and hymns glorifying God and Jesus as true saviors of mankind. In all these writings the vernacular was used, with punctuation, to facilitate easy reading and wide circulation. Some progressive writers today consider this plain style of writing a forerunner of the New Cultural Movement of the late 1910's and the early 1920's.

The Taipings held civil service examinations, too, in which the plain language was used in place of the classical style of writing required in the Ch'ing examinations. The theses in the Taiping examinations were not taken from the Confucian classics as in the Ch'ing examinations, but were selected from the Bible, Christian tracts, and Taiping proclamations, such as "God our Lord is the Only True Spirit" and "For Whom did God come to the Earth and why did Jesus sacrifice His Life?" The examinations, open to men and women alike, were at first given on the birthdays of Hung and his son, the crown prince; but later March 5 and 13 of the Taiping calendar were set aside for the annual examinations for the civil and military *hsiu-ts'ai* degree, respectively; May 5 and 15 for the civil and military *chü-jen* degree; and September 9 and 19 for the civil and military *chin-shih* degree.[16] Applicants for the examinations came from all walks of life, including fortunetellers and magicians. As might be expected, the standards of these examinations were not rigorous; it was said that in a certain Hupeh examination 800 out of 1,000 candidates passed. The examinations won the good will of many for this reason, but they compromised the original purpose of selecting talents for public service.

16. To be more accurate, the names of these degrees were considered improper and the Taipings changed *hsiu-ts'ai* (beautiful talent) to *hsiu-shih* (beautiful scholar), *chü-jen* (employable man) to *po-shih* (erudite scholar), and *chin-shih* (advanced scholar) to *ta-shih* (all-round scholar). The title *kuo-shih* (national scholar) was substituted for the Han-lin.

4. The New Calendar. The calendar adopted by the Taipings was unique in that it was neither lunar nor solar but somewhere in between. The year was divided into 366 days, with 31 days to each odd month (January and every other month thereafter) and 30 days to each even month. The defect of this calendar was that it created three superfluous days every four years, or 30 extra days every 40 years. To remedy this situation, a "year of adjustment" was scheduled for every 40 years, at which time each month was divided into 28 days, making a total of 336 days for the year, just 30 days short of the regular year. January 1 of the first year of the Taiping calendar was February 4, 1852.

5. Social Policies. Men and women were equal in the Taiping kingdom. Women were allowed to serve in the civil and military administration, and there were reportedly 100,000 female soldiers and officers under the command of Hung's sister. Women's Residential Halls (*Nü-kuan*) operated at Nanking in the early days of the Taipings for the young and unmarried, as well as for those women whose husbands had been killed in battle or were away. Governed by Hung's sister, they were relatively free of outside interference. Missionaries who visited Nanking were impressed with the freedom and ease with which members of the female sex walked or rode horses in the streets.

A number of social welfare measures were taken to support the disabled, the sick, the widowed and the orphaned. The egalitarian and ascetic spirit of the movement was also manifested, as noted earlier, in such policies as the prohibition of opium-smoking, foot-binding, slavery, and prostitution. In general, the Taiping society presented a marked contrast to the Ch'ing society.

FOREIGN NEUTRALITY

The rise of the Taipings coincided with a period of great difficulty between the foreign powers and the Ch'ing court. Sino-Western relations were being strained by such issues as the "Canton city question," the contumacy of the governor-general at Canton, the issue of treaty revision, and the legalization of the opium trade. Against this background the founding of the Taiping kingdom in Nanking provided the foreign powers with an exciting alternative to the Ch'ing court in Peking, and they began to wonder whether it might not be wise to recognize and support the Taipings against the troublesome Manchu dynasty, in return for friendly treatment and extended commerce.

The Taiping profession of Christianity evoked an early sympathy from foreigners, particularly the Protestant missionaries, although they were concerned about the new "Trinity," which smacked of blasphemy. Foreign traders were pleased with the prospect of extended commerce in the Taiping area, but were troubled by their strict prohibition of opium, which had become the single most lucrative article in the China trade. On the whole, foreign governments had mixed feelings about the Heavenly Kingdom of Great Peace, and the wise policy under such circumstances was to wait and see. The British plenipotentiary in China, Sir George Bonham, dispelled any impression of intended British aid to the Ch'ing army by announcing that Britain maintained neutrality in the Chinese civil strife and would not go beyond protection of the lives and properties of her subjects in Shanghai. For a firsthand knowledge of the Taipings, Bonham and his interpreter, Thomas T. Meadows, sailed in H.M.S. *Hermes* to Nanking in April 1853. The North King and the Assistant King granted an interview to Meadows and arranged for Bonham to see the East King, the prime minister. Bonham did not see him but sent a letter instead, in which he explained the British position of neutrality and asked the Taipings to recognize the British treaty rights and privileges. The Taiping reply was curiously condescending, stating that the Heavenly King, pleased with the coming of distant people from the "dependencies," graciously granted them permission to trade or to serve in Nanking. Accompanying the communication were several Taiping tracts which the British were asked to read to learn the Truth.

Bonham's visit, then, was not fruitful except in gathering information. He had come to ask for Taiping respect of British treaty rights, but the Heavenly King wanted to treat Britain as if she were an inferior state. Bonham went home, leaving a warning that if British lives and properties were violated, his government would take retaliatory measures such as they had a decade earlier in the Opium War. To London Bonham expressed doubt that the Taipings could replace the Ch'ing dynasty and recommended a policy of neutrality. Meadows' analysis of Taiping tracts and the movement as a whole sheds light on the mixed foreign feelings:

> The anthropomorphism displayed in the above pamphlet is very striking. The Deity is brought down from a state of distant superiority, and is represented as familiar with mortals, in a degree which to us appears somewhat revolting . . . There are some things good, very good, in the productions before us, leading us to infer that the authors were divinely taught, and to cherish the hope that not a few will,

through the medium of these truths, find the road to heaven. There are, however, some things of which we most highly disapprove; not the least of which are the pretensions to new and immediate communications from the Deity; some of which afford representations of the Divine Being far different from what we have been accustomed to in the Christian Scriptures, and made to serve the end of personal aggrandizement and ambition . . .

It would be sad to see Christian nations engaged in putting down the movement, as the insurgents possess an energy, and a tendency to improvement and general reform (as witness their calendar) which the Imperialists [Ch'ing] never have exhibited, and never can be expected to display. Questionable though it be, the form of Christianity which the insurgents profess is far better than the stupid idolatry hitherto practised by the Chinese; and it is possible that European nations, if engaged on the opposite side, would be going to war with some people in some respects better than themselves . . . The only policy that appears at present advisable, is to keep ourselves from being involved any further in the quarrel, and to avoid all Government connection with either party.[17]

The Americans also followed a policy of neutrality in the early years of the Taipings, although their sympathy was clearly not with the imperial government. Commissioner Humphrey Marshall wrote to the Secretary of State on April 28, 1853 that "from all I can learn the Government of China is fully employed by the rebels, and that everyday may bring forth the fruits of successful revolution, in the utter overthrow of the existing dynasty." The President of the United States, in his annual message on December 5, 1853, also reported: "The condition of China at this time renders it probable that some important changes will occur in that vast Empire which will lead to a more unrestricted intercourse with it. The commissioner to that country who has been recently appointed is instructed to avail himself of all occasions to open and extend our commercial relations, not only with the Empire of China, but with other Asiatic nations."[18] The commissioner in question was Robert McLane, who was appointed to China on October 18, 1853, to succeed Marshall. He was instructed that if China should be divided into several governments, he was to enter into diplomatic and treaty relations with all of them. This realistic approach was, of course, in line with the traditional American policy of recognizing whatever government was in *de-*

17. McNair, I, 345-46.
18. Tyler Dennett, *Americans in Eastern Asia* (New York, 1922), 212.

facto control of the land. Although McLane himself believed that the highest interests of the United States lay in sustaining the imperial government rather than in seeing China drift into a widespread anarchy, he followed his predecessor's policy of neutrality and "wait and see."

France, as protector and propagator of the Catholic faith abroad, was not favorably disposed toward the Taiping Protestant ideology. However, when the French minister to China, M. de Bourboulon, visited Nanking in December 1853, he was impressed with the order and discipline of the Taipings and he recommended a policy of neutrality to his government, too.

Russia, whose trade with China was mostly in the border areas of Sinkiang, Mongolia, and Manchuria, was less impressed with the Taiping movement. Politically, a Taiping success would mean a shift of gravity from Peking, where Russia maintained a semidiplomatic, religious mission, to Nanking and the south, where the British influence was strong. It was therefore in Russia's interest to sustain the imperial cause. However, for the time being, St. Petersburg also chose to stay neutral.

It has never been understood why the Taipings did not pursue an active policy of seeking foreign recognition; it is even more puzzling that on the one hand they professed equality of all men as God's children and on the other insisted on treating foreign representatives as delegates from inferior dependencies. Possibly the Taiping leaders distrusted foreigners and were afraid of their association. If the Taipings had had an active policy of foreign alignment against the Manchu government, with which the foreign powers were at odds, the future course of the revolution might have been different.

TSENG KUO-FAN AND THE HUNAN ARMY

The early Taiping success was a result of many factors. First, there was general sympathy toward their nationalistic-racial revolution against the alien Manchu rule, and the secret societies extended them considerable help. Secondly, the Taiping forces were an ideological army with a "Messianic" mission. The soldiers believed that Hung had been commissioned by God to exterminate the demons from earth, and that if they died for the cause they would rise to heaven and dwell in the bosom of God for eternity. Unafraid of death and ready to become martyrs, they fought with the single-minded devotion and bravery of a crusading army. Thirdly, the Taiping military organization was based on the tested methods of the famous Ming general, Ch'i Chi-kuang. Their well-disciplined troops showed much greater consideration toward the people than did the corrupt and debauched government forces. The bannermen and the Green Standard army had long lost their fighting spirit; when they met the zealous revolutionaries they went to pieces.

Under these conditions, the court resorted to organizing militia for local defense, such as it had done during the White Lotus Rebellion (1796-1804). When the Taipings swept into Hunan and besieged the provincial capital of Changsha in mid-1852, the much-harassed court hurriedly ordered the scholar-official, Tseng Kuo-fan, out of mourning to organize a militia force for the defense of his home province.

Tseng Kuo-fan (1811-72) of Hsiang-hsiang, Hunan, was a persistent if not a brilliant scholar, known for his tenacity of purpose. After winning the *chin-shih* degree in 1838, he rose gradually in the civil service and in 1849 became a junior vice-president of the Board of Rites. Thereafter he served as a junior vice-president of the Board of Punishments in 1851 and as an acting senior vice-president of the Board of Civil Office a year later. While living in Peking he made friends with leading Neo-Confucian scholars (Sung School) and from them acquired an appreciation of "quietude" (*ching*), "persistence" (*nai*), and "discipline" (*yüeh*), which, when applied to practical affairs, meant cool-headedness in emergency, fearlessness in the midst of difficulties, and realistic self-control. These qualities were to benefit him greatly in his later career.

In the middle of 1852 Tseng was made chief commissioner of the provincial examinations in Kiangsi. En route to this assignment he learned of his mother's death, and in accordance with the social convention he retired to his home town for a period of mourning. It was during this time that the court summoned him to organize a militia for Hunan. A filial son and a correct Confucianist, he did not wish to cut short the mourning period but was ultimately persuaded by friends and the governor to place the interests of the country above his familial obligations; thus he went to Changsha.

Tseng knew well that the Green Standard army and the militia could fight bandits but were no match for the well-organized Taiping revolutionary army. If he was to be effective, he would have to go beyond the imperial order and raise a new army. The Taipings were no White Lotus rebels, whom the militia had suppressed; they were an ideological army organized along the time-tested methods of the famed Ming general. To counter such a crusading force, it was necessary to turn the militia into a well-trained and well-indoctrinated army. For this purpose Tseng decided, interestingly enough, to adopt the military organization of the same Ming general, Ch'i Chi-kuang, and in addition to instill in his army a sense of mission: that of defending the Chinese cultural heritage in the tradition of Confucius and Mencius. Such an army would have an *esprit de corps* which could be assured by a careful recruitment policy based on common regional background.

With these ideas in mind, Tseng raised three battalions of troops, each comprising 360 men, making a total of 1,080. The officers were chosen from Confucian scholars, and the soldiers were selected from solid farm types rather than slick city dwellers. These officers and soldiers all came from the province of Hunan, as did Tseng himself—hence the name "Hunan army" (*Hsiang-chün*) or "Huan braves" (*Hsiang-yung*)— "braves" being the name for irregular troops or temporary recruits as opposed to the regular, standing army. Gradually the Hunan army was expanded into thirteen battalions, each enlarged to 500 men, in addition to 180 service personnel who performed sundry chores. The soldier's pay was 4.5 taels a month, ten times the wages of an ordinary house servant. The battalion commander received a salary of 50 taels monthly plus 150 taels more for expenses. Along with the army organization, Tseng also raised a navy—or rather a "water force"—of ten battalions totaling 5,000 men, to contend with the Taipings on the Yangtze. Two hundred forty war junks were made by the two dockyards which he established. Tseng derived the support of his Hunan army and navy from (1) the inland transit dues (*likin*) which theoretically were 0.1 per cent of the value of commodities but which actually amounted to 4 per cent to 10 per cent;[19] (2) customs dues; (3) Ch'ing treasury allocations; (4) contributions; (5) salt levies; (6) tribute grain; and (7) miscellaneous taxes.

The soldiers in the Hunan army were recruited by the officers, to whom they owed their allegiance; the officers in turn pledged their allegiance to Tseng, who had selected them. The Hunan army was therefore a private army. Up to this time no Ch'ing official, much less a private citizen, could maintain a personal army; the bannermen and the Green

---

19. In some provinces, it was as high as 20 per cent. *Likin* originally meant a surtax of "a thousandth" of the value of commodities, but the definition was never literally interpreted—not even by its originator, Lei I-hsien, who wrote: "The amount which has been collected is in general only one part in a hundred [i.e. one per cent of the value of the goods handled], and there are even cases in which it does not reach one part [in a hundred]." See Edwin George Beal, Jr., *The Origin of Likin* (Cambridge, Mass., 1958), 26.

Standard army all belonged to the central government. But now, due to the exigency of circumstances, Tseng Kuo-fan, a scholar and an official in mourning—and a Chinese at that—broke the precedent.

The court had repeatedly urged Tseng to send his forces to rescue Hupeh province from the Taipings, but he refused to leave Hunan until he had cleared away the local bandits and completed the training of his army and navy. Impatient with the delay, the emperor reprimanded him for partiality toward his native province without regard for the general situation. In early 1854 the Taipings once again threatened Wuchang, and the anxious court "begged" Tseng to aid Hupeh, authorizing him freedom of action without control from Peking. By February of that year, Tseng set out for Hupeh with a force of 17,000 men. In leaving their native province, the Hunan army and navy shed what little traces were left of a parochial militia and became a new fighting force of national stature. Tseng issued a proclamation in which he condemned the Taiping disruption of village life, the abolition of private ownership of land, the destruction of temples, and the violation of Confucian propriety and the Chinese way of life. The first two of these items, it is fairly evident, were meant for the peasants, and the last two were directed at the gentry. He skipped altogether the issue of nationalistic and racial revolution that the Taipings made much of, but stressed his own role as a defender of the cultural tradition. The literati flocked to his cause, not that they appreciated less the Taiping anti-Manchu stand, but that they loved more the preservation of Chinese heritage. Moreover, the Manchu dynasty had been established for more than 200 years, and the Chinese scholars had served it for all that time; were they to advocate racial revolution now, it would be unconvincing. In fact, the vested interest of the literati so intertwined with that of the dynasty that in supporting the imperial cause the literati were actually defending their own interests.[20] The peasants also responded to the call of Tseng because they were disheartened by the Taiping disruption of their peaceful country life and by the wanton destruction of the temples and shrines.

The initial encounter of the Hunan army and the Taipings was not encouraging for Tseng; he received several setbacks and was criticized by provincial authorities for having begun his campaign with a hollow bang. Sensitive and despondent, Tseng twice attempted suicide by drowning, but was saved both times by his loyal followers. A change for the

20. Lo Erh-kang, *Hsiang chün hsin-chih* (A new study of the Hunan army), (Shanghai, 1939), 66.

better came when his navy scored a major victory at Hsiang-t'an on May 1, 1854. Tseng's star began to rise and in October he recovered the important city of Wuchang, which had been occupied by the Taipings since June. The emperor was delighted with this turn of events and remarked: "I had not expected that the scholar Tseng Kuo-fan could achieve such a great feat!" A courtier whispered that the rapid rise in power of a Chinese might not be to the best interest of the dynasty. The emperor knew this only too well; but the gloomy fact remained that there was no other man who could stop the Taipings. He therefore vested Tseng with the unqualified authority to conduct the campaign against the rebels. This marked the beginning of the shift of military power from the Manchus to the Chinese.

The victorious and confident Hunan army then entered Kiangsi to besiege the important city of Kiukiang. The Taipings not only resisted effectively but in fact succeeded in cutting the Hunan forces in two, nailing down Tseng's men in a most uncomfortable and immobile situation. Now the Taiping fortune rose again. They took Wuchang for the third time in April 1855, and overran Hupeh and Kiangsi, with Tseng quarantined in Kiangsi. Meanwhile, the Taipings at Nanking broke out to destroy the Imperial Great Camps on the South and North of the (Yangtze) River in mid-1856, driving the imperial commissioner Hsiang-jung to suicide. The entire Yangtze valley fell to the revolutionaries, and the future indeed looked good for them. But at the crest of their success, a blow fell from within which was to cripple the movement beyond recovery.

THE TAIPING INTERNAL DISSENSION

In 1856 occurred a fratricidal conflict in Nanking which violently shook the Taiping kingdom. The basic cause of the trouble was the East King Yang's irrepressible ambitions, which had been evident from the start. He had joined Hung and Feng in the early days of the God Worshippers and was accorded the third place in the organization, but unsatisfied with this, he schemed to elevate himself to the second place. Having seen through the falsity of Hung's divine commission and his new Trinity, Yang began going into trances himself and claimed that God had favored him with visitations. Soon, Hsiao (later the West King) followed suit and claimed that he too received visitations from Jesus. The two of them formed a compact directly rivaling the original set of Hung and Feng.

Hung dared not expose their tricks for fear of reprisals; rather, he married his sister to Hsiao in an attempt to draw him away from Yang.

About six months before the revolution broke out at Chin-t'ien in January 1851, Yang suddenly fell sick, unable to speak or hear, and consequently unable to participate in the planning of the uprising. It was obvious that he was carrying out a passive resistance in order to force the other leaders to give him a higher place. For the sake of unity and the cause of the revolution, Feng voluntarily relegated himself to the third place, giving the second position over to Yang, whose illness was then miraculously cured through a "divine healing" on November 4, 1850. He became commander-in-chief of the armed forces, next only to Hung in the movement. From then on, it was he who decided strategies and issued orders. With the death of the South King (Feng) and the West King (Hsiao) in 1852, the position of the East King was made the more secure. As prime minister and commander-in-chief of the Heavenly Kingdom of Great Peace at Nanking, he made all the important decisions, issued orders, and controlled access to the Heavenly King, who was shrouded in mystery in the palace recess. During audiences, the East King alone remained standing, while all others knelt, and he addressed himself to the Heavenly King by the proud and intimate cognomen of "your minister and younger brother." People in Nanking knew more about Yang than about Hung. It is not surprising, then, that his name should be as familiar and that the Taiping movement was frequently called the Hung-Yang Rebellion.

So proud was he of his part in the Taiping success—and it was unquestionably great—that the East King entertained hopes of replacing Hung himself. To facilitate the operation he sent the North King (Wei) and the Assistant King (Shih) away from Nanking, the former to Kiangsi and the latter to Hupeh. The East King began going into trances more often and angrily scolding Hung in the name of God. The climax of his scheming came after the 1856 destruction of the Imperial Great Camp on the South of the River. Elated with this success and confident of his leadership, the East King decided that the time had come to depose the Heavenly King. He instigated his followers to honor him, the East King, as the "Lord of Ten Thousand Years," a designation reserved for the Heavenly King and used otherwise only by emperors of dynasties. Hung knew that the hour of reckoning was coming on fast. He secretly sent for the North King and Assistant King to rid the kingdom of the East King's menace. The North King hurried to Nanking by night, broke into the residence of the East King, and slaughtered him on September 2 along with some 20,000 followers. But the cure was worse than the disease, for the North King now behaved as overbearingly as the East King had done. When the Assistant King arrived and murmured about the unnecessary massacre, intimating that the guilt belonged to the East King alone and did not extend to his followers, the North King wanted to kill him, too. Although the Assistant King managed to escape under cover of darkness, his family and relatives were all slaughtered. Unable to bear the wanton killing, the Heavenly King had the North King executed, less than three months after the death of the East King. By now Hung had lost all faith in his associates; he turned over the reins of government to his two mediocre brothers, who could hardly keep the kingdom together. The Assistant King, the lone survivor of the original five kings under Hung, returned to Nanking to take charge of state affairs for a short while, but found himself distrusted by the Heavenly King. Uncertain of his safety and his future, the Assistant King left with a large following, roving through a number of provinces in the next seven years until he was finally killed in Szechwan in 1863.

The internecine strife of 1856 depleted the spirit and vigor of the Taiping movement so thoroughly that it was never able to recover. Hung gave himself over to indulgence in pleasure to forget his miseries, and leadership simply disappeared from his government. Many officers and men would have left but for the Ch'ing standing order that all Taipings who surrendered should be decapitated. A slight improvement in the morale came when Hung Jen-kan, a cousin and early convert of the Taiping leader, came to Nanking in 1859 after many years of sojourn at Hong Kong. He was made the Shield King (*Kan Wang*) and prime minister, but the decline of the regime was too far advanced to be arrested. Nonetheless, the ultimate downfall of the Heavenly Kingdom was delayed, largely because of the brilliant warfare waged by the young and talented general, Li Hsiu-ch'eng, better known as the Loyal King (*Chung Wang*).[21] It was he who destroyed the resuscitated Imperial Great Camp on the South of the River in May 1860 for the second time, relieving Nanking of a thorn in its side. Riding the tide of victory, he then swept all the way to the outskirts of Shanghai in August 1860, taking Soochow and Changchow on the way. Through him the Taipings recovered the entire province of Kiangsu, except for Shanghai and Chinkiang. It was a valiant effort of the Loyal King to keep the movement

21. Or Loyal Prince in Western literature.

from crumbling, but no one man could arrest the disintegration of a doomed kingdom.

THE TURNING POINT IN THE CAMPAIGN

Meanwhile, important changes were taking place in the Ch'ing command and in foreign attitude toward the Chinese civil war. The second Taiping destruction of the Great Camp put an end to the imperial fighting forces, and the court had to rely even more on the Hunan army. In May 1860 Tseng Kuo-fan was given the coveted title of imperial commissioner and governor-general of Liang-Kiang, and was put in complete command of the operations against the Taipings. He had been fighting for years but without being given any specific titles such as those he had just received, and for this reason local authorities had not felt called upon to support or cooperate with him; indeed, many obstructed his plans. But now, with his new titles and authorization, Tseng was able to work out a unified strategy. It was also fortunate for him that the influential Manchu president of the Li-fan yüan, Su-shun, supported him and served as his spokesman before the emperor.

Tseng's rise to a high position of responsibility marked a turning point in the campaign. His Hunan army had grown to a powerful fighting force of 120,000 men, commanded by a number of able scholar-generals. In his headquarters, there were numerous planners, strategists, advisers, and administrative assistants, all destined for greater glory in later years. Tseng was doubtless the most powerful man in Southeast China, with jurisdiction over the four key provinces of Kiangsu, Anhwei, Kiangsi, and Chekiang. Yet the Taipings under the Loyal King were still active and effective. They enjoyed another brief spell of success in Chekiang and Anhwei in mid-1861, dealing an almost shattering blow to Tseng at Ch'imen, Anhwei. It was not until Tseng's brother, Tseng Kuo-ch'üan, took the important city of Anking in September that the tide was once again turned. Thereafter the Hunan army and navy gained ascendancy, recovering a number of cities on the Yangtze until they pressed near Nanking. In recognition of his success, the court made Tseng Kuo-fan a junior guardian of the crown prince in 1861 and an assistant grand secretary a year later. Tseng now placed Li Hung-chang, one of his chief assistants, in charge of military affairs in Kiangsu, and Tso Tsung-t'ang, another able assistant, in charge of military operations in Chekiang. The coveted assignment of attacking Nanking was awarded to his brother, who, with the help of the Hunan navy, penetrated to the vicinity of Nanking in June 1862. With 20,000 men he began a long siege of the Heavenly Capital.

At about this time foreign attitude toward the Chinese civil war was undergoing a radical change. Foreigners had shown early sympathy toward the Taipings because of their supposed Christianity and the prospect of extended trade. But when they found the Taipings incapable of successful government, arrogant in their pretension of universal overlordship, adamantly opposed to opium importation, and continuously disturbing foreign trade and lives at Shanghai, they lost interest in the Heavenly Kingdom. Moreover, after the signing of the new treaties with the Ch'ing court in 1860, the Western powers realized that the enjoyment of the concessions was contingent on the continued existence of the dynasty. In fact, the French and Russian ministers had proposed military assistance against the Taipings. The offer was received with mixed feelings, partly because it hurt Chinese pride to accept aid from erstwhile enemies, and partly because the court and the provincial authorities such as Tseng feared that foreigners might become too proud and domineering to be controlled, creating worse complications than the Taipings. Yet, not to utilize the foreign offer was impractical, and to refuse it outright might offend foreign good will. A compromise formula was adopted whereby foreigners were to be used in the defense of Shanghai but not in the general war against the Taipings.

Against this improved Ch'ing-Western relationship, the Taipings put up a poor show. Not only did they make no effort to lure the foreigners from the imperial cause, but their army continuously harassed Shanghai, the center of foreign trade and residence. At the same time, life in Nanking had degenerated to a new low. Alexander Michie, an Englishman who visited the Heavenly Capital in March 1861, wrote:

> I have no hope of any good ever coming of the rebel movement. No decent Chinaman will have anything to do with it. They do nothing but burn, murder, and destroy. They hardly profess anything beyond that. They are detested by all the country people, and even those in the city who are not of the "brethren" hate them. They have held Nanking eight years, and there is not a symptom of rebuilding it. Trade and industry are prohibited. Their land-taxes are three times heavier than those of the Imperialists; they adopt no measures to soothe and conciliate the people, nor do they act in any way as if they had a permanent interest in the soil. They don't care about the ordinary slow and sure sources of revenue; they look to plunder, and

plunder alone, for subsistence, and I must say, I cannot see any elements of stability about them, nor anything which can claim our sympathy.[22]

Another description was furnished by the Rev. Issachar J. Roberts, who spent fifteen months in Nanking during 1861-62 at the invitation of the Heavenly King, who had formerly studied with him. His report of December 31, 1861 states, in part:

> As to the religious opinions of Tien Wang [Hung], which he propagates with great zeal, I believe them in the main abominable in the sight of God. In fact, I believe he is crazy, especially in religious matters, nor do I believe him soundly rational about anything . . . I do not believe they have any organized Government, nor do they know enough about Government to make one.
>
> He [Hung] wanted me to come, but it was not to preach the gospel of Jesus Christ and convert men and women to God, but to take office, and preach his dogmas, and convert foreigners to himself. I would as lief convert them to Mormonism, or any other *ism* which I believe unscriptural, and, so far, from the devil. I believe that in their heart they feel a real opposition to Gospel, but for policy's sake they grant it toleration . . . And hence I am making up my mind to leave them . . .[23]

In short, early foreign sympathy toward the Taipings had given way to disappointment and a determination to assist the imperial regime, whose existence was recognized as essential to foreign interests in China.

The first foreign intervention in the Chinese civil war took place in 1860 when the Loyal King attacked Shanghai. Rich merchants and businessmen in the city financed the organization of a "foreign legion" and the American adventurer from Salem, Massachusetts, Frederick T. Ward, was engaged by the wealthy banker Yang Fang, better known by his firm's name "Taki," to recruit foreign deserters and discharged seamen to form a "Rifle Squadron." By taking the city of Sungkiang, this foreign mercenary army diverted the Taiping forces from Shanghai and scored its first major victory. In September 1861, Ward revamped his squadron by drafting 4,000 to 5,000 Chinese soldiers, who were drilled and clad in the European fashion and were commanded by 100 European officers. In

22. McNair, I, 349.
23. McNair, I, 349-51.

addition, there were some 200 Filipinos in his army, which fought and pillaged in the Soochow-Sungkiang-T'ai-ts'ang area and won many battles. In March 1862, when they repulsed for the second time a Taiping attack on Shanghai, the emperor bestowed on them the flattering name the "Ever-Victorious army," and on Ward the rank of brigade-general. When Ward was fatally wounded on September 21, 1862 and died a day later, the leadership of the Ever-Victorious army went to another American adventurer, Henry A. Burgevine, a man of neither principle nor backbone. He argued with Taki for funds and forcibly seized 40,000 silver dollars. Consequently he was relieved of his duty and the English officer, the famous Charles G. (Chinese) Gordon, was installed as the new leader.

THE DOWNFALL OF THE TAIPING KINGDOM

On the recommendation of Tseng Kuo-fan, the court authorized Li Hung-chang to organize a new force to supplement the Hunan army. Tseng turned over 3,000 of his Hunan troops as the nucleus of the new army, while Li Hung-chang recruited several more thousand men, whom he organized after the fashion of the Hunan army. Since most of these recruits came from the Huai River area in Anhwei province, they became known as the Huai (or Anhwei) army.[24] During the Loyal King's second attack on Shanghai in 1862, Li led the Huai army to its rescue and scored a victory in the outskirts. Li was made governor of Kiangsu. In November 1863 the Huai army attacked the Taiping stronghold Soochow, backed up by the Ever-Victorious army which arrived from a different direction. Gordon succeeded in persuading eight Taiping defending kings and generals to surrender on terms of lenient treatment; but when taken to Li Hung-chang's headquarters, they were all slaughtered. The court rewarded Gordon with 10,000 taels and Li with the title of junior guardian of the crown prince. Popular Western and Chinese accounts report that Gordon was so incensed with the killing of the prisoners of war that he threatened to kill Li in return. But his wounded pride was soothed by Li's offer of 70,000 taels to be given to his Ever-Victorious army and by his (Li's) issuance of a public statement to the effect that Gordon was not present at the time of the killing, so to absolve him from any responsibility.

24. For a study of the rise of the Huai Army, see Stanley Spector, *Li Hung-chang and the Huai Army: A Study in Nineteenth-Century Chinese Regionalism* (Seattle, 1964), chapters 2-3.

Gordon pronounced himself satisfied, and his friendship with Li continued for life. The whole province of Kiangsu was now pacified, except for Nanking and a few small pockets.

Li's success in Kiangsu was paralleled by Tso Tsung-t'ang's in Chekiang; together they cut the sources of supply to the Heavenly Capital, which by now was under an ever-tightening siege—like "an iron barrel"—by Tseng Kuo-ch'üan. The Loyal King urged Hung to seek a new base in Kiangsi and Hupeh, but the latter replied that having been commissioned by God to be king on earth, he did not choose to leave. By early 1864 the food in Nanking had run out and the Heavenly King urged the people to subsist on "sweet dew," i.e. grass. Knowing that his cause was lost, Hung let state affairs lapse on the pretext of sickness, and muttered at times: "Since ancient times how can emperors be taken prisoners?" On June 1, 1864, he committed suicide at the age of fifty-two *sui*. His sixteen-year-old son Hung Fu was placed on the throne as the Young Heavenly King, with the Shield King as regent. On July 19, Tseng Kuo-ch'üan's army broke into Nanking and carried out a merciless massacre. Every Taiping officer and man resisted to the end and none surrendered. The Loyal King assisted the Young Heavenly King in a hasty flight from Nanking, and in the panic the young master's horse stumbled, throwing the rider to the ground. The Loyal King offered him his own horse, allowing himself to be captured. The Young Heavenly King managed to flee to Kiangsi, where he was ultimately discovered and executed. The Taiping Revolution came to an end in 1864.

In captivity the Loyal King was treated with courtesy by Tseng Kuo-fan, who had respect for his military talent. Tseng asked him to prepare an autobiographical deposition. From July 30 to August 7, 1864, he wrote several thousand words daily, recounting the history of the Taipings, pointing out the mistakes of the Heavenly King as well as those of the Ch'ing court, and praising the Tseng brothers and the Hunan army. The Loyal King also offered to induce the Taiping remnants to surrender, and suggested that the Young Heavenly King had already been killed.[25] Tseng sent to Peking an edited version of the deposition, omitting those portions that were critical of the Ch'ing court, while keeping the original in his family library.[26] At midnight of August 7, the Loyal King was

25. For an abridged English version of the deposition, see W. T. Lay (tr.), *The Autobiography of the Chung-wang* (Shanghai, 1865).
26. This original was published nearly a hundred years later under the title, *Li Hsiu-ch'eng ch'in-kung shou-chi* (Li Hsiu-ch'eng's personal deposition in his own hand-writing), (Taipei, 1962).

executed at the age of 40 *sui*. So ended the life of a military genius, who singlehandedly upheld a tottering empire for eight years after 1856. But for him the Heavenly Kingdom would have crumbled long before.[27]

Tseng was rewarded with the title of marquis first class, while his brother and Li were made count first class. Tseng was probably the most honored and powerful man in the empire at this point. His Hunan army and navy boasted of 120,000 to 130,000 men, and his entourage consisted of more than eighty of the most brilliant and capable advisers, strategists, planners, generals, and secretaries. A single order of his was obeyed by thousands of officials. Story has it that at the crest of success Tseng received a tiny slip of paper from someone bearing a secret message: "Your Excellency has already the entire southern half of the country in your hands, do you have any further idea?" Tseng's complexion, according to the story, turned ashen and he quickly swallowed the paper to destroy any evidence of seditious intention.[28] A correct Confucian and a loyal minister, he knew that any extraordinary power and fame enjoyed by a Chinese would be cause for suspicion by the Manchu overlords. Barely seventeen days after the recovery of Nanking, he was obliged to propose the disbandment of the Hunan forces, which had accomplished their original objectives and were beginning to show signs of fatigue. In statesmanship, in character, and in personal cultivation, Tseng had few equals. He was probably the most respected and the greatest scholar-official of 19th-century China. Yet today he is denounced in Communist China as

---

27. The Loyal King's behavior in captivity came under considerable criticism in Communist China during the centenary of the Taiping downfall in 1964. The historian Ch'i Pen-yu led the attack in anathematizing him as a shameless, treacherous traitor who begged for his life in captivity and ingratiated himself with his former enemies. On the other hand, Lo Erh-kang, a lifelong student of the Taiping movement, argued that the Loyal King made a "false surrender" in order to save the Taiping cause; that the deposition was a stratagem to fool Tseng Kuo-fan into believing that there was no urgent need to kill the Young Heavenly King and destroy the Taiping remnants. The party historians (Yüan Shu-i and Lu I-tzu) offered a qualified approval of the Loyal King by stating that although his plea for life was "counterrevolutionary and deplorable," it did no serious harm because the Taiping government had already fallen; that his earlier achievements outweighed his regrettable last act. What these critics did not know is the fact that the deposition on which they based their arguments is not the authentic version but the abridged one made by Tseng. Nowhere in the original version does the word "surrender" ever appear, and it is well known that the Loyal King was ready to die when he completed the deposition. For an interesting account, see Stephen Uhalley, Jr., "The Controversy over Li Hsiu-ch'eng: An Ill-timed Centenary," *The Journal of Asian Studies*, XXV:2:305-17 (Feb. 1966).
28. Hsiao I-shan, III, 779-80.

a traitor and executioner, who betrayed and massacred his fellow country-men in the interests of the alien Manchu rulers.[29]

CAUSES OF THE TAIPING FAILURE

The Taiping Revolution affected sixteen of the eighteen provinces in China proper and lasted for fourteen years. Its rise was as vigorous and promising as its end was pathetic and pitiful. Historical hindsight reveals several major reasons for the ultimate failure of the movement.

Strategic Blunder. The Taipings concentrated on forward movement and neglected to guard their rear. From their beginning at Chin-t'ien in Jan-uary 1851, the guiding principle in military operations was to take cities, seize provisions and treasuries, and move on to new conquests. They did not hold and administer the conquered areas. As important a place as Wuhan, the key communication and strategic center on the Yangtze, they gave up after looting, thus enabling the Hunan forces to use it as a rallying point from which to advance later to Nanking. In their pref-erence for swift movement, the Taipings skirted Changsha, the capital of Hunan, and in so doing they left Tseng Kuo-fan a base on which to raise the Hunan army. After the capture of Nanking, the Taipings should not have settled down for a soft life but rather should have taken ad-vantage of their impetus to sweep north all the way to Peking, when they might very possibly have dislodged the Manchu court. The northern ex-pedition which they did send under Lin Feng-hsiang was not a main Taiping force, but a thin column which erred in overextending itself in enemy territory, courting annihilation. The Ch'ing court, thus saved from the onslaught, was able to continue as the legitimate center of political power and the focal point of resistance.

Failing to take Peking, the Taipings should have at least concentrated on destroying the imperial Great Camps on the two sides of the Yangtze so completely as to allow no chance of resuscitation, in order to make Nanking safe. They should also have taken the entire province of Ki-angsu, including the important trading center of Shanghai, and estab-lished firm and friendly contacts with foreign representatives. It was a major mistake of Hung's to ignore the plea for assistance from the Small Sword Society, a branch of the Triad Society, which occupied the Chinese

29. Fan Wen-lan, *Han-chien kuei-tzu-shou Tseng Kuo-fan ti i-sheng,* (The life of the traitor and executioner Tseng Kuo-fan), (Shanghai, 1944).

walled city of Shanghai for a year and a half in 1853-54, thereby losing a chance to deprive the Ch'ing of an important point of contact with foreigners and a base for operations.

Ideological Conflict. The anti-Manchu appeal of the Taiping cause was compromised by its Christian ideology. The destruction of the temples and idols and the disruption of village life alienated the sympathies of the literati and peasants. The Taiping concept of all men being brothers and all women sisters contradicted the Confucian ideas of propriety and social hierarchy, and their prohibition against the cohabitation of husbands and wives ran counter to basic human relationships. Moreover, the unorthodox nature of the Taiping Christianity excited foreign antipathy. Indeed, their religious ideology alienated both Chinese and Westerner alike.

Initially, Hung had used religion to support his nationalistic revolution against the Manchus. He claimed divine commission and created a new Trinity so as to construct an invincible, supernatural aura around himself. He convinced the soldiers that they would rise to heaven if they were killed, and achieved a fearless army. By these manipulations, he successfully used religion as a means to advance his revolution. But later, when he became engrossed in religion and refused to cooperate with the secret societies because their members were not Christians, and when he refused to aid the Small Sword Society when it occupied Shanghai in 1853, he lost sight of his primary objective and placed religious considerations above the nationalistic revolution. Indeed, when he subordinated revolution to religion, he blurred his image as a nationalistic revolutionary, allowing himself to degenerate to the order of "religious bandits" (*chiao-fei*), like the White Lotus rebels.

Failure in Leadership. Of the original five leaders under Hung, the South and West Kings were lost in battles in 1852, and the East King and North King were killed in the fratricidal strife of 1856. Only the Assistant King survived, but he left Nanking to start a life of his own. Deprived of their support, Hung was lost. He had relied on the South King (Feng) for the organization of the God Worshippers and the initial uprising, as he had depended on the East King (Yang) for military operations and civil administration. After 1856, the only man of ability and courage was the Loyal King, but, as the Chinese described it, one pillar could not support a whole mansion. The Shield King, who came to

Nanking in 1859, was more a man of ideas than of practical ability, and he had the shortcoming of being jealous of other talents. His major claim to credit, if it can be called that, was a spontaneous program of modernization involving mining, banking, irrigation, trains, ships, post offices, publishing companies, and new communication lines. The Heavenly King approved of this project, but was unable to put it into practice because of the rapid decline of the Taiping fortune.

The paucity of genuine leadership placed Hung in a quandary. He could not evolve long-range constructive policies or over-all military strategy; nor could he guide a civil administration adequately, so he simply withdrew from all responsibility. It was no surprise that the missionary Roberts stated in 1861 that the Taiping "political system is about as poor as their theology. I do not believe they have any organized government, nor do they know enough about government to make one." In contrast, the opponents of Hung, such as Tseng Kuo-fan, Li Hung-chang, and Tso Tsung-t'ang, were all men of learning, ability, and rationality. Some have compared them to Hung as learned graduate advisers to a grade-school student.

Inconsistencies in Taiping Life. The revolutionaries preached the abolition of private ownership, but the leaders themselves accumulated vast wealth. They advocated the separation of husbands and wives into different quarters, the equality of the sexes, and monogamy as the correct form of marriage; but Hung himself kept 88 concubines, the East King kept 36, the North King 14, and the Assistant King 7. When the Women's Residential Halls were disbanded, the members were matched to officials according to their ranks—the higher the rank, the greater the number of women.

While Hung forbade people to read works of Confucius and Mencius, which were labeled "bogey books," he himself read them freely, borrowed ideas from the *Rites of Chou*, and explained his Christianity in Confucian terms. In his last years, Hung had become neurotic and was obsessed with superstition. He believed that God Almighty would solve all his problems and that he himself need do nothing. When Nanking was under the severe attack of Tseng Kuo-ch'üan and was about to fall, Hung announced that his "heavenly soldiers," more numerous than "water," would guard his city as an "iron barrel."

Poor Diplomacy. The Taipings enjoyed at first the sympathy of foreign powers. But instead of using it as a starting point for winning foreign recognition and assistance, they insisted on treating foreign powers as dependencies, an attitude that quashed all chances for good relations. When the foreign powers discovered that the Taipings were no more accommodating than the Manchus and were in fact hurting the foreign commerce at Shanghai, they withdrew their sympathy, shifting it after 1860 to the imperial government. The subsequent foreign defense of Shanghai in 1860 and 1862 prevented the Loyal King from taking this rich city, depriving the Heavenly Capital of an important source of supply and contributing to its final collapse.

THE LEGACY OF THE TAIPING REVOLUTION

Though it ended in failure, the Taiping experience had profound consequences in China. Politically, it affected the transfer of government power from the Manchus to the Chinese. Officers of the Hunan and Huai armies were awarded important assignments in the post-Taiping era, and key governor-generalships and governorships formerly occupied by the Manchus now passed into Chinese hands.[30] A few examples will illustrate this point. Tseng Kuo-fan, as governor-general of Liang-Kiang (1860-65) who also superintended military affairs in Chekiang, was in charge of four rich and important provinces (Kiangsu, Kiangsi, Anhwei, and Chekiang), while Li Hung-chang became governor of Kiangsu, and Tso Tsung-t'ang governor of Chekiang. All three in time rose to be grand secretaries of state. Li, in particular, as governor-general of Chihli and high commissioner of the Northern Ocean,[31] was China's virtual "prime minister" from 1870 to 1895. Tso also became governor-general, first of Chekiang and Fukien (1863-66), and then of Shensi and Kansu (1867-80), crowning his long career with the recovery of Sinkiang from the Moslem rebels in the 1870's. Even in the innermost organ of the court, the Grand Council, more and more Chinese were appointed until finally they outnumbered the Manchus. In short, the locus of power in the government had shifted from the Manchus to the Chinese.

30. During 1864-66 all fifteen governorships were occupied by Chinese and during 1867-69 by fourteen Chinese and one Manchu, as compared with seven Manchus and eight Chinese in 1840. Taking late Ch'ing (1851-1911) as a whole, 65.4 per cent of the governors-general and 77.8 per cent of the governors were Chinese, as compared with 34.6 per cent and 22.2 per cent Manchus (including Mongols and Chinese bannermen) respectively. See Lawrence D. Kessler, "Ethnic Composition of Provincial Leadership," 500, table 4; see also S. Y. Teng, "Some New Light on the Nien Movement," 65-66.

31. A post created in 1861 to take charge of the three northern ports of Tientsin, Newchwang (Yingkow), and Chefoo.

A corollary to this change was the growing influence of provincial officials in national affairs. Whereas in the early and middle Ch'ing periods the government was highly centralized, with the court deciding policies for the provinces, in the post-Taiping period the central power declined directly as the local power rose. The court often found it necessary to consult high provincial officials on national issues and defer to their opinions; not infrequently government offices in Peking solicited the views of local authorities in order to win support for their stands. At times powerful governors and governors-general would act independently of the central government. For instance, after the "Hundred-Day" Reform of 1898, Governor-general Liu K'un-i of Liang-Kiang vigorously opposed the empress dowager's plan of deposing the emperor; during the Boxer Rebellion of 1900 the provincial authorities in Southeast China refused to follow the court order of supporting the Boxers, and out of "self-preservation" independently entered into agreements with foreign powers. The most blatant instance of provincial independence occurred in 1911 when Dr. Sun Yat-sen's revolutionary army took Wuchang; the provincial authorities declared their support of the revolution and by so defying the court hastened the downfall of the Ch'ing dynasty.

Militarily, the Hunan and Huai armies were the forerunners of private armies that characterized the warlords of later periods. Tseng and Li recruited their officers on the four bases of (1) common provincial origin; (2) common scholastic background; (3) relatives and friends; and (4) teachers and students. The soldiers were raised and trained by the officers, to whom they owed undivided allegiance. "When the general dies, the army scatters. When the general lives, the army is complete"; so commented the author of the *Hsiang-chün chih* (A record of the Hunan army). This Tseng-Li tradition of the private army was inherited by Yüan Shih-k'ai, a onetime protégé of Li and later leader of the Peiyang warlords, who plagued China during the early years (1912-27) of the Republic.

Finally, the Taiping experience inspired later revolutionaries. The Taiping remnants who went underground to join the Heaven and Earth Society kept alive the idea of racial and nationalistic revolution against the Manchus. It became a source of inspiration to Dr. Sun Yat-sen (1866-1925), father of the Chinese Republic, who was born barely two years after the downfall of the Heavenly Kingdom. As a child he had heard stories about the Taipings and at the age of twelve decided to become a second Hung. His later revolution received support from the secret societies, and many of his early followers were members of the Ko-lao Brotherhood Association. Even his revolutionary philosophy—the Three People's Principles *(San Min Chu I)*—was influenced by the Taiping ideology. Sun believed Hung failed because he understood national independence but not popular sovereignty, and monarchy but not democracy. To repair these ideological defects, Sun advocated his first two principles of Nationalism *(Min-tsu)* and Democracy *(Min-ch'üan)*. His third principle, Socialism *(Min-sheng)*, which contained the ideas of "equalization of land" and "regulation of capital," was in part inspired by the Taiping land system and the communal ownership of property. The social revolution that the Taipings failed to realize was partly carried on by Dr. Sun and his followers.

Not only in China, but in Europe, the Taiping Revolution was a source of instruction. Disappointed by the failure of the 1848 revolution in Europe, Karl Marx found hopes in the Taiping movement and gained new perspective in the possibility of peasant revolution. Today, Chinese Communist historians hail the Taiping experience as the first peasant revolution in the history of Modern China.[32]

THE NIEN AND MOSLEM REBELLIONS

Although the Taipings had been suppressed by 1864, several other rebellions of a smaller order still raged over different parts of the country. The Nien Rebellion, which broke out in 1853 and lasted until 1868, focused its activities in the southern part of North China. The Moslem (Panthay) Rebellion in Yunnan lasted from 1855 to 1873, and the Tungan Rebellion in the northwest covered the period from 1862 to 1878. These long-lasting rebellions were extremely debilitating in their effects, but they established no rival governments to contest the court at Peking. They were not therefore as threatening as the Taipings.

"Nien" was the name for secret gangs in the Shantung, Honan, Kiangsu, and Anhwei area. The members were chiefly idlers, rascals, and bandits who lived off forced contributions and pillage. Several tens or sometimes several hundreds of them formed a "nien," which literally meant "band." They were proscribed during the Chia-ch'ing period (1796-1820). When the Taipings established themselves in Nanking in

32. However, a recent study by Vincent Y. C. Shih, *The Taiping Ideology: Its Source, Interpretations and Influences* (Seattle, 1967), argues that the Taiping movement was not a revolution, much less a peasant revolution.

1853, uncoordinated bands of Nien rebels rose in sympathetic response. The most powerful leader of these bands was Chang Lo-hsing, whose forces were joined by the remnants of the Taiping northern expeditionary army after its failure. Chang was invested with the title of King Wo by the Heavenly King, and his men wore long hair and attempted to imitate the Taiping military systems. Frequently the Nien and the Taipings co-operated in their military operations. In 1855 the poorly coordinated, decentralized Nien units were organized into five bands, distinguished by the different colors of their banners: red, yellow, blue, white, and black—a structure reminiscent of the early Ch'ing banner system.

Basically a conglomerate of peripatetic bands, the Nien rebels relied for their strength on the swift movement of their cavalry. They adopted the guerrilla tactics of avoiding frontal and direct confrontation with the imperial forces, while launching unexpected attacks when the enemy was off guard. With their fast-moving horsemen, they forced the Ch'ing army into a kind of shadowboxing. After years of inconclusive warfare, the court sent the fierce Mongolian general, Prince Seng-ko-lin-ch'in, to fight them, and he succeeded in killing the rebel leader Chang in 1863. But the Nien movement continued and, in fact, became stronger after 1864 when the Taiping remnants joined its cause. When Seng-ko-lin-ch'in was killed in action in 1865, the court asked Tseng Kuo-fan to take charge of the operations.

The rebel movement now split into two directions: the western band penetrated into Shensi and developed connections with the Moslem rebels, and the eastern band broke into Shantung, Hupeh, Honan, and Kiangsu. Tseng fought over a year without achieving results, coming under sharp criticism from the censors. Feeling the effects of age and distressed by the loss of vigor of his Hunan army, Tseng recommended Li Hung-chang to take over his assignment in early 1867. By the end of that year, Li's Huai army had succeeded in suppressing the eastern band of the Nien, while the western band had come under the severe attack of Tso Tsung-t'ang, who had been appointed imperial commissioner in charge of military affairs in Shensi and Kansu. In a last desperate attempt, the rebels thrust into the capital province of Chihli in early 1868, threatening Tientsin and Peking. However, under the joint attack of Tso and Li, the rebels received a series of shattering blows from which they never recovered. In August 1868, the Nien Rebellion was brought to an end.

The Moslem Rebellion in Yunnan, known in Western literature as the Panthay Rebellion—"Panthay" being a corruption of the Burmese term for Moslem—lasted from 1855 to 1873. It was generally believed that the Moslems in Yunnan had migrated from the Western Region (Sinkiang) during the Mongol period (1280-1368). They made up no more than 20 per cent or 30 per cent of the population of Yunnan, but being a closely knit group they represented a powerful minority. Despised by the Chinese and Manchus for their religion and different way of life, they were the object of social ostracism and political discrimination. Oppression by officials and infringement of rights by the Chinese people were frequent, and when the Moslems took their cases to court they were often denied justice. Officials and judges openly shielded the Chinese against the Moslems: there was a popular saying that when one Chinese was killed ten Moslems would be persecuted, and when ten Moslems were killed only one Chinese would be punished. It is therefore not surprising that the Moslems harbored a strong incentive for protest and revolt.

In 1855 an open rebellion broke out over the issue of some mining properties which the Chinese and the Moslems both claimed. The rebel leader, Tu Wen-hsiu, occupied Tali and proclaimed himself generalissimo and Sultan Suleiman of a new Moslem kingdom. Provincial military forces could not suppress him and the Manchu governor-general committed suicide. By 1868 Tu was in command, reportedly, of 360,000 men and 53 cities. It was not until 1872 that the government troops, under the leadership of new provincial authorities, were able to check him. Tu's son went to England and Turkey to seek aid, but to no avail. The rebellion, which lasted for eighteen years, came to an end in January 1873, when Tu, in despair, killed his family, took poison himself, and then surrendered.

There was yet another rebellion that troubled the Ch'ing court. The Moslems in the northwest, known as the Tungan, numbered six million in Shensi and eight million in Kansu. They were Chinese-assimilated, having adopted Chinese customs, language, and dress, but they still suffered social and political discrimination. Among them the adherents of the New Sect[33] (Hsin-chiao) were particularly militant. They maintained their headquarters in Chin-chi-pao, Ninghsia, and in Chang-chia-ch'üan, Kansu, as a rival counterpart to the Old Sect stronghold of Hochow. Resentment of social and political injustices, exacerbated by the conflict between the two sects themselves, led the New Sect to rebel in 1781 and

33. Founded by one Ma Ming-hsin in 1762. For details, see Immanuel C. Y. Hsü, *The Ili Crisis: A Study of Sino-Russian Diplomacy 1871-1881* (Oxford, 1965), 22-24.

1783, but on both occasions the government suppressed them mercilessly.

In 1862 when the Taipings invaded Shensi, the Moslems—some of whose leaders had participated in the Yunnan Revolt—rose again in response. One fanatic leader was Ma Hua-lung, who came from a direct line of the founder of the New Sect. The Ch'ing court, preoccupied with the Taiping campaign, could spare no able generals or troops to fight the Tungan. By 1864 the whole northwest was ablaze, with Kansu, Shensi, Ninghsia, and Sinkiang fallen to the rebels. The threat was intensified in 1866 when the western band of the Nien rebels broke into Shensi and joined forces with the Moslems. The harassed court appointed Tso Tsung-t'ang governor-general of Shensi and Kansu, with the specific assignment of clearing the two provinces of the rebels. He was, as noted before, then fighting the Nien rebels and was unable to take up the new assignment immediately. It was not until his suppression of the Nien rebels in August 1868, that he was able to turn his attention to the Moslem problem in Shensi and Kansu. Five years of hard campaigning ensued, and by 1873 he finally pacified the Moslem Rebellion in these two provinces.

With the suppression of these domestic rebellions, the Ch'ing government re-established its authority over most of the empire. The dynasty seemed to have reversed its downward course and experienced a restoration. The question is whether such an upturn marked the beginning of a second blossoming of the dynasty, or was simply a short respite during a general decline.

FURTHER READING

Bain, Chester A. "Commodore Matthew Perry, Humphrey Marshall, and the Taiping Rebellion," *Far Eastern Quarterly*, 10:3:258-70 (May 1951).

Beal, George E., Jr., *The Origin of Likin, 1853-1864* (Cambridge, Mass., 1961).

Boardman, Eugene P., *Christian Influence upon the Ideology of the Taiping Rebellion* (Madison, 1952).

Chiang, Hsing-te 蔣星德, *Tseng Kuo-fan chih sheng-p'ing chi shih-yeh* 曾國藩之生平及事業 (Tseng Kuo-fan's life and work), (Shanghai, 1935).

Chiang, Siang-tseh, *The Nien Rebellion* (Seattle, 1954).

Fan, Wen-lan 范文瀾, *T'ai-p'ing t'ien-kuo ko-ming yün-tung* 太平天國革命運動 (The revolutionary movement of the Heavenly Kingdom of Great Peace), (Hong Kong, 1948).

————, *Han-chien kuei-tzu-shou Tseng Kuo-fan ti i-sheng* 漢奸劊子手曾國藩的 一生 (The life of the traitor and executioner Tseng Kuo-fan), (Shanghai, 1949).

————, *et al.* (eds.), *Nien-chün* 捻軍 (The Nien Army), (Shanghai, 1953), 6 vols.

Hail, William J., *Tseng Kuo-fan and the Taiping Rebellion* (New York, 1964).

Hsiang, Ta 向達 *et al.* (eds.) *T'ai-p'ing t'ien-kuo* 太平天國 (The Taiping Heavenly Kingdom), (Shanghai, 1952), 8 vols.

Hsia, Nai 夏鼐, *T'ai-p'ing t'ien-kuo ch'ien-hou Ch'ang-chiang ko-sheng chih t'ien-fu wen-t'i* 太平天國前後長江各省之田賦問題 (Problems regarding the land tax in the provinces along the Yangtze River before and after the Heavenly Kingdom of Great Peace), *Tsing-hua hsüeh-pao*, 10:2:409-74 (April 1935).

Hsiao, I-shan, *Tseng Kuo-fan* 曾國藩 (Chunking, 1944).

Lo, Erh-kang 羅爾綱, *Hsiang-chün hsin-chih* 湘軍新誌 (A new study of the Hunan army), (Shanghai, 1939).

————, "T'ai-p'ing t'ien-kuo ko-ming ch'ien ti jen-k'ou ya-p'o wen-t'i 太平天國革命前的人口壓迫問題(The question of population pressure in the pre-Taiping Revolution years), *Chung-kuo she-hui ching-chi chi-k'an* (Collected writings on Chinese society and economics), Academia Sinica, 8:1:20-80 (Jan. 1939).

————, *T'ai-p'ing t'ien-kuo shih-kang* 太平天國史綱 (An outline history of the Taiping Kingdom), (Shanghai, 1937).

Lo Yü-tung 羅玉東, *Chung-kuo li-chin shih* 中國厘金史 (A history of *likin* in China), (Shanghai, 1936).

MacNair, H. F., *Modern Chinese History, Selected Readings* (Shanghai, 1927), I, chapter 9.

Meadows, Thomas T., *The Chinese and Their Rebellions* (London, 1856).

Michael, Franz, and Chung-li Chang, *The Taiping Rebellion: History and Documents* (Seattle, 1966), Vol. 1.

Pai, Shou-i 白壽彝 (ed.), *Hui-min ch'i-i* 回民起義 (The righteous uprising of the Moslems), (Shanghai, 1953), 4 vols.

P'eng, Tse-i 彭澤益, *T'ai-p'ing t'ien-kuo ko-ming ssu-ch'ao* 太平天國革命思潮 (The revolutionary thought-tide of the Heavenly Kingdom of Great Peace), (Shanghai, 1946).

Shen, Han-yin Chen, "Tseng Kuo-fan in Peking, 1840-1852: His Ideas on Statecraft and Reform," *The Journal of Asian Studies*, XXVII:1:61-80 (Nov. 1967).

Shih, Vincent Y. C., *The Taiping Ideology: Its Source, Interpretations and Influences* (Seattle, 1967).

————, "Interpretations of the Taiping Tien-kuo by Noncommunist Chinese Writers," *Far Eastern Quarterly*, X:3:248-57 (May 1951).

So, Kwan-wai, Eugene Boardman, and Ch'iu Ping, "Hung Jen-kan: Taiping Prime Minister," *Harvard Journal of Asiatic Studies*, 20:1-2:262-94 (June 1957).

Spector, Stanley, *Li Hung-chang and the Huai Army: A Study in Nineteenth-Century Chinese Regionalism* (Seattle, 1964).

Taylor, George, "The Taiping Rebellion, Its Economic Background and Social Theory," *The Chinese Social and Political Science Review*, 32:-545-614 (1932-33).

Teng, Ssu-yü, *New Light on the History of the Taiping Rebellion* (Cambridge, Mass., 1950).

————, *The Nien Army and Their Guerrilla Warfare, 1851-1868* (Paris, 1961).

————, *Historiography of the Taiping Rebellion* (Cambridge, Mass., 1962).

————, "Some New Light on the Nien Movement and Its Effects on the Fall of the Manchu Dynasty," *Symposium on Chinese Studies*, Commemorating the Golden Jubilee of the University of Hong Kong, 1911-1961, (Hong Kong, 1968), III, 50-69.

Teng, Yüan-chung, "The Failure of Hung Jen-kan's Foreign Policy," *The Journal of Asian Studies*, XXVIII:1:125-38 (Nov. 1968).

Wu, James T. K., "The Impact of the Taiping Rebellion upon the Manchu Fiscal System," *Pacific Historical Review*, 19:265-75 (Aug. 1950).

Yap, P. M., "The Mental Illness of Hung Hsiu-ch'üan, Leader of the Taiping Rebellion," *The Far Eastern Quarterly*, XIII:3:287-304 (May 1954).

PART III

Self-strengthening in an Age of Accelerated Foreign Imperialism

1861-95

11

The Dynastic Revival and
the Self-strengthening Movement

The peace settlement with Britain and France in 1860 and the suppression of the Taiping Revolution in 1864 eliminated two deadly threats to the dynasty, one external and the other internal. The Ch'ing court had forged a momentary reprieve, and in the period that followed displayed a remarkable spirit of resurgence, as manifested in the suppression of the Nien and Moslem rebellions, the restoration of the traditional order and the Confucian government, the maintenance of peace with foreign powers, and the initiation of the Self-strengthening Movement through adoption of Western diplomatic practices and military and technological devices. Arrested, if only temporarily, was the dynastic decline characterized by the twin evil of "internal rebellion and external invasion."

Scholars and statesmen of the 1860's and 1870's were quick to refer to this dynastic "second blossoming" as a "T'ung-chih Restoration" (*T'ung-chih chung-hsing*). Here, "restoration" lacks the same connota-tion as the Meiji Restoration of Japan, which meant the return of state powers from the military dictator (*shogun*) and the feudal lords (*daimyo*) to the emperor; it refers rather to efforts at restoring the traditional order through reaffirmation of the old morality and application of knowledge to practical affairs (*ching-shih chih-yung*). Measures were taken to rehabilitate the devastated agricultural areas and to search out men of talent for public service. The government remitted or reduced agricultural taxes in the countryside, distributed seeds and tools to assist in the recovery, and stressed a program of personal austerity. Private academies and libraries were reopened, and government examinations resumed, par-

317

ticularly in those areas that had not held them during the years of civil disorder. These examinations, while continuing to be literary, stressed the practical problems of the day. The court increased the quotas for degrees in the various provinces to reward military and financial contributions, while limiting the sale of ranks and offices. Within the bureaucracy stricter discipline was enforced and cases of corruption punished. Meanwhile, Peking exercised great care in foreign affairs to maintain peace and good relations with Western powers and to afford the country the chance to engage in reconstruction and self-strengthening.

Previous successful restorations in Chinese history[1] usually involved strong, brilliant, and virtuous rulers, but Emperor T'ung-chih (1862-74) was a minor during eleven of his thirteen reigning years and a weakling in the remaining two. The power of state was grasped firmly in the hands of his mother, the Empress Dowager Tz'u-hsi, who controlled the court for 48 years until her death in 1908. Considering Emperor T'ung-chih's personality, his reign certainly does not deserve the designation of restoration. Yet the emperor was more an institution than a personality; unusual accomplishments by able supporters, which caused a tidal change, can be considered the constituents of a restoration.[2]

Nonetheless, the T'ung-chih restoration definitely stood at a lower level of revival in Chinese history. While it did stem the decline for a while, it failed to regenerate the dynasty to a degree sufficient to allow survival with honor in the modern world. Its imitation of Western armament, technology, and diplomacy was a superficial gesture toward modernization; the finer aspects of Western civilization—political institutions, social theories, philosophy, fine arts, and music—went totally untouched. Historical perspective indicates that it was hardly more than a flash of rejuvenation in an eventide of waning dynastic fortune—an Indian Summer. Nonetheless, the immediate effect of the T'ung-chih Restoration was to signal a brave and reasonably successful effort at reviving the old order and to initiate the beginning of a new.

NEW LEADERSHIP AND THE COUP OF 1861

The emergence of a new political leadership at Peking played a vital role in forging a new era. As will be recalled, Prince Kung had been left

1. Such as those of Emperor Hsüan-wang (827-782 B.C.) of the Western Chou period, Emperor Kuang-wu (A.D. 25-57) of the Eastern Han period, and Emperor Su-tsung (A.D. 756-62) of the T'ang period.
2. Mary C. Wright, *The Last Stand of Chinese Conservatism: The T'ung-chih Restoration,* 1862-1874 (Stanford, 1957), 50.

in Peking to deal with Lord Elgin and Baron Gros in September 1860, when Emperor Hsien-feng fled to Jehol in the face of the advancing enemy. That the prince achieved a settlement with the barbarians and effected their withdrawal from the capital—all this without the support of an army or a navy—was considered by many Chinese and Manchus as nothing short of a miracle. They came to regard him as the savior of the dynasty and the foremost expert on barbarian management—one who knew how to deal with them and win their cooperation. Beyond doubt, Prince Kung had emerged as the new leader at Peking, while the court still cowered at Jehol.

Following the evacuation of foreign troops from Peking, Prince Kung led a number of high officials in requesting the return of the emperor. The sovereign was reluctant, partially out of shame at his unheroic flight, and partially out of fear that the enemy forces might return to coerce him into receiving their envoys without the kowtow. It was not until Prince Kung, in December 1860, successfully committed the British and French plenipotentiaries to desist from demanding the audience that the ruler finally announced, on February 11, 1861, that he would return the following month. But the journey was not to materialize: his health deteriorated, and he died prematurely.

Emperor Hsien-feng, who ascended the throne in 1851, had never been physically robust. When he first became ruler, he was determined to revive the dynastic fortune and avenge the foreign humiliations, as indicated in his hard policy toward the foreigners, the dismissal of Mu-chang-a, and the reliance on Governor-general Yeh at Canton. When his policy led to the second Anglo-Chinese war, at a time when the country was internally ravaged by the Taiping Revolution and other rebellions, he lost heart in state affairs, resigning himself to a life of carnal pleasures. In his refuge at Jehol, he tried to escape his misery and shame by frequenting the pleasure quarters, so much so that he became physically depleted and was prescribed deer's blood for sustenance. His frequent companions and mentors in these escapades were Prince I, Prince Cheng, and Assistant Grand Secretary Su-shun, the last in particular having developed a strong hold on him. On August 21, 1861, the emperor lapsed into a fatal illness; on his deathbed he named his son Tsai-ch'ün, aged six *sui*, the heir apparent.

Su-shun and the two princes presently produced a valedictory edict appointing themselves and five other high officials advisers on state affairs and members of a Council of Regents for the boy emperor. Prince Kung at Peking, who had expected to be the regent in light of his great service to the state, was left out in the cold. He was further snubbed when the Council of Regents rejected his request to attend the imperial funeral in Jehol. Equally abused were the two empresses of the late ruler—the 27-*sui* Tz'u-an, who was childless, and the 25-*sui* Tz'u-hsi who bore him a son, the present boy emperor. They were made empresses dowager on August 23, but were denied their legal authority to approve the edicts of the regents; Su-shun insisted that the regency deputed by the deceased emperor made consultation with them superfluous. An intense power struggle followed between the dowagers and the regents at Jehol, and the former decided to isolate the latter by joining forces with Prince Kung, who maintained a third power center at Peking.

Tz'u-hsi was a woman of remarkable ability and sinister schemes. During the late emperor's illness she had assisted him in drafting comments on memorials while concealing her secret jealousy of Su-shun's influence on him. Imbued with great personal ambition, she managed to retain the imperial seal upon the death of the emperor, and, suspicious of the authenticity of the valedictory edit produced by Su-shun, succeeded in persuading the other empress dowager to join her in assuming the reins of government themselves "behind a bamboo screen" for "self-preservation." A special emissary, reputedly the eunuch An Te-hai, was dispatched to Peking to sound out Prince Kung, who readily agreed to cooperate in hopes of utilizing the dowagers to establish himself in place of the Council of Regents. He now obtained permission from the dowagers to come to Jehol to attend the imperial funeral. All attempts by the regents to block him from seeing the dowagers failed, and their warning that the imperial uncle and sisters-in-law should avoid private interviews to allay suspicion went unheeded.

At the secret meeting, the dowagers and the prince decided that they should attempt no action in Jehol, where the regents held sway, but should act in Peking where Prince Kung had the upper hand; and that the coffin of the late emperor was to be returned to the capital, at which time swift action would be taken to arrest the regents. Tz'u-hsi was concerned about foreign reaction, but Prince Kung, apparently assured of foreign support, confidently announced that he would deter the alien powers from intervening.

Indeed, the British played a secret role in supporting the prince. As signer of the Conventions of Peking, Prince Kung had impressed the foreign representations with his good will, quick intelligence, fine manners, and willingness to cooperate in executing the treaties. The British came to regard him as a symbol of good relations and saw that it was in their interest to keep him in power. A dispatch from the British minister[3] to London on March 12, 1862, reveals the British role in this palace revolution: " . . . it is no small achievement within twelve months to have *created a party* inclined to and believing in the possibility of friendly intercourse, to have *effectually aided that party to power*. To have established satisfactory relations at Peking and become in some degree the advisers of a government with which eighteen months since we were at war." Prince Kung looked to the five or six thousand foreign troops in Tientsin as "a pillar of support . . . against his political opponents."[4]

On September 11, 1861, Prince Kung departed for Peking. Meanwhile, Grand Secretary Chou Tsu-p'ei and others in Peking, resentful of Su-shun's usurpation of power and conscious of the dowagers' desire to be regents themselves, asked the noted scholar Li Tz'u-ming to prepare a memorandum on the historical precedents for regency by the dowagers. Before Li had completed the study, a censor[5] had already seized the initiative by sending a memorial to Jehol, requesting the dowagers to expropriate the state administration and to appoint one or two princes of the blood to assist in the discharge of duties. Su-shun ridiculed the idea on the ground that there had never been the precedent of dowager administration in the Ch'ing dynasty. Arrogantly he declared that there was really no need to dispute with the dowagers about these high policy matters, since the Council of Regents was the logical organ of state to decide the issue. Such insult only inflamed the dowagers' ire and their determination to wrest the power from him.

Ignoring the strong opposition of the regents, the dowagers left for Peking with the boy emperor on October 26, accompanied by Princes I and Cheng, while the emperor's coffin set out shortly afterwards under the escort of Su-shun and Prince Chün. On November 1, the dowagers arrived in the capital and immediately received a joint memorial from Grand Secretary Chou Tsu-p'ei and the presidents of the Board of Revenue and Board of Punishment, requesting them to take charge of the state administration during the emperor's minority—apparently at the prompting of Prince Kung. They accused the eight regents of dominating

3. Frederick Bruce.
4. Masataka Banno, *China and the West: 1858-1861* (Cambridge, Mass., 1964), 241. Italics added.
5. Tung Yüan-chün.

rather than assisting the court. A day later, the dowagers summoned Prince Kung, the grand secretaries, and other high officials to the palace and announced the crimes of the eight regents and their immediate dismissal. Princes I and Cheng protested the illegality of the act, whereupon the dowagers issued a second edict stripping them and Su-shun of their nobility status and turning them over to the Imperial Clan Court for punishment. In a lightning movement, to forestall any armed opposition, Prince Kung's guards arrested the two princes, while Su-shun, who was accompanying the coffin to Peking, was accosted en route and thrown into the prison of the Imperial Clan Court. The two princes were allowed to hang themselves; Su-shun was decapitated on November 8; and the other five regents were dismissed.

Emerging victorious from this *coup d'état*, the dowagers and Prince Kung became co-regents. Actually it was against the Ch'ing imperial family law to allow a mother-empress to administer state affairs. During the minority of the first emperor, Shun-chih (1644-1661), his uncle Dorgan was made prince regent; and during the minority of Emperor K'ang-hsi (1662-1722) four regents under the leadership of Oboi assisted him. Never had there been any precedent of the imperial distaff serving as regent. But a lack of precedent could not deter the strong-willed Tz'u-hsi. She made Prince Kung her front man, with the titles of prince regent (*i-cheng wang*), grand councillor, chief minister of the Imperial Household, and head of the newly established Tsungli Yamen (Foreign Office).[6] The prince, on his part, needed the blessings of the dowagers to build his own power base. So they entered into an alliance founded in mutual expediency.

The reign title of the boy emperor, Ch'i-hsiang (Lucky), which was originally chosen by Prince I, was changed to T'ung-chih (Co-eval rule)— probably connoting the contemporaneous rule of the two dowagers— effective the following year, 1862. Tz'u-hsi did not like the designation of mother-empress (*mu-hou*), for it implied a status once removed from the legitimate source of power, preferring to be known as the Western Dowager, after the Western palace in which she lived. The other dowager, Tz'u-an, who lived in the Eastern palace, became known as the Eastern Dowager. Although both sat behind a bamboo screen while administering state affairs (*ch'ui-lien t'ing-cheng* 垂簾聽政) and receiving ministerial reports, it was usually the Western Dowager who read memorials, asked

6. An abbreviation of Tsung-li ko-kuo shih-wu ya-men (Office for the general management of affairs concerning the various countries).

questions, and made decisions. The Eastern Dowager, known more for her virtue than ability, was rather reticent in disposition.

Foreign reactions to the coup were generally favorable. The British minister in Peking informed London: "The downfall of the violent party, and the language of the decree of arrest amount to a real ratification of the Treaty of which the formal ratification was executed last year . . . I shall be certainly mortified, if the Prince [Kung] does not administer foreign affairs in a more reasonable and intelligent spirit than has hitherto characterized the proceedings of the Chinese Government." A. H. Layard, British Under-Secretary for Foreign Affairs, spoke before the House of Commons on March 18, 1862: "Within a very short time a great change had taken place; a coup d'état had been effected which led to a change of Ministers . . . Prince Kung and the two Empresses had called together a new Ministry and had inaugurated a new policy; for the first time a Chinese Government had admitted the rights of foreigners, and consented to treat them as equals."[7] Prince Kung and the Tsungli Yamen became symbols of progress and of good will toward foreigners. It was therefore incumbent upon the latter, in their own interest, to sustain the prince in the power struggle and to help stabilize the situation after the coup.

THE COOPERATIVE POLICY AND DIPLOMATIC MODERNIZATION

The bitter lesson of the 1860 peace settlement promoted a complete about-face in Prince Kung's attitude toward the foreigners. Whereas before this traumatic experience he was violently antiforeign, advocating unyielding resistance to foreign demands and the execution of Harry Parkes, after the settlement he arrived at a new conception of the barbarian problem. He came to respect and even admire the British power, convinced that China had no alternative but to learn to live with the West.

From his dealings with Lord Elgin and Baron Gros, Prince Kung had learned beyond doubt the superiority of Western weaponry. To his pleasant surprise, he discovered that the erstwhile enemies not only did not intend to deny China their military secret, but openly offered—as the French plenipotentiary did at a reception after the signing of the Convention of Peking—to help China train her army and manufacture weap-

7. Banno, 240-41.

ons after the Western fashion. The prompt evacuation of occupation troops from Peking after the peace further revealed that the foreign powers had no territorial designs on China and that they were not devoid of reason and good faith, as the Chinese were wont to depict them. Prince Kung came to the conclusion that if China kept her treaty obligations and treated foreigners with good will and open-mindedness, giving them no cause for complaints, peace would abound. In this roseate new light, the treaties which were formerly considered a disgrace now became a useful instrument to specify the maximum concessions beyond which China would make no grant and the foreigners could not legally go. From this realization the twenty-eight-year old prince evolved a new policy for China: diplomatically she would accommodate the West to gain a lasting period of peace in which to build up, with Western aid, her military strength. Thus, peace through diplomacy became the immediate objective (*piao*) of the government, while self-strengthening loomed as the ultimate goal (*pen*). This double-pronged approach was wholeheartedly supported by the Manchu Grand Councillor Wen-hsiang in the capital, and by several powerful leaders in the provinces—such as Tseng Kuo-fan, Tso Tsung-t'ang, and Li Hung-chang.

Prince Kung was not alone in charting a new course for China, for so had the Westerners. Foreign governments and private traders alike were satisfied with the new concessions of the recent treaties, and a feeling prevailed that one should not strangle the goose if it was to lay eggs. They recognized the fact that enjoyment of treaty rights was predicated upon the continued existence of the government granting these rights. The Western powers therefore decided to sustain the Ch'ing court and helped it modernize, in the belief that a stable China was more conducive to ever-increasing foreign trade. With this shift in policy, British neutrality changed to active, if limited, support of the imperial cause against the Taipings, as already seen in the last chapter.

Foreign diplomats, who had taken up residence in Peking, also gained a better understanding of the Chinese viewpoint, and unconsciously acquired a certain degree of Sinicization. The American minister, Anson Burlingame, and the British minister, Frederick Bruce, now championed a "Cooperative Policy" toward China, which expounded (1) cooperation among Western powers; (2) cooperation with Chinese officials; (3) recognition of China's legitimate interests; and (4) enforcement of the treaty rights.[8]

8. Wright, *The Last Stand*, 21-22.

The policy changes on the part of both China and the West resulted in a decade of relative peace, harmony, good will, and cooperation. It provided a good climate for the initiation of China's diplomatic and military modernization.

Diplomatic reform began with a recommendation by Prince Kung and Wen-hsiang on January 11, 1861, that a new office be established to direct foreign affairs; that a superintendent of trade be appointed at Tientsin to take charge of the three northern ports,[9] in addition to the one already stationed at Shanghai who took charge of the original five ports; that two linguists be sent from Canton and Shanghai for service in Peking; that intelligent Manchu boys below the age of thirteen or fourteen *sui* be selected from the bannermen's families to learn foreign languages; and that trade reports and foreign newspapers at the treaty ports be forwarded to the Tsungli Yamen. This state paper marked the beginning of the diplomatic phase of the Self-strengthening Movement.

The Tsungli Yamen. As noted in Chapter 3, the Ch'ing court had not previously established a foreign office, because China never accorded recognition to another state on an equal, diplomatic level, but only on a tributary or trading basis. The court dealt with these tributary and trading affairs through various state organs, obviating the need for a foreign office. During the pre-Opium War period, tributary affairs, which basically reflected a ritualistic relationship, were directed by the Board of Rites. Russian and frontier affairs were governed by the Li-fan yüan (Court of Colonial Affairs), and trade with the Western maritime countries was deputed to the governor-general at Canton, who "managed" the foreigners through the Hoppo and the hong merchants. During the period between the Opium and the Arrow wars, 1842-56, the governors-general at Canton and Nanking were, for all practical purposes, China's unofficial foreign and deputy foreign ministers, in the absence of a formal foreign office. After the Conventions of Peking in 1860 reaffirmed Western diplomatic residence in the Chinese capital, there was genuine need for a foreign office to centralize the direction of foreign affairs. Immediate attention was required of such matters as reception of foreign representatives, allocation of legation quarters, payment of indemnities, opening of the new ports, and a host of other questions relative to new treaty obligations. On recommendation of Prince Kung, the Tsungli Yamen (Office for General Management) was established in Peking on March 11, 1861. Though

9. Tientsin, Newchwang, and Chefoo.

commonly known to the foreigners as the Foreign Office, in reality it functioned more like a subcommittee of the Grand Council than a regular board of the government. Its organization and characteristics may be summarized as follows:

(1) It was intended to be a temporary office under the charge of a prince of the blood, supported by several ministers[10] who were concurrently high metropolitan officials—the grand councillors, grand secretaries, and presidents or vice-presidents of the boards. Under them were sixteen secretaries, divided equally between the Manchus and the Chinese. Prince Kung was the first and long-time presiding officer, while Wen-hsiang, grand councillor and vice-president of the Board of Revenue, was its principal minister until his death in 1876.

(2) As a government agency, it had no statutory (i.e. "constitutional") basis but was rather a makeshift creation necessitated by the exigency of circumstances. In theory it concerned itself only with the execution of foreign policy, not the making of it, since the ultimate power of decision rested with the emperor and his chief adviser, the Grand Council. In practice, however, the recommendations of the Tsungli Yamen were usually approved by the throne, Prince Kung and Wen-hsiang being both concurrently grand councillors.

(3) It was organized into five bureaus: Russian, British, French, American, and Coastal Defense. In addition, two other offices were attached to it: the Inspectorate-general of Customs and the language school called the T'ung-wen kuan.

(4) It engaged not only in foreign affairs but also in a number of modernization projects. Its promotion of modern schools, Western science, industry, and communication exposed it to frequent attacks by die-hard conservatives, while foreigners often criticized it for not progressing rapidly enough. Thus, the Tsungli Yamen occupied the uncomfortable position of a buffer between the two—accused by foreigners of procrastination and by xenophobes of selling out China's interest to the barbarians.

(5) It played an active role in the 1860's, but its influence waned after 1869-70, when the dowager T'zu-hsi chastised Prince Kung for the second time; when the Alcock Convention failed to win British ratification (next chapter); and when Li Hung-chang shouldered both the governor-generalship of Chihli and the superintendency of trade for the three northern ports. In this double capacity, he eclipsed the Tsungli Yamen (next section).

10. Usually 3 to 5 at first, but later increased to 9 to 11.

(6) Where it failed as an effective foreign office, the Tsungli Yamen succeeded reasonably well as a promoter of modernization. It was China's first major institutional innovation in response to the Western impact.[11]

The Superintendents of Trade. Besides the Tsungli Yamen, a superintendent of trade for the three northern ports was established at Tientsin, with the Manchu nobleman Ch'ung-hou as the first incumbent until his replacement by Li Hung-chang in 1870. This post was created to parallel the existing commissionership at Shanghai, which took charge of the affairs of the five original ports plus the new ports along the Yangtze River and along the seacoast to its south, opened by the recent treaties. In 1862 the commissioner at Shanghai received the title of Superintendent of Trade Affairs, a concurrent post for the governor of Kiangsu; later in 1866 it became a concurrent appointment for the governor-general at Nanking. These two superintendents of trade, one at Tientsin and one at Shanghai, became known respectively as the High Commissioner for the Northern Ocean (*Pei-yang ta-ch'en*) and High Commissioner for the Southern Ocean (*Nan-yang ta-ch'en*).[12]

One reason for the establishment of these trade superintendencies was to direct business away from Peking, in order to forestall much of diplomatic transactions in the capital. Knowing the court's fear and resentment of the imposed diplomatic residence in Peking, Prince Kung explained his secret motive in creating the new post: "If Tientsin can manage properly, then, even though the barbarian chieftains live in the capital, they must be depressed with having nothing to do and finally think of returning home."[13] So successful was the strategem that after Li Hung-chang undertook the Tientsin commissionership in 1870 he practically pre-empted the functions of the Tsungli Yamen. It was he who settled the case of the Tientsin Massacre in 1870, who recommended establishing an official relationship with Japan in 1871, and who settled the Margary murder incident in 1875-76 (next chapter). It was he, too, who conducted negotiations with the French over the Annamese question in 1884, and took charge of the opening of Korea in the early 1880's and negotiations with Japan after the war of 1894-95. Li's office at Tientsin became virtually China's foreign office for the quarter of a century following 1870. But foreign diplomats did not leave Peking.

11. Ssu-ming Meng, *The Tsungli Yamen: Its Organization and Functions* (Cambridge, Mass., 1962).
12. The word "Ocean" in these titles really means "ports."
13. Hsü, *China's Entrance*, 107.

The T'ung-wen kuan. Established in Peking in 1862 at the suggestion of Prince Kung, the T'ung-wen kuan, known to the foreigners alternately as the Interpreters College or the College of Foreign Languages, was originally intended as a school for the joint instruction of Western and Chinese languages, hence the name T'ung-wen (common languages). Initially it was created in response to the French and British Tientsin Treaty clauses specifying the English and French texts as the sole authentic versions of the treaties. China therefore needed to train able language experts to free herself from reliance on foreign interpreters and half-baked Canton linguists, who spoke only "pidgin" English.

Since no Chinese were qualified to instruct foreign languages, an English and a French missionary as well as a Russian interpreter at the legation initially were invited to teach their respective tongues at the T'ung-wen kuan; German was added later. Instruction in Chinese was also given.[14] In 1864 the American missionary-educator W. A. P. Martin joined the staff as professor of English. By 1866 astronomy and mathematics were introduced to the curriculum, over the opposition of the arch-conservative Grand Secretary Wo-jen; and in the following year the noted scholar-official Hsü Chi-yü was appointed director. The school gradually took on the appearance of a small liberal arts college.

In 1867 Martin returned to the United States for two years of advanced work in international law and political economy at the University of Indiana, where he earned a doctorate. Back in China in 1869, he was made president of the T'ung-wen kuan, with assurance of financial support from Robert Hart, the Inspector-general of Customs. Under Martin's direction, a variety of subjects were added to the eight-year curriculum, the first three being devoted to linguistic preparation and the next five to scientific and general studies. In 1879 the enrollment stood at 163, with 38 specializing in English, 25 in French, 15 in Russian, 10 in German, 33 in mathematics, 6 in astronomy, 7 in physics, 9 in international law, 12 in chemistry, and 8 in physiology.[15] The quality of students, however, was rather low, since few good Manchu or Chinese families would send their sons, with the result that a considerable portion of the student body consisted of middle-aged mediocrities enrolled for a pension.

Nonetheless, the T'ung-wen kuan marked the beginning of Western education in China. Since many of the foreign professors also engaged in translation with the help of their Chinese students, the school simulta-

14. By Professor Hsü Shu-lin.
15. W. A. P. Martin, *Calendar of the Tungwen College* (Peking, 1879), 10.

neously functioned as a prototype research institute for dissemination of foreign knowledge. In 1873 a small printing office was set up as a primitive sort of "university press," from which seventeen major publications were issued in the fields of international law, political economy, chemistry, physics, and natural philosophy.

Similar schools of foreign languages and Western studies were established at Shanghai in 1863 (*Kuang-fang-yen kuan*), at Canton in 1864, and at Foochow in 1866.[16] The T'ung-wen kuan at Peking lasted until 1902, when it was absorbed into the Imperial University. Among the more outstanding graduates of the Peking T'ung-wen kuan were two foreign ministers and a number of diplomats.

The Maritime Customs Service. As head of the Tsungli Yamen, Prince Kung appointed Horatio N. Lay as inspector-general of customs on April 7, 1861, charging him with the duty of "exercising a general surveillance over all things pertaining to the revenue, of aiding the Chinese superintendents to collect the revenue at the various ports, of preventing frauds upon the revenue, and of standing sponsor for the good conduct of the foreigners engaged in the Customs Service."[17] This appointment confirmed and institutionalized the foreign inspectorate of customs that had already been developed at Shanghai in 1854. It may be recalled that the Small Sword Society occupied the walled city of Shanghai in September 1853, and drove the Ch'ing customs superintendent[18] out of operation. Foreign traders gladly profited from this anarchy, paying no dues on their imports. However, the British consul in Shanghai, Rutherford Alcock, recalling Sir Henry Pottinger's instruction a decade earlier that British consuls see that their nationals pay the customs dues, cooperated with the American Commissioner in China, Humphrey Marshall, in devising a provisional system whereby the consuls of the two countries would collect customs dues from their respective countrymen for the Chinese government.

Attempts by the Chinese customs superintendent to re-establish himself in the international settlement at Shanghai, or even on a floating customs house, were resisted by Alcock in light of British neutrality in the Chinese civil war. The Chinese superintendent, not to be frustrated,

16. For details of T'ung-wen kuan and other schools at the Kiangnan Arsenal and the Foochow Dockyard, see an excellent study by Knight Biggerstaff, *The Earliest Modern Government Schools in China* (Ithaca, 1961).
17. Wright, *Hart and the Chinese Customs*, 151.
18. Wu Chien-chang, the former Canton hong merchant Samqua.

then imposed an inland tax on commodities before they reached Shanghai. Fearful of the possibility of trade being deflected elsewhere, the British, French, and American consuls opened discussion with the governor-general of Liang-Kiang and obtained an agreement that a foreign Board of Inspectors be established at Shanghai to aid in the equitable collection of customs dues from all foreign traders; in return the Chinese abolished the inland customs dues.

On July 12, 1854, Thomas Wade of Britain, Lewis Carr of the United States, and Arthur Smith of France were sworn in as inspectors of customs at Shanghai, with full approval of the Chinese customs superintendent. The bulk of the work fell on Wade, who alone among the three understood Chinese and the customs procedure. Finding the work too burdensome to permit his Sinological studies, Wade resigned a year later. Horatio N. Lay, a twenty-three-year-old acting British vice consul at Shanghai, then secured the job for himself on June 1, 1855. His vigorous supervision resulted in more customs revenue for the Ch'ing government than under the former imperial customs superintendent. After a leave of absence in order to serve with Lord Elgin during the Treaty of Tientsin negotiations in 1858, Lay returned to the inspectorate and laid the groundwork for a new customs service. The Shanghai-styled foreign inspectorate was to be extended to other treaty ports, each under the charge of a foreign inspector, or commissioner as he was later called, who took orders from the inspector-general at the head office in Shanghai, namely Lay himself. With this background, Prince Kung's appointment of Lay in April 1861 amounted to an official confirmation of a system already in operation.

Lay's response to the appointment was singularly curious and extremely insulting. He neither accepted nor rejected it, but took a trip to England on the grounds of poor health. During his absence, he designated G. H. FitzRoy, commissioner of customs at Shanghai, and Robert Hart, deputy commissioner of customs at Canton, as officiating inspectors-general until his return. Hart was sent to Peking to take Prince Kung's commands. In personality and manners, Hart was tactful and patient, the opposite of Lay. The Chinese responded to him much more warmly than to Lay, and when the latter proved to be too unruly and domineering over the Osborn flotilla issue (next section), Hart was named his replacement as inspector-general in 1863. Under Hart's leadership, an international customs service for China was developed, with 252 British and 156 other Western employees by 1875.

In a circular dated June 21, 1864, Hart spelled out what amounted to a "code of behavior" for the foreign employees. He suggested that they should learn Chinese, act with patience "without affectation of superiority," labor "to convince rather than to dictate," and "introduce remedies without causing the irritation that attends the exposure of defects." In decidedly clear terms he told them:

> ". . . it is to be distinctly and constantly kept in mind that the Inspectorate of Customs is a Chinese and not a Foreign Service, and that, as such, it is the duty of each of its members to conduct himself towards the Chinese, people as well as officials, in such a way as to avoid all cause of offence and ill-feeling . . . It is to be expected from those who take the pay, and who are the servants of the Chinese Government, that they, at least, will so act as to neither offend susceptibilities, nor excite jealousies, suspicion, and dislike. In dealings, therefore, with native officials, and in intercourse with the people, it will be well for the Foreign employees of the Customs to remember, that they are *the brother officers of the one*, and that they, to some extent, accepted certain obligations and responsibilities by becoming, in a sense, *the countrymen of the others*: the man who cherishes such an idea, will be led to treat the one class with courtesy, and the other with friendliness . . ."[19]

Hart's approach to proper behavior, his consideration, and his sense of proportion endeared him to the court, which took him into confidence as a trusted servant and an adviser on foreign affairs. As long as he lived, no other inspector-general was appointed; such was the regard of the Ch'ing court for its foreign employee, who on his part declined the position of British minister to China in the 1880's in order to remain with the customs service. Under his guidance many outstanding foreigners served in the Chinese international customs service; one of the more prominent was H. B. Morse, a graduate of Harvard in 1876, who after his retirement wrote several definitive and pioneer works on Chinese trade, administration, and foreign relations.

Introduction of International Law. Although before the Opium War Commissioner Lin Tse-hsü had asked the American missionary Peter Parker to translate three paragraphs of international law from Vattel, there was no complete text of the law of nations in Chinese. Ignorance

19. MacNair, I, 384-85. Italics added.

of international law led early Chinese negotiators into many blunders: they conceded easily on such significant issues as tariff autonomy, extraterritoriality, and the most-favored-nation treatment, while struggling bitterly against such common and innocuous practices and issues as diplomatic residence and audience without the kowtow. Witnessing China's need for a guide to diplomacy, W. A. P. Martin took upon himself a translation of a text of international law, which he considered the best and most mature fruit of Christian civilization. With the help of Chinese scribes, he began to translate Henry Wheaton's *Elements of International Law* in 1862, hoping to show that Westerners had principles to govern their international relations and were not totally dependent on brutal force, and hoping that his translation might bring the atheistic Chinese government to recognize the spirit of Christianity.

Prince Kung, in his eagerness to learn about Western diplomacy, was secretly anxious to know international law. Through the good offices of the American minister, Anson Burlingame, Martin's translation was presented to the Tsungli Yamen in 1864. As its style and diction were rough and unidiomatic, the manuscript was put through a thorough editing by four secretaries of the Tsungli Yamen.

While the manuscript was being edited, the Tsungli Yamen had a chance to test its usefulness. The new Prussian minister, von Rehfues, arriving in the spring of 1864 in a man-of-war, found three Danish merchant ships off Taku, and immediately ordered their capture as war prizes, Prussia and Denmark being at war in Europe. Prince Kung, armed with the new knowledge of international law, protested the extension of European quarrels to China and the seizure of ships in China's "inner waters," the Chinese expression for territorial waters. He refused to receive the Prussian minister before the redress was made and chided him for beginning his duties in such an unbecoming manner. Embarrassed, von Rehfues released the three ships and paid a compensation of $1,-500.[20] Having proven the utility of the translation, Prince Kung distributed three hundred copies of it to provincial authorities.

Wielding this new knowledge in combination with other measures of diplomatic modernization, China managed to maintain peaceful relations with the foreign powers throughout the decade of the 1860's, thus furnishing the country with a much needed respite to begin the Self-strengthening programs.

20. Hsü, *China's Entrance*, 133.

MILITARY MODERNIZATION AND
EARLY INDUSTRIALIZATION

Prince Kung's diplomatic modernization was-paralleled by his efforts to create a modern navy and by those of the provincial leaders—Tseng Kuo-fan, Tso Tsung-t'ang, and Li Hung-chang—to introduce military modernization through the adoption of foreign ships and guns, organization of supporting industries, and opening of new training schools. Their endeavors marked the beginning of the Self-strengthening Movement which lasted through three and a half decades to 1895. However, the idea of learning from the West predated these leaders by more than two decades.

The Pioneers. It was Commissioner Lin Tse-hsü who first championed the idea of learning about the West. Impressed with British ships and guns, he was anxious to obtain more information about the enemy. Orders were given to translate foreign newspapers from Macao, Singapore, and India, and gather information on Western geography, history, politics, and law. Under his sponsorship, passages of international law from Vattel were translated, and selections from Murray's *Cyclopaedia of Geography* were rendered into Chinese under the title of *Ssu-kuo chih* (A gazetteer of four countries) in 1841. With this rudimentary knowledge of the West, Lin developed a certain measure of respect for British power; and for all his outward hard-line approach to barbarian problems, he was secretly reluctant to precipitate a clash. The very fact that he purchased two hundred foreign guns to strengthen the Canton defense and ordered the translation of manuals of Western gun-making manifested his acute awareness of the superior barbarian weaponry and the need for China to unlock its mystery. Yet for political reasons, he did not openly advocate adoption of foreign armament.

The defeat in the Opium War, though a great national disgrace, was dismissed by most Chinese scholars and officials as an historical accident. Nonetheless, as noted briefly in Chapter 8, a few farsighted private scholars, associated with or influenced by Lin, sensed the advent of a new era in China's relations with the outside world. Foremost among them was Wei Yüan (1794-1856), to whom Lin had turned over the materials on foreign countries. Wei compiled them into a large work of fifty tomes (*chüan*) in 1844[21] entitled *Hai-kuo t'u-chih* (An illustrated gazetteer of

21. Enlarged to 100 *chüan* in 1852.

the maritime countries). The objective of the work was clearly explained in the preface: "Why did I compile this work? It is for the purpose of using barbarians to attack barbarians, using barbarians to negotiate with barbarians, and *learning the superior techniques of the barbarians* to control the barbarians."[22] The book falls into four parts: part one deals with the history, geography, and recent political conditions of Western countries; part two, the manufacturing and use of foreign guns; part three, shipbuilding, mining, and miscellaneous descriptions of the practical arts of the West; and part four, methods of dealing with the West, as suggested by the compiler and his contemporaries. It was the first significant Chinese work on the West.

Other pioneer works included a very complimentary account of the American political system, called *Ho-chung-kuo shuo* (On the United States), and a study of the recent foreign disturbance of China called *I-fen chi-wen* (A record of the barbarian miasma), both by Liang T'ing-nan. There followed the famous work of world geography by Hsü Chi-yü, entitled *Ying-huan chih-lüeh* (A brief survey of maritime circuit), and a vast compendium of eighty *chüan* on the geography, history, and politics of Russia and other northern countries called *Shuo-fang pei-sheng* (A manual for northern places) by Ho Ch'iu-t'ao. Except for the last-named, all the works stressed the importance of maritime defense against the Western sea powers. The essence of their message was that if China developed sufficient coastal defense, she could hold the enemy from the ocean at bay. There was little understanding or recognition of the fact that the overseas expansion of Europe and America, propelled by the forces of rising nationalism, capitalism, and rapid industrialization, could hardly be prevented by localized defense in China. This initial period of Western studies revolved around the limited subject of maritime defense, and the authors and compilers, being private scholars, had but a limited influence on their country.

The defeat in 1860 shocked the intelligentsia and officialdom into a greater awakening. Feng Kuei-fen (1809-74), also a onetime associate of Lin's, took the lead in promoting the idea of Self-strengthening (*Tzu-ch'iang*). In his famous work, *Protest from the Chiao-pin Studio* (*Chiao-pin-lu k'ang-i*), written about 1860-61, he realistically took notice of the vast difference between the old world that China had known in her past and the new world that had been thrust upon her, and urged that China adopt Western ships and guns, and construct dockyards and arsenals in

22. Italics added.

the trading ports. If the small country of Japan knew the need for forti-
fying herself along Western lines, he asserted, how much more China
should precipitate strengthening herself! Bearing in mind the recently
concluded peace with the Western powers, Feng warned that China
must utilize this heaven-sent opportunity to strengthen herself, or she
would live to regret missing the chance. As regards Wei Yüan's aspiration of using barbarians to control and negotiate with barbarians, Feng
found it an impossibility; difficulty of foreign languages and unfamiliarity
with their customs precluded China from sowing dissension among the
barbarians. "Only one sentence of Wei Yüan is correct: *learn the superior
techniques of the barbarians to control the barbarians.*"[23] This dictum
rang out as the motivating spirit of the Self-strengthening Movement
(*Tzu-ch'iang yün-tung*   自強運動) from 1861 until 1895.

Prince Kung and the Lay-Osborn Flotilla. The chief promoters of Self-
strengthening in the capital were Prince Kung and Wen-hsiang, who impressed upon the court that China lost the wars not because the soldiers
did not fight hard but because they were not properly equipped. To
guard against future humiliation, China must adopt Western firearms,
ships, and army training. A first step in this direction was taken in 1862
when the prince directed Acting Inspector-general of Customs Robert
Hart to commission Horatio Lay, then in England, to purchase and equip
a steam fleet. Lay acquired eight ships and engaged the service of Captain
Sherard Osborn of the Royal navy. Without the knowledge or prior approval of the court at Peking, Lay entered into an agreement with Osborn on January 16, 1863, whereby the latter was to be the sole commander-in-chief of this naval force as well as the native vessels manned
by Europeans, and that he was to accept orders from no one but Lay
as representative of the Chinese emperor. Behaving presumptuously in
this matter, Lay justified his action on the ground that he was not bound
by ordinary rules of conduct or normal procedure for transactions in
China. "My position was that of a foreigner engaged by the Chinese government to perform certain work *for* them, not *under* them. I need
scarcely observe that the notion of a gentleman acting *under* an Asiatic
barbarian is preposterous."[24] Lay had the vision of erecting himself as the
"First Lord of the Admiralty" in China and concurrently the Inspector-

23. Feng, Kuei-fen, *Chiao-pin-lu k'ang-i* (Protests from the Chiao-pin Studio) (Shanghai, 1897), 2:4b-6. Italics added.
24. Lay, *Our Interests in China*, 19.

general of Customs; the one would give him unrivaled military (naval) power, and the other, control of some seven million taels annual customs revenue. To befit his important status, he demanded a palace at Peking for residence. Needless to say, the Chinese found him unbearable.

Prince Kung informed Captain Osborn upon his arrival with the fleet in September 1863 that his official title was assistant commander-in-chief, with authority to control only the foreigners of the fleet, and that he must accept orders from the local governor-general and governor in whose jurisdiction he happened to be operating, i.e. Tseng Kuo-fan, the governor-general of Liang-Kiang, and Li Hung-chang, the governor of Kiangsu. Lay protested that he had come "to serve the emperor, not to be the servant of mere provincial authorities," especially under so "unprincipled an official" as Li. Prince Kung stood firm in his position. Under the circumstances Captain Osborn could do nothing but honorably recommend that the fleet be disbanded, lest it fall into the hands of the Taipings, or the hostile diamyos of Japan, or even the American Confederacy.

Tseng Kuo-fan understandably accepted the position that, rather than harboring an uncontrollable foreign navy which might cause unpredictable complications, China might best disband it and compensate the officers liberally. The American minister, Anson Burlingame, offered to mediate. Lay was pensioned off with £14,000, as pay and allowances for the period he was quarreling with the Chinese government. He was then replaced by Hart as inspector-general of customs. The Chinese government had spent a total of £550,000 purchasing and disbanding a fleet, from which it got absolutely nothing but headaches. The first attempt at a modern navy was a complete fiasco.[25]

The Beginning of Self-strengthening in the Provinces. The bulk of the Self-strengthening projects were promoted by provincial authorities such as Tseng Kuo-fan, Tso Tsung-t'ang, and Li Hung-chang. From their association with the Foreign Rifle Squadron and the Ever-Victorious army during the Taiping campaign, they had learned firsthand the superiority of Western guns and ships. But these contrivances were beyond the normal understanding of Confucian scholars and officials. Story has it that a contemporary of Tseng's, Hu Lin-i, was so astounded by the sight of two foreign steamers charging swiftly and effortlessly against contrary

25. For details, see John L. Rawlinson, *China's Struggle for Naval Development, 1839-1895* (Cambridge, Mass., 1967), 34-37; Morse, II, chapter 2.

river currents that he signed in resignation: "These are things we cannot comprehend!" The thought of facing such an unfathomable enemy in the future profoundly shocked him, and already weakened by overwork during the Taiping campaign, Hu died shortly afterwards.

If steamships made such a strong impact on Hu, he was not alone. To the farsighted, shipbuilding became a *sine qua non* for survival. Tseng Kuo-fan tried his hands at building one in Anking in 1862-63, but it could not move fast or freely. Baffled but not discouraged, he was the more determined to unveil the secrets of shipbuilding and gun-making in order to break the Western monopoly of power. In his diary of June 3, 1862 Tseng noted: "If we wish to find a method of self-strengthening, we should begin by considering the reform of government service and the securing of men of ability as urgent tasks; and then regard learning to make explosive shells and steamships and other instruments as the work of first importance. If only we could possess all their [barbarians'] superior techniques, then we would have the means to return their favors when they are obedient, and to avenge our grievances when they are disloyal."[26]

Under Tseng's sponsorship, the Kiangnan Arsenal was established at Shanghai in 1865, with machines purchased from the United States by Yung Wing, the first Chinese graduate of Yale (1854), who had joined Tseng's staff in 1863. The arsenal not only manufactured guns and cannon, but also constructed ships and maintained a translation bureau. Its first ship, 185 feet long and 27.2 feet wide, was successfully completed in 1868. The arsenal turned out a total of five ships, the last in 1872 with 400 horsepower and carrying 26 guns. Its translation bureau completed 98 titles of Western works in less than ten years, of which 47 were in the field of natural science and 45 on military affairs and technology. Doubtless, the Kiangnan Arsenal shone as a major accomplishment in the early phase of the Self-strengthening Movement.

If Tseng opened the way to Westernization, Tso and Li bore the torch unflaggingly. Tso had been a firm believer of the unity of knowledge and action, and, in his train of thinking, was influenced by Lin Tse-hsü and Wei Yüan. His first personal acquaintance with Western ships and guns came when he employed French officers and men in the recovery of Chekiang province from the Taipings in 1864. He too had attempted to manufacture a steamer by Chinese machines and methods, but it turned out to be very clumsy on its trial run at the West Lake in Hangchow.

26. Teng and Fairbank, *China's Response*, 62.

His continued interest in shipbuilding blossomed into the establishment of the famous Foochow Dockyard in 1866, with two Frenchmen, Prosper Giquel (1835-86) and Paul d'Aiguebelle (1831-75) as chief engineer and supervisor. It turned out a total of forty ships. Its naval school graduated a number of able officers, including the extremely adept and perceptive Yen Fu (1853-1921), who studied in Britain and, in later years, translated a number of important Western works on thought, sociology, logic, and jurisprudence (see Chapter 17). The Foochow Dockyard was the second most important achievement of the Self-strengthening Movement.

When Tso was transferred shortly afterwards to fight the Moslems, he placed the dockyard under the direction of Shen Pao-chen, a son-in-law of Lin Tse-hsü, while he himself continued to promote modernization in the Northwest: an arsenal in 1871, a gunpowder factory in 1875, and a woolen mill at Lanchow with German and other foreign employees. In 1878 he even attempted a modern bank and a mint for casting coins and silver dollars.

The leading spirit of the Self-strengthening Movement was Li Hung-chang. His association with the Ever-Victorious army and with foreign officers such as Ward and Gordon made him cognizant of the awesome power of guns and ships. He frankly conceded to Tseng Kuo-fan in May 1863 that the recovery of T'ai-ts'ang from the Taipings was entirely the result of Gordon's powerful cannon. In superlatives he praised the Western cannon and explosive shells as "matchless weapons for offensive and defensive in the whole world." He believed, somewhat naively, that possession of steamships and guns with explosive shells alone would suffice to stop foreign aggression. Li's adoration of the Western military system and arms is seen in a letter to Tseng in February 1863:

> I have been aboard the warships of British and French admirals and I saw that their cannon are ingenious and uniform, their ammunition is fine and cleverly made, their weapons are bright, and their troops have a martial appearance and are orderly. These things are actually superior to those of China. Their army is not their strong point, yet whenever they attack a city or bombard a camp, the various firearms they use are all non-existent in China. Even their pontoon bridges, scaling ladders, and fortresses are particularly well prepared with excellent technique and marvelous usefulness. All these things I have never seen before . . . I feel deeply ashamed that Chinese weapons are far inferior to those of foreign countries. Every day I warn and instruct my officers to be humble-minded, to bear the humiliation, to learn one

or two secret methods from the Westerners in the hope that we may increase our knowledge . . . If we encamp at Shanghai for a long time and cannot make use of nor take over the superior techniques of the foreigners, our regrets will be numerous![27]

In contrast to his admiration of Western guns and ships, Li deprecated his countrymen's impractical way of life and their lack of a sense of urgency:

Chinese scholars and officials have been indulging in the inveterate habit of remembering stanzas and sentences and practicing fine model calligraphy, while our warriors and fighters are, on the other hand, rough, stupid, and careless; so that what the scholars and officials use is not what they have learned, and what they have learned is not what they use. In peace time they sneer at the sharp weapons of foreign countries as things produced by strange techniques and tricky craft, which they consider it unnecessary to learn. In wartime, then, they are alarmed that the effective weapons of Western countries are so strange and marvelous, and regard them as something the Chinese cannot learn about. They do not know that for several hundred years the foreigners have considered the study of firearms as important as their bodies and lives . . .[28]

If China did not catch up in shipbuilding and gun-making, Li warned, Japan would soon imitate the West and take advantage of her. The urgency of the situation must compel China to institute Self-strengthening programs at once; she must not only learn to use foreign weapons but also to buy machines to make them herself. What China was facing, Li loudly pronounced in 1872, was *a totally unprecedented situation in her three thousand years of history*: the West had advanced step by step from India to Southeast Asia and to China. There was no way to stop the movement. China must meet this challenge head-on, determined to strengthen herself through adoption of Western guns and ships.

With Tseng Kuo-fan's death in 1872 and Tso Tsung-t'ang's involvement in the Moslem campaign in the Northwest and Sinkiang from 1868 to 1880, Li became the central spirit of Self-strengthening. His long tenure as governor-general of Chihli and as High Commissioner of the Northern Ocean for practically the quarter of a century after 1870 en-

27. Teng and Fairbank, *China's Response*, 69.
28. *Ibid.*, 70-71.

abled him to build up a substantial military and industrial empire in North China. Although a provincial authority, he actually performed a number of functions for the central government and served as a sort of "coordinator" of Self-strengthening programs throughout the country.[29] For thirty years he was the principal architect and instigator of "foreign matters" (*yang-wu*)[30] in China. Among his major achievements were the Nanking Arsenal in 1867, the China Merchants' Steam Navigation Company in 1872, a naval and a military academy at Tientsin in 1880 and 1885, respectively, and the Peiyang fleet in 1888.

However, Li's preoccupation with ships and guns and his total negligence of Western political systems and culture very much limited the scope of the Self-strengthening Movement. His attitude stemmed partially from his belief that China surpassed the West in everything except weaponry,[31] and partially from the fact that he was in charge of military training and coastal defense. He saw China's immediate need for military strength, but not the larger and more distant requirement for political and social reform. Defending his narrow approach in a letter to a friend-critic,[32] he wrote: "My humble duty is in military affairs, and therefore I must study military methods . . . Weapons are the most important thing for a nation; if we look to other larger and more far-reaching plans, we will hardly achieve our purposes. I can only try the best I can."

The Conservative Opposition. Limited as was the scope of the Self-strengthening Movement and its leaders' grasp of the problems facing China, the advocates of *yang-wu* were already far ahead of their fellow officials and scholars, who were mostly ignorant of the modern world and blind to modernization. When Prince Kung memorialized the throne in 1867 for permission to add a department of astronomy and mathematics at the T'ung-wen kuan and to invite foreign professors to teach these subjects to students of sound background in Chinese studies, he was vehemently attacked by the arch-conservative Grand Secretary Wo-jen (d.

29. K. C. Liu, "Li Hung-chang in Chihli: The Emergence of a Policy, 1870-1875." Paper read before the 18th annual convention of the Association for Asian Studies, New York, April 4, 1966; later published in Feuerwerker, Murphey, and Wright (eds.), *Approaches to Modern Chinese History*, 68-104.

30. Such as ships, guns, railroad, telegraph, and other Western-style enterprises, as distinguished from "foreign affairs."

31. Li wrote: "Everything in China's civil and military system is far superior to the West. Only in firearms is it absolutely impossible to catch up with them." Teng and Fairbank, *China's Response*, 71.

32. Kuo Sung-tao, China's first minister to England and France from 1876 to 1878.

1871), a leading Neo-Confucian scholar. How could the Chinese forget the disgrace of the foreign occupation of Peking and the burning of the Summer Palace, the latter demanded. How could anyone suggest shifting good Chinese scholars to barbarian studies?

> Your slave [i.e. servant] has learned that the way to establish a nation is to lay emphasis on propriety and righteousness, not on power and plotting. The fundamental effort lies in the minds of people, not in techniques. Now, if we seek trifling arts and respect barbarians as teachers regardless of the possibility that the cunning barbarians may not teach us their essential techniques—even if the teachers sincerely teach and the students faithfully study them, all that can be accomplished is the training of mathematicians. From ancient down to modern times, your slave has never heard of anyone who could use mathematics to raise the nation from a state of decline or to strengthen it in time of weakness. The empire is so great that one should not worry lest there be any lack of abilities therein. If astronomy and mathematics have to be taught, an extensive search should find someone who has mastered the technique. Why is it limited to barbarians; why is it necessary to learn from the barbarians?

Prince Kung's rebuttal was simple and pointed: if Wo-jen had a better way to save the country, let him show how:

> We merely continue our empty talk about moral principles and righteousness, and confusedly argue without end . . . If we remain contented with our ignorance, we are deeply concerned lest the situation will deteriorate like a stream running downhill every day . . . The grand secretary [i.e. Wo-jen] considers our action a hindrance. Certainly, he should have some better plans. If he really has some marvelous plan which can control foreign countries and not let us be controlled by them, your ministers should certainly follow the footsteps of the grand secretary . . . If he has no other plan than to use loyalty and sincerity as armor, and propriety and righteousness as a shield, and such similar phrases; and if he says that these words could accomplish diplomatic negotiations and be sufficient to control the life of our enemies, your ministers indeed do not presume to believe it.[33]

The Empress Dowager Tz'u-hsi, realizing the importance of Western learning but not wishing to offend the conservatives, approved the estab-

33. Teng and Fairbank, *China's Response,* 76-9.

lishment of the science department on the one hand, and on the other authorized Wo-jen to set up a separate department of Chinese studies in the school. It was her game of using the conservatives to checkmate the progressives, lest the latter become too powerful for her to control. Wo-jen, reluctant to associate with the T'ung-wen kuan, intentionally fell while riding to the school, thus providing himself with an excuse not to attend. The conservative Confucian society and officialdom were so ill-disposed toward innovations that the Self-strengtheners had to fight every inch of the way to launch the movement.

PERIODS OF SELF-STRENGTHENING

The First Period. According to the changing emphasis and the shifting philosophy, the Self-strengthening Movement can be divided into three periods. The first, roughly from 1861 to 1872, stressed the adoption of Western firearms, machines, scientific knowledge, and the training of technical and diplomatic personnel through the establishment of translation bureaus, new schools, and the dispatch of students abroad. Diplomatic innovations were introduced to insure good relations with Western powers so that China could discover their shipbuilding and armament secrets. As already indicated, the motivating force was the desire "to learn the superior *technique* of the barbarians in order to control the barbarians"; there was no recognition of the need for anything else from the West. The embattled leaders of this period were Prince Kung and Wen-hsiang in the capital, and Tseng, Tso, and Li in the provinces, and their main accomplishments were as follows:

1861   Establishment of the Tsungli Yamen at Peking and the Superintendencies of Trade at Tientsin and Shanghai at the suggestion of Prince Kung.

1862   Establishment of the T'ung-wen kuan (Interpreters College) at Peking at the suggestion of Prince Kung.
Creation of three gun factories at Shanghai by Li Hung-chang, who also assigned his men to learn the use of cannon with explosive shells from British officers and the use of rifles from German officers.

1863   Establishment of a foreign-language school (Kuang-fang-yen kuan) at Shanghai by Li.
The arrival of the Lay-Osborn flotilla.

  Dispatch of Yung-wing to the United States to purchase machines by Tseng.

1864 Creation of a small gun factory at Soochow by Li.

  Establishment of a foreign-language school (T'ung-wen kuan) at Canton.

1865 Establishment of the Kiangnan Arsenal at Shanghai by Tseng and Li, with a translation bureau attached.

1866 Establishment of the Foochow Dockyard at Ma-wei, outside Foochow, by Tso Tsung-t'ang, with machines purchased from France. Attached was a naval school in two divisions: one specializing in French and shipbuilding, and the other in English and navigation. Dispatch of the Pin-ch'un exploratory mission to Europe.

1867 Establishment of the Nanking Arsenal by Li.

  Creation of the Tientsin Machine Factory by Ch'ung-hou.

1868 Dispatch of Anson Burlingame as China's roving ambassador to the West, to assist the Manchu and Chinese co-envoys. (See next chapter.)

1870 Expansion of the Tientsin Machine Factory into four plants by Li.

1871 Planning for a Western-style fort at Taku.

1872 Dispatch of thirty teen-age students to the United States to study at Hartford, Connecticut on recommendation of Tseng and Li. A total of 120 boys were sent in four installments, 1872-81.

  Officers sent by Li to study in Germany.

  Request by Li to open coal and iron mines.

  The pre-eminent feature of this period of Self-strengthening was the emphasis on development of military industries, which had the following characteristics. First, they were all "government undertakings" (*kuan-pan*), which partook of all the usual bureaucratic inefficiency and nepotism of an official agency. They engaged in modern production but retained the old-styled managerial and administrative procedures. Secondly, they relied on foreigners for operation and materials. There seemed to be a blind faith in the ability of foreigners, regardless of their training and experience. The Nanking Arsenal was put under the direction of an Englishman, Halliday Macartney, a medical doctor by profession. The Foochow Dockyard was supervised by two Frenchmen, Giquel and d'Aiguebelle, who had never before in their lives built a ship. The materials for construction were all imported. Because of poor leadership and bureaucratic corruption, the ships and guns produced were nowhere comparable

in quality to their Western counterparts. Thirdly, these military industries formed the power bases of the provincial leaders sponsoring them,
and consequently smacked of a strong regional and "feudal" flavor. As
governor-general at Nanking, Li built the Nanking Arsenal; and as governor-general at Foochow, Tso constructed the Foochow Dockyard. There
was little concerted effort or coordination between the various regional
groups. Even after their transfer to other posts—Tso to the Northwest in
1868 and Li to North China (Tientsin), where they built up new power
bases—they continued to maintain personal connections with their former projects.[34]

The Second Period. As the Self-strengthening Movement progressed,
there was increasing recognition that wealth was the basis of power—one
had to be rich in order to be strong. Modern defense cost far more than
traditional defense; moreover, it had to be supported by better communication systems, industries, and enterprises. Li Hung-chang announced
in September 1876: "China's chronic weakness stems from poverty."
Therefore, in the second period, 1872 to 1885, while defense industries
remained a chief occupation, greater attention was directed to the development of profit-oriented enterprises such as shipping, railway, mining,
and the telegraph. These "foreign matters" (*yang-wu*) gradually came to
be regarded as "current affairs" (*shih-wu*), as they had been thrust forward as the pressing problems of state.

In addition to the "government-sponsored" (*kuan-pan*) military industries, there now appeared another type of enterprise, modeled in organization after the traditional salt administration: "government-supervised
merchant undertakings" (*kuan-tu shang-pan*).[35] Foremost among them
were the China Merchants' Steam Navigation Company, the K'ai-p'ing
Coal Mines, the Shanghai Cotton Cloth Mill, and the Imperial Telegraph Administration.[36] Capital for these undertakings came from private
sources, although the government as patron might initially supply some
funds or advance loans to be repaid later. But "profit and loss are entirely
the responsibility of the merchants and do not involve the government,"

34. Mou An-shih, *Yang-wu yün-tung* (The "foreign matters" movement), (Shanghai,
1961), 79-86.
35. Often translated, rather incorrectly, as "government supervision-merchant management."
36. Albert Feuerwerker, *China's Early Industrialization: Sheng Hsüan-huai* (1844-
1916) *and Mandarin Enterprise* (Cambridge, Mass., 1958), 9-10.

as Li Hung-chang decreed.[37] The merchant shareholders, who supplied the funds, were barred from the management, which was in the hands of government-appointed officials or private individuals (who might subscribe to shares later). For instance, the China Merchants' Steam Navigation Company's first promoter-manager was an official;[38] he was succeeded by a private individual who was the former compradore of the British firm of Jardine, Matheson and Company;[39] after 1884 it was again managed by an official.[40] These government-supervised merchant enterprises were a hybrid operation which smacked of strong official overtones and the usual bureaucratic inefficiency, corruption, and nepotism. Being profit-oriented, they discouraged private competition and tended to monopolize business through government favor or intervention. They also relied on foreign personnel for support: the "China Merchant" employed foreign marine superintendent, ship captains, and engineers.[41]

During this second period, Li Hung-chang ascended as the leading proponent of modern industries and enterprises, Tseng having died in 1872 and Tso being involved in the Northwest with the suppression of the Moslem Rebellion. Prince Kung had lost much of his influence with the Dowager Tz'u-hsi after his two chastisements in 1865 and 1869 (next chapter), while Wen-hsiang had died in 1876. Li emerged as the unrivaled leader of the Self-strengthening Movement, and though a provincial official—governor-general of Chihli—he performed a number of central government functions due to his proximity to Peking and the dowager's trust in him. Over 90 per cent of the modern projects were launched under his aegis.

1872   Inauguration of the China Merchants' Steam Navigation Company as a "government-supervised merchant undertaking," supported by Li.

1875   Plans to construct iron-clad ships.
      Dispatch of students from the Foochow Dockyard to study in France.

1876   Dispatch of seven officers by Li to Germany.

37. Kwang-ching Liu, "British-Chinese Steamship Rivalry in China, 1873-85" in C. D. Cowan (ed.), *The Economic Development of China and Japan* (London, 1964), 53.
38. Chu Ch'i-ang.
39. Tong King-sing.
40. Sheng Hsüan-huai.
41. Mou An-shih, 113-22.

Sending of thirty students and apprentices from the Foochow Dockyard to Britain and France.

Diplomatic mission to Britain and France, followed by those to other countries in the next years.

1877   Creation of the Bureau for the K'ai-p'ing Coal Mines at Tientsin by Li.

Establishment of a machine factory in Szechwan by Ting Pao-chen.

1878   Establishment of a textile factory in Kansu by Tso.

Establishment of the Shanghai Cotton Cloth Mill by Li.

1879   Inauguration of a telegraph line between Taku and Tientsin.

1880   Establishment of a naval academy at Tientsin by Li.

Request for permission to build railways by Li.

Adoption of a plan for a modern navy, and beginning of purchasing foreign warships.

1881   Inauguration of the Imperial Telegraph Administration.

Opening of the first telegraph line from Shanghai to Tientsin.

Creation of a railway of twenty *li* (six miles) north of Tientsin.

Dispatch of ten naval students abroad to study.

1882   Beginning of construction of a harbor and a shipyard at Port Arthur, by Li.

1884   Sending of thirteen naval students and four apprentices by Li to study shipbuilding in Britain, France, and Germany, and nine students to Britain to learn navigation.

The Third Period. From 1885 to 1895, while emphasis on the military and naval build-up continued, as witnessed by the organization of the Board of Admiralty (*Hai-chün ya-men*) in 1885 and the formal establishment of the Peiyang fleet in 1888, the idea of enriching the nation through light industry gained increasing favor; as a result textile and cotton-weaving gathered momentum. Li continued to dominate the scene, but he now faced rising competition from Governor-general Chang Chih-tung at Wuhan, and Governor-general Liu K'un-i at Nanking. Meanwhile, Prince Chün, father of the emperor and head of the newly established Board of Admiralty, emerged as a powerful figure in the capital, with Prince Kung's descent into political eclipse after the French war, 1884-85.

Organizationally, two new types of industrial and mercantile enterprises—"joint government and merchant enterprises" (*kuan-shang ho-pan*) and incipient "private enterprises" (*shang-pan*)—bid for existence in revolt against the dominant bureaucratic "government-supervised merchant undertakings." But these two failed to prosper because of traditional official discrimination against, and jealousy of, merchants. Among the larger "joint government and merchant undertakings" were the Kweichow Ironworks established in 1891 and the Hupeh Textile Company in 1894. In both cases the officials welcomed private capital but resented private control. The struggle for domination of the Hupeh Textile Company was so acute that the merchant capital was ultimately forced out, leaving the company entirely a government operation.[42] As regards private enterprises, they were very weak, representing but a small fraction of the total industrial effort and investment—a far cry from mobilizing private capital the way the Japanese did during the Meiji era. The major efforts of the decade from the mid-eighties to the mid-nineties included:

1885   Creation of a military academy at Tientsin by Li.
      Inauguration of the Board of Admiralty in Peking, with Prince Chün as head, assisted by Li.
1886   Establishment of a textile mill by Chang Chih-tung at Canton.
1887   Establishment of mints by Chang and Li at Canton and Tientsin respectively.
      Inauguration of the Mo-ho Gold Mines in Heilungkiang by Li.
1888   Establishment of the Peiyang fleet under Li's control.
1889   Creation of a cotton mill and an iron factory at Canton by Chang.
1890   Inauguration of the Ta-yeh Iron Mines, the Han-yang Ironworks, and the P'ing-hsiang Coal Mines by Chang.
1891   Establishment of the Lung-chang Paper Mill at Shanghai by Li.
      Establishment of the Kweichow Ironworks as a "joint government and merchant undertaking."
1893   Inauguration of a general office for machine textile manufacturing by Li.
      Establishment of four cotton and textile plants at Wuchang by Chang.
1894   Organization of two match companies in Hupeh province.
      Creation of the Hupeh Textile Company, as a "joint government and merchant undertaking."

LIMITATIONS AND REPERCUSSIONS OF THE
SELF-STRENGTHENING MOVEMENT

The preceding lists may present quite an impressive picture of endeavors, but they really represented very superficial attempts at modernization.

42. Mou An-shih, 158-63.

The scope of activity was limited to firearms, ships, machines, communications, mining, and light industries. No attempts were made to assimilate Western institutions, philosophy, arts, and culture. The Self-strengthening efforts barely scratched the surface of modernization, without achieving a breakthrough in industrialization. The basic weakness was exposed in the French war of 1884-85, when China, after twenty years of preparations, was unable to defend her tributary state, Annam. The failure of the movement was confirmed beyond doubt by the defeat in the Japanese war ten years later. Marxist historians stress the intrinsic contradiction in grafting modern capitalism and industry onto the agrarian Confucian social base. Perhaps the following points shed light on the lackluster performance of Self-strengthening.

1. *Lack of Coordination*. The central power of the Ch'ing dynasty had declined after the Taiping Revolution, so much so that apart from a flash of vigor during the T'ung-chih period (1862-74), there was hardly any direction in the government. The major brunt of modernization was borne not by the court at Peking, but by provincial authorities without central direction, planning, and coordination. Although Li Hung-chang after 1870 performed some central government functions, he was basically a regional official who could not take the place of the central government. The provincial promoters of Self-strengthening rivaled rather than cooperated with each other and regarded their achievements as the foundation of personal power. Their sense of regionalism and their eagerness for self-preservation persisted so strongly that during the French war of 1884 the Peiyang and Nanyang fleets refused to go to the rescue of the Fukien fleet under enemy attack, and during the Japanese war of 1894-95 the Nanyang fleet maintained "neutrality" while the Peiyang fleet alone fought the Japanese navy. The results of both wars were, of course, disastrous.

2. *Limited Vision*. The advocates of Self-strengthening promoted modern projects primarily to enable their country to resist foreign aggression, to suppress domestic unrest, and to fortify their own positions of power. They never dreamed of remaking China into a modern state. In fact, they strove to strengthen the existing order rather than to replace it. They had absolutely no conception of economic development, industrial revolution, and modern transformation. Consequently, their endeavors resulted in no more than a handful of isolated modern enclaves scattered

over an otherwise traditional country, in which the old institutions remained dominant.

Furthermore, the lack of popular participation restricted the scope of
modernization. The leadership in Self-strengthening operated from the
top down, with little grass-roots support as there was in Meiji Japan.
Shackled by traditions, the Chinese officials were unable to shake off the
age-old disdain for merchants, and continued to discourage private enterprise and competition. They also failed to instill private initiative in the
government industries or the government-supervised merchant undertakings, which continuously suffered from the usual bureaucratic inefficiency,
nepotism, and corruption.[43]

3. *Shortage of Capital*. China was a poor country with a limited supply
of capital. There was a shortage of bureaucratic as well as private capital,
which restricted the initiation and growth of industries and enterprises.
When the government raised taxes to support the new undertakings, it
weakened the people's all too limited resources for investment. One need
only note the same persons associated with the various enterprises—the
China Merchants' Steam Navigation Company, the Shanghai Cotton
Cloth Mills, the Imperial Telegraph Administration, and the Han-Yeh-
P'ing Mines—to know the small circle of entrepreneurs and the limited
funds at their disposal.[44] Moreover, capital formation was difficult in
these enterprises, since the profits, roughly 8 to 10 per cent a year, were
distributed to shareholders as dividends rather than reinvested for growth.

4. *Foreign Imperialism*. The generation of Self-strengthening coincided
with the period of intensified foreign imperialism, as evident in the Japanese invasion of Formosa in 1874 and annexation of the Liu-ch'iu Islands
in 1879; the British attempt to open Yunnan in 1875; the Russian occupation of Ili in Sinkiang, 1871-81; the French seizure of Annam and the
war of 1884-85; and the Japanese aggression in Korea and the war of 1894-
95. These cataclysmic events not only divided the attention of the government and the modernizers, but also incurred vast military expenses
and indemnities which siphoned away considerable sums that could
otherwise have been applied to Self-strengthening.

43. Ch'uan Han-sheng, "Chia-wu chan-cheng i-ch'ien ti Chung-kuo kung-yeh-hua
yün-tung" (China's industrialization movement before the Sino-Japanese War), *Li-
shih yü-yen yen-chiu-so chi-k'an*; Academia Sinica, 25 (June 1954), 74.
44. Feuerwerker, 249.

5. *Technical Backwardness and Moral Degradation.* Western machines and industrial management were alien to the traditional Chinese mentality. To overcome technical backwardness was a tremendous obstacle, the more so when the foreign advisers and teachers themselves were quite inexpert. The guns and ships turned out by the Self-strengthening projects were vastly inferior, necessitating continuous purchases from abroad. The nine large ships of the Peiyang fleet were all foreign-made, and the cannon at the Port Arthur and Weihaiwei naval bases were Krupp's products.

Moreover, men of talent and integrity usually steered clear of foreign matters and enterprises; only the lesser characters were willing to associate with the modernization projects, resulting in frequent cases of corruption and irregularity. Even Li Hung-chang himself was not noted for high morals and character—he reportedly left behind an estate of 40 million taels! His followers squeezed and milked the factories and enterprises under their charge mercilessly. The most scandalous of all was the misuse of 30 million taels of naval funds to construct the Summer Palace (*I-ho-yüan*) for the amusement of the dowager in retirement.

6. *Social and Psychological Inertia.* The great majority of the scholar-official class regarded foreign affairs and Western-style enterprises as "dirty" and "vulgar," beneath their dignity. So powerful was this conservatism that even the court could not ignore it. An excerpt from Li Hung-chang's letter to a friend[45] illustrates the difficulties of the modernizers:

> Ever since the discussion of coastal defense began in 1874, I have stated in detail the necessity of opening coal and iron mines, of building telegraph lines and railways, and of opening schools for pursuing Western knowledge and sciences in order to train men of ability. At that time Grand Councillor Wen-hsiang smiled in his eyes but kept silent, and in the court conference most of the participants were noncommittal except for two members who strongly objected to my suggestions. I had the honor of meeting Prince Kung and explained to him thoroughly the advantages of railways . . . Prince Kung agreed with my suggestion, but said that *nobody dared to promote such action.* I again begged him to watch for a chance to explain this point to the two dowager empresses, and he said that the two empresses could not initiate such a great plan either. Thereafter I spoke no more. . . .
>
> The gentry class forbids the local people to use Western methods

45. Kuo Sung-tao, minister to Britain and France, 1876-78.

and machines, so that eventually the people will not be able to do anything . . . Scholars and men of letters always criticize me for honoring strange knowledge and for being queer and unusual. *It is really difficult to understand the minds of some Chinese.*[46]

Cases of conservative opposition to modernization abound. In 1863 the British offer to build a railway from Shanghai to Soochow was rejected by local gentry. In 1874 the British-built short railroad from Shanghai to Woosung was ripped off its bed by mobs because the locomotive ran over a spectator. Two years later the governor-general was pressured by the local gentry to buy this foreign railway and have it totally wrecked. In 1872 when Tseng Chi-tse, son of Tseng Kuo-fan, took a steamer, a foreign contrivance, to Hunan to attend a family funeral, he was severely slandered by the gentry. In 1876 when Kuo Sung-tao went to Britain as a minister, the literati cruelly satirized him for leaving the land of the sages to serve the foreign devils. A pair of scrolls appeared as follows:

> Outstanding among his associates,
>   Elevated above his peers,
> Yet ostracized in the country of Yao and Shun.[47]
> Unable to serve men,
>   Why able to serve devils?
> Of what use to leave his fatherland!

Kuo's diary, which praised the Western civilization as having a history of two thousand years, was condemned by the conservatives as heresy, and they forced the government to destroy its printing block. These few instances suffice to lay bare the unfavorable social and political atmosphere within which the advocates of Westernization had to operate. Considering the tremendous odds against them, it is really a wonder that they dared to espouse such an unpopular cause and that they achieved the record, however imperfect, they did!

For all its shortcomings, the Self-strengthening Movement marked the beginning of industrialization and sowed the seeds of modern capitalism in China, with many significant repercussions. First, most of the arsenals, dockyards, machine factories, schools, and modern enterprises were located in the treaty ports and cities along the coast or on the river, where

46. Li Chien-nung, *The Political History of China*, 1840-1928 (New York, 1956), ed. and tr. by S. Y. Teng and J. Ingalls, 108-09. Italics added.
47. Legendary Sage-Emperors.

foreign help was most readily available. They contributed to the development of great metropolises such as Shanghai, Nanking, Tientsin, Foochow, Canton, and Hankow. Secondly, the farming population in nearby agricultural areas was drawn to these centers to become industrial workers or laborers, swelling the size of these cities and gradually giving rise to a new working class. Thirdly, the new industries and enterprises brought into being new professional men such as engineers, managers, and entrepreneurs, while those who had studied abroad returned home to become leaders in the army, navy, schools, and diplomatic service. They contributed to the rise of the new managerial and entrepreneurial class in China.

FURTHER READING

Banno, Masataka, *China and the West: 1858-1861: The Origins of the Tsungli Yamen* (Cambridge, Mass., 1964).

Bennett, Adrian A., *John Fryer: The Introduction of Western Science and Technology into Nineteenth-Century China* (Cambridge, Mass., 1967).

Biggerstaff, Knight, *The Eearliest Modern Government Schools in China* (Ithaca, N.Y., 1961).

Carlson, C. Ellsworth, *The Kaiping Mines, 1877-1912* (Cambridge, Mass., 1957).

Ch'en, Gideon, *Lin Tse-hsü, Pioneer Promoter of the Adoption of Western Means of Maritime Defense in China* (Peiping, 1934).

———, *Tseng Kuo-fan: Pioneer Promoter of the Steamship in China* (Peiping, 1935).

———, *Tso Tsung-t'ang, Pioneer Promoter of the Modern Dockyard and the Woolen Mill in China* (Peiping, 1938).

Ch'i, Ssu-ho 齊思和, "Wei Yüan yü wan-Ch'ing hsüeh-feng" 魏源與晚清學風 (Wei Yüan and the late Ch'ing intellectual climate), *Yen-ching hsüeh-pao*, 39: 177-266 (Dec. 1950).

Cohen, Paul A., "Wang T'ao's Perspective on a Changing World" in Albert Feuerwerker, Rhoads Murphey, and Mary C. Wright (eds.), *Approaches to Modern Chinese History* (Berkeley, 1967), 133-62.

Cowan, C. D., *The Economic Development of China and Japan* (London, 1964).

Ch'üan, Han-sheng 全漢昇, "Ch'ing-chi ti Chiang-nan chih-tsao-chü" 清季的江南製造局 (The Kiangnan Arsenal of the late Ch'ing period), *Li-shih yü-yen yen-chiu-so chi-k'an* 歷史語言研究所集刊 (Bulletin of the Institute of History and Philology, Academia Sinica), 23:1:145-59 (Taipei, 1951).

———, "Chia-wu chan-cheng i-ch'ien ti Chung-kuo kung-yeh-hua yün-tung" 甲午戰爭以前的中國工業化運動 (China's industrialization movement before the Sino-Japanese war), *Li-shih yü-yen yen-chiu-so chi-k'an*, (Bulletin of the Institute of History and Philology, Academia Sinica), 25:59-79 (June 1954).

———, "Ch'ing-mo Han-yang t'ieh-ch'ang" 清末漢陽鉄廠 (The Han-yang Iron and Steel Works at the end of the Ch'ing period), She-hui k'o-hsüeh lun-ts'ung (Journal of Social Sciences), 1:1-33 (April 1950).

Fairbank, John K., "The Provisional System at Shanghai in 1853-54," The Chinese Social and Political Science Review, 18:4:455-504 (Jan. 1935); 19:1:65-124 (April 1935).

———, "The Creation of the Foreign Inspectorate of Customs at Shanghai," The Chinese Social and Political Science Review, 19:4:496-514 (Jan. 1936); 20:1:42-100 (April 1936).

Feuerwerker, Albert, China's Early Industrialization: Sheng Hsüan-huai (1844-1916) and Mandarin Enterprise (Cambridge, Mass., 1958).

Giquel, Prosper, The Foochow Arsenal and Its Results, from the Commencement in 1867 to the End of the Foreign Directorate on the 16th February, 1874, tr. by H. Lang (Shanghai, 1874).

Hou, Chi-ming, Foreign Investment and Economic Development in China, 1840-1937 (Cambridge, Mass., 1965).

Hsü, Immanuel C. Y., China's Entrance into the Family of Nations: The Diplomatic Phase, 1858-1880 (Cambridge, Mass, 1968), Parts II and III.

Huang, I-feng 黃逸峰, and Chiang To 姜鐸, "Chung-kuo yang-wu yün-tung yü Jih-pen Ming-chih wei-hsin tsai ching-chi fa-chan shang ti pi-chiao" 中國洋務運動與日本明治維新在經濟發展上的比較 (A comparison of the Chinese "foreign matters" movement and the Japanese Meiji modernization from the standpoint of economic development), Li-shih yen-chiu (1963) 1:27-47.

Hung, William, "Huang Tsun-hsien's Poem: The Closure of the Educational Mission in America," Harvard Journal of Asiatic Studies, 18:50-73 (1955).

King, Frank H. H., Money and Monetary Policy in China, 1845-1895 (Cambridge, Mass., 1965).

La Fargue, Thomas E., "Chinese Educational Commission to the United States," Far Eastern Quarterly, I.59 71 (1941)

———, China's First Hundred (Pullman, Wash., 1942).

Liu, Hsiung-hsiang 劉熊祥, Ch'ing-chi ssu-shih-nien wai-chiao yü hai-fang 清季四十年外交與海防 (Forty years of diplomacy and maritime defense in the late Ch'ing period), (Chungking, 1943).

Liu, Kwang-ching, Anglo-American Steamship Rivalry in China, 1862-1874 (Cambridge, Mass., 1962).

———, "Li Hung-chang in Chihli: The Emergence of a Policy, 1870-1875," in Albert Feuerwerker, Rhoads Murphey, and Mary C. Wright (eds.), Approaches to Modern Chinese History (Berkeley, 1967), 68-104.

Meng, Ssu-ming, The Tsungli Yamen: Its Organization and Functions (Cambridge, Mass., 1962).

Mou, An-shih 牟安世, Yang-wu yün-tung 洋務運動 (The "foreign matters" movement), (Shanghai, 1961).

Pelcovits, Nathan A., *Old China Hands and the Foreign Office* (New York, 1948).

Spector, Stanley, *Li Hung-chang and the Huai Army* (Seattle, 1964).

Sun, Yü-t'ang 孫毓棠, "Chung-Jih Chia-wu chan-cheng ch'ien wai-kuo tzu-pen tsai Chung-kuo ching-ying ti chin-tai kung-yeh" 中日甲午戰爭前外國資本在中國經營的近代工業 (Modern industries operated by foreign capital in China before the Sino-Japanese War), *Li-shih yen-chiu*, 5:1-41 (1954).

Teng, Ssu-yü, and John K. Fairbank, *China's Response to the West* (Cambridge, Mass., 1954), I, chapters 5-14.

Tsiang, T. F., *Chung-kuo chin-tai-shih ta-kang* 中國近代史大綱 (An outline of Chinese modern history), (Taipei, 1959), chapter 3.

Wang, Hsin-chung 王信忠 , "Fu-chou ch'uan-ch'ang chih yen-ko" 福州船廠之沿革 (The origin and development of the Foochow Dockyard), *Tsinghua hsüeh-pao*, 8:1:1-57 (Dec. 1932).

Wilhelm, Hellmut, "The Background of Tseng Kuo-fan's Ideology," *Asiatische Studien*, 3:3-4:90-100 (1949).

———, "The Problem of Within and Without, a Confucian Attempt at Syncretism," *Journal of the History of Ideas*, 12:1:48-60 (Jan. 1951).

Wright, Mary C., *The Last Stand of Chinese Conservatism: The T'ung-chih Restoration, 1862-1874* (Stanford, 1957).

Wright, Stanley F., *Hart and the Chinese Customs* (Belfast, 1950).

12

Foreign Relations and Court Politics,

1861-80

During the period of the Self-strengthening Movement, China never lacked for advice and encouragement from foreign sources. Robert Hart, inspector-general of customs, and Thomas Wade, British minister at Peking, ceaselessly promoted "progress" in China. As a result of their constant urging, the Tsungli Yamen dispatched an exploratory mission to Europe in 1866.

The Pin-ch'un Mission, 1866. In 1865 Hart submitted a memorandum to the Tsungli Yamen entitled "Observations by an Outsider" (*Chü-wai p'ang-kuan lun*), in which he stressed the advantages of railways, steamships, the telegraph, mining, and Western diplomatic practices. The last was particularly important, because the establishment of Chinese embassies abroad would enable Peking to bypass the headstrong foreign diplomats in China and make direct representations to foreign governments. "I regard representation abroad as of paramount importance," Hart wrote, "and as, in itself, progress, for while I thought that I saw in it one of China's least objectionable ways of preserving freedom and independence, I also supposed it would constitute a tie which should bind her to the West so firmly and commit her to a career of improvement so certainly as to make retrogression impossible."[1] A year later (1866) Thomas Wade

1. Robert Hart, "Notes on Chinese Matters," in Frederick W. Williams, *Anson Burlingame and the First Chinese Mission to Foreign Powers* (New York, 1912), 285.

also presented a communication to Prince Kung, entitled "A Brief Exposition of New Ideas" (*Hsin-i lüeh-lun*), which placed similar emphasis on the need for railways, the telegraph, mining, steamships, modern schools, Western-style army training, and diplomatic representation abroad. He admonished the Chinese to look not to the past for guidance but to the future for inspiration. In short, the message of Hart and Wade was progress through adoption of Western devices and products.

A direct consequence of their prompting was the decision by the Tsungli Yamen to send an informal exploratory mission to Europe under the guidance of Hart during his furlough in 1866. The mission was put under the leadership of Pin-ch'un, a sixty-three-year-old ex-prefect who was Hart's secretary for Chinese correspondence at the time. He was given a temporary third civil service rank to add dignity to his mission, and was accompanied by several T'ung-wen kuan students. Prince Kung made it very clear that it was not a formal diplomatic mission, but only an informal information-gathering junket to the West. Being unofficial, it would obviate the touchy question of institutional propriety and avoid the high cost of a regular embassy. The mission visited London, Copenhagen, Stockholm, St. Petersburg, Berlin, Brussels, and Paris. Its novelty assured it a gracious welcome everywhere. Upon its return its members filled three diaries with detailed descriptions of what they had seen in Europe. Unfortunately their observations were mainly limited to Western social customs, tall buildings, the wonders of gaslight, elevators, and machines; only in passing did they touch upon the British Parliament and other political institutions. The mission signified China's first effort toward dispatching embassies abroad, but establishment of regular legations had to wait until 1877.

The Burlingame Mission and the Treaty Revision, 1868-70. While Western governments were committed to a "Cooperative Policy" in the 1860's, foreign traders and the Old China Hands in the treaty ports, especially Shanghai, never ceased to clamor for a more aggressive policy; they agitated to lay open all of China to Western commerce and to promote "progress" through adoption of railways, the telegraph, mining, and a host of other modern enterprises. Their pronouncements and the memoranda of Hart and Wade aroused fear in the Tsungli Yamen that the British might make many new demands on China during the forthcoming treaty revision—Article 27 of the Treaty of Tientsin with Britain specified that a revision might be made in ten years, i.e. 1868. To prepare for this ominous occasion, the Yamen anxiously polled the leading provincial authorities, who had become very powerful after the Taiping Revolution, for their views on such issues as were likely to arise: construction of telegraphs and railways, opening of mines, missionary activities, inland navigation, and Chinese diplomatic missions abroad.

Tseng Kuo-fan, the leading statesman of the period and governor-general at Nanking, suggested that China temperately but resolutely reject all foreign demands regarding railways, telegraphs, navigation of inland rivers, transportation of salt in Chinese waters, and opening of warehouses, because these activities would seriously hurt the livelihood of the Chinese people. On the other hand, mining was a potentially profitable venture, in which China might avail herself of foreign tools in the initial phase of operations. He definitely believed that China should open diplomatic missions abroad when suitable men and funds were available, but he showed no concern about missionary activities, believing that their alternate periods of success and decline—according to their funds, at the present on the ebb—made them generally ineffective and harmless. Tseng's views on these issues represented fairly well those of the more responsible and progressive officials.

Actually, the Tsungli Yamen's fear was unfounded. The British government looked without favor upon the Old China Hands' push for hasty and undue "progress" in China. On August 17, 1867 Lord Stanley, the foreign secretary, informed Minister Rutherford Alcock in Peking:

> We must not expect the Chinese, either the Government or the people, at once to see things in the same light as we see them; we must bear in mind that we have obtained our knowledge by experience extending over many years, and we must lead and not force the Chinese to the adoption of a better system. We must reconcile ourselves to waiting for the gradual development of that system, and content ourselves with reserving for revision at a future period, as in the case before us, any new arrangement which we may come to in 1868.[2]

The British government favored a "safe course" in China to consolidate the position already gained, and the use of moral influence, moderation, and patience to achieve future developments.

However, the Tsungli Yamen, without diplomatic agents in London, had no inkling of the British policy. But if it lacked intelligence reports,

2. Hsü, *China's Entrance*, 167.

its common sense suggested application of the old principle of *i-i chih-i* —playing off the barbarians against one another. Prince Kung and Wenhsiang, taking a hint from the retiring American minister Anson Burlingame that he would happily mediate as if he were China's envoy in cases of dispute with foreign powers, invited him to join a roving diplomatic mission[3] to the West to dissuade European and American governments from forcing the pace of Westernization in China. A born orator from Massachusetts, Burlingame declared: "When the oldest nation in the world, containing one-third of the human race, seeks, for the first time, to come into relations with the West, and requests the youngest nation through its representative, to act as the medium of such change, the mission is one not to be solicited or rejected."[4]

Burlingame, together with a Manchu and a Chinese co-envoy,[5] carried the mission to the United States in May 1868. The governor of California extended a warm welcome, describing Burlingame as "our guest, the son of the youngest, and representative of the oldest, government." In response Burlingame declared: "The hour has struck, the day has come" when China welcomed "the shining banners of Western civilization." In New York similar grandiloquence proclaimed the message that China was willing to invite missionaries to "plant the shining cross on every hill and every valley." Burlingame's eloquence and charm captivated the Americans, and perhaps himself; after a flattering audience with President Andrew Johnson, he signed a treaty with Secretary of State Seward on July 28, 1868—on his own authority, without the prior approval of the Chinese government. It committed the United States to a policy of noninterference in the development of China, and stipulated the sending of Chinese consuls and laborers to the United States, and reciprocal rights of residence, religion, travel, and access to schools in either country. Though not consulted in advance, Peking was too grateful to disown the treaty.

The mission moved on to London where it was received by Queen Victoria. Lord Clarendon, foreign secretary after Stanley, reaffirmed the policy of not forcing China "to advance more rapidly than was consistent with safety and with due and resonable regard for the feelings of her subjects," and of deprecating any European pressure for adoption of new systems in China.[6] At Berlin, Burlingame committed Prince Bismarck to a statement that the North German Confederation would deal with China

3. At a salary of £8,000 a year plus expenses.
4. *Foreign Relations of the United States*, 1868, I, 494.
5. Chih-kang and Sung Chia-ku.
6. Hsü, *China's Entrance*, 169.

in whatever manner Peking considered in its best interest. At St. Petersburg, after an audience with the tsar, Burlingame contracted pneumonia and died on February 23, 1869. The mission was then carried on by the two co-envoys, visiting Brussels and Rome and then returning to China in October 1870.

Insofar as its immediate objectives were concerned, Burlingame's mission was a great success, for it did commit Western powers to a policy of restraint and moderation in the forthcoming treaty revision. Yet from a long-range standpoint, it encouraged the growth of conservatism in China. The mandarins, who had spent 160,000 taels on the mission, came to believe that foreigners after all could be managed at a price. They became more complacent and less responsive to outside stimuli. The mission may have unwittingly produced a retarding effect on the modernization of China.

The actual negotiations on the treaty revision were carried out as between equals without the threat of guns and ships for the first time since the Opium War. The resultant Alcock Convention of 1869 allowed China to establish a consulate in Hong Kong, to increase the import duty on opium from 30 to 50 taels per picul (133⅓ lbs.) and export duty on silk from 10 to 20 taels, and to limit the most-favored-nation treatment so that the British must accept the conditions under which certain rights were granted to other powers, if they (the British) wished to claim the benefits of the same rights. These terms the British traders strongly opposed, especially the provision for the Chinese consul in Hong Kong, who was said to resemble a revenue officer and a spy. Great pressure subsequently led the British government to reject ratification of the Alcock Convention, an act which aroused deep Chinese disappointment and bitterness. The Tsungli Yamen felt betrayed in its trust in foreign good will, while conservatives and xenophobes were all too ready to point out that foreigners took but never gave, and that the minute a treaty slightly unfavorable to them was negotiated they disowned it. A new tide of antiforeignism rolled in as the decade of the 1870's opened.

The Tientsin Massacre, 1870. Even as Burlingame was inviting missionaries to plant the shining cross in every hill and every valley of China, a rash of anti-Christian activities broke out across the face of the country. Christianity, as a heterodox faith, was antithetical to Confucianism, and its practice of mixed congregations, which ran counter to the Chinese custom of avoiding open contact between men and women, instigated rumors of immoral and perverted behavior. Missionary protection of Chinese converts from local justice, and the construction of churches in disregard of time-honored concepts of geomancy (*feng-shui*) caused endless irritation to Chinese sensibilities.[7] Anti-Christian tracts appeared frequently; and a widely circulated one was entitled "A True Record to Ward Off Evil Doctrine" (*P'i-hsieh chi-shih*) written in the early 1860's by one who called himself "the most heartbroken man in the world."[8] Eruption of antimissionary activities under gentry instigation was common, eliciting a ready reprisal from foreign representatives. The British Minister at Peking, Rutherford Alcock, said pompously: "Demands once made, there is no retreat possible without serious loss of prestige and influence, on which everything depends in the East."[9] Thus, in August 1868, when a mob in Yangchow plundered and set fire to the new missionary station established by Rev. J. Hudson Taylor of the China Inland Mission, Alcock sent Consul W. H. Medhurst and four ships to Nanking to pressure Governor-general Tseng Kuo-fan to cashier the Yangchow officials and pay a compensation. In a similar fashion in November 1868, when a mob on Taiwan attacked foreign merchants seeking to break the camphor monopoly, British interpreter Gibson and Lieutenant T. P. Gurdon blew up the Chinese military installations at Anping and exacted 40,000 taels. Such gunboat policy and humiliating chastisement produced quick results but invariably inflamed the public feelings and excited xenophobic sentiments. Even London considered the Alcock-Medhurst action contrary to British policy and condemned the Gibson-Gurdon activity as "reprehensible" and "rash and inexcusable."[10]

The incident that touched off a major anti-Christian riot was the Tientsin Massacre of 1870. It is no coincidence that Tientsin was the scene of the outburst, for it had been twice occupied by foreign troops during the negotiations of the Treaties of Tientsin in 1858 and the Conventions of Peking in 1860. Even after the peace settlement, the British and the French continued to station five to six thousand troops there as a guarantee of China's fulfillment of treaty obligations. Although the French troops evacuated in November 1861 and the British in May 1862, portions

7. For a study of the missionary problem, see Paul A. Cohen, *China and Christianity: The Missionary Movement and the Growth of Chinese Anti-Foreignism, 1860-1870* (Cambridge, Mass., 1963), chapters 3-7.
8. John K. Fairbank, "Patterns Behind the Tientsin Massacre," *Harvard Journal of Asiatic Studies*, 20:3-4:501 (Dec. 1957).
9. *Ibid.*, 482-83.
10. *Ibid.*, 488.

of the Anglo-French forces remained in Taku until 1865. The presence of foreign troops was always a cause of irritation, and additional fuel came from the French seizure in 1860 of the imperial villa in Tientsin[11] for a consulate. Then, in 1869, the church Notre Dame des Victoires which ran an orphanage was constructed on the site of·a razed Buddhist temple. Because few Chinese would send orphans to a foreign establishment, the nuns offered a premium for each child, thereby giving incentive to rascals, known as the "child brokers," to kidnap children. Moreover, the nuns were particularly interested in baptizing the sick and dying children. The high mortality rate and the offer of premium inevitably aroused suspicion. Rumor spread that behind their high walls and closed gates, the foreigners bewitched the children, mutilated their bodies, and extracted their hearts and eyes to make medicine. An antiforeign riot loomed on the horizon. Ch'ung-hou, the superintendent of trade for the Three Northern Ports, inspected the orphanage and found no truth to the wild charges, but public feelings continued to run high. Then came the truculent French consul, Henri Fontanier, and his chancellor, M. Simon, armed with pistols, to demand justice for the sisters. Angry at the sight of the seething mob, which the district magistrate tried to disperse, Fontanier fired a shot which missed the magistrate but killed his servant. The mob boiled out of control, killed Fontanier and his assistant, and burned the church and the orphanage. Ten sisters, two priests, and two French officials lost their lives. Three Russian traders were killed by mistake, and four British and American churches were destroyed. This grave international crisis summarily dispersed a decade of good will and cooperation. Foreign gunboats quickly anchored off Tientsin, and strong protests from seven foreign ministers were lodged with the Tsungli Yamen, demanding redress and punishment of the rioters.

The court appointed its most venerable servant, Tseng Kuo-fan, now governor-general of Chihli, to investigate the case. On sick leave at Paoting, the sixty-year-old statesman doubted he had the stamina to survive the strenuous assignment. Nevertheless, he accepted the challenge and set out, ready to die if necessary in the service of his country. At Tientsin, he found the situation far more knotty than he had anticipated. The French chargé d'affaires, Count Julien de Rochechouart, demanded the lives of General Ch'en Kuo-jui and the Tientsin prefect and magistrate, while the conservative Chinese officials and literati clamored against any concession or appeasement. Tseng knew that to avoid a rupture with France he had

11. Wang-hai lou, "Sea-viewing Pavilion."

to be impartial in his investigation, but that to be impartial in this case was to invite attacks from the unrelenting conservatives. In short, he had to choose between integrity and loss of reputation. Here again Tseng's character and courage were manifest. Rather than cater safely to public sentiments, he risked his political future with the candid recommendation that the absolute truth of the case be established. He advised the court that Britain, the United States, and Russia be indemnified first, to dissociate them from the French cause. Next he made a personal inspection of the orphanage and learned firsthand from the one hundred and fifty children that they were not kidnapped but had been sent by their families voluntarily. Tseng asked the court to restore the reputation of the nuns by issuing a proclamation denying any truth to the rumor about the mutilation of bodies and extraction of hearts and eyes. Expressing his doubts that civilized Westerners could commit such barbarous crimes, Tseng attributed the rumor to the following facts: (1) the closed doors, the high walls, and the coal storage in the basement of the church excited popular suspicion that the kidnapped were kept in the cellar for untoward purposes; (2) children who visited the church hospital often chose to stay on, thereby arousing the suspicion that foreign drugs spellbound them; and (3) when deaths occurred, two or three bodies were put in one coffin because of a shortage of supply.

To settle the case, Tseng recommended heavy penalties for those involved in the riot: dismissal of the circuit intendant, the Tientsin prefect, and the district magistrate; capital punishment for fifteen chief instigators and banishment for twenty-one. If these arrangements would not satisfy the French, Tseng stated, greater punishment might be imposed.

The conservatives immediately branded Tseng a traitor. The Hunan Association in Peking felt so ashamed of his "appeasement" policy that it burned his calligraphy which had adorned its halls. Grand Secretary Wojen ridiculed the idea of bargaining with the French about the penalty, arguing pointedly that since the founding of the dynasty there had never been punishment without criminal evidence. The court, too, found Tseng's recommendations somewhat unpalatable. At this juncture, Li Hung-chang, governor-general at Wuhan, sent in a timely memorial adopting a median stance; he suggested that the civilized Christian state of France probably had no interest in imposing too heavy a penalty on Chinese officials, and that capital punishment of eight and exile of twenty would suffice. The court transferred Li to Tientsin to take over the investigation. Tseng was sent to Nanking as governor-general. Overwhelmed by a sense of personal

31. The interior of the Tsungli Yamen (Foreign Office)
with the leading ministers in discussion.

32. The Chinese Embassy to the United States with
its official guide, Anson Burlingame, in 1868.

33. Wei Yüan, an associate of Commissioner Lin and a leading Modern Text scholar.

34. Wen-hsiang.

35. Tseng Kuo-fan.

36. Tso Tsung-t'ang.

37. Chang Chih-tung, long-time
governor-general at Wuhan.

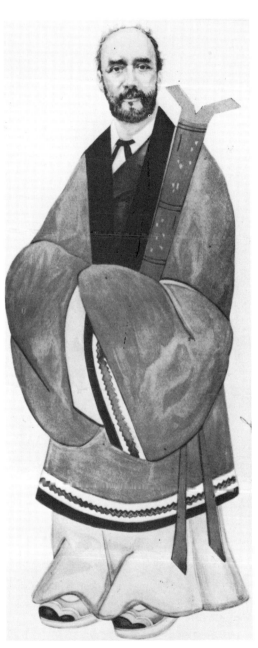

39. Sir Robert Hart
(*Vanity Fair*, 27 December 1894).

38. Marquis Tseng.

40. Sir Rutherford Alcock.

41. Dr. Martin A. P. Martin, president of T'ung-wen Kuan

42. Chinese students to the United States, 1872.

43. Chinese students' baseball club in front of the Chinese
Educational Mission in Hartford, Connecticut, 1878.

44. Li Hung-chang with British Prime Minister William Ewart Gladstone.

45. Empress Dowager Tz'u-hsi.

46. The Summer Palace (late Ch'ing dynasty, painting on paper).

inadequacy and hounded by the baying conservatives' accusations, the frustrated and embittered Tseng lapsed into a state of great distress and agony. When he wrote to friends he often inscribed on the envelope: "I fear public criticism without, and am conscience-stricken within."

Li Hung-chang speedily settled the case with the French, agreeing to pay a compensation of 400,000 taels for the loss of lives and properties, to send a mission of apology, to banish the Tientsin prefect and magistrate, and to sentence eighteen to capital punishment and twenty-five to hard labor on the frontier. The apology mission, led by Ch'ung-hou, reached France, only to find the French government too involved in the Prussian war to receive it. The official French explanation for delaying the reception was that China had failed to reciprocate to the French minister the same courtesy that Napoleon III had shown to Burlingame. Under these conditions, the Tsungli Yamen ordered Ch'ung-hou to dispense with the personal presentation of the Letter of Apology. On his way home via New York, however, Ch'ung-hou was summoned back to France, where the provisional president, M. Thiers, received him at Versailles on November 23, 1871. Thiers announced that France was not interested in decapitating the Chinese wrongdoers, but in lasting peace and order, and the case was officially closed with Thiers's acceptance of the Letter of Apology from the Chinese emperor.[12]

The Audience Question, 1873. Although foreign diplomats took up residence in Peking in 1861, they were continuously denied audience with the emperor. Prince Kung received them in his capacity as regent and explained that audience with the emperor was inadvisable during his minority, while that with the two dowagers would cause great inconvenience due to different social customs. Though agreeing among themselves that there was little point in demanding a meeting with a five-year old (*ciu sui*) boy emperor, foreign representatives announced that repeated delay of the audience was an act of unfriendliness. The real reason for the Chinese postponement, of course, was the fear that foreigners would not perform the kowtow, thus denying the myth of China's universal overlordship and of the tributary practice. The Tsungli Yamen knew that foreign diplomats would perforce claim immunity from kowtow under the 1858 Treaties of Tientsin, which explicitly provided that envoys not be required to perform ceremonies derogatory to their honor and dignity.

12. Knight Biggerstaff, "The Ch'ung Hou Mission to France, 1870-71," *Nankai Social and Economic Quarterly*, 8:3:633-47 (Oct. 1935).

Foreign ministers themselves had averred repeatedly that they would not perform the kowtow in any future audience.

The Tsungli Yamen's tactics put off, but did not solve, the question of audience, for the boy emperor would grow up. During the discussion of treaty revision in 1867, the Yamen solicited views from leading provincial authorities on the question, clearly noting that China would soon run out of time and excuse in postponing the audience, and that she would have difficulty obliging foreigners to follow her rituals and ceremonies. Nearly all the local authorities were content to sidestep the issue until the emperor's majority. Li Hung-chang, governor-general at Wuhan, declared that since Prince Kung was in touch with the foreign ministers, there was nothing that he could not transmit to the throne, and that if the ministers' requests were unreasonable, personal audience with the emperor would gain nothing. As to the ceremonies for future audiences following the emperor's majority, he stressed, foreign diplomats should be allowed to perform such rituals as they would before their own rulers. Tseng Kuo-fan, governor-general at Nanking, asserted that just as Emperor K'ang-hsi (1662-1722) had treated Russia as an enemy state on equal footing rather than as an inferior dependent state, the court should also regard foreign ministers as envoys from enemy states of equal status exempt from Chinese customs. One censor[13] perceptively observed that foreigners understood only profit and material gain, not proper human relationships, righteousness, filial piety, and rituals. Requiring them to observe Chinese ceremonies based on the Confucian Five Relations was as pointless as gathering a herd of sheep, dogs, horses, and pigs in a hall and making them dance to music. Foreigners' performance of the kowtow was no cause for joy, he evinced, just as their noncompliance was no cause for regret; hence, the kowtow should be dispensed with in future audiences. On the other hand, a number of conservative officials argued that China should not change her institutions and practices merely to suit the convenience of foreigners.

In 1872 the emperor reached his majority and was married, but no foreign diplomats were invited to take part in the celebration, thus avoiding protocol problems. In February of the following year he inaugurated his personal rule. Foreign representatives renewed their demand for an audience. Unable to defer the issue longer, the Tsungli Yamen conducted protracted discussions with the diplomats as to the proper rituals. They finally agreed that the foreign representatives should bow instead of kowtow dur-

13. Wu K'o-tu.

ing the audience. The Japanese foreign minister, Soejima Taneomi, who had arrived to exchange ratifications of the treaty of 1871 (next chapter), insisted that his ambassadorial rank entitled him to an audience before the Western diplomats, who all held the ministerial rank. It was an obvious attempt to impress others with Japanese mastery of European diplomatic practices and to assert Japanese equality with the Western powers.

On Sunday, June 29, 1873, the foreign diplomats were asked to convene at 5:30 a.m., but it was not until nine o'clock that they were received by Emperor T'ung-chih at the Pavilion of Violet Light. The Japanese foreign minister was received first, followed in order of seniority by the Russian minister (Vlangaly), the American minister (Low), the British minister (Wade), the French minister (de Geofroy), the Dutch minister (Ferguson), and the German interpreter (Bismarck). They laid their credentials on a table before the emperor, who expressed, through Prince Kung, his amicable feelings toward the foreign sovereigns represented there. The whole audience, for which the Westrn diplomats had waited twelve years, was over in half an hour.[14] It was an anticlimax, the more so when the foreign representatives later discovered that the pavilion in which they were received was also used for the reception of tributary envoys.[15]

The Margary Affair, 1875. The Great Depression in Europe in the early 1870's brought on by the tariff war adversely affected the China trade, which declined steadily after 1872. The Hong Kong and Shanghai Banking Corporation reported a loss and declared no dividend in 1874 and 1875 for the first time in its history. To brighten the trade prospects, the British concocted a scheme to open a back door to interior China by constructing a railway and trade route from Burma to Yunnan.

Captain Richard Sprye, a retired Indian army officer, first proposed the idea in 1858 to counter the Russian advance from the northwest and the American move from across the Pacific. London was cool to the suggestion, but Sprye kept the issue alive by repeating his proposal each time a new foreign secretary assumed office. When the correspondence became too bulky, Lord John Russell, foreign secretary in 1859, had a précis made,

14. For an interesting account of the audience, see *British Parliamentary Papers, China,* No. 1 (1874) *Correspondence respecting the Audience granted to Her Majesty's Minister and the other Foreign Representatives at Peking by the Emperor of China.*

15. Banquets were given there for the tributary envoys from Korea, Liu-ch'iu, Laos, Siam, and Annam in 1839-43, 1845-48, and 1864. See Fairbank (ed.), *The Chinese World Order,* 262.

with the remark: "Captain Sprye is a visionary who indulges in the wild-est notions and consumes an enormous quantity of Foolscap—there is a certain degree of interest attaching to his schemes but they are impracti-cable."[16] The Foreign Office generally believed that such a backdoor thrust would create troubles without a compensating commercial benefit. The matter might have rested there had not Lord Salisbury, the only high offi-cial to have fancied the project, become head of the India Office in the Disraeli ministry of 1874. He ordered the Indian government to under-take the survey of the proposed route and requested the Foreign Office to instruct the minister in Peking to seek Chinese permission for the entry of an exploratory mission from Burma.

Personally skeptical of the commercial possibilities of such a route, Wade found, to his surprise, that the Chinese government not only read-ily assented to his request but also agreed to let a British vice-consul, the twenty-eight-year-old Augustus Margary, travel up the Yangtze River to meet the mission. Though aware of the presence of guerrilla bands in the Chinese-Burmese border area and their hostility to foreigners, Margary ventured on to Bhamo on the frontier despite warnings by local Chinese officials, to await the mission from Burma under Colonel Horace A. Browne. There, on February 21, 1875, Margary was ambushed and killed.

International law provides that when a foreigner exposes himself to danger at his own risk, it is no responsibility of the host country to guar-antee his safety. The British government, however, obdurately held the Chinese government responsible for the murder and instructed Wade to obtain redress. Capitalizing on this occasion, the ambitious Wade de-manded an investigation of the murder, an indemnity for the bereaved family, another expedition, and trial of the acting governor-general of Yunnan and Kweichow in whose jurisdiction the incident took place; he also raised a number of extraneous issues such as the future audience procedure, transit dues, better etiquette in the treatment of foreign dip-lomats, and an apology mission to Britain. Peking readily assented to an investigation and an indemnity, but frowned on the other unrelated questions. Impetuously Wade withdrew his legation to Shanghai, threat-ening to break off relations. Rumor circulated that he had entered into a secret pact with the Russian minister, engaging a British army from India and a Russian advance from Ili in Sinkiang, which had been under Russian occupation since 1871 (next chapter). To avoid a rupture, the

16. Nathan A. Pelcovits, *Old China Hands and the Foreign Office* (New York, 1948), 115.

court on August 29, 1875, authorized the dispatch of an apology mission to Britain under the leadership of Kuo Sung-tao and sent its trusted foreign servant, Robert Hart, to Shanghai to persuade Wade to resume discussions. Hart tactfully intimated that if the negotiations were not reopened in China, Kuo might start diplomatic proceedings in London, where a settlement would exclude Wade from all claims to credit. Wade agreed to meet with Li Hung-chang at the summer resort of Chefoo. Li displayed considerable diplomatic skill in winning the sympathies of vacationing foreign diplomats, and Wade, feeling isolated, softened his stand. On September 13, 1876, the Chefoo Convention was concluded to settle the Margary case. Part I dealt with the dispatch of an apology mission to Britain and the payment of 200,000 taels to the bereaved family. Part II dealt with the preparation of an etiquette code between the Chinese government and foreign diplomats. Part III dealt with the opening of four new ports and the limitation of *likin*-free areas to treaty ports. However, this convention failed of British ratification until 1885, due to opposition from (1) the United States, Germany, France, and Russia, which criticized Britain's unilateral action; (2) the British mercantile communities, which clamored for a complete abolition of the *likin*; and (3) the Indian government, which protested the increase in opium tax.

The most significant outcome of the Margary incident was the dispatch of the mission of apology, which became the first resident Chinese legation abroad. The leader, Kuo Sung-tao, the progressive sixty-year-old friend of Li-Hung-chang, was given the title of vice-president of the Board of War prior to his departure for Britain. After the presentation of the emperor's Letter of Apology to Queen Victoria on February 8, 1877, he set up the first Chinese embassy in London. In the next two years, other legations were also established in Paris, Berlin, Spain, Washington, Tokyo, and St. Petersburg. By 1880 China had belatedly taken her place in the family of nations.

China's slowness in reciprocating the Western practice of diplomatic representation may be attributed to several causes. Institutionally, she had never dispatched permanent, resident embassies abroad but only *ad hoc* missions, which were sent out either in times of strength and prosperity to spread the prestige of the Son of Heaven and to bring outlying states into the tributary system, or in times of weakness and disorder to beg for peace or alliance with barbarian tribes. Psychologically, the majority of mandarins eschewed foreign affairs as beneath their dignity and foreign assignment as a form of banishment; men of keen political acumen strove to steer clear of foreign associations. Burlingame's two associates fared badly after their return: one was sent to an obscure post in western China, and the other spent his life on a Mongolian frontier, as if they had been contaminated by their foreign trip. The censors, the Hanlin scholars, and the conservative gentry and officials ceaselessly harped on the theme that historically barbarians were always transformed by Chinese ways, not the Chinese by barbarian ways. They promoted conservatism against modernization and condemned foreign association as disgraceful. To the question "Who among men of rectitude today excels in foreign affairs?" a grand secretary[17] replied: "Do men of rectitude care to engage in foreign affairs?" So powerful was the conservative atmosphere that the psychological inertia to innovation was immense. It took China more than fifteen years to overcome this barrier and reciprocate the Western practice of diplomatic representation.

THE IMPERIAL WOMAN AND HER POLITICS

For the nearly half-century from 1861 to 1908, the Empress Dowager Tz'u-hsi ruled supreme over China. She once proudly remarked that she had more power than Queen Victoria. Be that as it may, it is questionable whether or not she used the power for the good of the dynasty and the country. Endowed with large measures of determination, will power, ability for quick decision, and not a little native intelligence, still she was without much education and mental breadth, and was totally uninformed on the nature of the modern world that had been thrust upon China. Basically a narrow-minded, selfish woman, she placed her own interest above all else, irrespective of consequences to the dynasty and the state; her main concern at all times was to perpetuate her own power and position. To a large degree she must be held responsible for the failure to regenerate the dynasty and modernize the country. The question naturally arises as to how a single woman could wield such supreme power and remain at the pinnacle for so long, in contravention of dynastic laws and practices. The answer may partially be found in her consummate skill in political manipulation.

The Chastisements of Prince Kung. It has been stated in the previous chapter that the empress dowager and Prince Kung cooperated with each

17. Yen Ching-ming.

other out of expediency during and after the *coup d'état* of 1861. Using him as a front man in dealing with foreign powers and winning domestic sympathies, the dowager thus bought time to learn statecraft. The prince, of course, needed her to secure a powerful and exalted position. An ambitious man, he had actually aspired to be sole regent to the boy emperor T'ung-chih—much as Dorgan had been at the beginning of the dynasty when Emperor Shun-chih was a minor—and let the two dowagers nominally administer the state behind a bamboo screen. But Tz'u-hsi was too shrewd to let him be the only regent. Cleverly she showered him with high honors and offices, while jealously holding the ultimate power of state in her own hands. His dream frustrated, the prince could not help harboring some disappointment behind his mask of apparent success.

Prince Kung,[18] sixth son of Emperor Tao-kuang (1820-50) and a younger brother of the late emperor Hsien-fcng (1851-61), was a smart man with a quick but lightly cultivated intelligence. In childhood he was brash, arrogant, and flighty. As an admonition, his father gave him the title of *Kung*, meaning "Respect"—hence his designation Prince Kung—but it did not seem to influence his character much. After the coup of 1861, he rose to leadership in the government, enjoying the "trust," however fleeting, of the two dowagers and the support of foreign diplomats. His power and status, though not as great and exalted as Dorgan's at the beginning of the dynasty, was unrivaled at court. As prince regent, grand councillor, head of the Tsungli Yamen, and chief minister of the Imperial Household, he was the most sought-after man in Peking. Daily hundreds of officials and visitors queued up outside his office to await his decisions and favors, and not a few bribed their way into his circle. Elated with success and drunk in the enjoyment of power, his arrogance overrode his prudence, and even the dowagers found him overbearing during audiences. Attempts by friends to urge upon him caution, self-control, and restraint went unheeded, and an atmosphere of impending calamity encircled him. In 1865 a Hanlin compiler moved to impeach him, and the Dowager Tz'u-hsi, who felt capable enough in state administration by then, decided to chastise him. To the palace she summoned Grand Secretary Chou Tsu-p'ei and high officials of the boards of Civil Offices, Revenue, and Punishments to fix Prince Kung's guilt in accepting bribes, nepotism, usurpation of power, clique-formation, and overbearance. However, these officials dared not intervene in what they considered to be primarily a family quarrel between an imperial brother- and sister-in-law, and begged the

18. Personal name: I-hsin.

dowagers to decide the issue themselves. Tz'u-hsi, enraged at their timidity, drafted an edict herself—one noted for its countless wrong characters
—dismissing the prince from all official posts. Suddenly deprived of forceful leadership, the government's normal operations were seriously handicapped. Princes Tun and Chün, as well as other dignitaries, interceded
with the dowagers on Kung's behalf, pleading the importance of maintaining "family harmony" before the public. Tz'u-hsi, realizing that the
objective of chastisement had been achieved and that she still needed
Prince Kung to deal with the foreigners, restored him to the superintendency of the Tsungli Yamen. In this way, she demonstrated her leniency to
Kung, preserved the "face" of those who interceded, and showed her absolute power. When Prince Kung penitently went to the palace to thank her
for the partial restoration to favor, she in another gesture of generosity
reinstated him as grand councillor. The title of prince regent (*i-cheng
wang*), however, was withheld from him. Having been taught a lesson, the
deflated prince lost some of his zeal in state affairs and became more restrained in conduct.

A second blow struck him in 1869, in connection with the eunuch An
Te-hai, a confidant of Tz'u-hsi's since before the coup of 1861. It was he
who risked his life carrying her secret message to Prince Kung in Peking,
laying the groundwork for the later coup. Indebted, the dowager often
sought his counsel. As An's influence rose he became jealous of Prince
Kung, and not infrequently spoke ill of him before the dowager. It was no
secret that he had a hand in the decision to deny Prince Kung the title of
regent after the first chastisement. Kung became the more incensed by the
increasing numbers of opportunistic officials flocking to An's door to curry
favor. The chance for revenge came in 1869, when the eunuch in question
left Peking[19] on a purchasing mission for Tz'u-hsi, contrary to the dynastic
rule that no eunuch was allowed to leave the capital on pain of decapita-
tion. En route in Shantung, An was captured by Governor Ting Pao-chen,
who sent for instructions from the court. Tz'u-hsi was caught off guard,
while Tz'u-an, the other dowager, in consultation with the Grand Council
under Prince Kung, ordered his immediate beheading. Tz'u-hsi secretly
blamed Kung for maneuvering behind the scenes, straining their relations
more than ever. In frustration, Prince Kung resigned himself to a life of
relative inactivity. When his able assistant, Wen-hsiang, passed away in
1876, the government was deprived of vital leadership.

19. His destination, according to some accounts, was Kwangsi, and according to
others, Soochow.

With the death of the dowager Tz'u-an in April 1881—she was reputedly poisoned by Tz'u-hsi—Prince Kung lost a supporter and his position in government became even more tenuous. Story has it that during an audience with Tz'u-hsi, he was bluntly told: "You oppose me in every matter. Who do you think you are?" Kung replied: "I am the sixth son of Emperor Tao-kuang," to which the dowager rejoined: "I can strip you of . . ." The prince interrupted: "You may strip me of my princely rank but never of my status as the emperor's son!"[20] The dowager responded with cold silence. Her struggle with Prince Kung finally came to a head during the French war in 1884. The prince, accused by conservative officials of indecision, and four other grand councillors were summarily dismissed by her from the Grand Council at a stroke. After this third chastisement, Prince Kung totally lost heart for state affairs and went into an eclipse. Prince Li became the nominal ranking grand councillor, while Prince Chün, brother-in-law of the dowager, became head of the new Board of Admiralty (Hai-chün ya-men) in 1885. Both were men of inconsequential ability; henceforth the government drifted without able leadership and effective direction.

Manipulation of Imperial Succession. In 1872 Emperor T'ung-chih reached his majority and selected as his empress a young woman recommended by the dowager Tz'u-an, rather than the one chosen by his mother Tz'u-hsi. The latter resorted to all manner of devices to block the emperor from visiting with his empress, encouraging him instead to frequent the quarters of the consort of her choice. Annoyed by her meddling, the emperor retaliated by boycotting both his empress and the consort, finding consolation instead in outside pleasure quarters. In February 1873 he began his personal rule and, tired of his mother's interference, struck upon the idea of reconstructing the Summer Palace (Yüan-ming yüan), which Lord Elgin had burned in 1860, as a place for her retirement. Hoping to complete the project in time to celebrate her birthday in 1874, the emperor personally oversaw its designing and made daily inspection tours of the construction. In his total absorption he neglected state affairs, against all contrary exhortations. Ultimately, the construction was forced to a halt in September 1874 by a notorious scandal involving an opportunistic Canton merchant and a French lumber dealer. After the demise of his pet project, the disenchanted sovereign childishly turned his back on his responsibilities and spent his time at the operas and in the city's pleasure

20. Hsiao I-shan, III, 919.

quarters. Admonition from Prince Kung called forth the imperial wrath and an order dismissing him from all offices and relegating him to the status of a commoner—only to be rescinded a day later at the intercession of the two dowagers. Shortly afterwards, the young emperor became very ill; he died on January 12, 1875, at the early age of nineteen *sui*—officially of smallpox but unofficially of syphilis. During his illness, the dowager Tz'u-hsi did little to help him recover, but everything to hasten his end. The brief life of T'ung-chih was a sad and strange episode, which could be interpreted as a deliberate reaction to his mother's high-handed control.

Emperor T'ung-chih died without issue, although it was known that his empress was pregnant. The question of imperial succession became a matter of great delicacy and intrigue. Tz'u-hsi quickly saw her opportunity to regain the regency. Even before the late emperor's death she had begun her machinations, instigating court officials to request that the two dowagers again administer state affairs behind the bamboo screen. She realized that the choice of an adult prince for the throne would eliminate the need of a regent, while selection of a minor prince one generation below the deceased emperor would make her an "empress dowager-grandmother," i.e. twice removed from the legal source of power. Both courses of action had to be avoided. To maintain her regency, the new ruler had to be a minor, of the same generation as the late emperor, so that she would be just once removed. With these considerations, she rejected the late emperor's deathbed choice[21] and dismissed Prince Kung's suggestion that succession be delayed until after the empress had borne a child. At a council of twenty-seven princes on January 12, 1875, she autocratically announced her choice: her nephew, Tsai-t'ien, son of her sister and Prince Chün (I-huan), a boy of four *sui* of the same generation as the late emperor. The passing of the throne between members of the same generation violated the dynastic laws of succession, yet none dared to challenge her. Only a foolhardy Chinese secretary of the Board of Civil Offices, Wu K'o-tu, committed suicide in protest—an act known as the "death remonstration."

Ironically, the reign (1875-1908) of the new emperor was designated Kuang-hsü, or Glorious Succession. On January 15, 1875, the two dowagers graciously bowed to the "request" of the princes and high officials to serve as co-regents again during his minority. An edict was issued to the effect that the power of state would be returned to the emperor as soon as he came of age and that his future son would be adopted as the son of

21. Tsai-chu.

the late emperor. By this maneuvering, Tz'u-hsi assured herself of another term of regency, exercising the power of state behind the bamboo screen once more. But one thing she could not control: the growing up of the boy emperor.

In 1886 Emperor Kuang-hsü reached the age of sixteen *sui* and announced his intention to begin personal rule the following year. Knowing well the dowager's reluctance to renounce power, his father Prince Chün tactfully advised postponement of the take-over. On February 7, 1887, the emperor reached his long-awaited majority but was denied personal rule for two years, during which period he was to learn from the dowager the art of government (*hsün-cheng*). Finally, on March 4, 1889, the dowager officially "retired" to the Summer Palace, but no one doubted that she took with her the ultimate power of state. She forced the emperor to marry a cousin of her choice to insure her supervision of, and direct access to, policy matters. She maintained an iron control of the palaces through her confidant, the eunuch Li Lien-ying, and of the government through her trusted grand councillor, Sun Yü-wen. The emperor was but a figurehead without veto power over her decisions.

To free the court from her manipulations, Emperor Kuang-hsü and Prince Chün revived the project of reconstructing the Summer Palace (*I-ho yüan*) in all its splendor, hoping that she might enjoy herself there and relinquish her hold on state affairs. The funds for the construction, some 30 million taels, came from the budget of the Board of Admiralty, which Prince Chün headed. Because of this misuse of funds, no new ships were bought after 1888; not surprisingly the Chinese navy was disgracefully defeated in the Japanese war of 1894-95. Though enjoying the Summer Palace, the dowager continued to interfere with politics. Emperor Kuang-hsu's attempt at reform in 1898 lasted but a hundred and three days due to her intervention, and the Boxer Rebellion of 1900, which plunged China's international position to its nadir and incurred the eight-power occupation of Peking, was secretly patronized by her. Although she did carry out some halfhearted reform after 1901, her insincerity was only too obvious. When she died in 1908 the dynasty had already declined beyond salvation.

One may ask how one woman could wield such great power and why the officials did not refuse to obey her. Her success can be attributed to three stratagems. First, while violating dynastic laws and precedents herself, she obliged all other Manchus to follow them strictly. She governed the royal members inexorably with the imperial family law, and mercilessly sent offenders to the Imperial Clan Court for punishment. She treated them with severity to strike terror into their hearts and reduce them to abject submission. Secondly, to the Chinese officials she stressed the Confucian concepts of proper relationship between the ruler and the subjects and the importance of filial piety. She said in effect: if the two boy emperors obey and honor me so exactly, how much more should you officials! Thirdly, fully recognizing the Manchu degeneration, she relied on able Chinese such as Tseng Kuo-fan, Tso Tsung-t'ang, and Li Hung-chang, even though she was concerned about their rising power, their association with foreigners, and their control of the new army and navy and modern enterprises. To safeguard her position, she humored them with high positions and honors but kept them in check by secretly encouraging conservative forces to attack them. With these methods the dowager successfully dominated China for nearly half a century.[22] Yet her success was achieved at a high cost to the dynasty and the country. Under her autistic rule, the dynasty failed to achieve a regeneration, and China sank deeper and deeper into the slough of foreign imperialism.

It was rumored among the Chinese that the dowager's misrule was intentional. She came from the Yehe tribe of the Manchus which was ruthlessly subjugated by the founder of the Ch'ing dynasty, Nurhaci, in 1619. As an act of revenge, they speculated, she deliberately wrecked the dynasty by misgovernment. Be it rumor or fact, barely three years after her death the Ch'ing dynasty was overthrown.

FURTHER READING

Biggerstaff, Knight, "The Official Chinese Attitude Toward the Burlingame Mission," American Historical Review, 41:4:682-702 (July 1936).
———, "The First Chinese Mission of Investigation Sent to Europe," Pacific Historical Review, 6:4-307-20 (Dec. 1937).
———, "The Ch'ung Hou Mission to France, 1870-71," Nankai Social and Economic Quarterly, 8:3:633-47 (Oct. 1935).
Bland, J. O. P., and E. Backhouse, China under the Empress Dowager, Being the History of the Life and Times of Tzu Hsi (London, 1910).
British Parliamentary Papers, China, No. 1 (1874), Correspondence respecting the Audience granted to Her Majesty's Minister and the other Foreign Representatives at Pekin by the Emperor of China.
Buck, Pearl S., Imperial Woman: Story of the Last Empress of China (New York, 1955).

22. Li Fang-ch'en, 381-84.

Chih-kang 志剛, *Ch'u-shih t'ai-Hsi chi* 初使泰西記 (The first embassy to the West), 4 *chüan*, 1877.

Cohen, Paul A., *China and Christianity: The Missionary Movement and the Growth of Chinese Antiforeignism, 1860-1870* (Cambridge, Mass., 1963).

Der Ling, Princess, *Old Buddha* (New York, 1932).

Fairbank, John King, "Patterns Behind the Tientsin Massacre," *Harvard Journal of Asiatic Studies*, 20:3-4:480-511 (Dec. 1957).

Haldane, Charlotte, *The Last Great Empress of China* (Indianapolis, 1965).

Hsü, Immanuel C. Y., *China's Entrance into the Family of Nations: The Diplomatic Phase, 1858-1880* (Cambridge, Mass., 1968), Part III.

Latourette, K. S., *A History of Christian Missions in China* (New York, 1929).

Li, Shih-yüeh 李時岳, "Chia-wu chan-cheng ch'ien san-shih-nien chien fan-yang-chiao yün-tung" 甲午戰爭前三十年間反洋教運動 (The anti-foreign religion movement during the thirty years before the Sino-Japanese war), *Li-shih yen-chiu*, 6:1-15, (1958).

Lü, Shih-ch'iang 呂實強, *Chung-kuo kuan-shen fan-chiao ti yüan-yin, 1860-1874* 中國官紳反教的原因 (The causes of the anti-Christian movement among Chinese officials and gentry, 1860-1874), (Taipei, 1966).

Michie, A., *The Englishman in China during the Victorian Era, As Illustrated in the Career of Sir Rutherford Alcock K.C.B., D.C.L., Many Years Consul and Minister in China and Japan* (London, 1900) 2 vols.

Pelcovits, Nathan A., *Old China Hands and the Foreign Office* (New York, 1948).

Ross, John, *Chinese Foreign Policy* (Shanghai, 1877).

Tabohashi, Kiyoshi 田保橋潔, "Shin Dōchichō gaikoku kōshi no kinken" 清同治朝外國公使の觀見 (The audience of foreign ministers in the T'ung-chih period of the Ch'ing dynasty), *Seikyū gakuso*, 6:1-31 (Nov. 1931).

Tsiang, T. F., "Sino-Japanese Diplomatic Relations, 1870-1894," *The Chinese Social and Political Science Review*, 17:1:1-106 (April 1933).

Wang, S. T., *The Margary Affair and the Chefoo Convention* (New York, 1939).

Williams, F. W., *Anson Burlingame and the First Chinese Mission to Foreign Powers* (New York, 1912).

Wright, Mary C., *The Last Stand of Chinese Conservatism: The T'ung-chih Restoration, 1862-1874* (Stanford, 1957), chapters 10-11.

Yüan, Ting-chung 袁定中, "Na-la-shih fan-tung ti i-sheng" 那拉氏反動的一生 (The reactionary life of the empress dowager), *Li-shih yen-chiu*, 10:31-41 (1958).

13

Foreign Encroachment in Formosa, Sinkiang, and Annam

The last three decades of the 19th century in China constituted a period of accelerated foreign imperialistic encroachments. Europe, experiencing "a generation of materialism," was propelled by the forces of nationalism, evangelism, capitalism, and Darwinism into heightened activity in Asia, Africa, and the Middle East. Economically, not only had Britain and France succesfully industrialized, but also Germany, Italy, and the United States. This created a need for overseas markets for their surplus goods and a need for a source of raw materials. Culturally, Social Darwinism was the order of the day; it sanctioned overseas expansion with the philosophy that nations as well as species struggled to exist and that only the strongest was fit to survive. Religiously, the churches and denominations were fired with the sense of a divine mission to evangelize the heathens. To all this was added the proud, self-righteous feeling of racial superiority, reflected in the term the "White Man's Burden."[1]

To be sure, most of these forces had previously existed, but several developments in the 1860's gave them effective direction and impetus: the end of the Civil War in the United States in 1865, the Meiji Restoration in Japan in 1868, the unifications of Italy and Germany in 1870, and the rise of the Third Republic in France in the same year. These epochal events liberated centrifugal energies for externally oriented action, while the completion of the Suez Canal in 1869 further facilitated European expansion in Asia. Now not only the older aggressor nations—such as Brit-

1. For an excellent study of imperialism, see William Langer, *The Diplomacy of Imperialism, 1890-1902* (New York, 1950).

376

ain, France, and Russia—but also the latecomers—notably Japan and Germany—executed their imperialistic designs. In contrast, China under the empress dowager was making little headway in self-improvement and regeneration; the dynastic strength steadily declined after a brief upsurge during the T'ung-chih (1862-74) period. Taking advantage of China's weakness, foreign powers nibbled away the frontier areas and tributary states, following with frontal thrusts to the heart of the "Sick Man of Asia." By the close of the 19th century, China faced the ominous prospect of partition.

This chapter will discuss the Japanese advance in Formosa (Taiwan), the Russian occupation of Ili in Sinkiang, and the French seizure of the tributary state of Annam (Vietnam). The next chapter will deal with the Sino-Japanese war over Korea and the scramble for concessions in China during the postwar period.

JAPANESE AGGRESSION ON FORMOSA, 1871-74

Official Sino-Japanese relations had been held in abeyance for the three hundred years preceding 1871. Japan was a tributary state of China for a time during the Ming period (1368-1643). The Japanese shogun, Ashikaga Yoshimitsu, accepted the tributary status in order to enrich his coffers from trade—from 1433 to 1549 eleven tribute and trade missions sailed to China. Subsequently, however, nationalistic Japanese statesmen found such relations humiliating, and discontinued the practice after the middle of the 16th century, thus ending official contact with the mainland. But Japanese pirates, known as *Wako* (*Wo-k'ou* in Chinese, meaning "dwarf pirates"), continued to disturb the China coast and made themselves a nuisance to the Ming dynasty. After the establishment of the Ch'ing dynasty in 1644, no resumption of official relations was made; the Manchu rulers, unlike the Ming emperors, never attempted to bring Japan into the tributary system.

With the opening of China and Japan to Western commerce and diplomacy in mid-19th century, Japanese traders began to arrive in Shanghai on British and Dutch ships. By 1870 the Meiji government had decided to establish official relations with China, and sent Yanagiwara Sakimitsu to Peking to seek a treaty. The Tsungli Yamen, though inclined to permit trade, was reluctant to sign a formal treaty. Conservative officials, such as Governor Ying-han of Anhwei, opposed treaty relations on the ground that Japan was a former tributary state known as the Dwarf Nation and had a record of piracy along the China coast. Such a country, he warned, should not be treated in the same way as the leading Western powers, lest a precedent be set for other tributaries such as Korea and Annam. He felt that the Japanese arrival at the very time of the Tientsin Massacre was proof of their opportunism and inclination to take advantage of China in her times of trouble.

Progressive officials such as Li Hung-chang and Tseng Kuo-fan, on the other hand, favored treaty relations. Li opined that Japan, though a tributary state of the Ming dynasty, was never a Ch'ing tributary and her status was basically different from that of Korea and Annam. That Japan sought official relations without an introduction by, or the aid of, a Western power showed her independence and good will, and China should not begrudge her the request. If goaded into unfriendly relations, Li warned, Japan could cause worse trouble than the Western powers because of her proximity. Furthermore, one should not lose sight of the fact that China imported a considerable quantity of copper from Japan annually, and that there were large Chinese communities in Japan. On the basis of these considerations, Li recommended the establishment of equal treaty relations with Japan. Tseng Kuo-fan concurred in these views, stressing in addition the reciprocal nature of Sino-Japanese trade as opposed to the largely one-sided Sino-Western trade. He approved of treaty relations but recommended withholding the most-favored-nation treatment.

On the strength of their recommendations, the court authorized the conclusion of a commercial treaty with Japan on July 24, 1871, which contained the following important provisions: (1) nonaggression toward each other's territorial possessions; (2) mutual offer of good offices in case of conflict with a third power; (3) mutual consular jurisdiction; (4) trade and traiff in treaty ports only; and (5) no appointment of Japanese merchant consuls in China.

In 1873 the Japanese Foreign Minister Soejima came to Peking, ostensibly to exchange ratifications, but his real objective was to participate in the T'ung-chih audience and to sound out China's position on the Formosa incident. The latter involved the killing of 54 shipwrecked Ryū-kyūan sailors by the aborigines of Formosa late in 1871. Japan seized upon this occasion to assert her *exclusive* right to speak for the Ryūkyūans, and in doing so she precipitated the question of Ryūkyū's status, which had been wrapped in a shroud of mystery and ambivalence for two and a half centuries.

Ryūkyū, or Liu-ch'iu in Chinese, had been a regular tributary state of

China since 1372. During the Ch'ing period it paid tribute every other year and was one of the three most important tributary states—along with Korea and Annam. However, unknown to China, the Satsuma *han* (feudatory) of Japan subjugated Liu-ch'iu in 1609, putting the northern part under its direct administration while leaving the southern part to the Liu-ch'iuan king. Liu-ch'iu became a vassal of Satsuma, to which tribute was paid annually and also to the shogunal court at Edo (Tokyo) periodically. However, Satsuma directed that Liu-ch'iu continue its tributary relations with the Ch'ing dynasty so that Satsuma could reap the benefit of trade with China. Satsuma determined royal succession in Liu-ch'iu, but allowed the Chinese investiture mission to confirm the legitimacy of the king's rule. During the Ch'ing period a total of eight such missions came, the last in 1866, and throughout their stay in Liu-ch'iu, Satsuma took extreme care to remove its officials and things from sight, and to instruct the Liu-ch'iuans to answer Chinese queries in such a way as to hide the Japanese presence. Caught in double subordination, Liu-chi'iu regarded China as father and Japan as mother, using the Chinese calendar when dealing with China and the Japanese calendar when dealing with Japan. Although members of the Chinese investiture missions privately could not fail to detect some traces of Japanese influence on the islands, the Ch'ing court officially knew nothing of Liu-ch'iu's double status, and treated it as China's exclusive tributary state.[2]

Thus, when Soejima openly asserted the right to speak for the Liu-ch'iuans in 1873, the Tsungli Yamen pointedly told him that since Ryū-kyū was a Chinese tributary and Formosa part of China, the killing of the sailors of one by the aborigines of the other was no business of Japan. Moreover, China could not be held responsible for the behavior of the aborigines, because she had always allowed them large measures of freedom and never interfered with their internal affairs. Soejima countered that sovereignty over a territory was evidenced by effective control; since China did not control the Formosan aborigines, they were clearly beyond her jurisdiction. Hence any action by Japan to chastise them would not constitute a violation of Chinese jurisdiction. With the support of the Home Minister Ōkubo Toshimichi, Soejima persuaded the Tokyo government to send an expedition to Formosa. This move manifested on the

2. For details of Liu-ch'iu's double subordination, see two excellent articles: Robert K. Sakai, "The Ryūkyū (Liu-ch'iu) Islands as Fief of Satsuma," in Fairbank (ed.), *The Chinese World Order*, 112-34; Ta-tuan Ch'en, "Investiture of Liu-ch'iu Kings in the Ch'ing Period," *ibid.*, 135-64.

one hand the general Meiji foreign policy of expansion on the Asian main-land after the fashion of Western imperialism, and on the other a clever device to divert domestic demands for popular representative assemblies and to satisfy ex-samurais who had clamored for an expedition to Korea (next chapter). In April 1874 the Office of the Formosan Expedition was formed, with Ōkuma Shigenobu as director and Saigō Tsugumichi as commander-in-chief of the expeditionary force.

The Japanese army quickly landed in Formosa. Peking ordered Shen Pao-chen, director of the Foochow Dockyard, to defend the island. After careful examination of the situation with Li Hung-chang, Shen found effective defense impossible—the guns cast by Halliday Macartney in the Nanking Arsenals could fire nothing but salutes; real explosive shells would burst the gun, killing the gunner rather than the enemy. An agree-ment was arranged with the Japanese minister that exacted China's prom-ise to control Formosa effectively, to secure bonds from the aborigines against future mistreatment of shipwrecked sailors, and to permit Saigō to punish the aborigines in two villages. However, Saigō refused to honor this agreement; the Home Minister Ōkubo then came to Peking himself on September 10, 1874.

Aided by the French jurist Gustave Boissonade, Ōkubo argued that ab-sence of effective local Chinese administration on Formosa proved China lacked sovereignty. The Japanese landing, consequently, could not be con-strued as an invasion of Chinese territory. Prince Kung, however, insisted that Sino-Japanese relations be governed not by the general principles of international law, but by the specific treaty of 1871, which clearly stipu-lated nonaggression against each other's territorial possessions. To this Ōkubo retorted that the treaty concerned only Chinese-Japanese relations, not the Formosan aborigines who were beyond the pale of Chinese juris-diction. With neither side willing to concede, a diplomatic impasse en-sued. The British minister Thomas Wade offered mediation. Ōkubo's initial demand for an indemnity of $5 million was reduced to $2 million, a sum Wade considered not extravagant. After much dickering, the case was finally settled with Prince Kung agreeing to pay the aggressor half a million dollars, of which $100,000 was for the Ryūkyūan victims and $400,000 for the purchase of Japanese barracks that had been constructed on Formosa. In addition, China agreed not to condemn the Japanese ac-tion—a concession which implied recognition of Japan's claim to sover-eignty over Ryūkyū.[3] That China was willing to pay for being invaded—

3. In 1879 when China was involved with Russia over the Ili crisis in Sinkiang (next section), Japan annexed Ryūkū and renamed it Okinawa Prefecture.

as the British minister in Japan Harry Parkes sarcastically described the case—was a stark revelation of her weakness and an invitation to further foreign encroachment.

RUSSIAN OCCUPATION OF ILI, 1871-81

Ili was a Chinese prefecture (*fu*) governing nine cities in northern Sinkiang (Chinese Turkestan) near the border of Russian Turkestan. One of the nine, Ning-yüan (I-ning), was known to the Russians and Westerners as Kuldja, which they often wrongly designated a province. The Ili valley was agriculturally and minerally rich and strategically important; its Muzart Pass, soaring 12,208 feet, controlled communication with southern Sinkiang. Control of Ili had always facilitated control of all Sinkiang, and many Western military experts described Ili as the fortress of Chinese Turkestan. A place of such commercial and military potential naturally attracted the attention of strong neighbors. In 1851 the Russians secured the Treaty of Ili from China, which allowed them to establish consulates and duty-free trade at Ili and Chuguchak (Tarbagatai) on the Mongolian border. The Ili trade grew rapidly thereafter, reaching a million pounds sterling a year in the mid-1850's. The continuous expansion of the Russians in Central Asia brought them ever closer to Ili, and taking advantage of a Moslem rebellion in Sinkiang, General K. P. von Kaufman, the first governor-general of Russian Turkestan, sent troops to occupy Ili in 1871.

The Ch'ing Administration in Sinkiang and the Moslem Rebellions. The Moslem Rebellion in Sinkiang had its roots in the corrupt local Ch'ing administration. Ever since its conquest by Emperor Ch'ien-lung in 1759, Sinkiang had been governed as a military colony. The administration was headed by a military-governor at Ili, aided by a number of assistant military governors and imperial agents in various key points. Some 16,000 soldiers were deployed on the northern side of the Tienshan (Celestial) Mountains and 5,760 on the southern side. The high officials and officers were nearly entirely Manchus and bannermen, who ruled the local populace—mostly Turki-speaking, turban-wearing, Uighur Moslems—through 270 local chieftains known as the *begs*. The Manchu conquerors treated the subject Moslems with contempt, as if they were uncivilized aborigines, levying heavy taxes and exacting forced contributions to support their own unbridled extravagance. The discontent of the Moslems inspired a strong incentive to revolt, and their former rulers, the *khojas*, who had been banished by the Ch'ing to Khokand, were ever anxious to re-establish their personal rule. The *khojas* were the religious potentates who were descendants of the Prophet and ruled Kashgaria (southern Sinkiang) before the Ch'ing conquest in 1759. They perpetually encouraged their co-religionists in Sinkiang to revolt, while they themselves organized invasions. During the century since the Ch'ing conquest, no less than a dozen uprisings and invasions took place. In 1864, amid the dynastic decline and a Moslem rebellion in northwest China, the Moslems in Sinkiang struck again. Drained by its own corruption, the local Ch'ing administration was too weak to suppress them, while the central government in Peking was too preoccupied with the Taiping, the Nien, and other rebellions to undertake punitive measures.

During the disorder, Yakub Beg (1820-77), a Khokandian adventurer, entered Sinkiang in 1865, and through a series of military and political manipulations established himself by 1870 as the ruler of Kashgaria and part of northern Sinkiang. The British in India, to block the southern extension of the Russian influence, encouraged his empire-building and sent missions to cultivate amicable relationships. Fearful of a Yakub Beg invasion of Ili under British sponsorship, disturbed by the interruption of trade, and anxious to expand Russian influence into Chinese Turkestan, General Kaufman ordered the occupation of Ili in July 1871. Disclaiming to the world any territorial designs, the Russians insisted that safeguarding her borders from Moslem raids necessitated the occupation, and that as soon as the Chinese imperial authority was re-established in Sinkiang, Ili would be returned. A magnanimous impression was created that the Russian stewardship was an act of kindness to China during a period of disorder. It was obvious that Russia never believed that the effete Ch'ing dynasty could recover Sinkiang. To perpetuate disorder so as to prolong their occupation of Ili, the Russians signed a commercial treaty with Yakub Beg in 1872; the British followed suit a year later, both countries granting him recognition in exchange for trade privileges.

The Chinese could not reach Yakub Beg before they had suppressed the Moslem Rebellion in Shensi and Kansu. In 1866 the court appointed Tso Tsung-t'ang, governor-general of Fukien and Chekiang, as governor-general of Shensi and Kansu, with the specific assignment of suppressing the rebels there. However, before he assumed command, the court again transferred him to first fight the Nien rebels, as noted in Chapter 10. It was not until he had pacified the Nien Rebellion in 1868 that Tso was able to assume his earlier assignment. By efficient leadership, good strategy, and hard campaigning, he crushed the rebellion in these two provinces in 1873. The campaign had cost the government 40 million taels, and Tso's victorious army was poised to strike into Sinkiang. At this juncture, the Formosa crisis with Japan arose, and China's weakness as revealed in the settlement pointed up the urgent need for coastal defense. The nation now encountered the vexing question of whether it could support a bold naval program simultaneously with a costly Sinkiang campaign. A grand debate over the relative urgency and importance of the two ensued.

Maritime Defense versus Frontier Defense. Prince Kung and Wen-hsiang were the first to sound the note of alarm at the inadequacy of the coastal defense after a decade of Self-strengthening. To the court they gave warning: "If we continue to drift along passively and do not eagerly seek to improve ourselves and forge ahead, trouble in the future will be even more difficult to meet." High officials on the coast proposed the creation of a navy consisting of forty-eight ships, divided into three squadrons and stationed on the North, Central, and South China coasts. The threat of Japan, they felt, was more immediate than that of Russia. Li Hung-chang, leading spirit of this group, boldly asked the court to cancel the Sinkiang campaign and shift its funds to naval defense. He called for the purchase of foreign ships and guns, the training of officers and sailors, the recruitment of fresh talent by a new "foreign affairs" examination, the manufacture of munitions, and an increase in customs dues on opium imports to help pay for the naval expenses, estimated at 10 million taels annually.

The advocates of maritime defense advanced five arguments: (1) frontier defense was not as important and urgent as maritime defense, in view of Peking's proximity to the coast and Sinkiang's great distance from the capital; (2) financial exigency and the uncertainty of victory on the difficult terrain of Sinkiang compelled re-examination of the advisability of that campaign; (3) the barren land of Sinkiang, which was of little practical value to China, was not worth the cost of recovering it; (4) surrounded by strong neighbors, Sinkiang could not be effectively defended for long; and (5) to postpone the recovery of Sinkiang was not renunciation of territory conquered by former emperors, but simply a sensible way of preserving strength for the future.

On the other hand, many other officials, while not disputing the importance of naval defense, argued that it should not be undertaken at the expense of frontier defense. If China failed to suppress the rebels in Sinkiang, the Russians would continue their advance, and the Western powers might be encouraged to flare up along the coast in response. Russia, these officials argued, was a greater threat than Japan or any Western power because of her common frontier with China—Russia could reach China by land as well as by sea, whereas Japan and the Western countries could only reach her by sea. They compared the Russian trouble to a sickness of the heart, and the Western threat to that of the limbs. Tso Tsung-t'ang argued that Western powers fought for harbors, ports, and generally only commercial privileges, whereas Russia schemed to obtain both commercial and territorial concessions.

The advocates of frontier defense impressed upon the court five arguments, too: (1) Sinkiang was the first line of defense in the northwest; it protected Mongolia, which in turn shielded Peking. If Sinkiang were lost, Mongolia would be indefensible and Peking itself threatened; (2) the Western powers posed no danger of invasion at the moment, but the Russian advance in Sinkiang was an immediate threat; (3) the funds for frontier defense should not be shifted to coastal defense, since the latter had already been allocated its own standing fund; (4) the land conquered by the forefathers should not be given up; and (5) strategic spots such as Urumchi and Aksu should be recovered first. Tso Tsung-t'ang, the dominant figure of this group, warned that to halt the Sinkiang campaign now was to invite foreign domination of Sinkiang.[4]

The arguments of both groups were cogent and well reasoned. However, it was apparent that there was no immediate trouble along the coast, whereas there was a rebellion in Sinkiang, which needed to be suppressed, and an occupied Ili, which should be recovered. While not giving up the naval program, on April 23, 1875, the court appointed Tso imperial commissioner to conduct the Sinkiang campaign.

With headquarters at Lanchow, Kansu, Tso absorbed himself in an elaborate preparation for the campaign. His policy was "to proceed slowly but to fight quickly." By early 1876 he was ready to strike, and in March moved his headquarters to the advanced post of Suchow. General Liu Chin-t'ang struck hard and fast into Sinkiang, and by November had conquered its northern half. Yakub Beg, still established in southern Sinkiang, was apprehensive of his future; he sent an emissary to London in late spring 1877 to seek British mediation, indicating his willingness to accept the status of a tributary to China, like Burma. But Tso's army moved faster than discussions in London. Yakub Beg was soundly defeated and driven to suicide on May 29, 1877. His sons carried on the fight, but inter-

4. Immanuel C. Y. Hsü, "The Great Policy Debate in China, 1874: Maritime Defense vs. Frontier Defense," *Harvard Journal of Asiatic Studies,* 25:212-28 (1965).

necine strife among them precluded any effective resistance. By the end of 1877 all Sinkiang had been recovered except the small enclave of Ili, which was still under Russian occupation.

Having re-established the imperial authority in Sinkiang, China had fulfilled the Russian condition for the return of Ili. But the Russian minister in Peking[5] resorted to delaying tactics to postpone the issue. The Tsungli Yamen, then establishing Chinese legations abroad, charged the mission to Russia to negotiate for the return of Ili. The mission head, Ch'ung-hou, who had carried the apology to France in 1870, was given the title of imperial commissioner first class, i.e. ambassador, and authorized to act as he saw fit.

Ch'ung-hou's Mission and the Treaty of Livadia, 1879. Ch'ung-hou (1826-93), a pliable and pleasant Manchu noble of no great ability, embarked for Russia quite inadequately prepared for his task. Ignorant of Ili's geography and diplomatic intricacies, he arrived in St. Petersburg where Russian flattery apparently overwhelmed him and caused him to relax his vigilance. Moreover, he appeared anxious to conclude his business and return home. Speculation avers he feared the awesome Russians and earnestly desired to tend to urgent family affairs at home. His innocence and inattention allowed him to be duped into hastily signing the Treaty of Livadia, which returned Ili to China in name but ceded seven-tenths of the area to Russia, including the strategic Tekes valley and the Muzart Pass. In addition, it awarded to Russia an indemnity of five million rubles, the right to consulates in seven key places, and navigation on the Sungari River in Manchuria up to 600 *versts* (400 miles).[6] When these terms were telegraphed to Peking, the Tsungli Yamen was dumbfounded and cabled Ch'ung-hou not to sign the treaty. His curious reply was that the treaty had already been negotiated and the texts copied out; no changes or re-negotiation was possible. On October 2, 1879, on his own authority he signed the treaty and returned home without imperial authorization.

Chinese officialdom responded to the treaty with consternation. The Tsungli Yamen insisted that this type of restoral of Ili was worse than none. Tso Tsung-t'ang feared that the fruits of his arduous Sinkiang campaign were about to be snatched away by Ch'ung-hou's stupidity. He strongly urged the court to confront the Russians with a firm diplomacy supported by military readiness. "We shall first confront them [the Rus-

5. Eugene K. Butzow.
6. To Potuna.

sians] with arguments . . . and then settle it on the battlefield," he confidently announced.[7] On the other hand, Li Hung-chang, never sympathetic to the Sinkiang campaign and the policy of pressing Russia for the return of Ili, was only superficially critical of the treaty and did not advocate its rejection: "The present mission of Ch'ung-hou had its origin in an imperial edict endowing him with full powers to act as he saw fit. We cannot say that he had no power to negotiate a treaty settlement. If we give assent first and then repudiate it later, we are at fault. Since time immemorial, the first essential of international relations is to decide whether a cause is just. If our cause is unjust, we only ask for insult."[8]

Li was in the unpopular minority. The prevailing sentiment among scholars and officials was for war to avenge the humiliation, even though their country was not ready for it. Barrages of memorials poured into the court demanding severe punishment of the signer and rejection of the treaty. The most eloquent of these came from a young librarian of the Supervisorate of Imperial Instruction, Chang Chih-tung (1837-1909). In beautiful prose he announced: "The Russians must be considered extremely covetous and truculent in making the demands, and Ch'ung-hou extremely stupid and absurd in accepting them . . . If we insist on changing the treaty, there may not be trouble; if we do not, we are unworthy to be called a state."[9] He demanded that Ch'ung-hou be decapitated to show China's determination to reject the treaty, even at the price of war. Because he spoke the mind of the literati and officials, Chang immediately garnered great public fame.

The court appointed Marquis Tseng Chi-tse, minister to Britain and France and son of the great statesman Tseng Kuo-fan, head of a second mission to Russia, with the specific assignment of renegotiating the treaty. Meanwhile, Ch'ung-hou was sentenced to death by beheading after the Autumn Assizes. Strong protests were lodged by the representatives of Britain, France, Germany, and the United States over the inhumane treatment of a brother diplomat, and Queen Victoria even sent a personal plea to the empress dowager. On June 26, 1880, Ch'ung-hou was given a reprieve, but kept in prison to await the outcome of the second mission. Dissatisfied with this partial concession, Russia refused to treat with Tseng before Ch'ung-hou was granted a full pardon.

Irritated with China's denunciation of the treaty, her punishment of the signer, and her belligerent pronouncements, Russia sent twenty-three

7. Hsü, The Ili Crisis, 62.
8. Ibid., 64, with minor changes.
9. Ibid., 71, with minor changes.

warships to China as a naval demonstration.[10] War clouds hung low over Peking; there was great fear of a Russian naval attack along the coast in concert with an army thrust from Siberia overland to Manchuria and Peking. The court did not intend to precipitate a clash, but was pushed by public sentiments into taking a stronger position than it really wanted. To prepare for the eventuality of war, it installed the Hunan army officers of Taiping fame—rather than those of Li's Huai army—in key defense positions, and through its trusted foreign servant, Robert Hart, invited Charles Gordon to China to help its defenses.

Gordon, the former leader of the Ever-Victorious army and a legendary figure of Victorian England, had been secretary to the viceroy of India since the spring of 1880; but finding the life of a desk officer "a living crucifixion," he resigned, and two days later received the telegraphic invitation from Hart. Gordon immediately seized this opportunity. After a meeting with Li at Tientsin, Gordon agreed that China should not be led irresponsibly into a reckless war. He set out for Peking to warn that as long as it was the seat of government China could not afford to fight any first-rate power; the Taku forts could easily be taken from the rear, leaving Peking indefensible. If China must fight, he said, the court should move itself to the interior and be ready for a long war of attrition. Although such blunt counsels were unwelcome in the belligerent atmosphere of Peking, Gordon did make a powerful impression as to the inadvisability of war. He was used by Li both to discourage the war party from a disastrous venture and to show Russia that China did not lack friends in her hour of need.[11]

Marquis Tseng and the Treaty of St. Petersburg, 1881. As Gordon was counseling peace in China, Marquis Tseng was readying himself for the mission to St. Petersburg. To avoid his predecessor's mistakes, he had made extensive preparations for his diplomatic strategy and studied the maps of Ili exhaustively. Determined to hold firm on the boundary issue, bargain on the question of trade, and be conciliatory on monetary compensation, Tseng set out for Russia with assurance from the British foreign office of unofficial assistance, and the British ambassador at St. Petersburg[12] became his secret adviser.

The Russians at first refused to open negotiations at St. Petersburg, insisting on moving the site to Peking as a punishment for China's bellicose

10. Under Admiral S. S. Lesovskii.
11. Immanuel C. Y. Hsü, "Gordon in China, 1880," *Pacific Historical Review*, 23:2:147-66 (May 1964).
12. Lord Loftus Dufferin.

attitude. Fearful of negotiating under the threat of the enemy fleet, Peking desperately urged Tseng to use all means to keep the negotiations in Russia. The Russians finally acquiesced and opened the discussions in their capital, but negotiations progressed slowly because they could not find a way to return Ili without losing face. They knew they were in no position to wage a distant war, due to their depressed economy caused by the Turkish war of 1876-77 and their international isolation after the Congress of Berlin in 1878. Yet they could not extricate themselves from China gracefully. After nearly half a year's fruitless arguments, the tsar finally decided to end the quarrel by agreeing to return all of Ili, including the Tekes valley and the Muzart Pass, except for a few villages in the western portion for the settlement of those Moslem refugees who refused to return to China. The number of Russian consulates was reduced to two,[13] while the indemnity, dignified under the name of "military compensation," was increased to nine million rubles, about five million taels. Since the Treaty of Livadia had been emptied of contents, these terms were incorporated into a new agreement, the Treaty of St. Petersburg, on February 24, 1881.

The peace settlement, generally considered a Chinese diplomatic victory, created two important repercussions. First, it encouraged an upsurge of conservatism in China. The thought of having won a round from a powerful Western state stimulated self-confidence and complacency, in spite of Marquis Tseng's warning against pride, optimism, and arrogance. The literati, who freely and irresponsibly made high-flown speeches to express their views (ch'ing-i), were encouraged to believe that the victory resulted from their firm stand, and overconfidently trusted in their ability to untangle China's problems in foreign relations.

The second significant outcome of the settlement was the new status accruing to Sinkiang. Traditionally known as the Western Region (Hsi-yü), Sinkiang had never been an integral part of China but remained a frontier area held by her when she was strong, lost when she was weak. After the Treaty of St. Petersburg, the Ch'ing court accepted the recommendation of Tso Tsung-t'ang and turned it into a regular province in 1884, with Liu Chin-t'ang, the brilliant young general who contributed much to its reconquest, as its first governor. This unprecedented institutional innovation constituted a significant milestone in Chinese frontier history.[14]

13. At Turfan and Suchow.
14. Hsü, The Ili Crisis, 189-96.

THE SINO-FRENCH WAR OVER ANNAM, 1884-85

No sooner had the Ili crisis been settled than the problem of French encroachment in the tributary state of Annam loomed. Known in ancient times as Vietnam, Annam first came under Chinese influence in the 3rd century B.C., and its northern part was conquered by the Han Wu-ti (140-87 B.C.) in 111 B.C. Its name was derived from the An-nan (South-pacifying) protectorate established during the T'ang dynasty (618-907) to govern the area. Though independent after the fall of the T'ang, Annam remained under strong Chinese cultural and political influence. It was an important tributary state during the Ming (1368-1643) and Ch'ing (1644-1911) periods. Between 1664 and 1881 some fifty tribute missions came to Peking.

Western influence in Annam arrived with the Jesuits in 1615, but church work progressed slowly in this predominantly Confucian state The French East India Company had made an unsuccessful attempt at trade by the end of the 17th century. However, French influence began to wax by the end of the 18th century, when Nguyên Anh, the lone survival of the *ancien régime* that had been overthrown in 1788,[15] regained control of the country with the aid of some French officers. He was installed as Emperor Gia-Long of the Nguyên dynasty, which lasted from 1802 until 1945.[16]

The French Aggression. Gia-Long and his successors were conservative Confucianists, who promoted Chinese studies and institutions and countenanced xenophobic riots against the missionaries and converts. Louis Napoleon, in his ambition to build a French Indo-Chinese empire and pose as a champion of Catholicism abroad, sent troops to Saigon in 1859 to punish missionary incidents—troops that he had withdrawn from China after the Treaty of Tientsin of 1858. A treaty was imposed on Annam in 1862, by which the French secured an indemnity of $4 million, the rights to trade, to propagate religion, and to control Annamese foreign relations, as well as cession of three eastern provinces in south Annam, known to the French as Cochin China. Further discovery that the Red River in Tong-

15. By three Tây-son brothers: Nguyên Nhac, Nguyên Lu, Nguyên Huê.
16. For an outline of Vietnamese history of this and earlier periods, see D. G. E. Hall, *A History of Southeast Asia* (London, 1964), chapters 9 and 22; also Truong Buu Lam, "Intervention versus Tribute in Sino-Vietnamese Relations, 1788-1790" in Fairbank (ed.), *The Chinese World Order*, 165-79.

king was a better route than the Mekong to China's Yunnan province aroused French ambitions to seize north Annam. In 1874 a new treaty was signed which confirmed the French possession of Cochin China, the right to direct Annamese foreign relations, and navigation on the Red River. With this document France reduced Annam to a protectorate, although recognizing her independence in name. Preoccupied with the Formosa crisis and the Margary murder case, China took no positive action to stop the French advance; she merely refused to honor the treaty of 1874 on the ground that Annam had always been a Chinese dependency.[17]

French empire-building in the East met with German encouragement. At the Congress of Berlin in 1878, Bismarck is reputed to have told the French delegates that Germany would fight any French attempt at recovering the lost territory in Europe but would gladly assist their overseas aggrandizement. It was therefore no surprise that the French intensified their activities in Annam, and by 1880 had stationed troops in Hanoi and Haiphong and established fortresses along the Red River. To counter the French advance, the Annamese government strengthened its ties with China, despite French protests, by continuing the tribute in 1877 and 1881 and by seeking the aid of the irregular Chinese Black Flag army[18] which had established itself at the Annamese border. By 1882 the Black Flag army had begun engaging the French troops; and in the following year the Ch'ing court, wishing to defend its suzerainty over Annam, yet unwilling to fight the French openly, quietly dispatched regular troops into Tongking.

Li Hung-chang, governor-general at Tientsin and animating spirit of the Self-strengthening Movement, admonished against challenging France before completion of the Chinese naval program and coastal defense. With neither the power to invalidate the French treaties with Annam nor the strength to expel the French from Annam, Li argued, China should not lightly talk of war lest she court disaster. She should fight only when attacked. Even then, he warned, the prospect was bleak, for any Chinese victory could only bring a renewed French effort to prolong the war, while a French victory would drive Chinese troops back to China. Li therefore favored a quick settlement through negotiations. Prince Kung, head of the Tsungli Yamen and the leading member of the Grand Council, agreed that China should not prematurely challenge a first-rate Western power.

17. For French activities in Annam, see John F. Cady *The Roots of French Imperialism in East Asia* (Ithaca, N.Y., 1967), chapter 16; *Southeast Asia: Its Historical Development* (New York, 1964), chapter 18; Hall, chapter 34.
18. Under Liu Yung-fu, a Taiping remnant associated with the Heaven and Earth Society.

The Rise of the Ch'ing-i Party. The cautious attitude of Li and Kung was attacked and ridiculed as appeasement and defeatism by a coterie of young officials who were brilliant scholars and memorialists, former members of the Hanlin Academy, but who had had little practical experience or genuine knowledge of foreign and military affairs. They made ornate and fervid speeches to win public acclaim and imperial attention, and championed a belligerent course of action, as they did during the Ili crisis. They considered themselves the voice of the literati (*ch'ing-i*), calling themselves the party of the purists (*ch'ing-liu tang*). Two of the most vociferous members were Chang Chih-tung, who achieved instant fame during the Ili crisis, and Chang P'ei-lun, who emulated him in the present emergency.

The *ch'ing-liu* group disparagingly described France as a "spent arrow" and a country on the brink of bankruptcy. They advocated war to defend China's honor and her tributary state, and condemned appeasement as a sure way to encourage greater demands from the insatiable enemy. If China stood firm over Annam, they argued, the Japanese, the Russians, and the British would all be discouraged from adventures in Korea, Manchuria, and Burma. War was won, they pointed out, more by the human qualities of courage and virtue than by weapons: the spirit of men determined victory. They lashed at Li Hung-chang derisively: "The wily plans of the French are known even by lads and servants. Only Li Hung-chang does not know." "I fear that Li Hung-chang has been deluded by the French, and that the court has in turn been deluded by Li Hung-chang." Contemptuously they compared Li with the notorious historical traitor Ch'in Kuei (A.D. 1090-1155), and cowed other advocates of peace. Li complained to a friend: "I am plagued by the irresponsible talk of officials not in positions of authority . . . They discuss matters of policy, and after matters of policy, they discuss men. Most engage in bullying."[19]

The *ch'ing-liu group* entertained too much hope in China's moral strength, just as Li entertained too little because of her material weakness. The one that seemed to have a balanced grasp of the situation was Marquis Tseng, minister to Britain and France. He had attempted to negotiate a settlement in Paris, but was rebuffed by the French on the ground that they did not recognize China's right to speak for Annam. On the basis of his five-year sojourn in Europe and a cool-headed appraisal of French politics and her international position, Tseng came to the conclusion that France could not wage a far-flung foreign war. He warned Li

19. Lloyd E. Eastman, "Ch'ing-i and Chinese Policy Formation during the Nineteenth Century," *The Journal of Asian Studies*, XXIV:4:604-05 (Aug. 1965).

against timidity in dealing with the French for several reasons: (1) they despised the weak and respected the strong; they loved military glory but were easily frustrated by setbacks; hence they could not sustain a long war. The more was China determined to fight, the more was the likelihood of peace. Indecision, procrastination, and compromise could only lead to French gains, which would be difficult for China to recover later. (2) The French aspired to the coal mines in Kwangtung and the gold deposits in Yunnan; ceding to them Annam would not satisfy their appetite; it would only eliminate China's southern defensive frontier. (3) The loss of Tongking would make China a laughing stock for the world and encourage Britain and Russia to covet Tibet and Korea. (4) The political instability in France caused by partisan squabbles and cabinet changes, and her isolated position in European international politics would not permit her to wage a foreign war. For these reasons, Tseng warned against overcautiousness and urged a strong stance—the firmer China's position, the greater the chance for a favorable settlement.[20]

The Ch'ing court vacillated between war and peace. It was caught on the alternate horns of honor, which demanded defense of her tributary, and fear of fighting a leading Western power. A report from Robert Hart's agent in London[21] led the court to believe that the French troops in Annam probably would not precipitate a full-scale war; and that if Hanoi and the Red River were opened to trade and navigation, the basic cause of contention would be removed. The court therefore instructed Li Hungchang to open negotiations with the French minister, Bourée. The resultant agreement, which turned Annam into a joint protectorate of China and France, was immediately rejected by Paris, which decided to dispatch an expedition to Annam. Defeat of the Black Flag army and the regular Chinese troops in Tongking and fear of French attack on China herself caused great anxiety to the empress dowager, who angrily dismissed Prince Kung and four other members of the Grand Council.[22] She again ordered Li to seek a settlement. The subsequent arrangement between Li and the French naval captain, F. E. Fournier, in 1884 called for Chinese recognition of all French treaties with Annam, withdrawal of Chinese troops from Tongking, and a French promise of no demand for indemnity, no invasion of China, and no undignified reference to China in any future

20. Hsiao I-shan, III, 1070-71.
21. J. D. Campbell.
22. Lloyd E. Eastman, *Throne and Mandarins: China's Search for a Policy during the Sino-French Controversy, 1880-1885* (Cambridge, Mass., 1967), chapter 4.

treaties with Annam. The French parliament refused to ratify the agreement because the last condition resembled an implied recognition of Chinese suzerainty over Annam. On the other hand, the agreement so inflamed the *ch'ing-liu* party that forty-seven memorials poured into the court demanding Li's impeachment. Thus harassed, Li dared not report to the court the agreed-upon date of the withdrawal of Chinese troops from Annam.[23]

The Outbreak of War. Not having received orders to withdraw, the Chinese troops in Tongking rejected a local French demand that they evacuate Langson. Hostilities were renewed, and the Chinese inflicted some casualties on the French troops. Paris accused China of bad faith and sent an ultimatum on July 12, 1884, demanding a large indemnity and immediate execution of the Li-Fournier agreement. Some more negotiating was done but led nowhere. Fearing a French attack on China herself, the court transferred the two leaders of the *ch'ing-liu* party to key defense positions: Chang Chih-tung as governor-general at Canton to guard the southern border, and Chang P'ei-lun as commander of the Fukien fleet. On August 23, twelve French ships under Admiral Courbet launched an all-out attack on Foochow. Within an hour they sank and damaged eleven Chinese warships and destroyed the Foochow Dockyard, built with French aid in 1866. Watching the fight from a hilltop, Chang P'ei-lun was among the first to flee. But his report to the court was so distorted with ambiguous and florid terms that Peking thought China had won a naval battle! When the truth was known a few days later, he was exiled to the frontier. The court at last stopped wavering and declared war on France.

The Peace Settlement. The empress dowager supported war resolutely for three months, from August to November 1884. In early December she began to vacillate again, as a result of her distress over the indecisive military outcome in Tongking, the French blockade of the Yangtze River and key ports, and the stoppage of tribute grain from South China. The expected aid from Britain and Germany did not materialize; and there was also threat of renewed Russian activities on the northern frontier and a Japanese advance in Korea. The dowager's inclination toward peace was reciprocated by a similar desire in France, where unstable political conditions and the difficulty of supporting a distant military operation began to weigh on the government. Through the good offices of Hart's agents in Lon-

23. Eastman, *Throne and Mandarins,* chapter 5.

don, a preliminary peace was agreed upon in Paris, whereby China undertook to recognize the Li-Fournier agreement and France agreed to make no new demands. Fortuitously before this term was formalized into a treaty, the French army at Langson suffered a major defeat,[24] providing Peking with a good face-saving opportunity to pursue peace, and dampening the war spirit in France. In June 1885 Li Hung-chang and the French minister in China finally concluded a formal agreement: China recognized all the French treaties with Annam, and France evacuated her troops from Taiwan and the Pescadores. No indemnity was paid, but China suffered an economic loss in excess of 100 million taels and incurred some 20 million taels of debts.[25]

The indecision and vacillation of the court in the whole venture was pathetic. It had not wanted war but allowed itself to be harried into it by the ch'ing-liu party. If it had held firm from the very beginning and been determined for a long war, the French might not have dared to strike; and if it had followed a persistent policy of peace, the Fukien fleet and the Foochow Dockyard would have been spared. The price of ineffective leadership was the destruction of both and the loss of the tributary state of Annam. The ch'ing-liu pressure group must be held responsible to a large degree for espousing an unrealistic and emotional cause. Only one of them, Chang Chih-tung, survived the fiasco politically, while the rest faded into relative obscurity. Ironically, after a term of banishment Chang P'ei-lun returned to join Li Hung-chang's staff as his secretary, and later to become his son-in-law.

The loss of Annam after a short and unimpressive encounter with France signaled the failure of the twenty-year-old Self-strengthening Movement. The limited diplomatic, military, and technological modernization had not strengthened the country to a point where it could resist foreign imperialism. China's weakness prompted the British to emulate the French and detach Burma in 1885. A treaty was secured from China a year later, reducing Burma to a British protectorate but permitting her to continue paying tribute to Peking once every ten years. With the loss of these tributary states in the south, the fate of the leading tributary in the northeast, Korea, hung in a delicate balance, and this the Japanese were too astute not to notice.

24. By General Feng Tzu-ts'ai.
25. Shao Hsün-cheng, *Chung-Fa Yüeh-nan kuan-hsi shih-mo* (A complete account of Chinese-French relations concerning Vietnam), (Peiping, 1935).

FURTHER READING

Cady, John F., *Southeast Asia: Its Historical Development* (New York, 1964), chapters 12, 18.

————, *The Roots of French Imperialism in East Asia* (Ithaca, N.Y., 1967).

Ch'en, Ta-tuan, "Investiture of Liu-ch'iu Kings in the Ch'ing Period" in John K. Fairbank (ed.), *The Chinese World Order: Traditional China's Foreign Relations* (Cambridge, Mass., 1968), 135-64.

Ch'in, Han-ts'ai 秦翰才, *Tso-wen-hsiang-kung tsai Hsi-pei* 左文襄公在西北 (Tso Tsung-t'ang in the Northwest), (Chungking, 1945).

Eastman, Lloyd E., *Throne and Mandarins: China's Search for a Policy during the Sino-French Controversy, 1880-1885* (Cambridge, Mass., 1967).

————, "Ch'ing-i and Chinese Policy Formation during the Nineteenth Century," *The Journal of Asian Studies*, XXIV:4:595-611 (Aug. 1965).

————, "Political Reformism in China before the Sino-Japanese War," *The Journal of Asian Studies*, XXVII:4:695-710 (Aug. 1968).

Hall, D. G. E., *A History of Southeast Asia* (London, 1964), chapters 9, 22, 34-35.

Hsü, Immanuel C. Y., *The Ili Crisis: A Study of Sino-Russian Diplomacy, 1871-1881* (Oxford, 1965).

————, "The Great Policy Debate in China, 1874: Maritime Defense vs. Frontier Defense," *Harvard Journal of Asiatic Studies*, 25:212-28 (1965).

————, "British Mediation of China's War with Yakub Beg, 1877," *Central Asiatic Journal* (Leiden), 9:2:142-49 (June 1964).

Jelavich, Charles and Barbara, *Russia in the East, 1876-1880* (Leiden, 1959).

Kiernan, E. V. G., *British Diplomacy in China, 1880 to 1885* (London, 1939).

Lamb, Alastair, *Britain and Chinese Central Asia* (London, 1960).

Langer, William, *The Diplomacy of Imperialism* (New York, 1950).

Li, En-han 李恩涵, *Tseng Chi-tse ti wai-chiao* 曾紀澤的外交 (The diplomacy of Tseng Chi-tse), (Taipei, 1966).

McAleavy, Henry, *Black Flags in Vietnam* (New York, 1968).

Sakai, Robert K., "The Ryūkyū (Liu-ch'iu) Islands as Fief of Satsuma" in John K. Fairbank (ed.), *The Chinese World Order: Traditional China's Foreign Relations* (Cambridge, Mass., 1968), 112-34.

Shao, Hsün-cheng 邵循正, *Chung-Fa Yüeh-nan kuan-hsi shih-mo* 中法越南關係始末 (A complete account of Chinese-French relations concerning Vietnam), (Peiping, 1935).

————, *et al.*, (eds.) *Chung-Fa chan-cheng* 中法戰爭 (The Sino-French war), (Shanghai, 1955), 7 vols.

14

*Acceleration of Imperialism: the Japanese Aggression
in Korea and the "Partition of China"*

By virtue of its proximity to North China, Korea was regarded by the Chinese as a valuable "outer fence" and a leading tributary state during Ming and Ch'ing times. The Yi dynasty (1392-1910) of Korea annually sent three regular tribute missions to the Ming court and four to the Ch'ing, apart from the numerous smaller embassies.[1] During the two and one-half centuries from 1637 to 1894, no less than 507 Korean missions came to Peking, while 169 Chinese missions went to Korea. So important was Korea to China that the Ming dynasty, despite its dwindling treasury and military power, sent 211,500 men and spent 10 million taels to defend it against a Japanese invasion in 1592, and a comparable sum for a second defense in 1597. These exertions so strained the Ming dynasty that they contributed to its ultimate downfall. The Koreans were of course grateful and respectful toward China. Living under her political and cultural shadow, they modeled their institutions and way of life after China's, and described relations with her as "serving the great" (*sadae*), as distinguished from the more equal "neighborly relations" (*kyorin*) with Japan. Since 1637 the Koreans had closed their country and maintained virtually no foreign intercourse other than sending tributary missions to China and occasional delegations to Japan. To the Western world she came to be known as the Hermit Kingdom.

1. For details, see Hae-jong Chun, "Sino-Korean Tributary Relations in the Ch'ing Period" in Fairbank (ed.), *The Chinese World Order*, 90-111.

THE OPENING OF KOREA

Contact with the West first began in 1635 when a Dutch ship drifted to the Korean coast. Christianity began to spread during the second half of the 18th century, but was proscribed by the Korean court as a heterodox faith in 1786. In the following century, Christian missionaries and Korean converts suffered periodic persecution.

After the opening of China and Japan, the Hermit Kingdom came under increasing Western pressure for trade, religious propagation, and diplomatic relations. But, aside from caring for the shipwrecked, the Koreans refused to have any contact with the West. Jealously guarding their seclusion, they argued that their country was too small and too poor to engage in foreign trade and their people too "stupid" to understand Christianity. Korean intransigence was intensified after Taewongon (Great Lord of the Court), father of the minor king Kojong,[2] became regent in 1864. He promoted conservatism, resisted change, and in February 1866 renewed persecution of Christians, which resulted in a sweeping massacre of foreign priests. In October, the French minister in China, Bellonet, sent Admiral Roze on a punitive expedition of seven ships and 600 men. They captured Kangwha but suffered a defeat outside the city, sustaining three dead and 32 wounded. The French expedition, which was not authorized by Paris in the first place, then withdrew. In August of the same year, the American merchant ship, the *General Sherman*, charged up the Taedong River to P'yongyong to demand trade, but was burned by the Koreans when it ran aground during low tide; all the crew was lost. The Department of State authorized Frederick F. Low, minister in China, to investigate the case in 1871, accompanied by five ships under Admiral Rodgers. Refused negotiations off the Kangwha Island, Low forced his way to the Han River that leads to Seoul. The Korean shore battery opened fire, and the Americans retaliated by bombarding the city of Kangwha in full force on June 10 and 11. Subsequently, they also withdrew for lack of authorization to fight. The Koreans congratulated themselves for having repulsed both the French and the Americans.

The Tsungli Yamen in China, itself just learning to adjust to the changing international order in East Asia, was aware of China's inability to defend Korea against the Western advance. Beginning from 1867 it tactfully advised Korea to reach an accommodation with the West, but not until

2. Li Hsi in Chinese.

1879-1880 was positive action taken to urge Korea to enter into treaty relations with Western powers in order to counter the rising influence of Japan.[3]

Japanese relations with Korea during the Tokugawa period (1603-1867) had been under the charge of the feudal lords of the Tsushima Island,[4] but after the Meiji Restoration in 1868 the Tokyo government took upon itself the direction of policy. Three missions were dispatched to Korea to announce the political changes in Japan and to revise existing relations. Contemptuous of Japan's modernization and imitation of the West, Tae-wongon refused to alter relations and rejected as improper the Japanese state letter, in which the Japanese emperor, rather than following the shogunal practice of addressing himself as "Taikun" (Great Lord), assumed the title of "His Imperial Highness," which, Taewongon insisted, only the Chinese emperor could use.

To this deliberate insult the Japanese leaders[5] reacted with a decision in 1873 to send a punitive expedition to Korea. Such a course of action served many other purposes, too: (1) to provide an outlet for the disgruntled samurai at home and shift critical attention from domestic problems to a foreign issue; (2) to win their country a leading position in Asia by successfully challenging China's supremacy in Korea; (3) to forestall Britain and Russia in securing a foothold near Japan; and (4) to revenge the failure of Hideyoshi's invasions of Korea in 1592 and 1597. However, a group of prudent statesmen returning from abroad[6] reversed this decision on the grounds that Japan's backward domestic conditions did not permit a foreign venture at this time, and that internal development and consolidation had to precede overseas expansion.

Though the expedition was not sent, a surveying team, accompanied by gunboats, was dispatched in 1875. When attacked at Kanghwa Bay, the Japanese returned fire and destroyed the Korean forts. Tokyo followed up the victory by sending six more ships to Korea[7] and an emissary to Peking[8]

3. For a succinct study of Korean intransigence and Chinese adaptabiilty during this time, see Mary C. Wright, "The Adaptability of Ch'ing Diplomacy: The Case of Korea," *The Journal of Asian Studies*, XVII:3:363-81 (May 1958); for a study of China's involvement in Korea, leading to the war with Japan, see Wang Hsin-chung, *Chung-Jih Chia-wu chan-cheng chih wai-chiao pei-ching* (The diplomatic background of the Sino-Japanese war), (Peiping, 1937).
4. The Sō family.
5. Such as Saigō, Itagaki, and Soejima.
6. Such as Iwakura, Kido, and Itō.
7. Under Kuroda Kiyotaka and Inoue Kaoru.
8. Mori Arinori.

to sound out the Chinese response. Fearful of involvement, the Tsungli Yamen stated that though a tributary state Korea had always been allowed complete freedom in her domestic and foreign affairs. This timid disclaimer of responsibility encouraged the Japanese to force the opening of Korea, such as Commodore Perry did with Japan herself in 1854. Anxious to avoid a clash, the Ch'ing court, then engaged in the Margary affair, instructed Korea to enter into negotiations with Japan. On February 24, 1876, the Treaty of Kangwha was signed, stipulating: (1) recognition of Korea as an independent state on an equal footing with Japan; (2) exchange of envoys; (3) opening of three ports: Pusan (Fusan), Inchon, and Wonsan; and (4) Japanese consular jurisdiction in these ports. By not protesting the Korean independence, China in effect defaulted her exclusive claim to suzerainty.

Japan's forceful action in Korea was followed by her annexation of the Liu-ch'iu (Ryūkyū) Islands in 1879. Alarmed by these aggressive activities, the Chinese minister in Tokyo[9] and officials at home[10] urged the court that Korea be opened to Western powers to checkmate the rising Japanese influence. Thomas Wade, the British minister, also warned that if not opened to Western commerce, Korea might repeat the fate of Liu-ch'iu. The Ch'ing government then put Li Hung-chang in charge of Korean affairs, in place of the Board of Rites which had traditionally managed the tributary relations.

Li decided to throw Korea open to Western commerce and diplomacy. In 1882 he sent two of his subordinates, Ma Chien-chung, who had studied international law in France, and Admiral Ting Ju-ch'ang, to Korea in the company of three warships, to introduce Commodore R. W. Shufeldt of the United States for treaty negotiations. On May 22, 1882, the American-Korean treaty was signed, by which the two countries agreed to exchange diplomats, to establish consuls at trading ports, and to treat each other on the basis of equality. The United States recognized Korean independence, but the Koreans voluntarily issued a separate statement to the effect that Korea was a dependent state of China. Had this statement been included in the treaty, the United States Senate probably would not have ratified it.

In the next few years, Ma Chien-chung introduced British, French, and German representatives to sign treaties with the Koreans, too. The Hermit Kingdom was finally opened to the West, and it tardily began some mod-

9. Ho Ju-chang.
10. Such as Ting Jih-ch'ang, ex-governor of Fukien.

ernization after the Chinese fashion. Li's active diplomacy retrieved some of the ground lost by the Tsungli Yamen's *faux pas* in disclaiming responsibility over Korea.

DOMESTIC INSURRECTIONS AND INTERNATIONAL POLITICS

The Insurrection of 1882. After King Kojong began his personal rule in 1873, Queen Min gained increasing power at the expense of Taewongon. She supported reform and employed Japanese officers to train the army. Jealous and disgruntled, Taewongon was determined to curtail her influence and if possible eliminate her. The power struggle led to a head-on clash in 1882. Taewongon, capitalizing on the discontent of dismissed old soldiers who were victims of the queen's military reform, incited them to attack the palace and the Japanese legation. Queen Min narrowly escaped in disguise, while the Japanese legation was burned. Seven Japanese officers lost their lives, while the minister[11] fled home. The coup returned Taewongon to power.

The Chinese government once again sent Admiral Ting and Ma Chien-chung to investigate the situation. A Korean courtier confidentially informed Ma that the root of all the trouble was Taewongon, who insulated the king from outside contact and executed officials connected with foreign affairs. If Taewongon were not properly disposed of, he warned, the Japanese would probably take punitive action. Ma quickly arrested Taewongon and sent him to China for detention.

Meanwhile, more Chinese and Japanese ships had arrived. On advice of Ma, the Korean king reached a settlement with Japan, agreeing to pay an indemnity of $50,000 for the slain officers and $500,000 for the Japanese government, to send a mission of apology to Tokyo, and to allow Japan to station troops and construct barracks at her legation. The settlement represented a significant victory for Japanese diplomacy, for it gave Japan the right to send troops to Korea. This condition, an oversight of Ma's in spite of his training in international law, was to cause great trouble later.

After the insurrection of 1882, Li Hung-chang began to take positive steps to strengthen China's position in Korea. A commercial treaty between the two countries was signed, giving China extraterritoriality, while loans and gifts of foreign-style guns were extended to the Korean govern-

11. Hanabusa Yoshitada.

ment. Li arranged to appoint a Chinese commercial agent to supervise trade, and assigned a young officer, Yüan Shih-k'ai, to train the Korean army. Paul George von Mollendorf, the former German consul at Tientsin, was made customs commissioner in Korea and concurrently foreign affairs adviser. Six Chinese battalions were stationed in Korea to maintain order and to guard against future Japanese aggression. Chinese influence mounted to new heights in Korea under Li's positive policy.

The Insurrection of 1884. Yüan Shih-k'ai now allied himself with Queen Min to counter the rising Japanese influence. In the years that followed, struggle grew between the pro-Chinese and pro-Japanese Koreans. The head of the apology mission, having been warmly received in Tokyo, advised the Korean king to accept Japanese help in reform, and Kojong engaged two Japanese advisers. In a good-will gesture, Tokyo offered to reduce its troops in Korea and to return part of the indemnity for the reform of Korean administration. A new minister[12] was sent to Korea to promote friendship and guide the pro-Japanese group, now gathered under one Kim Ok-kyun.

The government of Korea at this point was dominated by Yüan Shih-k'ai and the pro-Chinese Koreans. In 1884, however, when China was at war with France and withdrew three battalions from Korea, the pro-Japanese group decided to stage a coup. At the inauguration dinner of the new post office at Seoul on December 4, 1884, all foreign representatives and high Chinese and Korean dignitaries were invited to attend, but the Japanese minister was conspicuously absent. Before the banquet was over, pro-Japanese Koreans set fire in the city, and aided by Japanese troops broke into the palace, captured the king, and wantonly killed pro-Chinese officials. But before the rebels and their Japanese advisers had decided what to do with the king—whether to send him to Japan or to Kanghwa Island—Yüan Shih-k'ai's troops rushed to the palace on appeal from Queen Min. The Chinese soldiers overwhelmed the rebels and the Japanese troops and rescued the king. The plot a failure, the Japanese minister burned his legation and escaped to a seaport,[13] while the chief Korean instigator, Kim, fled to Japan.

Tokyo lost no time in sending an expedition and a high emissary[14] to Korea, forcing the Korean government to pay $110,000 for the loss of lives

12. Takezoe Shinchirō.
13. Jinsen.
14. Inoue Kaoru.

and properties, send a letter of apology, and pay $20,000 for the recon-struction of the legation. In a concerted move, Itō Hirobumi went to Tientsin to confer with Li Hung-chang. Preoccupied with the French war, Li compromised readily and concluded a Tientsin Convention with him on April 18, 1884, stipulating that (1) China and Japan should withdraw their troops from Korea within four months; (2) neither country would train Korean troops but would jointly urge the Korean government to engage instructors of a third nationality; and (3) before dispatching troops to Korea in the future, the signatories should notify each other in advance, and after the restoration of order, withdraw the troops at once. This agreement virtually reduced Korea to a co-protectorate of China and Japan, eliminated China's claim to exclusive suzerainty, and con-firmed Japan's right to send troops. Li's concessions were to have grave consequences in the future.

International rivalry further confounded the situation. In 1885 Russia took ice-free Port Lazareff on the northeastern coast (lat. 39°N.), and the British retaliated by seizing Port Hamilton, an anchorage off the southern tip of Korea. Realizing the detrimental effect that Western in-fluence in Korea would have on her own interests, Japan adopted a new policy of encouraging China to strengthen her control, on the assumption that if China succeeded in curtailing foreign influences in Korea, Japan would have only her to deal with in the future. Oblivious to Japan's secret plans, Li Hung-chang proceeded to strengthen China's grip. He returned Taewongon to please the Koreans, and appointed Yüan Shih-k'ai Chinese Resident in Korea to direct all commercial and diplomatic af-fairs as well as to supervise the domestic administration. Young, energetic, and brash, Yüan quickly dominated the Korean court, the customs, the trade, and the telegraphic service. Expanding Chinese influence wherever and whenever possible, he rose to be the most powerful man in Korea from 1885 to 1893, all unaware that he was unwittingly serving Japan's interests. Neither he nor Li realized that this policy of exclusive control reversed their earlier policy of introducing Western influence to counter the Japanese. This period of Chinese supremacy in Korea coincided with the rapid economic and military growth in Japan, and by 1894 the Japanese had sufficiently modernized themselves to be ready to challenge China.

The incident that added fuel to the already tense situation was the as-sassination of Kim Ok-kyun, the pro-Japanese Korean leader of the 1884 coup who had fled to Japan. Repeated Korean requests to extradite him had been unsuccessful, but in March 1894 he was enticed—probably by one of Yüan's agents—to Shanghai, where he was assassinated by a Korean, son of a martyr of the 1884 coup. For want of a commercial steamship, the corpse was transported to Korea in a Chinese warship and there it was mutilated as a warning to traitors. The Japanese considered the incident a direct affront, and agitated for a war of chastisement. Foreign Minister Mutsu Munemitsu, however, explained in the Diet that the killing of one Korean by another in China did not legally concern Japan and could not constitute the *casus belli*. Nonetheless, Japanese feelings ran high, and secret societies such as the Genyōsha agitated for action. To create an excuse for sending troops, they encouraged the Tonghak rising in Korea.

The Tonghak Insurrection, 1894. The Tonghak movement was originally religious in nature, with some nationalistic cast but no political overtone; yet ultimately, because of official persecution, it took on political color. Its founder, Ch'oe Che-u (1824-64), was a frustrated scholar much like Hung Hsiu-ch'üan of the Taiping Revolution. Distressed by official oppression and the progress of Christianity at the expense of Buddhism and Confucianism, Ch'oe claimed, after years of meditation, to have received a "pill of immortality" and a commission to preach. The gospel he taught was supposedly a mixture of the quintessence of Buddhism, Confucianism, and Taoism, the three blending into a cult of "Eastern Learning" (*Tonghak*) as distinguished from Christianity, which was commonly dubbed the "Western Learning" (*Sohak*). Though Tonghak disciples emphasized "Eastern Learning," they also worshipped a divinity somewhat similar to that of the proscribed Catholics. The Korean government therefore banned the Tonghak as a heterodox sect intended to delude the minds of the people. In 1864 Ch'oe was arrested, given a trial, and decapitated. Although the cult went underground, it amassed some 100,000 secret adherents. Gradually, men with political ambitions also joined the organization. In 1892 the Tonghaks petitioned the government to lift the ban and clear the name of their founder, on the ground that the prohibition of Catholicism had been removed. The government not only did not comply, but ordered the dissolution of the sect.

Shortly afterwards, when a corrupt official who had embezzled public funds for a dam was attacked by a mob, the Tonghaks capitalized on the confusion to stage a rebellion. The Japanese secret society, Genyōsha, sent fifteen men to assist them. Unable to stem the tide of rebellion, the Korean court sent for help from Yüan. The Japanese minster, hoping to create an excuse for Japan to send troops, urged Yüan to take positive action against the rebels, giving the impression that Japan's sole interest was in safeguarding trade, without herself intending any military intervention. The Chinese minister in Tokyo also reported that the Japanese government was unlikely to start a war, as it had often been entangled in conflict with the Diet since the constitution came into effect in 1890. Li Hung-chang was therefore lulled into believing that Tokyo would not wage war, whereas in fact it was fully prepared to act the moment the Chinese moved their troops into Korea.

No sooner had the Chinese crushed the Tonghak uprising than 8,000 Japanese troops appeared in Korea. With the rebellion suppressed, the Japanese demanded reform of Korean internal administration. Li Hung-chang instructed the Korean government to stall the Japanese by declaring that reform might be carried out after the withdrawal of the Japanese troops.

THE OUTBREAK OF WAR

Determined to find a diplomatic solution, Li hoped to win Western sympathies and force Japan into a peace settlement. He had been assured by the Russian minister, Count Cassini, that St. Petersburg would intervene on China's behalf. However, the Russian government failed to act, having been warned by its minister in Tokyo that if Russia helped China, Britain might assist Japan. Li then turned to Britain for mediation. The latter suggested a simultaneous withdrawal of troops: the Chinese to the north and the Japanese to the south, leaving a neutral zone in the middle around the Korean capital. Tokyo rejected the proposal but assured the British that in the event of war the neutrality of Shanghai and British commercial interests in China would be respected. An American plea for peace also went unheeded, the Japanese being fully cognizant of the United States' weak posture in the Far East.

Li's diplomacy not only achieved nothing positive, but it delayed China's military preparations. Not until all hopes for a diplomatic settlement faded did he finally accede to Yüan's urgent request for reinforcement. Three British steamers were chartered to carry troops to Korea under the escort of three Chinese warships. The Japanese learned of this convoy through a bribe to a Chinese telegraphic clerk at Tientsin. On July 25, 1894, the Japanese navy sank the steamer *Kowshing* in the Korean Bay, drowning 950 Chinese soldiers. On August 1, China and Japan declared war on each other.

The war was, in effect, a significant contest between the two after a generation of modernization. On land the Japanese dealt a crushing defeat to Li's Huai army at P'yongyang, set up a puppet government under Taewongon, and declared Korea independent. At sea, the engagement was even more disastrous for China. Although the Chinese navy boasted 65 ships as compared with Japan's 32 and held eighth place to Japan's eleventh in the world, not all of China's fleets were mobilized.[15] Only Li's Peiyang fleet fought the Japanese, whereas the Nanyang fleet and the other two provincial squadrons[16] remained "neutral" for self-preservation. The Japanese mobilized 21 ships, nine of which were constructed after 1889, capable of 23 knots. The Peiyang fleet possessed 25 ships in 1888, when it was formally established; two of them were large ironclads of 7,000 tons, as compared with the largest 4,000-ton Japanese ships. However, the speed of the Chinese ships was only fifteen or sixteen knots. Adding to the debilitation of the Chinese navy, not a single ship had been added to the Peiyang fleet after 1888. In sum, the Chinese fleet was large, old, and slow, the Japanese, small, new, and fast.

The two fleets met on September 17, 1894, off the Yalu River in the Yellow Sea. Admiral Ting first adopted a formation of eleven ships in a wedge, with the two ironclads in front facing the twelve Japanese ships. The fighting had barely begun when Captain Liu of the flagship, who had studied in Britain and whom Admiral Ting relied upon, suddenly ordered a formation reverse into an inverted wedge, placing himself and the two ironclads in the rear, in the position safest from enemy attack. Additional confusion was created upon the first salvo from the flagship, which caused such a violent shock that the bridge collapsed, wounding Admiral Ting and his British adviser. And since Captain Liu was too terrified to fight, the flotilla was leaderless. The German adviser, C. von Hannecken, took over the command but was ineffectual because he was basically an army officer by training. After five hours of exchange, the Chinese had lost four ships and suffered casualties in excess of a thousand officers and men. The Japanese had lost but one ship.

The surviving seven Chinese ships retreated to Port Arthur for repair, and then on October 18 moved to the naval base at Weihaiwei. In November the Japanese occupied Dairen (Ta-lien) and Port Arthur from the landward side, rendering ineffectual the numerous cannon in the forts. Li had invested millions of taels in building up these naval bases but got

15. T. F. Tsiang, *Chung-kuo chin-tai shih ta-kang* (An outline of Chinese modern history), (Taipei, 1959), 139.
16. At Canton and Foochow.

no use out of them. At the time of their capture, the Port Arthur base which took sixteen years to construct had twenty-two forts and more than seventy Krupp guns, and the Dairen base which took six years to build had six forts and twenty-four Krupp guns. The fiasco was completed when the Japanese took Weihaiwei from the rear in February 1895, turning the guns in the forts on the Chinese ships in the harbor. Admiral Ting committed suicide, and his subordinates surrendered, turning over eleven ships to the Japanese.

The humiliating defeat on land and at sea after more than thirty years of Self-strengthening exposed Li to severe criticism and impeachment. His defense was that victory was impossible when only his Peiyang fleet and Huai army fought against the whole might of the Japanese nation. Be that as it may, Li was dismissed, disgraced, and deprived of the Yellow Jacket, a mark of imperial favor.

THE PEACE SETTLEMENT

Even before the total naval defeat, the court at Peking had initiated a peace move. In early November 1894, Prince Kung, reappointed head of the Tsungli Yamen, requested the American minister Denby to mediate, indicating that China was willing to pay an indemnity and recognize the independence of Korea. The Japanese government considered these two concessions insufficient but intimated its readiness to negotiate. By this time the Japanese army had taken Port Arthur and Dairen and crossed the Yalu River, threatening Manchuria and Liaotung. The court sent Chang Yin-huan, a minister of the Tsungli Yamen and vice-president of the Board of Revenue, on a peace mission to Japan, with the American ex-Secretary of State J. W. Foster as adviser. When Itō and Mutsu met with Chang at Hiroshima on February 1, 1895, they deliberately snubbed him, insisting that his full powers were insufficient to negotiate a settlement. They indicated a preference for someone more exalted, such as Prince Kung or Li Hung-chang. The Peiyang navy by this time had surrendered, and the Ch'ing court was desperate for peace. On February 13 it appointed Li envoy first class to Japan.

The peace terms presented by the Japanese government represented a composite demand of diverse circles. The army insisted on cession of the Liaotung peninsula, which would facilitate domination of Korea and Peking. The navy wanted Taiwan (Formosa) as a base for future advance to South Asia, as well as a lease on the Liaotung peninsula. The treasury asked for a large indemnity in the neighborhood of 200 million taels. The Progressive Party suggested, in view of the impending partition of China, that Japan take over Shantung, Kiangsu, Fukien, and Kwangtung provinces, while the Liberal Party urged the cession of Manchuria and Taiwan. The Japanese government synthesized these views into a ten-point proposal, stressing the independence of Korea, an indemnity, the cession of territory, and future commercial and navigational privileges.

At the opening of negotiations at Shimonoseki, Li urged the Japanese negotiators, Itō and Mutsu, to bear in mind the larger interest of Asia in the age of Western imperialism, and pleaded that China and Japan, with their common cultural and racial backgrounds, should not exploit each other. Li compared his age—73 *sui*—with Itō's 55 and Mutsu's 52, in an attempt to gain a psychological advantage over his opponents.[17] In the actual negotiations, however, he had a hard time inducing them to be lenient, particularly on the issue of the indemnity, which was set at 300 million taels. In this difficult situation, a "blessing in disguise" suddenly achieved what his diplomacy could not: returning from the conference one day, Li was shot by a Japanese fanatic. The bullet lodged below his left eye but was not fatal. The incident greatly embarrassed the Japanese government, which voluntarily declared an armistice. There was fear that Li might quit the peace talks and, capitalizing on his wound, obtain Western intervention on China's behalf. The Japanese emperor sent his personal doctor to treat Li's wound, and the Japanese newspapers changed their tone from criticism to eulogy of Li's accomplishments. On the morrow of the accident, Foreign Minister Mutsu went to see Li's son, an attaché in the delegation, and declared that "the misfortune of Li is also the fortune of the Great Ch'ing Empire. From now on peace terms will be more easily arranged, and the Sino Japanese war will be terminated."[18] In addition to the armistice, the Japanese government voluntarily reduced the indemnity to 200 million taels. When Li returned to the conference he pleaded for a further reduction of 50 million taels, but met with no success; he then "begged" for an abatement of 20 million, but still received no response. On April 17, 1895, the Treaty of Shimonoseki was signed. It provided for (1) recognition of Korean independence and termination of tribute to China; (2) an indemnity of 200 million taels to Japan; (3)

17. "Ma-kuan i-ho Chung-Jih t'an-hua lu" (Minutes of Sino-Japanese peace negotiations at Shimonoseki), opening section, in Ch'eng Yen-sheng (ed), *Chung-kuo nei-luan wai-huo li-shih ts'ung-shu* (A historical series on China's internal disorder and external trouble), (Shanghai, 1936), vol. 5.
18. Li Shou-k'ung, 464-65.

cession of Taiwan, the Pescadores, and the Liaotung peninsula; (4) the opening of Chungking, Soochow, Hangchow, and Sha-shih as ports; and (5) the right of Japanese nationals to open factories and engage in industries and manufacturing in China.

Back home the reaction was severely critical. Many Chinese scholars and officials accused Li and his son of selling out their country to preserve themselves. Chang Chih-tung, governor-general at Nanking, vigorously opposed the ratification of the treaty. On several occasions, hundreds of provincial graduates, gathering in Peking for the triennial metropolitan examinations, sent joint petitions to the court, urging rejection of the treaty, removal of the capital to the hinterland, and continuation of the fighting.[19] Despite all this display of anger, the court under Japanese pressure exchanged the ratifications on May 8, 1895.

The cession of Taiwan was met with strong resistance by the local populace. Taiwan, which had been made a province after the French war, had achieved considerable progress in modernization under its first governor[20] during 1885-91, and the Taiwanese now refused to cede their island to Japan. They declared independence on May 25, 1895, established a Republic of Taiwan, and offered the presidency to the incumbent governor.[21] On June 2, the Ch'ing court sent Li Ching-fang, son of Li Hung-chang, to Taiwan to turn over the island to Japan; large Japanese contingents also arrived to enforce the transfer. Finally, in October 1895 the local opposition was suppressed and the Republic of Taiwan went out of existence.

CAUSES OF THE CH'ING DEFEAT

In reappraising the preceding events, China's defeat appears inevitable for many reasons. First, Japan had become a modern state in which a nationalistic consciousness bonded the government and people into a unified body. The war was fought with the wholly consolidated might of the Japanese nation. In China, the state polity was still basically medieval, with the government and people forming separate entities. The war hardly affected the people at all; it was fought mostly by Li Hung-chang's Peiyang fleet and Huai army. Western observers pithily described the war as one between Li and Japan.

Second, there was no clear demarcation of authority, no unity of com-

19. They presented petitions seven times, the second on April 30 being the largest, involving 1,200 to 1,300 signatures.
20. Liu Ming-ch'uan.
21. T'ang Ching-sung.

mand, and no nationwide mobilization in China. Li Hung-chang had the responsibility for directing diplomatic and military affairs regarding Korea, but not the authority to decide policy matters or to control the ships and troops outside his Peiyang command and his Huai army. In foreign affairs, the Tsungli Yamen, the provincial authorities, and the irresponsible *ch'-ing-liu* officials, all holding different views, rendered the court indecisive and subjected Li to unwarranted pressures and criticism. In military affairs, he had no authority over the Nanyang and the two fleets at Canton and Foochow; nor could he command the provincial forces except through request to the throne. True, the poor showing of his Peiyang navy and Huai army was unforgivable after so many years of training and preparation, but there was much truth in Li's defense that victory was impossible when only his regional forces were pitted against the entire might of the Japanese empire.

Third, corruption at court and in the Peiyang command doomed the Chinese effort from the start. The dowager's misuse of the naval funds for the construction of the Summer Palace (*I-ho yüan*), her trust in the eunuchs, and the general degeneration of public morality predestined the defeat. For want of funds the British adviser's recommendation before the war that China purchase two fast ships went unheeded. Instead these two ships were purchased by Japan, and one of them, the *Yoshino*, established a splendid record in the naval battle.

Within the Peiyang command itself, corruption and irregularities were rampant. Li Hung-chang, himself not known for integrity and character, chose his subordinates on the basis of their personal loyalty and willingness to work rather than on their ability and uprightness. Many of his army and naval officers curried favor with the chief eunuch, Li Lien-ying, debasing themselves as his "disciples." They embezzled public funds to make presents to the eunuch, and he in turn protected their irregularities. The big ten-inch guns on the two ironclads, it was said, were allocated only three shells each, and the many smaller guns were assigned wrong size shot. The funds for the ammunition lined the pocket of the officer in charge of supply, none other than Li's son-in-law.[22] For all its outward brilliance—the newly painted ships and the neatly uniformed officers—the Peiyang was a comic-opera fleet good only for cruising the harbors, not fighting a modern war. Li knew its weakness only too well; hence he was reluctant to fight, relying instead on diplomacy to solve the Korean crisis.

Fourth, Li's diplomacy was limited by his obsession with the antiquated

22. Chang P'ei-lun.

policy of playing off the barbarians against one another (*i-i chih-i*). He allowed himself to be misled by Cassini into believing that the Russian government would intervene on China's behalf to force peace on Japan. When the promised intervention failed to materialize, Li desperately turned to Britain and the United States for mediation, neither of whom could effectively influence Japanese policy. Li's diplomacy was a complete failure because he did not understand the essentials of modern international politics, and because he overestimated his personal powers of persuasion. When he finally recognized the inefficacy of his diplomacy, much time had already been lost in making military arrangements.

All in all, the defeat was an irrefutable testimonial to the failure of the Self-strengthening Movement, already evidenced in the French war ten years earlier. The limited diplomatic, military, and technological modernization, without corresponding change in institutions and spirit, was incapable of revitalizing the country and transforming it into a modern state. China's loss seemed all but inevitable.

THE REPERCUSSIONS OF THE WAR

The defeat signaled the impending demise of the Ch'ing dynasty, and ushered in a period of accelerated foreign imperialism and domestic political movements. Among its more important repercussions were the following.

1. *Intensification of Imperialism.* The defeat exposed the decadence and helplessness of the Manchu dynasty and invited foreign powers to engage in a scramble for concessions (see next section). Foreign imperialists cut the China melon into leased territories and spheres of interest, within which they constructed railways, opened mines, established factories, operated banks, and ran all kinds of exploitive organizations. The intensification of imperialism plunged China ever deeper into a semi-colonial state, from which she was not freed until 1943.

2. *Oppression of Native Industries.* The right to establish factories and industries in China, won by Japan in the peace treaty, was extended to all treaty powers through the most-favored-nation clause. It enabled imperialists to manufacture locally and thus avoid customs duties and reduce transportation costs. Foreign investors and developers, with their vast capital, technical know-how, and privileged position, had a distinct ad-

vantage over the nascent Chinese industrialists and businessmen. Foreign economic imperialism inhibited the spontaneous growth of native capitalism and relegated Chinese industries to a position of subordination and vassalage.

3. *The Rise of Japan.* Japan replaced China as the leading state in East Asia. With Taiwan in the south and Korea in the north, Japan had secured a solid base for future advance in Southeast Asia and a convenient springboard to Manchuria. The war paved the way for her challenge to Russia in 1904, her rise to the great-power status, her future aggression in China, and her domination of Southeast Asia during World War II.

4. *New Political Movements in China.* The defeat demonstrated beyond doubt the inability of the Manchus to cope with the challenge of the times. Superficial modernization of the Self-strengthening type could not regenerate a rule deeply embedded in decadence. Furthermore, new crises of imperialism threatened the dismemberment of China. There was now a realization among thinking Chinese that China's salvation lay in a radical reform or even a revolution. The progressives advocated institutional reorganization after the fashion of Peter the Great and Emperor Meiji. The radicals demanded a revolution to replace the Manchu dynasty with a Chinese republic. These two currents constituted the main political movements in postwar China.

POSTWAR FOREIGN RELATIONS

The Triple Intervention. On April 23, 1895, barely six days after the signing of the Treaty of Shimonoseki, Russia, France, and Germany sent a joint note to Tokyo warning that the possession of the Liaotung peninsula by Japan would menace Peking, render illusory the independence of Korea, and threaten the general peace of the Far East. The instigator of this triple intervention was Russia, who felt threatened by Japan's acquisition of a foothold on the Asiatic mainland. In fact, the Russians themselves had cast covetous glances at the ice-free ports of Dairen and Port Arthur at the southern tip of Liaotung. Count Witte, Minister of Finance, openly stated that "it was imperative not to allow Japan to penetrate into the very heart of China and secure a footing in the Liaotung peninsula."[23] At the imperial conference of March 30, 1895, the

23. Abraham Yarmolinsky (tr. and ed.), *The Memoirs of Counte Witte* (New York, 1921), 83.

Russians decided to seek preservation of the status quo *ante bellum* in Liaotung; to advise Japan to desist from seizing it; and, if Japan should ignore this warning, to take whatever action necessary from the standpoint of Russia's national interest, including the bombardment of Japanese ports. To the outside world Russia was to announce a disclaimer of territorial designs in China.[24] France, a partner in the Dual Alliance, was committed to support Russia, and Germany, anxious to keep Russia occupied in the East so as to lessen her pressure in Europe, joined in the intervention. To give teeth to the admonition, the Russians recalled twenty-nine warships from the Chinese and Japanese harbors, declared Vladivostok a war zone, and gathered troops there. The Japanese consul and residents at Vladivostok were much alarmed by this sudden turn of events.

The possibility of a European intervention was very much in the air even before the final conclusion of the Sino-Japanese peace treaty. Itō and Mutsu urged that Japan refrain from territorial acquisitions on the Chinese mainland, but the military insisted that cession of land was necessary to vindicate the completeness of victory. In the end the Japanese high council included the demand on Liaotung in the peace terms. Now that the triple intervention had materialized, there were three alternatives before the Japanese: (1) to reject the warning at the risk of war; (2) to call an international conference on the Liaotung question; or (3) to accept the advice of the three powers. On April 24, 1895, the imperial conference decided on the second course of action, but when this information was relayed to the foreign minister Mutsu, who was absent because of sickness, he demurred for fear that the various Western powers might use the conference as an occasion to revise the other peace terms. To avoid complications, the Japanese government decided to return Liaotung to China at a price of 50 million taels, in addition to the original indemnity of 200 million taels. The three powers reduced the additional sum to 30 million taels, and on November 4, 1895, Li Hungchang and Hayashi, the Japanese minister in China, signed a formal agreement retroceding Liaotung.

The Russians became heroes in the eyes of the Chinese, and won further gratitude by offering loans to pay the Japanese indemnity. The first payment of 50 million taels was due within six months, and the second installment of a like sum in the following six months. The Ch'ing court, with an annual revenue of 89 million taels, was in no position to meet

24. *Ibid.*, 84.

these obligations except by contracting loans. For the first 50 million, plus the 30 million for the retrocession of Liaotung, Peking borrowed 400 million francs[25] from a Franco-Russian Banking Consortium[26] at 4 per cent interest. Count Witte, who arranged the loan, pledged Russia's resources as security. Later in 1896 and 1898, China twice borrowed from a British-German Consortium 16 million pounds sterling at 5 per cent and 4.5 per cent respectively.

The Sino-Russian Secret Alliance. Overwhelmed by the Russian tenderings of friendship, leading Chinese officials such as Chang Chih-tung and Liu K'un-i advocated an alliance with Russia as a safeguard against future Japanese and Western aggression. They won the support of Li Hung-chang, who, disappointed by the British failure to intervene on China's behalf during the war, more than ever considered an alliance with Russia as the cardinal principle of future Chinese diplomacy. Li had always been pro-Russian and anti-Japanese, as clearly indicated by his position during the great debate of 1874 and the Ili crisis in 1878-81. At length the empress dowager, too, fully sanctioned a Sino-Russian alliance.

On Russia's part, Count Witte welcomed closer relations with China in hopes of winning a concession to extend the Trans-Siberian Railway across Manchuria to Vladivostok, which, begun in 1891, had reached Transbaikalia. The question arose as to whether it should run to Vladivostok along the northern bank of the Amur River through some very difficult terrain, or whether it should cross over Manchuria at a saving of 514 *versts* (350 miles). Count Witte strongly favored the second alternative, to save time and money and to further his policy of *peaceful penetration* of China. However, Badmayev, the court physician who had great influence with the tsar, preferred an alternate route from Kiakhta to Peking. Count Kapnist, head of the Asiatic Department of the Foreign Office, feared that Witte's scheme would in effect mean Russian military occupation of Manchuria, which would certainly arouse opposition from other powers, and might even precipitate a partition of China. The Russian governor of the Amur province concurred with Kapnist. Nonetheless, Witte ultimately won over the tsar, who approved the idea of the shortest route between Russia and her Maritime Province. Cassini, Russian minister to China, was instructed to explain to Li Hung-chang that such a railway would facilitate Russian troop movement for the

25. About 100 million taels or 15,820,000 pounds sterling.
26. Including the Banque de Paris, Banque des Pays Bas, Crédit Lyonnais, and the Hotenger House.

defense of China. Some initial discussions apparently took place between the two, but no formal agreement was reached, despite the British *North China Daily News's* report of a "Cassini Convention."

The Russian desire for a railway concession and the Chinese desire for an alliance materialized at the coronation of Nicholas II in 1896. Peking had originally designated an official[27] who had gone to Russia earlier to attend the funeral of Alexander III, as the emissary for the coronation. Cassini quietly protested his low rank and lack of prestige, intimating that a dignitary with the rank of governor-general or a royal prince would be more appropriate to the occasion. The "governor-general" in question was of course Li Hung-chang, who had the prestige and rank to handle confidential matters. The tsar himself was said to have sent a telegram to the empress dowager assuring her that the appointment of Li would be most agreeable with him. So Li Hung-chang, who had been in disgrace after the war, was designated imperial commissioner first class and head of the Chinese congratulatory mission to Russia. At the grand old age of seventy-four *sui*, Li left for the West for the first time in his life, to participate in the coronation of the tsar and to visit the rulers of Britain, France, Germany, and the United States.

Though Li's appointment was requested by Russia, Witte had the "wit" to state in his *Memoirs* that "it seems fantastic that the first dignitary of China should be sent as an emissary to a foreign sovereign, and the unprecedented event caused a sensation."[28] So that Li could not visit other countries first, the tsar dispatched his confidant, Prince Ukhtomski, to "intercept" him at the Suez and to take him on the *Rossiya* to Odessa. "I . . . desired to prevent him [Li] from visiting any other European country before his arrival in Russia, for it was clear to me that while in Europe Li Hung-chang was bound to become the object of various intrigues on the part of the European statesmen."[29] At St. Petersburg Witte impressed upon Li that to uphold China's territorial integrity and render her armed assistance in case of emergency, Russia needed the shortest possible railway route from her European section to Vladivostok, across the northern section of Mongolia and Manchuria. Such a line, Witte assured his guest, would raise the productivity of the Chinese land it traversed and would not arouse Japanese opposition because it would serve to link Japan with Europe. Li raised some superficial arguments but

27. Wang Chih-ch'un.
28. Yarmolinsky, 85.
29. *Ibid.*, 87.

secretly welcomed the project. To the court at Peking he approvingly relayed the tsar's remark that such a route would benefit China and Russia alike in that it could block future British and Japanese advances. Witte and Li agreed on three principles:

1. China would grant Russia permission to construct a railway along a straight line from Chita to Vladivostok; the operation of the railway would be managed by a private organization called the Chinese Eastern Railway Corporation.
2. China would cede a strip of land sufficient for the building and operation of the railway; within the limit of the land the corporation should have complete authority of control, including the right of maintaining police. The railway might be redeemed by China after 36 years at 700 million rubles, but would pass free to her after 80 years.
3. China and Russia agreed to defend each other against any Japanese attack on China, Korea, or Russian Far Eastern possessions.

It was apparent that the Russian emphasis was on the first two conditions, and the Chinese, on the third.

The drafting of the treaty text was left to Foreign Minister Prince Lobanov-Rostovski, who inadvertently left out the words "par le Japon" (by Japan) in the clause dealing with the joint defense. Hence the altered version called for mutual defense against attack by any power rather by Japan alone. Such an omission would impose a disastrous burden on Russia, for she could not defend China against all powers, including France, who was a partner in the Dual Alliance. Upon Witte's urging, the tsar instructed the foreign minister to make the correction, but at the signing ceremony Witte discovered to his amazement that the change had not been made. Lobanov-Rostovski, striking his forehead, exclaimed, "I clearly forgot to tell my secretary to insert that paragraph in its formal wording." Tactfully he suggested to Li: "It is past noon. Let's take luncheon. We will sign the agreement afterwards."[30] Two secretaries then hurriedly recopied the text with the necessary changes, in time for the dignitaries to sign after the luncheon.

A rumor was circulated later that Li accepted a Russian bribe of $1.5 million, but Witte denied it. It appears that the bribery, even if a fact, was not decisive in Li's thinking, for he had come with the explicit secret

30. Yarmolinsky, 92-93.

mission of concluding a treaty of alliance. So proud was he of the policy of playing off the barbarians against one another—using Russia against Japan in this case—that he announced with satisfaction that the treaty would give China peace for twenty years.[31] But China was not to have peace for even two years.

The Scramble for Concessions. After the triple intervention, Germany asked the Ch'ing court for a naval base as a reward, on the ground that all other major powers had a base in the Far East: Britain in Hong Kong, France in Tongking, and Russia's winter harbor in Kiaochow, Shantung province. The Chinese rejected the request. Then, in 1897 when the kaiser visited Russia he asked the tsar whether he would object to German occupation of Kiaochow, an excellent naval base which Admiral Tirpitz had selected for acquisition. Finding himself in an awkward position to object, the tsar gave a vague assent, knowing that Russia herself preferred a naval base more to the north. The Germans then capitalized on the murder of two missionaries in Shantung, in November 1897, to seize Kiaochow and compel the Chinese government to lease it for 99 years, along with a concession to build two railways in Shantung. Encouraged by the German success, Russian Foreign Minister Muraviev proposed to occupy Port Arthur or Dairen—a scheme that won the tsar's approval over the protests of Witte, who argued the importance of honoring the pledge to respect Chinese territorial integrity, and of the naval minister, who preferred a base in Korea. In December 1897 the Russians took these two ports on Liaotung peninsula, under pretext of protecting China from the Germans. On January 1, 1898, when General A. K. Kuropatkin became Minister of War, he insisted on extending the occupation zone to the adjacent areas of these two ports as well. Russia then imposed an agreement on China in March, acquiring the right to lease Port Arthur and Dairen for 25 years and to construct a Southern Manchurian Railway from the two ports to the Chinese Eastern Railway, from which a further branch was to be constructed to Yingkow and the Yalu River. In this negotiation Witte later admitted having bribed the two Chinese negotiators, Li Hung-chang and Chang Yin-huan, with 500,-000 and 250,000 rubles apiece.[32] The Russians now appropriated the

31. T'ao-ch'i-yü-yin (ed.), "Li-fu-hsiang yu-li ko-kuo jih-chi" (A diary of State Minister Li's visit to the various countries), in Tso Shun-sheng (ed.), *Chung-kuo chin-pai-nien shih tzu-liao* (Materials relating to Chinese history of the last hundred years), supplementary volume, reprinted (Taipei, 1958), 387.
32. Yarmolinsky, 103.

Liaotung peninsula, which China had bought back from Japan three years earlier at 30 million taels.

With these precedents, the scramble for concessions raged like wild-fire. Not to fall behind the Germans and the Russians, the British leased Weihaiwei for 25 years and Kowloon (New Territories) for 99 years, in addition to securing a promise that China would not alienate the Yangtze valley to any other power, thus turning the area into a British sphere of influence. A similar commitment to nonalienation of the Fukien province was granted to Japan. The French leased Kwangchow Bay for 99 years and established a sphere of influence in Kwangtung-Kwangsi-Yunnan. Only the Italian demand for San-meng-wan in Chekiang province was rejected with impunity, on advice of the customs inspector-general, Robert Hart. The United States, then involved in the Spanish War and the Cuban rebellion, did not participate in this mad scramble, although her navy at one point did covet the Samsah Bay.

The cutting of the China melon threatened the partition of the Ch'ing empire. Indeed, the deepening foreign encroachment precipitated a reform movement domestically and the declaration of the Open Door Policy by the United States.

The Open Door Policy. Britain kept a sphere of special interests in China but she also wanted an open door for trade where other powers had special influence. Being a party to the scramble for concessions, she could hardly promote the idea of preventing the closing of other doors to British trade, which accounted for some 35 million pounds sterling out of a total of 55 million China trade in 1899. The British therefore turned to the United States, the only major power with a "clean" record. Sir Julian Pauncefote, the British minister in Washington, twice approached the Department of State, in March 1898 and January 1899, to suggest joint sponsorship of a movement for equal commercial opportunity in China. But he met with no success. The Americans, however, became more responsive after the Spanish War and the annexation of the Philippines. Meanwhile, the British kept promoting the Open Door idea. Lord Charles Beresford wrote *The Breakup of China* and toured the United States to advocate the cause. Another British Old China Hand, A. E. Hippisley, of the Chinese customs service, successfully impressed similar ideas upon his American friend, W. W. Rockhill, formerly minister in China and presently adviser to Secretary of State John Hay on Far Eastern affairs. On the basis of a Hippisley memorandum, Rockhill prepared a note embracing the idea of equal commercial opportunity in China, which Secretary Hay delivered to Britain, Germany, Russia, France, Italy, and Japan in September 1899. It contained three main points:

1. Within its sphere of interest or leasehold in China, a power would agree not to interfere with any treaty ports or the vested interest of other powers.
2. Within its sphere of interest or influence, no power would discriminate against nationals of other countries in matters of harbor dues or railway charges.
3. Within each sphere of foreign influence, the Chinese treaty tariff should apply and the Chinese government be allowed to collect customs duties.

None of the powers committed itself to this pronouncement, stating equivocally that its acceptance was contingent on that of others. Hay nevertheless declared on March 20, 1900, that their assent was "final and definite." Only Japan challenged the American interpretation. Later, during the Boxer Rebellion, when the activities of the powers appeared to threaten the Open Door principle, the United States made a second declaration on July 3, 1900, extending its scope to include the preservation of Chinese territorial and administrative entity. Being merely a statement of intention, it did not solicit an answer from the other powers.

The Open Door was a declaration of principles rather than a formal policy of the United States, which had neither the will nor the power to enforce it militarily. Strangely, the partition of China tapered off after the declaration, not so much because the imperialists respected the American call, but because they feared rivalry and conflict among themselves. The resultant equilibrium saved the Ch'ing empire from an immediate collapse.

FURTHER READING

Chang, Yin-lin 張蔭麟, "Chia-wu Chung-kuo hai-chün chan-chi k'ao" 甲午中國海軍戰績考(A study of the Chinese naval battle in 1894), *Tsing-hua hsüeh-pao*, 10:1 (Jan. 1935).
Ch'en, Jerome, *Yüan Shih-k'ai, 1859-1916* (Stanford, 1961), chapters 1-2.
Chun, Hae-jong, "Sino-Korean Tributary Relations in the Ch'ing Period" in John K. Fairbank (ed.), *The Chinese World Order: Traditional China's Foreign Relations* (Cambridge, Mass., 1968), 90-111.

Griswold, A. W., *The Far Eastern Policy of the United States* (New York, 1939).

Joseph, Philip, *Foreign Diplomacy in China, 1894-1900* (London, 1928).

Kennan, George, *American Diplomacy, 1900-1950* (Chicago, 1951).

Kim, C. I. Eugene, and Han-Kyo Kim, *Korea and the politics of Imperialism, 1876-1910* (Berkeley, 1967).

Langer, William, *The Diplomacy of Imperialism* (New York, 1950).

Limley, Harry J., "The 1895 Taiwan Republic," *The Journal of Asian Studies*, XXVII:4:739-62 (Aug. 1968).

Lin, T. C., "Li Hung-chang, His Korea Policies 1870-1885," *Chinese Social and Political Science Review*, 19:2:200-33 (1935).

"Ma-kuan i-ho Chung-Jih t'an-hua lu" 馬關議和中日談話錄 (Minutes of Sino-Japanese peace negotiations at Shimonoseki), in Ch'eng Yen-sheng 程演生 (ed.), *Chung-kuo nei-luan wai-huo li-shih ts'ung-shu* 中國內乱外禍歷史叢書 (A historical series on China's internal disorder and external trouble), (Shanghai, 1936), Vol. 5.

McCordock, R. Stanley, *British Far Eastern Policy, 1894-1900* (New York, 1931).

Mutsu, Munemitsu 陸奥宗光, *Kenkenroku* 蹇蹇錄 (Memoirs of Mutsu Munemitsu), (Tokyo, 1929).

Shao, Hsün-cheng 邵循正, *et al.* (eds.), *Chung-Jih chan-cheng* 中日戰爭 (The Sino-Japanese war), (Shanghai, 1956), 7 vols.

Spector, Stanley, *Li Hung-chang and the Huai Army* (Seattle, 1964).

T'ao-ch'i-yü-yin 桃谿漁隱 *et al.* (eds.), "Li-fu-hsiang yu-li ko-kuo jih-chi" 李傅相游歷各國日記 (A diary of State Minister Li's visit to the various countries), in Tso Shun-sheng 左舜生 (ed.), *Chung-kuo chin-pai-nien shih tzu-liao, hsü-pien* 中國近百年史資料續編 (Materials relating to Chinese history of the last hundred years), II, 387-415.

Tsiang, T. F., "Sino-Japanese Diplomatic Relations, 1870-1894," *Chinese Social and Political Science Review*, 17:1-106 (1933).

Varg, Paul A., *Open Door Diplomat: The Life of W. W. Rockhill*, Illinois Studies in the Social Sciences, 33:4 (Urbana, 1952).

Wang, Hsin-chung 王信忠, *Chung-Jih Chia-wu chan cheng chih wai-chiao pei-ching* 中日甲午戰爭之外交背境 (The diplomatic background of the Sino-Japanese war), (Peiping, 1937).

Wang, Yün-sheng 王芸生 (ed.), *Liu-shih nien-lai Chung-kuo yü Jih-pen* 六十年來中國與日本 (China and Japan during the last sixty years (1856-1916), II (Tientsin, 1932-33).

Wright, Mary C., "The Adaptability of Ch'ing Diplomacy: The Case of Korea," *The Journal of Asian Studies*, XVII:3:363-81 (May 1958).

Yao, Hsi-kuang 姚錫光, *Tung-fang ping-shih chi-lüeh* 東方兵事紀略 (A brief record of the war in the East).

Yarmolinsky, Abraham (tr. and ed.), *The Memoirs of Count Witte* (New York, 1921).

PART IV

Reform and Revolution

1898-1912

15

The Reform Movement of 1898

The frightful prospect of dismemberment precipitated a reform movement in China in 1898. The movement had actually been gathering momentum for ten years, for ever since China's defeat in the French war in 1885 the inadequacy of limited modernization had been obvious, and her defeat in the Japanese war in 1895 was irrefutable proof that the Self-strengthening Movement had failed. The need for a more extensive reform was recognized by scholars, officials, and even the emperor and the empress dowager, although they differed on the question of its nature, scope, and leadership. Li Hung-chang, the main figure in the Self-strengthening Movement, had gone into political eclipse; in his place rose Chang Chih-tung, the long-time (1889-94, 1896-1907) governor-general at Wuhan, and Weng T'ung-ho, the influential imperial tutor and president of the Board of Revenue (1886-98). Both advocated a conservative reform based on a limited administrative reorganization along with the adoption of Western methods to supplement the basic Chinese structure. A radical third force, advocating a drastic institutional change after the patterns of Peter the Great and Emperor Meiji, was led by the thinker-idealist K'ang Yu-wei. Emperor Kuang-hsü (1875-1908), first guided by Weng to his conservative reform, ultimately was won over by the dynamic K'ang. On the other hand, Empress Dowager Tz'u-hsi, who in principle was not opposed to a moderate reorganization, saw in the radical reform a threat to her own supremacy and threw her tremendous authority against it.

In this vortex of cross currents, one sees the power struggle between

423

the emperor and the dowager, the conflict between the conservatives and the progressives, the strife between the moderate reformers and the radicals, and the racial antipathy between the Manchus and the Chinese. The interplay of these forces was accentuated by the imminence of foreign partition of China. The Ch'ing empire in 1898 stood at a turning point in history: a successful reform might stave off the breakup, while failure could only foreshadow the extinction of the dynasty.

EARLY ADVOCATES OF REFORM AND
MISSIONARY INFLUENCE

The genesis of institutional reform may be traced to Feng Kuei-fen, whose *Protest from the Chiao-pin Studio* (*Chiao-pin-lu k'ang-i*) we have already briefly touched upon in Chapter 11. Feng argued that the new world which had been thrust upon China was drastically different from the world of ancient times, and that it behooved her to adopt the superior Western mathematics, physics, chemistry, and geography. She should initiate measures to reform her educational and examination systems, to abolish the eight-legged essay, to strengthen local political organizations, to encourage industrial manufacture, to reclaim virgin land, to open mines, and to improve agricultural tools. These farsighted views, first made after 1860, were too advanced for Feng's time. They were considered impracticable by Tseng Kuo-fan, and were only partially followed by Li Hung-chang when he established schools and translation bureaus and adopted Western military and technological devices in the Self-strengthening Movement.

Another advocate of progressive reform was Kuo Sung-tao, China's first minister to Britain and France (1876-78). His firsthand observation of the West resulted in an open, if unpopular, admission that Western countries had a distinctive history of their own of over 2,000 years and were in possession of illustrious political institutions and moral teachings. Deploring the limited scope of Self-strengthening, he praised the Japanese for sending students to Britain to study law and economics, and impressed upon Li Hung-chang the need to accept the Western educational system, political institutions, jurisprudence, and economics. These, rather than the military, Kuo argued, were the foundation of good government and a prosperous state. His plea went unheeded as Li insisted that having been entrusted with the country's defense he had no alternative but to stress the military aspect of modernization. If Kuo's progressive ideas were too liberal for Li, they were heresy in the eyes of Confucian moralists, who could not imagine any civilization unconnected with Confucius. To them Kuo was a betrayer of Chinese cultural heritage who rightfully deserved ostracism.

Among the nonofficials, Wang T'ao (1828-97) was remarkable for his progressive views. He had shown early sympathy toward the Taipings and had proffered them plans of taking Shanghai and dealing with the foreigners. Being suspect in the eye of the Ch'ing court, he escaped to Hong Kong in 1862 and became an editor of the foreign-sponsored *Hong Kong News*. Invited by James Legge to Scotland in 1867 to assist him in the monumental task of translating *The Chinese Classics*, Wang's two-year sojourn in Europe acquainted him with Western culture and institutions. Back in Hong Kong in 1870, he became editor of a newspaper (*Hsün-huan jih-pao*) and later contributed to the influential paper in Shanghai, the *Shen-pao*. From this vantage point Wang launched his campaign for reform. Like Kuo Sung-tao, he praised the Japanese imitation of Western institutions and urged his countrymen to alter their methods of civil service examinations, military training, education, and legal practice. He attacked corruption in the Ch'ing administration, the sinecure posts in government, and the *likin* tax. He proposed the opening of mines, the building of textile mills, the construction of steamers, railways, telegraph lines, and the development of a navy. He warned against leaning too much on the superficial, external mechanics of the West, whose strength he said lay in its law, justice, political system, popular election, and constitutional government. However, Wang was not a radical; he did not urge an outright Westernization of the age-old Chinese institutions, but a gradual grafting of useful Western elements onto the Chinese foundation.

After the Sino-Japanese War (1894-95) the idea of institutional reform caught on with scholars, publicists, writers, and officials. The more famous among them were Cheng Kuan-ying, the onetime compradore at the British firm of Butterfield and Swire Company, who had become a writer-modernizer and author of "Warnings to the Seemingly Prosperous Age" (*Sheng-shih wei-yen*), and Ho Ch'i, author of several works on the need for reform. They went so far as to urge the adoption of such foreign institutions as parliament and constitutional monarchy.

The general awakening to the need for reform was partially a result of missionary influence. Ever since the 1870's, a number of the more enlightened British and American Protestant missionaries had adopted the view that they should "secularize" their work and extend it beyond religious propagation to include an introduction to Western knowledge and culture. Whereas formerly the emphasis had been on "saving the heathen from the sufferings of hell," now the new concern was "to save the heathen from the hell of suffering in this world."[1] They established schools, gave public lectures, opened libraries and museums, and published newspapers and magazines—the last being a foreign privilege denied to the Chinese. The famous monthly *Wan-kuo kung-pao* (The Globe Magazine), published between 1875 and 1907 (except 1883-89) in Shanghai by Young J. Allen, devoted itself to "the extension of knowledge relating to geography, history, civilization, politics, religion, science, art, industry, and general progress of Western countries." By 1889 some 16,000 Chinese had studied at the mission schools.

With the establishment in 1887 in Shanghai of the *Kuang-hsüeh hui*, or Society for the Diffusion of Christian and General Knowledge among the Chinese (SDK), the missionaries reached out more effectively into the Chinese reading public and the upper class. Among the manifold activities in which the society engaged itself were an introduction of Western civilization through translations, promotion of the cause of reform, editorials on current topics, public addresses, and discussions conducted with scholars and officials. The leading members of the society, such as the Britishers Alexander Williamson and Timothy Richard, and the Americans Young J. Allen and W. A. P. Martin, all had a very good command of Chinese. In particular, Timothy Richard (1845-1919), secretary of the society since 1891 and its Peking representative in 1895, was dedicated to the cause of institutional reform. He published *New Views on Current Affairs* (*Shih-shih hsin-lun*), wrote on the works of Peter the Great and Emperor Meiji, and translated Robert MacKenzie's *The Nineteen Century: A History*. Through the missionary efforts, the mental horizons of Chinese intellectuals became broadened, and they developed a new respect for the foreigners. Timothy Richard was much sought after not only by prominent statesmen such as Prince Kung, Weng T'ung-ho, and Li Hung-chang, but also by such radical reformers as K'ang Yu-wei and Liang Ch'i-ch'ao. Many of K'ang's ideas on reform, in fact, came from the missionaries.[2]

1. Timothy Richard, *Forty-Five Years in China* (New York, 1916), 197.
2. K'ang admitted to a foreign interviewer: "I owe my conversion [to reform] chiefly to the writings of two missionaries, the Reverend Timothy Richard and the Reverend Doctor Young J. Allen." Cyrus H. Peake, *Nationalism and Education in Modern China* (New York, 1932), 15.

THE CONSERVATIVE REFORMERS: WENG AND CHANG

A powerful figure in Peking was Weng T'ung-ho (1830-1904), the imperial tutor who had emerged as an advocate of conservative reform. After the Japanese war, he and Chang Chih-tung had replaced Li Hung-chang as leaders of modernization, one in Peking and the other in the provinces. There was much in common in their family and educational backgrounds. Weng, the son of a grand secretary and winner of the first honor in the *chin-shih* examination of 1856, became a tutor to Emperor T'ung-chih and an expositor of classical and historical works to the two empress dowagers. In 1876 he was appointed tutor to the boy emperor Kuang-hsü, a post which he retained for twenty years and which enabled him to develop an intimate relationship with the ruler. Thus favorably placed, Weng was in a position to influence the emperor and to maintain good connections with the empress dowager, Tz'u-hsi. Deeply concerned with the future of the dynasty, which he saw was declining rapidly, and with the ever-deepening foreign encroachment which threatened the partition of China, Weng, a Confucian traditionalist, came to the reluctant conclusion that China could not survive without a reform. He was too clever a court politician not to see in the reform a chance to wrest the leadership of modernization from Li Hung-chang and Chang Chih-tung. To succeed in this venture, he knew that the support of both the emperor and the empress dowager was absolutely necessary. His every move hence was calculated to win their approval and to secure for himself the leadership in the movement. With his steep Confucian background and his eagerness to avoid irritating the conservative-minded dowager, Weng cautiously promoted a moderate reform, which would entail a limited administrative reorganization along with adoption of some Western "implements" in the Self-strengthening tradition. He was too proud a Confucianist, and too shrewd a politician, to admit that reform should go beyond that. In 1889 when the emperor assumed personal rule and the dowager formally retired to the Summer Palace, Weng presented to them copies of Feng Kuei-fen's *Protest from the Chiao-pin Studio* to promote the idea of conservative reform, but he made it clear that Chinese moral principles and ethical teachings must remain as the foundation of state, which needed to be supplemented, but by no means replaced, by Western learning. Drawn to the idea of reform, the emperor began to read Western translations in 1889 and to learn English in 1891 from two graduates of T'ung-wen kuan who were W. A. P. Martin's students.

Weng's rival, Chang Chih-tung, was also a moderate reformer, a thoroughbred Confucianist, and a superb scholar. He passed first in the *chü-jen* examinations in Chihli in 1852, and ranked third (*t'an-hua*) in the palace examinations for the *chin-shih* degree in 1863. Immersed in the Chinese cultural and ethical tradition, he was described by a missionary as "a Chinese to the backbone," to whom "there is no country like China, no people like the Chinese, and no religion to be compared with the Confucian."[3] Although he had initiated many projects of modernization in his jurisdiction, Chang never advocated the alteration of basic Chinese institutions and moral teachings. In fact, it was primarily to perpetuate the established institutions and way of life, rather than introduce progress, that he adopted foreign devices and implements, which he believed had made Western countries strong and wealthy.[4] Some administrative reorganization was necessary to raise efficiency, but the basic old order was not to be touched.

Chang wanted to save China by a renaissance of Confucianism, by education and industry, and by adoption of Western science and technical know-how. In his famous work, the *Exhortation to Learning* (*Ch'üan-hsüeh p'ien*), published in 1898, he impressed upon his countrymen the importance of "knowing" five things: (1) know the shame of having fallen behind Japan, Turkey, Siam, and Cuba; (2) know the fearful fate of Vietnam, Burma, Korea, Egypt, and Poland; (3) know the impossibility of improving the machines without first improving the "methods"; (4) know the essentials in Chinese and Western learning— the former being practical rather than antiquarian studies, and the latter being political systems rather than technology; and (5) know one's origin so as not to forget one's country when traveling abroad, not to ignore one's parents and relatives when becoming acquainted with foreign customs, and not to be so clever as to disregard the sages. The first two stressed the danger of foreign encroachment, the next two his approach to reform, and the last the importance of traditional morality. His message was essentially a reaffirmation of the superiority of China's moral tradition and the wisdom of supplementing, but not replacing, it with Western science and technology.

3. Hsiao Kung-ch'üan, "Weng T'ung-ho and the Reform Movement of 1898," *Tsinghua Journal of Chinese Studies*, New Series, 1:2:153 (April 1957).
4. Ch'en Ch'iu, "Wu-hsü cheng-pien shih fan-pien-fa jen-wu chih cheng-chih ssu-hsiang" (Political views of anti-reformers during the 1898 coup d'état), *Yen-ching hsüeh-pao*, 25:61 (June 1939).

Chang's idea of reviving Confucianism as the moral basis of state and adopting Western devices for practical use crystallized into a crisp slogan, "Chinese learning for the foundation (*t'i*), Western learning for application (*yung*)."[5] Here, Chang was actually manipulating rather than correctly interpreting the concepts of *t'i* (substance, principle) and *yung* (usefulness, application). Chinese and Western learning each had its own *t'i* and *yung*; a hybrid mixture as Chang had suggested could not endure, for the latter was bound to affect the former. Chang's formula, more clever than correct, was an effective shield against conservative attack; not even the die-hard could accuse him of disloyalty to Confucianism and Chinese heritage. Having established this unassailable position, Chang went on to argue for the need for change.

What was immutable, he said, was basic human relations and not laws and institutions; was the way of the sages and not machines and tools; was human mind and intention and not arts and crafts. There was no shame in learning from foreigners, for had not Confucius himself said that among three persons there must be one who could be his teacher? Chinese history itself was full of institutional changes: from feudal states to unified empire, from mercenary army to the *fu-ping* militia, from chariot warfare to cavalry and infantry warfare, from ancient script to modern script, and from barter trade to cash exchange. Reforms by Shang Yang (who died in 338 B.C.), Wang An-shih (A.D. 1021-86), and others in history were well-known, and even in the Ch'ing period innovations were not lacking. The early leaders relied on horsemen and archery when they were in Manchuria but shifted to cannon to suppress the Rebellion of the Three Feudatories. Emperor Ch'ien-lung (1736-95) partially modified the examination system, and Emperor Chia-ch'ing (1796-1820) created local militia outside the banner system and the Green Standard army. Other notable changes included the introduction of the *likin* (transit dues), the creation of the Yangtze naval force, the establishment of the Sinkiang province, the building of steamers, and the opening of telegraphic lines. All this showed that change could not be resisted. With this philosophy, reinforced by his powerful base at Wuhan, Chang challenged Weng T'ung-ho's leadership in a moderate reform.

The need for borrowing from the West, which appeared unavoidable, was artfully defended by many scholars and writers. They sought sanction from the past by dreaming up theories that Western science and culture actually had their origins in China. Ch'en Chih, in his noted work, *The Book of Utility* (*Yung-shu*), advanced the amusing thesis that

5. *Chung-hsüeh wei-t'i, Hsi-hsüeh wei-yung.*

during the disorder of the Ch'in period (221-206 B.C.) Chinese culture and institutions were transmitted to the Roman Empire via the Western Region (Sinkiang); that Moses' name was nothing but a corruption of the Chinese philosopher Mo-ti's, and that his exodus from Egypt was in fact Mo-ti's flight from China after his rejection by the Confucianists. Another scholar, Wang K'ai-yün of Hunan, went so far as to assert that Mo-ti was Jesus. Others insisted that the Christian ideas of heaven and hell originated in Buddhism, and that the modern Western institution of the republic might have evolved from the polity of the ancient Chou dynasty (1122-256 B.C.), which showed attributes of republicanism. These arguments for the Chinese origin of Western culture, though incredible to the point of absurdity, revealed the eagerness of the Chinese to explain away the disgrace of learning from the foreigners and so mollify the criticism of die-hard conservatives.

With the exception of the ultraconservatives, reform seemed to be the consensus of officials and scholars after 1895. As reactionary a figure as the Grand Secretary Hsü T'ung (1819-1900), a leader of the so-called "Northern Party" (*Pei-p'ai*) at court, conceded its usefulness and attempted to bring Chang Chih-tung to Peking to lead the movement. Weng T'ung-ho, a leader of the "Southern Party" (*Nan-p'ai*), successfully blocked the move to save the leadership for himself. To buttress his position, Weng sought out promising young scholars and officials far his junior in status and age to assist him, men who would not challenge his leadership. Among them was one K'ang Yu-wei, whom he brought to the attention of the emperor with the intention of making him his chief lieutenant in the moderate reform. But K'ang was of a very different breed than Weng had thought—he was, in fact, a radical reformer with a program of his own.

THE RADICAL REFORMERS: K'ANG AND LIANG

K'ang Yu-wei (1858-1927) was a most unusual man whose intellectual development swung dramatically from one extreme to the other. Born into a well-to-do scholarly family in Nan-hai, Kwangtung, he studied with his grandfather who was a famous teacher of Sung Neo-Confucianism (*Li-hsüeh*). K'ang was a child prodigy, composing essays in the classical style at the early age of seven *sui*. His devotion to the sages and his frequent citation of their teachings won him the sobriquet "The Sage Wei." At eighteen *sui*, he became a student of the great Cantonese Neo-Confucian scholar Chu Tz'u-ch'i, who stressed the political history of China and the importance of uniting scholarship with public affairs. K'ang sat at his feet for a number of years and gained a solid foundation of Neo-Confucianism.

After the death of his teacher, K'ang retired to a mountain[6] to meditate, hoping to develop a school of thought of his own. His intellectual background up to this point had been entirely traditional and free from Western influence. Emerging from the self-imposed seclusion after two years,[7] he went to Peking. On his return trip, he visited Shanghai (1882), as he had Hong Kong earlier. The orderliness and efficiency of the municipal governments in these British-dominated cities made a deep impression on him. If Western colonial administration could produce such good results, he wondered, how much more progressive must be the mother countries themselves! His interest in the West thus aroused, K'ang eagerly purchased and read all available translations of works put out by the Kiangnan Arsenal and missionary organizations, including the *Wan-kuo kung-pao*. Abruptly a totally new world was opened to him: he realized the backwardness of China and her dangerous position in the age of imperialism. He accepted the missionary view that progress as demonstrated by the Western nations was not only necessary but also desirable. Decisively he abandoned his plans to try for the civil service examinations in 1883, and turned his attention to new Western studies.[8]

In 1888, while yet a plebeian (i.e. without an official appointment), he attempted to present a memorial to the throne, in which he praised Japan's modernization along the lines of the Western powers, urged that China do likewise, and warned of the increasing threat of foreign encroachment. The Imperial College (*Kuo-tzu chien*), to which this memorial was submitted for transmittal to the throne, refused to forward it, suspecting its author to be insane. K'ang realized that to succeed in promoting reform he must (1) seize the intellectual leadership of the learned world, and (2) win over the emperor.

K'ang returned to Kwangtung to teach and write. His reputation as an unorthodox eccentric attracted young scholars, among whom was one Liang Ch'i-ch'ao (1873-1929), himself a child prodigy who attained the *chü-jen* degree at the age of seventeen *sui*. Liang was immediately impressed by K'ang and became his student. At the urging of his students,

6. Hsi-chiao shan.
7. Some accounts say four years.
8. Lo Jung-pang (ed.), *K'ang Yu-wei: A Biography and a Symposium* (Tucson, 1967), 38.

K'ang opened a school, the *Wan-mu ts'ao-t'ang* (The Grass Hut amid a Myriad of Trees) at Canton in 1891, in which he gave instruction in classical studies and promoted the idea of reform. Frequently he visited the library of the nearby Episcopal Mission to read books on representative government and constitutional monarchy.

The Modern Text Movement. K'ang's intellectual orientation by this time had undergone a radical change. Starting out as a Neo-Confucian scholar like many of his contemporaries, K'ang was now fired with the zeal for a Western-style political reform. The writings of Liao P'ing,[9] a proponent of the Modern Text school of classical learning, so impressed him with ideas useful to reform that he gave up all his past intellectual leanings. The Modern Text movement, he discovered, could be used as a vehicle to advance his cause.

"Modern Text" (*Chin-wen*) referred to the classics and their commentaries of the Ch'in (221-206 B.C.) and Han (202 B.C.-A.D. 220) periods, as opposed to the Ancient Text (*Ku-wen*) of earlier times. The book-burning of the First Emperor of Ch'in in 213 B.C. had supposedly destroyed all the ancient classics, and scholars of the succeeding dynasty, the Former Han, accepted classical texts written in the current script, the "seal characters," as authentic. These Modern Text scholars had dominated the intellectual world of the Former Han period, but toward the end of it a descendant of Confucius[10] claimed to have discovered, in the walls of his ancestral home, texts of the classics written in the ancient "tadpole characters." Although most scholars of the time doubted the authenticity of these Ancient Texts, one Liu Hsin (*ca.* 46 B.C.-A.D. 23) fought to establish them during the short-lived Hsin dynasty (A.D. 8-23) under the usurper Wang Mang. With the downfall of the Hsin dynasty and the restoration of the Han, now known as the Later Han (A.D. 25-220), the school of Ancient Texts declined. However, toward the end of the Later Han period, several great Ancient Text scholars appeared, including the master Cheng Hsüan (A.D. 127-200) who dominated the learned world. From then on, the Ancient Texts were ascendant at the expense of the Modern Texts.

The revival of antiquarian studies in the Ch'ing period and the concommitant interest in determining the authenticity of classical texts renewed the age-old issue of Ancient Texts versus Modern Texts. Several

9. Liao P'ing, *Chin-ku-hsüeh k'ao* (A study of Modern and Ancient Texts), (1886).
10. K'ung An-kuo.

famous scholars rose to promote the cause of Modern Texts. Chuang Ts'un-yü (1719-88) elucidated the "great principles hidden in esoteric language" of Modern Text scholars, and Liu Feng-lu (1776-1829) brought to light the meaning of some very unusual and bizarre expressions, which were characteristic of Modern Text scholars, such as the "Unfolding of the Three Epochs," "Going Through the Three Periods of Unity," and "Receiving Mandate to Reform Institutions." Wei Yüan (1794-1856) was another Modern Text scholar. A favorite subject on which the Ch'ing Modern Text scholars focused their attention was the *Kung-yang Commentary*, a lost subject for two thousand years.

K'ang Yu-wei determined to seize the leadership of the Modern Text movement, synthesize its key conceptions into works of his own, and invoke them to support his advocacy of institutional change. In 1891 he completed his first major book, A *Study of the Forged Classics of the Hsin Period* (*Hsin-hsüeh wei-ching k'ao*), in which he exposed as forgeries such classics as *The Rites of Chou*, the *Dispersed Rituals*, the *Tso Commentary*, and the *Mao Commentary on the Book of Odes*. Daringly K'ang argued: (1) the Ch'in book-burning did not impair the Six Classics; the Confucian texts had been transmitted intact to later generations; (2) consequently, there was no such thing as the Ancient Texts in the Former Han period; (3) the written character used at the time of Confucius was the same as that of the Ch'in and Han, namely the "seal character"; and (4) the so-called Ancient Texts were forged by Liu Hsin as part of a conspiracy to distort the Confucian "great principles hidden in esoteric language," with a view to helping Wang Mang usurp the Han throne.[11] Historical accuracy apart, K'ang's incisive argument, bold imagination, and piercing criticism struck the Ch'ing intellectual world like a hurricane. His attack on the Ancient Texts stimulated a spirit of doubt and pointed up the need for reappraising ancient books.

In 1897 his second book was completed, A *Study of Confucius on Institutional Reform* (*K'ung-tzu kai-chih k'ao*).[12] In it he boldly advanced the thesis that men in the past were mistaken to say that Confucius merely edited the Six Classics; he had, in fact, written them and had intended by them to promote institutional reform. Other philosophers of the Chou (1122-256 B.C.) and Ch'in (221-206 B.C.) had likewise advocated institutional reform—all of them, like the master, justifying their action on the pretext of imitating the past. They created an idealized

11. Liang Ch'i-ch'ao, *Intellectual Trends*, 92.
12. Often translated as *Confucius as a Reformer*.

golden past, irrespective of historical facts, to convince contemporary rulers of the wisdom of reform, as the ancient rulers Yao (2357-2256 B.C.) and Shun (2255-2206 B.C.) had done. By inference, K'ang in effect argued that since institutional reform had ben championed by the sage Confucius and other great philosophers of the past, it could scarcely be morally wrong. With this skilful twist, K'ang sought the sanction of the most honored master as a shield against the antireformers.

Certain cryptic ideas of the Modern Text School were fully exploited by K'ang to advance his cause. The conception of *T'ung san-t'ung,* or "Going through the Three Periods of Unity," he interpreted to mean that the three ancient great dynasties—Hsia (2205-1766 B.C.), Shang (1766-1122 B.C.), and Chou (1122-256 B.C.)—were quite distinct from each other; hence changes and reform were inherent in the very nature of history. Another expression, *Chang san-shih,* or "Unfolding of the Three Epochs," was interpreted by him to mean that the world progressed from "The Epoch of Disorder" (*Chü-luan shih*) to that of the "Rising Peace" (*Sheng-p'ing shih*) and ultimately to that of "Universal Peace" (*T'ai-p'ing shih*). In short, more changes, more progress. Actually, K'ang did not originate these ideas but borrowed them from Liao P'ing.[13] Nevertheless, he synthesized and elucidated the existing Modern Text ideas to strike the learned world with his unusual interpretations and to prove that changes and reforms were inevitable in human development. If his first book was a hurricane, the second was an earthquake. The literati were shocked by his unorthodox exposition: die-hard conservatives accused him of "deluding the world and deceiving the people," while correct Confucianists branded his interpretations "wild and foxy."[14] Be that as it may, K'ang's reputation soared as a leading proponent of the Modern Text school, although his second book was banned.

These two books were basically reinterpretations of ancient works, but another of K'ang's work, the *Ta-t'ung shu* (The book of universal commonwealth), completed earlier in 1887, was a creative piece of his own, very progressive in its contents. Many ideas in this book, however, were influenced by the ancient work, *The Evolution of Li* (*Li-yün*), which said in part:

13. Ku Chieh-kang, *Tang-tai Chung-kuo shih-hsüeh* (The study of Chinese history today), rev. ed., (Hong Kong, 1964), 42.
14. For all his unconventional views, K'ang remained within the framework of Confucian school; he was a Confucian revisionist rather than a traditionalist. See Hsiao Kung-chüan, "K'ang Yu-wei and Confucianism," *Monumenta Serica,* vol. XVIII (1957), 100, 200.

When the Grand Course was pursued, a public and common spirit ruled all under the sky . . . men did not love their parents only, nor treat as children only their own sons. A competent provision was secured for the aged till their death, employment for the able-bodied, and the means of growing up to the young. They showed kindness and compassion to widows, orphans, childless men, and those who were disabled by disease, so that they were all sufficiently maintained. Males had their proper work, and females had their homes. [They accumulated] articles [of value], disliking that they should be thrown away upon the ground, but not wishing to keep them for their own gratification. [They labored] with their strength, disliking that it should not be exerted, but not exerting it [only] with a view to their own advantage . . . This was [the period of] what we call the Grand Union [Universal Commonwealth].[15]

Inspired by these utopian ideas, K'ang envisaged an ideal world in which:

1. there should be no nations: the whole world should be divided into different regions under a single government;
2. the central and regional governments should be popularly elected;
3. there should be no family or clans but rather cohabitation of men and women for the duration of one year, after which everyone would change mates;
4. institutions for prenatal education should be established for pregnant women, and nurseries for babies;
5. children should go to school from kindergarten up according to age;
6. adults should be assigned by government to work in agriculture, industries, and other productive enterprises;
7. there should be hospitals for the sick and Old Folks Homes for the aged;
8. there should be public dormitories and dining halls for the enjoyment of all classes according to their working income;
9. there should be special rewards for inventors, discoverers, and those who serve with distinction in the establishments for prenatal education, the nurseries, the kindergartens, the hospitals, and the Old Folks homes;
10. the dead should be cremated and fertilizer factories erected in the neighborhood of the crematoria.[16]

15. James Legge, *The Sacred Books of China,* Part III, *The Li Ki* (Oxford, 1885), 364-66, with minor changes.
16. Liang Ch'i-ch'ao, 96-97.

This work of utopian socialism was shown to his students but kept from the public, as K'ang averred that the contemporary age was merely the disordered epoch, in which one could only speak of "Partial Security" (*Hsiao-k'ang*) and not "Universal Commonwealth" (*Ta-t'ung*). Students at the W*an-mu ts'ao-t'ang* were greatly excited by these new ideas and engaged in daily discussions of them.

K'ang's Drive for Recognition. K'ang had built up a resounding reputation for himself, but he still lacked the higher degrees that would qualify him for official appointment. His talented student Liang had already achieved the *chü-jen* degree in 1889, but K'ang did not win his until 1893. In 1895 the two of them went to Peking together for the triennial metropolitan examinations. It was a time of national humiliation, for Japan had defeated China and was dictating the peace at Shimonoseki. K'ang and Liang, in righteous anger, prepared a ten thousand-word memorial and gathered the signatures of 603 provincial graduates[17] to protest the peace treaty. The occasion, known as the *Kung-che shang-shu,* or public vehicles presenting a memorial—"public vehicle" being the nickname for the provincial graduates who had come to Peking by public transportation for the metropolitan examinations—was considered by some as the first "mass political movement" in Modern China. They urged the Ch'ing court (1) to reject the peace treaty; (2) to move the capital and continue the war; and (3) to initiate institutional reform. Pointedly they stated: "If the institutional reform had been undertaken earlier, there would have been no disaster today; if the institutional reform is undertaken now, it can avert future disaster; if not, the future disaster will be worse than the present one."[18] The Censorate, to whom this memorial was addressed, refused to present it to the throne because of its blunt language and emotional overtone.

K'ang's daring mobilization of the provincial graduates, his devastating views on the classics, and his advocacy of reform were highly irritating to the conservatives. At the metropolitan examinations Hsü T'ung, the chief examiner, was determined to flunk him. Since all the papers were anonymous, Hsü could only look for the one with an eccentric style and unorthodox views, for which K'ang was noted. When the examination results were announced, the paper which Hsü had rejected turned out to

17. Often incorrectly given as 1,200 or 1,300. See Liu Feng-han, *Yüan Shih-k'ai yü Wu-hsü cheng-pien* (Yüan Shih-k'ai and the *coup d'état* of 1898), (Taipei, 1964), 197.
18. Li Shou-k'ung, 591.

be Liang's, whereas K'ang's was a model of virtue in strict conformity with Confucian morality and Chinese traditionalism. Although K'ang and Liang had succeeded in fooling Hsü T'ung, at the palace examinations that followed, the examiner[19] deliberately discriminated against K'ang. Consequently, although he won the *chin-shih* degree, K'ang was not appointed to the coveted Hanlin Academy but to the Board of Public Works, the least of the Six Boards, as a "secondary secretary" (*chu-shih*). Too proud to take up the assignment, K'ang decided instead to concentrate on capturing the imperial attention through a barrage of memorials. Yet the mere position of a sixth-rank secretary did not qualify him to address the throne directly; he still had to request his Board, or some other office, to forward the memorials.[20]

K'ang's third memorial of May 29, 1895, suggesting methods of enriching the country, cultivating the people, educating students, and training the army, was forwarded by the Censorate to the throne on June 3. Impressed with the views expressed, the emperor ordered that copies be made for the empress dowager, the Grand Council, and the various provincial authorities. This marked the beginning of the imperial awareness of K'ang. However, his next memorial of June 30, 1895, suggesting the successive steps of reform and the opening of a parliament, was blocked by both the Censorate and the Board of Public Works.

K'ang and Liang now turned their attention to forming and participating in a number of "study societies" (*hsüeh-hui*) and newspapers. They joined the "Society for the Study of National Strengthening" (*Ch'iang-hsüeh hui*) in September 1895, other members including Sun Chia-nai, another imperial tutor and past president of several boards, Yüan Shih-k'ai, and several dozens of Britishers and Americans. The conservative reformers Weng T'ung-ho and Chang Chih-tung showed interest in the society, and Chang even made a contribution of 5,000 taels. The society sponsored lectures on reform every ten days, and engaged in a variety of other activities such as translation of Western and Japanese works, publication of newspapers, and establishment of libraries, museums, and an institute of politics. K'ang personally contributed funds toward the publication of a daily called the *Wan-kuo kung-pao*,[21] which had a circulation of 2,000 under the editorship of Liang. Many of the ideas in the paper relating to reform were borrowed from the publica-

19. Li Wen-t'ien.
20. His first two memorials, made in 1888 and 1895 as noted before, were not forwarded by the Imperial College and the Censorate to the throne.
21. Named after the missionary magazine as a tribute.

tions of the missionary organization *Kuang-hsüeh hui* (SDK). K'ang himself met with Timothy Richard while Liang offered to serve as his secretary, and there developed a degree of mutual support between SDK and the reformers' organization.

To extend the work of *Ch'iang-hsüeh hui*, K'ang went to Shanghai to establish a branch office, and secured Chang Chih-tung's blessing as well as a donation of 1,500 taels. Within a month, however, Chang withdrew his support when he found its publication, the *Ch'iang-hsüeh pao* (Journal of national strengthening), recorded dates not in the years of the reigning emperor but in those of Confucius. He quickly ordered its suspension and dissociated himself from the organization. Meanwhile, vehement accusation of *Ch'iang-hsüeh hui* as a subversive organization was made by die-hard conservatives, and on January 21, 1896, the court ordered it closed. The Peking *Ch'iang-hsüeh hui* had existed but four months, while the Shanghai branch had functioned barely a month. The undaunted members at Shanghai, however, used the unexpended 1,200 taels (from the original 1,500 donated by Chang) to launch a new weekly, *Current Affairs* (*Shih-wu pao*) in August 1896, to continue the cause of reform. Within a few months, its circulation rose to more than 10,000, while similar publications sprang up in other parts of the country. At Shanghai alone, as many as thirty newspapers and magazines were in circulation to promote reform, and at Tientsin in November 1897 there appeared the prestigious *Kuo-wen pao* (National review) under the editorship of Yen Fu (1854-1921), a famous graduate of the naval school of the Foochow Dockyard and a translator of Western works (see Chapter 17). Here he published his translation of Thomas Huxley's *Evolution and Ethics* to introduce the Darwinian ideas of struggle and the survival of the fittest. In Hunan province, the progressive governor Ch'en Pao-chen invited Liang to be the chief instructor in a newly established School of Current Affairs (*Shih-wu hsüeh-t'ang*) at Changsha. Liang's views on misgovernment, the need for reform, and popular sovereignty found full expression there. The progressives then established a China Reform Association to stimulate group discussion, and published The Hunan Daily (*Hsiang-pao*) and The Hunan Journal (*Hsiang hsüeh-pao*). The inland province of Hunan, long known for its conservatism, was transformed overnight into a progressive center.

As for K'ang himself, he traveled, lectured, and promoted the cause of reform in several provinces. Within three years, he had influenced the creation of many study societies, schools, and newspapers, most of which were in Hunan, Kiangsu, Kwangtung, and Peking.

The Rise of K'ang Yu-wei. The German lease of Kiaochow in 1897 and the subsequent scramble for concessions by other powers precipitated a new national crisis. The emperor tearfully told Prince Kung that he would not preside over the dismemberment of China and that unless he were given power to initiate reform he would abdicate. K'ang Yu-wei, on his part, hurried to Peking to present his fifth memorial, warning of the danger of partition and the pressing need for reform. He recommended that the emperor pursue three courses of action: (1) proclaim a national policy on reform after the fashion of Peter the Great and Emperor Meiji —"May your Highness adopt the heart of Peter the Great of Russia and the administration of Meiji of Japan!" (2) gather all the talents of the country to prepare for an institutional reorganization; and (3) allow provincial authorities to initiate institutional reform within their own jurisdictions. The memorial closed with a warning that any delay would invite further foreign encroachment and ultimate extinction of the dynasty. The president of the Board of Public Works refused to forward the memorial because of its bluntness; its contents, however, soon became common knowledge in Peking and Shanghai. Nonetheless, the memorial could not reach the throne. In disgust, K'ang thought of returning to the south but was persuaded to remain by Weng T'ung-ho, who, baffled by his own limited knowledge of foreign affairs and threatened by Chang Chih-tung's bid for leadership in the conservative reform, had secretly hoped to enlist K'ang as an aide in his own movement. Weng supported the recommendation of the Supervising Censor Kao Hsieh-tseng on January 11, 1898, that K'ang be granted an imperial audience, remarking to the emperor that K'ang's ability was a hundred times superior to his own and that it behooved the emperor to hear him (K'ang) on matters of reform. Emperor Kuang-hsu was then ready to grant K'ang an audience, but Prince Kung reminded him that court rules permitted no interviews for officials below the fourth civil rank. Reluctantly the emperor gave in, but ordered that K'ang be received by high officials at the Tsungli Yamen.

The celebrated interview, the first official airing of K'ang's views, took place on January 24, 1898. The highlights of the meetings, as given by K'ang himself, included the following exchanges:

> Jung-lu:[22] "The institutions of the ancestors cannot be changed."
> K'ang: "The institutions of the ancestors are used to govern the realm that had been theirs. Now we cannot preserve the realm of the ancestors; what is the use for their institutions? . . ."

22. Manchu general and a confidant of the dowager; president of the Board of War in 1895 and formerly commandant of the Peking Gendarmerie.

Liao Shou-heng, president of the Board of Punishment: "How should the institutions be reformed?"

K'ang: "We shall change the laws and regulations; the governmental system [*kuan-chih*] should be the first [to be reformed]."

Li Hung-chang: "Shall we, then, abolish all the Six Boards and throw away all the existing institutions and rules?"

K'ang: "The present is a time in which countries exist side by side; the world is no longer a unified one. The laws and governmental system [as they now exist in China] are institutions of a unified empire. It is these that have made China weak and will ruin her. Undoubtedly, they should be done away with. Even if we could not abolish them all at once, we should modify them as circumstances require. Only so can we carry out reform."[23]

The interview lasted until dusk. Jung-lu was the first to leave, apparently disgusted with what he had heard. Weng T'ung-ho, also present at the meeting and somewhat disturbed by K'ang's radical views, described him as "high-flown" and "very crazy."

When the report on the interview reached the emperor, he was eager to meet K'ang but was again blocked by Prince Kung. However, Kuang-hsü ordered on January 29 that K'ang be allowed to present memorials any time without obstruction or delay by court officials. K'ang's access to the ruler was thus assured. One of his earlier unforwarded memorials now reached the emperor, who was deeply moved by a blunt statement in it to the effect that without reform the sovereign might not even have the chance of becoming a commoner in the future, and might very well end up in the same pathetic way as the last emperor of the Ming dynasty who hanged himself. To the grand councillors the emperor remarked that only a man of complete devotion could have made such a straightforward statement at the risk of his life! Kuang-hsü's trust in K'ang rose steadily.

On January 29 K'ang presented his sixth memorial, in which he asked that the emperor decide on a national policy, select talents for public service, and create a "Bureau of Government Institutions" (*Chih-tu chü*) to assist in reform and to draft a constitution. In addition, twelve administrative bureaus, each resembling a European ministry, should be established: Jurisprudence, Finance, Education, Agriculture, Industry, Commerce, Railway, Postal Service, Mining, Cultural and International

23. Hsiao Kung-ch'üan, "Weng T'ung-ho," 175-76.

Exchange, Army, and Navy. In the provinces, a "Bureau of People's Affairs" (*Min-cheng chü*) should be created in each circuit, with branches in the districts. The director of the circuit bureau should have the equivalent status of the governor-general and governor, while the district branch officer should take charge of all administrative matters such as education, public health, agriculture, and police, leaving only lawsuits and revenue to the regular magistrate. Emperor Kuang-hsü, much impressed with these novel ideas, asked the princes and the ministers of the Tsungli Yamen to deliberate on them.

K'ang followed up with a seventh memorial in February 1898, repeating the suggestion that the emperor follow the examples of Peter the Great and Emperor Meiji. To acquaint the ruler with the reforms of foreign countries, K'ang presented his own works, "A Study of Meiji Reform" and "A Study of the Reform of Peter of Russia," as well as Timothy Richard's translation of "An Outline of New Western History" and other works on the reforms of the various countries. Reading these manuals daily, the emperor was more than ever determined to effect an institutional change.

Simultaneously with the barrage of memorials designed to persuade the emperor, K'ang strove to win public support. In April 1898, during the triennial metropolitan examinations at Peking, he organized a National Protection Society (*Pao-kuo hui*), which attracted several hundred provincial graduates and government officials. The society met three times and adopted the following objectives: (1) protect the people and religions of China; (2) protect the sovereignty and territory of China; (3) protect the independence of the Chinese race; (4) protect the continuation of Confucianism; (5) promote domestic institutional reform; (6) discuss foreign relations; and (7) promote the study of political economy. Branch "protection societies" quickly sprang up in the provinces. The conservatives attacked these organizations as subversive cliques and proposed investigations. The emperor simply remarked: "If these societies can protect our country, isn't it very good? Why should we investigate them?" However, most Manchu officials believed that the purpose of the National Protection Society was to protect China and not the Ch'ing dynasty. The vociferous conservative attack on the society resulted in poor attendance at its meetings.

On the death of Prince Kung on May 30, 1898, K'ang urged Weng T'ung-ho to forge ahead with reform at once. The latter, greatly annoyed by K'ang's fast-rising reputation and his growing influence with the emperor, now considered K'ang's dynamic personality and radical views a threat to his own position. Weng urged him to leave Peking to escape the conservative attack and impeachment, but K'ang was unconcerned, lest his departure encourage the ascendancy of the die-hard. On June 8 he presented his eighth memorial, followed by another shortly afterwards, requesting again that the emperor take the decisive step of proclaiming a national policy. On June 11, 1898, Emperor Kuang-hsü acceded to the request and issued the first reform decree, urging the princes, the officials, and the commoners alike to strive to learn the useful foreign knowledge without sacrificing the basic Chinese moral teachings. The Hanlin reader Hsü Chih-ching then recommended that the emperor receive K'ang in person. The audience took place on June 16. Some highlights of the five-hour interview, as given by Liang Ch-i-ch'ao, were as follows:

> After the emperor had asked about his [K'ang's] age and his qualifications, K'ang stated: "The four barbarians are all invading us and their attempted partition is gradually being carried out: China will soon perish."
>
> The emperor: "Today it is really imperative that we reform."
>
> K'ang: "It is not because in recent years we have not talked about reform, but because it was only a slight reform, not a complete one; we change the first thing and do not change the second, and then we have everything so confused as to incur failure, and eventually there will be no success."
>
>   "The prerequisites of reform are that all the laws and the political and social systems be changed and decided anew, before it can be called a reform. Now those who talk about reform only change some specific affairs, and do not reform the institutions."
>
> The emperor consented to K'ang's suggestions that a bureau be established to study the various systems, and stated: "Your reform program is very detailed."
>
> K'ang: "Your Majesty's sagacity has already noted it. Why not vigorously carry it through?"
>
> The emperor glanced outside the screen and then said, with a sigh, "What can I do with so much hindrance?"
>
> K'ang: "According to the authority which Your Majesty is now exercising to carry out the reforms, if he works on only the most important things, it will be sufficient to save China, even though

he cannot make a complete reform. Nevertheless, today most of the high ministers are very old and conservative, and they do not understand matters concerning foreign countries. If Your Majesty wishes to rely on them for reform it will be like climbing a tree to seek for fish."

After a long pause the emperor nodded and said, "You should withdraw and take a rest. . . . If you have something more to say you may prepare memorials to state your suggestions in detail and send them here."

As K'ang rose to leave, the emperor's eyes escorted him to the door. The palace attendants opined that there had never been an audience as long.[24]

On the same day, June 16, K'ang was appointed a secretary of the Tsungli Yamen. Three days later, he again presented a memorial, through the Yamen, requesting the adoption of a national policy on reform and the establishment of a bureau for governmental institutions. Completely won over by K'ang, the emperor ordered that hereafter he need not present memorials through any agency but should send them directly to the throne to save time. Furthermore, he asked for several of K'ang's works, "The Partition of Poland," "A Study of Reform in France," "A Study of Reform in Germany," and "A Study of Reform in Britain." Kuang-hsü was now fully convinced of the urgency of institutional change. At the age of forty, K'ang had captivated the emperor and become the leader of a radical reform.

THE "HUNDRED-DAY" REFORM

K'ang's views on reform, which had been evolved over a ten-year period prior to 1898, may be summarized as follows: The existing political institutions and administrative procedures of China, he believed, were designed at a time when she was a world in herself, free from involvement with Western powers. The primary consideration of the ruling dynasty then was to prevent domestic rebellion and uprising; hence the cumbersome system of checks and surveillance in central and local administrations and the impractical nature of the civil service examinations. Now that times had changed and internal security was no longer

24. Teng and Fairbank, *China's Response*, 177-79, with minor changes.

the sole concern of state, the old imperial system had become totally out-dated. The government must consider new problems of foreign relations and industrialization and modernize its structure accordingly. But to effect this basic change, the emperor must wrest power from the empress dowager, who in K'ang's view was the major obstacle to progress. As early as 1888, in his first memorial, K'ang had said, "The affairs of the empire remained in a sorry state as a result of the evil influences of eunuchs and palace maids." In his forth memorial of June 30, 1895, he again urged the emperor to tidy his administration and "make decisions according to his own sage wishes alone." The reforms of Peter the Great and Emperor Meiji were repeatedly cited as examples for Kuang-hsü; in particular, the Japanese experience was stressed as worthy of following in view of the geographical proximity and cultural and social affinity between China and Japan. In more concrete terms, K'ang proposed (1) revision of the ex-amination system and the legal code; (2) establishment of a govern-mental institution bureau and creation of twelve new bureaus to render useless the Grand Council, the Six Boards, and other existing offices; (3) establishment of bureaus of people's affairs in the circuits and branches in the districts as an embryonic form of local self-government; (4) crea-tion of a parliament in Peking; (5) establishment of a national assembly (*kuo-hui*); (6) adoption of a constitution and the principle of division of power between the executive, the legislative, and the judiciary. In short, K'ang envisaged a constitutional monarchy to replace the age-old "imperial Confucian" system.[25]

Such grandiose plans were far beyond the dream of the conservative reformers. Weng T'ung-ho was shocked beyond himself. Having lost to K'ang the leadership of reform and imperial patronage, Weng was even more distressed by the conservatives' attack on him for having introduced K'ang to the emperor. Weng therefore turned to block K'ang's work. On May 26, 1898, when the emperor asked him to gather together a set of K'ang's writings, Weng spoke derogatorily: "I do not associate with K'ang . . . this man's intentions are unpredictable." When the emperor asked why he had not mentioned this before, Weng replied: "Your servant discovered this recently upon reading his *Confucius as a Re-former*." The emperor could not understand Weng's sudden change of attitude and was deeply hurt by his contemptuous remarks about K'ang, for whom he, the emperor, had now developed a deep respect and fond-ness. The long, trusting, and affectionate relationship between Weng and

25. Hsiao Küng-ch'üan, "Weng T'ung-ho," 162-64.

his imperial pupil was discernibly strained. The emperor became receptive to the motion to dismiss him, engineered by K'ang's supporters to clear the way for their leader. They impeached Weng on charge of crimes ranging from accepting bribes to unconscionable behavior in the Board of Revenue, of which he was the long-time president. With the approval of the empress dowager, who hated Weng for having led the emperor astray and for having introduced K'ang to him, Weng was relieved of all official duties on June 15.

The emperor and K'ang now forged ahead in their bold program of reform. Kuang-hsü did not dare appoint K'ang to the all-important Grand Council for fear of the empress dowager, but he placed K'ang's assistants in several key positions: Liang Ch-i-ch'ao was given the sixth civil rank on July 3 to take charge of a translation bureau, and on September 5 four progressives—Yang Jui, Liu Kuang-ti, Lin Hsü, and T'an Ssu-t'ung —were given the fourth civil rank and made secretaries in the Grand Council. Two of them, Lin and T'an, were K'ang's students. These four secretaries became the link between the emperor and K'ang; they were the *de facto* executives of reform, drafting all important decrees and reading all important memorials relating to institutional changes, while the unsympathetic grand councillors were bypassed.

The spirit of the "New Deal" (*Hsin-cheng*) was manifested in the September 12, 1898, edict, which took the unprecedented and liberal view that the basic principles of government were the same in China as in the West and that reform was merely putting into effect those methods and principles that had proved sound, valid, and useful in the West:

> In revitalizing the various administrative departments our government adopts Western methods and principles. For, in a true sense, there is no difference between China and the West in setting up government for the sake of the people. Since, however, Westerners have studied [the science of government] more diligently (than we), their findings can be used to supplement our deficiencies. Scholars and officials of today whose purview does not go beyond China, [regard Westerners] as practically devoid of precepts or principles. They do not know that the science of government as it exists in Western countries has very rich and varied contents, and that its chief aim is to develop the people's knowledge and intelligence and to make their living commodious. The best part of that science is capable of bringing about improvements in human nature and the prolongation of human life.[26]

26. Hsiao Kung-ch'üan, "Weng T'ung-ho," 165.

For 103 days, from June 11 to September 20, some forty to fifty reform decrees were issued in rapid succession in the areas of education, government administration, industry, and international cultural exchange:

I. *Education.*
  A. Replacement of the eight-legged essay in the civil service examinations by essays on current affairs (June 23, 1898).
  B. Establishment of an Imperial University at Peking, (June 11, August 9).
  C. Establishment of modern schools in the provinces devoted to the pursuit of both Chinese and Western studies. Transformation of large private academies (*shu-yüan*) in the provincial capitals into colleges, of those in the prefectural capitals into high schools, and of those in the districts into elementary schools (July 10).
  D. Establishment of a school for the overseas subjects (August 6).
  E. Creation of a medical school under the Imperial University (September 8).
  F. Publication of an official newspaper (July 26).
  G. Opening of a special examination in political economy (July 13).
II. *Political Administration.*
  A. Abolition of sinecure and unnecessary offices, including:
    1. The Supervisorate of Imperial Instruction, the Office of Transmission, the Banqueting Court, the Court of State Ceremonial, the Imperial Stud, the Court of Sacrificial Worship, and the Court of Judicature and Revision.
    2. The governorships of Hupeh, Kwangtung, and Yunnan.
    3. The director-generalship of the Yellow River, the circuit intendants for grain transport, and the salt intendants. (August 30).
  B. Appointment of the progressives in government (September 5).
  C. Improvement in administrative efficiency by eliminating delays and by developing a new, simplified administrative procedure (June 26).
  D. Encouragement of suggestions from private citizens, to be forwarded by government offices on the day they are received (September 11).
  E. Permission for the Manchus to engage in trade (September 14).

III. *Industry*.
  A. Promotion of railway construction (June 25).
  B. Promotion of agricultural, industrial, and commercial developments (June 20).
  C. Encouragement of invention (July 5).
  D. Beautification of the Capital (September 5).
IV. *Others*.
  A. Tour of foreign countries by high officials (June 12).
  B. Protection of missionaries (June 12).
  C. Improvement and simplification of legal codes (July 29).
  D. Preparation of a budget (September 16).

Although Emperor Kuang-hsü and K'ang Yu-wei vigorously pushed the reform program, it was boycotted by most of the high officials in the central and provincial administrations. The abolition of the eight-legged essay met with strong opposition from the Board of Rites, which was in charge of the civil service examinations. The Tsungli Yamen, though more liberal, frowned upon the proposal of twelve new bureaus, and when ordered by the emperor to deliberate on it in conjunction with the Grand Council, they jointly rejected it. The exasperated ruler ordered them to re-examine it. It was only then that they approved a few minor points, but they did not change their attitude on the substance. As to the provincial authorities, all but the governor of Hunan, Ch'en Pao-chen, ignored or delayed the orders for reform. These central and local officials dared to challenge or disregard the emperor's orders in full knowledge of the fact that the real power of state was not in his hands but in those of the empress dowager, who was ill-disposed toward the reform.

THE EMPRESS DOWAGER AND THE COUP D'ÉTAT

Though in retirement at the Summer Palace since 1889, the Empress Dowager Tz'u-hsi still held the reins of government tightly. She had trained the emperor since his childhood to respect and fear her, and she saw to it that he reported to her on all important issues and all appointments above the second civil rank. No important decisions or appointments could be made without her approval. So conscious was she of her ultimate power that she once proudly remarked that her authority was greater than that of Queen Victoria. She could not tolerate any move —be it conservative or radical—to undermine her supreme power.

In fairness it must be recognized that she was not opposed to reform per se. She had been a supporter of the Self-strengthening Movement and had been favorably impressed with Feng Kuei-fen's *Protest from the Chiao-pin Studio*. It was only with her approval that Weng T'ung-ho introduced the idea of reform to the emperor, and she herself had stated that reform was her wish. The emperor launched the "New Deal" with her knowledge and kept her informed of all important measures during the early period of reform.

But the dowager was a conservative person, who favored accepting some foreign methods and devices to supplement the indigenous institutions, but not at the expense of Chinese cultural heritage, basic government structure, and traditional values. Any radical change in the political and social systems that affected the precepts of the Confucian ethical code, particularly the concept of filial piety, on which her position and authority rested, was a threat. She therefore warned against burning the "ancestral tablets," rash action, and imitating Japan—the last was simply too humiliating.[27] A conservative reform such as advocated by Weng T'ung-ho or Chang Chih-tung would be more to her taste, and the latter's attractive slogan, "Chinese learning for foundation, Western learning for practical application," suited her mentality. At the outset of the "Hundred-Day" Reform, she reportedly told the emperor: "So long as you keep the ancestral tablets and do not burn them, and so long as you do not cut off your queue, I shall not interfere."[28] In short, she would accept a moderate reorganization that did not upset the basic institutions or threaten her authority.

However, as the reform progressed, the dowager became alarmed by the abolition of the eight-legged essays, by the elimination of the sinecure offices and the three governorships, and by a host of other radical changes that swept away the ancestral institutions and traditional procedure in administration. She scolded the emperor for breaking the ancestral institutions, whereupon the latter rebutted: "If our ancestors were alive today, the institutions would have been different. I would rather break the institutions of the ancestors than lose their people and

27. Upon learning that the emperor was contemplating inviting the visiting Japanese statesman, Itō Hirobumi, to be his chief adviser in reform, the dowager became fearful lest the experienced and able Japanese turn the "New Deal" into a success and liberate the emperor from her control. She therefore insisted on sitting behind a hidden screen during the emperor's audience with Itō. Thus inhibited, the emperor could not discuss matters of substance but merely exchanged formalities with the visitor. See Hsiao I-shan, IV, 2,122-23.

28. Hsiao Kung-ch'üan, "Weng T'ung-ho," 142-43, 145.

their land." Intuitively she came to regard the reform as a concealed scheme of wresting power from her, which indeed was just what K'ang and the progressives intended it to be. The issue of reform now became a power struggle between the emperor and the empress dowager, and the conflict was sharpened after the death in June 1896 of the emperor's mother, the dowager's sister, who had served as a cushion between the two. With the dismissal in June 1898 of Weng T'ung-ho, who had attempted to reconcile the two, any hope of compromise was shattered. The dowager was determined to teach the emperor a lesson, and in this she was influenced by the chief eunuch, Li Lien-ying, whose corrupt practice at the inner palace would not be tolerated by the progressives.

It was generally accepted that Tz'u-hsi was supported by a *hou-tang* (the dowager's faction), composed of conservatives including Jung-lu, now governor general of Chihli who was in charge of the Peiyang forces, and Hsü T'ung, the arch reactionary grand secretary and a leader of the so-called "Northern Party" at court. Kuang-hsü, on the other hand, had the support of some less conservative elements who formed a *ti-tang* (the emperor's faction), including Ch'ang ling, a vice-president of the Board of Revenue, and Weng T'ung-ho, a leader of the "Southern Party." Radical reformers such as K'ang and Liang also rallied to the emperor's cause, though they were not "inside" members of the *ti-tang*. It was they who promoted the idea that the emperor as the legitimate source of power should exercise all necessary authority to carry out the reform and wrest control from the empress dowager.

The clash between the progressive and the conservative forces came to a head in August 1898. It was touched off by an incident involving the Board of Rites, which refused to present a memorial by its secretary, Wang Chao, who suggested that the emperor take a trip abroad. On September 1, the emperor, reputedly on K'ang's recommendation, dismissed the presidents and vice-presidents of the Board, commended Wang for his courage, and rewarded him with a button of the third civil rank. The wife of the ousted Manchu president of the Board tearfully complained to the dowager that all Manchus were in danger of dismissal. When it became known shortly afterwards that Li Hung-chang was relieved of his duties at the Tsungli Yamen (September 7), old and conservative officials became concerned about their future. Along with eunuchs and officials of the Imperial Household, they begged the dowager to stop the emperor's nonsense and take over the administration herself. When she declined to act, they went to see Jung-lu at Tientsin and hatched a plot, whereby the dowager was given a fabricated story that the emperor had secretly dispatched eunuchs to foreign legations to seek their support in eliminating her. The dowager fell into the trap. With the support of Jung-lu, she instigated a censor to request that she and the emperor review troops at Tientsin in October, at which time Jung-lu and his armed forces were to stage a *coup d'état* to depose Kuang-hsü.[29] The emperor vowed that he would not go to the review.

Rumor was rife in Peking that the emperor would soon be deposed. K'ang suggested that the emperor establish a new capital at Shanghai, cut his queue, change his attire, and adopt a different reign title to mark a new start. Plans were also made to approach Yüan Shih-k'ai, Jung-lu's subordinate who was training a new army of 7,000 men near Tientsin and who had previously shown sympathy toward reform and the *Ch'iang-hsüeh hui*. On September 14 Yüan arrived in Peking, and two days later was received by the emperor, who praised him for his accomplishments in army-training and sponsorship of new schools, and conferred on him the title of expectant vice-president, with a hint that hereafter he could act independently of Jung-lu.

On September 18 K'ang received an urgent message from the ruler to the effect that he had incurred the wrath of the dowager, that he might not keep the throne, and that the reformers should devise means to rescue him from the predicament:

> In view of the present difficult situation, I have found that only re-forms can save China, and that reforms can only be achieved through the discharge of the conservative and ignorant ministers and the ap-pointment of the intelligent and brave scholars. The empress dowager did not think so. Many times I have tried to persuade her, but she became angrier than ever. Now that I may not be able to keep the throne, you K'ang Yu-wei, Yang Jui, Lin Hsü, T'an Ssu-t'ung, and Liu Kuang-ti should secretly and quickly devise some safe measure to save me. In extreme worry and anxiety but with earnest hope, I am, The Emperor.[30]

On the same day, Jung-lu transferred troops to Tientsin and Peking, and ordered Yüan to return. Yüan temporized with a reply that he was

29. A recent study suggests that the story of deposing the emperor was fabricated by K'ang's party to discredit the conservatives. See Liu Feng-han, 169.
30. A recent study suggests that this decree, too, was fabricated by K'ang's party. See Liu Feng-han, 169.

still awaiting an audience with the emperor. Sensing the urgency of the situation, the reformers sent T'an Ssu-t'ung to see Yüan that night (September 18), urging him to protect the emperor at the forthcoming review. T'an prevailed upon Yüan (1) to besiege the Summer Palace, and (2) to kill Jung-lu, while he himself (T'an) would undertake to send assassins to dispose of the "Old Fogey" (i.e. dowager). Yüan tactfully parried any commitment, cautioning against hasty action, and stalled T'an with a vague suggestion that during the forthcoming review at Tientsin the emperor should hurry to his camp and give the order to kill Jung-lu.[31] When T'an informed K'ang of what transpired, it was clear that Yüan would not cooperate. K'ang decided to flee the capital.

On September 20, during an audience with Yüan, the emperor appears to have given him a very secret decree appointing him governor-general of Chihli after he had completed his mission. At three o'clock in the afternoon Yüan returned to Tientsin and unfolded the whole plot to Jung-lu, who quickly took the five-o'clock train for Peking.[32] Fearing that any delay might cause complication, the dowager's party advanced the date of the coup. On September 21, she raided the emperor's palace and intercepted all reform documents. Angrily she scolded him: "I brought you up for more than twenty years, and now you have listened to some small men to plot against me!" Too scared to reply, the emperor paused for a long while before uttering: "I have no such intention." Contemptuously she said: "Crazy boy! If I were done away with today, where would you be tomorrow?"[33] On that very day, September 21, she announced publicly that a serious illness had incapacitated the emperor, making it imperative that she take over the administration. For the third time in her life the dowager returned to administer state affairs behind a bamboo curtain, while the emperor was put under detention on a small island in the Imperial Garden west of the palace. The reform came to an abrupt end after 103 days.

Orders were quickly issued to arrest K'ang and the reformers. K'ang had already left Peking a day earlier, taking an English steamer from

---

31. Yüan later published his diary to whitewash himself, saying that he was too stunned to agree to T'an's suggestion of sending troops to besiege the Summer Palace and kill Jung-lu; that he temporized with T'an because the latter was a new dignitary and had come with a "protruding object" in his pocket, i.e. a pistol. Yüan implied that whatever promise he gave was exacted under duress. See Yüan Shih-k'ai, *Wu-hsü jih-chi* (My diary of 1898), (1909, 1922).
32. Liu Feng-han, 152, 172, 174-75.
33. Li Shou-k'ung, 564-65.

Taku to Shanghai. When the ship stopped at Chefoo on September 21, K'ang, still uninformed of the coup, went ashore for a walk and purchased some colored pebbles for which the place was famous. When the ship reached Shanghai on September 24, the local circuit intendant had received orders from Peking to arrest him. Meanwhile, the British government had instructed its consul at Shanghai to rescue K'ang. Under the protection of a British warship, he reached Hong Kong safely on September 29. From there he sailed for Japan, after having been assured of protection by the Tokyo government.[34] Liang Ch'i-ch'ao fled to the Japanese legation in Peking and with its help also managed to escape to Japan. T'an Ssu-t'ung, who could have fled, offered to be a martyr, declaring that since time immemorial no revolution had succeeded without bloodshed. The four reformers at the Grand Council, appointed only sixteen days earlier, as well as the censor Yang Shen-hsiu, and K'ang's younger brother K'ang Kuang-jen were all summarily executed without a trial. They were collectively known as the "Six Gentlemen" or "Six Martyrs" (*Liu chüntzu*). The progressive governor of Hunan, Ch'en Pao-chen, who recommended the appointment of the four reformers to the Grand Council, and Weng T'ung-ho, who had already been dismissed for having introduced K'ang to the emperor, were permanently disqualified for official appointments. A total of twenty-two reformers were arrested, imprisoned, dismissed, banished, and stripped of their properties. K'ang's writings were banned.

Most of the reform measures were reversed. The seven sinecure offices and three governorships abolished during the "Hundred-Day" Reform were reinstated; so was the eight-legged essay. The government press was closed; formation of societies was prohibited; and newspaper publishers and editors in Shanghai, Hankow, and Tientsin were ordered arrested. Private citizens were forbidden to submit memorials on state affairs.

However, there was to some degree a continuation of moderate reform. The Imperial University at Peking and the colleges at provincial capitals

34. On October 1, 1898, K'ang asked the Japanese consul in Hong Kong, Ueno, to inquire of his government whether he would be welcomed and protected in Japan. Premier Ōkuma cabled Ueno on October 9: "Inform K'ang that he will receive proper protection in Japan." Ueno in addition presented K'ang with the passage fare of 350 *yen*. See Teshirogi Kōsuke, "Bojutsu yori kōshi ni itaru kakumeiha to hempōha no kōshō—tōji no Nisshin kankei no ichi dammen" (The negotiations between the revolutionary party and the reform party from 1898 to 1900—an aspect of the then Japanese-Ch'ing relations), *Kindai Chūgoku kenkyū* (Studies on Modern China), Toyo Bunko, 7:175-76 (1966).

were allowed to continue, while the high schools and elementary schools at the prefectural and district levels could also operate if they suited local conditions. Provincial authorities were instructed to abolish or amalgamate superfluous offices and dismiss sinecure appointees. Some associates of Weng T'ung-ho were retained in important positions: Sun Chia-nai, president of the Board of Civil Office, was made associate grand secretary and put in charge of the Imperial University, and Wang Wen-shao, formerly governor-general of Chihli, was made a grand councillor, president of the Board of Revenue, and concurrently a minister of the Tsungli Yamen. Feng Kuei-fen's *Protest from the Chiao-pin Studio* was reprinted to spread the idea of a conservative, limited reform. The empress dowager made it clear that reform itself was not bad but that K'ang Yu-wei had carried it out badly.

Since the emperor had promoted a radical reform in total disregard of ancestral institutions, had relied on suspicious characters, and had attempted to wrest power from her, he must pay for his folly. Tz'u-hsi announced to the country that he was very sick and would appreciate recommendation of good doctors from the four corners of the empire. There was widespread speculation that the emperor would soon be done away with. Foreign diplomats in Peking warned that any untoward and underhanded incident involving the emperor would bring about an intervention. The British minister MacDonald declared: "Should the emperor die at this juncture of affairs, the effect produced among Western nations would be most disastrous to China." Under foreign pressure, the court admitted a French doctor to the emperor, and it was on his testimony that foreigners believed that the emperor was still alive. Still bent on revenge, the dowager solicited views from provincial authorities as to the advisability of deposing the emperor. Governor-general Liu K'un-i at Nanking vigorously opposed the idea with an incisive statement: "The relationship between the emperor and his ministers has already been fixed, while the mouths in and out of China cannot be easily silenced." Though frustrated, the dowager was undaunted. Another attempt at deposing the emperor was made in the following winter (1899) when, against all dynastic practices, she chose an heir apparent[35] for him. There was renewed fear for Kuang-hsü's life. Foreign diplomats boycotted her invitation to celebrate the choice, while 1,200 social leaders at Shanghai cabled the Tsungli Yamen to demand the protection of the emperor. All this, of course, greatly aggravated the Imperial Woman.

35. P'u-ch'ün.

CAUSES AND EFECTS OF THE FAILURE OF THE REFORM

Among the principal causes for the failure of the reform were the inexperience of the reformers and their ill-considered strategy, the reluctance of the empress dowager to give up power, and the powerful conservative opposition.

The Reformers' Inexperience. In 1898 K'ang Yu-wei was only forty and his chief supporter Liang Ch'i-ch'ao twenty-five, both without previous experience in government service. Neither had been abroad before the reform, and neither had more than a superficial understanding of Western culture and institutions. Their knowledge of the West was limited to what they read in the missionary publications and what they observed in the colonial administrations in Hong Kong and Shanghai. Small wonder that Chang Chih-tung ridiculed them for not having a real grasp of Western learning and institutions.

K'ang, in particular, was an idealist and philosopher rather than a practical statesman. He had very little knowledge of the reality of power politics and no power base from which to operate. He was able to win over the emperor as the legal source of power, but he ignored the obvious fact that the real power of state rested with the dowager. Impatient to achieve quick results, he hardly considered the effects of the reform decrees on others. Naively he believed that with the support of the emperor he could overcome all difficulties. Little did he realize that the radical reform was in effect a war on the whole Confucian state and society, one which could not but arouse strong opposition from many quarters. The abolition of the eight-legged essay hurt the future of all students who, having spent their lives preparing for the civil service examinations, suddenly discovered that what they learned was not what the government wanted. They vowed to "eat" K'ang. The elimination of sinecure offices and the three governorships, and the suggestion that twelve new bureaus be created caused fear of dismissal among all office holders. The decree which called for the appointment of men of practical knowledge instead of the promotion of incumbents on a seniority basis created insecurity in officialdom. The military reform jeopardized the privileges of the Manchu bannermen and the Chinese Green Standard army, and the attack on corruption doomed the practice of the squeeze, most avidly pursued by the chief eunuch, Li Lien-ying. The order to turn temples and shrines into schools irritated the monks and priests. The fact that all the reformers except the emperor were Chinese aroused fear among the Manchus. All these elements—scholars, officials, army officers, eunuchs, monks, and the Manchus in general—sought to undo the reform.

The progressives were not without inkling of the danger that lay in wait for them. K'ang's brother had urged him to quit before it was too late, but Weng T'ung-ho, determined to destroy K'ang, persuaded him to stay under the pretext that the emperor could not bear to see him leave. K'ang himself was too overwhelmed by the imperial favor to want to go, declaring that life and death were decided by Providence, beyond human control. K'ang's brother then planned with Liang to have him sent to Japan as envoy, but the emperor sent instead another progressive.[36] He was simply too dependent on K'ang to allow him to leave, and K'ang was too proud to quit halfway. The reform movement was in full swing for only 103 days, and then the dowager struck.

The Power of Tz'u-hsi. For thirty-seven years since 1861, the empress dowager had been the ultimate power of state. She was too experienced, and too well entrenched, to be uprooted by a handful of inexperienced reformers. Though in retirement since 1889, she was in firm control of political and military affairs. Her confidants in the Grand Council reported to her all policy decisions, the eunuchs in the palaces watched every move of the emperor, and Jung-lu, her henchman at Tientsin, was in charge of the Peiyang army. There was not a thing that escaped her notice. Jung-lu's troops, stationed at Taku, Tientsin, Tungchow, and the vicinity of Peking, were ready to defend her interest. These soldiers might be useless before foreign aggressors, but sufficient to frustrate any domestic venture by the reformers. Indeed, Jung-lu had been the bodyguard and protector of the dowager ever since the coup of 1861. The emperor and the idealistic reformers, without any army at their direct command, could turn only to Yüan Shih-k'ai, but the latter was too shrewd and opportunistic not to know the inevitable outcome of a contest between the emperor and the dowager. He chose the winning side and hastened the collapse of the reform.

The Conservative Opposition. In their self-appointed role as defenders of Confucian morality and traditionalism, conservative scholars[37] attacked

36. Huang Tsun-hsien.
37. Such as Yeh Te-hui and Wang Hsien-ch'ien.

the reformers of having respect for "neither the sovereign nor the fathers" (*wu-chün wu-fu*) and of confusing the basic Three Bonds of human relations when they advocated popular sovereignty and individual equality. K'ang's interpretation of Confucius as a reformer and his casting doubt on the authenticity of the classics were nothing less than blasphemy and heresy in the eyes of these guardians of Confucian virtues. One of them, Yeh Te-hui, accused K'ang of using the sage to advance his own interests, and sneered: "K'ang Yu-wei's face is Confucian . . . but his heart is barbarian . . . The Kung-yang [Modern Text] school of today is not the same as that of the Han period; the latter honored China whereas the former, the barbarians." Contemptuously he announced: "Even if [K'ang's] words might be accepted, he as a person should never be used."[38]

Even the moderate reformers and those who sympathized with the institutional change found it difficult to accept K'ang's interpretations. Weng T'ung-ho, who brought K'ang to the attention of the emperor, remarked of him after reading A *Study of the Forged Classics of the Hsin Period:* "truly a 'wild-fox' meditator among the commentators of the classics! No end to my astonishment." Ch'en Pao-chen, the progressive governor of Hunan, commented that K'ang's A *Study of Confucius on Institutional Reform* went beyond the usual academic interpretation of Confucian teachings, with dangerous and undesirable political implications. Sun Chia-nai, a sympathizer of reform and president of the Imperial University, was also critical of this work, as he informed the throne:[39]

> In the eighth *chüan* . . . there is a section entitled, "Confucius formed institutions and assumed the title of king." K'ang tries to establish, on questionable grounds, that Confucius assumed the kingly title when he projected his reforms . . . It is feared that if this view is taught [to scholars], every one [of them] would entertain the idea of altering the institutions, every one would believe that he could be a "su-wang" [uncrowned king]. As a consequence, schools which are established to educate talented men would instead confuse and poison the minds of the people. That would lead the empire into disorder.

Thus, while K'ang's intellectual exertion won him great fame as an exponent of the Modern Text school, it also alienated a number of moderate

38. Li Shou-k'ung, 546.
39. Hsiao Kung-ch'üan, "Weng T'ung-ho," 158, 174.

and prudent scholars, who simply could not accept the dangerous implications of his works. It is a poignant irony that K'ang's self-styled title
ch'ang-su, which he took after *su-wang* (the uncrowned king, i.e. Confucius), had the double meaning of "a constant follower of the uncrowned king," or simply "the permanently uncrowned."

All in all, K'ang was too much of a philosopher to be a practical statesman. His radical reform was a gallant attempt to save the dynasty, but
it also represented a sharp departure from the general trend of gradual
change that had begun since the Self-strengthening Movement of the
1860's. It was clearly too advanced for his time. Given the general decadence and senility of the dynasty, one wonders whether his program,
even if it were carried out in full, could have saved it.

The repercussions of the failure of 1898 were many and far-reaching.
First, it proved that progressive reform from the top down was impossible. Secondly, under the empress dowager and die-hard conservatives who
had returned to power, the court was totally incapable of leadership. It
encouraged antiforeignism and fostered the Boxer movement, which
incurred the eight-power occupation of Peking in 1900. It followed an
anti-Chinese policy to punish the reformers, and thereby widened the
cleavage between the Manchus and the Chinese. The reactionary grand
secretary, Kang-i, said: "Reform benefits the Chinese but hurts the Manchus. If I have properties, I would rather give them to my friends than let
the slaves share the benefit." Thirdly, an increasing number of the Chinese
came to feel that their future lay in the complete overthrow of the Manchu
dynasty, and that such an occurrence could not be realized by a peaceful
change; only a bloody revolution from below could effect it. Dr. Sun Yat-
sen took the lead in promoting this approach.

FURTHER READING

Burt, E. W., "Timothy Richard: His Contribution to Modern China," *International Review of Missions,* 293-300 (July 1945).

Cameron, Meribeth E., *The Reform Movement in China,* 1898-1912 (Stanford, 1931)

———, "The Public Career of Chang Chih-tung, 1837-1909," *Pacific Historical Review,* 7:3:187-210 (Sept. 1938).

Candler, W. A., *Young J. Allen* (Nashville, 1931).

Chang, Chih-tung 張之洞, *Ch'üan-hsüeh p'ien* 勸學篇 (An exhortation to learning), (1898), 2 *chüan.*

Ch'en, Ch'iu 陳鋆, "Wu-hsü cheng-pien shih fan-pien-fa jen-wu chih cheng-chih ssu-hsiang" 戊戌政變時反變法人物之政治思想 (Political views of anti-reformers during the 1898 coup d'état), *Yen-ching hsüeh-pao*, 25:59-106 (June 1939).

Ch'i, Ssu-ho 齊思和, "Wei Yüan yü wan-Ch'ing hsüeh-feng" 魏源與晚清學風 (Wei Yüan and the late Ch'ing intellectual climate), *Yen-ching hsüeh-pao*, 39:177-226 (Dec. 1950).

Chien, Po-tsan 翦伯贊, *et al.* (eds.), *Wu-hsü pien-fa* 戊戌變法 (The reform of 1898), (Shanghai, 1953), 4 vols.

Ch'ien, Mu 錢穆, "K'ang Yu-wei hsüeh-shu shu-p'ing" 康有為學術述評 (A critical study of K'ang Yu-wei's scholarship), *Tsing-hua hsüeh-pao*, 11:3:583-656 (July 1936).

Ch'üan, Han-sheng 金漢昇, "Ch'ing-mo ti Hsi-hsüeh yüan-ch'u Chung-kuo shuo 清末的西學源出中國說 (The late Ch'ing hypothesis of the Chinese origin of Western learning), *Ling-nan hsüeh-pao*, 4:2:57-102 (June 1935).

————, "Ch'ing-mo fan-tui Hsi-hua ti yen-lun" 清末反對西化的言論 (Anti-Westernization views at the end of the Ch'ing dynasty), *Ling-nan hsüeh-pao*, 5:3-4:122-66 (Dec. 1936).

Ho, Ping-ti, "Weng T'ung-ho and the 'One Hundred Days of Reform'," *Far Eastern Quarterly*, X:2:125-35 (Feb. 1951).

Hsiao, Kung-ch'üan, "Weng T'ung-ho and the Reform Movement of 1898," *Tsing Hua Journal of Chinese Studies*, New Series, 1:2:111-245 (April 1957).

————, "The Case for Constitutional Monarchy: K'ang Yu-wei's Plan for the Democratization of China," *Monumenta Serica*, XXIV:1-83 (1965).

————, "The Philosophical Thought of K'ang Yu-wei: An Attempt at a New Synthesis," *Monumenta Serica*, XXI: 129-93 (1962).

————, "K'ang Yu-wei and Confucianism," *Monumenta Serica*, XVIII:96-212 (1959).

Hu, Pin 胡濱, *Wu-hsü pien-fa* 戊戌變法 (The reform of 1898), (Shanghai, 1956).

Hummel, William F., "K'ang Yu-wei, Historical Critic and Social Philosopher, 1857-1927," *Pacific Historical Review*, 4:4:343-55 (Dec. 1935).

Levenson, Joseph R., *Confucian China and Its Modern Fate*, Vol. I: *The Problem of Intellectual Continuity* (Berkeley, 1958), chapters 5-6.

————, *Liang Ch'i-ch'ao and the Mind of Modern China* (Cambridge, Mass., 1953).

Liang, Ch'i-ch'ao 梁起超, *Wu-hsü cheng-pien chi* 戊戌政變紀 (An account of the 1898 coup).

————, *Intellectual Trends in the Ch'ing Period* (*Ch'ing-tai hsüeh-shu kai-lun*), tr. by Immanuel C. Y. Hsü (Cambridge, Mass., 1959), Part III.

Liu, Feng-han 劉鳳翰, *Yüan Shih-k'ai yü Wu-hsü cheng-pien* 袁世凱與戊戌政變 (Yüan Shih-k'ai and the coup d'état of 1898), (Taipei, 1964).

Liu, Jen-ta 劉仁達, "Wu-hsü pien-fa yün-tung chung K'ang Yu-wei so t'i-ch'u ti cheng-chih kang-ling" 戊戌變法運動中康有為所提出的政治綱領 (K'ang

Yu-wei's political platform for the reform movement of 1898), *Li-shih yen-chiu*, 4:1-10, (1958).

Lo, Jung-pang (ed.), *K'ang Yu-wei: A Biography and a Symposium* (Tucson, 1967).

Onogawa, Hidemi 小野川秀美, "Kō Yū-i no hempōron" 康有爲の變法論 (K'ang Yu-wei's ideas of reform), in *Kindai Chūgoku kenkyū* 近代中國研究 (Studies on modern China), ed. by the seminar on modern China, Toyo Bunko, Tokyo, 2:101-88 (1958).

Soothill, W. E., *Timothy Richard of China* (London, 1924).

T'ang, Chih-chün 湯志鈞, *Wu-hsü pien-fa chien-shih* 戊戌變法簡史 (A short history of the reform of 1898), (Peking, 1960).

Teng, Ssu-yü, and John K. Fairbank, *China's Response to the West* (Cambridge, Mass., 1954), I, chapters 15-18.

Thompson, L. G. (tr.), *Ta T'ung-shu: The One-World Philosophy of K'ang Yu-wei* (London, 1958).

Wang, Shu-huai 王樹槐, *Wai-jen yü Wu-hsü pien-fa* 外人與戊戌變法 (Foreigners and the Reform of 1898), (Taipei, 1965).

Woodbridge, Samuel I., *China's Only Hope: An Appeal by Her Greatest Viceroy, Chang Chih-tung* (New York, 1900).

Yüan, Shih-k'ai 袁世凱, *Wu-hsü jih-chi* 戊戌日記 (My diary of 1898), (1909, 1922).

16

The Boxer Uprising, 1900

The *coup d'état* of 1898 reversed the entire power structure, restoring reactionary Manchus to office at the expense of both radical and moderate Chinese. Jung-lu, Yü-lu, and Ch'i-hsiu entered the Grand Council, while the die-hard conservative grand secretary, Kang-i, gained increasing favor with the empress dowager, on whom he had developed an even greater hold than Jung-lu. Blind to the realities of international politics, these men rejected diplomacy and mutual accommodation, advocating instead a policy of hard resistance. Under their influence, the dowager determined to make no more concessions to foreign powers. The test came in February 1899 when the Italians demanded the cession of the Sanmen Bay in Chekiang. Ordering the governor of Chekiang to fight enemy landings without hesitation, she saw the new policy of intransigency vindicated when the Italians backed down in October. Proudly, the Imperial Woman instructed the provincial authorities on November 21, 1899, to entertain no more illusion of peace:

> It behooves our governors and governors-general throughout the country to unite forces and act in unison, without distinction or particularism of jurisdictions, to exhort and encourage their officers and soldiers to defeat the enemy and score victory. Never should the word "peace" fall from the mouths of our high officials, nor should they harbor it for a moment in their breasts. With such a country as ours, with her vast area, stretching out for several tens of thousands of *li*, her immense natural resources, and her hundreds of millions of inhabitants, if all would prove their loyalty to the emperor and love of their

country, what indeed is there to fear from any strong invader? Let us not think of making peace, nor rely solely upon diplomatic maneuvers.[1]

The dowager, indeed, had ample reasons for resenting the foreigners. Even before her rise to power, she had had to flee with the court to Jehol in the face of the Anglo-French advance to Peking in 1860. She supported the Self-strengthening Movement and the adoption of Western armament in order to throw the foreigners out when China was ready. But alas! The French and the Japanese wars dashed her dreams, and events in the postwar period were even more disheartening. First there was the scramble for concessions by foreign powers in 1897-98, and then the foreign sympathy for the reform of 1898. The meddling British facilitated K'ang Yu-wei's escape, the Japanese Liang Ch'i-ch'ao's, and the publication of the *Ch'ing-i pao* by these fugitives in Japan to continue the cause of reform irritated her no end. The behavior of the foreign ministers in Peking, too, had been downright insulting: they openly disapproved of her plot to depose the emperor and of her choice of Prince Tuan's son as heir apparent, as noted in the previous chapter. The enforced delay in the enthronement of the boy humiliated her and exasperated the prince, who was impatient to become the father of a new emperor. Frustrated by their inability to resist the foreign interference, they turned their support to a major antiforeign movement, the Boxer Uprising, which resulted in an unprecedented catastrophe and ultimately sealed the fate of the dynasty.

THE BACKGROUND OF THE BOXER MOVEMENT

Strong antiforeign sentiment permeated not only the court under the empress dowager, but the scholars, the officials, the gentry, and the people at large. Half a century of foreign humiliation, in war as well as in peace, had deeply wounded their national pride and self-respect. The presence of haughty foreign ministers, fire-eating consuls, aggressive missionaries, and self-seeking traders constantly reminded them of China's misfortune. This gnawing sense of injustice generated a burning desire for revenge until it burst out in a vast antiforeign movement. There were, of course, larger social, economic, political, and religious factors which contributed to such an outbreak.

1. Chester C. T'an, *The Boxer Catastrophe* (New York, 1955), 32, with minor changes.

Antipathy Toward Christianity. Imbued with the teachings of Confucianism, Taoism, and Buddhism, the Chinese resented the invasion of Christianity under the protection of gunboats. The Treaties of Tientsin in 1858 had allowed its free propagation in the interior, and the Conventions of Peking in 1860 granted missionaries the right to rent and buy land for the construction of churches. Protected by the flag and the treaties, the missionaries moved about freely in China, although they had great difficulty winning converts. They resorted to the practice of offering converts monetary subsidies and protection against official or unofficial interference and insult.[2] The Chinese disparagingly called these native Christians men who "eat by religion" (*ch'ih-chiao*)—i.e. they lived on income from the church. Indeed, those who accepted pecuniary compensation in exchange for their belief were seldom men of high purpose; most were poor material drawn from low social strata who sometimes took advantage of their association with the missionaries to bully their fellow countrymen and to evade the law. When these converts became involved in trouble and lawsuits, the missionaries often came to their aid, interceding with the magistrates on their behalf. The Tsungli Yamen summed up the situation in a report to the court: "During the several decades since we have handled church cases, never once have we come across an instance in which the missionaries reprimanded or punished the converts." The public demonstration by the missionaries of their protective power, influence, and wealth attracted the weak and the opportunistic to the church but repelled the strong and the proud.

The gentry were particularly antiforeign, since they regarded Christianity as a socially disruptive, delusive, heterodox sect. The converts' failure to kowtow to the idols, to worship Confucius and ancestors, and to participate in local festivals honoring the spirits greatly irritated the gentry. As self-appointed guardians of Confucian propriety, they resented the effrontery of inroads by any foreign religion or philosophy, and not infrequently they were the secret instigators of religious incidents. Folklore and rumor abounded, luridly portraying foreigners, behind the high church and conventual walls, raping Chinese women and extracting children's hearts and eyes to make medicine out of them. (See the Tientsin Massacre.) Indeed, Christianity, as a "heterodox" faith in China, became a basic cause and focus for antiforeignism.

2. *Hai-kuo t'u-chih* (An illustrated gazetteer of the maritime countries) mentioned 130 taels as the amount of business allowance for each convert, while the *Chung-Hsi chi-shih* (A record of Sino-Western affairs) reported subsistence subsidies of 4 taels apiece.

Public Anger over Imperialism. As the pace of foreign encroachment accelerated in 1897-98, a sense of imminent extinction grew. K'ang Yu-wei, speaking before the National Protection Society in Peking on April 17, 1898, warned of the danger of becoming a second Burma, Annam, India, or Poland. The progressives proposed national salvation through a radical institutional reform as noted in the last chapter, but the reactionaries and the ignorant simply yearned to vent their wrath by killing foreigners. The Big Sword Society (*Ta-tao hui*) of Shantung, devoting itself to exterminating foreigners and their Chinese collaborators, circulated posters in March 1898 calling for patriotic Chinese to rise and kill foreigners and "traitorous" natives at sight and burn their residences. It has been estimated that more than a thousand cases of conflict occurred over railways, mines, and churches in Shantung after the German occupation of Kiaochow, while countless incidents also erupted in other parts of the country, all testifying to the tremendous public anger over foreign encroachment.

Hardship of Life as a Result of Foreign Economic Domination. The influx of foreign imports after the Opium War created a depressant effect on the native economy, and the fixed 5 per cent ad valorem customs duty ruined China's protective tariff. Foreign cotton cloth sold for only one-third of the price of the Chinese cloth, driving native weavers and textile manufacturers into bankruptcy. Handicraft household industries fared especially badly in the face of foreign competition, casting many workers into unemployment. The hardships of life accelerated during the Taiping period; with widespread famine and starvation, destitute people became bandits, vagrants, or troublemakers. While many of those in extremity at first blamed their misfortune on the Taipings, they ultimately transferred their hatred to foreigners for having inspired the rebels with the alien Christian ideology.

In the post-Taiping era, further expansion of foreign trade resulted in an ever-increasing foreign domination of the Chinese markets, and during the Self-strengthening period (1861-95) large numbers of foreign-style enterprises and industries, as well as considerable foreign capital, were introduced. In 1899 China suffered a trade deficit of 69 million taels and a government budgetary imbalance of some 12 million taels (101 million expenditure versus 89 million revenue). To meet the deficit, the court increased taxes and solicited provincial contributions, the burden of which ultimately fell on the people. When life became unbearable for the all too hard-pressed people, they sought alleviation in banditry and secret societies.

Moreover, the foreign device of the railway worked havoc on the traditional communication systems. The two old north-south trunk lines—the Grand Canal and the land route from Hankow to Peking—lost out in competition with railways, and thousands of bargemen, carters, innkeepers, and businessmen were all thrown out of work. With the commutation of tribute rice from the south to cash payment in 1900, the Grand Canal became all but obsolete, effecting the decline of the cities and the livelihood of the people along its banks.

By the end of the 19th century, the country was beset by bankruptcy of village industries, decline of domestic commerce, rising unemployment, and a general hardship of livelihood. Many Chinese attributed this sorry state of affairs to evil foreign influence and domination of the Chinese economy. It was therefore not surprising that hostility developed toward foreigners and things foreign.

Natural Calamities. Added to the economic hardship, a series of natural disasters intensified further the difficulty of life. The Yellow River, which shifted its course from Honan to Shantung in 1852, and flooded frequently after 1882, broke loose again in 1898. It inundated hundreds of villages in Shantung, affecting more than a million people. Similar floods occurred in Szechwan, Kiangsi, Kiangsu, and Anhwei. As if the torrential suffering was not enough, a severe draught followed in 1900 in most of North China, including Peking. Victims of natural calamities as well as superstitious scholars and officials blamed the misfortune on the foreigners, who, they insisted, had offended the spirits by propagating a heterodox religion and prohibiting the worship of Confucius, idols, and ancestors. Foreigners were accused of damaging the "dragon's vein" (*lung-mai*) in the land when they constructed railways, and of letting out the "precious breath" (*pao-ch'i*) of the mountains when they opened mines. The gentry held foreigners responsible for destroying the tranquillity of the land and interfering with the natural functioning of the "wind and water" (*feng-shui*, geomancy), thus adversely affecting the harmony between men and nature. Such an evil influence, they argued, must be eliminated if China was to have a peaceful, good life. The question was, how could they rid the country of the foreigners who possessed big ships and powerful guns? As a poor and weak country, China could not possibly expel them by military means; but some naïvely clung to the notion that she could invoke the supernatural powers to neutralize the effect of guns!

It was in this atmosphere of superstition, economic depression, extreme privation, public anger over foreign imperialism, and resentment of the missionaries that a major antiforeign riot broke out in 1900.

THE ORIGIN OF THE BOXERS

"Boxers" was the name given by foreigners to a Chinese secret society called the I-ho ch'üan, or the "Righteous and Harmonious Fists," since members of this organization practiced old-style calisthenics. The I-ho ch'üan was an offshoot of the Eight-trigram Sect (*Pa-kua chiao*), which was associated with the White Lotus Sect, an anti-Ch'ing secret society, which as the reader will recall, fomented the rebellion of 1796-1804. The first official mention of I-ho ch'üan appeared in an edict of 1808, which described the appearance of sword carrying rascals in Shantung, Honan, and Kiangnan [Kiangsu and Anhwei] provinces, who gathered under the name of I-ho ch'üan and Pa-kua chiao, and set up gambling tents in markets and fairs to take advantage of the local people. Despite official prohibition, the I-ho ch'üan spread to Chihli province by 1818 and continued its activities. In the 1890's, this antidynastic secret body took on an antiforeign cast, vowing to kill foreigners and their Chinese collaborators. The conservative governor of Shantung, Li Ping-heng, encouraged their activities, and his second successor, Yü-hsien, equally reactionary, changed their name in 1899 to I-ho t'uan, the "Righteous and Harmonious Militia."[3]

3. This version of the Boxers' origin is based on the authoritative source, Lao Nai-hsüan, "I-ho ch'üan chiao-men yüan-liu k'ao" (A study of the origin of the Boxers), (1899). However, there is a new theory which advances the radical view that the I-ho t'uan of the 1890's had no connection with that of the early 19th century even though they shared a common name, and that it was in no way related to the Eight-trigram Sect or the White Lotus Sect. The Boxers, according to this theory, actually had their origin in a Ch'ing edict of 1853 which called for the organization of local militia to resist the Taipings. In response to this call, the governor of Shantung organized "good country folk" into a militia "to defend themselves and their families, to guard against robbers and thieves, and to effect mutual aid"—in short, a local self-defense unit without antiforeign or secret society overtones. Because of their calisthenic exhibitions during the plum blossom season, its members came to be known as the "Plum Fists." By 1887, they assumed an hostile attitude toward the missionaries and the Chinese converts, and by 1898 the group changed character because of participation by various unsavory characters, such as bandits, rascals, horse thieves, outlaws, beggars, and even prostitutes. In the spring of 1898 they replaced the name "Plum Fists" with that of Righteous and Harmonious Militia (*I-ho t'uan*). Hence, it was not Yü-hsien (who became governor in 1899) who gave them the new name, as is generally stated. See Tai Hsüan-chih, *I-ho t'uan yen-chiu* (A study of the I-ho t'uan), (Taipei, 1963), 10-16, 37, 73-75. In a review of this book, Philip Kuhn, who has

The Boxers were made up of several uncoordinated groups, such as the Ch'ien Fists, the K'an Fists, and the K'un Fists, each under its own leaders. They all honored the red color, although the Ch'ien Fists later preferred yellow. Their method of instruction differed with each group, but on the whole it was short and simple, completed within a day. Their organizational structure was also simple, usually formed in units of twenty-five, each under a leader with complete authority. The instructions of the K'an Fists called for the burning of incense, kowtowing to the spirits, standing straight and then prostrating on the ground, followed by jumping and dancing with a weapon in hand. The Ch'ien instructions required prostration on the ground with closed mouth until froth appeared, at which point the leader would shout: "The spirits have descended!" Immediately the learner rose and danced with a weapon, calling out a fictitious name for himself, usually that of a legendary or historical hero.

The Boxers called their head "Old Teacher" and the lesser leaders "First Elder Brothers" and "Second Elder Brothers." They dubbed foreigners "Primary Hairy Men" (*Ta mao-tzu*), Chinese Christians and those engaged in foreign matters "Secondary Hairy Men" (*Erh mao-tzu*), and those who used foreign articles "Tertiary Hairy Men" (*San mao-tzu*). All "Hairy Men" were subject to extermination.

The Boxer's pantheon included both legendary and historical figures, taken from fictions, novels, and superstitious stories such as *The Romance of the Three Kingdoms* (*San-kuo yen-i*), *Pilgrimage to the West* (*Hsi-yu chi*), and *The Enfeoffment of the Dieties* (*Feng-shen chuan*). Numbered among their gods were the Jade Emperor (Taoist diety), Kuan Kung (the god of war), Chu-ko Liang (the wise strategist) and Hsiang Yü (the Hegemon King of the Western Ch'u State).

Elemental in the Boxers' program, and of primary appeal to the superstitious populace, was the practice of magic arts, by which they claimed immunity to bullets after a hundred days of training, and the power to fly after four hundred days of work. They used charms, incantations, and rituals to invoke the supernatural powers. In the battlefield they burned a small yellow paper with the image of a footless man, while murmuring some magic formulae, which purportedly could bring down divine gen-

---

done extensive work on local militia of the Ch'ing period, remarks that "the weight of evidence lies against it [the new theory]" and that Tai "relies on negative and ambiguous evidence that is much too thin to offset Lao's conclusive identification of an I-ho ch'üan Sect in the Chia-ch'ing period." Cf. *The Journal of Asian Studies*, XXV:4:760-61 (Aug. 1966). It appears that Tai's new theory, while provocative and stimulating, needs further research and verification before it can be accepted.

erals and soldiers. Being antiforeign, the Boxers shunned the use of guns, preferring old-style swords and lances.

Originally anti-Ch'ing, the Boxers in the 1890's became prodynastic and antiforeign.[4] Yet not all the bands shared this spirit with equal conviction. The band that preferred the white color, which was closest to the orthodox White Lotus Sect, stubbornly held to the "anti-Ch'ing, revive-Ming" objective, while the others, being largely groups of bandits, vagrants, and the unemployed, maintained no definite views on this point. When the Boxers were summoned by the court to Peking in the summer of 1900, the "white" band continued to hold that their own "emperor" had the surname of Chu and that their own dynasty was the Ming. While they attacked the foreign legations, they also secretly gathered two thousand men in a futile attempt to kill the Manchu emperor and his officials.[5]

Despite their different stands on the Ch'ing rule, the various Boxer bands were at one in their determination to exterminate the foreigners and their Chinese collaborators. They vowed to get "one dragon, two tigers, and three hundred lambs"—the dragon signified Emperor Kuang-hsü who sponsored the reform of 1898, two tigers meant Prince Ch'ing and Li Hung-chang who engaged in foreign affairs, and the three hundred lambs denoted metropolitan officials who had anything to do with the foreigners. Only eighteen court officials, the Boxers claimed, deserved to live; these were, of course, the die-hard reactionaries who supported the Boxers.

THE COURT PATRONAGE OF THE BOXERS

In the 1890's the Boxers were particularly active under the name of the Big Sword Society (*Ta-tao hui*) in Shantung, where they received secret encouragement from the reactionary governor, Li Ping-heng. He cleverly shielded the incidents they created in a report to the court in July 1898: "The riots now stirred up by the secret societies have their origin in the conflicts between the people and the Christians . . . The reason they could not live together peacefully is that the Christians, with the support and protection of the missionaries, bullied and oppressed the common people."[6] Li recommended a policy of pacification rather than suppression

4. For a detailed study of this point, see Victor Purcell, *The Boxer Uprising* (Cambridge, 1963), chapters 9 and 10.
5. Li Shou-k'ung, 589.
6. T'an, 46.

of the Boxers. However, when two German missionaries were killed in 1897, the court was pressured by the German minister to dismiss Li.[7] It was this missionary case that gave Germany an excuse to demand the occupation of Kiaochow, thereby touching off a scramble for concessions by the other powers. Reacting to the humiliating behavior of German troops in Shantung, and suffering from the floods of the Yellow River, many of the despondent, destitute, and desperate people of Shantung became restless and joined the Boxer movement. Finally, in October 1898 the Boxers began to attack Chinese Christians.

In March 1899 Yü-hsien was appointed governor of the now thoroughly disturbed Shantung province. As antiforeign as Li Ping-heng, he continued to patronize the Boxers and the Big Sword Society, ordering prefects and district magistrates to ignore the petitions and complaints of the missionaries and converts as just so much wastepaper. Under his aegis, the Boxers raised the banner of support for the Ch'ing and extermination of the foreigners (fu-Ch'ing mieh-yang). The governor subsidized them with silver and invited them to set up training centers to teach his soldiers boxing. More than eight hundred such centers sprang into being, concentrating in the area west of the Grand Canal where people suffered most from the floods. As noted earlier, Yü-hsien dignified the Boxers with a new name, the I-ho t'uan, or the "Righteous and Harmonious Militia." Emboldened by official support, the Boxers stepped up their attacks on the missionaries and the converts. Yü-hsien's report to the court was decidedly less than impartial: "The conflicts between the people and the Christians in Shantung have had a long history. At first the common people looked down upon the Christians, but later when the foreigners were strong and we were weak, the Christians became increasingly arrogant. They domineered in the villages and bullied the good people. There is absolutely no such thing as maltreatment of the Christians."[8] The court accepted this interpretation, and its pronouncements thereafter assumed a more antiforeign tone.

However, in December 1899 foreign pressure again forced the court to remove Yü-hsien. He came to Peking praising the dependability of the Boxers and condemning any act of suppression as hurting China's own interests. Impressed with his presentation, the reactionary Prince Tuan, Prince Chuang, and Grand Secretary Kang-i recommended the use of the Boxers to the empress dowager, who, in her frustration with the foreign-

7. Shortly afterwards promoted to be governor-general of Szechwan.
8. T'an, 59.

ers, readily embraced the idea. Yü-hsien was rewarded with the governorship of Shansi; his successor in Shantung, the acting governor Yüan Shih-k'ai, who stood for a vigorous policy of suppression, was repeatedly admonished by Peking to refrain from punishing the Boxers. On December 7, 1899, the court ordered him not to "stubbornly stick to the policy of extermination, but should make a distinction between different cases, so that the people would not be forced to more desperate deeds." On January 3, 1900, it again instructed him to use persuasion and pacification rather than suppression, but Yüan refused to acquiesce, and the Boxers were suppressed in Shantung.

However, the court continued to favor the Boxers. On January 12, 1900, it decreed that people drilling themselves for self-defense and for protection of their villages should not be considered bandits.

> When peaceful and law-abiding people practice skill and calisthenics for the purpose of defending themselves and their families, or when they combine in village communities for the mutual protection of the rural population, this is only a matter of mutual help and collective defense . . . Let the governors and governors-general in the provinces give strict orders to the local authorities that in dealing with cases of this kind they should only inquire whether so-and-so is or is not a bandit, whether he has or has not stirred up strife, and let them not consider whether he belongs or not to a society, whether he is or is not an adherent of a religion.[9]

On April 17, 1900, the court again announced that organization of militia (t'uan) by peaceful and law-abiding villagers to preserve themselves and their families was in line with the ancient principle of "keeping mutual watch and giving mutual aid"; hence such activity should not be prohibited. Greatly heartened by these decrees, in May the Boxers killed sixty-eight Chinese Christians and burned seventy-five houses in Kaolo village, Chihli. The governor-general, Yü-lu, though dubious of the Boxers' claims to magic and supernatural powers, knew of the dowager's secret patronage of them. He proffered no chastisement, while the court also undertook no punitive measures on the pretext that "rash action may lead to catastrophes." The Boxers became more daring, burning and destroying railways and telegraph lines as symbols of foreign enslavement of China.

In early May 1900 the court contemplated organizing the Boxers into a militia, only to be blocked by Yü-lu and Yüan Shih-k'ai. The reactionaries in power would not give up; Kang-i repeatedly impressed upon the

9. T'an, 60-61, with minor changes.

dowager that the Boxers were favored by the gods and immune to bullets —exactly the type of men China should rely upon to expel the foreigners. The dowager secretly asked him to summon the Boxers to Peking and when their invulnerability to firearms was "confirmed" in a palace demonstration, she commended their leaders[10] and ordered court attendants, including the women, to learn boxing. The princes and nobles now invited the Boxers to their residences as guards and set up tables to burn incense to the Boxer gods. Half of the regular government troops joined the Boxers, and the distinction between the two was lost. Boxing had become a craze.

On May 28 the rising tide of antiforeignism alerted the foreign diplomats in Peking to the precautionary measure of calling in the legation guards from the ships off Tientsin harbor. First disapproving, then reluctantly assenting to the move, the Tsungli Yamen tried to limit the number of such guards to thirty for each legation. However, the first detachment that arrived in Peking on June 1 and 3 consisted of 75 Russians, 75 British, 75 French, 50 Americans, 40 Italians, and 25 Japanese.

The Boxers found encouragement in yet another court decree of May 29, which cautioned provincial officials not to attack them indiscriminately, for there were both good and bad elements among those who practised boxing. Their pride enkindled by such official approbation, the Boxers cut the railway between Peking and Tientsin on June 3, and the situation rapidly got out of control. Chang Chih-tung, governor-general at Wuhan, and Sheng Hsüan-huai, director of Railways and Telegraphs, unsuccessfully pleaded with the court to suppress them before it was too late. When the soldiers of General Nieh Shih-ch'eng killed some Boxers, his commander-in-chief, Jung-lu, received a veiled reprimand from the court on June 3: "Although there are good and bad elements among the Boxers, they are after all children of the court . . . The Grand Secretary [Jung-lu] must not act impetuously and dispatch troops to attack them and incite conflict. This is very important." Though having no sympathy for the Boxers, Jung-lu was unwilling to offend the dowager, and he administered a mild reproach to General Nieh: "The uniform of your troops makes them look like foreigners, and the ignorant villagers may mistake them for foreign troops. The Boxers are the children of China. You should earnestly explain to them and make every effort to disperse them."[11]

10. Li Lai-chung and Ts'ao Fu-t'ien.
11. T'an, 66.

By now, the court was completely dominated by the reactionaries. Prince Tuan had replaced Prince Ch'ing as head of the Tsungli Yamen, to which Hsü T'ung and Ch'i-hsiu were also appointed as ministers. Foreign diplomats came to the conclusion that the court intended to kill all foreigners in the capital. The British minister sent for urgent help from Admiral Seymour at Tientsin. An international force of 2,100 men left Tientsin by train on the morning of June 10, and encountered the Boxers at Lang-fang, halfway between Peking and Tientsin. Heavy fighting took place, blocking the foreign expedition. The telegraphic lines between Peking and Tientsin were cut, leaving the fate of the foreigners in the capital a mystery and a matter of grave concern. On June 10, the Boxers burned the British summer legation in the West Hills; a day later, the chancellor of the Japanese legation, Sugiyama, was killed by the troops of the reactionary Moslem general Tung Fu-hsiang, who earlier boasted to the dowager that he had no ability other than killing foreigners. The war dogs had been unleashed and would now, uncontrolled, run ravening and slavering about northern China.

On June 13 the court announced that since the embassies had been adequately protected by the legation guards, there was really no need for more foreign troops to come to Peking. It ordered Governor general Yü-lu and General Nieh to resist the advance of Admiral Seymour, and alerted the commander of the Taku Forts for any surprise attack by the foreigners. On the same day, large bodies of rampaging Boxers swarmed into Peking. They burned churches and foreign residences, and killed Chinese converts at sight or buried them alive. They even exhumed the graves of missionaries, including those of the early Jesuits such as Matteo Ricci, Schall von Bell, and Ferdinand Verbiest. So wild had the Boxers become that they even pillaged the residence of their supporter at court, the reactionary grand secretary Hsü T'ung, and dragged other high officials into the streets for public humiliation. On June 14 they made several attacks on the legation guards, and on June 20 killed the German minister, Clemens von Ketteler.

At Tientsin, the Boxers were equally uncontrollable. They burned churches and shops that sold foreign merchandise and books, and killed Chinese Christians. They broke into prison, released the inmates, and coerced the governor-general into allowing them a free pick of weapons from the government arsenals. Facing such fanatic disorder, foreign officers on the ships outside the harbor decided to take the Taku Forts, which they overpowered on June 16 and occupied a day later. Meanwhile the Seymour expedition, blocked from reaching Peking, decided to fight its way back to Tientsin.

Prince Tuan and Kang-i now advocated an all-out attack on the legations as the only way to expunge the national humiliations of half a century, and in this the dowager concurred. On June 16 the first of four imperial councils was called to deliberate on war or peace. Yüan Ch'ang, a director of the Court of Sacrificial Worship, pointing out the fake immunity of the Boxers to guns, cautiously opposed opening hostility against the legations. The dowager cut him short with the remark: "If we cannot rely upon the supernatural formulae, can we not rely upon the hearts of the people? China has been extremely weak; the only thing we can rely upon is the hearts of the people. If we lose them, how can we maintain our country?" The meeting was indecisive, but a decree was issued to recruit the "young and strong" Boxers into the army.

At the second imperial council on June 17, the dowager retailed an alleged four-point demand from the foreign powers: designate a special place of residence for the emperor; allow foreign ministers to collect provincial revenues; and permit them to direct Chinese military affairs. The fourth point, which she did not reveal, was said to be "restore the emperor to power." This four-point demand was actually fabricated by Prince Tuan to goad the dowager into declaring war on the powers. She fell into the trap, announcing: "Now that they [the foreigners] have opened hostilities, the extinction of our country is imminent. If we simply fold our arms and yield to them, I would have no face to see our ancestors after my death. If we must perish, why not fight to the death?" She ordered that the foreign ministers be informed that if their countries meant to fight they should go home. On June 18, the third imperial council was called but again reached no decision. On the following day, a belated report came from Yü-lu that foreigners had demanded the surrender of the Taku Forts. Assuming that fighting had formally broken out, the dowager called the fourth imperial council on the same day to announce the break-off of diplomatic relations. She had made up her mind to fight the powers with the help of the Boxers. Hsü Ching-ch'eng (1845-1900), ex-minister to Russia and a vice-president of the Board of Civil Office, was given the assignment of telling the foreign diplomats to leave Peking within twenty-four hours under Chinese military escort. Emperor Kuang-hsü, never sympathetic to the Boxers, held Hsü's hand, murmuring: "We should deliberate this matter more carefully." Immediately the dowager shouted: "The emperor release his hand. Do not spoil the situation!" On June 21, another memorial arrived from Yü-lu, giving an ambiguous but rather favorable picture of the first three days' fighting at Taku and Tientsin. Feeling confident, the court declared war on the foreign powers that day.[12]

The court now formally ordered provincial authorities to organize the Boxers to fight the foreign invasion. At Peking, the Boxers were officially designated as "righteous people" (*i-min*) and rewarded with a rice subsidy and silver. Prince Chuang and Kang-i assumed official command of some 30,000 Boxers, while Prince Tuan directed a total of 1,400 bands, each consisting of 100 to 300 men. Marshaling them together with the government troops under General Tung Fu-hsiang, they launched vehement attacks on the legations and the Northern Roman Catholic Cathedral. For each foreign male captured alive Prince Chuang offered a reward of 50 taels, for each female, 40, and for each child, 30. Kang-i announced: "When the legations are taken, the barbarians will have no more roots. The country will then have peace." The attack on the legations was made with the full knowledge and support of the dowager; needless to say, it afforded the reactionaries in and out of the government the greatest emotional satisfaction. They saw in the destruction of the legations a way to vent their wrath on the barbarians, to rid the capital of the foreign menace, to kill evidence of the court's sponsorship of the Boxers, and to stimulate general patriotism among the people.

In the legation grounds there were about 450 guards, 475 civilians including 12 foreign ministers, 2,300 Chinese Christians, and some 50 servants, who put up a stiff resistance. The Boxers, adopting the mannerisms and dress appropriate to their magical-supernatural associations, wore wild, loose hanging hair and moved with the formulated steps ascribed to witches. They carried "eight precious magic weapons" frequently described in Chinese legendary stories.[13] Peking was turned literally into the pandemonium of a witches' Sabbath.

INDEPENDENCE OF SOUTHEAST CHINA

Even before the formal declaration of war on June 21, it was clear that under the influence of the reactionaries the court was moving into a dangerous course of action that could only bring on a major catastrophe

12. Hsiao I-shan, IV, 2,196-98.
13. The soul-attracting banners, the sky-covering flags, the thunderbolt fans, the yin-yang bottles, the nine-ring chains, the all-purpose hooks, the fire-shields, and the flying swords.

and untold suffering. The only person who seemed capable of reversing the tide was Li Hung-chang, now governor-general at Canton, but he would not act. His rationale was this: "The imperial court has decided on appeasement [of the Boxers]; it is futile to memorialize . . . Jung-lu has under his command several tens of thousands of troops; there is no reason that he should sit back and let these small men gain control of the dowager."[14] The provincial authorities were caught in a dilemma: unable to change the court's policy, yet anxious to save their jurisdictions from the Boxer disturbance and the inevitable foreign punitive expedition.

When the court issued the declaration of war on June 21, the southeastern provincial authorities—Li Hung-chang at Canton, Liu K'un-i at Nanking, Chang Chih-tung at Wuhan, and Yüan Shih-k'ai in Shantung —collectively refused to recognize its validity, insisting that it was a *luanming,* an illegitimate order issued without proper authorization of the throne. They suppressed the declaration from the public, as they did the order of the same day that they should organize the Boxers to fight foreign invasion. Chang Chih-tung cleverly twisted an edict of June 20 which ordered that the governors-general "should be united together to protect their territories" to mean that they should cooperate to suppress the Boxers and protect the foreigners. On the suggestion of Sheng Hsüan-huai, director of Railways and Telegraphs, Chang and Liu—the Yangtze valley governors-general—entered into an informal pact with foreign consuls at Shanghai to the effect that they, as the highest authorities in their provinces, would protect foreign lives and properties and suppress the Boxers within their jurisdictions, while the foreign powers would refrain from sending troops into their regions. Li Hung-chang, Yüan Shih-k'ai, and the governor-general of Fukien and Chekiang subscribed to this agreement. Hence the whole of southeast China was exempt from the Boxer disturbance and foreign invasion.

These provincial leaders justified their independent course of action on the grounds that the Boxers and the reactionaries had seized control of the court and issued illegitimate orders; that the Boxers had to be suppressed; that war with several foreign powers was insanity; and that the lives of the foreign ministers in the legations had to be saved. They impressed upon the court that since time immemorial no government could rule by rebels, who killed and burned without regard to law; nor could a state fight six or seven foreign countries simultaneously. To mitigate the situation, they urged the court to assign well-disciplined troops

14. Hsia I-shan, IV, 2,203.

to protect the legations, and to continue to honor the foreign debts, amounting to some 1.1 million taels monthly. They appealed to Jung-lu, but his response was one of hopeless resignation: "Half of the entourage of Their Majesties [dowager and emperor] and the princes belong to the Boxer societies, as do the majority of Manchu and Chinese troops. Several tens of thousands of them swarm in the streets of the capital like locusts, and it is extremely difficult to control [them] . . . Heaven wills it; what can we do?"[15]

Sheng Hsüan-huai boldly suggested that Yüan Shih-k'ai march his troops from Shantung to Peking to purge the court of the undesirable elements and rescue the dowager and the emperor from their control, but Yüan was in no mood for such a venture—not so soon after the *coup d'état* of 1898. He declined with the statement: "Without authorization, if I should lead my troops northward to save the foreign ministers, I am afraid that I would be defeated first on the way. It is really difficult for me to comply."[16] On July 3 Liu K'un-i, in an effort to absolve the dowager of guilt, notified foreign consuls that the existing hostilities were "beyond the expectation of the imperial court." To all this flurry of activities the court's curt response was the issuance of a decree on July 3 ordering the provincial authorities to purge the word "peace" from their mouths.

The Allies held the Ch'ing government responsible for the foreign lives in the legations, while organizing an international force to relieve the siege. On July 14, foreign troops took Tientsin and threatened to march on Peking. On the same day, thirteen southeastern provincial authorities collectively urged the court to suppress the Boxers, protect the foreigners and compensate them for the losses sustained in the recent disturbance, and send a letter of apology to Germany for the death of von Ketteler. Under their pressure, the court turned somewhat conciliatory for a moment. The Tsungli Yamen was allowed to invite foreign diplomats and their families to move to the Yamen for safety, pending further arrangements for a safe return home. The suspicious foreign ministers replied that they could not understand "why they should be safer in the Yamen than in the legations." On July 18, Li Hung-chang was ordered by the court to ask the Chinese diplomats abroad to inform the respective governments that their representatives in Peking were safe. A day later, the apprehensive Tsungli Yamen renewed the offer to send

15. Li Fang-ch'en, 535.
16. Hsiao I-shan, IV, 2,229.

foreign ministers to Tientsin under Chinese military escort. Still suspicious, the foreigners asked the Yamen to explain "why, if the Chinese government cannot insure the protection of the foreign envoys in Peking, they feel confident of their power to do so outside the city, on the way to Tientsin."[17] They preferred to remain in the legation quarter to await the relief. On July 20 and 26, the Yamen twice sent cartloads of vegetables, watermelons, rice, and flour to the legations. During this brief period of conciliation (July 14-26), attacks on the legations were suspended for twelve days.

The war-storm broke again, however, with the arrival in Peking of the reactionary official, Li Ping-heng, on July 26. Encouraged by Kang-i and Hsü T'ung, he forcefully, and successfully, impressed upon the dowager that one could negotiate a settlement only when one could fight. The policy of war and extermination of foreigners was reaffirmed. High officials who dared to counsel peace met evil days, and five of them were executed.[18] The terrifying state of affairs is reflected in a telegram from Yüan Shih-k'ai to Sheng Hsüan-huai on August 2: "It is hopeless; better say less."[19]

Allied reinforcements arrived at Taku in late July, but due to mutual jealousy and differences of opinion, it was not until August 4 that they set out from Tientsin for Peking. This international force consisted of 18,000 men, of whom the Japanese numbered 8,000; the Russians, 4,800; the British, 3,000; the Americans, 2,100; the French, 800; the Austrians, 58; and the Italians, 53. The Germans arrived too late to join this international force. The powerful Allied forces stormed across the Tientsin-Peking route, driving and dispersing before it the erratic Boxers and government troops. So quickly and emphatically did the Western powers defeat the Chinese that Yü-lu and Li Ping-heng committed suicide in humiliation on August 6 and 11, respectively. The Allied forces charged into Peking on August 14 and relieved the beleaguered legations.[20] The fact that some 450 guards, 475 civilians, and 2,300 Chinese Christians were able to withhold the assault of an infinitely larger number of gov-

17. T'an, 102.
18. Hsü Ching-ch'eng, a vice-president of the Board of Civil Office and ex-envoy to Russia; Yüan Ch'ang, director of the Court of Sacrificial Worship; Hsü Yung-i, president of the Board of War; Lien-yüan, sub-chancellor of the Grand Secretariat, and Li Shan, president of the Board of Revenue.
19. T'an, 106.
20. Following their occupation of Peking, Allied troops, particularly the Russians, engaged in free looting and pillaging of the palaces and private residences. One Russian lieutenant general returned home with ten trunkfuls of valuables.

ernment troops and Boxers for nearly two months was a miracle. However, this miracle was made possible by Jung-lu, the commander-in-chief of the Peiyang forces, who had no sympathy for the Boxers but lacked the courage to oppose the dowager. He carried out the attack halfheartedly, firing noisy but empty guns and withholding the new and large-caliber cannon from use. As a result, the legation defense was not broken.

On the morrow of the Allied advance into Peking, the dowager, the emperor, and a small entourage fled in disguise. The emperor had actually wanted to remain in Peking to negotiate a peace with the powers and to take over the reins of government himself, but the dowager, shrewd as ever in her extremity, would not let him re-establish himself at her expense. She ordered, at the last minute of her departure, that the emperor's favorite consort,[21] who counseled him to stay, be thrown into a well, and forced the emperor to flee with her. Clad in coarse commoner's clothes to avoid identification, they escaped westward under pitiful conditions. After a long and hard journey, the court was re-established in Sian on October 23.

The Boxer catastrophe which had swept over North China, Inner Mongolia, and Manchuria, had at last been stilled, leaving in its wake 231 foreigners dead and many more Chinese Christians slain. Shansi, in particular, where Yü-hsien had become governor, had suffered greatly from the disturbance.

THE PEACE SETTLEMENT

In the aftermath of the Boxer Uprising, the venerable elder statesman Li Hung-chang was given the assignment of mending the situation. Li, as may be recalled, was disgraced after the Japanese war in 1895 but managed to make a partial comeback in December 1899, when he was appointed governor-general at Canton. There he spent the twilight of his life in a sort of semiretirement, when suddenly on June 18, 1900—three days before the declaration of war—he received a court summons to come to Peking. Initially disposed to respond affirmatively, Li changed his mind, deciding instead to stall, and if necessary to go only so far as Shanghai, there to await further developments. Witnessing the court's patronage of the Boxers' unrestrained behavior, he confessed to Liu K'un-i: "If Prince Ch'ing and Jung-lu could do nothing, how could I?" Twice, on July 3 and 6, the court urged him to come north without de-

21. Consort Chen.

lay, following, on July 8, with appointments as governor-general of Chihli and superintendent of trade for the northern ports, posts which previously he had held from 1870 to 1895. Only then, and tardily, did he sail for Shanghai, arriving on July 21. There he heard from Yüan Shih-k'ai that the court determined to continue the war and that the lives of foreign ministers in Peking were in great danger. Under such conditions, Li knew peace was impossible, and he accepted the British government's advice that he wait in Shanghai until the foreign ministers had been safely conducted to Tientsin. Then came the news that the five high officials who counseled peace had been executed. Totally discouraged, Li begged the court to grant a twenty-day sick leave. The request was denied; instead, on August 7, the court appointed him plenipotentiary to negotiate with the powers. Still he would not go north. During this point-counterpoint maneuvering, responsible officials and citizens anxiously looked to Li as the only man who could deal with the Allies. Governor-general Liu at Nanking telegraphed him on August 18: "The safety or peril of the country rests upon Your Excellency. If you do not go to Peking, no negotiation is possible. Not only will the situation remain unresolved, but also, it is feared, the powers may change their minds."

On August 20, the court in flight displayed signs of penitence by admitting responsibility for having brought on the misfortune. Repeatedly it "begged" Li to go to Peking to search for a settlement with the powers. During a three-month period, from June 18, no less than twelve decrees were issued, urging him to come north. Li's delaying tactics stemmed from the belief that the court would not follow his recommendation to suppress the Boxers and that, unless the siege of the legations be lifted and foreign ministers given safe conduct to Tientsin, there was no prospect for peace. Of some consolation was the knowledge that the powers did not consider themselves at war with China; they sent expeditionary forces merely to suppress the rebels. When Russia offered to withdraw her troops, diplomats, and citizens to Tientsin in preparation for the opening of negotiations, and indicated confidentially that she would set a tone of moderation at the conference to forestall excessive demands by the other powers, Li decided that it was time to go north, and he requested the court to appoint Prince Ch'ing and Jung-lu to join him in the peace endeavors. When the court complied, Li went north under Russian protection, arriving in Tientsin on September 18.

The court in exile still reigned under the influence of such reactionaries as Prince Tuan and Kang-i, who advocated a long drawn-out war of attrition. To checkmate them, Li petitioned that Jung-lu, who had been found unacceptable as a negotiator by the Allies because of his association with the attack on the legations, be allowed to join the court. On November 11, Jung-lu reached Sian and resumed his role as a member of the Grand Council.

Meanwhile, the Allied representatives in Peking declined to open negotiations before "the return of the court," by which they meant "the return of the emperor to power." They raised the issue not so much because they had any sentimental love for him (who, to be sure, was to be preferred to the dowager), but because they wanted to use it as a leverage to gain satisfaction of their other demands. The dowager, clinging to her power, refused to return on the grounds that she feared untoward treatment and unacceptable terms being imposed on her, indicating clearly that the court would return after, not before, the peace settlement. Chang Chih-tung informed the British consul at Hankow in no uncertain language that as long as foreign troops remained in Peking the dowager would not return. The southeastern provincial leaders now adopted the tactics of shifting the Allied attention to a different issue: that of punishing the guilty ministers. Particularly anxious for this approach was Yüan Shih-k'ai, who knew that the return to power of the emperor, whom he had betrayed during the 1898 reform, would be most detrimental to his own interests. These southeastern leaders, as well as Prince Ch'ing and Li Hung-chang, put great pressure on the court to accept the Allied demand for the punishment of nine pro-Boxer ministers plus Yü-hsien and General Tung Fu-hsiang, who led the attack on the legations. On November 9, 1900, a joint telegram succinctly evaluating the situation was sent to Jung-lu: "To punish the guilty ministers is in the interest of Their Majesties; to punish Tung Fu-hsiang is in the interest of Your Excellency." The court finally and reluctantly agreed to punish the guilty ministers but reserved its judgment on General Tung, who still commanded 15,000 troops near Sian. When unsatisfied Allied representatives insisted on the life of Tung, the southeastern authorities again urgently pressed Jung-lu for action. Liu K'un-i insinuatingly cabled him on November 22: "As Tung has been your protégé, I hope you will soon arrange to satisfy the public." Yüan Shih-k'ai also impressed on him that no wise statesman "would love a single man against the public opinion of the nation, not to mention against the interests of the people."[22] Finally, on December 3, 1900, the court reluctantly stripped Tung of his

22. T'an, 139, 141.

ranks and sent him to Kansu. During all the discussion of guilt, no mention was ever made of the two chief culprits; the dowager, who was most guilty, and Jung-lu, who probably could have prevented the rise of the Boxers, went unpunished.

During the Peking negotiations, the Allied representatives, working at cross purposes, had a hard time agreeing on the terms. In a vengeful spirit Germany demanded stern punishment. The kaiser spoke of a severe punitive action and even destruction of Peking; when dispatching a 7,000-man expedition, he declared: "May the name of Germany become known in such a manner in China that no Chinese will ever again even dare to look askance at a German."[23] Because of von Ketteler's murder, the Kaiser secured the appointment of Field Marshall Count von Waldersee, onetime assistant to Moltke on the Grand General Staff, as commander-in-chief of the Allied forces in China. Arriving in Peking on October 17, some two months after it had been occupied by the Allies, Waldersee took the dowager's palace, the I-luan t'ien, as his quarters. The British supported the Germans in an attempt to check the Russian advance in China, while the Russians ingratiated themselves with the Chinese in hopes of gaining concessions in Manchuria, which they (the Russians) had already occupied during the turmoil. The Japanese, disturbed by Russian ambitions too, adopted the policy of winning Chinese good will by offering to withdraw part of their troops to Tientsin. The French announced that they did not desire a break-up of China and entertained no secret designs on her. The United States announced the second Open Door Policy on July 3, 1900, supporting "Chinese territorial and administrative entity" and "permanent safety and peace."

After much niggling debate and argument among themselves, the Allies finally agreed on December 24, 1900, on a joint note of twelve articles. Confronted by the persistent pleading of Li Hung-chang that the terms were not renegotiable and that any delay might lead to a rupture, the court reluctantly accepted the note on January 16, 1901. On the basis of this note, discussions were conducted toward a final settlement, which consisted of the following main features:

(1) Punishment of the Guilty. The Allies had originally demanded the death penalty for twelve officials, including Princes Chuang and Tuan, Kang-i, Yü-hsien, Li Ping-heng, Hsü T'ung, and General Tung Fu-hsiang.[24] In the final settlement, Prince Chuang was ordered to commit

23. Morse, III, 309.
24. Others were Duke Lan, Yin-nien, Chao Shu-ch'iao, Hsü Ch'eng-yü, and Ch'i-hsiu.

suicide, Prince Tuan to be banished to Sinkiang for life imprisonment, and Yü-hsien to be executed. General Tung was deprived of office. Kang-i, Hsü T'ung, and Li Ping-heng, who had already died, received posthumous degradation.[25] In the provinces, a total of 119 officials received penalties ranging from capital punishment to mere reprimand.

(2) Indemnity. A penal compensation of 40 million pounds sterling was proposed on March 21, 1901, by the United States commissioner-plenipotentiary in Peking, W. W. Rockhill, but the German representative asked for 63 million pounds sterling instead. On April 25, the Allies fixed the indemnity at 67 million pounds to include the occupation cost up to July 1, 1901. On May 7 the figure was further revised to 67.5 million pounds, or 450 million taels. The payment was to be completed in 39 years (i.e. 1940) at 4 per cent annual interest, with the maritime customs, *likin*, native customs, and salt gabelle as security. To help meet the payment, it was agreed to increase the existing tariff from an *actual* 3.18 per cent to 5 per cent, and to tax hitherto duty-free merchandise. The detailed breakdown of the indemnity was as follows:

Russia	130,371,120 taels	29% of total
Germany	90,070,515	20%
France	70,878,240	15.75%
Britain	50,620,545	11.25%
Japan	34,793,100	7.7%
United States	32,939,055	7.3%
Italy	26,617,005	5.9%
Belgium	8,484,345	1.9%
Austria	4,003,920	.9%
Others	1,222,155	.3%

(3). Other Important Stipulations. In addition to the above two items, a number of other terms were agreed upon, including:

(a) Apology missions to Germany and Japan.

(b) Establishment of a permanent legation guard.

(c) Destruction of the Taku and other forts from Peking to the sea.

(d) Prohibition of the importation of arms for two years.

(e) Stationing of foreign troops in key points from Peking to the sea.

25. Duke Lan was sentenced to banishment to Sinkiang for life imprisonment; Ch'i-hsiu and Hsü Ch'eng-yu were executed, while Ying-nien and Chao Shu-ch'iao were asked to commit suicide.

(f) Suspension of official examinations for five years in some 45 cities, where the Boxers had been active.

These items were formalized into The Boxer Protocol of twelve articles and nineteen annexes, and signed by Li Hung-chang, Prince Ch'ing, and the representatives of eleven powers on September 7, 1901, a year and twenty-four days after the relief of the siege of the legations. The Allied troops evacuated Peking on September 17, though the court did not return until January 7, 1902.

RUSSIAN OCCUPATION OF MANCHURIA

Peace had finally been restored between the Allies and China, but the question of Russian occupation of Manchuria had yet to be resolved. Under the pretext of restoring order and suppressing the "rioters" in Manchuria, the Russians had sent 200,000 troops in July 1900, with the ambitious prospect of reducing it to a second Bukhara. Occupying Aigun on July 23, Tsitsihar on August 30, and Mukden (the subsidiary capital of the Ch'ing dynasty) on October 1, they gained control over all Manchuria through the course of three months of military operations. On November 30, Admiral Alexeiev, Russian governor-general of Liaotung Peninsula, coerced Tseng-ch'i, the Manchu military-governor of Mukden, into signing a nine-article "provisional agreement," which virtually pre-empted Chinese rule in Manchuria: Tseng-ch'i was to disarm and disband all his troops in Manchuria, surrender all munitions in the arsenals, dismantle forts and defenses, and agree to the appointment of a Russian Resident in Mukden. The Ch'ing court, angered, fearful, and humiliated, refused to recognize the validity of this agreement, which it insisted Tseng-ch'i had no authority to sign. It was only on Russian protest—that any punishment of the signer was an insult to the dignity of Russia— that the Manchu governor-general was retained in office.

Negotiations then opened in St. Petersburg. General Kuropatkin and Count Witte, ministers of War and Finance, advocated a separate Manchurian pact, independent of the general agreement then being negotiated at Peking, with the intention of excluding other foreign influence and investment from Manchuria and the areas beyond the Great Wall. On February 16, 1901, the Russians proposed a twelve-article treaty (to replace the Alexeiev-Tseng agreement), which returned Manchuria to China in name but which, in effect, legalized the occupation of Manchuria by Russian troops disguised as "railway guards." It prohibited China from sending arms to Manchuria, or granting railway and mining privileges to other powers without Russian consent. The culminating insult, however, was the stipulation that China pay for the Russian occupation costs and damages to railways and properties of the Chinese Eastern Railway Company, as well as granting Russia the right to construct a line from the said railway to the Great Wall in the direction of Peking.

The Russian aggression in Manchuria aroused grave apprehension among the powers, especially Japan, whose interests conflicted with those of Russia. The Japanese minister in Peking[26] warned Prince Ch'ing that any concession on the Russian occupation of Manchuria could lead to the partition of China: Britain was certain to follow with the occupation of the Yangtze valley, Germany with the Shantung province, and Japan would have no choice but to reserve to herself freedom of action. Admonitory messages also came from Britain and Germany against any separate territorial or financial treaty with Russia before the signing of the general agreement with the Allies in Peking. The United States, Austria, and Italy, too, urged China to resist the Russian demand. On the other hand, Witte threatened that a rejection of the proposed treaty would lead to Russian incorporation of Manchuria. The hapless Ch'ing court, still in exile at Sian, could come to no definite stand. It dared not offend either the powers or Russia; all it could do was to order Prince Ch'ing and Li Hung-chang to devise a way that would neither arouse the anger of the Russian court nor aggravate the indignation of the various powers. Li Hung-chang, instead of turning international jealousies to China's advantage, allowed his pro-Russian leanings to get the better of him, and advised the court to sign the treaty to avoid a perilous break. However, other powerful provincial figures, such as Chang Chih-tung and Liu K'un-i—the Yangtze governors-general—vigorously opposed the treaty. Liu argued that Russia would not return Manchuria whether China accepted the treaty or not, while Chang warned against a possible partition of China if she succumbed to the Russian threat. Caught between these opposing views, and pressured in diverse directions by Russia, Britain, and Japan, the court was totally incapable of making up its mind. It abjectly passed the decision to the Chinese minister in Russia, Yang Ju, who was authorized to act as he saw fit. Now Li asked him to accept the treaty, while Chang and Liu urged him to reject it, lest he become the target of public condemnation. Embroiled in this dilemma and in great anxiety, Yang seriously wounded his leg in an accident on March 22, 1901. On the following day he telegraphed the court that he

26. Komura Jutarō.

would not sign the treaty without its express instructions. By this time, Chinese ministers in Tokyo, London, and Berlin bombarded Peking with a barrage of admonitions against signing. Most emphatic was the diplomat in Japan who argued that Russia most assuredly dared not face the combined forces of Britain and Japan, and that any Chinese concession at this point could only earn British and Japanese enmity and complicate the pending general settlement at Peking. Under such pressure, the court finally decided on March 23 to reject the Russian treaty. Facing powerful international opposition, the Russians did nothing more than issue a disgruntled statement on April 6 that, much as they would like to evacuate Manchuria, the realities of international politics did not permit them to do so at the moment. The tense negotiations in St. Petersburg, having hung so perilously for months, suddenly ended in an anticlimax, without the much anticipated dire consequences to China.

Despite Chang Chih-tung's attack on his blind, pro-Russian policy, Li continued to espouse a separate settlement through direct negotiation. Count Witte, on the part of Russia, proposed as a prerequisite that China grant the Russo-Chinese Bank a contract which would give it railway, mining, and other industrial and commercial rights in Manchuria. Li counterproposed that the said contract be negotiated simultaneously with the issue of troop evacuation, to which Witte replied that the two must be treated as separate questions. Dunned by the Russians from without and ridiculed by his countrymen from within, Li Hung-chang, old, weak, and ashamed, passed away suddenly on November 7, 1901, at the age of 78.

Li's unfinished work was carried on by Prince Ch'ing and Grand Councillor Wang Wen-shao. The international situation was very much in Russia's disfavor, especially after the signing of the Anglo-Japanese alliance on January 30, 1902. Ultimately, the Russians signed an agreement with China on April 4, promising to evacuate Manchuria in three stages at six-month intervals. On her part, China agreed to protect the Russian-dominated Chinese Eastern Railway, its employees and properties, as well as all its allied enterprises. The first stage of evacuation was carried out on schedule, but when the second stage came due in April 1903, the Russians did not leave but resorted to the subterfuge of changing the uniforms of the troops to those of "railway guards." In addition, they demanded new monopolistic rights and reoccupied some of the evacuated cities, such as Mukden and Newchwang. This Russian incursion into Manchuria foreshadowed the war with Japan in 1904.

REPERCUSSIONS OF THE BOXER UPRISING

In retrospect, it becomes apparent that the Boxer movement was propelled by the combined forces of the reactionary Manchu court, the die-hard conservative officials and gentry, and the ignorant and superstitious people. It was a foolish and unreasoned outburst of emotion and anger against foreign imperialism, yet one cannot overlook the patriotic element inherent in it. Marxist historians today consider the Boxer movement a primitive form of a patriotic peasant uprising, with the right motive but the wrong methods.

The Boxer Uprising and its final settlement left behind many significant consequences: (1) The Allied occupation of Peking and the Russian advance into Manchuria threatened the partition of China and sharpened international jealousy and rivalry. There developed a growing fear among the powers of conflict between themselves, and a deep concern over the future of equal commercial opportunity in China, resulting in a general international desire to reduce tension and maintain the *status quo* in China. The United States declared the second Open Door Policy on July 3, 1900, with a view to preserving "Chinese territorial and administrative entity" and to safeguarding "for the world the principle of equal and impartial trade with all parts of the Chinese Empire." The declaration was followed by the Anglo-German agreement of October 16, 1900 (to which other powers were invited to adhere) which stipulated that the signatories would refrain from seizing territory in China. The subsequent stalemate in imperialistic activities prevented an immediate break-up of China. Nonetheless, her international position in the society of nations plummeted ignominiously to rock bottom. (2) The Boxer Protocol infringed upon Chinese sovereignty severely. Article 5 which stipulated the prohibition of the importation of arms, Article 8 which stipulated the destruction of the Taku and other forts, Article 7 which provided for stationing of foreign troops in the legation quarter, and Article 9 which gave foreign powers the right to deploy troops from Peking to the sea—all these compromised China's power of self-defense and restricted the free exercise of her sovereign rights. Article 10, which suspended government examinations in many parts of the country for five years as a punishment to the gentry class, was a blatant interference with the internal administration of China. (3) The indemnity of 450 million taels ($330 million) and its accrued interest over 39 years at 4 per cent annually amounted to a grand total of 982,238,150 taels, more than twice the original amount. The payments, which had to be made in foreign currencies rather than in Chinese taels, incurred an additional loss of several million taels annually in the exchange, especially during the years when the value of the silver suffered a sharp decline. For instance, in 1903 China had to pay 53.5 million taels instead of 42.5 million as originally agreed upon.[27] The outflow of such large capital inhibited, if not incapacitated, China's economic growth. (4) Foreign ministers in Peking now organized themselves into a powerful diplomatic corps, functioning above the Manchu court as a sort of super-government. The prestige of the Ch'ing dynasty sank to a nadir. (5) The barbarous conduct of the Boxers exposed China in an uncivilized light in the community of nations. On the other hand, the brutal demonstration of power by the foreign expeditionary forces created such an image of invincibility and superiority that Chinese pride and self-respect were shattered. The Chinese attitude toward foreigners swung from one of disdain and hostility to one of fear and toadying. (6) In a struggle for survival, the Manchu court instituted some halfhearted, superficial reform toward a constitutional government; while many Chinese, witnessing the hopelessness of the Manchu leadership, turned to revolution as the only hope for their country. Dr. Sun Yat-sen's advocacy of a forceful overthrow of the Ch'ing dynasty, hitherto regarded by respectable Chinese as an unlawful movement to eschew, now received increasing sympathy and support. His image reversed from that of a disloyal rebel to that of a high-minded, patriotic revolutionary. As a result, the pulse of revolution quickened, precipitating the ultimate downfall of the Manchu dynasty in 1911.

FURTHER READING

Campbell, Charles S., *Special Business Interests and the Open Door Policy* (New Haven, 1951).

27. It should be noted, however, that in an act of justice and good will, the United States, on recommendation of W. W. Rockhill, later returned the excessive portion of the indemnity. The total American private claims, amounting to only $2 million, had been paid by 1905, and in 1908 the United States government returned to China $10,785,286, while retaining $2 million for possible future adjustments. In 1924 the rest of the indemnity was waived. This Boxer refund was specified to be used for educating Chinese students in the United States. Remissions by other countries followed suit: Britain, 1922; Russia, 1924; France, 1925; Italy, 1925 and 1933; Belgium, 1928; Netherlands, 1933. See Chi-ming Hou, *Foreign Investment and Economic Development in China 1840-1937* (Cambridge, Mass., 1965) 26; also Paul A. Varg, *Open Door Diplomat: The Life of W. W. Rockhill* (Urbana, 1952), 48, 81-82.

Chien, Po-tsan 翦伯贊, *et al.* (eds.), *I-ho t'uan* 義和團 (The Boxer Movement), (Shanghai, 1951), 4 vols.

Fleming, Peter, *The Siege at Peking* (New York, 1959).

Hart, Robert, *These from the Land of Sinim, Essays on the Chinese Question* (London, 1903).

Ho, Ping-ti 何炳棣, "Ying-kuo yü men-hu k'ai-fang cheng-ts'e chih ch'i-yüan" 英國與門戶開放政策之起源 (Britain and the origin of the Open Door Policy), *Shih-hsüeh nien-pao*, 2:321-40 (1938).

Joseph, Philip, *Foreign Diplomacy in China, 1894-1900* (London, 1928).

Kuo, Pin-chia 郭斌佳, "Keng-tzu ch'üan-luan" 庚子拳乱 (The Boxer Rebellion of 1900), *Kuo-li Wu-han ta-hsüeh wen-che chi-k'an* (Quarterly Journal of Literature and Philosophy), National Wuhan University, 6:1:135-82 (1936).

Langer, William L., *The Diplomacy of Imperialism, 1890-1902* (New York, 1935).

Lo, Tun-yung 羅惇曧, "Keng-tzu kuo-pien chi" 庚子國變記 (The national crisis of 1900), in Tso Shun-sheng 左舜生 (ed.), *Chung-kuo chin-pai-nien shih tzu-liao, ch'u-pien* 中國近百年史資料初編 (Materials relating to Chinese history of the last hundred years), (Shanghai, 1926), I, 517-35.

Malozemoff, Andrew, *Russian Far Eastern Policy, 1881-1904* (Berkeley, 1958).

Purcell, Victor C., *The Boxer Uprising* (Cambridge, 1963).

Tai, Hsüan-chih, *I-ho t'uan yen-chiu* (A study of the I-ho t'uan), (Taipei, 1963).

T'an, Chester C., *The Boxer Catastrophe* (New York, 1955).

Varg, Paul A., *Open Door Diplomat: The Life of W. W. Rockhill* (Urbana, 1952), chapters 4 6.

———, *Missionaries, Chinese, and Diplomats: The American Protestant Missionary in China, 1890-1952* (Princeton, 1952).

———, "William W. Rockhill's Influence on the Boxer Negotiations," *Pacific Historical Review*, 18:3:369-80 (Aug. 1949).

———, *The Making of a Myth: The United States and China, 1897-1912* (East Lansing, 1968).

Wang, Wen-shao 王文韶, "Keng-tzu liang-kung meng-ch'en chi-shih" 庚子兩宮蒙塵紀實 (The true story of the flight of the empress dowager and the emperor in 1900), in Tso Shun-sheng 左舜生 (ed.), *Chung-kuo chin-pai-nien shih tzu-liao, hsü-pien* 中國近百年史資料續編 (Materials relating to Chinese history of the last hundred years), II, 501-04.

Wang, Yen-wei 王彦威, *Hsi-hsün ta-shih chi* 西巡大事記 (Journal of the imperial western tour), (Peiping, 1933).

Wehrle, Edmund S., *Britain, China, and the Antimissionary riots, 1891-1900* (Minneapolis, 1966).

Wu, Yung, *The Flight of An Empress* (New Haven, 1936).

Yün, Yü-ting 惲毓鼎, "Ch'ung-ling ch'uan-hsin lu" 崇陵傳信錄 (A true record of Emperor Kuang-hsü), in Tso Shun-sheng (ed.), *Chung-kuo chin-pai-nien shih tzu-liao, ch'u-pien* (Materials relating to Chinese history of the last hundred years), (Shanghai, 1926), I, 454-88.

17

Reform and Constitutionalism at the End of the Ch'ing Period

To the empress dowager, the Boxer catastrophe proved a traumatic experience. Following Allied occupation of Peking, she made a humiliating and hurried escape westward in a donkey cart, suffering hardship and privation for the first time in her life. She was without good food and comfortable lodging, and during the long flight she witnessed the deep suffering and relentless havoc that had been inflicted by the Boxers, facts which stimulated in her a sense of remorse and shame for having led her country into an unprecedented cataclysm. She often wept, and ruefully declared: "I had not expected to become the object of ridicule by the emperor!" Her astute political acumen and shrewd instinct dictated that it would be difficult for her to regain foreign esteem and domestic respect unless she showed some semblance of repentance and instituted measures of political reform. On August 20, 1900, while still in flight, she overcame pride, and issued a decree blaming herself for China's misfortune. After the court had been re-established at Sian, she proclaimed the desire to institute a reform of her own.

THE CH'ING REFORM, 1901-05

In a statement of January 29, 1901, the dowager solicited advice on reform from ministers of state, provincial authorities, and envoys abroad. It said in part:

> Now that peace negotiations are underway, we should realistically set aright all political affairs in order to become rich and powerful grad-

ually. . . . What has hurt the country is the word "selfishness" and what has troubled the state is the word "precedent." Of late there are those who have studied Western systems, but they have gone no further than the limited [fields] of the spoken and written languages, and the manufacture of machines and weapons. These are but the 'skin and hair' [i.e. superficial aspects] of Western technology, not the fundamental source of Western learning.

She admonished the high officials against continued adherence to mere superficiality, and allowed them two months in which to make detailed recommendations. They were to base their suggestions on Chinese and Western political systems, in order to indicate how best to renovate existing governmental institutions, administrative procedure, people's livelihood, methods of education, the military organization, and the financial system.

On February 14, 1901, the court reaffirmed its determination to institute reform, and accepted responsibility for the Boxer calamity. On April 21, a Superintendency of Political Affairs (*Tu-pan cheng-wu ch'u*) was instituted to formulate a legitimate program. Prince Ch'ing, Jung-lu, Li Hung-chang, and three others were appointed directors; while Chang Chih-tung and Liu K'un-i received appointment as associates.

The Yangtze governors-general, Chang and Liu, jointly presented three memorials in July 1901 in response to the court's call. In the first memorial, they stressed loyalty to the existing system, but indicated the need for educational reform to cultivate native talents, recommending:

1. the institution of modern schools at all levels, with a mixed curriculum of Chinese classics and Western history, geography, politics, science, and technology;
2. a change in the contents of the civil service examinations to include questions on both Chinese and Western subjects;
3. the termination of military examinations;
4. encouragement of foreign study and travel.

The memorial decisively concluded, in Chang's eloquent, pithy prose: "Unless we cultivate talents, we cannot expect to exist. Unless we promote education we cannot cultivate talents. Unless we reform civil and military examinations, we cannot promote education. Unless we study abroad, we cannot make up deficiencies of education [at home]."[1]

The second paper continued with a discussion of the essentials of good

1. Li Shou-k'ung, 707.

government, investigating methods of acquiring wealth and power. The memorialists recommended frugality, the recruitment of unusual talents, and an increase in the anticorruption subsidy to end irregularities in government. It also suggested termination of sales of office, and the reduction of the obsolete Green Standard army, as well as the dismissal of useless scribes and clerks in government offices.

The memorialists concluded their prospectus with a third paper which suggested the adoption of "Western methods," among which they recommended the expansion of military appropriations, the introduction of a foreign-style drill, promotion of agriculture, encouragement of industry and technology, and an organized compilation of regulations with regard to mining, railroad, and commerce. They also suggested adoption of the silver dollar, the use of an official revenue stamp, improvement of the postal service, and the active translation of foreign books. They tendered their proposals with a view to "redressing the Chinese system in order to implement the Western."

Predominantly on the basis of their recommendations, the dowager initiated an institutional reform, which differed little in content from the reform of 1898. It lasted over a more extended period, commencing in 1901 and terminating in 1905. The dowager reluctantly admitted that China could not be saved by patchy, piecemeal reform; and that complete reorganization and self-strengthening provided the only hope for the future. "Both the emperor and myself know that for the sake of the country and the people, there is no other way out," she conceded. Salient features of her program were:

I. *Abolition of old offices*
   A. Dismissal of useless clerks and attendants in government offices. (May 1901)
   B. Termination of the sale of office. (August 1901)
   C. Incorporation of the Supervisorate of Imperial Instruction (*Chan-shih fu*) into the Hanlin Academy. (August 1901)
   D. Abolition of the governorships of Yunnan and Hupeh (December 1904) and Kwangtung (July 1905), as well as the director-generalship of the Conservancy of the Yellow River and the Grand Canal. (February 1902)

II. *Creation of new offices*
   A. The Superintendency of Political Affairs. (April 1901)
   B. The Ministry of Foreign Affairs to replace the Tsungli Yamen. (July 1901)

    C. The Ministry of Commerce, which absorbed the old Bureaus of Railways and Mining. (August 1903)

    D. The Bureau of Military Training. (December 1903)

    E. The Ministry of Police. (October 1905)

    F. The Ministry of Education. (December 1905)

III. *Military reform*

    A. Termination of military examinations. (August 1901)

    B. Reduction of the Green Standard Army and Braves by 20 to 30 per cent within a year. (August 1901)

    C. Creation of provincial military academies. (August 1901)

    D. Training of the bannermen in Peking by T'ieh-liang and Yüan Shih-k'ai.

    E. Establishment of the Bureau of Military Training. (December 1903)

IV. *Educational reform*

    A. Opening of the state examinations in political economy for the Hanlin members above the compilers. (May 1901)

    B. Recruitment of Chinese students abroad for service at home by the envoys. (June 1901)

    C. Replacement of the "eight-legged essay" by current topics in provincial and metropolitan examinations, to begin in 1902. (August 1901)

    D. An order to transform provincial academies into colleges, prefectural schools into middle schools, and district schools into elementary schools, with a mixed curriculum, including the Confucian Four Books, Five Classics, Chinese history, as well as the study of foreign governments. (September 1901)

    E. Orders to provincial authorities to select students to study abroad. (September 1901, October 1902)

    F. An order to the Imperial Clan Court to select bannermen's children to study abroad. (January 1902)

    G. An order to Hanlin compilers and other holders of the *chin-shih* degree to study in the various departments of the Imperial University. (December 1902)

    H. Annual examinations for returned students from abroad. (July 1905)

    I. Abolition of the government examinations. (August 1905)

V. *Social reform*

    A. Permission for marriages between the Manchus and the Chinese. (February 1902)

    B. Liberation of women from foot-binding. (February 1902)

    C. Prohibition of opium. (September 1906)

VI. *Other reforms*

A. Revision of regulations on the tribute rice, and promotion of railway construction. (June 1901)

B. Provincial taxes on tobacco and liquor. (December 1903)

C. An order for drafting a commercial law. (December 1901)

D. Establishment of refugee camps to absorb vagrants and the unemployed. (June 1905)

E. Reduction of expenses in the palaces. (June 1904)

Though purportedly instituted in voluntary response to a changing social and political order, the program actually was a shrewd effort on the part of the dowager to disguise her shame over her role in the Boxer catastrophe. Her insincerity was revealed in the fact that while she openly asked for suggestions from officials in the central and provincial governments, she secretly intimated her profound distaste for things foreign. The Grand Council therefore tactfully advised officials not to speak freely of adopting Western ways. Distressed, Chang Chih-tung commented on imperial duplicity in a cable to a grand councillor, dated March 24, 1901: "I have heard that the inner circle [i.e. the dowager] does not like to speak of Western ways. Your telegram also advises us not to imitate the superficialities [lit. "skin and hair"] of Western methods so as to avoid criticism. I cannot but respond with a long sigh of resignation. If the situation is really so, then the two words 'institutional reform' have not yet hit the proper target. It is still useless, and ultimately, China will perish."[2]

The dowager's reform program was essentially a noisy demonstration without much substance or promise of accomplishment. Only three concrete improvements were actually made, namely (1) the abolition of the civil service examinations; (2) the establishment of modern schools; and (3) the sending of students abroad.

In addition to the dowager's insincerity, anti-Chinese discrimination and inept Manchu leadership also contributed to the ineffectiveness of the program. Important appointments were given to Manchus to an increasing extent. The Superintendency of Political Affairs,[3] for instance, was controlled by Jung-lu, a Manchu, and the newly formed Ministry of Foreign Affairs was placed under Prince Ch'ing, who controlled the

2. Li Shou-k'ung, 713. In the light of this evidence, it is hard to accept the thesis that the dowager was a sincere convert to reform, as advocated in Meribeth E. Cameron, *The Reform Movement in China, 1898-1912* (Stanford, 1931), chapter 3, "The Empress Dowager's Conversion," also pages 199, 201.

3. Although it had three Chinese and three Manchu directors.

Bureau of Military Training as well. The Ministry of Commerce and the Ministry of Education were both under Manchu leadership, together with a great number of other government agencies. This one-sided distribution of offices became even more evident after the deaths of the elder Chinese statesmen Li Hung-chang in 1901 and Liu K'un-i in 1902. Manchu domination of the government now prevailed. After the decease of Jung-lu in 1903, official leadership passed to Prince Ch'ing who proved vain, corrupt and incapable. The prospect for successful reform became even more remote.

THE CONSTITUTIONAL MOVEMENT, 1905-11

In 1905 a dramatic change occurred in the Ch'ing reform program, following Japan's spectacular victory over Russia. To many Chinese the defeat of the large autocratic Western power by a tiny Oriental constitutional monarchy was proof of the effectiveness of constitutionalism. They were further impressed by the discovery that nearly all the leading Western powers operated on the basic principles of constitutional government, and that the Russians themselves were moving in the direction of constitutionalism, with renewed popular demands for the convocation of the Duma (assembly). The floundering Chinese believed that at long last they had found a formula of survival. The famous scholar-turned-industrialist, Chang Chien, announced triumphantly that "the victory of Japan and the defeat of Russia are the victory of constitutionalism and the defeat of monarchism." He urgently besought Yüan Shih-k'ai (Li Hung-chang's successor as governor-general of Chihli) to assume vigorous leadership in promoting the cause of constitutionalism. The Chinese minister in Paris[4] also petitioned the court to adopt a constitution. The idea of constitutionalism suddenly caught fire and spread rapidly among intellectuals, social leaders, and the forward-looking governors-general and governors in the country.

The persuasive voice of the reformer Liang Ch'i-ch'ao greatly contributed to the national clamor for constitutionalism. In exile in Japan since the failure of the "Hundred-Day" Reform, Liang came into contact with Japanese modernizers and widely read translations of Western philosophy and political thought. He fervently embraced nationalism and such concepts as liberty and equality as the inalienable rights of the people. Persistently he expounded these ideas in his journals, *The Public*

4. Sun Pao-ch'i.

Opinion (*Ch'ing-i pao*), 1898-1902, and *The New People's Miscellany* (*Hsin-min ts'ung-pao*), 1902-1907, in an attempt to instill his countrymen with these ideas. His diagnosis of China's weakness showed that the Chinese people owed personal allegiance to the ruler, but not to the state; that Confucianists talked about universal rule without first providing effective emphasis on the importance of the Chinese nation; that despotism and autocracy lay at the roots of corruption and weakness of China. He ardently insisted that the Chinese had to accept nationalism as a prerequisite to the exercise of such rights as equality, liberty, and sovereignty. However, he did not believe that the China of his time was ready for a truly democratic and representative government, but considered constitutional monarchy more effective as an immediate target. He advocated gradual political change and deprecated violent revolution. Liang employed a mixture of classical and colloquial diction in a new style of writing which won an immediate following among the reading public. His journals were eagerly pursued by young students who rushed to bookstores for recent issues, in order to imbibe such new concepts as people's sovereignty, nationalism, and constitutionalism. Liang rose to become a glittering star of Chinese journalism and political philosophy during the early years of the twentieth century.[5]

Radicals under Dr. Sun Yat-sen, however, launched a powerful counterattack to Liang's concepts of constitutional monarchy. They forcefully contended that it was essential for China to overthrow the Manchu dynasty and establish a republic in order to inaugurate a new era. They founded *The People's Tribune* (*Min-pao*) in 1905 to debate with Liang, providing such editorials as "A Refutation of the Recent Statement in *The New People's Miscellany* on the Inadvisability of Revolution" and "A Refutation of the Statement that Revolution Can Incur Partition," in defense of their position. The younger generation found such sweeping views extremely refreshing and stimulating.

The empress dowager, whose hatred for revolution exceeded her distaste for constitutionalism, determined to lend support to the constitutional movement, which she considered a lesser evil. She readily assented to Yüan Shih-k'ai's recommendation in July 1905 that the court send Manchu princes and nobles abroad to investigate foreign political systems as a prelude to introducing a constitution. She knew that this undertaking would prove time-consuming, and therefore work in her favor.

An investigatory mission of five members was created under the leader-

5. Liang Ch'i-ch'ao, 102.

ship of Tsai-tse, a Manchu noble. Three of the members were to visit Japan, Britain, France, and Belgium, while two others were to proceed to the United States, Germany, Austria, and Italy. On the day of their departure from Peking, August 26, 1905, a revolutionary[6] set off a bomb in the railway station, terrifying two members into withdrawing. A reconstituted delegation set out on December 11, 1905, in two groups, returning home the following July.

The mission reported favorable impressions of the British and German systems of government, but concluded that the Japanese constitution was more suitable to China because of greater similarity between the two countries. The Manchu leader of the mission, Tsai-tse, personally proposed adoption of a constitution within five years, impressing upon the dowager the threefold advantages of such a move: it would preserve the Ch'ing dynasty, reduce friction with foreign powers, and facilitate the repression of internal rebellion. He indicated, moreover, that a well-designed constitution could become an instrument of executive power, providing concentrated leadership in the central government. "When a constitution is established," he stated, "the powers of the governors and governors-general in the provinces and of the high officials at court will not be as great as before." The recommendation was approved by a royal commission, and endorsed by the dowager on September 1, 1906. But she shrewdly neglected to specify the date of promulgation.

Divergent views with regard to the constitution were held by different factions in government. The dowager considered it a convenient device by which to conciliate the public without actually compromising her own power. The Manchus saw in it a chance to centralize government control and exclude the Chinese from inner circles, thereby wresting power from the provincial governors-general, who were predominantly Chinese. Thus constitutionalism became an anti-Chinese device of the Manchus. On the other hand, to many Chinese constitutionalism provided hope of liberation from unfair, oppressive Manchu discrimination and domination.

Having assented to the principle of constitutionalism, the court appointed a group of officials to deliberate on the reform of governmental institutions on September 2, 1906, as a first step toward establishment of a constitutional monarchy. Conflict of interests and fear of criticism led to the decision to exclude five offices from discussion: the Grand Council, the Department of Imperial Household, the Eight Banners, the Hanlin Academy, and the eunuchs. A report on administrative reorganiza-

6. Wu Yüeh.

tion, which was finally submitted, stressed concentration of responsibility, elimination of inveterate governmental weakness, and the increase of efficiency. On the grounds of this study, the court issued a decree of reform on November 7, 1906, proposing that

1. The Grand Council, the Grand Secretariat, the Ministry of Foreign Affairs and the Ministry of Education would remain unchanged, along with the Hanlin Academy, the Imperial Clan Court, the Imperial Board of Astronomy, the Imperial Department of Equipage, and the Imperial Medical Department.
2. The Board of Civil Offices would become the Ministry of Civil Offices.
3. The Board of Revenue would become the Ministry of Finance.
4. The Ministry of Police would become the Ministry of Civil Affairs.
5. The Board of War would become the Minstry of the Army, absorbing the Bureau of Military Training, and the Imperial Stud (*T'ai-p'u ssu*).
6. The Board of Punishments would become the Ministry of Justice.
7. The Board of Public Works and the Ministry of Commerce would be enlarged into a Ministry of Agriculture, Industry, and Commerce.
8. The Ministry of Rites would absorb the Court of Sacrificial Worship (*T'ai-ch'ang ssu*), the Banqueting Court, (*Kuang-lu ssu*) and the Court of State Ceremonial (*Hung-lu ssu*).
9. The Court of Judicature and Revision (*Ta-li ssu*) would become the Supreme Court (*Ta-li yüan*).
10. A new ministry of Posts and Communications was to absorb the several agencies of steamship, railway, telegraph, and postal service.
11. The Court of Colonial Affairs (*Li-fan yüan*) would become the Ministry of Dependencies.
12. A National Assembly (*Tzu-cheng yüan*) would be inaugurated to give expression to public opinion, and an Audit Department (*Shen-chi yüan*) would examine public expenditure.

The reorganization constituted a power coup which achieved little more than expanding Six Boards into eleven modern-sounding ministries. It created the image of modern constitutionalism but retained the essence of the old governmental procedure. It provided an institutional reshuffle, which was actually retrogressive in that it increased Manchu power in proportion to that of the Chinese. The new proposals simply eliminated the previous equal distribution of offices between the two ethnic groups, providing a new ratio which distinctly favored the ruling Manchus. The thirteen leaders in the Grand Council and the eleven ministries[7] now contained seven Manchus, four Chinese, one Mongol and one Chinese bannerman. Since the last two usually followed Manchu leadership, the Chinese accounted for less than one-third of the top echelons in government after the reorganization. The widened schism between Manchus and Chinese disappointed many proponents of constitutionalism.

Manchu power consolidation took place in local government, too. The court curbed the powers of the governors-general and governors in 1907 by directly appointing provincial judicial, police, and agricultural-industrial-commercial commissioners. Carefully worked out measures then followed to withdraw the two most coveted powers of local authorities when the court appointed provincial financial commissioners and transferred provincial forces to the new Ministry of Army. Yüan Shih-k'ai lost four of his six Peiyang divisions. The court delivered a coup de grace on August 1907, when it transferred the two most powerful Chinese governors-general, Chang Chih-tung and Yüan Shih-k'ai, to Peking as grand councillors, with the latter serving concurrently as minister of foreign affairs. Under the guise of constitutionalism, the Manchus successfully carried out their anti-Chinese policy and achieved unprecedented concentration of power.

A few promising aspects of the constitutional movement existed, however. These provided for the establishment of a Bureau of Constitutional Compilation, in August 1907; the dispatch of three officials, in September 1907, to Japan, Britain, and Germany to study constitutionalism; the appointment of two individuals, one Chinese and one Manchu, to inaugurate a National Assembly; and the order to establish provincial, prefectural, and district assemblies.

The reformers of 1898, still in exile in Japan, were apparently heartened by developments in China. Hoping to be invited to join the constitutional movement, Liang Ch'i-ch'ao suspended publication of his *New People's Miscellany* and proceeded to organize a Political Information Society (*Cheng-wen she*) in Japan, to promote (1) responsible parliamentary government; (2) legal reform to insure judiciary independence;

---

7. Foreign Affairs, Civil Affairs, Internal Affairs, Finance, Education, War, Justice, Rites, Agriculture-Industry-Commerce, Posts and Communications, Dependencies.

(3) local self-government and clear demarcation of authority vis-à-vis the central government; and (4) cautious diplomacy to strive for equal rights in the international community. Members of the society showed interest in cooperating with the Ch'ing court, but Yüan Shih-k'ai who betrayed the reformers in 1898 refused to have anything to do with them; so did the dowager, who hated K'ang and Liang.

Revolutionaries under Dr. Sun Yat-sen, on the other hand, ridiculed Liang and associates for their flirtation with the reactionary court. Rejected by both the court and the revolutionaries, the Political Information Society was left in midstream. Some members of the society, however, secretly returned to China in an attempt to goad social leaders, students, and overseas groups into demanding the early establishment of parliament and the immediate promulgation of a constitution. In response, the court prohibited student participation in political movements and public speech-making on December 25, 1907, and on July 25, 1908, it banned the activities of the society. By this time the government had completely failed to muzzle the hue and cry of the constitutionalists. Dozens of so-called "Constitution-Protection Clubs" sprang up in the provinces, and waves of delegates came to Peking to petition for the early promulgation of the constitution. The tide became so powerful that even Manchu bannermen joined the cause. Under such pressure, the court, on August 27, 1908, issued an "Outline of Constitution" (*Hsien-fa ta-kang*), a parliamentary law, and prescribed a nine-year tutelage period before the constitution became effective.

The empress dowager never genuinely contemplated introducing any constitutional monarchy in China. The Ch'ing "Outline" actually gave the throne even greater power than the Japanese model. It specified that executive, legislative, and judiciary power resided in the emperor, who, sacred and inviolable, would continue to rule the empire in the unbroken line of ten thousand generations. Parliament could consider, but not decide, questions of government; the laws and regulations passed by it would not become effective without the approval of the sovereign. Furthermore, provisions with regard to the rights and duties of the citizens were little more than meaningless formalities. The "Outline of Constitution" was an instrument of imperial procrastination, in the attempt to consolidate dynastic power and prolong the Manchu rule. In no way did it benefit the Chinese people. In spite of these safeguards, the dowager was still reluctant to put the "Outline" into practice, and sought to delay the introdutcion of a constitution in China during her lifetime by requiring a nine-year gestation period, following the Japanese pattern.[8] During this time certain measures were to be gradually instituted. Among them were the following:

> First year, 1908-09: organization of provincial assemblies.
> Second year, 1909-10: inauguration of provincial assemblies.
> Third year, 1910-11: inauguration of the national assembly.
> Fourth year, 1911-12: organization of an auditing system and investigation of the budget of the empire.
> Fifth year, 1912-13: implementation of local self-government.
> Sixth year, 1913-14: adoption of a budget for the empire.
> Seventh year, 1914-15: strict adherence to the budget; literacy rate: 1 per cent of the populace.
> Eighth year, 1915-16: abolition of distinction between the Manchus and the Chinese; literacy rate: 2 per cent of the populace.
> Ninth year, 1916-17: issuance of constitution, parliamentary law, election regulations for the two houses; election for the two houses; and literacy rate: 5 per cent of the populace.[9]

The dowager, already 73, apparently had great confidence in her longevity and delaying tactics; but a serious illness hit her in less than three months and ended her life on November 15, 1908. An announcement regarding the strangely coincidental death on the preceding day of the 37-year-old emperor, Kuang Hsü, followed the dowager's demise. Despite accounts of his having Bright's disease, court sources close to the emperor concurred that he had enjoyed excellent health and had seldom been sick in his life. Legend reveals that he secretly, if imprudently, rejoiced over the dowager's impending death. The Imperial Woman then vengefully vowed: "I cannot die before him!" Indications point to the possibility that she poisoned him the day before she died. Widespread rumor circulated that Yüan Shih-k'ai participated in the plot because he had betrayed the emperor in 1898 and dreaded his return to power, but there was no evidence to substantiate this story.

The dowager's three-year-old grandnephew, P'u-i,[10] succeeded to the throne, with his father, the second Prince Chün,[11] acting as regent. The prince appeared bent on eliminating Yüan for his betrayal of the late

8. In 1881 the Japanese emperor promised a Diet (parliament) in 1890.
9. Full details in Cameron, 205-7.
10. Later known as Henry Pu-yi.
11. Tsai-feng, half-brother of the late Emperor Kuang-hsü.

emperor, but was restrained by fear of mutiny among the Peiyang forces. The Chinese statesman Chang Chih-tung also reportedly cautioned him against killing high officials during the period of imperial mourning. Prince Chün then insisted that Yüan was suffering from a leg ailment, from which he needed to recuperate in quiet retirement. On January 2, 1909, Yüan was forced out of the government.

Having successfully avenged the late emperor's betrayal and enforced an inherently anti-Chinese policy, Prince Chün now posed, purportedly, as the instrument of constitutional monarchism. On February 17, 1909, he ordered the establishment of provincial assemblies, which were inaugurated October 14. With the creation of these popular bodies, the demand for the convocation of parliament gained rapid momentum. Three times in the following year—on January 26, June 22, and October 3, 1910—representatives of sixteen provinces went to Peking to petition the early convening of parliament. Even though they were supported by massive signatures on the order of 200,000, 300,000, and 25,000,000, respectively, the court turned a deaf ear to their request. It reprimanded them for interfering with state affairs and insolently ordered them to go home. Thus insulted, these representatives, mostly chairmen and vice-chairmen of their respective provincial assemblies, met in a secret conclave and reputedly decided to throw their sympathies quietly to the revolutionaries.[12] In spite of the tremendous pressure from the provincial assemblies and private constitutionalists, all Prince Chün did was to announce on November 4, 1910, that he would shorten the period of constitutional preparation from nine to six years. At the same time, he furthered his anti-Chinese policy by organizing a "Royal Cabinet" on May 8, 1911, with five imperial relatives among the thirteen appointees. There were eight Manchus and one Mongol bannerman, but only four Chinese, in this cabinet. When provincial assemblies protested against royal domination of the cabinet, they were pointedly reminded by Prince Chün of the throne's absolute control of appointments, designated in the "Outline of Constitution." The Chinese became increasingly convinced that genuine constitutionalism was impossible under Manchu leadership.

Disillusion and disappointment generated mounting anti-Manchu sentiment and swung public feeling toward the revolutionary cause. Within a few months, Dr. Sun Yat-sen's party swept the Ch'ing dynasty into the oblivion of history.

12. P'eng-yüan Chang, "The Constitutionalists," Mary C. Wright (ed.), China in Revolution, 160-70.

FURTHER READING

Bland, J. O. P., *Recent Events and Present Policies in China* (Philadelphia, 1912).

——, and E. Backfouse, *China under the Empress Dowager* (Philadelphia, 1910).

Cameron, Meribeth E., *The Reform Movement in China, 1898-1912* (Stanford, 1931).

Chang, P'eng-yüan 張朋園, *Liang Ch'i-ch'ao yü Ch'ing-chi ko-ming* 梁啓超與清季革命 (Liang Ch'i-ch'ao and the late Ch'ing revolution), (Taipei, 1964).

Ch'en, Jerome, *Yüan Shih-k'ai, 1859-1916* (Stanford, 1961), chapters 3-7.

Chu, Samuel C., *Reform in Modern China: Chang Chien, 1853-1926* (New York, 1965).

Der Ling, Princess, *Old Buddha (Empress Tzu Hsi)* (London, 1929).

Franke, Wolfgang, *The Reform and Abolition of the Traditional Chinese Examination System* (Cambridge, Mass., 1960).

Haldane, Charlotte, *The Last Great Empress of China* (Indianapolis, 1965).

Kent, Percy Horace, *The Passing of the Manchus* (London, 1912).

Levenson, Joseph R., *Liang Ch'i-ch'ao and the Mind of Modern China* (Cambridge, Mass., 1953).

Reid, John G., *The Manchu Abdication and the Powers, 1908-1912* (Berkeley, 1935).

Sun, E-tu Zen, "The Chinese Constitutional Missions of 1905-1906," *Journal of Modern History*, 24:3:251-68 (Sept. 1952).

T'ai, Hung-tz'u 戴鴻慈, *Ch'u-shih chiu-kuo jih-chi* 出使九國日記 (Diary of my diplomatic mission to nine countries), (Peking, 1906).

Tsai-tse 載澤, *K'ao-ch'a cheng-chih jih-chi* 考察政治日記 (My diary of political studies abroad), (Peking, 1908).

18

Late Ch'ing Intellectual, Social, and Economic Changes, with Special Reference to 1895-1911

The late Ch'ing was a period of drastic transformation, with the pace of change accelerating after 1895. There occurred not only radical political reorganization as described in the previous chapter—from autocracy to constitutional monarchy, from a government of Six Boards to that of multiple ministries—but also great changes in intellectual, social, and economic life. Intellectually, in addition to the aforementioned Modern Text Movement (Chapter 15), there was a fundamental reorientation of outlook and activity as a result of shifting trends in traditional learning and the influx of Western ideas. Socially, the individual emerged as the basic unit of society, replacing the family and the clan, while two new classes, the compradores and militarists, gained prominence, and the cities grew enormously. Economically, there was an increasing stricture upon government finances, a growing trade imbalance, and a deepening foreign control of the modernized section of Chinese economy. Seldom had China seen such drastic socioeconomic and intellectual changes in so short a time.[1]

INTELLECTUAL REORIENTATION

The Metamorphosis of Traditional Learning. Late Ch'ing intellectual trends differed markedly from the middle period. The double challenge of domestic rebellion and foreign invasion forced the scholars to reexamine their role in society. The Han School of Empirical Research (*K'ao-cheng hsüeh*), with its preoccupation with antiquarian studies and its

1. The idea of a rapidly changing China after 1900 has been convincingly presented in Mary C. Wright (ed.), *China in Revolution, The First Phase, 1900-1913* (New Haven, 1968), 1-63, "Introduction: The Rising Tide of Change."

pride in pursuing knowledge for the sake of knowledge, struck a discordant note in the rapidly changing times. This school, as noted in Chapter 4, had reached its zenith during the middle Ch'ing period, with its methodology firmly established and its scope of investigation clearly defined. By the Chia-ch'ing period (1796-1820) it had exhausted nearly all the principal subjects, and its latter-day followers sought the baubles of trivia and minutiae, wrangling over the undefinable nomenclature of artifacts and esoteric technical terms and institutions of ancient times. Yet they behaved as if they were the oligarchs of learning. As a consequence the school suffered a growing inner decay. A further blow was struck during the Taiping era when its major centers of activities—Anhwei, Chekiang, and Kiangsu—experienced the worst devastation. Scholars either fled or joined the military and government services; there were simply not enough able men left to uphold the school. Staggered by the blows from within and without, the school found itself unable to maintain its leadership in the learned world.

The breakdown of the Han domination liberated other schools from their subservient status. The Sung school of Neo-Confucian studies regained respectability, with T'ang Chien and Wo-jen as the leading exponents. The T'ung-ch'eng (Anhwei) School of Ancient-Style Writing, the lone opponent of Han orthodoxy at its height, gained increasing popularity and drew such men as Tseng Kuo-fan in his earlier years. The Modern Text Movement arose, emphasizing the unity of scholarship and politics and culminating in K'ang Yu-wei's reform movement. The "New Scholars" also emerged, taking a strong interest in Western learning. The scope of late Ch'ing intellectual trends, indeed, exceeded the framework of the traditional scholarship of the past two thousand years.

Through this changed intellectual atmosphere flowed two parallel currents: the revival of the idea of "practical statesmanship" (i.e. unity of knowledge and practice) and the trend toward intellectual tolerance and integration. At a time when the country was hard pressed with the vital problems of foreign invasion and domestic upheaval, the scholars felt a moral obligation to contribute their share to social and political stabilization. Even the Han scholars renounced their traditional apathy toward public affairs. All late Ch'ing scholars—be they classicists, historians, Sung scholars, Han scholars, T'ung-ch'eng scholars, Modern Text scholars, novelists, or translators of Western works—shared the conviction that they had an integral role to play in public affairs.

Moreover, with the collapse of the Han orthodoxy, the schools no longer jealously guarded their boundaries. Scholars tended to take interest in a broad spectrum of subjects and approaches. Those who bullheadedly clung to a single school or a narrow approach no longer could command respect. Thus, the T'ung-ch'eng writers adopted ideas from both the Han and the Sung schools, just as the Neo-Confucian scholars took to Ancient-Style Writing to rival the Han empirical researchers. For instance, the great statesman Tseng Kuo-fan had an early interest in the T'ung-ch'eng School, whence he moved to Neo-Confucian studies and Han textual criticism, finally ending up with a remarkable public career. He had, in fact, attempted to integrate (Sung) philosophy, (Han) textual criticism, literature, and practical statesmanship into one comprehensive, basic learning, called the *li-hsüeh*, to reflect the Confucian concept of *li*, or propriety. K'ang Yu-wei moved from Neo-Confucian studies to Modern Texts and to Western works of political reform. Broad interest in and a syncretic approach to learning characterized the age. Hence, the late Ch'ing intellectual world, having moved from the dominance of one school (Han) to the juxtaposition of many, moved again from division toward integration. In this process, the mental horizon of Ch'ing scholars was rendered much broader than before, reaching out of the traditional boundary into Western studies.[2]

The "New Learning." The influx of Western ideas began with the translation of the Bible and religious tracts in the pre-Opium War period. Of the 795 titles translated by Protestant missionaries between 1810 and 1867, 86 per cent were in religion, and only 6 per cent in the humanities and sciences. During the 1861-95 Self-strengthening Movement, translations extended into diplomacy, military arts, science, and technology. Of 567 works translated between 1850 and 1899, 40 per cent were in applied sciences, 30 per cent in natural sciences, 10 per cent in history and geography, 8 per cent in social sciences, and about 3.5 per cent in religion, philosophy, literature, and the fine arts.[3] During this stage, emphasis was on science and technology, the chief sources of information being Anglo-American works, which accounted for 85 per cent of all translations as opposed to 15 per cent from Japanese texts.

After the Japanese war of 1894-95 the trend shifted. The narrowness of China's modernization program became fully apparent: men of fore-

2. Hsiao I-shan, IV, 1,746, 1,748, 1,951-60.
3. Tsuen-hsiun Tsien, "Western Impact on China through Translations," *Far Eastern Quarterly*, XIII:3:311, 315 (May 1954).

sight realized clearly that she must broaden her understanding of the West beyond merely military and industrial techniques to include studies of political institutions, economic systems, social structures, and scientific as well as philosophical thought. Translations of Western works in these fields became a paramount prerequisite to reform and renovation. K'ang Yu-wei and Liang Ch'i-ch'ao indefatigably urged massive translations of Western and Japanese works, and Liang was appointed to organize an official translation bureau during the "Hundred-Day" Reform. But the project failed to materialize, due to the lightning success of the conservative coup. After the Boxer Rebellion, the Peking Imperial University absorbed the old T'ung-wen kuan translation bureau, completing a number of translations and compilations of textbooks in mathematics, physics, trigonometry, education, and philosophy. In 1907 the Ch'ing court formally created a Bureau of Translation and Compilation, to which many proud products of the old literary examinations were appointed. Among them was Wang Kuo-wei, a solid scholar who took great interest in Kant, Schopenhauer, and Nietzsche. On the whole, however, the official translation bureaus had less impact on China's culture than did the private translators. Among the latter, two were particularly remarkable: Yen Fu and Lin Shu.

Yen Fu (1854-1921) of Hou-kuan, Fukien, pioneered a new direction in China's endeavor to understand the modern West. The first Chinese to sustain a serious introduction of Western thought, he attempted as few before him to delve into Western theories, law, sociology, and philosophy, and to make a comparative study of Western and Chinese civilizations.

Having received in childhood a thorough grounding in the Chinese classics, and having become acquainted with both the Han and Sung approaches to learning, at fourteen Yen entered the naval academy at the Foochow Dockyard; there he acquired a new education in English, arithmetic, algebra, geometry, trigonometry, physics, chemistry, mechanics, geology, astronomy, and navigation. He graduated with high honors in 1871 and was immediately assigned to active service, which took him to Japan, Malaya, the Philippines, and Taiwan. Selected in 1876 to study in an English naval academy, he arrived in the British Isles the following year at a time when the great masters and thinkers—Darwin, Huxley, and Spencer—were shaking the world with their ideas of evolution and the social application of the struggle for survival. Yen's immediate attraction to Darwinism came not so much from its biological import as its stress on the assertive energy of men and the "actualization of potentialities within a competitive situation."[4] Not surprisingly, Yen began to examine China's problems and her position in the world in the light of social Darwinism.

Eager to discover the sources of Western (particularly British) wealth and power, Yen Fu diligently studied the British political systems, economic institutions, social philosophy, and legal concepts. This broad interest in Western civilization, rather than just the narrow subject of the navy, and his penetrating grasp of China's plight in the modern world brought him to the attention of the liberal Chinese minister in London, Kuo Sung-tao, who, as we may recall, had repeatedly urged Li Hung-chang to broaden the scope of Self-strengthening to include the study of Western political, social, and legal systems, much as the Japanese students and visitors in Britain were doing. Kuo's voice had gone unheeded by Li, but now found a sympathetic listener in Yen. The two of them, despite wide divergences in age and position, often engaged in long discussions on the differences between Chinese and Western civilizations. Above all Kuo was impressed with his youthful friend's assertion that the basis of British power was the legal concept of impartial justice.[5]

Yen returned home in 1879 and was made dean of instruction at Li Hung-chang's Peiyang Naval Academy at Tientsin, where he remained for nearly twenty years. Though he rose to its superintendency in 1890, he was never taken into confidence by Li, and his naval career never truly blossomed; while his Japanese contemporaries in Britain, such as Itō and Tōgō, all became leaders of a modernization which turned their country into a powerful state.[6] Frustrated by his inability to help his country, especially after the Peiyang fleet's fiasco in the Japanese war, in which many of his former colleagues and students were casualties, Yen began to lash out at China's weakness through writing and translation. In this he finally found his true vocation as a publicist, free and able to air his pent-up ideas.

A key to Western development, he loudly proclaimed to his countrymen, was the "different vision of reality" which involved ideas and values; it was thought, not military power, which made a country strong and

4. Benjamin I. Schwartz, *In Search of Wealth and Power: Yen Fu and the West* (Cambridge, Mass., 1964), 46.
5. *Ibid.*, 29.
6. Itō Hirobumi became premier, while Tōgō Heihachirō rose to be an admiral and distinguished himself in the Sino-Japanese and Russo-Japanese wars. See Edwin Albert Falk, *Togo and the Rise of Japanese Sea Power* (New York, 1936).

wealthy. In order to acquaint his people with firsthand knowledge of Western ideas, he spent the next fifteen years translating a number of important works, including T. H. Huxley's *Evolution and Ethics* (1900), J. S. Mill's *On Liberty* (1903) and *Logic* (1905), Herbert Spencer's *A Study of Sociology,* Montesquieu's *De l'esprit des lois* (1909), Edward Jenk's *A History of Politics,* and William S. Jevon's *Logic.* For the first time the Chinese met the ideas of evolution, free trade, the principles of sociology, and the division of power in government.

The crux of Yen's message in all his writings was that the basic difference between China and the modern West lay in their dissimilar attitudes toward human energy. The West exalted action, assertiveness, struggle, and dynamism in order to actualize the unlimited human potentialities. Government and society provided favorable conditions—liberty, rising equality of opportunity, self-government, public spirit, and impartial justice—to facilitate the liberation of the individual's inner energies, and channeled them toward collective goals. The government promoted rather than suppressed the individual's constructive self-interest, so that the public and private interests reinforced each other. Thus, when Britain fostered ideas, values, and proper environment for the fulfillment of human potential, and when she elevated her people's capability, intelligence, and morality, she became rich and powerful.[7]

In China, he contended, the opposite held true. The ways of the Sages discouraged the development of the people's capacities and inhibited the free flow of their vital energies. The traditional rulers since the Ch'in dynasty (221 B.C.-206 B.C.) had all been "robbers," skimming off the cream of the populace and failing to elevate their intelligence. This was the basic trouble of China, Yen pointed out in a ten-thousand-word memorial which he prepared for, but did not have time to submit to, Emperor Kuang-hsu during the short-lived 1898 reform. He bluntly announced that 70 per cent of China's troubles were internal, only 30 per cent external. What China needed was not a piecemeal improvement, but a radical change in her view on domestic peace and order. The traditional rulers, he insisted, had always tried to keep the people weak and ignorant so as to facilitate their control of the country. They deprecated competition and innovation and admonished men to follow ancestral paths in order to achieve stability. They encouraged thrift and discouraged the development of resources. They honored antiquity and despised modernity. They deplored aggressiveness and promoted contentment, and

7. Schwartz, 70-75, 238-43.

they inculcated in the people a habit of meekness to forestall rebellion. All this, Yen proclaimed, reversed the Western promotion of progress and improvement through competition, release of energies, and elevation of human capacity and intelligence.[8]

Yen's exaltation of Western assertiveness and dynamism, and his deprecation of Chinese passivity and enervation led later to the description of Western civilization as activity-oriented (*tung-te wen-hua*) and Chinese civilization as stability-oriented (*ching-te wen-hua*).

If the traditional Chinese methods of maintaining domestic order led to poverty, ignorance, and weakness, Yen argued, discard them, even though they were the work of the Sages. On the other hand, he insisted, if Western methods could alter the deplorable situation, adopt them; for knowledge knows no national boundary. China must change her old ways and compete for survival in the modern world. She must develop patriotism and nationalism, foster universal technical and scientific education, promote popular economic self-interest, and create "the organs of a rationalized national state."[9] This in essence was Yen's message to his countrymen.

Yen was noteworthy not only for his ideas but also for his excellent writing style. In his translation he followed the threefold criteria of faithfulness (*hsin*), comprehensiveness (*ta*), and elegance (*ya*). Because of the syntactical differences between Chinese and Western languages, Yen's translations were basically not literal renditions but summations or paraphrasings of the original. His method was to immerse himself in the original, capture its spirit and quintessence, and then communicate its meaning in idiomatic, classical Chinese. For instance, he conveyed the essential meaning of "the struggle for existence" and "the survival of the fittest" by rendering them as: "Things struggle; nature selects. The superior is victorious; the inferior vanquished."

His lofty, abstruse, terse, and elegant style was very much in the tradition of the T'ung-ch'eng school of Ancient Style. At the completion of a piece of work he would always ask for comment from his mentor, Wu Ju-lun, an Ancient-Stylist and protégé of Tseng Kuo-fan. Wu had nothing but high praise for his contributions and literary elegance, but unfortunately Yen's high style militated against popular acceptance, appealing to only a small group of educated elite, such as Liang Ch'i-ch'ao. Consequently his influence had too little circumference. Nonetheless, Yen

8. Hsiao I-shan, IV, 2,021-24.
9. Schwartz, 185.

Fu lived to become a monument in the annals of Sino-Western cultural exchange. It was he who first made a penetrating, comparative study of the two diverse civilizations and came up with bold answers to the perennial questions: "What does the West have that China does not?" and "What are the sources of Western power and wealth?"

Contemporary with Yen Fu was Lin Shu (1852-1924), another great translator, who excelled in rendering Western novels. Born into a humble family in Nan-t'ai, near Foochow, Lin grew up under extreme hardship. His father having gone to Taiwan to seek employment when Lin was only four, the family subsisted on an income from needlework done by his mother and elder sister. However, Lin began his education at ten with a local teacher, who drew him to the works of past masters, such as the T'ang essayists Han Yü and Ou-yang Hsiu and the poet Tu Fu. From them he acquired the terse, pithy style that characterized his lifelong work. Having attained the first and second literary degrees in 1872 and 1882, but having repeatedly failed the examinations for the coveted third degree, he resigned himself, a disgruntled literatus, to teaching.

A tubercular, Lin was characteristically sensitive, tense, sentimental, and impulsive. A series of family deaths—his mother in 1895, his wife in 1897, and two of his children in the next two years—threw him into despondency and loneliness. To raise him from despair, a friend,[10] who had been a cadet at the Foochow Naval Academy and a law student at the University of Paris, suggested that they jointly translate Alexander Dumas's *La Dame aux camélias*. Aware of Lin's unfamiliarity with foreign languages, this friend translated orally as Lin composed it into acceptable Chinese. So successful was this "oral translation" that it set the pattern for Lin's later projects. Lin moved his pen extremely fast, often completing his written version simultaneously with the oral rendition.[11] The scope of his translation was vast, ranging from romantic fiction to social novels, fables, biographies, plays, and detective stories. His most famous translations included the above-mentioned *La Dame aux camélias*; Charles Dickens's *Oliver Twist, David Copperfield, The Old Curiosity Shop, Dombey and Son*, and *Nicholas Nickleby* (all published between 1907 and 1908); H. Rider Haggard's *King Solomon's Mines, Montezuma's Daughter*, and *Beatrice*; Sir Walter Scott's *Ivanhoe, The Talisman*, and *The Betrothed*. In his lifetime Lin completed no less than 159 titles, in 12 million words.

10. Wang Tzu-jen.
11. Two of his most constant collaborators were Wei I and Tseng Tsung-kung.

Though readily admitting the inaccuracies of oral translation, Lin, because of his sensitivity and excellent literary endowment, was able to grasp the spirit, mood, and humor of the original by instinct. Hence he came remarkably close to the essence of the novels he translated. He achieved the result by spontaneously merging himself with the characters, as he explained: "People in a book become at once my nearest and dearest relatives. When they are in difficulties, I fall into despair; when they are successful, I am triumphant. I am no longer a human being but a puppet whom the author dangles on his strings."[12] He attained such success in communicating the original feeling in a restrained, classical style that at times his translations were considered superior to the originals. Arthur Waley, a leading contemporary English translator of Eastern works, remarked after comparing Lin's versions with Dickens's own works: "The humor is there, but is transmuted by a precise, economic style; every point that Dickens spoils by uncontrolled exuberance, Lin Shu makes quietly and effectively."[13] On the other hand, errors and distortions were also present in Lin's editions—for instance, when he rendered some of Shakespeare's plays into prose narratives. On the whole, however, his translations convey more of the original spirit of the Western literature than a beginning Chinese student of foreign languages could possibly attain from a direct reading.

Lin couched his translations in the cogent, ancient style of the T'ung-ch'eng school, although he himself denied any formal association with it. The fact that the famed ancient stylist Wu Ju-lun praised his works is evidence enough of the close affiliation. Indeed, so dedicated was Lin to the classical form that he contemptuously derided Liang Ch'i-ch'ao's new style of writing as journalistic and spurious ("wild fox"), and chided the "Plain Language" (*Pai-hua*) of the late 1910's and the 1920's as the output of street peddlers.

Through Lin, Western literature was first introduced into China, and through his translations the Chinese for the first time gained invaluable insights into Western customs, social problems, literary currents, ethical concepts, familial relations, and the glittering world of literature itself. In addition to the translations, Lin often promoted patriotism, nationalism, social progress, and better human relationships in the prologues and introductions of his works. His influence on the younger generation

12. Leo Ou-fan Lee, "Lin Shu and His Translations: Western Fiction in Chinese Perspective," *Papers on China*, East Asian Research Center, Harvard University, 19: 186 (December 1965).
13. *Ibid.*, 187.

cannot be overemphasized. Though his tenacious adherence to the ancient style caused him to lag behind the times, his contributions rank him with Yen Fu as one of the twin luminaries in the firmament of Chinese translators at the turn of the century.

Japanese Translations. In addition to Western works, numerous Japanese translations of Western subjects were also rendered into Chinese. K'ang Yu-wei and Liang Ch'i-ch'ao, during the "Hundred-Day" Reform, vigorously promoted the use of the Japanese media as a convenient short cut to the essentials of Western learning, since the Japanese had already translated many of the more important Western masterpiecs, and because learning Japanese was easier than learning a Western language. In a preface to a catalogue of Japanese works to be translated, K'ang humorously stated: "I regard the West as a cow, and the Japanese as the farmhand, while I myself sit back and enjoy the food!"

Although the failure of the reform program obviated en masse translation of Japanese works, K'ang and Liang continued to provide the idea during their exile in Japan, and they influenced a vast number of Chinese students in that country. The Ch'ing court, as well as provincial authorities and private parties, had been sending increasing numbers of students to Japan, until the count had reached some 13,000 in 1906. The students not only delivered into Chinese a great variety of Japanese books and translations of Western works, but also borrowed many Japanese terms for key subjects, such as *che-hsüeh* (philosophy), *ching-chi-hsüeh* (economics), and *she-hui-hsüeh* (sociology). The late Ch'ing new educational system was modeled upon that of Japan, as were most of the textbooks. Between 1902 and 1904 translations from Japanese sources accounted for 62.2 per cent of the total 573 works, while British sources dwindled to 10.7 per cent, and American to 6.1 per cent. Of the total, social sciences occupied 25.5 per cent, history and geography 24 per cent, natural science 21 per cent, applied sciences 10.5 per cent, philosophy 6.5 per cent, and literature 4.8 per cent.[14] Clearly Japan had replaced Britain and the United States as the chief supplier of information, and the emphasis had shifted from science and technology to social sciences, philosophy, and literature. China's interest in the West had definitely moved from military science to social studies and the humanities.

The translation of Western and Japanese works resulted in widespread dissemination of foreign ideas among the educated Chinese. Democracy,

14. Tsuen-hsuin Tsien, 319.

parliamentary government, constitution, division of power, liberty, equality of the sexes, Darwinism, and a host of other imported concepts invaded the discussions and idiom of the intelligentsia. Such ideas could not but exert a considerable impact upon the society.

SOCIAL CHANGES

The kinship society of China, with its age-old customs, values, and emphasis upon the family and clan as basic units, was shaken to its foundations during the last decade of the dynasty. The Confucian concepts of family loyalty, filial piety, chastity, Three Bonds, and Five Relationships gave way to Western ideas of individualism, freedom, and equality of the sexes. Realization grew that the individual was more a member of the society and state than of the family, vested with inalienable rights upon which nobody, not even the family elders, could infringe. Young Chinese began to assert their independence from their families and to condemn Confucian teachings on proper relationships as obsolescent and feudal. The omnipotence of the family head was challenged.

The Disintegration of the Family-centered Society. Until the late Ch'ing, the traditional Chinese family resembled a miniature kingdom in which the head occupied the place of the sovereign, with authority to enact family law and make life and death decisions for the members. The government, recognizing this familial omnipotence, never intervened in the domestic relations between father and son, husband and wife, and brother and sister. However, with the influx of foreign doctrines and political philosophy, New Scholars of Western Learning began to promote the radical notion that the power of the family head logically belonged to the state, that the inalienable rights of the individual were beyond the control of the family head, and that as basic components of the state, male and female should be equal. These ideas, striking at the very roots of family relations, won currency among the young. Furthermore, the opening of modern schools at the turn of the century in effect meant that the government had taken over from the family the responsibility for educating the youth. Thus, when the state intervened in family relationships, it struck away the political prop for a kinship society.

Concomitantly, the legal support of the family-centered society also crumbled. The old juridical system, devised to support the kinship social structure, recognized the special position of the family head, the inequality of the sexes, the inability of women to inherit property, the exclusion of sons of concubines and illegitimate marriages from family succession, the collective punishment of family members for crimes committed by one, and the so-called Ten Unpardonable Crimes.[15] It inflicted heavier punishment upon wives than husbands involved in fighting, and sanctioned the Confucian teaching that father and son should shield each other from justice. Reflecting as they did feudal social relationships, they were clearly out of tune with the rapidly changing times. When the new legal codes of the late Ch'ing,[16] as well as those of the early republican period, took into consideration the inalienable rights of the individual, the equality of the sexes, the right of women to inherit property, etc., the old juridical basis of the kinship society was shattered.

Similarly, the economic foundations of the old society tottered. The influx of foreign commodities under preferential customs and the right of foreigners after 1895 to engage in local manufacturing disastrously affected the native handicraft industries and agrarian economy. Foreigners dominated Chinese public utilities, communication, mining, banking, and other modern enterprises. Their factories, by virtue of vast capital and mass production, outsold Chinese rivals even in distant villages. As common an agricultural product as cotton was marketed by foreigners more cheaply than the Chinese could produce it. Farm women who traditionally weaved as a secondary vocation were thrown out of work, and farmers had increasing difficulty eking out a living.

Such economic distress created an adverse impact on familial relationships. The clan and family could no longer provide help and comfort to those members who became unemployed, sick, and destitute. The displaced handicraft worker or the peasant left for the city, where he slipped from family and clan control; if lucky enough to find a new life, his meager income hardly sufficed to support his own dependents, let alone the clansmen. The ties between such a man and his clan became attenuated. Very often the wife and children of such a man were forced to work in a different city just to scrabble out a living, thereby scattering further not only clansmen but even immediate family members. Little wonder that old familial relationships broke down under the impact of the foreign economic invasion.

Shorn of its political, legal, and economic props, the kinship society

15. Parricide, unfilial behavior, incest, lack of harmony, insubordination, rebellion, conspiracy against the ruler, treason, inhuman offenses, and sacrilege.
16. Enacted under leadership of Sun Chia-pen.

simply could not survive. At the same time, it became socially fashionable and economically expedient to adopt the Western style small family system. The big-family system and kinship society gradually passed out of existence as China moved from an agrarian, premodern state toward a proto-industrial, modern society.[17]

The New Classes. The second major social change was the rise of two new social forces, the compradores and the militarists. The former were the new rich, the latter the new power. Both threatened to eclipse the influence of the scholar-official class. Hence the traditional social stratification of the four classes—scholar-official (*shih*), farmer (*nung*), artisan (*kung*), and merchant (*shang*)—could no longer adequately reflect the principal functional orders of society.

The forerunner of the compradore was the "linguist" of pre-Opium War days, who was employed by the foreign trader to transact business with the hong merchant. The compradores subsequently assumed the function of business agents or managers for foreign establishments. Their familiarity with local conditions, as well as their language facility, made them indispensable to foreign banks, trading companies, industrial concerns, and factories. They assisted their foreign employers in finding business sites, recruiting factory workers, selling finished goods, buying raw materials, making investments, and arranging loans to the Chinese government and private parties. They were compensated with a handsome salary and lucrative commissions on a contractual basis. As middlemen they were able to manipulate the terms of transaction between the foreigners and Chinese, reaping a quick and handsome profit. Maintaining wide connections in official and private circles, they led the high life of the former hong merchants. Their association with influential foreign firms, their power to manipulate, their connections and new wealth made them a new social force compelling recognition.

In their business transactions the compradores were contractually bound to work for the benefit of their foreign employers; not infrequently they had to work against the interests of their own country and people. They helped foreign banks to make loans to the Chinese at usurious rates; they opposed any patriotic movement to boycott foreign imports; and they helped the foreigners to squeeze the utmost profit from the Chinese market. Consequently, the compradore class has been dealt much scathing criticism by modern Chinese historians and Marxist scholars alike as un-

17. Hsiao I-shan, IV, 1,455-59.

patriotic, traitorous, and parasitic. Yet many of them, once having acquired sufficient capital and managerial skill, turned to promoting modern industries and enterprises themselves.[18] Obviously one cannot lightly dismiss the compradores as a class of sinners and parasites, for many did contribute to their country's economic development.

The second new social force was that of the militarists. In traditional Chinese society soldiers were held in contempt, as reflected in the popular saying: "Just as good iron is not made into nails, so good men do not become soldiers."[19] However, a new military type arose by the close of the Ch'ing period—men who had received some modern military training and were not illiterate and foolhardy in the traditional image. These were connected with the new army the court had trained after the collapse of Li Hung-chang's Huai army in the Japanese war. Among the leading trainers was Yüan Shih-k'ai, organizer of a new army of 7,000 men fashioned more or less on the German model at Hsiao-chan, some 70 li (23 miles) from Tientsin. His officers, largely chosen from Tientsin Military Academy graduates, owed him personal allegiance. His reputation as an able officer soared when, as governor of Shantung in 1900, he kept that province free from Boxer disturbances. Upon the death of Li Hung-chang in 1901, Yüan succeeded to the important governor-generalship of Chihli. And even though he was later forced by Manchu jealousy to shed command of his new army, his loyal subordinates retained control of these forces. Numbered among these officers were Tuan Ch'i-jui, Feng Kuo-chang, Chang Hsün, and Ts'ao K'un, all destined to be leading power-holders in the late 1910's and 1920's. Yüan and his cohorts, known as the Peiyang clique, exercised tremendous political influence through their military power. That Yüan's original brigade produced five future presidents or acting chief executives, one premier, and most of the warlords in North China testifies to the rise of the militarists as a new social and political class. Appropriately, Yüan was dubbed "father of the warlords."[20]

The Growth of the Cities. A third new social phenomenon was the rise of the great metropolises. The government sponsored Self-strengthening projects centered mostly along the coast and in the treaty ports where foreign assistance was most readily available. Foreigners and their

18. As in the case of Tong King-sing.
19. *Hao-t'ieh pu ta ting, hao-nan pu tang ping.*
20. Ralph C. Powell, *The Rise of Chinese Military Power, 1895-1912* (Princeton, 1955), 76-80.

establishments—such as banks, trading companies, and factories—also located mainly in these ports and leased territories. The greater safety of these places and the concentration of foreign capital therein induced Chinese businessmen to migrate there, while displaced peasants also came to the cities seeking employment, usually ending up in factories operated by foreigners or Chinese entrepreneurs. Increasingly the treaty ports became the financial, industrial, and population centers of China. Such sites as Shanghai, Nanking, Canton, Hankow, and Tientsin expanded into urban centers of considerable size and wealth. The growth of cities and city-centered industries delineates the emerging capitalism of modern China.

ECONOMIC PLIGHT

Budgetary Deficit. Government finances in the late Ch'ing presented a totally different picture from early and middle Ch'ing, when revenue usually exceeded expenditures. In the K'ang-hsi period (1662-1722), in spite of repeated tax remissions totaling in excess of 120 million taels, there was a treasury surplus of 8 million. The Ch'ien-lung period (1736-95) saw the reserve increase to 70 million, despite vast spending and costly military campaigns.

Beginning with the 19th century, however, the situation deteriorated. Domestic rebellions, foreign wars, drought, floods, opium importation, and silver outflow reduced the treasury reserve to a mere 8 million taels by 1850, which was further cut two years later to 3 million taels as a result of military expenses against the Taipings. Normal channels of revenue could no longer sustain the costly campaign, so a new commercial transit tax, the *likin*, was instituted in 1853, with an annual yield of 10 to 20 million taels. In the ensuing two decades, a total of 70 million taels was expended suppressing the Taiping, the Nien, and the Moslem rebellions. These extraordinary outlays set government finances so far back that budgetary imbalance became the order of the day. By the T'ung-chih period (1862-74), the average deficit had grown to 10 million annually—60 million income against 70 million expenditure.

During the Kuang-hsü period (1875-1908), even though the government income increased rapidly, its expenditures grew even more rapidly, causing an ever-widening gap. This sharp increase in expenditures resulted from foreign wars, indemnities, costs of foreign loans, and new Self-strengthening projects. A few major outlays of funds illustrate the burden of the government: military expenses in Sinkiang from 1875-1881, 52 million taels; the Ili indemnity, 5-6 million; the French war of 1884-85, 30 million; the Japanese war of 1894-95, 60 million; the Japanese indemnity, 230 million; the Boxer indemnity, 450 million; river conservancy, 10 million; natural disaster relief, 30 million; and sundry other reparations for "church incidents" and damages to foreign properties. In addition, there was the naval expense on the order of 5 million a year. In 1899, the government expenditure rose to 101 million, against an income of 88.4 million:[21]

1899

Revenue		Expenditures	
Land-poll tax	24 million	Provincial administration	9.1
Wastage allowance	2.5	Interest and payment of	
Tribute grain commuta-		foreign loans	24.0
tion and allowance	2.5	New Army	18.0
Salt gabelle and salt		Green Standard Army	
likin	13.5	and bannermen	13.0
Likin	16.5	Navy	5.0
Customs	26.6	Customs, lighthouses, etc.	3.6
Native opium tax	1.8	River Conservancy	2.5
Others	1.0	Frontier defense	2.0
TOTAL	88.4	Imperial household	1.0
		Legations	1.0
		Railways	.8
		Other central government expenses and military training	21.0
		TOTAL	101.0

The cost and payment of foreign loans, 24 million taels, amounted to 30 per cent of the revenue, 88.4 million. After the Boxer Rebellion, China incurred further the enormous responsibility of 450 million taels of indemnity, of which a total of 225 million was paid between 1902 and 1910. During the same period, considerable sums were spent on new domestic projects, such as the Imperial University, educational system, police, and army. To meet the expenditures, the government attempted a variety of devices, including a tax increase, sale of office, and forced contributions.

21. Hsiao I-shan, IV, 1,534-36; Chi-ming Hou, *Foreign Investment*, 239-40.

Still it had to subsist on foreign loans. From 1874 to 1911, 171.4 million pounds sterling[22] in loans were contracted, of which only 32.3 million pounds sterling had been paid off by the end of the dynasty in 1911, with 139 million still outstanding. The practice of borrowing money to pay former debts plunged the government into a hopeless mire, leaving the new republican government a tremendous financial burden at its birth in 1912.

Trade Imbalance. Foreign trade provides an equally discouraging picture. Imports continuously exceeded exports, causing a steady outflow of capital. The following chart gives a bird's-eye view of foreign trade at ten-year intervals:

Year	Import	Export	Balance
1865	55,715,458 taels	54,103,274	−1,612,184
1875	67,803,247	68,912,929	+1,109,682
1885	88,200,018	65,005,711	−23,194,307
1895	171,696,715	143,293,211	−28,402,504
1905	447,100,082	227,888,197	−219,212,549
1911	471,503,943	377,338,166	−94,165,777

Within the short period of half a century, imports rose nearly nine times, from 55 million taels to 471 million, and exports seven times, from 54 million to 377 million. Except for the short span from 1872 to 1876 when there was a slight favorable balance between 2.5 and 10 million, the entire late Ch'ing period suffered from trade imbalance, with 1905 at the worst when the deficit reached 219 million taels.[23]

The rapid growth of the trade figures did not necessarily indicate a corresponding increase in actual value or volume of the trade, because of the continuous rise in commodity prices and the sharp drop in silver value vis-à-vis the gold. Prices in late Ch'ing, in general, doubled every fifteen years. For instance, a chest of opium, which cost 378 taels in 1890, rose to 792 taels in 1903, a 100 per cent increase in thirteen years. Prices of raw silk also more than doubled from 2.8 taels to 5.7 each picul (133⅓ lbs.). The price fluctuation was partially caused by the drastic change in the exchange rate between silver and gold. The pound sterling which was worth 3 taels in 1871 was good for 7.5 in 1903. Thus, a chest of

---

22. One pound was equal to U.S. $4.86 at that time.
23. Chi-ming Hou, 231-32; Yu-kwei Cheng, *Foreign Trade and Industrial Development of China* (Washington, D.C., 1956), 258-59.

imported opium costing 91 pounds and 8 shillings in 1890 was sold in China for 378 taels; when it was sold for 792 taels in 1903, its original cost was still 92 pounds.

The imbalance of payment was somewhat relieved by remittance from Chinese overseas subjects, amounting to some 50 million annually, and by the spending of foreign legations and missionaries and other organizations, totaling 10 million in 1893, 26 million in 1894, and 30 million in 1895, with the average thereafter at 10 to 15 million annually.[24] Thus, the ill effects of the late Ch'ing trade deficit was partially cushioned by these remittances.

Foreign Investment and Domination. An unusual, if not abnormal, development in late Ch'ing economy was the dominating role exercised by foreigners in modern Chinese industries and enterprises. Their degree of control and scope of activities is seldom seen in independent states; hence late Ch'ing economy has been appropriately dubbed "semicolonial." The following brief survey delineates the foreign participation in several key sections of modern Chinese economy.

(1) Banking. The old-style Chinese banks, or money shops, never financed foreign trade, so foreign banks and their branches in the treaty ports monopolized the financing of imports and exports in China for nearly half a century—from her opening in 1842 to the establishment of the first modern Chinese bank in 1898. The first foreign bank in China was the British-chartered Oriental Banking Corporation, which established a branch in Hong Kong in 1845 and another in Shanghai in 1848. The most powerful foreign banks were the Chartered Bank of India, Australia, and China, and the Hong Kong and Shanghai Banking Corporation—which began their operations in 1853 and 1864-65 respectively. These two British banks exercised a virtual monopoly over China's foreign trade financing until 1889, when the Deutsch-Asiatische Bank entered upon the scene. Not to be excluded from the rewards, other foreign banks soon followed suit: the Japanese-owned Yokohama Specie Bank at Shanghai in 1892; the Russo-Chinese Bank (founded in 1895 to finance the construction of the Chinese Eastern Railway in Manchuria); the American-owned Cathay Company (dominated by the Guaranty Trust of New York) and the International Banking Corporation;[25] and, of course, French, Belgian, and Italian banks, too.

24. Hsiao I-shan, IV, 1,591.
25. Later, after 1927, known as the National City Bank of New York.

These enterprising foreign institutions performed not only the normal banking functions, but assumed more unusual roles as well, such as serving as treasury agents for their respective governments, receiving deposits of the Chinese maritime customs and salt gabelle that had been pledged as security against foreign loans, and even issuing their own bank notes. The latter were issued without any explicit permission of China, but the foreign banks insisted that their extraterritoriality entitled them the right, and the feeble Ch'ing court was helpless to stay them. In reality, the notes were nothing more than promissory notes, "an interest free loan from the Chinese public to the foreign banks."[26] Playing both ends against the middle, with these notes the foreign banks bought Chinese commodities, and with the Manchu and Chinese private and official deposits the banks made highly profitable investments in China. Naturally, when bankruptcy occurred, as during World War I, the bank notes became useless and Chinese deposits were lost. It has been estimated that by 1910 the total amount of foreign bank notes in circulation was between 35 and 100 million Chinese silver dollars.[27]

To compete with foreign banks, the Ch'ing court approved, in 1898, the creation of a private Chinese bank, the Commercial Bank of China (*Chung-kuo t'ung-shang yin-hang*),[28] with an initial capital of 5 million taels. In 1905 the Hu-pu Bank (*Hu-pu yin-hang*) began operations with a capital of 10 million taels; three years later it changed its name to Ta-Ch'ing Bank (*Ta-Ch'ing yin-hang*), and again, after the establishment of the Republic in 1912, changed its name to Bank of China. In 1907 the Bank of Communications was organized by the government, and by 1914 there were 59 Chinese banks.[29]

(2) Shipping. In conjunction with trade, foreign firms often established shipping companies, which led to a rapidly expanding and highly competitive international industry in Chinese coastal and inland waters —a right usually denied to foreigners in an independent state, but forced upon China by the unequal treaties. The first such outfit, the Shanghai Steam Navigation Company, was founded in 1862 by the American firm of Russell and Company, with an initial capital of one million taels (U.S. $1,356,000), and for fifteen years it was the largest shipping company in China.

26. Chi-ming Hou, 57.
27. *Ibid.*, 58.
28. Originally called the Imperial Bank of China.
29. L. S. Yang, *Money and Credit in China* (Cambridge, Mass., 1952), 90; Frank M. Tanaga, *Banking and Finance in China* (New York, 1942), 35-37.

However, the largest share of foreign shipping was British. Butterfield and Swire Company invested 970,000 taels in the China Navigation Company in 1872, followed by Jardine, Matheson and Company's investment of 325,000 taels a year later in the China Coast Steam Navigation Company. The fast, large, efficient foreign ships quickly pre-empted much of the business from the slower, older Chinese junks. To protect national interests, in 1872 Li Hung-chang sponsored the creation of the China Merchants' Steam Navigation Company, which had an initial investment of 476,000 taels, and in 1877 it acquired the entire American fleet of Shanghai Steam Navigation Company. Facing heightened competition, Jardine, Matheson and Company established two more shipping firms, the Yangtze Steam Navigation Company in 1879, and the Indochina Steam Navigation Company in 1881—the first with a capital of 300,000 taels, the second with 1,370,000 taels.[30] The Japanese entered as a late but vigorous competitor by consolidating, in 1907, four shipping companies into the giant Nishen Kisen Kaisha under heavy government subsidy. The Japanese and German shares of shipping grew rapidly after 1900, while the British maintained a consistent lead throughout the late Ch'ing period, and the Americans commanded a respectable position only during 1868-76:[31]

Foreign Shipping in China

Year	Tonnage (in millions)	Britain	U.S.	Japan	Germany	Others
1868	6.4	52.2%	35%	0.1%	7.3%	5.4%
1872	8.5	46.8	41.1	0.1	7.2	4.9
1877	8.0	81.1	6.9	1.4	6.2	4.3
1892	22.9	84.4	0.3	2.8	6.4	6.1
1902	44.6	60.4	1.1	16.5	16.1	5.9
1907	63.4	52.5	1.6	24.6	10.5	10.8

As a consequence of increasing foreign domination, the Chinese share of shipping declined drastically from 30.4 per cent in 1880 to 19.3 per cent in 1900.[32]

(3) Railways. The frenzied scramble for railway concessions after the Japanese war was probably the most blatant form of economic imperial-

30. K. C. Liu, *Anglo-American Steamship Rivalry in China, 1862-1874* (Cambridge, Mass., 1962), 11.
31. Chi-ming Hou, 61.
32. *Ibid.*, 138.

ism. Unable to resist, in 1895 Peking granted France the right to construct a 289-mile line from Indochina to Yunnan. In the following year
Russia obtained rights for construction of the Chinese Eastern Railway
across Manchuria as an extension of the Trans-Siberian Railway to Vladivostok, totaling 1,073 miles. Two years later she extorted another concession to build a 709-mile branch to Port Arthur and Darien under the
name of Southern Manchurian Railway, which was transferred to Japan
after Russia's defeat in 1905. Germany, too, was no laggard, acquiring
the rights in 1897 to construct 285 miles of rail-line between Kiaochow
and Tsinan in Shantung province. These four major foreign railways
alone totaled 2,356 miles of track, or 41 per cent of the entire railway
mileage in China in 1911.[33] In addition, many Chinese lines were built
with foreign loans, and were therefore not free from foreign control or
influence.[34]

Added to the insult of imperialism was the injury of economic loss:
the foreign powers obtained their rights as concessions, hence paying
nothing and permitting no Chinese government agency to collect taxes
on the railway properties and income. Not only were foreign-owned railways instruments of economic imperialism, but also they were political
and military bludgeons to further foreign influence and facilitate troop
movements in times of conflict.

(4) Mining and Manufacturing. Foreigners in China did not limit
themselves to banking, shipping, and railway operations, but also engaged
in mining and manufacturing. Among the largest and best known of
foreign-operated mines were the Japanese-dominated (since 1902) Han-
Yeh-P'ing Mines and Ironworks, and the British-dominated (since 1900)
Kaiping Coal Mine in Chihli, which in 1912 amalgamated with the Chi-
nese-operated Lanchow Mining Company to form the Kailan Mining
Administration. As regards foreign manufacturing and allied activities, the
best illustration is the multifarious Jardine, Matheson and Company,
which, besides foreign trade, was engaged in tea-processing, silk-reeling,
ship-repairing, engineering, breweries, cotton textile, insurance, packing,
cold storage, and loans—indeed a ubiquitous industrial and economic

33. Chi-ming Hou, 65.
34. The Peking-Hankow railway: a Belgian loan of £4.5 million in 1899 at 5 per cent
interest, and two Anglo-French loans of £5 million at 5 per cent in 1908 and £450,000
at 7 per cent in 1910; the Shanghai-Nanking Railway: a British loan of £2.9 million
at 5 per cent in 1904-7; the Canton-Hankow Railway: a British loan of £1.1 million at
4½ per cent in 1905; the Shanghai-Ningpo Railway: a British loan of £1.5 million at
5 per cent in 1908; and the Tientsin-Pukow Railway: two Anglo-German loans of £5
million in 1908-9 and £3 million in 1910, both at 5 per cent. Morse, III, 449.

47. A Boxer poster.

48. Imprisoned Boxers after the lifting of the blockade by the expeditionary forces.

49. Portrait of the young Emperor Kuang-hsü.

50. Yüan Shih-k'ai.

51. Prince Ch'ing.

52. Prince Chün.

53. K'ang Yu-wei.

54. Liang Ch'i-ch'ao.

55. Timothy Richard.

56. Huang Hsing.

57. Yüan Shih-k'ai, center, as provisional president of the Republic of China, 1912.

58. Wu P'ei-fu, left, with two of his generals.

59. Sun Yat-sen with Madame Sun Yat-sen, a graduate of the
University of California at Berkeley and Wellesley.

60. Pu-yi in 1922.

61. Chang Tso-lin.

62. Dr. Sun with his second wife, Soong Ching-ling,
during a journey in 1924 to Peking.

complex! Other foreign activities included shipbuilding and repairing, textile manufacturing, sugar-refining, spinning and weaving, tobacco, and public utilities. Not a single phase of China's modern economy was immune to the encroachment of foreign capital, influence, and control. And out of a total of 636 foreign firms in business in China by 1897, more than half, 374, were British.[35]

Foreign control extended even to the postal service in China for more than a quarter of a century. The inefficiency of the traditional Chinese postal stations led the foreigners in 1860 to establish their own service in the treaty ports, even though the Ch'ing government never granted them the right. As China yawned wider before the increasing alien inroads, the foreign postal service extended along the coast and into the interior. It was not until 1896 that the Manchu court established the Imperial Postal Service under the charge of the inspector-general of Maritime Customs, Sir Robert Hart. Finally in 1911 the new Ministry of Posts and Communications took over general direction of postal functions; only then did China divest the postal service of foreign control.

Two Sides of Imperialism. The total foreign investment in China reached U.S. $788 million in 1902 and U.S. $1,610 million in 1914.[36] The degree of foreign domination is seen in the fact that 84 per cent of shipping, 34 per cent of cotton-yarn spinning, and 100 per cent of iron production were under foreign control in 1907, while 93 per cent of railways were foreign-dominated in 1911. The scope of foreign influence was as wide as the modern sector of Chinese economy, which had been reduced to "semicolonial." Nationalistic Chinese historians and economists, as well as Marxist scholars, point to such a high degree of foreign dominance as proof of naked imperialism. They charge that foreigners stifled the native industry and exercised a depressant and oppressive effect on the Chinese economy. They expostulate on the unfair advantages that foreigners had over their Chinese competitors due to their vast capital, technical knowledge, special privileges under unequal treaties, and immunity from Chinese laws, taxes, and official interference. All this, of course, is true. Foreigners invested in China to make money; few thought in terms of aiding China's economic development. The fact that they reaped profit to the extent of better than 10 per cent annually and controlled most of the modern

35. Chi-ming Hou, 103.
36. Other estimates: U.S. $1,509.3 million in 1902 and U.S. $2,255.7 million in 1914. See Chi-ming Hou, 211, 235.

sector of China's economy, certainly made it difficult for the Chinese to make money and win their rightful place in business.

Yet imperialism is not without its beneficial side effects. Foreign investors introduced modern technology and the entrepreneurial spirit, and financed many modern industries. Their success created an environment in which profit from industrial undertakings was demonstrably possible, thereby prompting the Chinese to follow their example. Additionally, the employment and training of Chinese in foreign factories and business establishments produced a native pool of technical knowledge of production and managerial skills which later were to be profitably tapped by and for the Chinese. It was not unusual for the compradores, after having learned foreign business methods and having accumulated considerable capital, themselves to invest in industry or serve in government-sponsored enterprises. Such a one was Tong King-sing, the director of the China Merchants' Steam Navigation Company, and formerly compradore with Jardine, Matheson and Company. Nor should one lose sight of the fact that foreign-leased areas and treaty ports provided a certain degree of peace and order necessary for industrial growth; and that foreign establishments had already borne most of the cost of "social overhead," such as public utilities, roads, and communication facilities, which eased the development of Chinese industry. Clearly, foreign investment produced an "imitation" effect on the Chinese and provided the preconditions essential for the economic modernization of China.[37]

In sum, imperialism is both baneful and beneficial. On the one hand it inhibits the growth of native industry, on the other it stimulates patriotism—by inciting a desire for national economic protection and competitive equality—and provides the incentive for economic modernization. Corroboration for the latter aspect is evident in the fact that during the height of imperialism many Chinese factories and enterprises were born. In 1904-8, 227 modern Chinese companies were registered with the government, and by 1912 there were 20,749 native factories in operation, though the majority were of small or medium size, and only 750 employed workers in excess of a hundred.[38] While it is true that they had to struggle for survival in the shadow of the giant foreign firms, the fact remains that they emerged under foreign stimulation.

The decade and a half following the Japanese war was a very turbulent era, in which the old intellectual, social, and economic order passed away

37. Chi-ming Hou, 217, 221.
38. Feuerwerker, 3-5.

and the new struggled toward birth. The rapid transition presaged a major political upheaval in the offing. The Manchu dynasty, already two and a half centuries old, stood at a critical point in history. If it could not keep abreast of the times and offer an alternative to violent change, it would be doomed to extinction.

FURTHER READING

Brière, O., S.J., *Fifty Years of Chinese Philosophy, 1898-1950* (London, 1956).

Chou, Ku-ch'eng 周谷城, *Chung-kuo she-hui chih pien-hua* 中國社會之變化 (Changes in Chinese society), (Shanghai, 1931).

Chu, Samuel C., *Reform in Modern China: Chang Chien, 1853-1926* (New York, 1965).

Feuerwerker, Albert, *China's Early Industrialization: Sheng Hsüan-huai (1844-1916) and Mandarin Enterprise* (Cambridge, Mass., 1958).

Hou, Chi-ming, *Foreign Investment and Economic Development in China, 1840-1937* (Cambridge, Mass., 1965).

Lee, Leo Ou-fan, "Lin Shu and His Translations: Western Fiction in Chinese Perspective," *Paper on China*, Harvard East Asian Research Center, 19:159-93 (Dec. 1965).

Levy, M. J., and Shih Kuo-heng, *The Rise of the Modern Chinese Business Class* (New York, 1949).

Liang, Ch'i-ch'ao, *Intellectual Trends in the Ch'ing Period (Ch'ing-tai hsüeh-shu kai-lun)*, tr. by Immanuel C. Y. Hsü, (Cambridge, Mass., 1959), Part III.

Liu, Kwang-ching, *Anglo-American Steamship Rivalry in China, 1862-1874* (Cambridge, Mass., 1962).

Lo, Yü-tung 羅玉東, "Kuang-hsü ch'ao pu-chiu ts'ai-cheng chih fang-ts'e" 光緒朝補救財政之方策 (The government policies of meeting the financial crisis during the Kuang-hsü period (1875-1908)), *Chung-kuo chin-tai ching-chi-shih yen-chiu chi-k'an* 中國近代經濟史研究集刊 (Studies in modern economic history of China), 1:2:189-270 (May 1933).

Morse, H. B., *The International Relations of the Chinese Empire*, Vol. III, *The Period of Subjection* (London, 1918).

Powell, Ralph L., *The Rise of Chinese Military Power, 1895-1912* (Princeton, 1955).

Schwartz, Benjamin I., *In Search of Wealth and Power: Yen Fu and the West* (Cambridge, Mass., 1964).

Sun, E-tu Zen, *Chinese Railways and British Interests, 1898-1911* (New York, 1954).

Sun, Yü-t'ang 孫毓棠, "Chung-Jih Chia-wu chan-cheng ch'ien wai-kuo tzu-pen tsai Chung-kuo ching-ying ti chin-tai kung-yeh" 中日甲午戰爭前外國資本在中國經營的近代工業 (Modern industries operated by foreign capital in China before the Sino-Japanese War), *Li-shih yen-chiu*, 5:1-41, (1954).

Tamagna, Frank M., *Banking and Finance in China* (New York, 1942).

Tsien, Tsuen-hsuin, "Western Impact on China Through Translations," *Far Eastern Quarterly*, XIII:3:305-27 (May 1954).

Vevier, Charles, *The United States and China, 1906-1913: A Study of Finance and Diplomacy* (New Brunswick, 1955).

Wang, Tsao-shih 王造時, "Chung-Hsi chieh-ch'u-hou she-hui-shang ti pien-hua" 中西接觸後社會上的變化 (Social changes after the Sino-Western contact), *Tung-fang tsa-chih*, 31:2:31-40 (1934).

Wang, Y. C., *Chinese Intellectuals and the West, 1872-1949* (Chapel Hill, 1966).

Yang, Lien-sheng, *Money and Credit in China* (Cambridge, Mass., 1952).

19

The Ch'ing Period in Historical Perspective

The foregoing survey of Ch'ing history inevitably raises the question as to the significance, accomplishments, and failings of the period. Indeed, historical perspective affords the Ch'ing, the last in a succession of twenty-five imperial dynasties, a distinctive and crucial position in Chincsc history. It proves to have been the most durable period of foreign rule in China, spanning 268 years as opposed to the Yüan (Mongol) dynasty's 89. It saw the rise of the second largest empire in Chinese history, next only to the Yüan, and provided the country with a prolonged period of peace and prosperity. This *Pax Sinica* precipitated, among other things, an unprecedented population growth from 100 million in 1650 to 430 million in 1850. These territorial and demographic legacies underlay the bases of Communist China's strength.

Moreover, the Ch'ing period witnessed the epochal transition from traditional China to its modern counterpart. The Confucian state and society and the old ways of life which persisted during the early and middle stages of the dynasty went through a radical transformation under the Western impact after the mid-19th century. The labored emergence of a new order can only be understood through a knowledge of the Ch'ing history, thereby facilitating comprehension of China's supreme difficulty in adjusting to the modern world.[1]

The Ch'ing dynasty provided China with both brilliant accomplish-

1. Ping-ti Ho, "The Significance of the Ch'ing Period in Chinese History." Paper read before the 18th annual convention of the Association for Asian Studies, New York, April 4, 1966. Later published in *The Journal of Asian Studies*, XXVI:2:189-95 (Feb. 1967).

ment and ignominious disaster. But on the whole their rulers seem to have performed better than their Ming counterparts.[2] The conclusive lesson which emerges from historical analysis of the Ch'ing period indicates that survival hinges on the ability to respond constructively and creatively to the challenge of the times. Manchu success during the 17th century appears to have been largely a result of such adaptation; while its failure, two and a half centuries later, appears to have resulted from a lack of parallel adjustment.

The Manchus seized power through the enterprise of outstanding leaders like Nurhaci and Abahai, who appeared at the critical moment when the reigning Ming dynasty was beset by political corruption, eunuch dominance, heavy taxation, and debilitating rebellions. Weary of squalor and confusion, the people were ready for change; and the Manchus turned popular dissatisfaction to their advantage. Under the pretext of restoring peace and order for the Ming, they entered China in response to national discontent. Their leaders were flexible enough to overcome Manchu tribal mentality and organization, enlisted Chinese collaboration, and incorporated existing Ming institutions. A succession of farsighted and able rulers followed the formal establishment of the dynasty in 1644, and K'ang-hsi, Yung-cheng, and Ch'ien-lung inaugurated wise and far-reaching policies.

A prolonged period of peace, affluence, and military glories was ushered in. The Confucian order was retained, perceptively, as it was conceived to be essential to the success of alien rule. In addition, a system of governmental dyarchy was instituted, providing the appointment of both Manchus and Chinese to positions of administrative responsibility in an attempt to absorb Chinese talent and reduce racial antipathy, and simultaneously introducing a system of mutual checks and balances. As it emerged, the new Ch'ing empire rested upon the foundations of an administrative system inherited from the Ming with supplementary Manchu innovations such as the Li-fan yüan and the Grand Council. Neo-Confucianism was promoted, with proper emphasis on such concepts as loyalty and maintenance of the *status quo*, for the primary purpose of stabilizing existing society. The Manchus strove to preserve their own identity within the larger circumference of Chinese society, specifically creating institutions such as the Imperial Clan Court to keep a close watch over Manchu nobles. They also prevented Chinese immigration to their Manchurian homeland. Intermarriages were banned, whether

2. Hsiao I-shan, *Ch'ing-tai shih* (A history of the Ch'ing dynasty), 312.

Chinese-Manchu or Chinese-Mongol. Power was centralized in the hands of the sovereign to an unprecedented degree, and divisive tendencies were forestalled by thwarting movements toward feudalism among Manchu nobles and by forbidding them and bannermen to develop provincial connections. The rise of eunuchs was banned, the influence of imperial distaff curbed, and official cliques and factions prohibited. Furthermore, through literary inquisitions the Ch'ing struck terror into recalcitrant Chinese scholars on the one hand and enticed them on the other to enter government service whenever possible through literary examinations and attractive appointments.

Such exertions contributed to a successful consolidation of the Manchu position in China. Following the overthrow of Ming loyalist opposition on Taiwan in 1683, the nation enjoyed a century of peace, prosperity, and unprecedented population growth. This era of *Pax Sinica* saw China emerge as one of the largest, most illustrious empires on earth, with impressive advances in culture and scholarship. The court patronized learning and sponsored the publication of vast encyclopedias, while private scholars engaged in extensive empirical research on ancient works and carried out a brilliant re-examination of the Chinese cultural heritage.

Yet the height of fortune is also the beginning of decline—"When the sun reaches midday it begins to set, and when the moon is fullest it begins to wane," the Chinese saying goes. The scintillation and the splendor of Ch'ien-lung's reign already contained the seeds of decay. China had indulged excessively in luxury, neglecting essential problems. Population growth outpaced land increase, resulting in a decrease of per capita acreage. Military training was lax. Corruption and irregularity became widespread within the imperial bureaucracy, contributing to the recurring historical phenomena known as the "dynastic cycle." By 1800, the Ch'ing dynasty had begun its downward course.

Experience dictates that internal decay invites both domestic rebellion and foreign invasion; and in Chinese history they often occurred simultaneously when imperial power declined. True to dictum, the diminution of Ch'ing authority witnessed the outbreak of the White Lotus Rebellion (1796-1804), as well as an intensified Western drive to open China to trade and diplomacy. The double threat, both internal and external, plagued the imperial court throughout the 19th century. The dynasty was able to quell domestic rebellion, a known quantity, but completely failed to stem Western intrusion, an unknown quantity. Dynastic disintegration intensified after the Taiping Revolution (1850-64), witnessing a shift in political power from the capital to the provinces, and from Manchu to Chinese dominance. The future of the Ch'ing dynasty was doomed, even though the T'ung-chih Restoration (1862-74) temporarily arrested the downward drift.

The ultimate failing of Ch'ing rule lay in its incapacity to adequately cope with the Western impact by initiating far-reaching reform in order to swiftly transform China into a modern state. Whereas in the 17th century Manchu leaders showed flexibility, adopting Chinese institutions and the Confucian order, their late 19th- and early 20th-century descendants were totally inept and unable to transcend tradition. They could not successfully innovate an alternative to revolution in creative response to contemporary challenge. Indeed, political mismanagement, domestic rebellion, and foreign humiliation had so degraded the Ch'ing dynasty that its impending fall appeared evident in the late 19th century, just as the imminent fall of the Ming had seemed inevitable in the early 17th century. After 268 years, the Manchu dynasty lost its "Mandate of Heaven" and reached what the Chinese call its "preordained finale."

The Ch'ing experience presents a sharp and notorious contrast to the experience of Meiji Japan, affording opportunity for much discussion and a variety of interpretations from conflicting points of view. The more obvious reasons for China's hampered advance appear to have been factors which restricted the dissemination of new ideas, such as vast territorial jurisdiction, poor communications, self-sufficiency, an almost total lack of tradition of borrowing from abroad, and the conservative intellectual posture. Among other reasons for Ch'ing decay, the following are worth consideration.

1. *Feeble Leadership and Faulty Institutions.* The Ch'ing autocracy concentrated state power in the person of the emperor, making dynamic leadership mandatory. Resourceful rulers like K'ang-hsi, Yung-cheng, and Ch'ien-lung inaugurated eras of brilliance, providing China with much splendor and accomplishment. Mediocre emperors followed in trepidation, exerting themselves to preserve, rather than magnify, past glory. Unfortunately for China and the Ch'ing dynasty, powerful and creative leadership failed to appear when it was most needed. The last of the great emperors, Ch'ien-lung, was followed by Chia-ch'ing and Tao-kuang, both methodical and average men. Hsien-feng's eleven-year reign was disrupted by the debilitating Taiping Revolution and the humiliation of the *Arrow* War with Britain and France. T'ung-chih and Kuang hsü were two

boy emperors during whose reigns state power rested with the empress dowager, Tz'u-hsi, who ruled supreme for nearly half a century. While not without native intelligence and decisiveness, she was basically ignorant, conservative, venal, and selfish, placing her own interests above those of the dynasty and the country at large. She supported the Self-strengthening Movement not with a view to transforming China into a modern state, but to preserving the old order and her own position. All she sought from the Movement was to suppress domestic revolt and resist foreign imperialism. She permitted piecemeal improvement instead of full-scale regeneration, partly because she feared subversion by those Chinese who were in charge of modernization. Tz'u-hsi was therefore responsible, to a large extent, for failing to provide constructive leadership.

Ineffective imperial leadership might have been offset by vigorous, far-sighted statesmanship on the part of the central bureaucracy. In a Confucian state, though ministers were supposed to serve and not lead the emperor, they could offer counsel and influence official policy. During the late Ch'ing period, however, the majority of scholars and officials were a "saturated class," too content with their privileges and vested interests to want to change the existing order. Advisers and advocates on "foreign matters" (yang-wu) were lone exceptions in the conservative officialdom. These progressives did not combine to form a "creative minority" (to quote Toynbee), but appeared as isolated individuals who sought to adopt Western devices in answer to the challenge of the times. They did not function as a closely knit group, as in the case of Meiji Japan, but responded separately without reference to a centrally coordinated master plan. Of the early Self-strengthening leaders, only Prince Kung and Wen-hsiang were in the central government, while Tseng Kuo-fan, Tso Tsung-t'ang, and Li Hung-chang were all provincial personalities. The slender thread of central direction disappeared after the dowager's repeated chastisements of Kung and Wen-hsiang's death in 1876. Li Hung-chang became, to some extent, a "coordinator" of modernization projects, performing some functions of the central government after his appointment in 1870 as governor-general of Chihli and imperial commissioner in charge of the northern ports. Nevertheless, he faced jurisdictional restrictions, receiving no authority to command provinces other than his own. Later modernizers, Chang Chih-tung and Liu K'un-i, also conducted their projects in piecemeal fashion within their own provinces. In short, there was regional but not national planning, contrary to governmental policy in Meiji Japan. Moreover, these regional efforts were largely directed from the top down, with little popular participation, thereby precluding wide proliferation of modern industries and ideas.

Without the benefit of either effective imperial leadership or a creative liberal minority, it became increasingly difficult, if not impossible, to channel national energy toward the collective goal of rejuvenating the country.

2. *Manchu Suspicion of the Chinese.* Despite the announced court policy of nondiscrimination and appointment of both Chinese and Manchus to governmental office, the Manchus in reality remained conquerors and the Chinese were merely tolerated as "outsiders." Until the time of the Taiping Revolution, key appointments, both civil and military, went to the Manchus, and even those positions allotted to the Chinese could be filled by Manchus, but not vice versa. Although the practice relaxed after the Taiping era, Manchu suspicion of the Chinese never abated. The life of Tseng Kuo-fan provides an excellent illustration. Among imperial commanders, he alone scored victories over the Taipings at first, and though the emperor was pleased, he became apprehensive when warned by a courtier that the spectacular success and popularity of a Chinese scholar might work against the best interests of Manchu rule. Tseng was therefore denied command of the campaign until several years later when no Manchu could manage the situation. In 1862, when there was contention over the disposal of the Lay-Osborn flotilla, the court sold it to a foreign power rather than turn it over to Tseng, lest he inadvertently use it as an instrument of power. Tseng became so fearful of Manchu jealousy and suspicion that after the downfall of the Taipings, he proposed to disband his Hunan army, and during the remainder of his tenure as governor-general at Nanking, he led a relatively inactive life in semi-Taoist retirement. He retained little of his ambition to modernize China. Although such an attitude was not unnatural for a man who felt that his mission had been accomplished, it was for the most part in reaction to Manchu suspicion.

Tseng's junior colleague and successor, Li Hung-chang, who became the leading spirit of the Self-strengthening Movement, met with opposition and frustration from all sides. He was constantly ridiculed by conservatives for betraying his country's interest to foreigners. The empress dowager realized the need for his services, but feared his growth in stature at the expense of the court. She therefore halfheartedly supported his modernization projects, allowing reactionaries to attack him with impunity. She also resorted to the strategy of divide and rule by permitting or even encouraging conservative literati opinion (ch'ing-i) to stall the progressives. In 1874, when Li asked Prince Kung to speak to the two dowagers about the desirability of railways, Kung replied that even they could not reach a decision on the matter because of powerful popular opposition.[3] When a Board of Admiralty was organized in 1885, the directorship went to an ignorant Manchu, Prince Chün, instead of to a more capable Chinese like Li Hung-chang or Tseng Chi-tse. Manchu fear of Chinese subversion and Chinese fear of Manchu jealousy precluded effective cooperation between the two, and far-reaching reform became impossible. K'ang Yu-wei's program for institutional reform in 1898 was condemned by the Manchus as a plot to benefit the Chinese at their expense. The last decade of the Ch'ing rule saw an intensified effort on the part of the Manchus to curb Chinese influence. Grand Secretary Kang-i announced: "When the Chinese become powerful, the Manchus extinguish; when the Chinese are tired, the Manchus grow fat."[4] Ethnic antipathy impeded genuine modernization, because the Manchus contended that reform and constitutionalism would undermine their power. Doubtless, the Manchu-Chinese schism precluded engendering an effective joint enterprise to regenerate the nation.

3. *Ignorance of the Nature of the Western Challenge.* The Western advance was characterized by factors such as ships and guns, trade and evangelism, and imperialism and nationalism. It was sustained by a modern, dynamic civilization, superior to the Chinese in many respects. It introduced novel phenomena into China, understood by few. The unprecedented challenge caught China ill-prepared, and unable to achieve a solution. Until the time of the reform in 1898, the majority of scholars and officials drew instruction from Chinese history, where barbarian invasion had always been transitory. Hence the 19th-century Western advance, which figured in this category, was merely regarded as unfortunate and passing. Even China's repeated defeat by the West was interpreted as accidental. The actual nature, extent, and scope of the Western impact thus were misunderstood, even by progressive advocates of Self-strengthening measures. Li Hung-chang, for instance, recognized that the situation was without parallel in 3,000 years of Chinese experience, and yet he continued to exhibit an exceedingly limited view of the Western poten-

3. Hsü, *China's Entrance*, 205.
4. Sun Chen-t'ao, *Ch'ing-shih shu-lün* (A critique of Ch'ing history), (Hong Kong, 1957), 128.

tial. His modernization programs concentrated largely on military and diplomatic improvement. Even a liberal like Kuo Sung-tao, China's first minister to the West, took the shallow view that foreign relations meant meeting emergencies when and where they arose. As regards the imperial court, it engaged in the Self-strengthening program in a defensive manner. When foreign pressure subsided, action slowed down, and a long-range platform, expressing national and foreign policy, failed to emerge. Ch'ing efforts were haphazard, like patching old clothes with new cloth and filling old bottles with new wine. They produced piecemeal endeavors which fell short of accomplishing a major breakthrough in economic development. Evidently modern capitalism and political reform could not be successfully grafted onto an outdated Confucian foundation.

Ch'ing ignorance of the contemporary world is not hard to understand when one considers the general mentality of scholars and officials prior to the 1898 reform. The majority of them lived in the past. They existed in a dream world of Chinese "culturalism," looking to antiquity for guidance instead of to the future for inspiration. Ancient ways were glorified and contemporary example despised. Machines, ships, guns, and telegraphic and railroad communications were considered artful contrivances beneath their dignity. They revealed ethnocentric pride, but little nationalistic spirit, citing historical sayings to justify the attitude that it was well and proper to Sinicize barbarians, but outrageous to imitate their ways. It was inconceivable to them that China, the Celestial Empire, should be transformed in the image of the West.

It was precisely against such narrow, retrogressive views that Yen Fu agitated for the adoption of new values in life, suggesting a "different vision of reality" through the study of Western thought. Similarly, Liang Ch'i-ch'ao advocated a "renovation" of China, after the turn of the century. Their exertions provided the seeds of future intellectual fermentation.

4. National and International Turmoil, and Insufficient Capital. Modernization and economic development require extended peace and adequate capital, but both factors were lacking in late Ch'ing China. The country was constantly plagued by internal rebellion, foreign conflict, missionary incidents, and natural calamity, causing a widespread breakdown of law and order, and sharp increases in government expenditure. After 1830, China went through the Opium War; the *Arrow* War; the Taiping Revolution; the Nien Rebellion; the Panthay (Moslem) Rebellion; the Tungan (Moslem) Revolt; the Tientsin Massacre; the Formosa crisis; the Margary Murder; the Ili crisis; the French war; the Japanese war; and the Boxer Rebellion. Peace and stability scarcely existed.

In addition to continuous disturbance which inhibited economic development, war expenses and indemnities caused the continual outflow of capital. Fiscal welfare became dependent upon foreign loans and funds extracted from the provinces. From 1842 to 1895, China paid out a total of 300 million taels for indemnities and interest. For the Boxer indemnity of 450 million taels, the Chinese government paid 225 million taels between 1902 and 1910, of which 164 million (72 per cent) came from provincial assessments, 33 million (16 per cent) from maritime customs, and 27 million (12 per cent) from the national treasury. Such drainage of resources naturally impeded economic development, and the prospect of successful modernization grew increasingly dimmer with the growing fiscal stringency of the central government, as discussed in the last chapter.[5]

5. *The Foreign Role.* Inasmuch as foreign influence was a major shaping force in late Ch'ing China, it requires at least a general analysis. Foreign governments and their representatives, while they wished to see China move in the direction of "progress," and while they continually impressed on imperial agencies the urgency of accepting Western institutions and products, they nevertheless implicitly shared the view that China should be kept dependent on the West. A moderately progressive and prosperous but weak China, dependent on foreign advice, good will, trade, and aid would be much more to the interest of the West than a completely independent and assertive China. China must not be allowed to modernize too far and acquire the strength to repel the West. Sir Thomas Wade, British minister to China, for example, made a policy statement with regard to the role of the Chinese Maritime Customs under Sir Robert Hart, in support of this attitude, stating:

> . . . in the well-being of which [Foreign Inspectorate of Customs] we, the English, are specially concerned, not only for its regulation of trade, but as the one instrument by which progress is being introduced into China, as it were, unknown to herself, and therefore without provoking her suspicion; and lastly, *unless I am greatly mistaken, for every measure of precaution possible against her [China's] acquisition of a fleet or her organization of an army.*[6]

5. Feuerwerker, 45; Chi-ming Hou, 164.
6. Foreign Office, 418/1/242, Wade to Granville, *very confidential*, July 25, 1880, Public Record Office, London. Italics added.

If this view sheds light on British policy toward China, one is not surprised at the perennial weakness of Ch'ing forces. It lends credence to the Marxist view that, by relying on foreign collaboration instead of struggling against it, the Ch'ing dynasty failed to achieve genuine strength.[7]

These domestic and foreign factors subverted successful modernization. Both Manchu and Chinese leaders were to be blamed for not circumventing obstacles, and the price of failure was the extinction of the dynasty. Lord Macartney's prophetic words, spoken in 1794, after his visit to the court of Ch'ien-lung, now became doubly meaningful. He stated:

> The Empire of China is an old, crazy, first-rate Man of War, which a fortunate succession of able and vigilant officers have contrived to keep afloat for these hundred and fifty years past, and to over-awe their neighbours merely by her bulk and appearance. But, whenever an insufficient man happens to have command on deck, adieu to the discipline and safety of the ship. She may, perhaps, not sink outright; she may drift some time as a wreck, and will then be dashed to pieces on the shore; but she can never be rebuilt on the old bottom.

Indeed, she could not be rebuilt on the old foundation; only a revolution could hope to regenerate her.

FURTHER READING

Feuerwerker, Albert, *China's Early Industrialization: Sheng Hsüan-huai (1844-1916) and Mandarin Enterprise* (Cambridge, Mass., 1958).

Ho, Ping-ti, "The Significance of the Ch'ing Period in Chinese History." Paper read before the 18th convention of the Association for Asian Studies, New York, April 4, 1966. Later published in *The Journal of Asian Studies*, XXVI:2:189-95 (Feb. 1967).

Hou, Chi-ming, *Foreign Investment and Economic Development in China, 1840-1937* (Cambridge, Mass., 1965).

Hsü, Immanuel C. Y., *China's Entrance into the Family of Nations: The Diplomatic Phase, 1858-1880* (Cambridge, Mass., 1960), chapter 13, "The Imperial Chinese Tradition in the Modern World."

7. Huang I-feng and Chiang To, "Chung-kuo yang-wu yün-tung yü Jih-pen Ming-chih wei-hsin tsai ching-chi fa-chan shang te pi-chiao" (A comparative study of China's "Foreign Matters" Movement and Japan's Meiji modernization from the standpoint of economic development), *Li-shih yen-chiu* (Historical Research), 1:40 (1963).

Hu, Shih, *The Chinese Renaissance* (Chicago, 1934).

Huang, I-feng 黃逸峰 and Chiang To 姜鐸, *"Chung-kuo yang-wu yün-tung yü Jih-pen Ming-chih wei-hsin tsai ching-chi fa-chan shang ti pi-chiao"* 中國洋務運動與日本明治維新在經濟發展上的比較 (A comparative study of China's 'foreign matters' movement and Japan's Meiji modernization from the standpoint of economic development), *Li-shih yen-chiu*, (1963), 1:27-47.

Meng, Shen 孟森, *Ch'ing-tai shih* 清代史 (The Ch'ing history), (Taipei, 1960).

Sun, Chen-t'ao 孫甄陶, *Ch'ing-shih shu-lun* 清史述論 (A critique of Ch'ing history), (Hong Kong, 1957).

20

Revolution, Republic, and Warlordism

The pressing question facing China after the Japanese war was what she could do to achieve national salvation in the face of accelerating foreign imperialism and dynastic decline. Two major political movements developed, each representing a different approach to the problem. One was the progressive reform of 1898, led by K'ang Yu-wei, from which evolved the Ch'ing reform and constitutional movements of the 1900's, as seen in the previous chapters. The other was a revolutionary movement led by Western-trained Dr. Sun Yat-sen, who advocated the complete overthrow of the Manchu dynasty. At first, the progressive reformers played the more prominent role. However, as Ch'ing endeavors proved insincere and discriminatory against the Chinese, the revolutionaries gained increasing support from the younger intellectuals, the secret societies, and the overseas Chinese communities. The momentum of their movement grew steadily until it finally swept the age-old imperial institution out of existence and replaced it with a republic—an epochal change in the long Chinese history.

BACKGROUND AND CHARACTERISTICS OF THE REVOLUTION

Ch'ing Decadence. Ever since the mid-19th century, Chinese history was largely one continuous record of national humiliation. The long list of unequal treaties from the Treaty of Nanking in 1842 to the Boxer Protocol of 1901, the loss of the tributary states in the 1880's and the 1890's, and the lack of vigor in domestic administration testify to the utter

538

Ch'ing inability to defend China's honor in the modern world. What formerly had been the proud Middle Kingdom was now reduced to a semicolony. The Manchus, who had entered China in 1644 as conquerors, had completely lost face before the Chinese public. The death knell was sounded when the court, in a desperate struggle for survival, carried out an anti-Chinese policy under the pretext of reform and constitutionalism. Such a flagrant show of discrimination amidst rapid dynastic decline only served to exacerbate opposition from the ruled.

The Tradition of Nationalistic Revolution. Anti-Manchu sentiment never disappeared throughout the 268-year dynasty. Chinese thinkers in the early Ch'ing period such as Ku Yen-wu and Wang Fu-chih ceaselessly promoted the "anti-Ch'ing, revive Ming" idea. Although their activities did not result in an outright overthrow of the alien rule, the germ of revolution was kept alive in underground organizations and secret societies. The various Ming loyalist movements, the Revolt of the Three Feudatories, the activities of the Heaven and Earth Society, the White Lotus Rebellion, and the Taiping Revolution demonstrate the unending thread of nationalistic-racial protest. Dr. Sun's revolution was to be very much in the tradition of the continuous fight against the alien rule.

Foreign Influence. The great revolutions of the modern West—the Glorious Revolution of England, the American Revolution, and the French Revolution—all exerted a profound influence upon the Chinese. The ideas of democracy, independence, human rights, equality, and freedom swept through the minds of young Chinese. Moreover, the success of the national unification movements of Italy and Germany in 1870 served as shining examples for forward-looking Chinese, prompting them to take similar action. Nationalism, democracy, and republicanism now became the motivating forces for revolutionary change in China.

Need for Political Innovation. The monarchical institution of China, in the view of Dr. Sun, was responsible for the succession of imperial dynasties in the past 2,000 years without ever changing the substance of government. Chinese history revolved around the cycle of division, disorder, unification, and despotism, noted Sun, and each period of disorder was followed by a lengthy and merciless struggle for the throne by many contenders until one ultimately won out. In the process the country and the people suffered needlessly and the historical pattern repeated itself periodically. To break this cycle and to give a proper outlet to the ambitions of men, it was necessary to replace the monarchy with a republic— a federal republic—in which all could fulfill their dreams, exercise their rights, and become leaders of the provinces and the nation. To achieve this goal, Sun urged all freedom-loving people of China to participate in a National Revolution to bring about the downfall of the imperial system and the Manchu dynasty, and to introduce a modern republic, free from foreign intervention and interference.

Three Revolutions in One. For all their prosperity, independence, and democracy, the Western powers, observed Dr. Sun, were beset with the problems of industrialism. Labor-management disputes, strikes, demands for higher wages, and the unequal distribution of wealth between the capitalist minority and the worker majority foreboded a social revolution. Though China had not been industrialized enough to witness these same problems, the seeds of capitalism had been sown ever since the Self-strengthening Movement in the 1860's, when many modern industries, enterprises, and foreign establishments and investments came into being. To forestall the evils of capitalism, Sun proposed the regulation of capital to prevent the concentration of wealth among the few.

Moreover, in view of the perennial land problem caused by the faster pace of population increase over land accretion, Sun advocated a program of land equalization to the end that the ancient utopian dream, "land to the tiller," might be fulfilled.

In short, Sun envisioned a three-in-one revolution propelled by all the people of China: a nationalistic revolution to overthrow the Manchu dynasty and the imperial institution, a democratic revolution to establish a republic and popular sovereignty, and a social revolution to equalize the land rights and to prevent the ills of capitalism. Seldom had any revolution in the world been conceived in such a grandiose manner.

DR. SUN AND THE REVOLUTION

Sun Yat-sen (1866-1925),[1] father of the Chinese Revolution, was born on November 12, 1866, in Hsiang-shan, near Canton, of peasant parentage. He was one of six children, of whom two boys and two girls sur-

1. His personal name was Wen, while Yat-sen was his style (secondary name). In China he is better known by his other name, Chung-shan, the Chinese pronunciation of the Japanese name, Nakayama, which he adopted while a political refugee there at the age of 31.

vived. Because of the poor soil, the people of Hsiang-shan had a tradition of seeking their livelihood away from home. At the age of fifteen, Sun's elder brother (Sun Mei) left for Honolulu where he was to build up a prosperous business. Sun himself entered school at six and had studied the traditional primers and the Confucian Four Books and the Five Classics by the age of twelve. Yet because of the family's poverty, he did not receive a thorough grounding in Chinese classical studies. Born only two years after the downfall of the Taiping kingdom, Sun in his childhood often heard the stories of the revolution and secretly aspired to be a second Hung Hsiu-ch'üan.

The Influence of Honolulu and Hong Kong. In 1879 Sun went with his mother to Honolulu to join his brother. For the first time the boy saw the wonders of ships, the prosperous good life, and the fair taxes of the islands. He entered the Anglican missionary Iolani School and later graduated from Oahu College in 1883 at the age of seventeen. His ambition to continue his studies in the United States was thwarted by his brother, who feared for his conversion to Christianity. Sun returned to China and after spending a year at the Diocesan Home in Hong Kong to improve his English, he transferred to the Queen's College, where he was Christianized after all. In 1885 he married, and after a short trip to Honolulu he returned in time to witness China's defeat by France. Thoroughly disgusted with the Ch'ing decadence, he began to develop ideas about overthrowing the dynasty.

At twenty Sun enrolled in the Po-chi Medical School at Canton, while improving his Chinese studies by reading the twenty-four dynastic histories. Among his schoolmates was one Cheng Shih-liang, who had wide connections with the secret societies. The two of them frequently engaged in lengthy discussion about the need for a revolution, and Cheng volunteered to enlist help from his underground friends. In 1887 Sun transferred to the College of Medicine for Chinese in Hong Kong because of its better curriculum and the freedom that the British colony afforded for revolutionary activity. While on the one hand Sun received a sound training in science and medicine from the strict English dean, Dr. James Cantlie, on the other he used the school as the headquarters for his revolutionary activities, traveling back and forth between Hong Kong and Macao to promote the cause. After five years of study, he graduated first in his class and began practice in Macao in 1892. A year later, he moved to Canton, freely donating his services and medical supplies to the needy in order to win friends and to make new contacts. Here he ran into an old Taoist priest, a onetime follower of the Opium War hero Lin Tse-hsü, who advised him that for the revolution to succeed he must seek the help of the secret societies. From him Sun learned of the organization and the locations of these secret bodies, and Cheng Shih-liang was instructed to develop contacts with them.

It is apparent, then, that Hawaii and Hong Kong had a strong influence on Sun during the formative period of his life. What he saw in these places, and the contrasts they presented to his native district of Hsiang-shan, could not help but make a deep impression upon his young mind. Hawaii during his stay (1879-83), still an independent island kingdom, was rapidly being invaded by American influence, bringing with it the ideas of democracy, a modern legal system, modern schools, and the need for industrial development. The progressives of the islands were advocating the overthrow of the monarchical system in favor of an American-style democracy, while the conservatives rejected foreign intrusion and republicanism. Hawaii was experiencing problems not unlike those confronting China. Although Hawaii did become a republic in 1893, it was constantly under the threat of American annexation.[2] From this historical lesson Sun became convinced that it was insufficient to merely overthrow the Manchu dynasty and establish a republic; it was imperative to instill in the people a strong sense of nationalism with which to reconstruct the country and preserve their independence.

Hong Kong was no less a source of inspiration and instruction. The efficiency of the British colonial administration, the clean streets, the modern hygienic developments, and the orderliness provided a sharp contrast to Sun's native place. Why should they be so different when they were only fifty miles apart, he asked. Later he was to discover that the provincial capital and the metropolis of Peking were even more corrupt than his home district—the higher the official the more irresponsible he became. For all her 4,000 years of civilization, China had no cities as well governed as Hong Kong which had been under the British rule for only a few decades. The contrast kindled in Sun's heart a burning desire to overthrow the inefficient Ch'ing government.

However, Dr. Sun was a realist endowed with a large measure of "tactical flexibility" and a "proficiency at focusing simultaneously upon conflicting goals."[3] Before 1894, while planning for the overthrow of the

2. It did take place in 1898.
3. Harold Z. Schiffrin, Sun Yat-sen and the Origins of the Chinese Revolution (Berkeley, 1968), 27.

Manchu dynasty, he also considered reform as a possible means of saving China. Influenced by two respected reformists, the famous journalist Wang T'ao and the founder of his medical college, Ho Ch'i (Ho Kai), Sun entertained the idea of joining the reformist group. As an ex-peasant and a Christian convert who had a Western education but no traditional degree, Sun realized only too well that he was an "outsider" barred from the inner circles of the traditional society. But joining the camp of the gentry-reformists would enable him to drive a wedge into the elitist establishment. Twice between 1890 and 1892 he approached Cheng Tsao-ju, a former minister to Japan and the United States, and Cheng Kuan-ying, the noted compradore-turned-publicist, but in either case he elicited no significant response. Then he decided to reach Li Hung-chang, the epitome of gentry-reformists.

In the summer of 1894 Sun and a companion, Lu Hao-tung, went north to see the state of affairs in the capital and to seek an interview with Li. In a letter Sun advised Li that the wealth and power of European states were not achieved by battleships and cannon but by the full development of human talents, the full exploitation of the earth's resources, the full utilization of material devices, and the free exchange of goods. China must develop her talents through universal free education, vocational guidance, and promotion of science and agriculture. Describing himself as one who had traveled abroad and studied foreign languages, literature, politics, mathematics, and medicine, Sun went on to say: "I paid particular attention to their [the West's] methods of achieving a prosperous country and a powerful army and to their laws for reforming the people and perfecting their customs."[4] Li Hung-chang, however, was too preoccupied with the Japanese war either to see him or accept his service. The deep disappointment that ensued, coupled with the firsthand observation of the Manchu decadence in Peking, more than ever strengthened Sun's determination to overthrow the dynasty.

The Revive China Society, 1895. Sun resolved to return to his original goal of revolution and seek aid from those whom he knew best—the Chinese overseas, the secret societies, the Christian converts, and the missionaries—men existing on the fringes of Chinese society.[5] He went to Honolulu in the fall of 1894. With the help of his brother he organized the Revive China Society (Hsing-Chung hui) on November 24,

4. Schiffrin, 37.
5. Schiffrin, 40.

1894, with an initial membership of 112. Planning to expand his activities to the United States, Sun was urgently called back to China to take advantage of the war situation. He returned to Hong Kong and established a headquarters for the Revive China Society there on February 21, 1895, with branches in the provinces. Members of the Society took an oath to "expel the Manchus, restore the Chinese rule, and establish a federal republic."[6] And with that, the first revolutionary body was born.

On March 16 the Revive China Society set out to raise 3,000 men to capture Canton in order to establish it as their revolutionary base. Lu Hao-tung designed a "Blue Sky-White Sun" flag for the revolutionaries, which has since become the national flag of the Republic of China. Canton at the time was seething with unrest, caused by the sudden disbandment of troops that had been raised to reinforce the Japanese war. Sun developed connections with the San-yüan-li militia and scheduled an uprising on October 26. However, the plot was discovered, resulting in the loss of munitions and forty-eight lives, including that of Lu Hao-tung —the first martyr of the revolution.

Sun fled to Hong Kong, only to find that the British authorities had complied with a Ch'ing request to ban him for five years. Following the advice of Dr. Cantlie, Sun and a follower, Ch'en Shao-po, escaped to Japan. Upon their arrival at Kobe, they were pleasantly surprised by the local journalistic description of the Canton uprising as a "revolution" rather than an unlawful revolt. Flattered, Sun ordered that henceforth all uprisings should be called "revolutions." At Yokohama a Revive China Society branch was established, and the revolutionaries began developing connections with Japanese sympathizers, among whom were Sone Toshitora and the Miyazaki brothers (Yazō and Torazō). Sun was a changed man; he cut off his queue, took up Western attire, and left for Honolulu to promote the revolution.

The London Kidnap. The trip to Honolulu proved unfruitful. Many of Sun's supporters had grown indifferent after the abortive Canton uprising. To the United States Sun went to seek support from the Chinese communities, only to find them even less politically conscious. Their Hung League organizations had degenerated to a point where they had totally forgotten their original "anti-Ch'ing, revive Ming" objectives. They had become little more than fraternal and social societies. It was not until

6. A recent survey disputes this oath, wich is said to have been added retroactively. See Chün-tu Hsüeh, *Huang Hsing and the Chinese Revolution* (Stanford, 1961), 29.

after repeated lectures by Sun that these organizations revived their old dedications to revolution.

Arriving in London on October 1, 1896, Sun was lodged at the Gray's Inn as arranged by Dr. Cantlie. On October 11, on his way to church, Sun was lured to the Chinese legation, where he was kidnapped and detained on the third floor. The Ch'ing minister had already secured the approval of Tsungli Yamen to send him home secretly on a chartered ship at a cost of £7,000. Sun, however, was able to slip a message out to Dr. Cantlie via the English attendant of the legation. Having unsuccessfully sought intercession from Scotland Yard, Cantlie brought the case to the Foreign Office, and *The London Globe* in striking headlines exposed the illegal kidnap on October 22. Shocked by the incident, the Foreign Office obliged the Ch'ing legation to release Sun the next day. The kidnap had the unexpected result of making him world famous overnight. It was, in a way, a blessing in disguise.

Sun remained in Europe for about two years to study firsthand the recent political and social developments. Witnessing the growing trend toward social reform and revolution in the various industrialized countries, Sun wanted to save China from similar problems of strikes and labor-capital disputes in the future. In 1897 he developed the idea of a social revolution to complement his earlier nationalistic and democratic revolution. Here was the basis of his famous Three People's Principles (*San-min chu-i*)—People's National Consciousness, or Nationalism (*Min-tsu*); People's Rights, or Democracy (*Min-ch'üan*); and People's Livelihood, or Socialism (*Min-sheng*)—which Sun frequently and proudly compared with the famous Lincolnian expression "of the people, by the people, and for the people."

The Three People's Principles subsequently became the revolutionary philosophy for Sun and his followers. The first principle, nationalism, called for not only the overthrow of the alien Manchu rule, but also the removal of the foreign imperialistic yoke. The second principle, democracy, aimed at achieving the Four Rights for the people—initiative, referendum, election, and recall—and the Five Powers for the government: executive, legislative, judicial, control (supervisory), and examination—the last two reflecting the traditional functions of the censorate and the civil service examinations. The third principle, socialism, stressed the need for regulating capital and equalizing land. Here we see traces of the ancient Chinese utopian idea of "land to the tiller" as well as the influence of the Taiping land revolution. But more immediately and positively, it was from the famous Single Taxer Henry George and John Stuart Mill that Sun gained the idea that all increment in land value after it had been fixed (after the revolution) should go to the government. Thus, Sun's idea of a social revolution, first conceived in 1897 in an embryonic form, became a full-fledged third principle of his revolution by 1905-06.[7] These Three People's Principles are still the abiding creed of the Nationalist government on Taiwan today.

A Difficult Period, 1896-1900. Sun had built up fame and had evolved a revolutionary philosophy, but still lacked concrete success. Realizing the small numbers of Chinese students and merchants in Europe, he returned in mid-1897 to Japan, where the overseas Chinese communities were much larger and where it was more convenient to direct the revolutionary work on the mainland. Befriended by Inukai Ki, leader of the Japanese Liberal Party, Sun was introduced to Premier Ōkuma Shigenobu and Soejima Taneomi, vice-president of the Privy Council. Other private figures, notably the Miyazaki brothers and Hirayama Shū, became devoted supporters of Sun.

These Japanese and Sun shared the common feeling of Asia's grievance against Western imperialism. Many of them believed that China, once a great civilization, was only in temporary doldrums from which she could lift herself if proper outside help and a new leadership were available. Japan, having achieved modernization first, must repay her ancient cultural debt to China by assisting her to reform, modernize, and gain freedom from foreign imperialism. These ideas, persuasively set forth in the so-called Ōkuma Doctrine of 1898, won wide currency among the Japanese *shishi*—"men of high purpose"—many of whom considered Sun the man of destiny to regenerate China in the cause of Pan-Asianism.[8]

In contrast to these warmhearted Japanese sympathizers, the Chinese communities in Japan were largely apolitical and conservative. Out of 10,000, only a hundred or so supported Sun. Revolutionary work in China progressed even more slowly because of the general fear of involvement in anti-Manchu activity. Although the secret societies were an exception, they lacked the necessary education, cohesion, and sense of direction to offer any leadership.

To add to the frustration, there was the hostile influence of the Emperor-Protection Society (*Pao-huang tang*) under the leadership of

7. Martin Bernal, "The Triumph of Anarchism over Marxism, 1906-1907" in Mary C. Wright (ed.), *China in Revolution*, 103-04.
8. Marius B. Jensen, *The Japanese and Sun Yat-sen* (Cambridge, Mass., 1954), 53.

K'ang Yu-wei and Liang Ch'i-ch'ao, who had fled to Japan after the ill-fated "Hundred-Day" Reform. They and their followers vehemently attacked the ideas of revolution and republicanism. Sun took a rather conciliatory attitude toward K'ang, since they were both political refugees in a foreign country. However, his proposal for cooperation was contemptuously rejected by K'ang, who still regarded himself as an imperial tutor too dignified to associate himself with any rebel. Inukai's good-will mediation succeeded no further than arranging a meeting between the two, but at the appointed time K'ang did not show up. Liang, on the other hand, was far less arrogant and showed a receptiveness to revolutionary ideas, but was kept from cooperating by his teacher. The monarchist reformers and the revolutionaries clashed like "water and fire." It was not until K'ang was ordered by the Japanese government to leave the country that a change took place. Liang and Sun began discussing cooperation and even the possible amalgamation of the two groups, with Sun as director and Liang vice-director. K'ang, then traveling in Britain and Canada, quickly transferred Liang to Hawaii to take charge of the local branch of the Emperor-Protection Society. Still inclined toward reconciliation, Liang proposed that Emperor Kuang-hsü be made president of the future republic—an interesting idea but totally unacceptable to Sun.

In order to accelerate revolutionary activities and to fight off the rising influence of the Emperor-Protection Society which threatened to appropriate the revolutionary bases in Yokohama, Honolulu, and the United States, Sun initiated a three-pronged program of action: Ch'en Shao-po was sent to Hong Kong to inaugurate the China Daily (*Chung-kuo jih-pao*) in 1899; Shih Chien-ju and Hirayama went to the Yangtze area to strengthen ties with secret societies; and Cheng Shih-liang opened a reception center in Hong Kong, to which seven Ko-lao Brotherhood Association leaders came to pledge their support.

Taking advantage of the Boxer Rebellion in 1900, Sun dispatched Cheng Shih-liang to organize an uprising at Waichow (Hui-chou), north of Hong Kong, while Shih Chien-ju went to Canton to plot a sympathetic movement. Sun himself planned to go to Hong Kong in the company of a dozen or so Japanese supporters and officers, in the hopes of leading a revolutionary army northward. Unfortunately, the plot was again discovered and with Hong Kong authorities still refusing him admission, Sun fled to Formosa. Once there, he was befriended by the Japanese governor, Kodama, who promised help. Meanwhile, the revolutionaries had initiated activities along the coastal areas of Kwangtung, aided by the secret societies. They met with initial successes, but were stalled while anxiously waiting for reinforcements and supplies from Sun and the Japanese. Quite unexpectedly, there was a sudden change of government in Japan, and the new premier, Prince Itō, banned officers from serving in Sun's revolutionary army and ordered Governor Kodama to halt all assistance. Sun was not even allowed to leave Formosa. Without the reinforcements and supplies, the revolutionary army could not hold out for long; it ultimately disbanded and its leader, Cheng, fled to Hong Kong. The lone Japanese participant, Yamada, was captured and killed by the Ch'ing forces—the first foreigner lost in the Chinese Revolution. Meanwhile, Shih Chien-ju's attempt to blow up the governor-general's office at Canton led to his capture and loss of life at the tender age of twenty-one. Thus, the Waichow uprising ended in a fiasco.

Almost simultaneously, another uprising broke out in Central China under the leadership of T'ang Ts'ai-ch'ang, a onetime follower of K'ang Yu-wei. With support from the secret societies and the revolutionaries, T'ang's Independent army (*Tzu-li chün*)—so named because of its objective to create an independent state to replace the Ch'ing—was scheduled to attack Wuhan on August 23, 1900, at the height of the Boxer Rebellion. The plot was exposed prematurely, and T'ang was executed. The failure, partially caused by K'ang's unfulfilled promise of funds and reinforcements, discredited the Emperor-Protection Society, and worked unwittingly in favor of the revolutionaries.

Sun's image changed dramatically at this point. The mismanagement of the Ch'ing court during the Boxer catastrophe led many to look to him with encouragement. He was no longer regarded as a rebel or an outlaw, but rather as a patriotic, devoted revolutionary working for the betterment of his country and people. Students at home and in Japan enthusiastically supported him. Those in Japan published the *Citizen's Tribune* (*Kuo-min pao*) and the *Twentieth Century China* to promote the revolutionary cause and to advocate the assassination of Ch'ing officials. Back home several well-established scholars published the *Kiangsu Tribune* (*Su-pao*), and a young revolutionary, Tsou Jung, contributed a 20,000-word treatise, "The Revolutionary Army" (*Ko-ming chün*) in 1903, attacking the Ch'ing court and favoring revolution. The editor of *Su-pao*, Chang Ping-lin, was imprisoned for two years and the author died in jail at only twenty years of age.

In addition to these publications, a number of societies sprang up to support the revolution. At Shanghai, a prominent scholar, Ts'ai Yüan-p'ei, organized the Recovery Society (*Kuang-fu hui*), and at Changsha, Huang Hsing, who had secretly studied military arts in Japan, formed the China Revival Society (*Hua-hsing hui*) in 1903 with an initial membership of 500, including Sung Chiao-jen who later distinguished himself as a leading revolutionary figure. The constituents of this latter organization were mostly intellectuals and secret societies, particularly the Ko-lao Brotherhood Association which enrolled more than 100,000 men. After an abortive attempt to seize Changsha in 1904, Huang escaped to Japan, where he built up a strong following.

The T'ung-meng hui, 1905. The fortunes of the revolution turned considerably for the better during the period 1902-5, providing a sharp contrast to the dark days of the immediate past. Sun traveled widely in Vietnam, Japan, Honolulu, and the United States rallying support for his cause. Encouraged by the enthusiastic response of Chinese students in Japan, he developed the idea of forming a revolutionary party.[9] Many of these students had aspired to military studies but were prevented by the Ch'ing embassy. However, through Sun and Inukai, two Japanese officers were engaged to give instructions secretly to a group of fourteen students in the methods of weapon-making, military tactics, and guerrilla warfare. The students took an oath before Sun to "expel the Manchus, restore the Chinese rule, establish a republic, and equalize the land."

In Honolulu, since the Emperor-Protection Society had appropriated much of his former power base, Sun adopted the advice of his maternal uncle[10] to enter the Hung League (*Hung-men*), and was elected the "Hung Rod," i.e. generalissimo. With this new title and stature, he was warmly welcomed into the Hung League in the United States in 1904 as "Elder Brother Sun." He succeeded in revising the charter of the League by stressing its original anti-Ch'ing objective while interpolating the new purpose of "expelling the Manchus, restoring the Chinese rule, establishing a republic, and equalizing the land." In doing so, he swayed the Chinese communities in the United States over to his side from the Emperor-Protection Society.

In the spring of 1905 Sun was invited by Chinese students in Europe for a visit. Mutual discussion led to the decision of not only seeking support from students and the secret societies but also from the Ch'ing New

9. Leonard S. Hsü, *Sun Yat-sen: His Political and Social Ideals* (Los Angeles, 1933), 61.
10. Yang Wen-na.

Army. At Brussels Sun initiated thirty students into a revolutionary society, and at Berlin and Paris he initiated twenty and ten more, respectively, all pledging the four objectives mentioned above. However, the
largest revolutionary organization was in Tokyo, where several hundred
students were recruited, representing seventeen of the eighteen provinces
of China—Kansu having sent no students to Japan at that time. The seeds
of a new revolutionary party were sown, and Sun was encouraged to believe that the revolution would succeed in his lifetime.[11]

Through the intercession of Miyazaki, who praised Sun as a most remarkable man whose equal could not be found in the Western or Eastern hemispheres, Huang Hsing and Sung Chiao-jen met with Sun on July
28, 1905, at the office of their magazine, the *Twentieth Century China*.
Sun stressed the need for unifying all revolutionary groups into one
organization to avoid duplication of efforts and a struggle for power
among themselves. After several meetings, they decided to join hands
in a unified organization, The Chinese United League (*Chung-kuo
T'ung-meng hui*), or T'ung-meng hui in abbreviation, on August 20,
1905. Sun, 37, was elected chairman; Huang Hsing, 31, became chief of
the executive department with the authorization to act for the chairman
during his absence; and Sung Chiao-jen, 23, was made a member of the
judicial department. About seventy persons joined the T'ung-meng hui
at its inauguration. After taking an oath to pledge their support of the
four principles already mentioned, they were instructed by Sun in the
secret handshake and three sets of passwords: "Chinese, Chinese things,
and world affairs." Sun then shook hands with each, congratulating happily: "From now on you are no longer subjects of the Ch'ing dynasty!"
Just as he was speaking, the wooden partition of the room fell with a
bang. Sun quipped: "This symbolizes the downfall of the Manchus!"

Sun worked out a detailed procedure for his revolution. Initially, there
should be a military rule of three years in the areas liberated by the revolutionary forces. During this period the military government would control all military as well as civil affairs at the district (*hsien*) level. Meanwhile it would cooperate with the local people toward eliminating the
old political and social evils, such as slavery, foot-binding, opium-smoking,
and bureaucratic corruption. The second stage would be a period of
political tutelage, lasting not more than six years, during which time local
self-government should be instituted and popular elections for local assemblies and administrators would be held. However, the military gov-

11. Leonard S. Hsü, 62-63.

ernment would still retain control of the central government. During this period, there would be a provisional constitution to specify the rights and duties of the military government and the people. When the period of tutelage ended, the military government would be dissolved and the country would be governed by a new constitution. In short, Sun envisioned a three-stage revolution to lead the country into constitutionalism.

Sun's Three People's Principles were accepted as the revolutionary philosophy of the T'ung-meng hui, although the majority of the members focused only on the first two principles of nationalism and democracy. This was because the China Revival Society and the Restoration Society, both of which emphasized the overthrow of the Manchus and the establishment of a republic, contributed most of the members, while Sun's direct followers constituted but a small percentage. Huang Hsing now emerged as the strong man of the party, his name often appearing alongside that of Sun's as co-leaders. The membership of T'ung-meng hui grew rapidly to 963 by 1906, of whom 863 joined in Japan, the rest coming from Europe, Hawaii, Hong Kong, and Malaya.[12] Branches were established in China as well as in key overseas communities.

Huang Hsing turned over his *Twentieth Century China* as the official publication of the T'ung-meng hui. It engaged in heated debates with Liang Ch'i-ch'ao, who deprecated the ideas of revolution and republicanism in favor of constitutional monarchy. Not long afterwards, the *Twentieth Century China* was banned because it offended the sensitivity of the Japanese government by publishing an article entitled "The Japanese Politicians' Exploitation of China." The revolutionaries changed the name of the publication to the *People's Tribune* (*Min-pao*), with the first issue appearing on November 26, 1905. It boasted many gifted contributors, such as Chang Ping-lin, Hu Han-min and Wang Ching-wei. Their aggressive enthusiasm and combined talents overwhelmed Liang, who, for all his persuasive pen and flowing style, simply could not hold the ground alone for the Emperor-Protection Society. Moreover, Liang was secretly sympathetic with the revolutionary cause. His stress on the need for a constitution exposed the ineptness of the Manchu government, thereby indirectly advancing the revolutionary cause.[13] More and more, the younger generation turned to the side of the revolution.

12. Chün-tu Hsüeh, 44.
13. Chang P'eng-yüan, *Liang Ch'i-ch'ao yu Ch'ing-chi ko-ming* (Lian Ch'i-ch'ao and the late Ch'ing revolution), (Taipei, 1964), 325-26, 330-33.

The founding of the T'ung-meng hui constituted a milestone in the Chinese revolution, for it materially changed the character and style of the revolution. No longer did Sun operate on the periphery of society; he had moved into the "main stream of Chinese nationalism," receiving new support from the returned students, disaffected literati, and progressive army officers—groups that traditionally provided the leadership in China. The social base and potential areas of operations had been substantially enlarged. The T'ung-meng hui was multiprovincial and multiclass, as compared with the predominantly Cantonese makeup of the earlier Hsing-Chung hui, capable of instigating uprisings along the coast as well as in the *interior* of China. Above all, it provided a unified central organization that resembled a modern political party, which served as a rallying point for all revolutionary and progressive forces in the country.[14] As such, it fittingly received the tribute "the mother of the Chinese revolution."

The pulse of the revolution now quickened. One uprising followed another between 1906 and 1911—six times in Kwangtung and one each in Kwangsi and Yunnan, making a total of ten, counting the first two attempts at Canton and Waichow in 1895 and 1900. The last revolutionary attempt in April 1911, aiming at capturing the important provincial caiptal of Canton, created such a sensation and shock to the Ch'ing court that it presaged the success of the next attempt at Wuchang half a year later. This tenth failure produced the famous seventy-two martyrs, many of whom were students who had returned from Japan. They were later buried at the Yellow Flower Mound (*Huang-hua kang*) in the northern suburb of Canton.[15]

THE RISE OF THE REPUBLIC

The ten unsuccessful attempts at revolution all took place in the south and the southwest, where proximity of Hong Kong and Hanoi offered greater freedom of plotting and organization. However, powerful elements within the T'ung-meng hui now advocated to skip these peripheral areas and hit where it hurt the dynasty most—either in Peking or in the heartland of Central China along the Yangtze. If the tri-cities of Wuhan could be captured, they reasoned, the revolutionaries would be in a good

14. Schiffrin, 8-9.
15. The common expression, "Huang-hua kang 72 martyrs" who died on "March 29" is inexact. Actually, more than 82 revolutionaries lost their lives on April 27, 1911, which was the 29th day of the third lunar month. See Chün-tu Hsüeh, 93.

position to respond to action in the south or to advance north to the capital. Thus, on July 13, 1911, a Central China Bureau of the T'ung-meng hui was established in Shanghai with Sung Chiao-jen as leader. The central provinces of Hupeh and Hunan emerged as the prime target.

In Hupeh there existed already two organizations affiliated with, but not a part of, the T'ung-meng hui. One was the Common Advancement Society (*Kung-chin hui*), which was founded in August 1907, and consisted largely of returned students from Japan and secret society members. The other was the misnamed Literary Society (*Wen-hsüeh hui*), an offspring of the Military Study Society (*Chen-wu hsüeh-she*), which came into being on January 30, 1911, and consisted generally of members of the Ch'ing New Army in Hupeh who had been won over to the revolutionary cause. Of the two groups, the former was more prestigious, while the latter was more powerful due to its infiltration of the New Army. On June 1, 1911, the two societies agreed to cooperate in a joint action at Wuchang, and invitations were extended to Huang Hsing and Sung Chiao-jen in Shanghai—Sun being abroad—to come to direct the revolution. So quick and so successful was the subversion of the New Army that an immediate outbreak was irrepressible; the occasion that touched it off was the turmoil created by the railway controversy.

Nationalization of the Railways. Railways construction, which ran into such opposition in the 1870's and 1880's, became a craze after the Sino-Japanese War, and Sheng Hsüan-huai was appointed by the court as director-general of a new railway company in 1896. He had hoped to raise funds from government and private sources as well as from foreign loans, but since the first two were unable to contribute much, the major supply of capital came from the foreigners. In the decade that followed, a number of lines were constructed with foreign loans, the most famous being the Peking-Hankow and the Shanghai-Nanking railways. In 1898 a loan with the American-owned China Development Company was negotiated to construct the Canton-Hankow line. However, strong gentry and merchant opposition led Chang Chih-tung, governor-general at Wuhan, in 1905 to redeem the right from the American company with a payment of U.S. $6.75 million, financed by a new £1.2 million loan from the Hong Kong government. The people of Kwangtung, Hunan, and Hupeh, through whose provinces the proposed line would cross, were allowed to build it themselves; in addition the people of Szechwan were given the right to construct the line from Hankow into their province.

Provincial ability and resources, however, proved inadequate. In spite of new taxes on land, rice, property, and salaries, Hunan was able to raise only five million taels against a 60-million-tael construction cost. Kwangtung gathered only half of the needed amount. The Szechwan gentry and merchants found few subscribers to the shares of their railway company, and the situation was further confused by a two-million-tael embezzlement among the directors of the company. Under such conditions, the court in 1908 put Chang Chih-tung in charge of the Canton-Hankow Railway as well as the Hupeh portion of the Szechwan-Hankow line. In June 1909 he began negotiations for a £6 million loan from the British-French-German-American banking consortium, but progress was delayed by his death four months later on October 5.

In line with its policy of centralizing power as noted in Chapter 17, the Ch'ing government in the spring of 1911 approved the proposal of a junior metropolitan censor[16] that the main railways be nationalized while the minor or branch lines be left to private operations. On May 9, the court formally ordered the nationalization of the Canton-Hankow and Szechwan-Hankow lines, and on May 20 Sheng Hsüan-huai signed a contract with the four-power banking consortium for a 40-year loan at 5 per cent interest.

The gentry and the people of the four provinces vigorously protested the nationalization policy and the invasion of foreign capital. Having invested considerable, if still insufficient, sums in these lines, they organized "railway-protection clubs" to defend their vested interests and mobilized the provincial assemblies to fight for their rights. Delegations were dispatched to Peking to appeal to the court, and demands were made to dismiss Sheng for selling out China's interests to foreigners. So powerful was the sense of injustice that popular uprisings in Szechwan and Hunan were all but inevitable.

On June 17 the court offered to indemnify those people who had invested in the railways: for Hunan and Hupeh, a 100 per cent compensation; for Kwangtung, 60 per cent, with the remaining 40 per cent to be paid in government bonds redeemable within ten years after the railway had become profitable; for Szechwan, due to the proven embezzlement, the government would give only redeemable bonds at 6 per cent interest to cover the railway capital of 7 million taels and the actual construction cost of 4 million taels. The treatment of the four provinces was thus un-

16. Shih Ch'ang-hsin. He was supported by Sheng Hsüan-huai, now Minister of Posts and Communications.

equal; Hunan and Hupeh received the best terms, Kwangtung next, and Szechwan the worst. Small wonder that the people of Szechwan were incensed, while those of the other three provinces were less agitated!

The Provincial Assembly of Szechwan, representing the interests of the gentry, the rich landlords, and the wealthy merchants, took the lead in protesting this unfair treatment. It attacked Peking for betraying the interests of Szechwan to the foreigners, and reacted strongly against the high-handed, despotic manner in which the government negotiated the loan and proclaimed the nationalization policy without first consulting the provincial assemblies. Aroused by Yüan Shih-k'ai's special emissary, T'ang Shao-i, and encouraged by the secret sympathy of the ex-governor-general, Wang Jen-wen, the leaders of the Provincial Assembly organized a mass movement of students and people to demand postponement of the nationalization project and the impeachment of Sheng Hsüan-huai.[17] On August 24, 1911, more than 10,000 Szechwanese staged a rally in the provincial capital of Chengtu. Overcome by emotion, they wailed and screamed; they resolved to stop tax payments, to sponsor strikes at the schools and markets, and to mourn before the placard of the late Emperor Kuang-hsü who had granted them the right to construct the railway. The new governor-general, Chao Erh-feng, anxious to please the court and keep his position, ordered the arrest of gentry representatives, and an open conflict broke out between the troops and the demonstrators, resulting in thirty-two deaths among the latter. Thereafter, fighting between the people of Szechwan and the government troops intensified.

It must be noted that at this point although the Szechwan gentry agitated against the court, they did so to protect their own interests without any idea of overthrowing it—most of the members of the Provincial Assembly believed in constitutional monarchy.[18] But when their demands were ignored by the government, they turned their sympathy to the revolutionaries. A Szechwanese leader[19] declared: "Domestic politics is hopeless, and the government apparently does not care for the people. To save the country there is no other way but revolution. We Szechwanese have already made proper preparation, and would coordinate with other provinces for joint action."[20] The railway controversy and the revolution now fused into one pressing issue.

17. Chūzō Ichiko, "The Railway Protection Movement in Szechuan in 1911," *Memoirs of the Research Department of the Toyo Bunko*, Tokyo, 14:50-57 (1955).
18. Chūzō Ichiko, 68-69.
19. Liu Sheng-yüan or perhaps P'u Tien-chün.
20. Li Shou-k'ung, 736-37.

The Wuchang Revolution. To control the unrest in Szechwan, the court transferred part of the Hupeh New Army there—an act which placed the strategic city of Wuchang in a vulnerable position, which the revolutionaries were quick to take advantage of. Huang Hsing, still in Shanghai, had hoped to take action by the end of October, but on October 9 a bomb accidentallly exploded in the revolutionary headquarters located in the Russian Concession of Hankow. Subsequent police raids resulted in the arrest of thirty-two revolutionaries and the seizure of weapons, explosives, and important documents including the lists of names of the members of the New Army who had been won over. To protect themselves, the engineering and artillery battalions of the New Army decided to strike the following day.

On the morning of October 10, the engineering unit took the lead in seizing the government munition depot in Wuchang, and the artillery joined in a combined attack on the office of the governor-general who fled along with the military commander.[21] The New Army rebels met little resistance and had complete control of the city by noon. Having no genuine revolutionary leaders present—Sun being abroad and Huang still in Shanghai—they drafted the reluctant Ch'ing brigade commander, Li Yüan-hung, to be the military governor of Hupeh. Meanwhile, T'ang Hua-lung, the former chairman of the Hupeh Provincial Assembly who had long shown sympathy with the revolution, was appointed the civilian executive chief of the revolutionary government, charged with the duty of setting up an initial administrative body. It was he who on the one hand sent out telegrams to the other provinces urging them to declare independence of the Ch'ing court, and on the other successfully convinced the foreign consuls in Hankow that they should stay neutral during the turmoil. Thus, when the escaped Ch'ing governor-general requested the foreign consuls to call in gunboats to bombard the revolutionaries, the French and Russian consuls simply replied that the situation was totally different from the Boxer Rebellion, while other consuls proclaimed strict neutrality.[22] On October 12, Hanyang and Hankow fell to the revolutionaries.

The quick success was indeed "providential," as Dr. Sun later recalled, for if the Manchu governor-general had not been scared away, the military commander would have stayed and probably would have crushed the

---

21. Jui-cheng and Chang Piao, respectively.
22. P'eng-yüan Chang, "The Constitutionalists" in Mary C. Wright (ed.), *China in Revolution*, 175-76.

thin revolutionary forces, estimated at a little more than 2,000 men. Foreign neutrality, of course, helped the revolutionary cause. What was most encouraging was the rapid succession of declarations of independence by the provinces and important municipalities: Changsha, October 22; Yunnan, October 31; Shanghai, November 3; Chekiang, November 5; Fukien and Kwangtung, November 9; and Szechwan, November 27. Within a month and a half, fifteen provinces, or two-thirds of all China, seceded from the Ch'ing dynasty.

In order to appease the public anger, the court dismissed Sheng Hsüan-huai on October 26 and released the imprisoned Szechwanese gentry. Meanwhile, counterattacks by the government's Peiyang forces had succeeded in recovering Hankow on November 2 and Hanyang on November 27. However, these temporary Ch'ing victories were more than offset by the loss to the revolutionaries of Shanghai in early November and Nanking on December 4, 1911. At the latter place, a provisional revolutionary government was established, electing Huang Hsing generalissimo and Li Yüan-hung vice-generalissimo. However, both declined the appointments, awaiting Sun's return from abroad.

Traveling in Denver, Colorado, Sun learned of the success of the Wuchang revolution from a local newspaper account. His first thought was to rush home as fast as he could to have the personal satisfaction of directing the revolution, but his better judgment dictated that he engage in diplomacy instead. Knowing that British support was essential to the future of the revolution, he traveled east to New York, from whence he sailed for London. Successfully he committed the British government to stop all loan negotiations with the Ch'ing government, to prevent Japan from aiding the Peking regime, and to lift the ban on his entering British territories and possessions so that he could return home freely. A promise was also secured from the president of the four-power banking consortium that as soon as the revolutionary government was recognized by the powers, the consortium would negotiate with it. With these diplomatic accomplishments, Sun went to France, where he was warmly greeted by Premier Clemenceau and the French people. Back in Shanghai on December 25, Sun was elected four days later by a nearly unanimous vote of the provincial delegates to be the provisional president of the Republic of China.[23] Li Yüan-hung became the provisional vice-president, and Huang Hsing the minister of war. The new government adopted the

23. Sun received sixteen out of seventeen possible votes, and Huang Hsing received one.

solar calendar in place of the lunar one, and designated January 1, 1912, as the first day of the republic. After some twenty-seven years of struggle,[24] Sun's lifelong dream came to a glorious fulfillment. The question now facing the Nanking government was how to terminate the Ch'ing dynasty and achieve national unification.

The Manchu Abdication. In a dying struggle for survival, the court sent Minister of War Ying-ch'ang and Admiral Sa Chen-ping to chastise the revolutionaries at Wuchang, and appointed Yüan Shih-k'ai governor-general of Hunan and Hupeh. Still smarting under his summary dismissal in 1908 and dissatisfied with the limited appointment, Yüan refused to end his retirement on the grounds that his "leg ailment"—the Ch'ing pretext for his forced retirement—had not yet recovered. Ying-ch'ang's army, commanded by officers who were mostly former subordinates of Yüan, fought halfheartedly and suffered repeated defeats, while Admiral Sa was persuaded by Li Yüan-hung to defect on November 11. Under these conditions, the court had no choice but to turn to Yüan once again. Yüan demanded (1) inauguration of a national assembly in a year; (2) organization of a responsible cabinet; (3) pardon to the revolutionaries; (4) lifting the ban on parties; (5) full power to control the army and the navy; and (6) guarantee of sufficient military funds. The first four of these terms were aimed at mollifying the public and the revolutionaries, while the next two were designed to make Yüan the most powerful man in the country. By item two—perhaps the most important of all—Yüan did not really mean a genuine "responsible" cabinet; it was his subterfuge to pre-empt the power of the regent, Prince Chün, who had retired him earlier and to eliminate the "Royal Cabinet."

Under the pressure of military defeat and rapid secession of the provinces, the regent had no choice but to give in. On October 27, 1911 Yüan was appointed imperial commissioner in full charge of the army and the navy, and his two chief lieutenants, Feng Kuo-chang and Tuan Ch'i-jui, were given command of the First and Second armies respectively. Still unsatisfied, Yüan continued to bargain and refused to come out of retirement. However, to show his power and ability to control the situation, he ordered Feng to deal a severe blow to the revolutionaries, which he did by taking Hankow on November 2.

About this time, a dramatic event developed in North China. On

24. Since 1885.

October 29, two leaders[25] of the Ch'ing 20th Division stationed at Launchou (halfway between Mukden and Peking) demanded of the court the inauguration of a constitutional monarchy within a year. Fully expecting a rejection which would give them an excuse to march on Peking and effect a "central revolution," they found to their surprise that the court, stunned by the secession of Shansi on the same day, meekly bowed to their demand. Prince Chün declared himself unfit to govern as regent and Prince Ch'ing resigned as premier. On November 1, Yüan was made premier; it was only then that he came out of retirement and went south to take charge of the campaign against the revolutionaries. Two days later the court hurriedly promulgated a nineteen-article "principle of constitution" in an attempt to appease the public.

The appointment of Yüan as premier, which was, in a way, a Ch'ing device to keep him from joining the revolutionaries, did not please the 20th Division commanders; they refused to recognize his appointment. Rumors circulated that they intended to seize Peking immediately. Many dependents of high Ch'ing officials fled to the foreign concessions in Tientsin, while the court itself at one point contemplated moving to Jehol, only to be halted by Yüan who did not want to lose control over it. The commanders of the 20th Division then entered into a secret plot with the commander of the 6th Division[26] and the Shansi revolutionary leader[27] to organize a joint march on Peking so as to prevent Yüan's return to the capital. The commander of the 6th Division commented: "The main obstacle to the revolution is the Ch'ing slave Yüan Shih-k'ai. To complete the revolution Yüan must be prevented from entering Peking. Once he reaches Peking it would be bad for the revolution and all of us."[28] If this joint attack had materialized, the Ch'ing dynasty would have been toppled immediately and Yüan would have lost his instrument of control and bargaining power. Moreover, his own position would have been caught between the revolutionaries in the south and the rebel divisional commanders in the north, spelling an end to his dreams of glory and aggrandizement. For a man of Yüan's ambitions, treachery, and manipulation, such a situation could never be allowed to develop. So he simply had the chief instigator, the commander of the

25. Chang Shao-tseng and Lan T'ien-wei, both graduates of a Japanese military academy and secret members of the T'ung-meng hui.
26. Wu Lu-chen, also a secret member of the T'ung-meng hui.
27. Yen Hsi-shan.
28. Hsiao I-shan, IV, 2,654.

6th Division, assassinated on November 7.[29] He assumed the premiership, formed his cabinet, and placed his henchmen in full control of the capital area and the imperial guards. On December 4 the regent was retired at an annual pension of 50,000 taels. What was left of the Ch'ing court was merely the boy emperor and the widowed dowager.[30] With them as his puppets, Yüan started to flirt with the revolutionary forces for his personal future.

Three times before November 10 he sent emissaries to Li Yüan-hung to propose peace talks, while his son, Yüan K'o-ting, went to see Huang Hsing, the commander-in-chief of the revolutionary forces at Hanyang, suggesting collaboration and joint action. However, both attempts failed because the revolutionaries knew well Yüan's favorite trick of playing both ends against the middle. Thus snubbed, Yüan ordered his troops to shatter the revolutionaries' defense at Hanyang, which fell on November 27. Having shown his power, he halted any further attack to show his leniency, and persuaded the British minister, John Jordan, to instruct the British consul at Hankow to mediate a truce, which was arranged on December 1. His peace emissary, T'ang Shao-i, then went to Shanghai to negotiate with the revolutionary representative, Wu Ting-fang. Huang Hsing now cabled Yüan that if he would support the republic and force the abdication of the Ch'ing emperor, the future presidency of the republic would be his. So eager was he for this new position that when Sun was elected provisional president on December 29, Yüan was incensed and broke off peace negotiations.

Strangely enough, most of the revolutionaries at this point considered Yüan indispensable: he was the only man who could save the country from a civil war and who could force the Ch'ing court out of existence. Sun did not favor compromise but as an idealist he cared little whether he or Yüan were president, as long as the Manchu dynasty was overthrown and the principle of a republic was firmly established. Furthermore, he was a bit irked with his own followers, who ignored his three-stage revolutionary procedure and his principles of democratic reconstruction and people's livelihood. They emphasized only nationalism to overthrow the Manchus. With this state of mind and the knowledge of Yüan's superior military power, Sun was willing to step down. He humored Yüan with

29. Some accounts hold the Ch'ing court responsible for the assassination. However, a recent work states categorically that Yüan "bribed an officer under Wu's command to assassinate Wu." See Jerome Ch'en, *Yüan Shih-k'ai, 1859-1916: Brutus Assumes the Purple* (Stanford, 1961), 113.
30. Lung-yü, wife of the late emperor Kuang-hsü.

the explanation that he had accepted the *provisional* presidency in order to keep the *regular* presidency for him. Still unpacified, Yüan ordered more than forty of his generals to oppose the republic in favor of a constitutional monarchy, and under the pretext of raising military funds to fight the revolutionaries, he exacted 80,000 ounces of gold from the helpless dowager. Sun had to reassure Yüan that if he could avert the civil war, a "just reward" would be awaiting him. When a group of Ch'ing diplomats abroad[31] urged the abdication of the throne on January 3, 1912, Yüan knew that the days of the dynasty were numbered. He informed the Nanking government that he would induce the voluntary abdication of the Ch'ing throne if the presidency of the republic was offered to him. To guard against duplicity on the part of Yüan, Sun specified, through the news media, the procedure for the transfer of power: (1) Yüan must notify foreign ministers or consuls of the Ch'ing abdication; (2) Yüan must publicly declare his support of the republic; (3) Sun will resign upon receiving notifications from the diplomatic or consular corps of the Ch'ing abdication; (4) the parliament will elect Yüan provisional president; and (5) Yüan must pledge to honor the constitution to be prepared by the parliament, and until he does so he will not be given military power.

Yüan mobilized his friend Prince Ch'ing to impress upon the court that rather than losing everything, it would be wise to abdicate gracefully under the favorable conditions that the revolutionaries were willing to offer. Between January 17 and 19, three imperial conferences were held to deliberate the question; most of the Manchu and Mongol princes were opposed to abdication. Yüan then instigated some fifty[32] of his generals to announce their support of the republic. Tuan Ch'i-jui went so far as to inform the court that if the Manchu nobles had doubts about the republic he would bring troops to Peking to argue with them. Feng Kuo-chang also spoke openly to his troops in favor of the republic. In collaboration with these moves, Yüan's emissaries visited the palace repeatedly to urge an early abdication. They tactfully advised the dowager that since Emperor Kuang-hsü started, but did not live to see, the constitutional movement, it behooved her to carry on his work and to accept republicanism. The dowager is reported to have answered: "I know that the country is public property and not the private possession of the Manchus, but since the Manchus have a heritage of more than 200 years, I only ask

31. Under the leadership of Lu Cheng-hsiang, minister to Russia.
32. Some accounts say forty-two. See Jerome Ch'en, 127.

that the tomb of Emperor Kuang-hsü be maintained and repaired, and that the status of the imperial family be not degraded." On January 30 Prince Chün and Prince Ch'ing, the former regent and premier, advised that "since the government troops have lost the will to fight, it would be better to abdicate under favorable conditions." On February 1, 1912, the dowager summoned Yüan to the palace and sobbingly announced: "I leave the various matters to your judgment and have no request other than the preservation of the dignity and honor of the emperor."[33]

The Nanking government offered to treat the deposed Ch'ing emperor with the same courtesy as a foreign sovereign, subsidize him with 4 million taels annually,[34] and allow him to live in the Summer Palace with the usual number of guards and attendants. On February 12, Sun warned that these favorable terms would be withdrawn if the abdication did not take place within two days. On that very day, Yüan made public the previously prepared imperial rescript, countersigned by himself as premier and all the cabinet ministers, announcing the formal abdication of the Ch'ing throne. And with that the 268-year Ch'ing rule, the last of China's twenty-five dynasties, came to an end.

The imperial rescript contained a statement which authorized Yüan to organize a provisional republican government and to negotiate for a national unification with the revolutionaries. Such a statement did not appear in the original version, prepared by the famous scholar Chang Chien for the Nanking government and accepted by Yüan, but was later secretly inserted by Yüan to show that he derived the provisional presidency from the deposed Ch'ing emperor and not from the Nanking regime. Sun was exasperated but could do nothing about it since it was already published.

On the same day Yüan pledged his support of the republic, which was a prerequisite to his assumption of the presidency: "The republic is universally recognized as the best form of state . . . Now that the Ch'ing emperor has clearly announced his abdication in a rescript which has been countersigned by me, the date of such announcement is the end of the imperial administration and the beginning of the republic. Let us henceforth forge ahead and endeavor to reach a state of perfection. *Never shall we allow the monarchical system to reappear in China.*"[35] On February 13, Sun resigned as the provisional president of the republic and recommended that Yüan be named his successor, contingent upon the

33. Hsiao I-shan, IV, 2,725, 2,727.
34. To be changed to 4 million silver dollars after the new currency was issued.
35. Italics added.

latter's acceptance of three conditions: (1) that Nanking remain the capital; (2) that he come to Nanking to assume the provisional presidency; and (3) that he observe the provisional constitution to be drafted by the provisional parliament. On the following day, the provisional parliament formally elected Yüan the provisional president and Li Yüan-hung the provisional vice-president. However, it voted to make Peking the national capital; it was only through the intervention of Huang Hsing that the decision was reversed in favor of Nanking.[36] A delegation of eminent leaders was then dispatched to Peking on February 18 to welcome Yüan to Nanking.

Yüan was in no mood to leave his power base in the North for the South, where the revolutionaries were strong. He instigated riots by his soldiers to justify the need for his continued presence in Peking. The revolutionary leaders had no choice but to allow him to inaugurate in Peking, which took place on March 10. A day later, Sun promulgated the Provisional Constitution of fifty-six articles—the first such document in China. On April 1, 1912, Sun formally relinquished his duties as provisional president, and by a vote of the parliament on April 5 Peking was made the national capital. The United States was the first to recognize the new republic of China, followed by Brazil, Peru, Austria, Portugal, and others.

The Significance. The rise of the republic was an epochal event in Chinese history, for it spelled an end to more than two thousand years of imperial dynasties. China no longer belonged to any "Son of Heaven" or any imperial family but to all the people. The success of the revolution fulfilled not only the dreams of the two-and-a-half-century nationalistic revolutionary tradition, but went beyond narrow racial considerations to liberate political power from one ethnic group, the Manchus, and extend it to all the people of China: the Chinese, the Manchus, the Mongols, the Moslems, and the Tibetans. The rapidity of the success—from the Wuchang Revolution of October 10, 1911, to the establishment of the republic on January 1, 1912, a total of eighty-three days—was seldom equaled by any other great revolutions of the world.

Yet the revolution was an incomplete one with many unfortunate repercussions, much to the chagrin of Sun. Most of his followers devoted themselves to the overthrow of the Manchus and the establishment of the republic; few paid attention to the more important task of demo-

36. Chün-tu Hsüeh, 135.

cratic reconstruction and the problem of people's livelihood. When the dynasty was overthrown and the republic established, they felt that their prime objectives had been achieved. So anxious were they for peace that they were willing to compromise with so unprincipled a man as Yüan, over the opposition of Sun, who, outvoted, was regarded as an impractical idealist. Of the Three People's Principles, they discarded the second and third totally and accepted only part of the first—nationalism against the alien Manchu rule—without realizing that after the establishment of the republic they must continue to struggle against foreign imperialism. They ignored Sun's three-stage revolutionary program altogether. Their readiness to cooperate with the old elements, and their favorable treatment of the deposed emperor, paved the way for future warlordism and attempts to revive the imperial system—by Yüan in 1915 and by Chang Hsün in 1917. Sun's disillusionment with his own party was a major cause for his resignation as provisional president. He asked, "Without revolutionary reconstruction, what's the use of a revolutionary president?"

YÜAN'S BETRAYAL OF THE REPUBLIC

Once elected the provisional president, Yüan started to make a travesty of the republic. In this first cabinet, the four substantive ministries—Foreign Affairs, Internal Affairs, War, and Navy—all went to his henchmen, while the four lesser ministries—Education, Justice, Agriculture, and Forestry—were allocated to the T'ung-meng hui members. Huang Hsing, the choice of the revolutionaries for the Ministry of War, was merely made the resident-general of Nanking, and since Yüan refused to pay his 50,000 troops, Huang was soon obliged to disband them. The premier, T'ang Shao-i, one of the boys who went to the United States to study in 1872, genuinely desired to lead the nation toward the rule of law, in apparent contradiction with Yüan's secret wishes. To humiliate him, Yüan dismissed the military governor-general of Chihli[37] and sent him to help disband the troops in Nanking without the premier's countersignature as required by the provisional constitution. T'ang resigned in protest on June 16, 1912, as did the four T'ung-meng hui cabinet ministers.

The next premier was an ineffective diplomat, Lu Cheng-hsiang, a former minister to Russia. His lack of policy and sense of direction led to his impeachment by the parliament, and after July 27 Lu stopped going to

37. General Wang Chih-hsiang.

the office on the pretext of illness. Yüan's confidant Chao Ping-chün, the minister of internal affairs, served as acting premier and later became premier on September 24. Under him, the cabinet was nothing but a puppet of the president. Within five months, Yüan had succeeded in reducing the "responsible cabinet" to a shambles.

However, to the southern revolutionary leaders Yüan displayed a great outward deference, cordially inviting Sun and Huang to visit him. They accepted the invitation but did not go together, for fear of being trapped simultaneously. Sun went first and during his 26-day stay in Peking was warmly welcomed by Yüan, who thirteen times listened attentively to his views on land reform, the single tax theory, the importance of transferring capital from Peking to the interior, and the need for constructing 200,000 miles of railway. On September 9, Yüan appointed Sun director of railways with the full power to draw up a plan for a national railway system. Sun went away with the belief that Yüan was a man of ability and sincerity, "indispensable to the presidency in the next ten years."[38] Then came Huang Hsing, "the Napoleon of the Chinese Revolution," who was given the same cordial treatment and the same airing of his views on a variety of subjects, including his exposition of the need for industrial development and the usefulness of an efficient parliamentary system. Huang was appointed director-general of the Canton-Hankow and Szechwan railways. Having pacified the two revolutionary leaders, Yüan became bolder than ever in his search for dictatorial powers.

The Second Revolution. According to the provisional constitution, a parliament was to be elected within six months of the formation of the government. Election laws and regulations on the organization of the parliament were promulgated by the provisional government in August 1912, including the adoption of a bicameral system. By the time of the election in December, the T'ung-meng hui had absorbed four splinter parties to form the Nationalist Party (*Kuomintang*) under the effective guidance of Sung Chiao-jen. Sung had studied parliamentary theories in Japan, had won the support of Huang Hsing, and was respected by prominent constitutionalists outside the party. Though not opposed to Yüan's election as president, he strongly advocated party government and a responsible cabinet to guide the country into constitutionalism and to check the abuse of the president.

Against the Nationalist Party were a number of smaller parties, such

38. Chün-tu Hsüeh, 141.

as the Unification Party (*T'ung-i tang*), the Republican Party (*Kung-ho tang*), and the Democratic Party (*Min-chu tang*), the last under the chairmanship of Liang Ch'i-ch'ao. The elections gave the Nationalists a landslide victory, taking 269 seats out of a total 596 in the Lower House, and 123 out of 274 in the Upper House. The Nationalist Party commanded more votes than the other three parties combined, which now merged into one Progressive Party (*Chin-pu tang*), in general support of the Yüan government.

The Nationalist victory was largely the work of Sung Chiao-jen. His organizing ability and frequent public advocacy of using the responsible cabinet and the loyal opposition systems to check the excesses of the president irritated Yüan greatly. Failing to win him over by bribery Yüan decided to eliminate him through assassination, and Chao P'ing-chün, fearful of losing the premiership to Sung, joined in the plotting. On March 20, 1913, just as he was leaving the Shanghai railway station to take up his new assignment as the Nationalist representative in Peking, Sung was shot; he died two days later, at the age of thirty-one. The confession of the captured assassin and the subsequent investigations implicated Premier Chao and possibly President Yüan. However, before the formal trial at the Shanghai Mixed Court, the assassin died suddenly in prison. Premier Chao refused to be subpoenaed to the court on the pretext of illness. He was later transferred to the governor-generalship of Chihli, where he mysteriously died by poisoning on February 17, 1914. Others involved in the case were either killed or poisoned, and the trial dragged on inconclusively, without ever reaching a clear verdict. It was nevertheless generally assumed that Yüan was behind the Sung assassination.

To bolster his position against the Nationalists, in April 1913 Yüan negotiated a so-called "reorganization loan" of £25 million from the Five-Power Banking Consortium.[39] Sun and Huang Hsing urged the parliament to reject this "illegal" loan, whereupon Yüan's acting premier, Tuan Ch'i-jui, surrounded the parliament building with troops and declared presumptuously: "It being a *fait accompli*, there is no need for further discussion!" When the Nationalist members of the parliament impeached the government, an irreparable schism developed between Yüan and the revolutionaries. In a lightning manner, Yüan dismissed the Nationalist military governors in Kiangsi, Kwangtung, and Anhwei, and his army readied for an attack on the south.

39. Britain, France, Germany, Russia, and Japan.

On July 12, 1913, the military governor of Kiangsi[40] declared independence and in less than a month six other provinces followed suit,[41] starting what is known as the "Second Revolution." Yüan had little trouble crushing these poorly equipped southern armies. Within a couple of months, the fight was over; Yüan's generals took over control of the Yangtze area as provincial warlords.

In retrospect, Sun blamed the failure of the Second Revolution more on the internal dissension within his party than on Yüan's military power. He had preferred an uncompromising stand toward Yüan, but Huang Hsing insisted on resolving the differences through legal means. He had wanted to conduct a revolt at Nanking, but ultimately deferred to Huang due to his military experience; yet Huang gave up Nanking easily for the lack of funds. Moreover, Li Yüan-hung of Hupeh unexpectedly joined forces with Yüan and opened the way for the Peiyang army to make a decisive thrust southward. Another contributing cause was the assistance Yüan received from the British Minister, John Jordan, who arranged loans, supplied munitions, and barred Sun and Huang from Hong Kong. Above all, the people were weary of fighting and of bloodshed; they wanted peace at all costs and could not see why, after the establishment of the republic, there was still the need for a second revolution.

Yüan's Monarchical Dream. The easy suppression of the Second Revolution elated Yüan, whose personal ambitions now knew no limits. No longer satisfied with the title of provisional president, he yearned for it to be changed to president with a lifelong tenure, preparatory to his ultimate goal of emperorship. In his dream for glory, Yüan had completely swept aside his 1912 inauguration pledge that he would uphold the republic against any reappearance of the monarchy.

The first step in Yüan's scheme was to prompt the parliament to issue the presidential election law on October 5, 1913, before the completion of the constitution. A day later, the two houses of the parliament held the presidential election, amidst the hue and cry of the so-called "citizen corps"—Yüan's disguised soldiers, police, and plainclothesmen—who besieged the building, shouting: "If you do not elect the president we want, do not expect to leave." In spite of the threat, Yüan failed to win the necessary votes on the first two ballots,[42] and it was only on the third

40. Li Lieh-chün.
41. Kiangsu, Anhwei, Kwangtung, Fukien, Hunan, and Szechwan.
42. Receiving 471 votes on the first ballot and 497 on the second, out of a total 759 parliamentarians present.

that he was elected by a plurality vote. On October 10, 1913, Yüan was formally inaugurated as president, and the provisional government became the regular government.

Within three weeks, on October 31, the parliament promulgated the T'ien-t'an Constitution, which adopted the cabinet rather than the presidential system, to check Yüan's powers. Incensed, Yüan asked his generals to attack it as a document incompatible with the national conditions and as a Nationalist device to dominate the parliament. When the parliament stood firm, Yüan simply dissolved the Nationalist Party on November 4 and revoked the credentials of 358 of its parliamentarians (eighty more later) on the pretext of their involvement in the Second Revolution. As 1914 opened, the parliament could not meet for lack of a legal quorum. Having brushed aside the constitution, the parliament, and the opposition party, Yüan achieved a virtual dictatorship.

Mindful of the importance of legality, Yüan called a national conference on March 18, 1914, to revise the 1912 provisional constitution. Each of the twenty-two provinces contributed two delegates, while four each came from the capital and the national chamber of commerce, and eight from Mongolia, Tibet, and Chinghai, making a total of sixty. The upshot of the conference was the shift from the cabinet to the presidential system and the authorization of the president and the parliament to prepare a new constitution. The new document, known as the Constitutional Compact, was promulgated on May 1, 1914, and extended the presidential term to ten years, renewable by re-election without limit. Moreover, the president had the right to nominate his own successor. With this constitution Yüan was assured of the lifelong tenure as well as the right to pass it on to his offspring. For all intents and purposes he had become an emperor, without the title. Yet he was still unsatisfied. He wanted to be a *de facto* as well as a *de jure* monarch. His eldest son, Yüan K'o-ting, anxious to become the crown prince and future sovereign, did his best to fan his father's vanity and desire for glory. By 1915 Yüan was fully prepared to betray the republic, much as Napoleon III did France.

To forestall foreign opposition Yüan agreed to accept the infamous Twenty-one Demands from Japan,[43] and signed agreements with Russia and Britain recognizing their special interests and positions in Outer

---

43. In five groups: 1. recognition of Japan's position in Shantung; 2. special position for Japan in Manchuria and Inner Mongolia; 3. joint operation of China's iron and steel industries; 4. nonalienation of coastal areas to any third power; and 5. control by Japan of China's several important domestic administrations. For details, see next chapter.

Mongolia and Tibet, respectively. He was further heartened by an intriguing, if noncommittal, statement of the Japanese premier, Ōkuma, to the effect that should China become a monarchy her political system would be identical with Japan's; that since Yüan was already in full control of China's political power a change to the monarchy would bring the situation more in accord with reality. Yüan took it to mean a Japanese endorsement of his monarchical dreams.

Yüan's American adviser on constitutional matters, Dr. Frank J. Goodnow, who was later to be president of Johns Hopkins University, published an article in which he stated that Americans had long doubted the fitness of a republic in China, where the tradition of autocracy would make constitutional monarchy a far more suitable institution, if it met no opposition. Yüan's Japanese adviser also stressed constitutional monarchy as the source of national strength, as in Japan and Britain. With these expert endorsements, the hush-hush monarchical movement broke out into the open. Yang Tu, chief organizer of the movement, publicly advocated national salvation through constitutional monarchy, and on August 21, 1915, the Peace-Planning Society (*Ch'ou-an hui*) was organized to draft Yüan for emperor. The famous translator of Western thought, Yen Fu, who had doubts about China's readiness for democracy, was listed, against his will, as one of the six directors. The movement quickly swept into full swing, although Yüan himself remained conspicuously aloof, denying continuously any imperial aspirations. To a Japanese newsman he announced self-righteously that during the 1911 revolution he had declined the throne offered by the Manchu imperial family. "If I took it now, I would be inhuman and unrighteous, taking advantage of the orphan [boy emperor] and the widow [dowager]. How could I bear it?"

Nevertheless, the monarchical movement grew more pronounced every day. Numerous "petitions" reached the government favoring change in the national polity. The National People's Representative Assembly, which was called to deliberate the issue, approved monarchy by an overwhelming majority on November 20, 1915. On December 11, representatives of the provinces petitioned, in the name of the people, that Yüan consent to become the emperor of China. After a polite declination on the grounds that he lacked virtue and merit, Yüan "reluctantly" acceded to the second petition on December 12. A day later he decreed that the next year, 1916, would mark the start of his new reign, called ironically the Glorious Constitution (*Hung-hsien*).

Like many dictators before and after him, Yüan was overtaken by megalomania, too confident to know when to stop. He did not seem to see that in spite of all the uncertainties in the early republican period, one thing was definite: the imperial system could never return. His betrayal of the republic and his shameless drive toward the emperorship went beyond the point of tolerance by his countrymen—not only his critics but even his own followers.

Sun had, in the meantime, fled to Japan after the failure of the Second Revolution. Convinced that the internal disunity was a major cause for his defeat, he reorganized the Nationalist Party into a tighter structure under the name of Chinese Revolutionary Party (*Chung-kuo ko-ming tang*) on July 8, 1914. Members were required to owe him personal allegiance and to fingerprint their written pledge. Sun retained strict control of the central and branch organizations as well as the power of appointments at all levels—the embryo of a principle later known as "democratic centralism." Now appointed generalissimo of a Chinese Revolutionary army, Sun set out to fight Yüan's illegal destruction of the parliament, the provisional constitution, and his abject betrayal of the republic. With the assassination of Yüan's Shanghai commander[44] on November 10, 1915, and the seizure of the government warship *Chao-ho*[45] on December 5, the war against Yüan formally began.

In Yunnan, a National Protection army came into being to fight the monarchist movement, under a group of revolutionaries including the former military governor Ts'ai Ao. Ts'ai had been lured to Peking by Yüan in September 1913 and was detained there, but on November 11, 1915, he managed to escape and returned to Yunnan via Japan and Vietnam. He and his former teacher, Liang Ch'i-ch'ao, vowed to fight Yüan, one with guns and the other with the pen, in order to save the republic and to preserve the honor and character of China's 400 million people. The Yunnan revolutionaries dedicated the National Protection army (*Hu-kuo chün*)[46] to the "elimination of the country's thief, defense of the republic, upholding democracy, and developing the spirit of popular sovereignty." On December 23, an ultimatum was delivered to Yüan, allowing him two days to cancel his monarchist movement. When Yüan refused, Yunnan declared its independence on December 25, and the National Protection army, some 10,000 strong, set out in a three-direction campaign. On December 27 Kweichow declared independence. Pressed

44. Cheng Ju-ch'eng.
45. By the revolutionaries under Ch'en Ch'i-mei.
46. Coincidentally, the name of the monastery where they met happened to be *Hu-kuo ssu*.

by these developments, Yüan delayed his scheduled enthronement on January 1, 1916. Two of his leading generals, Tuan Ch'i-jui and Feng Kuo-chang, each declined an appointment as commander of the expedition against the National Protection army on the pretext of illness. On March 15, Kwangsi declared independence, while a separate antimonarchist army rose in Shantung. The Japanese government served notice that in view of Peking's inability to keep domestic peace and to win support of the powers, it had forfeited its right to represent China, and that henceforth Japan would treat the north and the south as equal belligerent parties.

Facing these disappointing domestic and foreign developments, Yüan had no choice but to forsake his monarchical dream and the reign of "Glorious Constitution" on March 22, 1916. Yet he still hoped to hang on to his presidency by reviving the cabinet system to appease the revolutionaries. However, events moved too fast for him: Kwangtung declared its independence on April 6 and Chekiang on April 12. By May 5, the various revolutionary groups had unified into one Military Affairs Council, which refused to recognize Yüan as president, as did prominent citizens of nineteen provinces. Even K'ang Yu-wei twice urged him to retire and take a trip abroad.[47] By then Yüan's cause was all but lost; his followers one after another began to disown him. When he asked Feng Kuo-chang to mobilize generals and military governors to support him for the presidency, Feng simply asked him to resign. On May 9 Shensi declared its independence, followed by Szechwan on May 22 and Hunan on May 27.[48] Deserted by his henchmen and overcome with shame, anxiety, and grief, Yüan suddenly died of uremia on June 6, 1916, at the age of fifty-six. The tragicomic drama of monarchism came to an abrupt end.

Commenting on the life of Yüan, Liang Ch'i ch'ao remarked that he (Yüan) knew no distinction between men and animals, assuming that all could be bought with gold and intimidated by the sword. His mockery of the constitution, his illegal manipulation of the parliament, his methods of bribery, coercion, murder, and enslavement were an irreparable affront to public character and morale, and laid the groundwork of lawlessness and disorder in the decade that followed.

47. Pai Chiao, *Yüan Shih-k'ai yu Chung-hua min-kuo* (Yüan Shih-k'ai and the Chinese Republic), (Shanghai, 1936), 341-42, 350-71.
48. It was said that Yüan fainted upon reading the telegram from his confidant governor of Szechwan, Ch'en Huan, which said: "From today, Szechwan severs all relations with Yüan Shih-k'ai." Yüan later sighed: "Now, even Ch'en Huan is like this. What is there for me to say! Please reply to him and tell him that I will retire." See Jerome Ch'en, 232.

PERIOD OF WARLORDISM, 1916-27

The disappearance of a strong power-holder generated centrifugal forces, plunging the country into a period of chaos and disorder. The warlords fought against each other for power and self-aggrandizement without any sense, logic, or reason, rendering this period the darkest in republican history.

On June 7, 1916, Vice-President Li Yüan-hung took over the presidency. A question of "legality" immediately arose as to whether he had *succeeded* to the office according to the 1912 constitution of *acted* for the deceased president in accordance with Yüan's 1914 constitution. In short, which of the two constitutions was valid? The revolutionaries in the south insisted on the former, arguing that the very purpose of the antimonarchist movement and the civil war was to protect the legality of the 1912 constitution, whereas Premier Tuan Ch'i-jui in Peking favored continuation of the 1914 constitution which had been in effect for two years. The conflict was resolved when the naval commander at Shanghai[49] declared independence of the Peking regime on June 25, throwing his support to the south. Feng Kuo-chang, who had built up a power base at Shanghai and was fearful of losing it, put pressure on Pe king to restore the 1912 constitution. On August 1, President Li complied with the request, re-established the old parliament that had been dissolved illegally by Yüan on January 10, 1914, and renamed Tuan premier according to the 1912 constitution. The revolutionaries agreed to abolish their Military Affairs Council in the interest of national unification.

Restoration of the Manchu Emperor, 1917. The question of whether China should enter the war against Germany now loomed large. Premier Tuan, under American prodding, declared war on Germany on May 14, 1917, without the approval of the president and the parliament. To disarm parliamentary opposition, he employed Yüan's tactics of instigating some 3,000 "citizens" from business, political, and military circles to surround the parliament and demand passage of the war declaration. Tuan's generals and military governors bluntly demanded that President Li dissolve the parliament, while the latter in retaliation urged Li to relieve Tuan of the premiership. On May 23, Li took the bold step of dismissing Tuan, only to find a rash of declarations of independence by his

49. Li Ting-hsin.

henchmen in the provinces—Shensi, Shansi, Chekiang, Shantung, Chihli, Fukien, etc. They organized a general staff at Tientsin and decided to march on Peking. In desperation President Li sought the good office of Chang Hsün, the military governor of Anhwei. Chang came to the capital with 5,000 soldiers on June 7, 1917, but he demanded the dissolution of the parliament as a prerequisite to mediating. Li had no choice but to comply on June 12, in full knowledge of its illegality according to the 1912 constitution.

Once established in Peking, Chang, with the support of K'ang Yu-wei and secret concurrence of the Peiyang leaders Tuan and Feng, restored the last Manchu emperor, P'u-i, to the throne on July 1.[50] Ch'ing institutions were revived and ranks and appointments were awarded. Chang Hsün was made the chief minister of the cabinet and concurrently governor-general of Chihli, a post taken from the warlord Ts'ao K'un, while Tuan was left out of the distribution of offices. Feeling deceived, Tuan and Ts'ao gathered their Peiyang forces against the 20,000 long-queued soldiers of Chang, driving them out of Peking on July 12 and quickly ending the restoration movement.

The Civil War Among the Warlords. Once again Tuan was the premier, supported by the so-called Research Clique (*Yen-chiu hsi*) under Liang Ch'i-ch'ao, who was now the finance minister. The Research Clique argued that since the restoration movement had officially put an end to the republic, it behooved the country to construct a new republic under the leadership of Tuan, and the first step in that direction was to call a new provisional parliament. When Tuan did so on November 10, rather than reconvene the old parliament dissolved by President Li on June 12, the revolutionaries in the south accused him of violating the 1912 constitution. Sun Yat-sen once again established a military government at Canton to launch a Constitution Protection Movement (*Hu-fa yün-tung*).

To crush domestic opposition, Tuan negotiated foreign loans under the pretext of entering the world war. Using methods reminiscent of Yüan's, he manipulated the provisional parliament to revise the election and organization laws of the 1912 constitution, and organized an An-Fu (Anhwei-Fukien) Club[51] to rally the support of his military and civilian

50. For an intimate and interesting account of the life of P'u-i after his abdication in 1912, see his autobiography which appears in English under the title, *The Last Manchu*, tr. by K. Y. P. Tsai and ed. by Paul Kramer (New York, 1967), chapters 1-8.
51. Named after the An-Fu Street in Peking.

followers. In the re-elected parliament which convened on August 12, 1918, the An-Fu Clique controlled more than 330 votes, and the Research Clique about 20. This "An-Fu Clique Parliament" easily passed the resolution to declare war on Germany on August 14 as Tuan wanted, enabling him to negotiate the so-called "Nishihara loans"[52] of some 145 million yen under the pretext of sustaining China's war effort.

Thus replenished, Tuan set out to destroy the southern military government. Troops were sent to Hunan to exert pressure on the revolutionaries in Canton, and to Szechwan to check any possible revolt by Yunnan. In doing so Tuan precipitated another civil war. However, President Feng Kuo-chang, successor to Li Yüan-hung, favored a peaceful solution to the domestic squabble. His clash with Tuan, a former colleague under Yüan, split the Peiyang Clique in two: the group under Tuan of Anhwei became known as the Anhwei Clique, and the one under Feng of Chihli became known as the Chihli Clique. Feng's followers sabotaged Tuan's campaign against the Constitution Protection army, causing a failure of Tuan's military policy and his resignation on November 22. What followed was a period of mad fighting between the two cliques. The Chihli group ultimately won out with the support of yet another clique from Manchuria—the Fengtien army under the leadership of a former bandit, Chang Tso-lin.

The Chihli Clique, boasting eight divisions and four brigades, won control of the seven provinces in North and Central China, including Peking, while the Fengtien—with five divisions, twenty-three brigades, and three brigades of cavalry—dominated Manchuria, Inner Mongolia, and the area north of Peking. In April 1922, fighting broke out between the two groups themselves, resulting again in the victory of the Chihli Clique. However, Chang Tso-lin was able to retain control of Manchuria, independent of the Peking regime.

The victorious Chihli Clique offered the presidency to Li Yüan-hung in the hopes of achieving national unification through a peaceful settlement with the Canton government. It encountered opposition from a powerful wing within the clique, and by the middle of 1922 a split took place: (1) the Lo-yang faction under Wu P'ei-fu favored a military conquest of China and support of President Li; and (2) the Tientsin-Paoting faction which opposed Wu favored Ts'ao K'un for president. In the end, President Li was driven out of office in a most demeaning manner, and

52. Named after the Japanese negotiator, Nishihara. The Japanese yen was worth about one-half of the American dollar at the time.

Ts'ao K'un had himself elected president in October 1923 by bribing some 500 members of the parliament with a payoff of an alleged 5,000 Chinese dollars apiece. Public morale hit rock bottom, and the people were disgusted with politics in the north. The only hope lay with the revolutionary government at Canton.

Yet Sun had enough troubles of his own in the south. His Constitution Protection Movement had made little progress, for ever since the establishment of the military government at Canton on August 25, 1917, he had been handicapped by not having direct control of the armed forces, despite his title of generalissimo. The real power of command lay with the southwestern provincial leaders such as Lu Jung-t'ing of Kwangtung and Kwangsi. With ambitions of his own, Lu had forced Sun out of the military government in May 1918. Fleeing to Shanghai in deep disappointment and frustration, Sun led a life of resignation, engaging mostly in writing his "Outline of National Reconstruction" (*Chien-kuo fang lüeh*) and planning the reorganization of the party. On October 10, 1919, he tightened the Chinese Revolutionary Party and renamed it the Chinese Nationalist Party (*Chung-kuo kuo-min-tang*). To chastise the rebels at Canton rather than to fight Tuan in the north, Sun directed his forces southward. Through a series of maneuverings, he was able to recover Canton and to revive the military regime; the formal establishment of a republican government followed on April 2, 1921, with Sun as president, in rival existence with the warlord government in Peking.

On February 3, 1922, Sun set out northward to continue his Constitution Protection campaign, only to be turned back by an unexpected mutiny in Canton, led by a former supporter, Ch'en Chiung-ming. Caught in his presidential headquarters under heavy bombardment, Sun narrowly escaped to a loyal warship, and later with British and Russian help, he reached Shanghai. Thus, his Constitution Protection campaign really never got off the ground.

Following Ts'ao K'un's disgraceful election to the presidency in October 1923, the warlords again were embroiled in a series of mad fighting. War broke out in September-October of 1924 between Kiangsu[53] and Chekiang,[54] ending with a victory for Kiangsu. Under the pretext of aiding Chekiang, the Fengtien forces advanced from Manchuria toward Peking, precipitating a second Chihli-Fengtien war. Most unexpectedly,

53. Under Ch'i Hsi-yüan of the Chihli Clique.
54. Under Lu Yung-hsiang of the Anhwei Clique.

when the commander-in-chief[55] of the 170,000-man Chihli army went to the front, his Third Army commander Feng Yü-hsiang mutinied and occupied Peking on October 23, 1924, bringing about a total collapse of the Chihli forces. Supported by his own "National People's army" (*Kuomin chün*), Feng reorganized the cabinet and forced President Ts'ao K'un out of office on November 2, 1924.

Now, in the interest of national unification, the "National People's army," the Fengtien Clique, and the Anhwei Clique jointly asked Tuan Ch'i-jui to be the executive of a provisional government, and invited Sun Yat-sen to Peking to discuss the problem of peace and unification. Though his health was failing, Sun made the trip and arrived in Peking on December 31, 1924. He was heartened by the warm welcome of more than 100,000 people, though annoyed with Tuan's apparent insincerity. His condition turned worse after January 20 and death overtook him on March 12, 1925. At the last minute, he was still murmuring "peace, struggle . . . save China." A will, signed by him a day earlier, urged his comrades to carry on his unfinished work. So ended the career of the father of the Chinese Revolution, who had devoted forty years of his life to the betterment of his country and his people.

Sun died a disappointed man. The revolution and the republic had not brought the anticipated peace and order: if anything, the republican period saw more misery and lawlessness than before. It resembled the traditional disorder and chaos that always followed the fall of a dynasty. Yet Sun had laid the foundation for progress, from which his disciples could carry on. In 1926, a young general, Chiang Kai-shek, resumed the unfinished "Northern Expedition" against the warlords and succeeded to a large extent in his mission. In 1928 a Nationalist government was established in Nanking, and the long eluded objective of unification was finally achieved, even if only superficially.

FURTHER READING

Cantlie, Sir James, and C. Sheridan Jones, *Sun Yat-sen and the Awakening of China*, (New York, 1912).

Ch'ai, Te-keng 柴德賡, *et al.* (eds.), *Hsin-hai ko-ming* 亥辛革命 (The revolution of 1911), (Shanghai, 1957), 8 vols.

Chang, Ch'i-yün 張其昀, *Chung-hua min-kuo ch'uang-li shih* 中華民國創立史 (A history of the founding of the Chinese Republic), (Taipei, 1953).

Chang, P'eng-yüan 張朋園, *Liang Ch'i-ch'ao yü Ch'ing-chi ko-ming* 梁起超與

55. Wu P'ei-fu.

清季革命(Liang Ch'i-ch'ao and the late Ch'ing revolution), (Taipei, 1964).

Chen, Stephen, and Robert Payne, *Sun Yat-sen* (New York, 1946).

Ch'en, Jerome, *Yüan Shih-k'ai, 1859-1916* (Stanford, 1961).

Feng, Tzu-yu 馮自由, *Chung-hua min-kuo k'ai-kuo ch'ien ko-ming shih* 中華民國開國前革命史(A history of the revolution before the establishment of the Chinese Republic), (Chungking, 1944), 3 vols.

Gasster, Michael, *Chinese Intellectuals and the Revolution of 1911* (Seattle, 1969).

Gillin, Donald G., *Warlord Yen Hsi-shan in Shansi Province, 1911-1949* (Princeton, 1967).

Hsü, Leonard S., *Sun Yat-sen: His Political and Social Ideals* (Los Angeles, 1933).

Ichiko, Chūzō, "The Railway Protection Movement in Szechuan in 1911," *Memoirs of the Research Department of the Toyo Bunko*, Tokyo, 14:47-69 (1955).

Ikei, Masaru, "Japan's Response to the Chinese Revolution of 1911," *The Journal of Asian Studies*, XXV:2:213-27 (Feb. 1966).

Jensen, Marius B., *The Japanese and Sun Yat-sen* (Cambridge, Mass., 1954).

Kuo, Pin-chia 郭斌佳, "Min-kuo erh-tz'u ko-ming shih" 民國二次革命史 (The second republican revolution), *Kuo-li Wu-han ta-hsüeh wen-che chi-k'an* 國立武漢大學文哲季刊 (Quarterly Journal of Literature and Philosophy), National Wu-han University, 4:3 (1935).

Leng, Shao-chuan, and Norman D. Palmer, *Sun Yat-sen and Communism* (New York, 1960).

Levenson, Joseph R., *Confucian China and Its Modern Fate*, Vol. II: *The Problem of Monarchical Decay* (Berkeley, 1964).

Li, Nai-han 黎乃涵, *Hsin-hai ko-ming yu Yüan Shih-k'ai* 辛亥革命與袁世凱 (The revolution of 1911 and Yüan Shih-k'ai), (Shanghai, 1949).

Li, Tien-yi, *Woodrow Wilson's China Policy, 1913-1917* (Lawrence, Kansas, 1952).

Liang, Chin-tung, *The Chinese Revolution of 1911* (New York, 1962).

Linebarger, Paul, *Sun Yat sen and the Chinese Republic* (New York, 1925).

———, *The Gospel of Chung Shan* (Paris, 1932).

MacNair, H. F., *China in Revolution* (Chicago, 1931).

Pai, Chiao 白蕉, *Yüan Shih-k'ai yü Chung-hua min-kuo* 袁世凱與中華民國 (Yüan Shih-k'ai and the Chinese Republic), (Shanghai, 1936).

Powell, Ralph L., *The Rise of Chinese Military Power, 1895-1912* (Princeton, 1955).

Price, Frank W. (tr.), *San Min Chu I* (Three People's Principles), (Shanghai, 1927).

P'u-i, Henry, *The Last Manchu: The Autobiography of Henry Pu Yi, Last Emperor of China*, tr. by Kuo Ying Paul Tsai, and edited with an introduction by Paul Kramer (New York, 1967).

Scalapino, Robert A., "Prelude to Marxism: The Chinese Student Movement in Japan, 1900-1910" in Albert Feuerwerker, Rhoads Murphey, and

Mary C. Wright (eds.), *Approaches to Modern Chinese History* (Berkeley, 1967), 190-215.

Schiffrin, Harold, "Sun Yat-sen's Early Land Policy: The Origin and Meaning of 'Equalization of Landrights'," *The Journal of Asian Studies*, XVI:549-64 (1957).

————, *Sun Yat-sen and the Origins of the Chinese Revolution* (Berkeley, 1968).

Sharman, Lyon, *Sun Yat-sen, His Life and Its Meaning* (New York, 1934).

Shen Tsu-hsien, *et al.* (eds.), *Jung-an ti-tzu chi* 容庵弟子記 (An account of Yüan Shih-k'ai by his disciples), reprinted (Taipei, 1962).

Sheridan, James E., *Chinese Warlord, the Career of Feng Yü-hsiang* (Stanford, 1966).

Wright, Mary (ed.), *China in Revolution: The First Phase, 1900-1913* (New Haven, 1968).

————, "Introduction: The Rising Tide of Change," *China in Revolution*, 1-63.

Wu, Yü-chang, *The Revolution of 1911* (Peking, 1962).

Young, Ernest P., "The Reformer as a Conspirator: Liang Ch'i-ch'ao and the 1911 Revolution" in Albert Feuerwerker, Rhoads Murphey, and Mary C. Wright (eds.), *Approaches to Modern Chinese History* (Berkeley, 1967), 239-67.

————, "Yüan Shih-k'ai's Rise to the Presidency," *Orbis*, XI:4:419-42 (Winter 1968).

Yu, George T., *Party Politics in Republican China: The Kuomintang, 1912-1924* (Berkeley, 1966).

21

The Intellectual Revolution, 1917-23

The founding of the republic had not brought peace, order, and unity. Instead, the early republican years had been among the worst in modern Chinese history, characterized by moral degradation, monarchist movements, warlordism, and intensified foreign imperialism. "What is wrong with China, and what can be done to save her?" queried the intellectuals. Obviously, political face lifting through the adoption of the republican institution was insufficient to regenerate the nation; something far more fundamental was needed to awaken the country and the people.

The new intellectuals, Western-trained or Western-influenced, advocated a radical change in the philosophical foundations of national life. They called for a critical re-evaluation of China's cultural heritage in the light of modern Western standards, a willingness to part with those elements that had made China weak, and a determination to accept Western science, democracy, and culture as the foundation of a new order. At the same time, they launched a campaign to introduce a new literature based on the vernacular language instead of the classical. This intellectual outburst dealt a shattering blow to Confucianism—including traditional ethics, customs, human relations, and social conventions—and ushered in a new iconoclastic attitude toward China's past. In terms of depth and scope, the intellectual transformation that resulted surpassed that of the 1895-1911 period (Chapter 18). Indeed, in the opinion of some, nowhere in Chinese history since the Spring and Autumn and the Warring States periods (722-221 B.C.) had social and intellectual changes been so drastic and fundamental.[1]

1. Kuo Chan-po, *Chin-wu-shih-nien Chung-kuo ssu-hsiang shih* (A history of Chinese thought during the last fifty years), reprinted, (Hong Kong, 1965), 1.

This intellectual revolution, taking place somewhere between 1917 and 1923, hailed a New Cultural Movement which has sometimes been described, perhaps erroneously, as a "Chinese Renaissance." A high point in this turbulent period was the gigantic student demonstration in Peking on May 4, 1919, which quickly evoked nationwide response. Hence this period is also commonly known as that of the May Fourth Movement.

THE BACKGROUND

Yet this stirring age of intellectual ferment could not have come to pass without certain significant developments abroad and at home. Externally, sentiments of nationalism and democracy were particularly strong during World War I, and the Wilsonian ideals of national self-determination and abolition of secret diplomacy appealed to Chinese intellectuals. Moreover, rolling events of epochal significance were occurring in different parts of the world: the Bolshevik Revolution in Russia in 1917; the socialist revolts in Finland, Germany, Austria, and Hungary; and the rice riots in Japan in 1918. In contrast, China was plagued by chaos and warlordism. Chinese intellectuals felt deeply committed to revive their strife-ridden and civil war-torn country.

These intellectuals approached the task with fiercely nationalistic and patriotic sentiments, stimulated partly by Japan's humiliating Twenty-one Demands of 1915.[2] Divided into five groups, the first four called for Japanese control of Shantung, Manchuria, Inner Mongolia, the southeast coast of China, and the Yangtze valley. The fifth, the most sinister of all, required employment of Japanese advisers in Chinese political, financial, military, and police administrations, as well as the purchase of at least 50 per cent of China's munitions from Japan.

These terms inflamed the Chinese public. Newspapers denounced the demands and promoted anti-Japanese sentiments. Nineteen governors urged Yüan Shih-k'ai to stand his ground and numerous petitions flooded his office begging him not to yield. Yet under the pressure of a Japanese ultimatum on May 7, 1915, Yüan accepted the first four groups while putting a reservation on the fifth. Then, without the consent of the parliament, he concluded a treaty with Japan on May 25.

In protest, groups of Chinese students in Japan returned home, while

2. Delivered by the Japanese minister, Hioki Eki, to President Yüan Shih-k'ai on January 18, 1915.

merchants in China organized a widespread boycott of Japanese goods. The people vowed to "externally resist the great powers and internally expel the traitors." The Twenty-one Demands had the unexpected effect of precipitating a fear of imminent extinction and a consequent outburst of nationalism.

Contributing to the rise of the new nationalism was the rapid emergence of a politically conscious merchant-enterpreneur class and a labor force which numbered between two and three million by 1919. Indeed, the World War I period had witnessed an unprecedented expansion of Chinese industry and commerce—especially in the fields of textiles, flour mills, silk, matches, cement, cigarettes, and modern banks and joint-stock corporations—as a result of favorable internal and external conditions. Domestically, the replacement of the imperial dynasty by a new republic in 1912 marked the inauguration of a new era. No longer did the government regard industrialists and merchants as suspect; and no longer did it prohibit the formation of private "cliques" and associations as under the Ch'ing. The scholar-turned-industrialist Chang Chien, as minister of agriculture and industry, promulgated a series of regulations to encourage and protect industrial and commercial development. In cooperation, private organizations with similar objectives sprang up one after another in 1912: the Chinese Industrial Development Association, the Chinese Enterprise Society, various provincial industrial and commercial development organizations, and chambers of commerce in the key cities. Private interests won legal and official recognition as well as patronage.

Externally, the World War I period witnessed a rapid decline of Western imperialism in China. The war had so adversely affected European industries and trade with Asia that it created a golden chance for China's native industries to develop unhindered. Between 1913 and 1918, British imports fell from 96 million taels to 49 million; French imports, from 5.2 million to 1.5; and German imports, from 28 million to 0. In reverse proportion, the Chinese foreign trade deficit was cut from 166 million customs taels in 1913 to 16 million in 1919, while silk export rose from 87,517 *tan* in 1914 to 131,506 *tan* in 1919.[3] Similarly, native industries and commerce grew by leaps and bounds: textile companies rose from 22 in 1911 to 54 in 1919, and 109 in 1921; flour mills from 67 in 1916, to 86 in 1918; modern banks from 7 in 1911, to 131 by 1923; steamships from 893 (total tonnage 141,024) in 1913, to 2,027 (236,622 tons)

3. Tan = one picul = 133⅓ lbs.

in 1918; coal production from 12.8 million tons in 1913, to 20.1 in 1919; and iron from 1 million tons in 1914, to 1.8 million in 1919.[4]

These new industries and enterprises gave rise to new merchant and labor classes, which, unlike the old-style apolitical tradesmen and inert peasants, were sensitive to China's predicament under imperialism. They were determined to defend their country's interests. Most of them lived in the cities, where they contributed to the expansion of the urban centers and their economy. Peking, Shanghai, Wuhan, Nanking, Tientsin, and Canton all became large metropolises which nourished the growth of a new intelligentsia. From 1907 to 1917 at least 10 million members of these classes had received some sort of modern education, and were imbued with a strong nationalist determination "to save their country" (chiu-kuo) from the double scourge of foreign imperialism and domestic disorder.

The returned students—those who had studied abroad—were particularly aware of China's plight and were eager to introduce reforms. From 1903 to 1919, 41.51 per cent of these students studied in Japan, 33.85 per cent in the United States, and 24.64 per cent in Europe.[5] France, as the cradle of modern Western civilization, attracted a considerable number of Chinese work-study students (ch'in-kung chien-hsüeh) during World War I and a large labor force of some 200,000 by 1918-19. The latter group worked on roads, docks, factories, and munition dumps, and at least 28,000 of them were educated. The United States, which had a tradition of educating Chinese youths since 1872, drew some 1,200 by 1915. But Japan, because of geographic proximity and lower costs of living, attracted the largest numbers of Chinese students—13,000 by 1906.[6]

Among the most prominent returned students were Ch'en Tu-hsiu and Ts'ai Yüan-p'ei from France, Kuo Mo-jo and Lu Hsün (Chou Shu-jen) from Japan, and Hu Shih and Chiang Monlin from the United States. Ch'en, Ts'ai and Hu, in particular, rapidly became the guiding spirit of the intellectual revolution.

Ch'en Tu-hsiu (1879-1942) of Anhwei had received a thorough train-

4. Chou Hsiu-luan, Ti-i-tz'u shih-chieh ta-chan shih-ch'i Chung-kuo min-tsu kung-yeh ti fa-chan (The development of Chinese national industries during World War I), (Shanghai, 1958), chapters 1-2.
5. Tse-tsung Chow, The May Fourth Movement: Intellectual Revolution in Modern China (Cambridge, Mass., 1960), 26, 31.
6. Estimates range from 8,000 to 13,000. See Robert A. Scalapino, "Prelude to Marxism: The Chinese Student Movement in Japan 1900-1910" in Feuerwerker, Murphey, and Wright (eds.), Approaches to Modern Chinese History, 192.

ing in Chinese classical studies in youth and had passed the first Ch'ing civil service examinations in 1896. In 1902 and 1906 he traveled to Japan, staying only for a short time. He went to France in 1907 and came strongly under her political and literary influence. Returning home in 1910 he participated in the republican revolution, though not a T'ung-meng hui member. Later, as a result of his involvement in the Second Revolution, he fled to Japan. In 1915 he returned home in protest to the Twenty-one Demands.

Ts'ai Yüan-p'ei (1876-1940) of Chekiang, after winning the second and third degrees (in 1889 and 1892, respectively) and a coveted membership in the Hanlin Academy, went to Germany to study at the University of Leipzig in 1907. Four years later he returned home in time to take part in the republican revolution and was appointed minister of education in Dr. Sun's government, a post from which he resigned after Yüan Shih-k'ai took over the presidency. In the summer of 1912 he again went to Germany where he stayed for about a year. His next three years were spent in France, where he took charge of the work-study program of Chinese students and laborers. In 1916, after declining the governorship of Chekiang, he returned home to become chancellor of the National University of Peking.

Hu Shih (1891-1962), a scion of the famous early Ch'ing scholar Hu Wei (1633-1714), also received a classical education in his youth. After graduating from the Chinese Public Institute in 1909, he won a government scholarship to study in the United States, earning the B.A. (1915) and Ph.D. (1917) in philosophy from Cornell and Columbia universities, respectively. Influenced by John Dewey and Thomas Huxley, he firmly believed in pragmatism, scientific methods of thought, and the evolutionary improvement of society. His seven-year sojourn in the United States thoroughly exposed him to American literary and social movements, for it was a time of liberation, characterized by a craze for new things: new humanism, new nationalism, new history, new art, new poetry, and new women. Influenced by Harriet Monroe's *Poetry: A Magazine of Verse*, which promoted verse-writing in plain language, Hu's own idea of substituting the vernacular language for the classical in literary writing[7] assumed greater importance in his mind. While still a student at Cornell in 1915, he and Y. R. Chao boldly started a movement to introduce the *pai-hua* (plain language) style of writing.

7. First conceived during his high school days at the Chinese Public Institute from 1906 to 1909.

These new intellectuals were products of a transitional period—all thoroughly grounded in Chinese classical studies and yet well acquainted with Western civilization. Liberalism, socialism, pragmatism, science, and democracy had left their indelible mark. When they returned home— Ch'en in 1915, Ts'ai in 1916, and Hu in 1917—they functioned as leaven in transforming the literary and intellectual personality of China. Their call for a critical re-evaluation of the national heritage and the introduction of Western thought and ideologies sparked an intellectual revolution which dealt a shattering blow to traditionalism and ushered in the period of the New Cultural Movement.

THE UNFOLDING OF THE NEW CULTURAL MOVEMENT

Ch'en Tu-hsiu and the New Youth. Back from Japan in 1915, Ch'en Tu-hsiu founded a monthly periodical in Shanghai, the *Youth Magazine* (*Ch'ing-nien tsa-chih*), later renamed the *New Youth* (*Hsin ch'ing-nien*) or *La Jeunesse.* It was dedicated to arousing the youth of the country to destroy the stagnant old traditions and forge a new culture. In the first issue Ch'en called on the young generation to struggle against the old and rotten elements of society and to reform their thought and behavior in order to achieve a national awakening:

> The Chinese compliment others by saying, "He acts like an old man although still young." Englishmen and Americans encourage one another by saying, "Keep young while growing old." Such is one respect in which the different ways of thought of the East and West are manifested. Youth is like early spring, like the rising sun, like the trees and grass in bud, like a newly sharpened blade. It is the most valuable period of life . . . I do not wish to waste my fleeting time in arguing with them [the old generation] on this and that and hoping for them to be reborn and thoroughly remodeled. Tearfully, I merely place my plea before the fresh and vital youth, in the hope that they will achieve self-awareness, and begin to struggle. What is this self-awareness? It is to be conscious of the value and responsibility of one's young life and vitality, to maintain one's self-respect, which should not be lowered. What is the struggle? It is to exert one's intellect, discard resolutely the old and the rotten, regard them as enemies and as a flood of savage beasts, keep away from their neighborhood and refuse to be contaminated by their poisonous germs.[8]

8. Tse-tung Chow, 46, with minor changes.

The youth were asked to choose the fresh, vital elements from all the civilizations of the world, in order to create a new culture for China. In this monumental task, Ch'en suggested six guiding principles: (1) to be independent and not servile; (2) to be progressive and not conservative; (3) to be aggressive and not retrogressive; (4) to be cosmopolitan and not isolationist; (5) to be utilitarian and not impractical; and (6) to be scientific and not visionary.

Ch'en vehemently attacked conservatism and traditionalism as the roots of China's evils. Confucianism, in particular, fared badly in his writings. It was, he said, the product of an agrarian and feudal social order, totally incompatible with modern life in an industrial and capitalistic society. Confucianism must be rooted out because (1) it advocated "superfluous ceremonies and preached the morality of meek compliance," making the Chinese people weak and passive, unfit to struggle and compete in the modern world; (2) it recognized the family and not the individual as the basic unit of society; (3) it upheld the inequality of the status of individuals; (4) it stressed filial piety which made men subservient and dependent; and (5) it preached orthodoxy of thought in total disregard of freedom of thinking and expression.[9] Loudly Ch'en called for the destruction of conservatism in order to make room for constructing a new culture.

> We indeed do not know which of our traditional institutions may be fit for survival in the modern world. I would rather see the ruin of our traditional "national quintessence" than have our race of the present and future extinguished because of its unfitness for survival . . . The world continually progresses and will not stop. All those who cannot change themselves and keep pace with it are unfit for survival and will be eliminated by the processes of natural selection. Therefore, what is the good of conservatism?[10]

Ch'en's bold attack on traditionalism opened a new vista in the musty intellectual world, and quickly won him an enthusiastic following among the educated youth.

Ts'ai Yüan-p'ei and the Peita. The New Cultural Movement received a great impetus when Ts'ai Yüan-p'ei took over the chancellorship of the National University of Peking, or Peita in abbreviation, in December

9. Tse-tsung Chow, 302; Kuo Chan-po, 103.
10. Tse-tsung Chow, 46.

1916. This government-supported institution of higher learning had a conservative tradition, with its professors drawn mostly from the official-dom. Students did not take their education seriously, but regarded it as a stepping stone to official appointments. The frivolous atmosphere of the university and the loose morals of students and faculty were notorious.

Upon assuming the chancellorship, Ts'ai admonished them that the university was a place of learning and not a short cut to wealth and position. His administration rested upon three principles: (1) the university should be an institution of research—dedicated not merely to the introduction of Western civilization but to the creation of a new Chinese culture; not to the preservation of national quintessence but to its re-evaluation by scientific methods; (2) a university education was not a substitute for the old civil service examinations; and (3) absolute academic freedom was to be allowed, and free expression of divergent theories and viewpoints guaranteed, as long as they could be sustained on rational grounds.

Under Ts'ai's guidance, the Peita became an exciting institution of higher learning, with professors of different political persuasions—liberals, radicals, socialists, anarchists, conservatives, and reactionaries—composing the faculty. The university boasted of an incredibly productive and intellectual life, as the most vital and promising scholars of the country flocked to join the staff. In 1917 Ch'en Tu-hsiu was made dean of the School of Letters, and Hu Shih, returning from the United States, became a professor of literature. The next year, Li Ta-chao was appointed librarian, and in his employ was a young assistant named Mao Tse-tung.

Hu Shih and His Contributions. Hu Shih was an energetic proponent of scientific thinking, pragmatism, and the vernacular style of writing. Because of the Huxley and Dewey influences, the main sources of Hu's inspiration were agnosticism and pragmatism, which became his principal approaches in evaluating traditional ethics and ideas. Truth, according to the pragmatist, is changeable in proportion to its utility based on experimentation. Such an attitude, distinctly a product of an industrial capitalistic society, was diametrically opposed to the Confucian concept that truth is eternal and unchangeable. Confucianism was therefore in Hu's eyes totally out of touch with the realities of the modern world.[11] He invented the perjorative phrase "Confucius and Sons Incorporated," and his followers shouted "Down with Confucianism."

11. Kuo Chan-po, 124-25.

If Hu was against Confucianism, he was for liberalism, individualism, science, and democracy. Drawing from pragmatism, he preached a gradual, bit-by-bit improvement of society through study of its problems, experimentation, and solution. Under his aegis, "Mr. Science" and "Mr. Democracy" became the catchwords of the age. Since both originated in the West, Hu in effect advocated a complete Westernization. "Go West!" was his message.

Hu's philosophy is best explained in his own words:

> The spirit of the new thought tide is a critical attitude. The methods of the new thought tide are the study of problems and the introduction of academic theories. . . . The attitude of the new thought tide toward the old civilization is, on the negative side, to oppose blind obedience and to oppose compromise, and on the positive side, to reorganize our national heritage with scientific methods. What is the sole aim of the new thought tide? It is to recreate civilization.[12]

Hu Shih's most important single contribution was perhaps the introduction of plain language (*pai-hua*) in writing. Condemning the traditional emphasis on style rather than on substance, he maintained that the classical style of writing was dead and that a dead language could not produce a living literature. He proposed to write in the vernacular language, and succeeded in creating a very lucid, vivid style, which won immediate acceptance among liberal and forward-looking men. He advised students to shun classical allusions, time-worn literary phrases, and parallel sentences; to avoid imitating the ancients; and to write with meaning, substance, and genuine feelings.

Conservative opposition was not lacking. Upholders of traditionalism published *The National Heritage* (*Kuo-ku*) to defend the classical style of writing, but the magazine had little appeal and ceased to exist after only four issues. Nevertheless, Yen Fu and Lin Shu, the two famous translators around the turn of the century, continued to boycott the movement. In a letter to Chancellor Ts'ai, Lin ridiculed the vernacular style of writing as the work of "roadside peddlers." Yen chided the substitution of "vulgar" vernacular for the elegant classical style as retrogression, which could not survive the law of evolution and competition. Ts'ai's reply was remarkable for its simplicity: the plain language differed from the classical only in form and not in content; the works of Huxley,

12. Tse-tsung Chow, 219.

Montesquieu, and Adam Smith, as well as the fiction of Dickens, Dumas fils, and Hardy—which Yen and Lin translated—all appeared in the plain language. Could they say, in all fairness, that the translations, which appeared in the classical style, surpassed the originals?

The conservatives were fighting a losing battle because nearly all the proponents of the plain language had received thorough classical training themselves and now were composing beautiful essays in the vernacular style. Ch'en's writings were noted for their passion and power; Hu's for their clarity and lyricism; and novelist Lu Hsün's for their satiric sharpness. Most of the contributors to the *New Youth* wrote in the plain language. The case for the *pai-hua* was officially vindicated when the government in 1920 adopted it for use in school.

From the historical standpoint, the success of the plain-language movement stemmed, at least partially, from the fact that after the abolition of the "eight-legged essay" in 1901, students in China lacked definite models to follow. In their search for the new and unusual, they were first briefly attracted to Liang Ch'i-ch'ao's semiclassical and semicolloquial journalistic style. But with the advent of *pai-hua* they readily joined the new trend.

In 1918, students at Peita organized a magazine called the *New Tide* (*Hsin-ch'ao*), which was governed by three criteria: a critical spirit, scientific thinking, and a reformed rhetoric. The *New Youth* and the *New Tide*, along with a host of others including the *Weekly Critic* (*Mei-chou p'ing-lun*),[13] launched an all-out attack on the bastions of traditionalism —old literature, old ethics, old human relations, and Confucianism. These magazines ridiculed old patterns of thought, old customs, personal loyalty of officials, filial piety, superstition, the double standard of chastity for men and women, the big family system, and above all, monarchism and warlordism. They attacked the unquestioned acceptance of the national heritage and demanded a critical reappraisal of all the classics and ancient works, and the creation of a new culture. Science, democracy, technology, agnosticism, pragmatism, liberalism, parliamentarianism, and individualism found new favor with them.

These magazines were an intellectual bombshell. For the first time in China important national and social problems were being publicly discussed and debated. The youth of the country could not wait to read each new issue. John Dewey, upon visiting China in 1919, commented:

13. Under the editorship of Hu Shih.

"There seems to be no country in the world where students are so unanimously and eagerly interested as in China in what is modern and new in thought, especially about social and economic matters, nor where the arguments which can be brought in favor of the established order and the status quo have so little weight—indeed, are so unuttered."[14] The explosive nature of this social and intellectual ferment sparked a massive national outburst.

THE MAY FOURTH MOVEMENT, 1919

On May 4, 1919, about 5,000 students in Peking held a huge demonstration against the verdict of the Versailles Peace Conference on Shantung. It was at once an explosion of public anger, an outburst of nationalism, a deep disappointment in the West, and a violent indictment of the "traitorous" warlord government in Peking. So powerful and so far-reaching was this incident that it evoked an immediate national response and pressured the Chinese delegation at Versailles to reject the peace treaty. Nationalism, public opinion, and mass demonstration had emerged as new forces in Chinese politics. Some historians today hail the May Fourth incident as the first genuine mass movement in modern Chinese history.

It will be recalled that in 1898 Germany leased from the Ch'ing government the naval base of Kiaochow in Shantung province for 99 years. When World War I broke out, China was a neutral, while Japan joined the Allies and ousted the Germans from Kiaochow; subsequently she took over most of Shantung. To legalize her occupation, Japan included in the Twenty-one Demands provisions which recognized her position in Shantung, and to further bolster her claim she entered into a series of treaties with the great powers. By the Russo-Japanese agreement of February 20, 1917, Russia recognized the Twenty-one Demands, while Japan agreed to recognize the Russian gains in Outer Mongolia during 1912-15. The Anglo-Japanese agreement of a day later obligated Britain to support the Japanese position in Shantung at the forthcoming peace conference and to second her claims to German possessions in the Pacific north of the equator; in return Japan agreed to support the British claims to German islands in the Pacific south of the equator. Similar secret agreements were made with France and Italy. Then, in November 1917, the Lansing-Ishii Agreement was concluded by which the United States recognized that "geographical propinquity creates special relations be-

14. Tse-tsung Chow, 183.

tween nations"—i.e. Japan had a special position in China—while Japan paid lip service to the Open Door Policy.

The *coup de grâce* was the secret pacts of September 1918 between Peking and Tokyo. By granting the Chinese warlord government a loan of 20 million yen, Japan won the right to build two railways in Shantung, to station troops at various key points, and to train and direct Chinese railway guards. Under instructions from Peking, the Chinese minister in Tokyo, Chang Tsung-hsiang, "gladly agreed" (*hsin-jan t'ung-i*) to these terms.

Armed with these secret treaties, the Japanese came to Versailles confident of winning their case on Shantung. Needless to say, retention of Shantung would indirectly acknowledge the validity of the Twenty-one Demands and the viability of the secret treaties with the Peking regime, agreements which gave Japan far greater concessions in Manchuria and other parts of China than in Shantung. The Japanese repertoire of treaties evinced a pragmatic approach to international relations which appeared in stark contrast to the naive Chinese faith in Western ideals.

The Chinese delegation[15] had come to what they believed a just tribunal dedicated to the principles of democracy, self-determination, and protection of the weak. Indeed, Wilsonian idealism and the Fourteen Points had caught the Chinese fancy; many believed that the long awaited age of world democracy had finally arrived, and that Wilson was about to forge a new world out of the fragments of the old. On November 17, 1918, 6,000 Chinese paraded in Peking to celebrate the victory of Western democracy over German despotism and militarism. It was in this state of high expectation that the Chinese delegation had come to Versailles, pledged to seek the recovery of Shantung and the complete abolition of the unequal treaties. But their exuberant optimism rapidly turned to dismay. They were coldly told that the peace conference had not been called to adjust all the international grievances of the past, but to settle problems arising from the conclusion of the war. Consequently, only Shantung belonged on the agenda.

The Chinese delegation pleaded that Shantung, the birthplace of Confucius and Mencius, was the Holy Land of China—and that the German rights which the Japanese had claimed to inherit had ceased to exist when China entered the war in 1917 and abrogated all treaties with Germany. Moreover, Article 5 of the 1898 agreement on Kiaochow stipulated that

15. Consisting of members from both the Peking and Dr. Sun's Canton governments in order to give an appearance of national unity.

"Germany engages at no time to sublet the territory leased from China to another power." Similarly, the Twenty-one Demands were invalid because the Chinese parliament had never ratified them. Moreover, China's entry into the war in 1917 had so changed her status—from a neutral to a belligerent—that she was qualified to invoke the international law principle of *rebus sic stantibus*[16] to nullify the Twenty-one Demands. In rebuttal, the Japanese delegation calmly divulged the 1918 secret agreements with Peking, pointing out that they had been "gladly agreed" to by China *after* her entry into the war. No amount of Chinese argument could alter this fact, and the fate of Shantung was sealed.

The Allies were bound by secret treaties to support the Japanese position, which left Wilson as the lone champion of the Chinese cause. Japan threatened to raise the issue of racial equality for discussion and to withdraw from the conference if her demands were not met. It was clear that Japan could not be denied on both the Shantung and the racial issues. Ultimately, Wilson was persuaded by the Allied representatives as well as his own advisers[17] that it was important to first establish the League of Nations with Japan in it, and to secure justice for China later. On April 28, 1919, the peace conference adjudicated the Shantung question in favor of Japan.

When news of the Paris decision reached Peking, Chinese faith in Wilson and the tenets of his idealism was shattered. Enraged by what they saw as Western betrayal, students vowed to defend Shantung by blood. The influential newspaper *Shen-pao* editorialized: "At the outset of the Paris Conference, we heard a lot of what was called 'the triumph of right and justice,' 'the upholding of the rights and privileges of small and weak nations,' but what do we get? Whoever expects help from others is doomed to be disappointed. Let our countrymen understand today once and for all that their only course is to act by themselves. Had our countrymen not abandoned their own interests, who could have infringed upon them?"[18]

On May 4, several hundred returned students met to discuss what they could do in this period of national crisis and humiliation. They decided to send telegrams to the Versailles Conference to protest the unjust verdict and to the Chinese delegation to urge the rejection of the treaty if the terms on Shantung were not revised. It was also resolved to stage a

16. This principle suggests that when the objects of a treaty, or the conditions under which it is concluded, no longer exist, the treaty becomes null and void.
17. Such as Colonel House.
18. *North China Herald*, May 17, 1919, p. 415, with minor changes.

mass demonstration and to present petitions to the foreign legations for transmittal to Paris.

The demonstration was joined by large groups of students from the thirteen universities and colleges in Peking, swelling the number to 5,000. The demonstrators distributed handbills informing spectators of the disgraceful development at Paris and calling for their open support. Huge banners floated above the crowd with such inscriptions as "Reclaim Kiaochow unto death," and "Punish the traitor Ts'ao Ju-lin."[19] The orderliness of the parade evaporated when it passed the house of Ts'ao, at which time the students went out of control and broke into it. Since Ts'ao had escaped, they beat up his houseguest—who was none other than the Chinese minister to Japan who had "gladly agreed" to the 1918 pacts—and set fire to the house. With the belated arrival of the police, most of the demonstrators had gone; only ten of them were arrested.

The immediate response to the arrest was a general strike by all students in Peking and the resignation of Ts'ai as chancellor of Peita. The strike quickly spread to students in other major cities, and was joined by shopkeepers, industrial workers, and employees in commercial establishments all over the country. A concerted boycott of Japanese goods followed; people stopped buying Japanese products and taking Japanese steamers, and dockhands refused to unload Japanese goods. Under increasing pressure from the public, the Peking regime released the students on May 7.

Meanwhile, thousands of telegrams were sent to the Chinese delegation at Paris, asking them to reject the treaty and threatening them with punishment if they did not. Perhaps most representative was the one sent by the Society for China's Salvation: "The whole nation is indignant over the failure of the Shantung question. Never sign the treaty. We demand your immediate withdrawal from the Conference. Better to have forced occupation than voluntary submission. Otherwise sole responsibility rests on you."[20] The Peking warlord regime, confused and unable to take a definite stand, left the decision of signing to the delegation itself. Lest the delegates yield under foreign pressure or secret government order, Chinese students in Paris organized an around-the-clock vigil to see that none of them left their quarters. At the signing ceremony on June 28, there were no Chinese representatives. Visibly distressed, President Wilson was heard muttering: "That is most serious. It will cause grave com-

19. The foreign minister.
20. *North China Herald*, May 17, 1919, p. 413.

plications . . . this is most unfortunate, but I don't know what we can do."[21]

Wilson sacrificed China in order to lure Japan into the League of Nations; yet he was unable to get his own country into the international organization. Ironically, Japan was among the first to withdraw from the League, in 1933. As to China, although she rejected the peace treaty with Germany, she signed the treaty with Austria, and by virtue of that act automatically became a member of the League of Nations.

EXPANSION OF THE NEW CULTURAL MOVEMENT

The May Fourth incident served as a catalyst for the intellectual revolution in China. While interest in the West continued in the days that followed, as evidenced by invitations to a number of famous foreign philosophers and thinkers to visit China, a split appeared among Chinese intellectuals. Those who were bitterly disappointed by the Versailles Conference began to turn to Marxist socialism under the influence of the Bolshevik Revolution; others who were tradition-bound blamed Western materialism as the cause of World War I and suggested Chinese spiritualism as an antidote. These different strands of thought—together with the grand debates on the relative value of Eastern and Western civilizations, of science and metaphysics, and attempts to re-evaluate the Chinese national heritage by modern methods and standards—propelled the New Cultural Movement to greater heights.

Foreign Visitors. John Dewey and his wife visited China from May 1, 1919, to July 11, 1921. With Hu Shih as interpreter, Dewey gave a number of public lectures on his social and political philosophy of pragmatism; on his own ideas about education, methods of thought, and ethics; and on his views of the three leading contemporary philosophers: Bergson, Russell, and James. His lecture halls were always packed with large crowds, including high school and college students. Everywhere there was a thirst for new knowledge and a curiosity for novel solutions to China's problems. Dewey told his audiences: "China could not be changed without a social transformation based upon a transformation of ideas. The political revolution was a failure, because it was external, formal, touching the mechanism of social action but not affecting conceptions of life, which really control society."[22] Impressed with the eagerness of Chinese

21. *Foreign Relations of the United States,* 1919, XI, 602.
22. John Dewey, "New Culture in China," *Asia,* XXI:7:581 (July 1921).

youth to listen to his exposition of philosophy and social ideas which seemingly only bored American students, Dewey enthusiastically reported: "There is an eager thirst for ideas—beyond anything existing, I am convinced, in the youth of any other country on earth."[23]

Bertrand Russell stayed for the better part of a year, from October 1920 to July 1921. With Y. R. Chao interpreting, he gave a series of public lectures, but the tenor of his message was quite different from Dewey's. Rather than telling the Chinese what they should do to get along in the modern world, Russell, an avid pacifist, extolled the value of the tranquil, humane, tolerant, and pacific Chinese outlook on life. The Confucian concept of filial piety, he said, in spite of its many shortcomings, was "less harmful than its Western counterpart, patriotism," which led more easily to imperialism and militarism.[24] He was attracted to the Taoist ideas of "production without possession, action without self-assertion, [and] development without domination," which approximated his own ideas of promoting creative impulses while eliminating the possessive tendency. Apologetically he commented: "In so far as there is a difference of morals between us and the Chinese, we differ for the worse, because we are more energetic, and can therefore commit more crimes *per diem*." The essence of Russell's message was that the West should learn from China "the just conception of the ends of life," while China should "acquire Western knowledge without acquiring the mechanistic outlook" —by which was meant taking men as raw material to be molded by scientific manipulation.[25]

Russell's advice did not strike a very responsive note with Chinese intellectuals, who, in their eagerness to be modern, wanted to be patriotic, nationalistic, and action-prone rather than pacific, filial, and passive. They were more anxious to destroy Confucianism and to promote Westernization than to teach the West how to acquire the Chinese humane conception of life. The latter was a yoke upon their efforts to be part of the moving, dynamic West, and had to be thrown off in the name of progress. There was no place in the velocity and rhythm of Western-style change for the tranquillity of the Confucian past.

Other visitors included the American educator Paul Monroe in 1921, the German philosopher Hans Driesch in 1922, and the Indian Nobel prize laureate R. Tagore in 1923. Plans to invite Bergson and Eucken did not materialize.

---

23. Dewey, 586.
24. Bertrand Russell, *The Problem of China* (London, 1922), 41.
25. *Ibid.*, 81-82, 192-94.

In addition to the contributions of foreign visitors, Western thought and ideologies were also eagerly pursued by Chinese intellectuals themselves, whose taste reflected a gradual shift from Anglo-American to German-Russian sources. Apart from the philosophies of Dewey and Russell which were already introduced, the works of the French philosopher Bergson, were transmitted by Carsun Chang, and those of the German philosophers Schopenhauer and Nietzsche by Wang Kuo-wei. Ch'en Tu-hsiu and Li Ta-chao introduced Marx and Engel, while Li Ta wrote on the dialectical methods and the thought of Lenin, Bukharin, and Plekhanov. Li Shih-tseng introduced the Russian anarchist Kropotkin, and popularized his ideas on "mutual assistance" and "unity" as the basic forces of progress—in direct refutation of Darwin's idea of "struggle." Many Chinese intellectuals and scholar-politicians readily adopted anarchist views, and after the May Fourth incident Marxism and Bolshevism gained increasing favor among the radicals. A grand debate soon erupted over the relative merits of gradual social reforms versus rapid fundamental changes.

Problems and "Isms." Hu Shih, the high priest of pragmatism in China, vigorously advocated an evolutionary "drop-by-drop" improvement of society through the study and solution of specific, practical problems. Li Ta-chao, and shortly afterwards Ch'en Tu-hsiu, argued for an immediate and thoroughgoing sociopolitical transformation, after the Soviet fashion. In an article entitled "More Study of Problems and Less Talk of "Isms',"[26] Hu Shih urged his countrymen to shun the high-sounding, all-embracing "isms" as nothing but "the dreams of self-deceived and deceptive persons, iron-clad proof of the bankruptcy of Chinese thought, and the death-knell of Chinese social reform!" Forcefully he argued:

> Civilization was not created *in toto*, but by inches and drops. Evolution was not accomplished overnight but in inches and drops. People nowadays indulge in talk about liberation and reform, but they should know that there is no liberation *in toto*, or reform *in toto*. Liberation means the liberation of this or that system, or this or that idea, or of this or that individual; it is reform by inches and drops. The first step in the re-creation of civilization is the study of this or that problem. Progress in the re-creation of civilization lies in the solution of this or that problem. [27]

26. Appeared in the July 20, 1919, issue of the *Weekly Critic*.
27. Maurice Meisner, *Li Ta-chao and the Origins of Chinese Marxism*, (Cambridge, Mass., 1967), 107.

Hu cautioned against blind activism and rudderless revolutions, proposing instead spontaneous and gradual reform to eliminate the five enemies of social progress—poverty, sickness, illiteracy, corruption, and disorder.

Li Ta-chao, the leading convert to Marxism, replied that "isms" were necessary to provide a "common direction" in solving social problems. Speaking in equally forceful terms, he argued: "It is first necessary to have a fundamental solution, and then there will be hope of solving concrete problems one by one. Take Russia as an example. If the Romanoffs had not been overthrown and the economic organization not reformed, no problems could have been solved. Now they are all being solved."[28]

Hu's rebuttal was that there was no panacea for all the ills of China; each must be attacked and solved individually, and "isms" were only romantic hypotheses for solving social problems. Though conceding to this last point, Li nevertheless championed political action: "The solution of the economic problem is the fundamental solution. As soon as the economic problem is solved, then all political and legal problems and the problems of the family system, women's liberation, and the workers' liberation can be solved."[29] Ch'en Tu-hsiu, less committed to Marxism than Li in mid-1919, conceded that "it is better to promote the practical movement of education and emancipation of workers than vaguely to talk anarchism and socialism." But by the end of 1920 he too became a firm convert to Bolshevism and to the efficacy of political action, arguing that "isms" in social reforms provided the same necessary function as the destination in a voyage. Still, he acknowledged that revolution and social reforms could not be accomplished *in toto* overnight.[30]

On the surface, the debate ended in Hu's favor. Yet it was a hollow victory, for it was the vogue among youth to discuss "isms," and even Hu himself constantly spoke of liberalism, pragmatism, experimentalism, etc. A witty critic described Hu and the pragmatists as saying: "You should give up all 'isms' and accept our 'isms,' because, according to our 'ism,' no 'ism' should be accepted as a creed."[31]

Paradoxically, after preaching "more study of problems," Hu and his followers delved into the less practical pursuits of textual criticism, ancient history, and archeological investigations in the 1920's, at a time when social and political problems pressed for urgent and immediate

28. Meisner, 107.
29. *Ibid.*, 111.
30. Tse-tung Chow, 220.
31. Tse-tsung Chow, 222.

solution. On the other hand, many advocates of "isms" and fundamental change went to the peasants and workers and studied their problems first-hand. It is apparent that Hu failed to see that pragmatism was the product of a stable American society that permitted free examination of problems and the implementation of reforms, whereas China of the warlord period totally lacked the sociopolitical conditions prerequisite to experimentation and gradual reform. A recent study perceptively commented: "Hu had fallen victim to the same error that he had perceived in his more radical colleagues, the error of importing foreign theories without paying sufficient attention to the social environment in which these theories had been created."[32]

Go East! Go West! The vast destruction wrought by World War I had greatly disillusioned many Chinese. Liang Ch'i-ch'ao blamed Western imperialism and blind worship of science as the roots of conflict and suggested that Chinese spiritualism might redress the imbalance. Liang Sou-ming, author of *East and West: Their Civilizations and Philosophies*, also argued against science and democracy in an effort to defend the integrity of the Chinese civilization. The life of a people depends on their basic spirit, he declared; to sacrifice China's own spirit in favor of a foreign ethos and institutions was to undermine her destiny. Rather, she should develop her forte solely from her own standpoint.[33] The two Liangs deprecated Western materialistic civilization in direct proportion to their eulogy of Chinese spiritual civilization. They urged their countrymen: "Go East!"

In opposition, Hu Shih and other advocates of Westernization said: "Go West!" Wu Chih-hui berated Liang Sou-ming as a "useless creature of the 17th century." Hu Shih announced that China was behind the West not only in science and technology, but also in everything else—politics, literature, music, arts, morality, and even physical structure.[34] Nevertheless, the advocates of Westernization still demonstrated interest in a scientific and critical re-evaluation of the Chinese cultural heritage. Utilizing Western approaches and methods of research, Hu completed *An Outline History of Chinese Philosophy*, in which he advanced the bold and unprecedented thesis that the School of Logicians in ancient China was not strictly a school and that each of the Hundred Schools

32. Meisner, 108-9.
33. Kuo Chan-po, 317.
34. *Ibid.*, 318.

had its own methods of logical thinking. In a similar example of modern scholarship, Liang Ch'i-ch'ao re-examined the work of the ancient philosopher, Mo-tzu, and authored, among other works, *The Political Thought of the Pre-Ch'in Period*, and *Intellectual Trends in the Ch'ing Period*.[35] Also noteworthy were the "Antiquity-doubters" (*I-ku p'ai*) at Peita,[36] who after exhaustive studies of ancient classics and history raised doubt as to their authenticity and rejected the traditional view that Confucius was their editor. Needless to say, the re-evaluation of the national heritage constituted another major achievement of the New Cultural Movement and expanded its scope and dimensions.

CONCLUDING REMARKS

The intellectual revolution of 1917-23 represents China's third stage of response to the Western impact. The first stage—the Self-strengthening Movement from 1861 to 1895—saw superficial attempts at diplomatic and military modernization, and the second—the era of reform and revolution from 1898 to 1912—witnessed the acceptance of Western political institutions. The intellectual awakening of 1917-23 marked a further shift away from the traditional Chinese base to complete Westernization. By 1920 China was very much a part of the modern world.

Appraisals of the significance of the New Cultural Movement varied according to different viewpoints. Liberals proclaimed it as a movement of emancipation from old thought, old ethics, old values, and affirmation of human rights. The birth of a new literature with a new style of writing, and the official adoption of the Plain Language encouraged some to regard the May Fourth Movement as a Chinese Renaissance. Conservatives, however, attacked the movement for its corrupting influence on the youth and lack of respect for traditionalism, although they conceded its usefulness in stimulating nationalism. Radicals eulogized the movement. Li Ta-chao praised it as not only a patriotic movement but "a part of human liberation," and Mao Tse-tung describes it as essentially an "anti-imperialist and anti-feudal bourgeois-democratic revolution of China," propelled by a united front of workers, students, and national bourgeoisie under the leadership of the intelligentsia.[37] Mao also claims, perhaps exaggeratedly, that the May Fourth Movement formed part of

35. For an English rendition of the latter work, see translation by Immanuel C. Y. Hsü (Harvard University Press, 1959).
36. Such as Ch'ien Hsüan-t'ung (classics) and Ku Chieh-kang (history).
37. Tse-tsung Chow, 347, 349.

Lenin's world revolution. Similarly, the Chinese Communist Party and its historians regard May 4, 1919, as the watershed which separated the eighty-year period of the "Old Democracy" from the period of "New Democracy." During this latter period, the proletariat had become a conscious, independent political force, and communism had developed into an increasingly powerful ideological tool in the social, political, and cultural revolution of China.

Regardless of these different viewpoints, the fact remains that the May Fourth Movement was essentially a socio-politico-intellectual revolution aimed at achieving national independence, individual emancipation, and creation of a new culture through a critical and scientific re-evaluation of the national heritage as contrasted with foreign civilizations. Leaders of the movement regarded a radical change in the "thought base" as a prerequisite to successful modernization and national regeneration. Old ethics, customs, literature, social relations, and economic and political institutions came under disparaging attack to make way for the new. Yet a new culture was slow to emerge. The May Fourth Movement had been far more effective at destroying the past than at constructing the future.

Nonetheless, three main achievements are indisputable. First, the literary revolution led to the establishment of the Plain Language in 1920 and the rise of a new literature in vernacular style—based on humanitarianism, romanticism, realism, and nationalism. Literature now assumed a didactic role of instilling social consciousness in the public—"from literary revolution to revolutionary literature."

Secondly, the influx of diverse foreign ideas and ideologies caused the emergence of two opposing views on social reconstruction and national regeneration: the pragmatic, evolutionary method expounded by Hu Shih and later partially accepted by the Nationalist Party; and the Marxist revolutionary approach adopted by the Chinese Communist Party. The contemporary history of China from 1921 onward is primarily a story of the struggle between these two parties and their different approaches.

Thirdly, the intensification of nationalism stimulated the rise of a Young China, extremely sensitive to her perilous position in the modern world and jealous of guiding her own destiny. Such an attitude generated psychological reconstruction and national confidence which partially compensated for the sense of inadequacy and inferiority that had built up over the decades. The result was a violent reaction against foreign imperialism and an intense drive to end the unequal treaties.

Yet, in historical perspective, for all its bombastic characteristics, the intellectual revolution succeeded primarily in introducing Western thought and destroying Chinese traditionalism, rather than creating new systems of thought and new schools of philosophy.[38] The avowed purpose of forging a new culture through a critical re-evaluation of Chinese and Western civilizations stirred up a series of debates and polemics without really creating a new culture as such. Nonetheless, a foundation had been laid to adapt foreign ideas and institutions creatively to the Chinese situation. Whether by the evolutionary or revolutionary route, the ultimate goal remained the same: national salvation through the creation of a New China—thoroughly Westernized, yet distinctly Chinese.

FURTHER READING

Boorman, Howard L., and Richard C. Howard, *Biographical Dictionary of Republican China*, Vols. I and II (New York, 1967 and 1968).

Brière, D., S.J., *Fifty Years of Chinese Philosophy, 1898-1950* (London, 1956).

Ch'en, Tuan-chih 陳端志, *Wu-ssu yün-tung chih shih ti p'ing-chia* 五四運動之史的價評 (A historical review of the May 4th Movement), (Shanghai, 1936).

Chiang, Monlin, *Tides from the West: A Chinese Autobiography* (New Haven, 1947).

Ch'ien, I-shih 錢亦石, *Chin-tai Chung-kuo ching-chi shih* 近代中國經濟史 (Modern Chinese economic history), (Chungking, 1939).

Chou, Hsiu-luan 周秀鸞, *Ti-i-tz'u shih-chieh ta-chan shih-ch'i Chung-kuo min-tsu kung-yeh ti fa-chan* 第一次世界大戰時期中國民族工業的發展 (The development of Chinese national industries during World War I), (Shanghai, 1958).

Chow, Tse-tsung, *The May Fourth Movement: Intellectual Revolution in Modern China* (Cambridge, Mass., 1960).

De Francis, John, *Nationalism and Language Reform in China* (Princeton, 1950).

Dewey, John, *Letters from China and Japan* (New York, 1921).

———, "Old China and New," *Asia*, XXI:5:445-56 (May 1921).

———, "New Culture in China," *Asia*, XXI:7:581-86 (July 1921).

Feng, En-jung 馮恩榮, *Ch'üan-p'an Hsi-hua yen-lun hsü-chi* 全盤西化言論續集 (A supplementary collection of articles on complete Westernization), (Canton, 1935).

Fifield, Russell H., *Woodrow Wilson and the Far East, The Diplomacy of the Shantung Question* (New York, 1952).

38. Ch'ien Mu, "Wu-shih nien-tai chung chih Chung-kuo ssu-hsiang chieh" (Fifty years of Chinese intellectual world), in *Wu-ssu yun-tung lun-ts'ung*, (A collection of articles on the May 4th Movement), (Tapei, 1961), 1.

Hu, Shih, *The Chinese Renaissance* (Chicago, 1934).

Hua Kang, 華崗, *Wu-ssu yün-tung shih* 五四運動史 (A history of the May 4th Movement), (Shanghai, 1951).

Huang, Sung-k'ang, *Lu Hsün and the New Cultural Movement of Modern China* (Amsterdam, 1957).

King, Wunsz, *China at the Paris Peace Conference in 1919* (New York, 1961).

Kuo, Chan-po 郭湛波, *Chin-wu-shih-nien Chung-kuo ssu-hsiang shih* 近五十年中國思想史 (A history of Chinese thought during the last fifty years), reprinted (Hong Kong, 1965).

Kwok, D. W. Y., *Scientism in Chinese Thought* (New Haven, 1965).

Levenson, Joseph R., *Liang Ch'i-ch'ao and the Mind of Modern China* (Cambridge, Mass., 1953).

————, *Confucian China and Its Modern Fate*, Vol. I: *The Problem of Intellectual Continuity* (Berkeley, 1958), chapters 8-9.

Lü, Hsüeh-hai 呂學海, *Ch'üan-p'an Hsi-hua yen-lun chi* 全盤西化言論集 (A collection of articles on complete Westernization), (Canton, 1934).

Meisner, Maurice, *Li Ta-chao and the Origins of Chinese Marxism* (Cambridge, Mass., 1967).

Russell, Bertrand, *The Problem of China* (London, 1922).

Sakai, Robert K., "Ts'ai Yüan-p'ei as a Synthesizer of Western and Chinese Thought," *Papers on China*, Harvard University, 3:170-92 (May 1949).

Wang, Y. C., *Chinese Intellectuals and the West, 1872-1949* (Chapel Hill, 1966).

Wu-ssu yün-tung lun-ts'ung 五四運動論叢 (A collection of articles on the May 4th Movement), (Taipei, 1961).

22

National Unification Amidst Ideological Ferment
and Anti-imperialistic Agitation

In the wake of the intellectual revolution, two major political events developed as a repercussion of the Bolshevik Revolution in Russia. One was the rise of the Chinese Communist Party, and the other the reorganization of the Nationalist Party. Both developments played a major role in shaping the course of the contemporary history of China.

THE BIRTH OF THE COMMUNIST PARTY, 1921

Chinese awareness of Marxism probably began around 1905 when the *Min-pao* published a biography of Karl Marx in its second issue. In early 1908 the anarchist journal, *T'ien-i pao* (Journal of natural justice), founded less than a year earlier, published translations from the Japanese of Friedrich Engels's 1888 "Introduction to the Communist Manifesto," the first chapter of the *Manifesto* itself, and excerpts from Engels's *The Origin of the Family*. Although there was an incipient recognition of Marx and Engels as the founding fathers of "scientific socialism," the influence of Marxism remained small until the May Fourth period when the success of the Bolshevik Revolution dramatized the power of such an ideology. Many Chinese intellectuals had lost faith in the West after the Versailles pronouncement on Shantung, and found it difficult to accept the West as teacher and oppressor simultaneously. Therefore, ideas and ideologies critical of the West found new favor, and powerful elements among the intellectuals were drawn to the utopian socialism of Saint-Simon, the anarchism of Kropotkin and Bakunin, and the revolutionary philosophy of Marx. Socialism was appealing because it provided a practical philosophy with which to reject "both the traditions of the Chinese past and the Western domination of the present."[1] Moreover, it represented a goal as yet unrealized in western Europe and America, and its acceptance in China would put her ideologically ahead of the capitalist states. This subtle psychological satisfaction, buttressed by a general disappointment with the West and a secret desire to surpass it, made Marxism especially attractive.

The intellectual and psychological appeal of Marxism was further strengthened by the practical Soviet offer of friendship and the enticing Leninist theory of imperialism. Anxious to win friends and create a new image, Moscow twice announced—in 1918 and 1919[2]—its readiness to renounce the old tsarist special rights and privileges in China. Although it altered its position somewhat in 1920 and proposed to *negotiate* the abolition of the unequal treaties—as a means to win Chinese recognition —the Soviet overture nevertheless created a favorable impact, for it represented an unsolicited, unilateral expression of friendship and a radical departure from the haughty and rapacious behavior of imperialist powers.

Added to this olive branch was the encouraging Leninist theory of imperialism. Lenin had proclaimed that imperialism was the inevitable product of the last stage of capitalism; when capitalism grew to a high point, as in the late 19th and early 20th centuries, it had to seek overseas markets to sell its surplus goods and to buy raw materials. At this point mutual jealousy and rivalry among the capitalist states would inevitably lead them into conflict and eventual extinction. The downtrodden people of Asia and other underdeveloped areas should thus rise against foreign imperialism and hasten the passing away of the foreign yoke. This Leninist theory offered comfort to the Chinese intellectuals, for not only did it blame the West for China's ills and predict the imminent demise of capitalism, but it also gave Asia a place in the world revolution—in refutation of the previous stand of most European Marxists who insisted that the problems of the world could be solved only in and by the West.

In effect, the intellectual appeal of Marxism-Leninism, the voluntary offer of friendship by the Soviet regime, and the practical success of the Bolshevik Revolution combined to create a powerful ideological impact in China. Marxist and Leninist study groups began to spring up, and the

1. Bernal, 111, 137; Meisner, 100.
2. Through Foreign Commissar G. V. Chicherin on July 4, 1918, and Assistant Foreign Commissar Leo Karakhan on July 15, 1919.

National University of Peking, where intellectual curiosity and freedom of expression were most pronounced, became a hotbed of radicalism. As early as the middle of 1918, the librarian Li Ta-chao professed his conversion to Marxism and hailed the Bolshevik Revolution as a "great, universal, and elemental force" comparable in importance to the French Revolution. But he envisaged an even greater experience of rebirth in China, and founded the New Tide Society (*Hsin-ch'ao she*) in the autumn of 1918, followed shortly by the Marxist Research Society. Li celebrated "The Victory of Bolshevism" in the November 1918 issue of *New Youth,* and edited a whole issue of it on Marxism in 1919. His library office humorously became known as the "Red Chamber" (*Hung-lou*), frequented by young and eager followers including his students Ch'ü Ch'iu-pai, Chang Kuo-t'ao, and his library assistant Mao Tse-tung—all destined to be the future leaders of the Chinese Communist movement.

No less potent than the Marxist impact was the stunning effect of the May Fourth incident on the Chinese intellectuals. Whereas formerly many of them embraced Western democracy, liberalism, and internationalism without being overly concerned with the question of imperialism, they now decisively cut off their dependence on the West and vowed to take China's fate into their own hands. Political activism was the new catchword. Among those rudely awakened and fervently militant intellectuals, the foremost was Ch'en Tu-hsiu. Deeply struck by the student role in the May Fourth incident, he committed himself to subsequent demonstrations and was landed in prison on June 11, 1919. After his release in September, Ch'en resigned from the university under conservative pressure. Making Shanghai his new home, he became increasingly absorbed in Marxism. By mid-1920 his faith in the West was completely demolished, and democracy to him was no more than a tool used by the bourgeoisie "to swindle mankind in order to maintain political power."[3] Ch'en became the second most important convert to Marxism, and organized a Marxist Study Society in May 1920 and a Socialist Youth Corps in August, which were the forerunners of the Chinese Communist Party.

Meanwhile, in Peking, another group was gathering around Li Ta-chao, whose Marxist Research Society was replaced by the Society for the Study of Socialism in December 1919. By March 1920 the various Marxist groups in Peking had united to form the Peking Society for the Study of Marxist Theory. Two Russians, A. A. Muller and N. Bortman, had

3. Meisner, 113.

offered Li help in 1919 but concrete steps toward forming a party did not begin until the arrival in early 1920 of Grigorii Voitinsky, an agent of the Third (Communist) International, or Comintern in abbreviation. In March he conferred with Li about organizing a party, and shortly afterwards left for Shanghai to confer with Ch'en. The upshot of these critical conferences was the decision to establish a branch party in Shanghai by Ch'en and another in Peking by Li. Only the consolidation of these two branches remained for the unification of communism in China.

In July 1921 the founding meeting of the Chinese Communist Party—since called the First Congress of the Party—was held secretly at a girls' boarding school[4] in the French Concession of Shanghai. It was attended by twelve delegates[5] representing fifty-seven members, but neither Ch'en nor Li was present—Ch'en was at Canton and his group was represented by Chou Fu-hai, while Li's group was represented by Chang Kuo-t'ao. In spite of their absence, Ch'en and Li, 41 and 32 respectively, were honored as the co-founders of the party. Although the central party headquarters was set up in Shanghai, Li's Peking group maintained virtual independence. The expression, "Ch'en in the south, Li in the north" (*Nan-Ch'en pei-Li*), underscored the absence of a tight unified party organization at birth.

Not only did they form two regional foci, but Ch'en and Li also differed considerably on the revolutionary role of the workers and the peasants. Ch'en subscribed to the general European Marxist emphasis on the workers and the implicit disdain toward the inert peasant mass. He believed that the progressive urban elements should spearhead the movement while the backward peasantry follow meekly: "The peasants are scattered and their forces are not easy to concentrate, their culture is low, their desires in life are simple, and they easily tend toward conservatism . . . These environmental factors make it difficult for the peasants to participate in the revolutionary movement."[6] Ch'ü Ch'iu-pai likewise rejected the idea that the agrarian sector could take the lead in reforming the Chinese society. On the other hand, Li Ta-chao, imbued with a more romantic attitude toward social change, took the opposite view to stress the importance of the peasantry: "In economically backward and semi-colonial China, the peasantry constitutes more than ninety per cent of the population; among the whole population they occupy the principal

4. Po-wen Middle School for Girls.
5. Including Mao Tse-tung, but not Chou En-lai who was in France, or Chu Teh who was in Germany.
6. Meisner, 242.

position, and agriculture is still the basis of the national economy. Therefore, when we estimate the forces of the revolution, we must emphasize
that the peasantry is the important part."[7] Impassioned by an innate love
for the purity of the countryside and a deep aversion to the corruption
of city life, Li urged young intellectuals to go to the villages to liberate
the peasants and stimulate their revolutionary energies, in the spirit of
the Russian Populist (*narodnik*) movement. Indeed, he saw in the liberation of the peasantry the liberation of China.[8]

Although the party supported Ch'en's position, Li's views offered a
powerful alternative and strongly influenced the thinking of his young
assistant, Mao, whom he introduced to Marxism in 1918 and whom he
successfully inspired with the Populist, nationalistic views on the peasant role in the revolution. After Li's execution by the warlord Chang
Tso-lin on April 28, 1927, it was Mao who carried on the peasant struggle
and put his mentor's ideas into practice.

THE NATIONALIST PARTY REORGANIZATION, 1923-24

The Bolshevik Revolution not only influenced the establishment of the
Chinese Communist Party (CCP), but also prompted the reorganization of the Nationalist Party, or Kuomintang (KMT). Dr. Sun, father
of the Chinese Revolution, had long been disappointed by the lack of
unity and discipline within his party, and by the Western reluctance to
assist him in developing China. Ever since the founding of the republic
in 1912, he had encountered obstruction and disobedience within his
party and precious little cooperation. Nor was the latter quality any
more prevalent after two major reorganizations: from the T'ung-meng
hui to the Chinese Revolutionary Party (*Chung-kuo ko-ming-tang*) in
1914, and to the Chinese Nationalist Party (*Chung-kuo kuo-min-tang*)
in 1919. Sun was continuously frustrated by flagrant acts of insubordination such as Ch'en Chiung-ming's mutiny in 1922 and the open obstruction of the southwestern military governors who had earlier pledged
their allegiance.

Equally annoying was the Western support of the warlords and their
lack of interest in Sun's international development plan for China. As
early as 1913 the Western imperialists had patronized Yüan Shih-k'ai
with a £25 million loan from the Five-Power Banking Consortium with
which he crushed the Second Revolution. The British minister in par-

7. Meisner, 239.
8. *Ibid.*, 81.

ticular, John Jordan, supplied Yüan with munitions and barred Sun and Huang Hsing from landing in Hong Kong. After Yüan's death, the imperialists supported the various warlords, fomented civil strife, and turned a deaf ear to Sun's pleas for assistance. The Paris Peace Conference, which ignored China's rightful claims in Shantung, and the Washington Conference of 1922 (p. 624), which smoothed Anglo-American relations with Japan more than it solved China's problems, were further proof of Western insincerity.

Throughout the republican period, Sun was plagued by the threefold problem of foreign imperialism, party disunity, and civil strife, from which he could find no escape and solution. In his frustration, he found the sparkling success of the Bolshevik Revolution doubly inspiring, and the Soviet offer of friendship and abolition of the unequal treaties gratifying and refreshing. Just as he attributed the Russian success to good party organization and strict discipline, Sun blamed his failure on poor discipline, slack organization, and inadequate indoctrination. He was anxious to reorganize the KMT after the successful Soviet model and to seek Soviet aid to his National Revolution.

Two other factors also influenced him. One was the founding of the Chinese Communist Party, which had developed close ties with labor and agrarian organizations, and the other was the fervent nationalism and buoyant public spirit of the younger generation after the May Fourth incident. Since both forces shared his objectives of "anti-imperialism and anti-warlordism," he was ready to introduce new blood into his somewhat aged organization.

However, Sun had to wait to learn the secrets of Soviet success and to reorganize his party. As head of the revolutionary regime at Canton rather than that of the legal government at Peking, he was not the first choice of Moscow. The Russians had sent M. I. Yurin and A. K. Paikes to Peking in 1920 to negotiate a treaty, but the warlord government was advised by the British and the Japanese to decline the overture. The Soviets next turned to the powerful warlord Wu P'ei-fu, whom they conveniently transformed into a "bourgeois nationalist," but under British pressure Wu also proved unresponsive. It was only then that the Soviets "rediscovered" Sun, who had reputedly sent congratulations to Lenin in 1918 which heartened that Bolshevik leader.[9]

9. C. Martin Wilbur and Julie Lien-ying How, Documents on Communism, Nationalism, and Soviet Advisers in China, 1918-1927: Papers Seized in the 1927 Peking Raid (New York, 1956), 138.

In the spring of 1921 the Comintern's Dutch agent, H. Maring, met with Sun in Kwangsi and was most impressed with his nationalist spirit and ideas of revolution. Sun, on his part, was gratified to learn of the Soviet New Economic Policy which he likened naively to his own Industrial Plan (*Shih-yeh chi-hua*). Maring soon became convinced that the KMT was the mainstream of Chinese nationalism and that the nascent CCP should expand its influence through utilizing the established base of the KMT. He urged the CCP members to join the KMT on the grounds that it was not a bourgeois party per se but a coalition of all classes. Ch'en and Li reluctantly gave in to his pressure, and in August 1922 the CCP Central Committee resolved to permit individual Communists to enter the KMT. Li Ta-chao took the lead in joining the Nationalist Party through the introduction of its senior member, Chang Chi.

Sun was willing to accept the Communists for a number of reasons. Idealistically, he felt that *all* Chinese, including the Communists, had a right to participate in his National Revolution (*Kuo-min ko-ming*). Practically, he wanted to utilize the CCP's ties with the labor and agrarian movements and Soviet aid in reorganizing the KMT. Furthermore, he very realistically believed that any rapid, independent growth of the CCP under the Soviet aegis, with its commitment to class struggle, would ultimately undermine his own cause of National Revolution; it would therefore be wise to absorb them into his party and assimilate them in time. Lastly, Sun had considerable concern about possible Soviet aid to some warlords not friendly to him; Li Ta-chao and Ch'en Tu-hsiu had been instructed by the Soviets to develop connections with Wu P'ei-fu and Ch'en Chuing-ming, both avowed enemies of the National Revolution. A policy of friendship and alliance with the Soviets and the CCP would undercut these warlords.[10]

The Comintern dispatched Adolf Joffe to China to work out the basis of Soviet-KMT-CCP cooperation. Arriving in Peking on August 12, 1922, Joffe received a most cordial welcome from the New Tide Society and thirteen other organizations, much to the jealousy of the Western consular corps and the displeasure of the warlord government. Subsequently, he engaged in lengthy correspondence and negotiations with Sun, who by this time had decided on the policy of "alliance with the Soviets; admission of the Communists" (*Lien-O yung-Kung*). This policy, approved by fifty-three Nationalist leaders at a Shanghai conference on September

10. Chiang Yung-ching, *Pao-lo-t'ing yü Wu-han cheng-ch'üan* (Borodin and the Wuhan regime), (Taipei, 1963), 2-3.

4, 1922, became the cardinal principle in the reorganization of the KMT. A nine-man committee including Ch'en Tu-hsiu was appointed to take charge of the reorganization, and a manifesto drafted by Hu Han-min was announced on January 1, 1923.

On January 12, the Comintern instructed the Chinese Communists to enter the Nationalist Party and take part in Sun's *bourgeois democratic* revolution. Ch'en accepted the order most reluctantly, for he feared for the KMT's corrupting influence on the worker and peasant members of the CCP. "It was only due to the pressure of the Third Internationale that the Chinese Communist Party grudgingly recognized the necessity of carrying on its activities within the Kuomintang," remarked Ch'en.[11] However, the CCP itself was not dissolved; the Communists entered the KMT as individuals rather than as a bloc and they agreed to accept the order and discipline of the Nationalist leaders. Publicly, the CCP acknowledged the KMT as the leader and central force of the National Revolution.

The Sun-Joffe negotiations led to a joint manifesto on January 26, 1923, which included four main points: (1) it is not possible to carry out Communism or the Soviet system in China at present; (2) the Soviet government reaffirms its earlier announcement of September 27, 1920, regarding the renouncement of special rights and privileges in China; (3) a mutual understanding is reached with regard to the future administration and reorganization of the Chinese Eastern Railway; and (4) the Soviets disavow any imperialistic intentions or policies in Outer Mongolia.[12]

In his negotiations with Joffe, Sun demonstrated hardheaded practical statesmanship. For all his eagerness to seek Soviet aid, he refused to substitute Communism for his Three People's Principles; nor would he surrender the power of leadership to Marxist discipline and order. He left no doubt that the KMT occupied the leadership position in the National Revolution, and that it was the Communists who entered the Nationalist Party, not vice versa. Moreover, they had entered as individuals, not as a group, so as to avoid the embarrassing situation of "bloc within" or a "party within a party." From all appearances Sun had achieved his objectives very much on his own terms.

Following the Sun-Joffe agreement, the Soviets sent Mikhail Borodin

11. Benjamin I. Schwartz, *Chinese Communism and the Rise of Mao* (Cambridge, Mass., 1958), 53, 60.
12. Complete text in Conrad Brandt, Benjamin I. Schwartz, and John K. Fairbank, *A Documentary History of Chinese Communism* (London, 1952), 70-71.

(Grusenburg), an experienced diplomat, to help Sun reorganize the KMT, and General Galen (Blücher) to help train a party army. In addition, some forty Soviet advisers came with them. In August 1923, Sun dispatched a young general, Chiang Kai-shek, to study firsthand the Soviet military system, the political indoctrination of the Red army, and the methods of discipline in the Bolshevik Party. After a three-month visit, Chiang returned home where he was soon commissioned by Sun to found the Whampoa Military Academy outside Canton.

At the first National Congress of the KMT held from January 20 to 30, 1924, and attended by 165 delegates, Sun stressed the importance of party unity and the development of a strong organization for national unification and reconstruction. He called on the members to sacrifice their personal freedom and contribute their talents unselfishly to the revolutionary objectives. It was during the meeting that the news of Lenin's death on January 25 arrived, and the Congress, to show its grief and respect, recessed for three days—a public affirmation of the new policy of friendship and alliance with the Soviet Union.

There were, of course, KMT members who, though not averse to the Soviet alliance, were reluctant to accept the CCP. To smooth the path of cooperation, Sun patiently explained that since both the KMT and the CCP were committed to anti-imperialism and anti-warlordism, it behooved them to join hands in the common struggle. On January 28, 1924 Li Ta-chao tactfully declared that members of his party had entered the KMT in order to devote themselves to the revolution, without any ulterior motives to advance the Communist cause. Moreover, they entered as individuals, not as a bloc; therefore one could not accuse them of forming "a bloc within" the KMT party, even though they held double memberships. Li reiterated that as long as the Communists remained in the KMT, they would obey the latter's orders and accept its disciplinary action. He emphatically disclaimed any intention of infiltrating or subverting the KMT from within.[13] In spite of his explanation, the fact remained that the Communist Party did not dissolve itself, nor did its members who entered the KMT lose their Communist membership. There was, in fact, a Communist bloc within the Nationalist Party.

Sun had admitted Communists in the interest of the revolution without seeming to realize all the implications of his action. Still idealistic, he assumed that since the Comintern had favored such a collaboration it would help him control the Communist members, and perhaps even in-

13. Wilbur and How, 149.

struct them to obey him. He also entertained some hopes that in due course the small number of Communists might be effectively submerged within the substantially larger Nationalist ranks. What he did not realize was that the real intention of Moscow was to graft the young CCP onto the established body of the KMT so that it could subvert it from within, seize the proletarian hegemony, and squeeze out the rightists like "lemons."[14]

Meanwhile, the Congress had created a Presidium of five members, including Li Ta-chao.[15] It closed with a manifesto of three parts, emphasizing its anti-imperialist and anti-warlord stand, its dedication to the Three People's Principles and the Five-Power Constitution, and its determination to abolish the unequal treaties externally and to establish local self-government internally.

In the reorganized Kuomintang, the Central Executive Committee, which exercised power for the National Party Congress when the latter was not in session, was the most powerful organ. Three of its twenty-four regular members were Communists;[16] so were six of the seventeen alternate members.[17] Under the Central Executive Committee was the Central Party Headquarters (*Chung-yang tang-pu*) composed of a secretariat and eight departments; two of the departments (Organization and Farmers) were headed by Communists,[18] and one (Workers) had a Communist secretary-general. Thus the Communists won a number of key appointments and assumed direction of some very strategic offices of the Nationalist Party.

The KMT-CCP collaboration was an uneasy marriage of convenience, each needing but distrusting the other. The KMT desired Soviet aid in revitalizing the party, in developing a party army, and in carrying out the National Revolution; it also aspired to the utilization of Communist ties with the workers, peasants, and the masses. On the other hand, the Comintern and the CCP wanted to use the KMT base to expand their influence and eventually to subvert it from within. In this tenuous relationship, cooperation lasted as long as it was in the interest of both; each hoped to emerge the victor when the other had outlived his usefulness. Sun's stature and prestige were decisive factors in holding together the

14. Schwartz, 80.
15. Others included Sun himself, Hu Han-min, Wang Ching-wei, and Lin Shen.
16. Li Ta-chao, T'an P'ing-shan, and Yü Shu-te.
17. Mao Tse-tung, Ch'ü Ch'iu-pai, Chang Kuo-t'ao, Lin Tsu-han, Yü Fang-chou, and Han Lin-fu.
18. Under T'an P'ing-shan and Lin Tsu-han, respectively.

various elements, but once he passed away, divisive forces were unleashed and loomed increasingly large on the horizon.

THE NORTHERN EXPEDITION AND THE KMT-CCP SPLIT

Having reorganized the party, Sun was eager to resume the much-delayed Northern Expedition to wipe out the warlords and frustrate their imperialist supporters. Taking advantage of a civil war in the North which broke out in September 1924, he quickly organized a campaign, but no sooner had his expedition gotten off the ground than the warlord alliance in the North became suddenly shattered by the mutiny of Feng Yü-hsiang, as noted in Chapter 20. Feng occupied Peking, overthrew the Ts'ao K'un government, and invited Sun to a conference of national unification. It was during this conference that Sun fell seriously ill. Worried about his unfinished work, he bade farewell to his followers with this message: "The revolution is not yet complete; comrades must strive on!" On March 12, 1925, he passed away.

Sun's political mantle fell on Wang Ching-wei and Hu Han-min, the left- and right-wing leaders of the KMT, respectively. But the military power rested with Chiang Kai-shek, the superintendent of the Whampoa Military Academy who was in charge of developing an officer corps to staff the new party army. His cadets were given political indoctrination as well as military training so that they could correctly instruct the soldiers in the political mission of the revolution. Within the academy, Sun's confidant Liao Chung-k'ai served as the chief party representative, while Ho Ying-ch'in was the head military instructor. All orders and regulations in the academy and in the party army, to be valid and enforceable by the superintendent, had to be countersigned by the party representative. The deputy head of the Political Education Department at the academy was none other than the young Communist Chou En-lai, and among the students of the fourth graduating class was one Lin Piao.

The cadets rapidly became a powerful military factor. They suppressed the Hong Kong-Canton Merchants' Volunteers Uprising in October 1924,[19] drove away the rebel governor Ch'en Chiung-ming, and frustrated the various southwestern warlords. With Canton relatively safe from hostile forces, a Nationalist Government was established on July 1, 1925,

19. Organized by Ch'en Lien-po, a compradore of the Hong Kong and Shanghai Banking Corporation.

in rival existence with the Peking warlord government, and Wang Ching-wei was made president. A series of pacification campaigns followed in Kwangtung and Kwangsi, and by February 1926 all opposition in the two provinces had been suppressed. Determined to resume the Northern Expedition, the Nationalist Government on June 25 appointed Chiang Kai-shek commander-in-chief of the National Revolutionary army, consisting of 6,000 Whampoa cadets and 85,000 troops. On July 27 Chiang set out on his celebrated campaign against the northern warlords, who were deployed as follows:

1. The Chihli warlord Wu P'ei-fu had control of Honan, Hupeh, part of Chihli and Hunan, and the Peking-Hankow Railway.
2. The Fengtien (Manchurian) warlord Chang Tso-lin had established himself as generalissimo in Peking, controling Manchuria, Chihli, Shantung, and the Fengtien-Peking and Tientsin-Pukow railways.
3. Sun Ch'uan-fang, who had seceded from the Chihli Clique, was established at Nanking, dominating the five southeastern provinces of Kiangsu, Chekiang, Fukien, Kiangsi, and Anhwei.

In addition, two independent forces were established in the Northwest which belonged neither to these warlord groups nor to the revolutionary army, although they were somewhat sympathetic to the latter:

1. Feng Yü-hsiang's "National People's Army" had retreated to the Northwest under the pressure of the Chihli and Fengtien forces.
2. Yen Hsi-shan had established a firm base in Shansi, without participating in the civil strife.

Chiang's strategy was to attack Wu P'ei-fu first, and then Sun Ch'uan-fang and Chang Tso-lin. Strengthened by Soviet supplies[20] and aided by CCP advance agents who mobilized peasant and worker organizations and fomented strikes and sabotage in the cities, the Northern Expeditionary forces struck a blitzkrieg from Canton to Central China, taking Wuhan in September 1926, Nanchang in November, Foochow in December, and Shanghai and Nanking in March 1927. Within nine months the southern half of China was conquered. The campaign had been a spectacular success; the future indeed looked bright. But at this point an

20. Soviet supplies to the KMT reached two million roubles from October 1924 to December 1925. See Wilbur and How, 169.

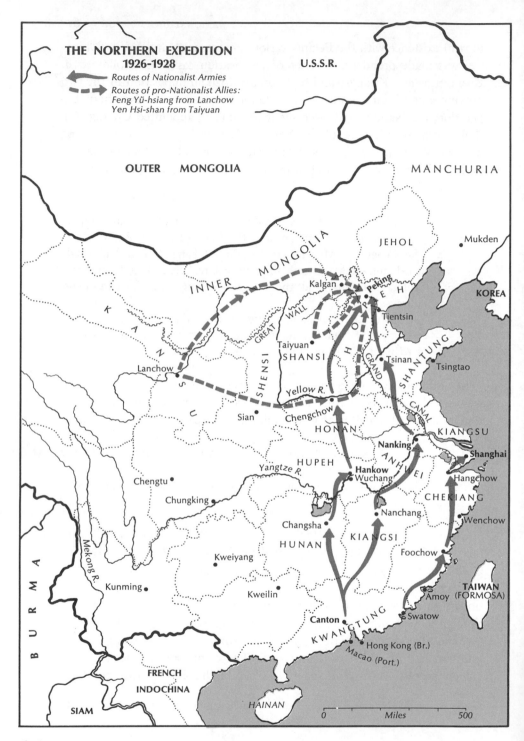

THE NORTHERN EXPEDITION
1926-1928

→ Routes of Nationalist Armies
⇢ Routes of pro-Nationalist Allies:
Feng Yü-hsiang from Lanchow
Yen Hsi-shan from Taiyuan

U.S.S.R.

OUTER MONGOLIA

MANCHURIA

INNER MONGOLIA

KANSU

JEHOL

Mukden

KOREA

Kalgan
GREAT WALL
Peking
Tientsin
Taiyuan
SHANSI
SHENSI
Lanchow
Yellow R.
Chengchow
Sian
HONAN
Tsinan
Tsingtao
SHANTUNG
GRAND CANAL
KIANGSU
Nanking
ANHWEI
Shanghai
HUPEH
Yangtze R.
Hankow
Wuchang
Chengtu
Chungking
Nanchang
Hangchow
CHEKIANG
Changsha
Wenchow
HUNAN
KIANGSI
Foochow
Kweiyang
Kunming
Kweilin
TAIWAN
(FORMOSA)
Amoy
Canton
KWANGTUNG
Swatow
Hong Kong (Br.)
Macao (Port.)
FRENCH
INDOCHINA
Mekong R.
BURMA
SIAM
HAINAN

0   Miles   500

616

ominous KMT-CCP split developed, which threatened to wreck the party and interrupt the Northern Expedition.

The collaboration of the two parties had been a delicate matter from the start. It was held in balance by Sun's immense prestige and the feeling of mutual needs, but many members in both camps had grave doubts about the wisdom of such an alliance. Chiang Kai-shek, for one, never believed in Soviet sincerity in aiding China's revolution. Returning from Russia in late 1923, he informed Liao Chung-k'ai, Sun's close associate and an advocate of "alliance with Russia, admission of [Chinese] Communists," that the real intention of Moscow's policy was to seize the leadership position for the CCP from within the KMT. In this context, "world revolution" and "internationalism" were nothing but a subterfuge for Soviet imperialism, no different from other forms of exploitation practiced by the West and Japan. Chiang was therefore deeply concerned with the future of the KMT-CCP collaboration.

On their part, the Communists also felt increasingly restricted in their operation within the KMT framework. Their tactics of strikes, sabotage, domination of the mass organizations, splitting the KMT left from the right, etc. encountered endless obstruction, as Ch'en Tu-hsiu described the situation: "Our cooperation with the Kuomintang is becoming more precarious day by day. Superficially, we seem to be in conflict about various, separate problems but actually what they want is complete hegemony. There are now only two roads open to us—either we abandon the fight for hegemony or break with them!"[21]

The bone of contention from the outset was the question of dual membership and its corollary of the "bloc within." The Nationalists had admitted the Communists as individuals and expected them to accept the KMT leadership and obey its orders, but the Communist Party demanded that its members take orders from itself and form a secret bloc within the KMT. Holders of dual membership, in short, were expected to be nominal KMT members but real CCP members. Conflict of orders naturally led to friction which involved the sensitive question of discipline. When confronted by a group of troubled KMT Supervisory Committee members on June 25, 1924, Borodin glibly maintained that the old Kuomintang had died, and that the contradictions between the CCP and KMT members was a healthy phenomenon which might lead to the emergence of a "central group" at the core of the party. He further argued that the KMT-CCP collaboration had in fact benefited the Na-

21. Schwartz, 60.

tionalists more than the Communists.[22] Disturbed by this line of thinking, the KMT Supervisory Committee members became deeply worried about the "bloc within" and the future of collaboration. Yet during Sun's lifetime, no open break took place, although tension continued to rise.

After the assassination of Liao Chung-k'ai in August 1925,[23] some fifteen rightist KMT Executive and Supervisory Committee members[24] left Canton for Western Hill (Hsi-shan), outside Peking, to hold a Fourth Central Executive Committee meeting on November 23 in front of Sun's coffin. Here, they issued a proclamation calling for the expulsion of the Communists from the KMT and the dismissal of Borodin as adviser. The KMT left wing at Canton accused the Western Hill group of lacking the legal quorum to pass valid resolutions. It called its own Fourth Central Executive Committee meeting, and adopted resolutions to censure the Western Hill faction and to call a Second National Congress on January 1, 1926. At this congress, Borodin's domination was formidable. The Communists won new memberships on the KMT Supervisory Committee and increased memberships on the Central Executive Committee. Of the latter's nine-man Standing Committee, three were Communist and three were fellow travelers. At least five or six of the nine ministries of the KMT central party headquarters came under Communist control: Organization, Propaganda, Workers, Farmers, Overseas, and Youth.[25] Facing these developments, the Western Hill group set up its own party headquarters in Shanghai, to signify a split with Canton.

Another ingredient added to the tension was the "Warship *Chung-shan* incident" of March 20, 1926. On that day the captain of *Chung-shan*, under Communist influence, unsuccessfully attempted to kidnap Chiang Kai-shek, who in return dismissed the captain and all Soviet advisers and party representatives in the First Army and its affiliated military establishments. It was in a sense the first step in Chiang's break with the Communists, yet in the interest of the impending Northern Expedition no open schism was announced. Nonetheless, some restrictive measures were quickly taken against the Communists. On May 15, 1926, the KMT Central Executive Committee passed nine resolutions to limit

22. Li Fang-ch'en, 870-71.
23. Reputedly by KMT rightists under the secret patronage of the British Hong Kong authorities. Hu Han-min's younger brother, Hu I-sheng, was implicated. See Wilbur and How, 165.
24. Including Tai Chi-t'ao. Lin Shen, Chü Cheng, Chang Chi, Tsou Lu.
25. Chiang Yung-ching, 10-11.

Communists to no more than a third of all committee memberships, to exclude them from department directorships in the central party head-quarters, and to prohibit KMT members from accepting Communists memberships. Although the CCP Central Executive Committee rejected these decisions and resolved to organize its own military forces, Stalin, not wishing to precipitate a split at this point, ordered it to tolerate the resolutions in order to remain within the KMT.[26]

It was only after the Nationalists had successfully imposed these re-strictions on the Communists that Chiang set out on his Northern Expe-dition in July 1926. His troop movement was fast, as noted before, and having pacified Central China, the KMT decided to move the govern-ment from Canton to Wuhan by January 1, 1927. Meanwhile, the CCP received an order from Stalin dated November 30, 1926, instructing it to intensify the political work in the revolutionary army, and to improve its military knowledge so as to be readied for important positions in the army.

When the KMT left wing and the Communists moved to Wuhan in December 1926, the right wing refused to go, proceeding instead to Nan-chang, Kiangsi, where they proposed to establish a separate government; in the end, however, they did join the Wuhan government to avoid a split. The Wuhan government was dominated by Borodin and the KMT left wing, and the two important ministries of workers and farmers were put under the charge of the Communists.[27] The latter actively carried out Stalin's new order of March 3, 1927, calling for the intensification of mass movements, arming the workers and peasants, and mobilizing the masses to embarrass and attack the KMT rightists. These stepped-up activities were most evident in the areas under the control of Wuhan, which included Hupeh, Hunan, and Kiangsi.

At the same time Chiang Kai-shek, conducting a successful military campaign, was rapidly building a power base in Eastern and Southeastern China. He had deliberately disregarded Borodin's advice to skip Shanghai in favor of the North, driving instead straight to the gates of that financial center. There the Communist-dominated General Labor Union had al-ready staged a debilitating strike, mobilized its armed pickets, fought the local garrison, and won control of the city from within. Not knowing whether they should cooperate with Chiang, they waited for orders from

26. Conrad Brandt, *Stalin's Failure in China, 1924-1927* (Cambridge, Mass., 1958), 76.
27. Su Chao-cheng and T'an P'ing-shan respectively.

Moscow. Still hoping to prevent a split, Stalin asked the Shanghai workers to "bury their weapons" and to "avoid any clashes" with Chiang, whose troops thus entered the city unopposed on March 22.[28] Riding the tide of victory, the Northern Expeditional forces went on to conquer Nanking on March 24 and won domination of Fukien, Chekiang, and greater parts of Kiangsu and Anhwei. It was apparent that Wuhan and Nanking formed two power centers within the KMT hierarchy, and that a split was imminent. Though ready to break with the CCP and send Borodin home, Chiang was temporarily dissuaded by Wang Ching-wei, who had just returned from abroad via the Soviet Union. Wang, however, did not stay with Chiang, but went to Wuhan to join Borodin.

With the support of the Shanghai-Nanking financial circles, Chiang became more determined to persecute the Communists. A "purge committee" (ch'ing-tang) was organized on April 10, 1927, and orders were issued to dissolve the political department of the National Revolutionary army. From April 12 on, wholesale liquidation of the Communists began —first in Shanghai, and then in Nanking, Hangchow, Foochow, Canton, and other places. Nationalist troops, police, and secret agents raided Communist cells, shot down suspects at sight, disarmed the workers' pickets, and eliminated the labor unions. When they had finished, a devastating blow had been dealt to China's proletarian vanguard.[29] Surprisingly, during all this time, Chiang continued to profess friendship with Moscow—his quarrels were only with the local Communists.

Buffeted by Communist protest, the Wuhan government on April 17 dismissed Chiang as commander-in-chief of the National Revolutionary army. Chiang could not have cared less; with the help of Hu Han-min he organized his own Nationalist government at Nanking a day later. The split between the two power centers had widened into an unbridgeable gulf.

To counter Chiang's success at Shanghai and Nanking, Borodin proposed that Wuhan itself launch a "Second Northern Expedition"[30] to Peking and sought the collaboration of Feng Yü-hsiang and Yen Hsishan. Borodin's strategy called for a swift strike by the Wuhan forces into Honan to destroy the Fengtien army and to open a way for Feng to enter from Shensi, while Yen's forces, coming down from Shansi, were to attack the retreating Fengtien troops from behind and join forces with

28. Brandt, 112-113.
29. Brandt, 114.
30. The campaign from Canton to Wuhan was considered the "First Northern Expedition."

Feng in a combined drive to take Peking. The Wuhan forces were then to return to the home base in preparation for an "Eastern Expedition" to clear Kiangsi, Fukien, and Kwangtung of hostile elements.

The plan was opposed by M. N. Roy, the new Comintern representative, on the ground that it was too risky to depend on the support of Feng and Yen. He proposed instead consolidation of the base through an intensified land revolution in Hunan and Hupeh, and then launch an expedition to the southeast. The CCP Central Committee, which was inclined to Roy's view, passed a resolution on April 16 to postpone the Second Northern Expedition. Sharp and derogatory exchanges took place between Roy and Borodin. On April 18, the Wuhan government under Wang Ching-wei decided on a double-barrel approach of launching the Northern Expedition first, to be followed by an Eastern Expedition. The military plans projected the occupation of Peking three months after the Wuhan army joined forces with Feng on the Peking-Hankow Railway.[31]

As planned, the Wuhan forces struck successfully into Honan, inflicted heavy casualties on the Fengtien army, and met Feng at the important railway center of Chengchow. Once established in Honan, however, Feng proved to be far more independent than Borodin had expected. Yen was even more of a problem; he refused to cooperate altogether on the ground that Wuhan represented the Communist regime while Nanking was the true Nationalist government. Meanwhile, Chiang Kai-shek carried on his own Northern Expedition successfully along the Tientsin-Pukow Railway, taking Hsuchow on June 2, 1927.

Feng now proposed a joint Northern Expedition by Chiang, Wuhan, and himself. To Borodin and Ch'en Tu-hsiu, joint expedition meant "joint extermination of the CCP," and they spurned the proposal outright. Feng then visited Chiang at Hsuchow on June 20-21, ostensibly to attempt a reconciliation between Nanking and Wuhan but actually to concert action against communism.[32] The conference ended with Feng's public demand that Wuhan expel Borodin and the Communists.

Feng's apostasy and Yen's refusal to collaborate not only shattered Borodin's Northern Expedition but also placed Wuhan in a pocket of hostile forces. Compounding the plight was the effect of Stalin's power struggle with Trotsky. In the wake of Chiang's success, Trotsky had accused Stalin of flawed leadership in China and violation of a cardinal Leninist principle that temporary agreement or even alliance with bour-

31. Chiang Yung-ching, 196-99; 202.
32. Chiang Yung-ching, 381.

geois elements was permissible, only if the Communists retained their organizational independence and freedom of action. In the KMT-CCP collaboration, Trotsky asked, where was the Communist freedom of action? To vindicate his China policy, Stalin badly needed a victory. On June 1, 1927, he sent a telegram to Borodin and the CCP asking them (1) to organize a new armed force of 20,000 Communist members and 50,000 workers and peasants; (2) to reorganize the KMT at Wuhan; (3) to increase the worker and peasant members in the KMT Central Committee; (4) to confiscate land at the local level without waiting for the orders of the Wuhan government; and (5) to set up a KMT special court to try the counterrevolutionaries without involving the Communists. It was, in effect, a call to raise a separate army and to transform the Wuhan regime into a Communist dictatorship under the intended puppet Wang Ching-wei. Realizing the impossibility of the order, Borodin and Ch'en Tu-hsiu asked Roy to execute it. On June 5, Roy revealed to Wang the telegram in an attempt to show his good will and complete trust. Not until then did Wang realize Stalin's real intention to destroy the KMT left wing and turn the Wuhan regime into a Communist puppetry. Yet he took no immediate action to stop the plot. Instead, he went to see Feng at Chengchow on June 6; Feng offered to mediate between Wang and Chiang.

On July 13, Borodin announced that in view of Wuhan's inability to cope with Feng's apostasy, the Communists would leave the regime, though not the KMT party. The CCP moved its headquarters to Kiukiang, Kiangsi, and stepped up its attack on Wuhan. Wang retaliated by announcing on July 14 that Communist members of the KMT guilty of violating Nationalist policies and ideology by word or by deed would be punitively sanctioned. Two days later he further announced that if the Communists left the Wuhan government, they might as well leave the KMT party, army, and all levels of government.

Although Wang seemed to have split with the Communists, he was still tolerant of them. There was no immediate liquidation, nor forcible dismissal of Communists from the KMT party and army. It was not until July 26 that the Wuhan presidium, under increasing Communist excoriation, ordered the ousting of Communists from KMT party and government posts unless they resigned from their CCP membership. They were also ordered to stop obstructing the National Revolution. Meanwhile, no KMT members were allowed to take membership in other parties. Under these adverse conditions, Borodin had no choice but to leave Wuhan on July 27, 1927, returning to Russia via Mongolia.

The final *coup de grâce* fell after the Nanchang Uprising of August 1, which was carried out by the Communists under the name of the Nationalist left wing. Wang finally ordered an all-out liquidation of the Communists and reorganization of the front organizations such as the General Labor Union, the Farmers' Association, the Women's Association, and the Merchants' Association.

Now that Nanking and Wuhan had both liquidated the Communists, the Western Hill faction at Shanghai proposed reconciliation. A special Central Committee was established at Nanking to exercise the power of the party headquarters, and on December 10 all differences between Wuhan and Nanking were formally resolved: Chiang was reappointed commander-in-chief of the National Revolutionary army, while Wang announced plans to go abroad.

The Wuhan government was dissolved in February 1928, although a branch Political Council continued to exist. With the domestic conflict finally resolved, Chiang resumed his Northern Expedition. Though blocked by Japanese troops at Tsinan in Shantung province, Chiang was able to surmount the obstacle. With the help of Feng Yü-hsiang and Yen Hsi-shan, he marched on Peking, then occupied by the Fengtien warlord Chang Tso-lin. Fleeing to Manchuria, Chang was killed in a train explosion at Huangkutun, near Mukden, engineered by the Japanese, on June 4, 1928.[33] His son, the Young Marshal Chang Hsüeh-liang, pledged allegiance to the Nationalist Government in July, and later, on December 31, he endorsed the Three People's Principles, "renounced" his regional control of Manchuria, and signified his support of the Nationalist Government by accepting its flag. As the year 1929 opened, China, or the greater part of it, was united by Chiang Kai-shek, after thirteen dismal years of civil anarchy. With Nanking as the new seat of government, the old capital Peking was renamed Peiping, Northern Peace.

In retrospect, one cannot but conclude that the KMT-CCP split testified to the complete failure of Stalin's policy in China. He had wanted to seize the proletarian hegemony within the KMT and squeeze out the rightists like "lemons," but little did he realize that the reorganized KMT

33. The mastermind of the plot was the Kwantung Army's Lt. Col. Kōmoto Daisaku, who wanted to forge a new political order in Manchuria out of the confusion. Tokyo was not informed of the plot in advance. When notified of the incident, Premier Tanaka sighed: "What fools! They [the Kwantung army] behave like children. They have no idea what the parent has to go through." Takehiko Yoshihashi, *Conspiracy at Mukden: The Rise of the Japanese Military* (New Haven, 1963), 50-51.

was no longer the loose, inefficient collectivity he once knew. The party structure had been revitalized by Borodin, and the party army had been trained with the assistance of Galen. Above all, Stalin failed to see that the CCP did not control the army. Moreover, Chiang's political acumen appeared to be at its height and he acted with speed and decisiveness, squeezing out the Communists before Stalin, thousands of miles away, had a chance to strike.[34] Commenting on the event a decade later, Mao Tse-tung told an American journalist that Borodin was indecisive, Roy was a dunce who talked but did not act, and Ch'en Tu-hsiu was guilty of rightist opportunism.[35]

THE DIPLOMACY OF NATIONALISM

The era of ideological and political ferment was also the age of surging nationalism in China. In diplomacy as well as in domestic front, Chinese behavior was dominated by a vigorous outburst of nationalistic sentiment. At the Washington Conference of 1921-22, the Chinese fought hard for independence and international respect, and in the post-conference period they struggled ceaselessly with the imperialist powers for tariff autonomy, revocation of extraterritoriality, and relinquishment of foreign concessions. Their intense drive to eliminate these national stigmas led to numerous clashes with foreign police and mercenaries, who reacted all too frequently with highhanded and needlessly harsh measures of repression, with the result that the decade of the 1920's was filled with what the Chinese outrageously called "cases of atrocious murder" (ts'an-an). Nationalism, the moving spirit of 19th-century Europe, had finally caught fire with the Chinese, and propelled them forward in a new mission of saving their country from the double scourge of imperialism and warlordism.

The Washington Conference. The failure of the Paris Peace Conference to settle the Shantung question equitably and to tackle many problems of the Pacific weighed heavily on the Americans. In his report to the American people, President Wilson condemned the European powers and Japan for their unjust verdict on Shantung and their insistence on maintaining their concessions and leased territories in China. His successor, President Harding, also attacked the Shantung decision as "the

34. Schwartz, 80.
35. Edgar Snow, *Red Star Over China* (New York, 1938), 165.

rape of the first great democracy of the Orient . . . the colossal blunder of all time." To rectify the wrongs and resolve the unfinished business of the Paris Conference, the United States began making plans in 1920 for another international meeting, which materialized in the Washington Conference of November 12, 1921-February 6, 1922. It was attended by nine powers which had interests in the Far East and the Pacific: Britain, the United States, France, Italy, Japan, China, Belgium, the Netherlands, and Portugal.

The Chinese delegation came with high expectations. It presented a nine-point proposal which asked the participants to honor China's territorial integrity and political independence, to desist from concluding treaties among themselves that would affect China, to respect her rights of neutrality in future wars, to remove all limitations on her political, jurisdictional and administrative freedom, to review all foreign special rights, immunities, and concessions in China, and to set time limits to her commitments. The proposal evoked a warm and sympathetic response from the American and European delegations. France and Britain offered to relinquish their leased territories of Kwangchow Bay and Weihaiwei respectively, provided other powers would do the same. However, Japan's strenuous opposition to discussing leased territories and concessions obtained before 1920 on the ground that they did not properly belong to the agenda absolved them from the commitments while keeping Chinese good will.

Under the sponsorship of the United States, the Chinese proposal was consolidated into four general principles which ultimately found expression in a Nine-Power Treaty of February 6, 1922. The signatories agreed to respect China's territorial integrity and political independence, to renounce further attempts to seek spheres of influence, to respect her neutrality in time of war, and to honor equal commercial opportunity for all. Separately, the powers agreed to close on January 1, 1923, all foreign post offices in China except those in the leased territories, and to let China increase the import tariff from the actual 3.5 per cent to 5 per cent ad valorem.

As regards Shantung, direct negotiations between the Chinese and Japanese took place under the good offices of the United States and Britain. World public opinion, particularly official and unofficial American pressure, obliged Japan to relinquish Shantung while retaining some economic rights. She was allowed to keep certain properties in Shantung needed by the Japanese community there, such as consular buildings, public schools, cemeteries and shrines. Japanese nationals were to be appointed advisers in various utilities, stockyards, and vital enterprises; they were also to serve for five years as the chief engineer, the traffic manager, and the chief accountant of the Tsingtao-Tsinan Railway, which the Chinese were to purchase with a Japanese loan. All in all, China accomplished most of her objectives although she did not score a clean sweep.

Elsewhere in the Conference, two important international agreements were concluded. By the Four-Power Treaty of December 13, 1921, intended to replace the Anglo-Japanese Alliance, Britain, the United States, Japan, and France agreed to settle disputes in the Pacific by peaceful consultation. By the Five-Power Naval Treaty of February 5, 1922, these four powers and Italy agreed to maintain a military *status quo* in the Far East and refrain from building new fortifications and naval installations east of the 110th meridian east longitude. The naval ratio of capital ships of the five powers was fixed at 5 for Britain and the United States each, 3 for Japan, and 1.75 each for France and Italy. This ratio entitled Britain and the United States to 15 capital ships of 525,000 tons each, Japan 9 ships of 315,000 tons, and France and Italy 175,000 tons apiece.

On the surface this naval ratio seemed to favor Britain and the United States at the expense of Japan, but it actually benefited the latter, too, in several ways. For one thing, both Britain and the United States maintained two fleets in the Atlantic and in the Pacific, whereas Japan maintained only one fleet in the Pacific. Moreover, at the time of the treaty the Japanese naval strength was 50 per cent of that of the United States; the ratio of 5:3 actually allowed Japan a 10 per cent increase in sea power.[36] All in all, the naval treaty assured Japan of a dominant position in the western Pacific and relative security from British or American attack. Nonetheless, the treaty was denounced by Japanese militarists and extremists as a national disgrace, and was used by them as an issue to overthrow the civilian party government later.

Upsurge of Chinese Nationalism. The Nine-Power Treaty was basically an expression of good will on the part of the signatories toward China's *future* development, but it lacked enforcement power. It neither invalidated the existing privileges of the powers in China, nor bound them to defend the Open Door or Chinese independence by force, and as such it did little to alleviate China's sense of injury and self-respect. For-

36. Tang Tsou, *America's Failure in China, 1941-50* (Chicago, 1963), 17.

eigners continued to bestride the Chinese scene with haughty arrogance, and filled high posts in the Chinese Maritime Customs, the Salt Revenue, and the Postal Service. Foreign settlements and municipal concessions existed as usual, and Chinese in the Shanghai International Settlement paid taxes without representation on the Municipal Council. The Japanese still ran the Southern Manchurian Railway and used it as an instrument of encroachment, and the British continued to dominate South China trade through Hong Kong. To Chinese patriots, these humiliating signs of imperialism were a constant irritant and a reminder of China's semicolonial status, which should no longer be endured. Fired with nationalism, they set out to "save their country" (*chiu-kuo*) from imperialism, capitalistic exploitation, and warlordism. In this endeavor, the young students and the growing labor class in the large cities played a major role; they vowed to eliminate these foreign and domestic evils by force if necessary.

Foremost among the nationalistic outbreaks was the "May 30th Incident" of 1925, which had its origin in a Chinese workers' strike in February of that year in protest of low wages at a Japanese cotton weaving mill in Shanghai. Mediation by the Chamber of Commerce and other civic bodies resulted in a preliminary settlement, which the Japanese owner subsequently rejected. The workers went on a second strike, and on May 15 sent eight representatives to negotiate with the management. The confrontation ended in a violent clash, resulting in the killing of one worker[37] and wounding of the other seven. The British-dominated Shanghai Municipal Council not only did not persecute the Japanese who opened fire, but arrested a number of Chinese workers on charges of disturbing peace and order. On May 22, a large body of college students and workers held a public memorial service for the slain and engaged in roadside speeches attacking the Japanese owner. The arrest of many of them by the police incited a 3,000-student demonstration on Nanking Road on May 30, to protest British and Japanese atrocities. At this critical point, a British police lieutenant[38] ordered his men to open fire, killing eleven Chinese and wounding several dozens. In addition, some fifty students were arrested.

This "May 30th Atrocious Incident" (*Wu-san ts'an-an*) provoked nationwide protests, strikes, and boycotts by students, workers, and merchants alike. Not until December, when the British police inspector-

37. Ku Cheng-hung.
38. Everson.

general and his lieutenant were fired and the Municipal Council paid an indemnity of Ch$75,000 to the deceased and the wounded, did the public anger subside.

Following the May 30th incident, a rash of nationalistic agitation broke out in different parts of the country, and clashes with the imperialists occurred in many places: (1) the Hankow incident of June 10-11, 1925, resulted in the killing of 14 and wounding of 100 Chinese by British and Japanese militia; (2) the Shaki-Shameen incident at Canton on June 23 caused the deaths of 52 and the wounding of 117 Chinese by Anglo-French soldiers, precipitating a general strike by Chinese workers in Hong Kong; (3) the Nanking incident of July 31 resulted in the loss of four Chinese workers in a British factory; and (4) the Chungking incident of July 2 involved the killing of four Chinese by British sailors. A number of other incidents also occurred in Ningpo, Amoy, Chinkiang, and Wan-hsien, Szechwan.

Amid these outbursts, the Chinese in the Shanghai International Settlement strenuously protested "taxation without representation." In 1926 the foreign voters conceded with a resolution permitting three Chinese to be elected to the Municipal Council, which had hitherto been dominated by nine foreigners. The offer was not accepted until the Chinese membership was increased to five in 1930, while the foreign membership remained the same.

In other areas of anti-imperialistic activity, the Chinese succeeded in recovering a number of foreign municipal concessions and to a large extent the tariff autonomy (see next chapter). By the end of the 1920's, the nationalistic revolution had made considerable progress: foreign imperialism had been dealt a severe blow and domestic warlordism considerably reduced by the Northern Expedition.

THE NANKING GOVERNMENT

With the successful completion of the Northern Expedition in 1928, the military phase of Dr. Sun's three-stage revolution was completed, and the second stage of political tutelage was due to be introduced. On October 3, 1928, the KMT Central Executive Committee adopted a provisional constitution called "An Outline of Political Tutelage" (*Hsün-cheng kang-ling*), which legalized the party's guidance of the government. The KMT was entrusted with the double duty of tutoring the people in the exercise of their four rights—election, recall, initiative, and referendum—and of supervising the government's exercise of its five powers—executive, legislative, judicial, control, and examination. The highest organ of the party was the National Party Congress, which when not in session delegated its powers to the Central Executive Committee, which in turn maintained a Standing Committee—the real seat of power. In juxtaposition with the Central Executive Committee was the Central Supervisory Committee, which was concerned with matters of discipline and supervision of the finances.

The dominant feature of the government was its five-yüan structure[39] under the president of the republic. Of the five the most important was the Executive Yüan (*Hsing-cheng yüan*), the highest organ of administration commonly dubbed the "cabinet." It consisted of ten ministries,[40] each headed by a minister and two vice-ministers, and a number of special commissions in charge of national reconstruction, overseas affairs, Tibetan-Mongolian affairs, etc. Contrary to Western practice, the Executive Yüan was not responsible to the legislative branch of government, but to the party and the president of the republic.

The Legislative Yüan (*Li-fa yüan*) was composed of 49 to 99 members chosen for two years on a more or less geographical basis. It was not a counterpart of the Western parliament or congress, but was essentially a law-drafting organization which translated the legislative principles adopted by the KMT Central Executive Committee into law. Its duties included deliberations on laws, budget, amnesty, declaration of war, and treaties of peace.

The Judiciary Yüan (*Ssu-fa yüan*) was the highest judicial organ of state and was in charge of interpreting laws and orders, initiating pardons, reprieves, and restitution of civil rights, and coordinating the court systems. However, it could not interfere with the court decisions.

The Examination Yüan (*K'ao-shih yüan*) was made a separate branch of the government largely because of the tradition of the civil service examinations. Included under its administration were two structures: an Examination Commission which conducted different types of government examinations, and a Ministry of Personnel which took charge of civil service ratings.

The Control Yüan (*Chien-ch'a yüan*) approximated in function the old Censorate. It was composed of 19 to 29 members who supervised

39. Created on recommendation of Hu Han-min in accordance with Dr. Sun's "Outline of National Reconstruction."
40. Internal affairs, foreign affairs, war, finance, agriculture and mining, industry and commerce, education, communication, railway, and hygiene.

government operations, audited the budget, and impeached derelict officials.

Each of these five yüan was headed by a president and a vice president who were usually senior members of the KMT. The initial slate of key appointments in the National Government was as follows:

> President of the republic: Chiang Kai-shek (Chiang Chung-cheng).
> Executive Yüan: T'an Yen-k'ai, president; Feng Yü-hsiang, vice-president.
> Legislative Yüan: Hu Han-min, president; Lin Shen, vice-president.
> Judiciary Yüan: Wang Ch'ung-hui, president; Chang Chi, vice-president.
> Examination Yüan: Tai Chi-t'ao, president; Sun Fo (Sun K'o), vice-president.
> Control Yüan: Ts'ai Yüan-p'ei, president; Ch'en Kuo-fu, vice-president.

The new government was dedicated to the fulfillment of Dr. Sun's legacy—The Three People's Principles, the Five-Power Constitution, the Fundamentals of National Reconstruction, and Sun's deathbed admonition: "The revolution is not yet complete; comrades must strive on!" Pledging to carry on the unfinished work of revolution, it vowed externally to fight for the complete abolition of the unequal treaties and win for China a position of equality with the leading powers, and internally to initiate democratic reconstruction and social reforms. Hopefully, by the end of the Period of Political Tutelage, which was fixed to last six years from 1929, the country would be ready for the introduction of a constitution.

The challenge of the threefold revolution—nationalistic, democratic, and social—was indeed great, and the responsibility of the government heavy. It remained to be seen whether its ability was equal to its task.

FURTHER READING

Borg, Dorothy, *American Policy and the Chinese Revolution, 1925-1928* (New York, 1947).

Brandt, Conrad, *Stalin's Failure in China, 1924-1927* (Cambridge, Mass., 1958).

———, Benjamin Schwartz, and John K. Fairbank, A *Documentary History of Chinese Communism* (London, 1952).

Chapman, H. Owen, *The Chinese Revolution, 1925-27* (London, 1928).

Ch'en, Kung-po, *The Communist Movement in China* (New York, 1966).

Ch'en, Jerome, "The Left Wing Kuomintang—a Definition," *Bulletin of the School of Oriental and African Studies*, University of London, XXV: Part 3: 557-76 (1962).

Chiang, Kai-shek, *China's Destiny* (New York, 1947).

———, *Soviet Russia in China: A Summing Up at Seventy* (New York, 1957).

Chiang, Yung-ching 蔣永敬, *Pao-lo-t'ing yü Wu-han cheng-ch'üan* 鮑羅廷與武漢政權 (Borodin and the Wuhan regime), (Taipei, 1963).

Ch'ien, Tuan-sheng, *The Government and Politics of China* (Cambridge, Mass., 1950), chapters 6-8.

Ho, Kan-chih, *A History of the Modern Chinese Revolution* (Peking, 1959).

Houn, Franklin W., *A Short History of Chinese Communism* (Englewood Cliffs, 1967), chapters 1-2.

Hu, Ch'iao-mu, *Thirty Years of the Communist Party of China* (Peking, 1951).

Isaacs, Harold R., *The Tragedy of Chinese Revolution* (Stanford, 1951).

King, Wunsz, *China at the Washington Conference, 1921-1922* (New York, 1963).

Landis, Richard B., "The Origins of Whampoa Graduates Who Served in the Northern Expedition," *Studies on Asia*, 149-63 (1964).

Linebarger, Paul M. A., *The Political Doctrines of Sun Yat-sen* (Baltimore, 1937).

MacFarquhar, Roderick L., "The Whampoa Military Academy," *Papers on China*, Harvard University, Vol. 9 (1955).

Malraux, André, *Man's Fate*, tr. by H. M. Chevalier (New York, 1934).

Meisner, Maurice, *Li Ta-chao and the Origins of Chinese Marxism* (Cambridge, Mass., 1967).

North, Robert C., *Kuomintang and Chinese Communist Elites* (Stanford, 1952).

———, *Moscow and Chinese Communists* (Stanford, 1953).

———, and Xenia J. Eudin, *M. N. Roy's Mission to China* (Berkeley, 1963).

Roy, M. N., *My Experience in China* (Calcutta, 1945).

———, *Revolution and Counter-Revolution in China* (Calcutta, 1946)

Schwartz, Benjamin I., *Chinese Communism and the Rise of Mao* (Cambridge, Mass., 1958).

Snow, Edgar, *Red Star over China* (New York, 1938).

T'ang, Leang-li, *The Inner History of the Chinese Revolution* (London, 1920).

———, *The Suppression of Communist Banditry in China* (Shanghai, 1934).

Trotsky, Leon, *Problems of the Chinese Revolution*, third edition (New York, 1966).

Tsui, Shu-ch'in, "The Influence of the Canton-Moscow Entente upon Sun Yat-sen's Revolutionary Tactics," *The Chinese Social and Political Science Review*, 20:1:101-39 (April 1936).

Whiting, Allen S., *Soviet Policies in China 1917-1924* (New York, 1954).

Wilbur, C. Martin, and Julie Lien-ying How (eds.), *Documents on Communism, Nationalism, and Soviet Advisers in China, 1918-1927: Papers Seized in the 1927 Peking Raid* (New York, 1956).

Willoughby, W. W., *China at the Conference* (Baltimore, 1922).

Wu, Hsiang-hsiang 吳相湘, *O-ti ch'in-lüeh Chung-kuo shih* 俄帝侵略中國史 (A history of the Russian imperialist aggression in China), (Taipei, 1957), Vol. 2, chapters 1-2.

Wu, Tien-wei, "Chiang Kai-shek's March Twentieth Coup d'état of 1926," *The Journal of Asian Studies*, XXVII:3:585-602 (May 1968).

Yoshihashi, Takehiko, *Conspiracy at Mukden: The Rise of the Japanese Military* (New Haven, 1963).

23

The Nationalist Government:

A Decade of Challenges, 1928-37

From its inception in 1928 to the outbreak of the Sino-Japanese War in 1937, the Nationalist government at Nanking hardly enjoyed a day of peace from domestic squabbles and foreign aggression. No sooner had it been established as the legal government of China than it found itself challenged by dissident politicians within the KMT and by the rebellious "new warlords." Compounding the disorder were the two larger threats of rising Communist opposition in the southeast and Japanese aggression in Manchuria, Shanghai, and North China. The decade in question was indeed fraught with "internal troubles and external invasion" (*nei-yu wai-huan*), as the traditional phrase has it. Partly because of the overwhelming circumstances, the Nationalists failed to carry out the much-needed social and economic reforms to alleviate the plight of the peasant—a negligence which was to have far-reaching consequences a decade later. Yet, in spite of all odds the government was able to score some progress in modernization—particularly in the fields of finance, communication, education, defense, and light industry. While a definitive account of this Nationalist decade has yet to be written, pending the opening of new archival materials, the key developments of the period can be traced with some perspective and accuracy.

THE "NEW WARLORDS" AND THE DISSIDENT POLITICIANS

The unification achieved by the Northern Expedition was more apparent than real, for although many of the northern warlords had been wiped

633

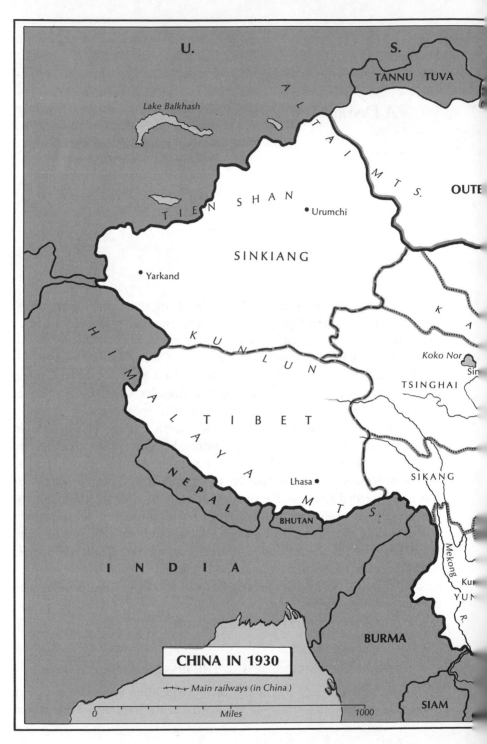

CHINA IN 1930

╪╪╪╪ Main railways (in China)

0   Miles   1000

S. R.

Lake Baikal

HEILUNGKIANG

Amur R.

Ulan
Bator

Harbin

MONGOLIA

MANCHURIA

KIRIN

Vladivostok

MONGOLIA

CHAHAR

JEHOL

LIAONING

Mukden

Kalgan

Peking

Tientsin

Dairen (Jap.)

KOREA

JAPAN

SUIYUAN

HOPEH

Taiyuan

SHANSI

SHANTUNG

Tsingtao

nchow

Yellow R.

SHENSI

Kaifeng

KIANGSU

Sian

HONAN

Nanking

ANHWEI

Shanghai

engtu

Yangtze R.

HUPEH

Hankow

CHEKIANG

CHWAN

Ichang

gking

Nanchang

Wenchow

Changsha

KWEICHOW

HUNAN

KIANGSI

weiyang

FUKIEN

Foochow

Kweilin

Pacific

KWANGSI

KWANGTUNG

Amoy

TAIWAN
(FORMOSA)

Canton

Swatow

Macao
(Port.)

Hong Kong (Br.)

Ocean

NCH

OCHINA

HAINAN

PHILIPPINE IS.

RYUKYU IS.

635

out, a number of others had maintained themselves by nominally supporting the Expedition. In his eagerness to achieve a national unification, Chiang Kai-shek negotiated with them for a mutual accommodation, granting them appointments which confirmed their semi-independent regional status while receiving in return their recognition of Nanking as the central government of China.

Some of these warlords were in fact quite "progressive" in outlook, promoting modernization in their own jurisdiction. But they lacked the sense of national commitment that would make them surrender their semi-independence. Cooperation with Nanking was possible as long as their interests did not collide; if they did the warlords would act as they saw fit or perhaps challenge Nanking to a contest. Dubbed the "New Warlords," they maintained their regional power bases as follows:

1. Li Tsung-jen and Li Chi-ch'en headed the Kwangsi Clique which dominated the provinces of Kwangsi, Kwangtung, Hunan, and Hupeh.
2. Feng Yü-hsiang and his "National People's Army" occupied a preponderant position in the northern and northwestern provinces of Shantung, Honan, Shensi, Kansu, Chinghai, and Ninghsia.
3. The Young Marshal Chang Hsüeh-liang controlled the Northeast (Manchuria) and Jehol.
4. Yen Hsi-shan had established a strong base in Shansi, reaching out into Hopeh, Suiyuan, and Chahar.

Each of them maintained a large army for territorial aggrandizement as well as for self-protection; collectively, they drained a good portion of the country's meager resources desperately needed for national reconstruction. Although they agreed in principle to military reduction, they refused to cooperate in August 1928, when Nanking proposed to cut the total number of troops in the country from two million to 800,000. In March 1929 the KMT Third National Congress again called for the amalgamation of splinter military groups into one national command, the reorganization of all troops into one national army, and the centralization of local financial administrations to prevent the provinces from siphoning off receipts that legally belonged to the central government. The new warlords saw in these resolutions nothing but artful devices to reduce their power and demanded that Nanking take the first step in military cut. But Chiang considered his Whampoa-trained staff and troops the backbone of a new national army and insisted that any cuts should start with the provincial forces. The obstinance of the one side merely reinforced the intransigence of the other and the resolutions of the Congress were rendered inoperative from the beginning.[1]

Quite apart from the problem of the new warlords, the KMT was plagued with factional strifes. The right wing, led by party elder Hu Han-min and the West Hill group,[2] was in constant conflict with the left wing headed by Wang Ching-wei.[3] Meanwhile Chiang Kai-shek, the new strong man holding the military power, represented a third force. Junior to both Hu and Wang in party status, Chiang charted his course alternately favoring each with his support according to the dictates of political necessity and expediency. In his new government at Nanking, Chiang collaborated with Hu, who was made president of the Legislative Yüan, while Wang and his left-wing followers were out of office. The latter group retaliated by accusing Chiang of betraying the principles and ideas of Sun, and demanded a reorganization of the KMT in the spirit of the 1924 manifesto—hence their nickname "The Reorganizationists." Being the "out" group, they attacked the government and not infrequently formed alliances with the new warlords against Chiang.

Though the military reorganization was nipped in the bud, there was considerable restlessness among the new warlords, especially the Kwangsi group. It should be remembered that after the dissolution of the Wuhan regime in 1928, a branch Political Council continued to exist at Wuhan under the chairmanship of Li Tsung-jen, who had penetrated into Central China from his home base in Kwangsi during the last stage of the Northern Expedition. The Council remained hostile toward Nanking, and in February 1929 dismissed the governor of Hunan,[4] who was loyal to the central government. When Nanking overruled the order and initiated an investigation, the Kwangsi warlords took it as a personal affront and a prelude to attack. After rapidly transferring troops to Changsha, the capital of Hunan, and after receiving support from another Kwangsi leader, Pai Ch'ung-hsi, the Wuhan Political Council formally rebelled. Although this "Hunan Revolt" was quickly crushed and the Political Council abolished, the core of the rebel forces escaped destruction and Kwangsi remained a semi-independent base of Li and Pai.

No sooner had the Hunan incident been resolved than another revolt broke out in May 1929 under the sponsorship of Feng Yü-hsiang. Assum-

1. Ch'ien Tuan-sheng, *The Government and Politics of China* (Cambridge, Mass., 1950), 101.
2. Including Wu Chih-hui, Chang Chi, Sun Fo, Lin Shen, and Tai Chi-t'ao.
3. Including Madame Sun Yat-sen and Eugene Ch'en.
4. Lu Ti-p'ing.

ing the title of commander-in-chief of a 300,000-man "Party-protecting National Salvation army of the Northwest," Feng attacked the government forces and destroyed sections of the Peiping-Hankow and Lung-Hai railways. Although Nationalist counterattack, coupled with "advice" from two of his lieutenants,[5] forced Feng into "retirement," twenty-seven of his generals jointly denounced Nanking and stirred up yet another rebellion in October 1929. It was not until December that Chiang, after mobilizing 300,000 troops, was able to clear Honan and Hopeh of rebel forces.

At this juncture, a strange alliance slowly emerged between the dissident KMT politicians and several of the new warlords. In February 1930 Wang Ching-wei, still abroad, condemned the KMT Third Congress's resolutions on military and financial reorganization, and evoked a sympathetic response from Yen Hsi-shan. Yen sent troops into Peiping and Tientsin, and encouraged by Li Tsung-jen declared himself commander-in-chief of all the armed forces of China, with Feng Yü-hsiang as his deputy. Paradoxically, they received support from both the KMT extreme right and left—the West Hill group and the Reorganizationists —who were at odds with Chiang. The fragile peace could not withstand the rising tide of belligerency and in May a large-scale civil war erupted in Central China.

Wang Ching-wei hurried home to lend his support to the antigovernment forces. On July 13, 1930, he called an "Expanded Session" (of the KMT Central Executive Committee) at Peiping which resolved to create a separatist regime and another KMT organization, with Yen as the chairman of a seven-man presidium, in open rivalry with Nanking. Fortunately for Chiang, the Young Marshal Chang Hsüeh-liang disapproved of Wang's scheme and quickly sent his troops to Peiping and Tientsin, driving the separatist regime to seek refuge at Taiyuan, Yen's home base. Meanwhile, Chiang's forces had scored victories in Hupeh and Hunan, forcing Yen and Feng to announce their "retirement."

With the quick exit of his "Expanded Session" at Peiping, Wang Ching-wei hastily departed for Hong Kong to continue his opposition. When Nanking called a KMT national congress to deliberate on the provisional constitution for the Tutelage Period (*Hsün-cheng yüeh-fa*), Wang, along with Eugene Ch'en and others, protested with the creation of another separatist government at Canton in May 1931. In their demand for the resignation of Chiang, they received support from General

5. Han Fu-chü and Shih Yu-san.

Shih Yu-san in Hopeh, who provoked a new civil war. Once again, the Young Marshal came to Nanking's aid, and their combined forces dealt a crushing blow to Shih in July, forcing him to "retire." But the Canton regime continued its opposition. However, military operations by the government were suspended in September, due to Japanese invasion of Manchuria (see next section). In the following month, representatives of Nanking and Canton met to explore the possibility of reconciliation in the face of the foreign crisis. An agreement was reached whereby a Fourth KMT National Congress would be called simultaneously at the two capitals. Confronted by a split government and hostile public opinion, Chiang resigned in December as president of the Nanking government. He was replaced by the mild elder statesman, Lin Shen, while Sun Fo (Dr. Sun's son) became the head of the Executive Yüan. With this reorganization, the Canton regime agreed to dissolve itself. The new leaders now pleaded with Chiang and Wang to compose their differences in the interest of the country, and the two of them met at Hangchow and went to Nanking jointly to symbolize a *rapprochement*. On January 25, 1932, Sun Fo resigned the presidency of the Executive Yüan in favor of Wang, while Chiang accepted the chairmanship of the Military Commission. It is noteworthy that the Wang-Chiang reconciliation was possible only because the latter had split with Hu Han-min in March 1931.[6]

The political realignment restored some peace within the KMT, but not the country. The year 1933 witnessed another insurrection in Fukien, engineered by the commanders[7] of the Cantonese Nineteenth Route army, which had heroically fought the Japanese at Shanghai the year before (see next section). This army had been transferred to Fukien to fight the Communists after the Shanghai truce in May 1932, but once there, its commanders were won over by Communist propaganda and by ambitious southern politicians.[8] The army leaders created a "People's Revolutionary Government" at Foochow, renamed their forces the "People's Revolutionary Army," and in November 1933 rebelled against the central government. They called for war with Japan and collaboration with the Communists and the Soviet Union. Despite its leftist orientation, the movement failed to receive aid from the Communists who themselves were hard pressed by the Nationalists (section below). Thus deprived of critical support, the Fukien insurrection was suppressed in Jan-

6. Over the question of the provisional tutelage constitution, which Chiang wanted but which Hu insisted was unnecessary.
7. Generals Ts'ai T'ing-k'ai and Chiang Kuang-nai.
8. Li Chi-ch'en and Ch'en Ming-shu.

uary 1934, and the Nineteenth Route army was reorganized as the Seventh National army.

Barely two years later, another mutiny broke out in the two southern provinces of Kwangtung and Kwangsi. In June 1936, under the pretext of fighting the Japanese, Ch'en Chi-t'ang and Li Tsung-jen, leaders of the two provinces respectively, established a "Southwestern Political Council," with Ch'en as commander of the "Federated Japan-Resisting Patriots' Armies" and Li as his deputy. Boldly, they advanced their troops northward to challenge the central authority. Disaffection set in, however, and several of Ch'en's generals[9] were persuaded by Nanking's agents that resistance against Japan could not be effective unless it was directed by the central government. When they defected to Nanking along with nine Cantonese airplanes in July 1936, the fighting spirit of the Kwangtung wing of the rebellion was broken and Ch'en left for Hong Kong. Having resolved half of the "Incident of the Two Kwangs," the government was in a better position to deal with Kwangsi through the combined use of military pressure and sugar-coated persuasion. A new National Defense Committee was created to include Li and other rebel leaders in order to symbolize Nanking's acceptance of their demand for fighting the Japanese. On their part, the Kwangsi leaders agreed to stop military operations on the condition that they retain special privileges in provincial military, political, and financial affairs. They received nominal appointments from Nanking to confirm their status as provincial authorities, but Kwangsi remained outside the "direct" control of the central government. Nonetheless, the myth of national unity was preserved intact.

From the above survey it is clear that throughout its first decade of existence, the Nanking government was seriously beset with internal strife and civil wars. Though it survived these crises, its energy and resources, which could otherwise have been devoted to the urgent task of national reconstruction, had been much spent. The fate of the government would have been very different had it not been for the help it twice received from the Young Marshal. Yet in transferring troops to North China, Chang Hsüeh-liang left Manchuria in a vulnerable position. Of this, the Japanese were quick to take notice.

JAPANESE AGGRESSION IN MANCHURIA

Manchuria, the rich Northeast of China, is noted for its abundant agricultural products and mineral resources. Japan had coveted the area ever since her defeat of China in 1895, and her ambitions were further

9. Such as Generals Yü Han-mou and Li Han-hun.

aroused by the acquisition of the former tsarist rights in Manchuria after the Russo-Japanese War. With the annexation of Korea in 1910, many Japanese came to regard Manchuria as the next "logical" target for conquest. Three times—in 1912, 1916, and 1928—they schemed to foment a "Manchuria-Mongolia Autonomous Movement," and although these attempts failed, the idea that "to conquer the world it is necessary to conquer China first, and to conquer China it is necessary to conquer Manchuria and Mongolia first,"[10] gained increasing momentum.

Japanese activists generally assumed that chaos and disorder in China would facilitate their scheme; hence any attempt at unification had to be prevented. This explains their military intervention in Shantung in April 1928, and when that venture failed to block the Northern Expedition, their intense effort to dissuade the Young Marshal from joining forces with Chiang Kai-shek. Three times in the summer of 1928 Premier Tanaka's agents prevailed upon him not to collaborate with the "shaky" and "Communist-tinged" Nanking government, and pledged that Japan would extend military and financial aid should Chiang attack him. Under extreme pressure, the Young Marshal agreed to postpone decision for three months, but in the end he spurned the Japanese overture by hoisting the Nationalist flag over all Manchuria on December 29, 1928, to signal his acceptance of the central government.

Japanese disappointment was intensified by concern over the rising tide of nationalism in China which was creating the prospect of a united country. Japan's prestige and trade were hurt by numerous anti-Japanese demonstrations and "don't buy Japanese goods" movements in various parts of China, while in Manchuria the Young Marshal was rapidly developing an air force, a naval base, and railways competing with existing Japanese lines. Feeling threatened, Japanese residents in Manchuria urged their government to take a strong stand, and a number of the more active ones, particularly the lower echelon personnel of the Southern Manchurian Railway, organized a Manchurian Youth League (*Manshū Seinen Renmei*) in 1928 to promote a "Manchuria-Mongolia Autonomous State." In this, they received the sympathy and encouragement of the Kwantung army.

The Kwantung army was something of an anomaly in the Japanese

10. Often attributed to the "Tanaka Memorial" of 1927, which actually did not exist; however, the ideas contained in the alleged memorial were quite common among the Japanese. In fact, the Dairen Conference of 1927 adopted resolutions that contained these ideas. Cf. Liang Ching-tun, *Chiu-i-pa shih-pien shih-shu* (A historical account of the September 18, 1931, Incident), (Hong Kong, 1964), 2-3, 197, 199, 218.

military establishment. Its origin can be traced to the period immediately after Japan's defeat of Russia in 1905. As part of the peace settlement, Japan took over the Russian leasehold in the Liaotung Peninsula and tsarist railway and economic rights in Manchuria. In 1906, the Japanese renamed the southern base of Liaotung, including Port Arthur and Dairen, the Kwantung Leased Territory, to be administered by a governor-general whose jurisdiction included the railway zone in Manchuria. For thirteen years, the position of governor-general was held by a general who simultaneously served as commander of the local army, but in 1919 the office of the governor-general became a civilian administration, with a separate Kwantung Army Command to guard the leased territory and the Manchurian railway zone. Following the Russian trick of posing as "railway guards," the Kwantung army firmly established itself in Manchuria—so firmly, in fact, that it moved its headquarters from Port Arthur to Mukden in 1928. Virtually free from home control, the Kwantung army enjoyed a semiautonomous status and took upon itself the task of wresting Manchuria from China.[11]

This self-appointed mission of the Kwantung army received a new impetus with the arrival of Lt. Colonel Ishiwara Kanji in October 1928 and Colonel Itagaki Seishirō in July 1929. These two strategists quickly became the ideological and political mentors of the Kwantung army, relegating the commanding general and the chief of staff to nominal leadership. Itagaki and Ishiwara openly advocated the occupation of Manchuria, which they proposed to use as a bulwark against a Soviet southern advance and as a supply base in the event of war with the United States. Moreover, Manchuria's vast territory and natural wealth could alleviate the crowded conditions and limited resources of Japan, provide business opportunities, and relieve the unemployment problem at home. To justify the seizure, they argued that the thirty million suffering people of Manchuria were eagerly awaiting Japanese liberation from the misrule of warlords and greedy bureaucrats.[12] Although their long-range deadline was 1936, they considered 1931 propitious for action. China was deeply mired in domestic turmoil and natural disaster. The Nanking government had been entangled in one civil strife after another, and the politician Wang Ching-wei had twice attempted to establish a rival regime. The Communist threat loomed large, and the central government was involved in

11. Sadako N. Ogata, *Defiance in Manchuria: The Making of Japanese Foreign Policy, 1931-1932* (Berkeley, 1964), 3-4; Takehiko Yoshihashi, *Conspiracy at Mukden*, 37, 130-31.
12. Ogata, 42-45.

a succession of costly campaigns (next section). Aggravating the plight were the devastating floods of the Grand Canal and the Yangtze and Huai rivers, which drowned 140,000 and left 250,000 homeless in the ten central provinces.

Internationally, the situation was no less favorable. The Western powers, hard hit by the Depression, were too involved with domestic problems to block Japanese aggression, and the League of Nations was too powerless to intervene. The Nine-Power Treaty of 1922 which guaranteed China's political and territorial integrity, and the Kellogg-Briand (Paris) Pact of 1928 which outlawed war as an instrument of national policy, had all but become mere paper shorn of the power to enforce their idealistic goals. The fact that neither the League nor any Western power intervened in the Sino-Soviet clash in 1929-30 over the control of the Chinese Eastern Railway was sufficient proof of the weakness of international sanction. The Kwantung army believed that it could seize Manchuria with impunity.

Within Japan itself, ominous signs of economic and social distress were appearing even before depression hit the country. Industry, which had undergone vast expansion in the 1920's, was suffering the effects of overproduction, which caused business failures and rising unemployment. In 1927, thirty-five banks including the large Bank of Taiwan went out of business, and between July 1929 and June 1930 some 660,000 men were thrown out of work.[13] Furthermore, the world-wide Depression had sharply reduced Japan's trade with the United States, Britain, and China. Capitalizing on the economic and social unrest thus generated, many expansionists advocated that the conquest of Manchuria would lift the country out of its predicament, and they received the endorsement of the army and the zaibatsu (financial-industrial overlords).

Until the 1920's the militarists had traditionally remained aloof from politics. But with the election of General Tanaka Giichi as president of the Seiyūkai (Political Friends Association) in 1925 and his assumption of the premiership in 1927, the military leaders emerged as a powerful force in national policy at the expense of party government. They accused the civilian leaders of incompetency as shown in their acceptance of the "humiliating" naval ratio of 5:5:3 at the Washington Conference (1922) and in their ratification of the London Naval Agreement (1930) which reaffirmed that ratio. They criticized, ridiculed, and bullied the civilian government, and loudly clamored for a positive policy that would

13. Yoshihashi, 12, 116.

lead to Japan's domination of China and ultimately the world. The first step, they insisted, was the conquest of Manchuria. Inasmuch as 75 per cent of foreign investment there was already Japanese, the *zaibatsu* also favored intensified activity, although they preferred peaceful penetration to outright military conquest.

Tokyo's military authorities had set the spring of 1932 as the target date for the occupation of Manchuria, but the Kwantung army would not wait. Their sense of urgency was in some measure precipitated by the possibility of the routine reassignment of Itagaki and Ishiwara in the summer of 1931. In June, Major Hanaya Tadashi, dispatched to Tokyo to plead for an immediate invasion of Manchuria, succeeded in winning the approval of the most influential members of the military establishment; their decision, however, was kept secret. In August the newly appointed commander of the Kwantung army, General Honjō Shigeru, and his chief of staff, Miyake Mitsuharu, were invited to attend a second closed conference. Conspicuously absent were the minister of war, General Minami Jirō, and the chief of the General Staff, Kanaya Hanzo—the two men directly responsible to the emperor. At the conference it was decided that the two heavy field guns at Port Arthur were to be moved to Mukden to facilitate the breeching of the city wall, and that the Japanese commander in Korea was to reinforce the Kwantung army once hostilities broke out. Rumor was soon rife in Tokyo that a Manchurian expedition would take place in August or September.

During the summer of 1931, two incidents occurring in Manchuria played into the hand of the Kwantung army. The first, in July, was a clash over property rights between Chinese farmers and Korean settlers at Wan-pao-shan near Changchun, resulting in the killing of hundreds of Chinese by Japanese police. The second was the murder in August of Captain Nakamura Shintarō and three companions while traveling in disguise to disaffect the Inner Mongolians. These incidents brought the already overcharged atmosphere of Manchuria to a new pitch, and the Kwantung army, anxious to strike, began to hold nightly exercises. Itagaki and Ishiwara secretly set September 28 as the date for a railway explosion plot to provoke an incident that would give Japan an excuse to occupy Manchuria.

Worried about the military's unruly behavior, the Japanese emperor repeatedly urged prudence and restraint on September 10 and 11. On the 15th, Minister of War Minami dispatched General Tatekawa Yoshisugu of the General Staff to Mukden to "caution the Kwantung army against rash action and to warn that support could not be expected from the government." When word of this mission was secretly transmitted to the Kwantung army by the Second Division of the General Staff, Itagaki and Ishiwara abruptly decided to advance the target date and schedule the incident before the emissary could deliver his restraining message. Arriving in Mukden on September 18, Tatekawa was immediately whisked off to a lavish dinner party by the wily Itagaki, and then wined and dined into a state of complete intoxication. Story has it that in secret sympathy with the Kwantung army's plot, Tatekawa allowed himself to be tricked into delaying the delivery of the message.[14]

At 10:00 p.m. a bomb exploded on the Southern Manchurian Railway track outside Mukden. The damage was actually so minimal that it did not disrupt normal railway service, but the Japanese patrol claimed that Chinese soldiers opened fire from the fields after the explosion and that it had no choice but to fight back in "self-defense." By 3:40 the following morning the walls of Mukden had been breeched and the city occupied. The Japanese consul general at Mukden, Hayashi Hisajirō, pleaded with Itagaki for a diplomatic settlement since China had already declared a policy of nonresistance, but the latter insisted that "the prestige of the Japanese nation and army was at stake."[15] Orders were given to attack and advance. Changchun was taken on September 19, Antung and Yingkow the 20th, and Kirin the 21st.

Both Tokyo and Commander Honjō knew of the contrived invasion plot but took no action to stop it, thus allowing field-grade officers of the Kwantung army to take the fate of Japan into their own hands and lead it onto the road of militarism, conquest, and ultimately, destruction. In the view of many, the Mukden Incident of September 18, 1931, sowed the seeds of World War II.

News of the incident reached Tokyo at 2:00 a.m. September 19. The government was split on a future course of action. The Minister of War and the General Staff urged the support of the Kwantung army on the ground that the patriotism of its officers should not be blunted. The civilian cabinet under Wakatsuki in principle opposed the military conquest of Manchuria and was distressed at the headstrong conduct of the Kwantung army, but was unable to counter it. An irrevocably divided situation emerged at midday on Septemper 19 when just as the cabinet declared a policy of nonaggression, the Minister of War announced that

14. Ogata, 58-59.
15. Yoshihashi, 8.

the army need not consult the cabinet about future measures but would rely on the discretion of the Kwantung army. Although the cabinet denied Honjō's request for three reinforcement divisions and prohibited the Korean Command to send troops to Manchuria, the Kwantung army continued to advance on its own, while the Korean Command defiantly dispatched reinforcements to Manchuria on September 21. Wakatsuki struggled briefly to withhold funds from the Korean expedition but gave in to army pressure on September 23, thus in effect approving the Manchurian incident. At a time when the country was in desperate need of political leadership, Wakatsuki failed to provide it.[16] What followed was a period of "credibility gap," with the civilian government repeatedly pronouncing its policy of nonexpansion of hostilities, while the military continued to advance in Manchuria. Step by step Wakatsuki was made to accept the *fait accompli* of the army, and the embarrassment that followed led to the cabinet's downfall in December 1931.

International sanction was slow to come. The new British government, in office but a month, was beset with domestic problems. British public opinion was surprisingly lenient toward Japan, whose action in Manchuria it considered not "entirely unjustified." The London *Times* stated that "Japan had a strong case, but had put herself regrettably and unnecessarily in the wrong." The United States took the easy position that Tokyo could not be held responsible for the violation of the Paris Pact since the Kwantung army had acted without its authorization. The Soviet Union also took no action as long as her Siberian border remained unviolated.[17] Thus, China was left to face the enemy alone.

Actually, the Japanese attack was not entirely unexpected in China. On September 11, 1931, Chiang Kai-shek warned the Young Marshal not to engage the Japanese, and on September 15 the bulk of the Northeastern forces at Mukden were transferred. When hostilities broke out on September 18, the Young Marshal again asked for instructions from Peking, where he lay sick, and was told once more not to resist. Deeply embroiled in civil strife, Chiang Kai-shek could not afford a foreign war. He decided to appeal to the League of Nations, with full knowledge that it was powerless to intervene and that the Western powers were disinclined to help, yet he could find no other source of support. By appealing to the international organization for justice, he hoped to gain time to organize his defense and await a favorable turnabout in Japanese domestic

16. Ogata, 65-69; Yoshihashi, 9, 235.
17. Ogata, 71-73.

politics. For some unknown reason, he did not pursue direct negotiations with Tokyo. The policy of the Nanking government, so often oversimplified as one of nonresistance, was actually a combination of "nonresistance, noncompromise, and nondirect negotiation." In retrospect, one cannot help feeling that such a negative approach could hardly achieve positive results. If the government had authorized the Northeastern army to resist the invader, the glamour of aggression might have been dimmed, thus providing a chance for the more moderate civilian government in Tokyo to have had a greater voice in the China affair. Moreover, if Nanking had pursued an active policy of negotiations with Tokyo, it might have reaped more positive results.[18] Unfortunately, it followed neither course. Instead, it placed its reliance on protests to Tokyo and on appeals to the League of Nations.

On September 23, the League asked both China and Japan to limit hostilities, and a day later the United States urged the two countries to suspend military operations in honor of the Nine-Power Treaty. To these warnings the Japanese turned a deaf ear. When the League on October 25 again pleaded with Japan to evacuate Manchuria, this time before November 16, the Japanese army advanced faster than ever, taking Tsitsihar two days later. Facing such intransigence, the international organization on December 10 decided to dispatch an investigatory mission to Manchuria.

The United States, on its part, announced on January 7, 1932, the "Non-Recognition Doctrine" through Secretary of State Henry Stimson. By the terms of this statement, the United States declared that it would not recognize any situation, treaty, or agreement created by means contrary to the covenants and obligations of the Kellogg-Briand (Paris) Pact of 1928, which outlawed war as an instrument of national policy. Isolationist President Herbert Hoover stated categorically: "Neither our obligation to China, nor our own national interest, nor our dignity requires us to go to war over these questions which arose out of Japan's aggression in Manchuria."[19]

Without effective international sanction and concerted Chinese resistance, the Japanese army overran Manchuria in five months. The only flicker of Chinese heroism came from a local general—Ma Chan-shan, acting governor of Heilungkiang—who stubbornly resisted the enemy in spite of all the odds against him. His ability to frustrate the invader

18. Liang Ching-tun, prefaces, iii, vi.
19. Tang Tsou, 18.

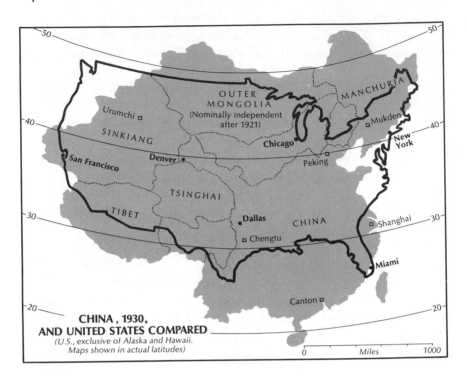

CHINA , 1930,
AND UNITED STATES COMPARED
(U.S., exclusive of Alaska and Hawaii.
Maps shown in actual latitudes)

inspired the rise of local militia and "righteous volunteers" who fought the Japanese as best they could. Yet in the end these sporadic, uncoordinated resistance movements failed to stop the enemy.

On January 28, 1932, the Japanese opened a second front at Shanghai to divert international attention from Manchuria. There they ran into stiff resistance by the Cantonese Nineteenth Route army and Nanking's modernized Fifth army. But after holding the enemy at bay for more than a month, the Chinese defenses crumbled, and the Nanking government retreated to Loyang in Central China. Later, through international mediation a truce was arranged on May 5, 1932, by which the Japanese agreed to evacuate the occupied areas of Shanghai and Woosung.

To legitimize their naked aggression, the Japanese on March 9, 1932, created the puppet state of Manchukuo—the Manchu state—to impress the forthcoming International Commission of Inquiry with the "local character" of the Manchurian incident. The last Ch'ing emperor, P'u-i, deposed in 1912, was made Chief Executive, with a group of leftover old literati as ministers.[20] The Commission, led by the Acting Viceroy of India, Lord Lytton, spent six weeks (April 21-June 4) in Manchuria, and in September submitted its report. Undeceived by the façade, it condemned Japan as an aggressor and rejected her claim that Manchukuo was a spontaneous development of the Manchus. The report refuted the Japanese argument that military operations in Manchuria were necessitated by self-defense, and branded Manchukuo a puppet state under the domination of Japanese military and civilian officials. As a result, the League refused to recognize the legality of Manchukuo; but apart from this moral sanction, it could do nothing else.

The Japanese reaction was singularly arrogant and insulting: the Kwantung army stepped up military operations in Jehol and attacked the various passes of the Great Wall in January 1933. Two months later, in an ultimate act of defiance, Japan withdrew from the League.

The Japanese advance was finally brought to a halt by the T'ang-ku Truce on May 31, 1933, which turned Eastern Hopeh into a demilitarized zone, from which both Chinese and Japanese troops were to be evacuated. In effect, the defense of Peiping and Tientsin was lost by default.

Having completed the conquest of the four Northeastern provinces of China, the Japanese enthroned P'u-i on March 1, 1934, with a reign title of "K'ang-te," Prosperity and Virtue.

The successes of the Manchurian campaign had only whetted the appetite of the Japanese expanionists. Hardly had the smoke cleared from the last battle when new plans of conquest were swept into action. The Japanese scheme now called for the detachment of North China piece by piece through fomenting "autonomous movements"; in this regard, Doihara Kenji, chief of the Kwantung army's secret service, played an active role.

THE COMMUNIST CHALLENGE

Even as the Nationalist government was threatened by Japanese invasion from without and dissident politicians and new warlords from within, it was confronted by a much greater and more fundamental challenge from the Communists. The latter, after their split with the KMT in 1927, had bifurcated into two distinct entities: the party's Central Politburo under the leadership of Moscow-trained Chinese Communists went underground in Shanghai, while Mao Tse-tung pursued an independent

20. Including Cheng Hsiao-hsü, the poet and calligrapher, as premier.

course in the countryside of Hunan and Kiangsi. The Politburo followed the Comintern tactics of strikes, sabotage, and uprisings in the cities, but Mao organized peasant support and developed Soviet areas far away from KMT control. Mao's unorthodox approach placed him in the position of "opposition" vis-à-vis both Moscow and the CCP Politburo; yet of all the tactics used by the Communists, his eventually reaped the greatest success.

The Comintern Policy. The CCP revolutionary strategy was largely determined by Stalin several thousand miles away, and his orders were at times a product of fantasy and at times a result of his feud with Trotsky. After the KMT-CCP split, Trotsky announced that the Chinese revolutionary tide had receded to a low ebb which required a cautious policy of peaceful penetration. Stalin, however, insisted that China was experiencing a high revolutionary tide which justified armed uprisings, seizure of power, and establishment of the Soviets. Stalin's triumph over Trotsky in the Soviet power struggle assured the dominance of his line, and orders were issued to the CCP to carry out armed insurrections.

With the support of a newly organized 15,000-man peasant-worker army, a group of Communists[21] staged a coup at Nanchang, Kiangsi on August 1, 1927. They seized control of the city for three days, and then the Nationalists closed in on them. On August 5 the rebels broke the siege and fled to the border areas of Kwangtung, Kiangsi, and Fukien. The Nanchang uprising, a brainchild of Stalin's, had been a total failure.

At this time, a radical reshuffling of the CCP leadership was taking place. At an emergency meeting in Hankow on August 7, 1927, Ch'en Tu-hsiu was dismissed from the party leadership because of his "surrenderism," and Ch'ü Ch'iu-pai, a Stalin protégé, took over as secretary-general of the Central Politburo, a new organ which had superseded the Central Committee. Li Li-san, another choice of Stalin's, was put in charge of propaganda. Under the guidance of the new Comintern representative, B. Lominadze, these leaders accepted Moscow's diagnosis that China was ripe for armed insurrections and creation of the Soviets. Ch'en Tu-hsiu, in disgrace, organized his own Third Party with the support of T'an P'ing-shan.

Mao Tse-tung on his part had entered Hunan to foment popular resentments which culminated in the Autumn Harvest Uprising of September 7, 1927. Under his inspiration and direction, the rebellious peas-

21. Including Ho Lung, Chu Teh, and Chou En-lai.

ants destroyed sections of the Canton-Hankow Railway, seized control of a number of places in the province, and carried out "liquidation struggles" and land revolution. This first uprising of Mao's, however, fell far short of success. Under the attack of government troops, Mao was obliged to flee to Ching-kang-shan in the border area of Kiangsi and Hunan to regroup his forces. Unsympathetic to the peasant movement, Ch'ü Ch'iu-pai sponsored a resolution at the November meeting of the Central Politburo stating that "a purely peasant uprising without the leadership and help of the working class cannot achieve conclusive victories."[22] The failure of the Autumn Harvest Uprising cost Mao his membership in the Politburo.

To step up armed uprisings, Moscow sent Heinz Neumann[23] to China, and under his guidance an insurrection broke out in Canton on December 11, 1927.[24] The Communists won control of the city for three days, and established a "Canton Commune" and a Soviet regime. But the success was short-lived. Under the joint attack by government troops and workers from the city labor union, the uprising was abruptly suppressed.

As these urban uprisings failed one after another, Mao's activity in the countryside began to assume importance. At Ching-kang-shan he was joined by Chu Teh and Ch'en Yi on January 23, 1928, and their combined forces formed the Fourth Red army, with Chu as the commander and Mao as the "party" representative. Here was the birth of the celebrated Chu-Mao leadership. In July they moved their headquarters to Juichin, Kiangsi, where a Soviet regime was established.[25] In Shensi, another Communist base was being created by Liu Chih-tan and Kao Kang. These two centers in the border areas operated outside the jurisdiction of the CCP Central Politburo.

At the CCP Sixth Party Congress in July 1928—held in Moscow partly to avoid the KMT raid and partly to coordinate with the Comintern's International Congress which had been called to eliminate the Trotskyite influence—Ch'en Tu-hsiu was condemned for his "rightist opportunism," while Ch'ü Ch'iu-pai was attacked for his "leftist deviationism." The Congress called for (1) the overthrow of the Nationalist govern-

22. Schwartz, *Chinese Communism*, 104.
23. A German agent, alias A. Neuberg.
24. Led by Chang T'ai-lui and Yeh T'ing.
25. This was, however, not the first Soviet government in China. The earliest was established in November 1927, in the Hailufeng area near Canton. See Etō Shinkichi, "Hai-lu-feng: The First Chinese Soviet Government," *The China Quarterly*, 8:163-83 (Oct.-Dec. 1961); 9:149-81 (Jan.-March 1962).

ment and the destruction of its military power: (2) the establishment of Soviets in China; (3) land revolution and confiscation of the holdings of landlords; and (4) the unification of China through the expulsion of the imperialists. Chu-Mao activities in the Kiangsi-Hunan hinterland were recognized as legitimate though not models for the Chinese Communist movement. Instead, the Congress elected Hsiang Chung-fa and Li Li-san new leaders, with the former serving as secretary-general and the latter director of propaganda. The party headquarters remained in underground Shanghai.

Of the two, Li was more lively and eloquent. He emerged as the strong man of the party between June 1929 and September 1930. In October 1929 he was told by the Comintern that he should ready himself for the advent of a new revolutionary tide. Not long afterward, a large-scale civil war broke out in Central China in July 1930, and taking advantage of the situation Li fomented strikes and sabotage, sending the newly organized Red army under P'eng Te-huai to attack Changsha, the capital of Hunan. The city was taken, but the success again was fleeting. Within three days the government troops recovered Changsha and inflicted heavy losses on the rebels. The failure of the precipitous "Li Li-san line" led the Comintern representative, Pavel Mif, who resented Li's iron control of the party, to ask Moscow to dismiss him. The Comintern dispatched Ch'ü Ch'iu-pai to investigate the case, but he could not attack Li without criticizing the Kremlin's policy. Caught on the horns of a dilemma, Ch'ü's attack was half-hearted and ineffectual. However, the Comintern and the "Returned Student Clique" (see below) launched a devastating campaign against Li, accusing him of (1) "opportunist passivity" because of his reliance on the prospect of world revolution; (2) "petty bourgeois chauvinism" and "great Chinaism" because of his exaggeration of the importance of the Chinese revolution; (3) "adventurism" because of his misunderstanding of the meaning of "upsurge" and "direct revolution"; and (4) Trotskyite proclivity because of his reference to the imminent transformation of the Chinese Revolution into a socialist revolution.[26] A victim of Stalin's failure in China, Li was sent to Moscow for recantation. There, he was severely condemned by the Presidium of the Executive Committee of the Comintern and sent to Lenin University to study and correct his mistakes. Ch'ü Ch'iu-pai fared even worse; he was attacked for his double-dealing, factionalism, "wily oriental diplomacy," and wrong views on agrarian and peasant questions under the in-

26. Schwartz, 151-63.

fluence of Borodin, Ch'en Tu-hsiu, and other undesirable characters.[27] As a result of this attack, Ch'ü was dropped from the CCP Politburo a month later.

The party leadership now fell to Wang Ming (Ch'en Shao-yü) and Po Ku (Ch'in Pang-hsien), who headed the "international wing" (kuo-chi pai) of the CCP consisting of twenty-eight returned students who had studied at the Sun Yat-sen University at Moscow from 1926 to 1930. Returning home in early 1930, they became known as the "Twenty-eight Bolsheviks" and "China's Stalin Section."[28] They were not particularly welcomed by Li Li-san, but with his fall in late 1930 they rose to take over the Politburo in January 1931, with the support of Mif, the Comintern representative and the former rector of Moscow's Sun Yat-sen University. In February, Wang Ming published a famous article, "The Two Lines," in which he attacked Li and the old cadres for their failure to see the Chinese capitalists as counterrevolutionaries and for their unforgivable advocacy of forming alliances with capitalist and bourgeois reformers. Any Communist, Wang asserted, who favored cooperation with any other party, army, or organization against the imperialists and landlords was a right deviationist and a two-faced double-dealing compromiser.

Mao's Independence. Operating outside the jurisdiction of the CCP central organization, Mao and Chu were relatively unaffected by the party squabble. They had developed an independent and comparatively unorthodox activity by organizing the peasants and creating Soviets in the hinterland of Kiangsi and Hunan. They had practiced guerrillaism to perfection and initiated a rather "egalitarian" land revolution by parceling out the redistributed land to the rich and poor peasants alike. They had evolved a self-sufficient territorial base without relying on the help or guidance of the Comintern or the party leaders at Shanghai, with whom they maintained an attitude of "outward obedience and inward disobedience." The CCP Central Politburo never really approved of Mao's activity, while Moscow merely tolerated it because all other CCP-led uprisings had failed. Mao's growing power and independence contrasted sharply with the state of the party central organization, which was plagued by unstable leadership, lack of financial support from the Soviet

27. John E. Rue, *Mao Tse-tung in Opposition, 1927-1935* (Stanford, 1966), 241.
28. *Ibid.,* 7-8; Tso-liang Hsiao, *Power Relations within the Chinese Communist Movement, 1930-1934* (Seattle, 1961), 125.

Union which itself was absorbed in economic reconstruction, and Nationalist persecution. The KMT raids had become so devastating that the Communist secret service chief in Hankow[29] was arrested and forced to divulge names. This led to the capture and subsequent execution of the secretary-general, Hsiang Chung-fa, on June 24, 1931. The party fortunes had fallen to a low ebb.

Sensing the desperation of the Politburo, Mao boldly invited its members to attend the First All-China Congress of the Soviets to be held in Juichin on November 7, 1931. The Twenty-eight Bolsheviks condescendingly arrived in Mao's capital, not with the intention of supporting his movement but of chastising his unorthodox conduct. Prior to the Congress, they called a party conference which adopted resolutions to condemn Mao for his failure to adopt a strong "class and mass line," for his guerrilla tactics, and for his "rich peasant" mentality in the land revolution. They chided his narrow empiricism, his "opportunistic pragmatism," and his "general ideological poverty." The conference closed with a call for the proletarian leadership in agrarian reforms, the expansion of the Red army, and the adoption of the regular warfare in place of guerrillaism. Starkly, the Twenty-eight Bolsheviks rejected the Maoist approach and intended to replace his machine.[30]

However, at the Congress the Maoists completely dominated the scene. Having defeated the first two KMT campaigns (see below), they were flushed with success and confidence. With their control of the majority votes, they easily outmaneuvered the Twenty-eight Bolsheviks. Mao was elected chairman of the Central Executive Committee of the All-China Soviet Government and retained his position as Chief Political Commissar of the First Front Red army. A number of the former party leaders were absorbed into his government, while the Twenty-eight Bolsheviks were deliberately left in the cold during the distribution of offices. Only three of them, including Wang Ming who was absent, were given places on the Central Executive Committee, while Po Ku was not appointed to anything.

In this power struggle, Mao was able to score an impressive victory and won increased recognition of his activity, not because of Soviet patronage but because of a very realistic strategy he had evolved himself on the basis of five important elements: (1) the peasant mass support; (2) a party and government apparatus of his own; (3) an independent

29. Ku Shun-chang.
30. Rue, 247-48.

military force; (4) a secure territorial base far away from KMT control; and (5) self-sufficiency.[31] But Mao's success was not complete; the Twenty-eight Bolsheviks retained their iron control of the Politburo to which he could gain no admission. Mao remained an "outsider," in opposition to the CCP central organization. After the Congress, Po Ku and most of the other Politburo members returned to Shanghai, in preparation for the next round of dueling with Mao.

The Bolsheviks and the Maoists split over a number of issues too fundamental to be reconciled. On the question of land reform, Mao favored equal distribution of all grades of land to small landlords, rich peasants, and poor peasants alike, whereas the Politburo members insisted on complete deprivation of the landlords, and relocation of land to favor the poor at the expense of the rich. They condemned the Maoists of backward peasant mentality, with unsteady and weak class consciousness. On military strategy, Mao opted for the mobile guerrilla tactics of luring the enemy deep into the base area where the Red army could "amass superior forces to attack the enemy's weak spots" and assure elimination of "a part, small or large, of the enemy's forces by picking them off one at a time." By "circling around in a whirling motion," the Red army could confuse the enemy and win the battle.[32] The Politburo, on the other hand, insisted on positional warfare, holding the Communist base, and invading the enemy territory rather than waiting for him to invade the Red territories. On the sensitive issue of Japanese aggression, Mao announced his readiness to form a United Front and a coalition army of all military forces willing to fight the enemy, whereas the Politburo rejected collaboration with reformist groups, and argued for the rapid expansion of the Red army so that it could perform the sublime duty of safeguarding the Soviet Union against imperialist attack, should the need arise. So wide was the gulf between the Maoists and the Bolsheviks that a *rapprochement* seemed impossible.

Mao's problem was not the Politburo alone; he had to fight the KMT invasion, too. Indeed, Chiang Kai-shek was relentlessly organizing expeditions against the Communists.

The KMT Campaigns. Since his dismissal of the Russian military advisers in 1927, Chiang increasingly sought to obtain German aid for the development of his army. Beginning with the appointment of Colonel Max Bauer, an associate of General Ludendorff during World War I,

31. Schwartz, 189-90.
32. Rue, 272.

as his adviser in 1928, a German military mission in China gradually took shape. In 1933 the famous strategist General Hans von Seeckt arrived to coordinate the campaign against the Communists and in the following year he assumed the direction of the mission. When poor health obliged him to resign in March 1935, the mission leadership then went to General Alexander von Falkenhausen. Through the efforts of these advisers, Chiang developed a German-style Central army of more than half a million men.

From 1930 to 1934 Chiang launched a total of Five Campaigns of Encirclement and Extermination against the Communists.[33] The first and the second, lasting from December 19, 1930, to January 3, 1931, and from April 1 to May 31, 1931, respectively, ended in rapid failure. The third, opened by Chiang himself on July 1, 1931, with 130,000 men, achieved some initial progress but was cut short by the Japanese invasion of Manchuria in September. The period that followed was extremely trying for the Nationalists. Not only did the Japanese continue to advance in Manchuria, but they opened a second front in Shanghai on January 28, 1932. Domestically, the Maoists were fast gaining strength, establishing a Soviet Republic at Juichin, Kiangsi, on November 7, 1931. There was endless popular demand for cessation of the civil strife and for war with Japan. Chiang, however, decided on a policy which gave priority to domestic consolidation, insisting that he could not wage an effective foreign war without first achieving internal peace. On January 1, 1933, he inaugurated the fourth campaign with 153,500 men. But the time was ill-chosen. In March, the Japanese took Jehol and penetrated as far as the Great Wall, threatening Peiping and Tientsin. Transfer of part of the Nationalist forces to the North and defection of some other units to the Communists placed Chiang in a vulnerable position. The subsequent Communist offensive terminated the fourth campaign in another failure on April 29, 1933.

At this point, a critical power struggle developed within the Communist camp. In late 1932 or early 1933, Po Ku and other CCP Politburo members arrived in Juichin in the company of a Comintern military adviser, Li T'e,[34] with the intention of discrediting Mao and replacing his

---

33. The dates of these campaigns and the strength of the Nationalist troops employed vary with different accounts. My information has been largely drawn from the official Nationalist source; see Wang Chien-min, Chung-kuo Kung-ch'an tang shih-kao (A draft history of the Chinese Communist Party), (Taipei, 1965), II, chapter 20.
34. His real name is Otto Braun, now living in East Germany; see Stuart Schram, Mao Tse-tung (New York, 1966), 166.

men in the army and the party. Excoriating Mao's rather "egalitarian" approach, they pressed for a radical land investigation drive to eliminate the landlords, attack the rich peasants, neutralize the middle peasants, and ally the poor peasants and the landless laborers with the party. The funds realized from this campaign were to be used for the expansion of the Red army. Mao reluctantly acquiesced as he could not dispute the need for funds to support and expand the army.

Meanwhile, the Nationalists, having signed the T'ang-ku Truce with the Japanese in May 1933 which temporarily stemmed the enemy advance, were organizing a fifth campaign, which was opened in October with 700,000 men. Counseled by his German advisers, Chiang adopted a "strategically offensive but tactically defensive" posture, moving his troops gingerly and relying on encirclement and progressive economic strangulation. His troops constructed fortresses and pillboxes as they advanced, tightening the blockade ever more until all outside supplies to the Red areas were cut off. Proclaiming the Communist problem as "70 per cent political, 30 per cent military" in nature, Chiang stressed rural reconstruction and neighborhood organization (pao-chia) in the reconquered areas. The campaign progressed slowly but steadily until it was interrupted a month later by the Fukien Revolt, as noted before.

The Fukien rebels had earlier reached a preliminary "Anti-Japanese, Anti-Chiang Pact" with the Communists on October 26, 1933, but failed to receive Communist aid after they had established a People's Revolutionary Government in Foochow on November 20. Mao had hoped to work out some sort of cooperation with the Fukien regime, but the Politburo refused to take a stand, thereby losing a chance to force the KMT to fight on two fronts. The Fukien rebels, left alone, were quickly suppressed on January 20, 1934, and Chiang was able to resume his campaign against the Communists.

Mao faced an extremely critical situation at this point of his career—not only were the Nationalists hitting hard, but the Politburo members were doing their best to destroy him from within. At the Second All-China Soviet Congress, he nearly lost his grip on the Chinese Communist movement. Though re-elected chairman of the Soviet government in January 1934, he lost control of the Central Executive Committee which was placed under a seventeen-man presidium dominated by the Twenty-eight Bolsheviks, one of whom, Chang Wen-t'ien, took over from Mao the chairmanship of the Council of People's Commissars—a sort of premiership in the Soviet government. Although Mao retained the chairmanship of the Central Executive Committee, the post was reduced to something of an honorary title by the Bolsheviks, who intended to make Mao a figurehead. The final *coup de grâce* came in July 1934 when Po Ku at Juichin and Wang Ming in Moscow conspired to obtain an order from the Comintern that Mao be put on probation and barred from party meetings. For three months from July he was imprisoned or placed under house arrest at Yü-tu, some sixty miles west of Juichin. It was not until the Long March began in October that he was released.[35]

The Long March. The KMT Fifth Campaign was a great success which finally routed the rebels from their seven-year-old base in Kiangsi. The Communist defeat was largely the result, from a military standpoint, of Li T'e's wrong strategy of positional warfare instead of Mao's test-proven guerrilla warfare. Throughout the first half of 1934 the Red army suffered incalculable losses and by the midyear it was nearly crushed. Mao wanted the Red Army to break through the siege and split into small groups to fight guerrilla war, but the Revolutionary Military Council under the dominance of Li T'e ordered the Red Army to break through the siege as a united force and not split into smaller guerrilla groups. With Po Ku as interpreter, Li T'e took charge of the general evacuation. The able-bodied were allowed to join the exodus, while the wounded and dependent were ordered to stay behind. On October 15, 1934, the Long March officially began with 85,000 soldiers, 15,000 government and party officials, and 35 women who were wives of high leaders. A number of Maoists and ex-party leaders unacceptable to the Twenty-eight Bolsheviks were left behind to defend the base, including Su Yü, Ch'en Yi, and Ch'ü Ch'iu-pai. Mao's two children were also left behind. On November 10, 1934, Juichin fell to the Nationalists.

At the outset of the march, the Twenty-eight Bolsheviks and the Whampoa Faction[36] dominated the army and the party. The morale of the troops was predictably low, and as they fled westward they came under the merciless pounding of the KMT forces. When they reached Tsunyi in northern Kweichow in January 1935, Mao had gathered enough support from the dissident military leaders, who had developed sufficient doubts about Li T'e's ability, to demand an enlarged Politburo conference. At this crucial meeting, Mao bitterly attacked the Po Ku group for their failure to support the Fukien Revolt and for their wrong

35. Rue, 263-64.
36. Headed by Chou En-lai, then chairman of the Revolutionary Military Council, and Yeh Chien-ying.

decision to fight a positional warfare. The Twenty-eight Bolsheviks could hardly argue against the stark fact of defeat. The Maoists won the day, and Mao took over the chairmanship of the reorganized Revolutionary Military Council, from which Li T'e's influence was totally eliminated. The guerrilla strategy was revived. Mao became head of the CCP Politburo and Secretariat.

The Tsunyi Conference marked the end of the dominance of the Twenty-eight Bolsheviks and the rise of Mao as the leader of the Chinese Communist Party. He assumed direction of the march and selected as its ultimate destination northern Shensi, where Kao Kang and Liu Chih-tan had built up another Soviet base. However, in July 1935 when the march reached Maoerhkai near the Szechwan-Sikang border, the party "elder," Chang Kuo-t'ao, challenged the choice of the terminus, proposing instead to establish a Red base in Sikang, or Tibet, or even Sinkiang. The clash that developed resulted in Chang's decision to lead a column of his own for Sikang,[37] while Mao and his group continued their trek toward northern Shensi under extremely difficult and trying conditions, finally reaching Wuch'icheng in Paoan County in October 1935. At the end of this epic 25,000 *li* (actually 6,000 miles) Long March, Mao's column could count only 8,000 survivors. Along with the local Red Fifteenth Army Corps of 7,000 men, Mao commanded about 15,000 men at this point. Later, the arrival of other units under Ho Lung, Chang Kuo-t'ao, and Chu Teh swelled the total strength to 30,000.[38] In December 1936 the Communists moved their headquarters to Yenan, which they had seized. There, Mao engaged in rebuilding the party machine by pulling around himself those leaders that had survived the purges of the Twenty-eight Bolsheviks. At long last, Mao rose to the pinnacle of the Chinese Communist Movement, but Moscow did not publicly acknowledge his position until 1938.[39]

Reminiscing about the Kiangsi defeat with an American journalist (Edgar Snow) sometime later, Mao reiterated the dual Politburo mistakes of not aiding the Fukien Revolt and of fighting the positional warfare with the Nationalists. These were, of course, important immediate causes of the fiasco, but there were other larger factors at work too. For one thing, the Nationalist improvement of the communication system

37. The rift was to lead to a formal break between Mao and Chang and the latter's defection from the CCP in 1938.
38. Schram, 176; Jerome Ch'en, *Mao and the Chinese Revolution* (London, 1965), 199.
39. Rue, 4, 272.

THE LONG MARCH
1934-1935

||||| Communist areas, 1934-1936

⬅ Route of main Communist forces
    from Juichin area

⬅ Route of Communist forces
    from other areas

U.S.S.R.

OUTER   MONGOLIA

MANCHUKUO
(MANCHURIA)

INNER   MONGOLIA

JEHOL

• Mukden

KANSU

• Kalgan

Peking

KOREA

TSINGHAI

Lanchow •

• Taiyuan

SHANSI

Tientsin

• Yenan

SHENSI

• Tsinan

Tsingtao •

• Sian

Yellow R.

Nanking

SZECHWAN

Yangtze R.

Hankow

•Shanghai

• Chengtu

Ichang •

SIKANG

Chungking •

Changsha

HUNAN

• Nanchang

KIANGSI

FUKIEN

Tsunyi •

KWEICHOW

• Juichin

Mekong R.

Kweiyang •

TAIWAN
(FORMOSA)

BURMA

Kunming •

• Kweilin

Amoy •

YUNNAN

KWANGSI

Canton

KWANGTUNG

Swatow •

FRENCH
INDOCHINA

Hong Kong (Br.)

Macao (Port.)

SIAM

HAINAN

0   Miles   500

in and near Kiangsi had altered the isolated character of the Soviet region, whose self-sufficiency had been destroyed by the Nationalist economic blockade. Even more detrimental was the Politburo's ruthless drive for the land revolution and class struggle, which drove nearly all classes of peasants—rich, middle, and poor—into desperation and apathy. They endeavored to avoid the Red army and the party to such a degree that the former was rendered incapable of recruitment, expansion, and proper mobilization. Without the mass support, it is doubtful that the Communists could have successfully fought a guerrilla war against the Nationalists, even if this strategy had been adopted.[40]

SIAN INCIDENT AND THE UNITED FRONT

The radical change in the position of the Chinese Communists coincided with a basic shift in the Comintern's world revolutionary strategy. Facing the rise of Nazi Germany and Fascist Italy in Europe and militarist Japan in Asia, the Comintern at its Seventh Congress in August 1935 adopted a resolution urging the various national Communist parties to form alliances with leftist and anti-Fascist groups against the threat of these avowed enemies of Bolshevism and Marxism. In the case of China, a policy of the United Front would have the added benefit of relieving the Communists of Nationalist attacks.

Beginning in 1936, the CCP started to promote collaboration with all parties, groups, and armies in a grand alliance against Japan. Under its sponsorship, popular organizations such as "The National Liberation Anti-Japanese Association," "The People's Anti-Japanese League," and "The National Salvation Society" sprang into existence. New persuasive slogans such as "Chinese must not fight Chinese" and "Immediate war with Japan; stop fighting the Communists" were widely circulated to evoke a sentimental response among patriotic Chinese, especially the youth in Peiping, Nanking, and Shanghai. Popular pressure mounted feverishly demanding an end to the civil war and the turning of guns against the Japanese.

The Nanking government, as noted before, had decided on a policy of domestic consolidation before an external war. With the Communists pushed into a pocket in the Northwest, Chiang Kai-shek was anxious to finish with them once and for all. Confidently, he ordered the Northeast-

40. Shanti Swarup, *A Study of the Chinese Communist Movement* (Oxford, 1966), 258-66.

ern army[41] under Chang Hsüeh-liang and the Northwestern army under Yang Hu-ch'eng to mount an offensive against the Communists. But the morale of the troops was extremely low, and the fighting was ineffective. Homesick and weary of a civil war, the Northeastern officers and men became susceptible to the United Front propaganda. Communist agents began to infiltrate the Northeastern officers' training corps, and by the summer of 1936 contact had been made with Chang and Yang. The two commanders were won over to the United Front.

On December 3 Chiang flew to Sian, the headquarters of Chang and Yang, with a view to stabilizing the restless situation and increasing the effectiveness of the campaign. There, at daybreak on December 12, a mutiny broke out, engineered by the Northeastern 105th division and the second battalion of Chang's personal guard. With Chiang as his captive, the Young Marshal named eight demands:

1. Reorganization of the Nanking government to include all parties and groups responsible for national salvation.
2. Termination of all civic strife.
3. Immediate release of patriotic leaders who had been arrested in Shanghai.
4. Release of all political prisoners.
5. Protection of the people's right to assembly.
6. Freedom to organize the people's patriotic movement.
7. Faithful fulfillment of Dr. Sun's will.
8. Immediate convocation of a National Salvation Conference.

On December 14, the Northeastern, Northwestern, and Communist forces formed a United Anti-Japanese command headed by a Military Commission. That Chang served as the chairman of the Commission implied that he might have had some secret ambitions to head the United Front.

The Sian mutiny and the kidnap of Chiang stunned the country and the world. Right-wing Nationalist leaders at Nanking quickly decided upon a punitive expedition and sent its airplanes to Sian in a demonstration of power. The country was once again on the verge of a civil war. At this point the Communists discovered that the mutineers were more anti-Chiang than anti-Japanese, and came to the conclusion that any large-scale Nationalist attack would inevitably involve them (the Com-

41. It had moved from the Peiping-Tientsin area to Shensi after the T'ang-ku Truce, 1933.

munists) and hurt their cause. Moscow also realized that disorder in China could only benefit Japan and that Chiang should be spared to lead the fight against Japan. A Sino-Japanese war would surely relieve Japanese pressure on the Soviet Union and the Nationalist pressure on the Communists. Prompted by these considerations, Chou En-lai emerged from behind the mountains to offer mediation. The Communist position was shifted overnight from "anti-Chiang against Japan" to "ally with Chiang against Japan."

Bewildered by this change, and pressured by public opinion, the Young Marshal reconsidered his mutiny and finally agreed to release his prized prisoner. On Christmas day, 1936, Chiang flew back to Nanking in the company of his erstwhile captor, who had offered himself up for punishment. A special military court sentenced him to ten years' imprisonment and five years' loss of civil rights, but through Chiang's intercession on the basis of Chang's quick repentence, the sentence on imprisonment was remitted. Nevertheless, he was put under house arrest.[42]

Although Chiang insisted that he did not sign any agreement as to the conditions of his release, he did promise that the Communists could participate in the future war against Japan if they pledged their support of the Three People's Principles. The anti-Communist campaign was terminated, though the government blockade of the Red area in the Northwest continued.

The Sian incident might be considered a blessing in disguise. It helped unite the country and put an end to the civil strife. No longer was Chiang considered the obstacle to fighting the Japanese, but a national hero with a new mandate of leading the country in a United Front against the aggressor.

SUCCESS OR FAILURE: A DECADE IN REVIEW

Saddled though it was with endless domestic and foreign problems, the Nationalist government struggled to carry out Dr. Sun's legacy of national reconstruction. The record at the end of the first decade revealed some progress in the fields of finance, communication, industrial development, and education. On the other hand, the government neglected the much-needed basic social and economic reforms, and carried on an irresponsible fiscal policy of deficit spending—both of which left far-reaching consequences of a very fundamental nature which ultimately

42. Now living on Taiwan, reputedly in freedom.

proved disastrous. The following is a quick review of the achievements and failures of the decade.[43]

Financial Reform. The outstanding accomplishments were the substitution of the silver dollar (*yüan*) for the tael (*liang*) and the introduction of paper currency, *fa-pi*, as the legal tender. Although the silver dollar had been introduced in 1914 as a basic unit of currency, the tael was continuously used in commercial transactions because of tradition and supposed convenience. The juxtaposition of the two media of exchange caused confusion and complications, since their exchange rates varied with places and seasons. On April 4, 1933, the government decisively abolished the tael and substituted for it the silver dollar at an exchange rate of 0.715 (tael) for 1 (dollar).

No sooner had this reform been introduced than a new problem arose: the sharp rise in silver value in the world market was causing a rapid outflow of the metal from China, undermining the very basis of the new currency. The imposition of an export tax on silver on October 15, 1934, failed to stem the tide and actually encouraged silver-smuggling. The continuous drain caused a host of unhealthy economic phenomena such as inflation, high interest rates, tight money, decline in the stock market, stagnancy in real estate, and bankruptcies of enterprises. On November 3, 1935, the government finally took the bold step of nationalizing silver and introduced a new paper money, *fa-pi*, to be issued by four national banks on 25 per cent silver reserve. Later, in February 1936, a decimal system of nickel coins in denominations of 5, 10, and 20 cents, as well as copper coins of ½ and 1 cent, were circulated to supplement the paper currency.

The four national banks were assigned different duties. The largest of them, The Central Bank, with a capital of 100 million Chinese dollars in 1934,[44] became the central bank of the nation charged with maintaining currency stability. The Bank of China, with a capital of Ch$40 million, directed foreign exchanges, and the Bank of Communication, with a capital of Ch$20 million, was entrusted with assisting domestic industries and enterprises. The Farmers' Bank of China handled farm credit and land mortgages up to Ch$50 million. The first three banks were

43. Information in this section is largely extracted from *K'ang-chan ch'ien shih-nien chih Chung-kuo* (China during the ten years before the Sino-Japanese War, 1937), compiled by Chung-kuo wen-hua chien-she hsieh-hui (China cultural reconstruction association), reprinted (Hong Kong, 1965).
44. Original capital was Ch$20 million in 1928.

authorized to buy and sell foreign currencies in unlimited amounts in order to stabilize the rates of exchange. Thus, for the first time in Chinese history, foreign exchanges were controlled by government banks.

Tariff Autonomy. The fixed tariff of 5 per cent ad valorem, imposed after the Opium War, had been a constant reminder of China's semicolonial status and a major irritant in the rising national consciousness of her people. Abolition of the tariff restriction had been a cardinal goal of the Nationalist government since its inception. Indeed, even before the country was completely unified, the Nanking regime on July 20, 1927, announced tariff autonomy as of September 1, with the new rates generally imposing 7.5 per cent ad valorem on ordinary articles, 13-25 per cent on luxury items, and 57.5 per cent on tobacco and liquor. Simultaneously, the *likin* transit dues—first introduced in 1853—together with other commodity levies would be abolished. But the political uncertainty in August 1927, generated by the resignations of Hu Han-min as president of the Nanking government and Chiang Kai-shek as commander-in-chief of the armed forces, afforded Japan and other foreign powers an excuse to oppose strenuously the new tariff. Similarly, with the Northern Expedition far from completed and the recent split with the CCP still reverberating in its domestic policy, Nanking could hardly force the issue.

But once the Northern Expedition was brought to a successful conclusion, the government renewed its fight for tariff autonomy. Supported by rising nationalism among its people, it announced on July 7, 1928, two guiding principles in which treaties and agreement that had expired should be replaced by new ones, while those not yet expired should be abolished and renegotiated according to legal procedures. The United States was the first to enter into an equal and friendly tariff agreement with China on July 24, followed swiftly by Germany (August 17), Belgium (November 22), Italy (November 27), Britain (December 20), France (December 22), and Japan (May 6, 1929). With these agreements, the great powers recognized China's tariff autonomy and, furthermore, agreed *in principle* to give up their consular jurisdiction.

Recovery of Foreign Concessions. In concert with the struggle for tariff autonomy, the Nationalists, aided by the success of the Northern Expedition and public outburst of nationalistic agitation, succeeded in revoking a number of foreign municipal concessions. The British, who bore the major brunt of Chinese pressure, finally agreed to relinquish their concessions at Hankow and Kiukiang in February 1927, at Chinkiang in February 1929, at Weihaiwei in April 1930, and at Amoy in September of the same year. The Belgian concession at Tientsin was also recovered in January 1931. However, restitution of China's lost rights was not complete until 1943 when the United States and Britain took the lead in voluntarily abolishing all unequal treaties with China, thereby ending the century-old national humiliation.

Communication. Improvement of the communication systems was another positive accomplishment of the government. In 1928 a Ministry of Railways was established to direct the improvement of existing lines and the construction of new ones. Among the most prominent projects were the extension of the Lung-Hai Railway—the East-West trunk line— to Sian in 1934 and to Pao-chi in 1935, and the completion in 1936 of the Canton-Hankow Railway—the major south-central trunk line. Other noteworthy achievements included the development of the ferry system at Nanking, which linked the Tientsin-Pukow and the Shanghai-Nanking railways, and the construction of the iron bridge over the Ch'ien-t'ang River in 1937, wihch connected the Chekiang-Kiangsi and the Shanghai-Hangchow-Ningpo lines. These national accomplishments were matched in the provinces by completion of a number of smaller projects. From 1928 to 1937, the railway network grew from 8,000 kilometers to 13,000.

Even more impressive was highway construction, due to its lower costs —about one-twentieth that of the railway. In 1936 the highway network accounted for 115,703 kilometers, as compared with a mere 1,000 in 1921.

Modern airlines were also initiated. The China National Aviation Corporation was organized in 1930 with Chinese and American capital,[45] and it operated four lines between Shanghai and Chengtu, Shanghai and Peiping, Shanghai and Ch'üan-chou, and Szechwan and Kunming. The second largest was the Eurasia Aviation Corporation, a Sino-German enterprise[46] which opened for business in 1931. It also operated four lines between Shanghai and Sinkiang, Peiping and Canton, Peiping and Lanchow, and Sian and Chengtu. A third company, the Southwestern Aviation Corporation, was established by the Southwestern provincial authorities in 1933, running flights in Kwangtung and Kwangsi, and from there to Kunming and Foochow.

45. The American interests were owned by the Aviation Exploration Inc., a subsidiary of the Curtiss Company.
46. The German interests were owned by the Lufthansa Company.

Postal service and telecommunication were much improved and expanded during the decade. In 1921 post offices numbered less than 10,-000 over 400,000 *li* of postroad. By 1935-36 they had increased to 14,000 over 584,800 *li*. Telegraph lines, which had suffered severe damage during the warlord period, underwent rapid restoration and construction; by 1936 they totaled 95,300 kilometers. Correspondingly, long-distance telephone lines grew from 4,000 kilometer in 1925 to 52,200 in 1937.

Industrial Development. There was a general recognition on the part of the government and the people that economic development was essential to the creation of a modern state. Consequently, the official promotion of industrialization evoked a warm popular response. Despite the loss of Manchuria and the Japanese attack on Shanghai, which wrought havoc with foreign trade at that key port, the importation of heavy machinery never abated. Over a ten-year period between 1927 and 1937, the total importation of industrial equipment reached Ch$500 million, which, though small by Western standards, represented considerable effort in a war-torn, poverty-stricken country. Although no spectacular breakthrough was achieved in industrialization, good progress was scored in a number of light industries such as cotton weaving, flour production, matches, cement, and chemical manufacturing.[47]

Education. Notable progress was also achieved in the field of education. The Ministry of Education reorganized and amalgamated a number of public universities, colleges, and professional schools into thirteen national universities,[48] five technical colleges, and nine provincial universities. It extended subsidies to private institutions of higher learning[49] for the dual purpose of establishing new professorships and purchasing equipment. Of the 20 private universities and 33 private colleges, 32 received this help in 1934 and 1935, and 40 in 1936. Not to be outdone, secondary education underwent a four-to-fivefold growth during the decade.

47. In the cotton industry, the number of weaving machines grew from 13,459 in 1927 to 23,955 in 1936, and the quantity of land devoted to cotton-production increased from 27.6 million *mou* to 56.2 million. In flour production, 150 factories in 13 provinces turned out 75 million bags annually at a value of Ch$200 million. Cement output rose from 2.14 million barrels (375 lbs. each) in 1925 to 3.56 million in 1934. New chemical factories included 12 acid-manufacturing companies, 7 alkali-producing plants, and a number of ammonia plants.
48. The most famous were Peking, Tsing-hua, and Central universities.
49. The most famous were Yenching, Soochow, Shanghai, Lingnan, and St. John's universities, all Christian institutions.

By 1937 there were 2,042 middle schools, 1,211 normal schools, and 370 professional schools, with a total enrollment of 545,207.

The New Life Movement. To revitalize the moral fibre of the people and achieve a spiritual awakening, the government in 1934 promoted a New Life Movement, which stressed hygienic practices, promptness, truthfulness, courtesy, and the four traditional virtues of politeness (*li*), righteousness (*i*), integrity (*lien*), and self-respect (*ch'ih*). Scholars and officials were urged to read the writings of the 19th-century statesman Tseng Kuo-fan for their spirit of loyalty and devotion to public service. Although the young generation did not take to these old virtues too seriously,[50] the New Life Movement and the related activities such as military training for the able-bodied and military instructions at schools did provide something of a psychological uplift and the feeling of doing something in the face of Japanese aggression.

The World of Literature. Literary activities were extremely lively during the decade under review, with most of the creative writings reflecting social realities of the times. A powerful organization was the League of Chinese Left-wing Writers, founded in 1930 under the auspices of the CCP with a view to capturing the literary scene of China. Members of the League attacked the Nationalist government, scorned the rightist writers and lovers of the traditional art and literature, criticized the Anglo-American school of writers, and eulogized Soviet literature and leftist programs. The guiding spirit of the League was none other than Ch'ü Ch'iu-pai, the deposed party leader, although its spokesman was the famous writer Lu Hsün. Through its numerous publications,[51] it succeeded to a considerable extent in dominating the literary circles.

However, two groups stood out adamantly in opposition and won acclaim through their own merits. One was led by Lin Yü-t'ang, whose humorous, satirical, and somewhat playful publications, *The Analects, This Human World,* and *The Cosmic Wind* continuously enjoyed public fa-

---

50. A famous joke about the New Life Movement was its admonition that one should always walk on the left side of the street. The warlord Han Fu-ch'ü, governor of Shantung, reputedly remarked: "If everybody walks on the left side, who walks on the right?"
51. *World Culture, Sprout, The Pathfinder, The Big Dipper, Modern Fiction, Mass Literature, Literature Monthly, Literature News,* and *Literature* (Wen-hsüeh). Cf. C. T. Hsia, *A History of Modern Chinese Fiction, 1917-1957* (New Haven, 1961), 125.

vor. The second group which centered mostly around the faculty members of the universities and colleges in Peiping, published the *Literature Quarterly*[52] and the *Literary Supplement* of the *Ta Kung Pao*.[53] They enjoyed wide circulation because of their avant-garde, critical attitude and their use of the advanced techniques and strategies of Western writers. The crosscurrents of these three major groups contributed to an unusually lively literary atmosphere, making the decade "the richest literary period in modern China."[54]

The foremost writer of the decade was Lu Hsün (1881-1936),[55] although he had perhaps passed his peak of creativity. Known for his sharp, satirical indictment of the decadence and injustice of the old as well as the existing order, he attacked the hypocrisy and cruelty of the traditional life in a short story, "The Diary of a Madman." The protagonist, a man with a persecution complex, castigated the past as "cannibalism" even though the historical record was full of "benevolence, righteousness, truth, and virtue." The irony was that after his recovery the "madman" sought an official appointment, and in so doing collaborated with the "old game of cannibalism."[56]

Lu Hsün's most famous work was perhaps "The True Story of Ah Q," in which the hero symbolized a national disease. Ah Q, a crude country lad of a very low social status who lived at the end of the Ch'ing dynasty, was continuously bullied by his fellow villagers. Unable to fight them, he developed a dream world for himself. Whenever humiliated, he would put on an air of superiority and pretend to have won a "spiritual victory." In an attempt to boost his prestige, he went to town to engage in thievery, boasting to the villagers upon his return of his new association with the revolution. When the real revolutionaries came to the village, they collaborated with the gentry and put Ah Q on trial for robbery. The moral of the story was that Ah Q epitomized China's national disease and that the revolution had compromised with the old elements at the expense of its professed goals of social improvement.

Another major leftist writer was Mao Tun (1896-   ),[57] editor of *The Short Story* and author of a number of novels, including the trilogy of *Disillusion*, *Vacillation*, and *Pursuit*. His major work, *The Twilight*,

52. Edited by Cheng Chen-to.
53. Edited by Shen Ts'ung-wen.
54. Hsia, 138-39.
55. Real name: Chou Shu-jen.
56. Hsia, 32-33.
57. Real name: Shen Yen-ping.

described the futile effort of a nationalistic industrialist in Shanghai, who, facing economic recession and business failures in the wake of Communist uprisings, plunged into the stock market to recoup his losses. Outmaneuvered by a foreign-supported compradore, he ended in a dismal failure that sent him into bankruptcy. By his inability to grasp the Marxist oracle, the author inferred, the industrialist was doomed to failure.[58]

If Mao Tun looked to Marxism for solution to China's problems, Lao She (1898-   ),[59] believed in patriotism and individual duty. Having spent five years (1925-30) in London, he was influenced by English writers. The best known of his works was *Camel Hsiang-tzu* (1937), or *Ricksha Boy* in English, which portrayed the endless struggle of a ricksha-puller who dreamed of improving his station through sheer personal effort—hard work, marrying the boss's daughter, etc.—only to find the social obstacle too great to overcome. Dejected and resigned to his fate, he took up smoking and drinking, and finally made peace with the old order by living the degenerate life of a funeral mourner. The moral of the story was clear: in a sick society individual endeavor was futile; only collective action could alleviate the life of the poor.

Another famous non-leftist writer was Pa Chin (1904-   ),[60] a prolific writer with a dozen novels and four collections of short stories to his credit by 1937. Born into a well-to-do Szechwanese family, Pa Chin wrote with sentimentalism, frequently employing such themes as love versus revolution, good versus evil, heroes versus weaklings, and bravery versus cowardice. His *Love Trilogy—Fog, Rain*, and *Lightning*—made an immediate hit with the younger generation, while his autobiographical trilogy —*Family* (1937), *Spring* (1938), and *Autumn* (1940)—won wide acclaim for its moving descriptions of the tribulations of the younger members of a large family who struggled to break away from their elders, only to court stubborn opposition and tragic outcomes. In this work the author drove home the message that the bad systems in China must be held responsible for the evils of the society.

Regardless of their political persuasions, the writers of the 1930's had two things in common: they were imbued with a strong sense of their didactic functions, and their works reflected social realism. With satire, sarcasm, and pity, they portrayed the decadence and backwardness of the

58. Hsia, 156-57.
59. Real name: Shu Ch'ing-ch'un.
60. Real name: Li Fei-kan. The pen name Pa Chin was made up of the Chinese renditions of the first and last syllables of the Russian anarchists, *Ba*kunin and Kro-*potkin*. Cf. Hsia, 238.

old society. Perhaps, in a transitional period when revolutionary changes were taking place and when tradition constantly fought with modernity, it was inevitable that the writers involve themselves in social issues. From this standpoint, their works represented a legitimate indictment and a social protest of the existing order.

Neglect of Social and Economic Reforms. Against the record of accomplishments in finance, communication, tariff autonomy, industrial development, and education, the Nationalist government was seriously remiss in ignoring the age-old problem of landlordism and the misery of the peasant, who constituted more than 80 per cent of the total population. This failure was in part a result of compromise with the "new warlords" after the Northern Expedition. Chiang Kai-shek, in his eagerness to win a quick victory and unify the country, negotiated with the more "progressive" warlords and absorbed them into his system. These warlords had little concern for the welfare of the masses and the suffering of the peasants. Their inclusion in the KMT hierarchy diluted its social consciousness. Moreover, a considerable percentage of the KMT generals and officials were themselves connected with the landed interest; hence they were not anxious for any radical reform that would jeopardize their own position. The middle class—mostly merchants, traders, businessmen, and usurers—was no better motivated in this regard. Living in the treaty ports or operating in the villages as loan sharks, they were the beneficiaries of the existing order and hardly desired any change that would rock the boat. It was these people—the warlords, the generals, the officials, the merchants, the traders, and the money-lenders—upon whom the Nationalist government relied for support. Small wonder that it could not implement its professed social and economic programs. In fact, a general feeling prevailed over many complacent KMT personnel that since the peasant had suffered for ages, it mattered little if they were asked to wait a little longer—until the government had solved the more pressing problems of domestic insurrections and foreign aggression.

But the plight of the peasant had reached the point of desperation. A League of Nations study revealed that tenant and semitenant farming comprised 60-90 per cent in South China, and in addition to paying 40-60 per cent of the annual crops as rental, they had to pay for their landlords' regular land tax and surtax as well—the latter varying from 35 per cent to 350 per cent of the former.[61] The peasant had been exploited to

61. Swarup, 52.

the limit; only a revolution could give him relief. Yet all the KMT did was to pass a resolution in 1930 to reduce the land rent to 37.5 per cent of the main crops, and even this modest step was never really put into practice. Dr. Sun's ideal of "land to the tiller" was never fulfilled.

Fiscal Irresponsibility. That the Nationalist government was indifferent to the land problem is again seen in the fact that it relegated the land tax, the most basic of revenues in the old dynastic days, to provincial administrations, while relying on customs revenues and commercial taxes for its own sustenance. Established in the coastal areas and using Western-trained financiers such as T. V. Soong and H. H. Kung to chart the country's economic course, the Nanking government was never close to the peasant and the soil, and probably did not care about or understand the severity of the land problem. From 1928 to 1935, the government derived 42.23 per cent of its income from customs revenues, 17.13 per cent from the salt tax, and 9.16 per cent from commodity taxes. Yet the total receipts covered only 80 per cent of the expenditures, which largely consisted of military expenses (40.3 per cent) and debts service (25-37 per cent).[62] Throughout these years, the government never achieved a fiscal balance but subsisted on deficit spending. The chronic ill of budgetary imbalance led to abusive issuance of notes, which later was to cause severe inflation during the Japanese and civil wars and precipitated the economic collapse of the government in 1949.

On balance, at the end of its first decade the Nationalist government appeared stronger than it really was. On the surface, it looked as though it were forging a new order out of chaos—having pacified or reached working arrangements with the new warlords and the dissident politicians, quarantined the Communists in the Northwest, trained a German-style Central army, carried out some modernization programs in the several fields mentioned above, and formed a United Front with the various parties and groups against Japanese aggression. A superficial observer might readily say that a new China was emerging on the horizon. Yet beneath the veneer of progress lay the serious fundamental problems of social and economic injustices and the chronic ill of deficit spending. Of the three goals it set out to achieve in 1928—nationalistic revolution, democratic reconstruction, and social reform—the government by 1937 had made considerable progress toward the first, modest advance toward the second, but failed miserably in the third. Moreover, its extension of the

62. Shun-hsin Chou, *The Chinese Inflation, 1937-1949* (New York, 1963), 40-42.

Political Tutelage Period beyond the original six years from 1929, under the pretext of foreign invasion and domestic insurrections, disenchanted the liberals, who came to regard the delay as an artful device of the Nationalists to prolong their monopoly of power at the expense of constitutionalism.

The decade under review may be summed up in a neat Chinese expression, *wai-ch'iang chung-kan*, which suggests that the government was "strong on the outside but weak inside."

FURTHER READING

Bertram, James M., *China in Crisis: the Story of the Sian Mutiny* (London, 1937).

Bisson, Thomas A., *Japan in China* (New York, 1938).

Borg, Dorothy, *The United States and the Far Eastern Crisis of 1933-1938* (Cambridge, Mass., 1964).

Ch'ien, Tuan-sheng, *The Government and Politics of China* (Cambridge, Mass., 1950), chapters 7-10.

Christopher, J. W., *Conflict in the Far East: American Diplomacy in China from 1928-33* (Leiden, 1950).

Clubb, O. Edmund, *20th Century China* (New York, 1964), chapters 5-6.

———, *Communism in China, as Reported from Hankow in 1932* (New York, 1968).

Crow, Carl, (ed.), *Japan's Dream of World Empire, The Tanaka Memorial* (London, 1943).

Etō, Shinkichi, "Hai-lu-feng: The First Chinese Soviet Government," *The China Quarterly*, 8:160-83 (Oct.-Dec. 1961); 9:149-81 (Jan.-March 1962).

Friedman, I. S., *The Relations of Great Britain with China, 1933-1939* (New York, 1939).

Gillin, Donald G., *Warlord Yen Hsi-shan in Shansi Province, 1911-1949* (Princeton, 1967).

Houn, Franklin W., *A Short History of Chinese Communism* (Englewood Cliffs, 1967), chapter 3.

Hsia, C. T., *A History of Modern Chinese Fiction, 1917-1957* (New Haven, 1961).

Hsia, T. A., *The Gate of Darkness* (Seattle, 1968).

———, "Ch'ü Ch'iu-pai's Autobiographical Writings: The Making and Destruction of a 'Tender-Hearted' Communist," *The China Quarterly*, 25: 176-212 (Jan.-March 1966).

Hsiao, Tso-liang, *Power Relations within the Chinese Communist Movement, 1930-1934* (Seattle, 1961).

Hsü, Kai-yü (tr. and ed.), *Twentieth Century Chinese Poetry, An Anthology* (New York, 1963).

Hsüeh, Chün-tu, and Robert C. North, "The Founding of the Chinese Red Army," *Contemporary China* (Hong Kong), VI:59-82 (1962-64).

Hu, Ch'iao-mu, *Thirty Years of the Communist Party of China* (Peking, 1951).

Isaacs, Harold R., *The Tragedy of the Chinese Revolution*, revised (Stanford, 1951).

Israel, John, "Kuomintang Policy and Student Politics, 1927-1937" in Albert Feuerwerker, Rhoads Murphey, and Mary C. Wright (eds.), *Approaches to Modern Chinese History* (Berkeley, 1967), 289-303.

————, *Student Nationalism in China, 1927-37* (Stanford, 1966).

Jones, F. C., *Manchuria Since 1931* (London, 1949).

K'ang-chan ch'ien shih-nien chih Chung-kuo 抗戰前十年之中國 (China during the ten years before the Sino-Japanese War, 1937), compiled by Chung-kuo wen-hua chien-she hsieh-hui 中國文化建設協會 (Chinese cultural reconstruction association), reprinted, (Hong Kong, 1965).

Kiang, Wen-han, *The Chinese Student Movement* (New York, 1948).

Lattimore, Owen, *Manchuria, Cradle of Conflict* (New York, 1935).

League of Nations, *Report of the (Lytton) Commission of Enquiry* (1932).

Liang, Ching-tun 梁敬錞, *Chiu-i-pa shih-pien shih-shu* 九一八事變史述 (An historical account of the September 18, 1931, incident), (Hong Kong, 1934).

Linebarger, Paul, *Government in Republican China* (New York, 1938).

Liu, F. F., *A Military History of Modern China, 1924-1949* (Princeton, 1956).

North, Robert C., *Moscow and Chinese Communists* (Stanford, 1963).

Ogata, Sadako N., *Defiance in Manchuria: the Making of Japanese Foreign Policy* (Berkeley, 1964).

Paauw, Douglas S., "The Kuomintang and Economic Stagnation, 1928-1937," *The Journal of Asian Studies*, XV:213-20 (1957).

Quigley, Harold S., *Far Eastern War, 1937-1941* (Boston, 1942).

Rappaport, Armin, *Stimson and Japan, 1931-33* (Chicago, 1963).

Rue, John E., *Mao Tse-tung in Opposition, 1927-1935* (Standford, 1966).

Schram, Stuart, *Mao Tse-tung* (New York, 1966).

Schwartz, Benjamin I., *Chinese Communism and the Rise of Mao* (Cambridge, Mass., 1958), chapters 4-13.

Scott, A. C., *Literature and the Arts in Twentieth Century China* (New York, 1963).

Smith, Sara M., *The Manchurian Crisis, 1931-1932* (New York, 1948).

Stimson, Henry J., *The Far Eastern Crisis* (New York, 1936).

————, and McGeorge Bundy, *On Active Service in Peace and War* (New York, 1948).

Strong, Anna Louise, *China's Millions: the Revolutionary Struggles from 1927 to 1935* (New York, 1935).

Swarup, Shanti, *A Study of the Chinese Communist Movement* (Oxford, 1966).

Tang, Tsou, *America's Failure in China, 1941-50* (Chicago, 1963).

Thornton, Richard C., "The Emergence of a New Comintern Strategy for

China: 1928," *The Comintern: Historical Highlights,* ed. by M. M. Drachkovitch and B. Lazitch (New York, 1966), 66-110.

————, *The Comintern and the Chinese Communists, 1928-1931* (Seattle, 1969).

Tong, Hollington K., *Chiang Kai-shek, Soldier and Statesman* (Shanghai, 1937), 2 vols.

Tsao, V. Y., *The Constitutional Structure of Modern China* (Melbourne, 1948).

Tso-liang Hsiao, *Power Relations Within the Chinese Communist Movement, 1930-34* (Seattle, 1961); Vol. II, *The Chinese Documents* (Seattle, 1967).

————, *The Land Revolution in China, 1930-1934* (Seattle, 1969).

Tung, William L., *The Political Institutions of Modern China* (The Hague, 1964).

Wang, Chi-Chen (tr.), *Ah Q and Others: Selected Stories of Lusin* (New York, 1941).

————, *Contemporary Chinese Story* (New York, 1953).

Wang, Chien-min 王健民, *Chung-Kuo Kung-ch'an-tang shih-kao* 中國共產黨史稿 (A draft history of the Chinese Communist Party), (Taipei, 1965), 3 vols.

Wang, Kan-yu, *The Local Government of China: A Study of the Administrative Nature of Local Units* (Chungking, 1945).

Willoughby, W. W., *The Sino-Japanese Controversy and the League of Nations* (Baltimore, 1935).

Wright, S. F., *China's Struggle for Tariff Autonomy: 1843-1938* (Shanghai, 1938).

Yakhontoff, Victor A., *The Chinese Soviets* (New York, 1934).

24

The Sino-Japanese War, 1937-45

The prospect of a China united against foreign aggression worried the Japanese militarists and extremists, who feared for the future of their expansion policy on the continent. As in 1931, those anxious to strike before China became too strong were again the young officers of the Kwantung army; encouraged by the easy conquest of Manchuria, by the lack of international sanctions, and by the rise of Nazism and Fascism in Europe, they were eager to turn North China into a second Manchukuo and there build up a continental base for Japan. Barely half a year after the Sian incident and the adoption of the United Front policy in China, these officers manufactured an incident at the Marco Polo Bridge (Lukou-ch'iao) about ten miles west of Peiping, on July 7, 1937, precipitating a clash with the Chinese garrison. Once hostilities began and all hope for a peaceful settlement had faded, the Chinese government became fiercely determined to fight for its survival to the bitter end. What the Japanese had intended to be a short war to conquer North China turned out to be a long war of attrition which lasted until 1945. This second Sino-Japanese war in less than half a century[1] produced serious and far-reaching repercussions in both countries: it led to the defeat of Japan for the first time in her modern history and thoroughly exhausted the Nationalist government in China, thus opening the way for the seizure of power by the Communists in 1949.

1. The first was fought in 1894-95.

THE RISE OF THE JAPANESE MILITARISTS

Though it appeared on the surface as a locally inspired affair master-minded by the Kwangtung army, the "China Incident" of 1937 was actually a well-planned, premeditated plot climaxing a series of clashes between the Japanese military and the civilian government, as well as between the different groups of the military itself. Ever since their successful venture in Manchuria, the militarists had catapulted themselves into national politics at the expense of the civilian government. Ignoring the traditional admonition that the military should refrain from meddling in politics, the young officers openly attacked party politicians for their mishandling of the affairs of state which was said to have lowered Japan's international status. Spurred by chauvinistic zeal, they ridiculed the bureaucrats for their inefficiency and corruption, and censured the *zaibatsu* for their alleged role in bringing about the depression. As the self-appointed saviors of the country, the young officers vowed to eliminate these evil elements and to effect a "Showa Restoration" whereby the emperor, through the army, would re-establish a direct relationship with the farmers and the people at large. So "sacred" was this mission that the young officers succeeded in creating an image that nothing could stand in their way and nothing could be allowed to undermine the prestige and position of the army. Their ruthless drive for power, their open advocacy of expansion, and their ready recourse to conspiracies, plots, intimidation, and assassinations bespoke a certain type of "abnormal behavior."[2] Indeed, their unruly, unrestrained behavior was hard to swallow even for the older, well-disciplined officers. Yet the young officers could not be stopped, for they claimed to represent the voice of the people and the future of Japan, and they enjoyed the support of extremist politicians and secret societies. Throughout the period of 1932-36 the militarists rose steadily in national politics until they totally eclipsed the party government. It was a tragedy for modern Japan.

The Coup of May 15, 1932. The meteoric rise of the militarists was achieved partially through the brutal methods of coup and assassination. Following two abortive coups in the spring of 1931, the young officers

---

2. For an illuminating study of Japanese behavior of this period, see Maruyama Masao, *Gendai seiji no shisō to kōdō* (Contemporary political thoughts and actions), I (Tokyo, 1961), 7-148.

employed political assassination as a tool and effectively eliminated the former finance minister and governor of the Bank of Japan as well as the leader of the Mitsui *zaibatsu*[3] in the spring of 1932. Then, on May 15, 1932, a group of army and navy officers attacked Tokyo's police station, banks, and party headquarters and succeeded in murdering Premier Inukai Tsuyoshi, who had disapproved of the military action in China and had favored a negotiated settlement. In brazen defiance of the consequences, the assassins then voluntarily surrendered themselves to the police. The trial that followed turned out to be a public airing of the conspirators' philosophy—to save the country through the elimination of the weak politicians, corrupt bureaucrats, and selfish *zaibatsu*. The argument evoked widespread sympathy to the point where even the prosecutor and the newspapers treated the conspirators as heroes rather than assassins. The party government, in existence since 1918, was dealt a mortal blow from which it did not recover until after World War II.

The choice of the next two premiers testified to the powerful influence of the militarists. The Seiyūkai had put forward its titular leader, Dr. Suzuki Kisaburō, for nomination, but the army insisted on Baron Hiranuma Kiichirō, head of the extremist National Foundation Society (*Kokuhōn sha*). The Elder Statesman Saionji was obliged to pick a compromise candidate in Admiral Saitō Makoto, whose government lasted for two years until July 1934.[4] The next government was again headed by a naval officer, Admiral Okada Keisuke, who remained in office until the coup of 1936. During these two cabinets, the militarists and political extremists continued to gain ascendancy and pushed the country further down the road of fascism and totalitarianism.

The Coup of February 26, 1936. The army, though united in its struggle against civilian rule, had its own inner conflicts. A number of older, more responsible officers subscribed to the traditional injunction to shun politics, but many others had become political-minded and meddlesome; among these latter were two groups. One was the Imperial Way Faction (*Kōdō ha*), consisting of young activist, field-grade officers under the leadership of Minister of War Araki, vice-chief of the General Staff Mazaki, and commander-in-chief of the Gendarmerie Hata. They demanded a military dictatorship, control of the national budget, expansion of the army and the navy, nationalization of the essential industries, territorial

3. Inoue and Baron Dan respectively.
4. It fell in July 1934 in the wake of a financial scandal involving the minister of commerce and industry, Baron Nakajima.

aggrandizement in Asia, and direct action in China. The other group was the Control Faction (*Tōsei ha*), consisting of older and better disciplined high-ranking officers, such as Generals Nagata Tetsuzan, Abe Nobuyuki, and strangely enough, Tōjō Hideki. They too wanted a firm foreign policy and expansion of Japan's hegemony in Asia, but they disapproved of direct action and terroristic methods, preferring to gain influence through legal means and proper channels.

The inner conflicts of the army generated instability and turmoil. In July 1933 a coterie of young officers, disappointed with Admrial Saitō's inability to carry out the reforms demanded by the Imperial Way Faction, plotted to kill all cabinet ministers and party leaders. Although this fantastic conspiracy was uncovered in time to prevent a vast bloodshed, the forty-four defendants, amid the rising tide of militarism and chauvinism, escaped trial until 1937 and were released in 1941. Nonetheless, the failure of this coup enabled the Control Faction to score a point in the power struggle. General Araki was replaced by General Hayashi Senjūrō as minister of war. In an attempt to reduce tension between the two groups, Hayashi replaced in July 1935 General Mazaki as inspector-general of military education with a milder, more amenable officer, Lieutenant General Watanabe Jutarō. The mastermind of this reshuffle was General Nagata of the Control Faction, whose moments of glory lasted but a month—on August 12, 1935, a young military radical, Lieutenant Colonel Aizawa, assassinated him. However, the sentence of death for the assassin hardly blunted the razor-sharp fanaticism of the young officers. When the minister of finance slashed the army budget in January 1936, they decided to strike again.

On February 26, a group of young officers and 1,400 soldiers, led by Captain Ando Teruzo, seized control of central Tokyo, occupying the Diet building, the police headquarters, and the War Department. They invaded the premier's residence, killing his brother-in-law by mistake. Others that were killed included a former premier,[5] the minister of finance,[6] and the inspector-general of military education.[7] It was not until the loyal troops had surrounded the mutineers and proclaimed the emperor's order that they return to their camps that the coup was finally brought under control. The subsequent trial sent thirteen young officers to execution and Generals Araki and Mazaki to the reserves.

With the resignation of Admiral Okada as premier in March 1936,

5. Admiral Saitō.
6. Takahashi.
7. General Watanabe.

Hirota Kōki took over the helm of government. He had been foreign minister since autumn 1933 and was known for his extremist connections and aggressive China policy. Supported by the militarists, he promised to "reform" the government and appointed many army-approved personnel to his cabinet.[8]

Hirota's China Policy. Hirota's foreign policy aimed at isolating China from the rest of the world so as to coerce her into submission, and improving relations with the West while preventing it from expanding its influence in Asia. In an attempt to bind China, Japan, and Manchukuo together in a political and economic union, he proposed in October 1935 to adjust Sino-Japanese relations on the basis of three conditions: (1) Chinese recognition of Manchukuo and friendly relations between China and Japan; (2) economic cooperation between China, Japan, and Manchukuo in developing North China; and (3) joint defense against communism. What he essentially wanted was to force Nanking to recognize the *fait accompli* in Manchuria, the various Japan-sponsored autonomous movements in North China, and the necessity of making a common cause with Japan against the Soviet Union. The Chinese government refused to accept these terms; instead it issued three counterproposals: (1) complete Chinese territorial integrity; (2) nonimpairment of China's sovereignty; and (3) Sino-Japanese relations based on equality. Not surprisingly, no concrete results came from these exchanges.

Japanese activities in North China had become all but intolerable. They sponsored an autonomous movement of the five northern provinces of Hopeh, Chahar, Suiyuan, Shansi, and Shantung, and in December 1935 created an Eastern Hopeh Autonomous Council. The Chinese government countered it with the establishment of a Hopeh-Chahar Political Council with its headquarters in Peiping. But, friction mounted as Japanese *ronin* (rascals) as well as Koreans and Formosans continued to openly engage in large-scale silver- and narcotics-smuggling. To all appearances, North China was beginning to look like a second Manchuria. Meanwhile, Japanese-inspired incidents in other parts of China broke out one after another. In June 1935 a Japanese vice-consul at Nanking suddenly disappeared, giving the militarists a pretext for threatening to oc-

8. For instance, his minister of finance, Baba Eiichi, was an army stooge. The new president of the Privy Council, Baron Hiranuma, was an avowed facist and extremist. His army and navy ministers, General Terauchi and Admiral Nagano, were both expansionists.

cupy part of the city as a prerequisite for negotiations. Tensions were temporarily relieved when the vice-consul in question reappeared in the city a few days later—he had gone to the hills to commit suicide but could not endure the hardship of hunger. Another incident involved the unauthorized establishment of a Japanese consulate in Chengtu, Szechwan, in 1936. Amid the resulting popular indignation, Chinese mobs killed four Japanese newspapermen, who were mistaken for consuls. The case was settled when two of the rioters were sentenced to death.

Against this turbulent background, Chinese popular demands for resistance against Japan mounted daily, and a nationwide boycott of Japanese imports succeeded in cutting trade by two-thirds. Hirota, acting on the wishes of the Diet which had a Minseitō (Democratic Party) majority, reopened negotiations with China in the summer of 1936, proposing: (1) an end to anti-Japanese activities in China; (2) recognition of Japan's special position in North China; (3) Sino-Japanese collaboration against communism, especially in Outer Mongolia; (4) Sino-Japanese economic cooperation; and (5) Japanese advisers in all branches of the Chinese government. These terms, especially the last which smacked of the Twenty-one Demands of 1915, were flatly rejected by the Chinese government, which counterproposed: (1) termination of Japanese, Korean, and Formosan smuggling; (2) withdrawal of Japanese troops from Hopeh and Chahar; and (3) suppression of the Japanese-sponsored autonomous movements. Negotiations broke down in December 1936.

Internationally, Hirota had adopted a policy oriented toward isolating the Soviet Union, preparing for war against the United States and Britain, and collaborating with Germany and Italy. Japan signed the Anti-Comintern Pact with Germany in 1936, and with Italy a year later. Under Hirota, Japan had become a totalitarian state, moving ever closer to the brink of war.

Hirota's government fell in December 1936, and in February of the following year General Hayashi became premier. The new foreign minister, Sato Naotake, proposed a *rapprochement* with China through the restoration of economic relations and an initial settlement of minor issues; North China, however, was to be maintained as a special area. China at this time had already been committed to a United Front and was in no mood for further concessions. The Hayashi cabinet fell after four months; the next administration under Prince Konoe Fumimaro was entirely dominated by the army. General Tōjō, chief of staff of the Kwantung Army, advocated the application of force against China. Although his ideas were rejected by Tokyo, the Japanese army in North China decided to go ahead on its own and provoked a clash on July 7, 1937.

THE UNDECLARED WAR, 1937

Invoking the Boxer Protocol of 1901 which permitted foreign signatories to station troops between Peking (Peiping) and the sea, the Japanese garrison in North China in early July 1937 held a field exercise outside Peiping, near the Marco Polo Bridge. On the pretext that a soldier was missing, the Japanese demanded to enter the nearby city of Wanping before midnight of July 7 to conduct a search. When refused by the local Chinese garrison—the 29th Army under General Sung Che-yüan—the Japanese army bombarded the city and occupied it at 4:30 a.m. on the morning of July 8, thus precipitating an undeclared war between the two countries.

Strictly speaking, the Japanese claim to the right of field exercises under the Boxer Protocol was untenable. While Article 9 of the Protocol provided twelve places between the Chinese capital and Shanhaikuan for the stationing of fixed numbers of foreign troops—1,350 each for Britain, France, Germany, and Japan, 500 for Italy, 300 for Russia—the Marco Polo Bridge and Wanping were not among them.[9] Indeed, the Japanese garrison by July 1937 had quadrupled the alloted figure. Not only were the Protocol stipulations violated, but the Japanese had deviated from the precedents of field exercise. Foreign powers in the past generally had held exercises in the Shanhaikuan area—the farthest from Peking (Peiping)—to avoid irritating Chinese sensibilities. Moreover, the very applicability of the Protocol in 1937 was doubtful from the legal standpoint, since the Chinese capital had moved from Peking (Peiping) to Nanking; the stipulation on free passage from the capital to the sea had become all but meaningless.[10]

Once hostilities began, Japanese reinforcements from Manchuria and the home islands poured into North China, occupying all the strategic points outside Peiping. Obviously, the Marco Polo Bridge incident was but the beginninng of a much larger design. The Nanking government, having committed itself to the United Front against Japanese aggression,

9. These twelve places were Huang-tsun, Lang-fang, Yang-tsun, Tientsin, Chun-liang-cheng, T'ang-ku, Lu-tai, Tang-shan, Luan-chou, Chang-li, Chin-wang-tao, and Shan-haikuan.

10. Shuhsi Hsü, *How the Far Eastern War Was Begun* (Shanghai, 1938), 19-33.

63. General Chiang Kai-shek and Yen Hsi-shan.

64. Part of the former members of the First Division of the First Corps of the Worker-Peasant Revolutionary Army, first formed after the Autumn Harvest Uprising of 1927 (Yenan, 1937, Mao third from left).

65. President Roosevelt greeting China's Finance Minister, T. V. Soong.

66. Feng Yü-hsiang.

67. Hu Shih as head of the Academia Sinica, *circa* 1960.

68. Sun Fo.

was determined to fight. On July 17, 1937, at a summer conference at Kuling, Chiang Kai-shek resolutely announced that when pushed to the ultimate extreme, China had no choice but "to throw the last ounce of energy" into "a struggle for national survival." However, to leave no stone unturned, he named four minimum conditions upon which peace talks might be initiated:

1. No settlement infringing upon the territorial integrity and sovereignty of China.
2. No illegal alteration of the Hopeh-Chahar Political Council headed by General Sung Che-yüan.
3. No removal of local officials appointed by the central government, such as the chairman of the said council, by outside pressure.
4. No restriction upon the position of the 29th Army.

Chiang made it clear that China desired peace but not at all costs; that she did not seek war, but if it was thrust upon her she had no choice but to fight to the end, with no thought of compromise. He earnestly called upon the people and the country to unite in a holy struggle: "Let there be no distinction between North and South, age or youth, but let all implicitly and with iron discipline follow the guidance of the government."[11] The war of resistance, delayed since 1931, finally assumed coherence and meaning. The Chinese people and the various parties—the KMT, the CCP, the Youth, etc. all enthusiastically pledged their support of the war.

If China was prepared for a long fight, Japan had no intention of becoming bogged down on the Asiatic mainland; Russia was still the principal enemy in the minds of the General Staff. Japan wanted a quick victory to seize North China and force Nanking into economic cooperation. Disparaging China's ability and will to wage a full-fledged war, the Japanese military allowed three months to conclude the China affair. From a strictly military point of view, it looked as if their prediction was accurate.

The modernized Japanese army proved more than a match for the Chinese. Having inflicted heavy losses on the 29th Army, the Japanese were poised to attack Peiping in late July. Any effective defense of this city of ancient treasure and culture would undoubtedly have caused untold damage to the priceless historic relics and art objects. The Nationalists decided to spare Peiping this terrible fate and ordered its evacuation on July 28. Two days later Tientsin was also lost.

On August 13 the Japanese opened a second front in Shanghai, the

11. Shuhsi Hsü, 56, 61-64.

financial center of the nation, to destroy China's economic capacity for war. There, unexpectedly, Chiang threw in some of his best German-trained troops—the 87th and 88th divisions—which succeeded brilliantly in stalling the enemy advance for three months. The casualties on both sides were heavy, and some military critics considered Chiang's decision too costly to be wise. Nonetheless, the valiant resistance proved that China could frustrate the aggressor if she applied herself firmly, and such a revelation was a tremendous boost to Chinese morale. But the Japanese tactic of outflanking the defender ultimately worked, causing an unexpectedly rapid disintegration of the Chinese defenses. The road to Nanking was left wide open, and the enemy swiftly advanced to the gates of the Chinese capital. At this point, Germany offered mediation.

Berlin had not favored the Japanese invasion of China. Not only did it fear that such a commitment of troops would relieve Japanese pressure on Russia, but it was also concerned that China might be driven to seek Soviet aid. Nor did Berlin overlook the sensitive issue of German advisers training Chinese troops against the invader, who was paradoxically an ally of Germany in the Anti-Comintern Pact. For these reasons, Berlin instructed its ambassador in China, Oscar P. Trautmann, to forward a Japanese proposal of peace to Chiang in November 1937: (1) autonomy for inner Mongolia; (2) extension of the demilitarized zone in North China, where China could retain her administrative power but not appoint anti-Japanese officials; (3) extension of the demilitarized zone at Shanghai; (4) termination of anti-Japanese activities in China; and (5) effective measures against communism in China, and customs revision in favor of Japan.

Chiang was advised by his generals to consider the peace terms seriously, but so swift was the Japanese juggernaut that Nanking fell on December 12, 1937, before any diplomatic talks took place. The Japanese militarists now demanded that Tokyo discontinue the negotiations or revise the terms. On December 20 the Japanese government made a second proposal through the German ambassador, demanding that China agree (1) to abandon her anti-Japanese policy and unite with Japan and Manchukuo in a joint anti-Communist front; (2) to pay a reparation to Japan; (3) to sign a treaty of economic cooperation with Japan and Manchukuo; and (4) to accept demilitarized zones with autonomous agencies in them.

Tokyo warned that rejection of these terms would force Japan to reevaluate the war from a radically new standpoint; hence the second proposal was tantamount to an ultimatum. General Falkenhausen, Chiang's

German adviser, was instructed by Berlin to impress upon the Chinese leader of the inadvisability of a prolonged war. As Chiang weighed the various alternatives and delayed his decision, the Japanese made an even harsher third proposal of nine points, which the German ambassador hesitated to forward.[12] Meanwhile, Chiang had independently come to the decision of rejecting the peace overture. He moved his capital to Chungking, Szechwan, where the rugged terrain, the precipitous gorges, and the rapid currents in the narrowing Yangtze would make it all but impossible for the enemy to penetrate. Chiang himself, as commander-in-chief of the Chinese forces, remained in strategic Wuhan to direct military operations, while schools, factories, and other establishments in the occupied areas were encouraged to migrate inland. The southwest became a new base of resistance which dashed the Japanese dream of a quick settlement.

The fall of Nanking was followed by the indiscriminate massacre of approximately 100,000 civilians, accompanied by innumerable cases of molestation of women. So notorious was "The Rape of Nanking," as it came to be known, that even the Japanese militarists concealed it from the public at home. When the facts were finally revealed in the postwar International War Crimes Tribunal in Tokyo, the Japanese people were deeply shocked and ashamed of the atrocities.

After their conquest of Nanking, the main Japanese forces moved northward along the Tientsin-Pukow Railway, while other columns moved southward from North China in a pincer movement to seal off the important communication junction of Hsuchow. But at T'ai-erh-chuang, near Hsuchow, they encountered heroic resistance by Chinese forces in late March and early April of 1938, sustaining 30,000 casualties. This was a major Chinese victory since the fall of Nanking, but ultimately Hsuchow had to be evacuated on May 19. Later, in June, the Chinese broke the Yellow River dikes to slow the enemy advance.

The next major battle was fought at Wuhan, where Chiang had established his headquarters and where twelve Japanese divisions had closed in from two directions along the Yangtze and the Huai rivers. After several hundred large and small encounters over a period of four and one-half months, Wuhan was finally relinquished on December 25, 1938. Its loss, coupled with the fall of Canton on October 21, drove some of the unfirm Nationalist leaders to despair and despondency, but Chiang carried on the fight as he had pledged.

12. James T. C. Liu, "German Mediation in the Sino-Japanese War, 1937-38," *Far Eastern Quarterly*, VIII:2:157-71 (Feb. 1949).

The fall of Wuhan marked the end of the first phase of the war, which lasted sixteen months. During this period the Chinese traded space for time and enticed the enemy deep into the hinterland. Correspondingly, the Japanese strategy for quick victory bogged down, mired deep in the abdomen of China from which it could not extricate itself.

The next stage of war—from the fall of Wuhan in December 1938 to the Pearl Harbor attack in December 1941—was basically one of attrition, where the Japanese occupied most of the cities and communication lines in the eastern half of China, while the Chinese pursued a scorched-earth policy followed by strategic withdrawals and guerrilla warfare. Numerous seesaw battles were fought, but on the whole the situation gradually became stabilized, with the Japanese dominating the key *points* on the map such as cities and communication centers, and the Chinese holding the vast *areas* in the countryside, often only a few miles from the enemy. Thus, "point warfare" and "area warfare" characterized the respective Japanese and Chinese strategies.

The masses of civilians were gravely affected by the war, and their tribulations were exacerbated by the particularly atrocious conduct of the enemy. The Japanese bombed noncombatants, torpedoed fishing boats, strafed civilians, bayoneted ex-soldiers tied in batches of fifty, and burned, looted, and raped. So wild and reckless were they that they sometimes attacked neutrals; the American gunboat *Panay* was sunk by Japanese planes outside Nanking on December 12, 1937. International sanctions were slow in coming, for Europe itself was threatened by Nazism and Fascism, and the United States still clung to her neutrality. Yet, in spite of everything, the Japanese could not quickly win the war. Tokyo finally resigned itself to a stalemate; it adopted the policy of living off the conquered land with the help of puppet governments. On October 29, 1937, a Mongolian Autonomous Government was created in Chahar and Suiyuan, with the Inner Mongolian Prince Teh as the figurehead ruler. On December 14, another puppet "provisional government" was established in Peiping, with Wang K'e-ming as the front man; it governed the five northern provinces of Hopeh, Chahar, Suiyuan, Honan, and Shantung. On March 28, 1938, a third puppet government was set up at Nanking under the formal leadership of Liang Hung-chih, with jurisdiction over the three eastern provinces of Kiangsu, Chekiang, and Anhwei. But none of the three leaders had the national stature necessary to achieve unification; so the Japanese intensified their search for a man of greater prominence.

WANG CHING-WEI'S PEACE MOVEMENT

On November 3, 1938 in commemoration of the birthday of Emperor Meiji, Prince Konoe, premier of Japan, proclaimed a "New Order in East Asia," based upon six principles: (1) permanent stability for East Asia; (2) neighborly amity and international justice; (3) joint defense against communism; (4) economic cooperation; (5) creation of a new culture; and (6) world peace. It was a kind of Japanese "Monroe Doctrine," manifesting the historical Japanese aspiration to dominate Asia as reflected in Hideyoshi's attempts to conquer Korea and China in the late 16th century, in the Pan-Asiatic ideas among Japanese leaders in the early 20th century, and in the alleged "Tanaka Memorial" of 1927.[13]

To those Chinese politicians who had been frustrated by the absence of prospects for victory or peace, by the progressive inflation,[14] and by the mounting difficulties of life, the Konoe statement appeared to offer a ray of hope for a quick settlement. Wang Ching-wei, among others, found the Japanese idea intriguing and was ready to explore it. After an unsuccessful attempt to persuade the governor of Yunnan[15] to secede with him, he flew out of Chungking to Hanoi on December 18, 1938, to start a peace movement. Four days later, Konoe announced Japan's decision to destroy the Nationalist government and to adjust Sino-Japanese relations with a "new" Chinese regime on the basis of (1) friendship and amity: not only would Japan make no demands of territory or indemnity but she would return to China all concessions and leased territories and abolish extraterritoriality; (2) mutual defense against communism in the same spirit as the anti-Comintern Pacts between the Axis powers; and (3) economic cooperation without any intention on the part of Japan to monopolize China's economy.

Considering these terms to be more favorable than the proposals tendered through the German ambassador earlier, Wang urged the Chungking government to accept them as the basis for a settlement. Chiang dismissed the notion summarily and persuaded the KMT to expel Wang. The latter then proceeded to organize his own government and signed eight agreements with Japan, including recognition of Manchukuo and

13. Kenneth Colegrove, "The New Order in East Asia," *Far Eastern Quarterly,* I:1:5-24 (Nov. 1941).
14. The wholesale prices during 1937-1941 rose 4.7 per cent monthly in Shanghai and 6.8 per cent in Chungking. Shun-hsin Chou, 21.
15. Lung Yün.

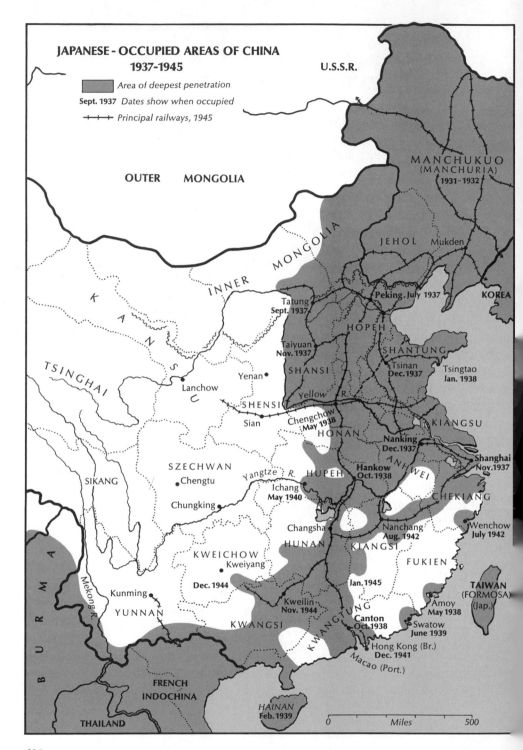

JAPANESE - OCCUPIED AREAS OF CHINA
1937-1945

Area of deepest penetration
Sept. 1937 Dates show when occupied
┼┼┼┼ Principal railways, 1945

U.S.S.R.

OUTER   MONGOLIA

MANCHUKUO
(MANCHURIA)
1931-1932

I N N E R   MONGOLIA

JEHOL   Mukden

K A N S U

Tatung
Sept. 1937

Peking, July 1937

KOREA

HOPEH

TSINGHAI

Taiyuan
Nov. 1937

SHANTUNG

Tsinan
Dec. 1937

Tsingtao
Jan. 1938

SHANSI

Lanchow

Yenan

Yellow R.

SHENSI

Sian

Chengchow
May 1938

HONAN

KIANGSU

Nanking
Dec. 1937

Shanghai
Nov. 1937

SZECHWAN

Chengtu

Yangtze R.

HUPEH

Hankow
Oct. 1938

ANHWEI

CHEKIANG

SIKANG

Ichang
May 1940

Chungking

Changsha

Nanchang
Aug. 1942

Wenchow
July 1942

HUNAN

KIANGSI

FUKIEN

KWEICHOW

Kweiyang

Dec. 1944

Jan. 1945

TAIWAN
(FORMOSA)
(Jap.)

Kunming

YUNNAN

Kweilin
Nov. 1944

KWANGSI

KWANGTUNG

Amoy
May 1938

Canton
Oct. 1938

Swatow
June 1939

B U R M A

Mekong R.

Hong Kong (Br.)
Dec. 1941

Macao (Port.)

FRENCH
INDOCHINA

HAINAN
Feb. 1939

THAILAND

0   Miles   500

688

permission for Japan to station troops in China in order to facilitate a joint defense against communism. Other aspects of the agreements acknowledged Japanese control over China's natural resources in an act of "economic cooperation," and Japanese authority to appoint advisers in Chinese education and cultural affairs.

To rationalize his collaboration with the enemy, Wang told his countrymen that China must recognize Japan's ability to wage a long war. Since two years of fighting had produced no concrete results, it would be a prudent course to end hostilities so as to save the Asiatic civilization from destruction. Stressing the fact that Dr. Sun had been a firm believer in Pan-Asianism and Sino-Japanese cooperation, Wang called upon his countrymen not to fight but to befriend Japan. Similarly, he announced, Sino-Japanese collaboration could provide a bulwark against communism and thereby save the country from the ravages of civil war. Euphemistically, Wang's followers compared his peace movement to the "appeasement policy" of Tseng Kuo-fan and Li Hung-chang during the Self-strengthening period (1861-95).

It should be noted, however, that although Sun was pro-Japanese in his early revolutionary career, he grew bitter about Japanese intervention later and became ardently pro-Soviet after 1920. How could Wang claim to be a loyal follower of Sun and still be anti-Communist? To explain away this apparent contradiction, Wang went to great length to distinguish Marxism from original communism and Sun's Principle of People's Livelihood. Communism, he announced, at the "Sixth National Congress" of his "own" KMT, originated in ancient Greece as a political idea not unlike the utopian notion of *Ta-t'ung* in ancient China; it bore no relation to Marxism which was based on dialectical materialism and class struggle. When Sun equated his Principle of People's Livelihood with communism, Wang insisted, he was referring to the original communism in a broad sense and not to Marxist communism, as evidenced by his 1923 joint communiqué with Joffe which clearly stated that communism was not fit for China. Hence Wang could be opposed to communism and still be a loyal disciple of Sun.

In March 1940, under Japanese aegis, Wang set up a five-yüan government in Nanking, which absorbed the older puppet regimes at Peiping and Nanking. The regime was recognized by Manchukuo, and the three Axis powers and their satellites,[16] but not by any of the major Western powers.

16. Such as Rumania, Bulgaria, and Denmark.

The question naturally arises as to why Wang, the close follower of Sun and the second-ranking member in the Nationalist Party and government, should want to defect to the enemy and risk his reputation? It appears that first of all he was driven by defeatism to conclude that China could not win the war; it would be more realistic to negotiate a peace before total defeat. Secondly, he had been engaged in a power struggle with Chiang whom he thought had usurped his place as successor to Dr. Sun. Thirdly, he was concerned about the welfare of the people in the Japanese-occupied areas. A fourth and intriguing interpretation was offered by his chief aide, Chou Fu-hai, who artfully explained in a news conference that Wang's movement could not hurt China; if Chiang won the war, Wang's agreements with Japan would naturally be nullified; if Chiang could not win the war, his future settlement with Japan could not possibly surpass the terms achieved by Wang. Then, in a move calculated to evoke sympathy, Chou asked the searching question: If Wang had not offered his services, who would have taken care of the teeming millions in the occupied areas? One may surmise that Wang, driven by defeatism and jealousy of Chiang, decided to offer himself as a buffer between the harsh Japanese conquerors and the helpless people of China. Perhaps he truly believed that his peace mission could not hurt China in the long run and could actually reduce a good deal of misery in the short run. The truth of his motivation may never be known, for he died a few months before Japan's surrender in 1945. Though he was spared a public trial, his senior followers were shot as traitors soon after the war.

THE NATIONALIST PROGRAM OF RESISTANCE AND RECONSTRUCTION

During the early years of the war, a number of important developments took place within the KMT and the government. In 1937 a National Defense Advisory Council was created to include social leaders and members of parties other than the KMT to symbolize national unity. This creation was followed by the reorganization of the Supreme Military Command in January 1938, which placed the Military Commission directly under the government and provided for its administration by a chairman (Chiang) and seven to nine members. Of greater significance was the convocation at Wuhan of the KMT Provisional National Congress in April 1938 and its adoption of four major resolutions: (1) creation of the new post of Director-general (*Tsung-ts'ai*) as the party Leader, with

Chiang as the first appointee; (2) creation of a Three People's Principles Youth Corps to train young men as a basic force in the war of resistance and national reconstruction; (3) creation of a People's Political Council to replace the National Defense Advisory Council, as the highest wartime popular organ of state; and (4) adoption of an "Outline of Resistance and Reconstruction."

The "Outline" stressed the importance of the Three People's Principles and of national unity in prosecuting the war under the leadership of Chiang and the KMT. It also manifested a number of fundamental goals as follows:

1. Establishment of local government in preparation for the ultimate introduction of a constitution;
2. Independent diplomacy and alliance with countries opposed to aggression against the imperalists;
3. Military training of the people and intensification of the political indoctrination of soldiers in order to give them a better understanding of the meaning of resistance;
4. Adoption of a planned economy with a view to integrating national defense and people's livelihood; encouragement of the removal of factories from the occupied zones to free China, and development of new plants in the free areas;
5. Recognition of education as the foundation of resistance and reconstruction; encouragement of the removal of universities and colleges from occupied territories to free China, and elevation of Chinese traditional studies as well as modern scientific education.

The "Outline" received the enthusiastic support of the National Social Party on April 13, 1938, and of the Youth Party on April 21. The Communist Party, which had its own program, gave it its tacit consent.

Following the KMT Congress, a People's Political Council was organized, comprised of members of all political persuasions including Mao Tse-tung and a number of other Communist leaders. Its inaugural meeting, convened at Wuhan between July 7 and 15, 1938, was attended by 162 delegates who staunchly pledged that all Chinese, regardless of parties, religions, creeds, and professions, were committed to supporting the war until the final victory was won.

The country was united in the struggle against Japan, yet behind the brave façade of national solidarity were critical cleavages and the seeds of discord, especially with regard to the question of the Communist Party.

THE UNITED FRONT AND ITS DECLINE

As may be recalled, the Communists had re-established relations with the Nationalists after the Sian incident of December 1936. In January of the following year Wang Ming and other members of the Comintern arrived in Yennan to help formulate the strategy of the United Front. They urged the CCP to convince the Nanking government of its sincerity in cooperation, to win Anglo-American sympathy, to expand the Red army to its full capacity, to impress upon Chiang of its readiness to reconsider the question of the Chinese Soviets in case of war with Japan, and to establish popular fronts in the five provinces of Shensi, Kansu, Ninghsia, Chinghai, and Sinkiang. On the basis of these guidelines, the CCP began negotiations with Nanking in February 1937 about the details of the United Front. Shortly after the outbreak of the Sino-Japanese War, the CCP issued on September 22, 1937, an appealing manifesto entitled, "Together We Confront the National Crisis" (*Kung-fu kuo-nan*), to explain its position during the war:

1. The CCP will struggle to fulfill completely Dr. Sun's Three People's Principles which best answer China's needs today.
2. The CCP will abolish the policy of sabotage and Sovietization which aims at the overthrow of the KMT government, and will stop the forcible confiscation of the holdings of landlords.
3. The CCP will abolish all existing Soviets in favor of democratic government, so as to achieve unified political administration throughout the country.
4. The CCP will abolish the name and insignia of the Red Army, which is to be reorganized as the National Revolutionary Army and is to be subject to control by the government's Military Commission; it is ready to march forward and fight the Japanese at the front.[17]

Welcoming the Communist pledges, Chiang expressed the pious hope that the CCP would prove its sincerity through actual contribution to the war and to the cause of National Revolution. The 30,000-man Red army was reorganized as the 8th Route army—later renamed the 18th Route army—under the command of Chu Teh and P'eng Te-huai. One of its

17. The basis of this manifesto was contained in a telegram of February 10, 1937, from the CCP Central Committee to the KMT Central Executive Committee. See Schram, 183.

three divisional commanders was Lin Piao, destined to rise to greater fame in later years. The army was sent to fight the Japanese in northern Shansi. Later, in December 1937, Communist units south of the Yangtze were organized as the New Fourth army under the command of Yeh T'ing and Hsiang Ying, with a strength of 10,000 men. A further symbol of the KMT-CCP *rapprochement*, as already noted, was the election of Mao and other Communist leaders to the newly created People's Political Council in 1938. Thus, the two parties once again collaborated in the face of Japanese aggression.

Yet this alliance, like the earlier one of 1923-27, was ill-fated. From the beginning the Communists regarded it as nothing more than a means to carry out the orders of the Comintern, to be freed from Nationalist attacks, and to build up strength during the war. Lest any member of his party misunderstand these secret objectives, Mao admonished the cadres that they should fully utilize the opportunity of the Japanese war for self-expansion. "Our fixed policy," he said, "should be 70 per cent expansion, 20 per cent dealing with the Kuomintang, and 10 per cent resisting Japan."[18] The cadres were asked to act accordingly if they lost contact with the party headquarters. Mao made it very clear that temporary co-operation with the KMT was not a betrayal of one's principles, nor a surrender to the enemy, but a realistic way to heal the battle fatigue and preserve the revolutionary strength for the future. He reassured his followers that reorganizing the Red army into a National Revolutionary army and substituting border governments for the Soviet regimes were merely changes in form and not in substance. Collaboration with the KMT, in short, afforded the CCP a chance to recoup, to expand, and to initiate a new approach in place of the old one that had not proved very successful.

So that the United Front might be exploited to full advantage, Mao mapped out a three-stage strategy: first, to achieve a compromise with the KMT in order to safeguard the existence of the CCP; second, to struggle for parity with the KMT; and third, to infiltrate into central China and build up a new base from which to launch a counterattack and seize the supreme power of state.

In an October 1937 report entitled "The Future of the War of Resist-

---

18. This statement has been quoted frequently. See F. F. Liu, A *Military History of Modern China, 1924-1929* (Princeton, 1956), 206; Chiang Kai-shek, *Soviet Russia in China: A Summing-Up at Seventy* (New York, 1957), 85; and Arthur N. Young, *China and the Helping Hand, 1937-1945* (Cambridge, Mass., 1963), 58.

ance and the Chinese Communist Line," Mao made an illuminating analysis of the prospects of the party in light of the war. Should China win, the Nationalists would be so exhausted and the Communists so strengthened that the victory could actually bring about an "October Revolution" in China. On the other hand, should China be defeated but not totally crushed, the country most likely would be divided into three spheres, with the Japanese in Manchuria and North China, the Nationalists in the Southwest, and the Communists in the Northwest. If China lost the war totally, then the Nationalists would be wiped out, while the Communists would go underground. Since military power was a decisive factor in Chinese politics, it behooved the CCP to fully utilize the war to expand its military strength in preparation for the ultimate seizure of power.

In light of these explanations, it is not hard to see why the Communist forces, after some initial encounters with the Japanese, avoided "hard fighting" but instead concentrated on self-development and expansion, striving toward the goal of "a million Red soldiers and a million party members."[19] Their manual for the cadres, entitled "The Strategy in Working with Friendly Armies," called for infiltration of the KMT troops through the planting of secret agents and cells to sow dissension, to instigate clique-formation, and to foster defection and rebellion. In March 1939 the Communists created their own Shensi-Kansu-Ninghsia border government, and later established the Shansi-Hopeh-Chahar-Suiyuan border government. Clashes between the Communist and Nationalist forces began to occur with increasing frequency.

The growing tension between the KMT and the CCP was catalyzed by rapidly shifting international alignments. The signing of the German-Soviet Non-Aggression Pact in August 1939—followed by the Japanese-Soviet Neutrality Pact in April 1941—had removed the doctrinal basis and expediency of the United Front. Conflict between the KMT and CCP became more serious. The situation was particularly critical in western Shantung and in Kiangsu where the New Fourth army was sta-

---

19. On April 24, 1945, Mao Tse-tung claimed that during 1943 and 1944 his troops engaged 64 per cent and 56 per cent of the Japanese forces, respectively, and 95 per cent of the "puppet army." Cf. Mao Tse-tung, III, 1,043-44. However, in a postwar interview, Marshal Hata Shunroku, the Japanese commander in China, "disparaged Communist operations against the Japanese, dismissing them by saying the 'Chinese Communists merely resorted to guerrilla warfare and planned the expansion of the area under their influence and the weakening and disintegration of the Nationalist Forces through the war against Japan.'" Young, 343.

tioned. When the government on October 19, 1939, ordered the transfer of that army to north of the Yellow River, it refused to obey; instead it expanded its operations in Kiangsu. On January 5, 1941, a major clash took place between the New Fourth army and the Nationalist 40th division, resulting in the government decision, on January 17, to disband the New Fourth Army and to arrest its commander for court martial. The CCP simply appointed another commander[20] and retaliated by increasing the strength of the New Fourth army to seven divisions. This "New Fourth army incident" all but destroyed the United Front, and Communist members of the People's Political Council refused to attend. Resumption of talks between the two parties took place in March 1943, only to break down again over Communist demands for legal status and military expansion to four armies of twelve divisions. By the end of 1943 the CCP negotiator, Chou En-lai, had left Chungking.

When talks were begun once more on May 4, 1944, in Sian, the Communists renewed their demands for twelve divisions, legal status, and recognition of the Shensi-Kansu-Ninghsia border region. In addition they asked for a constitutional coalition government. After some preliminary exchanges, the site of negotiations was moved to Chungking. It was a time of a Japanese general offensive which weakened the position of the Nationalist government, and the Communists were quick to exploit the situation. They raised their demands from twelve divisions to sixteen, recognition of all CCP-controlled areas in North, Central, and South China, and the convocation of a National Affairs Conference to deliberate on the question of a coalition government. But the Nationalists adamantly refused to consider these demands.[21]

Throughout the remaining period of the war, the KMT-CCP conflict was never resolved. Although Chiang repeatedly announced that the Communist problem, being political in nature, should be solved only by political means,[22] he sent a large body of his best troops to blockade the Communist areas in the Northwest, with the intention of using them in the event of a civil war following the Japanese war. On their part, the Communists ceaselessly expanded their military forces and popular organizations while posing as democratic agrarian reformers rather than radical revolutionaries. In their border governments they took care to see that only one-third of the offices were filled by Communists, with the

20. Ch'en Yi.
21. Jerome Ch'en, *Mao and the Chinese Revolution* 265-66.
22. *United States Relations with China, With Special Reference to the period 1944-1949* (Washington D.C., 1949), 135.

other two-thirds equally divided between the representatives of the peasants and the landlords. Consequently, an impression was successfully created among Westerners that Chinese Communists were different from Russian Communists. Even President Roosevelt's special emissary in China, Patrick Hurley, who visited the Communist capital of Yenan on November 7, 1944, remarked that the Chinese "Communists are not in fact Communists; they are striving for democratic principles," just as the Nationalists were not Fascists as many described them.[23] Indeed, the shrewd strategy of the CCP had won it a quasi "international recognition" and a vast expansion of its military forces. By April 1945 the Red army had reached a strength of 910,000 men.[24]

WARTIME DIPLOMACY AND U.S. INVOLVEMENT IN CHINA

From the outbreak of war in July 1937 to the Japanese attack on Pearl Harbor in December 1941, China fought alone. While she received sympathy, moral support, and some small loans from the Western powers, the Soviet Union was the only country that extended her substantial material aid. Relieved of direct Japanese pressure because of the China war, the U.S.S.R. offered China a nonaggression pact in August 1937, sent "volunteer" pilots, and granted three loans totaling U.S. $250 million—U.S. $50 million each in 1937 and 1938 and U.S. $150 million in 1939—at the very low interest rate of 3 per cent. By the end of 1939, the Soviet Union had supplied 1,000 planes and dispatched some 2,000 pilots and 500 military advisers. In fact, some of Russia's best military talent was connected with the China aid program.[25]

Western aid during the same period was pitifully small—a result of isolationism in the United States and troublesome developments in Europe. Of the total Western contribution of U.S. $263.5 million—which barely surpassed Russia's U.S. $250 million—the United States provided U.S. $120 million for nonmilitary purchases and U.S. $50 million for currency stability, while Britain and France provided a meager U.S. $78.5 million and $15 million respectively. However, American purchase of Chinese silver before and after the outbreak of war in 1937, amounting to 350 million ounces at U.S. $252 million, indirectly helped to alleviate the crushing burden of war expenses. Yet, paradoxically, until

23. Herbert Feis, *The China Tangle* (Princeton, 1953), 222.
24. Mao Tse-tung, III, 1039.
25. Such as Marshal Klimenti Voroshilov, General Georgi Zhukov, and General Vassily Chuikov, all destined to win fame during World War II.

the termination of the Japanese-American commercial treaty in July 1939, the United States was a heavy purchaser of Japanese silk and a major supplier of oil, scrap iron, and automobile parts; it also met nearly 40 per cent of Japan's total needs for metals, cotton, and wood pulp.[26] There can be no doubt that Japan's access to the American market directly and indirectly supported her war efforts in China.

The outbreak of the war in Europe in September 1939, however, substantially altered the foreign aid picture. Russian assistance to China slackened and finally ceased, while France and Britain leaned backward to avoid irritating Japan. Under Japanese pressure, France discontinued the rail service from Vietnam to Yunnan in June 1940, and Britain closed the Burma Road a month later, thus totally isolating China from the outside world. The situation was somewhat improved as United States aid to China gathered momentum in the wake of worsening Japanese-American relations. In March 1941, President Roosevelt made the Lend-Lease available to China, and although the amount was only U.S. $26 million in 1941, or 1.7 per cent of the total to all countries, it represented a significant start. In addition, a number of other American and British credits were extended to help stabilize Chinese currency and foreign exchange.

The attack on Pearl Harbor changed the character of the China war and transformed the foreign aid picture. Anglo-American declarations of war against Japan and similar Chinese action against the Axis powers turned the war in Asia into part of a world-wide struggle against aggression and totalitarianism. The Allied powers established a China-Burma-India theater of war, with Chiang Kai-shek as the supreme commander of the China theater, effective January 5, 1942. General Joseph Stilwell, who had been a language officer in Peiping earlier, was sent to Chungking as Chiang's chief of staff. Moreover, the group of American volunteer pilots —the Flying Tigers—who had been operating in Kunming since August 1941 were incorporated into the United States Fourteenth Air Force on July 4, 1942, with General Claire L. Chennault as commander. American aid from then on expanded substantially. From 1942 to the end of the war in 1945, United States credits to China reached the unprecedented mark of U.S. $500 million. Correspondingly Lend-Lease aid rose to U.S. $1.3 billion, which when combined with the U.S. $26 million in 1941 and U.S. $210 million in 1946, made a grand total of U.S. $1.54 billion, or 3 per cent of the total Lend-Lease to all countries.[27]

26. Young, 206-7, 440-41, 144.
27. Young, 350, 441.

During the early phase of the Pacific war, the Japanese achieved spectacular successes, taking Hong Kong, Singapore, Burma, and the Philippines one after another. The lackluster Allied performance contrasted sharply with the long Chinese resistance which now gained new Western respect. Secretary of War Henry Stimson told Roosevelt that "the brilliant resistance to aggression which the Chinese have made and are making, and their contribution to the common cause, deserve the fullest support we can give." Not only did Washington grant China a $300 million loan for currency stabilization, but it persuaded London to issue a joint renunciation of all unequal treaties of the past century on January 11, 1943. Furthermore, Roosevelt and Secretary of State Cordell Hull were determined to make China one of the Big Four despite British and Soviet opposition. British Foreign Minister Anthony Eden "did not like the idea of the Chinese running up and down the Pacific," while the Soviet Foreign Minister, V. Molotov, argued that China had no admissible interest in Europe. In the end they both bowed to American persuasion and accepted China as one of the cosigners of the Moscow Declaration of November 1, 1943. This critical document was a pledge by the Four Powers to prosecute the war unceasingly until the final victory was won; it expressly disavowed any intention of signing separate peace treaties with the enemies.[28]

Cairo Conference, 1943. Roosevelt was fond of personally meeting with world leaders and making major decisions on war aims and future peace plans. Likewise, the various national leaders were eager to meet with him in order to secure greater American aid. In this context, Roosevelt was anxious to talk with Chiang and Stalin, but the Chinese leader was reluctant to face the Russian counterpart, embittered as he was with the Japanese-Soviet Neutrality Pact of 1941 and the alleged Soviet support of the Chinese Communists. Chiang asked that he be given the first chance to see the President separately, and if this could not be arranged he would rather postpone the meeting. Roosevelt and Churchill then arranged two meetings, with Chiang at Cairo and with Stalin at Teheran.

In the Allied grand strategy, Europe came first, the Pacific second, and China third. Apprehensive lest the President's fondness for China might sway him into making extensive promises to Chiang at the expense of the European war, Churchill asked to hold prefatory discussions with Roosevelt first. Fearful that such a move would arouse Chinese and Russian

28. Feis, 20-21, 96, footnote.

suspicion, Roosevelt went straight to Cairo. With Madame Chiang, a Wellesley graduate who has a remarkable command of English, as interpreter, Chiang and Roosevelt held lengthy and cordial talks, to the chagrin of Churchill, who remarked: "The talks of the British and American staffs were sadly distracted by the Chinese story. . . . The president . . . was soon closeted in long conferences with the Generalissimo [Chiang]. All hopes of persuading Chiang and his wife to go see the Pyramids and enjoy themselves until we return from Teheran fell to the ground, with the result that the Chinese business occupied first instead of last place at Cairo."[29] Chiang's request for the prompt return of all lost territories won Roosevelt's endorsement and was later subscribed to by Churchill and Stalin. The President further agreed to increase supply shipments to China over the Hump (Himalayas), carry out long-range bombing of Japan, and give China a high place in the future United Nations organization. By giving her a handsome reward, the President felt, China would fight harder in the war.

The Cairo Declaration of December 1, 1943, demanded for the first time the "unconditional surrender" of Japan, the complete restoration of Chinese territories lost to Japan, and the return of Japanese possessions outside Japan proper, i.e., Sakhalin and Kurile islands to Russia and some of the Japanese mandatories in the Pacific to the United States. In his Christmas message to the American people, the President warmly announced: "Today we and the Republic of China are closer together than ever before in deep friendship and in unity of purpose."[30]

The Stilwell Crisis. A thorn in the side of Sino-American relations was the personality of General Stilwell, Chiang's American chief of staff. Nicknamed "Vinegar Joe," Stilwell was blunt and stubborn, lacking the qualities of a military diplomat that his office demanded. Influenced by a coterie of liberal and somewhat leftist advisers, he became increasingly critical of Chiang's conduct of the war and the Nationalist policy toward the Communists. Not only did he strain the relations with his host-superior, but got himself deeply involved in Chinese politics when on September 6, 1943 he made the suggestion—politically sensitive, if militarily sound—that Chiang lift the military blockade of the Communist areas in the Northwest and permit the 18th Route army to fight the Japanese alongside the Nationalist troops. The American embassy in

29. Feis, 103.
30. *United States Relations with China,* 37.

Chungking estimated that at least twenty divisions, or perhaps as many as 400,000 of Chiang's best troops, were relegated to blockading the Communist areas when they could have been fighting the Japanese. Incensed by Stilwell's meddling in Chinese politics, Chiang was ready to ask for his recall but was dissuaded by Madame Chiang on grounds that such a move would be unpopular in the United States. The strained relations between the two were exacerbated by disagreements over strategy in Northern Burma, where Stilwell had been training Chinese soldiers to open a new supply line to Free China.[31] The bickering came to a head in the face of a Japanese general offensive in 1944 which had the avowed purpose of clearing the "continental corridor" from North to South China and Indochina. In this drive, the enemy penetrated to the important city of Kweilin in Kwangsi province. Not only were American airbases lost—earlier used by the B29's for raids on Japan—but Chungking itself was threatened. Stilwell renewed his proposition to use the Communist troops, while Chiang stubbornly refused, fearful as he was of the unreliability of the CCP troops and of sinister Soviet designs on Manchuria, Mongolia, and Sinkiang. The relations between the two had deteriorated beyond repair.

Deeply concerned with the Communist question in China and the overall Sino-Soviet relationship, Roosevelt sent Vice-President Henry Wallace to China and instructed Ambassador Averell Harriman in Moscow to impress upon Stalin the need for friendly relations with China. Stalin and Molotov rejoined that the Chinese Communists were not real Communists, but "margarine Communists," "cabbage Communists," and "radish Communists"—meaning red on the outside but white inside.[32] When told of these descriptions, Chiang laughingly remarked that the Chinese Communists posed as innocent agrarian democrats when in fact they were more communistic than the Russians. He assured Wallace that he would use political means to solve the Communist question, while hoping that the CCP would give up its independent army and territory and merge into the Nationalist government. Regarding Sino-Soviet relations, he pledged that he would go more than halfway to meet Stalin if President Roosevelt agreed to serve as an "arbiter" or "middleman."[33]

31. Largely due to Stilwell's efforts, the Lido and Burma roads were finally completed in January 1945; they were renamed the "Stilwell Road."
32. Feis, 140-41, 180.
33. United States Relations with China, 558.

Chiang complained bitterly of Stilwell's lack of cooperation and judgment. In an attempt to establish a direct contact with the White House, he requested that the President send a special personal representative to Chungking.[34] By this maneuver he hoped to bypass the State and War departments, which had sustained Stilwell. Wallace noted: "I am deeply moved by the cry of a man in distress."

As the Japanese offensive rolled closer to Chungking, the United States Joint Chiefs were persuaded by Stilwell to get the President to ask that Chiang hand over the command of all Chinese troops, including the Communist forces, to Stilwell. His pride deeply wounded, Chiang told Roosevelt that he would accept this "exacting but sincere" suggestion if three conditions were met: (1) a clear definition of Stilwell's authority; (2) noninclusion of the Communist troops in his command; and (3) complete control and distribution of the lend-lease by Chiang himself. The President noted to the Joint Chiefs: "There is a good deal in what the Generalissimo says."[35]

General Patrick Hurley, secretary of war in the Hoover Administration, was sent to Chungking as the presidential emissary to harmonize Stilwell's relations with Chiang and facilitate the former's installment as commander of the Chinese troops. Suave and persuasive, Hurley secured Chiang's consent to turn over the command to Stilwell, although the Generalissimo insisted on retaining the final say on major strategic decisions so that Stilwell would have no greater power than he. At this point—September 19—"Vinegar Joe" arrived at the Chinese leader's quarters and delivered, against Hurley's advice, a strongly worded, reproving message from Roosevelt which asked Chiang to give Stilwell "unrestricted command" of Chinese forces at once or assume "personal responsibility" for the rapidly deteriorating military situation in China. The message struck Chiang as if he "had been hit in the solar plexus," observed Hurley.

Chiang told the President that while he would accept an American commander and reorganize his military chain of command, he could not assign such a heavy responsibility to Stilwell, who wanted to command rather than cooperate with him. Chiang bluntly asked for Stilwell's recall. Awed by the prospect of losing his command, Stillwell softened his stand and agreed to drop the use of Communist forces. But the die was cast; Chiang would not alter his position.

34. Churchill kept a personal representative in Chungking, Gen. Carton de Wiart.
35. Feis, 153, 172.

Although the Joint Chiefs continued to sustain Stilwell in this controversy, whatever doubts the President may have had were dissolved by a masterly report from Hurley, who wrote that he believed Chiang was open to persuasion and leadership but that Stilwell was convinced that the Generalissimo would not act except under force; hence every move of Stilwell's was calculated to subjugate rather than to collaborate with Chiang. "There is no issue between you and Chiang except Stilwell," Hurley shrewdly told the President; "my opinion is that if you sustain Stilwell in this controversy, you will lose Chiang Kai-shek and possibly you will lose China with him." The report closed with the belief that if another American general were appointed to replace Stilwell, Chiang would cooperate with him and devise a way to stop the Japanese advance. Hurley's advice proved to be decisive and Stilwell was recalled on October 19, 1944.[36]

Stilwell's replacement, Lieutenant General Albert C. Wedemeyer, was made commanding general of American forces in China and chief of staff to Chiang, but not commander of the Chinese forces. Wedemeyer's mild and conciliatory manner, which provided quite a contrast to Stilwell's headstrong behavior, won him immediate acceptance by Chiang, and Sino-American relations changed for the better overnight. Strangely, the Japanese offensive also tapered off by itself during this time, as a result of the transfer of troops to fight the American campaign in the Pacific. Thereafter, Japanese forces in China mounted no further offensives of great magnitude.

Hurley's Mediation, 1944-45. Since the KMT-CCP friction compromised China's war efforts and threatened future national unity and reconstruction, Hurley sought ways to bring about a reconciliation between the two parties. On November 7, 1944, with the approval of Chiang and the American general staff, he flew to Yenan for a two-day conference with Mao. Impressed with his initiative in making the trip, the Communists gave him a warm welcome. Rapport was established when Hurley, anxious to please his host, reciprocated the "harvest dance" of a local welcoming party with an Indian dance and let out his Choctaw war whoop: "Ya-hoo!" The ensuing discussions led to a Five-Point Draft Agreement on November 10. It called for the formation of a coalition government, representation of the CCP on a United National Military Council, legal status for the CCP, civil and political freedoms, and unification of all

36. Feis, 191, 198.

armed forces under a coalition national government.[37] Mao signed it as chairman of the CCP Central Committee, and Hurley did so as the "personal representative of the President of the United States," although the Department of State later insisted that he had signed merely as a "witness."[38] Showing his appreciation of the American effort, Mao wrote to Roosevelt on November 10: "It has always been our desire to reach an agreement with President Chiang Kai-shek which will promote the welfare of the Chinese people. Through the good offices of General Hurley we have suddenly seen hope of realization."[39] Hurley's visit to Yenan convinced him that "there is very little difference, if any, between the avowed principles of the National Government the Kuomintang and the avowed principles of the Chinese Communist Party."[40]

However, Chiang Kai-shek looked at the Communist issue from an entirely different angle. To him, a coalition government implied a failure of KMT tutelage and opened the door for Communist infiltration of the government. His rejection of the Five-Point Draft Agreement was unmistakable when he set forward his own Three-Point Plan, which asked the Communists to accept Dr. Sun's Three People's Principles and turn over their troops to the Nationalist government, which in return would grant the CCP a legal status, a place on the National Military Council, and some political and civil liberties. In short, he asked Mao to turn over his guns and confide in Nationalist sincerity during the future redistribution of political power. Too shrewd to accept this kind of offer, Mao commented in his *Coalition Government:*

> These people [i.e. Chiang and his followers] said to the Communists: "If you give up your army, we shall give you freedom." If these words were sincere, then the parties which had no army should have enjoyed freedom long ago . . . yet neither of them enjoyed any freedom . . . Just because they [the workers, peasants, students, intellectuals and bourgeoisie] had no army, they lost their freedom.[41]

As a result of this impasse, the Communist representative in Chungking, Chou En-lai, left for Yenan on December 9. Not until January 20, 1945,

37. Details in *United States Relations with China,* 74-75.
38. Tang Tsou, 290; Jerome Ch'en, *Mao,* 266.
39. *Foreign Relations of the United States, China* (Washington, D.C., 1967), vol. 6 (1944), 689.
40. *Foreign Relations of the United States, China,* 748. Hurley to Secretary of State Stettinius, Dec. 24, 1944.
41. Mao Tse-tung, III, 1073; Carsun Chang, *The Third Force in China* (New York, 1952), 136; Tang Tsou, 292.

after repeated urgings from Hurley, did he return to Chungking to re-open negotiations.

Pressured by public opinion and American advice, Chiang agreed to call a National Affairs Conference, which was to be composed of repre-sentatives of all parties and independents. Ostensibly, the conference would study problems relating to the termination of the KMT tutelage, the introduction of a constitution, the preparation of a common political program, and the participation of all parties in government *before* the inauguration of the constitution. In actuality, however, coalition govern-ment was anathema to Chiang and the KMT; they secretly contrived ways to block it. On March 3, 1945, without prior consultation with the Communists, the Nationalist government announced the convocation of the National Assembly on November 12 to adopt a new constitution. Since the delegates to this assembly had been elected in 1936 under Nationalist sponsorship, Chiang could count on the adoption of a constitution favor-able to the KMT. Chou En-lai denounced the Nationalist move as "de-ceitful," and Mao refused to recognize the legality of the 1936 National Assembly. Deadlocked, negotiations broke down again.[42]

Hurley, who was appointed ambassador on November 17, 1944, fol-lowing the resignation of Ambassador Clarence E. Gauss, did not enjoy complete support of the embassy staff, many of whom had grown openly critical of Chiang and his regime. They urged Washington to bypass the Nationalist government and work directly with the CCP and the other parties in fighting the Japanese. The idea was overruled by the President, who supported Hurley's policy of exclusive and unconditional support of Chiang. By May 1945, however, the idea of bringing pressure to bear on Chiang to reach a settlement with the Communists and thereby to broaden his government was meeting with greater favor in Washington. Meanwhile, important decisions were being made at the international level regarding the climax of the war against Japan.

The Yalta Conference, 1945. By the end of 1944, Germany's defeat was in sight and the Allied leaders shifted their strategic focus to Japan. Washington had decided to attack Japan directly from the Pacific rather than from China as previously planned. The Joint Chiefs estimated that the defeat of Japan could be achieved within eighteen months after the defeat of Germany, which was predicted to occur somewhere between July 1 and December 1, 1945. This overestimation of Japanese strength led to the decision to invite the U.S.S.R. into the war so as to shorten it

42. Jerome Ch'en, *Mao*, 269.

and save Allied lives. General MacArthur, having reconquered the Philippines, estimated that as many as sixty Soviet divisions would be needed to destroy the Japanese army in Manchuria. To fix the terms of the Soviet entry into the Pacific war, a meeting between the Big Three was called at Yalta in February 1945.

There, Stalin agreed to enter the war against Japan within two or three months after Germany's defeat, on the condition that all former Russian rights violated by the Japanese attack in 1904, as well as Russian privileges in Manchuria, be restored to the Soviet Union. Specifically, he asked for the Kurile Islands, Southern Sakhalin, warm-water ports such as Dairen and Port Arthur, the Chinese Eastern Railway and the Southern Manchurian Railway, and support of the *status quo* in Outer Mongolia. "It is clear," he told Roosevelt, "that if these conditions were not met, it would be hard for him and Molotov to explain to the Soviet people why Russia was entering the war against Japan."[43] Since many of the conditions touched upon the sovereignty of China, which was not represented at the conference, it devolved upon Roosevelt to secure Chiang's approval of these terms. On his part, Stalin agreed to respect Chinese sovereignty in Manchuria and to sign a treaty with Chiang recognizing him as the sole leader of China.

Already ill and very tired, Roosevelt did not drive a hard bargain at Yalta. He felt that he had accomplished the main objectives of the conference, namely Stalin's agreement (1) to enter the war three months after Germany's defeat; (2) to support Chiang as the Chinese leader; and (3) to recognize Chinese sovereignty in Manchuria. Nonetheless, he did "sign away" sovereign Chinese rights in Manchuria without authorization. British Foreign Secretary Anthony Eden maintained that there was no need to pay Russia such a high price for intervention since she would probably enter the war on her own anyway. However, his advice against signing the Yalta Agreement was ignored by Churchill, who desired to manifest his faith in the President's judgment and to safeguard British interests in the Far East.

The exact terms of the Yalta Agreement were kept from Chiang and Hurley, although both had learned something about them indirectly. Feeling bypassed and insulted, Hurley decided to confront the President when he (Hurley) returned to Washington in March 1945. To his great astonishment, Hurley found Roosevelt's hand, when stretched out for greeting, to be nothing but "a very loose bag of bones," and the skin on his face "seemed to be pasted down on his cheekbones." "As you know,"

43. Feis, 243.

Hurley testified later, "all the fight that I had in me went out."[44] On April 12, Roosevelt died and Harry Truman assumed office in complete ignorance of the Yalta Agreement, which was kept in Admiral Leahy's special file.

The Soviet Union had notified Japan on April 5 that the 1941 neutrality pact between them had lost its meaning; hence the "impossibility" of its continuation. Actually, by the terms of the pact, it was to remain in force for one year after such notice had been served, but it was obvious that the U.S.S.R. was not going to wait. Events now moved rapidly. Hitler committed suicide on May 1, and Germany surrendered a week later. Soviet troops began to move from Europe to Asia.

Chiang sent his brother-in-law, T. V. Soong, to Moscow to work out an agreement with Stalin before the Soviet troops poured into Manchuria. Stalin offered China a thirty-year treaty of friendship and alliance against future Japanese aggression. He promised to support Chiang as the leader of China, to abstain from aiding his enemies, to begin evacuating Soviet troops in Manchuria three weeks after Japan's surrender, and to complete this withdrawal in two or three months. In return, China was to grant the U.S.S.R. many vital concessions in Manchuria: the right to station naval and air forces in a military zone including Port Arthur, Dairen, and adjacent areas, ownership of the Manchurian railways and connected enterprises, and Chinese recognition of the independence of Outer Mongolia. Before the terms were written into a formal treaty, Stalin left for Potsdam to meet with Churchill and Truman. Significantly, he left with the knowledge that Japan, on July 6, had requested him to mediate for a settlement with the Allies.

On the evening of the first day of the Potsdam Conference, July 16, 1945, the news reached Truman of the successful detonation of the first atomic bomb in New Mexico.[45] The President, who had felt insecure before Churchill and Stalin, was "tremendously pepped up by it [the news] . . . and said that it gave him an entirely new feeling of confidence." Learning of the bomb, Churchill spoke in poetic grandeur: "What was gunpowder? Trivial. What was electricity? Meaningless. This atomic bomb is the second coming in wrath."[46] The British leader was convinced that the war would be over in one or two violent shocks and that there was no more need to ask the Soviets to enter the war. The American

44. Feis, 279.
45. A plutonium bomb of the implosion type, called the "Fat Boy."
46. Herbert Feis, *Japan Surrendered: The Atomic Bomb and the End of the War in the Pacific* (Princeton, 1961), 72-73, 75.

military chiefs concurred but maintained that the Soviet entry would end the war sooner with a corresponding saving of lives. At any rate, a feeling persisted that Soviet control of Manchuria could not be prevented unless the United States was willing to go to war to defend it; barring this, the Americans had best allow the Russians to earn their reward.

The Potsdam Declaration of July 26, 1945, demanded Japan's "unconditional surrender or prompt and utter destruction." When Tokyo ignored the warning, the first atomic bomb was dropped on Hiroshima on August 6. Two days later the Soviet Union entered the war. On August 9, the second atomic bomb fell on Nagasaki, and a day later the Japanese government made a conditional acceptance of the Potsdam Declaration. On that day Stalin warned T. V. Soong that if the treaty of alliance were not signed soon, Manchuria would be in danger of falling to the Chinese Communists; the treaty was therefore signed on August 14.[47] The terms were similar to those already discussed except for minor variations. The Soviet Union agreed to give the Chinese central government under Chiang moral, military, and material aid; to respect Chinese sovereignty in Manchuria; to evacuate troops from Manchuria within three weeks of Japan's defeat and to complete the move in three months; to refrain from intervention in Sinkiang; and to acknowledge the political independence and territorial integrity of Outer Mongolia. On her part, China agreed to allow self-determination for Outer Mongolia by means of a plebiscite, and to acknowledge joint control with the U.S.S.R. of the Chinese Eastern Railway and the Southern Manchurian Railway for thirty years, after which time they would automatically revert to China without compensation. Dairen was to be a free port for all treaty nations for thirty years, while Port Arthur was to become a joint naval base for China and the Soviet Union.

The treaty, though costly, was accepted by Chiang with satisfaction, for it secured peace for China on her northern border, and committed the Soviet Union to recognition of Chinese sovereignty in Manchuria and Sinkiang and to nonsupport of the Communists against the Nationalist government. Indeed, peace with Russia was essential to China's postwar reconstruction, and Chiang felt that if the Soviets failed to observe their obligations, the treaty could be used as a yardstick to judge their behavior.[48]

47. Signed not by Soong, who feared for his political future, but by Foreign Minister Wang Shih-chieh for China.
48. Chiang Kai-shek, 228.

On August 14, 1945, the Japanese emperor issued an imperial rescript to end the war, and on September 2 the Instrument of Surrender was signed on board the U.S.S. *Missouri* in Tokyo Bay. After eight years of fighting, China had finally emerged victorious. Chiang's prestige was never higher, for he had led the country through the darkest days of war to ultimate victory. China's international position was also never more honorable—she had fought the longest fight against aggression and totalitarianism.

The country rejoiced over the end of war and eagerly looked forward to a period of peace and reconstruction. Yet under the veneer of jubilation and excitement there was a deep concern over the still unresolved Communist problem and its ominous implications. Indeed, Mao Tsetung had waited out the war, quietly gathering strength to make his bid for power.

THE WAR CONSEQUENCES

The war had generated far-reaching repercussions in China, Japan, and East Asia. Among the most important were the following.

1. *A New International Order in Asia.* The end of the Pacific war ushered in a new day in East Asia. Through her long years of struggle against aggression, China replaced Japan as the leading power. She emerged from her prewar semicolonial status to become one of the Big Five and a chartered member of the United Nations, with a permanent seat and veto power in the Security Council. Never before in her modern history was her international prestige higher than at this point. In contrast, Japan ceased to be a major force in international politics and turned inward toward social reconstruction under American occupation and guidance. The old European colonial powers—Britain, France, and the Netherlands —though victors in war, were shorn of much of their former prestige, as they had been expelled from their Asian possessions by the Japanese during the war. Their former colonies, India, Burma, Indochina, and Indonesia, all clamored for independence. The age of European colonialism in Asia, which began in the 16th century, finally came to an end. On the other hand, by virtue of her dominant role in defeating Japan, the United States had emerged as the most powerful state on the Pacific. This turn of events heralded a totally new chapter in the evolution of international relations in Asia.

2. *Nationalist Exhaustion.* Although the victory over Japan was primarily won by the Americans, China's contributions could not be overlooked. Throughout the war she had pinned down a substantial percentage of the Japanese armed forces, which might otherwise have been employed elsewhere. From 1937 to 1941 when she fought alone, China engaged between 500,000 and 750,000 enemy troops in China proper—roughly half of the total Japanese strength—in addition to the 200,000- to 700,000-man Kwantung army in Manchuria. At the end of the war in 1945, 1.2 million out of a total 2.3 million overseas Japanese armed forces were tied down in China. The China campaigns consumed 35 per cent of total Japanese war expeditures—U.S. $12 billion out of a total U.S. $34 billion—and resulted in 396,040 Japanese killed and a much larger number wounded.[49] On her part, China mobilized 14 million men, sustained total casualties of 3,211,419 —including 1,319,958 killed, 1,761,355 wounded, and 130,126 missing— and incurred an awesome war debt of Ch$1,464 billion.[50] Civilian casualties and property losses were incalculable. The Nationalist government, which bore the major brunt of the fighting, was so depleted physically and spiritually that it was manifestly incapable of coping with the new challenges of the postwar era.

3. *Economic Distress.* The chronic ill of deficit spending, which had plagued the Nationalist government since its inception in 1928, exacerbated during the war as a result of mounting military expenditures and the loss of customs revenues from the coastal provinces that had fallen to the enemy. The vast discrepancy between income and expenditures is alarmingly evident in the following statistics of three typical years:[51]

	War Costs	*Revenues*
	(million Ch$)	
1937	1,167	870
1941	10,933	2,024
1945	1,268,031	216,519

There was no way for the government to bridge the gap except through the admittedly unwise course of increasing note issues, with the full knowledge that such a measure would inevitably bring on inflation. The

49. Young, 417-18.
50. Chiang Kai-shek, 131.
51. Young, 435.

note issues rocketed from Ch$1.9 billion at the outset of war in 1937 to Ch$15.81 billion by the end of 1941, and to Ch$1,031.9 billion in 1945. The consequence of the abusive issue of paper money was rampant inflation and the rapid rise in average retail prices:[52]

	Retail Price Rise (per cent)
1937 (first 9 months after the war)	29
1938	49
1939	83
1940	124
1941	173
1942	235
1943	245
1944	231
1945 (to August)	251
1945 (from August to end of year)	230

Ultimately, inflation damaged army morale, destroyed administrative efficiency, ruined civilian lives, and reduced the middle class to destitution. The economic distress caused by inflation alienated large segments of the Chinese people, especially the intellectuals, who blamed the government for mismanagement and irresponsibility. If inflation was a necessary evil to sustain the war, it had become a curse in the postwar period and undermined the very economic foundations of the government.

4. *Psychological Weariness.* Having patiently endured all hardships during eight years of war, the Chinese people were too weary to undertake any kind of struggle once the victory had been won—least of all a civil war between the Nationalists and the Communists. They longed for peace and recuperation, and when these eluded them they blamed the government and the party in power. Mao Tse-tung, who had correctly predicted this turn of events in the early phase of the war, was quick to exploit this mass discontent. No sooner had peace returned than he began to challenge Nationalist supremacy. Civil war clouds once again hovered ominously on the horizon, portending a future fraught with turmoil for the exhausted nation.

52. Young, 436.

FURTHER READING

Bisson, Thomas A., *Japan in China* (New York, 1938).

Borg, Dorothy, *The United States and the Far Eastern Crisis of 1933-1938* (Cambridge, Mass., 1964).

Chang, Kia-ngau, *The Inflationary Spiral: The Experience in China, 1939-1950* (New York, 1958).

Chiang, Kai-shek, *China's Destiny* (New York, 1947).

———, *Soviet Russia in China: A Summing Up at Seventy* (New York, 1957).

Ch'ien, Tuan-sheng, *The Government and Politics of China* (Cambridge, Mass., 1950).

Chou, Shun-hsin, *The Chinese Inflation, 1937-1949* (New York, 1963).

Clifford, Nicholas R., *Retreat from China: British Policy in the Far East, 1937-1941* (Seattle, 1967).

Clubb, Edmund O., *20th Century China* (New York, 1964), chapters 6-7.

Colegrove, Kenneth, 'The New Order in East Asia," *Far Eastern Quarterly*, I:1:5-24 (Nov. 1941).

Compton, Boyd, *Mao's China: Party Reform Documents, 1942-1944* (Seattle, 1952).

Fairbank, John K., *The United States and China* (Cambridge, Mass., 1958).

Feis, Herbert, *The China Tangle* (Princeton, 1953).

———, *Japan Surrendered: The Atomic Bomb and the End of the War in the Pacific* (Princeton, 1961).

Fishel, W. R., *The End of Extraterritoriality in China* (Berkeley, 1952).

Houn, Franklin W., *A Short History of Chinese Communism*, chapter 4.

Hsü, Shuhsi, *How the Far Eastern War Was Begun* (Shanghai, 1938).

———, *The War Conduct of the Japanese* (Shanghai, 1938).

Jones, F. C., *Manchuria Since 1931* (London, 1949).

Linebarger, Paul M. A., *The China of Chiang K'ai-shek; A Political Study* (Boston, 1941).

Liu, James T. C., "German Mediation in the Sino-Japanese War, 1937-38," *Far Eastern Quarterly*, VIII:2:157-71 (Feb. 1949).

———, "Sino-Japanese Diplomacy during the Appeasement Period, 1933-1937" (Ph.D. thesis, University of Pittsburgh, 1950).

McLane, Charles, *Soviet Policy and the Chinese Communists, 1931-1946* (New York, 1958).

Miles, Milton E., U.S.N. *A Different Kind of War: The Little Known Story of the Combined Guerrilla Forces Created in China by the U.S. Navy and the Chinese during World War II* (Garden City, N. Y., 1967).

North, Robert, *Moscow and the Chinese Communists* (Stanford, 1953).

Romanus, C. F., and R. Sunderland, *Stilwell's Mission to China* (Washington, D.C., 1953).

Rosinger, Lawrence K., *China's Wartime Politics, 1937-1944* (Princeton, 1945).

Snow, Edgar, *Red Star over China* (New York, 1938).

———, *Random Notes on Red China, 1936-1945* (Cambridge, Mass., 1957).

White, Theodore H., (ed.), *The Stilwell Papers* (New York, 1948).

———, and Annalee Jacoby, *Thunder Out of China* (New York, 1946).

Young, Arthur N., *China and the Helping Hand, 1937-1945* (Cambridge, Mass., 1963).

PART VI

The Rise of the Chinese People's Republic

25

The Civil War, 1945-49

The collapse of Japan, after two atomic shocks, had come much sooner than expected. It left the Nationalist government totally unprepared for the consequences of the sudden termination of war. A number of pressing problems now clamored for Chiang Kai-shek's immediate attention, and foremost among them was the Communist threat to move into the Japanese occupied territories and take over the enemy arms. No less ominous was the situation in Manchuria where Soviet forces had plunged deep into the hinterland and refused to stop with the Japanese surrender. Despite Stalin's promise of evacuation in three months, their intentions remained shrouded in secrecy. Thus, the end of the war had created an extremely critical military situation for the Nationalists.

Following the Japanese surrender, a mad race took place between the KMT and CCP forces, each trying to reach the occupied territories first to receive the Japanese surrender and thereby harvest the vast quantity of enemy arms and military supplies. In the contest the Communists seemed to enjoy a distinct geographical advantage. They were in control of eighteen "liberated areas" in North, South, and Central China, with a population of 100 million, and boasted of one million regular troops and two million militiamen,[1] who were deployed in the countryside of the Yellow, Yangtze, and Pearl river valleys. The big metropolises of Peiping, Tientsin, Shanghai, Nanking, Hankow, and Canton, which were located in these valleys, became urban islands in a Communist-dominated rural

1. Mao Tse-tung, *Mao Tse-tung hsüan-chi* (Selected works of Mao Tse-tung), (Peking, 1963), IV, 1157.

715

ocean. To make full use of this favorable situation, Mao Tse-tung declared on August 9, 1945—a day after the Soviet entry into the war—that the collapse of Japan was in sight and that the hour had arrived for the CCP to mount a general offensive. On August 10, Chu Teh, commander-in-chief of the People's Liberation army (PLA), ordered his troops to seize all towns, cities, and communication centers under Japanese occupation, and to receive the enemy's surrender and military supplies. On August 11, Lin Piao led a 100,000-man army along the Peiping-Mukden Railway, striking into Manchuria. Within two weeks of the Japanese surrender, the Communists expanded their territory from 116 to 175 counties.[2]

The Nationalist forces, scattered along the several battlefronts and in Western China, were less favorably situated in the race, but Chiang was determined not to let the fruits of victory slip from his fingers. On August 10 he appealed to the Communist leaders to refrain from independent actions, and ordered the Japanese and puppet forces to hold out against non-Nationalist troops. Denouncing Chiang's action as "beneficial to the Japanese invader and traitors," Chu Teh directly asked the Japanese commander-in-chief in China, Okamura Yasuji, to surrender to the Communist representatives. To overcome the Communist geographical advantage, Chiang requested American help to airlift and sealift his troops to the occupied areas.

The United States quickly came to the aid of the Nationalists. She authorized the transportation of their troops to the occupied areas and the landing of 50,000 American marines in key ports and communication centers to await the arrival of Nationalist forces. Three government armies were airlifted to Peiping, Tientsin, Shanghai, and Nanking, and subsequently a total of half a million troops were transported to the various parts of the country. In addition, Washington's General Order No. 1 to Tokyo explicitly required that the surrender of Japanese forces in China (exclusive of Manchuria),[3] Taiwan, and French Indochina north of the 16° parallel be made to Chiang and his representatives. On August 15 Chiang himself ordered Okamura to maintain order and keep all military supplies inside occupied territory until further instructions from him. On August 22 Okamura was further told to allow passage only of Nationalist troops to the occupied territory. The Japanese commander complied fully.

With American assistance and Japanese cooperation, the Nationalists

2. Mao Tse-tung, III, 1,119; Jerome Ch'en, *Mao*, 261.
3. In Manchuria, the Soviet forces were authorized to receive the Japanese surrender.

won the first round of competition with the Communists. The government regained control of nearly all the important cities and communication centers in Central, East, and South China, while the Communist forces temporarily retreated to the countryside. Yet in spite of this setback, the CCP managed to score some gains during the first two weeks of contest, winning control of fifty-nine cities and vast countryside, especially in North China.[4]

Manchuria presented a particularly explosive picture. The Soviet forces under Marshal Rodion Malinovsky had swept in with amazing speed on August 8 and were joined by additional striking forces from Outer Mongolia two days later. The Soviet advance did not stop with the Japanese surrender on August 14; nor did it halt at the geographical limit of Manchuria. It penetrated deep into Jehol and Chahar, and facilitated the entry of the CCP forces into Manchuria, where the Soviets turned over to them large quantities of surrendered Japanese arms.[5]

In an effort to resolve these knotty problems and effect a *rapprochement* with the CCP, Chiang three times invited Mao to a conference in Chungking. Though hesitant and fearful of a Nationalist ruse, Mao ultimately decided to come, after the American envoy, Patrick Hurley, had gone to Yenan to vouch for his safety. On August 28, 1945, Mao flew to Chungking. The people of China, both eager and weary, held their breath for this historic meeting between Chiang and Mao, praying for an amicable outcome so that a civil war might be averted.

MAO IN CHUNGKING

Mao's strategy in the negotiations had been carefully worked out before he left Yenan. Despite the initial Nationalist success in regaining control of the big cities, Mao was confident that the CCP would eventually dominate the areas north of the Lower Yangtze and Huai rivers, most of Shantung, Hopeh, Shansi, Suiyuan, all of Jehol and Chahar, and part of Liaotung. However, for the immediate future he foresaw many difficulties; therefore he decided to adopt a flexible and conciliatory course of action in Chungking but hold firm on matters of basic importance.[6] Consequently, during his stay in the Nationalist wartime capital, Mao made

4. Mao Tse-tung, IV, 1,151. Report of Mao on August 26, 1945.
5. Mao Tse-tung, IV, 1,134; Tang Tsou, 315-16. 300,000 rifles, 138,000 machine guns, 2,700 pieces of artillery, etc.
6. Mao Tse-tung, IV, 1,151-54.

every effort to appear reasonable and willing to make concessions—a posture calculated to win world public opinion and the sympathy of the middle-of-the-roaders. Wearing a new tunic and a pair of new shoes, he appeared every bit an amiable, warm human being rather than a tough, fire-eating revolutionary. He accepted Nationalist hospitality and the use of a car, went to Chinese operas, attended dinner parties, and drank toasts to Chiang's long life. He received numerous visits from young people and even allowed a married woman to kiss his hand. Outwardly, there was an expression of friendliness and civility on the part of both the host and the guest, which buoyed popular hopes for reconciliation and peace.

In the formal negotiations, Mao cultivated the image of being reasonable and ready to accommodate. No longer did he insist on the coalition government, but asked instead for the calling of a National Affairs Conference[7] which would study the problems relating to the formation of such a coalition, the convocation of a National Assembly, and the introduction of a constitution.

On the issue of the relative strength of the KMT and CCP forces and their integration into a national army, Mao initially demanded 48 divisions for the CCP but agreed to reduce it to 43—as opposed to the KMT's 263—so as to maintain a ratio of 1:7. Finding the Nationalists unreceptive, Mao finally offered to keep only 20 to 24 divisions if the KMT agreed to cut its forces to 120 divisions.[8]

On the question of political control of the liberated areas, Mao essentially wanted a free hand in North China, Inner Mongolia, and some important cities. When the Nationalists balked at the idea, he proposed a temporary *status quo* of the liberated areas pending the adoption of a constitution, which would stipulate popular election of the local government. It was clear that Mao strove to maintain control of local affairs, but on this point the Nationalists stubbornly refused to yield.

As regards the question of receiving the Japanese surrender, there was also a gulf between the two parties. The Nationalists insisted on the exclusive right to disarm the enemy, while the Communists claimed similar privileges in areas where they had been active or where they had already encircled the enemy. No agreement was reached on this point either.

Six weeks of negotiations left no doubt that little progress had been made. Despite Mao's conciliatory appearance, he would not yield on

7. Later to be called the Political Consultative Conference.
8. Mao-Tse-tung, IV, 1,155-64.

those basic points that touched the fundamental position of the CCP. On the other hand the Nationalists, negotiating from a position of strength, stubbornly refused to compromise their privileged status. Chiang's prestige was at its zenith, having led the country to victory against seemingly insuperable odds. Furthermore, he enjoyed American aid and support and had signed a treaty of friendship and alliance with Stalin, in addition to maintaining a vastly superior military strength over his enemy.[9] He was hardly interested in the kind of "transient arrangements" for peace that Mao was willing to make at this juncture.

Chiang had endured the hardships of retreat for eight years and now demanded most, if not all, of the fruits of victory. He saw no point in sharing his glory with the Communists. Perhaps if Hurley had played a more active role in persuading Chiang to accept a *modus vivendi* along Mao's lines, the Communists could have been confined to North China. But Hurley chose to be a passive peacemaker and scrupulously maintained his neutrality; the most he would do was to urge both leaders to strive for agreement on the "basic over-all principles" first and work out the "details" later. But it was precisely on these matters of details that the two parties were unable to come together.

The final communiqué, issued by Chiang and Mao on October 10, stressed their agreement on the convocation of a Political Consultative Conference and on the importance of peaceful reconstruction. The depth of their disagreement was not communicated to the public, but it was obvious that the talks had not produced concrete results. Upon his return to Yenan, Mao called upon his followers to redouble their efforts for "peace" by mobilizing the masses and expanding the people's army to build a new China. His emboldened posture was in part an outcome of new developments in Manchuria.

SOVIET OPERATIONS IN MANCHURIA

Soviet activities in Manchuria completely belied Stalin's promise at Yalta and at the Sino-Russian treaty negotiations that he would evacuate troops from Manchuria within three weeks of the occupation and complete the withdrawal within three months. It appears that when he made the promise in February and July-August 1945, he had not expected the imminent rise of the Chinese Communists to power. He did not seem to mind American mediation in China, and had in fact advised Mao to work

9. Allegedly 11 to 1, according to the Nationalist minister of war.

out some agreement with Chiang. Mao superficially heeded Stalin's admonition, but secretly decided to proceed with the military contest with the Nationalists.[10] On his own, Stalin later admitted his mistaken diagnosis of the China situation.[11]

Apparently, Stalin's position underwent a radical change shortly after the war, when the vigor and resourcefulness of the CCP strongly impressed him. Once the special rights and privileges in Manchuria—granted by the Yalta Agreement and the Sino-Soviet treaty—had been confirmed by actual Soviet occupation, Stalin saw no need to honor his promise. The Soviet forces looted the Manchurian industrial plants and moved their valuable equipment to Russia as "war booty" at a replacement cost of $2 billion.[12] They employed all kinds of pretexts designed to prevent the entry of Nationalist troops into Manchuria.

In October 1945, Nationalist troops carried in American ships were refused admission to Dairen by Soviet authorities on grounds that it was a commercial port not authorized for the transportation of soldiers. Malinovsky suggested three other ports—Hulutao, Yingkow, and Antung —for alternative landing sites. Chagrined, the Nationalists went to the first two ports, only to find that they had already come under Chinese Communist control. Finally, after five weeks' delay the Nationalist forces landed in a North China port, Chinwangtao, from whence they fought their way into Manchuria. Harassed and delayed by Communist attacks, it was not until November 26 that the government troops occupied the first strategic city in Manchuria, Chinchow.

Permission for air transport of Nationalist troops into Manchuria was continuously denied by Soviet commanders, who allowed only security forces and gendarmes to be so lifted into Manchurian cities three to five days before the Soviet evacuation. With so little time allowed, no regular government troops could arrive to take over. On other occasions, the Soviet commanders would notify the Nationalists of their withdrawal from a certain place so late that when the latter arrived the place had already fallen to the Chinese Communists. By these tactics the Soviet forces effectively blocked the entry of substantial government troops into Manchuria, while facilitating the movement of the Chinese Communist

10. Lin Piao recalled in 1960: "Some well-intentioned friends at home and abroad [i.e. Stalin] . . . were worried about us," but Chairman Mao correctly assessed the situation and branded all reactionaries "paper tigers." See Tang Tsou, 326.
11. To Eduard Kardelj, an aide to Tito.
12. According to the estimates made by Edwin Pauley, American member of the Inter-Allied Reparation Commission.

army, equipping it with captured Japanese arms and allowing it to absorb puppet military units. Three times the Soviet troops delayed their withdrawal under various pretexts, and when they finally did leave in May 1946, Manchuria was all but in the hands of the Chinese Communists.

Chiang was determined to recover Manchuria, which he said was the *raison d'être* of China's eight-year war with Japan. General Wedemeyer, doubting the Nationalist capacity to take Manchuria, had advised him to first consolidate the areas south of the Great Wall and north of the Yangtze and safeguard the communication lines in North China. Rejecting the counsel, Chiang committed nearly half a million of his best-equipped troops to Manchuria—a decision he was to regret later.[13] Finally, the Soviet commanders allowed Nationalist units to be airlifted into major Manchurian cities, and government forces entered Changchun on January 5, 1946, and Mukden three weeks later. By then the CCP forces had almost completely dominated the vast countryside outside of these pockets, thus confronting the Nationalists with an untenable position. The country braced itself as the threat of civil war loomed large once more.

MARSHALL IN CHINA

By November 1945 Washington had adopted a new policy which called for continuing American support of the Nationalist government, on the condition that it not employ American arms to conduct a civil war and that it strive to reach a settlement with the Communists. In effect, this shift represented a repudiation of the former policy which had espoused unconditional support of Chiang's government. Disillusioned, Hurley resigned in protest on November 27, charging career officials of the State Department with plotting behind his back and siding with the Chinese Communists. President Truman then appointed General George C. Marshall, the most distinguished American soldier of World War II, as a special presidential ambassador to China.[14] He was instructed to assist the Nationalist government in re-establishing its authority as far as possible, including Manchuria, but not to involve the United States in any direct military intervention. He was also to urge Chiang to call a national conference of all major parties to deliberate on the cessation of the civil

13. Chiang Kai-shek, 232-33.
14. On suggestion of the secretary of agriculture, Clinton Anderson, in the November 27, 1945 cabinet meeting.

war and the unification of the country, to the end that a "strong, united, and democratic China" might emerge. Finally, he was told to make clear to Chiang that large-scale American aid was contingent on the achievement of a truce and national unity.[15]

Arriving in China in mid-December 1945, Marshall found both parties receptive to his mediation and prepared to endorse his three immediate objects: (1) a cease-fire in the civil war; (2) the convocation of a Political Consultative Conference to deliberate the formation of a coalition government; and (3) the integration of the KMT and CCP forces into a national army. The polite welcome and the pledge of support by the contending parties were heartening gestures, but it was evident that they could not have done otherwise. Marshall's high prestige, his apparent sincerity, his professed goal of helping China achieve peace, unity, and democracy, and above all the enormous power of his country were sufficient inducements for cordial behavior by both the KMT and the CCP. Nonetheless, beneath the veneer of warmth and appreciation, the extremists in both parties harbored feelings of antipathy toward what they considered an example of American meddling.

Deeply distrustful of each other, the Nationalists, with at least a five-to-one military superiority over the Communists in early 1946, were confident of their ability to crush the enemy in a quick bout. On the other hand, the Communists sneered at the Nationalist "paper tiger" which they felt sure could be torn apart in a prolonged contest. Each of the two insisted on a different set of conditions for collaboration. The Nationalists demanded that the Communists surrender their troops[16] *before* the establishment of the constitutional government, whereas the Communists insisted that such integration should come *after* its establishment. The KMT advocated the presidential system in the coalition government; the CCP argued for a cabinet system. Since the KMT would most likely dominate the central government, especially its executive branch, the CCP adamantly demanded a large degree of provincial autonomy and a strong legislature to checkmate the executive. If the rising spirit of belligerency was to be contained, these key issues had to be thrashed out to the satisfaction of both sides.

Marshall's active mediation achieved rapid and impressive results. On January 10, 1946, he committed the KMT and the CCP to calling a

15. *United States Relations with China,* 133, 605-7.
16. Under the euphemism of "unity of military command," i.e., the integration of the CCP forces *into* the KMT forces.

Political Consultative Conference, an immediate cease-fire, and a restoration of communications. A tripartite Executive Headquarters was created, consisting of one Nationalist, one Communist, and one American member, with the last-mentioned as chairman; its decisions required unanimous agreement. To supervise the cease-fire, teams reflecting a similar three-party composition were sent into the field.

The Political Consultative Conference was convened between January 10 and 31 during the truce and was composed of thirty-eight members: eight from the KMT, seven from the CCP, nine from the Democratic League, five from the Youth Party, and nine independents. Its lengthy deliberations resulted in the resolution that the supreme organ of state should be a multiparty State Council vested with both legislative and executive powers. The Council was to consist of forty members, of whom one half would be nominated by the KMT and the other half by the other parties and the independents. Decisions of the State Council involving a change in the resolutions of the Political Consultative Conference (PCC) would require ⅔ votes; hence any party or group able to muster ⅓ votes—14 to be exact—enjoyed a veto power. The Communists and their sympathizers, notably the Democratic League, were confident that they could line up the necessary votes to block any KMT attempts at revision.

The PCC adopted the cabinet system of government in which the Executive Yüan was to be responsible to the Legislative Yüan. It further resolved that the future constitution should recognize the province as the highest organ of local government, with a popularly elected governor and a constitution of its own to insure the proper division of power between the central and provincial governments.

The work of the PCC, more favorable to the Communists than to the Nationalists, reflected the general desire for peace and democratic rule. Though he did not take part in its deliberations, Marshall approvingly described its work as "a liberal and forward-looking charter." For the first time since the end of the war, there appeared a ray of hope for peace and reconstruction.

A further monumental achievement by Marshall was the agreement on February 25, 1946, regarding the relative strength of the KMT and the CCP forces and the integration of the two into a national army. It was resolved that within a year the KMT forces were to be reduced to 90 divisions and the CCP forces to 18, followed in the next six months by a further reduction of forces to 50 and 10 divisions respectively. These military cuts were distributed as follows: Manchuria: 14 KMT divisions to 1 CCP division; North China: 11 KMT divisions to 7 CCP divisions; Central China: 10 KMT divisions to 2 CCP divisions; South (including Formosa) and Northwest China: 6 and 9 KMT divisions respectively, and no Communist forces.[17] Obviously, the Nationalists came out very well in this military arrangement, as Communist influence was drastically reduced in Manchuria and North China. Similarly, the Nationalists were enabled to take over the Communist base in the Northwest, thus blocking direct contacts between the Chinese Communists and their Soviet comrades.

Marshall's quick success led President Truman to announce on February 25, 1946, the establishment of a United States Military Mission in China, staffed by 1,000 officers and men under General Wedemeyer. It was understood, from Marshall's earlier promise, that the Communist forces would be included in American training programs and would receive American equipment before their integration into the Nationalist forces. On March 11, 1946, a relieved and satisfied Marshall returned to the United States to arrange a loan of $500 million from the Export-Import Bank. It was during his brief absence from China that the sincerity of the Nationalists and the Communists was put to a severe test.

Neither the KMT nor the CCP really trusted each other since both were revolutionary parties committed to different causes and were unaccustomed to compromise. Cooperation between them was nearly impossible, except on a temporary and expedient basis. While Marshall's early success was largely a result of his active persuasion and respected stature, it was also true that the two contending parties found it bad politics not to play along with him. Secretly, the extremist elements in both parties found him standing in their way to victory. The CC Clique[18] in the Nationalist Party—dubbed by Marshall as the "selfish irreconcilables"—strongly felt that the agreements with the Communists were imposed upon the KMT by Marshall, and that without his intervention the Nationalists could have scored a victory over the enemy long before. The Communists, on their part, temporized with Marshall as long as the agreements were basically in their favor or not insufferably detrimental, but they never diminished the secret expansion of their army and areas

17. *United States Relations with China* 141. However, Chiang had serious doubts as to the Communist willingness to put the military reorganization plans into practice. To Marshall he described the integration of KMT-CCP forces as a task "as difficult to achieve as 'to negotiate with the tiger for its skin.'" Chiang Kai-shek, 162.
18. Named after its leaders, Ch'en Li-fu and Ch'en Kuo-fu.

of operation. Only Marshall's presence kept the two parties from ripping apart the façade of cooperation. But once he was out of sight, they ignored the truce and scrambled to improve their positions on the battlefield, so that they would be better situated should the final settlement fall short of realization. What began as local clashes soon grew into large-scale fighting in April 1946. The resolutions of the Political Consultative Conference remained unfulfilled dreams.

Fighting in Manchuria was particularly bitter. Having legally recovered it from the Japanese after eight years of war, Chiang was determined not to lose it again to the Russians or the Chinese Communists. In spite of the obvious unfavorable military situation there, Chiang dispatched a large portion of his troops to Manchuria. There, the CCP forces, favored by the Soviet occupation authorities, dealt a crushing blow to the Nationalist army and occupied the strategic city of Changchun on April 18, 1946. With this major victory, the CCP demanded an upward revision of the military deployment ratio in Manchuria from one to five CCP divisions vis-à-vis KMT's fourteen. Angrily rejecting the demand, Chiang ordered an all-out attack which resulted in the recovery of Changchun in May. Fighting would have rapidly gotten out of hand but for the remonstrance of Marshall, now back in China. A fifteen-day truce was arranged on June 6. But war fever had gripped both parties and the feeling was gaining ground that Marshall obstructed their ultimate victory. In early July 1946, Chiang told him that "it was first necessary to deal harshly with the Communists, and later, after two or three months, to adopt a generous attitude." On another occasion he said: "If General Marshall were patient, the Communists would appeal for a settlement and would be willing to make the compromises necessary for a settlement."[19] The Communists, on their part, were equally confident of an ultimate victory. Accusing the United States of playing the double role of aiding the Nationalists while posing as an impartial mediator, they demanded the withdrawal of all American troops. It appears that sometime in mid-1946, both the KMT and the CCP had decided to embark upon a new course of action irrespective of Marshall, whose influence had fallen to a nadir.

Riding the tide of victories, the Nationalist government announced unilaterally on July 4, 1946, that they would convoke the National Assembly on November 12, in open disregard of the PCC resolution that no such Assembly should be called before the formation of the coalition

19. Tang Tsou, 425.

government. As expected, the CCP and the Democratic League proclaimed their boycott of this "illegal" Assembly; in addition Mao called for a war of self-defense. The split had widened into an unbreachable gulf. Marshall appealed to the Chinese people to exert their pressure on both parties for a compromise, but it was a lone cry in the wilderness which won much sympathy but no results. His warning to Chiang of possible economic collapse and a Communist victory had little effect. The Generalissimo still believed that the inflation, though fierce and threatening, would not bring on an economic disaster, because the agrarian economy of China was governed by forces different from those of the industrial Western states.[20]

From July to September 1946, Chiang's forces won practically every battle, a fact which seemed to strengthen the view that Marshall had delayed the Nationalist victory. The Communists, in temporary retreat, openly accused the United States of using mediation as a smoke screen while underwriting Chiang's civil war. With his integrity thus questioned, Marshall warned Chiang on October 1 that unless the fighting stopped he would terminate the mediation and return home. Still winning in the battlefield, Chiang refused to stop. Then, in a grand gesture of magnanimity he called off the offensive on November 8—a few days before the convocation of the National Assembly—to allow the Communist Party and the Democratic League to reconsider their position. So confident was he of the justness of his cause and of his ability to win that he told Marshall on December 1, 1946, that the enemy forces could be wiped out in eight to ten months.[21]

Marshall realized that he had failed miserably in his mission. On January 6, 1947, President Truman announced his recall. In his farewell message to the Chinese people, a bitterly disappointed Marshall blamed the KMT "irreconcilable groups" for their "feudal control of China" and lack of interest in implementing the PCC resolutions; he also criticized the Communists for their "unwillingness to make a fair compromise." China's hope lay with the liberals, he said, but they lacked the power to exercise a "controlling influence."[22] The prospect for peace and unity was indeed bleak, and on this note the American dream of mediation in China came to an end.

20. *United States Relations with China*, 212.
21. *United States Relations with China*, 212.
22. "Personal Statement by the Special Representative of the President (Marshall), Jan. 7, 1947," in *United States Relations with China*, 686-89.

Marshall returned to the United States to become the secretary of state, but embittered by his recent experience he was incapable of evolving a positive China policy. "When I came back, I was hard put to find a long-view conclusion in the matter because of the failing structure of the Kuomintang and the determination, organization, and the discipline of the Communist group and their undoubted advice and possible support that would occur later from the Soviet group."[23] In this confused state of mind, Marshall's attitude was basically one of "wait and see," hoping that things might work themselves out in China. The only flicker of positive action was the dispatch of Wedemeyer on a fact-finding mission in July 1947, at the suggestion of Republican Congressman Walter Judd, a former medical missionary in China and a staunch supporter of Chiang Kai-shek. Wedemeyer stayed in China for a month, tried in vain to impress Chiang with the need for reform, and came back with a report that recommended "sufficient and prompt military assistance" to the Nationalist government under the supervision of 10,000 American officers and men. Further, the report called for economic aid for five years, and a five-power guardianship of Manchuria under the United States, the Soviet Union, France, Britain, and China, or failing that, a United Nations "trusteeship" for Manchuria. The report was politely received and quietly shelved by Marshall, who was unable to see how the United States could spare 10,000 men when rapid demobilization had left only one and one-third divisions in the country.[24] It was sadly apparent that the Wedemeyer mission had made little impression on either Chiang or Marshall.

THE CIVIL WAR

Chiang opted to resolve the Communist problem by military means after mid-1946, in order to prove that he could easily wipe out the enemy if unimpeded by American mediation. A victory would vindicate the correctness of his judgment and prove the impracticality of the romantic American dream of a coalition government in China. In spite of repeated warnings that the United States would not underwrite his civil war, Chiang could not persuade himself to believe that Washington would prefer the Communists to himself. There was a feeling among the Nationalists that the United States could not afford to see China slip to the

23. Marshall's testimony in the MacArthur hearings. Tang Tsou, 445.
24. Out of a total strength of 925,163 men in June 1947. Cf. Tang Tsou, 459.

Communists; therefore, her warning could not be taken at face value. If the situation grew desperate enough the Americans would have no choice but to come to the aid of the Nationalists.

In the early phase of the civil war, the government troops reaped victories at every encounter. Enjoying at least a 3:1 military superiority in mid-1946, the Nationalists were confident of a quick triumph. On the other hand, the Communists foresaw many difficult days ahead before a final victory and conducted their struggle accordingly. Mao predicted in 1946 that it would take five years to settle accounts with Chiang, and General P'eng Te-huai conceded the likelihood of a stalemate: "We cannot be defeated, but it is possibly true that we cannot win."[25] Though unshakably loyal to their faith in the ultimate and "inescapable" victory, the Communists were prepared for a long and hard campaign.

From July to December 1946, the Nationalists captured 165 towns and 174,000 square kilometers of territory from the Communists. The crowning success came in March 1947 when they seized the Communist capital of Yenan. Chiang confidently told the American ambassador, Leighton Stuart, that the enemy could be totally defeated or driven to the hinterland by August or September. Indeed, Mao and the CCP central organization found themselves in temporary retreat. They evacuated Yenan on March 18 and fled into hiding, hotly pursued by some 400,000 Nationalist troops.[26] At the end of the first year of civil war in June 1947, the Communist "liberated areas" had shrunk by 191,000 square kilometers and 18 million population.[27]

Buoyed by the chain of military victories, Chiang confidently launched his political offensive. The National Assembly was convened on November 15, 1946, despite the boycott of the Communist Party and the Democratic League. Its 1,744 delegates adopted a new constitution on Christmas Day, consisting of fourteen chapters and 175 articles. This document, promulgated on New Year's Day, 1947, reaffirmed the Three People's Principles as the basic philosophy of the state, the five-yüan government, and the people's four rights—initiation, referendum, election, and recall. The president of the republic was to be elected by the National Assembly for a six-year term. Also stipulated in the document was the right of the chief executive to appoint the president of the Executive Yüan with the consent of the Legislative Yüan, as well as the ministers in the Executive

25. Mao Tse-tung, IV, 1,364; Jerome Ch'en, *Mao*, 291-92.
26. *United States Relations with China*, 238; Jerome Ch'en, *Mao*, 283-84.
27. Jerome Ch'en, *Mao*, 299-300.

Yüan on the recommendation of the Yüan president. Members of the Legislative Yüan were to be elected on geographical and professional bases for a three-year term. The Judicial Yüan enjoyed the right to interpret the constitution, thus establishing the viability of judicial review in the Chinese legal system. Essentially, this government structure followed neither the presidential nor the cabinet system exclusively but was a mixture of both. The Executive Yüan, for instance, with the consent of the president of the republic, could veto the resolutions of the Legislative Yüan, but if the latter overruled the veto by a ⅔ vote, the Executive Yüan had to accept it or resign. With regard to local government, provisions were made for the popular election of provincial governors and district (*hsien*) magistrates.

As expected, the Communists loudly attacked the constitution as illegal. Unruffled by these charges, the Nationalists proceeded with the election of a new National Assembly and the selection of members of the Legislative Yüan in November 1947. The Assembly, convened on March 29, 1948, elected Chiang Kai-shek president of the republic on April 19, with Li Tsung-jen as vice-president. With this election, the twenty-year political tutelage of the KMT—which was originally scheduled to last only six years—formally came to an end. But even as Chiang accepted the mantle of office, the civil war had entered a critical stage for the Nationalists.

Mid-1947 seemed to mark a turning point in the fighting. The victory-laden Nationalist military machine began to sputter, partly because of increased assignment of soldiers to garrison duties in reconquered areas, with a corresponding reduction in the actual fighting force. In contrast, the Communist army had been expanding steadily, reaching 1.95 million in June 1947 as compared with KMT's 3.73 million.[28] The Communists went on a general offensive in the second half of 1947, scoring victories in Honan and northern Hopeh.

By far the severest blow to the Nationalists occurred in Manchuria, where, against American advice, Chiang had committed half a million of his best troops. Within three months of Christmas 1947, Lin Piao's army had inflicted losses of 150,000 on the crack Nationalist army. The remainder were pressed into a small triangular area between Mukden,

28. By June 1948, the CCP forces reached 2.8 million vs. KMT's 3.62. In November, the CCP forces actually surpassed the KMT: 3 million vs. 2.9 million. In June 1949, the CCP had achieved an overwhelming superiority over the Nationalists: 4 million vs. 1.5 million. Cf. Jerome Ch'en, *Mao*, 374.

Changchun, and Chinchow, which represented less than 1 per cent of Manchuria. It was hopeless to hold such an untenable position, yet Chiang decided to fight to the bitter end. By mid-1948 Lin had so tightened the encirclement that he practically smothered the Nationalist defenders. Having destroyed another 100,000 government troops, he conquered Chinchow on October 14, Changchun on October 18, and Mukden on November 2. The Manchurian campaign cost Chiang 470,000 of his best troops[29] and dealt a mortal blow to the morale of the entire government army. In the opinion of General David Barr, it "spelled the beginning of the end" for the Nationalist cause.[30]

Operating simultaneously with the Manchurian battles, another Communist field army under Ch'en Yi conquered Shantung after fierce fighting at Tsinan on September 26, 1948. This accomplished, the CCP forces, 550,000 strong, moved on to attack the historic battle site of Hsuchow, at the junction of the Tientsin-Pukow and Lung-Hai railways. Chiang had deployed 400,000 of his mechanized troops, equipped with tanks, heavy artillery, and armored cars to defend this gateway to Nanking. But many of his officers had become demoralized under the relentless hammer blows of the enemy. They were further frustrated by rain, snow, and sleet which immobilized their mechanized units. No sooner had the Battle of Huai-Hai[31] begun in October 1948 than two entire Nationalist divisions defected. From November 11 to 22, 100,000 government troops were destroyed. Hsuchow fell on December 15. By the time the Battle of Huai-Hai was over in January 1949, the Nationalists had lost no less than 200,000 men and two well-known commanders,[32] who were captured by the enemy. Flushed with victory, Mao confidently predicted victory in one year.[33] His forces now pressed toward Nanking, the seat of the Nationalist government.

Meanwhile, Lin Piao's 800,000-man army, freed from Manchurian engagements, together with the Communist North China Army Group,[34] formed a pincer movement against Peiping-Tientsin in December 1948. The Nationalist defender, General Fu Tso-yi, who had formerly defeated Communist forces in Suiyuan, had 500,000 men under his command. But

29. The Nationalists admitted to a loss of 300,000 men.
30. *United States Relations with China*, 335. General Barr was head of the American Army Advisory Group in China.
31. The combined names of *Huai* River and *Lung-Hai* Railway.
32. Generals Tu Yü-ming and Huang Wei.
33. Mao Tse-tung, IV, 1,164.
34. Under General Nieh Jung-chen.

all expectations of resistance evaporated when his defense plans were stolen by a Communist agent operating in his headquarters.[35] Deprived of their strategy and hopelessly outnumbered, the garrisons of Tientsin and Peiping capitulated on January 15 and 23, 1949, respectively. General Fu himself surrendered, along with 200,000 troops. From September 1948 to January 1949 the government had lost one and one-half million men.[36] Under such staggering losses, the Nationalist forces simply collapsed.

What of the future of the government? Chiang was forced by the peace faction within his party to resign on January 21, 1949, while Vice-President Li Tsung-jen took over the reins of government as acting president. Still hoping to hold the southern half of China below the Yangtze, Li engaged in negotiations with the Communists, but to no avail. With victory so close at hand, Mao saw no reason to compromise. On April 21, his forces crossed the Yangtze, and three days later occupied Nanking, driving the refugee government to seek asylum in Canton. The Communist advance now accelerated in all directions and simply could not be stopped. Even before all China had been conquered, Mao proclaimed the establishment of the People's Republic on October 1, 1949. When the Nationalist government fled from Canton to Chungking on October 13 and to Taiwan on December 8, the Communist conquest of mainland China was complete. After twenty-eight years (1921-49) of struggle, Mao rose to the pinnacle of power.

THE ROLE OF THE UNITED STATES

What did the United States do during the Chinese civil war and what were her "sins" of commission or omission? It must be stated at the outset that when he dispatched Marshall to China in December 1945, President Truman made it very clear that large scale aid to China was to be contingent on the achievement of national unity. Marshall himself had repeatedly warned Chiang in mid-1946 that the United States was not prepared to underwrite a Chinese civil war and that the spiraling inflation might precipitate an economic collapse. When Chiang ignored these warnings and went ahead with the fighting, the die was cast.

Washington's chief mistake was its inability to evolve a positive policy toward China. It neither disowned the Nationalist regime nor extricated itself entirely from China, but followed a course of partial withdrawal

35. Teng Pao-san.
36. Jerome Ch'en, *Mao*, 307.

and limited assistance to the Nationalist government—such as the granting of $27.7 million for economic aid in October 1947 and the establishment of a small Army Advisory Group to offer Chiang counsel. This policy of drift prompted Chiang's friends in Washington and the "China Lobby" to engineer a move to block the European Recovery Program unless a meaningful China aid program was initiated. Republican Congressman Walter Judd declared in November 1947: "(We) have got to win in Asia, too, or we will ultimately lose in Europe. I cannot myself vote to put some $20,000,000,000 into holding the line on one front and then ignore another front vital to our future." To him loss of China would lead to the eventual loss of all Asia. While not advocating the dispatch of American boys, he urged substantial military assistance to the Nationalists to clear the area south of the Great Wall and to hold Manchuria. In the same vein, General MacArthur pressed for greater China aid and sneered at the American pressure for KMT reforms while fighting a civil war: "The two issues are as impossible of synchronization as it would be to alter the structural design of a house while the same was being consumed by flame."[37]

In response to an urgent Nationalist request by the end of 1947 for a four-year aid program of $1.5 billion—of which $500 million of economic aid and $100 million of military aid were to be administered for the first year—Truman recommended on February 18, 1948, a grant-in-aid of $570 million for fifteen months to retard the Chinese economic collapse. It was a time of critical fighting in Manchuria and North China, where the Nationalists were being beaten badly. Only a direct American military expedition could have saved the situation—at least temporarily—but Marshall, contending that the China problem was "practically insoluble," refused to commit American troops, thereby sacrificing *the last chance* for armed intervention. The China aid bill, however, limped through Congress with a 13 per cent cut at $400 million, but was not implemented until the second half of 1948 when the Nationalist cause was all but lost. The aid was too little and too late. On July 30, 1948, Mao declared the demise of the KMT regime "not too far away." On August 13 Marshall was reported to have said: "I wash my hands of the problem which has passed altogether beyond my comprehension and my power to make judgments."[38]

The misfortune of the Nationalists was compounded by their entangle-

37. Tang Tsou, 466, 468.
38. Tang Tsou, 473, 478, 446.

ment in American politics during an election year. Disappointed with the Democratic Administration, Nationalist diplomats cultivated the Republicans on the assumption that the 1948 election would result in a change of administration. Governor Thomas Dewey of New York, the Republican candidate for the Presidency, declared on June 25, 1948, that if elected he would extend massive financial and military aid to China. But Truman confounded the world—and Chiang—with a resounding victory in the election. As president, he twice turned down Nationalist pleas for aid in November and December 1948.[39] Moreover, sensing the passing of the Kuomintang mandate, Washington withdrew what little evidence of support it still maintained for the Nationalists by evacuating the Army Advisory Group. The feeling was strong in Washington, after Chiang's resignation in January 1949, that the United States ought to get out of China as fast as possible. A final plea for $700 million by General Chennault in May 1949 to support the Southwestern and Northwestern provincial authorities against the Communists also fell on deaf ears in Washington.

In retrospect, one is inclined to the view that the United States was "guilty" of many acts of omission and inaction, but it cannot be held responsible for the "loss of China." Chinese Communism had been an internal development spanning thirty years of history and no foreign intervention could have altered its course. Active American armed intervention before the spring of 1948 might have delayed the Communist advance but probably could not have stopped it for good. Such an intervention would have required, in the view of one China expert,[40] 150,000 American boys, although a million soldiers would seem to be more realistic in the light of the later Korean and Vietnamese experiences. Even then, the most that could be expected was a temporary delay in the rise of the Communists which perhaps would have provided the Nationalists with a respite to work out their own salvation. The question then arises, how long could and would American soldiers have stayed in China, when demobilization and return to normalcy were the order of the day at home? In effect, then, the United States could not have prevented the rise of the Chinese Communists, but her policy of drift and her denial of aid to the Nationalists at a time when they needed it most dealt a severe blow to Chiang and made his cause seem hopeless, thus indirectly hastening the

39. First request for an American military mission; second request for an aid program of $3 billion for three years, tendered by Madame Chiang herself.
40. Nathaniel Peffer, a professor at Columbia University.

collapse of his regime. In that sense, the United States shared some responsibility for the downfall of the Nationalists.

CAUSES OF THE NATIONALIST DEFEAT

For an event as important as the fall of the Nationalist government on mainland China, historians have the unshirkable responsibility of assessing its causes. While a definitive study may be premature, pending a more complete opening of the archives, some tentative interpretations may be offered at the risk of oversimplification and stating of the obvious. To this writer the single most important cause for the downfall of the Nationalists was the eight-year Japanese war, which completely exhausted the government militarily, financially, and spiritually. Had there been no Japanese war, the situation in China would have been very different. Hence, many of the disastrous repercussions of the war discussed in the last chapter continued to plague the Nationalists during their struggle with the Communists. The price the Nationalists paid to win the Japanese war was also the first installment toward its eventual downfall.

1. *Deceptive Military Strength.* Although the Nationalist army emerged from the Japanese war better equipped and trained than ever before, it was a tired and weary force. Already exhibiting signs of fatigue during the last stage of the Japanese war, it was held together by nationalism, patriotism, and the prospect of an imminent Allied victory. Japan's surrender gave the troops a sense of relief and a feeling of having accomplished the mission, and they longed for a rest. The thought of fighting another civil war was abhorrent to them. Though they fought when ordered, their spirit was unwilling and their flesh weak. Their credible performance before mid-1947 represented a last desperate thrust before the final collapse.

The Communists, on the other hand, did not bear the major brunt of fighting during the Japanese war and had vastly expanded their military forces. The end of war was also the hour of recognition for them, now fresh, vigorous, and confident of the future. Their contest with the Nationalists was not unlike that between a young strapping lad and a tired old squire. Ideologies apart, the difference in stamina contributed to the outcome of the bout.

Leaving aside the question of war weariness, the Nationalist strategy also left much to be desired. Against American advice, Chiang sent large bodies of his troops to Manchuria, only to have 470,000 of them slaughtered or captured, when he should have concentrated his men to defend areas south of the Great Wall. The ill-fated decision to take Yenan and pursue the fleeing Communist leaders to the strategically unimportant mountainous Northwest drained another 400,000 troops. The battles of Huai-Hai and Tientsin-Peiping were poorly directed, causing yet another irreparable loss in manpower. In the short period from September 1948 to January 1949, the Nationalists lost well over one million men; the heart of their army was destroyed and what was left could no longer fight.

2. *Inflation and Economic Collapse.* Even more disastrous than war weariness and mistakes in strategy was the galloping inflation which was already rampant during the Japanese war, and became completely uncontrollable after the war. The single most important cause of this inflation was the flagrant increase in note issues which grew from 1.3 billion yüan in January 1937 to a fantastic 24,558,999 billion by the end of 1948, with the result that prices increased by 30 per cent per month during 1945-48. In August 1948 the legal paper money, *fapi*, was replaced by a gold yüan note at the exchange rate of three million to one, but within six weeks all controls broke down and inflation resumed its runaway course. During the brief span from August 1948 to April 1949, note issues increased by 4,524 times, and the Shanghai price index rose an astronomical 135,742 times. The conversion of gold yüan notes to silver yüan notes in July 1949, redeemable in actual silver and coins, served to further distort the financial picture and hasten the economic collapse.[41] Inflation and financial mismanagement destroyed the livelihood of hundreds of millions of Chinese and totally discredited the government. Small wonder that the majority of the people were not averse to, and even looked forward to, a change in administration.

3. *Loss of Public Confidence and Respect.* In addition to fiscal irresponsibility which brought on rampant inflation, the obnoxious conduct of Nationalist officials who returned to the Japanese-occupied areas after the war did permanent damage to the government prestige. They returned as conquerors and treated the people with contempt, as if they had been disloyal citizens or traitors. The officials were more interested in taking over enemy properties for selfish purposes than for the welfare of the people who had suffered so grievously during the Japanese occupation.

41. Shun-hsin Chou, 21-27, 273.

They monopolized profitable commodities and enterprises in open competition with the people, and publicly auctioned relief materials for personal gains. Worst of all, they forced the conversion of the Japanese-supported puppet currency in South and Central China into *fapi* at the exorbitant rate of 200 to 1, when a more equitable rate would have been half that much.[42] When the savings and cash reserves of the people were so suddenly and drastically reduced, their immediate reaction was deep resentment, the more so when a few years earlier the puppet government had forced them to convert their *fapi* to the puppet currency at the rate of two to one. The two conversions slashed the cash reserves of the people by 400 times! These citizens within occupied territories, who had waited for eight years for the return of Nationalist rule, were so mercilessly milked and so contemptuously treated that they wondered whether life would have been better under the Japanese. The net result of the misbehavior of the Nationalist officials was the alienation of millions of suffering people.

4. Failure of American Mediation and Aid. The course of events in postwar China could have been different if the United States had followed a different course during the Japanese war. First, had her China aid been more substantial during the first four years of the war, 1937-41, it might have beefed up Nationalist finances to the point where inflation could have been checked in its early stages. By nipping the trouble in the bud, the later runaway situation might never have occurred, thus avoiding the ultimate economic collapse. Secondly, if the United States had retained the original strategy of attacking Japan from the Chinese mainland, American soldiers would have landed in the coastal provinces of China, seizing territory from the Japanese and turning it over to the Nationalist government, thereby reducing the chances for a Communist occupation. The plan was discarded, however, by a change in the Allied strategy in 1944, which called for the invasion of Japan from the Pacific, thus bypassing China altogether. This decision placed Nationalist China in a strategically insignificant position, and when the war suddenly ended she was caught ill-prepared to face the consequences of the unexpected peace.

Quite apart from these economic and military considerations of what might have happened, the United States lost at least three chances to exert a decisive influence in China diplomatically. First, if Hurley had played a more active role of mediation during Mao's visit to Chungking

42. Shun-hsin Chou, 24.

in August-October 1945, he might have prevailed upon Chiang to accept the "transient arrangements" that Mao was offering, thereby averting the immediate outbreak of the civil war. This was a golden chance carelessly thrown away. Secondly, if Marshall had been more forceful in "pressuring" the KMT and Chiang into honoring the Political Consultative Conference resolutions, hostilities might have been checked. Thirdly, when the Nationalists were in a critical retreat during the spring of 1948, the United States had the last chance to intervene militarily but she did not choose to do so. In retrospect, it seems that the United States lost all these chances by default.

The failure of American mediation stemmed partially from the naive notion that the Chinese Communists were merely agrarian reformers different from the Russian Communists, when in fact the former were far more radical than the latter, as recent events have shown. There was also the American cliché that the Nationalists were fascist, dictatorial, and feudal, whereas in fact they hardly enjoyed a day of peace to put into practice their program of democratic reconstruction since their rise to power in 1928. The pet American idea of a coalition government in China did not work because it failed to take into consideration the fact that the KMT and the CCP were both revolutionary parties not given to compromise except on a very temporary basis, as shown in the 1923-27 and 1937-40 alliances. Coalition government might have averted an immediate civil war, but chances were slim that it could have postponed it indefinitely.

Because of the failure of mediation and the complete disillusionment that followed, the United States gave the Nationalist government only limited aid in 1947-48—too little and too late. In the last analysis, the Nationalists lost the gamble in assuming that the United States could not afford to see them go down the drain.

5. *Retardation of Social and Economic Reforms.* Aside from these immediate causes of the Nationalist downfall, a far more fundamental failing was the continuous retardation of badly needed social and economic reforms. This neglect might have been partially caused by a host of overwhelming circumstances beyond Nationalist control. Throughout its two-decade rule the Nanking government faced one pressing problem after another, each sapping its resources and leaving it no peace. From the outset, it was challenged by the "new warlords" and dissident politicians, and hardly had it resolved these problems when it was deluged by the

mounting threats of Japanese aggression and Communist insurrection. It took all the energy, resources, and skills the Nationalists could muster to fend off a war with Japan while launching five campaigns against the Communists. There was little time or inclination left to tackle the seemingly less imminent, if more basic, problems of economic justice and social reforms. Not only was the Principle of People's Livelihood—regulation of capital and equalization of land—never implemented, but even the far more moderate resolution of farm rent reduction to 37.5 per cent of the yearly crop never materialized. Dr. Sun's ideal of "land to the tiller" remained only a fond dream. Once the Japanese war broke out, military affairs took precedent over all others, relegating the long-overdue social reforms further to the background.

Despite these overwhelming circumstances, it was nevertheless correct to say that the Nationalists lacked the necessary motivation to initiate social and economic reforms. Established in the coastal regions far away from the hinterland, the Nanking government relied on customs dues and city commercial taxes for its sustenance, paying little attention to agrarian problems. It did not understand the peasants, saw no urgency in solving their problems, and was unsympathetic to their plight. Ironically, the Nationalist officials continued to live under the shadow of the Confucian distinction between the rulers and the ruled, and looked down upon the peasants as an inert nonentity. They failed to see the revolutionary potential of the peasant masses and consequently never attempted to organize them. It was precisely in this area of neglect that the talent of Mao found its highest and most successful expression. The stone that one builder had rejected became the cornerstone of the other's house.

FURTHER READING

Belden, Jack, *China Shakes the World* (New York, 1949).

Beloff, Max, *Soviet Policy in the Far East, 1944-1951* (London, 1953).

Chang, Carsun, *The Third Force in China* (New York, 1952).

Chang, Kia-ngau, *The Inflationary Spiral: The Experience in China, 1939-1950* (New York, 1958).

Chassin, Lionel M., *The Communist Conquest of China: A History of the Civil War, 1945-49* (Cambridge, Mass., 1965).

Ch'en, Jerome, *Mao and the Chinese Revolution* (London, 1965).

Chiang, Kai-shek, *Soviet Russia in China: A Summing Up at Seventy* (New York, 1957).

Ch'ien, Tuan-sheng, "The Role of the Military in the Chinese Government," *Pacific Affairs*, 21:239-51 (1948).

Chou, Shun-hsin, *The Chinese Inflation, 1937-1949* (New York, 1963).

Clubb, Edmund O., *20th Century China* (New York, 1964), chapter 8.

Griffith, Samuel B., II, *The Chinese People's Liberation Army* (New York, 1967).

Ho, Kan-chih, *A History of the Modern Chinese Revolution* (Peking, 1959).

Houn, Franklin W., *A Short History of Chinese Communism*, chapter 5.

Hu, Ch'iao-mu, *Thirty Years of the Communist Party of China* (Peking, 1951).

Johnson, Chalmer A., *Peasant Nationalism and Communist Power, The Emergence of Revolutionary China* (Stanford, 1962).

Koen, Ross Y., *The China Lobby* (New York, 1960).

Liao, Kai-lung, *From Yenan to Peking* (Peking, 1954).

Liu, F. F., *A Military History of Modern China, 1924-1949* (Princeton, 1956).

Loh, Pichon P. Y., *The Kuomintang Debacle of 1949: Conquest or Collapse?* (Boston, 1965).

Mao, Tse-tung, *Mao Tse-tung hsüan-chi* (Selected works of Mao Tse-tung), (Peking, 1963), III and IV.

Melby, John F., *The Mandate of Heaven: Record of a Civil War, China 1945-49* (Toronto, 1968).

Porter, Brian, *Britain and the Rise of Communist China, 1945-1954* (London, 1967).

Tsou, Tang, *America's Failure in China, 1941-50* (Chicago, 1963).

United States Relations with China, With Special Reference to the Period 1944-1949 (Washington, D. C., 1949).

Van Slyke, Lyman P. (ed.), *The Chinese Communist Movement: A Report of the U.S. War Department, July 1945* (Stanford, 1968).

Wedemeyer, Albert (General), *Wedemeyer Reports!* (New York, 1959).

Young, Arthur N., *China and the Helping Hand, 1937-1945* (Cambridge, Mass., 1963).

———, *China's Wartime Finance and Inflation, 1937-1945* (Cambridge, Mass., 1965).

26

The People's Republic

With the conquest of the country nearly complete, Mao Tse-tung summoned a People's Political Consultative Conference on September 12, 1949, to prepare for the formation of a new government. A total of 662 delegates from forty-five units were selected by the CCP to attend. They met for twelve days and adopted an Organic Law of the Central People's Government, a Common Program which was basically a statement on national purposes, and a national flag consisting of a red background with a large yellow star in the upper left corner surrounded by four smaller stars. The large star symbolized CCP leadership and the smaller ones represented the four-class coalition of workers, peasants, petty bourgeois, and national bourgeois. On October 1, the Chinese People's Republic was formally established, with a capital in Peiping, now renamed Peking. It was recognized by the Soviet Union a day later and by the other Communist states in a rapid succession.[1] Among the non-Communist countries that granted recognition were India, Burma, Pakistan, Ceylon, Britain, and France.[2] The United States, however, has steadfastly refused to recognize the new government.

The theory and practice of statecraft by the regime reflected to a large extent ideas expressed in Mao's *New Democracy* and the Rectification (or Intra-Party Struggle) Movement (*Cheng-feng*) developed in Yenan.

---

1. Bulgaria and Rumania, October 3, 1949; Czechoslavakia, Poland, Hungary, and Yugoslavia, October 4; East Germany, October 27; and Albania, November 23.
2. As of 1968, 51 countries have recognized Communist China, while 65 have recognized Nationalist China.

The *New Democracy,* a major theoretical work of 1940, was a creative adaptation of Marxism-Leninism to the Chinese situation during the critical transition from semicolonialism and semifeudalism to socialism. It stipulated that the economic structure should consist of three sectors: the state economy, in which the government should control big industries, mines, enterprises, and public utilities; the agricultural economy, in which individual farms should develop into collective farms; and the private economy, in which the middle and small capitalists should be allowed to operate. Of the three, the state sector was to assume the position of leadership and strive to increase production faster than the private sector so as to eliminate possible competition. It was also to be responsible for guiding the other sectors toward socialism. As regards the political structure, the work set forth the principle of "Democratic Centralism" and the coexistence of the four classes under the leadership of the proletariat and its party, the CCP. Culturally, Mao favored the development of a scientific, antifeudal, mass culture. Selective acceptance of useful elements of foreign cultures was desirable but the culture of the New Democracy should be national and anti-imperialistic, able to advocate the dignity and independence of the Chinese nation. "It belongs to our nation and bears the characteristics of our nation."[3]

Mao's second theoretical contribution during the Yenan period was the Rectification Movement of 1942, to combat (1) subjectivism and unorthodox tendencies; (2) sectarianism within the party ranks; and (3) formalism in literature. It was a drive aimed at inculcating on the party members a correct understanding of Marxism-Leninism, the thought of Mao, and the general party line in order that they might avoid "leftism" and "rightism." The struggle was one of principle and not of personality, with a view to winning back deviants to orthodoxy through indoctrination, thought reform, and realization of mistakes.[4] With this process of ideological rectification, the Chinese Communists hoped to avoid the permanent purge that had characterized the Soviet experience.

POLITICAL ORGANIZATION

The Organic Law of 1949 made it very clear that the Chinese People's Republic was not a "Dictatorship of the Proletariat" as in the Soviet Union, but a "Democratic Dictatorship" led by the CCP on the basis

3. Mao Tse-tung, II, 655-704.
4. Mao Tse-tung, III, 813-30.

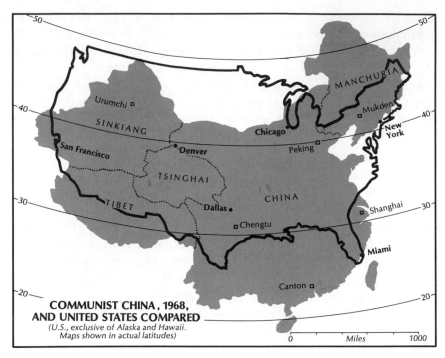

**COMMUNIST CHINA, 1968,
AND UNITED STATES COMPARED**
(U.S., exclusive of Alaska and Hawaii.
Maps shown in actual latitudes)

of a four class alliance. The coexistence of the four classes endowed the government with a "democratic" character, while its uncompromising and unyielding attitude toward the counterrevolutionaries gave it the attribute of a "dictatorship." A cardinal principle followed by the new government was "Democratic Centralism," which provided for popularly elected bodies at different levels of government. These assemblies would elect their own representative officials, pending the approval of the higher authorities. The "election" part of this process was "democratic," while obedience to higher authorities suggested "centralism." By extension, the term also came to mean free discussion in the formation of a policy and tight, unswerving compliance to that decision once it had been made, regardless of one's original stand.

The Government Structure. Under the Organic Law the supreme organ of state was the Central People's Government Council which exercised executive, legislative, and judicial powers. It met twice a month to deliberate on high policies of state. Its members included the chairman (Mao), the six vice-chairmen,[5] and fifty-six others elected by the People's Political

5. Including Liu Shao-ch'i and Madame Sun Yat-sen.

Consultative Council. When not in session its powers were delegated to a State Administrative Council, whose twenty-odd members constituted a sort of cabinet responsible to the Government Council or, when the latter was not in session, to the chairman of the state, Mao. The State Administrative Council was headed by a premier (*tsung-li*), Chou En-lai, and a number of vice-premiers; under them were four committees: Political and Legal Affairs, Finance and Economics, Culture and Education, and People's Supervision. Each of these committees directed a determined number of the thirty various ministries, commissions, and boards.

On a par with the State Administrative Council were three other important organs: the People's Revolutionary Military Council, the People's Supreme Court, and the Procurator-general's Office.

Under the central government but above the provincial administrations were six unique Great Administrative Areas,[6] each with jurisdiction over several provinces. Presumably, these intermediate setups were created to help consolidate the central government's hold on the provinces, but, as it later turned out, they developed centrifugal tendencies at the expense of the central power. Subsequently, they were abolished in 1953, and the political structure of the nation reverted to the three traditional tiers of national, provincial, and district (or county) administrations.

The Organic Law remained in force for five years while steps were undertaken to introduce a constitution. In 1953 a census was taken and an election law promulgated, allowing voting privileges to all citizens of eighteen and above, except landlords and counterrevolutionaries. In early 1954 elections were held, with the village and township congresses electing their representatives to the district congresses, which then elected their delegates to the provincial congresses, which in turn elected their delegates to the All-China People's Congress. The last-named body was convened between September 15 and 28, and adopted a new constitution of four chapters and 106 articles. Chapter 1 reiterated the principle of "Democratic Centralism" and the alliance of the four classes, as well as the four types of ownership: state, cooperative, individual, and capitalist. Chapter 2 described the government structure, purposely omitting the Great Administrative Areas. Chapter 3 was the usual bill of rights, with the exception that the government reserved the right to "reform traitors and counterrevolutionaries"—thus voiding the legal guarantees for those who had the misfortune of disagreeing with the government. Chapter 4

6. The Northeast, North China, East China, Central-South China, Northwest China, and Southwest China.

designated Peking as the capital and described the national flag, as mentioned before.

Under the new constitution, the highest organ of state is the All-China People's Congress, which is supposed to meet briefly each year to ponder major policy decisions and elect top government officials. The position of the chairman of the republic (Mao) has emerged stronger than before, since the six vice-chairmanships have been reduced to one (Chu Teh). Other major central offices include a State Council (*Kuo-wu yüan*), a National Defense Council, a Supreme People's Court, and a Supreme People's Procuratorate. Below the central government are provincial and district (or county) administrations.

Political Parties. The leading party is of course the CCP, which claimed a membership of 4.5 million in 1949, 17 million in 1961, and possibly 26 million in 1967.[7] The party is organized in four channels: representative, executive, administrative, and control. According to the 1956 party constitution, the highest organ in the representative sector is the National Party Congress, which convenes once a year and whose members are elected for five-year terms. In the executive sector, there is the powerful Central Committee,[8] also elected for five years, which is headed by a chairman and four vice-chairmen; in 1958 a fifth vice-chairman was added. Convened twice a year, the Central Committee when not in session delegates its powers to the Politburo,[9] which in turn maintains a Standing Committee of China's seven most powerful men. Until the recent Cultural Revolution, these seven included the Central Committee's chairman (Mao), five vice-chairmen (Liu Shao-ch'i, Chou En-lai, Chu Teh, Ch'en Yün, and Lin Piao), and the party general secretary (Teng Hsiao-p'ing).[10] The Central Committee maintains six regional bureaus and a number of departments such as Organization, Training, Propaganda, and Social Affairs.

7. Peter S. H. Tang and Joan M. Maloney, *Communist China: The Domestic Scene, 1949-1967* (South Orange, N.J., 1967), 145.
8. 43 regular and 27 alternate members in 1957; grew to 96 and 94, respectively, in 1960.
9. 17 full and 6 alternate members in 1960.
10. Franz Schurmann, *Ideology and Organization in Communist China* (Berkeley, 1966), 143, 146. It is to be noted that Liu, Teng, Chu, and Ch'en had fallen in power during the Cultural Revolution in 1966, and the Ninth Party Congress of April 1969 elected Mao chairman of the party and the Central Committee, with Lin Piao as his deputy and Chou En-lai as general secretary. See the section on Cultural Revolution.

In the administrative sector of the party, there is the Central Secretariat, and in the control sector, the Central Control Commission. An over-all view of the party structure appears in the following chart.

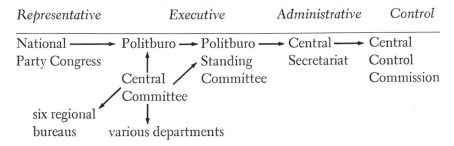

Representative	Executive	Administrative	Control

National ⟶ Politburo ⟶ Politburo ⟶ Central ⟶ Central
Party Congress ↑ ↗ Standing   Secretariat   Control
        Central ╱ Committee   Commission
      ╱ Committee
six regional ╱ ↓
bureaus   various departments

Significantly, party and government are closely interlocked, and all important party members fill key positions in government as well as in semiofficial organizations such as trade unions, farm groups, and mass organizations. Mao in 1949 held the chairmanships of the CCP Central Committee, the Politburo, the Central Secretariat, the People's Government, the Revolutionary Military Council, and the National People's Congress. After the 1956 party reorganization, however, he relinquished the chairmanship of the Central Secretariat; in 1959 he resigned from the chairmanship of the People's Government (State Chairmanship) in favor of Liu Shao-ch'i, who concurrently held the position of first vice-chairman of the CCP Central Committee.

As a "People's Democratic Dictatorship" rather than a "Dictatorship of the Proletariat," the Chinese People's Republic permits a number of non-Communist parties to exist. The most important ones include (1) the KMT Revolutionary Committee, which consists of a group of leftist KMT members under the titular leadership of Madame Sun Yat-sen, who chose to stay in mainland China rather than join Chiang on Taiwan; (2) the Democratic League, which had always sympathized with the CCP during its struggles with the KMT; (3) the Third Party, which had unsuccessfully attempted to effect a reconciliation between the KMT and the CCP; (4) the Chih-kung tang—constituted largely of Chinese overseas—which has antecedents in the secret Hung-men Society of old; (5) the Democratic Reconstruction Association; and (6) the People's Salvation Association, of anti-Japanese fame in the 1930's.

The juxtaposition of these parties serves many purposes. Not only does it broadcast the alleged leniency and democratic spirit of the new regime and the public support it enjoys, but it also enables the CCP to preserve its purity by obviating the need of absorbing them. However, since a Communist dictatorship—no matter how democratic it claims to be—recognizes neither the concept of a "loyal opposition" nor the freedom associated with political parties as understood in the West, these non-Communist parties are essentially window dressing. They possess only the right to agree and cooperate with the CCP and the government. Once their usefulness is outlived, their future is doomed. The attempt by the Red Guards on August 24, 1966, to disband them within seventy-two hours, though it met with no success, indicated the direction in which the wind was blowing.

Uniqueness of Chinese Communism. The differences in the Chinese and Russian revolutionary experiences accounted for many unique features of Chinese Communism. First of all, the Chinese Revolution was led to success by a group of professional revolutionaries who received wide support from the peasantry; in Russia, it was the urban workers who gave decisive support to the professional revolutionary leaders. The Chinese leaders were mostly of intellectual and middle-class backgrounds; those who were of true proletarian origin accounted for a very small fraction. The success of the Chinese experience suggests that possession of correct doctrine is more important than formal organic ties with the proletariat. Nonetheless, the CCP leaders insist that they are spiritual, if not social, proletarians.[11]

Secondly, the classical Marxist pattern of societal development from feudalism to capitalism to socialism does not apply in China, for the stage of capitalism did not properly exist there. In its place the Chinese Communists have substituted a semifeudal, semicolonial period, from which China moved into an intermediary stage called the New Democracy before advancing to the ultimate stage of socialism.

Thirdly, during New Democracy four classes coexist and non-Communist parties are permitted to operate, albeit in a limited fashion. In contrast, the dictatorship of the proletariat in the Soviet Union permits only one class and one party.

Fourthly, the Chinese Communist seizure of power had its base in the countryside and achieved success after a prolonged period of struggle. The Russian Revolution was characterized by strikes, sabotage, and uprisings

11. Benjamin I. Schwartz, "On the 'Originality' of Mao Tse-tung," *Foreign Affairs*, (Oct. 1955), 74.

in urban centers, and won victory in a much shorter time than the Chinese.

Fifthly, in place of the Soviet permanent purge which accounted for the killing of 70 per cent of the Central Committee members elected in 1934,[12] the Chinese stressed ideological remolding and thought reform. Until the Cultural Revolution in the mid-1960s, the Chinese leadership had been remarkably stable and closely knit. The only purge of note was connected with the antiparty activity in 1953-54 of Kao Kang, party boss of Manchuria, and Jao Shu-shih, party first secretary in East China, who schemed to usurp the positions of Liu Shao-ch'i and Chou En-lai in government. When exposed, Kao committed suicide and Jao was imprisoned. It should also be noted that the dismissal of Minister of Defense P'eng Te-huai in 1959 due to policy difference with Mao was neither a purge nor a liquidation.

The success of the Chinese Communist Revolution led Mao to assert that the Chinese experience should provide a prototype of revolution in Asia. By implication he denied the universal applicability of the Soviet model and reduced it to a European variety. The Chinese claim was sure to cause far-reaching consequences in Sino-Soviet relations, as we will soon see in a later section; it may even have inadvertently inspired the Eastern European satellite countries' assertion of "different paths to socialism."

ECONOMIC DEVELOPMENT

The government in 1949 had inherited a badly disrupted economy following the civil war and the Japanese war that preceded it. Inflation had rocketed beyond control; floods had affected 30-40 per cent of the arable land; and industrial and food output had plummeted to 56 per cent and 70-75 per cent of the prewar peak, respectively. Thus, the first order of business was to rehabilitate the economic life of the nation and to restore industrial and agricultural production to prewar heights.

To promote financial stability, the Communists had earlier issued a People's Currency (*Jen-min p'iao*) in May 1949 and banned the circulation of foreign currencies as a medium of exchange. Strenuous efforts were made to achieve price and wage stabilization through a drastic reduction of the paper money in circulation and the introduction of a "wage-point"

12. Chün-tu Hsüeh, "The Cultural Revolution and Leadership Crisis in Communist China," *Political Science Quarterly*, LXXXII:2:184 (June 1967).

system for payment of workers, which operated on the basis of the prices of five basic items—rice, oil, coal, flour, and cotton cloth. As the prices of these articles fluctuated from week to week, the "wage-point" rose and fell accordingly, so that the average salary of workers varied in money value but not in actual purchasing power. Similar methods were used to safeguard savings and bank deposits. Furthermore, concerted efforts were undertaken by the Liberation Army to restore communication lines in order to facilitate the exchange of commodities. Also put into practice was a new taxation system involving agricultural, industrial, commercial, sales and income taxes. With these measures, inflation was stamped out in 1950 and the government budget balanced.

Land Revolution and Agricultural Collectivization. In addition to efforts to eliminate inflation and restore fiscal stability, the government launched a vigorous agrarian revolution in an attempt to cure China's age-old problem of landlordism. Since 70-80 per cent of the land was owned by 10 per cent of the farm population—the landlords[13] and rich peasants— the government promulgated in June 1950 the Agrarian Reform Law, which called for the abolition of the "land ownership system of feudal exploitation" and the confiscation of landowners' holdings and farm implements for redistribution to landless peasants. The agrarian popula- tion was classified into five categories: (1) landlords: those who possessed large land properties and who did no manual work themselves but lived on usury and the exploitation of others; (2) rich peasants: those who owned land but worked on it themselves while also hiring farm hands, lending money, and renting part of the land to poor peasants; (3) middle peasants: those who owned land but worked on it themselves without exploiting others; (4) poor peasants: those who owned little land or farm implements, who had to sell part of their land to make ends meet, and who had to rent land from others; and (5) hired hands: those who owned no land and had to live on labor or loans.

Theoretically, the government allowed the landlords to keep their por- tions of the redistributed land, and exempted from confiscation the rich peasants' land that they themselves cultivated. But in practice many in- justices and acts of violence were committed in local "accusation meet- ings," where virulent denunciations of landlords and rich peasants took

---

13. Actually the average landlord's holding was only forty acres. See T. J. Hughes and D. E. T. Luard, *The Economic Development of Communist China, 1949-1960* (London, 1962), 143.

place under the guidance of overzealous party cadres and vengeful peasants. Both landlords and rich peasants suffered grievous losses at these meetings, and many were summarily shot after a brief public trial. The gentry, formerly the dominant elite and the backbone of the traditional society, was destroyed, and in its place we find the party.[14]

By December 1952 the agrarian revolution had been completed, and some 700 million *mou* (1/6 acre) of land had been redistributed to 300 million peasants. On the average, in East and South China—where the population density was the highest—each head received one *mou*; in Central China, 2 to 3 *mou*; in North China, 3 *mou*; and in Manchuria, 7 *mou*.[15] On the whole, the land revolution favored the poor peasants and the hired hands at the expense of the landlords and the rich peasants, while the middle peasants were affected least of all.

No sooner had the land revolution been completed in December 1952 than the government started a second phase of agrarian reform—a drive toward collectivization in 1953, with a view to raising production, preventing the re-emergence of rich peasants, achieving greater agricultural specialization, and proceeding faster toward the goal of socialist transformation. Collectivization involved several stages, the lowest being the "mutual aid" teams where the peasants pooled or loaned their implements and worked jointly and seasonally, as during the spring planting and the autumn harvest. The second stage was the semisocialist agricultural producers' cooperatives, in which the members pooled not only their implements and labor but land as well, although theoretically retaining individual ownership. The third stage was the fully socialized cooperative, similar to the Soviet collective farm, in which all members collectively owned the land. By the end of 1956, some 96 per cent of all peasant households had officially become members of the semisocialist producers' cooperatives. When the collectivization campaign was completed in 1957, there were a total of 760,000 to 800,000 cooperative farms, each averaging 160 families, or 600 to 700 persons. A further move toward socialist transformation was the introduction of the people's communes, which will be discussed shortly.

Industrial Expansion. Lenin stated, "There is only one real foundation for a socialist society, and it is large industry." Recognizing the critical role of industrialization in building a socialist state, the CCP spared no effort

14. Schurmann, 497.
15. Hughes and Luard, 145-46.

to achieve this goal. By 1952 not only had the prewar industrial and agricultural peaks been matched, but those of 1949 surpassed by 77.5 per cent. The time had arrived for a First Five-Year Plan. Preparatory work began in 1951, and in the autumn of the following year a State Planning Committee was established under the direction of Kao Kang, chairman of the Northeast Administrative Area. This Five-Year Plan was supposed to start in 1953, but inexperience and lack of statistical knowledge, planning technique, and machinery plagued it with delay and constant revision. When the Plan was finally put into practice in February 1955—some two years after the official beginning—it was in effect only a Two-and-a-half-Year Plan. It called for the construction of 694 industrial projects, of which 156 plants were to be built with Soviet aid. At the end of the planned period, the industrial output was supposed to double, the introduction of the cooperative farms was to be effected, and the incorporation of private industry and commerce into state organizations was to be completed, so that a "socialist transformation" might become a reality. Of the total outlay of capital, 58.2 per cent was earmarked for industrial construction, 19.2 per cent for transport, posts, and telecommunication, 7.6 per cent for agriculture, forestry, and water conservancy, and 7.2 per cent for culture, education, and public health.

The year 1956 marked a spectacular advance in industrial output that topped the previous year by 25 per cent, matched by an increase of 60 per cent in capital investment. Although the pace slowed down somewhat in 1957, the First Five-Year Plan still overfulfilled the original targets by 17 per cent according to the "fixed prices of 1952." Steel production reached 5.2 million tons, iron 5.8 million tons, electric power 19,030 million kwh—each representing a 25 per cent increase over the original quotas. The coal production of 122 million tons was an 8 per cent overfulfillment, while grain output was 11.6 per cent above quota.

The success of the First Five-Year Plan prompted the government to launch a more ambitious Second Five-Year Plan for 1958-62. It called for an overall increase of 75 per cent in both industrial and agricultural production by 1962 and a 50 per cent increase in national income. A sample of the target figures for key industries and agricultural products indicates the confidence of the planners: coal, 190-210 million tons; steel, 10.5-12 million tons; electricity, 40,000-43,000 million kwh; crude oil, 5-6 million tons; grain, 275 million tons; and cotton, 2.4 million tons.[16]

In harmony with the rapid economic growth, the government radically

16. Hughes and Luard, 31, 64-65.

revamped the system of higher education with a view to producing larger numbers of engineers and technicians in a shorter time. Liberal arts education was discouraged in favor of technical education, and many technical institutes were created at the expense of general universities. The curriculum was revised, and departments within the universities and institutes were reorganized to allow the student greater concentration on a specialty rather than diverting his time and energy between a variety of subjects. Thus, specialized knowledge in a narrow field was preferred to general education.[17] According to the study of a noted American scientist, 90 per cent of China's quarter of a million scientists and engineers in 1960 had been trained since the Communist take-over in 1949, and in 1960, China graduated about 75 per cent as many engineers as the United States.[18]

The "Great Leap" and the Commune. No sooner had the Second Five-Year Plan begun than the government plunged ahead in a new feverish drive to accelerate the expansion of the already overheated economy. In early February 1958, the National People's Congress announced a "Great Leap Forward" Movement for the next three years, calling for a 19 per cent increase in steel production, 18 per cent in electricity, and 17 per cent in coal output for 1958. The Chinese Communists rosily anticipated catching up with or even surpassing the British industrial capacity in fifteen years, i.e., 1972. Buoyed by optimism, the exhuberant planners repeatedly revised the production targets upward in the ensuing months in hopes of achieving an unprecedented rate of growth. The steel quota was raised from 6.2 million tons in February 1958 to 8-8.5 million in May and to 10.7 million in August. A general increase of 33 per cent in industrial output was confidently predicted for the year.[19] To achieve this phenomenal development record, everyone was urged to participate in industrial production, and in so doing everybody, regardless of his background— government official, peasant, student, professor, worker, etc.—became a proletarian. By the fall of 1958, some 600,000 backyard furnaces had sprung up all over the country.

Along with this frenzied drive for industrialization, the government took a further step toward socialist transformation by announcing the

17. Immanuel C. Y. Hsü, "The Reorganization of Higher Education in Communist China, 1949-61," *The China Quarterly* (July-Sept. 1964), 128.
18. John A. Berberet, *Science and Technology in Communist China* (Santa Barbara, 1960), 3.
19. Hughes and Luard, 66-69.

creation of People's Communes. Actually, in the spring of 1958, piecemeal amalgamation of agricultural producer's cooperatives had already begun in Hopeh, Honan, and parts of Manchuria; by July the movement reached a "high tide," and the term "People's Commune" formally appeared. Mao together with other high government officials visited some of the early models in Honan and Hopeh, and on August 29 the CCP Central Committee officially announced the birth of People's Communes.[20] The movement quickly spread to different parts of the country. By November 1958 there were 26,000 communes embracing 98 per cent of the farm population. On the average each rural commune consisted of some thirty cooperatives of about 5,000 households, or 25,000 people. It assumed the administrative functions of the villages; controlled the area's agricultural as well as industrial resources; collected taxes; and operated schools, banks, nurseries, public kitchens, old folks homes, public cemeteries, etc. It took over all private properties such as land, houses, and livestock. By January 1959, 99 per cent of the peasants had joined the communes, each of which maintained numerous production brigades and teams to increase agricultural and industrial output.

In parallel existence with rural communes were urban communes, of which the Red Flag Commune of Chengchow in North China stood out as a model. It was created in August 1958 with 4,134 households—comprising 18,729 people—and centered around the Chengchow Spinning and Weaving Machinery Factory. Collective living began with the moving of the workers to the factory area, around which the commune developed clothing stores, public dining halls, child care centers, nurseries, hospitals, schools, parks, banks, and movie theatres. There were also old folks homes, savings banks, and farms where vegetables were grown and pigs and poultry were raised for the public mess halls. Since 80 per cent of the women were employed, "livelihood service stations" and neighborhood service units were indispensable. They were run mostly by elderly persons, who performed chores for a small fee, such as paying bills, mending clothes, cleaning the houses, baby-sitting, and caring for the sick. Organizationally, the head of the Chengchow Spinning and Weaving Machinery Factory served also as the head of the commune, while the CCP branch at the factory was concurrently the party committee of the commune, over which it maintained close control. The various departments of the commune included industry, agriculture, finance, planning, civil security, welfare, sanitation, and culture. There were, of course, pro-

20. Schurmann, 474-78.

duction teams—organized along military lines as regiments, battalions, and platoons—to raise industrial, agricultural, and every other aspect of output.[21]

Historically, only two commune experiments had ever been attempted and both soon expired as ignominious failures. They were the Paris Commune of 1871, which lasted seventy-three days from March 17 to May 28, and the peasant communes in the Soviet Union during the early revolutionary period. In 1930 Stalin pronounced communes unfit for the socialist present, though ideal for the distant future. Mao was of course not unaware of these experiences, but he seems to have been more influenced by the late Ch'ing reformer K'ang Yu-wei's work, *Ta-t'ung shu* (The Book of Universal Commonwealth), which was inspired by the ancient work "The Evolution of Li" (*Li-yün*) of the *Book of Rites* (*Li-chi*). In the *Ta-t'ung shu*, K'ang argued for the creation of a utopia in which there would be no private property, no private ownership, no sale of land, no private industry, no private commerce; in which there would be public hospitals, public maternity wards, public welfare, public education, public homes for the aged, and public cemeteries. A basic feature of this utopia was the destruction of the family and the emancipation of woman from servitude in the kitchen.[22] It was no coincidence, therefore, that Mao described the characteristic of the commune as *ta* (grand) and *kung* (public), which were the key concepts in the opening passage of the "Evolution of Li": "When the *Grand* Course was pursued, a *public* and common spirit ruled all under the sky."[23] Hailing the introduction of the commune as "the morning sun above the broad horizon of East Asia," the Chinese Communists confidently boasted that "the attainment of communism in China is no longer a remote event."[24]

As a result of the Great Leap and the introduction of the communes, the government proudly announced at the end of 1958 that industrial production for the year had surpassed that of 1957 by 65 per cent. Machine tools had trebled; coal and steel had doubled; oil had increased by 50

21. Janet Salaff, "The Urban Communes and Anti-city Experiment in Communist China," *The China Quarterly* (January-March 1967), 82-110.

22. For contents of the *Ta-t'ung shu*, see Liang Ch'i-ch'ao, *Intellectual Trends*, 95-98. For K'ang's influence on Mao, see Wen-shun Chi, "The Ideological Source of the People's Communes in Communist China," *Pacific Coast Philogy*, II (April 1967), 62-78.

23. Translation by James Legge, *The Sacred Books of China*, Part III, *The Li Ki* (Oxford, 1885), 364. Italics added.

24. Benjamin I. Schwartz, "China and the Communist Bloc: A Speculative Reconstruction," *Current History*, 35:208:326 (Dec. 1958).

per cent and electricity by 40 per cent. Even taking into consideration the unavoidable exaggeration of the figures, one still has to admit that considerable success had been achieved. Yet, much of the quality was sacrificed for quantity as the government itself later admitted. In August 1959, 3 million of the 11 million tons of steel produced in 1958 was pronounced unfit for industrial use—backyard furnaces simply did not perform the same function as the giant steel mill. Amid the utopian dreams of instant development, a new feeling of pragmatism began to emerge which stressed realism in planning and expertise in technological operations. It was becoming apparent that authentic economic progress needed far more than ideological power to be a reality.

SOCIAL AND PSYCHOLOGICAL CONTROL

A basic ingredient of Maoism is the continuous organization of mass movements for the attainment of specific objectives predetermined by the party. Indeed, chronic surges of mass campaigns punctuated the daily rhythm of life in Communist China, and the Chinese people, once described as a pile of loose sand, are now more tightly organized than any other national population in the world. Practically everybody belongs to some mass organization through which the party and the government exercise their control and carry out national policy. In addition, their monopoly of the communications media and the omnipresence of their security police and party cadre have combined to turn the society into a watertight compartment unprecedented in the history of China. Under such totalitarian control freedom has become an anathema except when it has served the interests of the state.

The mass organizations were actually semigovernmental bodies of gigantic size. Foremost among them in 1953 were the All-China Federation of Democratic Youth, which boasted a membership of 18 million; the All-China Federation of Trade Union, 10.2 million; the All-China Democratic Women's Federation, 76 million; and the All-China Students' Federation, 3.29 million. In addition, there were the Young Pioneers, which included children between the ages of 9 and 14 and claimed a membership of 8 million, and the Democratic Youth League, which spanned the age group 14 to 25 and boasted 12 million. By way of these gigantic organizations, the government indoctrinated the people and organized them for demonstrations, parades, and drives, such as the Resist-America Aid-Korea Campaign in 1951, the Three-Anti (San-fan) Movement in 1951 to combat corruption, waste, and bureaucratism, and the Five-Anti (*Wu-fan*) Movement in 1952 to fight bribery, tax evasion, fraud, theft of government property, and leakage of state economic secrets. The greatest of all mass campaigns was perhaps the organization in 1966 of hundreds of thousands of students into the Red Guards to combat the Anti-Maoists.

The New Socialist Man. The new society under the Communists encouraged the forging of a new style of life (*tso-feng*) and the creation of a new Socialist Man. People were urged to mind not only their own business but to check on one another's thoughts and actions, to attend numerous political gatherings, and to participate in "learning" and "struggle" sessions. The Socialist Man was supposed to have no regard for face, be prepared to make public confessions, and, most important, revere the state before his family. His whole being was irrevocably dedicated to advancing the cause of the proletarian revolution rather than to seeking individual advancement or bringing honor to his family and home town, as in the feudal past. Article 42 of the Common Program clearly demanded that the new man was to have Five Loves—love of the fatherland, love of people, love of labor, love of science, and love of public property. Although there was fear that such a Socialist Man might be too austere and too unnatural—one worthy of awe more than of love—this misgiving was somewhat relieved by the discovery that the Soviet comrades in China still retained some vestiges of humanness.

Psychological Control. In connection with the molding of a new style of life, there developed a subtle if devastating indoctrination program known in journalistic jargon as "brainwashing" (*hsi-nao*).[25] It was a process of psychological coercion based on Pavlov's theory that environmental conditioning could alter human will and remold the character of the individual. Thus, brainwashing was used not only to convert enemies and extract confessions, but also to indoctrinate party cadres and transform intellectuals so that they could be of use to the state rather than be liquidated as in postrevolutionary Russia.

The indoctrination process usually lasts from several months to a year, depending on the intensity of the objective, but in all cases it takes place in a faraway controlled camp where the individual, completely isolated

25. Edward Hunter, *Brainwashing in Red China* (New York, 1951); Richard L. Walker, *China under Communism: The First Five Years* (New Haven, 1955), chapter 3; Robert J. Lifton, *Thought Reform and the Psychology of Totalism: A Study of "Brainwashing" in China* (New York, 1961).

from the outside world, is deprived of all sense of security. Upon arriving at the camp, the trainees are grimly impressed with the impossibility of retreat. They are divided into small groups, each under the guidance of an activist. They are assigned heavy physical labor to insure fatigue, thereby weakening their will to resist. In this condition they study and criticize the background and the life history of one another. During this initial period of about two months, food and living quarters are very poor.

In the next stage of three or four months, food and living conditions improve, while physical exertion is somewhat reduced but remains sufficient to guarantee fatigue at the end of the day. There are more study sessions and group meetings, where the insignificance of the individual and the omnipotence of the party are stressed. The works of Marx, Lenin, Stalin, and Mao become the new Bible. The past is depicted as dark, corrupt, and decadent, while the new life under the Communist regime represents liberation and progress and provides chances for a new and meaningful existence. Class struggle and the inevitability of ultimate party victory are continuously pounded into the minds of the trainees.

At the end of the second period, the trainee in all likelihood experiences an emotional crisis, whereupon he comes to the conclusion that there is no point in hiding or resisting; the party will win anyway. So he seeks liberation by releasing his feelings and accepting wholeheartedly the party and what it represents. With this, a heavy burden is lifted and he is reborn. He finds new meaning in the Communist jargon and propaganda, and is anxious to help others to find the same experience, partly to justify his own conversion. Consolidation of this state of mind requires about four months. When the indoctrination is completed, a quarter of the graduates are sent for further schooling, while the remainder go into society to organize and lead the public. The whole society, in fact, is a laboratory of mass control.

Through mass organizations, secret police, mass communications media, and indoctrination, the government has succeeded in controlling and remolding the society and the people to an extent unknown in Chinese history. The once individualistic Chinese have been transformed into the most regimented people in the world.

FOREIGN RELATIONS

Though deeply committed to international communism, Mao and his followers were national communists at heart, keenly aware of China's misfortunes of the past century. Like all Chinese of all persuasions, they were fired with a burning desire to restore China's rightful position under the sun, to achieve the big-power status denied her since the Opium War, and to revive the national confidence and self-respect that had been lost during a century of foreign humiliation. The new regime from its inception adopted a bold stance toward the Western powers, to show that it was not afraid of them as were the Manchu and the Nationalist governments, which meekly bowed before the imperialist gunboats.

This attitude was reflected in a number of cases. After their conquest of Manchuria the Communists held the American, British, and French consular officers at Mukden incommunicado. In early 1950 they requisitioned the French, Dutch, and other Western consular properties. Soon afterwards, the British consul-general at Mukden, Stevenson, and his American counterpart, Angus Ward, were openly abused. The British consul at Urumchi was expelled on charges of espionage, and the French vice-consul at Kunming was asked to leave. More recently, the British and Soviet diplomats in Peking were subjected to harassment and humiliation by the Red Guards during the Cultural Revolution. These incidents might seem trivial on the surface and in some cases may have appeared as sheer nonsense and bad taste, but they manifest the covert drive to demonstrate that New China is different from Old China and that she dares to challenge foreign powers with impunity—no more are there foreign gunboats sailing up the Peiho or the Yangtze to demand apologies as in the past. Doubtless, these acts were calculated to foster the prestige of the government and instill self-confidence and self-respect in the people. For all intents and purposes, the government has succeeded in transmitting the message that under the Communist rule foreign imperialism has passed out of China.

A major source of strength during the early years of the People's Republic was its close ties with the Soviet Union. In 1949 Mao unequivocally announced his "lean to one side" policy: "The Chinese people must lean either to the side of imperialism or to the side of socialism. There can be no exception. There can be no sitting on the fence; there is no third path." Such a policy was prompted not only by ideological affinity but also by practical considerations: the infant People's Republic needed Soviet aid and protection to forestall Western intervention, such as that which occurred in Siberia after the Bolshevik Revolution. Small wonder that Mao went to the Soviet Union shortly after his rise to power in 1949—his first trip abroad—to seek a treaty of friendship and alliance.

The Moscow-Peking Axis, which formally came into being after the treaty was signed on February 14, 1950, became the cornerstone of the People's Republic's foreign policy during the greater part of its first decade. Stalin granted Mao a military alliance, $300 million of credit, and a promise to provide experts to help with Chinese industrialization and military modernization. Mao in 1952 eulogized the Axis as "lasting, unbreakable, and invincible," while Liu Shao-ch'i paid tribute to it in the following glowing terms: "There is no deceit, competition, mutual exclusion or extortion between each other, or oppression and plunder of the one by the other—as is inherent among the capitalist countries."[26] Despite their own urgent needs, the Soviets dispatched to China large numbers of scientists, technicians, and military advisers: 1,000 to 25,000 each in the Chinese air force and navy, 5,000 to 10,000 in the Chinese army in 1953, and some 400,000 in various industrial enterprises and plants by February 1954. When Khrushchev and Bulganin visited Peking in 1954 they agreed to help build 156 production enterprises. By 1955 Moscow accorded China the position of associate leader in the international Communist movement, as Foreign Minister Molotov noted before the Council of Ministers: "The most important result of the Second World War was the organization, side by side with the world capitalist camp, of the world camp of socialism and democracy headed by the Soviet Union—to speak more truly, headed by the Soviet Union and the Chinese People's Republic."[27]

The mutual profession of friendship and cordiality was reflected in many ways. The Soviet Union promoted China's interests by allowing her to play a major role in Asian affairs. Peking was chosen as the site for the Asian and Australasian Trade Union Conference in 1949, the Asian and Pacific Peace Conference in 1952, and the World Federation of Democratic Youth in 1954. Ho Chih-minh's Democratic Republic of Vietnam was first recognized by Communist China and then by the Soviet Union. At the Geneva Conference of 1954 China played the leading role in championing the cause of Ho and insisting on the division of Vietnam at the 17th parallel, which awarded to Ho the fertile area of the Red River and the port of Haiphong. Other acts of Soviet friendship included the return to China of the Manchurian "loot" in 1952, of the Soviet share of the joint ownership of the Chinese Eastern Railway in 1953, the renunciation of the Soviet right to use Port Arthur as a naval base, and the

26. Peter S. H. Tang, Communist China Today (New York, 1957), 378-81.
27. Peter S. H. Tang, 383.

abandonment of Soviet "joint stocks" in Sinkiang enterprises in 1955. A further expression of generosity was made in 1957 when the Soviets agreed to assist China in her nuclear development, and a year later sent a heavy-water-type reactor. Peking, on its part, helped maintain Soviet primacy in the socialist bloc by mediating the differences between Moscow and its East European satellites in 1956, as we will see in a later section.

Peking's relations with other Asian states reflected her intense drive for leadership in Asia. In this respect, China's historical relations with the smaller states on her periphery, especially Korea and Vietnam (Annam) —which had been the leading tributary states during the Ming and Ch'ing periods—had left an indelible mark on Mao and his associates. They unhesitatingly sent a million "volunteers" to aid North Korea against the American "invasion" in 1950 when they themselves had barely set up their government. They played the role of a "big brother" to North Vietnam at the 1954 Geneva Conference, and have extended to it substantial aid in its recent war against the South Vietnamese and the Americans, despite their own preoccupation with the Cultural Revolution.

As regards the non-Communist states of Asia, such as India, Pakistan, Indonesia, Burma, Laos, and Cambodia, Peking attempted to neutralize them by harping on the theme of coexistence: (1) mutual respect for each other's territory and sovereignty; (2) mutual nonaggression; (3) mutual noninterference in each other's domestic affairs; (4) equality of relationships and mutual benefit; and (5) peaceful coexistence. With these five principles, Peking succeeded to a large extent in keeping these states from aligning with the West. The theme of peaceful coexistence was repeated at the Bandung Conference of twenty-nine Afro-Asian states in 1955, where Chou En-lai won recognition as the upholder of Asian-African nationalism against Western imperialism. The Geneva and Bandung conferences, in effect, accorded China big-power status and leadership position in the Afro-Asian bloc. As the underdog who has found a viable formula not only to reverse its destiny but to achieve quick and spectacular success in economic development and elevation of national status, Peking has become a glittering inspiration to underdeveloped nations.

FIRST SIGNS OF STRAIN

While the first decade of the People's Republic abounded in accomplishments, it was not without stress and strain. The first notes of discord were struck in 1953-54, when two powerful regional authorities challenged the second- and third-ranking leaders in the central government. Kao Kang, party boss of Manchuria,[28] and Jao Shu-shih, chairman of the East China Military and Administrative Committee,[29] jointly espoused the adoption of the Soviet system of economic development, the separation of party officials from industries, and the adoption of a "single director" system at all levels of industrial management. The proposal was in effect an indictment of the current policy of the party and government leaders, Liu Shao-ch'i and Chou En-lai. The latter countered with the proposition of "collective leadership" in industrial management. The clash was climaxed by the challengers' demand that they and the party general secretary, Teng Hsiao-p'ing, resign. The three defendants, with the help of the mayor of Peking, P'eng Chen, then managed to have the challengers expelled from the Central Committee in 1954 on charges of anti-party activities. This first power struggle ended with Kao committing suicide and Jao thrown into prison.

A second challenge to the state came in 1956 from the public. The seven strict years of Communist rule had generated considerable resentment and repressed emotion, which burst out after the Hungarian Revolt. "Tens of thousands of persons went out to the street to oppose the People's Government," as Mao described it.[30] Partly to afford the people a chance to let off steam—lest there be a Hungarian-type revolt in China —and partly to ferret out the real critics, Mao cleverly declared: "Let hundred flowers blossom; let hundred schools contend!" Many intellectuals naively mistook the statement to mean a liberation of expression and spoke their minds. The severe criticism that was made went far beyond the government's expectation. Finding it unbearable and detrimental, the party and government leaders pressured Mao to clamp down with lightning speed. The critics were caught and although they regretted their imprudence, it was too late to recant. Many were sent to corrective camps or were forced to sign a "socialist self-reform pact" to renew their pledge of allegiance. In the wake of this antirightist campaign, the government in 1957 initiated a "socialist education movement" among the industrial and agrarian population, followed by the dispatch of military and civil leaders to physical labor as an example to the people. The im-

28. Concurrently a vice-chairman of the People's Republic and the chairman of the important State Planning Committee.
29. Also director of the Organization Department of the CCP's Central Committee.
30. Gene T. Hsiao, "The Background and Development of 'The Proletarian Cultural Revolution'," *Asian Survey*, VII:6 (June 1967), 393.

portance of "redness," i.e., ideology over "expertise," was very much emphasized.

On balance, the first decade of the People's Republic closed with considerable success. Domestically, it had consolidated the control of the country, scored an economic breakthrough denied to previous governments, suppressed opposition, and in a way brought the country to the threshold of communism. Externally, it had maintained close ties with the Soviet Union and the East European satellite states, fought the United Nations' forces in Korea to a standstill (which was a sort of victory), played the big-power role at Geneva and Bandung, and mediated between the Soviets and the satellites. Nuclear development had also begun and the future looked bright. It was in this state of satisfaction and high expectation that Mao confidently launched the Great Leap Forward Movement and spoke of surpassing the British industrial output in fifteen years. It was also in this rosy state of euphoria that he introduced the communes in hopes of putting China on a higher ideological plane than the Soviet Union and, eventually, of overtaking her in the race toward the portals of true communism.

Yet beneath this veneer of pride and success, internal dissension over economic policy and divisive tendencies in the Moscow-Peking Axis were already appearing. As the second decade opened in 1959, the government faced the double challenge of worsening relations with the Soviets and an incipient power struggle among its top leaders.

THE SINO-SOVIET SPLIT

The Moscow-Peking Axis underwent a rapid deterioration toward the end of the decade. What was once described as the "lasting, unbreakable, and invincible" relationship had degenerated into a bitter feud which threatened to split the Communist bloc. The source of the trouble could be traced to Khrushchev's denunciation of Stalin and attack on his "personality cult" at the 20th Congress of the Soviet Communist Party in 1956. Mao, who himself practiced Stalinism and the "personality cult," did not take the attack too kindly, although on the surface he cooperated by reorganizing the CCP Central Committee into a sort of "collective leadership" after the Soviet fashion. The façade of Axis collaboration was maintained, but Mao was convinced that he, not the Russians, was the true bearer of Marxism-Leninism and that only the Chinese experience provided the prototype of revolution in Asia. By implication, he reduced the Soviet path to socialism to a local or European variety without universal validity. Mao was determined to make himself the ideological leader of international communism and Peking a new center in the Socialist bloc. The lack of an effective, all-round Soviet leader after Stalin facilitated his scheme, while the unrest in the East European satellite states in the wake of de-Stalinization provided him with a golden opportunity to maneuver. The Hungarian Revolt of 1956, ruthlessly crushed by the Soviets, was followed by the Polish assertion of "different paths to socialism," with which Khrushchev was unable to cope. Seizing the chance to play the role of bloc mediator and harmonizer, Mao sent his ebullient premier and foreign minister, Chou En-lai, on a fence-mending trip to East Europe, stressing on the one hand the need for socialist solidarity under Soviet leadership in the face of the capitalist threat, and on the other the importance of recognizing the different conditions in the satellite countries. The Maoist approach, though merely a stopgap device, arrested the disintegrative tendency in the Communist world, and maintained Soviet primacy in the bloc. By thus taking Moscow's chestnuts out of the fire, Peking extended its influence for the first time beyond Asia and provided something of an alternative voice to Moscow. Encouraged by this success, Mao followed up with a vehement attack on Tito's revisionism in 1957, making himself the defender of Marxist-Leninist doctrinal purity. By 1958, Mao had gained the status of an ideological leader of world communism with Peking as an alternative center to Moscow. The monolithic structure of the Socialist camp that existed under Stalin had crumbled, and with it the undisputed leadership of the Soviet Union.

The rise of Mao and the challenge of Communist China to Soviet supremacy raised the question whether the socialist world could tolerate two leaders and two centers. Perhaps the answer is yes, but not without tension between the two. The strain and stress in the Moscow-Peking Axis soon grew into an open fight, precipitated by Khrushchev's change of heart with respect to China's nuclear development. By the agreement of October 15, 1957, he had promised to furnish the Chinese with a sample atomic bomb, scientific data, and technical personnel to help develop the bombs. After sending a heavy-water type reactor in 1958, Khrushchev regretted his promise, reputedly out of fear of China's growing stature. As a result, not only was the sample bomb never given but in 1959 Khrushchev started to restrict the flow of scientific information and to withdraw Soviet personnel. Deeply embittered, Mao accused him of having fallen prey to American propaganda, of following "revisionism," and of holding heretical views on the nature of war and the grand strategy of world revolution. By implication, he questioned Khrushchev's fitness to lead the international communist movement.

The Chinese Communists subscribed to the classical Marxist-Leninist concept that war between the socialist and capitalist worlds was inevitable. In Peking's view, war enhanced rather than hindered the cause of communism. World War I, they said, made possible the rise of Communist Russia; World War II made possible the rise of Communist China; and World War III would bring communism to power in the United States and spell an end to the capitalist world.

Peking claimed that it was not afraid of war; although a nuclear holocaust might kill 300 million Chinese out of a population of 600 million, the more advanced industrial nations of the West would fare worse. Reportedly, Chou En-lai had stated that after the next war there would be "twenty million Americans, five million Englishmen, fifty million Russians, and three hundred million Chinese left."[31] Such a bold stance was probably designed to forestall all fears of war and the dampening of the revolutionary spirit of the world communist movement.

Khrushchev disputed the Chinese view. He argued that war had become too devastating to be inevitable and that World War III would decimate the earth, leaving no room for the victory of communism. On the other hand, because of its superior system, the socialist camp could outproduce the capitalist world and score a victory through peaceful competition. To Peking, these views sounded like heresy. In April 1960, the Chinese vehemently accused Khrushchev of "emasculating, betraying, and revising" Marxism-Leninism—acts which could only lead the international communist movement to disaster. Stung, Khrushchev accused Mao of "being like Stalin, of being oblivious ot any interests but his own, of spinning theories detached from the realities of the modern world." He called Mao "an ultra-leftist, an ultra-dogmatist, and a left revisionist."[32] Tension between Moscow and Peking reached such a pitch that a grand conference of eighty-one Communist parties was called at Moscow in November 1960 to adjudicate the dispute.

The Chinese delegation ridiculed the idea of peaceful coexistence as

31. Zbigniew K. Brzezinski, *The Soviet Bloc: Unity and Conflict* (Cambridge, Mass., 1960), 403.
32. Donald S. Zagoria, "The Future of Sino-Soviet Relations" *Asian Survey*, 1:2:3-14 (April 1961); Edward Crankshaw, "Khrushchev and China," *The Atlantic Monthly* (May 1961), 43-47.

a mirage, argued for increased support for the wars of liberation and national independence movements, and belittled the chances of a peaceful take-over. The Soviets retorted that the dangers of global war were too great and that since the Communist bloc had not achieved a decisive strategic superiority it should act with caution. Moreover, the economic race would be the decisive factor, and time was on the side of the socialist camp.[33] The final communiqué of the conference, issued on December 6, 1960, endorsed the Soviet view on peaceful coexistence, with only minor changes to appease the Chinese. Peking reluctantly subscribed to the communiqué to preserve bloc solidarity, but beneath the surface, bitterness remained. Although the Soviets seemed to have scored a victory at the conference, it became manifestly clear that Peking could challenge Moscow without the risk of expulsion from the bloc. The day of Soviet hegemony was over.

Sino-Soviet relations were further strained, as time went on, by Moscow's unilateral action during the Cuban missile crisis in 1962 and by its acceptance of the nuclear test ban treaty without consulting the Chinese.[34] The feud had become so bitter that in 1964, when completion of a Chinese nuclear device seemed imminent, Khrushchev toyed with the idea of destroying Peking's atomic installations with a Soviet missile. The scheme was too fantastic for other Soviet leaders, who quickly notified the Chinese leadership. Mao threatened to invade Outer Mongolia to prove that the U.S.S.R. could not protect its satellites in Asia. A clash was averted at the last minute, when the more pragmatic Soviet leaders, Brezhnev and Kosygin, on October 15, 1964, succeeded in mustering enough support in the Central Committee to relieve Khrushchev as chairman of the Council of Ministers.[35] A day later the first Chinese atomic device exploded in Sinkiang—a feat achieved by China's own scientists after the withdrawal of Soviet personnel.

Although Sino-Soviet relations temporarily took a turn for the better, it soon became evident that the new Soviet leadership had not deviated basically from the course followed by Khrushchev. Peking renewed its attack on Soviet revisionism. The split continued to widen until it seemed too deep to be bridged. A number of Communist parties around the

33. For a penetrating analysis of the Moscow Conference, see Donald S. Zagoria, *The Sino-Soviet Conflict*, 1956-1961 (Princeton, 1962), chapter 15.
34. Statement by Foreign Minister Ch'en Yi to a group of Scandinavian newsmen, as reported by *The Christian Science Monitor*, May 27, 1966.
35. Harold C. Hinton, *Communist China in World Politics* (New York, 1966), 478-482.

world evinced sympathy for Peking's dynamic stance, while others became seriously splintered into pro-Chinese and pro-Russian factions. Soviet attempts to read the Chinese out of the international communist movement have so far met with little success. The 23rd International Congress of Communist Parties held in Moscow in April 1966 was boycotted by the parties of New Zealand, Albania, Japan, and China. At about the same time, a Ceylonese Communist leader openly declared that the ideological center of world communism had shifted from Moscow to Peking. In February 1968, the Soviets made another attempt to expel the Chinese from the bloc during the Budapest conference, but thirteen Communist parties from Asia, Europe, and Latin America[36] refused to attend, while the Rumanian delegates walked out of the conference in protest. In June 1969, at the Moscow summit conference of seventy-five Communist parties, the Soviets made yet another move to anathematize and oust Communist China, but again to no avail. The Italian and Rumanian delegates openly deplored the Soviet attack on Peking, and fourteen of the participants either refused to sign or signed with reservations the final declaration of the conference on imperialism. These fourteen included some of the very powerful Communist parties of the world, such as the Italian, the Cuban, the Swedish, the British, the Australian, the Swiss, the Spanish, and the Rumanian. Needless to say, Communist China and its staunch ally, Albania, boycotted the conference as did North Korea, North Vietnam, and Yugoslavia.

With renewed border clashes in Manchuria[37] and Sinkiang in the spring and summer of 1969, Sino-Soviet relations have been rapidly worsening, and there are segments in the Soviet leadership who are not averse to a "pre-emptive" strike against Communist China. The danger of war seems to have sobered some of the more responsible leaders in Peking and Moscow, who may have arrived at the similar view that ideological differences need not preclude resumption of relations at the "state level" in order to avoid a complete break. Consequently, preliminary diplomatic proceedings have been initiated to explore ways of settling the border disputes. On October 1, 1969, the twentieth anniversary of the founding of the People's Republic, the *People's Daily* and the *Red Flag* both declared their support for the settlement of border conflicts by negotiation,

36. Communist China, North Korea, North Vietnam, Japan, Burma, Malaysia, Thailand, Indonesia, Albania, Cuba, the Netherlands, Sweden, and Yugoslavia.
37. Over Chen-pao (Damansky) Island in the Ussuri River and Pa-cha (Goldinsky) Island in the Amur River.

and Lin Piao openly announced that "if others don't attack us, we will not attack others. If others attack, we shall counterattack." Out of the diplomatic détente, however tenuous at the moment, some normalization of state relations may emerge, but ideological *rapprochement* remains distant.

THE GREAT PROLETARIAN CULTURAL REVOLUTION

In view of the close Sino-Soviet relations in the first decade of the People's Republic, any progressive deterioration of the Axis could not but have a profound impact on the domestic politics of China. Mao's handling of the Sino-Soviet dispute was not immune from criticism, for the pragmatic party leaders still considered Russian aid important in China's economic, military, and nuclear development. This feeling was strengthened by their growing disillusionment with the breakneck pace of agricultural collectivization and industrial expansion, the overemphasis on ideology ("redness") instead of expertise in technology and weaponry, and the incessant mass campaigns which tended to accomplish a certain objective at the expense of all others. As long-time associates of Mao, in actual control of the daily operations of the party and the government, these pragmatists were deeply concerned with the irrational, careening course which their aging leader was charting toward the socialist transformation.

These leaders had acquired great influence over the years, especially after the party reorganization in 1956. As may be recalled, after Krushchev's denunciation of Stalin's "personality cult" in February 1956, a "collective leadership" prevailed over the Soviet hierarchy. In response, the Chinese Communist Party called its 8th National Congress in September and adopted resolutions to tone down the practice of the "Mao cult" and to reorganize the party structure in line with Soviet developments. The new 1956 party constitution omitted the reference to Mao's thought as the guide of the CCP as described in the 1949 version. The party reorganization called for a collective leadership to replace the previously dictatorial position of Mao, who was at once chairman of the CCP Central Committee, the Politburo, and the Secretariat. The reorganization created four vice-chairmanships of the Central Committee, a Standing Committee of the Politburo, and a general secretaryship of the party. The chairman of the Central Committee was no longer the concurrent head of the Secretariat, which was put under the supervision of the party general secretary. The Politburo's Stading Committee, the seat of power, was made up of the chairman and the four vice-chairmen of the Central Committee plus the party general secretary—representing a collective leadership of six. Mao retained the chairmanship of the Central Committee, but Liu Shao-ch'i became the first vice-chairman who exercised certain functions for the chairman, and Teng Hsiao-p'ing was appointed party general secretary. With this reshuffle, Mao retreated to the "second line" while advancing Liu and Teng to the "first line" to enhance their prestige and status so that, as Mao stated ten years later (1966), "When I have to see God, the country can avoid great chaos."[38]

With their newly elevated positions, Liu and Teng, both less idealistic and more pragmatic than Mao, felt confident to voice their opinions on the country's urgent economic and foreign dilemmas. They favored a less precipitous course of action in order to cultivate a more stable social order, and were in favor of legal guarantees of the people's freedom, promulgation of criminal and civil codes, and priority for industrial development over agricultural collectivization. Mao, on his part, continued to push for mass movements, increased speed in collectivization, the Great Leap, and the communes. By 1958 the Central Committee had very much come under the control of Liu and Teng, and it soon found the idea of commune "unsound." At its 6th Plenum on December 10, 1958, two resolutions were adopted, one to amend the commune system, and the other to "accept" Mao's request not to be the State Chairman (i.e. chairman of the People's Republic) for another term, on the ground that he needed more time to pursue the theoretical works of Marx and Lenin and to devote himself to party and state affairs. Every effort was made to convey the impression that Mao had made the move voluntarily, but the fact remained that Liu had quietly "eased him out" of the state chairmanship. Mao himself commented on the event in October 1966. "I was extremely discontented with that decision, but I could do nothing about it."[39]

The year 1959 was particularly critical for the politics of economic development. The results of the Great Leap and the Communes, which had become fully evident, were deeply discouraging. Indigenous production methods entailed an enormous waste of materials, a high cost of operation, and a low quality of products. The steel turned out by the backyard blast furnaces could not meet industrial requirements, and,

38. Gene T. Hsiao, 392.
39. Gene T. Hsiao, 395.

more disheartening was the fact that many of these makeshift furnaces dissolved in rainstorms. Agricultural production was adversely affected by deficient water conservation projects and faulty re-alkalinization of the land. Intensive use of machinery without proper maintenance, in order to keep up with the high production quotas, resulted in rapid deterioration and damage to the tools, while eager recruitment of inexperienced workers caused managerial problems.[40] The communes were responsible for lower, not higher, industrial and agricultural output, although the published figures were inflated to meet the preset targets. All in all, the results of the first year of the Great Leap and the Communes were disastrous, and there was great discontent among the populace.

Facing this situation, the pragmatists grew increasingly critical of the Maoist policies. They felt that Mao ran the country with a guerrilla mentality out of tune with the changing times, and that he was more effective in his earlier role of a revolutionary than as the chief administrator of a large state. Tactful allusions to his failing faculties began to appear. Indeed, the economic disruptions and the social turmoils stirred up by the "Three Red Banners Campaign"—the General Line of the Party (i.e. Mao's will), the Great Leap Forward Movement, and the Commune—cast increasing doubts in the minds of the pragmatists as to the correctness of the Maoist approach. Boldly, they espoused an alternative course, even at the risk of offending the Leader.

The Dismissal of P'eng Te-huai. At the Lushan Conference of the Central Committee in August 1959, Ch'en Yün, the fifth-ranking party member and a leading economic planner, argued for several major changes, including a return from communes to cooperatives, a more realistic schedule of economic development, cooperation with the Soviets—whose technical aid and strategic protection China still needed—and greater emphasis on technical expertise rather than on political dogmatism or "redness." Ch'en's statement probably had the prior approval of Liu Shao-ch'i, but it was not known whether the latter spoke out for him at the conference.[41]

A more blunt critic of the government policy was Defense Minister P'eng Te-huai, an old comrade-in-arms of Mao's and a leading soldier in the country who had just returned from a trip to the Soviet Union, where

40. Kang Chao, "Economic Aftermath of the Great Leap in Communist China," *Asian Survey*, IV:5:851-58 (May 1964).
41. Henry G. Schwartz, "The Great Proletarian Cultural Revolution," *Orbis*, (Fall 1966), 813-14.

he presumably had talked with the Russian leaders, including Khrushchev. In an 80,000-word memorandum which he circulated among the conference members, P'eng lashed out at Mao's policies. He equated the Great Leap with "petty bourgeois fanaticism" and called it "a rush of blood to the brain . . . a high fever" of unrealism—an unmistakable allusion to Mao's failing mental faculties. P'eng ridiculed the idea of surpassing the British industrial output in fifteen years and deprecated China's economic "blunder after blunder." He attacked party control of the army and asked for the creation of a modern professional army with up-to-date equipment. By implication he questioned Mao's views on the "people's war" and decried the constant diversion of soldiers to political works. Severe as his criticisms were, however, P'eng did not ask for the removal of Mao but only a revision of his policy. Apparently, P'eng had counted on the support of Liu and Teng, but when neither spoke out for him, his cause was lost.[42] Mao dismissed P'eng as defense minister and named Lin Piao as his successor.[43]

The confrontation at Lushan ended in victory for the Maoists, who opted ever more vigorously for a radical economic policy, the supremacy of ideology over weaponry, the preference for "redness" over "expertise," and a tough stance toward Soviet revisionism. As the new minister of defense, Lin Piao championed the study of the thought of Mao which he praised as the "creative application and development of Marxism-Leninism." Loyalty to Mao had transcended the realm of political obedience to become a process of deification.

Nevertheless, the dismissal of P'eng was to have continuous repercussions. Party intellectuals and writers began to produce articles and stories satirizing the top leadership, while the pragmatists in high authority quietly applied brakes to the Maoist push during the three difficult years of 1959-61, when the country was hard hit by poor harvests. They supported an expansion of peasants' plots for private use, extension of a limited free market, increase of small enterprises, and restoration of some degree of individual economy. In foreign affairs, they urged some form of reconciliation with the modern revisionists (U.S.S.R.) and a reduction of aid to other national independence movements. It was be-

42. For an interesting account of the meeting, see David A. Charles, "The Dismissal of Marshal P'eng Teh-huai," *The China Quarterly*, (Oct.-Dec. 1961), No. 8, pp. 63-76; also Robert S. Elegant, "Mt. Lu Meeting Paved Way for Turbulence in China," *Los Angeles Times*, Dec. 17, 1967.

43. P'eng's associate, Huang K'o-ch'eng, the army chief-of-staff, was replaced by Lo Jui-ch'ing, a secret service man.

cause of this new line that the country began to recoup in 1962. But, in the eyes of Mao, these pragmatists were working against his policy of rapid and complete socialization. Fearful of the rise of bourgeois and revisionist tendencies, of the increasing bureaucratization of the party, of the lack of revolutionary experience among the youth, and of the unhealthy atmosphere in arts and literature, Mao launched a new socialist education movement in September 1962, stressing the importance of class struggle in an attempt to rectify the current ills in cultural circles. When the latter did not respond constructively, Mao criticized them repeatedly during 1963-64 for their failure to produce new works that reflected the socialist transformation. Again, the admonition fell on deaf ears. Then, all of a sudden, on November 10, 1965, the Shanghai *Wen-hui Pao* published an article to attack the historical play "Hai Jui Dismissed from Office" (*Hai Jui pa-kuan*), written by Wu Han, the deputy mayor of Peking and a former university professor.[44]

The Black Gang. Wu Han first wrote a story, "Hai Jui Scolds the Emperor," under a pseudonym in the *People's Daily* on June 16, 1959, not long before the dismissal of Defense Minister P'eng. Hai Jui, a mid-16th-century official of the Ming court, was supposed to have reprimanded the ruler in these words: "For a long time the nation has not been satisfied with you. All officials, in and out of the capital, know that your mind is not right, that you are too arbitrary, that you are perverse. You think that you alone are right; you refuse to accept criticism; and your mistakes are many."[45] The article was later rendered into a historical play entitled "Hai Jui Dismissed from Office," which appeared in the January 1961 issue of the *Peking Literature and Art*. In this new version, Hai Jui was portrayed as an honest official who lost his governorship because the emperor disliked his advocacy of returning to the peasants land that had been seized by rich landlords. It required little imagination to see that the author implied the emperor to be Mao and the dismissed official to be P'eng.

Two other members of the Peking Municipal Government were even more scathing in their criticism of the government leadership. They were Teng T'o, secretary of the Peking Municipal Committee, editor of its theoretical journal, the *Frontline*, and former editor-in-chief of the *People's Daily* (1954-59); and Liao Mo-sha, director of the United Front

44. Not a CCP member, but one of the Democratic League.
45. Chün-tu Hsüeh, "The Cultural Revolution," 173.

69. Mao Tse-tung and Chu Teh reviewing their troops after the capture of Peking, 1949.

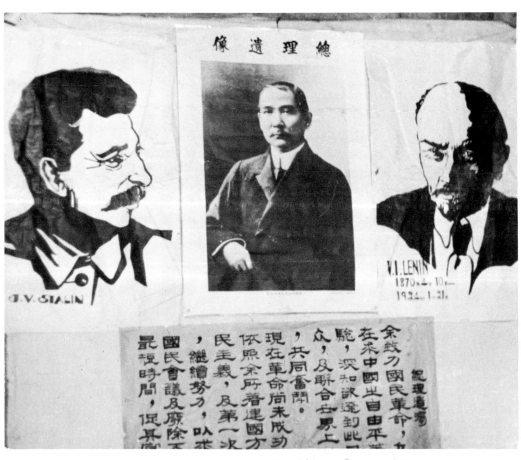

70. Russian influence among the Chinese Communists.

71. Chen Yi.

72. Peng Te-huai.

73. Chou En-lai at the Geneva Conference in 1954.

74. Lin Piao, heir apparent to Mao.

75. Chiang Ch'ing (Mrs. Mao) and Chou En-lai.

76. Chairman Mao, Liu Shao-ch'i, and Soong Ching-ling (Madame Sun Yat-sen).

77. China's largest blast furnace, completed in 4 months and 26 days.

78. Members of the Heifen commune in Kansu Province.

79. Red Chinese "provocation" on the Russian-Chinese border.

80. A Red Chinese and an Indian soldier face each other at the border
between Indian-protected Sikkim and Red Chinese-held Tibet.

81. Chiang Kai-shek leads a group of high officials to pay homage
to the heroes who died for the cause of Nationalist China.

82. A. N. Kosygin with Mao Tse-tung in Peking, 1965.

Department in the Peking Municipal Committee. Under the pseudonym Wu Nan-hsing,[46] Wu Han and the two of them jointly published sixty-seven articles in the *Frontline* between October 10, 1961, and July 1964, criticizing the Leader by direct implications or historical analogies. Particularly outspoken was Teng, who alone wrote 153 articles in the *Peking Evening News* between March 1961 and September 1962 under the general title, "Evening Chats at Yenshan." One of these "Evening Chats," dated June 15, 1961, sarcastically compared, by allusion, the Great Leap with building a castle in the air. Another article, entitled "Special Cure for Amnesia," which appeared in the *Frontline* of July 25, 1962, read in part:

> There are all sorts of illness in this world . . . one of which is called "amnesia." Anyone who has this disease has a lot of trouble, because it cannot easily be cured . . . The man who has this illness . . . often forgets what he has said or done. Gradually he will become temperamental . . . easily angered, and finally mad . . . Another symptom is that he often faints. If not cured in time, he will become an idiot. Once one of these two symptoms is discovered, he must take a full rest and stop talking or doing things, otherwise the result will be disastrous. [47]

Another poem of his, published in the *Peking Daily* of November 10, 1961, satirized the "great empty talks" of a child in his neighborhood, who imitated styles of past poets and composed doggerels like this:

> The heaven is our father,
> The great earth is our mother,
> The sun is our nurse,
> The East wind is our supporter
> The West wind is our enemy.[48]

The frequent appearance of sarcastic writings which used historic analogies or allusions to criticize Mao and his policies suggested a coordinated effort directed by individuals very high in authority. Since all

46. Wu for Wu Han; Nan for Nan-tsun, Teng's pen name; and Hsing for Fan Hsing, Liao's pen name.
47. Chün-tu Hsüeh, "The Cultural Revolution," 175.
48. Henry G. Schwartz, 807. It should be noted that for years Communist poets and writers have eulogized Mao as the sun and the father, while Mao himself has stated that the East Wind has prevailed over the West Wind.

three contributors were members of the Peking Municipal Government, the inference was clear that the mayor, P'eng Chen, or someone higher in the party hierarchy, was behind them. Mao was ready to launch a counterattack but for the fact that Peking was so tightly controlled by its mayor that he, Mao, could not find room "to put in a needle."[49] In the summer of 1965, he disappeared to Shanghai, the regional base of Chou En-lai, and there at a branch meeting of the Central Committee in September he called for attacks on "reactionary bourgeois ideology." The groundwork was laid for a gigantic counteroffensive. Under his instructions, the editor-in-chief of the Shanghai branch of the *Liberation Army Daily*, Yao Wen-yüan, fired the opening salvo of Cultural Revolution on November 10, 1965, when he published in the *Wen-hui Pao* an article, "Comment on the Newly Composed Historical Play 'Hai Jui Dismissed from Office.'" Wu Han was attacked for his "humanism" and lack of "class view," since he held that Hai Jui of the official ruling class could understand and help the members of another class—namely, the peasants. Other attacks quickly descended on Wu Han, Teng T'o, and Liao Mo-sha, now dubbed the "Black Gang." They were accused of having falsified historical figures to satirize the present Leader, of deceiving people into learning the virtues of the feudal past, of blurring the class struggle, and of urging the restoration of land and private economy. Teng, in particular, was blacklisted for having defended Khrushchev in 1963.

Mao's selection of Wu Han as the first target was well thought out. As deputy mayor of Peking and a leading intellectual whose writings were associated with Teng and Liao, Wu's implication would inevitably lead to the involvement of the other two and perhaps even Mayor P'eng Chen himself. If it could be proved that P'eng was part of this "counterrevolutionary and revisionist" gang, then his patron, Liu Shao-ch'i, could be implicated. Since their criticism of the Maoist mismanagement of the economy and the practice of the "personality cult" resembled Krushchev's denunciation of Stalin, their implication would justify Mao's branding them as revisionists. Thus, what started as a literary and cultural revolution quickly expanded into a bitter power struggle among the top leaders. The army under Lin Piao sided with Mao, while the party remained under the firm control of Liu and Teng.[50]

49. Mao's own expression, in Gene T. Hsiao, 397.
50. According to a Nationalist intelligence report, in 1966 Mao was in control of only 30 per cent of the Central Committee.

The Purge. Under mounting pressure, Wu Han recanted on December 30, 1965, admitting that he had failed to use Mao's theory of class struggle in his play. Unsatisfied, the Maoists insisted on getting at the "truth." Apparently unconscious of the depth of the attack and confident of his hold on the party machinery, Liu left Peking on March 26, 1966, on a prescheduled state visit to Pakistan and Afghanistan. On that very day, Mayor P'eng Chen, who was also a vice-premier and the eighth-ranking member of the Politburo, disappeared. He had been purged.

On April 18, the *Liberation Army Daily* editorialized: "Hold High the Great Red Banner of Mao Tse-tung's Thought and Actively Participate in the Great Socialist Cultural Revolution." It was a clear declaration of the army's support of Mao and his policy. Taking advantage of Liu's absence, the Maoists moved fast to overwhelm the opposition. They closed in on the Peking Municipal Party Committee and extracted confessions from the Black Gang trio.[51] In early May, Mao's spokesman in Shanghai, Yao Wen-yüan, charged that the Liu faction had intended to replace Premier Chou En-lai with P'eng Chen and to rehabilitate former Defense Minister P'eng Te-huai and his revisionist line at the expense of Lin Piao. On May 16, an article in the *Red Flag*, edited by Mao's private secretary Ch'en Po-ta, asked: "Who has been sheltering Teng T'o and his group?" And on June 1, the Maoist forces seized control of the *People's Daily*, which then belatedly joined the Cultural Revolution. On June 4 it editorialized: "No one who dares to oppose Chairman Mao . . . can escape denunciation by the whole Party and the whole nation, whoever he may be, whatever high position he may hold and however much of a veteran he may be."[52] On the same day, the Maoists took over the Peking Municipal Party Committee and reorganized its various publications.

Out of the struggle, Lin Piao rose to be the new strong man, next only to Mao. Lin had been diligently building his power base since becoming the defense minister in 1959. By promoting the study and application of the thought of Mao and by emphasizing ideology and politics over military weapons and technical expertise, he had won increasing favor with the aged leader. In 1964 Lin succeeded in creating army-controlled political departments in the industries, trade unions, educational and scientific organizations, and government offices, to promote the daily "devotional" study of Mao's works as a weapon against the inroads of bourgeois ide-

51. All three reportedly committed suicide after arrest.
52. Quoted in Tang and Maloney, 220.

ology and revisionism. He succeeded in getting military men appointed as secretaries of the Central Committee's six regional bureaus, thereby extending the army's influence into the party and reversing the party practice of infiltrating the army. Just as he had praised Mao as having *creatively applied* and *extended* Marxism-Leninism, Lin's followers increasingly pictured him as one who had "*creatively applied* the thought of Mao Tse-tung." With his publication in September 1965 of the famous 20,000-word essay, "Long Live the Victory of the People's War," Lin's prestige soared beyond the military ranks. Cleverly exploiting the Maoist idea of organizing the peasants against the bourgeois, Lin advanced the thesis that the underdeveloped countries in the "countryside" of the world could encircle and defeat the capitalist industrial states in the "city" areas. With this article, Lin rose to be a theorist of the first order, and the interpreter and propagator of the thought of Mao.[53] He needed only a formal proclamation from the Leader to be named the heir apparent.

The moment of glory came when Mao returned to Peking on July 18, 1966. On August 1, at the 11th Plenum of the Central Committee, Mao promoted Lin to be the first vice-chairman of the Central Committee, i.e., the second-ranking member in the hierarchy, while Liu fell to the eighth. Side by side, Mao and Lin reviewed the Red Guards (then being formed), while the former addressed the latter as his "closest comrade-in-arms." On August 5, Mao wrote the first wall poster: "Bomb the (Liu-Teng) Headquarters!"

The party conference adopted several key resolutions. It spelled out the targets of attack as "those within the party who are in authority" and who were "taking the capitalist road." It announced the creation of the Red Guards (*Hung-wei ping*) as a "shock force" to carry out the movement from the capital to the provinces—thus bypassing altogether the party machinery and its Youth League, which were under the control of Liu. It called for the establishment of permanent "cultural revolutionary groups, committees, and congresses" at all levels, and the application of Mao's ideas on the mass line, the class struggle, and the theory of contradictions. On November 22, 1966, a seventeen-member Central Cultural Revolutionary Committee was formed, with Mao's private secretary Ch'en Po-ta (editor of the *Red Flag*) as chairman, and Mao's wife, Chiang Ch'ing, as one of the vice-chairmen. Their selection suggests that Mao could trust no one except those closest to him personally. This

53. Chu-yüan Cheng, "Power Struggle in Red China," *Asian Survey*, VI:9:472-74 (Sept. 1966).

Revolutionary Committee, together with the Military Committee under Lin Piao, and the State Council under Chou En-lai, became the new ruling triumvirate.

The Red Guard Movement. Historically, the Red Guards in China first appeared in eastern Hunan in 1927 under the guidance of Wang Chen, and a year later Mao also used the name for his units. The term was probably borrowed from the Russian *Krasnaya Gvardia* which was in use in 1917. Now, in 1966, Mao and Lin revived the term, recruited high school and college students as Red Guards, and imbued them with a new mission. With this development, the Cultural Revolution entered a second phase.

The youthful Red Guards envisioned themselves as "revolutionary successors" and "revolutionary rebels," dedicated to the elimination of the old thought, old culture, old customs, and old habits. Vowing to uphold the thought of Mao, they were determined to make their country safe from bourgeois influences and revisionist tendencies. They wrote big-character wall posters (*ta-tzu pao*), ransacked private properties, rampaged the cities, renamed streets, attacked those with modern attire and haircuts, and humiliated foreign diplomats. They attacked Liu Shao-ch'i as a revisionist and a Chinese Krushchev, and pressured him and his wife into public self-criticism. Reportedly, Liu confessed to his "right leaning" in 1962 and 1964, his "bourgeois world outlook," his failure to appreciate "the meaning of Chairman Mao's thought," and his mistake of not understanding the Cultural Revolution. He praised Lin Piao as a far more distinguished comrade who set an example for him in learning the thought of Mao. In spite of these alleged recantations, the attack on Liu did not let up. In April 1967 his famous work, "How to be a Good Communist," which had first appeared in 1939, was excoriated for its failure to incorporate, in its 1962 edition, comments on the importance of the thought of Mao and the need for opposing imperialism and modern revisionism.[54] Thousands of Red Guards marched by his house to demand his dismissal. However, Liu was not immediately dismissed but put under house arrest, for to strip him of the state chairmanship would require an act of the People's National Congress, over which the Maoists exercised no control. However, in October 1968 an editorial in the *Red Flag* announced that Liu had finally been "deprived of all powers and positions."[55] In

54. Tang and Maloney, 114-15.
55. *The Christian Science Monitor,* Oct. 18, 1968.

November the CCP Central Committee confirmed that Liu had been ousted from all party and government posts. The dismissal was strictly unconstitutional; it merely underscored the fact that Liu had been out of power for some time—probably since August 1966.

Other prominent victims of the Cultural Revolution who had been attacked, humiliated, dismissed, and purged included Chou Yang, deputy director of the CCP Propaganda Department; Lu Ting-i, vice-premier and minister of culture; Lo Jui-ch'ing, chief of staff of the People's Liberation Army; Po I-po, vice-premier and chairman of the State Economic Commission; Chu Teh, a founder of the Red Army; Yang Hsien-chen, a former president of the Central Marxist-Leninist Institute;[56] and Lu P'ing, president of the Peking University. However, the enigmatic personality, Premier Chou En-lai, who remained with the Maoists but showed conciliation toward the Liu group, survived unscathed, as usual. It was he who tried to salvage the nation and the sagging economy from the rampaging Red Guards. By spring 1967 the Red Guard Movement seemed to have waned somewhat. The students were ordered to return to school, and the various educational institutions were reopened in the fall of 1967. The army was given the task of creating some order out of disorder.

As of January 1968, the Maoists had succeeded in winning control of ten "administrative units,"[57] about a third of the country, while the rest seemed to be still under the control of individuals appointed by Liu, who had supervised the training and organization of the party for over two decades. Many of these local authorities countered the Maoists by adopting "economism" and offering material incentives to the workers and peasants. By increasing their wages and granting them allowances, these authorities organized them to sabotage production and to resist the attack of the Red Guards. Consequently, violent street fighting and bloodshed occurred in many parts of the country. Even though a full-scale civil war did not break out, the country had already suffered extremely serious setbacks politically, economically, and ideologically.

By September 1968 the Maoists claimed to have seized control of the entire twenty-nine provinces, autonomous regions, and municipalities, but their hold on these areas was not uniformly firm. There were reports of continued resistance to the Maoist revolutionary committees in Chekiang, Kiangsu, Honan, Yunnan, and Manchuria. Schism was also said to

56. Yang, removed in 1964, was probably the first victim of the Cultural Revolution.
57. Heilungkiang, Kweichow, Shantung, Shansi, Tsinghai, Kiangsi, Shanghai, Peking, Tientsin, and Inner Mongolia.

exist within the revolutionary committee in Hunan, Mao's home province, while bitter fighting broke out in Canton between the rival factions of the Red Guards—the "Red Flag" versus the "East Wind"—during the summer of 1968. It is possible that the anti-Maoists had infiltrated these organizations. The net result of all these clashes—between the Maoists and the anti-Maoists, and between the Maoist factions themselves—was more disorder and greater misery for the people.

The violence and chaos wrought by the Red Guards may have gone too far for their original organizers. By fall 1968 the central authorities seemed to have decided to curb their influence. Mao is reported to have said that he could not rely on "young intellectuals and students" to carry on the revolution and that they should go to the interior to learn from the peasants and the workers. Meanwhile, intensive preparations were made for the convocation of a party congress, the first since 1958. The Ninth Party Congress, which finally opened in April 1969, unanimously elected Mao chairman of the party and the Central Committee, with Lin Piao as vice-chairman and Chou En-lai as secretary-general. The new party constitution reaffirms the thought of Mao as the guilding policy of the party and the state, and designates Lin as Mao's successor. The Central Committee has been enlarged to include 170 regular members and 109 alternates, a very substantial percentage of whom are army commanders and leaders of the Cultural Revolution. Apart from Mao, Lin, and Chou, the top leadership now includes Ch'en Po-ta (Mao's secretary), Kang Sheng, Chiang Ch'ing (Mao's wife), Yao Wen-yüan, and Hsieh Fu-chih (security chief). It is generally assumed that with the convocation of the congress the Cultural Revolution came to an end.

While it is too early to draw definitive conclusions from the Cultural Revolution, it is nevertheless possible to venture a few tentative observations. First, though the Maoists and the anti-Maoists engaged in a bitter struggle, they differed only in means but not in ends. The former followed a precipitous course of socialist transformation and insisted on rejecting Soviet revisionism, while the anti-Maoists argued for a more pragmatic approach to economic reconstruction and some reconciliation with the Soviet Union. Actually, in foreign relations, the anti-Maoists were more hard-boiled than the Maoists. The former preferred stepping up aid to North Vietnam in cooperation with the Soviets; the latter preached a "do-it-yourself" revolution in Asia, with China offering moral and economic support and perhaps strategic guidance, but no direct military intervention.

Secondly, although the Cultural Revolution unfolded in 1965, its genesis can be traced to 1959 when P'eng Te-huai and Ch'en Yün spoke out against the Maoist policies. Their dismissals did not end criticism of the top leadership by party intellectuals, writers, and playwrights, who apparently enjoyed the tacit patronage of the pragmatic leaders, Liu Shao-ch'i and Teng Hsiao-p'ing. Since the latter had firm control of the party machinery, Mao had no alternative but to establish separate channels of command by creating "revolutionary committees" and the Red Guards, and by calling for the aid of the army. Thus, the army emerged as a decisive factor in Chinese politics. This rise of military influence, along with the new importance of Mao's wife and his private secretary, does not bode well for the future of the regime. For one thing, the army may grow out of control. For another, the rise of imperial distaff and relatives has always been anathema in traditional Chinese history; in any case, it has revealed the ruler's lack of confidence in any except his trusted intimates.

Thirdly, the failure of the Great Leap and the Commune, and the continuous criticism of his policies tarnished Mao's image. It has become necessary, therefore, to rebuild it through an intensified campaign of deification. Conscious efforts have been made since 1964 to place Mao even above Marx, Engels, Lenin, and Stalin as one who has *creatively developed* Marxism to new peaks.[58] In this vein, an editorial of the *Liberation Army Daily* dated May 28, 1966, paid Mao the highest tribute: "The thought of Mao Tse-tung is the sun in our heart, the root of our life, and the source of all our strength. Through it one becomes unselfish, daring, intelligent, and able to do anything; no difficulty can conquer him while he can conquer any enemy. The thought of Mao Tse-tung transforms man's ideology, transforms the fatherland . . . Through it the oppressed people of the world will rise." Another editorial of the same paper dated June 7, 1966, credited Mao with "the gifts of genius, creatively and comprehensively developing Marxism-Leninism."[59] A no less glowing eulogy was offered by Lin Piao in 1967:

> It is Comrade Mao Tse-tung, the great teacher of the world proletariat of our time, who in the new historical conditions, has systematically summed up the historical experience of the dictatorship of the proletariat in the world, scientifically analyzed the contra-

58. *People's Daily*, March 17, 1965.
59. Tang and Maloney, 87.

dictions in socialist society, profoundly shown the laws of class struggle in socialist society and put forward a whole set of theory, line, principles, methods and policies for the continuation of the revolution under the dictatorship of the proletariat. With supreme courage and wisdom, Chairman Mao has successfully led the great Proletraian Cultural Revolution in history. This is an extremely important landmark, demonstrating that *Marxism-Leninism has developed to the stage* of Mao Tse-tung's thoughts.[60]

In 1967 alone, 350 million copies of "Quotations from Chairman Mao Tse-tung" and 86.4 million sets of Mao's *Selected Works* were published. Yet, in the final analysis, the deification process is a defensive measure designed to restore the sacrosanct image of a failing leader.

Fourthly, what began as honest disagreement on policy matters between long-time comrades-in-arms turned into a bitter and ruthless power struggle that led to hundreds of leaders being arrested, dismissed, humiliated, imprisoned, or killed. The once tightly knit leadership of the CCP, which has often been considered a characteristic of Chinese Communism, has been damaged beyond repair.

Fifthly, until 1966 the turmoil in China did not seem to have seriously affected China's industrial and nuclear development. The rates of increase in industrial output for 1964, 1965, and 1966 were 15 per cent, 11 per cent, and 15 per cent, respectively—still respectable, though slower than the pace of the 1950's.[61] Nuclear development in fact made giant strides. During 1966, three tests were conducted on May 9, October 29, and December 29; during 1967, one on June 17; during 1968, one on December 27; and during 1969, two in late September—the last five being tests of hydrogen bombs.[62] However, the fate of the Third Five-Year Plan, which belatedly started in 1966, seems doomed because of the disruptions caused by the Cultural Revolution and the Red Guards.

Lastly, the Maoists have won the struggle for the present, but Mao and Maoism will never be the same in the eyes of the Chinese people. Once he is gone, elements of pragmatism are likely to return, perhaps even among his loyal supporters of today.

60. *Peking Review*, Nov. 10, 1967, 7. Italics added.
61. Chu-yüan Cheng, "The Cultural Revolution and China's Econmoy," *Current History*, (Sept. 1967), 150-52.
62. The explosions of June 17, 1967, and December 27, 1968, had a yield of three megatons each, or three million tons of TNT.

FURTHER READING

Boorman, Howard L., *et al.* (eds.), *Moscow-Peking Axis: Strengths and Strains* (New York, 1957).

Brzezinski, Zbigniew, *The Soviet Bloc: Unity and Conflict* (Cambridge, Mass., 1960).

———, "The Challenge of Change in the Soviet Bloc," *Foreign Affairs*, 39:3:430-43 (April 1961).

Chao, Kang, "Economic Aftermath of the Great Leap in Communist China," *Asian Survey*, IV:5:851-58 (May 1964).

Charles, David A., "The Dismissal of Marshal P'eng Teh-huai," *The China Quarterly*, 8:63-76 (Oct.-Dec. 1961).

Ch'en, Theodore H. E., *Thought Reform of the Chinese Intellectual* (Hong Kong, 1960).

———, "New Citizens for a New Society," *Current History*, 155-63 (Sept. 1965).

———, "A Nation in Agony: The Cultural Revolution in Communist China," *Problems of Communism* (Nov.-Dec. 1966).

Cheng, Chu-yüan, "Power Struggle in Red China," *Asian Survey*, VI:9:469-83 (Sept. 1966).

———, *The People's Communes* (Hong Kong, 1959).

———, "The Cultural Revolution and China's Economy," *Current History*, 148-54, 176-77, (Sept. 1967).

———, "The Root of China's Cultural Revolution: The Feud Between Mao Tse-tung and Liu Shao-ch'i," *Orbis*, XI:4:1160-78 (Winter 1968).

Chi, Wen-shun, "The Ideological Source of the People's Communes in Communist China," *Pacific Coast Philogy*, II:62-78 (April 1967).

Clubb, O. Edmund, *20th Century China* (New York, 1964), Part III.

Cohen, Jerome A., *The Criminal Process in the People's Republic of China, 1949-1963: An Introduction* (Cambridge, Mass., 1968).

Cohen, Arthur A., *The Communism of Mao Tse-tung* (Chicago, 1964).

Crook, Isabel and David, *The First Years of Yangyi Commune* (London, 1966).

Dai, Shen-yu, "Chinese Communist Ideology," *Current History* (Jan. 1957), 26-32.

Eckstein, Alexander, "Sino-Soviet Economic Relations: A Re-appraisal" in C. D. Cowan (ed.), *The Economic Development of China and Japan* (London, 1964), 128-59.

———, *Communist China's National Income* (New York, 1961).

———, *Communist China's Economic Growth and Foreign Trade* (New York, 1966).

Elegant, Robert S., *The Center of the World, the Mind of China under Communism* (New York, 1962).

Fitzgerald, Charles P., *Revolution in China* (New York, 1952).

Gray, Jack, and Patrick Cavendish, *Chinese Communism in Crisis: Maoism and the Cultural Revolution* (New York, 1968).

Halpern, A. M., "Communist China and Peaceful Co-existence," *The China Quarterly* (July-Sept. 1960), 16-30.

———, "The Chinese Communist Line on Neutralism," *The China Quarterly*, (Jan.-March 1961), 90-115.

Hintin, Harold C., *Communist China in World Politics* (Boston, 1966).

Ho, Kan-chih, *A History of the Modern Chinese Revolution* (Peking, 1959).

Houn, Franklin W., *A Short History of Chinese Communism*, chapters 6-13.

Hsiao, Gene T., "The Background and Development of the Proletarian Cultural Revolution," *Asian Survey*, VII:6:389-404 (June 1967).

Hsieh, Alice L., *Communist China's Strategy in the Nuclear Era* (Englewood Cliffs, 1962).

Hsü, Immanuel C. Y., "The Reorganization of Higher Education in Communist China, 1949-61," *The China Quarterly* (July-Sept. 1964), 128-60.

Hsüeh, Chün-tu, "The Cultural Revolution and Leadership Crisis in Communist China," *Political Science Quarterly*, LXXXII:2:169-90 (June 1967).

Hughes, T. J. and D. E. T. Luard, *The Economic Development of Communist China, 1949-1960* (London, 1961).

Hunter, Edward, *Brainwashing in Red China* (New York, 1951).

Johnson, Chalmers, "Building a Communist Nation in China" in Robert A. Scalapino (ed.), *The Communist Revolution in Asia* (Englewood Cliffs, 1965), 47-81.

———, "Lin Piao's Army and Its Role in Chinese Society," *Current Scene: Developments in Mainland China*, (July 1, 1966), 1-10; (July 15, 1966), 1-10.

———, "China: The Cultural Revolution in Structural Perspective," *Asian Survey*, VIII:1:1-15 (Jan. 1968).

Lewis, John Wilson, *Leadership in Communist China* (Ithaca, N. Y., 1963).

Li, Choh-ming, *Economic Development in Communist China: An Appraisal of the First Five Years of Industrialization* (Berkeley, 1959).

Lifton, Robert J., *Thought Reform and the Psychology of Totalism: A Study of "Brainwashing" in China* (New York, 1961).

Liu, Ta-chung, *The Economy of the Chinese Mainland: National Income and Economic Development, 1933-1959* (Princeton, 1965).

Liu, William T., *Chinese Society under Communism: A Reader* (New York, 1967).

Lowe, Donald M., *The Function of "China" in Marx, Lenin, and Mao* (Berkeley, 1966).

MacFarquhar, Roderick, *The Hundred Flowers Campaign and the Chinese Intellectuals* (New York, 1960).

Mao, Tse-tung, *New Democracy* (New York, 1945).

———, *Selected Works of Mao Tse-tung* (London, 1954).

Mu, Fu-sheng, *The Wilting of the Hundred Flowers: The Chinese Intelligentsia under Mao* (New York, 1962).

Munro, Donald J., "Chinese Communist Treatment of the Thinkers of the Hundred Schools Period," *The China Quarterly*, (Oct.-Nov. 1965), 119-40.

Rostow, W. W., et al. (eds.), *The Prospects for Communist China* (New York, 1954).

Salaff, Janet, "The Urban Communes and Anti-City Experiment in Communist China," *The China Quarterly*, (Jan.-March 1967), 82-110.

Schram, Stuart R., *The Political Thought of Mao Tse-tung* (New York, 1963).

―――, *Mao Tse-tung* (New York, 1966).

Schurmann, Franz, *Ideology and Organization in Communist China* (Berkeley, 1966).

Schwartz, Benjamin I., "On the 'Originality' of Mao Tse-tung," *Foreign Affairs*, (Oct. 1955), 67-76.

―――, "Ideology and the Sino-Soviet Alliance" in H. L. Boorman (ed.), *Moscow-Peking Axis* (New York, 1957).

Schwartz, Henry G., 'The Great Proletarian Cultural Revolution," *Orbis*, (Fall 1966), 803-22.

Tang, Peter S. H., *Communist China Today* (New York, 1957).

―――, *The Commune System in Mainland China* (Washington, D.C., 1961).

―――, and Joan M. Maloney, *Communist China: The Domestic Scene, 1949-1967* (South Orange, N.J., 1967).

Thomas, S. B., *Government and Administration in Communist China* (New York, 1953).

Townsend, James R., *Political Participation in Communist China* (Berkeley, 1967).

Walker, Richard L., *China under Communism: The First Five Years* (New Haven, 1955).

Whiting, Allen S., *China Crosses the Yalu: The Decision to Enter the Korean War* (Stanford, 1968).

Wu, Yüan-li, *An Economic Survey of Communist China* (New York, 1956).

―――, *The Economy of Communist China* (New York, 1965).

Yang, C. K., *A Chinese Village in Early Communist Transition* (Cambridge, Mass., 1959).

―――, *The Chinese Family in the Communist Revolution* (Cambridge, Mass., 1959).

Yin, Helen and Y. C., *Economic Statistics of Mainland China, 1949-1957* (Cambridge, Mass., 1960).

Young, Kenneth T., *Negotiating with the Chinese Communists: The United States Experience, 1953-1967* (New York, 1968).

Zagoria, David S., *The Sino-Soviet Conflict, 1956-1961* (Princeton, 1962).

―――, "The Future of Sino-Soviet Relations," *Asian Survey*, I:2:3-14 (April 1961).

27

The Nationalist Rule on Taiwan

In bitter rivalry with the Communist regime on the mainland is the Nationalist government on Taiwan, each hotly disputing the other's claim of being the legal government of China. For the Communists, it is a matter of lasting regret that Taiwan eluded their conquest, but for the Nationalists, the island offers a second lease on life and a base of resistance from which a counterattack against the mainland may eventually be staged. Thus, Taiwan, at one time the base of Ming loyalist opposition to the Ch'ing,[1] has become, once again, the citadel of a new resistance movement.

Taiwan, or Formosa in Portuguese ("beautiful"), lies about 100 miles from the mainland and 695 miles south of Japan. The island measures 240 miles long and 98 miles wide at the broadest points, covering an area of 13,844 square miles—larger than the Netherlands, a trifle smaller than Switzerland, and about the size of Massachusetts, Rhode Island, and Connecticut combined.[2] Ceded to Japan by the Ch'ing court after the war of 1894-95, Taiwan was restored to China in 1945 in accordance with the terms of the Cairo Declaration that Manchuria, Formosa, and the Pescadores be returned to China after the defeat of Japan.

With the rapid deterioration of the military situation on the mainland toward the end of 1948, Chiang Kai-shek looked to Taiwan as a possible refuge. To prepare for this eventuality, he appointed General

1. Under the leadership of Cheng Ch'eng-kung, better known as Koxinga, and his son, from 1661 to 1683. See Chapter 2.
2. Chiao-min Hsieh, *Taiwan: ilha Formosa* (London, 1964), 3-6.

Ch'en Ch'eng, a confidant, as governor of Taiwan on December 29, 1948. After his own resignation from the presidency on January 21, 1949, Chiang retired to his home town,[3] near Ningpo, to make contingency plans for a withdrawal to the island. He could do so because, though officially out of the government, he retained the KMT director-general-ship and control of the government troops and funds. With the fall of Nanking in April 1949, all indications pointed to an imminent Nationalist collapse, and Chiang quickly ordered the evacuation of troops and military equipment as well as the removal of U.S. $300 million of gold reserves and foreign currencies to Taiwan, there to establish a new base of resistance. He assumed *de facto* leadership on Taiwan even though the acting president, Li Tsung-jen, remained officially the head of state on the mainland. When the Nationalist government finally moved to Taiwan in December 1949, Li did not come along but went to the United States for "medical treatment." Chiang then resumed his post as president of the republic on March 1, 1950.

To bolster the defense of Taiwan, Chiang made "strategic" withdrawals from several outposts. In April and May 1950, troops were evacuated from the Hainan and the Chusan islands, and in 1953-54 Nationalist guerrilla units stranded in North Vietnam and the Yunnan-Burmese border region were repatriated. Added strength came when 14,209 Chinese Communist prisoners of war, captured during the Korean War, joined the Nationalists in January 1954. A year later, in January 1955, a considerable number of civilians and troops on the Ta-ch'en Islands off the Chekiang coast were repatriated. Aided by these withdrawals and new programs of military training and recruitment, Taiwan developed a respectable force of 600,000 troops, a fifth of whom are stationed on the offshore islands of Quemoy and Matsu, a few miles from the mainland.

UNITED STATES POLICY TOWARD TAIWAN

United States policy toward the Nationalists on Taiwan has gone through a complete about-face, from indifference to active support. In the latter half of 1949, witnessing the Nationalist collapse on the mainland, Washington was resigned to the fall of Taiwan sometime in 1950. President Truman announced the policy of noninvolvement on January 5, 1950:[4]

3. Ch'i-k'ou.
4. Quoted in Joseph W. Ballantine, *Formosa: A Problem for United States Foreign Policy* (Washington, D. C., 1952), 120.

The United States has no predatory designs on Formosa or on any other Chinese territory. The United States has no desire to obtain special rights or privileges or to establish military bases on Formosa at this time. Nor does it have any intention of utilizing its armed forces to interfere in the present situation. The United States Government will not pursue a course which will lead to involvement in the civil conflict in China.

Similarly, the United States Government will not provide military aid or advice to Chinese forces on Formosa.

In a similar vein, on January 12, 1950, Secretary of State Dean Acheson delineated the American defense perimeter in the Pacific as running from the Aleutians to Japan, Ryūkyū (Okinawa), and the Philippines—leaving out Taiwan altogether. Areas within this defense perimeter, he declared, "must and will be held," but "so far as the military security of other areas in the Pacific is concerned, it must be clear that no person can guarantee these areas against military attack . . . Should such an attack occur . . . the initial reliance must be on the people attacked to resist it and then upon the commitments of the entire civilized world under the Charter of the United Nations."[5] Thus, from October 1948 to June 1950, Washington did not consider it necessary to defend Taiwan against Communist conquest.

However, this policy was negated by the North Korean attack on South Korea on June 25, 1950. President Truman declared on June 27 that "communism has passed beyond the use of subversion to conquer independent nations and will now use armed invasion and war . . . In these circumstances the occupation of Formosa by Communist forces would be a direct threat to the security of the Pacific area and to the United States forces . . . in that area."[6] He ordered the Seventh Fleet to defend Taiwan against any Communist invasion, and meantime urged the Nationalists to desist from attacking the mainland so as to prevent the enlargement of hostilities. With this change of policy, Washington dispatched a chargé d'affaires to Taipei on July 28, 1950, and three days later General MacArthur visited Chiang Kai-shek to discuss joint defense plans. On August 4, MacArthur's deputy chief of staff[7] arrived in Taipei to set up a permanent liaison with the Nationalist government.

The outbreak of the Korean War thus marked a turning point in

5. Ballantine, 125.
6. *Ibid.*, 127.
7. Major General Fox.

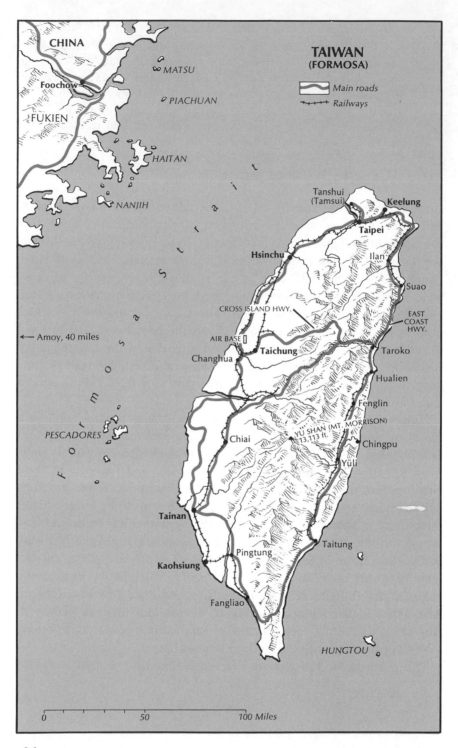

TAIWAN
(FORMOSA)

Main roads
Railways

CHINA

Foochow

FUKIEN

MATSU

PIACHUAN

HAITAN

NANJIH

Tanshui
(Tamsui)

Keelung

Taipei

Hsinchu

Ilan

Suao

CROSS ISLAND HWY.

EAST
COAST
HWY.

AIR BASE

← Amoy, 40 miles

Taichung

Taroko

Changhua

Hualien

Fenglin

PESCADORES

YU SHAN (MT. MORRISON)
13,113 ft.

Chiai

Chingpu

Yüli

Tainan

Taitung

Kaohsiung

Pingtung

Fangliao

HUNGTOU

0   50   100 Miles

786

United States-Nationalist relations. The former "hands-off" policy of Washington was jettisoned in favor of one of "neutralizing" Taiwan while preventing it from becoming a Communist trophy. A further stiffening of the United States position followed the entry of the Chinese Communist "volunteers" into the Korean War in October 1950. Steadfastly, Washington boycotted the recognition of the People's Republic and objected to its admission to the United Nations. Meanwhile, American military shipments to Taiwan were resumed, and economic aid also began, amounting to $98 million from June 1, 1950, to June 30, 1951.[8] In addition, a 116-man Military Assistance Advisory Group was established on Taiwan in April 1951 under Major General William C. Chase, and by May 1952 the mission had grown to 400. Taiwan had acquired a new strategic importance in the United States defense plans, and General MacArthur described the island as "an unsinkable aircraft carrier and submarine tender ideally located to accomplish offensive strategy and at the same time checkmate defensive or counteroffensive operations by friendly forces based on Okinawa and the Philippines."[9] A further boost to the Nationalist cause came when Japan decided on April 28, 1952, to sign a peace treaty with the government of the Republic of China on Taiwan rather than with the Communist regime in Peking. Taking into consideration the Nationalist claim to legal jurisdiction over all China, the Japanese specified in the treaty that its terms were applicable to all territories now, as well as those "which may hereafter be," under Nationalist control.

The growing stature of Taiwan was reflected in the elevation of the United States chargé-d'affaires to the ambassadorial rank in January 1953[10] and in the signing of a mutual defense pact with the United States in December 1954. Attempts by the Communists to take Quemoy and Matsu in autumn 1954 and 1958 were repeatedly frustrated by Nationalist resistance under American encouragement. President Eisenhower accepted the Nationalist view that giving up these offshore islands, whatever their military value, was tantamount to an abject surrender. President Kennedy announced that should any attack on these islands constitute, in the opinion of the United States, a prelude to an attack on Taiwan itself, Washington would take appropriate actions for its defense.

8. Economic aid in 1951-52: $81 million; 1952-53: 105 million; 1953-54: 116 million; 1954-55: 138 million; 1955-56: 79 million; 1956-57: 90 million; 1957-58: 61 million; 1958-59: 74 million; 1959-60: 70 million; 1961-62: 134 million.
9. Quoted in Ballantine, 153.
10. First ambassador, Karl L. Rankin.

Thus, Taiwan's international position was made secure. The Nationalist government still represents China at the United Nations, and repeated attempts by the Soviets and other states to oust its representatives have been unsuccessful. Today, the government of the Republic of China on Taiwan is recognized by sixty-five states, including the United States, Japan, Canada, and most of the Latin American states except Cuba.

POLITICAL STRUCTURE

With the surrender of Japan in August 1945, Taiwan was restored to China and was made a province, with Ch'en Yi[11] as governor. The choice was unfortunate, for Ch'en was hardly a conscientious administrator. Corrupt and discriminatory, his term was marked by numerous scandals including lucrative public auctions of Japanese properties that he had taken over, and by outrageous practice of discrimination against the Taiwanese, who were treated as colonial subjects unfit for executive and managerial posts in the government or in the large enterprises. The Taiwanese who at first had welcomed the Nationalist take-over quickly lost faith in Ch'en's administration, which they came to regard as worse than the Japanese colonial rule. Public indignation finally could no longer be contained and in late February of 1947, a violent uprising erupted. Ch'en temporized a bit to gain time while calling for reinforcements from the mainland, and when they arrived he carried out a ruthless massacre of the Taiwanese. Although his subsequent dismissal[12] mollified the situation to some extent, his misrule did great damage to the Nationalist cause and served to embitter the Taiwanese against the mainlanders.[13] It was not until after Ch'en Ch'eng became governor in January 1949 that the acrimonious relationship began to improve, largely through increased participation of Taiwanese in provincial and local governments, although high appointments in the central government continued to elude them. By June 1950 Taiwanese accounted for 53,024 of the total 81,000 persons in the provincial administration. Among these Taiwanese civil servants, 55 filled senior posts out of a total 316 openings in this category; 780

11. Not to be confused with the Communist foreign minister, Ch'en Yi, whose personal name is composed of a different character but has a similar pronunciation.
12. Later shot in January 1949 for conniving and colluding with Communist agents.
13. The ratios between the Taiwanese and the mainlanders are: 5.9 million vs. 47,551 in 1945; 6.8 million vs. 524,940 in 1950; 9.5 million vs. 1.27 million in 1960, and approximately 10 million vs. 3 million in 1968. Chiao-min Hsieh, 206.

filled second class jobs out of a total 3,118; and 15,476 occupied third class posts out of 24,635.[14]

The Nationalist government on Taiwan is headed by a president, assisted by a secretary-general and a chief of staff who helped him with civil and military affairs. The five-yüan structure is maintained, although the functions and the legal positions of some of the yüans have changed. The powers of the Legislative Yüan have been expanded at the expense of the Executive Yüan. The appointment of the president (premier) of the Executive Yüan is subject to the approval of the Legislative Yüan, which also has the right of interpellation. Members of the Legislative Yüan are elected, and they choose their president and vice-president from among themselves. The Legislative Yüan can initiate legislation, interpellate ministers, review the budget, and conduct independent investigations—a far cry from the old Legislative Yüan of the Political Tutelage period, which was hardly more than a law-drafting bureau of the KMT Central Executive Committee.

The composition of the Judiciary Yüan has also been changed considerably. It is composed of (1) A Council of Grand Judges, whose duty it is to interpret the constitution, laws, and decrees. The Council has seventeen members, all appointed by the president of the republic with the concurrence of the Control Yüan; (2) the Supreme Court; (3) the Administrative Court; and (4) the Disciplinary Commission.

The president and vice president of the Control Yüan are elected from among the members of the Yüan itself, who are in turn elected for six years by provincial and municipal assemblies. The Examination Yüan has a president and a vice-president and nineteen commissioners, also elected for six years.

Except for the ministries of foreign affairs and national defense, the five-yüan government duplicates much of the functions of the provincial government, which has its own departments of civil affairs, finance, education, agriculture and forestry, communication, public health, public safety, etc. From the standpoint of administrative efficiency, the presence of two governments on Taiwan is a luxury which the small island can ill afford. Yet the juxtaposition is a political necessity, for the existence of the central government gives substance to its claim to legal jurisdiction over all China and offers hope for an eventual return to the mainland.

A sensitive issue in the otherwise peaceful, if somewhat pedestrian, political life on Taiwan was the presidency of Chiang Kai-shek. The con-

14. Fred W. Riggs, *Formosa Under Chinese Nationalist Rule* (New York, 1952), 49.

stitution specifices that a president is elected for six years and may be re-elected for a second term. Chiang, elected president in Nanking in 1948, was re-elected on Taiwan in 1954. As 1960 approached, the delicate question of the third term arose. Since Chiang himself disfavored an amendment of the constitution, the question was resolved—after much discussion from various angles—by a vote of the National Assembly in February 1960, which suspended the application of the constitutional stipulation on presidential terms during the period of "general mobilization and rebellion-suppression." On March 21, 1960, Chiang was elected to a third term, with Ch'en Ch'eng as vice-president, and in 1966, to a fourth term, with Yen Chia-kan as vice-president and premier.

ECONOMIC AND SOCIAL DEVELOPMENT

The bitter lesson of defeat on the mainland taught the Nationalists that they could not ignore the pressing problems of social and economic reform. Once established on Taiwan, they endeavored to succeed where earlier they had failed. With determination, American advice (through the Joint Commission on Rural Reconstruction [JCRR]), and considerable concentration of brainpower and technical skill, they successfully carried out a three-stage land reform and thereby fulfilled Dr. Sun's ideal, "land to the tiller."

The moving spirit in this agrarian program was Governor Ch'en Ch'eng, who began the first stage of reform in 1949 with a compulsory reduction of the annual land rent from the prevailing 50-70 per cent to 37.5 per cent of the main crop.[15] In places where the existing rent was below 37.5 per cent it was to remain as it was. Moreover, the time-honored practice of giving an "oral lease," which offered no legal protection to the tenants, was replaced by a written lease valid for at least six years. Buttressed by these measures, the livelihood of 300,000 farm families was substantially improved, and the increased income enabled them to purchase cattle and houses which were facetiously dubbed "37.5 cattle" and "37.5 houses."[16]

The second stage began with the sale of 430,000 acres of public land in June 1951. This property, representing 20 per cent of the arable land on Taiwan, had originally been set aside by the Japanese colonial ad-

15. This rate of 37.5 per cent was first adopted by the KMT in 1930 but was never implemented.
16. W. G. Goddard, *Formosa: A Study in Chinese History* (East Lansing, Michigan, 1966), 191.

ministration for the settlement of Japanese immigrants. Now the Nationalist government allowed each farmer to purchase a sufficient amount of acreage to support a family of six: seven acres of paddy land or fourteen acres of dry land. The purchase price was set at two and one-half times the annual yield of the main crop, repayable in twenty semiannual installments at 4 per cent interest. No single installment, however, was to exceed the prevailing rent. This second stage of agrarian reform enabled 139,688 farmers to become landowners.[17]

The third stage was launched in January 1953 with the compulsory sale of private and tenanted land to the government, which resold it to farmers at the same price while charging a 4 per cent annual interest. No less than 193,823 families benefited from these measures, bringing the total number of land-owning families to 400,000—or two and one-half to three million individuals. The completion of the agrarian reform program reduced tenancy from 39 per cent to 15 per cent on all farmland.[18] By early 1968 tenants operated only 10 per cent of the land, while 90 per cent was tilled by owners.[19]

As a result of the land reform, production of main crops increased substantially. Rice climbed from 1.8 million tons in 1953 to 2.3 million in 1962; vegetables from 685,577 tons to 925,549 tons; tea from 13,093 tons to 21,728 tons; and pineapple from 75,318 tons to 101,537 tons.[20] The general well-being of the farmers is reflected in the large number of houses they have constructed or repaired and the impressive quantity of bicycles and sewing machines they have purchased.

No less impressive has been the rate of industrial development. After an initial period (1945-52) concerned with rehabilitating war-torn industrial machinery, the government launched a Four-Year Economic Development Plan for 1953-56, in which it took the lead in promoting medium- and small-size basic industries which required no great outlay of capital and which utilized local raw materials. It encouraged cottage and handicraft industries which could improve employment in the rural communities. Backed by technical and managerial personnel from the mainland, American economic assistance, and a fierce determination to make Taiwan a showcase in the Pacific, the First Four-Year Plan was a remarkable success. Progress was scored in nearly every line of industrial activity:

17. Goddard, 192; Chiao-min Hsieh, 285-86.
18. Goddard, 193; Chiao-min Hsieh, 286.
19. *Free China Weekly*, Taipei, Feb. 4, 1968.
20. Chiao-min Hsieh, 266.

aluminum, alkali, textiles, electricity, leather, chemicals, paper, jute, sugar, pineapples, mushrooms, handicraft, etc. By the end of 1956 some 2,000 factories were in operation, a third of which were built after 1952. The number of industrial workers increased from 274,000 to 340,000 during this period, while the production index in 1956 was more than double that of 1951. Per capita income rose by 42 per cent in 1956 over 1953.[21]

The success of the First Four-Year Plan prompted the government to launch its Second, Third, and Fourth Plans, each a success story. Available statistics show that by 1963 Taiwan had achieved an 86 per cent increase in industrial production over 1957, a 42 per cent increase in agricultural output, 50 per cent in national income, and 22 per cent in per capita income.[22] Since 1963 Taiwan has experienced, on the average, an annual economic growth of 9.7 per cent, with 1964 the highest at 14.2 per cent and 1966 the lowest at 8.07 per cent—all surpassing the original target of 7 per cent a year. The Gross National Product (GNP) for 1967 reached U.S. $3.11 billion as compared with U.S. $1.2 billion in 1952.[23] Nationalist officials proudly announced in 1967 that Taiwan had achieved the second highest per capita income[24] in Asia, trailing only Japan, while in terms of individual daily caloric intake (2,422) Taiwan ranked first in all Asia." With a GNP growth rate of 10.3 per cent in 1968 and an industrial expansion of 19.8 per cent in the first half of 1969, Taiwan has achieved a remarkable economic viability[25]—this, in spite of the phasing out of American aid in mid-1965. Needless to say, Taiwan has benefited greatly from increased United States procurement for the Vietnam War since 1965. In 1969 the government began its Fifth Four-year Plan, setting the annual growth rate at 7 per cent while expecting to surpass it with ease.

CULTURAL LIFE

Taiwan had attained the remarkably high literacy rate of 97.15 per cent by 1967. This impressive record was made possible by a constitutional requirement that 15 per cent of the national budget, 25 per cent of the provincial's, and 35 per cent of the district's be devoted to education. Beginning with the fall term of 1968, free education was extended from six to nine years. Nearly a quarter of the total population of 13 million on Taiwan were students at the end of 1967, distributed in 2,115 elementary

21. Chiao-min Hsieh, 309-10.
22. Chiao-min Hsieh, 311.
23. Free China Weekly, Nov. 5, 1967; April 21, 1968.
24. U.S. $209.
25. Free China Weekly, Aug. 6 and Dec. 17, 1967; May 25 and Sept. 28, 1969.

schools, 555 middle schools, and 74 universities and colleges. The number of educational institutions alone underscored the vast improvement since the end of the Japanese rule; in 1945 there were only 1,100 elementary schools, 75 middle schools, and one university and four colleges.[26]

In harmony with the burgeoning growth of Taiwan's educational system is the increasing attractiveness and quality of its research organizations. The National Taiwan University, the leading institution of higher learning, maintains a number of graduate programs and since 1960 has been awarding the doctorate in conjunction with the Ministry of Education. Among the pure research organizations, the most prestigious is the Academia Sinica located at Nankang, outside Taipei. Its beautiful site and idyllic surroundings provide a haven for serious scholars. It maintains a number of institutes, such as Mathematics, History and Philology, Chemistry, Zoology, Ethnology, and Modern History. The last-named institute, one of the youngest, was formed in 1955 and has since turned out a number of sound monographs by able young historians under the general guidance of its director, Kuo Ting-yi. Among other research organizations of note are the Tsing-hua University Atomic Research Institute and the Chiao-t'ung University Electronics Research Institute.

Scholars on Taiwan like to consider the island the repository of Chinese cultural heritage. Indeed, many of the art collections formerly housed in the museums of Peking and Nanking had been removed to Taiwan. From the Peking Palace Museum came 231,910 pieces of exquisite art work and rare books, and from the Central Musuem at Nanking came 11,729 priceless artifacts. Exhibitions of this treasury of national art are made regularly at the museums at Tai-chung and Taipei.

This rapid survey of major developments on Taiwan points up the fact that the Nationalist government, which failed miserably on the mainland, has succeeded in turning the island into a "model" province and a showcase in Asia. Materially, the people enjoy a general well-being and a high standard of living unequaled in Chinese history. Nationalist officials proudly proclaim that the per capita income on Taiwan is three times as high as that on the mainland.[27] Yet, for all its apparent prosperity, Taiwan is a small island with limited possibilities. It is not the spiritual home of China, and the refugee mainlanders rarely consider it more than a waiting station before the eventual return to the continent. They feel socially rootless, intellectually isolated, and spiritually empty. Young

26. Report of the Chinese cultural attaché at the Washington embassy, Chang Nai-wei, in *Chinese Students News Bulletin*, April 1968, Nos. 97-98.
27. *Free China Weekly*, Aug. 6, 1967.

men are discouraged by the lack of outlets for their talents, and older men feel hemmed in by the restrictive environment. Not surprisingly, this lack of hope, opportunity, and future has generated a terrific sense of frustration. The refugees long to return to the mainland, yet the practical-minded know that it is a dream not easily realizable in the near future—perhaps never in their lifetime. Apart from repeating the slogan "Going Back to the Mainland" to keep hope alive, the government increasingly has come to regard Taiwan as a "treasure island" (*pao-tao*), which, though small and confining, serves a useful purpose in history. The coexistence of economic prosperity and spiritual discontent is a modern phenomenon which once again testifies to the biblical truth that man does not live on bread alone. In the last analysis, he needs hope in order to live a meaningful life.

FURTHER READING

Ballantine, Joseph W., *Formosa: A Problem for United States Foreign Policy* (Washington, D.C., 1952).

Barclay, George W., *Colonial Development and Population in Taiwan* (Princeton, 1954).

Bate, H. Maclear, *Report from Formosa* (London, 1952).

Goddard, W. G., *Formosa: A Study in Chinese History* (East Lansing, 1966).

——, *The Makers of Taiwan* (Taipei, 1963).

Han, Lih-wu (Hang, Li-wu), *Taiwan Today* (Taipei, 1951).

Hsieh, Chiao-min, *Taiwan: ilha Formosa* (London, 1964).

Huang, Chia-mo, *Mei-kuo yü Tai-wan, 1784-1895* (America and Taiwan, 1784-1895), (Taipei, 1966).

Joint Commission on Rural Reconstruction, *A Decade of Rural Progress, 1948-1958* (Taipei, 1958).

Kerr, George, "Formosa's Return to China," *Far Eastern Survey* (Oct. 15, 1947).

——, "Formosa: the March Massacres," *Far Eastern Survey* (Nov. 5, 1947).

——, *Formosa Betrayed* (Boston, 1965).

Lien, Heng 連橫, *Tai-wan t'ung-shih* 台灣通史 (A general history of Taiwan), (Shanghai, 1947), 2 vols.

Mancall, Mark (ed.), *Formosa Today* (New York, 1964).

Rankin, Karl L., *China Assignment* (Seattle, 1964).

Riggs, Fred W., *Formosa under Chinese Nationalist Rule* (New York, 1952).

Shieh, Milton J. T., *Taiwan and the Democratic World* (Taipei, 1951).

United States Relations with China, with Special Reference to the Period 1944-1949 (Washington, D.C., 1949), 307-10, 923-38.

VanderMeer, Canute and Paul, "Land Property Data on Taiwan," *The Journal of Asian Studies*, XXVIII:1:144-50 (Nov. 1968).

28

Epilogue: Historical Perspective

Modern China defies comparison with the China of previous ages, for the changes which distinguish modern China from its traditional counterpart are both fundamental and far-reaching. Politically, the dynasty and the imperial institution have passed out of existence, and with them the educated bureaucracy based on literary excellence. Economically, the age-old system of land tenure characterized by landlordism has been destroyed for good. Socially, the gentry no longer provide the backbone of society, while the old four-class stratification and the position of the family as the basic unit of society have been shattered. Intellectually, Confucianism, Buddhism, and Taoism have gone bankrupt. So broad and so deep have been the changes that they have affected virtually every phase of Chinese life. Indeed, more changes have been wrought in the short span of modern China than in all the previous history of the country. The only period of old with which it might possibly be compared is that of the Warring States period (481-221 B.C), during which time drastic political, intellectual, social, and economic changes took place, culminating in the first unification of China by the Ch'in state and the end of feudalism. Yet the two cases were essentially dissimilar, for change in ancient China was an outgrowth of domestic conditions, while the transformation of modern China was precipitated, to a large extent, by influence from abroad.

The metamorphosis of modern China was prolonged and painful. From the self-sufficient universal empire of 1600-1800, China has evolved into

795

a modern national state, passing through a number of intermediate stages en route: diplomatic and military innovations during the Self-Strengthening period of 1861-95, political reform and revolution from 1898 to 1912, intellectual revolution from 1917 to 1923, and the struggle for supreme power between the Nationalists and the Communists since 1921, leading to the rise of Mao Tse-tung and the People's Republic in 1949.

Each step in China's transformation was a struggle, which in the final analysis represented an intellectual decision as to what extent Old China had to be jettisoned in order to make room for the introduction of modern Western elements. The reluctance to yield has all too frequently been criticized as proof of China's backwardness, lack of initiative, and inability to innovate and respond creatively to the challenges of time. Yet one should not lose sight of the fact that the conquest of the mind is by its very nature a slow process, especially when the indigenous civilization is durable and strong. Although it imposes a heavy burden, slowness to Westernize in a sense testifies to cultural strength rather than weakness. It is no coincidence that China and India, two of the oldest and most illustrious civilizations of the world, were among the slowest to modernize. But once the mind is convinced of the need for change, the scope and depth of its transformation can be very great—not infrequently exceeding the degree of change in countries where response to outside stimuli is quick. Given the momentum of change, it is still too early to say whether the metamorphosis of modern China is over. More likely than not, the process will go on for some time.

In accepting the West—whether through democracy or socialism— Chinese leaders always seem to have harbored a secret desire to adulterate and Sinicize the innovation, so as to make it less completely foreign. Sun Yat-sen accepted the republican form of government but rejected the traditional three-way division of power in favor of a five-yüan government. Mao Tse-tung, for all his devotion to Marxism-Leninism, championed his own New Democracy, whereby the dictatorship of the proletariat is replaced by the alliance of the four classes. Regardless of their ideological persuasions, the great Chinese leaders have always seemed inclined to seek a new order that is thoroughly modern yet distinctly Chinese. Moreover, they have exhibited an innate desire to surpass the West in various subtle ways: Sun preached the Principle of People's Livelihood long before any leading Western countries turned socialist, while Mao, striving to be more "communistic" than his Soviet comrades, boasts of having brought his country closer to the true portals of communism than the Soviet Union.

HISTORICAL CONTINUITY AND DISCONTINUITY

Two questions are frequently raised: first, how "Chinese" and how "Marxist" is Communist China, and second, can recent developments in China be explained in the light of her history? Communist China exhibits many qualities which can be regarded as having some historical antecedents, while many others, because of their foreign origins, cannot be so viewed. The mixture of historical continuity and discontinuity makes it extremely difficult to interpret China purely on the basis of her past. A knowledge of the modern West, including that of the socialist camp, is necessary for a more meaningful grasp of the turn of events in China.

Historical continuity manifests itself in many ways. The once sacrosanct imperial ruler is replaced by a deified party leader, and the old bureaucracy by party elite and cadre. Political indoctrination to ensure conformity of thought can be construed as a modern variation of the ideological orthodoxy of Confucianism. The "Mandate of Heaven," which fictitiously gave the ruling dynasty the authority to govern, is now reflected in the "will" of the people as expressed by their vanguard, the party. The classics have been replaced by works of Marx, Lenin, and Mao, while the little Red Book, the *Quotations of Chairman Mao*, has supplanted the *Analects* and the *Three-Word Classics*. The tradition of large-scale public works—the Great Wall and the Grand Canal—is manifested by the numerous gigantic material accomplishments of the Peking regime. The Middle Kingdom concept is furthered by Communist China's intense drive toward big-power status, ideological leadership of the socialist camp, and atomic parity with the United States and the Soviet Union. The maintenance in Peking of dozens of foreign "peace delegations" which enjoyed free transportation and accommodations suggests the continuing ascription to others of tributary status. Korea and Vietnam (Annam), traditionally China's most important tributary states, are precisely the countries with which Peking has endeavored to keep the closest ties.

On the other hand, just as many instances of historical discontinuity may be discovered. The ideas of dialectical materialism, class struggle, democratic centralism, and democratic dictatorship have no antecedents in China's past. Mass organizations, psychological remolding, control of the communication media, and the endless upsurge of mass campaigns and mass demonstrations are all alien to the Chinese tradition. The idea of progress has superseded the cyclical concept of history, and political and social activism has become the new creed of the country. The breakneck rate of industrialization, rapid agricultural collectivization and communization, and crash programs of atomic development have replaced the tranquil, serene, and somewhat passive life of old. The vicious denunciation of old thought, old customs, old habits, and old culture contrasts sharply with the Confucian respect for age and longing for the golden past. Family honor, individual heroism, filial piety, and "face" are all discarded as feudal vestiges; in their place have arisen the new concepts of the labor hero, public confession, criticism and self-criticism, and the denunciation of parents by children. Families and townships have been absorbed into communes, and the new alliance between workers, peasants, and the petty and national bourgeoisie has replaced the old stratification of scholar-official, farmer, artisan, and merchant.

The juxtaposition of elements of both historical continuity and discontinuity dictates that only a judicious balance between a knowledge of China's past and that of the West can provide a proper perspective.

COMMUNIST CHINA: A HISTORICAL INEVITABILITY?

My interpretation of Chinese Communism as the fourth phase of modern China's development should not be taken as a suggestion that such an occurrence is a historical inevitability. While it is true that Chinese Communism, which is an outgrowth of the intellectual revolution of 1917-23, must be considered a very likely—and perhaps even logical—development, its ultimate triumph in 1949 was not necessarily a historical necessity. Had it not been for the exhaustion of the Nationalist government by the Japanese war and the widespread discontent which the government's failure to implement social and economic reforms generated, the Communist influence could have been checked and its rise to power delayed or perhaps prevented. A less aggressive Japan and a more progressive Nationalist Party could have enabled the Nanking government to remain in power, although nobody can say how long.

Despite their recent outbursts against American imperialism, Soviet revisionism, and their own cultural heritage, the mainland Chinese are basically a peace-loving, hard-working, law-abiding people of notable intelligence and common sense. Their revolt against the outside world, as well as their own past, bespeaks an atypical behavior not uncommon during a revolutionary and transitional age when the fluid state of affairs frequently neutralizes usual norms of conduct. But once China's sense of injury at the hands of foreign powers is mollified by the achievement of big-power status, industrialization, and nuclear power, a more responsible and more realistic appraisal of her position vis-à-vis the rest of the world will be in order. Hopefully, pragmatism and common sense will return to guide the country into a rightful position in the community of nations.

FURTHER READING

Fairbank, John K., *The United States and China* (Cambridge, Mass., 1958), chapters 1 and 17.

————, *China: The People's Middle Kingdom and the U.S.A.* (Cambridge, Mass., 1967).

————, "China's Foreign Policy in Historical Perspective," *Foreign Affairs*, 47:3:449-63 (April 1969).

Fitzgerald, Charles P., *Revolution in China* (New York, 1952).

Levenson, Joseph R., *Modern China and Its Confucian Fate*, Vol. III: *The Problem of Historical Significance* (Berkeley, 1965).

List of Illustrations and Acknowledgments

Tseng-shih Wen-hsien, Taipei, 1965. 36. Tso T'sung-t'ang. From Gideon Chen, *Tso Tsung-t'ang,* Peking, 1938. 37. Chang Chih-tung, long-time governor-general at Wuhan. From Wright, *Hart and the Chinese Customs.* 38. Marquis Tseng. Radio Times Hulton Picture Library. 39. Sir Robert Hart (*Vanity Fair,* 27 December 1894). Radio Times Hulton Picture Library. 40. Sir Rutherford Alcock. Radio Times Hulton Picture Library. 41. Dr. Martin A. P. Martin, president of T'ung-wen Kuan. From William A. P. Martin, *A Cycle of Cathay,* New York and Chicago, 1896. 42. Chinese students to the United States, 1872. From Thomas E. La Fargue, *China's First Hundred,* Pullman, Washington, 1942. 43. Chinese students' baseball club in front of the Chinese Educational Mission in Hartford, Connecticut, 1878. From La Fargue, *China's First Hundred.* 44. Li Hung-chang with British Prime Minister William Ewart Gladstone. Charles Phelps Cushing. 45. Empress Dowager Tz'u-hsi. The Freer Gallery of Art. 46. The Summer Palace (late Ch'ing dynasty, painting on paper). The Metropolitan Museum of Art, gift of Franklin Jasper Walls, 1948.

Following page 522
47. A Boxer poster. From Alexander H. Smith, *China in Convulsion,* Edinburgh and London, 1901. 48. Imprisoned Boxers after the lifting of the blockade by the expeditionary forces. The Bettmann Archive. 49. Portrait of the young Emperor Kuang-hsü. The Metropolitan Museum of Art, anonymous gift, 1942. 50. Yüan Shih-k'ai. The Bettmann Archive. 51. Prince Ch'ing. From Conger, *Letters from China.* 52. Prince Chün. The Bettmann Archive. 53. K'ang Yu-wei. Charles Phelps Cushing. 54. Liang Ch'i-ch'ao. From Timothy Richard, *Forty-five Years in China,* New York, 1916. 55. Timothy Richard. From Richard, *Forty-five Years.* . . . 56. Huang Hsing. From Percy Horace Kent, *The Passing of the Manchus,* New York and London, 1912. 57. Yüan Shih-k'ai, center, as provisional president of the Republic of China, 1912. Radio Times Hulton Picture Library. 58. Wu P'ei-fu, left, with two of his generals. Radio Times Hulton Picture Library. 59. Sun Yat-sen with Madame Sun Yat-sen, a graduate of the University of California at Berkeley and Wellesley. Radio Times Hulton Picture Library. 60. Pu-yi in 1922. Charles Phelps Cushing. 61. Chang Tso-lin. Radio Times Hulton Picture Library. 62. Dr. Sun with his second wife, Soong Ching-ling, during a journey in 1924 to Peking. Eastfoto.

Following page 682
63. General Chiang Kai-shek and Yen Hsi-shan. Radio Times Hulton Picture Library. 64. Part of the former members of the First Division of the First Corps of the Worker-Peasant Revolutionary Army. Eastfoto. 65. President Roosevelt greeting China's Finance Minister, T. V. Soong. Radio Times Hulton Picture Library. 66. Feng Yü-hsiang. Eastfoto. 67. Hu Shih as head of the Academia Sinica, *circa* 1960. Courtesy of the Academia Sinica. 68. Sun Fo. Charles Phelps Cushing.

Following page 770
69. Mao Tse-tung and Chu Teh reviewing their troops after the capture of Peking, 1949. Eastfoto. 70. Russian influence among the Chinese Communists. Harrison Forman. 71. Chen Yi. Harrison Forman. 72. Peng Te-huai. Harrison Forman. 73. Chou En-lai at the Geneva Conference in 1954. Radio Times Hulton Picture Library. 74. Lin Piao, heir apparent to Mao. Eastfoto. 75. Chiang Ch'ing (Mrs. Mao) and Chou En-lai. Eastfoto. 76. Chairman Mao, Liu Shao-ch'i, and Soong Ching-ling (Madame Sun Yat-sen). Eastfoto. 77. China's largest blast furnace, completed in 4 months and 26 days. UPI. 78. Members of the Heifen commune in Kansu Province. UPI. 79. Red Chinese "provocation" on the Russian-Chinese border. The Soviet news agency Novosti via UPI. 80. A Red Chinese and an Indian soldier face each other at the border between Indian-protected Sikkim and Red Chinese-held Tibet. UPI. 81. Chiang Kai-shek leads a group of high officials to pay homage to the heroes who died for the cause of Nationalist China. UPI. 82. A. N. Kosygin with Mao Tse-tung in Peking, 1965. UPI.

Index

0   500   1000 Miles

U.   S.

Irkutsk

Yenisey R.

Irtysh R.

MONGOLIAN

Lake Balkhash

Alma Ata

ALTAI   MTS.

TIEN   SHAN

Urumchi

Hami

PAMIR MTS.

Tarim R.

S I N K I A N G

Yarkand

Lop Nor

K A N S

KASHMIR

KUNLUN   MTS.

TSINGHAI

Koko Nor

Sining

Lanchow

H
I
M
A
L
A
Y
A

T I B E T

NEPAL

Shigatse

Lhasa

CHAMDO

SZEC

Chengtu

Ganges R.

SIKKIM

BHUTAN

Brahmaputra R.

M T S.

Mekong R.

I N D I A

E. PAKISTAN

Kunming

YUNNAN

BURMA

L
A
O

COMMUNIST CHINA, 1970

▏▎▏▎ Autonomous Regions

┼┼┼┼ Main railways (in China and Russia)

THAILAND